I0130994

Anonymus

Educational Endowments (Ireland) Commissioners

Annual report, 1888-89, minutes of evidence and appendices

Anonymus

Educational Endowments (Ireland) Commissioners
Annual report, 1888-89, minutes of evidence and appendices

ISBN/EAN: 9783742811141

Manufactured in Europe, USA, Canada, Australia, Japa

Cover: Foto ©Suzi / pixelio.de

Manufactured and distributed by brebook publishing software
(www.brebook.com)

Anonymus

Educational Endowments (Ireland) Commissioners

EDUCATIONAL ENDOWMENTS (IRELAND) COMMISSION.

48 & 49 *Vic.*, *Ch.* 78.

ANNUAL REPORT

OF THE

COMMISSIONERS,

FOR THE YEAR

1888-89,

TOGETHER WITH

ABSTRACT OF THE MINUTES OF THE COMMISSION, MINUTES OF EVIDENCE, AND APPENDICES.

Presented to both Houses of Parliament by Command of Her Majesty.

DUBLIN:
PRINTED FOR HER MAJESTY'S STATIONERY OFFICE
BY
ALEXANDER THOM & CO. (LIMITED).
And to be purchased, either directly or through any Bookseller, from
EYRE and SPOTTISWOODE, East Harding-street, Fetter-lane, E.C., or 32, Abingdon-street, Westminster, S.W.; or ADAM and CHARLES BLACK, 6, North Bridge, Edinburgh; or HODGES, FIGGIS, and CO., 104, Grafton-street, Dublin.

1889.

TABLE OF CONTENTS.

FOURTH REPORT

OF THE

EDUCATIONAL ENDOWMENTS (IRELAND) COMMISSION.

TO HIS EXCELLENCY LAURENCE, EARL OF ZETLAND.

LORD LIEUTENANT GENERAL AND GENERAL GOVERNOR OF IRELAND.

MAY IT PLEASE YOUR EXCELLENCY,

We, the Commissioners appointed under the Educational Endowments (Ireland) Act, 1885, have the honour to submit to your Excellency the following Report of our proceedings during the fourth year in which the Act has been in operation, that is, from October 1, 1888, to September 30, 1889.

The number of meetings which we have held during the year for the transaction of the business of the Commission has been as follows:

120 Meetings of the full Commission.
39 Meetings of the Judicial Commissioners.
33 Meetings of the Assistant Commissioners.

Total, 192 Meetings.

A Return of the attendances at these Meetings is annexed; *infra* p. xlix.

We have also individually taken part in the drafting of Schemes, and have attended at the Office of the Commission for the transaction of routine business. The annexed abstract of our minutes, *infra* pp. l–cxxvii, contains a summary of our proceedings during the year.

Public Sittings of the Commission.

During the year we held the following public sittings for the purpose of taking evidence respecting the amount and character of the endowments, the efficiency of the schools, and the state of education in each locality; or of considering objections and amendments in cases where Schemes had been already published:—

MULLINGAR.—At the Court House, Monday, October 8, 1888.

Hevey's Institution, Mullingar.
Wilson's Hospital, Multyfarnham.
Farra School, Bunbrosna (Incorporated Society).
Meath and Ardagh Diocesan Free School.
Westmeath Protestant Orphan Society.
Belvedere Orphan Institution, Tyrrellspass.
Loreto Convent Intermediate School, Mullingar (Visit).

SLIGO.—At the Court House, Tuesday, October 9, 1888.

Erasmus Smith's School, Sligo.
Ballinorly National School, Calry, Sligo.
Diocesan Free School, Sligo.
Primrose Grange School (Incorporated Society).
College of the Immaculate Conception, Sligo. (No appearance.)
Castleconnor and Kilglass Schools (Valentine Endowment).
National School, Manorhamilton (Masterson Endowment).

BOYLE.—At the Court House, Wednesday, October 10, 1888.

Boyle Academical Institution.

ELPHIN.—At the School, Wednesday, October 10, 1888.

Bishop Hodson's Grammar School, Elphin.

NEWTOWNFORBES.—At Lisnaboe School, Thursday, October 11, 1888.

Lisnaboe Endowed School, Newtownforbes.
Clonguish School (West Endowment).

ROSCOMMON.—At the School, Thursday, October 11, 1888.

The Ranelagh School, Roscommon (Inspection).

GALWAY.—At the Court House, Friday, October 12, 1888.

Ilserton School, Kilcreest (Persse Endowment). (No appearance.)
Erasmus Smith's Grammar School, Galway.
Lombard Street National Schools, Galway.
St. Ignatius' College, Galway.
St. Joseph's Seminary, Nun's Island, Galway.
Christian Brothers Schools, Clarenbridge, Galway. (No appearance.)
Rockfield Institution, Ballinakill, Clifden.

TUAM.—At the Court House, Saturday, October 13, 1888.

Diocesan Free School, Tuam.
St. Jarlath's College, Tuam.

LONDONDERRY.—At the Court House, Friday, October 19, 1888.

Robertson Endowments, Co. Donegal. (Objections.)
Londonderry Academical Institution. (Objections.)

COLERAINE.—At the Town Hall, Saturday, October 20, 1888.

Irish Society's Schools, Beresford Place, Coleraine.
Camus School, Castleroe.

MAGHERAFELT.—At the Court House, Monday, October 22, 1888.

Rainey's School, Magherafelt. (Objections.)

BALLYMENA.—At the Court House, Tuesday, October 23, 1888.

Guy's Free School, Ballymena. (Objections.)
Ballymena Collegiate School. (Objections.)

HOLYWOOD.—At the Court House, Wednesday, October 24, 1888.

Sullivan Schools, Holywood. (Objections.)

BANGOR.—At the Court House, Wednesday, October 24, 1888.

Endowed School, Bangor.
Charitable Endowment, Bangor.
Ballygrainey National School, Bangor.
Ballymullan (Crawfordsburn) National School, Bangor.
Ballysallagh National School, Bangor.
Ballyvester School, Bangor.

DONAGHADEE.—At the Court House, Thursday, October 25, 1888.

Mount Alexander Endowed School, Donaghadee.
National School (No. 1), Donaghadee.
Admiral Leslie's Free School, Donaghadee.
Carrowdore (Woburn) National School.

BALLYWALTER.—At the Court House, Thursday, October 25, 1888.

Joseph Brown's Endowment, Co. Down.
Tubberspadderig National School, Inishargy.
Tully Cavey National School, Grey Abbey.
Mountstewart Erasmus Smith's School, Grey Abbey.

BELFAST.—In the Grand Jury Room, Friday, October 26, 1888.

Application from the Diocesan Council of Down Connor and Dromore for the incorporation of a Diocesan Governing Body for Educational Endowments of "The Church of Ireland."
Application from the Elementary Education Committee of the General Assembly for the incorporation of Governing Bodies for Educational Endowments connected with the Presbyterian Church in Ireland.
Brown Street Schools, Belfast.
Charitable Bequest of Samuel Ledley, for the purpose of erecting a School in Ballymacarett.
Presbyterian Orphan Society of Ireland.
St. Enoch's National Schools, Belfast (Inspection).

CARRICKFERGUS.—At the Court House, Saturday, October 27, 1888.

Parochial School, Carrickfergus.

LARNE.—At the Court House, Saturday, October 27, 1888.

Grammar School, Larne.

DOWNPATRICK.—At the Court House, Monday, October 29, 1888.
Blue School, Downpatrick (Southwell Endowment).
Parochial Schools, Downpatrick.
Killough National School, Downpatrick.
Shrigley National School, Killyleagh.
Carrickinab National School, Tyrella.

CLANE.—At the School, Saturday, November 10, 1888.
Hewetson's School, Clane.

CELBRIDGE.—At the Institution, Saturday, November 10, 1888.
Celbridge Institution, Incorporated Society (Inspection).

DUBLIN.—At the Office of the Commission, Saturday, May 4, 1889.
Ulster Royal School Endowments. (Deputation from the General Synod.)

ROCHFORT BRIDGE.—At the Convent National Schools, Tuesday, May 14, 1889.
The Field Charity, Rochfort Bridge.

DUBLIN.—At the Four Courts, Friday, May 31, 1889.
Ulster Royal School Endowments.—Revised Draft Scheme. (Objections.)

BALTINGLASS.—At the Court House, Monday, July 1, 1889.
Stratford Lodge Schools, Baltinglass.
Erasmus Smith's School, Kiltegan. (No appearance.)

KILTEGAN.—At the School, Monday, July 1, 1889.
Erasmus Smith's School, Kiltegan. (Inspection.)

RATHVILLY.—At the School, Tuesday, July 2, 1889.
D'Israeli's School, Rathvilly.

NEW ROSS.—At the Court House, Wednesday, July 3, 1889.
Endowed School, New Ross.
Ballyanne Schools, New Ross (Bolger Endowment). (No appearance.)
Hill's School, New Ross (Tottenham Endowment).
Whitechurch, Rochestown (Paul Endowment).
Whitechurch Parochial School (Glascott Endowment).

WEXFORD.—At the Court House, Thursday, July 4, 1889.
The Tate School, Wexford.
Erasmus Smith's School, Wexford.
Ferns Diocesan School.
St. Peter's College, Wexford.
Duncormick School (Richards Endowment).
Kennedy Endowment, Rathaspeck.
Application from the Diocesan Council of Ferns for the Incorporation of a Diocesan Governing Body for Educational Endowments of "the Church of Ireland."

CARYSFORT, AUGHRIM.—At the Royal School, Friday, July 5, 1889.
Carysfort Royal School Endowment.
Macreddin National School. (Inspection.)

ARKLOW.—At the Court House, Friday, July 5, 1889.
Carysfort Royal School Endowment. (Application for Transfer to Arklow for Industrial Education).
The Incorporated Society's School, Arklow.

WICKLOW.—At the Court House, Saturday, July 6, 1889.
Grattan Endowed School, Ashford.
Diocesan School, Wicklow.
Wicklow Free School.
Trevelan Orphan School (Waldron Endowment).

DUBLIN.—At the Office of the Commission, Monday, July 8, 1889.
Hewetson's School, Clane. (Objections.)

DUBLIN.—At the Office of the Commission, Thursday, July 11, 1889.
Rainey School, Magherafelt. (Deputation from the General Assembly and the Presbytery of Magherafelt.)

ANAHILT.—At the School, Tuesday, July 23, 1889.
Endowed School, Anahilt.

Publication of Draft Schemes.

The following Tables contain a list of the Draft Schemes already completed and published as prescribed by the Act, section 31, those which have been framed by consent being so marked; with the dates of the several stages through which they have passed, the value of the endowments dealt with, and the estimated amount to be annually administered under each Scheme. Forty Schemes have been finally approved by the Lord Lieutenant in Council, and are now in operation, four have been provisionally approved but not yet finally approved, three have been signed by the Judicial Commissioners and are now awaiting His Excellency's consideration, and thirty Draft Schemes have been published and await consideration of the objections and amendments received by us. Scheme No. 3, which has been remitted to us by the Lord Lieutenant in Council with a declaration, is still under our consideration as to a portion of the Endowments comprised therein; Scheme No. 34, for the reconstitution of "The Commissioners of Education in Ireland," and for the future government of the Ulster Royal Schools, is at present under revision, with the object of carrying out the declaration with which it has recently been remitted to us.

TABLE I.—DRAFT SCHEMES already published, and stages through which each Scheme has passed:—

Number of Scheme	Endowment. County.	Locality.	Name.	Draft Scheme [illegible] published.	Scheme signed by Judicial Commissioners.	Scheme [illegible] by the Lord Lieutenant in Council.	[illegible] approved by Lord Lieutenant in Council.	Scheme finally approved by Lord Lieutenant in Council.
1	Dublin,	[illegible]	[illegible] Borough Schools,	[illegible]	[illegible]	Oct. [illegible]	[illegible]	—
[illegible]	"	"	[illegible]	—	May [illegible]	May [illegible]	Aug. [illegible]	Oct. [illegible]
[illegible]	"	Dublin,	Church of Ireland Training College and [illegible]	[illegible]	Sept. [illegible]	Oct. [illegible]	April [illegible]	June [illegible]
[illegible]	"	[illegible]	[illegible]	June [illegible]	Sept. [illegible]	Oct. [illegible]	[illegible]	—
[illegible]	"	Dublin,	[illegible] Female Orphan School,	Aug. [illegible]	Nov. [illegible]	Nov. [illegible]	March [illegible]	June [illegible]
[illegible]	"	[illegible] and [illegible]	[illegible] Parochial [illegible]	Aug. [illegible]	[illegible]	Dec. [illegible]	May [illegible]	[illegible]
[illegible]	"	Dublin,	[illegible] Presbyterian Church [illegible]	[illegible]	May [illegible]	May [illegible]	July [illegible]	Oct. [illegible]
7	Antrim,	Belfast,	[illegible]	[illegible]	May [illegible]	May [illegible]	August [illegible]	Oct. [illegible]
8	"	"	Ulster Society for the Education of the Deaf and Dumb, and the Blind,	[illegible]	May [illegible]	May [illegible]	[illegible]	—
	"	"	Ulster Society (Amended Scheme),	—	Feb. [illegible]	Feb. [illegible]	[illegible]	[illegible]
	"	"	Ulster Society (Further amended Scheme),	—	July [illegible]	July [illegible]	[illegible]	[illegible]
9	Dublin,	Dublin,	St. Patrick's Cathedral Schools [illegible]	[illegible]	May [illegible]	May [illegible]	July [illegible]	[illegible]
10	"	"	[illegible] College and [illegible] School,	[illegible]	May [illegible]	May [illegible]	July [illegible]	[illegible]
11	[illegible]	[illegible]	[illegible] School,	June [illegible]	[illegible]	[illegible]	[illegible]	May [illegible]
12	Dublin,	Dublin,	[illegible] Society,	June [illegible]	[illegible]	[illegible]	[illegible]	May [illegible]
13	Armagh,	Lurgan,	[illegible] Endowed School,	June [illegible]	Oct. [illegible]	Nov. [illegible]	[illegible]	May [illegible]
14	Dublin,	[illegible]	National Association for Promoting the Education of the Deaf and Dumb,	June [illegible]	Oct. [illegible]	[illegible]	[illegible]	May [illegible]
15	Antrim,	Belfast,	Royal Belfast Academical Institution,	June [illegible]	Feb. [illegible]	Feb. [illegible]	[illegible]	—
	"	"	Royal Belfast Academical Institution (Amended Scheme),	—	July [illegible]	July [illegible]	[illegible]	[illegible]
16	"	"	[illegible] College [illegible]	June [illegible]	Oct. [illegible]	Nov. [illegible]	[illegible]	May [illegible]
17	[illegible]	[illegible]	[illegible] School, [illegible] School, and [illegible] School,	June [illegible]	Oct. [illegible]	Nov. [illegible]	[illegible]	May [illegible]
18	Dublin,	[illegible]	[illegible] School,	June [illegible]	Feb. [illegible]	Feb. [illegible]	April [illegible]	July [illegible]
19	Monaghan,	[illegible]	[illegible] School,	June [illegible]	Oct. [illegible]	Nov. [illegible]	[illegible]	May [illegible]
20	Londonderry,	Coleraine,	Academical Institution,	June [illegible]	Oct. [illegible]	Nov. [illegible]	[illegible]	May [illegible]

TABLE I.—DRAFT SCHEMES already published and stages through which each Scheme has passed—continued.

Number of Scheme.	Endowment. County.	Locality.	Name.	Draft Scheme first published.	Scheme signed by Judicial Commissioners.	Scheme first published by the Lord Lieutenant in Council.	Scheme provisionally approved by Lord Lieutenant in Council.	Scheme finally approved by Lord Lieutenant in Council.
				[illegible].	[illegible].	[illegible].	[illegible].	[illegible].
[illegible]	Antrim,	Lisburn,	[illegible] Endowment ([illegible] School),	June [illegible],	Feb. [illegible],	Feb. [illegible],	Remitted, Aug. [illegible]	—
	"	"	[illegible] Endowment (Amended Scheme),	—	Aug. [illegible],	Aug. [illegible],	[illegible]. Feb. [illegible],	April [illegible]
							[illegible].	[illegible].
[illegible]	"	Belfast,	Ladies' Industrial School,	June [illegible],	Feb. [illegible],	Feb. 11,	April [illegible],	July [illegible].
[illegible]	Londonderry,	Londonderry,	Magee Presbyterian College (Classical School),	June [illegible],	Feb. [illegible],	Feb. 11,	April [illegible],	July [illegible].
[illegible]	"	"	Gwyn's Charitable Institution and Young Endowment.	June [illegible],	—	—	—	—
[illegible]	"	"	Creggan School,	June [illegible],	[illegible]. Oct. [illegible],	[illegible]. Dec. [illegible],	Mar. [illegible],	May [illegible].
[illegible]	Dublin,	Dublin,	Dublin Working Boys' Home and Harding Endowment.	Aug. [illegible],	[illegible]. Feb. [illegible],	[illegible]. Feb. [illegible],	April [illegible],	July [illegible].
[illegible]	"	"	[illegible] Female Orphan School,	Aug. [illegible],	[illegible]. Aug. [illegible],	[illegible]. Aug. [illegible],	—	—
[illegible]	Antrim,	Belfast,	Belfast Royal Academy,	Aug. [illegible],	[illegible]. Feb. [illegible],	[illegible]. Feb. [illegible],	Remitted, May [illegible].	—
	"	"	Belfast Royal Academy (Amended Scheme),	—	June [illegible],	July [illegible],	Oct. [illegible],	Dec. [illegible].
[illegible]	Dublin,	Dublin,	[illegible] Sunday and Daily Schools,	Aug. [illegible],	—	—	—	—
[illegible]	Cavan,	Tullyvin and [illegible],	Tullyvin and [illegible] Schools,	Aug. [illegible],	Feb. [illegible],	Feb. [illegible],	April [illegible],	July [illegible].
[illegible]	Fermanagh,	[illegible],	[illegible] School,	Aug. [illegible],	[illegible] [illegible],	[illegible] [illegible],	April [illegible],	July [illegible].
[illegible]	Dublin,	Dublin,	St. [illegible] Schools and [illegible]'s School (Classical School),	Aug. [illegible],	Feb. [illegible],	Feb. [illegible],	April [illegible],	July [illegible].
[illegible]	Londonderry,	Coleraine,	Laurel Hill School,	Aug. [illegible],	Feb. [illegible],	Feb. [illegible],	April [illegible],	July [illegible].
				[illegible].	[illegible].	[illegible].	[illegible].	
[illegible]	Armagh,	Armagh,	Royal School,	April [illegible],	June [illegible],	July [illegible],	Remitted, [illegible].	—
	Tyrone,	Dungannon,	Royal School,					
	Fermanagh,	Enniskillen,	Royal School,					
	Cavan,	Cavan,	Royal School,					
	Donegal,	Raphoe,	Royal School,					
	King's,	Banagher,	Royal School,					
	Wicklow,	Carysfort,	Royal School,					
								[illegible].
[illegible]	Donegal,	[illegible],	The [illegible] Endowment,	June [illegible],	April [illegible],	May [illegible],	Aug. [illegible],	Oct. [illegible].
[illegible]	Armagh,	Lurgan,	[illegible] National School,	June [illegible],	April [illegible],	May [illegible],	July [illegible],	Oct. [illegible].
[illegible]	Cork,	Cork,	High School for Girls,	June [illegible],	June [illegible],	June [illegible],	Aug. [illegible],	Oct. [illegible].
[illegible]	"	Baltimore,	The Baltimore Fishery School (Classical School),	June [illegible],	April [illegible],	May [illegible],	Aug. [illegible],	Oct. [illegible].
[illegible]	Dublin,	Dublin,	The Royal Irish Academy of Music and the Coulson Endowment.	June [illegible],	April [illegible],	May [illegible],	July [illegible],	Oct. [illegible].
[illegible]	Londonderry,	Londonderry,	Londonderry Academical Institution,	June [illegible],	April [illegible],	May [illegible],	Remitted, Aug. [illegible].	—
	"	"	Londonderry Academical Institution (Amended Scheme).	—	Aug. [illegible],	Aug. [illegible],	Oct. [illegible].	—
[illegible]			The Church of Ireland Victoria Jubilee Fund (Classical Schools).	July [illegible],	April [illegible],	May [illegible],	July [illegible]	Oct. [illegible].
[illegible]	Limerick,	Limerick,	The Villiers' Charitable Institutions,	July [illegible],	June [illegible],	July [illegible],	Oct. [illegible].	—
[illegible]	Antrim,	Ballymena,	Guy's Free School,	July [illegible],	—	—	—	—
[illegible]	"	"	Ballymena Collegiate School,	July [illegible],	—	—	—	—
[illegible]	Tipperary,	Clonmel,	Clonmel Grammar School,	July [illegible],	Aug. [illegible],	Aug. [illegible]	—	—
[illegible]	Kilkenny,	Kilkenny,	Kilkenny College,	Aug. [illegible],	—	—	—	—
[illegible]	Cork,	Cork,	Cork Parochial Schools, Green Coat Hospital, Cork Grammar School, and [illegible]'s Charity (Classical Schools).	Aug. [illegible],	June [illegible],	July [illegible]	Oct. [illegible].	—

TABLE I.—DRAFT SCHEMES already published, and stages through which each Scheme has passed—*continued*.

Number of Scheme	Endowment: County	Endowment: Locality	Endowment: Name	Draft Scheme first published	Scheme signed by Judicial Commissioners	Scheme first published by the Lord Lieutenant in Council	Scheme provisionally approved by Lord Lieutenant in Council	Scheme finally approved by Lord Lieutenant in Council
				[illegible]	[illegible]	[illegible]	[illegible]	[illegible]
[illegible]	Londonderry,	Magherafelt,	Rainey's School, ...	Aug. 11.	—	—	—	—
[illegible]	Kilkenny, .	Thomastown,	Parochial School, ...	Aug. [illegible]	April [illegible]	May 1,	Aug. [illegible]	Oct. [illegible]
[illegible]	Armagh, .	Armagh, .	The [illegible], Mall, and College-street Schools, and "Primate Robinson's Loan Fund."	Aug. [illegible]	April [illegible]	May 1,	Aug. [illegible]	Oct. [illegible]
[illegible]	Down, . .	Holywood, .	The Sullivan Schools, ...	Aug. [illegible]	April [illegible]	May 1,	Aug. [illegible]	Oct. [illegible]
[illegible]	Cork, . .	Cork, . .	The [illegible] Seminary, ...	Aug. [illegible]	April [illegible]	May 1,	July [illegible]	Oct. [illegible]
				[illegible]				
[illegible]	Waterford, .	Waterford, .	[illegible] School, ...	Mar. [illegible]	June [illegible]	July [illegible]	Oct. [illegible]	—
[illegible]	Limerick, .	Limerick, .	[illegible] Road School (General Scheme), .	Mar. [illegible]	—	—	—	—
[illegible]		Diocese of Meath.	The Parochial Schools of the Diocese of Meath; and the Preston School, Navan (General Scheme)	Mar. [illegible]	—	—	—	—
[illegible]	Meath, .	Oldcastle, .	The Gilson Schools, ...	Mar. [illegible]	—	—	—	—
[illegible]	Kildare, .	Clane, . .	[illegible] School (General Scheme), . .	Mar. [illegible]	Aug. [illegible]	Aug. 14,	—	—
[illegible]			The Presbyterian Orphan Society of Ireland (General Scheme)	Mar. [illegible]	June [illegible]	June [illegible]	Aug. [illegible]	Oct. [illegible]
[illegible]	Tipperary, .	Cashel, .	Cashel Corporation School Endowments, .	April [illegible]	—	—	—	—
[illegible]	" .	" .	Cashel Deanery Schools, ...	April [illegible]	—	—	—	—
[illegible]	Antrim, .	Larne, .	Larne Grammar School (General Scheme), .	April [illegible]	—	—	—	—
[illegible]	Cork, . .		The Munster Dairy School and Agricultural Institute.	April [illegible]	—	—	—	—
[illegible]	Down, . .	[illegible]	The [illegible] School Endowment, . . .	May [illegible]	—	—	—	—
[illegible]		[illegible]	The Endowments of and belonging to Congregations under the care of the Presbytery of [illegible]	May [illegible]	—	—	—	—
[illegible]	Cork, . .	Cork, . .	St. Stephen's Hospital (General Scheme), .	May [illegible]	—	—	—	—
[illegible]		Dioceses of Cork, Cloyne, and Ross.	The Parochial Schools of the Dioceses of Cork, Cloyne, and Ross, and Bishop [illegible] School, Cloyne (General Scheme).	May [illegible]	—	—	—	—
[illegible]	Cork, . .	Kinsale, .	The [illegible] School Endowment, . .	May [illegible]	—	—	—	—
[illegible]	[illegible], .	[illegible] Bridge.	The [illegible] Charity (General Scheme), . .	June [illegible]	—	—	—	—
[illegible]	Roscommon,	Elphin, .	Bishop Hodson's Grammar School, . .	June [illegible]	—	—	—	—
[illegible]		Belfast, .	The Orphan Society in the Association of Irish Non-Subscribing Presbyterians and other Free Christians (General Scheme).	June [illegible]	—	—	—	—
[illegible]	Tyrone, .	Strabane, .	The Strabane Academy, ...	June [illegible]	—	—	—	—
[illegible]			The Sabbath School Society for Ireland in connection with the Presbyterian Church (General Scheme).	June [illegible]	—	—	—	—
[illegible]		Diocese of Ferns.	The Parochial Schools of the Diocese of Ferns (General Scheme).	Aug. [illegible]	—	—	—	—
[illegible]	[illegible], .	[illegible],	The [illegible] Charity and the Parochial Schools (General Scheme).	Aug. [illegible]	—	—	—	—
[illegible]		Presbytery of Ballybay.	The Endowments of and belonging to Congregations under the care of the Presbytery of Ballybay (General Scheme).	Aug. [illegible]	—	—	—	—
[illegible]		Diocese of [illegible].	The Parochial Schools of the Diocese of [illegible] (General Scheme).	Aug. [illegible]	—	—	—	—
[illegible]		Diocese of Leighlin.	The Parochial Schools of the Diocese of Leighlin (General Scheme).	Aug. [illegible]	—	—	—	—
[illegible]		Presbytery of Banbridge.	The Endowments of and belonging to Congregations under the care of the Presbytery of Banbridge (General Scheme).	Aug. [illegible]	—	—	—	—
[illegible]	[illegible], .	The [illegible], .	Joseph [illegible]'s Endowment, ...	Aug. [illegible]	—	—	—	—

TABLE II.—ENDOWMENTS of the several Institutions for which Draft Schemes have been published, with the estimated Income of these Institutions from fees, subscriptions, and other sources.

No. of Scheme.	Endowment. County.	Locality.	Name.	Valuation of School Buildings and Premises.	Annual Income of Endowment. From Houses and Lands.	From Fund Funds.	Additional Annual Income from Fees, Subscriptions and other Sources.	Total Annual Amount to be administered under Scheme.
				£ s. d.	£ s. d.	£ s. d.	£ s. d.	£ s. d.
1	Dublin,	Swords,	Swords Old Borough Schools,	[illegible]	—	[illegible]	—	[illegible]
			Swords New Borough Schools,	[illegible]	—		[illegible]	
2	"	Dublin,	Church of Ireland Training College,	[illegible]	—	[illegible]	[illegible]	[illegible]
3	"	Castleknock,	Morgan's School,	[illegible]	[illegible]	[illegible]	—	[illegible]
			Mercer's School (exempted except [illegible]),	—	—	—	—	—
4	"	Dublin,	Methodist Female Orphan School,	[illegible]	—	[illegible]	[illegible]	[illegible]
5	"	[illegible],	[illegible] Parochial School,	[illegible]	—	—	—	[illegible]
		[illegible],	[illegible] Parochial School,	[illegible]	—	[illegible]	—	
6	"	Dublin,	Ormond-quay Presbyterian Church Endowments,	[illegible]	[illegible]	[illegible]	[illegible]	[illegible]
7	Antrim,	Belfast,	[illegible]-street Schools,	[illegible]	[illegible]	—	[illegible]	[illegible]
8	"	"	Ulster Society for the Education of the Deaf and Dumb, and the Blind,	[illegible]	—	[illegible]	[illegible]	[illegible]
9	Dublin,	Dublin,	St. Patrick's Cathedral (Choristers') School,	[illegible]	—	—	[illegible]	[illegible]
			St. Patrick's Deanery Schools,	[illegible]	—	—	—	
			Knight's Endowed School,	[illegible]	[illegible]	—	—	
			[illegible] Endowment,	—	[illegible]	—	—	
10	"	"	Alexandra College,	[illegible]	[illegible]	—	[illegible]	[illegible]
			Alexandra School,	—	—	—	[illegible]	
11	Antrim,	Belfast,	[illegible] School,	[illegible]	[illegible]	[illegible]	[illegible]	[illegible]
12	Dublin,	Dublin,	Hibernian Marine Society,	[illegible]	[illegible]	[illegible]	[illegible]	[illegible]
13	Armagh,	Lurgan,	Watts's Endowed School,	[illegible]	—	[illegible]	[illegible]	[illegible]
14	Dublin,	[illegible],	National Association for the Education of the Deaf and Dumb,	[illegible]	[illegible]	[illegible]	[illegible]	[illegible]
15	Antrim,	Belfast,	Royal Belfast Academical Institution,	[illegible]	[illegible]	[illegible]	[illegible]	[illegible]
16	"	"	Methodist College,	[illegible]	[illegible]	[illegible]	[illegible]	[illegible]
17	Donegal,	Lifford,	[illegible] School,	[illegible]	—	[illegible]	[illegible]	[illegible]
			[illegible] School,	[illegible]	[illegible]	[illegible]	[illegible]	
			[illegible] School,	[illegible]	—	[illegible]	[illegible]	
18	Dublin,	Dublin,	[illegible] Tailors' School,	[illegible]	[illegible]	[illegible]	—	[illegible]
19	Monaghan,	Monaghan,	Collegiate School,	[illegible]	—	—	[illegible]	[illegible]
20	Londonderry	Coleraine,	Academical Institution,	[illegible]	—	[illegible]	[illegible]	[illegible]
21	Antrim,	Lisburn,	[illegible] Endowments,	[illegible]	—	[illegible]	—	[illegible]
22	"	[illegible],	Ladies' Industrial School,	[illegible]	[illegible]	[illegible]	[illegible]	[illegible]
23	Londonderry	Londonderry,	Magee College,	[illegible]	—	[illegible]	[illegible]	[illegible]
24	"	"	Gwyn's Charitable Institution,	[illegible]	[illegible]	[illegible]	—	[illegible]
			Young Endowment,	—	—	[illegible]	—	
25	"	"	Creggan School,	[illegible]	—	—	—	[illegible]
26	Dublin,	Dublin,	Dublin Working Boys' Home,	[illegible]	—	—	[illegible]	[illegible]
			Harding Endowment,	—	—	[illegible]	—	
27	"	"	[illegible] Female Orphan School,	[illegible]	[illegible]	[illegible]	—	[illegible]
28	Antrim,	Belfast,	Belfast Academy,	[illegible]	[illegible]	—	[illegible]	[illegible]
29	Dublin,	[illegible],	[illegible] Day and Daily Schools,	[illegible]	[illegible]	[illegible]	[illegible]	[illegible]
30	Cavan,	Tullyvin,	Tullyvin and [illegible] Schools,	[illegible]	—	[illegible]	—	[illegible]
31	Fermanagh,	Lisnaskea,	[illegible] School,	[illegible]	[illegible]	—	[illegible]	[illegible]
			Carried forward,	[illegible]	[illegible]	[illegible]	[illegible]	[illegible]

* Exclusive of School Fees which do not come into the hands of the Governing Body, but are paid directly to the Masters.
† Exclusive of [illegible] Endowment of £[illegible] for [illegible].
Exclusive of [illegible] Endowment not yet fallen into possession.
§ [illegible]

TABLE II.—ENDOWMENTS of the several Institutions for which Draft Schemes have been published, with the estimated Income of these Institutions from fees, subscriptions, and other sources—continued.

No. of Scheme.	Endowment. County.	Locality.	Name.	Valuation of School Buildings and Premises.	Annual Amount of Endowment. From Estates and Lands.	From Trust Funds.	Estimated Annual Income from Fees, Subscriptions, and other Sources.	Total Annual Amount to be administered under Scheme.
				£ s. d.	£ s. d.	£ s. d.	£ s. d.	£ s. d.
			Brought forward,	[illegible]	[illegible]	[illegible]	[illegible]	[illegible]
[illegible]	Dublin,	Dublin,	St. Peter's School,	[illegible]	[illegible]	[illegible]	[illegible]	[illegible]
			Rev. Wray's School,	—	—	[illegible]		
[illegible]	Londonderry,	Coleraine,	Laurel Hill School,	[illegible]	[illegible]	—	—	[illegible]
[illegible]	Armagh,	Armagh,	Royal School,	[illegible]	[illegible]	[illegible]	—	[illegible]
	Tyrone,	Dungannon,	Royal School,	[illegible]	[illegible]	[illegible]	—	
	Fermanagh,	Enniskillen,	Royal School,	[illegible]	[illegible]	[illegible]	—	
	Cavan,	Cavan,	Royal School,	[illegible]	[illegible]	[illegible]	—	
	Donegal,	Raphoe,	Royal School,	[illegible]	[illegible]	—	—	
	King's,	Banagher,	Royal School,	[illegible]	[illegible]	—	—	
	Wicklow,	Carysfort,	Royal School,	[illegible]	[illegible]	[illegible]	—	
[illegible]	Donegal,	—	The Robertson Endowments,	[illegible]	—	[illegible]	—	[illegible]
[illegible]	Armagh,	Lurgan,	[illegible] National School,	[illegible]	—	—	[illegible]	[illegible]
[illegible]	Cork,	Cork,	High School for Girls,	[illegible]	—	—	[illegible]	[illegible]
[illegible]	"	Baltimore,	The Baltimore Fishery School,	[illegible]	—	—	[illegible]	[illegible]
[illegible]	Dublin,	Dublin,	The Royal Irish Academy of Music,	[illegible]	[illegible]	[illegible]	[illegible]	[illegible]
			The Coulson Endowment,	—	—	[illegible]	—	
[illegible]	Londonderry,	Londonderry,	Londonderry Acad. Institution,	[illegible]	—	—	[illegible]	[illegible]
[illegible]		Whole of Ireland,	The Church of Ireland Widows' Relief Fund,	—	[illegible]	[illegible]	—	[illegible]
[illegible]	Limerick,	[illegible]	Villiers' Charitable Institutions,	[illegible]	[illegible]	[illegible]	—	[illegible]
[illegible]	Antrim,	Ballymena,	Guy's Free School,	[illegible]	—	[illegible]	—	[illegible]
[illegible]	"	"	Ballymena Collegiate School,	[illegible]	—	—	[illegible]	[illegible]
[illegible]	Tipperary,	Clonmel,	Clonmel Endowed School,	[illegible]	[illegible]	—	—	[illegible]
[illegible]	Kilkenny,	Kilkenny,	Kilkenny College,	[illegible]	[illegible]	—	—	[illegible]
[illegible]	Cork,	Cork,	St. Finn Barr's Parochial Schools,	[illegible]	[illegible]	—	—	[illegible]
			St. Luke's Parochial Schools,	—	—	—	[illegible]	
			St. Mary Shandon Parochial School,	[illegible]	—	[illegible]	[illegible]	
			St. Nicholas' Parochial and Industrial Schools,	[illegible]	—	[illegible]	[illegible]	
			St. Peter's Parochial Schools,	[illegible]	[illegible]	[illegible]	—	
			Christ Church Parochial Schools,	[illegible]	[illegible]	[illegible]	[illegible]	
			Green Coat Hospital,	[illegible]	[illegible]	[illegible]	—	
			Grammar School,	[illegible]	—	—	[illegible]	
			[illegible] Charity,	[illegible]	[illegible]	[illegible]	—	
[illegible]	Londonderry,	Magherafelt,	Rainey's School,	[illegible]	[illegible]	—	[illegible]	[illegible]
[illegible]	Kilkenny,	Thomastown,	Parochial School,	[illegible]	—	[illegible]	[illegible]	[illegible]
[illegible]	Armagh,	Armagh,	The Drelincourt School,	[illegible]	[illegible]	—	—	[illegible]
			The Mall School,	[illegible]	[illegible]	—	[illegible]	
			The Callan-street Schools,	[illegible]	—	—	—	
			Primate Robinson's Loan Fund,	—	—	[illegible]	—	
[illegible]	Down,	Holywood,	The Sullivan Schools,	[illegible]	—	[illegible]	[illegible]	[illegible]
[illegible]	Cork,	Cork,	The [illegible],	[illegible]	—	[illegible]	[illegible]	[illegible]
			Carried forward,	[illegible]	[illegible]	[illegible]	[illegible]	[illegible]

* The School Fees do not come into the hands of the Governing Body, but are paid directly to the [illegible].
† There is an [illegible] in the hands of the [illegible] in a [illegible] of the French Government [illegible].
‡ The Fees are paid directly to the masters, with the exception of the fees for Modern Languages, which are retained by the Governors, who pay [illegible] a year to the Modern Languages Master.
§ Rev. Mr. King, the present master, holds [illegible] under Irish Church Act, 1869.
‖ These schools are about to be rebuilt.
¶ Estimated, the school-house not appearing in valuation books.

TABLE II.—ENDOWMENTS of the several Institutions for which Draft Schemes have been published with the estimated Income of those Institutions from fees, subscriptions, and other sources,—*continued*.

No.	Endowment. County.	Locality.	Name.	Valuation of School Buildings and Premises. £ s. d.	Annual Income of Endowment. From Rents and Lands. £ s. d.	From Trust Funds. £ s. d.	Estimated Annual Income from Fees, Subscriptions and other Sources. £ s. d.	Total Annual Amount to be administered under Scheme. £ s. d.
			Brought forward,	[illegible]	[illegible]	[illegible]	[illegible]	[illegible]
53	Waterford,	Waterford,	[illegible] School,	[illegible]	—	—	—	[illegible]
54	Limerick,	Limerick,	[illegible] School,	[illegible]	—	[illegible]	[illegible]	[illegible]
55		Diocese of Meath.	The Parochial Schools of the Diocese of Meath.	[illegible]	[illegible]	[illegible]	[illegible]	[illegible]
			The Preston School, Navan,	[illegible]	[illegible]	[illegible]	—	
56	Meath,	Oldcastle,	The Gilson Schools,	[illegible]	—	[illegible]	[illegible]	[illegible]
57	Kildare,	Clane,	[illegible] School,	[illegible]	[illegible]	[illegible]	[illegible]	[illegible]
58			The Presbyterian Orphan Society of Ireland.	[illegible]	[illegible]	[illegible]	[illegible]	[illegible]
59	Tipperary,	Cashel,	Cashel Corporation School Endowments.	[illegible]	[illegible]	—	—	[illegible]
60	"	"	Cashel Nunnery Schools,	[illegible]	[illegible]	[illegible]	[illegible]	[illegible]
61	Antrim,	Larne,	Larne Grammar School,	[illegible]	—	[illegible]	[illegible]	[illegible]
62	Cork,		The Munster Dairy School and Agricultural Institute.	[illegible]	—	[illegible]	[illegible]	[illegible]
63	Down,	[illegible]	The [illegible] School Endowments.	—	—	[illegible]	—	[illegible]
64		Presbytery of Dublin.	The Endowments of and belonging to Congregations under the care of the Presbytery of Dublin.	[illegible]	—	—	[illegible]	[illegible]
65	Cork,	Cork,	St. Stephen's Hospital,	[illegible]	[illegible]	[illegible]	—	[illegible]
66		Dioceses of Cork, Cloyne, and Ross.	The Parochial Schools of the Dioceses of Cork, Cloyne, and Ross.	[illegible]	[illegible]	[illegible]	[illegible]	[illegible]
			Bishop Crowe's School, Cloyne,	[illegible]	[illegible]	[illegible]	[illegible]	
67	Cork,	Kinsale,	The Southwell School Endowment.	[illegible]	[illegible]	—	—	[illegible]
68	Westmeath,	[illegible] Bridge.	The [illegible] Charity,	[illegible]	[illegible]	—	[illegible]	[illegible]
69	Roscommon,	Elphin,	Bishop Hodson's Grammar School,	[illegible]	[illegible]	—	[illegible]	[illegible]
70		Belfast,	The Orphan Society of the Association of Irish Non-Subscribing Presbyterians and other Free Christians.	—	—	[illegible]	[illegible]	[illegible]
71	Tyrone,	[illegible]	The [illegible] Academy,	[illegible]	—	—	—	[illegible]
72			The [illegible] School Society for Ireland in connection with the Presbyterian Church.	—	—	[illegible]	[illegible]	[illegible]
73		Diocese of [illegible]	The Parochial Schools of the Diocese of [illegible]	[illegible]	[illegible]	[illegible]	[illegible]	[illegible]
74	Down,	Downpatrick,	The [illegible] Charity,	[illegible]	[illegible]	[illegible]	—	[illegible]
			The Parochial Schools,	[illegible]	—	—	[illegible]	
75		Presbytery of Ballybay.	The Endowments of and belonging to Congregations under the care of the Presbytery of Ballybay.	[illegible]	—	—	[illegible]	[illegible]
76		Diocese of Kilmore.	The Parochial Schools of the Diocese of Kilmore.	[illegible]	[illegible]	[illegible]	[illegible]	[illegible]
77		Diocese of Leighlin.	The Parochial Schools of the Diocese of Leighlin.	[illegible]	[illegible]	[illegible]	[illegible]	[illegible]
78		Presbytery of Banbridge.	The Endowments of and belonging to Congregations under the care of the Presbytery of Banbridge.	[illegible]	[illegible]	—	[illegible]	[illegible]
79	Down,	The Ards,	Joseph Brown's Endowment,	—	[illegible]	[illegible]	—	[illegible]
			Total,	[illegible]	[illegible]	[illegible]	[illegible]	[illegible]

* The School Fees do not come into the hands of the Governing Body, but are paid directly to the [illegible].
† This does not include farm produce.
Estimated.

Objections and Amendments

During a period of two months from the first publication of each Draft Scheme, objections may be lodged, and amendments may be proposed, under section 32 of the Act, by any public body or person interested. In accordance with this provision, objections were lodged and amendments were proposed during the past year by the several public bodies and persons mentioned in the following list:—

Draft Scheme No. 54. The Roxborough Road School, Limerick.

1. Rev. James Fitzgerald Gregg, M.A.
2. Most Rev. Dr. O'Dwyer, Bishop of Limerick.

Draft Scheme No. 55. The Parochial Schools of the Diocese of Meath; and the Preston School, Navan.

1. Diocesan Council of Meath.
2. Down, Connor and Dromore Church Education Society.
3. Rev. James E. H. Murphy, M.A., Rector of Rathcore.

Draft Scheme No. 56. The Gilson Schools, Oldcastle.

1. James Lenox Naper, Esq., D.L., one of the existing Trustees.
2. Diocesan Council of Meath.
3. Rev. Laurence Gaynor, P.P., Oldcastle, one of the existing Trustees.
4. Mrs. M. J. De Vere, Principal Teacher of Female School.
5. R. H. Connellan, Assistant Master.

Draft Scheme No. 57. Howetson's School, Clane.

1. Existing Trustees of the School.
2. Rev. S. O. Cotton, Rector of Carogh.

Draft Scheme No. 58. The Presbyterian Orphan Society.

1. Existing Governing Body.

Draft Scheme No. 59. The Cashel Corporation School Endowment.

1. Town Commissioners of Cashel.
2. Thomas Laffan, M.D., and Andrew Mulcahy, Citizens of Cashel.

Draft Scheme No. 60. The Cashel Deanery Schools.

1. Incorporated Society for promoting English Protestant Schools in Ireland.
2. Town Commissioners of Cashel.
3. Thomas Laffan, M.D., and Andrew Mulcahy, Citizens of Cashel.

Draft Scheme No. 61. The Larne Grammar School.

1. Existing Trustees of the School.

Draft Scheme No. 62. The Munster Dairy School and Agricultural Institute.

1. Commissioners of National Education in Ireland.
2. Existing Local Committee of the School.
3. Mayor of Cork and other persons in the City and County of Cork.

Draft Scheme No. 63. The Lalloy School Endowments.

1. Ven. Charles Seaver, M.A., Archdeacon of Connor.

Draft Scheme No. 64. The Endowments of and belonging to Congregations under the care of the Presbytery of Dublin.

1. Presbytery of Dublin.
2. Congregational Committee of Christ Church, Rathgar.

Draft Scheme No. 65. St. Stephen's Hospital, Cork.

1. Existing Trustees of the Hospital.

Draft Scheme No. 66. The Parochial Schools of the Dioceses of Cork Cloyne and Ross, and Bishop Crowe's School, Cloyne.

1. Proposed Governing Body.
2. Diocesan Synod of Cork, Cloyne, and Ross.
3. Very Rev. H. T. Fleming, M.A., Dean of Cloyne.
4. Rev. Robert St. J. Ashworth, M.A., Rector of Athnowen.
5. Rev. Louis E. Fleury, M.A., Rector of Kilworth.
6. Rev. Robert F. Clarke, Rector of [illegible].
7. Ven. Henry J. Woodruffe, M.A., Archdeacon of Ross, and Rector of Lislee.
8. Rev. G. R. Swanton, Rector of Aghadown.
9. Rev. S. MacDonnell, Rector of Kilmocomoge.
10. Rev. G. M'Fetridge, M.A., Rector of Kilgariffe.
11. Rev. Walter Lamb, Rector of Desertserges.
12. Colonel W. St. L. Alcock Stawell, D.L.
13. R. U. Penrose Fitzgerald, Esq., M.P.
14. W. D'Esterre Parker, Esq.

Draft Scheme No. 67. The Southwell School Endowment, Kinsale.

1. Select Vestry of the Parish of Kinsale.
2. Rev. J. Canon Cotter, P.P., Kinsale, on behalf of the Roman Catholic Community of Kinsale.

Draft Scheme No. 68. The Shiel Charity, Rochfort Bridge.

1. Most Rev. Dr. Nulty, Bishop of Meath.

Draft Scheme No. 69. Bishop Hodson's Grammar School, Elphin.

1. Very Rev. W. Warburton, D.D., Dean of Elphin.
2. Chapter of the Cathedral, Elphin.
3. Diocesan Synod of Elphin.
4. Select Vestry of St. John's Parish, Sligo.
5. Inhabitants of Ougham Parish.
6. Inhabitants of the Town and neighbourhood of Elphin.
7. Inhabitants of the Town and neighbourhood of Strokestown.
8. Sir Robert A. Hodson, Bart.

Draft Scheme No. 70. The Orphan Society of the Association of Irish Non-Subscribing Presbyterians and other Free Christians.

1. Existing Directors and General Purposes Committee of the Association.

Draft Scheme No. 71. The Strabane Academy.

1. Existing Managing Committee of the Academy.
2. Æneas Kerr, M.A., Principal.

Draft Scheme No. 72. The Sabbath School Society for Ireland in connection with the Presbyterian Church.

1. Existing Executive Committee of the Society.

Draft Scheme No. 73. The Parochial Schools of the Diocese of Ferns.

1. Rev. James P. M. French, Rector of Clonegal.
2. Rev. Charles L. M. Jones, Rector of Preban and Moyne.
3. Rev. J. Meredith, LL.D., Rector of Killegney.
4. Rev. J. K. Latham, D.D., Rector of Wexford.
5. Rev. W. W. Carroll, M.A., Rector of Bannow.

Draft Scheme No. 74. The Southwell Charity, and the Parochial Schools, Downpatrick.

1. Committee of Representatives of original Subscribers of £50 to the Parochial Schools, of present Subscribers to the Schools, and of the Select Vestry.
2. Very Rev. Edward Maguire, D.D., Dean of Down.
3. Wm. Johnston, J.P., existing Trustee.
4. John R. M'Dowell, Manager of the Parochial Schools.
5. Dr. J. Wykeham Olphert.
6. Robert Stewart, Master of "The Blue School," Downpatrick.

Draft Scheme No. 75. Joseph Brown's Endowments, County Down.

1. Existing Trustees of the Endowment.
2. Remonstrant Synod of Ulster.
3. Managers of the Schools situated in the Districts defined by the Will of the late Joseph Brown.
4. Rev. L. M'Kenna, P.P., Manager of Ballyroney National School.
5. Minister and Members of Ballyhemlin Remonstrant Congregation.
6. Wm. Watson, Agent over the Ayle Estate.

After the consideration of objections and amendments lodged to the Draft Scheme No. 84, for the reconstitution of "The Commissioners of Education in Ireland," and for the future Government of the Royal School Endowments, a Revised Draft Scheme was published, to which further objections and amendments were received from the following public bodies and persons interested, and were considered at a Public Sitting held on May 31, 1889:—

The existing Governing Body—

1. Commissioners of Education in Ireland.

Bodies representing Religious Denominations—

2. "General Synod of the Church of Ireland."
3. Diocesan Councils of Armagh, Derry and Raphoe, Kilmore, and Clogher.
4. Intermediate Education Committee of the General Assembly of the Presbyterian Church in Ireland.
5. Presbytery of Raphoe.

Persons representing Religious Denominations—

6. Most Rev. Dr. Logue, Archbishop of Armagh.
7. Most Rev. Dr. Donnelly, Bishop of Clogher.
8. Most Rev. Dr. M'Gennis, Bishop of Kilmore.
9. Very Rev. B. M'Namee, P.P., V.F., Omagh.
10. Very Rev. Thos. Byrne, P.P., Dungannon.
11. Very Rev. Canon Donnelly, P.P., Magherafelt.

Local Bodies, Public Meetings, &c.—

12. Local Committee of Protestant Denominations in the County of Fermanagh.
13. Raphoe proposed Local Boards (Protestant and Roman Catholic).

14. Schoolmasters Association.

Persons claiming Vested Interests—

15.	Rev. W. M. Morgan, LL.D., Armagh,	Head Masters of the Royal Schools
16.	Rev. F. H. Ringwood, LL.D., Dungannon,	
17.	Rev. W. Steele, D.D., Enniskillen,	
18.	Rev. J. A. Weir, LL.D., Raphoe,	
19.	Rev. W. P. Moore, M.A., Cavan,	
20.	T. Gordon, Esq., M.A., Armagh,	Assistant Masters in the Royal Schools
21.	W. H. Gunning, Esq., B.A., Dungannon, M. Beckett, Esq., B.A., Dungannon, T. G. Gambier, Esq., Dungannon, C. Henzie, Esq., Enniskillen,	
22.	W. J. Valentine, Esq., Enniskillen.	
23.	W. Brown, Cavan.	

Other Persons—

24. A. Nelson, Armagh.
25. Rev. John Knox Leslie, The Manse, Cookstown.

Draft Schemes in Preparation.

The following is a list of Endowments appearing to come within the jurisdiction of the Commission with respect to which preliminary inquiries were held before September 30, 1889. It includes the cases of Endowments in which application for the settlement of Schemes has been made by the existing governing bodies, but which would otherwise be exempt from the jurisdiction of the Commission under the provisions of section 7 of the Act.

In some of the cases on the following list Draft Schemes are in preparation; in others the expediency of publishing Schemes is under consideration, or further inquiries are in progress.

A. (1). Endowments under the control of the Commissioners of Education in Ireland:—

Banagher Royal School.
Carysfort Royal School.

The Diocesan Free School Endowments of—

Leighlin and Ossory.
Meath and Ardagh.
Tuam, Killala, and Achonry.

Endowments of private foundation—

Eyrecourt School, Co. Galway.
Midleton School, Co. Cork.
Ballyroan School, Queen's County.

(2). The Endowments under the management of the Incorporated Society for promoting English Protestant Schools in Ireland.

(3). The Endowments of the Schools founded by Erasmus Smith.

(4). The Parochial Schools of "The Church of Ireland" in the following Dioceses:—

Armagh.
Clogher.
Derry.
Down, Connor, and Dromore.
Tuam.
Killala and Achonry.
Dublin.
Glendalough.
Kildare.
Killaloe, Ross.
Clonfert and Kilmacduagh.
Ardfert and Aghadoe.

(5). The Endowments belonging to Congregations under the care of the following Presbyteries:—

Ahoghill.
Ards.
Ballymena.
Belfast.
Carrickfergus.
Coleraine.
Connaught.
Newry.
Rathfriland.

B. Endowments classified according to Provinces and Counties, as follows:—

Province of Leinster—

County of Carlow—

D'Israeli's School, Bough, Rathvilly.

City of Dublin—

Gardiner's Charity.
Infant School, Trinity Place.
Love's Charity.
Queen's Institute.
The Ralph Macklin School.
Schools formerly in connection with the Unitarian Congregation, Strand Street.
School formerly known as "[illegible] Street School."
Lowten Apprenticeship Fund.

County of Dublin—

Rathmines Township Schools.
The Drummond Institution, Chapelizod.

County of Kilkenny—

[illegible] School, Kilkenny.

County of Longford—

[illegible] Endowed School, Newtownforbes.
[illegible] School (West Endowment).

County of Louth—

Blue School, Drogheda.
Endowed School, Ardee.
Endowed School, Dundalk.
Grammar School, Dundalk (Erasmus Smith's).

County of Wexford—

Ballymore Schools, New Ross (Hodge Endowment).
Duncormick School (Richards Endowment).
Endowed School, New Ross.
Erasmus Smith's School, Wexford.
Hill School, New Ross (Tottenham Endowment).
The Tate School, Wexford.
Whitechurch Parochial School (Glascott Endowment).
Whitechurch, Stokestown (Peel Endowment).

Province of Leinster—*continued*—

County of Wicklow—

Crofton Endowed School, Ashford.
Erasmus Smith's School, Kiltegan.
Stratford Lodge Schools, Baltinglass.
Diocesan School, Wicklow.
Free School, Wicklow.
Tomriland Orphan School, (Waldron Endowment).

Province of Munster—

City of Cork—

Lapp's Charity.
Cork School of Science, Art and Music.

County of Cork—

Aghada National School.
Cove National Endowed Boys School.
Crofton School, Churchfield, Macroom.
Endowed School, Bandon.
Endowed School, Charleville.
Endowed School, Youghal.
Erasmus Smith's School, Bandon.
Fermoy College.
Girls Industrial School, Bandon.
Rahan School, Mallow (Custer Endowment).

County of Limerick—

Leamy's Free School, Limerick.
Mungret Agricultural School, Limerick.

County of Tipperary—

Charleville School, Clonmel.

County of Waterford—

Alcock's Apprenticeship Endowment, Waterford.
Endowed School, Lismore.
Blue School, Waterford (Mason Endowment).
Protestant Orphan School, Waterford.
School of Industry, Lady Lane, Waterford.

Province of Ulster—

County of Antrim—

Brown Street Schools, Belfast.
English School, Ballymena (formerly Erasmus Smith's).

Province of Ulster—*continued*—

County of Down—

Admiral Leslie's Free School, Donaghadee.
Ballywalter School, Bangor.
Ballymaconnell National School, Bangor.
Ballyrobert (Crawfordsburn) National School, Bangor.
Ballysallagh National School, Bangor.
Carrickmannan National School, Tyrella.
Carrowdore (Woburn) National School.
Camberwell Endowment, Bangor.
Endowed School, Annahilt.
Endowed School, Bangor.
Killough National School, Downpatrick.
Mount Alexander Endowed School, Donaghadee.
Mountstewart Erasmus Smith's School, Grey Abbey.
No. 1 National School, Donaghadee.
Shrigley National School, Killyleagh.
Tubber-na-Carrig National School, Inishargy.
Tullycavey National School, Grey Abbey.

County of Fermanagh—

Anne Hall's Endowment for Agricultural Education.

County of Londonderry—

Anne Hall's Endowment for Agricultural Education.
Camus School, Coleraine.
Foyle College, Londonderry.
Irish Society's Schools, Beresford Place, Coleraine.

Province of Connaught—

County of Galway—

D'Arcy School, Kilchreest (Persse Endowment).
Rockfield Institution, Ballinahill, Clifden.

County of Leitrim—

National School, Manorhamilton (Kesterson Endowment).

County of Roscommon—

Academical Institution, Boyle.
Anne Hall's Endowments.

County of Sligo—

Castleconnor (Ardvally and Scurmore), and [illegible] Schools (Valentine Endowment).
Ballinvally National School, Calry, Sligo.
Erasmus Smith's School, Sligo.

Exempt Endowments.

In the following cases, which have been declared exempt upon public inquiry, no application for the settlement of a Scheme has been made by the present governing bodies, and we therefore have at present no jurisdiction to proceed further:—

Province of Leinster—

City of Dublin—

Bethesda Female Orphan School, Upper Dorset Street.
Christian Brothers Schools, Basin Lane.
Girls Almshouse, Great Britain Street.
Female Orphan House, North Circular Road.
Pleasants' Asylum, Lower Camden Street.
St. Brigid's Catholic Ragged Schools.
St. Catherine's National Schools, Meath Street.
St. James's National School, Basin Lane.
St. Michan's National School, North Anne Street.
SS. Michael and John's National Schools, Essex Street.
St. Saviour's Orphanage, Dominick Street.
St. Thomas' Orphanage, Gloucester Street.
Strahan School, in connexion with the Unitarian Church, St. Stephen's Green.
Wesley College, St. Stephen's Green.

County of Dublin—

Parochial Schools, Castleknock.
Parochial School, Finglas.

County of Kilkenny—

Chapel Lane School, Kilkenny.
St. Kieran's College, Kilkenny.

County of Louth—

Christian Brothers Schools, Drogheda.
Christian Brothers Schools, Dundalk.
St. Mary's College, Dundalk.

County of Meath—

St. Finian's Seminary, Navan.

County of Westmeath—

Belvedere Orphanage, Tyrrellspass.
Westmeath Protestant Orphan Society.
Wilson's Hospital, Multyfarnham.

County of Wexford—

St. Peter's College, Wexford.

Province of Munster—

County of Clare—

Christian Brothers Schools, Ennis.
Killaloe Diocesan College, Ennis.

City of Cork—

Christian Brothers Schools, Cork.
Presentation Brothers School, Cork.
St. Finn Barr's Seminary, Cork.
St. Vincent's Orphanage, Cork.

County of Cork—

Carmelite Seminary, Kinsale.
Christian Brothers Schools, Charleville.
Christian Brothers Schools, Youghal.
Convent National School, Youghal.
St. Colman's College, Fermoy.
St. Joseph's Convent School, Kinsale.

County of Limerick—

Cathedral Grammar School, or Blue School, Limerick.
Christian Brothers Schools, Limerick.
Mount St. Vincent School, Limerick.
Sacred Heart College, Limerick.

County of Tipperary—

Christian Brothers Schools, Clonmel.
Rockwell College, Cahir.

County of Waterford—

Bishop Foy's Endowment, Waterford.
Bishop Foy's Apprenticeship Fund, Waterford.
Christian Brothers Schools, Waterford.
Friends School, Newtown, Waterford.
St. John's College, Waterford.

Province of Ulster—

County of Antrim—

Friends Agricultural School, Brookfield.
Friends Provincial School, Lisburn.
St. Malachy's College, Belfast.

County of Armagh—

Jackson's Schools, Forkhill.
St. Patrick's College, Armagh.

County of Cavan—

Christian Brothers Schools, Cavan.
St. Patrick's College, Cavan.

County of Fermanagh—

Vaughan Charter School, Tubrid.

County of Londonderry—

St. Columb's College, Londonderry.

County of Monaghan—

St. Macartan's Seminary, Monaghan.

Province of Connaught—

County of Galway—

Christian Brothers Schools, Clarenbridge.
Lombard Street Schools, Galway.
St. Ignatius College, Galway.
St. Jarlath's College, Tuam.
St. Joseph's Seminary, Nun's Island, Galway.

County of Sligo—

College of the Immaculate Conception, Sligo.

In the cases of Dempsey's Schools, Kells, and Hevey's Institution, Mullingar, the Judicial Commissioners, upon consideration of the circumstances of the endowments, have not thought it expedient to frame Schemes.

Consent Schemes.

In dealing with the ordinary cases of endowments exempt from our jurisdiction, it has been our practice to publish a Draft Scheme when requested to do so by the governing body, and to postpone requiring the formal consent in writing required under section 7 of the Act, until the governing body has had an opportunity of considering the Scheme in print. Where it is proposed to include a large number of exempt endowments in the same Scheme, as, for example, in the Schemes for Dioceses and Presbyteries, we have acted upon the request of the representatives of the denominations to which the schools belong, so far as to introduce the separate endowments into the schedules of the Draft Scheme with an intimation that, before signing the Scheme, we require to be furnished with the written consent of the existing governing body or owner of each endowment found to be exempt, and that if this consent be not furnished, the endowment will be struck out. In a few instances after the publication of the Draft Scheme we have been requested to strike out exempt endowments, but a much larger number of applications have been received to insert additional schools and endowments. As the advantages of placing endowments of similar character under the care of a permanent governing body have become known, the number of applications for Schemes dealing comprehensively with such endowments has increased.

Mixed Endowments.

We have had before us several cases of endowments applicable or applied partly to educational purposes, and partly to charitable purposes other than educational, and we have dealt with some of these, under the powers conferred by section 8 of the Act, by vesting the property constituting these mixed endowments in the governing bodies incorporated for administering the educational trusts of the Schemes.

Several applications have been received from persons and bodies interested in the non-educational portions of mixed endowments to vary trusts which have been found ineffective or unsatisfactory, and we have acceded to these applications so far as we could, having regard to the provisions of section 8 of the Act. In some cases power has been given to the governing bodies of mixed endowments, with the sanction of the Commissioners of Charitable Donations and Bequests, to apply funds held upon non-educational trusts to educational purposes, if at any time they should cease to be beneficially applicable for those purposes to which they were originally devoted.

In Scheme No. 47 we have included a number of endowments connected with "The Church of Ireland" in the city and liberties of Cork, including the endowments of the Parochial Schools, those of the Cork Grammar School and Green Coat Hospital, an endowment founded by Roger Brettridge, and several non-educational endowments belonging to different parishes.

Under this Scheme a comprehensive denominational system of Primary Schools, District Schools, and Intermediate Schools, under the supervision of a central representative Governing Body, with provisions for the advancement of deserving pupils, has been established for the locality.

The non-educational endowments dealt with by the Scheme consist of alms-houses connected with some of the parishes, an annual sum of £112, portion of the Brettridge endowment applicable for the benefit of poor old men unable to work, and William Masters' endowment founded to provide loans to Protestant tradesmen. In some of these cases, upon the application of the parties interested, we have altered obsolete or inconvenient trusts, so as to enable the new central governing body to extend the usefulness of the endowments.

In Scheme No. 60, dealing with the remaining Parochial Schools of the Dioceses of Cork Cloyne and Ross, we were enabled, in the first instance, with the assistance of the diocesan authorities, to include in the schedule upwards of one hundred schools, with their buildings and endowments, and also Bishop Crowe's Grammar School, Cloyne, which it is proposed to utilize as an Intermediate School for the advancement of promising pupils selected by competition from the elementary schools included in the Scheme.

Inspection of Schools.

In all our Schemes we have provided, as prescribed in Section 17 of the Act, for the inspection of every school sharing in the endowments, by an Inspector to be appointed by the Lord Lieutenant. In the cases of schools already subject to inspection as National Schools, we have provided that until an Inspector is appointed by the Lord Lieutenant, the Inspector appointed by the Commissioners of National Education shall be deemed to be the Inspector under the Act. By this means the Governing Body may be saved the cost of a second inspection, which would have to be borne by the endowments.

In the Scheme for the Magee Presbyterian College, Londonderry, which has been in force since July 6, 1888, as the College is in connection with the Royal University, and has a Theological Department under the immediate supervision of the General Assembly, we made a special provision as to inspection. The Scheme permits the General Assembly to select annually three persons of experience in education, not connected with the College or its endowments, and to submit their names to the Lord Lieutenant, who may appoint one of them as Inspector, or may, for cause stated in the minute of appointment, appoint any other person His Excellency may think fit; the Scheme also provides that, until the appointment of an Inspector by the Lord Lieutenant, the Moderator of the General Assembly for the time being shall be deemed to be the Inspector.

We have received communications from many of those interested in endowments, complaining that the cost of inspection may place upon their funds a burden which they are badly able to bear; and the governing bodies of many small endowments which are exempt from our jurisdiction have made the provision for inspection a reason for declining to take advantage of the Act. There is in many cases a fear that as the Act does not define the nature of the proposed inspection, it may interfere unduly with the management of the Schools, and may also involve unnecessary expenditure. It is the general opinion that any inspection which would involve the formal examination of all the pupils of each School would be too costly, and considering the number of examinations to which pupils are already subject, it would in our opinion be injurious to the interests of education. On this subject we would refer to Section 17 of the Act, which appears to indicate that the object of the statutory inspection is to secure that the provisions of the Scheme are efficiently carried out by the Governing Body. We think it most desirable that the arrangements for the inspection required by the Act should be completed as soon as possible, and we may add that, if they prove as satisfactory and inexpensive as those which have been made by the Local Government Board for the audit of accounts under our Schemes, objections and apprehensions now interfering with the beneficial working of our Act will be removed.

The Royal School Endowments.

App. p. 117. Revised Draft Scheme, which was published on April 30, 1889, and sent to all parties interested, with an intimation that further observations upon it would be received and considered before the Scheme was finally settled.

We thought it advisable to omit from this Scheme the provisions of the original Draft relating to the Banagher and Carysfort Royal School Endowments, reserving them to be dealt with separately. The present Scheme is confined to the re-constitution of "The Commissioners of Education" and the future management of the Ulster Royal School Endowments. Pending the settlement of other Schemes, the newly constituted body of Commissioners will continue to hold and administer the Banagher, Carysfort and other Endowments as if the constitution of the Commissioners of Education had not been altered.

App. p. 152. Upon the publication of the Revised Draft Scheme, we received the objections and
App. p. 152. amendments mentioned *supra* p. xv. We held a Public Sitting in Dublin, on May 31, 1889, at which the parties interested were represented, and the objections to the Revised Draft Scheme were fully discussed. The report of the proceedings at this sitting will be found in the Appendix, p. 152. The objections and amendments to the Revised Draft Scheme having been carefully considered, the Scheme was further revised, and having
infra p. xxii. been signed by the Judicial Commissioners on June 28, 1889, it was submitted in due course for the approval of the Lord Lieutenant in Council.

Objections to this Scheme were lodged with the Clerk of the Privy Council, and we were requested to submit our observations upon them for the consideration of the Council. The more important of these objections, with our observations upon them, will be found *infra*, p. xxii. The Scheme was considered by the Judicial Committee of the Privy Council, on October 24 and 25, 1889, and was remitted to us by the Lord Lieutenant in Council on November 6, 1889, with the following declaration:—

1. That the Scheme should provide for the final distribution of the Endowments of each District between the two Local Boards, in the same proportion and on the same conditions as those by which the Scheme proposes to distribute the minimum grants.

2. That the Commissioners of Education should consist of twenty members only, namely, ten Commissioners appointed by the Lord Lieutenant, and ten Commissioners appointed by the Local Boards; and that as regards the appointment of Commissioners by the Lord Lieutenant, the following words be omitted from the end of paragraph 3 of Clause 1 of the Scheme, "and of the five Protestants, one at the least shall be a member of the said Church, one at the least shall be a Presbyterian, and one at the least shall be a Methodist."

3. That the Council are of opinion:—

(a.) That the Armagh Protestant Local Board should consist of eight representatives of "The Church of Ireland," and one representative of the Methodist Church, from the Armagh and Tyrone Districts.

(b.) That the Tyrone Protestant Local Board should consist of eight representatives of the Presbyterian Church, and one representative of the Methodist Church, from the Tyrone and Armagh Districts.

(c.) That the Protestant share in the Armagh School premises be assigned to the Armagh Protestant Local Board, and that the Protestant share in the Dungannon School premises be assigned to the Tyrone Protestant Local Board; subject in both cases to any just claim for compensation by reason of portions being erected by "Church of Ireland" or Presbyterian benefactors.

(d.) That the revenues from the Armagh and Dungannon Royal School Endowments, after crediting the Armagh Protestant Local Board with all private endowments given by donors belonging to "The Church of Ireland," and the Tyrone Protestant Local Board with all private endowments given by donors belonging to the Presbyterian Church, should be allocated equally between the two Boards, and should be applicable according to the Scheme throughout both districts.

4. That more explicit provision should be made for preserving such rights as the assistant masters may have until retirement.

The Judicial Commissioners are now engaged in preparing an Amended Scheme in obedience to the foregoing declaration.

Munster Dairy Farm and Agricultural Institute.

On the occasion of our visit to Cork, in the autumn of 1887, we held an inquiry as to the Munster Agricultural and Dairy School. The school is managed by a Local Committee under the control of the Commissioners of National Education. It is maintained partly by payments made by the Commissioners, partly by pupils' fees and public subscriptions, and shortly before our visit a grant of £3,000 had been obtained by the Local Committee from the Lords Commissioners of Her Majesty's Treasury. We found that the Dairy School was doing very efficient work, and largely attended by young women, who came not only from the county of Cork, but from distant parts of Ireland. The Agricultural School was much less successful, and was attended by a comparatively small number of pupils. We were asked, on the part of the Local Committee, to incorporate a Governing Body consisting in the main of the present Local Committee, as representing the subscribers, and representatives of the Grand Juries of the province, who were expected to contribute to the maintenance of the institution. It appeared to us that by framing a suitable Scheme the Dairy School, which has hitherto been so successful, might be placed on a more permanent and secure foundation.

and that at the same time facilities might be given for the subsequent development of an Agricultural Institute for the South of Ireland. Accordingly we prepared a Draft Scheme which was published on April 29, 1889.

Since the date of our visit we have received a memorial, signed by the Mayor of Cork and other persons of influence in the City and County of Cork, which will be found in Appendix B, p. 362, objecting to the Scheme, partly on the ground that "the proposed Munster Dairy School and Agricultural Institute is not at present desirable nor for the public advantage," and partly on the ground that the proposed constitution of the Governing Body was not satisfactory. We also, on September 6, 1889, received the following resolution from the Local Committee:

> "That having been informed by the Honorary Secretary of the result of his interview with the Chief Secretary for Ireland, on the subject of the establishment of the proposed Munster Dairy and Agricultural Institute, the Committee of the Munster Dairy School regret very much that the refusal of the Chief Secretary to apply to the Treasury for any extension of Government aid for the purpose of affording agricultural instruction to the sons of farmers in the South of Ireland, has the effect of precluding all present hope of developing the existing Dairy Farm into the proposed Munster Agricultural Institute, and consequently the Committee of the Dairy School are reluctantly compelled, at present, to abandon the Scheme, which they believe would have had the effect of doing for the sons of farmers the good which has hitherto been accomplished for their daughters."

We were nevertheless unwilling to abandon the Scheme, and in any case could not do so without ascertaining the wishes of all parties interested. We, therefore, wrote on October 8, 1889, to the Local Committee pointing out that if they were incorporated under our Scheme they would be able at least to carry on the work which they are at present doing, and would be placed in a more favourable position to take advantage of any opportunity that might offer for the further development of the institution. We received a further reply from them on October 9, 1889, enclosing the following resolution:—

> "That the Committee are prepared to accept some simple form of incorporation, if the connexion at present existing between the Local Committee and the Boards of National Education and Public Works can be maintained, until such time as sufficient funds are provided to enable the new governing body to carry out a complete system of agricultural education."

We have since informed them that we will consider their resolution as soon as our other business permits, but that we do not feel ourselves at liberty to undertake the proposed alteration in the Scheme without giving an opportunity, by a further public inquiry, to those interested to state their views.

We are very desirous to proceed with the Scheme, as we believe its completion would be of public advantage, and we hope that the difficulties may be removed which have for the present interrupted its progress.

Technical and Industrial Education.

In all the Schemes admitting of such a provision, we have introduced a clause authorising the Governing Bodies to place their Schools in connection with the Department of Science and Art. Under this clause they will be able, not only to obtain aid from that Department for the teaching of Science and Art, but also to apply to the Local Authorities for grants towards technical education, in accordance with the Technical Instruction Act passed in the last Session of Parliament. We have also given power to the Governing Bodies, in all cases where the nature of the endowments allowed it, to apply a portion of their own funds to the promotion of such branches of technical and industrial education as they may, from time to time, find most suited to the wants of the locality, and to the capacity of the pupils.

All which we have the honour to submit for Your Excellency's consideration as our Report in the premises.

Witness our hands, this Thirteenth day of November, 1889.

GERALD FITZGIBBON.
JOHN NAISH.
GERALD MOLLOY.
ANTHONY TRAILL.
J. B. DOUGHERTY.

WM. EDWARD ELLIS, Secretary.
Office of the Commission, 23, Nassau-street, Dublin.

ULSTER ROYAL SCHOOL ENDOWMENTS.

Portions of the Scheme framed by the Judicial Commissioners, and submitted to Lord Lieutenant in Council, which vary from the corresponding provisions of the Revised Draft Scheme, *infra*, p. 313, or which were the subject of Objections lodged with the Clerk of the Privy Council.

These Objections, with the Observations of the Commissioners thereon, appear *infra*, p. xxxi.

Those portions of the text which are affected by the Declaration of the Lord Lieutenant in Council are printed in italics.

See *ante*, p. xx., *post*, pp. 148, 152, 300, 313, and 323.

Recitals—

The Ulster Royal Schools.
Carysfort Royal School.
Banagher Royal School.
14 & 15 *Charles II.*, c. 10.

The Commissioners of Education in Ireland.

53 *George III.*, c. 107.
3 *George IV.*, c. 79.
17 & 18 *Vic.*, c. 24.

And whereas the said Commissioners have from time to time caused certain sums of money, portion of the funds of other Ulster Royal Schools, remaining after defraying the expenses of the said Schools and paying the Masters thereof, to be applied to the maintenance of the Royal School of Raphoe, whose funds stood and still stand in need of such aid, and the sums so applied, amounting to the sum of £1,880 and upwards, are entered in the accounts of the said Commissioners as due and owing by the Royal School of Raphoe, whose funds are insufficient to repay the same, to the other Ulster Royal Schools:

General Recitals.

1.—*Interpretation of Terms.*

PART I.—THE COMMISSIONERS OF EDUCATION IN IRELAND.

Reconstitution of Commissioners.

2. From and after the date of this Scheme, "The Commissioners of Education in Ireland" shall be reconstituted in manner hereinafter provided, and as so reconstituted shall continue to be a Body Corporate, with perpetual succession and a common seal, and power to acquire and hold property, real and personal, for the purposes of this Scheme, and shall, for the purposes of this Scheme, continue to have hold exercise and enjoy all the powers, jurisdiction, privileges, and authority which at the date of this Scheme shall be vested in or capable of being exercised or enjoyed by the Commissioners, under the hereinbefore recited Acts or otherwise howsoever.

From and after the date of this Scheme, subject to the provisions hereinafter contained as to the continuing Commissioners, the said Body Corporate shall consist of the members following, that is to say—

(*a*) Ten Commissioners appointed by the Lord Lieutenant, as hereinafter provided.

(*b*) Ten Commissioners elected by the Local Boards, as hereinafter provided.

(*c*) *Two Commissioners elected by the Council of the University of Dublin, as hereinafter provided.*

(*d*) *Two Commissioners elected by the Senate of the Royal University of Ireland, as hereinafter provided.*

(*e*) *Two Commissioners elected by the Governing Body of the Institution known as "The Catholic University of Ireland," as hereinafter provided.*

(*f*) *Two Commissioners elected by the Intermediate Education Board for Ireland, as hereinafter provided.*

(*g*) *One Commissioner elected by the Council of Studies of the Royal College of St. Patrick, Maynooth, as hereinafter provided.*

(*h*) *One Commissioner elected by the Faculty of The Magee Presbyterian College, Londonderry, as hereinafter provided.*

From and after the date of this Scheme, subject to the provisions hereinafter contained as to the continuing Commissioners, no person shall be entitled to be, to continue, or to become a Commissioner by virtue of any office whatsoever.

3. *Continuing Commissioners.*

Appointment of Commissioners by Lord Lieutenant.

4. The Commissioners appointed by the Lord Lieutenant shall be appointed in manner following, and shall hold office during the pleasure of the Lord Lieutenant. Immediately after the date of this Scheme, and from time to time thereafter, as occasion shall require, the Lord Lieutenant shall appoint such and so many persons resident in Ireland to be Commissioners as, with the continuing Commissioners, shall make up the number of ten Commissioners so appointed.

With the view of ensuring that the Commissioners shall be persons having the confidence of the several religious denominations entitled to benefit from the Endowments, the Lord Lieutenant shall provide so far as is consistent with the retention of office by the continuing Commissioners, that five of the ten Commissioners appointed by the Lord Lieutenant shall be Protestants and five shall be Roman Catholics, *and of the five Protestants, one at least shall be a member of the said Church, one at the least shall be a Presbyterian, and one at the least shall be a Methodist.*

[The remainder of this clause is identical with the corresponding part of clause 4 of the Revised Draft Scheme, *infra* p. 313–14.]

Election of Commissioners.

5. At a meeting of each Local Board, to be held after due notice, and within two months after the date of this Scheme, the members present shall elect one person to be a Commissioner. Each Commissioner so elected shall hold office until the last day of the calendar year first ending more than twelve months after the date of this Scheme. At a meeting of each Local Board to be held in the month of November or December in such year and in every year thereafter, the members present shall elect one person to be a

Commissioner. Each Commissioner so elected shall enter upon office on the first day of January following his election, and shall hold office until the thirty-first day of December next ensuing, or until the election of his successor, whichever shall last happen, or until he shall vacate his office as hereinafter provided.

As soon as conveniently may be after the date of this Scheme, and subsequently from time to time as occasion shall require, the other bodies entitled to elect Commissioners shall respectively elect the number of Commissioners hereinbefore prescribed. The elections shall be held at such times, and the Commissioners elected shall hold office for such periods, as the bodies so entitled to elect Commissioners shall respectively prescribe from time to time.

The several Local Boards and other bodies entitled to elect Commissioners may elect Commissioners from among their own number, or may elect such other suitable persons, resident in Ireland, as they shall respectively think fit.

Every outgoing elected Commissioner, if otherwise qualified, shall be eligible for re-election.

Whenever any elected Commissioner shall die, or resign by writing under his hand, or become bankrupt, or refuse to act, or become incapable of acting, or shall cease to reside in Ireland, or shall be removed from office by a resolution, passed after due notice, of the body by which he was elected, his office shall thereupon become vacant, and the fact of the vacancy, with the cause thereof, shall be recorded in the minutes of the body by which he was elected, and such body may thereupon elect a qualified person to fill the vacancy; every Commissioner so elected shall hold office so long only as the Commissioner in whose place he shall have been elected might have held the same.

6. *Vesting of Endowments and Continuance of Powers.*
7. *Officers, Superannuation, and Expenses.*
8. *Chairman, Quorum, and Honorary Officers.*
9. *Committees.*
10. *Meetings.*
11. *Minutes, Books, and Documents.*
12. *By-laws and Regulations.*
13. *Accounts and Audit.*
14. *Annual Report.*
15. *Inspection.*
16. *Additional Endowments.*
17. *Management of Estates.*
18. *Leasing Powers.*
19. *Powers of Investment.*

PART II.—THE ULSTER ROYAL SCHOOLS.

Ulster Local Boards of Education.

20. From and after the date of this Scheme, a Protestant Board of Education and a Roman Catholic Board of Education shall be constituted as hereinafter provided, for the administration of Educational Endowments in each of the following Districts:—

- The Armagh District, consisting of the County of Armagh.
- The Tyrone District, consisting of the County of Tyrone with so much of the County of Londonderry as is included in the Diocese of Armagh.
- The Fermanagh District, consisting of the County of Fermanagh with the County of Monaghan, being part of the Diocese of Clogher.
- The Cavan District, consisting of the County of Cavan.
- The Donegal District, consisting of the County of Donegal.

The several Local Boards shall be respectively designated as follows:—

- The Armagh Protestant Board of Education.
- The Armagh Roman Catholic Board of Education.
- The Tyrone Protestant Board of Education.
- The Tyrone Roman Catholic Board of Education.
- The Fermanagh Protestant Board of Education.
- The Fermanagh Roman Catholic Board of Education.
- The Cavan Protestant Board of Education.
- The Cavan Roman Catholic Board of Education.
- The Donegal Protestant Board of Education.
- The Donegal Roman Catholic Board of Education.

Each of the said several Local Boards shall constitute a Body Corporate, with perpetual succession and a common seal, and power to acquire and hold property, real and personal, for the purposes of this Scheme.

Functions of Local Boards.

21. The functions of the Local Boards shall be as follows:—

(1.) To establish or aid in establishing, and to maintain or aid in maintaining, such School or Schools in their several Districts as they shall think expedient.

(2.) To administer and apply such share of the Endowments included in this or any other Scheme framed under the Act as shall be vested in or received by them.

(3.) To exercise such supervision and control over the Schools sharing in the Endowments administered by them as may be necessary to ensure compliance with the provisions of this or of any other Scheme framed under the Act, and applicable to such Schools.

(4.) To elect Commissioners and to do all other acts necessary to give effect to the provisions of this Scheme.

(5.) To take, acquire, receive, hold, and administer grants, conveyances, and other or additional donations, subscriptions, devises, bequests, and endowments, real or personal, for the purposes of this Scheme, or for any objects or purposes not inconsistent with or calculated to impede the efficient working of the provisions hereof. All property and moneys so held or received shall be administered by the several Local Boards in accordance with any special trusts lawfully affecting the same, and shall be included in the accounts to be kept by the respective Local Boards under this Scheme. Each Local Board shall have and exercise, with respect to all Endowments held or received by them, the same and the like powers of management, leasing, sale, exchange, and investment respectively, and the like powers for the purposes of this Scheme relating to such Endowments, which the Commissioners might have and exercise with respect to such Endowments if vested in or received by them under this Scheme.

(6.) To promote Intermediate Education in their several Districts by such means, consistent with the provisions of this Scheme, as shall from time to time appear expedient.

22. *Constitution of Local Boards.*

The Protestant Local Boards.

Armagh Protestant Board.

23. *Five* members of the Armagh Protestant Board of Education shall represent the Diocesan Council of Armagh; *three* shall represent the *General Assembly*; and one shall represent the Methodist Conference.

Tyrone Protestant Board.

24. *Four members of the Tyrone Protestant Board of Education shall represent the Diocesan Council of Armagh; one shall represent the Diocesan Council of Derry and Raphoe; four shall represent the General Assembly;* and one shall represent the Methodist Conference.

Fermanagh Protestant Board.

25. Five members of the Fermanagh Protestant Board of Education shall represent the Diocesan Council of Clogher; three shall represent the General Assembly; and one shall represent the Methodist Conference.

Cavan Protestant Board.

26. Three members of the Cavan Protestant Board of Education shall represent the Diocesan Council of Kilmore; two shall represent the Select Vestry of the Parish of Cavan; three shall represent the General Assembly; and one, representing the other Protestant Denominations of the District, shall be elected by the other members of the Board as hereinafter provided.

Donegal Protestant Board.

27. Three members of the Donegal Protestant Board of Education shall represent the Diocesan Council of Derry and Raphoe; five shall represent the General Assembly; and one, representing the other Protestant Denominations of the District, shall be elected by the other members of the Board as hereinafter provided.

28. *Casual vacancies.*

Election of Members.

29. The members of the several Protestant Local Boards hereinbefore named, other than the Archbishop and Bishops aforesaid, shall hold office until the 31st day of December first happening more than twelve months after the date of this Scheme, or until the election of their respective successors, whichever shall last happen, or until they shall vacate their office as hereinbefore provided. Before the said thirty-first day of December and once in every year thereafter, each of the several bodies entitled to elect representatives upon the said several Boards may elect such representatives. The elections shall be held, once in each year, at such times as the several bodies entitled to elect representatives shall respectively prescribe from time to time. The members so elected shall hold office until the election of their respective successors. Every outgoing member, if otherwise qualified, shall be eligible for re-election.

At the first meeting in each calendar year commencing more than twelve months after the date of this Scheme, the Protestant Local Boards of Cavan and Raphoe shall each elect one suitable person resident in the District and willing to act, who shall be a member of a Protestant Denomination not otherwise represented upon the Board, and each person so elected shall hold office as a member of the Board until the election of his successor, or until he shall vacate his office as hereinbefore provided. Every such outgoing member, if otherwise qualified, shall be eligible for re-election provided he shall have attended at the least one-third of the meetings of the Board held during his term of office, but not otherwise.

Appointment of Deputies.

30. The Archbishop and each of the Bishops aforesaid, for the time being, if unable or unwilling to act as a member of the Local Board to which he belongs, may, from time to time, by writing under his hand, nominate a qualified person to act in his place, for such period as may be in such writing specified.

The Roman Catholic Local Boards.

31. *Constitution of Roman Catholic Boards.*
32. *Armagh Roman Catholic Board.*
33. *Tyrone Roman Catholic Board.*
34. *Fermanagh Roman Catholic Board.*
35. *Cavan Roman Catholic Board.*
36. *Donegal Roman Catholic Board.*
37. *Appointment of Ecclesiastical Members.*

Appointment of Lay Members.

38. If at the date of this Scheme any of the lay members of the several Roman Catholic Boards hereinbefore named shall be unable or unwilling to act, and whenever thereafter any lay member shall die, or resign by writing under his hand, or become bankrupt, or refuse to act, or become incapable of acting, or shall cease to reside in the District or portion of a District represented by him, or shall fail to attend at the least one-third of the meetings of the Board held in any one year, his office shall thereupon become vacant, and the fact of the vacancy, with the cause thereof, shall be recorded in the minutes of the Board; and, as soon as conveniently may be after the occurrence of such vacancy, the remaining lay members of the Board shall co-opt a qualified person resident in such district or portion of a district to fill the vacancy.

Appointment of Deputies.

39. The Archbishop and each of the Bishops aforesaid, for the time being, if unable or unwilling to act as a member of the Local Board to which he belongs, may, from time to time, by writing under his hand, nominate a qualified person to act in his place, for such period as may be in such writing specified.

General Provisions as to Local Boards.

40. *Chairman, Quorum, and Honorary Officers.*
41. *Meetings.*
42. *Minutes, Books, and Documents.*
43. *Byelaws and Regulations.*
44. *Accounts and Audits.*
45. *Committees.*
46. *Estates Committees.*

School Committees.

47. Each Local Board may from time to time establish or appoint such School Committee or School Committees as they shall think fit, to aid in the supervision and management of any School or Schools *situated in the District*, and qualified to share in the Endowments administered by the Local Board. The Local Board may fix the constitution and define the functions of such School Committee which they may so establish or appoint. The Governing Body for the time being of any School or Schools *situated in the District*, and qualified to share in the Endowments administered by the Local Board, may be recognised as a School Committee for the purposes of this Scheme. Each School Committee established, appointed or recognised under this Scheme shall consist of not less than three persons, each of whom shall be a member of the Local Board of the District, or of the Governing Body or Teaching Staff of the School, or a Manager of the School. Every School for which a School Committee shall be established, appointed or recognised as aforesaid, shall be deemed to be a School managed by a Local Board for the purposes of this Scheme, and shall from time to time be visited by the Local Board for the purpose of ascertaining that it is conducted in accordance with the provisions of this Scheme.

48. *Annual Reports.*

Powers of Local Boards.

49. *Subject to the provisions of this Scheme, each Local Board may maintain or aid any School or Schools within the District qualified as hereinafter provided, in such manner as may, from time to time, seem best calculated to promote Intermediate Education in the District; provided that the Commissioners may prevent any School from sharing in the Ulster Royal School Endowments which the Inspector appointed by*

the Lord Lieutenant shall report not to be qualified as hereinafter provided, and they may prevent any application of the Endowments administered by any Local Board which is not in accordance with the provisions of this Scheme.

No person appointed after the date of this Scheme to any paid office or employment under a Local Board, or becoming entitled to any salary or emolument out of the Endowments administered by the Local Board, shall be capable of becoming, or shall continue to be a member of the Board.

Supervision of Schools and Appointment of Masters and other Officers.

50. Subject to the provisions of this Scheme, each Local Board, directly or through a School Committee, shall have and exercise general supervision and control over every School sharing in the Endowments administered by the Board, shall determine the various branches of education to be taught, shall regulate the fees to be charged in each School, shall fix the terms and vacations, and shall make such rules and regulations for the management of each School, as to the Local Board or School Committee, as the case may be, shall seem expedient. Subject as aforesaid, each Local Board, directly or through a School Committee, shall from time to time fix the number, salaries, and emoluments of the Masters and other members of the teaching and domestic staff to be employed, and shall define their several and respective duties. The Local Board, directly or through a School Committee, shall appoint the Head Master of each School, and shall provide for the appointment, through the Head Master or after conference with him, of such teaching and domestic staff and other officers and servants as may in each case be required.

Subject to the provisions hereinafter contained as to the vested interests of individuals holding office at the date of the passing of the Act, every person in the employment of a Local Board or of a School Committee may be removed by the Local Board or by the School Committee, as the case may be, for such cause as they shall deem adequate, or upon reasonable notice, or upon payment of a reasonable sum, not exceeding six months' salary, in lieu of notice: provided that no Head Master shall be removed except upon a resolution of the Local Board or of the School Committee, as the case may be, passed at a special meeting convened on due notice, at which not less than one-half of the members for the time being shall be present, and confirmed at a subsequent meeting held at an interval of not less than one week nor more than five weeks after the first meeting.

61. *School Fees, and Boarding arrangements.*

52. *Functions of Head Masters.*

Powers of Protestant Local Boards to allocate Endowments.

53. Each Protestant Local Board, with the sanction of the Commissioners, may allocate the Endowments administered by the Board among the different Protestant Denominations of the District, and may, with the like sanction, allocate a share or shares of such Endowments to any School or Schools placed under the control of a Governing Body consisting of or including any three or more members of the Board, or under the control of a School Committee, representing any one or more of such Denominations, upon such terms, and subject to such conditions, and in such manner, as, having regard to the relative numbers of the members of the several Protestant Denominations entitled to benefit from the Endowments of the District, shall in each case seem just.

Any two or more Protestant Local Boards, with the like sanction, may join in exercising the powers conferred by this clause, as if for the purposes of this clause the said Boards had been one Local Board, and as if their several Districts and the Endowments administered by the said Boards had been united and amalgamated.

Provided that every exercise of the powers conferred by this clause shall be sanctioned by a resolution passed at a meeting of the Local Board or Boards concerned, specially convened for the purpose, and attended by not less than two-thirds of the full number of members of each Local Board concerned: provided also that no such resolution shall be passed if any three members of any Local Board concerned shall object to the same by writing under their hands: provided also that all Endowments allocated under this clause shall be administered in accordance with the provisions of this Scheme.

Allocation by Armagh and Tyrone Protestant Boards.

54. *The Armagh and Tyrone Protestant Local Boards, with the sanction of the Commissioners, may unite and amalgamate the Armagh and Tyrone Districts, and the Endowments administered by the said Boards, in accordance with the following provisions, and upon such further terms, and subject to such further conditions, and in such manner, as the said Boards, with the sanction aforesaid, may agree upon:—*

(a.) *All moneys payable by the Commissioners to the said Boards respectively from the Ulster Royal School Endowments other than the School premises, and excepting moneys received upon claims established under the Second Schedule hereto, shall be divided in equal shares between two Denominational Committees constituted as hereinafter provided.*

(b.) *One Denominational Committee shall be constituted of the several members of the said Boards for the time being representing the Diocesan Councils of Armagh and of Derry and Raphoe respectively, with two additional members to be co-opted by them from time to time as hereinbefore provided. The other Denominational Committee shall be constituted of the several members of the said Boards for the time being representing the General Assembly and the Methodist Conference respectively.*

(c.) *All interest in the Armagh Royal School premises, or in the value or produce thereof, or in any moneys derived therefrom, which would otherwise belong to or be receivable by the Armagh Protestant Local Board under the provisions of this Scheme, shall belong to and shall be received and administered by the Denominational Committee first above mentioned. All interest in the Dungannon Royal School premises, or in the value or produce thereof, or in any moneys derived therefrom, which would otherwise belong to or be receivable by the Tyrone Protestant Local Board under the provisions of this Scheme, shall belong to and shall be received and administered by the Denominational Committee secondly above mentioned; subject, however, to the payment to the Denominational Committee first above mentioned, by way of annual occupation rent or of purchase money, as the case may require, of any proportion, to be ascertained as hereinafter provided, of the value of the Dungannon Royal School premises which may be proved to be attributable to the expenditure of private moneys thereon by any benefactor or benefactors belonging to the said Church.*

(d.) *Each of the said Denominational Committees, when constituted, shall be deemed to be, for all the purposes of this Scheme, a Protestant Local Board for the Armagh and Tyrone Districts conjointly, and may exercise all the powers of a Local Board throughout the said Districts, and all Endowments received by either of the said Committees shall be administered in accordance with the provisions of this Scheme.*

The powers conferred by this clause may be exercised at any time between the date of this Scheme and the expiration of six months after this Scheme shall have come into operation with respect to the Royal School Endowments of both the Armagh and Tyrone Districts, but not afterwards: provided that every exercise of the said powers shall be sanctioned by a resolution passed at a joint meeting of both the above-mentioned Boards, specially convened for the purpose, attended by not less than two-thirds of the full number of each of the said Boards, and that every such resolution may, at any time be rescinded or may from time to time be varied, with the sanction of the Commissioners, by a like resolution: provided also that no such resolution shall be passed rescinded or varied, unless with the concurrence of a majority of the full number of Members of each of the said Boards, for the time being. The Commissioners may make all rules and regulations, and may do and sanction all acts, necessary for carrying out the provisions of this clause, if and whenever the powers aforesaid shall be exercised.

Distribution of Ulster Royal School Endowments.

Application of Endowments for first Three Years.

*55. Subject to the other provisions of this Scheme, and after providing for all proper and necessary outgoings charges and liabilities, and for any retiring annuities payable under this Scheme out of the several Endowments, the income received by the Commissioners from each of the Ulster Royal School Endowments, other than the School premises, *during the period from the date at which this Scheme shall come into operation with respect to each of the said Endowments respectively until the end of the third complete calendar year next following, which period is hereinafter called the first three years*, shall be paid by the Commissioners, in equal shares, to the two Local Boards of the District, and the moneys so paid shall be applied by the several Local Boards for the following purposes, or for such and so many of them as the said Boards respectively shall deem expedient:—

(a.) To aid, maintain, or improve any existing Intermediate School or Schools situated in the District, and managed in accordance with the provisions of this Scheme;

(b.) To establish, or aid in establishing, in the District, any Intermediate School or Schools to be managed as aforesaid;

(c.) To invest and accumulate a capital fund, of which the principal and interest may from time to time be applied by the Local Board, as they shall deem expedient, in aiding, maintaining, improving, or establishing any Intermediate School or Schools in the District, to be managed as aforesaid;

(d.) To make provision, in such other manner as the Local Board shall deem expedient, for promoting Intermediate Education in the District so as to enable the Local Board after the first three years to avail themselves of the provisions of this Scheme.

Provided that if the Local Board of any District shall think it more advantageous to apply the moneys paid to them under this clause, in aid of any Intermediate School or Schools in another District, managed in accordance with the provisions of this Scheme, they may, with the sanction of the Commissioners, so apply the same.

Application of Endowments after first Three Years.

*56. Subject to the other provisions of this Scheme, and after providing for all proper and necessary outgoings charges and liabilities, the income received by the Commissioners, after the expiration of the first three years, from the several Ulster Royal School Endowments with respect to which this Scheme shall have come into operation, shall be distributed by the Commissioners among the several Local Boards, and shall be applied by the Local Boards for the purposes of Intermediate Education as hereinafter provided.

Minimum Grants.

57. For each calendar year commencing after the expiration of the first three years, the Commissioners shall in the first instance pay to each Local Board a minimum grant calculated as follows:—

To each of the Armagh Local Boards, twenty-five per cent. of the net income received during the year from the Armagh Royal School Endowments, other than the School premises.

To each of the Tyrone Local Boards twenty-five per cent. of the net income received during the year from the Dungannon Royal School Endowments, other than the School premises.

To each of the Fermanagh Local Boards, twenty-five per cent. of the net income received during the year from the Enniskillen Royal School Endowments, other than the School premises.

To each of the Cavan Local Boards, thirty per cent. of the net income received during the year from the Cavan Royal School Endowments, other than the School premises.

To each of the Donegal Local Boards, fifty per cent. of the net income received during the year from the Raphoe Royal School Endowments, other than the School premises.

The net income of each of the said several Endowments, for the purposes of this clause, shall be the amount received during the year from the lands and reversion belonging to the same respectively, after providing for all proper and necessary outgoings charges and liabilities, exclusive of any retiring annuities payable under this Scheme. So long as any retiring annuity shall be payable out of the income of any of the said Endowments respectively, the payment of the full amount of the minimum grant aforesaid shall be a charge upon the said income in priority to any payment under the next succeeding clause of this Scheme, but after payment of such retiring annuity.

Distribution of Residue among Qualified Schools.

58. After payment of any retiring annuities payable under this Scheme, and of the above-mentioned minimum grants, the residue of the income received by the Commissioners from the several Ulster Royal School Endowments with respect to which this Scheme shall have come into operation, during each calendar year commencing after the expiration of the first three years, shall be treated as a common fund, out of which the Commissioners shall first pay the amounts necessary to provide the free places hereinafter required to be provided by the Commissioners, and they shall then distribute the remainder of the income aforesaid among the several Local Boards for the benefit of the several Schools fulfilling the conditions prescribed in the First Schedule hereto, hereinafter referred to as qualified Schools, for which claims shall have been made and established in accordance with this Scheme. The distribution shall be made in proportion to the number of pupils receiving Intermediate Education in the said Schools, ascertained in the manner prescribed in the Second Schedule hereto.

Each Local Board may in the first instance select, according to their own discretion, the qualified School or Schools in their District for which they will claim a share of the aforesaid residue, but the Governing Body of any School claiming to be qualified, or to be qualified in all respects save being managed by the Local Board, and for which the Local Board shall not have made a claim, may appeal to the Commissioners, who shall thereupon inquire and determine whether it is for the benefit of Intermediate Education in the District

* In the Draft Amended Scheme which the Judicial Commissioners are preparing, in obedience to the Declaration of the Lord Lieutenant, cc. 55, 56, 59 and 60 have, in addition to considerable alterations necessary by the Declaration, undergone some modification and compression.

that the School should be admitted to share in the said grant, and may, by special resolution, admit the School accordingly. Provided that, in every such case, the Commissioners shall require, as a condition of admission, that the School shall be placed under the management of the Local Board, either directly, or through a School Committee, which shall be constituted as hereinbefore prescribed, and shall be established, appointed or recognised by the Local Board of the District or by the Commissioners, and, before admitting any School, the Commissioners shall also satisfy themselves that the School in all other respects fulfils the prescribed conditions.

Evidence of Qualification and Claims.

*59. The Commissioners may accept the certificate of the Inspector appointed by the Lord Lieutenant as sufficient evidence, in the case of any School or of any pupil or pupils, that the prescribed conditions have been fulfilled, or they may require such further or other evidence as they may think necessary. If any question shall arise, or shall be raised by any Local Board, as to the fulfilment of the prescribed conditions by any School, or by any pupil or pupils, the same shall be inquired into and determined by the Commissioners, who may charge the expenses of the inquiry against any Local Board or Boards concerned, or may order the same to be otherwise defrayed, as they shall think just.

The Commissioners shall prescribe the manner and form in which claims shall be made and established under the provisions of this Scheme, and they may prescribe the manner and form in which the register of pupils, the time table of studies, the record of attendance of teachers and pupils, and any other evidence required to show that any School is a qualified School, or to verify any claim against the above-mentioned residue, shall be kept in or furnished by such School. The decision of the Commissioners upon every question arising in respect of the qualification of any School, or in respect of any claim, or of any pupil or examination, shall be final.

Free places provided by Schools sharing Minimum Grants.

60. Every School sharing in the minimum grant received by any Local Board shall be required, besides fulfilling the other prescribed conditions, to provide, to the satisfaction of the Commissioners and of the Inspector appointed by the Lord Lieutenant, free education for pupils selected by competition in accordance with the following conditions:—

(a.) One free place, at the least, in each School sharing in the minimum grant received by any Local Board, shall be offered in each year by the Local Board for competition by examination among all candidates qualified as hereinafter mentioned.

(b.) Each candidate shall, during each of the two years next before the day appointed for the examination, have made not less than one hundred attendances as a pupil at a public Elementary School in the District; shall not on the day of examination exceed the age of fourteen years; shall be of good conduct and character; and shall be in such circumstances as to need, and in be capable of taking full advantage of free Intermediate Education in a qualified School.

(c.) The examination for each District shall be held at a time and place, and in a course, to be appointed and publicly announced not less than six months previously by the Local Board, subject to the approval of the Commissioners, and shall be conducted by an Examiner or Examiners appointed by the Local Board, subject to the like approval. All the candidates for the free places offered by each Local Board shall be examined at the same time and place, in the same course, and under the same conditions.

(d.) The subjects of examination shall be those of Elementary Education, and not below the standard of the Fifth Class, as defined by the Rules and Regulations of the Commissioners of National Education for the time being, and may include any extra or optional subjects taught in National Schools.

(e.) The name and address of every candidate, with a statement of his or her circumstances, and a certificate of attendance signed by the Manager of the Elementary School or Schools attended by him or her, and such further evidence of qualification as the Local Board may reasonably require, shall be furnished to the Local Board not less than one month before the examination. If any question shall arise as to the qualification of any candidate, the same shall be inquired into and determined by the Examiner or Examiners, whose decision and report upon all such questions, and upon the merits of the candidates, shall, subject to the approval of the Commissioners, be final. No free place shall be awarded to any candidate whom the Examiner or Examiners shall not report to have shown sufficient merit.

(f.) Each candidate to whom a free place shall be awarded shall be entitled, subject to removal for misconduct or failure to make satisfactory progress, to receive Intermediate Education as a day pupil at a School sharing in the minimum grant received by the Local Board offering the free place, in all the ordinary subjects taught in the School, free of charge, for the two School years next following the examination; or, if admitted as a boarding pupil, shall, subject as aforesaid, be entitled to a reduction at the rate of ten pounds per annum in the fee usually charged in the School for a boarding pupil of the same age.

Free places provided from Residue.

61. *Every School receiving benefit from the minimum grant of any Local Board, or from the residue of the Ulster Royal School Endowments, shall be required, besides fulfilling the other prescribed conditions, to provide, to the satisfaction of the Commissioners and of the Inspector appointed by the Lord Lieutenant, free education for pupils holding places to be provided by the Commissioners in accordance with the following conditions:—*

(a.) *In addition to the free places to be provided under the preceding clause, ten free places to be provided by the Commissioners shall be offered in each year by each Local Board for competition among all the qualified candidates admitted to the examination to be held under the preceding clause.*

(b.) *Each candidate to whom a free place provided by the Commissioners shall be awarded, shall be entitled, subject to the conditions in the preceding clause mentioned, to receive Intermediate Education as a day pupil at any qualified School selected by the candidate, in all the ordinary subjects taught in the School, free of charge, for the two School years next following the examination; or, if admitted as a boarding pupil, shall, subject as aforesaid, be entitled to a reduction at the rate of ten pounds per annum in the fee usually charged in the School for a boarding pupil of the same age.*

(c.) *The Local Board conducting such examination may allocate the free places awarded under the preceding clause and this clause respectively, among the successful candidates, so as to secure, so far as possible, to each successful candidate, a free place in the qualified School which such candidate can most advantageously attend.*

(d.) *Upon production of such evidence as may be reasonably required that the holder of such free place awarded under this clause has, during the preceding half-year, received, in a qualified School, the education to which he or she was entitled, the Commissioners shall pay the sum of five pounds, out of the abovementioned residue, to the Managers or towards the support of the School in which such education was given.*

Application of the Endowments by the Local Boards.

*62. Subject to the other provisions of this Scheme, and to any special trusts or conditions upon which any part thereof may be received, the moneys received by the Local Boards under or for the purposes of this Scheme shall be expended and applied by them for or towards the following purposes, or for or towards such and so many of them as to the Local Boards respectively shall seem expedient:—

(a.) To maintain the buildings, furniture, appliances, and premises of the several qualified Schools managed by them, in good order and condition, and to make such additions thereto, and such improvements therein, as may be required from time to time,

(b.) To pay rents, taxes, cost of insurance, and other charges, necessarily or properly payable out of or for the School premises, and to defray the necessary working expenses of the qualified Schools, and the cost of management. Provided that no money shall be expended by any Local Board out of the Royal School Endowments upon or for any School premises, unless the premises are vested in the Local Board or in the Commissioners, for the purposes of this Scheme, for a perpetual estate of freehold, or for a term of which not less than one hundred years shall be unexpired.

(c.) To provide for the education of the pupils: for this purpose the several Local Boards may, directly or through School Committees, employ and pay such Masters, Teachers, and other educational staff, as they may deem it expedient to engage for the instruction of the pupils in the qualified Schools managed by them.

(d.) To provide prizes for the most deserving pupils of the qualified Schools; such prizes may be awarded in money, or in remission of school fees, or in such other manner as the several Local Boards may deem best calculated to stimulate the industry, reward the diligence, or promote the progress of the pupils, or may be so given as to enable or encourage deserving and capable pupils from elementary Schools in the District to obtain Intermediate Education free, or at a reduced cost, in the qualified Schools.

(e.) To establish in connection with any qualified School or Schools, exhibitions or scholarships, which shall in each case have such value, and shall be awarded upon such examination, and shall be held subject to such conditions as the Local Board establishing the same shall think fit. These exhibitions and scholarships may be given so as to enable their holders to Intermediate Education free, or at a reduced cost, at any qualified School or Schools, or may be tenable at any University, College, or other place of higher education elsewhere, as the Local Board establishing the same may from time to time determine.

Schools entitled to Minimum Grants and Residue.

63. *The amount of the minimum grant received by each Local Board shall be expended by them for the purposes of one or more Schools to be selected by the Board from the qualified Schools within the District, or if there be no qualified School in the District, shall be expended by them for the purposes of any one or more Schools selected by the Board receiving the grant from the qualified Schools in the other Districts. The minimum grant may be applied by each Local Board for the purposes of any qualified School or Schools, or for the benefit of the pupils of any qualified School or Schools, in such proportions and in such manner as the Local Board shall think expedient, but every share of the residue of the Ulster Royal School Endowments received by a Local Board upon a claim established under the provisions of the Second Schedule hereto shall be applied for the benefit of the School for which such claim shall have been established, or for the benefit of the pupils of that School.*

64. *Aid from Public Sources.*

65. *Religious Instruction.*

School Buildings and Premises.

66. The buildings of each of the Ulster Royal Schools, and the lands held and occupied therewith at the date of this Scheme, described in the Fourth Schedule hereto, hereinbefore and hereinafter called the School premises, shall be regarded as part of the capital of the Royal School Endowments of the Districts in which they are respectively situated, and from and after the date at which this Scheme shall come into operation with respect to each of the said Endowments respectively, the School premises, and the value and produce thereof, and any moneys derived therefrom, shall in each case be applied exclusively for the educational benefit of the District, and, subject to the provisions as to private endowments hereinafter contained, shall be treated as belonging in equal shares to the two Local Boards of the District. Subject to the provisions hereinafter contained, the income derived from the School premises during the first three years may be applied in the same manner as the moneys received under Clause 55 of this Scheme, and after the first three years shall be applied to the same purposes as the minimum grants hereinbefore mentioned, or in addition to the said minimum grants. Subject as aforesaid, the capital derived from the School premises shall be held and applied as a Building Fund, as hereinafter provided.

67. *Armagh School Premises.*

As soon as conveniently may be after this Scheme shall come into operation with respect to the Armagh Royal School Endowments, the Commissioners shall proceed, on notice to the Armagh Local Boards, to ascertain and declare the proportion, if any, of the then value of the Armagh School premises which may be proved to be attributable to the expenditure of private moneys on the said premises by any Protestant benefactor or benefactors. When such proportion has been declared, the Commissioners shall offer the said premises to the Armagh Protestant Local Board, to be used for the purposes of a School managed by the Board in accordance with the provisions of this Scheme, at a rent fixed by estimating the fair occupation rent of the whole of the said premises at £200 per annum, and deducting from that sum, as belonging exclusively to the said Board, the proportion thereof, if any, which has been proved to be attributable to the expenditure of the private moneys aforesaid. If the said Board shall take the said premises on the said terms, the Commissioners shall deliver the possession thereof to the Armagh Protestant Local Board, and shall permit them to occupy the same on the said terms so long as the said premises shall be used for the purposes aforesaid. If the said Board shall not take the said premises upon the terms aforesaid, or having taken them, shall at any time cease to use them for the purposes aforesaid, the Commissioners shall sell or let the said premises to the best advantage, and shall dispose of the proceeds thereof as herein provided.

68. *Cavan School Premises.*

[Similar to corresponding clause in the Revised Draft Scheme, the valuation being fixed at £1,000 instead of £2,000.]

69. *Dungannon School Premises.*

As soon as conveniently may be after this Scheme shall come into operation with respect to the Dungannon Royal School Endowments, the Tyrone Local Boards shall meet and consider, or shall appoint a joint Committee to meet and consider, whether it would be more advantageous to employ the Dungannon School premises for the purposes of education, or to dispose of them by sale or letting, or to dispose of certain portions by sale or letting, and to employ other portions for the purposes of education. They shall also consider whether it would be desirable, if the premises should be employed for the purposes of education, that they should be taken jointly or in several portions, by the two Local Boards, or should be taken wholly or partly by one Board, for the purposes of a School or Schools to be managed by such Board or Boards, in accordance with the provisions of this Scheme, and they shall consider the terms and conditions on which the said premises may be most advantageously and justly dealt with, having due regard to the interest of both Local Boards therein, and treating any proportion of the value of the said premises which may be proved to be attributable to the expenditure of private moneys on the said premises, by any Protestant benefactor or benefactors, as belonging exclusively to the Tyrone Protestant Local Board.

[The remainder of this clause is similar to the corresponding clause in the revised Draft Scheme, *infra*, p. 318.]

Enniskillen School Premises.

70. As soon as conveniently may be after this Scheme shall come into operation with respect to the Enniskillen Royal School Endowments, the Commissioners shall offer the Enniskillen School premises to the Fermanagh Protestant Local Board at the estimated capital value of £7,000. If the said Board shall take the said premises on the said terms, and shall, out of funds contributed for the purpose, pay to the Commissioners, within six months after this Scheme shall come into operation as aforesaid, the sum of £3,500, the Commissioners shall thenceforth hold the said premises upon trust for the Fermanagh Protestant Local Board, and shall deliver the possession thereof to the said Board, and shall permit them to occupy the same so long as the said premises shall be used for the purposes of a School, managed by the said Board in accordance with the provisions of this Scheme. If the said Board shall afterwards at any time cease to use the said premises for the purposes aforesaid, the Commissioners shall sell or let the said premises to the best advantage, and shall hold and dispose of the proceeds thereof as belonging exclusively to the Fermanagh Protestant Local Board, and as part of the endowment to be applied by the said Board in accordance with the provisions of this Scheme. The Commissioners shall invest, hold, and apply the said sum of £3,500, if paid as aforesaid, as a Building Fund for the purposes of the Fermanagh Roman Catholic Local Board as hereinafter provided.

If the Fermanagh Protestant Local Board shall not take the said School premises, and raise and pay the said sum of £3,500, within the period above mentioned, the Commissioners, as soon as conveniently may be after the expiration of the said period, shall give public notice of their intention to dispose of the Enniskillen School premises to the best advantage, and shall invite tenders for the same within a limited time. Special notice of the intention to dispose of the said premises shall be given to Her Majesty's Secretary of State for War, and also to the Fermanagh Local Boards, either or both of whom may offer to take all or any part of the said premises to be used for purposes of education. As soon as the time limited for receiving tenders shall have expired, the Commissioners shall consider the tenders received, and shall determine whether it would be more advantageous to sell or let the said premises, or to permit all or any part of them to be used by either or both of the Fermanagh Local Boards for purposes of education, and shall dispose of the said premises or of the proceeds thereof accordingly.

71. *Raphoe School Premises.*

72. *General Provisions relating to disposal of School Premises.*

73. *Building Funds.*

Vested Interests.

74. *Saving of Vested Interests of Head Masters.*

75. *Retiring Annuities and Payments to Head Masters.*

76. *Removal of Head Masters.*

77. *Agreement for Retirement of Head Masters.*

Assistant Masters and others.

78. From and after the date at which this Scheme shall come into operation with respect to each of the Ulster Royal School Endowments, the services of the Assistant Masters and of all other persons then employed in the Royal School of the District, or receiving any salary or emoluments out of the Endowments thereof, shall be discontinued. Upon such discontinuance, the Commissioners shall grant to each of the Assistant Masters and other persons named in the Third Schedule hereto, if then still holding the same office which he held at the date of the passing of the Act, during his life, a retiring annuity equal in amount to one-thirtieth part of the amount of the salary payable to him out of the respective Royal School Endowments at the date of the passing of the Act, for each completed year during which he shall have held office at the date of the discontinuance of his services, not exceeding the full amount of the salary aforesaid, as stated in the Third Schedule hereto.

79. *Engagement of Assistants by Local Boards.*

80. *Payment of Retiring Allowances.*

[Clauses 79 and 80 are similar to Clause 51 of the Revised Draft Scheme.]

81. *Exhibitions and Scholarships.*

Balance of Cash Accounts of Ulster Royal Schools.

82. As soon as conveniently may be after the thirtieth day of June or thirty-first day of December next following the date of this Scheme, the Commissioners shall make up and balance the current cash accounts of the several Ulster Royal School Endowments up to that day. Every balance then appearing due upon any of the said accounts, except the account of the Raphoe Royal School Endowments, shall be treated as the first charge upon the capital of the Endowments from which the same shall be owing, and as thenceforth bearing interest at the rate of four per cent. per annum. Any balance then appearing due upon the cash account of the Raphoe Royal School Endowments shall be discharged, by an equal percentage rate, out of any balances then appearing to credit upon the cash accounts of the other Ulster Royal School Endowments, and, after discharge thereof, the balance remaining to credit upon each of the said accounts, so far as it consists of net income for the current calendar year after payment of current expenses, shall be treated as current income, and so far as it consists of accumulations or other moneys, it shall be treated as part of the capital of the Endowments to which it belongs.

83. *Payment of Charges.*

84. *Future Accounts of Ulster Royal School Endowments.*

[Clauses 83 and 84 are similar to the last two paragraphs of Clause 56 of the Revised Draft Scheme.]

PART III.—GENERAL PROVISIONS.

85. *Other Endowments administered by Commissioners.*

Reference to Commissioners.

86. If any doubt or question shall arise as to the proper application or construction of any of the provisions of this Scheme, any Local Board concerned may apply to the Commissioners for their direction or opinion thereon, and the direction or opinion of the Commissioners upon any such doubt or question, given by special resolution, shall be final.

87. *Payment of Expenses.*

88. *Printing of Scheme.*

Alteration of Scheme.

89. This Scheme may be altered from time to time by the Commissioners of Charitable Donations and Bequests for Ireland, in any matter whatsoever, upon

the application of the Commissioners, founded upon a special resolution specifying the alteration required, which resolution shall be passed by a majority consisting of not less than two-thirds of the Commissioners present at a meeting held on due notice for the consideration thereof, and shall be afterwards confirmed by a special resolution of the Commissioners passed at a subsequent meeting held after not less than six days' notice for the consideration thereof. Except upon such application as aforesaid, no alteration shall be so made, and no alteration shall be made contrary to anything contained in the Act.

SCHEDULES REFERRED TO IN THE FOREGOING SCHEME.

FIRST SCHEDULE.—*Qualified Schools.*

The conditions to be fulfilled by a School in order that it shall be qualified to receive awards from the subsistence grant of any Local Board, or from the residue of the income of the Ulster Royal School Endowments, after the first three years mentioned in the Scheme, shall be as follows:—

(*a.*) The School shall be an Intermediate School conducted in accordance with the provisions of this Scheme, and shall be managed by the Local Board of the District in which it is situated, either directly or through a School Committee, established, appointed, or recognised as prescribed in the Scheme.

(*b.*) Instruction shall be regularly given in the School, throughout each School year for which a payment is made, in the following subjects at the least:—

In a School for Boys—Latin, Greek, English, French or German, Ancient and Modern History, Geography, Arithmetic, Algebra, Geometry, and Physical Science or Drawing.

In a School for Girls—Latin, English, French or German, Ancient and Modern History, Geography, Arithmetic, Algebra or Geometry or Physical Science, and Music or Drawing.

In a School for Boys and Girls—Latin, Greek, English, French or German, Ancient and Modern History, Geography, Arithmetic, Algebra, Geometry, and Drawing.

(*c.*) The School, throughout the School year for which a payment is made, shall have regularly afforded Intermediate Education, in the subjects specified in the Second Schedule hereto at the least, to not less than twenty pupils, each of whom shall have made not less than one hundred attendances as a pupil at the School on different days in the School year, and not less than seven of those pupils shall, during the School year, have passed the Examinations of the Intermediate Education Board for Ireland, in the subjects specified in the Second Schedule hereto at the least. The date at which the School year shall terminate for the purposes of this and the following Schedule to this Scheme, shall be the first day of August in each year; no attendance of any pupil shall be counted at more than one School in the same School year, and no pupil shall be counted who at the last day of the School year shall be less than twelve or more than nineteen years of age.

(*d.*) The Inspector appointed by the Lord Lieutenant shall satisfy himself by sufficient examination and inquiry, and shall report and certify, that throughout the School year for which a payment is made, the buildings, appliances, and premises of the School have been sufficient and suitable for an efficient Intermediate School, and have been maintained in good order, that a competent staff for the efficient teaching of the subjects specified in this Schedule has been employed in the School, and that Intermediate Education has been regularly afforded to the required number of pupils of the prescribed age, in the subjects specified in the Second Schedule hereto at the least.

Provided that in any case in which a School may be prevented, by any temporary or accidental cause, from fulfilling all the conditions aforesaid in any School year, the Commissioners may, for such year, dispense with the fulfilment of any one or more of the said conditions, upon being satisfied that the School is likely to fulfil the same in the next succeeding year, but such a dispensation shall not be made for the same School for two consecutive years.

The Schools fulfilling the conditions specified in this Schedule, and none others, shall be qualified Schools for the purposes of this Scheme.

SECOND SCHEDULE.—*Distribution of Residue.*

The residue of the income of the Ulster Royal School Endowments to be distributed under Clause 89 of the foregoing Scheme, shall be annually divided among the several Local Boards in proportion to the number of marks obtained by the several qualified Schools for which claims shall have been made and established in accordance with the following provisions:—

(1.) *One mark shall be allowed for every pupil who, throughout the School year for which the payment is claimed, shall have regularly received Intermediate Education in a qualified School, in the subjects hereinafter specified at the least, and who shall have made not less than one hundred attendances as a pupil at the School on different days in the School year, and who, on the last day of the School year, shall not be less than twelve nor more than nineteen years of age. Provided that the number of pupils for whom marks shall be allowed to any School in any year under the foregoing provisions shall not exceed four times the number of the pupils for whom marks shall be allowed to the same School in the same year under the next following provision.*

(2.) *One additional mark shall be allowed for every pupil included in the foregoing number, who, during the same School year or within one calendar month after its expiration, shall have passed the Examinations of the Intermediate Education Board for Ireland, in the Junior Grade, in the subjects hereinafter specified; two additional marks shall be allowed for every like pupil passing in the Middle Grade; and three additional marks shall be allowed for every like pupil passing in the Senior Grade.*

(3.) *The subjects in which each pupil is required to receive Intermediate Education, or to pass the abovementioned Examinations, as the case may be, shall be the following subjects at the least:—*

For Boys.—English; Latin; Greek or French or German; and two Mathematical subjects, or one Mathematical subject and Drawing.

For Girls.—English; Latin; French or German; and two Mathematical subjects, or one Mathematical subject and Drawing or Music.

In the Programme of the abovementioned Examinations, Arithmetic, and any subject including Arithmetic, shall be regarded as a Mathematical subject.

(4.) *No mark shall be allowed for the same pupil to more than one School in the same School year.*

(5.) *Whenever a claim has been established for any School in two or three consecutive years, the marks allowed to the School in ascertaining the payment to be made shall be the average number obtained by the School in accordance with the foregoing provisions in the two or three consecutive years, as the case may be, ending with the year for which the payment is made.*

THIRD SCHEDULE.—*Vested Interests.*

FOURTH SCHEDULE.—*Royal School Premises.*

EDUCATIONAL ENDOWMENTS (IRELAND) COMMISSION.

ULSTER ROYAL SCHOOL ENDOWMENTS.

OBJECTIONS

Lodged with the CLERK of the PRIVY COUNCIL to the SCHEME framed under the Educational Endowments (Ireland) Act, 1885, for altering the constitution of the COMMISSIONERS of EDUCATION, and for the future Government and Management of the ULSTER ROYAL SCHOOL ENDOWMENTS.

OBSERVATIONS

OF THE EDUCATIONAL ENDOWMENTS COMMISSIONERS UPON THE FOREGOING OBJECTIONS.

OBJECTIONS.

I. *The Diocesan Councils of Armagh, Derry and Raphoe, Kilmore, and Clogher.*

1. They object to the inconsistent provisions of the Scheme (clause 10) with regard to the areas entitled to benefit from the Royal School Endowments. They submit, that in accordance with the founder's intentions the area in each case should be the county, and not the diocese; and that, consequently, Monaghan should not be added to Fermanagh, nor a portion of the County of Londonderry to Tyrone.

2. They object to the constitution in the Scheme of one mixed Protestant Board in each district, while a separate Board, equal to it in numbers and in weight in the decision of common questions, has been conceded to the wishes of the Roman Catholics. They cannot understand on what grounds this privilege should have been conceded to the Roman Catholics and withheld from them. Without entering into any question of the relative importance of the differences which separate the various bodies of Christians from each other, it seems enough to point out that the bodies with which the Scheme proposes to associate the Church of Ireland feel it their duty to maintain their existence as separate communions, with distinct places and forms of worship, distinct orders of ministers, and distinct standards of faith.

They claim in the first instance a separate Board in each county for the Church of Ireland, with its due share of the endowment, and with power to unite *subsequently* with any other Protestant Local Board or Boards, on such terms as may be agreed on by the Boards concerned. On all grounds they consider it essential that provision should be made for a final division of the entire available endowments among the several Denominational Boards on the principle admitted in clause 43 of the Scheme. The tables drawn up by the Educational Endowments Commission, from the Census returns of 1881, show the following *per centages* of the literate population belonging to the several denominations in each county.

—	Roman Catholics.	Church of Ireland.	Presbyterians.	All Others.
Armagh,	37	33	25	5
Tyrone,	45	22	30	3
Fermanagh,	47	42	8	6
Cavan,	75	20	5	—
Donegal,	63	18	15	3

They submit that in each county the several Denominational Boards should receive their shares of the entire net annual income of the county endowment in the foregoing proportions, on the principle already adopted in the Scheme for the Strabane Borough School Endowment. They urge this claim with the more confidence as clause 51 of the Scheme expressly provides for the continuance of boarding departments in the several schools, whereas the Strabane Endowment is applied for the primary education of day pupils only.

Moreover, they feel convinced that the "minimum" grants as proposed in the Scheme (clause 57) would be wholly inadequate for the proper maintenance of the premises and the teaching staff of the existing Royal Schools, especially as heavy rents would be payable for the buildings by the Local Boards.

They would also observe that the apparent preservation to the Church of Ireland of the value of former gifts of her members will be illusory unless the endowments are *first* "allocated among the different Protestant denominations." [See clause 72 (b)].

3. While maintaining the above fundamental objection to the mixed Local Boards of the Scheme, they further object that in the proposed constitution of these Boards, the representation of the Church of Ireland is wholly inadequate from every point of view. In some of the districts in question are the members of the Church of Ireland fewer than the Presbyterians. Yet on each of the proposed mixed Boards for Tyrone and Donegal there are five Presbyterians and only three Churchmen, and on the Boards for Fermanagh and Cavan the Church of Ireland has not the representation to which her members are entitled, and from this disparity serious practical injustice may result in the appointment of Committees for the allocation of endowments under clauses 52 and 54, and in the treatment of competing schools in the various districts, and also from the hopeless minority in which the Church of Ireland would find herself in negotiations with Roman Catholic Local Boards.

They therefore submit that so as to correspond as nearly as possible with the above per centages the representation on the mixed Local Boards should have been as follows:—

—	Church of Ireland.	Presbyterians.	All other Protestants.
Armagh,	5	3	1
Tyrone,	4	4	1
Fermanagh,	7	1	1
Cavan,	7	2	0
Donegal,	4	4	1

4. They also object to the inadequate provision for the Church of Ireland in the proposed reconstitution of the Commissioners of Education (clause 2). While of the ten Commissioners appointed by the Lord Lieutenant five must be Roman Catholics (clause 4), the Church of Ireland cannot count on having more than one representative, equal provision being made for the Presbyterians, and even for the small number of Methodists in the counties concerned. They, therefore, claim a provision that of the ten Commissioners to be appointed by the Lord Lieutenant three shall be members of the Church of Ireland, so as to secure the representation to which she is entitled under the above returns, viz., three-fifths of the entire number (five) of Protestant Commissioners.

They object to the representation of Universities, as the functions of the Central Board will be mainly fiscal, and as the proposed arrangements for such elections will, in all probability, disturb the balance of denominational representation.

They specially protest against the admission of formal representatives of Roman Catholic and Presbyterian Divinity Schools (Maynooth and Magee College), while there is no corresponding provision for the Church of Ireland.

5. They are strengthened in their conviction that a *fixed* division of the endowments upon equitable principles is the only satisfactory mode of treatment, by finding that under clause 58 "the distribution of the residue shall be made in proportion to the number of pupils receiving intermediate education in the qualified schools." Apart from a uniform examination, no satisfactory test of "results" can be applied, and even with the restriction provided in Schedule II., mere numbers may, and probably will, outweigh merit in the calculation of "results fees." The conse-

quence will be that the greater part of the "residue" will be absorbed by large elementary schools, in which a handful of pupils (seven will suffice) will succeed in passing the Intermediate Examinations, while four times that number will serve to mask, each for results fees, without even such a qualifying examination by a State Inspector as the National Board requires. And even if the Local Boards should refuse to admit such schools to the competition, an appeal is provided to the Commissioners, whereas no appeal is allowed, even to the other Local Boards of the district, against the admission of schools not truly intermediate.

6. They consider that any application under clause 80 for an alteration of the Scheme should be founded on a resolution passed by a majority consisting of not less than two-thirds of the whole number of Commissioners for the time being.

Dated this 13th day of August, 1889,

HENRY T. DIX & SONS,
Solicitors for said Diocesan Councils,
61, Upper Sackville-street, Dublin.

II. *The Committee representing the various Protestant Denominations of County Fermanagh.*

Proposed by Mr. William Galt and seconded by Mr. William Carson, J.P.—

"That we object to section Seventy, in which '*The Fermanagh Protestant Board*' is required to provide the sum of £3,000 as a condition without which they cannot use the school premises for the purposes of education."

We hereby certify that the above resolution was passed unanimously by the meeting held this day.

CHARLES T. OVENDEN, Chairman.
E. CUTHBERT MITCHELL, Hon. Secretary.

Enniskillen, 22nd July, 1889.

OBSERVATIONS OF THE COMMISSIONERS

upon the OBJECTIONS made to SCHEME No. 24, for altering the constitution of the COMMISSIONERS of EDUCATION, and for the future government and management of THE ULSTER ROYAL SCHOOL ENDOWMENTS.

In obedience to the request of The Clerk of The Privy Council, dated September 10, 1889, the Commissioners respectfully submit the following Observations for the consideration of His Excellency The Lord Lieutenant in Council:—

Preparation of the Scheme.

"The Commissioners of Education in Ireland," pursuant to the Educational Endowments (Ireland) Act, 1885, Sec. 20, on January 30, 1886, submitted a Draft Scheme for altering their constitution, and extending their powers, and for the re-organization of the Royal Schools.

On June 21, 1886, the same Commissioners, pursuant to the Act, Sec. 27, requested that their Draft Scheme should be submitted to the Lord Lieutenant in Council, which has been done accordingly.

For Draft Scheme of "The Commissioners of Education," see Educ. End. Com. Rep. I., p. 403.

On March 1, 3, and 5, 1886, the Educational Endowments Commissioners held a public inquiry in Dublin to consider the above-mentioned Draft Scheme, and to afford an opportunity to those interested in the Royal School Endowments of presenting their views.

For Report of this Inquiry, see Rep. I., pp. 26; 40; 68.

The Commissioners afterwards held public inquiries at Cavan, October 1 and 3, 1887; Enniskillen, October 4 and 5, 1887; Raphoe, October 6, 1887; Dungannon, October 18, 1887; and Armagh, October 19 and 20, 1887. At these inquiries evidence was taken, and the parties interested were heard, personally and by Counsel.

For Report of these proceedings, see Rep. II., pp. 1; 20; 49; 154; and 170.

After consideration of the Draft Scheme submitted by "The Commissioners of Education," and of the evidence taken at the public inquiries, the Educational Endowments Commissioners, pursuant to the Act, prepared a Draft Scheme for the reconstitution of the Commissioners of Education, and the future management of the Royal School Endowments, which was published on April 30, 1888: it was accompanied by a Memorandum explaining the principles upon which it was framed.

Objections to this Draft Scheme were received from "The Commissioners of Education," and from persons and bodies representing various local, denominational, and other interests; also from the Head Masters, and others claiming vested interests in the Endowments.

For the Draft Scheme originally published with the Objections thereto, see Rep. III., pp. 507; 536.

For the consideration of these Objections the Commissioners held a further public inquiry in Dublin, on August 2, 3, 4, and 7, 1888, at which the subject was fully discussed.

For Report of this Inquiry, see Rep. III., p. 381.

The Commissioners afterwards reconsidered the Draft Scheme, and on March 30, 1889, they published a Revised Draft Scheme, which was furnished to all the parties interested who were requested to submit their further Objections and proposed Amendments, if any, before May 13, 1889; several Objections and proposed Amendments were furnished accordingly.

For the Revised Draft Scheme, and the Objections and proposed Amendments thereto, see Rep. iv., pp. 313; 323.

On May 4, 1889, the Commissioners received a Deputation from "The General Synod of the Church of Ireland," who presented the views of that body regarding the Revised Draft Scheme.

For Report of the proceedings of May 4, 1889, see Rep. iv., p. 148.

The Commissioners then held a Final Public Inquiry on May 31, 1889, for the discussion of the matters remaining in controversy upon the Revised Draft Scheme.

For Report of the proceedings of May 31, 1889, see Rep. iv., p. 162.

The Judicial Commissioners, in conference with their colleagues, then carefully discussed and finally settled the Scheme, amending the Draft in several material respects, and on June 26, 1889, they signed it, and submitted it for the approval of the Lord Lieutenant in Council.

The Commissioners deem it necessary to refer to the Reports of the foregoing proceedings, in the course of which Objections similar to those now submitted to His Excellency, with others, were discussed, and to give a summary of the facts and principles upon which the Scheme has been framed in its present shape.

Amount and Particulars of the Endowments.

The Ulster Royal School Endowments consist of three classes of property:—(a.) The School Estates. (b.) Money Funds, including Cash and Government Stock. (c.) The School Premises.

(a.) THE ULSTER ROYAL SCHOOL ESTATES.

The following is an account of the Average Income and Expenditure of the Estates of the five Ulster Royal Schools for the past five years, extracted from the Annual Reports of "The Commissioners of Education."

ULSTER ROYAL SCHOOLS ESTATES.—*Average Income and Expenditure*; 1884–8.

—	Rents Received.	Outgoings and Estate Expenses.	Townland Schools.	Rents, Taxes, and Repairs, School Premises.	Net Sum available for Royal Schools.
	£ s. d.	£ s. d.	£ s. d.	£ s. d.	£ s. d.
ARMAGH,	1,580 17 5	323 5 7	65 13 7	770 2 10	[illegible] 0 5
CAVAN,	425 0 4	187 1 8	None.	64 19 10	[illegible] 0 6
DUNGANNON,	2,004 13 10	420 17 0	30 5 5	64 16 10	[illegible] 10 4
ENNISKILLEN,	1,667 4 3	303 13 0	None.	188 10 1	1,155 [illegible] [illegible]
RAPHOE,	330 10 1	134 11 5	40 4 8	46 19 5	40 11 0
TOTALS,	6,001 16 1	1,460 [illegible] 8	179 11 0	430 11 0	3,115 [illegible] 11

(b.) MONEY FUNDS.

"The Commissioners of Education" have kept separate accounts for the five Ulster Royal Schools. They have expended upon the Armagh and Raphoe Schools sums in excess of the receipts from their endowments, debiting those Schools with the amounts advanced. The funds of the other Schools were credited with the full income derived from their estates. "The Commissioners of Education" also hold certain sums of Government Stock in trust for the Schools, derived partly from accumulations of income, and partly from sales of land. The following is a statement of the Cash and Stock, on December 31st, 1888, estimating the Stock at par.

—	Cash Balance.		Government Stock.	Total.	
	Debit.	Credit.		Debit.	Credit.
	£ s. d.	£ s. d.	£ s. d.	£ s. d.	£ s. d.
ARMAGH,	1,616 19 5	–	1,617 10 7	...	[illegible]
CAVAN,	–	1,899 [illegible] 4	4,316 18 8	–	6,[illegible] 0 0
DUNGANNON,	–	769 13 4	300 0 0	–	[illegible] 3 0
ENNISKILLEN,	–	3,307 4 8	2,[illegible] 16 4	–	6,[illegible] 1 0
RAPHOE,	1,576 11 5	–	None.	1,576 11 8	–
TOTAL,	3,[illegible] [illegible] [illegible]	5,901 [illegible] [illegible]	9,004 17 6	–	12,[illegible] 14 8

(a) The School Premises.

The following is a summary of the extent and valuation of the School Premises. The buildings have been kept in good repair by "The Commissioners of Education," and in each case include a residence for the Head Master and Assistants, in addition to accommodation for the number of pupils specified. The premises are held in fee-simple; except in the cases of Armagh, where part of the land is held in fee-farm at a rent of £40 7s. 0d.; and of Dungannon, where a small plot is held for [illegible] years at a rent of £1.

—	Lands.		Buildings.			Total Valuation.
	Extent within Mearings.	Valuation.	Accommodation.		Valuation.	
			Boarders.	Boarders and Day Pupils.		
	A. R. P.	£ s. d.			£ s. d.	£ s. d.
Armagh, ...	15 0 0	[illegible] 0 0	[illegible]	140	[illegible] 0 0	[illegible] 0 0
Cavan, ...	10 [illegible] 15	[illegible] 10 0	[illegible]	[illegible]	70 0 0	[illegible] 10 0
Dungannon, ...	10 2 18	21 0 0	[illegible]	130	140 0 0	171 0 0
Enniskillen, ...	64 1 5	[illegible] 0 0	100	150	130 0 0	[illegible] 0 0
Raphoe, ...	[illegible] 0 4	[illegible] 0 0	40	70	57 0 0	[illegible] 0 0

The financial position of the Raphoe Royal School has for several years been very embarrassed, and "The Commissioners of Education" have stated that but for the pendency of the Scheme they would have had to reduce the school expenditure very considerably. The present debt of £1,270 11s. 3d. could not be paid out of the Raphoe Endowment without closing the school. The Scheme proposes to discharge it rateably out of the cash balances standing to the credit of the Cavan, Dungannon, and Enniskillen Endowments. This course seems justified by the Act 3 Geo. IV., cap. 79, sec. 6, which enables "The Commissioners of Education" to apply the surplus funds of any of the Royal Schools in aid of the funds of any other school standing in need of assistance.

After making this provision, the accounts of the several endowments available for the educational purposes of the Scheme when fully brought into operation would appear to be approximately as follows, but the Scheme will not take effect in any case until the determination of the Head Master's vested interest, and the available income will be afterwards subject to reduction by the amount of the retiring allowances provided by the Scheme, so long as such allowances continue payable.

—	Money Funds.		Annual Value of School Premises.	Net Annual Rents.	Total Net Annual Value of Endowments.
	Capital.	Income at 3½ per cent.			
	£ s. d.	£ s. d.	£ s. d.	£ s. d.	£ s. d.
Armagh, . . .	None.	None.	[illegible] 0 0	[illegible] 0 0	673 0 4
Cavan, . . .	5,171 0 0	180 19 7	[illegible] 10 0	[illegible] 0 0	[illegible] 11 0
Dungannon, . . .	[illegible] 0 0	33 10 0	171 0 0	[illegible] 13 4	1,[illegible] 0 4
Enniskillen, . . .	4,[illegible] 0 0	150 17 4	[illegible] 0 0	1,[illegible] 0 0	1,[illegible] 19 4
Raphoe, . . .	None.	None.	[illegible] 0 0	45 11 0	107 11 0

With this statement of the present condition of the Endowments, the Commissioners proceed to deal with the Objections to the Scheme.

I. Objection of the Diocesan Councils of Armagh, Derry and Raphoe, Kilmore, and Clogher.

Area entitled to benefit from the Royal School Endowments.

The Draft Scheme of "The Commissioners of Education" proposed forthwith to discontinue the Royal Schools of Raphoe, Cavan, and Enniskillen, and to apply the Endowments as a common fund for the maintenance of four denominational Schools, namely:—one at Armagh, one at Dungannon, one in Munster, and one in Leinster; "the School at Armagh to be presided over by a Head Master professing the faith of the Church of Ireland; the School at Dungannon by a Head Master professing the faith of the Presbyterian Church of Ireland; and the two Schools in Munster and Leinster by Head Masters professing the Roman Catholic faith." Power was reserved to subsidize Schools in the districts in which the existing Royal Schools were discontinued, but so that the aggregate of all such subsidies should in no event exceed £400 per annum. Rep. I., 434.

Earl Belmore, on the part of "The Commissioners of Education," stated their view to be that each of these four Schools should have £1,000 per annum: that the Roman Catholics should have half the endowment, and the other two denominations divide the other half, reserving power to Ib. 22.

vary these proportions, "if one School was only half availed of, and another was fail." Having regard to their Act, sec. 13, and to the trusts affecting the endowments, the Judicial Commissioners did not feel justified in depriving three of the present districts of their Schools, or in applying the funds to maintain Schools in Leinster or Munster.

[illegible] In the Letter directing the foundation of the Ulster Royal Schools King James I. declared his intention to endow the Endowments to the Archbishop and Bishops in whose Dioceses the lands should be allotted. The direction that there should be one Free School at least appointed in each of the Counties of Armagh, Tyrone, Donegal, Fermanagh, and Cavan is contained in an Order of the Irish Privy Council.

The Statute 14 & 15 Charles II., cap. 10, which is still in force, enabled the Lord Lieutenant, with the assent of the Privy Council, and the approbation of the Archbishop of the Province and Bishop of the Diocese, to remove the several Royal Schools "from one town to another more convenient *within the same Diocese wherein the School was formerly kept*," and to "divide the possessions of any one of the said schools into two or more, where they should find cause."

The Statute 3 Geo. IV., cap. 79, sec. 8, also still in force, enabled the surplus funds of any of the Royal Schools to be applied to the purposes of any others of the schools needing aid. The Judicial Commissioners, therefore, were of opinion that the inhabitants of the Dioceses in which the schools were situated—namely, the Dioceses of Armagh, Kilmore, Clogher, and Raphoe—were within the scope of these Endowments, and that the counties in which the schools were situated had not an exclusive claim. They also thought that the Act of 1885 authorised the employment of a portion of the funds of one district in another, for purposes of Intermediate Education, if due regard were had to the needs and circumstances of each locality, and the amount of the endowments.

In the case of Armagh, the county had hitherto almost exclusively enjoyed the benefits of the Endowment, and was almost wholly within the Diocese of Armagh; and the endowment appeared capable of full utilisation within the County of Armagh, which the Scheme therefore adopted as the Armagh District.

In the cases of Cavan and Raphoe, the Counties of Cavan and Donegal were, for similar reasons, adopted as the School Districts.

Rep. iv., 163. In the case of Tyrone, the Commissioners found that a small part of the Diocese of Armagh, including the town of Magherafelt, was, at the date of the King's letter directing the foundation of the Royal Schools, part of the County of Tyrone, but was afterwards transferred to the County of Londonderry. The Commissioners did not see any reason to exclude it from the School District. The effect of its inclusion will be to enable the Tyrone Local Boards, if they should at any time think fit, to aid Intermediate Education at Magherafelt. All except one of the members of these Boards represent the County of Tyrone, and an extension of the endowment beyond the limits of the county is therefore not likely to take place without urgent reasons.

The Commissioners venture to doubt that the objection to the inclusion of Magherafelt would be now pressed but for its bearing upon the more important question of including the County of Monaghan in the Fermanagh District.

[illegible] The whole County of Monaghan is included in the Diocese of Clogher, which also includes the greater part, but not the whole, of the County of Fermanagh. The Enniskillen Endowment is larger than any of the others in amount, and for many years the Commissioners of Education have not fully expended it upon Portora Royal School, which is the only public "Superior School" returned in the Census, or of which any pupils appear to have passed the examinations of the Intermediate Education Board, from the County of Fermanagh.

[illegible] The Roman Catholic College for the Diocese of Clogher is established at Monaghan, and educates a considerable number of pupils from the County of Fermanagh, for whom no other Intermediate School is equally available. It was erected at a cost of over £20,000, but its annual endowment is only £110.

The Diocesan School established under the Statute 12 Elizabeth, cap. 1, for the Diocese of Clogher, and formerly under the management of "The Commissioners of Education," was also situated at Monaghan. It lost its Endowment by the operation of the Irish Church Act, 1869, in the year 1878, when Dr. M. C. Hime, the last Diocesan Schoolmaster, was appointed to Foyle College.

[illegible] Up to that time, it was a very successful school, having upwards of 100 pupils. It was closed by "the Commissioners of Education" until 1882, when it was re-opened as a Collegiate School by a Local Protestant Committee, who raised upwards of £600 0s. 0d., which they expended upon the buildings. The School has since steadily increased, and is now vested in a Local Governing Body constituted by a Scheme approved by the Lord Lieutenant under the Educational Endowments Act, 1885. Within the last three years twenty-eight of its pupils, some of whom are boarders from the Counties of Fermanagh, Cavan, Armagh, and Tyrone, have passed the Intermediate Examinations. It has no endowment except the school premises.

[illegible] Under these circumstances, the Judicial Commissioners were of opinion that the inhabitants of the County of Monaghan, being within the Diocese of Clogher, had a claim to participate in the Enniskillen Royal School Endowment at least as meritorious as that of the inhabitants of the other Royal School Districts. The effect of excluding Monaghan would have been to deprive the pupils from Fermanagh, now receiving their education at Monaghan, of the benefit of the endowment, and either to exclude the Roman Catholics from availing themselves of the endowment, or to oblige them to establish a new Intermediate School within the County of Fermanagh, at the same time depriving the Protestant Local Board of the power to claim the share of the Royal School Endowments to which the success of the Monaghan Collegiate School would otherwise entitle them under the Scheme

Claims were made to extend the area of the Scheme to the Counties of Antrim and Down, and the remaining portion of Londonderry, outside the Diocese of Armagh. These claims were supported by Dr. Traill, but were rejected by the Judicial Commissioners as unwarranted by the terms of the foundation, and also because the amount of the Endowments was so small that the admission of the large educational establishments of Derry, Coleraine, and Belfast would leave the Schools of the present districts without adequate or even substantial pecuniary support. Rep. [illegible] Rep. [illegible]

For these reasons the Commissioners submit that the proposal of the Diocesan Councils to deprive portions of their own Dioceses of the benefits of the Scheme should not prevail.

Separation of the Protestant Denominations.

Throughout the inquiries of the Commission, it was conceded by all concerned that the Roman Catholics entertained insurmountable objections to avail themselves of Schools under undenominational management, and that the administration of whatever funds were to be made available for them must be entrusted exclusively to members of their own Church. It may be observed that there was no instance in Ulster of the successful management of an educational institution by a body including both Roman Catholics and Protestants.

The Commissioners felt themselves bound, from the public character of the Royal School Endowments, to distribute them in just proportions among all denominations, upon terms to which none could reasonably take exception upon conscientious grounds. Separate Roman Catholic Local Boards were therefore formed.

It is a principle of the Scheme to secure that each Local Board thereby constituted shall receive in the first instance, as "its due share of the endowment," a minimum grant sufficiently large to afford substantial aid to at least one Intermediate School. Under the Scheme, this minimum grant consists, in each case, of a fixed percentage of the receipts from the School Estate, with a provision for School premises, either from the existing lands and buildings, or from an equivalent capital sum. The Endowments are insufficient to make such a provision for more than two Local Boards in any of the districts; the existing School premises could not in any case be divided into more than two parts; and Dungannon and Enniskillen are the only cases in which any division of them could be made. Rep. [illegible] Rep. [illegible]

The evidence given to the Commissioners satisfied them that the great majority of the Protestants of Ulster, including the majority of the members of "The Church of Ireland," though maintaining "their existence as separate Communions" in other respects, desired to unite in the management of the schools attended by their children.

The successful Protestant Schools of Ulster, almost without an exception, have been established, and are managed by mixed Local Boards.

As examples, the Commissioners would mention the Royal Belfast Academy; the Royal Belfast Academical Institution; Foyle College, Londonderry; the Londonderry Academical Institution; the Coleraine Academical Institution; the Strabane Academy; Waring Endowed School, Lurgan; and the Monaghan Collegiate School. Except the Methodist College, Belfast, the Commissioners do not know of any Intermediate School in Ulster equally efficient or successful with those which they have mentioned, which is under the exclusive management of the members of any single Protestant denomination.

The claim for separate Boards for "The Church of Ireland" was first made in Dublin, by "The Standing Committee of the General Synod," and was discussed at the inquiries held in the localities of the several Royal Schools with the following results. Rep. [illegible] Rep. [illegible]

At Cavan a Memorial was presented on behalf of the different Protestant denominations by the Right Rev. Samuel Shone, D.D., Bishop of Kilmore. It was signed by 627 persons belonging to all the Protestant denominations. The memorialists claimed the Royal School premises, with a subsidy adequate to maintain a good classical school, and sufficient to meet the just requirements of the district, and they advocated such a change in the management of the present Royal School as would place it on a broader and more popular basis. Rep. [illegible]

This Memorial was supported by the Rev. William H. Hutchinson, M.A., Diocesan Secretary, and by a number of witnesses of other Protestant denominations. The formation of a corporate body, with the Bishop at its head, on which all Protestant denominations should be represented, was advocated. Rep. [illegible]

The Bishop in giving evidence respecting the Tullyvin School near Cavan, stated his belief that if a mixed body were formed, there was a prospect of their being able to give a higher education to the boys of the neighbourhood. A joint Board was subsequently formed by Scheme No. 30, for the Tullyvin Endowment, and in Dublin, on May 4, 1889, the Bishop stated that so far as they had gone it had worked well in Cavan. Rep. [illegible] Rep. [illegible]

At Enniskillen a Local Committee was formed to represent "The Church of Ireland, the Presbyterian Church, and the Methodist Church," and the Rev. S. Cuthbert Mitchell, Presbyterian Minister of Enniskillen, appeared as Honorary Secretary of that Committee to represent "the whole Protestant community." He stated that he did not anticipate the slightest difficulty in establishing or managing a School, for both Boarders and Day Boys, to which all denominations of Protestants might come; that the Local Committee were convinced that they could manage the Portora School if they had control of it themselves; and he desired it to be left to each denomination to select their own representatives. Rep. [illegible] [illegible] [illegible]

These views were supported by other witnesses, members of the Committee, including the Rector of Enniskillen, the Rector of the adjoining Parish of Rossory, in which Portora is situated, and the Methodist Minister of Enniskillen. [illegible] [illegible]

Rep. 8, 34. The Right Rev. Charles M. Stack, D.D., Bishop of Clogher, advocated the proposal of the Committee, as being exactly the same as that which had succeeded in Monaghan, viz., a Board composed of all the Protestant denominations, who, he was quite certain, would prefer to make a joint effort in Enniskillen to maintain a School.

The Commissioners asked the Committee to furnish them with the heads of the Scheme which Ib. 323. they desired, and the Bishop subsequently, on October 20, 1886, forwarded a statement, signed by all the Protestant witnesses who had appeared at Enniskillen, including himself. This document contained the following passage:—

> "In reference to the *Constitution of the proposed Local Board*, we desire that the Board should consist of the following gentlemen:—The Right Rev. Charles Stack, D.D., Lord Bishop of Clogher, and his successors; the Rector of the Parish of Enniskillen; the Rector of the Parish of Rossory, Enniskillen; the Presbyterian Minister of Enniskillen; the Superintendent Minister of the Enniskillen Methodist Circuit; one Layman elected by the Select Vestry of Enniskillen Parish; one Layman elected by the Select Vestry of Rossory Parish; one Layman elected by the Committee of the Enniskillen Presbyterian Congregation; and one Layman elected by the Quarterly Meeting of the Enniskillen Methodist Circuit."

The Committee proposed that this Board should hold, in trust for the benefit of Protestants of all denominations in the district, the Portora School premises, and any other moneys or property of a public or private nature that might at any time be entrusted to the Board for educational purposes; and they specified a number of provisions which they desired to introduce into the Scheme.

At the further Inquiry on August 3, 1888, upon the hearing of Objections to the original Draft Scheme, Counsel for the Committee representing the various Protestant denominations of Fermanagh strongly opposed the views of the Diocesan Councils. He stated that the Bishop of Clogher Rep. 48, 191. was at the head of the Committee; that they were all in favour of all the Protestant denominations being united, and saw no difficulty in their working. He put forward many objections to separation; stated that the separate denominations had no schools in existence; that all those denominations felt that their only chance of having any efficient schools equipped in a proper way, and having competent masters, was to have a united school in each district; that if the Protestant share of the endowment was to be disintegrated into fragments, it would be perfectly impossible to have any good schools at all; that splitting the Endowment into fragments was quite inconsistent with the basis that had been laid down of giving a minimum to each efficient school in the first instance; and that a permanent division of the endowments among the different religious communities would produce hostility among the different sections of the Protestant community, and would be a disastrous thing upon all considerations.

Rep. 16, 172. Ib. 189. At the final Inquiry on May 31, 1889, Counsel for the Fermanagh Protestant Committee stated that, so far as Enniskillen and Fermanagh were concerned, they were all united; they had got a common mixed Board, and they were perfectly content to have it; and they were content, too, that the amount coming to each of these bodies, Episcopalian, Presbyterian, and Methodist, should be put into a common fund. Though the Committee thought that the proportion of each body should be allocated in separate shares, they knew they could not maintain Portora in an efficient condition unless they administered all their shares as one; they were all agreed about that.

Report, 8, 23. At Raphoe a public meeting was convened by the Magistrates, and a Local Committee was appointed to endeavour to secure the maintenance of the Raphoe Royal School.

This Committee consisted of the Rector of Raphoe, the Master of the Royal School, the Ministers of the two leading Presbyterian Congregations of Raphoe, two lay members of "the Church of Ireland," and three lay Presbyterians.

The Honorary Secretary of this Committee informed the Commissioners at Raphoe that the only way in which there was the slightest hope of the school being well managed was by having a Local Rep. 8, 23. Board, which should be fairly representative of the religious denominations of the people in proportion to their numbers. Statistics were given of the pupils available for the Royal School, if conducted on the system recommended by the Committee, and of these more than three-fourths were Presbyterians. The Secretary stated that if there was to be a school there at all, it must be supported by the people of the Presbyterian Church; and that the Episcopalians and Presbyterians had never found the slightest difficulty in working together.

Rep. C, 23. Colonel Montgomery, D.L., representing the Episcopalians, stated that they wished to co-operate with their Presbyterian brethren; that it would be a great misfortune if there was anything done that would raise anything like a sectarian principle in the school; and that a joint management would be much better.

Ib. 26. The Rev. K. H. Thompson, Incumbent of the neighbouring Parish of Convoy, stated that there was no reason to suppose that any difficulty would arise from the joint composition of the Board of Management, but that the number of Church people in the district entitled them to have representation on the Board, which he was certainly satisfied to take in proportion to their numbers.

Ib. The Rev. W. A. E. Murphy, Incumbent of Mevagh, a former pupil of the School, anticipated no difficulty in the working of the Committee; stating that it would be in the hands of the Presbyterians, naturally, from their superior numbers.

Ib. 23. Of fourteen pupils attending the Raphoe Royal School in October, 1883, thirteen were Presbyterians.

The Donegal Protestant Local Board proposed by the Scheme is constituted in the exact proportions of the various Protestant denominations desired by the Raphoe Committee, and the Rev. Canon Babington, a Member of the Deputation of the General Synod, though desiring that separate Boards should be formed in the first instance, informed the Commissioners in Dublin, on May 8, 1889, as follows:—

"As far as we are concerned, in the one particular instance in which I am interested, we would join, and join without difficulty." [illegible]

At Dungannon, a Local Committee was appointed at a public meeting convened by Lord Ranfurly, and well attended by all the Protestant bodies. [illegible]

The Rev. Dr. Ringwood, Head Master of the Royal School, stated that he had found no difficulty with the Presbyterians, and thought that if a school were formed at Dungannon in which the Governing Body included Episcopalians, Presbyterians, and Methodists, and they chose the Masters, it would succeed. [illegible]

Robert Stevenson, Esq., Chairman of the Local Committee, informed the Commissioners that a Local Committee was of vital importance to the school; and that it would be much better for all the people that the Protestant denominations should act together, and that the school should be under a mixed Board. He presented a written statement as to the urgent necessity for a classical school in Dungannon, setting forth proposals for its management, recommending a Local Board consisting of the Rector of the parish, the Presbyterian and Methodist Ministers, and representative Laymen, and he considered such a joint management scheme very much better than the proposal of "the Commissioners of Education," to divide the schools among the different Protestant denominations. [illegible] [illegible]

At Armagh opinion was divided.

The Rev. W. M. Morgan, LL.D., Head Master of Armagh Royal School, was against a mixed Board having the management of a denominational school. [illegible]

His Grace the Lord Primate claimed the right of appointment of the Master of Armagh School for the Archbishop of Armagh and his successors; a claim which the Judicial Commissioners, having regard to the "Irish Church Act, 1869," sec. 30, found themselves unable to admit. He also expressed an opinion that no attempt to create a mixed body to govern a boarding school would be attended with success. [illegible]

The Very Rev. C. A. Chadwick, D.D., Dean of Armagh, feared that a mixed Board would be dangerous to the school, "speaking of boarding schools purely;" he was in favour of having in one place a Presbyterian school and in another place a Church school, and did not believe it possible to work a boarding school satisfactorily on the mixed principle, though, if the boarding department were free from interference by persons representing different religious persuasions, he "would be very glad to see the town represented." As regards the day school, if the boarding school could be independent of it, he did not see why some such scheme should not be carried out. [illegible]

Upon this point, the Commissioners may remark that the Scheme, sections 50, 51, and 53, are specially framed to enable the Local Boards to make arrangements of the character indicated by the Dean of Armagh. Each Local Board may recognise and aid schools under the exclusive management of members of any one denomination, and may make arrangements for separate Boarding Departments.

On the other hand, at Armagh, Robert G. M'Crum, Esq., High Sheriff of the County, representing the Presbyterian laity, suggested the formation of a Local Board of Management consisting of Representatives of the different Protestant denominations. [illegible]

The Rev. Jackson Smyth, D.D., and the Rev. John Elliott, Presbyterian Ministers of Armagh, preferred combining with other Protestant denominations, and the latter proposed a Representative Board, with the Primate at the head of it, composed both of Clergy and Laymen. He stated that he should be very sorry to see an exclusive Board at the head of either Armagh or Dungannon School, thought it would be moving in the wrong direction, and was quite sure there would not be the least difficulty with a local Board comprising several denominations, as the Governing Body of the School. [illegible]

Thomas G. Peel, Esq., Clerk of the Armagh Town Commissioners, presented a memorial from twenty members of that Body, praying that the Armagh Royal School should not be disturbed, that its endowments should continue to be applied as heretofore, and that no change should be made. He stated, however, that if any change were made, he would not object to a Local Committee such as had been suggested by the High Sheriff, so as, if possible, to make the School more useful than it was. In that case, he did not object to a mixed body of Protestant denominations, and would admit one Presbyterian Minister to "balance" the Primate. [illegible]

When the Commissioners came finally to revise the Scheme, they thought, upon the foregoing evidence, that the Armagh district was the only one in which there was a desire on the part of any section of the Protestant inhabitants for the formation of separate Local Boards. It also appeared to them that a most favourable opportunity existed in the case of the Armagh and Tyrone districts of endeavouring to form such boards, and, recognising the importance of satisfying all reasonable objections, they took measures to enable the representatives of "the Church of Ireland" to carry out the views now advocated by the Diocesan Councils.

The circumstances of the Armagh and Dungannon Schools and Endowments exceptionally facilitated the formation of separate Protestant Boards in those districts.

The Endowments were both of substantial amount.

The Schools, from their position, were competing Schools, and both had never been successful at the same time. Taking the Armagh and Tyrone districts together, the Episcopalians were almost equal in numbers to the other Protestants, and the aggregate numbers of Episcopalian and Presbyterian representatives on the proposed Local Boards were the same.

[illegible] On May 4, 1889, the Commissioners directed the attention of the deputation from the General Synod to these circumstances, and suggested that they should endeavour to come to an agreement before the completion of the Scheme; at the final hearing on May 31, 1889, the Commissioners formally offered to provide by the Scheme for a Presbyterian School and Board at Dungannon, and a Church Board and School at Armagh, with power to work denominationally over the two districts, if any practicable arrangement to that effect could be made, and the Dean of Armagh undertook to open negotiations without the loss of a day.

On June 1, 1889, the Commissioners addressed a circular letter to the members of the proposed Armagh and Tyrone Protestant Boards, and to the bodies representing the denominations concerned, containing proposals for leaving it to the determination of those interested whether mixed or separate Protestant Boards should be formed.

Attention is respectfully directed to this letter, which will be found Rep. iv., p. 337.

The Dean of Armagh and the Rev. H. B. Wilson, D.D., were requested to assist in obtaining such an expression of opinion as might be a guide to the Commissioners in dealing with the subject.

In the result the majority preferred the proposals of the Scheme to the formation of separate Boards, but there was a minority who would prefer the latter alternative, provided the funds were equally divided between Armagh and Tyrone.

The Methodist representatives were very unfavourable to the proposal to divide the Protestant Local Boards.

With one exception, the Presbyterians were strongly opposed to Denominational Boards, as they thought injury would be done thereby to both schools.

The Very Rev. James Byrne, D.D., Dean of Clonfert, preferred the mixed Boards proposed by the Commissioners to an arrangement which would in practice come to a Presbyterian Board for Dungannon, and a Church Board for Armagh. The establishment of exclusive Boards seemed to him "to assume that the Church and other Protestants could not beneficially work together a system of Intermediate Education," which assumption he regarded as an exaggeration of religious difference not corresponding to the actual sentiments which prevailed between the religious bodies themselves. Both Schools would, he thought, have more pupils under mixed Boards, and would, in consequence, be more vigorous and efficient in every way, and it would, in his view, be matter for deep regret that sectarianism should be stamped on the Higher Education of the country.

The weight of this opinion was enhanced, not only by Dean Byrne's position in his Church and in the locality, but by his experience as a former Fellow of Trinity College, Dublin.

Of the lay members of the proposed Local Boards, all but one were opposed to the formation of separate Boards, in the interests of Education.

[illegible] The Armagh Diocesan Council, with three of its clerical members and two of its lay members, and the Rev. H. B. Wilson, D.D., who were individually consulted as members of the proposed Local Boards, supported the proposal for separate Boards.

Under these circumstances the Commissioners introduced Sec. 53 of the Scheme, to enable the Armagh and Tyrone Boards to form separate Boards, and to divide their share of the Endowment, upon just terms, if they should at any time so desire, but they felt bound to adhere to the principle of forming united Protestant Boards in the first instance, as being not only in consonance with the wishes of all Protestant Denominations in four of the five districts, but also supported by the general preponderance of argument and opinion.

They would again observe that the Scheme, while enabling the Protestant Local Boards to act together upon all common questions, in no way precludes the establishment of schools, or of separate boarding or other departments, under the exclusive management of the members of distinct denominations. The Objection of the Diocesan Councils seems to misapprehend the effect of the Scheme in this respect, as, under its provisions, the Endowments will be applied to Schools under the direct management of mixed Boards only where the Local Board, in each case, think it inexpedient to recognise, or impossible to maintain separate Schools.

Final Division of the Endowments.

The Commissioners must observe that they never drew up any tables making the division of the literate population, or showing the percentages, set forth in the Objection.

The percentages stated are not accurately calculated from any tables known to the Commissioners, and the Objection omits the separate return of Methodists, which is contained in the Census, and was referred to throughout the proceedings.

The tables referred to as having been drawn up by the Commission, were prepared by Dr. Traill upon calculations based on Table 144 of the General Census. Though the Commissioners believe them to be accurately computed, they were not made the basis of the Scheme.

As the objection proposes to divide the endowments in proportion to the percentages of "the literate population" appearing from the Census, the Commissioners have now extracted the following Table from the Census Returns, 1881, Table xxx., for the separate counties, showing the numbers of each denomination who "read and write," and their percentages in each district.

TABLE showing the Numbers and Percentages of the "Literate Population," according to Religious Professions, in the undenominational Counties and Districts, from the Census 1881: Table xxx.

County and District.	R.C.		Protestant Episcopalians.		Presbyterians.		Methodists.		All Others.		Total.	
	Number.	Per Cent.	Number.	Per Cent.	Number.	Per Cent.	Number.	Per Cent.	Number.	Per Cent.	Number.	Per Cent.
1. Armagh District,	28,634	57·68	27,848	54·[illegible]	17,884	21·[illegible]	2,859	[illegible]	9,988	0·78	51,877	100
Tyrone County,	44,271	45·1	24,330	24·63	25,300	26·12	7,621	7·64	1,089	1·11	98,384	100
Armagh Diocese in Derry County.	3,840	33·51	8,651	75·49	3,725	34·71	46	·43	151	1·39	10,738	100
2. Tyrone District,	46,451	44·68	27,894	26·71	20,848	25·67	6,367	6·44	1,438	1·39	103,467	100
Fermanagh County,	21,088	46·73	19,188	42·20	1,908	4·41	3,697	8·1	56	·12	44,189	100
Monaghan County,	33,366	64·16	8,735	16·87	8,965	18·26	477	·81	514	1·	52,808	100
3. Fermanagh District.	54,386	56·30	27,571	28·55	10,507	10·85	4,084	4·2	580	·6	97,548	100
4. Cavan District.	51,046	75·19	12,680	18·42	3,177	4·68	940	1·38	294	·43	67,848	100
5. Donegal District.	47,330	61·49	13,808	17·96	13,705	17·83	1,428	1·89	680	·9	76,970	100
Total,	[illegible]	52·53	109,[illegible]	[illegible]	78,384	17·05	19,985	2·89	8,808	1·81	432,671	100

The Methodists are at least as distinct from any branch of the Presbyterian Church as they are from "The Church of Ireland." Their numbers, position, and exertions for education seemed to give them a claim to distinct representation in dealing with the public endowments.

The "Reformed Presbyterian Church," the "United Presbyterians," the "Seceding Presbyterians," the "Non-Subscribing Presbyterians," the "Covenanters," and other denominations adopting the Presbyterian system of Church government, form the bulk of those included among "All other Denominations" in the Census. If these are not to be separately recognised, they must be classified as "Presbyterians" in estimating the "percentages of the literate population."

The Commissioners are of opinion that if separate Boards be formed for "The Church of Ireland" and the "Presbyterians," similar provision should be made for the Methodists, and therefore the creation of at least four denominational Boards, and the division of the Endowments into at least four shares, would follow if the Objection be allowed.

In that case the principle that the minimum grant secured to each Local Board should be sufficient to afford substantial aid to at least one Intermediate School in each district must be abandoned, as the endowments are insufficient to provide such grants for more than two Boards.

In most cases, the proposed division would break up the endowments into shares so small as to be useless, and would deprive those districts where the endowments are not large, and those denominations who are in any district proportionally few, of all chance of substantial aid.

The difficulty of dividing the School premises, or of allocating their value among more than two Boards, appears insurmountable, and no suggestion has been put forward upon this point which is consistent with the treatment of the School premises as a part of the public endowments, and subject to the claims of all denominations.

The annexed Tables contrast the mode of distribution proposed in the Scheme with the results of a "final division" upon the principle proposed in the Objection.

f

TABLE showing the Distribution of the NET CASH INCOME of the Royal School Estates and Money Funds, in proportion to the "PERCENTAGES OF THE LITERATE POPULATION," as proposed in the OBJECTIONS.

Schools.	Roman Catholics.		"Church of Ireland."		Methodists.		Presbyterians and "All Others."		Total for each School.
	Percentage.	Amount.	Percentage.	Amount.	Percentage.	Amount.	Percentage.	Amount.	
		£ s. d.		£ s. d.		£ s. d.		£ s. d.	£ s. d.
1. Armagh, ...	37·43	[illegible] 8 0	11·26	[illegible] 1 0	[illegible]	37 4 0	[illegible]	104 17 0	[illegible]
2. Cavan, . . .	75·10	[illegible] 19 [illegible]	13·47	97 15 0	1·34	5 10 10	[illegible]	[illegible] 19 1	47[illegible] [illegible]
3. Donegal, . . .	[illegible]	[illegible] 0 1	[illegible]	6 8 8	1·43	0 10 8	1[illegible]	8 10 7	46 [illegible]
4. Fermanagh District,	[illegible]	[illegible] 5 [illegible]	[illegible]	[illegible] 17 [illegible]	[illegible]	84 17 0	[illegible]	[illegible] 0 0	[illegible]
Fermanagh County, .	[illegible]	[illegible] 5 1	[illegible]	[illegible]	9·1	[illegible] 15 [illegible]	[illegible]	[illegible]	[illegible]
5. Tyrone District, .	14·26	4[illegible] 0 0	[illegible]	[illegible] 0 0	[illegible]	[illegible] 4 0	[illegible]	[illegible] 7 4	[illegible]
Tyrone County, . .	[illegible]	[illegible]	[illegible]	[illegible]	[illegible]	[illegible]	[illegible]	[illegible]	[illegible]
Total Districts, . .		3,7[illegible] 19 0		[illegible] 0 10		1[illegible] [illegible]		[illegible] 7 0	[illegible]
Total Counties, . .		[illegible] 13 7		[illegible]		104 15 11		[illegible]	[illegible]

TABLE showing the Distribution of the ROYAL SCHOOL ENDOWMENTS as proposed in the SCHEME.

Schools.	Minimum Grant to each Local Board.							Residue.	Total for Annual Amount.
	Share of						Total Minimum Grant.	Residual Contribution to Residue.	
	School Property.		Money Funds.		Share of Surplus Income.				
	Percentage.	Annual Value.	Percentage.	Annual Sum.	Annual Amount.				
		£ s. d.		£ s. d.	£ s. d.		£ s. d.	£ s. d.	£ s. d.
1. Armagh. Protestant Board, . .	[illegible]	(a) 1[illegible] 0 [illegible]	[illegible]	None.	170 17 [illegible]		[illegible] 17 4	[illegible] 14 7	[illegible]
Roman Catholic Board, .	[illegible]	[illegible]	[illegible]	None.	[illegible] 17 [illegible]		[illegible] 17 4		
2. Cavan. Protestant Board, . .	[illegible]	(b) [illegible] 15 [illegible]	[illegible]	[illegible]	[illegible]		1[illegible] 0 0	[illegible]	[illegible]
Roman Catholic Board, .	[illegible]	None.	[illegible]	[illegible] 1 [illegible]	[illegible]		1[illegible] 0 0		
3. Donegal. Protestant Board, . .	[illegible]	(c) [illegible]	[illegible]	None.	7[illegible] 15 [illegible]		[illegible] 15 0	None.	[illegible]
Roman Catholic Board, .	[illegible]	[illegible]	[illegible]	None.	[illegible] 14 [illegible]		53 10 0		
4. Fermanagh. Protestant Board, . .	[illegible]	(d) [illegible]	[illegible]	[illegible] 14 [illegible]	[illegible] 7		4[illegible] 14 11	[illegible] 10 [illegible]	1,0[illegible]
Roman Catholic Board, .	[illegible]	[illegible]	[illegible]	[illegible] 14 [illegible]	[illegible] 7		[illegible] 14 11		
5. Tyrone. Protestant Board, . .	[illegible]	(e) [illegible]	[illegible]	[illegible]	[illegible]		[illegible] 10 10	470 [illegible]	[illegible]
Roman Catholic Board, .	[illegible]	[illegible]	[illegible]	[illegible]	[illegible]		[illegible] 10 10		
Total, . .		[illegible]		[illegible] 1 [illegible]	3,010 10 [illegible]		[illegible] 10 [illegible]	1,[illegible] 15 [illegible]	[illegible]

Total annual amount secured to Local Boards, as Minimum Grants, £2,[illegible] 16 [illegible]
Total annual amount distributable as Residue, ... £1,[illegible] 15 [illegible]

(a.) The value of the Armagh School Premises is fixed by the Scheme, sec. 67, at £[illegible] per annum.

(b.) The value of the Cavan School Premises is taken at £[illegible] 10s. 0d. per annum, being 3½ per cent. upon £[illegible] allotted to the Roman Catholic Board as an equivalent for the existing School premises, which may be taken by the Protestant Board under the Scheme, sec. 68. Rep. [illegible]

(c.) The value of the Donegal School premises is taken at the Government Valuation.

(d.) The value of the Enniskillen School premises is taken at £193 10s. 0d. per annum, being 3½ per cent. upon £7,000, the purchase money offered by the War Office, and fixed by the Scheme, sec. 78, as the estimated value for the purpose of pre-emption by the Protestant Board. [illegible]

(e.) The Tyrone Local Boards are in negotiation to divide the existing School premises, as they are considered sufficient to accommodate two Schools. Their value is taken at the Government Valuation. [illegible]

The share of the Protestant Local Board in the value of the School premises, as shown in the foregoing table, will be increased in any case where a claim in respect of private benefactions is established; and, during the first three years after the Scheme comes into operation in each District, the whole net income of the endowments will be divided between the Local Boards, to aid them in making effective arrangements for Intermediate Education in their several districts. Scheme, sec. 73 (b.) [illegible]

For some time after the Scheme comes into force, there will, however, probably be a considerable charge upon the funds for the retiring allowances of the present masters. [illegible]

Even if any basis of distribution, defensible on principle, could have been found, the Commissioners would have thought it most inexpedient to make a final division of the entire endowments.

Such a division would destroy the stimulus to exertion supplied by the provision for giving proportionate benefits to the schools doing the largest amount of educational work. It would leave the more poorly endowed districts, and the denominations whose numbers in any district are proportionately few, with shares useless in themselves, and insufficient to induce others, "voluntarily" to unite on fair terms with those entitled to them. Unless the terms of union are fixed by the Scheme, dissensions are likely to arise, and the more poorly endowed parties to the arrangements will certainly be placed at a disadvantage.

Again, a final division would attach endowments to districts in which there is no guarantee for their efficient employment. For example, the Enniskillen endowment, consisting of school premises worth £7,000, money funds amounting to £[illegible], and an estate producing a net income of £[illegible] per annum, would be permanently appropriated to the County of Fermanagh, in which the Enniskillen Royal School, from which only five pupils in all passed the examinations of the Intermediate Education Board during the last four years, appears to be the *only public Intermediate School*. [illegible]

The history of the Royal Schools appears to furnish a strong argument against giving fixed endowments to particular schools, or making educational grants without regard to the work done in return. The numbers of the pupils have always been subject to extreme fluctuation, though the expenditure upon the Schools has always been very large, and has for many years remained about the same. [illegible]

The Commissioners further found it impossible to discover any principle upon which the "due share of the endowment," to which any denomination was entitled, could be finally or permanently ascertained. The total population, the "literate population," rating qualifications, the numbers returned in the Census as attending "Superior Schools," and the number passing the Intermediate Examinations, were all suggested as the basis of division, and in every instance appeared to be met by valid objections. [illegible]

The Commissioners accept the principle that the claims upon the Royal School Endowments are proportionate to the relative numbers of those who require the class of education to which these Endowments have been devoted. The Commissioners believe them to be required, and to be legally appropriated, for the highest class of Intermediate Education—namely, education which includes the teaching of Greek and Latin, Modern Languages, and the other subjects of instruction in advanced Schools. The Scheme has been framed with the object of confining the benefit of these Endowments to Schools of that character. It appears impossible to estimate at any one time even the aggregate number of pupils likely in the future to need Grammar School Education in any locality. It is hopeless to attempt to estimate the relative numbers of such pupils belonging to different religious denominations, or to different districts. Therefore the Scheme proposes to prescribe strict conditions as to the class of education to which the funds must be applied, to give the whole available Endowment to the Local Boards of each district for a period of three years, to be expended in establishing a system of Grammar School education in whatever manner each Board thinks best suited to its own locality, and afterwards permanently to secure to each Board a definite sum which ought, if properly employed, to be substantially useful to at least one School, with a share of the residue proportionate to the amount of Grammar School education actually given in the qualified School or Schools which it maintains.

In this way only, as it seemed to the Commissioners, could those denominations which claim larger shares than their numbers seem to warrant, prove their title to their just proportion.

If the arguments be well founded which are advanced to show that the number of pupils seeking Grammar School education preponderate in any particular denomination, or in any particular district, the Scheme will proportionately increase their claim upon the Endowments.

The impossibility of adopting the statistics of any fixed period as a just or satisfactory basis for permanent division is apparent. Some of those who represented "the Church of Ireland" at one time proposed to accept the numbers passing the examinations of the Intermediate Education [illegible]

f 2

Board as the basis of division, yet, according to this test, the proportion assignable to the Protestant Schools, for the whole area of the Scheme, would in 1885 have been 53 per cent., and would have been 65 per cent. in 18[illegible], while the total numbers passing from the Schools of particular counties or districts were, in several cases, so small that accidental changes in individual Schools in successive years completely altered the percentages, and rendered the results, as between the different districts and the different denominations, wholly untrustworthy for the purpose of any permanent division.

Rep. iv., [illegible]. Rep. iv., 172.

A division of the endowments separately as proposed in the Objection, if made in proportion to the relative numbers of the pupils passing the Intermediate Examinations in the several counties, would have most anomalous results.

Rep. iv., [illegible]. For example, the whole of the Fermanagh Endowment, worth £1,580 per annum, would fall to the Protestant share, for few pupils, and 82 per cent. of the Cavan Endowment would fall to the Roman Catholics, for 18 pupils, in four years, while the Protestant Schools of Armagh, passing 819 pupils during the same period, would be entitled to only 54 per cent. of an endowment of £978 per annum, or, if boys only were taken into account, would be reduced to 50 per cent., amounting to £489 per annum, including the value of the school premises.

Assuming the average numbers of pupils passing the Intermediate Examinations during the last four years to represent the proportions in which the Royal School Endowments should be shared, the following Table will show the annual amount which would be payable to each Local Board, in addition to its Minimum Grant, if the Residue were so divided.

The results of a division under the Scheme would, however, be proportionately more favourable to those Local Boards which exerted themselves to establish the best Schools during the period of three years allowed for that purpose, as none but considerable Schools could participate, and then only in respect of pupils receiving Intermediate Education in Latin, and at least one Modern Language, in addition to English and two other subjects.

TABLE showing the DISTRIBUTION OF THE RESIDUE in proportion to the Numbers and Percentages of Pupils passing the INTERMEDIATE EXAMINATIONS from Schools in the ROYAL SCHOOL DIVISIONS during the FOUR YEARS, [illegible].

Division.	Pupils passing Intermediate Examinations. Numbers. Boys only. Prot.	R.C.	Boys and Girls. Prot.	R.C.	Percentages. Boys only. Prot.	R.C.	Boys and Girls. Prot.	R.C.	Distribution of Residue. Annual Amounts. Boys only. Prot.	R.C.	Boys and Girls. Prot.	R.C.	Total.
									£ s. d.	£ s. d.	£ s. d.	£ s. d.	£ s. d.
1. Armagh,	173	149	319	143	[illegible]	[illegible]	[illegible]	[illegible]	[illegible]	[illegible]	[illegible]	[illegible]	
2. Cavan,	4	15	5	16	[illegible]	[illegible]	[illegible]	[illegible]	[illegible]	[illegible]	[illegible]	[illegible]	
3. Donegal,	[illegible]	7	79	3	7	[illegible]	[illegible]	[illegible]	[illegible]	[illegible]	[illegible]	[illegible]	
4. Fermanagh,	[illegible]	[illegible]	[illegible]	117	[illegible]	7	[illegible]	[illegible]	[illegible]	[illegible]	[illegible]	[illegible]	
5. Tyrone,	148	[illegible]	201	129	[illegible]	[illegible]	[illegible]	[illegible]	[illegible]	[illegible]	[illegible]	[illegible]	
	[illegible]	[illegible]	[illegible]	[illegible]	[illegible]	[illegible]	[illegible]	40	[illegible]	[illegible]	[illegible]	[illegible]	[illegible]

Scheme No. 1. The principle adopted in the [illegible] Scheme referred to in the objection is that of the Minimum Grants in the Royal Schools Scheme. The [illegible] Endowment was applicable for the education of all the children of poor inhabitants of the Borough, and was placed under the management of two Local Boards, Protestant and Roman Catholic, as the Governing Bodies of separate National Schools.

The [illegible] Scheme recites that a division of the income in proportion to the number of pupils likely to attend the respective Schools would not give the Protestant School a sufficient sum to maintain it in efficiency. The minimum sum adequate to maintain it efficiently was ascertained by the Scheme at £115, which was secured to the Protestant Local Board in the first instance, and the pupils of both schools were admitted to compete for a further sum of £150 per annum.

Ib. sec. 13. Ib. sec. 16.

The endowment was ample to provide for both Schools, being supplemented by aid from the National Board. No difficulty existed, and no question was raised as to the character of the education to be given, the distribution of the fund among different districts, or the claims of separate Protestant denominations.

Private Benefactions.

Rep. ii., 178, 182. Rep. [illegible]. The only private benefactions to the Royal Schools of which evidence was given, consisted of expenditure by former Archbishops of Armagh upon the erection of certain portions of the Armagh and Dungannon School Buildings.

It was mentioned that at Raphoe a similar claim might exist respecting part of the school building formerly used as a Diocesan Library.

The Scheme, sec. 72 (b.), recognises an exclusive right to the value of private benefactions in the members of the denomination to which the donor belonged, but the Commissioners believe it impossible to ascertain the amount of any such claim until the buildings upon which the expenditure was made come under the operation of the Scheme. This will not occur while the present Head Masters hold office. Rep. iv., 183.

When the Scheme comes into operation the condition of the buildings and the proportion of their value attributable to private outlay may not be the same as now, but can then be easily ascertained.

When the buildings are taken over by the Local Boards, or are sold, the then value of any private benefactions must be ascertained, and credited to the denomination to which the benefactor belonged.

In any case in which a Protestant Local Board takes the buildings and devotes them to the purposes of a School under their own management, the Commissioners do not see how it can be necessary to deal separately with the claim.

In every other case, and whenever any Protestant Local Board allocates its funds among different Protestant denominations, the Scheme will enable the representatives of the Church of Ireland to establish their claim. It contains careful provision for the settlement of all disputed questions, and the Commissioners cannot think these provisions "illusory." In the course of settling the Scheme they asked the representatives of "the Church of Ireland" to suggest amendments, and none were put forward. Scheme, secs. 34, 65, 67, 71, 72. Ib. secs. 64, 66. Rep. iv., 183.

Representation of "The Church of Ireland."

The only figures brought before the Commissioners to show that the Scheme did not assign the majority upon each Protestant Local Board to the Denomination which includes the largest number of the "literate population" in the district, proved, on investigation, to have been arrived at from the Census by a process of calculation which treated *all children under five years of age as "literate."* Except in Donegal, where the Episcopalians and Presbyterians are almost absolutely equal in the County, the Scheme gives a clear majority upon each Board to the Denomination which is most numerous among the "literate" population. The Commissioners felt it to be most inexpedient that the single representative of the smallest Denomination should hold the scale between the larger bodies upon any Board. Nine members being adopted as the most convenient number, it followed that five of these must belong to the largest Denomination, and one being assigned to the smallest Denomination, but three remained to represent the Denomination standing second in order of numbers. Rep. iv., 183. Ib. 183.

In Armagh the Board is formed in proportions admitted to be just.

In Tyrone the "literate" Presbyterians are more numerous than the Episcopalians, both in the County and in the District; they were therefore entitled to five members, and one being assigned to the Methodists, the remaining three were allotted to "the Church of Ireland," upon the same principle which was adopted in Armagh. supra, and

In Fermanagh the Local Committee representing all the Protestant Denominations proposed that the Board should consist of five members of "the Church of Ireland, two Methodists, and two Presbyterians, and that the County of Fermanagh alone should form the District. Counsel for the Methodists afterwards stated that if Monaghan were included, they would claim but one member, and that a third should be given to the Presbyterians. Counsel for the Fermanagh Committee stated that he was not instructed to object to the representation of five, three, and one. The relative majority of "the Church of Ireland" in the united district is much less than in the County of Fermanagh alone, where the Church representatives themselves proposed that they should be only five in number. Rep. ii., 401. Rep. i., 420, 424.

For Cavan also the Board was formed in proportions which were accepted by the Local Committee representing all Protestant denominations, and to which no objection was made by the Diocesan Council of Kilmore upon the publication of the original Draft Scheme. Rep. ii., 433.

In Donegal, though the Episcopalians and Presbyterians in the whole County are as nearly as possible equal, the evidence already referred to showed that the Presbyterians greatly preponderated in the locality of the Royal School, and all who appeared before the Commissioners agreed in assigning the majority upon the Local Board to that denomination. Rep. ii., 41.

As it is objected that in the proposed constitution of the Protestant Local Boards "the representation of the Church of Ireland is *wholly inadequate from every point of view,*" the Commissioners think it right to observe that the net annual value of the Royal School Endowments in the three districts of Armagh, Cavan, and Enniskillen, in each of which the members of "the Church of Ireland" have a clear majority upon the Board, amounts to the sum of £3,187 2s. 6d., and the minimum grants secured to these Boards amount to £952 5s. 0d., while in the two districts of Tyrone and Donegal, where the Presbyterians have the majority, the annual value of the Endowments is £1,225 14s. 4d., and the minimum grants amount to £377 5s. 4d.

Constitution of the Commissioners of Education.

The Draft Scheme of the Commissioners of Education proposed to reduce their number to eight, who were to be appointed by the Lord Lieutenant. It provided that in their selection regard should be had to the religious denominations of the classes from which pupils might reasonably be expected [illegible] to attend the Schools placed under their government. This provision was generally objected to, and accordingly the original Draft Scheme provided that of ten Commissioners to be appointed by the Lord Lieutenant five should be Roman Catholics and five should be Protestants. The Methodists thereupon urged a claim that one Commissioner at the least should be a Methodist, as they could

Rep. ii., 683 not secure any representation through the Local Boards.

The Commissioners then inserted the present provision in their Revised Scheme.

If it be just and expedient that three-fifths of the Protestant Commissioners should at all times be members of "the Church of Ireland" the object can be attained in making the appointments.

The Commissioners thought it most desirable that "the Commissioners of Education" should include direct representatives of the Universities and other Bodies engaged in Higher and Intermediate Education. They must dispute the assertion that the functions of the Central Board will

Scheme, secs. 63, 19, 56, 69, 88. Sched. I. be "mainly fiscal." The maintenance of a proper standard of Intermediate Education among the Schools and pupils claiming benefit from the endowments; the admission of Schools to share in those endowments; the decision whether the Schools claiming participation are suitably maintained and equipped as efficient Intermediate Schools, and whether due provision is made for awarding the free scholarships; the regulation of the arrangements for restricting the endowments to really qualified schools, and the jurisdiction to decide all questions arising in respect of any claim, or of any pupil, or examination, or with reference to the due application of the Endowments in accordance with the Scheme, all rest with the Commissioners, who are also charged with the management of the property, and the distribution of the funds. They have important duties to perform respecting the disposal

Ib. secs. 17, 18, 23. Ib. secs. 68, 72. of the School premises, the expenditure of the Building Funds, and the general administration of the Scheme.

There are also other Endowments throughout Ireland, not included in the present Scheme, which are under the government of the Commissioners.

It further appeared to be of the highest importance that the Commissioners should be in direct communication with the other educational Institutions of Ireland, and that the Scheme should be administered by persons acquainted with the requirements of pupils preparing for the Examinations of the Intermediate Education Board, and of the Universities, or for the Learned Professions. For these reasons the Scheme proposes the appointment of ten representatives of important educational bodies. The Representatives of Maynooth College, and the Magee Presbyterian College, were added, not because these Institutions have a Theological faculty, but because a large proportion of the pupils of the chief Roman Catholic Schools, and many of the Presbyterian pupils receiving their Intermediate Education, in the Royal School Districts, are preparing to become Students of these Colleges.

The nearest "corresponding provision" which it appeared possible to make was that for the election of two Commissioners to represent the University of Dublin, with which the Divinity School of "the Church of Ireland" is connected.

"The balance of denominational representation" has not been overlooked in the arrangements proposed.

Distribution of the Residue.

The objection to the proposed distribution of the residue of the Ulster Royal School Endowments appears to rest upon a misapprehension of the Scheme, of which sec. 38 is not fully or correctly quoted. That clause provides that the distribution shall be made in proportion to the number of pupils receiving Intermediate Education in the *qualified* Schools, *ascertained in the manner prescribed in the Second Schedule* of the Scheme.

No School can be "qualified" to receive any benefit, either from a minimum grant or from the residue, unless it fulfils the following among other conditions:—

Scheme, Sched. I It must be an *Intermediate School* conducted in accordance with the provisions of the Scheme.

Instruction must be regularly given in the School in subjects which in all cases include Latin, French or German, Ancient and Modern History, and Physical Science or Drawing, besides Greek for boys, in addition to the ordinary subjects of an English and Mathematical Education.

Not less than twenty pupils, each making at least 100 attendances, must have been regularly afforded Intermediate Education throughout the School year, and seven at the least of those pupils must have passed the Examinations of the Intermediate Education Board, in *at least five specified subjects*; including in every case, Latin, and at least one Modern *Language*, in addition to English and Mathematics.

The Inspector appointed by the Lord Lieutenant must satisfy himself by sufficient examination and inquiry, and must report and certify, that all these conditions have been fulfilled; also that the School is properly maintained and suitably equipped as an efficient Intermediate School, employing a competent staff for the teaching of all the prescribed subjects, and giving the prescribed education to the required number of pupils within the ages of eleven and nineteen years.

No "Elementary School," large or small, can receive any part whatever either of the residue or of any minimum grant under the Scheme.

The Commissioners have endeavoured to provide every possible protection against the diversion of these Endowments from their legitimate purpose, namely:—the support of a limited number of Schools providing a high class of Intermediate Education for considerable numbers of pupils.

Rep. iv. 179. Considerations of expense, and the recognised inexpediency of introducing a new system of examinations, deterred the Commissioners from requiring the Inspector to examine every individual pupil, as the National Board requires, but it will be his duty to satisfy himself of the fulfilment of the prescribed conditions in the case not only of each School, but of each pupil for whom a claim is made.

"The Commissioners of Education" are empowered by the Scheme to prescribe the mode of keeping the records of attendance and of studies, and the manner in which claims must be made and verified, and, though they may accept the certificate of the Inspector, they may call for such other evidence as they think necessary. Scheme, sec. 63

The objection is mistaken as to the power of appeal to the Commissioners; sec. 63 provides that the Commissioners must investigate and determine every question arising, *or raised by any Local Board*, as to the fulfilment of the prescribed conditions *by any school or by any pupil*.

Every one of the Local Boards will be directly interested in preventing the admission of any school "not truly intermediate," and the Scheme makes every possible provision to ensure full compliance with its requirements.

The condition that seven pupils must pass the Intermediate Examinations in at least five specified subjects was fully discussed and considered, and the Commissioners regard it as very stringent. The number was reduced from ten to seven at the instance of the Counsel for the Presbyterians, who feared that otherwise many of the Protestant Schools would be excluded. Ev. iv, 157 / ib. 178.

It should be remembered that these pupils must not merely pass the Intermediate Examinations; they must pass in *five* subjects at least, of which two must be Latin and a Modern Language other than English. The importance of this restriction appears from the fact that of 4,096 pupils who "passed the Intermediate Examinations" in 1888, only 1,282 passed in Latin. Int. Edu. Com. Rep., 1888.

Every Intermediate School capable of passing seven pupils yearly in these subjects will almost certainly have a larger number under instruction preparing for the examinations of future years, besides a further number who, after passing the Intermediate examinations, will be pursuing their school education for at least another year in preparation for their Colleges or Universities, or for public examinations, such as those required for admission to the Public Service, or the Learned Professions. Ev. iv, 174, 178.

The instruction of both these classes of Intermediate pupils, preparatory and advanced, appeared to the Commissioners to give a most legitimate claim upon the Royal School Endowments, and it was found impossible to test the credit which ought to be allowed for school work of this description, otherwise than by ascertaining the proportion which such pupils ought to bear in a first class Intermediate School to those actually passing the Intermediate Examinations. The proposal to fix this proportion by the Scheme was first made by the Presbyterian Intermediate Education Committee, and was generally approved of. Ev. iv, 238 / ib. 178.

The Commissioners availed themselves of the best attainable information upon this subject before fixing the limit at three additional pupils under instruction for each one passing the Intermediate Examinations.

At the final inquiry on May 31, 1889, the Rev. Dr. Morgan gave "about thirty per cent." as his estimate of the proportion passing the examinations. Mr. Wilkins, Head Master of the Dublin High School, representing the Protestant Schoolmasters' Association, stated that one in four would be in his experience about right. The Commissioners subsequently got detailed information on the subject, and obtained returns of the actual numbers from the High School, Dublin, which, in 1888, stood first as regards distinctions of the Protestant Schools of Ireland; and also from six of the leading Roman Catholic Intermediate Schools, including Clongowes College and the Blackrock College, which have successively stood first at the Intermediate Examinations. Ev. iv, 174 / ib. / p. 330

The Commissioners also obtained returns tending to show that a very large proportion of the pupils who enter the Universities with distinction, and who therefore represent the highest standard of Intermediate Education, have remained at School for at least a year after passing the Intermediate Examinations. In the four years 1886–1889, of the 66 pupils who gained Entrance Exhibitions at Trinity College, Dublin, from Irish Schools, no less than 52 had previously passed the Intermediate Examinations, and of these 46 had remained at School for at least a year after so passing.

In the Royal University during the same period, of 116 pupils from Irish Schools who obtained distinctions at Entrance, 107 had previously passed the Intermediate Examinations, and no less than 103 of these had remained at School for at least a year afterwards.

Upon this information the Commissioners entirely satisfied themselves that an efficient Intermediate School passing seven pupils in five Grammar School subjects at the Intermediate Examinations in any year, might fairly be expected to have in attendance four or even five other pupils receiving the same class of instruction. They fixed the limit at one in four, and they gave additional marks for pupils passing in the several grades upon a scale which renders any such consequence as the objection suggests perfectly impossible. Seven pupils passing the Intermediate Examinations even in the Junior Grade would entitle their School to fourteen marks, and the largest number of additional marks for which the School could obtain credit in respect of other pupils could not exceed twenty-one, which number the seven pupils would obtain if they passed in the Senior Grade. Scheme, Sched. 2 (B.)

The tests imposed by the Scheme incline, in the opinion of the Commissioners, towards excessive strictness, and their only doubt is whether during the preparatory period of three years all the Local Boards will succeed in reaching the prescribed standard. If any Local Board should fail to maintain at least one qualified School in its own district, its share of the Royal School Endowments must be applied in aid of a qualified School to be selected from those of the other districts. ib. sec. 41

The object of the whole Scheme, namely:—to secure the effective application of the Endowments for the assistance of really efficient Grammar Schools, can, in the opinion of the Commissioners, be attained only by imposing conditions sufficiently stringent to limit the number of the participating schools, and to prevent the division into a large number of small shares of an income which on the most favourable calculation, cannot exceed £4,000 per annum. The best standard of Intermediate Education can be maintained only in Schools sufficiently large to employ an extensive and highly qualified staff, and the Scheme is framed so as to oblige each of the Local Boards to use its best exertions, and to devote its funds, in the first instance, to the establishment and maintenance of a single School qualified to satisfy the stringent requirements of the Scheme. When this is accomplished it can increase the number of its Schools, but each of them must come up to the required standard.

The Commissioners do not believe that the maintenance of such Schools can be secured if the Endowments be either finally distributed in fixed amounts without regard to the efficiency of their application, or be divided among a number of denominations in shares many of which would be too small to afford substantial aid even to a single School.

Alteration of the Scheme.

Ed. End. Ir. Act, 1885, s. 15. Having regard to the large number of the Commissioners, and to the fact that the Representatives of the Local Boards may probably not be resident in Dublin, a condition that two-thirds of the whole number should actually attend, and should be unanimous in supporting any application or alteration of the Scheme, appears tantamount to nullifying the power of alteration contained in the Act, sec. 15.

Scheme, cl. 68. The Scheme requires two successive special resolutions, each passed *after due notice*, and the concurrence of a *two-thirds majority of the Commissioners present*, before any application for alteration can be made, and the alteration must afterwards be sanctioned by the Commissioners of Charitable Donations and Bequests.

The Commissioners submit that the further restriction suggested in the Objection ought not to be imposed.

II. OBJECTION OF THE COMMITTEE REPRESENTING THE VARIOUS PROTESTANT DENOMINATIONS OF THE COUNTY OF FERMANAGH.

Appx., B. The Enniskillen School premises consist of buildings of which the tenement valuation is £168 0s. 0d., and of land containing 54A. 1R. 3P., valued at £98 0s. 0d. The Buildings contain accommodation for at least 150 pupils, including 100 boarders, with residences for the Head Master and teaching staff. The average expense of maintaining them has been £125 0s. 0d. per annum. They appeared too costly and extensive for the requirements of any School likely to be established in them. The lands have been let by the Head Master, who stated that he derived an income of £150 per annum from them.

Min. iv., 613. Her Majesty's Secretary of State for War proposed to purchase these premises for £7,000.

Rep. iv., 318. The Revised Draft Scheme proposed that if no larger amount could be realised, this offer should be accepted, and that the purchase money should be divided equally between the Fermanagh Local Boards, enabling each Board to apply its share in providing School premises.

Rep. iii., 462. Rep. iv., 172. Rep. iv., 453. The Commissioners were of opinion that for £3,500 the Fermanagh Protestant Local Board could provide premises more suitable to their purposes than the existing buildings, but they were prepared to give the Protestant Local Board an opportunity of attempting to maintain the school at Portora, and not to divert the premises from educational purposes.

The Roman Catholic Local Board offered to take the land as an equivalent for the buildings, and Counsel for the Protestant Local Board stated that the buildings, with a garden and playground for the school, were all that they wanted. A written proposal, dated September 6, 1888, was made on behalf of the Roman Catholics of the Diocese by the Most Rev. Dr. Donnelly, Bishop of Clogher, to take over the land on behalf of the Roman Catholics, and leave the buildings to the Protestant Board, who should also be at liberty to retain any portion of the land required for their school, either by purchase or at a rent based on the Government valuation.

Rep. iv., 172. At the Final Hearing, Counsel for the Protestant Local Board still urged their claim to a right of pre-emption, for educational purposes, and £7,000 being offered by the War Office, the Commissioners felt themselves justified in taking that sum as the selling value, and in giving the right of pre-emption at that sum.

Accordingly, though doubting the prudence of the Protestant Board in undertaking the charge of these expensive buildings, the Commissioners introduced the provision for pre-emption contained in Clause 70 of the Scheme, but especially having regard to the fact that the lands produced an actual income of £150 per annum, and to the offer to accept them as equivalent to the buildings, they thought it reasonable to require that the Roman Catholic share of the purchase money, £3,500, should be provided by the Protestant Local Board and not taken from the endowments.

Ibid., 186. The matter was fully discussed at the Final Hearing, and the Commissioners understood these terms to be accepted.

The Commissioners are of opinion that if the Protestant Local Board are to have any reasonable prospect of efficiently maintaining the Portora School, the amount of their minimum grant should not be reduced by setting off their share of the value of the school premises against it, and that their ability to raise £3,500 in order to purchase the School premises, will be some guarantee of their determination to maintain the School.

This involves much less exertion on the part of those interested in maintaining Portora School than has been shown in other places under less favourable circumstances. As examples—the Commissioners would mention, among Protestant Schools, the Monaghan Collegiate School, the Strabane Academy, and the Londonderry and Coleraine Academical Institutions, all of which have been established by local and voluntary efforts. The Roman Catholic Intermediate Schools have been very costly, and the Diocesan College at Monaghan was erected at an expense of £20,000, almost wholly contributed by the Roman Catholic inhabitants of the Counties of Monaghan and Fermanagh.

ABSTRACT OF THE MINUTES OF THE COMMISSIONERS.

PART I.

SUMMARY OF MEETINGS AND ATTENDANCES.

(A.) TABLE showing MEETINGS held during the Year ending September 30, 1889.

[illegible]	Number of Meetings held.	Number of these Meetings which were Public Inquiries.	Number of [illegible] of Full Commission.
The Full Commission,	120	33	14
The Judicial Commissioners,	35		—
The Assistant Commissioners,	83	—	—
Total,	194	83	14

(B.) TABLE showing the ATTENDANCES of the COMMISSIONERS at the Meetings during the Year ending September 30, 1889.

NAMES OF COMMISSIONERS	Full Commission, Meetings.	Full Commission, [illegible]	Judicial Commissioners' Meetings.	Assistant Commissioners' Meetings.	Total.
JUDICIAL COMMISSIONERS:					
Lord Justice FitzGibbon,	118	1	30	—	158
Lord Justice Naish,	102	1	39	—	142
ASSISTANT COMMISSIONERS:					
Very Rev. Dr. Molloy,	108	10	—	32	150
Dr. Traill,	83	8	—	13	104
Professor Dougherty,	94	1	—	31	126

PART II.

MINUTES OF THE FULL COMMISSION.

October 1, 1886.

Meeting of the Commission held this day at the Office, 13, Nassau-street, Dublin.

Present:—Lord Justice FitzGibbon, Rev. Dr. Molloy.

Minutes of the two preceding meetings, and of the statutory attendances of September 10, September 24, and September 27, read and confirmed.

Letters read:—

Rev. James B. Keane (August 6), as to a Scheme for the Meath Diocesan Endowments.

The existing Trustees of the [illegible] Endowed School, sending Heads of Scheme for that Endowment.

George Emery (August 17) (September 28), objecting to the Draft Scheme published for the Drelincourt, Mall, and College-street Schools, &c., Armagh.

The Clerk of the Salters' Company (August 18), acknowledging letter sent with the Draft Scheme published for the Rainey School, Magherafelt.

Wm. J. Fleming, Clerk, Commissioners of Education Office (August 21), as to his vested interests under the proposed Scheme for the reconstitution of the Commissioners of Education.

James M. Weir, B.A., Head Master (August 21) (September 17), objecting to the Draft Scheme published for Kilkenny College.

Thomas Anderson (August 23), approving of the Draft Scheme published for Guy's Free School, Ballymena.

The Right Rev. Dr. Walsh, Lord Bishop of Ossory (August 31), objecting to the Draft Scheme for Kilkenny College.

Andrew Brown (August 30), suggesting amendments to the Draft Scheme published for the Rainey School, Magherafelt.

Rev. George Webster, D.D. (August 6), enclosing leases as to the buildings belonging to St. Nicholas' Schools, Cork.

Rev. Stephen Moxley, LL.D. (August), as to the Ballymena Endowment.

The Most Rev. Dr. Donnelly, Lord Bishop of Clogher (September 9), and Rev. W. H. Hutchinson (September 21), as to the Draft Scheme for the Royal School Endowments.

Rev. W. de Montmorency (September 17), enclosing objection on behalf of the Marquis of Ormonde to the Draft Scheme published for Kilkenny College.

Rev. Thomas Jordan, D.D. (Sept. 19), enclosing objection on behalf of His Grace the Lord Primate to the Draft Scheme published for the Rainey School, Magherafelt.

Thomas Turpin (September 20), as to the removal of [illegible] School to Maryborough.

J. Whiteside Dane (September 7), enclosing returns as to the valuations of the holdings of Protestants and of Roman Catholics in Counties Fermanagh and Monaghan.

W. J. De Vere and Rev. T. O. Dardis, as to meetings of the Trustees of the [illegible] Endowed School.

The Right Rev. Dr. Gregg, Lord Bishop of Cork (September 27), suggesting amendments to the Draft Scheme published for the Bandon Academy, Cork.

Thomas H. Jermyn, Secretary, Bennett's Trusts (September 27), suggesting amendments to the Draft Scheme published for the Cork Parochial Schools.

Letter (September 18) read from Rev. W. Prior Moore, M.A., as to a proposal purported to be made to him in his evidence before the Commission.

A reply, as drafted, ordered to be sent.

Letter (September 21) read from the Right Hon. the Earl Belmore, suggesting an amendment in the recitals of the Draft Scheme for the Royal School Endowments.

To be informed that the correction will be made.

Letters (September 12 and 20) read from the Rev. S. Cuthbert Mitchel, as to the Portora Royal School Endowment.

A reply, as drafted, directed to be sent.

Letter (August 21) read from Very Rev. P. J. Byrne, P.P., V.G., as to the formation of the Tyrone Roman Catholic Local Board.

A letter, as drafted, was directed to be sent in reply, and the Secretary was also directed to send the Archbishop of Armagh, the Bishop of Derry, the Bishop of Clogher, and the Rev. B. M'Namee, a copy of the letter to the Very Rev. P. J. Byrne and of his reply thereto, when received. [This direction was subsequently countermanded.]

Letter (September 14) read from Rev. B. M'Namee, Omagh, as to the formation of the Tyrone Roman Catholic Local Board.

A reply, as drafted, directed to be sent.

Letter (September 26) read from Alexander Livingstone, as to the visit of the Commissioners to Lismabee School, Newtownforbes.

A reply, as drafted, ordered to be sent.

Letter (September 27) read from Joseph O'Doherty, Harvey's Institution, Mullingar, asking if he should give evidence at the Inquiry to be held in Mullingar.

A reply, as drafted, ordered to be sent.

Letters as to the incorporation of Governing Bodies to hold Educational Endowments in the several Dioceses were read from:—

Rev. John Finlay, as to the Diocese of Leighlin.
Rev. C. Ormsby Wiley, M.A., as to the Diocese of Killala and Achonry.
John G. Peamish, as to the Diocese of Ferns.
Thomas Keogh, as to the Diocese of Ossory.
Joseph J. Murphy, as to the Diocese of Down and Connor and Dromore.

Replies, as drafted, directed to be sent.

Letter (September 24), read from Rev. H. B. Wilson, D.D., Convener, General Assembly of the Presbyterian Church in Ireland, as to the incorporation of Governing Bodies to hold Educational Endowments belonging to that Church.

A reply, as drafted, ordered to be sent.

Letter (September 28), read from Very Rev. the Dean of Killala, asking if he should attend Inquiry into the Castleconnor and Kilglass Schools, to be held at Sligo.

A reply, as drafted, ordered to be sent.

The Draft Annual Report for the year 1887–8 was considered.

The Commissioners adjourned.

GERALD FITZGIBBON,

October 5, 1888.

Wm. Edward Ellis, Secretary.

October 3, 1888.

Meeting of the Commission held this day at the Office, 23, Nassau-street, Dublin.

Present:—Lord Justice FITZGIBBON, Rev. Dr. MOLLOY, Professor DOUGHERTY.

Letter (October 1), read from Rev. C. J. M'Alester, Holywood, objecting to the Draft Scheme published for the Sullivan Schools, Holywood.

Letter (October 2), read from E. H. Poe Hosford, asking when the objection lodged by James M. Weir, Head Master, Kilkenny College, will be considered.

A reply, as drafted, ordered to be sent.

Letter (October 2), read from R. L. Scott, Clerk of the Salters Company, asking for three copies of the Draft Scheme published for the Rainey School, Magherafelt.

Copies ordered to be sent.

The Draft Annual Report for the year 1887–8 was considered.

The Commissioners adjourned.

GERALD FITZGIBBON,

October 5, 1888.

Wm. Edward Ellis, Secretary.

October 5, 1888.

Meeting of the Commission held this day at the Office, 23, Nassau-street, Dublin.

Present:—Lord Justice FITZGIBBON, Lord Justice NAISH, Rev. Dr. MOLLOY, Professor DOUGHERTY.

Minutes of the two preceding meetings read and confirmed.

Letters read:—

L. A. Beamish (October 3), sending names for the proposed Governing Body for the Munster Agricultural School.

Hermann Unna (October 4), as to his vested interests as Assistant Master of Erasmus Smith's Grammar School, Galway.

Letter (October 4) read from the Very Rev. William C. Townsend, D.D., Dean of Tuam, as to the Tuam Diocesan Free School.

A reply, as drafted, ordered to be sent.

The Commission made arrangements for the holding of Public Sittings, commencing October 19, in the following localities:—Londonderry, Coleraine, Magherafelt, Ballymena, Holywood, Bangor, Donaghadee, Ballywalter, Belfast, Carrickfergus, Larne, and Downpatrick: and instructions were given to the Secretary to have the following advertisements inserted in the Dublin papers, and also, so far as they concern the districts, in the Belfast and Londonderry papers:—

NOTICE is hereby given that the Commissioners will hold Public Sittings at the following places, on the days and at the hours named, for the purpose of taking evidence, and considering objections to published Schemes, respecting the undermentioned Endowments:—

LONDONDERRY, at the Court House.

Friday, October 19, at 1 o'clock, P.M.

(To consider objections to published Schemes).

Robertson Endowments, Co. Donegal.
Londonderry Academical Institution.

COLERAINE, at the Town Hall.

Saturday, October 20, at 11.30 A.M.

Irish Society's Schools.
Castle (Coleraine) School.

MAGHERAFELT, at the Court House.

Monday, October 22, at 11 o'clock, A.M.

(To consider objections to published Schemes).

Rainey's School, Magherafelt.

BALLYMENA, at the Court House.

Tuesday, October 23, at 11 o'clock, A.M.

(To consider objections to published Schemes).

Guy's Free School.
Ballymena Collegiate School.

HOLYWOOD, at the Court House.

Wednesday, October 24, at 10.30 o'clock, A.M.

(To consider objections to published Schemes).

Sullivan's Schools, Holywood.

BANGOR, at the Court House.

Wednesday, October 24, at 3 o'clock, P.M.

Bangor Endowed School.
Bangor Charitable Endowment.
Ballymaconnell National School.
Ballymullan (Crawfordsburn) National School.
Ballymullagh National School.

DONAGHADEE, at the Court House.

Thursday, October 25, at 10.30 o'clock, A.M.

Donaghadee Endowed School.
Donaghadee National School.
Carrowdore, Woburn, National School.

BALLYWALTER, at the Court House.

Thursday, October 25, at 3 o'clock, P.M.

Brown's Endowment, Ballyhalbert.
Inishargy, Tubber-na-Carrig, National School.
Grey Abbey, Tully Cavey, National School.
Grey Abbey, Mountstewart, Erasmus Smith's School.

BELFAST, in the Grand Jury Room, Court House.

Friday, October 26, at 11 o'clock, A.M.

Application from the Diocesan Council of Down and Connor and Dromore for the incorporation of a Diocesan Governing Body for Educational Endowments of "The Church of Ireland."

Application from the Elementary Education Committee of the General Assembly for the incorporation of Governing Bodies for Educational Endowments connected with the Presbyterian Church in Ireland.

Brown-street Schools, Belfast.
Charitable Bequest of Samuel Ledley, for the purpose of erecting a School in Ballymacarrett.

CARRICKFERGUS, at the Court House.

Saturday, October 27, at 10.30 o'clock, A.M.

Carrickfergus Parochial School.

LARNE, at the Court House.

Saturday, October 27, at 3 o'clock, P.M.

Larne Grammar School.

DOWNPATRICK, at the Court House.

Monday, October 29, at 12.30 P.M.

Downpatrick Blue School.
Killough National School.
Killyleagh, Shrigley, National School.
Tyrella, Carrickmab, National School.

At the abovementioned sittings the Commissioners will receive evidence with respect to these and other endowments from persons interested in education.

The Commissioners had an interview with Sir Thomas Brady with regard to the Draft Scheme published by the Commission for the future government and management of the Baltimore Fishery School.

The Draft Annual Report for the year 1887-8, was further considered.

The Commissioners adjourned.

GERALD MOLLOY,
November 2, 1888.

Wm. Edward Ellis, Secretary.

October 8, 1888.

Meeting of the Commission held this day.

Present:—Lord Justice FITZGIBBON, Lord Justice NAISH, Rev. Dr. MOLLOY, Dr. TRAILL, Professor DOUGHERTY.

Letter read from the Moderator of the General Assembly, and others, with regard to the Draft Scheme for the Rainey School, Magherafelt.

A reply, as drafted, ordered to be sent.

Letter read from T. H. Montgomery, Agent for the Irish Society, as to the Irish Society's Schools, Coleraine.

A reply, as drafted, ordered to be sent.

Letter read from Rev. Andrew Phelan, P.P., Maryborough, as to his publishing his evidence in a local paper.

A reply, as drafted, ordered to be sent.

The Commissioners adjourned.

JOHN NAISH,
October 9, 1888.

N. D. Murphy, Junr.,
Chief Clerk and Assistant Secretary.

October 8, 1886.

PUBLIC SITTING.

Meeting of the Commission held this day at the Court-house, Mullingar.

Present:—Lord Justice FitzGibbon, Lord Justice Naish, Rev. Dr. Molloy, Dr. Traill, Professor Dougherty.

Mr. James B. Macartney, Shorthand Writer, was in attendance.

Lord Justice FitzGibbon made an opening statement.

Hevey's Institution, Mullingar.

The following witnesses were sworn and examined:—

The Most Rev. Dr. Nulty, Lord Bishop of Meath.
Rev. Dr. Edward V. Casey.

It was ruled:—That, although the Endowment was not exempt from the jurisdiction of the Commission, the Commissioners do not deem it expedient or necessary to frame a Scheme for its management.

Wilson's Hospital, Multyfarnham.

The Rev. H. Wilson White, LL.D., was sworn and examined.

It was ruled:—That the Act does not apply to this Endowment, unless with the consent in writing of the Governing Body.

Farra School, Bunbrosna (Incorporated Society).

The following witnesses were sworn and examined:—

T. G. Foster, M.A., Head Master.
Rev. John Beamish, M.A., Catechist.

Meath and Ardagh Diocesan School.

The Very Rev. Francis Swift, M.A., Dean of Clonmacnois, was sworn and examined.

Westmeath Protestant Orphan Society.

S. E. Mason, Solicitor, was sworn and examined.

The following witnesses made statements:—

Rev. R. Dowse, M.A., Hon. Sec.
Very Rev. Francis Swift, M.A., Dean of Clonmacnois.
Rev. J. Beamish, M.A.

Belvedere Orphanage, Tyrrellspass.

The following witnesses were sworn and examined:—

Rev. R. Dowse, M.A., Hon. Sec.
S. E. Mason, Solicitor.

The Commissioners adjourned. Subsequently they visited Hevey's Institution, Farra School, and Wilson's Hospital, and the Loretto Convent Intermediate School, Mullingar.

John Naish,
October 9, 1886.

N. D. Murphy, Junr.,
Chief Clerk and Assistant Secretary.

October 9, 1886.

PUBLIC SITTING.

Meeting of the Commission held this day at the Court-house, Sligo.

Present:—Lord Justice FitzGibbon, Lord Justice Naish, Rev. Dr. Molloy, Dr. Traill, Professor Dougherty.

Mr. James B. Macartney, Shorthand Writer, was in attendance.

Manorhamilton National School.

Rev. I. Coulter, M.A., was sworn and examined.

Calry School, Ballincoely.

William Clarke and the Rev. J. F. Berry, M.A., were sworn and examined.

PRIMROSE GRANGE SCHOOL (INCORPORATED SOCIETY).

W. A. Shackleton, M.A., Head Master, and Rev. F. J. Hamilton, were sworn and examined.

CASTLECONNOR AND KILGLASS SCHOOLS (VALENTINE ENDOWMENT).

The Very Rev. William Skipton, M.A., Dean of Killala, was sworn and examined.

SLIGO DIOCESAN SCHOOL.

William G. Eades, M.A., Head Master, was sworn and examined.

The Commissioners adjourned, and visited Primrose Grange School, the Sligo Model National School, and the Calry National School.

JOHN NAISH,
October 9, 1888.

N. D. Murphy, Junr.,
Chief Clerk and Assistant Secretary.

October 9, 1888.

Meeting of the Commission held this day at the Royal Hotel, Boyle.

Present:—Lord Justice FITZGIBBON, Lord Justice NAISH, Rev. Dr. MOLLOY, Dr. TRAILL, Professor DOUGHERTY.

Minutes of the three preceding meetings read and confirmed.

It was agreed:—That the Commissioners should visit the Ranelagh School, Roscommon, on Thursday, October 13, and the Assistant Secretary was directed to give notice to the Head Mistress of the School of the Commissioners' intended visit.

The Commissioners adjourned.

JOHN NAISH,
October 21, 1888.

N. D. Murphy, Junr.,
Chief Clerk and Assistant Secretary.

October 10, 1888.

PUBLIC SITTING.

Meeting of the Commission held this day at the Court-house, Boyle.

Present:—Lord Justice FITZGIBBON, Lord Justice NAISH, Rev. Dr. MOLLOY, Dr. TRAILL, Professor DOUGHERTY.

Mr. James S. [illegible], Shorthand Writer, was in attendance.

Lord Justice FITZGIBBON made an opening statement.

BOYLE ACADEMICAL INSTITUTION.

Rev. John Watson, B.A., Secretary, was sworn and examined.

The following witnesses made statements:—

Rev. F. B. Clarke, LL.D., Rector of Boyle.
Lieut.-Colonel Fielding, J.P.
Rev. Canon Burke, M.A.

The Commissioners adjourned and proceeded to visit the Institution.

JOHN NAISH,
October 21, 1888.

N. D. Murphy, Junr.,
Chief Clerk and Assistant Secretary.

October 10, 1888.

PUBLIC SITTING.

Meeting of the Commission held this day at the Grammar School, Elphin.

Present:—Lord Justice FitzGibbon, Lord Justice Naish, Rev. Dr. Molloy, Dr. Traill, Professor Dougherty.

Mr. James S. Macartney, Shorthand Writer, was in attendance.

Bishop Hodson's Grammar School, Elphin.

The following witnesses were sworn and examined:—

The Very Rev. Wm. Warburton, D.D., Dean of Elphin.
Rev. Edward Irwin, Head Master.
Colonel Cooper, [illegible]

The following made statements:—

John Scott.
Thomas Byrne.

The Commissioners adjourned.

Previous to the Public Sitting the Commissioners visited the School.

John Naish.

N. D. Murphy, Junr., October 21, 1888.
Chief Clerk and Assistant Secretary.

October 11, 1888.

PUBLIC SITTING.

Meeting of the Commission held this day at the *[illegible] School, Newtownforbes.*

Present:—Lord Justice FitzGibbon, Lord Justice Naish, Rev. Dr. Molloy, Dr. Traill, Professor Dougherty.

Mr. James S. Macartney, Shorthand Writer, was in attendance.

Lord Justice FitzGibbon made an opening statement.

[illegible] Endowed School.

The following witnesses were sworn and examined:—

H. Ross Dyas, J.P.
Rev. G. R. Peyton, B.A., Rector of Clongish.
Alexander Livingstone, Head Master.

Rev. F. Potterton, LL.D., made a statement.

Clontumpher School (West Endowment).

The Rev. G. R. Peyton, B.A., was sworn and examined.

Edward Byrne, Schoolmaster, made a statement.

The Commissioners adjourned.

After the Public Sitting, the Commissioners proceeded to Roscommon, and visited the Ranelagh School (Incorporated Society's).

John Naish.

N. D. Murphy, Junr., October 21, 1888.
Chief Clerk and Assistant Secretary.

October 11, 1888.

Meeting of the Commission held this day at the Royal Hotel, Galway.

Present:—Lord Justice FitzGibbon, Lord Justice Naish, Rev. Dr. Molloy, Dr. Traill, Professor Dougherty.

The papers received from the Commissioners of Charitable Donations and Bequests referring to the Rockfield Institution, Ballinaskill, Clifden, were perused and considered.

A letter was read from the Clerk of the Salters Company, with regard to the Rainey School, Magherafelt.

The Commissioners adjourned.

John Naish.

N. D. Murphy, Junr., October 21, 1888.
Chief Clerk and Assistant Secretary.

October 13, 188[illegible].

PUBLIC SITTING.

Meeting of the Commission held this day at the Courthouse, Galway.

Present:—Lord Justice FitzGibbon, Lord Justice Naish, Rev. Dr. Molloy, Dr. Traill, Professor Dougherty.

Mr. James S. Macartney, Shorthand Writer, was in attendance.

Lord Justice FitzGibbon made an opening statement.

St. Ignatius' College, Galway.

The Very Rev. P. Hughes, S.J., President, was sworn and examined.

It was ruled:—That the Act does not apply to this Endowment, unless with the consent in writing of the Governing Body.

St. Joseph's Seminary, Nun's Island.

Rev. Br. J. P. Lynch was sworn and examined.

It was ruled:—That the Act does not apply to this Endowment, unless with the consent in writing of the Governing Body.

Lombard Street National Schools.

The Rev. P. Dooley, P.P., was sworn and examined.

It was ruled:—That the Act does not apply to this Endowment, unless with the consent in writing of the Governing Body.

Illerton School (Fisher Endowment).

In this case there was no appearance, and the Assistant Secretary was directed to telegraph to Mr. F. Joyce, Agent of the landowner on whose property the annuity constituting the Endowment is charged, to make it his convenience to attend at the Courthouse, Tuam, at 12 o'clock, to-morrow.

Rockfield Institution, Ballinakill, Clifden.

Lord Justice FitzGibbon made an introductory statement.

Rev. Canon Fleming, was sworn and examined.

Ven. J. O'Sullivan, D.D., Archdeacon of Tuam, made a statement.

Erasmus Smith's Grammar School, Galway.

The following witnesses were sworn and examined:—

Richard Biggs, M.A., LL.D., Head Master.
Hermann Dunn, Assistant Master.

The following witnesses made statements:—

Redmond A. M'Donagh, M.A., Solicitor (on behalf of the Rev. P. Dooley, P.P., Galway).
Rev. J. G. Clarke.

The Commissioners adjourned.

Previous to the Public Sitting the Commissioners visited the Erasmus Smith's Grammar School.

John Naish
October 21 188[illegible].

R. D. Murphy, Junr.,
Chief Clerk and Assistant Secretary.

h

October 12, 1889.

PUBLIC SITTING.

Meeting of the Commission held this day at the Court-house, Tuam.

Present:—Lord Justice FITZGIBBON, Lord Justice NAISH, Rev. Dr. MOLLOY, Dr. TRAILL, Professor DOUGHERTY.

Mr. James S. Moriarty, Shorthand Writer, was in attendance.

TUAM DIOCESAN FREE SCHOOL.

The Very Rev. W. C. Townsend, D.D., Dean of Tuam, was sworn and examined.

ST. JARLATH'S COLLEGE, TUAM.

The Very Rev. P. Kilkenny, D.D., Ex-President, and the Very Rev. M. O'Connell, President, were sworn and examined.

It was ruled:—That the Act does not apply to this Endowment, unless with the consent in writing of the Governing Body.

CHRISTIAN BROTHERS SCHOOLS, TUAM.

Rev. Br. Ignatius Delany was sworn and examined.

It was ruled:—That the Act does not apply to this Endowment, unless with the consent in writing of the Governing Body.

The Commissioners adjourned.

JOHN NAISH.
October 21, 1889.

N. D. Murphy, Junr.,
Chief Clerk and Assistant Secretary.

October 15, 1889.

Meeting of the Commission held this day at the Office, 28, Nassau-street, Dublin.

Present:—Lord Justice FITZGIBBON, Lord Justice NAISH, Rev. Dr. MOLLOY, Dr. TRAILL, Professor DOUGHERTY.

Letters read:—

Wm. Davidson [Oct. 9], as to the removal of the Ballymena Endowments to Abbeyleix.

Rev. S. Cuthbert Mitchell [Oct. 9], as to the buildings and premises of the Portora Royal School.

Thomas B. Montgomery [Oct. 11], as to the inquiry to be held by the Commissioners at Coleraine.

John C. Pounden [Oct. 8], as to the incorporation of a Governing Body to hold Educational Endowments in the Diocese of Ferns.

The Most Rev. Dr. O'Donnell, Bishop of Raphoe [Oct. 12], as to the Raphoe Royal School buildings.

Rev. G. B. Hurley [Oct. 13], correcting an error in the Schedule to the Draft Scheme for the Cork Parochial Schools.

H. H. Bottomley, Sub-sheriff [Oct. 13], as to accommodation in the Court-house, Belfast.

Rev. Wallace M'Mullen [Oct. 15], as to representation of the Methodist Body on the Central Board to be formed for the management of the Royal School Endowments.

Rev. James Stewart [Oct. 15], asking for any Scheme framed for the Hon. the Irish Society Schools in Coleraine.

Objections received from the following persons and public Bodies against the Draft Schemes published on August 12, were laid before the Commission:—

No. 46. KILKENNY COLLEGE.

John H. Nunn, Solicitor, on behalf of the Provost, Fellows, and Scholars of Trinity College, Dublin.

Thos. F. M'Elroy, on behalf of the Parents of the pupils (past and present) of Creighton's School, Kilkenny.

No. 47. CORK PAROCHIAL SCHOOLS.

Right Rev. Dr. Gregg, Lord Bishop of Cork, on behalf of himself and the other proposed Governors.

Rev. George Webster, D.D., Incumbent of St. Nicholas' Parish.

Ven. Mervyn Archdall, D.D., Archdeacon of Cork.

No. 49. The Rainey School, Magherafelt.

Rev. W. Todd Martin, D.D., on behalf of the Intermediate Education Committee of the General Assembly of the Presbyterian Church.

Rev. P. Canon Donnelly, P.P., and others, Magherafelt.

M. F. Kincaid, Head Master, Rainey School.

No. 50. The Drelincourt, Callan, and Mall-street Schools, Armagh.

Very Rev. Geo. Chadwick, D.D., Dean of Armagh, on behalf of the Select Vestry of the Parish of Armagh.

Rev. James M'Neece, on behalf of the Select Vestry of the Parish of Clonfeacle.

George Strong, Head Teacher in Drelincourt School.

No. 51. Sullivan Schools, Holywood.

Adam Speers, Esq., B.Sc., Head Master.

Letter [Oct. 8] read from Very Rev. P. J. Byrne, P.P., V.G., in answer to the letter written to him as directed in the minutes of October 1, with regard to the Tyrone Roman Catholic Board.

To be informed that his letter will receive due attention from the Commissioners.

The directions given (Oct. 1, 1885) to the Secretary with reference to Dean Byrne's letter (Aug. 31) were countermanded.

Letter [Oct. 8] read from Rev. M. Le B. Kennedy, M.A., Head Master, Clonmel Endowed School, asking when the objections and amendments lodged against the Draft Scheme framed for the management of that School will be heard.

A reply, as drafted, was directed to be sent.

Letter [Oct. 9] read from Rev. John Jackson, as to an Endowment in the Parish of Ramoan, Co. Antrim, called "Sharpe's Bequest."

To be informed that the case of the Endowment referred to by him will be inquired into by the Commissioners in due course.

Letters read from Rev. Henry F. Macdonald, Hon. Sec. (October 10), and from W. H. Porter, one of the proposed Governors of the Robertson Endowments, Co. Donegal, asking for copies of the objections and amendments lodged against the Draft Scheme published for these Endowments.

To be informed that the objections, which are voluminous in detail, have not been printed, but at the public sitting to be held at Londonderry on October 19, an opportunity will be afforded to all parties of inspecting them.

Letter [Oct. 8] read from William Eccles, Coleraine, as to the proposed inquiry by the Commission into the Hon. the Irish Society's Schools in Coleraine.

A reply, as drafted, directed to be sent.

Letter [Oct. 9] read from the Clerk of the Privy Council, Dublin Castle, as to the method by which Schemes framed under the Educational Endowments Act are to be published when finally approved by the Lord Lieutenant in Council.

To be requested to have the goodness to give the necessary directions to the Queen's Printer to secure that the copies issued and sold by him shall bear the imprint necessary to render them legal evidence, as in the majority of cases the copies hitherto issued by the Queen's Printer to the public do not bear any imprint, and are, therefore, useless as evidence.

Letter [Oct. 13] read from Rev. S. Walker, as to the particular Schools at Donaghadee, into which inquiries will be held by the Commissioners on October 23.

A reply, as drafted, directed to be sent.

Letter [Oct. 9] read from the Secretary, Commissioners of Education, enclosing objection to the Draft Scheme published for the Clonmel Endowed School.

A reply, as drafted, ordered to be sent.

Letter [Oct. 10] read from F. W. Leeper, as to the incorporation of a Governing Body to hold Educational Endowments in the Diocese of Glendalough.

That the same reply be sent as in the case of Diocesan applications mentioned in the Minutes of October 1.

Letter [Oct. 11] read from D. De la Cherois, D.L., as to the inquiry to be held by the Commissioners at Donaghadee, on October 23, and asking that the Lord Bishop of Down should be informed of the inquiry.

That a reply, as drafted, be sent to Mr. De la Cherois, and also that the Secretary should give notice of the inquiry to the Lord Bishop of Down.

Letter [Oct. 13] read from Rev. John Nolan, C.C., asking for particulars as to the Larne Grammar School.

That extracts bearing on the subject, which can be obtained from previous Reports, be forwarded to him.

Letter [Oct. 18] read from the Hon. Somerset Ward, asking for particulars as to the (Clanbrassil) Endowment, Bangor.

Same instructions given as in the case of the preceding letter.

The draft Annual Report for the year 1887–8, was further considered and amended.

The Commissioners adjourned.

GERALD MOLLOY,
November 8, 1888.

Wm. Edward Ellis, Secretary.

October 19, 1888.

PUBLIC SITTING.

Meeting of the Commission held this day at the Court-house, Londonderry.

Present:—Lord Justice FITZGIBBON, Lord Justice NAISH, Rev. Dr. MOLLOY, Dr. TRAILL, Professor DOUGHERTY.

Mr. David Pressley, Shorthand Writer, was in attendance.

OBJECTIONS AND AMENDMENTS TO THE DRAFT SCHEME FOR THE ROBERTSON ENDOWMENTS, CO. DONEGAL.

The following persons made statements:—

Rev. Henry P. MacDonald, M.A., Secretary.
Rev. Canon Baillie, M.A.
Rev. Samuel G. Cochrane, M.A.
Sir Samuel Hayes, Bart., D.L.
Rev. F. Carre.
William H. Porter, J.P.

OBJECTIONS AND AMENDMENTS TO THE DRAFT SCHEME FOR THE LONDONDERRY ACADEMICAL INSTITUTION.

Professor J. R. Leebody, and A. M'Vicker, made statements.

The Commissioners adjourned.

JOHN NAISH,
October 31, 1888.

N. D. Murphy, Junr.,
Chief Clerk and Assistant Secretary.

October 19, 1888.

Meeting of the Commission held this day.

Present:—Lord Justice FITZGIBBON, Lord Justice NAISH, Rev. Dr. MOLLOY, Dr. TRAILL, Professor DOUGHERTY.

The Draft Report for the year 1887–8 was considered and amended.

A letter, as drafted, was directed to be sent with regard to the printing of the Appendices to the Report.

The Commissioners adjourned.

JOHN NAISH,
October 31, 1888.

N. D. Murphy, Junr.,
Chief Clerk and Assistant Secretary.

October 20, 1888.

PUBLIC SITTING.

Meeting of the Commission held this day at the Town Hall, Coleraine.

Present:—Lord Justice FitzGibbon, Lord Justice Naish, Rev. Dr. Molloy, Dr. Traill, Professor Dougherty.

Mr. David Pressley, Shorthand Writer, was in attendance.

THE IRISH SOCIETY'S SCHOOLS, COLERAINE.

The following witnesses were sworn and examined:—

C. M. Longbridge, Head Master.
Rev. Henry S. O'Hara.
Rev. James Stewart.
Rev. R. Wallace.
Rev. John Carroll.
Daniel Taylor, J.P.

Rev. R. B. Wylie made a statement.

CAMUS (CASTLEROCK) SCHOOL.

The following witnesses were sworn and examined:—

Rev. F. S. Gardner.
James Hamhill.
Daniel Brown.
Francis Givens.

Rev. F. Torrens made a statement.

The Commissioners adjourned.

Previous to the Public Sitting the Commissioners visited the Irish Society's Schools.

John Naish,
October 21, 1888.

N. D. Murphy, Junr.,
Chief Clerk and Assistant Secretary.

October 20, 1888.

Meeting of the Commission held this day.

Present:—Lord Justice FitzGibbon, Lord Justice Naish, Rev. Dr. Molloy, Dr. Traill, Professor Dougherty.

The Report for the year 1887–8 was further considered and amended, and Dr. Traill handed in an addition to the Report, which was ordered to be printed and attached to the Report.

The Commissioners adjourned.

Anthony Traill,
November 16, 1888.

N. D. Murphy, Junr.,
Chief Clerk and Assistant Secretary.

October 21, 1888.

Meeting of the Commission held this day at the Northern Counties Hotel, Portrush.

Present:—Lord Justice FitzGibbon, Lord Justice Naish, Rev. Dr. Molloy, Professor Dougherty.

Minutes of the meetings at Boyle, Elphin, Newtownforbes, Galway, Tuam, Londonderry, and Coleraine, read and confirmed.

Letter read from Very Rev. Wm. Warburton, D.D., Dean of Elphin, as to Bishop Hodson's Grammar School, Elphin.

The Assistant Secretary was directed to reply to same, in terms as drafted, and to return, as requested, the Agent's letter.

The Report for the year 1887–8 was further considered and amended.

The Commissioners adjourned.

Anthony Traill,
November 16, 1888.

N. D. Murphy, Junr.,
Chief Clerk and Assistant Secretary.

October 22, 1888.

PUBLIC SITTING.

Meeting of the Commission held this day at the Court-house, Magherafelt.

PRESENT:—Lord Justice FITZGIBBON, Lord Justice NAISH, Rev. Dr. MOLLOY, Dr. TRAILL, Professor DOUGHERTY.

Mr. John M'Bride, Shorthand Writer, was in attendance.

OBJECTIONS AND AMENDMENTS TO THE DRAFT SCHEME FOR THE RAINEY SCHOOL, MAGHERAFELT.

P. O. Gaussen, B.L., appeared for H. B. Kincaid, Head Master.

D. S. Henry, B.L., appeared for the Roman Catholics of Magherafelt.

The Rev. Thomas Jordan, D.D., made a statement and was examined, having been previously sworn.

The following witnesses were sworn and examined:—

Samuel Porter, J.P.
Arthur Bracken.
H. B. Kincaid, Head Master.

The following made statements:—

Campbell Gaussen, J.P.
Rev. A. Minnis.
Rev. Thomas Fisher.
Andrew Brown.
Rev. H. B. Wilson, D.D.
D. S. Henry, B.L.
P. O. Gaussen, B.L.
Alex. Johnston.
John Glover, Solicitor.
Rev. Joseph J. Quinn, C.C.

The Commissioners adjourned.

Previous to the Public Sitting the Commissioners visited the various National Schools in Magherafelt, and also the Rainey School.

ANTHONY TRAILL,
November 16, 1888.

N. D. Murphy, Junr.,
Chief Clerk and Assistant Secretary.

October 23, 1888.

PUBLIC SITTING.

Meeting of the Commission held this day at the Court-house, Ballymena.

PRESENT:—Lord Justice FITZGIBBON, Lord Justice NAISH, Rev. Dr. MOLLOY, Dr. TRAILL, Professor DOUGHERTY.

Mr. John M'Bride, Shorthand Writer, was in attendance.

OBJECTIONS AND AMENDMENTS TO THE DRAFT SCHEME FOR GUY'S FREE SCHOOL, BALLYMENA.

The following witnesses were sworn and examined:—

John Alexander, Head Master.
Rev. Charles Davey.
John Patrick, J.P.
Very Rev. J. W. Murray, LL.D., Dean of Connor.

The following witnesses made statements:—

Rev. John Gibson, Clerk of the Ballymena Presbytery.
Rev. Thomas Eaton.
William Orr Wilson.
Rev. David M'Meekin.

OBJECTIONS AND AMENDMENTS TO THE DRAFT SCHEME FOR THE BALLYMENA COLLEGIATE SCHOOL.

The following witnesses were sworn and examined :—

Rev. Thomas Eaton.
Captain Perry.
Rev. Robert King.

The following witnesses made statements :—

Rev. John Gibson.
Rev. S. Moffett.
Rev. D. M'Meekin.
Alexander Carson, Solicitor.

The Commissioners adjourned.

Previous to the Public Sitting the Commissioners visited Guy's Free School, Ballymena Collegiate School, and the Ballymena Model National School.

ANTHONY TRAILL,

November 16, 1888.

N. D. Murphy, Junr.,
Chief Clerk and Assistant Secretary.

October 23, 1888.

Meeting of the Commission held this day at the Royal Hotel, Belfast.

Present :—Lord Justice FITZGIBBON, Lord Justice NAISH, Rev. Dr. MOLLOY, Dr. TRAILL, Professor DOUGHERTY.

The Report for the year 1887-8 was further considered and amended.

The Commissioners adjourned.

ANTHONY TRAILL,

November 16, 1888.

N. D. Murphy, Junr.,
Chief Clerk and Assistant Secretary.

October 24, 1888.

PUBLIC SITTING.

Meeting of the Commission held this day at the Town Hall, Holywood.

Present :—Lord Justice FITZGIBBON, Lord Justice NAISH, Rev. Dr. MOLLOY, Dr. TRAILL, Professor DOUGHERTY.

Mr. John M'Bride, Shorthand Writer, was in attendance.

OBJECTIONS AND AMENDMENTS TO THE DRAFT SCHEME FOR SULLIVAN'S SCHOOLS, HOLYWOOD.

The following witnesses were sworn and examined :—

Rev. C. J. M'Alester.
Adam Speers, B.Sc., Head Master, Sullivan Upper Schools.

The following witnesses made statements :—

J. Anderson, J.P.
R. L. Patterson, J.P.

The Commissioners adjourned.

ANTHONY TRAILL,

November 16, 1888.

N. D. Murphy, Junr.,
Chief Clerk and Assistant Secretary.

October 24, 1888.

PUBLIC SITTING.

Meeting of the Commission held this day at the Court-house, Bangor.

Present:—Lord Justice FITZGIBBON, Rev. Dr. MOLLOY, Dr. TRAILL, Professor DOUGHERTY.

Mr. John M'Bride, Shorthand Writer, was in attendance.

BANGOR ENDOWED SCHOOL.

The following witnesses were sworn and examined:—

The Hon. Somerset Ward, J.P.
James H. Rainey, Head Master.

The following witnesses made statements:—

Very Rev. E. Maguire, D.D., Dean of Down.
The Hon. R. E. Ward.
Rev. W. Clarke.

BALLYMACONNELL, BALLYGRAINEY, AND BALLYMALLAGH NATIONAL SCHOOLS.

The following witnesses made statements:—

Very Rev. E. Maguire, D.D., Dean of Down.
Rev. John Quarry.

KILLOUGH AND BALLYCULTER SCHOOLS.

The Hon. Somerset Ward was examined.

The Commissioners adjourned.

Previous to the Public Sitting the Commissioners visited Bangor Endowed School, and the Ward National Schools.

ANTHONY TRAILL,
November 16, 1888.

N. D. Murphy, Junr.,
Chief Clerk and Assistant Secretary.

October 25, 1888.

PUBLIC SITTING.

Meeting of the Commission held this day at the Courthouse, Donaghadee.

Present:—Lord Justice FITZGIBBON, Rev. Dr. MOLLOY, Dr. TRAILL, Professor DOUGHERTY.

Mr. John M'Bride, Shorthand Writer, was in attendance.

MOUNT ALEXANDER ENDOWED SCHOOL, DONAGHADEE.

The following witnesses were sworn and examined:—

Daniel De la Cherois, D.L.
J. W. Charles, Master of the School.
Rev. R. H. Crane, Rector of Donaghadee.

It was ruled:—That the Act does not apply to this Endowment unless with the consent in writing of the Governing Body.

ADMIRAL LESLIE'S FREE SCHOOL, DONAGHADEE.

Daniel De la Cherois, D.L., was examined.

Georgina Taylor was sworn and examined.

DONAGHADEE No. 1 NATIONAL SCHOOL.

John Malcom was sworn and examined.

CARROWDORE NATIONAL SCHOOL.

Rev. R. A. Cooper, B.D., was sworn and examined.

It was ruled:—That the Act does not apply to this Endowment unless with the consent in writing of the Governing Body.

The Commissioners adjourned.

Previous to the Public Sitting the Commissioners visited the Endowed School and the National Schools.

ANTHONY TRAILL,
November 16, 1888.

N. D. Murphy, Junr.,
Chief Clerk and Assistant Secretary.

October 25, 1888.

PUBLIC SITTING.

Meeting of the Commission held this day at Ballywalter National School.

Present:—Lord Justice FITZGIBBON, Rev. Dr. MOLLOY, Dr. TRAILL, Professor DOUGHERTY.

Mr. John M'Bride, Shorthand Writer, was in attendance.

BROWN'S ENDOWMENTS, CO. DOWN.

The following witnesses were sworn and examined:—

Frederick Saunderson.
Rev. S. A. Lyle, M.A.

INISHARGY (TUBBER-NA-CARRIG) SCHOOL.

Rev. S. A. Lyle, M.A., was sworn and examined.

It was ruled:—That the Act does not apply to this Endowment unless with the consent in writing of the Governing Body.

GREY ABBEY, TULLYCAVEY, NATIONAL SCHOOL.

The following witnesses were sworn and examined:—

George Allen.
John Moran.
Thomas Boyd.

The Commissioners adjourned.

ANTHONY TRAILL,
November 16, 1888.

N. D. Murphy, Junr.,
Chief Clerk and Assistant Secretary.

October 26, 1888.

PUBLIC SITTING.

Meeting of the Commission held this day at the Court-house, Belfast.

Present:—Lord Justice FITZGIBBON, Rev. Dr. MOLLOY, Dr. TRAILL, Professor DOUGHERTY.

Mr. John M'Bride, Shorthand Writer, was in attendance.

APPLICATION from the DIOCESAN COUNCIL of DOWN and CONNOR and DROMORE for the INCORPORATION of a DIOCESAN GOVERNING BODY for EDUCATIONAL ENDOWMENTS of "THE CHURCH OF IRELAND."

The following deputation attended on behalf of the Diocesan Council:—

Very Rev. Theophilus Campbell, D.D., Dean of Dromore.
Ven. Charles Seaver, D.D., Archdeacon of Connor.
Rev. E. J. Hartrick, M.A.
Alexander Tate, C.E.
Joseph John Murphy, Hon. Secretary.
David Manson, Assistant Secretary.

The following witnesses made statements:—

Very Rev. T. Campbell, D.D., Dean of Dromore.
Joseph John Murphy.
Rev. E. J. Hartrick.

SAMUEL LESLEY'S CHARITABLE BEQUEST.

James M'Ildowie, B.L. (instructed by Messrs. M'Ildowie and Sons), appeared on behalf of the trustees, and made a statement.

G. H. Todd, Master of Ballymacarrett School, was sworn and examined.

The following witnesses made statements:—

Rev. T. W. Roe, LL.D.
Rev. Hugh Hanna, D.D.
Ven. Charles Seaver, D.D., Archdeacon of Connor.
W. Quartus Ewart, J.P.
Rev. E. J. Hartrick, M.A.
James Major.
Joseph John Murphy, J.P.

APPLICATION from the ELEMENTARY EDUCATION COMMITTEE of the GENERAL ASSEMBLY for the INCORPORATION of GOVERNING BODIES for EDUCATIONAL ENDOWMENTS connected with the PRESBYTERIAN CHURCH in IRELAND.

The following witnesses made statements:—

Rev. H. B. Wilson, D.D.
Rev. W. Johnston, D.D.
Rev. Hugh Hanna, D.D.

BROWN STREET SCHOOLS, BELFAST.

Rev. William Johnston, D.D., was sworn and examined.

PRESBYTERIAN ORPHAN SOCIETY.

Rev. William Johnston, D.D., was examined, having been previously sworn.

The Commissioners adjourned, and visited the Brown-street National Schools, St. Enoch's National Schools, and the Presbyterian Orphanage.

ANTHONY TRAILL,
November 16, 1886.

N. D. Murphy, Junr.,
Chief Clerk and Assistant Secretary.

October 27, 1886.

PUBLIC SITTING.

Meeting of the Commission held this day at the Court-house, Carrickfergus.

Present:—Lord Justice FITZGIBBON, Rev. Dr. MOLLOY, Dr. TRAILL, Professor DOUGHERTY.

Mr. John M'Bride, Shorthand Writer, was in attendance.

CARRICKFERGUS PAROCHIAL SCHOOL.

Rev. George Chamberlain was sworn and examined.

The Commissioners adjourned, and visited the School.

ANTHONY TRAILL,
November 16, 1886.

N. D. Murphy, Junr.,
Chief Clerk and Assistant Secretary.

October 27, 1886.

PUBLIC SITTING.

Meeting of the Commission held this day at the Larne Grammar School.

Present:—Rev. Dr. MOLLOY, Dr. TRAILL, Professor DOUGHERTY.

Mr. John M'Bride, Shorthand Writer, was in attendance.

LARNE GRAMMAR SCHOOL.

The following witnesses were sworn and examined:—

Rev. James Kennedy, Secretary.
R. M. Jones, M.A., Head Master.
Rev. T. P. Morgan, Rector of Larne.
Rev. John Nelson, C.C.
John A. Bowman.

The Commissioners adjourned, and visited the School.

ANTHONY TRAILL,
November 16, 1886.

N. D. Murphy, Junr.,
Chief Clerk and Assistant Secretary.

October 19, 1888.

PUBLIC SITTING.

Meeting of the Commission held this day at the Court-house, Downpatrick.

Present:—Rev. Dr. Molloy, Dr. Traill, Professor Dougherty.

Mr. John M'Bride, Shorthand Writer, was in attendance.

Downpatrick Blue School.

The following witnesses were sworn and examined:—

J. Marland, Solicitor.
John R. M'Connell, Steward of the Charity.
Colonel William Brownlow Forde, D.L.
Robert Stuart.
Rev. T. Blackwood Price, M.A.

William N. Wallace, D.L., made a statement.

Killough National School.

Hugh Finlay, former teacher of the School, was sworn and examined.

Rev. Godfrey Brennan made a statement.

Killyleagh, Shrigley, National School.

Lachlan MacLaine, J.P., manager, was examined.

The Commissioners adjourned.

Previous to the Public Sitting, the Commissioners visited Downpatrick Blue School.

Anthony Traill,
November 16, 1888.

N. D. Murphy, Junr.,
Chief Clerk and Assistant Secretary.

November 2, 1888.

Meeting of the Commission held this day at the Office, 23, Nassau-street, Dublin.

Present:—Lord Justice FitzGibbon, Lord Justice Naish, Rev. Dr. Molloy, Professor Dougherty.

Minutes of Meeting of October 5, read and confirmed.

Letters read:—

The Clerk of the Privy Council, Dublin Castle [Oct. 15], enclosing objections lodged against the amended Scheme for Nicholson Memorial School, Lisburn, for observations of the Commissioners thereon.

Wm. J. De Vere [Oct. 15], enclosing resolution passed at a meeting of the Trustees of the Oldcastle Endowed School.

Rev. T. R. S. Collins, M.A. [Oct. 17], enclosing a further amendment to the Draft Scheme published for the Church of Ireland Victoria Jubilee Fund.

James Mitchell, Clerk of the Monaghan Union [Oct. 17], sending returns of the number of Protestants and Roman Catholics rated at various amounts in that Union.

Rev. Charles Davis, P.P. [Oct. 9], enclosing objections and amendments to the Draft Scheme published for the Baltimore Fishery School, Cork.

Rev. Abraham Jagoe, M.A. [Oct. 20], as to the Newspaper Report of the sitting in Londonderry on October 16, 1888.

Rev. Br. John P. Lynch, Christian Schools, Galway [Oct. 21], as to the Erasmus Smith Endowment.

James E. Pugh [Oct. 21], as to the Scheme for the Sullivan Schools, Holywood.

H. E. Kinnaird, Head Master, Rainey School [Oct. 20], enclosing copy of a letter which he has written to the Salters Company with reference to his vested interests.

Rev. S. L. Brakey [Oct. 20], as to the incorporation of a Governing Body to hold Educational Endowments in the Diocese of Clogher.

Alex. Gareth [Oct. 25], sending names of subscribers to the funds of the Ballymena Collegiate School in addition to those mentioned in the Schedule to the Draft Scheme published for that Endowment.

Letter [Oct. 19] read from the Most Rev. Dr. M'Gennis, Bishop of Kilmore, as to the Cavan Royal School buildings.

To be informed that his letter will receive due attention from the Commissioners.

Letter [Oct. 31] read from the Secretaries, Commissioners of Charitable Donations and Bequests, suggesting an amendment to the Draft Scheme published for the Drelincourt, College, and Mall-street Schools, and Primate Robinson's Loan Fund, Armagh.

That the Secretaries be thanked, and also be informed that the Commissioners will act on the suggestion of their Board.

Letter [Oct. 31] read from Major G. B. Knapp, Hon. Sec., Cork Grammar School, asking when the Scheme for that Institution will come into operation.

A reply, as drafted, directed to be sent.

Letter [Oct. 30] read from the Right Hon. Viscount De Vesci, enclosing memorial of certain inhabitants of Abbeyleix, asking that the Endowment of the Ballyroan Endowed School should be transferred to Abbeyleix, and guaranteeing certain funds in case of the transfer being granted.

A reply, as drafted, directed to be sent.

Letter [Oct. 31] read from Rev. Joseph J. Quinn, C.C., Magherafelt, asking that certain corrections be made in the evidence given by him at the sitting at Magherafelt on October 23, 1888.

To be informed that a copy of his evidence, when printed, will be sent him, in which he can introduce the corrections mentioned.

Letter [Oct. 31] also read from Rev. Joseph J. Quinn, C.C., asking that the Commissioners will frame a Scheme for the proposed new Convent Schools, Magherafelt.

A reply, as drafted, directed to be sent.

Letter [Oct. 31] read from J. B. Lyons, Head Master, Ballyroan Endowed School, as to his emoluments.

To be informed that he should state what are his emoluments from all sources.

The Commissioners arranged to visit the following Institutions on Saturday, November 10, at the hours mentioned:—

Incorporated Society's School, Celbridge, at 10 o'clock, A.M.
Hewetson's School, Clane, at 12 o'clock, noon.
Clongowes Wood College, Naas, at 1.30, P.M.

Notice was directed to be sent to the parties interested, in terms as drafted.

It was ordered:—

I. That the following Schemes be prepared for immediate signature by the Judicial Commissioners:—

No. 35.—"The Robertson Endowments" for Schools in the Diocese of Raphoe and County of Donegal.
No. 34.—"The Queen-street National School, Lurgan."
No. 37.—"The High School for Girls, Cork."
No. 38.—"The Baltimore Fishery School."
No. 39.—"The Royal Irish Academy of Music, and the Coulson Endowment."
No. 41.—"The Church of Ireland Victoria Jubilee Fund"; for the Education of Children of the Clergy.
No. 42.—"The Villiers' Charitable Institutions, Limerick."
No. 4?.—"The Thomastown Parochial School."
No. 43.—"The Rochelle Seminary, Cork."

II. That the following Schemes be prepared next after above for signature by the Judicial Commissioners:—

No. 40.—"The Londonderry Academical Institution."
No. 43.—"Guy's Free School, Ballymena."
No. 44.—"Ballymena Collegiate School."
No. 46.—"Kilkenny College."
No. 47.—"The Parochial Schools of the City of Cork; The Green Coat Hospital, Cork; The Cork Grammar School; and Bretridge's Charity, Cork."
No. 48.—"Rainey's School, Magherafelt."
No. 50.—The Drelincourt, Mall, and College-street Schools, Armagh and "Primate Robinson's Armagh Loan Fund."
No. 51.—"The Sullivan Schools, Holywood."
No. 5.—"Morgan's School, Castleknock."
No. 54.—"Gwyn and Young Endowments, Londonderry."
No. 57.—"Bertrand Female Orphan School, Dublin."
No. 58.—"Phibsborough Sunday and Daily Schools, Dublin."
No. 64.—"The Royal School Endowments, &c."

III. That the following Draft Schemes be prepared for first publication:—
"Oldcastle Endowed School."
"Meath Parochial Schools, and Navan Endowed School."

"Waterford Corporation Free Grammar School."
"Cashel Corporation School Endowment."
"The Incorporated Society."
"Munster Dairy School and Agricultural Institute."

The Draft Report for the year ending September 30, 1888, was adopted and signed, subject to procuring Dr. Traill's signature to same.

The Commissioners, having fixed a stated attendance on Wednesday, November 7, at 4 o'clock, p.m., adjourned.

JOHN NAISH,

November 7, 1888.

Wm. Edward Ellis, Secretary.

November 7, 1888.

Stated attendance of the Commissioners held this day at the Office, 39, Nassau-street, Dublin.

Present:—Rev. Dr. MOLLOY, Dr. TRAILL.

Letter [Nov. 1] read from Rev. L. O'Sullivan as to the incorporation of a Governing Body to hold Educational Endowments in the Diocese of Killaloe (East).

A reply, as drafted in similar cases, ordered to be sent.

Communication read from Lieut.-Col. William Rowan as to the incorporation of a Governing Body to hold Educational Endowments in the Diocese of Ardfert and Aghadoe, and as to the representation of the several Dioceses of the Church of Ireland on the Governing Body to be appointed for the Incorporated Society.

A reply, as drafted in similar cases, ordered to be sent in answer to the first portion of the letter, and stating that the second portion will receive the consideration of the Commissioners.

Letter [Nov. 6] read from Rev. B. M'Namee, P.P., Omagh, as to the formation of the Tyrone Roman Catholic Local Board.

That, subject to the approval of the Judicial Commissioners, the original directions given in the minutes of October on this subject be carried out.

Letter [Nov. 6] read from Rev. Edward Lewis, Grammar School, Elphin, as to his vested interests.

To be informed that his letter will receive due consideration from the Commissioners in the preparation of a Scheme for the above Endowment.

Letter [Nov. 3] read from Rev. The Superior-General of the Patrician Brothers, Mountmellick, as to the Ballyroan Endowment.

A reply, as drafted, directed to be sent.

JOHN NAISH,

November 9, 1888.

Wm. Edward Ellis, Secretary.

November 9, 1888.

Meeting of the Commission held this day at the Office, 39, Nassau-street, Dublin.

Present:—Lord Justice FITZGIBBON, Lord Justice NAISH, Rev. Dr. MOLLOY, Dr. TRAILL, Professor DOUGHERTY.

Minutes of the preceding Meeting, and of the stated attendance of November 7, read and confirmed.

Letter [Nov. 8] read from Thomas Cooke-Trench, J.P., as to the inquiry to be held into Hewetson's School, Clane.

Letter [Nov. 7] read from the Rev. William C. Ledger as to the payment of the Treasury costs incurred in the publication of the Scheme for the Moat School, Lisburn.

The Secretary was directed to write to the agent to the Representatives of the late Archibald Hamilton in terms as drafted with regard to same.

The Commissioners adjourned.

ANTHONY TRAILL,

November 16, 1888.

Wm. Edward Ellis, Secretary.

November 10, 1888.

PUBLIC SITTING.

Meeting of the Commission held this day at Hewetson's School, Clane.

Present:—Lord Justice FitzGibbon, Lord Justice Naish, Rev. Dr. Molloy, Dr. Traill, Professor Dougherty.

Hewetson's School, Clane.

The following witnesses were sworn and examined:—

Thomas Cooke-Trench, J.P.
Rev. William Sherlock, M.A., *Incumbent of Clane.*
John Lemon, Master of the School.

The Commissioners adjourned.

Previous to the Public Sitting the Commissioners visited the Incorporated Society's Institution, Celbridge, and afterwards Clongowes Wood College, Naas.

John Naish,
July 11, 1889.

N. D. Murphy, Junr.,
Chief Clerk and Assistant Secretary.

November 14, 1888.

Stated attendance of the Commissioners held this day at the Office, 13, Nassau-street, Dublin.

Present:—Dr. Traill.

Letters read:—

Rev. L. O'Sullivan [Nov. 10] acknowledging receipt of letter written by direction of minute of November 7.

The Most Rev. Dr. Logue, Lord Archbishop of Armagh [Nov. 12], as to the formation of the Tyrone Roman Catholic Local Board.

Mrs. Crawford [Nov. 10] enclosing list of the Schools from which the girls at the Incorporated Society's School, Celbridge, came.

J. B. Lyons, Head Master, Ballyroan School [Nov. 8], as to his emoluments.

Messrs. Bell, Stewarts, and May, solicitors [Nov. 6], enclosing objection on behalf of Sir Hugh Adair, to the Draft Scheme published for Guy's Free School, Ballymena.

Letter [Nov. 10] read from Rev. James Mitchell as to the Annahilt Endowed School, near Hillsborough, county Down, endowed by the will of a Mr. Jamieson.

That Rev. Mr. Mitchell be asked to forward a copy of the will mentioned.

Letter [Nov. 8] read from Rev. F. A. Sanders as to the payment of the Treasury costs incurred in the publication of the Schemes for the Tullyvin and Bunbawn Schools, and stating that the funds of the Moore Charity have not yet been transferred by the Commissioners of Education to the new Governing Body.

The Secretary was directed to write to the Commissioners of Education on the subject.

Letter [Nov. 7] read from Rev. Robert F. Clarke as to the preparation of a Scheme for the Brinny Parochial School, Cork.

A letter, as drafted, directed to be sent.

Anthony Traill,
November 16, 1888.

Wm. Edward Ellis, Secretary.

November 16, 1888.

Meeting of the Commission held this day at the Office, 13, Nassau-street, Dublin.

Present:—Lord Justice FitzGibbon, Rev. Dr. Molloy, Dr. Traill, Professor Dougherty.

Minutes of the meetings in the North of Ireland, from October 20 to October 29, inclusive, of November 9, and of the stated attendance of November 14, read and confirmed.

Letters read:—

Very Rev. Dean Byrne, P.P., Dungannon [Nov. 15], as to the formation of the Tyrone Roman Catholic Board.

Rev. Thomas Jordan, P.P. [Nov. 15], asking for a copy of the evidence recently taken at Magherafelt, as to the Rainey School.

Letter [Nov. 15] read from the Secretary, Board of Works, Dublin, asking for what further period after January 1 next, the Educational Endowments Commissioners will require the Offices at 23, Nassau-street, Dublin.

A reply, as drafted, directed to be sent.

Questions connected with the Draft Schemes for the Parochial Schools of the Diocese of Meath, and for the Munster Dairy School and Agricultural Institute, were discussed.

The Secretary was directed to write to the Secretary, Representative Church Body, asking him to call the attention of that Body to the letter of the Commission of the 5th July last with reference to a draft Scheme for the Parochial School Endowments of the Diocese of Meath.

The Commissioners, having fixed a stated attendance for Wednesday, November 21, at 4 o'clock, P.M., adjourned.

JOHN NAISH,
November 23, 1888.

Wm. Edward Ellis, Secretary.

November 21, 1888.

Stated attendance of the Commissioners held this day at the Office, 23, Nassau-street, Dublin.

Present:—Lord Justice FITZGIBBON, Lord Justice NAISH, Rev. Dr. MOLLOY, Dr. TRAILL.

Letters read:—

Rev. John Gilmore [Nov. 15] as to the objection of the Ballymena Presbytery to the Draft Scheme published for Guy's Free School, Ballymena.

Rev. S. L. Brakey [Nov. 16 and 17] as to the incorporation of a Governing Body to hold Educational Endowments in the Diocese of Clogher.

Rev. A. H. Barton, D.D., Rector of Cavan [Nov. 17] as to the letting value of the Cavan Royal School buildings and land attached.

Thomas Cooke-Trench, J.P. [Nov. 19], on behalf of the Trustees of the Newtown's Charity, Clane, asking that a Scheme be prepared by the Commission for that Charity on certain lines stated.

Letter [Nov. 16] read from Rev. Joseph J. Quinn, C.C., on behalf of the Very Rev. Canon Donnelly, Magherafelt, enclosing a letter dated November 7, from the Salters Company, with regard to their proposed Endowment to the Rainey School.

To be informed, that in accordance with an understanding come to at Magherafelt, the settlement of the Scheme for the Rainey School will be deferred until all those interested have an opportunity of seeing the printed report of the evidence then taken, and with reference to his statement that the Salters Company have thrown upon this Commission the responsibility of doing what is just and fair, that the Scheme of the Salters Company with reference to their proposed endowment has not left it open to this Commission to apply that endowment for the benefit of all religious denominations upon conditions which they would consider satisfactory.

Letter [Nov. 18] read from the Rev. J. A. Weir, LL.D., as to the Scheme for the Royal School Endowments.

A reply, as drafted, directed to be sent.

JOHN NAISH,
November 23, 1888.

Wm. Edward Ellis, Secretary.

November 23, 1888.

Meeting of the Commission held this day at the Office, 23, Nassau-street, Dublin.

Present:—Lord Justice FITZGIBBON, Lord Justice NAISH, Rev. Dr. MOLLOY, Dr. TRAILL, Professor DOUGHERTY.

Minutes of the preceding meeting, and of the stated attendance of November 21, were read and confirmed.

Letters read:—

Rev. H. B. Wilson, D.D., Convener of the General Assembly's Education Committee [Nov. 21] asking for copies of the Scheme framed for the Ormond Quay Presbyterian Church Endowments, Dublin.

Letter [Nov. 21] read from Rev. Josias Mitchell, enclosing extract from Mr. Jamieson's Will, relating to the Anahilt Endowed School, County Down.

A letter, as drafted, ordered to be sent.

Letter [Nov. 22] read from Rev. John Finlay, Secretary to the Diocesan Council of Leighlin, asking if it comes within the functions of the Educational Endowments Commission to appoint a Governing Body to hold any future Educational Endowments when at present there are no existing endowments to invest in the Governing Body.

To be informed that the functions of the Commission do not extend to the points in question.

It was agreed that the Draft Scheme for the Waterford Corporation Free Grammar School be brought up for discussion before the full Commission, but not to be published until the Incorporated Society's Scheme is published.

The Commissioners adjourned.

GERALD FITZGIBBON,
November 24, 1888.

Wm. Edward Ellis, Secretary.

November 24, 1888.

Meeting of the Commission held this day at the Office, 13, Nassau-street, Dublin.

Present:—Lord Justice FITZGIBBON, Lord Justice NAISH, Rev. Dr. MOLLOY, Dr. TRAILL, Professor DOUGHERTY.

Minutes of the preceding meeting read and confirmed.

Letters read:—

Rev. A. J. Moore [Nov. 23] with regard to the petition lodged with the Privy Council against the amended Scheme for the Nicholson Memorial School.

Thomas Greene, M.A., Secretary, Representative Church Body [Nov. 23] as to the letter of the 5th July from this Commission, relating to the Parochial Schools of the Diocese of Meath.

The objections lodged with the Privy Council against the Amended Scheme for the Nicholson Memorial Schoolhouse, Lisburn, were considered, and also the observations of the Commissioners on same.

The Draft Scheme for the Royal School Endowments and the objections lodged against same, were considered.

The Commissioners, having fixed a stated attendance for Wednesday, November 28, at 3 o'clock, P.M., adjourned.

GERALD MOLLOY,
November 28, 1888.

Wm. Edward Ellis, Secretary.

November 28, 1888.

Stated attendance of the Commissioners held this day at the Office, 13, Nassau-street, Dublin.

Present:—Rev. Dr. MOLLOY, Dr. TRAILL.

Letter [Nov. 27] read from Rev. Josias Mitchell, enclosing copy of Jamieson's Will, relating to the Anahilt Endowed School, Hillsborough, co. Down.

That Rev. Mr. Mitchell be thanked for his letter and its enclosure, and that the Will be returned to him after a copy of same has been made.

The observations of the Commissioners on the objections lodged with the Privy Council against the Amended Scheme for the Nicholson Memorial School, Lisburn, were further considered and amended.

GERALD MOLLOY,
November 28, 1888.

Wm. Edward Ellis, Secretary.

November 30, 1888.

Meeting of the Commission held this day at the Office, 23, Nassau-street, Dublin.

Present:—Lord Justice FITZGIBBON, Lord Justice NAISH, Rev. Dr. MOLLOY, Dr. TRAILL, Professor DOUGHERTY.

Minutes of the preceding meeting, and of the stated attendance of November 28, read and confirmed.

Letter (Nov. 29) read from Rev. B. M'Namee, P.P., Omagh, as to the Tyrone Roman Catholic Local Board.

Letter (Nov. 29) read from Rev. Canon B. Babington, with reference to the appointment of Trustees to hold Diocesan Endowments.

A reply, as drafted, directed to be sent.

Letter (Nov. 30) read from Messrs. Wm. Mooney and Sons, asking if the Commissioners will undertake the preparation of a Draft Scheme for Shell's Charity, co. Westmeath.

A reply, as drafted, directed to be sent.

Letter (Nov. 29) read from Colonel Marsh, C.R.E. in Ireland, with reference to the purchase of the buildings and land of Portora Royal School, by Her Majesty's Secretary of State for War.

A reply, as drafted, ordered to be sent, and a copy of Colonel Marsh's letter was directed to be sent to the Most Rev. Dr. Donnelly, Lord Bishop of Clogher; to the Rev. S. Cuthbert Mitchel, Honorary Secretary, Local Protestant Committee at Enniskillen, asking them for their observations on same.

The Secretary was directed to write to Messrs. H. T. Dix and Son, Solicitors to the Incorporated Society, asking them for the original Deed from the Mayor, Sheriff, and Citizens of the County of the City of Waterford, to the Society, dated the 1st day of July, 1743.

The observations of the Commissioners on the objections lodged against the amended Scheme for the Nicholson Memorial School, Lisburn, were further amended, and finally approved, and the Secretary was directed to forward same to the Clerk of the Privy Council.

The Commissioners adjourned.

JOHN NAISH,
December 1, 1888.

Wm. Edward Ellis, Secretary.

December 1, 1888.

Meeting of the Commission held this day at the Office, 23, Nassau-street, Dublin.

Present:—Lord Justice FITZGIBBON, Lord Justice NAISH, Rev. Dr. MOLLOY, Dr. TRAILL, Professor DOUGHERTY.

Minutes of the preceding meeting read and confirmed.

Letter (Nov. 28) read from Rev. J. Kennedy, asking if the Commissioners will prepare a Scheme for the Larne Grammar School, county Antrim.

A reply, as drafted, directed to be sent.

The Commissioners had under consideration the objections to the Scheme for the Royal School Endowments, and in reference to the question of the disposal of the School buildings, the Secretary was directed to write letters, as drafted, to the following:—

Most Rev. Dr. Logue, Archbishop of Armagh.	As to Armagh.
Rev. W. Moore Morgan, LL.D., Very Rev. Dean Byrne, Dungannon, Colonel J. C. J. Lowry, James Brown, Esq.,	As to Dungannon.
Most Rev. Dr. O'Donnell, Bishop of Raphoe.	As to his estimate of the value of the Raphoe Buildings.

The Draft Scheme for the Meath Parochial Schools and the Navan Endowed School was considered, and the Secretary was directed to write, in terms as drafted, to Mr. John J. Preston, one of the existing Trustees, as to the appointment of future Head Masters of Navan Endowed School.

The Commissioners having fixed a stated attendance for Wednesday, December 5, at 3 o'clock, adjourned.

GERALD FITZGIBBON,
December 7, 1888.

Wm. Edward Ellis, Secretary.

December 5, 1888.

Stated attendance of the Commissioners held this day at the Office, 23, Nassau-street, Dublin.

Present :—Lord Justice FITZGIBBON, Rev. Dr. MOLLOY, Dr. TRAILL.

Letters read :—

Rev. Canon Babington (December 3), enclosing original Deeds as to the property to be incorporated in the proposed Diocesan Trustees for the United Dioceses of Derry and Raphoe.

The Most Rev. Dr. O'Donnell, Lord Bishop of Raphoe (Dec. 3), as to the letting value of the buildings and lands belonging to the Raphoe Royal School.

GERALD FITZGIBBON,

Wm. Edward Ellis, Secretary. December 7, 1888.

December 7, 1888.

Meeting of the Commission held this day at the Office, 23, Nassau-street, Dublin.

Present :—Lord Justice FITZGIBBON, Lord Justice NAISH, Rev. Dr. MOLLOY, Dr. TRAILL, Professor DOUGHERTY.

Minutes of the preceding meeting, and of the stated attendance of December 5, read and confirmed.

Letters read :—

Rev. W. Moore Morgan, LL.D. (Dec. 4), in reference to the proposed consultation with regard to the Armagh Royal School buildings.

Colonel J. C. J. Lowry (Dec. 5), stating he has asked the Rector of Dungannon to act in his place in reference to the proposed consultation with regard to the Dungannon Royal School buildings.

Very Rev. Dean Byrne, P.P. (Dec. 5), enclosing letters from the persons interested, as to the formation of the Tyrone Roman Catholic Local Board.

The Clerk of the Privy Council, Dublin Castle (Dec. 3), stating that the Annual Report of the Commissioners for the year 1887–8, has been circulated.

Rev. R. Cuthbert Mitchell (Dec. 3), with reference to the Portora Royal School buildings.

F. W. Leeper (Dec. 5), enclosing copy of Resolutions adopted at the recent Sessions of the Synods of Dublin, Glendalough, and Kildare respectively.

L. A. Dominick addressed to Lord Justice FitzGibbon, with reference to the Munster Agricultural and Dairy School.

Letter read from Rev. A. Richards, Rector of Dungannon, asking if he should act in place of Colonel Lowry at proposed conference with reference to the Dungannon Royal School buildings.

A reply, as drafted, directed to be sent.

Letter (Dec. 3) read from the Under Secretary, Dublin Castle, asking for an estimate of the expenses of the Commission in 1889–90, and for a statement as to the probable duration, present progress, &c., of the Commission.

The Secretary was directed to draft a reply.

The Draft Scheme for the Gilson Schools, Oldcastle, was considered, and instructions were given to write to the following :—The Roman Catholic Bishop of Meath, to name one representative; the Board of Guardians, to name two representatives; and the Resident Commissioner of National Education, to name one representative; the names and addresses of the first representative Governors to be inserted in the Draft Scheme.

The Secretary was directed to write to the Archdeacon of Meath, asking him, after conference with the Bishop of Meath, to supply the names of four clergymen and six laymen to be named on the Governing Body for the management of the Parochial Schools of the Diocese of Meath and the Navan Endowed School.

The Scheme for the Royal School Endowments, and the objections lodged against same were further considered.

The Commissioners adjourned.

JOHN NAISH,

December 18, 1888.

Wm. Edward Ellis, Secretary.

December 8, 1888.

Meeting of the Commission held this day at the Office, 23, Hume-street, Dublin.

Present :—Lord Justice FitzGibbon, Lord Justice Naish, Rev. Dr. Molloy, Dr. Traill, Professor Dougherty.

Letters read :—

The Most Rev. Dr. Logue, Lord Archbishop of Armagh (Dec. 7), with reference to the Armagh Royal School buildings.

Rev. James Dowd (Dec. 7), enclosing a Schedule of all the Educational Endowments in the Diocese of Limerick to be incorporated under diocesan trustees.

Letter (Dec. 6) read from Rev. William Johnston, D.D., Honorary Secretary, asking the Commission to prepare a Scheme for the Presbyterian Orphan Society.

To be informed that the materials which he has already forwarded will be sufficient to enable the Commissioners to prepare the first draft of a Scheme, as to which they will be glad to consider the views of the existing Governing Body before formally publishing it.

The Schemes for the Royal School Endowments, and the objections lodged against same, were considered.

Questions relating to the Draft Scheme to be prepared for the Blue Coat School, Cork, were discussed.

The Commissioners having fixed a stated attendance for Tuesday, December 11, at 4 o'clock, P.M., adjourned.

John Naish,
December 13, 1888.

Wm. Edward Ellis, Secretary.

December 11, 1888.

Stated attendance of the Commissioners held at the Office, 23, Hume-street, Dublin.

Present :—Rev. Dr. Molloy, Dr. Traill.

Letters read :—

Rev. James B. Keene (Dec. 10), stating that the Schedule of Parochial Schools will be ready in a few days.

Rev. W. Sherlock, Rector of Clane (Dec. 8), returning draft of the Scheme for Hewetson's School, Clane, together with suggestions and amendments by the existing trustees of the School.

John Naish,
December 13, 1888.

Wm. Edward Ellis, Secretary.

December 13, 1888.

Meeting of the Commission held this day at the Office, 23, Hume-street, Dublin.

Present :—Lord Justice FitzGibbon, Lord Justice Naish, Rev. Dr. Molloy, Dr. Traill, Professor Dougherty.

Minutes of the two preceding meetings, and of the stated attendance of December 11, read and confirmed.

Letters read :—

Very Rev. Dean Byrne (Dec. 11),
James Brown (Dec. 11),
Rev. L. Richards (Dec. 12), } As to the Dungannon Royal School Buildings.

That the Secretary write to each thanking him for his letter, and stating that same will be of great assistance to the Commissioners in revising the Scheme for the Royal School Endowments.

Letter (Dec. 12) read from Rev. David Wilson, D.D., asking that the book containing extracts from Wills relating to the Villiers' Charitable Institution, Limerick, be returned to him.

Ordered :—That the book be returned, as requested.

Letter (Dec. 11) read from the Clerk of the Privy Council, Dublin Castle, stating that a sitting of the Privy Council has been fixed for Thursday, December 20, to hear the objections lodged against the Amended Scheme for the Nicholson Memorial School, Lisburn.

The Secretary was directed to send a further letter, as drafted, to Colonel North, C.R.E. in Ireland, with reference to the offer of the War Department to purchase the premises of Portora Royal School.

The Commissioners adjourned.

JOHN NAISH,
December 15, 1888.

Wm. Edward Ellis, Secretary.

December 13, 1888.

Stated attendance of the Commissioners held at the Office, 23, Nassau-street, Dublin.

Present:—Dr. TRAILL, Professor DOUGHERTY.

The Heads of a Scheme for the Incorporated Society for promoting English Protestant Schools in Ireland were considered.

JOHN NAISH,
December 15, 1888.

Wm. Edward Ellis, Secretary.

December 15, 1888.

Meeting of the Commission held this day at the Office, 23, Nassau-street, Dublin.

Present:—Lord Justice FITZGIBBON, Lord Justice NAISH, Rev. Dr. MOLLOY, Dr. TRAILL, Professor DOUGHERTY.

Minutes of the preceding meeting, and of the stated attendance of December 13, read and confirmed.

Letter (Dec. 14) read from the Most Rev. Dr. Nulty, Lord Bishop of Meath, as to the Draft Scheme for the Oldcastle Endowed School.

To be informed that as soon as the Draft Scheme is published a copy will be sent to his Lordship, and the Commissioners will be glad to receive and consider any objections or amendments his Lordship may think fit to make.

Points in connection with the Draft Scheme for the Cashel Corporation School Endowment were considered.

Directions were given as to the special provisions to be introduced into the Scheme for the Incorporated Society with regard to the Endowments held by the Society from the Waterford Corporation under lease dated 1st July, 1748.

The Commissioners adjourned.

JOHN NAISH,
December 20, 1888.

Wm. Edward Ellis, Secretary.

December 19, 1888.

Stated attendance of the Commissioners held at the Office, 23, Nassau-street, Dublin.

Present:—Rev. Dr. MOLLOY.

Letter (Dec. 14) read from Ven. G. Nugent, M.A., Archdeacon of Meath, giving names of the Governing Body to be formed for the management of the Parochial Schools of the Diocese of Meath, and the Navan Endowed School.

Letter (Dec. 15) read from the Town Clerk of Cashel, enclosing resolution of the Town Commissioners of Cashel as to the proposed Governing Body for the administration of the Cashel Corporation Endowment.

A reply, as drafted, subject to the approval of the Commissioners at their next meeting, directed to be sent.

Letter (Dec. 17) read from Messrs. Wm. Mooney & Son, Solicitors, as to Shiel's Charity, Co. Westmeath, and asking when the Commissioners intend to visit the locality.

A reply, as drafted, subject to the approval of the Commissioners at their next meeting, directed to be sent.

Letter (Dec. 18) read from Rev. L. Graham, P.P., Oldcastle, asking for a copy of the proposed Draft Scheme for the Oldcastle Endowed School.

A reply, as drafted, directed to be sent.

GERALD FITZGIBBON,
December 20, 1888.

Wm. Edward Ellis, Secretary.

December 20, 1888.

Meeting of the Commission held this day at the Office, 13, Nassau-street, Dublin.

Present :—Lord Justice FitzGibbon, Lord Justice Naish, Rev. Dr. Molloy, Dr. Traill.

The minutes of the preceding meeting, and of the stated attendance of December 19, read and confirmed.

ROYAL IRISH ACADEMY OF MUSIC AND COULSON ENDOWMENT.

George Cree, Esq., M.A., and D. R. Drury, LL.D., attended as a deputation from the Royal Irish Academy of Music, to confer with the Commissioners concerning the revised Scheme framed by the Judicial Commissioners for the above-named Endowments.

Letter (Dec. 18) read from the Clerk of the Oldcastle Union, asking for a copy of the proposed Draft Scheme for the Oldcastle Endowed School.

A reply, as drafted, was amended and approved, and ordered to be sent.

The Commissioners adjourned.

GERALD FITZGIBBON,
January 16, 1889.

Wm. Edward Ellis, Secretary.

January 8, 1889.

Meeting of the Commission held this day at the Office, 13, Nassau-street, Dublin.

Present :—Lord Justice FitzGibbon, Lord Justice Naish.

Letters read :—

Right Hon. Sir P. J. Keenan, K.C.B., Resident Commissioner of National Education (Dec. 20), nominating a Governor for the Governing Body of the Oldcastle Endowed School.

The Secretary Representative Church Body (Dec. 21), as to Diocesan Endowments generally.

Rev. P. M'Glone, P.P. (Dec. 22), on behalf of the Most Rev. Dr. Donnelly, Lord Bishop of Clogher, as to the valuation of the Portora Royal School premises and land.

Charles J. Battersby (Dec. 27), as to the incorporation of a Governing body to hold endowments in the Diocese of Ardagh.

Rev. Jas. B. Keene (Dec. 28), sending Schedule of the Parochial Endowments in the Diocese of Meath.

George Cree, Hon. Sec., Royal Irish Academy of Music (Dec. 31), asking that a copy of the suggestions made by the Academy on the revised Scheme for the Academy and the Coulson Endowment, be sent to the Corporation of Dublin.

The Town Clerk of Waterford (Jan. 1), sending information as to the premises belonging to the Waterford Corporation Grammar School.

The Clerk of the Privy Council, Dublin Castle (Jan. 5), sending copies of Schemes Nos. 6, 15 and 23, finally approved by the Lord Lieutenant in Council.

George Harrison (Dec. 28), as to the objections made by the existing Governing Body to the Draft Scheme for the Cork High School for Girls.

The Commissioners adjourned.

GERALD FITZGIBBON,
January 16, 1889.

Wm. Edward Ellis, Secretary.

January 11, 1889.

Meeting of the Commission held this day at the Office, 13, Nassau-street, Dublin.

Present :—Lord Justice FitzGibbon, Lord Justice Naish.

Letters read :—

The Secretary, Commissioners of Education (Jan. 8), as to application of Mr. Fleming that his full salary should be paid by Treasury.

Messrs. Hassard and Son, Solicitors (Jan. 8), asking when the Scheme for the Rainey School will be settled by the Judicial Commissioners.

The Clerk of the Oldcastle Union (Jan. 8), sending the names of two representatives of the Board of Guardians to be inserted on the proposed Governing Body for the Oldcastle Endowed School.

James W. Drury (Jan. 9), as to the proposed amendments by the Royal Irish Academy of Music to the revised Scheme for the Royal Irish Academy of Music and the Coulson Endowment.

John Mackintosh (Jan. 7), asking for a copy of the revised Scheme for the Raphoe Endowments, county Donegal.

Colonel Marsh, C.R.E. in Ireland (Dec. 26), with reference to the offer of the War Department to purchase the premises of the Portora Royal School.

The Commissioners adjourned.

GERALD FITZGIBBON,
January 16, 1889.

Wm. Edward Ellis, Secretary.

January 16, 1889.

Meeting of the Commission held this day at the Office, 23, Nassau-street, Dublin.

Present:—Lord Justice FITZGIBBON, Lord Justice NAISH, Dr. TRAILL.

Minutes of the three preceding meetings read and confirmed.

Letters read:—

The Town Clerk of Cashel (Jan. 11), sending names of two representatives of the Cashel Corporation to be named on the proposed Governing Body for the Cashel Corporation Endowment.

The Town Clerk of Dublin (Jan. 11), as to the proposed amendments of the Royal Irish Academy of Music to the revised Scheme for the Academy and the Coulson Endowment.

Sir W. S. B. Kaye (Jan. 11), as to the circulation of Parliamentary papers among Members of Parliament.

John W. Jennings (Jan. 11), as to the death of Mr. Gibson Black, one of the Trustees of the Herbert Endowment attached to the Phibsborough Sunday and Daily Schools, Dublin.

Rev. James B. Keene (Jan. 15), enclosing copy of the Will of Joseph Kinsey.

H. L. Scott, Clerk of the Salters Company (Jan. 14), acknowledging receipt of letter dated January 11, directed to be sent by the Judicial Commissioners.

Letter (Dec. 1) read from Rev. E. A. Lyle, asking when the Commissioners intend to settle a Scheme for Brown's Endowment, Ballyhalbert.

A reply, as drafted, directed to be sent.

The Commissioners adjourned.

GERALD FITZGIBBON,
January 18, 1889.

Wm. Edward Ellis, Secretary.

January 18, 1889.

Meeting of the Commission held this day at their Offices, 23, Nassau-street, Dublin.

Present:—Lord Justice FITZGIBBON, Lord Justice NAISH, Dr. TRAILL.

Minutes of the preceding meeting read and confirmed.

Letter (Jan. 10) read from Rev. Joseph J. Quinn, C.C., as to the evidence taken at Magherafelt on October 22, 1888.

A reply, as drafted, directed to be sent.

The Secretary was directed to write to Rev. N. W. Carre, asking him for the name of the new Trustee of the Herbert Endowment attached to the Phibsborough Sunday and Daily Schools, and also whether the transfer has been made of the Stock.

The Commissioners adjourned.

JOHN NAISH,
January 23, 1889.

Wm. Edward Ellis, Secretary.

January 23, 1889.

Meeting of the Commission, held this day at the Office, 23, Nassau-street, Dublin.

Present:—Lord Justice FITZGIBBON, Lord Justice NAISH, Dr. TRAILL.

Minutes of preceding meeting read and confirmed.

Letters read:—

The Secretaries, Commissioners of Charitable Donations and Bequests (Jan. 16), as to the revised Schemes for the Royal Irish Academy of Music, and the Coulson Endowment.

Rev. Thomas Browne, P.P., Loughmore, Limerick (Jan. 18), enclosing correspondence he has had with the Commissioners of National Education in the matter of the late Mungret Agricultural Model Farm.

Rev. N. W. Carre (Jan. 21), giving name of the new Trustee appointed for the Herbert Endowment attached to the Phibsborough Sunday and Daily Schools.

The Secretary was directed to write to the Parish Priest of Cashel, and to the Town Clerk of Cashel, as to the co-option of the Governors to be named in the Draft Scheme for the Cashel Corporation Endowment, and stating that the Commissioners would be glad if the Roman Catholic Archbishop of Cashel, the Parish Priest of Cashel, and his senior Curate, and the two proposed elected Governors, Dr. Laffan and Mr. Wood, would, after conference, suggest the names of say, two or three gentlemen, from whom the Commissioners might make a selection, after ascertaining that they would be willing to act.

The Commissioners adjourned.

GERALD FITZGIBBON,
January 25, 1889.

Wm. Edward Ellis, Secretary.

January 25, 1889.

Meeting of the Commission held this day at the Office, 23, Nassau-street, Dublin.

Present:—Lord Justice FITZGIBBON, Lord Justice NAISH, Dr. TRAILL.

Minutes of preceding meeting read and confirmed.

Letter (Jan. 23) read from Rev. James B. Keene, as to the Schedules of the Draft Scheme for the Meath Parochial Schools.

The Commissioners adjourned.

JOHN NAISH,
February 1, 1889.

Wm. Edward Ellis, Secretary.

January 30, 1889.

Stated attendance of the Commissioners held this day at the Office, 23, Nassau-street, Dublin.

Present:—Lord Justice FITZGIBBON.

Letter (Jan. 28) read from Dr. Laffan, Cashel, as to the Draft Scheme for the Cashel Corporation Endowment.

Letter (Jan. 26) read from the Controller of H.M. Stationery Office, as to the supply of Parliamentary Papers to the Department from which such papers emanate.

JOHN NAISH,
February 1, 1889.

Wm. Edward Ellis, Secretary.

February 1, 1889.

Meeting of the Commission held this day at the Office, 23, Nassau-street, Dublin.

Present:—Lord Justice FITZGIBBON, Lord Justice NAISH, Professor DOUGHERTY.

Minutes of preceding meeting, and of the stated attendance of January 30, were read and confirmed.

Letter (Jan. 28) read from Very Rev. Dean Kinane, P.P., Cashel, as to the proposed Governing Body for holding the Cashel Corporation Endowments.

Letter (Jan. 29) read from Messrs. M'Ildowie and Sons, Solicitors, asking when a Scheme will be prepared for the Lesley Bequest, co. Down.

A reply, as drafted, ordered to be sent.

Letter (Jan. 30) read from Rev. R. Montgomery, as to the incorporation of a Governing Body to hold Educational Endowments belonging to the Presbytery of Belfast.

A reply, as in the case of Diocesan Councils, ordered to be sent.

The Secretary was directed to write to Charles E. Robson, Agent to the Earl of Roden, asking him to be good enough to furnish the Commissioners with the Trust Deed relating to the Dundalk Grammar School.

The Commissioners adjourned.

JOHN NAISH,
February 6, 1889.

Wm. Edward Ellis, Secretary.

February 6, 1889.

Meeting of the Commission held this day at the Office, 23, Nassau-street, Dublin.

Present:—Lord Justice FitzGibbon, Lord Justice Naish, Dr. Traill.

Minutes of preceding meeting read and confirmed.

Letter (February 1) read from Rev. John Gibson, as to the incorporation of a Governing Body to hold Educational Endowments belonging to the Presbytery of Ballymena.

A reply, as in the cases of Diocesan Councils, ordered to be sent.

The Commissioners adjourned.

Gerald FitzGibbon,
February 8, 1889.

Wm. Edward Ellis, Secretary.

February 8, 1889.

Meeting of the Commission held this day at the Office, 23, Nassau-street, Dublin.

Present:—Lord Justice FitzGibbon, Dr. Traill.

Minutes of the preceding meeting read and confirmed.

Letters read:—

James W. Drury (February 7) as to the revised Scheme for the Royal Irish Academy of Music and the Coulson Endowment.

Rev. James M'Cully, Presbytery of Ballybay (February 6),
Rev. David Parks, Presbytery of Banbridge (February 7),
Rev. W. Irwin, Presbytery of Coleraine (February 7),
as to the incorporation of Governing Bodies to hold Educational Endowments belonging to the several Presbyteries above named.

A reply, as drafted in similar cases, ordered to be sent.

The Commissioners adjourned.

Gerald FitzGibbon,
February 13, 1889.

Wm. Edward Ellis, Secretary.

February 13, 1889.

Meeting of the Commission held this day at the Office, 23, Nassau-street, Dublin.

Present:—Lord Justice FitzGibbon, Lord Justice Naish, Dr. Traill.

Minutes of preceding meeting read and confirmed.

Letter (February 7) read from Rev. S. Edgar Stewart as to the incorporation of a Governing Body to hold Educational Endowments belonging to the Presbytery of Carrickfergus.

A reply, as drafted in similar cases, directed to be sent.

Letter (February 9) read from Charles E. Robson, Agent to Lord Roden, as to an agreement between the late Lord Limerick and the Corporation of Dundalk re Dundalk Grammar School.

To be informed that the Commissioners will be obliged if he can let them have a copy of the agreement.

Letter (February 9) read from Messrs. Mayland and Co., Downpatrick asking that certain documents in the possession of the Commission may be returned to them.

To be asked to leave the documents with the Commissioners until they can prepare a draft Scheme for the Downpatrick Blue School.

Letter (February 8) read from the Clerk of the Salters Company as to the proposed endowment to be given by the Company for the Rainey School, Magherafelt.

The Secretary was directed to send copies of this letter, with a letter as drafted, to the following parties interested:—His Grace the Lord Primate; Very Rev. Canon Donnelly, P.P., Magherafelt; Messrs. Maxwell and Son, Solicitors; Mr. H. E. Kinnaird, Head Master, Rainey School; Mr. Campbell Gunning; and Mr. S. Brown, for the Magherafelt Market Trustees.

The Commissioners adjourned.

Gerald FitzGibbon,
February 15, 1889.

Wm. Edward Ellis, Secretary.

February 15, 1889.

Meeting of the Commission held this day at the Office, 23, Nassau-street, Dublin.

Present:—Lord Justice FitzGibbon, Lord Justice Naish, Dr. Traill.

Minutes of preceding meeting read and confirmed.

The observations of the Trustees of Harrison's School, Clare, on the Draft Scheme for that Institution were considered, as were also some points with regard to the Draft Scheme for the Munster Dairy School and Agricultural Institute.

The Commissioners adjourned.

John Naish,
February 20, 1889.

Wm. Edward Ellis, Secretary.

February 20, 1889.

Meeting of the Commission held this day at the Office, 23, Nassau-street, Dublin.

Present:—Lord Justice FitzGibbon, Lord Justice Naish, Dr. Traill.

Minutes of preceding meeting read and confirmed.

Letter (February 18) read from His Grace the Lord Primate as to the proposed Endowment to be given by the Salters Company to the Rainey School, Magherafelt.

The Commissioners adjourned.

Anthony Traill,
February 23, 1889.

Wm. Edward Ellis, Secretary.

February 23, 1889.

Meeting of the Commission held this day at the Office, 23, Nassau-street, Dublin.

Present:—Lord Justice FitzGibbon, Rev. Dr. Molloy, Dr. Traill.

Minutes of preceding meeting read and confirmed.

Letter (February 20) read from Campbell Cameron as to the proposed Endowments to be given by the Salters Company to the Rainey School, Magherafelt.

Letter (February 19) read from Rev. H. F. Macdonald asking when the revised Scheme for the Robertson Schools will be published.

A reply, as drafted, directed to be sent.

The Secretary was ordered to send a reply as drafted to the letter of Dr. Laffan Cashel, dated January 25, 1889, as to the proposed Governing Body for the administration of the Cashel Corporation Endowment.

The Secretary reported that the Rev. Alexander Gordon and the Rev. C. J. M'Alester had an interview with him with reference to a consent Scheme which the existing Governing Body of the Orphan Society of Non-Subscribing Presbyterians are anxious to have for the future management of that Institution.

The Commissioners adjourned.

Gerald FitzGibbon,
February 27, 1889.

Wm. Edward Ellis, Secretary.

l

February 27, 18[illegible].

Meeting of the Commission held this day at the Office, 23, Nassau-street, Dublin.

Present :—Lord Justice FITZGIBBON, Lord Justice NAISH, Rev. Dr. MOLLOY, Dr. TRAILL, Professor DOUGHERTY.

Minutes of preceding meeting read and confirmed.

Letters were read from the following persons as to the proposed Endowment to be given by the Salters Company to the Rainey School, Magherafelt :—

H. E. Kincaid, Head Master, Rainey School (Feb. 25).
Rev. Thomas Jordan, D.D. (Feb. 27).
Samuel Porter, J.P. (Feb. 26).

Letter (Feb. 24), read from Thos. Laffan, M.D., declining to act on the proposed Governing Body for the future management of the Cashel Corporation Endowment.

The Secretary was directed to write in terms as drafted to the Town Clerk of Waterford asking him to give the names of two representatives of the Corporation of Waterford to be named on the proposed Governing Body for the Stephen-street School, Waterford.

The Secretary was also directed to write to the Resident Commissioner of National Education in terms as drafted with respect to the nomination by him of one of the Governors of the Gilson Schools, Oldcastle.

It was ordered :—

I. That the following Schemes should be advanced with a view to being signed by the Judicial Commissioners at an early date, in the order in which they stand :—

34. The Royal School Endowments.
35. The Robertson Endowments.
36. The Queen-street National School, Lurgan.
37. The Cork High School for Girls.
38. The Baltimore Fishery School.
39. The Royal Irish Academy of Music and the Graham Endowment.
40. The Londonderry Academical Institution.
41. The Church of Ireland Victoria Jubilee Fund.
45. The Clonmel Grammar School.
47. The Cork Parochial Schools, &c.
48. The Dunmanway Parochial School.
51. The Sullivan Schools, Holywood.
52. The Rochelle Seminary, Cork.
27. The Bertrand Female Orphan School, Dublin.
42. The Villiers' Charitable Institutions, Limerick.
50. The Drelincourt, Mall, and Callan-street Schools, and Primate Robinson's Loan Fund, Armagh.
29. The [illegible] Sunday and Daily Schools, Dublin.
24. The Gwyn and Young Endowments, Londonderry.
44. Ballymena Collegiate School.
46. Kilkenny College.
43. Rainey's School, Magherafelt.

II. That the following Schemes be advanced with a view to first publication on the last Monday in March :—

53. The Meath Parochial Schools and the Haven Endowed School.
54. The Gilson Schools, Oldcastle.
55. The Stephen-street School, Waterford.
56. The Roxborough-road School, Limerick.
57. Hewetson's School, Clane.
58. The Presbyterian Orphan Society.

III. That the following Schemes be advanced with a view to first publication on the last Monday in April :—

59. The Incorporated Society.
60. The Cashel Corporation Endowment.
61. The Cashel Parochial Deanery Schools.
62. The Munster Dairy School and Agricultural Institute.
63. The Larne Grammar School.
64. The Cork Blue School.

The letter from the Clerk of the Salters Company of the 8th instant was considered, and the final settlement of an answer to same was postponed to the next meeting.

The Commissioners adjourned.

GERALD MOLLOY,
March 8, 18[illegible].

Wm. Edward Ellis, Secretary.

March 1, 1889.

Meeting of the Commission held this day at the Office, 23, Nassau-street, Dublin.

Present :—Lord Justice FITZGIBBON, Lord Justice NAISH, Rev. Dr. MOLLOY, Dr. TRAILL.

Minutes of preceding meeting read and confirmed.

Letters were read from the following persons as to the proposed Endowment to be given by the Salters Company to the Rainey School, Magherafelt.

Andrew Brown (Feb. 26).
Very Rev. Canon Donnelly (Feb. 27).

The Secretary was directed to write, in terms as drafted, in reply to the letter date 5th ultimo, from the Clerk of the Salters Company.

The Commissioners adjourned.

J. B. DOUGHERTY,
March 8, 1889.

Wm. Edward Ellis, Secretary.

March 6, 1889.

Stated attendance of the Commissioners held this day at the Office, 23, Nassau-street, Dublin.

Present :—Rev. Dr. MOLLOY.

Letters read :—

Rev. J. Kennedy, Secretary (Feb. 28), enclosing copy of Trust Deed of Larne Grammar School.

Very Rev. W. Warburton, D.D., Dean of Elphin (Mar. 1), as to a Governing Body for the Elphin Grammar School.

Very Rev. Canon Donnelly (Mar. 4), as to the proposed Endowment of the Salters Company to the Rainey School.

The Clerk of the Salters Company (Mar. 4), acknowledging the receipt of Commissioners letter of March 2.

T. R. G. Jozé, Secretary (Mar. 5), as to the proposed amendment to Clause 14 of the revised Scheme for the Royal Irish Academy of Music and the Coulson Endowment.

Letter (Mar. 1) read from Rev. M. Le B. Kennedy asking when the Scheme for the Clonmel Grammar School will be signed by the Judicial Commissioners.

A reply, as drafted, ordered to be sent.

J. B. DOUGHERTY,
March 6, 1889.

Wm. Edward Ellis, Secretary.

March 8, 1889.

Meeting of the Commission held this day at the Office, 23, Nassau-street, Dublin.

Present :—Lord Justice FITZGIBBON, Lord Justice NAISH, Rev. Dr. MOLLOY, Dr. TRAILL, Professor DOUGHERTY.

Minutes of preceding meeting and stated attendance of March 6, read and confirmed.

Letters read from :—

Rev. J. Kennedy, Secretary, Larne Grammar School (Mar. 6).

T. R. G. Jozé, Secretary (Mar. 7) as to the revised Scheme for the Royal Irish Academy of Music and the Coulson Endowment.

R. H. Todd, Solicitor, Magherafelt (Mar. 6), on behalf of the Market Trustees, Magherafelt, as to the proposed Endowment of the Salters Company to the Rainey School.

Rev. Isaac Coulter (Feb. 26), asking that a Scheme may be prepared for the Masterson Charity, Sligo.

Letter (Mar. 7) read from Rev. John Kinghan asking if the Presbyterian Sabbath School Society could be dealt with under the Educational Endowments (Ireland) Act.

A reply, as drafted, ordered to be sent.

Letter (Mar. 6) read from Patrick Kent, Solicitor, Waterford, stating that Messrs. Harvey and Son of Waterford, could give the information required as to the Stephen-street School, Waterford.

That the Secretary write to Messrs. Harvey and Son for the information required.

Letter (Mar. 1) read from Rev. Hill Wilson White, LL.D., asking that a certain alteration may be allowed in the evidence taken as to Wilson's Hospital, Multyfarnham.

To be informed that the alteration will be made.

Letter (Mar. 5) read from Rev. David Parks, Presbytery of Banbridge, asking if teachers' residences would be considered as an Educational Endowment.

A reply, as drafted, ordered to be sent.

The Draft Schemes for the Stephen-street School, Waterford, and for the Roxborough-road School, Limerick, were considered and amended, and finally approved, subject to their being signed for press by the Assistant Commissioners in charge of same.

The Commissioners adjourned.

Gerald Molloy,
March 16, 1889.

Wm. Edward Ellis, Secretary.

March 9, 1889.

Meeting of the Commission held this day at the Office, 23, Nassau-street, Dublin.

Present:—Lord Justice Fitzgibbon, Lord Justice Naish, Rev. Dr. Molloy, Dr. Traill, Professor Dougherty.

Letter (Mar. 6) read from Rev. Canon Gregg, giving the name of a clergyman to be named on the proposed Governing Body for the Roxborough-road School, Limerick.

The Secretary was directed to write to the Rev. Canon Gregg, asking him whether the above School is situated in the County, City, or Liberties of Limerick.

Letter (Mar. 8) read from the Secretary to the Treasury, asking if any further sums have been received from Governing Bodies in payment for the publication of Draft Schemes.

A reply, as drafted, ordered to be sent.

Letter (Mar. 5) read from Rev. Canon Donnelly, P.P., Magherafelt, asking for copies of the suggestions made by parties interested in reply to the letter of the Commissioners, dated February 14, 1889.

The Secretary was directed to write to Joseph Vaughan, Athlone, asking for particulars in reference to certain Non-educational Endowments in the Parish of St. Mary, Athlone.

The Secretary was also directed to write to Rev. William Johnston, D.D., asking for a full description of the property belonging to the Presbyterian Orphan Society.

The Commissioners adjourned.

Gerald Molloy,
March 16, 1889.

Wm. Edward Ellis, Secretary.

March 13, 1889.

Stated attendance of the Commissioners held this day at the Office, 23, Nassau-street, Dublin.

Present:—Rev. Dr. Molloy, Dr. Traill.

Letters read:—

Rev. Canon Gregg (Mar. 8), stating that the Roxborough-road School is situated in the City of Limerick.

Alexander Livingstone, Master, [illegible] Endowed School, Newtownforbes (Mar. 12), suggesting that in a new Scheme for that School leave might be given the teacher to keep boarding pupils.

Gerald Molloy,
March 15, 1889.

Wm. Edward Ellis, Secretary.

March 16, 1889.

Meeting of the Commission held this day at the Office, 13, Nassau-street, Dublin.

Present:—Lord Justice FitzGibbon, Rev. Dr. Molloy, Dr. Traill, Professor Dougherty.

Minutes of the two preceding meetings, and of the stated attendance of March 13, read and confirmed.

Letters read:—

Messrs. Harvey and Son, Waterford (Mar. 15), as to the tenure by the Corporation of Waterford of the premises belonging to the Stephen-street School.

Rev. J. C. Clarke (Mar. 8), as to an Intermediate School for girls lately established in Galway.

Letter (Mar. 16) read from Rev. Henry S. O'Hara, Coleraine, asking that his memorial to the Irish Society, handed in and read by Lord Justice FitzGibbon at the sitting in Coleraine, be printed in the Report of the Commissioners.

Ordered:—That the memorial be printed.

The Rev. J. M. Hamilton, Donore, Rev. George Hanson, Rathgar, and Rev. C. H. Irwin, Bray, had an interview with the Commissioners with reference to a common Scheme which the Presbytery of Dublin desire to have for the future management of the Endowments belonging to that Presbytery.

The Commissioners adjourned.

John Naish,
March 18, 1889.

Wm. Edward Ellis, Secretary.

March 18, 1889.

Meeting of the Commission held this day at the Office, 13, Nassau-street.

Present:—Lord Justice FitzGibbon, Lord Justice Naish, Rev. Dr. Molloy, Dr. Traill, Professor Dougherty.

Minutes of preceding meeting read and confirmed.

Letters read:—

The Town Clerk of Waterford (Mar. 16), giving names of two representatives of the Corporation of Waterford to be inserted in the Draft Scheme for the Stephen Street School, Waterford.

The Secretary to the Treasury (Mar. 16), transmitting receivable orders for sums to be obtained from the Governing Bodies of the following Institutions for the cost of publication of Draft Schemes:—

No. 8. Ulster Society, Belfast.
No. 15. Royal Belfast Academical Institution.
No. 22. Belfast Royal Academy.

The Draft Scheme for the Gilson Schools, Oldcastle, was considered and amended, and finally approved, subject to its being signed for press by the Assistant Commissioner in charge of same.

The Commissioners adjourned.

Gerald FitzGibbon,
March 19, 1889.

Wm. Edward Ellis, Secretary.

March 19, 1889.

Meeting of the Commission held this day at the Office, 13, Nassau-street, Dublin.

Present:—Lord Justice FitzGibbon, Lord Justice Naish, Rev. Dr. Molloy, Dr. Traill.

Minutes of preceding meeting read and confirmed.

Letter (Mar. 18) read from Rev. S. A. D. Campbell, sending resolution of Select Vestry of St. Mary's, Athlone, as to the Ranelagh Endowment.

To be informed that same will receive the consideration of the Commissioners.

Letter (Mar. 18) read from Rev. F. H. Ringwood, LL.D., Royal School, Dungannon, as to the Revised Scheme for the Ulster Royal School Endowments.

A reply, as drafted, ordered to be sent.

The Revised Draft Scheme for the Ulster Royal Schools was considered.

The Commissioners adjourned.

Gerald FitzGibbon,
March 21, 1889.

Wm. Edward Ellis, Secretary.

March 21, 1889.

Meeting of the Commission held this day at the Office, 23, Nassau-street, Dublin.

Present:—Lord Justice FitzGibbon, Lord Justice Naish, Rev. Dr. Molloy.

Minutes of preceding meeting read and confirmed.

Letter (Mar. 18) read from John Burgess, Hon. Sec., Select Vestry of St. Mary's Parish, Athlone, as to the Ardkeenan Endowment in that Parish.

A reply, as drafted, directed to be sent.

Letter (Mar. 20) read from the Most Rev. Dr. Logue, Lord Archbishop of Armagh, as to the valuation of the buildings and premises of the Royal School, Armagh.

Ordered:—That His Grace be thanked for his letter, and also be informed that it will receive consideration.

The Draft Schemes for the Parochial Schools of the Diocese of Meath, and the Preston School, Navan, and for Hewetson's School, Clane, were considered and amended and finally approved.

It was ordered:—

That the following Draft Schemes be first published on March 26, 1889:—

No. 53. "The Stephen Street School, Waterford."
No. 54. "The Roxborough Road School, Limerick."
No. 55. "The Parochial Schools of the Diocese of Meath and the Preston School, Navan."
No. 56. "The Gilson Schools, Oldcastle."
No. 57. "Hewetson's School, Clane."
No. 58. "The Presbyterian Orphan Society for Ireland."

and instructions were given as to the mode of publication.

The Commissioners adjourned.

John Naish,
March 23, 1889.

Wm. Edward Ellis, Secretary.

March 23, 1889.

Meeting of the Commission held this day at the Office, 23, Nassau-street, Dublin.

Present:—Lord Justice FitzGibbon, Lord Justice Naish, Rev. Dr. Molloy, Dr. Traill.

Minutes of preceding meeting read and confirmed.

Letter (March 21) read from Rev. F. H. Ringwood, LL.D., Royal School, Dungannon, as to the revised Scheme for the Ulster Royal Schools.

A reply, as drafted, ordered to be sent.

Letter (March 20) read from Rev. Thomas Jordan, D.D., asking when the Scheme for the Rainey School, Magherafelt, will be forwarded to the Lord Lieutenant in Council.

A reply, as drafted, ordered to be sent.

Letter (March 21) read from Sir Patrick Keenan, K.C.M.G., Resident Commissioner of National Education, as to the proposed Governing Body for the Gilson Schools, Oldcastle.

A reply, as drafted, ordered to be sent.

The Revised Draft Scheme for the Ulster Royal School Endowments was considered.

The Draft Scheme for the Presbyterian Orphan Society for Ireland was considered and amended and finally approved, subject to its being signed for press by the Assistant Commissioner in charge.

The Commissioners adjourned.

John Naish,
March 28, 1889.

Wm. Edward Ellis, Secretary.

March 23, 1889.

Meeting of the Commission held this day at the Office, 63, Nassau-street, Dublin.

Present:—Lord Justice FITZGIBBON, Lord Justice NAISH, Rev. Dr. MOLLOY, Professor DOUGHERTY.

The Revised Draft Scheme for the Ulster Royal School Endowments was further considered.

The Secretary was directed to communicate with the Bishop of Cork, Cloyne, and Ross, sending him a copy of the Meath Diocesan Scheme, and stating that the Commissioners are prepared to undertake, with a view to publication on May 27 next, the preparation of a Scheme on similar lines for the United Dioceses of Cork, Cloyne, and Ross, retaining Bishop Crowe's School, Cloyne, as an Intermediate School, and that to effect this object it would be necessary that all suggestions, and a list of endowments to be provisionally included in the Scheme, should be sent to the Commissioners not later than April 20; also informing his Lordship that the Commissioners are engaged in revising, amongst others, the Cork City Parochial Scheme, which, it is hoped, will be submitted to the Lord Lieutenant about the 22nd prox.; and that, therefore it is to be remembered that the Cork City and Districts, being included in the existing Scheme, should not be included in that now in preparation.

It was ordered:—

That the following Schemes be advanced with a view to first publication on the last Monday of May:—

Ballyroan School, Queen's County.
Bishop Hodson's Grammar School, Elphin.
Ledley Bequest, County Down.
Kinsale Endowed School, County Cork.
The Endowments belonging to the Presbytery of Belfast.
The Parochial Schools of the United Dioceses of Cork, Cloyne, and Ross, and Bishop Crowe's School, Cloyne.

The Commissioners adjourned.

JOHN NAISH,
March 26, 1889.

Wm. Edward Ellis, Secretary.

March 26, 1889.

Meeting of the Commission held this day at the Office, 63, Nassau-street, Dublin.

Present:—Lord Justice FITZGIBBON, Lord Justice NAISH, Rev. Dr. MOLLOY, Professor DOUGHERTY.

Minutes of two preceding meetings read and confirmed.

Letters addressed to Lord Justice FitzGibbon read, from:—

Rev. R. S. D. Campbell (March 21) as to the Ranelagh Endowment, Athlone.
Rev. Br. John O'Brien (March 21) as to an Endowment to be given to the Christian Schools, Kells.

The Revised Draft Scheme for the Ulster Royal School Endowments was further considered.

The Commissioners adjourned.

JOHN NAISH,
March 28, 1889.

Wm. Edward Ellis, Secretary.

March 28, 1889.

Meeting of the Commission held this day at the Office, 63, Nassau-street, Dublin.

Present:—Lord Justice FITZGIBBON, Lord Justice NAISH, Rev. Dr. MOLLOY, Professor DOUGHERTY.

Minutes of preceding meeting read and confirmed.

Letters read:—

Rev. J. M. Hamilton, M.A. (Mar. 25), as to the incorporation of a Governing Body to hold Educational Endowments, belonging to the Presbytery of Dublin.
Right Rev. Dr. Day, Lord Bishop of Cashel (March 25), stating he received a copy of the Draft Scheme for the Meath Parochial Schools.

Letter (Mar. 26) read from Rev. Joseph J. Quinn, C.C., Magherafelt, as to the proposed endowment by the Salters Company for the Rainey School, Magherafelt.

A reply, as drafted, ordered to be sent.

The Revised Draft Scheme for the Ulster Royal School Endowments was further considered.

The Commissioners adjourned.

JOHN NAISH,
March 29, 1889.

Wm. Edward Ellis, Secretary.

March 29, 1889.

Meeting of the Commission held this day at the Office, 23, Nassau-street, Dublin.

Present:—Lord Justice FITZGIBBON, Lord Justice NAISH, Rev. Dr. MOLLOY, Professor DOUGHERTY.

Minutes of preceding meeting read and confirmed.

The Revised Draft Scheme for the Ulster Royal School Endowments as finally settled, after being compared with proof by the Secretary and signed for press not later than Thursday April 4, was directed to be sent to those interested not later than Saturday, April 6, the mode of publication to be the same as in the case of the Draft Scheme.

A letter as drafted with regard to the premises of the Royal School, Raphoe, was directed to be sent to the following parties interested:—

The Most Rev. Dr. O'Donnell, Lord Bishop of Raphoe.
The Rev. W. L. Berkeley, M.A.
The Rev. Henry F. Macdonald, M.A.

The Commissioners adjourned.

GERALD FITZGIBBON,
April 15, 1889.

Wm. Edward Ellis, Secretary.

April 1, 1889.

Stated attendance of the Commissioners held this day at the Office, 23, Nassau-street, Dublin.

Present:—Lord Justice FITZGIBBON.

Letter (29 Mar.), read from John C. Porteous, Secretary, Diocesan Council of Ferns, addressed to Mr. Ellis, asking some questions in reference to a Scheme for the Endowments of the Diocese of Ferns.

An unofficial reply was directed to be sent.

GERALD FITZGIBBON,
April 15, 1889.

Wm. Edward Ellis, Secretary.

April 2, 1889.

Stated attendance of the Commissioners held this day at the Office, 23, Nassau-street, Dublin.

Present:—Rev. Dr. MOLLOY.

Letter (April 1), read from Rev. J. Kennedy, giving particulars of the Larne Grammar School premises, funds, &c.

Letter (April 2), read from Rev. James B. Keene, as to the manner of obtaining the consent of the present Trustees that the endowments should be dealt with under the Act, of the various schools mentioned in the Schedule to the Meath Diocesan Scheme.

A reply, as drafted, ordered to be sent.

Letter (March 28), read from Rev. Thomas H. Fleming, enclosing copy of a Resolution passed by the Managing Committee of the Rockfield Institution, county Galway.

To be informed that same will receive the careful consideration of the Commissioners.

GERALD FITZGIBBON,
April 15, 1889.

Wm. Edward Ellis, Secretary.

April 10, 1889.

Stated attendance of the Commissioners held this day at the Office, 63, Nassau-street, Dublin.

Present:—Rev. Dr. Molloy.

Letters read:—

Rev. John Cairns (April 4), as to the incorporation of a Governing Body to hold Educational Endowments belonging to the Presbytery of Connaught.

W. H. Porter (April 8), asking when the Scheme for the Robertson Endowments, co. Donegal, will be approved by the Lord Lieutenant in Council.

Rev. F. H. Ringwood, LL.D. (April 9), as to the revised Scheme for the Ulster Royal School Endowments.

Letter (April 8) read from P. King Joyce, Head Master, Banagher Royal School, as to the omission of that School from the Revised Scheme for the Ulster Royal School Endowments.

A reply, as drafted, ordered to be sent.

Letter (April 9) read from Rev. Frederick Buick, as to the incorporation of a Governing Body to hold Educational Endowments belonging to the Presbytery of Ahoghill.

A reply as drafted in similar cases ordered to be sent.

Gerald FitzGibbon,
April 15, 1889.

Wm. Edward Ellis, Secretary.

April 15, 1889.

Meeting of the Commission held this day at the Office, 63, Nassau-street, Dublin.

Present:—Lord Justice FitzGibbon, Lord Justice Naish, Rev. Dr. Molloy.

Minutes of preceding meeting, and of the stated attendances of April 1, April 3, and April 10, read and confirmed.

Letters read:—

Rev. Henry F. Macdonald (April 11),
Rev. Abraham Jagoe (April 11),
Sir Samuel H. Hayes (April 11),
as to the revised Scheme for the Robertson Endowments, co. Donegal.

L. A. Renwick (April 13), as to the Scheme for the Munster Dairy School and Agricultural Institute.

Letter (April 9) read from Rev. C. Ormsby Wiley, as to the preparation of a Scheme for Endowments in the Dioceses of Killala and Achonry.

A reply, as drafted, directed to be sent.

Letter (April 11) read from Messrs. Morland and Co., Solicitors, asking that certain papers in the possession of the Commissioners may be returned to them.

A reply, as drafted, directed to be sent.

Letter (April 11) read from Rev. Peter Fagan, P.P., asking when the Commissioners intend to visit Killucan in order to take evidence with regard to Shiel's Charity.

A reply, as drafted, directed to be sent.

Letter (April 13) read from the Clerk of the Salters Company, as to the proposed endowment to be given by the Company for the Rainey School, Magherafelt.

A reply, as drafted, directed to be sent, and copies of the letter of the Salters Company and of the reply thereto directed to be sent to all parties interested.

Sir Henry Cartwright, late Agent, and R. L. Sands, Clerk of the Salters Company, had an interview with the Commissioners with reference to the correspondence between the Commissioners and the Salters Company.

The Commissioners adjourned.

John Naish,
April 16, 1889.

Wm. Edward Ellis, Secretary.

April 16, 18[illegible].

Meeting of the Commission held this day at the Office, 13, Nassau-street, Dublin.

Present:—Lord Justice FITZGIBBON, Lord Justice NAISH, Rev. Dr. MOLLOY.

Minutes of preceding meeting read and confirmed.

Letter (April 16) read from Robert Davis, Enniskillen, as to School Scholarships and Exhibitions in the Ulster Royal Schools under the revised Scheme.

A reply, as drafted, ordered to be sent.

Letter (April 15) read from the Right Hon. Viscount De Vesci as to the Scheme in preparation for the Ballyroan Endowment.

Lord Justice FitzGibbon undertook to send an unofficial reply to same.

Letter (April 15) read from Rev. S. Leslie Brakey, asking for extension of time to send in the observations on the revised Scheme for the Ulster Royal School Endowments.

A reply, as in previous cases, ordered to be sent.

Letter (April 16) read from the Right Rev. Dr. Gregg, Lord Bishop of Cork, as to the incorporation of a body to hold Educational Endowments in the Dioceses of Cork, Cloyne, and Ross, and enclosing schedule of such Endowments.

Ordered:—That his Lordship be thanked for his letter and its enclosure.

The Draft Schemes for the Cashel Corporation School Endowment, and for the Cashel Deanery Schools, were considered and amended.

The Secretary was directed to write to the Very Rev. A. H. Leech, D.D., Dean of Cashel, asking him for the names of two or three of his leading Parishioners to be named on the proposed Governing Body for the Cashel Deanery Schools, in addition to the Incumbent and Churchwardens.

The Commissioners adjourned.

JOHN NAISH,
April 18, 18[illegible].

Wm. Edward Ellis, Secretary.

April 18, 18[illegible].

Meeting of the Commission held this day at the Office, 13, Nassau-street, Dublin.

Present:—Lord Justice FITZGIBBON, Lord Justice NAISH, Rev. Dr. MOLLOY.

Minutes of preceding meeting read and confirmed.

Letters read:—

The Most Rev. Dr. O'Donnell, Lord Bishop of Raphoe (April 16), as to the Raphoe Royal School premises.

Rev. Alexander Gordon (April 17), giving particulars of funds belonging to the Irish Non-Subscribing Presbyterian Orphan Society.

Rev. David Humphrys (April 17), as to the Erasmus Smith's Endowments.

Ven. W. E. Meade, D.D., Archdeacon of Armagh (April 17), stating that the extension of time granted for sending in observations on the revised Draft Scheme for the Ulster Royal School Endowments will be sufficient.

Letter (April 17) read from Rev. William Wright, as to the incorporation of a Governing Body to hold Educational Endowments belonging to the Presbytery of Ards, co. Down.

A reply as drafted in similar cases ordered to be sent.

Letter (April 17) read from Messrs. J. Marland and Co., asking that an agreement relating to the Downpatrick Blue School be returned to them.

Ordered:—That a copy be made and that the original be returned as requested.

The Draft Scheme for the Cashel Corporation School Endowment was considered and finally approved.

The Draft Schemes for the Cashel Deanery Schools and the Munster Agricultural Dairy School were considered and amended.

The Secretary was directed to write to L. A. [illegible], Honorary Secretary, asking for the names in which the Stock belonging to the Munster Dairy School stands.

The Commissioners adjourned.

GERALD FITZGIBBON,
April 23, 18[illegible].

Wm. Edward Ellis, Secretary.

April 23, 1889.

Meeting of the Commission held this day at the Office, 23, Nassau-street, Dublin.

Present :—Lord Justice FitzGibbon, Lord Justice Naish, Rev. Dr. Molloy, Professor Dougherty.

Minutes of preceding meeting read and confirmed.

Letters read :—

Rev. E. L. Eves (April 16), as to a meeting held at Maryborough with reference to the Ballyroan Endowment.

Very Rev. A. H. Leech, Dean of Cashel (April 23), sending names for proposed Governing Body of the Cashel Deanery Schools.

H. B. Kincaid (April 23), acknowledging receipt of a copy of the letter, dated April 18, from the Clerk of the Salters Company.

Questions were discussed relating to Larne Grammar School; Cashel Corporation School Endowment; Cashel Deanery Schools; and Munster Dairy School and Agricultural Institute; and also with regard to some of the Schemes about to be signed by the Judicial Commissioners.

The Commissioners adjourned.

Gerald FitzGibbon,
May 1, 1889.

Wm. Edward Ellis, Secretary.

April 24, 1889.

Meeting of the Commission held this day at the Office, 23, Nassau-street, Dublin.

Present :—Lord Justice FitzGibbon, Lord Justice Naish, Rev. Dr. Molloy, Professor Dougherty.

Letters read :—

Rev. S. Cuthbert Mitchell (April 22), as to the revised Scheme for the Ulster Royal School Endowments.

Rev. J. J. Sherrard (April 23), giving consent of the trustees of Rynagh Parochial School-house that it should be dealt with under the Meath Diocesan Scheme.

Rev. M. Le B. Kennedy (April 23), as to the objection of the Commissioners of Education to the Draft Scheme for the Clonmel Endowed School, and as to his vested interests.

Letter (April 20) read from James Gregg and J. G. Johnson, Assistant Masters in the Raphoe Royal School, claiming vested interests under the Scheme for the Ulster Royal School Endowments.

A reply, as drafted, directed to be sent.

Questions were discussed with reference to the Scheme for the High School for Girls, Cork.

The Commissioners adjourned.

Gerald FitzGibbon,
May 1, 1889.

Wm. Edward Ellis, Secretary.

April 26, 1889.

Meeting of the Commission held this day at the Office, 23, Nassau-street, Dublin.

Present :—Lord Justice FitzGibbon, Lord Justice Naish, Rev. Dr. Molloy, Professor Dougherty.

Letters read :—

Rev. P. Canon Donnelly (April 23), as to preparing a Scheme for the Convent Schools, Magherafelt.

Most Rev. Dr. M'Gennis, Lord Bishop of Kilmore (April 24), as to the revised Scheme for the Ulster Royal School Endowments.

L. A. Beamish (April 24), sending particulars of the funds belonging to the Munster Dairy School and Agricultural Institute.

Rev. J. A. Weir, LL.D. (April 25), as to the revised Scheme for the Ulster Royal School Endowments.

James Gregg and T. C. Johnson (April 26), with regard to their vested interests as Assistant Masters in the Raphoe Royal School.

Mr. J. L. Napier had an interview with the Commissioners with reference to the Scheme for the Gibson Schools, Oldcastle.

The Secretary was directed to apply for the date of the appointment of James Gregg and T. G. Johnson, as Assistant Masters, in the Raphoe Royal School.

The Draft Schemes for the Cashel Deanery Schools; the Larne Grammar School; and the Munster Dairy School and Agricultural Institute, were amended and finally approved.

It was ordered :—

That the following Draft Schemes be first published on April 29, 1889 :—

No. 59. The Cashel Corporation School Endowments.
No. 60. The Cashel Deanery Schools.
No. 61. The Larne Grammar School.
No. 62. The Munster Dairy School and Agricultural Institute.

and instructions were given as to the mode of publication.

The Commissioners adjourned.

GERALD FITZGIBBON,
May 1, 1889.

Wm. Edward Ellis, Secretary.

May 1, 1889.

Meeting of the Commission held this day at the Office, 63, Nassau-street, Dublin.

Present :—Lord Justice FITZGIBBON, Lord Justice NAISH, Rev. Dr. MOLLOY, Dr. TRAILL.

Minutes of three preceding meetings were read and confirmed.

Letters read :—

Rev. James Morell (April 26), sending list of the Endowments belonging to the Presbytery of Ballybay.
Rev. W. Todd Martin (April 24), as to the proposed Endowment of the Salters Company to the Rainey School, Magherafelt.
Rev. S. G. Cotton (April 27), objecting to the Draft Scheme published for Hewetson's School, Clane.
Robert Gregg, Solicitor, Cork, with regard to the Draft Scheme published for the High School for Girls, Cork, and to the objection of the Proprietors to same.
Rev. Peter Fagan (April 29), as to the inquiry to be held with regard to Shiel's Charity, Co. Westmeath.
Rev. Edward L. Ewen (April 29), as to the Ballyroan Endowment.
The Clerk of the Privy Council, Dublin Castle (April 30), stating that the Scheme for the [illegible] School, Lisburn, has been finally approved by the Lord Lieutenant in Council.

Letters containing observations on the Revised Scheme for the Ulster Royal School Endowments were read from :—

The Commissioners of Education (April 25).
W. J. Valentine, Assistant Master (April 29).
Rev. R. M'Keown, v.g., p.p. (April 24).
Rev. A. Nelson (April 27).
Most Rev. Dr. O'Donnell, Lord Bishop of Raphoe, } April 28.
Rev. W. L. Berkeley, } April 28.
Very Rev. Dean Byrne (April 29).
Rev. P. Canon Donnelly (April 29).
W. H. Gunning, and other Assistant Masters (April 29).
The Honorary Secretaries of the General Synod of the Church of Ireland (May 1).

The Secretary was directed to write to the Honorary Secretaries of the General Synod, in terms as drafted, stating that the Commissioners will attend on Saturday next at 12 o'clock at their office to meet the deputation which the General Synod desire to send to them with reference to the resolutions set forth in the above-named letter; also to write to the Editors of the Dublin Newspapers, informing them that the proceedings on Saturday will be open to the Press.

The Commissioners adjourned.

JOHN NAISH,
May 3, 1889.

Wm. Edward Ellis, Secretary.

May 3, 1889.

Meeting of the Commission held this day at the Office, 23, Nassau-street, Dublin.

Present :—Lord Justice FitzGibbon, Lord Justice Naish, Rev. Dr. Molloy, Dr. Traill, Professor Dougherty.

Minutes of the preceding meeting read and confirmed.

Letter [May 1] read from the Secretaries, National Education Board, stating that the public inquiry as to Shiel's Charity may be held in the Rochfort Bridge National Convent Schools.

Letter [May 2] read from Rev. John J. Robinson, as to a grant for a Parochial School-house in the Parish of Delgany, Co. Wicklow.

A reply, as drafted, directed to be sent.

The principles on which a Draft Scheme for the Crofton School, [illegible], should be prepared were provisionally agreed to.

The Commissioners adjourned.

John Naish,
May 8, 1889.

Wm. Edward Ellis, Secretary.

May 4, 1889.

PUBLIC SITTING.

Meeting of the Commission held this day at the Office, 23, Nassau-street, Dublin.

Present :—Lord Justice FitzGibbon, Lord Justice Naish, Rev. Dr. Molloy, Dr. Traill, Professor Dougherty.

Mr. Henry Bond, Shorthand Writer, was in attendance.

Revised Scheme for the Ulster Royal School Endowments.

This sitting was for the purpose of receiving a deputation from the General Synod of the Church of Ireland, and the deputation consisting of the following persons attended :—

1. His Grace the Lord Primate.
2. The Lord Bishop of Derry.
3. The Lord Bishop of Clogher.
4. The Lord Bishop of Kilmore.
5. Very Rev. the Dean of Armagh.
6. Ven. the Archdeacon of Clogher.
7. Rev. Precentor Ovenden.
8. Rev. W. Moore Morgan, LL.D.
9. Rev. W. H. Hutchinson, LL.D.
10. Rev. Canon Babington.
11. Colonel Phillips, R.E.

Statements were made by each of the above with the exception of Ven. the Archdeacon of Clogher and Rev. Dr. Hutchinson.

PRIVATE MEETING.

Letters read from :—

Most Rev. Dr. Donnelly, Lord Bishop of Clogher, as to the Revised Scheme for the Ulster Royal School Endowments.

Right Rev. Dr. Walsh, Lord Bishop of Ossory [May 4], enclosing resolution passed by Diocesan Council of Ossory as to the Ballyroan Endowment.

Rev. M. Le B. Kennedy [May 3], as to his objection to the Draft Scheme published for the Clonmel Endowed School.

The Commissioners adjourned.

John Naish,
May 8, 1889.

Wm. Edward Ellis, Secretary.

May 8, 1889.

Meeting of the Commission held this day at their Offices, 23, Nassau-street, Dublin.

Present :—Lord Justice FITZGIBBON, Lord Justice NAISH, Rev. Dr. MOLLOY, Dr. TRAILL.

Minutes of two preceding meetings read and confirmed.

Letters read :—

Wm. J. De Vere, Head Master, Gilson Schools, Oldcastle [May 4], objecting on behalf of Mrs. De Vere, to the Draft Scheme published for the above schools.

Rev. E. L. Eves [May 7], as to the Ballyroan Endowment.

Horace Turpin [May 7], as to the Ballyroan Endowment.

Rev. George Shaw [May 7], asking that a Scheme may be prepared for the Presbyterian Sabbath School Society.

Letter [May 3] read from Rev. William Irwin, asking questions with regard to school committees and repairs of school buildings under the proposed Scheme for the Endowments belonging to the Presbytery of Ballybay.

A reply, as drafted, ordered to be sent.

Letter [May 4] read from Ven. The Archdeacon of Meath, asking for extension of time to send in objections and amendments to the Draft Scheme for the Meath Parochial Schools and the Preston School, Navan.

A reply, as drafted, ordered to be sent.

Letter [May 4] read from W. P. Chapman, Secretary, Incorporated Society for promoting English Protestant Schools in Ireland, asking for the consent of the Commissioners that certain alterations should be carried out at the Primrose Grange Institution, Sligo.

A letter, enclosing the written consent of the Commissioners, ordered to be sent.

Letter [May 4] read from Rev. F. A. Macnamara, as to certain particulars mentioned about Clara Parochial School in the Draft Scheme published for the Meath Parochial Schools, &c.

A reply, as drafted, ordered to be sent.

The letter dated May 7, sent in reply to a telegram from Rev. E. L. Eves, asking the Commissioners to receive a deputation from Maryborough as to the Ballyroan Endowment, was approved.

The hearing of the objections to the revised Scheme for the Ulster Royal School Endowments was provisionally fixed to be held on the 20th May and following days.

The Right Honourable the Earl of Courtown had an interview with the Commissioners with regard to a Scheme for the Parochial Endowments of the Diocese of Ferns.

The Commissioners adjourned.

GERALD FITZGIBBON,

May 10, 1889.

Wm. Edward Ellis, Secretary.

May 10, 1889.

Meeting of the Commission held this day at the Office, 23, Nassau-street, Dublin.

Present :—Lord Justice FITZGIBBON, Lord Justice NAISH, Rev. Dr. MOLLOY, Dr. TRAILL, Professor DOUGHERTY.

Minutes of preceding meeting read and confirmed.

Letters read :—

Rev. James Mitchell [May 8] as to the Annahilt Endowed School, County Down.

Michael Carey, *Leinster Express Office* [May 8], as to the Ballyroan Endowment.

Letter [May 8] read from Rev. David Parks, sending particulars of the Endowments belonging to the Presbytery of Banbridge.

Letter [May 9] read from the Most Rev. Dr. O'Dwyer, Lord Bishop of Limerick, objecting to the Draft Scheme published for the Roxborough-road School, Limerick.

A reply, as drafted, directed to be sent.

Letter [May 9] read from Rev. John Healy, LL.D., as to an Endowment for founding a Widows' Alms-house, in the Parish of St. Columba's, Kells, County Meath.

A reply, as drafted, directed to be sent.

Directions were given to write to the Right Rev. Dr. Gregg, D.D., Bishop of Cork, asking for a name to be substituted for that of Mr. R. C. Hall, deceased, in the City of Cork Parochial Schools Scheme, also for the names to be given as the Governing Body in the Scheme now in preparation for the Dioceses of Cork, Cloyne, and Ross, and for the Schedules to the same.

The Commissioners adjourned.

JOHN NAISH,
May 16, 1889.

Wm. Edward Ellis, Secretary.

May 14, 1889.

PUBLIC SITTING.

Meeting of the Commission held this day at the Convent National Schools, Rochfort Bridge.

Present:—Rev. Dr. Molloy, Dr. Traill, Professor Dougherty.

Mr. George K. Magee, Shorthand Writer, was in attendance.

Rev. Dr. Molloy made an introductory statement.

THE SHEIL ENDOWMENT, ROCHFORT BRIDGE.

The following witnesses were sworn and examined:—

Rev. P. Fagan, P.P.
Wm. Mooney, J.P., Solicitor for the Trustees.

The Commissioners adjourned.

Previous to the Public Sitting, the Commissioners visited the Convent National Schools, and inspected the house and grounds of Gortamloe.

JOHN NAISH,
July 6, 1889.

N. D. Murphy,
Chief Clerk and Assistant Secretary.

May 15, 1889.

Meeting of the Commission held this day at the Office, 13, Nassau-street, Dublin.

Present:—Lord Justice Naish, Rev. Dr. Molloy, Dr. Traill, Professor Dougherty.

Minutes of meeting of May 10, read and confirmed.

Letter [May 15] read from the Secretary, Commissioners of Education, asking for the consent of the Commissioners that a bridge should be built on their Cavan Estate.

A letter, enclosing the written consent of the Commissioners, ordered to be sent.

Questions as to the Scheme for the Ledley Endowment, Ballymacarrett, were discussed

The Commissioners adjourned.

GERALD MOLLOY,
May 20, 1889.

Wm. Edward Ellis, Secretary.

May 20, 1889.

Meeting of the Commission held this day at the Office, 33, Nassau-street, Dublin.

Present:—Lord Justice FitzGibbon, Lord Justice Naish, Rev. Dr. Molloy, Dr. Traill, Professor Dougherty.

Minutes of preceding meeting read and confirmed.

Letters read:—

J. L. Napier [May 16], submitting objections to the Draft Scheme published for the Gilson Schools, Oldcastle.

Rev. Canon Gregg [May 15], submitting objections to the Draft Scheme published for the Roxborough Road School, *Limerick*.

Rev. Thomas P. Morgan [May 16], as to the Draft Scheme published for the Lorne Grammar School.

Rev. Peter Fagan, P.P. [May 19], enclosing Lease relating to Rochfortbridge Convent Schools.

Messrs. M'Elwee and Sons [May 13], as to the present amount of the Ledley Endowment, Ballymacarrett.

The Town Clerk, Kinsale [May 16], giving description of the premises known as the Kinsale Endowed School.

The existing Trustees of the Endowments belonging to Christ Church, Rathgar, in the Presbytery of Dublin [May 15], giving their consent that the Endowments should be dealt with under the Act.

Rev. George Shaw [May 17], asking the Commissioners to prepare a Scheme for the Presbyterian Sabbath School Society for Ireland.

Observations on the revised Draft Scheme for the Ulster Royal School Endowments were submitted from the following persons:—

Rev. A. G. Lecky [May 15], on behalf of the Presbytery of Raphoe.

James Henry, Solicitor [May 16], on behalf of the Committee of the General Assembly of the Presbyterian Church.

Messrs. H. T. Dix and Sons [May 17], on behalf of the Diocesan Councils of Armagh, Derry and Raphoe, Kilmore, and Clogher.

Messrs. Kelly and Lloyd [May 18], on behalf of Rev. W. Prior Moore and of Rev. William Moore Morgan.

A. Callton, Solicitor [May 18], on behalf of Rev. J. A. Weir.

Letters read from the following persons, asking for copies of the observations received by the Commissioners on the revised Draft Scheme for the Ulster Royal School Endowments:—

Very Rev. Dean Byrne, Dungannon [May 18].
Rev. W. L. Berkeley [May 18].
Most Rev. Dr. O'Donnell, Lord Bishop of Raphoe [May 18].

Ordered:—That copies of the observations be forwarded when ready, together with the notes of the Public Sitting held on May 4, to each applicant.

Letter [May 16] read from Rev. James E. H. Murphy, objecting to the Scheme for the Parochial Schools of the Diocese of Meath in reference to the clause respecting "Religious Instruction."

A reply, as drafted, ordered to be sent.

Letter [May 16] read from Rev. F. H. Ringwood, Dungannon, stating that Drill-Master Sergeant Whelan had died, and asking whether his widow would receive the compensation due to Sergeant Whelan under the Scheme for the Ulster Royal School Endowments.

A reply, as drafted, ordered to be sent.

Letter [May 16] read from Rev. S. Cuthbert Mitchel, asking if the Commissioners would receive a deputation with regard to the revised Draft Scheme for the Ulster Royal School Endowments.

It was ordered:—

I. That the following Schemes be advanced, with a view to publication at the end of May:—

St. Stephen's Hospital, Cork.
Ballyroan Endowment, Queen's County.
Ledley Endowment, Ballyjamesduff.
Southwell School Endowment, Kinsale.
Presbytery of Dublin Endowments.
Cork, Cloyne, and Ross Diocesan Scheme.
Crofton Endowment, Macroom.

II. That the following Schemes be advanced, with a view to publication at the end of June:—

Bishop Hodson's Grammar School, Elphin.
Shell Endowment, Rashfort Bridge.
Strabane Academy.
Brown's Endowments, County Down.
Non-Subscribing Presbyterian Orphan Society.
Anne Hall Endowment for Agricultural Education.

III. That the following Schemes be advanced, with a view to publication at the end of July:—

Incorporated Society.
Mungret College, Limerick.
Limerick Diocesan Scheme.
Ardfert and Aghadoe Diocesan Scheme.
Morgan's School, Castleknock.

The Draft Schemes for the Ledley Endowment and for the Southwell School Endowment, Kinsale, were considered and amended.

The Commissioners adjourned.

JOHN NAISH,
May 21, 1889.

Wm. Edward Ellis, Secretary.

May 21, 1889.

Meeting of the Commission held this day at the Office, 23, Nassau-street, Dublin.

Present :—Lord Justice FITZGIBBON, Lord Justice NAISH, Rev. Dr. MOLLOY, Dr. TRAILL, Professor DOUGHERTY.

Minutes of preceding meeting read and confirmed.

Communication read from the Under Secretary, Dublin Castle, submitting for report a Parliamentary Question of which notice had been given by Mr. T. M. Healy, M.P., with reference to a Scheme for the Erasmus Smith's Endowments.

The Secretary was directed to forward report as drafted.

The Draft Schemes for the Crofton Endowment, Macroom, for the Educational Endowments belonging to the Presbytery of Dublin, and for the Parochial Schools of the Diocese of Cork, Cloyne, and Ross, were considered.

The Commissioners adjourned.

JOHN NAISH,
May 24, 1889.

Wm. Edward Ellis, Secretary.

May 24, 1889.

Meeting of the Commission held this day at the Office, 23, Nassau-street, Dublin.

Present :—Lord Justice FITZGIBBON, Lord Justice NAISH, Rev. Dr. MOLLOY, Dr. TRAILL, Professor DOUGHERTY.

Minutes of preceding meeting read and confirmed.

Letters read :—

Rev. Michael Ahern [May 21], giving description of the Gurrane Male and Female National Schools, Macroom.

Rev. Wm. Johnston, B.D. [May 23], enclosing objections to the Draft Scheme published for the Presbyterian Orphan Society.

George Harrison, Secretary, Cork High School for Girls [May 24], sending back the revised Scheme for that School.

Letter [May 23], read from John C. Ferguson, as to a Scheme for the Endowments belonging to the Diocese of Ferns.

A reply, as drafted, ordered to be sent.

The Commissioners adjourned.

JOHN NAISH,
May 27, 1889.

Wm. Edward Ellis, Secretary.

May 27, 1889.

Meeting of the Commission held this day at the Office, 23, Nassau-street, Dublin.

Present :—Lord Justice FITZGIBBON, Lord Justice NAISH, Rev. Dr. MOLLOY, Dr. TRAILL.

Minutes of preceding meeting read and confirmed.

Letters read :—

Rev. James B. Keene [May 24], on behalf of the Meath Diocesan Council, objecting to the Draft Scheme published for the Meath Parochial Schools.

Rev. Jas. B. Keene [May 24], on behalf of the Meath Diocesan Council, objecting to the Draft Scheme published for the Gilson Schools, Oldcastle.

Rev. Laurence Grehan, P.P. [May 24], objecting to the Draft Scheme published for the Gilson Schools, Oldcastle.

Peter Hinde (May 23),
David B. Jack, M.D.,
Rev. Edmund L. Swan (May 25), } as to the Ballyroan Endowment.

Letter [May 25], read from Joseph J. Murphy, Secretary, Diocesan Council of Down and Connor and Dromore, as to the preparation of a Scheme for the Parochial Schools of those Dioceses.

A reply, as drafted, ordered to be sent.

c

The Draft Scheme for St. Stephen's Hospital, Cork, was considered, amended, and passed, and the Secretary was directed to write to the Bishop of Cork asking his Lordship to name one clergyman and one layman as the first representatives of the Diocesan Council, and one clergyman and one layman as the first representatives of the City of Cork Church School Board.

A circular, as drafted, was directed to be sent in the case of each Draft Scheme published for a Diocese or Presbytery to the Clergyman of each Parish or the Clerk of the Presbytery inquiring as to any additional Endowments that it might be desired to include in the Scheme.

The Commission then adjourned.

GERALD FITZGIBBON,

Wm. Edward Ellis, Secretary. May 29, 1889.

May 29, 1889.

Meeting of the Commission held this day at the Office, 12, Nassau-street, Dublin.

Present:—Lord Justice FITZGIBBON, Lord Justice NAISH, Rev. Dr. MOLLOY, Dr. TRAILL.

Minutes of preceding meeting read and confirmed.

Letters read:—

The Secretary, Local Government Board [May 25], as to the audit of accounts of endowments for which Schemes have been finally approved.

Rev. J. A. Weir [May 28] as to his objections to the revised Scheme for the Ulster Royal School Endowments.

Letter [May 27] read from the Under Secretary, Dublin Castle, asking for information with regard to the Scheme for the Munster Dairy School and Agricultural Institute.

A reply, as drafted, ordered to be sent.

Letter [May 27] read from Rev. W. Moore Morgan, LL.D., asking as to the order in which the objections to the revised Scheme for the Ulster Royal Schools will be heard on the 31st instant.

A reply, as drafted, ordered to be sent.

Letter [May 20] read from Rev. J. Kennedy, Secretary, Larne Grammar School, asking as to cost under the Scheme for inspection and audit.

A reply, as drafted, ordered to be sent.

Letter [May 28] read from Rev. C. J. M'Alester, as to the reading of Clause 23, in the Scheme framed for the Sullivan Schools, Holywood.

A reply, as drafted, ordered to be sent.

The Secretary was directed to send the memorandum received from Wm. N. Wallace, D.L., with reference to the Southwell Endowment, Downpatrick, to Messrs. Murland and Sons, Solicitors for John Mulholland, Esq., with a letter as drafted.

The Secretary was directed to write in the cases of all Dioceses, Presbyteries, or other bodies for which the Commissioners are about to prepare Schemes, forwarding extracts from the Schedules to the Report of the Endowed Schools Commission of 1879-80, regarding Endowments which appear to come within the scope of the proposed Schemes, and to inquire with respect to each of them whether it may be included in the Draft Scheme.

Directions were given as to the Draft Schemes to be published at the end of June, and meetings were fixed for the consideration of the same.

It was ordered:—

That the following Draft Schemes be first published on May 31, 1889:—

No. 63.—"The Lailey School Endowments, Ballymacarrett."

No. 64.—"The Educational Endowments of and belonging to Congregations under the care of the Presbytery of Dublin."

No. 65.—"St. Stephen's Hospital, Cork, founded by William Worth."

No. 66.—"The Parochial Schools of the Dioceses of Cork, Cloyne, and Ross, and Bishop Crowe's School, Cloyne."

No. 67.—"The Southwell School Endowment, Kinsale."

and instructions were given as to the mode of publication.

The Commissioners adjourned.

JOHN NAISH,

Wm. Edward Ellis, Secretary. June 5, 1889.

May 31, 1889.

PUBLIC SITTING.

Meeting of the Commission held this day at the Court of Chancery, Four Courts, Dublin.

Present :—Lord Justice FitzGibbon, Lord Justice Naish, Rev. Dr. Molloy, Dr. Traill, Professor Dougherty.

Mr. Henry Bond, Shorthand Writer, was in attendance.

THE REVISED DRAFT SCHEME PUBLISHED BY THE COMMISSIONERS FOR ALTERING THE CONSTITUTION OF "THE COMMISSIONERS OF EDUCATION," AND FOR THE FUTURE GOVERNMENT AND MANAGEMENT OF THE ULSTER ROYAL SCHOOL ENDOWMENTS.

ON THE CONSIDERATION OF THE OBJECTIONS AND AMENDMENTS PROPOSED TO THE ABOVE DRAFT SCHEME.

Lord Justice FitzGibbon made an introductory statement.

The following Bodies and Persons were represented as under, or appeared in person :—

The Commissioners of Education in Ireland, by Jeffrey M'Dowell, Secretary, pro tem.

The General Synod of the Church of Ireland, and the Diocesan Councils of Armagh, Derry, and Raphoe, Kilmore, and Clogher, by E. T. Bewley, Q.C. (instructed by Messrs. H. T. Dix and Sons, Solicitors).

The Intermediate Education Committee of the General Assembly of the Presbyterian Church in Ireland, by James J. Shaw, LL.D. (instructed by James Henry, Solicitor).

The Most Rev. Dr. Logue, Lord Archbishop of Armagh, by Rev. H. M'Neece.

The Most Rev. Dr. Walsh, Lord Archbishop of Dublin.

The Most Rev. Dr. Donnelly, Lord Bishop of Clogher, by R. P. Carton, Q.C. (instructed by William F. Wray, LL.B., Solicitor).

The Most Rev. Dr. M'Gennis, Lord Bishop of Kilmore, by Michael Drummond, Esq. (instructed by H. P. Kennedy, Solicitor).

The Very Rev. B. M'Namee, P.P., V.F., Omagh.

Very Rev. Dean Byrne, P.P., Dungannon.

The Local Committee of Protestant Denominations in the County of Fermanagh, by R. M. Dane, Esq. (instructed by J. W. Dane, Solicitor).

The Schoolmasters Association, by William Wilkins, M.A., Vice-Chairman.

Rev. William Moore Morgan, LL.D., Rev. F. H. Ringwood, LL.D., Rev. W. Steele, D.D., by Right Hon. Samuel Walker (instructed by Messrs. Kelly and Lloyd, Solicitors). Mr. James M'Ivor, B.L., also appeared on behalf of Dr. Steele.

Rev. James A. Weir, LL.D., by A. Colles, Solicitor.

Thomas Gordon, Esq., B.A., by John Harley, LL.D. (instructed by Messrs. H. T. Dix and Sons, Solicitors).

The Commissioners adjourned.

John Naish,
June 5, 1889.

Wm. Edward Ellis, Secretary.

June 1, 1889.

Meeting of the Commission held this day at the Office, 28, Nassau-street, Dublin.

Present :—Lord Justice FitzGibbon, Lord Justice Naish, Rev. Dr. Molloy, Dr. Traill, Professor Dougherty.

Letters read :—

Joseph John Murphy, Hon. Secretary, Diocesan Council of Down and Connor and Dromore [May 30], as to a Scheme for the Parochial Schools of these Dioceses.

John C. Pounden, Diocesan Secretary [May 31], enclosing a Draft Scheme for the Parochial Schools of the Diocese of Ferns and Schedules of the property to be included in the Scheme.

Rev. John Finlay [May 31], sending list of Parochial Schools in Diocese of Leighlin.

The Secretary was directed to write a letter, as drafted, with reference to the establishment of denominational Protestant Boards for the Armagh and Tyrone districts as defined in the Scheme for the Ulster Royal School Endowments, and to send same to the members of the proposed Armagh and Tyrone Protestant Boards, and to those who have represented the denominations concerned before the Commission, viz :—The Standing Committee of the General Synod, the Presbyterian Intermediate Education Committee, the Methodist Conference, the Raphoe and Dungannon Local Committees, the Commissioners of Education, and the several Diocesan Councils concerned.

The Commissioners adjourned.

John Naish,
June 5, 1889.

Wm. Edward Ellis, Secretary.

June 6, 1889.

Meeting of the Commission held this day at the Office, 23, Nassau-street, Dublin.

Present:—Lord Justice FitzGibbon, Lord Justice Naish, Rev. Dr. Molloy, Dr. Traill, Professor Dougherty.

Minutes of three preceding meetings read and confirmed.

Letters read:—

The Town Clerk of Cashel (June 3), enclosing objections on behalf of the Town Commissioners of Cashel to the Draft Scheme published for the Cashel Corporation School Endowment.

Rev. W. Reid (May 31), enclosing resolutions of the Presbytery of Magherafelt, as to the Rainey School Endowment.

M. F. Parke (June 3), as to the Endowment of the Kilfinane Classical School, County Limerick.

Rev. James K. H. Murphy (June 5), objecting further to the Draft Scheme published for the Meath Parochial Schools.

Ven. C. Beaver, Archdeacon of Connor (June 4), objecting to the Draft Scheme published for the Lodge School Endowments, Ballymoney.

Letter (June 3) read from Rev. M. Le B. Kennedy as to his position as Head Master of the Clonmel Endowed School.

A reply, as drafted, directed to be sent.

Letter (June 3) read from Rev. S. G. Cotton, asking when the Commissioners intend hearing the objections lodged to the Draft Scheme for Hewetson's School, Clane.

Ordered:—

That a copy of Rev. Mr. Cotton's letter be transmitted to the Rev. Wm. Sherlock, asking him to inform the Commissioners whether Mr. Cooke-Trench has yet returned to Ireland, and stating that they would be prepared to have a sitting at the office for the consideration of the objections in this case on any afternoon at 4 o'clock that may be convenient to the parties interested.

Letter (June 4) read from Rev. W. Moore Morgan, asking for extension of time for sending in the observations of the Armagh Diocesan Council, and also asking questions with regard to certain parts of the Scheme for the Ulster Royal School Endowments.

A reply, as drafted, ordered to be sent.

The Secretary was directed to write to Dr. Morgan, Armagh, and to Dr. Steele, Portora, in terms as drafted, with respect to their vested interests as Head Masters of the Royal Schools.

The Secretary was directed to prepare a circular letter, as drafted, with reference to a Scheme for the Crofton School Endowment, co. Cork, and to send copies of the same to the Protestant Incumbent of the Parish of Macroom, the Parish Priest of Clondrohid, the representatives of the Testatrix, and the surviving Trustee of the school; and also to enclose a copy to Sir P. J. Keenan, K.C.M.G., Resident Commissioner of National Education, with a letter saying that the circular has been sent to the persons mentioned above, and to him as he had been kind enough to furnish the Commissioners on a former occasion with valuable information concerning the Endowment, and that the Commissioners would be obliged if, after reading the circular, he would favour them with his observations on the subject.

The Draft Scheme for the Ballyroan Endowed School was considered.

At Dr. Traill's request, the Commission agreed to insert in the Minutes, as follows, a copy of his "protest" against the Scheme for the Southwell School Endowment, Kinsale:—

I protest against the Scheme for the following reasons:—

1. Because this Endowment was left by a Protestant to Trustees who were at that time necessarily Protestants. In the absence of the original document it must be assumed that one of the conditions laid down by the founder was that the Schoolmaster should be a Protestant, because he has always been not only a Protestant, but a clergyman of the then Established Church.

2. Because the endowment has been illegally taken hold of by the Town Commissioners of Kinsale, who, on the death of the last Protestant Schoolmaster, Rev. John Fordon, appointed a Roman Catholic Schoolmaster, under whose auspices the school finally became defunct.

3. Because, though there is no doubt that Roman Catholic boys were always at liberty to use the School, and as a matter of fact did receive their education there, it is most unjust that when they refuse to use the School, owing to the pressure of their ecclesiastical authorities, a claim should be put forward on behalf of the Roman Catholics to have the Endowment divided.

4. Because the Protestants of Kinsale and its neighbourhood require the entire amount of the Endowment to do themselves justice in the matter of education.

Anthony Traill.

The Commissioners adjourned.

John Naish,
June 13, 1889.

Wm. Edward Ellis, Secretary.

June 7, 1889.

Meeting of the Commission held this day at the Office, 24, Nassau-street, Dublin.

Present:—Lord Justice FitzGibbon, Lord Justice Naish, Rev. Dr. Molloy, Dr. Traill, Professor Dougherty.

Letter (June 6) read from the Most Rev. Dr. M'Gennis, Lord Bishop of Kilmore, as to the Cavan Royal School buildings and premises.

To be informed that his letter will receive the careful consideration of the Commissioners.

Letter (June 4) read from Andrew Brown enclosing a Memorial from the Presbyterian inhabitants of Magherafelt with regard to the Rainey School, Magherafelt.

To be informed that the Memorial will receive the careful consideration of the Commissioners.

The Secretary was directed to write a letter, as drafted, with reference to a Scheme for the Ballyroan Endowed School, Queen's Co., and to send same to the Protestant Incumbent of the Parish of Maryborough, the Parish Priest of Maryborough, the Protestant Incumbent of the Parish of Abbeyleix, and to the Right Honorable Viscount De Vesci.

The Secretary was directed to write in terms as drafted to Messrs. J. Murland & Co., solicitors to John Mulholland, Esq., D.L., asking for particulars of arrears of the rentcharge of £283 16s. constituting portion of the Southwell School Endowment, Downpatrick, and payable by Mr. Mulholland.

The Commissioners adjourned.

John Naish,
June 13, 1889.

Wm. Edward Ellis, Secretary.

June 13, 1889.

Meeting of the Commission held this day at the Office, 24, Nassau-street, Dublin.

Present:—Lord Justice FitzGibbon, Lord Justice Naish, Rev. Dr. Molloy, Dr. Traill, Professor Dougherty.

Minutes of the two preceding meetings read and confirmed.

Letters read:—

Rev. M. Le B. Kennedy, Head Master, Clonmel Endowed School (June 10), as to his vested interests.

Rev. Alfred T. Harvey (June 11), enclosing consent of Lord Darnley that the Parochial School buildings and premises in Athboy and Killochonnigan should be dealt with by the Scheme for the Meath Parochial Schools.

Messrs. Wm. Mooney and Son, Solicitors (June 12), enclosing copy of deed dated March 4, 1887, appointing new trustees, and other documents relating to Shiel's Charity, county Westmeath.

Thos. Pakenham Law (June 13), as to a subscription on the townland of Coolure, mentioned in Schedule to Meath Parochial Schools.

Letters read from the following persons in reply to the letter directed to be sent with reference to a Scheme for the Ballyroan Endowed School, Queen's County:—

The Parish Priest of Maryborough (June 8).
The Incumbent of Abbeyleix (June 11).
Right Hon. Viscount De Vesci (June 13).

Letters were read from the following persons in answer to the communication with reference to the formation of denominational Protestant Boards for the Armagh and Tyrone Districts, as defined in the Scheme for the Ulster Royal School Endowments:—

Rev. Wallace M'Mullen (June 8), representing the Methodist Conference.

Very Rev. The Dean of Clogher (June 9), as a member of the Tyrone Protestant Local Board.

Very Rev. The Dean of Armagh (June 10), on behalf of himself, Venerable the Archdeacon of Armagh, and the Rev. Benjamin Wade, as members of the Armagh Protestant Local Board.

Wm. Paul (June 11), as a member of the Armagh Protestant Local Board.

Rev. H. B. Wilson (June 11), as Secretary of the Conference between the members of the Protestant Local Boards of Armagh and Tyrone Districts.

Ven. The Archdeacon of Armagh (June 11), on behalf of the Diocesan Council of Armagh.

James H. Stronge (June 11), as a member of the Armagh Protestant Local Board.

Letters also read:—

Rev. Joseph T. Quinn (June 11), as to the revised Scheme for the Ulster Royal School Endowments.

Thos. Goold-Trench (June 6).

Rev. S. G. Cotton (June 12),

as to a sitting for hearing the objections to the Draft Scheme published for the Hewetson's School, Clane.

Letter [June 7] read from the Under Secretary, Dublin Castle, as to the opportunities afforded for discussing the Scheme for the Munster Dairy School and Agricultural Institute before it is finally approved.

A reply, as drafted, directed to be sent.

Letter [June 10] read from Rev. Wm. Steele, D.D., as to his retiring allowance under the Scheme for the Ulster Royal School Endowments.

A reply, as drafted, directed to be sent.

The Secretary was directed to write to Messrs. J. Murland and Co., Solicitors, asking them to reply to the letter of the Commissioners dated May 30, not later than the 19th instant.

HEWETSON'S SCHOOL, CLANE.

A sitting was fixed to be held at the office at 3 o'clock, P.M., on Monday, July 8, for the purpose of considering the objection of the Rev. S. G. Cotton to the Draft Scheme for Hewetson's School, Clane, and notice was directed to be sent to parties interested.

The Draft Scheme for Bishop Hodson's School, Elphin, was considered and amended.

The Commissioners adjourned.

GERALD FITZGIBBON,

June 14, 1889.

Wm. Edward Ellis, Secretary.

June 14, 1889.

Meeting of the Commission held this day at the Office, 43, Nassau-street, Dublin.

Present:—Lord Justice FITZGIBBON, Lord Justice NAISH, Rev. Dr. MOLLOY, Dr. TRAILL, Professor DOUGHERTY.

Minutes of preceding meeting read and confirmed.

The Draft Scheme for The Shiel Charity, County Westmeath, was considered and finally approved.

The Commission made arrangements for the holding of Public Sittings, commencing July 1, in the following localities:—Baltinglass, Rathvilly, New Ross, Wexford, Carysfort, Aughrim, Arklow, and Wicklow; and instructions were given to have the following advertisement inserted in the Dublin papers, and also, so far as it concerns the district, in the Wexford papers:—

Notice is hereby given that the Commissioners will hold Public Sittings at the following places, on the days and at the hours named, for the purpose of taking evidence respecting the under-mentioned Endowments:—

BALTINGLASS.—At the Court-house:—

Monday, July 1, at 1 o'clock, P.M.

Stratford Lodge Schools.

Kiltegan (Brabazon Smith's) School.

RATHVILLY.—At the School:—

Tuesday, July 2, at 10.15 o'clock, A.M.

D'Israeli's School, Baugh, Rathvilly.

NEW ROSS.—At the Court-house:—

Wednesday, July 3, at 12 o'clock, noon.

New Ross Endowed School.

Ballyanne Schools, New Ross (Bolger's Endowment).

Hill's School, New Ross (Tottenham's Endowment).

Whitechurch, Brickstown (Pool's Endowment).

Whitechurch Parochial School (Glascott's Endowment).

WEXFORD.—At the Court-house :—

Thursday, July 4, at 11.45 o'clock, A.M.

The Free School, Wexford.
Erasmus Smith's School, Wexford.
Ferns Diocesan School.
St. Peter's College, Wexford.
Duncormack School (Richards' Grant).
Kennedy Endowment, Rathaspeck.

CARYSFORT, AUGHRIM.—At the Royal School :—

Friday, July 5, 10.30 o'clock, A.M.

Royal School, Carysfort.

ARKLOW.—At the Court-house :—

Friday, July 5, at 2.30 o'clock, P.M.

Carysfort Royal School Endowment. Application for transfer to Arklow for Industrial Education.
The Incorporated Society's School, Arklow.

WICKLOW.—At the Court-house :—

Saturday, July 6, at 10.45 o'clock, A.M.

Crofton Endowed School, Ashford.
Wicklow Diocesan School.
Wicklow Free School.
Wicklow Protestant Orphan School (Waldron's Bequest).

At the above-mentioned sittings the Commissioners will receive evidence with respect to these and other endowments from persons interested in education.

The Commissioners adjourned.

ANTHONY TRAILL,
June 17, 1889.

Wm. Edward Ellis, Secretary.

June 17, 1889.

Meeting of the Commission held this day at the Office, 28, Nassau-street, Dublin.

Present :—Lord Justice FITZGIBBON, Lord Justice NAISH, Rev. Dr. MOLLOY, Dr. TRAILL, Professor DOUGHERTY.

Minutes of preceding meeting read and confirmed.

Letters read :—

The Lord Bishop of Cork, Cloyne, and Ross [June 14], sending name to be substituted for that of Mr. R. G. Hall, as representing the Grammar School in the City of Cork Parochial School Scheme.
Rev. W. H. Green [June 14], Carrigaline,
Rev. S. MacConnell [June 14], Kilmeaden,
Rev. G. H. Sweetman [June 15], Aghadown,
Rev. L. H. Henry [June 15], Kilworth,
Rev. F. Connor [June 14], Ballybeely,
Rev. H. T. Townsend [June 14], Kilcoe,
with reference to the Scheme for the Parochial Schools of the Dioceses of Cork, Cloyne, and Ross.
Rev. E. L. Even [June 15],
J. Loftus Bland [June 16],
as to Ballyroan Endowed School.
Rev. J. L. Darling [June 15], as to the Draft Scheme published for Kilmacow Endowed School.

The Secretary was directed to write in terms, as drafted, to the Rev. W. M. Morgan, LL.D., in reply to his letter of 7th instant, as to his vested interests as Head Master of Armagh Royal School.

The Draft Scheme for Bishop Hodson's Grammar School, Elphin, was considered, amended, and finally approved.

The Commissioners adjourned.

J. B. DOUGHERTY,
June 19, 1889.

Wm. Edward Ellis, Secretary.

June 19, 1889.

Meeting of the Commission held this day at the Office, 23, Nassau-street, Dublin.

Present:—Lord Justice FitzGibbon, Lord Justice Naish, Rev. Dr. Molloy, Dr. Traill, Professor Dougherty.

Minutes of preceding meeting read and confirmed.

The following letters read:—

Rev. J. Lalor, Abbeyleix [June 17], as to Ballyroan Endowed School.
Thomas Laffan and Andrew Mulcahy, as to Cashel Corporation School Endowment.
Rev. D. H. Powell [June 17], as to William Masters' Endowment, Cork.
William Mooney, Solicitor [June 13], as to The Kidd Charity, Rochfortbridge.
Messrs. H. T. Dix and Sons [June 18], enclosing objection of Incorporated Society to Draft Scheme for Cashel Diocesan Schools.

Letter read from E. Davidson, Sub-Sheriff to Wicklow, giving the Commissioners the use of the Court-houses at Baltinglass, Arklow, and Wicklow, for the Public Sittings fixed at these places.

The Secretary was directed to write and thank him.

Letter [June 17] read from Rev. R. C. Hallowes, asking as to the proposal made with regard to Carysfort Royal School Endowment.

The Secretary was directed to send extracts from Archbishop Walsh's evidence, in which the proposal was made.

Letter [June 15] read from Rev. C. Davis, P.P., Baltimore, as to the Scheme for Baltimore Fishery School.

A reply, as already directed to be sent by Lord Justice FitzGibbon, approved.

Letter read from A. J. Nicolls, LL.B., Secretary Loan Fund Board, as to the Scheme for the Thomastown Parochial School.

A reply, as drafted, directed to be sent.

Letter [June 17] read from the Secretary of the Commissioners of Charitable Donations and Bequests, as to the Scheme for Royal Irish Academy of Music and Coulson Endowment.

A reply, as drafted, directed to be sent.

Letter [June 8] read from Messrs. George M'Ildowie and Sons, as to the Draft Scheme published for the Ledley Endowment.

A reply, as drafted, directed to be sent.

The proposed amendments to be made in the revised Scheme for the Ulster Royal School Endowments were considered.

The Secretary was directed to write to Rev. Dr. Galway, or the Treasurer of the Green Coat Hospital, Cork, asking for information regarding the William Masters Endowment.

The Commissioners adjourned.

John Naish,
June 21, 1889.

Wm. Edward Ellis, Secretary.

June 21, 1889.

Meeting of the Commission held this day at the Office, 23, Nassau-street, Dublin.

Present:—Lord Justice FitzGibbon, Lord Justice Naish, Rev. Dr. Molloy, Dr. Traill, Professor Dougherty.

Minutes of preceding meeting read and confirmed.

Letters read:—

Rev. W. Moore Morgan [June 19], as to his vested interests.
James Earl [June 19], as to D'Israeli's School, Rathvilly.
Andrew Browne [June 19], as to the Rainey School, Magherafelt.
The Hon. Secs., Standing Committee of the General Synod [June 20], as to "Church Education" Schools.
The Hon. Secs., Standing Committee of the General Synod [June 20],
The Secretary, Commissioners of Education [June 20],
as to the revised Scheme for the Ulster Royal School Endowments.

Letters read from the following, and in each case a reply, as drafted, was directed to be sent:—

Rev. Dr. Jordan [June 19], as to Rainey School, Magherafelt.
Rev. J. R. Latham [June 18], as to sittings at Wexford.
Rev. Luke Doyle [June 19], as to St. Peter's College, Wexford.
J. C. Pounden [June 20], as to sittings in County Wexford.
Rev. J. H. Orr [June 20], Clerk of the General Assembly, as to Rainey School, and asking the Commissioners to receive a deputation, which they consented to receive at an hour convenient to the deputation, on Thursday, July 11.
Rev. T. W. Roe [June 20], enclosing amendments to Ledley School Scheme.

The proposed amendments to be made in the revised Scheme for the Ulster Royal School Endowments were further considered and amended.

The Commissioners adjourned.

GERALD MOLLOY,
June 24, 1889.

Wm. Edward Ellis, Secretary.

June 24, 1889.

Meeting of the Commission held this day at the Office, 13, Nassau-street, Dublin.

Present:—Lord Justice FITZGIBBON, Lord Justice NAISH, Rev. Dr. MOLLOY, Dr. TRAILL, Professor DOUGHERTY.

Minutes of preceding meeting read and confirmed.

Letter [June 21] read from L. A. Beamish, Esq., stating objections of Governing Body of Munster Dairy School to the Draft Scheme for that School.

Letters were also read from the following, and replies were directed to be sent as drafted:—

The Lord Bishop of Ossory [June 21], as to Baugh School, Rathvilly.
Thomas Wilkinson [June 21], granting the Commissioners the use of Courthouses at New Ross and Wexford.
Rev. W. J. Wilson [June 22], as to Irish School, Whitegate, County Cork.
Rev. W. Steele, D.D., as to his vested interests under the Scheme for the Ulster Royal School Endowments.

The Secretary was directed to write to R. U. Penrose Fitzgerald, M.P., asking if he wishes Corkbeg School to be included in the Cork Diocesan Scheme.

The Scheme for the Ulster Royal School Endowments was further considered and amended.

The Commissioners adjourned.

JOHN NAISH,
June 26, 1889.

Wm. Edward Ellis, Secretary.

June 26, 1889.

Meeting of the Commission held this day at the Office, 13, Nassau-street, Dublin.

Present:—Lord Justice FITZGIBBON, Lord Justice NAISH, Rev. Dr. MOLLOY, Dr. TRAILL, Professor DOUGHERTY.

Minutes of preceding meeting read and confirmed.

Letter read from the Assistant Under Secretary, Dublin Castle [June 22], as to Munster Agricultural School.

The Secretary was directed to reply stating that the final consideration of the Draft Scheme would be postponed until the Treasury have an opportunity of considering it, adding that the office closes for vacation on the 10th August, and that if the proposed communication reaches the office before the 30th July it would facilitate the early settlement of the Scheme.

The Secretary was also directed to write to L. A. Beamish, Esq., Hon. Sec. of the School, informing him of the purport of the above correspondence.

Letter [June 24] read from the Rev. J. H. Orr, Clerk of the General Assembly, as to the deputation with reference to Rainey School.

To be informed that the Commissioners will receive the Deputation at 12 o'clock, noon, on Thursday, July 11.

Letters read:—

Rev. R. C. Hallowes [June 24] as to Incorporated Society School, Arklow.
Rev. J. R. Latham [June 25] as to certain Draft Schemes for which he asks.
Rev. G. O. Greene [June 26] as to the endowments at New Ross.

The Scheme for the Ulster Royal School Endowments was further considered and amended.

The Commissioners adjourned.

GERALD FITZGIBBON,
June 28, 1889.

Wm. Edward Ellis, Secretary.

June 28, 1889.

Meeting of the Commission held this day at the Office, 23, Nassau-street, Dublin.

Present:—Lord Justice FitzGibbon, Lord Justice Naish, Rev. Dr. Molloy, Dr. Traill, Professor Dougherty.

Minutes of preceding meeting read and confirmed.

Letters read:—

Rev. M. Ahern, P.P., Clondrohid [June 26], as to the proposed Scheme for the Crofton Endowment.

R. U. Penrose Fitzgerald, M.P. [June 26], as to the Corkbeg School, County Cork.

R. G. M'Fetridge [June 27] suggesting amendments to the Cork Diocesan Scheme.

Henry B. Minchin [June 27] as to the proposed Scheme for the Crofton Endowment.

Letter [June 26] read from Rev. F. Dobbin as to the clause regarding religious instruction in the Cork Diocesan Scheme.

A reply, as drafted, directed to be sent.

Letter [June 27] read from Rev. W. Reid, asking if the Commission will receive a deputation from the Presbytery of Magherafelt with regard to the Rainey School, Magherafelt.

To be informed that the Commissioners will receive the deputation on the same occasion as they have arranged to receive a deputation from the General Assembly.

The Scheme for the Ulster Royal School Endowments was finally considered, and copies were ordered for signature by the Judicial Commissioners.

The Draft Schemes for the Strabane Academy, for the Irish Non-Subscribing Presbyterian Orphan Society, and for the Presbyterian Sabbath School Society, were finally approved.

It was ordered:—

That the following Draft Schemes be first published on (this day) June 28, 1889:—

No. 68.—"The Shiel Charity, Bushfort Bridge" (Common Scheme).

No. 69.—"Bishop Hodson's Grammar School, Elphin."

No. 70.—"The Orphan Society of the Association of Irish Non-Subscribing Presbyterians and other Free Christians" (Common Scheme).

No. 71.—"The Strabane Academy."

No. 72.—"The Sabbath School Society for Ireland in connexion with the Presbyterian Church" (Common Scheme).

Instructions were given as to the mode of publication.

The Commissioners adjourned.

Gerald FitzGibbon,
July 3, 1889.

Wm. Edward Ellis, Secretary.

July 1, 1889.

PUBLIC SITTING.

Meeting of the Commission held this day at the Court-house, Baltinglass.

Present:—Lord Justice FitzGibbon, Lord Justice Naish, Rev. Dr. Molloy, Dr. Traill, Professor Dougherty.

Mr. James H. Macartney, Shorthand Writer, was in attendance.

Lady Stratford's Schools, Baltinglass.

The following witnesses were sworn and examined:—

Messrs. G. Dennis.
Claude H. Sweeney.
E. P. O'Kelly.
Mrs. Roberts Kavanagh.

The Commissioners adjourned and visited the present School premises of Lady Stratford's Schools, and the site of the proposed new Schoolhouse; subsequently they proceeded to Kiltegan and inspected the Erasmus Smith's Schoolhouse.

John Naish,
July 5, 1889.

N. D. Murphy,
Chief Clerk and Assistant Secretary.

July 2, 1889.

PUBLIC SITTING.

Meeting of the Commission held this day at D'Israeli's School, Rongh, Rathvilly.

Present:—Lord Justice FitzGibbon, Lord Justice Naish, Rev. Dr. Molloy, Dr. Traill, Professor Dougherty.

Mr. James S. Macartney, Shorthand Writer, was in attendance.

D'Israeli's School, Rathvilly.

Paul A. Brown, Solicitor, appeared for the Rev. J. Phelan, P.P., Rathvilly, and made a statement.

The following witnesses were sworn and examined:—

The Right Rev. The Lord Bishop of Ossory.
James Earl, Master of the School.
Rev. Somerset Quintin.

The Commissioners adjourned.

Previous to the Public Sitting, the Commissioners inspected D'Israeli's School.

John Naish,
July 3, 1889.

N. D. Murphy,
Chief Clerk and Assistant Secretary.'

July 3, 1889.

PUBLIC SITTING.

Meeting of the Commission held this day at the Court-house, New Ross.

Present:—Lord Justice FitzGibbon, Lord Justice Naish, Rev. Dr. Molloy, Dr. Traill, Professor Dougherty.

Mr. James W. Macartney, Shorthand Writer, was in attendance.

Lord Justice FitzGibbon made an opening statement.

New Ross Endowed School.

Henry G. Hinson, Solicitor, appeared on behalf of the Trustees, and made a statement.

J. R. Colfer, Solicitor, appeared on behalf of the Rev. M. Kavanagh, P.P., New Ross, and made a statement.

The following witnesses were sworn and examined:—

Rev. Francis Le Hunte, Incumbent of New Ross.
Rev. Godfrey G. Grome, B.A., Head-master.

Hill School, New Ross.

John T. E. Boyd, Solicitor, appeared on behalf of Colonel Tottenham, and made a statement.

The following witnesses were sworn and examined:—

Rev. F. Le Hunte.
William Cobbe, Master of the School.

The Paul Endowment, Stokestown.

The following witnesses were sworn and examined:—

Joseph W. Deane.
Bryan Todd, Master of the School.
Rev. M. W. Fulham.

J. R. Deane-Drake, Esq., was examined.

The Commissioners adjourned and visited the Endowed School, the Stokestown School, and the Hill School.

John Naish,
July 5, 1889.

N. D. Murphy,
Chief Clerk and Assistant Secretary.

July 4, 1889.

PUBLIC SITTING.

Meeting of the Commission held this day at the Court-house, Wexford.

Present :—Lord Justice FITZGIBBON, Lord Justice NAISH, Rev. Dr. MOLLOY, Dr. TRAILL, Professor DOUGHERTY.

Mr. James S. Macartney, Shorthand Writer, was in attendance.

Lord Justice FitzGibbon made an introductory statement.

THE TATE SCHOOL, WEXFORD.

R. W. Elgee, Solicitor, appeared on behalf of the Trustees, and made a statement.

Michael F. O'Connor, Solicitor, appeared on behalf of the Most Rev. Dr. Browne, Lord Bishop of Ferns.

The following witnesses were sworn and examined :—

Ven. John G. Ardagh, M.A., Archdeacon of Ferns.
R. P. Caldwell, Head Master.
Rev. James K. Latham, B.D.
Benjamin Hughes.

FRANCIS SMITH'S SCHOOL, WEXFORD.

R. W. Elgee, Solicitor and Rev. J. K. Latham made statements.

FERNS DIOCESAN SCHOOL.

R. W. Elgee, Solicitor, made a statement.

ST. PETER'S COLLEGE, WEXFORD.

Very Rev. Luke Doyle, President, was sworn and examined.

DUNCORMACK SCHOOL.

The following witnesses were sworn and examined :—

Rev. R. H. Deane.
Rev. T. Roche, C.C., Duncormack.

Rev. J. Alexander, M.A., made a statement.

THE EDMONDS ENDOWMENT, RATHASPECK.

R. W. Elgee, Solicitor, and Rev. J. K. Latham made statements.

FERNS DIOCESAN SCHEME.

John C. Pounden, Secretary, Ferns Diocesan Council, was sworn and examined, and presented an amended Draft Scheme, which he stated would be satisfactory to the Diocesan Council.

The Commissioners adjourned, and visited the Tate School and St. Peter's College.

JOHN NAISH,
July 5, 1889.

N. D. Murphy,
Chief Clerk and Assistant Secretary.

July 5, 1889.

PUBLIC SITTING.

Meeting of the Commission held this day at Carysfort Royal School, [illegible].

Present :—Lord Justice FITZGIBBON, Lord Justice NAISH, Rev. Dr. MOLLOY, Dr. TRAILL, Professor DOUGHERTY.

Mr. James S. Macartney, Shorthand Writer, was in attendance.

Lord Justice FitzGibbon made an opening statement.

ROYAL SCHOOL, CARYSFORT.

There were present :—

The Most Rev. Dr. Walsh, Lord Archbishop of Dublin.
Rev. John O'Brien, P.P., Aughrim.
Rev. C. J. Hickson, Incumbent of [illegible].
Rev. James Dunphy, P.P., Arklow, and
The Tenants of the Carysfort [illegible]

The following witnesses were sworn and examined:—

Rev. John O'Brien, P.P.
Rev. G. J. Hinkson, M.A.
William Carter.
Thomas Acton.
James Just.
Thomas Stephenson.
William Cheney.

The Lord Archbishop of Dublin made a statement.

The Commissioners adjourned.

Previous to the Public Sitting the Commissioners visited Macreddin National School.

JOHN NAISH,
July 5, 1889.

N. D. Murphy,
Chief Clerk and Assistant Secretary.

July 5, 1889.
PUBLIC SITTING.

Meeting of the Commission held this day at the Court-house, Arklow.

Present:—Lord Justice FITZGIBBON, Lord Justice NAISH, Rev. Dr. MOLLOY, Dr. TRAILL, Professor DOUGHERTY.

Mr. Jas. S. Macartney, Shorthand Writer, was in attendance.

Lord Justice FitzGibbon made an opening statement.

CARYSFORT ROYAL SCHOOL ENDOWMENT.—APPLICATION FOR TRANSFER TO ARKLOW FOR INDUSTRIAL EDUCATION.

Robert Philpott made a statement and handed in the resolutions of the Town Commissioners and of a Public Meeting.

The following witnesses were sworn and examined:—

Rev. James Dunphy, P.P., Arklow.
Rev. R. G. Hallowes, Incumbent of Arklow.
Rev. Wm. Morgan.
John Storey, T.C.
Daniel Condren, C.T.C.
James Tyrrell.
Alexander Taylor.

ARKLOW PAROCHIAL SCHOOL (INCORPORATED SOCIETY).

The following witnesses were examined:

Rev. R. G. Hallowes.
Alexander Taylor.
John Redmond.

The Commissioners adjourned.

JOHN NAISH,
July 6, 1889.

N. D. Murphy,
Chief Clerk and Assistant Secretary.

July 5, 1889.

Meeting of the Commission held this day at the Woodenbridge Hotel, Woodenbridge.

Present:—Lord Justice FITZGIBBON, Lord Justice NAISH, Rev. Dr. MOLLOY, Dr. TRAILL, Professor DOUGHERTY.

Minutes of the previous Public Sittings read and confirmed.

Letter read from Sir Patrick J. Keenan, K.C.M.G. (June 29), as to the proposed Scheme for the Grafton School Endowment.

Letter (June 29) read from W. F. Littledale as to the inquiry at Carysfort Royal School.

Letter read from Rev. D. O'Sullivan (June 29), as to the proposed Scheme for the Grafton Endowment.

A reply, as drafted, ordered to be sent.

Letter (June 28) read from Rev. Jas. B. Keane asking that the sitting to hear the objections lodged against the Draft Scheme for the Gilson Schools, Oldcastle, may be deferred until after September 1.

A reply, as drafted, ordered to be sent.

It was ordered :—

I. That the following Schemes should be advanced with a view to being signed by the Judicial Commissioners on August 11, 1889 :—

No. 37. The Bewand Female Orphan School.
No. 34. The Gwyn and Young Endowments. Revise to be sent to parties interested for their observations.
No. 39. The Phibsborough Sunday and Daily Schools.
No. 43. Guy's Free School, Ballymena.
No. 44. Ballymena Collegiate School.
No. 45. Clonmel Endowed School.
No. 46. Kilkenny College. Revise to be sent to parties interested for their observations.
No. 57. Hewetson School, Clane.
No. 63. The Ledley School Endowments, Ballymacarrett.
No. 67. The Southwell School Endowment, Kinsale.

II. That the following Schemes be advanced with a view to first publication on August 10.

The Preston School, Abbeyleix.
The Downpatrick Blue School.
The Grafton School, Clondrohid.
The Incorporated Society.
The Parochial Schools of the Diocese of Limerick.
The Parochial Schools of the Diocese of Ardfert and Aghadoe.
Brown's Endowment, Ballyhalbert.
The Parochial Schools of the Diocese of Ferns.
The Educational Endowments belonging to the Presbytery of Ballybay.
The Educational Endowments belonging to the Presbytery of Banbridge.

The Commissioners adjourned.

GERALD FITZGIBBON,
July 8, 1889.

Wm. Edward Ellis, Secretary.

July 6, 1889.

PUBLIC SITTING.

Meeting of the Commission held this day at the Court-house, Wicklow.

Present :—Lord Justice FITZGIBBON, Lord Justice NAISH, Rev. Dr. MOLLOY, Dr. TRAILL, Professor DOUGHERTY.

Mr. James S. Macartney, Shorthand Writer, was in attendance.

CROFTON ENDOWED SCHOOL, ASHFORD; WICKLOW DIOCESAN SCHOOL; WICKLOW FREE SCHOOL.

Rev. Henry Rooke, M.A., and Mr. Joseph Smith, were examined.

WICKLOW TYRRELLIAN ORPHAN SCHOOL.

Joseph Smith and Joseph M'Carroll were examined.
The Commissioners adjourned.

JOHN NAISH,
July 11, 1889.

N. D. Murphy,
Chief Clerk and Assistant Secretary.

July 8, 1889.

Meeting of the Commission held this day at the Office, 23, Nassau-street, Dublin.

Present :—Lord Justice FITZGIBBON, Lord Justice NAISH, Rev. Dr. MOLLOY, Professor DOUGHERTY.

Minutes of June 29 and July 6 read and confirmed.

Letter, as drafted, was ordered to be sent to W. G. Brooke, Esq., Chief Clerk to the Lord Chancellor, with reference to the Charities Bequest.

Letters read :—

Messrs. C. M'Dowell and Sons (July 5), enclosing resignation of Edward Rice as Trustee of the Ledley School Endowments.
Rev. T. Harman (July 8), giving consent that the School-house, &c., in the Parish of Templebready should be dealt with under the Cork Diocesan Scheme.

Questions regarding the Leamy School and Mungret College, Limerick, were considered.
The Commissioners adjourned.

JOHN NAISH,
July 11, 1889.

Wm. Edward Ellis, Secretary.

July 6, 1889.

PUBLIC SITTING.

Meeting of the Commission held this day at the Office, 13, Nassau-street, Dublin.

Present:—Lord Justice FitzGibbon, Lord Justice Naish, Rev. Dr. Molloy, Professor Dougherty.

Mr. Charles Ryan, Shorthand Writer, was in attendance.

Hewetson's School, Clane.

On the consideration of the objections lodged against the Draft Scheme published by the Commissioners for this Endowment:—

Thomas Cooke-Trench, J.P., and Rev. William Sherlock, Rector of Clane, appeared in support of the objections of the existing Governing Body of the Endowment.

Rev. S. G. Cotton, appeared in support of his own objection.

The Commissioners adjourned.

John Naish,
July 11, 1889.

Wm. Edward Ellis, Secretary.

July 11, 1889.

Meeting of the Commission held this day at the Office, 13, Nassau-street, Dublin.

Present:—Lord Justice FitzGibbon, Lord Justice Naish, Rev. Dr. Molloy, Dr. Traill, Professor Dougherty.

Minutes of the meeting at Clane on November 10, 1888, of the meeting at Wicklow on July 6, 1889, and of the two preceding meetings, read and confirmed.

Letters read:—

R. K. Connellan, Assistant Master, Gilson Schools, Oldcastle (July 4), as to his vested interests.

C. W. Osborne (July 5), on behalf of the owner of the Crofton Estate, as to the proposed Scheme for the Crofton School, [illegible].

Rev. S. G. Cotton (July 9), as to the Scheme for the Parochial Schools of that Diocese.

John C. Fox (July 9), as to a Scheme for the Parochial Schools of the Diocese of Ferns.

Rev. T. Jordan, D.D. (July 9), enclosing Examiner's Report for the year 1888, on the Rainey School, Magherafelt.

William Thompson (July 10), as to inquiry to be held at [illegible] Endowed School.

Thomas Acton, D.L. (July 10), as to the Carysfort Royal School Endowment.

Letter (July 9) read from Rev. S. Clarke, as to the position of the Minister and Churchwardens of a parish under the Cork Diocesan Scheme.

A reply, as drafted, ordered to be sent.

The Secretary was directed to inform the Rev. H. Le B. Kennedy, Head Master, Clonmel Endowed School, that the Commissioners propose to sign the Scheme for that Endowment, with others, on August 12, 1889.

Questions regarding the following Limerick Endowments were considered:—

Mungret College.
Leamy's Free School.
Diocesan School (£30 per annum).

The letters to be published in the Annual Report with reference to the Scheme for the Ulster Royal School Endowments were settled.

Gerald FitzGibbon,
July 12, 1889.

Wm. Edward Ellis, Secretary.

July 11, 1889.

PUBLIC SITTING.

Meeting of the Commission held this day at the Office, 23, Nassau-street, Dublin.

Present :—Lord Justice FITZGIBBON, Lord Justice NAISH, Rev. Dr. MOLLOY, Dr. TRAILL, Professor DOUGHERTY.

Mr. Charles Ryan, Shorthand Writer, was in attendance.

RAINEY SCHOOL, MAGHERAFELT.

Deputations consisting of the following persons attended on behalf of the General Assembly of the Presbyterian Church, and of the Presbytery of Magherafelt :—

REPRESENTING THE GENERAL ASSEMBLY.

Right Rev. The Moderator of the General Assembly.
Rev. John H. Orr, D.D., Clerk of Assembly.
Rev. H. B. Wilson, D.D., Cookstown.
Rev. J. M. Hamilton, M.A., Dunean.

REPRESENTING THE PRESBYTERY OF MAGHERAFELT.

Rev. W. Reid.
Rev. George Gillespie.

Statements were made by each of the above with regard to the Draft Scheme published for the above named Endowment.

The Commissioners adjourned.

GERALD FITZGIBBON,
July 12, 1889.

Wm. Edward Ellis, Secretary.

July 12, 1889.

Meeting of the Commission held this day at the Office, 23, Nassau-street, Dublin.

Present :—Lord Justice FITZGIBBON, Rev. Dr. MOLLOY, Dr. TRAILL, Professor DOUGHERTY.

Minutes of the two preceding meetings read and confirmed.

Letter [July 13] read from Colonel W. D. Marsh, C.R.E., in Ireland, as to the purchase of the Portora Royal Schools Buildings by the War Department.

The reply as already sent was approved.

Letter [July 10] read from Mr. John M'Laughlin, Caretaker, at Portora Royal School, as to his vested interests, if any.

A reply, as drafted, directed to be sent.

Questions regarding the Crofton Endowment, Clondrohid, County Cork, and the Ballyroan Endowment, Queen's County, were discussed.

The Commissioners adjourned.

JOHN NAISH,
July 15, 1889.

Wm. Edward Ellis, Secretary.

July 15, 1889.

Meeting of the Commission held this day at the Office, 23, Nassau-street, Dublin.

Present :—Lord Justice FITZGIBBON, Lord Justice NAISH, Rev. Dr. MOLLOY.

Minutes of preceding meeting read and confirmed.

Letters read :—

W. G. Brooke, Chief Clerk to Lord Chancellor (July 13), as to the Charlton Trust.
Rev. J. W. Aitkin (May 2), as to the Barry Baldwin Bequest, Clonakilty.

Letter [June 29] read from Joseph John Murphy, Secretary, Diocesan Council of Down and Connor and Dromore, as to certain Endowments belonging to the Magdalene Church Schools, Belfast, and to the Cork Church Education Society.

A reply, as drafted, directed to be sent.

A letter, as drafted, was directed to be written to the Registrar of Erasmus Smith's Board asking if his Board desire that certain Parochial School buildings and premises in the Diocese of Ferns vested in the Erasmus Smith's Board, should be transferred to a Diocesan Body to be incorporated under a Scheme framed by the Commission.

The Secretary was directed, in the cases of the Dioceses of Leighlin and Limerick, to write a letter as drafted to the Bishop and Diocesan Secretary, asking in each case for a list of names from whom the Commissioners might select the first clerical and lay representative Governors to be named in the Scheme.

Questions regarding the following Limerick Endowments were considered :—

Mungret College.
Leamy's Free Schools.
Diocesan Schools (£20 per annum).

The Commissioners adjourned.

GERALD FITZGIBBON,
July 19, 1889.

William Edward Ellis, Secretary.

July 19, 1889.

Meeting of the Commission held this day at the Office, 63, Nassau-street, Dublin.

Present :—Lord Justice FITZGIBBON, Lord Justice NAISH, Rev. Dr. MOLLOY, Professor DOUGHERTY.

Minutes of preceding meeting read and confirmed.

Letters read :—

The Clerk of the Privy Council, Dublin Castle (July 16), as to the Draft Scheme published for the Munster Dairy School and Agricultural Institute.

The Clerk of the Privy Council, Dublin Castle (July 18), sending notice of Public Sitting on July 30, to hear the objections lodged with the Privy Council against the following schemes :—

No. 35. The Robertson Endowments.
No. 38. The Baltimore Fishery School.
No. 40. The Londonderry Academical Institution.
No. 48. The Thomastown Parochial School.
No. 50. The Drelincourt, Mall, and Callanstreet Schools, Armagh.
No. 51. The Sullivan Schools, Holywood.

Letter (July 17) read from Jas. W. Deane as to Paul's Endowment, New Ross.

A reply, as drafted, ordered to be sent.

Letter (July 16) read from the Secretary, Commissioners of Education, asking for the consent of the Educational Endowments Commissioners to certain proposed improvements and repairs being made at the Mullaghmore School House.

Letter enclosing the written consent of the Commissioners ordered to be sent.

Letter (July 16) read from Rev. F. H. Ringwood, LL.D., Head Master, Royal School Dungannon, asking how soon he could retire from that position.

A reply, as drafted, ordered to be sent.

Letter (July 18) read from Rev. Alexander Gordon, Hon. Sec., Orphan Society of the Association of Irish Non-Subscribing Presbyterians and other Free Christians, enclosing objections and amendments to the Draft Scheme published for the Society, and asking if the Commissioners would have an interview with him with regard to same.

A reply, as drafted, directed to be sent.

The Secretary was directed to write letters in terms as drafted :—

To the Secretaries, Commissioners of Charitable Donations and Bequests, in reply to Mr. Gernon's inquiry about Anne Hall's Charity.

To the Secretary of the Incorporated Society, for list of existing Committee of Fifteen, and also as to the changes, if any, in the list of members of the Society for the past years.

In the case of Brown's Trust, Ballyhalbert, for the names of the existing Trustees of the Will, and for particulars of the Endowments.

To the Clerk of the Presbytery of Banbridge asking for the names of six laymen to be named as lay Trustees on the proposed Governing Body of the endowments belonging to or under the care of congregations of the Presbytery of Banbridge.

To the Secretary of the Bank of Ireland, inquiring whether he could arrange to check in his office the particulars which have been furnished to the Commissioners of Government Stock belonging to the Endowments dealt with by their Schemes.

The Draft Schemes for the Endowments of the Presbytery of Ballybay, and for the Endowments of the Diocese of Ferns, were considered and finally approved.

The Commissioners adjourned.

JOHN NAISH.
July 26, 1889.

Wm. Edward Ellis, Secretary.

July 23, 1889.

PUBLIC SITTING.

Meeting of the Commission held this day at the Endowed School, Antrim.

Present:—Rev. Dr. MOLLOY, Dr. TRAILL, Professor DOUGHERTY.

Mr. John M'Bride, Shorthand Writer, was in attendance.

ANTRIM ENDOWED SCHOOL.

Professor DOUGHERTY made an introductory statement.

The following witnesses were sworn and examined:—

David W. Shaw, *Secretary*.
Robert Gillespie.
Rev. A. Millar.
Rev. James Mitchell.
Andrew Clements, *Head Master*.
Miss Maria Harding.
Dr. William Thomson.

The Commissioners adjourned.

Previous to the Public Sitting the Commissioners visited the School.

ANTHONY TRAILL,
November 12, 1889.

N. D. Murphy,
Chief Clerk and Assistant Secretary.

July 26, 1889.

Meeting of the Commission held this day at the Office, 83, [illegible]-street, Dublin.

Present:—Lord Justice FITZGIBBON, Lord Justice NAISH, Rev. Dr. MOLLOY, Professor DOUGHERTY.

Minutes of the meeting of July 19, read and confirmed.

Letters read:—

The Secretaries, Commissioners of Charitable Donations and Bequests (July 23), as to Anne Hall's Charity, County Fermanagh.

Rev. G. J. Hickson (July 16), as to the Carysfort Royal School Endowment.

W. P. Chapman, Secretary, Incorporated Society (July 24), sending list of present members of the Society.

The Right Rev. The Lord Bishop of Limerick (July 25), sending names for Governing Body for the Limerick Parochial School Endowments.

The Right Rev. The Lord Bishop of Ossory (July 22), sending names for the Leighlin Parochial School Endowments.

Letters read:—

Thomas Laffan (July 24), as to objections lodged against the Draft Scheme for the Cashel Corporation School Endowment.

Ven. W. C. Gorman, M.A., Archdeacon of Ossory (July 24), as to the Scheme for the Thomastown Parochial School.

Rev. W. Moore Morgan (July 24), asking on behalf of the Lord Primate for a copy of the evidence taken at the sitting held on July 11, 1889, with reference to the Rainey School, Magherafelt.

W. Quartus Ewart (July 23), asking for extension of time to send objections to Draft Scheme for the Ladley School Endowments.

The replies already sent by direction of Lord Justice FitzGibbon, approved.

Letters read:—

Rev. A. Millar (July 24), enclosing letters of appointment of Trustees of the Antrim Endowed School.

The Right Hon. The Earl of Courtown (July 22), as to certain clauses in the proposed Ferns Diocesan Scheme.

The Right Rev. Dr. Gregg, Lord Bishop of Cork (July 23), sending observations on and objections to the Draft Scheme published for the Dioceses of Cork, Cloyne, and Ross.

Rev. W. Moore Morgan (July 23), asking if a School building with a special trust can be vested in the proposed Diocesan Board for the Diocese of Armagh.

Thomas H. Jermyn, Secretary to the Trustees of St. Stephen's Hospital, Cork (July 23), enclosing objections to the Draft Scheme published for that Institution.

Rev. Edward J. Hartrick, Hon. Secretary Down and Connor and Dromore Church Education Society (July 18), enclosing Resolution of the Society as to clauses 18, 19, 20, and 21 of the Draft Scheme published for the Parochial Schools, &c., of the Diocese of Meath.

Replies as drafted ordered to be sent.

The Scheme for the Clonmel Endowed School, and the Draft Scheme for the Southwell Endowment, Downpatrick, were considered and amended, and ordered for final approval at the next meeting.

The Draft Schemes for the Parochial Schools of the Diocese of Limerick, for the Parochial Schools of the Diocese of Leighlin, and for the endowments belonging to the Presbytery of Ballybay, were finally approved, subject to completion of the Schedules to each.

The Secretary was directed to write again to Rev. David Parks, asking for the names of six laymen to be named on the Governing Body for the Endowments of the Presbytery of Banbridge.

The Commissioners, having fixed the Agenda for Friday, August 2, and for Wednesday, August 7, adjourned.

JOHN NAISH,
August 2, 1889.

Wm. Edward Ellis, Secretary.

August 2, 1889.

Meeting of the Commission held this day at the Office, 23, Nassau-street, Dublin.

Present :—Lord Justice FITZGIBBON, Lord Justice NAISH, Rev. Dr. MOLLOY, Dr. TRAILL, Professor DOUGHERTY.

Minutes of preceding meeting read and confirmed.

Letters read :—

Edward P. Brennan, Registrar, Erasmus Smith's Board (July 27), as to the School buildings in the Diocese of Ferns vested in his Board.

Thomas H. Jermyn (July 27), acknowledging receipt of letter of the Commission with regard to objections lodged by the Trustees of St. Stephen's Hospital, Cork.

Rev. D. O'Sullivan (July 29), as to the Crofton Endowment, Clondrohid, county Cork.

Rev. James Dowd (August 1), returning Schedule corrected for the Scheme for the Parochial Schools of the Diocese of Limerick.

The Secretaries, Commissioners of Charitable Donations and Bequests (July 30), as to Anne Hall's Charity.

Rev. Wm. W. Carven (August 1), sending correction to Schedule of Ferns Diocesan Scheme.

Letters read from the following in reference to the Draft Scheme published for the Parochial Schools of the Dioceses of Cork, Cloyne, and Ross :—

Rev. Walter Lamb (July 26), Donoughmore.
Ven. Archdeacon of Ross (July 29), Lisle.
Rev. Robert F. Clarke (July 29), Brinny.
Rev. S. MacConnell (July 30), Kilbrogan.
Rev. Wm. H. Powell (July 30), } Riversdale School.
J. W. Alcock-Stawell (July 31), }
Rev. Robert St. J. Ainsworth (July 30), Athnowen.
Rev. A. D. Macnamara (July 30), Ballymoney.
Rev. R. H. Meade (August 1), Rincurran.

Letters read :—

Thomas Laffan (July 29), as to the hearing of the objections lodged against the Draft Scheme published for the Cashel Corporation School Endowment.

Very Rev. Wm. Warburton, Dean of Elphin (July 27), as to the Draft Scheme published for Bishop Hodson's Grammar School, Elphin.

Joseph John Murphy, Secretary, Down, Connor and Dromore Diocesan Council (July 30), as to the conscience clause in the Ferns Diocesan Scheme.

A reply, as drafted, ordered to be sent.

Letters read from the following, sending objections to the Draft Scheme published for the Endowments of and belonging to Congregations under the care of the Presbytery of Dublin :—

Rev. J. M. Hamilton, Clerk of the Dublin Presbytery (July 31).
Walter Warrick, Secretary to Committee of Christ's Church, Rathgar (July 30).

Letter (July 26) read from Rev. J. Canon Cotter, P.P., Kinsale, objecting to the Draft Scheme published for the Southwell School Endowment, Kinsale.

The Secretary was directed to write, in terms as drafted, to the Rev. J. Canon Cotter, and to the Rev. J. L. Darling, from whom objections have been received to the Draft Scheme, enclosing to each copy of the objection made by the other.

Letter (July 30) addressed to Lord Justice FitzGibbon, read from Rev. Francis Le Hunte, with reference to conscience clause in proposed Ferns Diocesan Scheme.

The Commission approved of the answer proposed to be sent by Lord Justice FitzGibbon.

The Draft Scheme for the Southwell Charity, and the Parochial Schools, Downpatrick, for Joseph Brown's Endowments, county Down, and for the Endowments of and belonging to Congregations under the care of the Presbytery of Banbridge, were considered and finally approved.

The Scheme for the Clonmel Grammar School was considered.

Mr. Henry T. Dix had an interview with the Commissioners in reference to the revised Scheme for the Bertrand Female Orphan School, Dublin.

The Commissioners adjourned.

J. B. Dougherty,
August 8, 1889.

Wm. Edward Ellis, Secretary.

August 8, 1889.

Meeting of the Commission held this day at the Offices 23, Nassau-street, Dublin.

Present :—Lord Justice FitzGibbon, Lord Justice Naish, Rev. Dr. Molloy, Professor Dougherty.

Minutes of preceding meeting read and confirmed.

Letters read :—

H. T. Dix, Solicitor, one of the Governors of the School (Aug. 3), and the Secretaries, Commissioners of Charitable Donations and Bequests (Aug. 3), as to the Scheme for the Bertrand Female Orphan School, Dublin.

Thomas H. Jermyn (Aug. 3), sending objections of Trustees to the Draft Scheme, published for St. Stephen's Hospital, Cork.

Joseph W. Deane (Aug. 6), enclosing documents relating to Ford's Charity, New Ross.

R. A. Miller (Aug. 3), sends Bank book, accounts, &c., of Jackson's Endowment attached to the Forkhill Endowed School.

J. W. Alcock Sewell (Aug. 6), stating that he does not want Riverdale School to be included in the Cork Diocesan Scheme.

The Hon. Somerset Ward (Aug. 7), sending Conveyances, &c., relating to Bangor Endowed School.

John G. Fenwick (Aug. 7), returning proposed Draft Scheme for the Parochial Schools of the Diocese of Ferns, approved by the Ferns Diocesan Council.

Rev. David Purdy (Aug. 6), sending names for Governing Body for the Presbytery of Banbridge Schemes.

Letters read :—

Rev. John Kinghan (Aug. 5), as to the Inspection Clause in the Draft Scheme published for the Presbyterian Sabbath School Society.

Joseph J. Murphy, Secretary, Diocesan Council of Down, Connor, and Dromore (Aug. 3 and 5), as to the Conscience Clause in Schemes already published for Parochial Schools.

C. E. D. Black, Secretary, Royal Commission on Deaf and Dumb and the Blind (Aug. 6), enclosing paper prepared unofficially by the Assistant Secretary, at the request of the late Dr. Robert M'Donnell, and asking if it should be published in the Report of his Commission, as emanating from the Educational Endowments (Ireland) Commission.

Replies, as drafted, ordered to be sent.

The Draft Scheme for the Parochial Schools of the Diocese of Ferns was considered and finally approved.

The Secretary was directed to return the original Lease of Mungret College to the Very Rev. Thomas Head, S.J., Rector of Mungret College.

The Memorandum drawn up by the Commission as to the Limerick Endowments was considered, amended, and finally approved.

Copies of same ordered to be sent to the following :—

The Right Rev. Dr. Graves, Lord Bishop of Limerick.
The Most Rev. Dr. O'Dwyer, Lord Bishop of Limerick.
The Right Hon. Lord Emly.
Rev. Thomas Head, S.J.
All the Trustees of Mungret College.
All the Trustees of Leamy School.
Very Rev. The Dean of Limerick.
Rev. Canon Gregg, M.A.
All witnesses at Limerick Inquiry.
The Commissioners of Education.
The Commissioners of National Education.
The Commissioners of Charitable Donations and Bequests.

It was ordered :—

That the following Draft Schemes be first published on August 10, 1889 :—

No. 73.—"The Parochial Schools of the Diocese of Ferns" (Common Scheme).
No. 74.—"The Southwell Charity and the Parochial Schools, Downpatrick" (Common Scheme).
No. 75.—"The Endowments of and belonging to Congregations under the care of the Presbytery of Ballybay" (Common Scheme).
No. 76.—"The Parochial Schools of the Diocese of Limerick" (Common Scheme).
No. 77.—"The Parochial Schools of the Diocese of Leighlin" (Common Scheme).
No. 78.—"The Endowments of and belonging to Congregations under the care of the Presbytery of Banbridge" (Common Scheme).
No. 79.—"Joseph Brown's Endowments, county Down."

And instructions were given as to the mode of publication.

The Commissioners adjourned.

GERALD FITZGIBBON,
October 1, 1889.

WM. EDWARD ELLIS, Secretary.

September 24, 1889.

Meeting of the Commission held this day at the Office, 23, Nassau-street, Dublin.

Present :—Lord Justice FITZGIBBON, Dr. MOLLOY, Professor DOUGHERTY.

Objections and amendments to the following Draft Schemes were submitted :—

No. 69. BISHOP HODSON'S GRAMMAR SCHOOL, ELPHIN.

Very Rev. The Dean of Elphin (Aug. 20 and 21).
Very Rev. The Dean of Elphin (Aug. 13), enclosing resolution of Chapter of Cathedral, Elphin.
Very Rev. The Dean of Elphin (Aug. 24), enclosing copy of resolution passed at meeting of St. John's Select Vestry, Sligo.
Very Rev. The Dean of Elphin (Aug. 24), enclosing two memorials.
W. T. Davidson, Hon. Sec. (Aug. 15), sends objections of St. John's Select Vestry, Sligo.
Very Rev. The Dean of Elphin (Aug. 27), enclosing memorial of inhabitants of Croghan.
Very Rev. The Dean of Elphin (Sept. 3), sends some additional names for preceding memorial.
Very Rev. The Dean of Elphin (Sept. 16), as to meeting of Diocesan Synod.
Sir Robert Hodson, Bart. (Aug. 27).
Venerable The Archdeacon of Elphin (Sept. 23).

No. 70. ORPHAN SOCIETY OF IRISH NON-SUBSCRIBING PRESBYTERIANS AND OTHER FREE CHRISTIANS.

Rev. Alexander Gordon, M.A. (Aug. 23), on behalf of the Association.

No. 71. THE STRABANE ACADEMY.

Moses Kerr, Principal (Aug. 17).
The Committee of the Academy (Aug. 10).
Rev. John Irwin, Secretary (Sept. 4).

No. 72. THE SABBATH SCHOOL SOCIETY FOR IRELAND, IN CONNEXION WITH THE PRESBYTERIAN CHURCH.

Rev. George Shaw, D.D. (Sept. 9), on behalf of the Society.

No. 73. Parochial Schools of the Diocese of Ferns.

Rev. Charles L. [illegible] (Aug. 16), amendment to Schedule.
Rev. Jas. F. M. [illegible] (Aug. 17), wants [illegible] School and [illegible] School struck out of Schedule.
Rev. William W. Cowan (Aug. 27 and Sept. 6), wants Schools added to Schedule.

No. 74. Southwell Charity and the Parochial Schools, Downpatrick.

Dr. J. Wybrants Olphert (Aug. 13 and 21).
John B. M'Connell (Aug. 15 and Sept. 11), amendment to Schedule.
Very Rev. The Dean of Down (Aug. 20).

No. 75. Endowments, &c., of Presbytery of Ballybay.

Rev. James Morell (Aug. 12), addition to Schedule.
Rev. James [illegible] (Aug. 13), amendment to Schedule.
Rev. R. R. Drysdale (Aug. 13), " "
Rev. James M'Kee (Sept. 6), " "
Rev. R. H. Smythe (Sept. 7), " "
Rev. Samuel Lowden (Sept. 9), " "
Rev. James M'Gully (Sept. 14), stating the Presbytery of Ballybay approve of the Scheme itself, but send amended Schedule.

No. 77. Parochial Schools of the Diocese of Leighlin.

Rev. John Finlay (Sept. 21), stating the Diocesan Council approve of the Scheme, subject to a slight alteration in Clause 23, but send an amended Schedule.

Letters read :—

The Clerk of the Privy Council (Aug. 10), returning the Scheme for the Londonderry Academical Institution, with a declaration.

Rev. J. W. Fisher (Aug. 14), as to getting consent that a certain School in his parish should be dealt with in Leighlin Diocesan Scheme.

Rev. J. Lindsey Darling (Aug. 16 and Sept. 4), and Rev. J. Canon Cotter (Aug. 20 and Sept. 18), as to the objections already lodged to the Draft Scheme, published for the Southwell School Endowments, Kinsale.

W. D. Reeves Parker (Aug. 17), asking that Glenbrook School should be included in the Cork Diocesan Scheme.

Rev. F. R. S. Read (Aug. 19), as to Kilfinane School, in the Diocese of Limerick.

The Secretaries, National Education Board (Aug. 23), as to the Draft Scheme for the Munster Dairy School and Agricultural Institute.

Rev. John Haines (Aug. 27), as to Endowments to be vested in Diocesan Board of Cork, Cloyne, and Ross.

Right Hon. Lord Emly, and other Trustees of Mungret College, as to the Memorandum drawn up by the Commission with reference to Limerick Endowments.

Rev. J. K. Leliane (Sept. 5), enclosing suggestions of the Trustees of Tate's School, Wexford, as to including the School in Ferns Diocesan Scheme.

Letter (Aug. 10) read from Joseph J. Murphy, Secretary, Diocesan Council of Down and Connor and Dromore, as to certain clauses in the Ferns Diocesan Scheme.

Reply as already sent by direction of Lord Justice FitzGibbon approved.

Letters read :—

Rev. Henry W. Hallam (Aug. 18), as to certain Endowments in his Parish (Mossey).

Joseph J. Murphy, Secretary, Diocesan Council of Down and Connor and Dromore (Aug. 20), as to the wording of certain clauses in the Ferns Diocesan Scheme.

L. A. Beamish, Honorary Secretary (Sept. 7), enclosing resolutions of the Committee of the Munster Agricultural and Dairy School, and of the County Kerry Grand Jury, with reference to the Draft Scheme published for the above Institution.

Rev. James Dowd, Secretary, Diocesan Council (Sept. 11), stating he has not information to fill up "Form of Income."

James Orgam, Secretary, Congregational Union of Ireland (Sept. 12), asking that copies of Schemes, as published, may be sent to him.

Rev. Frederick Dobbin (Sept. 18), asking as to the reading of Clause 20 of the Cork Diocesan Scheme.

Rev. James Dowd, Secretary, Limerick Diocesan Council (Sept. 18), as to the Expenses Clause of the Scheme published for the Parochial Schools of the Diocese of Limerick.

Replies, as drafted, directed to be sent.

Letter (Aug. 15) read from Very Rev. The Dean of Cloyne, as to an Endowment for Almshouses in his parish.

The Secretary was directed to write for particulars as to foundation.

Letter (Aug. 21) read from Rev. George Shaw, asking for extension of time to send in objections to the Draft Scheme published for the Presbyterian Sabbath School Society.

Reply as already sent at direction of Professor Dougherty approved.

Letter (Sept. 3) read from Rev. Henry Roche, asking for information as to a grant from Lord Chesterfield for a School at Wicklow.

The Secretary was directed to find out particulars of it.

Letters (Sept. 9 and 16) read from Rev. Thomas Browne, asking that papers lodged by him with reference to Mungret Agricultural School should be returned.

Ordered:—That the papers be returned, and that for the other documents he be referred to the Commissioners of National Education, in whose custody they appear to be.

Letter (Sept. 16) read from Rev. John Stewart, asking that a Scheme be prepared for the Endowments of the Presbytery of Ballymena, on the same lines as the one published for the Banbridge Presbytery.

Reply, as usual in similar cases, ordered to be sent.

Letter (Sept. 17) read from Wm. J. De Vere, Secretary, Gilson Schools, Oldcastle, asking that the Chancery Scheme for those Schools lodged by him in the office, be returned.

Ordered:—That the Scheme be returned as requested.

Letters read:—

Rev. A. Miller (Sept. 21), asking that Bank Book of Jamieson's Charity be returned.

Messrs. L'Estrange and Brett (Sept. 21), asking for copies of letters written at direction of Commission on January 18, 1889.

J. G. Rainsford (Sept. 3), asking that a letter from Lord Roden to him which he lodged in the office be returned to him.

Ordered:—That the several applications be complied with.

The Secretary was directed to write to the Solicitors of the Gwyn and Young Endowments in terms as drafted, asking them for corrected particulars of the funds, and the names of the present annuitants and the amount of the annuities still payable.

The Commissioners adjourned.

GERALD FITZGIBBON,
October 1, 1889.

Wm. Edward Ellis, Secretary.

September 24, 1889.

Meeting of the Commission held this day at the Office, 13, Nassau-street, Dublin.

Present:—Lord Justice FITZGIBBON, Dr. MOLLOY, Professor DOUGHERTY.

Letters read:—

Very Rev. Thomas Head, S.J., Rector, Mungret College (Sept. 24), sending printed copies of pamphlet drawn up by Rev. Wm. Rowan, S.J., as to the recommendations of the Commissioners on the Limerick Endowments.

Rev. M. F. Barke (Sept. 23), asking for an Endowment for St. Andrew's Seminary, Kilfinane, County Limerick.

Rev. J. M. Hamilton, Clerk of the Dublin Presbytery (Sept. 23), enclosing original Deeds:—(1) relating to School, Church, and Manse of Drogheda Congregation. (2) relating to site on which are erected the Church and School of Tullamore Congregation, and also letter of consent of A. L. Eckford, only remaining Trustee of latter Congregation.

Letters (Sept. 21 and 23) read from B. Bagwell as to the Scheme signed by the Judicial Commissioners for the Clonmel Grammar School.

That the letters be returned to Mr. Bagwell with a statement that he is under a mistake in sending them to the Commissioners, as the Scheme is now before the Privy Council, and any observations and amendments should be forwarded to the Clerk of the Privy Council.

Letter (Sept. 13) addressed to the Assistant Secretary, read from Rev. Br. John P. Lynch, Galway, asking for certain documents relating to the Erasmus Smith Endowments, and also for a copy of the Commissioners' Report for the year 1887.

That the documents asked for be sent if they are in the Office.

The Draft Annual Report for the year ending September 30, 1889, was considered.

The Commissioners adjourned.

GERALD FITZGIBBON,
October 1, 1889.

Wm. Edward Ellis, Secretary.

PART III.

MINUTES OF THE JUDICIAL COMMISSIONERS.

October 5, 1888.

Meeting of the Judicial Commissioners held this day at the Office, 23, Nassau-street, Dublin.

Minutes of preceding meeting read and confirmed.

Mr. John M'Bride was appointed to take a shorthand report of the Sittings of the Commission to be held at Londonderry, Coleraine, Magherafelt, Ballymena, Holywood, Bangor, Donaghadee, Ballywalter, Belfast, Carrickfergus, Larne, and Downpatrick, from October 19 to October 29, inclusive.

GERALD FITZGIBBON.
November 23, 1888.

Wm. Edward Ellis, Secretary.

November 19, 1888.

Meeting of the Judicial Commissioners held this day at the Four Courts, Dublin.

The Scheme for the Royal Irish Academy of Music and the Coulson Endowment was considered.

GERALD FITZGIBBON,
November 23, 1888.

Wm. Edward Ellis, Secretary.

November 23, 1888.

Meeting of the Judicial Commissioners held this day at the Office, 23, Nassau-street, Dublin.

Minutes of the two preceding meetings read and confirmed.

The Scheme for the Royal Irish Academy of Music and the Coulson Endowment was further considered.

GERALD FITZGIBBON,
November 30, 1888.

Wm. Edward Ellis, Secretary.

November 30, 1888.

Meeting of the Judicial Commissioners held this day at the Office, 23, Nassau-street, Dublin.

Minutes of preceding meeting read and confirmed.

The Scheme for the Royal Irish Academy of Music and the Coulson Endowment was further considered and revised.

The Secretary was directed to send a proof of the revised Scheme to the parties interested, together with a letter, as drafted.

GERALD FITZGIBBON,
December 13, 1888.

Wm. Edward Ellis, Secretary.

December 13, 1888.

Meeting of the Judicial Commissioners held this day at the Office, 23, Nassau-street, Dublin.

Minutes of preceding meeting read and confirmed.

Arrangements were made for the closing of the Office during the usual Christmas holidays.

GERALD FITZGIBBON,
January 8, 1889.

Wm. Edward Ellis, Secretary.

January 3, 1889.

Meeting of the Judicial Commissioners held this day at the Office, 23, Nassau-street, Dublin.

Minutes of preceding meeting read and confirmed.

Letter (Jan. 4) read from Rev. N. W. Carre, stating that one of the Trustees of the Phibsborough Sunday and Daily Schools, Dublin, has died.

The Secretary was directed to send a copy of the letter addressed by the Commissioners to the Salters Company, to all parties interested in the Rainey School, Magherafelt.

GERALD FITZGIBBON,
January 16, 1889.

Wm. Edward Ellis, Secretary.

January 16, 1889.

Meeting of the Judicial Commissioners held this day at the Office, 23, Nassau-street, Dublin.

Minutes of preceding meeting read and confirmed.

Letter (Jan. 17), read from Sir Francis W. Brady, Hon. Sec. Royal Irish Academy of Music, as to the revised Scheme for the Academy, and the Coulson Bequest.

A reply, as drafted, ordered to be sent, and a letter was also directed to be sent to Alderman V. B. Dillon on the subject.

The Scheme of the Royal Irish Academy of Music and the Coulson Bequest was further considered.

GERALD FITZGIBBON,
February 15, 1889.

Wm. Edward Ellis, Secretary.

February 15, 1889.

Meeting of the Judicial Commissioners held this day at 10, Merrion-square, Dublin.

Minutes of the preceding meeting read and confirmed.

The Scheme for the Ulster Royal School Endowments was revised and the objections to same considered.

GERALD FITZGIBBON,
March 21, 1889.

Wm. Edward Ellis, Secretary.

March 21, 1889.

Meeting of the Judicial Commissioners held this day at the Office, 23, Nassau-street, Dublin.

Minutes of preceding meeting read and confirmed.

The Secretary was directed to write in terms as drafted to the Manager of the Freeman's Journal, Limited, with reference to the rate at which advertisements of Draft Schemes should be inserted.

GERALD FITZGIBBON,
March 29, 1889.

Wm. Edward Ellis, Secretary.

March 29, 1889.

Meeting of the Judicial Commissioners held this day at the Office, 23, Nassau-street, Dublin.

Minutes of preceding meeting read and confirmed.

The Scheme for the Robertson Endowments, County Donegal, was considered and revised.

The Secretary was directed to send copies of the revised Scheme to the Secretary of the Robertson Trustees, saying that the Draft Scheme has been revised with due regard to the objections received and to the evidence taken at Londonderry; that some amendments suggested by the Meath Diocesan Scheme (copy enclosed) have been introduced, and that the Scheme, with any further observations, be returned not later than April 17; also asking for a certificate of the correctness of the Schedules, specially noting the necessity for including all Schools aided by Robertson Funds, and correctly describing the premises.

The Scheme for the Lurgan Queen-street National School was considered.

GERALD FITZGIBBON,
April 16, 1889.

Wm. Edward Ellis, Secretary.

April 16, 1889.

Meeting of the Judicial Commissioners held this day at the Office, 23, Nassau-street, Dublin.

Minutes of preceding meeting read and confirmed.

It was ordered :—

That the offices of the Commission be closed at Easter.

GERALD FITZGIBBON.
April 18, 1889.

Wm. Edward Ellis, Secretary.

April 17, 1889.

Meeting of the Judicial Commissioners held this day at the Four Courts, Dublin.

The Scheme for the Lurgan Queen-street National School was amended and finally approved.

GERALD FITZGIBBON,
April 18, 1889.

Wm. Edward Ellis, Secretary.

April 18, 1889.

Meeting of the Judicial Commissioners held this day at the Office, 23, Nassau-street, Dublin.

Minutes of the two preceding meetings read and confirmed.

The Schemes for the following Endowments were considered and amended :—

No. 38.—The Baltimore Fishery School.
No. 39.—The Royal Irish Academy of Music and the Coulson Endowment.
No. 40.—The Londonderry Academical Institution.
No. 41.—"The Church of Ireland Jubilee Fund," for the Education of Children of the Clergy.
No. 42.—The Thomastown Parochial School.
No. 50.—The Drelincourt, Mall, and Callan-street Schools, Armagh; and Primate Robinson's Armagh Loan Fund.
No. 51.—The Sullivan Schools, Holywood.
No. 52.—The Rochelle Seminary, Cork.

GERALD FITZGIBBON,
April 23, 1889.

Wm. Edward Ellis, Secretary.

April 23, 1889.

Meeting of the Judicial Commissioners held this day at the Office, 23, Nassau-street, Dublin.

Minutes of preceding meeting read and confirmed.

The Schemes for the following Endowments were further considered and finally approved :—

No. 35.—The Robertson Endowments.
No. 38.—The Baltimore Fishery School.
No. 39.—The Royal Irish Academy of Music and the Coulson Endowment.
No. 40.—The Londonderry Academical Institution.
No. 41.—"The Church of Ireland Jubilee Fund," for the Education of the Children of the Clergy.
No. 49.—The Thomastown Parochial School.
No. 51.—The Sullivan Schools, Holywood.
No. 52.—The Rochelle Seminary, Cork.

GERALD FITZGIBBON,
April 24, 1889.

Wm. Edward Ellis, Secretary.

April 24, 1889.

Meeting of the Judicial Commissioners held this day at the Office, 23, Nassau-street, Dublin.

Minutes of preceding meeting read and confirmed.

Schemes framed by the Judicial Commissioners for the future government and management of the following Endowments were duly signed :—

No. 33.—The Robertson Endowments and other Endowments in the Diocese of Raphoe.
No. 34.—The Queen-street National School, Lurgan.
No. 35.—The Baltimore Fishery School.
No. 39.—The Royal Irish Academy of Music, and the Coulson Endowment.
No. 40.—The Londonderry Academical Institution.
No. 41.—"The Church of Ireland Jubilee Fund"; for the Education of Children of the Clergy.
No. 42.—The Thomastown Parochial School.
No. 50.—The Drelincourt, Mall, and College-street Schools, Armagh, and "Primate Robinson's Armagh Loan Fund."
No. 51.—The Sullivan Schools, Holywood, County Down.
No. 52.—The Rochelle Seminary, Cork.

The Secretary was directed to forward the above Schemes to the Chief Secretary to the Lord Lieutenant for his Excellency's approval, with the usual letter.

The Secretary was directed to write in terms as drafted to Robert Gregg, Esq., Solicitor, South Mall, Cork, as to the interests of the Proprietors in regard to the Cork High School for Girls.

Gerald FitzGibbon,
May 1, 1889.

Wm. Edward Ellis, Secretary.

May 1, 1889

Meeting of the Judicial Commissioners held this day at the Office, 23, Nassau-street, Dublin.

Minutes of the preceding meeting read and confirmed.

Mr. Henry Boyd appointed to take a Shorthand Report of the sitting of the Commission, to be held on Saturday, May 4, 1889.

Gerald FitzGibbon,
May 4, 1889.

Wm. Edward Ellis, Secretary.

May 4, 1889.

Meeting of the Judicial Commissioners held this day at the Office, 23, Nassau-street, Dublin.

Minutes of the preceding meeting read and confirmed.

The Scheme for the High School for Girls, Cork, was considered and amended.

A copy of the Revised Scheme was directed to be sent to the Secretary of the School, for the observations of the Proprietors.

Gerald FitzGibbon,
May 8, 1889.

Wm. Edward Ellis, Secretary.

May 8, 1889.

Meeting of the Judicial Commissioners held this day at the Office, 23, Nassau-street, Dublin.

Minutes of the preceding meeting read and confirmed.

Mr. George K. Magee appointed to take a Shorthand Report of the sitting of the Commission, to be held at Rochfort-bridge National Convent Schools, County Westmeath, on Tuesday, May 14, 1889.

Gerald FitzGibbon,
May 20, 1889.

Wm. Edward Ellis, Secretary.

May 9, 1889.

Meeting of the Judicial Commissioners held this day at the Four Courts, Dublin.

The Secretary was directed to write a letter, as drafted, to the Clerk of the Privy Council, with reference to an accidental omission in the *First Schedule*, Part I., to the Scheme for the Drelincourt, Mall, and Callan-street Schools, Armagh, signed on April 24, and enclosing amended signed copies to be substituted for those already sent.

GERALD FITZGIBBON,

Wm. Edward Ellis, Secretary. May 20, 1889.

May 20, 1889.

Meeting of the Judicial Commissioners held this day at the Office, 23, Nassau-street, Dublin.

Minutes of the two preceding meetings read and confirmed.

Mr. Henry Bond appointed to take a Shorthand Report of the sitting of the Commission to be held in the Court of Chancery, Four Courts, Dublin, on Friday, May 31, 1889.

GERALD FITZGIBBON,

Wm. Edward Ellis, Secretary. May 24, 1889.

May 24, 1889.

Meeting of the Judicial Commissioners held this day at the Office, 23, Nassau-street, Dublin.

Minutes of the preceding meeting read and confirmed.

Letter (Oct. 23) read from George Harrison, Secretary, Cork High School for Girls, returning the Revised Scheme with the observations of the existing Proprietors thereon.

The Scheme for the Cork High School for Girls was considered.

GERALD FITZGIBBON,

Wm. Edward Ellis, Secretary. May 27, 1889.

May 27, 1889.

Meeting of the Judicial Commissioners held this day at the Office, 23, Nassau-street, Dublin.

Minutes of the preceding meeting read and confirmed.

The Scheme for the Presbyterian Orphan Society was considered and amended.

GERALD FITZGIBBON,

Wm. Edward Ellis, Secretary. June 1, 1889.

June 1, 1889.

Meeting of the Judicial Commissioners held this day at the Office, 23, Nassau-street, Dublin.

Minutes of the preceding meeting read and confirmed.

The Scheme for the Presbyterian Orphan Society considered and finally approved.

GERALD FITZGIBBON,

Wm. Edward Ellis, Secretary. June 3, 1889.

June 3, 1889.

Meeting of the Judicial Commissioners held this day at the Office, 23, Nassau-street, Dublin.

Minutes of the preceding meeting read and confirmed.

Schemes framed by the Judicial Commissioners for the future government and management of the following Endowments, were duly signed:—

No. 57.—The High School for Girls, Cork.
No. 58.—The Presbyterian Orphan Society.

The Secretary was directed to forward the above Schemes to the Chief Secretary to the Lord Lieutenant for His Excellency's approval, with the usual letter.

GERALD FITZGIBBON,

Wm. Edward Ellis, Secretary. June 7, 1889.

June 7, 1889.

Meeting of the Judicial Commissioners held this day at the Office, 23, Nassau-street, Dublin.

Minutes of preceding meeting read and confirmed.

It was ordered :—

That the offices of the Commission be closed at Whitsuntide.

The Scheme for the Stephen-street School, Waterford, was considered and amended.

GERALD FITZGIBBON,

Wm. Edward Ellis, Secretary. June 14, 1889.

June 11, 1889.

Meeting of the Judicial Commissioners held this day at the Four Courts, Dublin.

The Scheme for the Villiers' Charitable Institutions, *Limerick*, was considered and revised.

The Secretary was directed to send two copies of the Scheme, as revised by the Judicial Commissioners, to the Trustees, and to request that they will return one copy signed by them, with their observations, not later than the 20th inst.

The Scheme for the Parochial Schools, &c., of the City of Cork, was considered and revised.

The Secretary was directed to send a copy of the Revised Scheme to the Right. Rev. Dr. Gregg, Bishop of Cork, asking for His Lordship's observations thereon before its being signed by the Judicial Commissioners.

GERALD FITZGIBBON,

Wm. Edward Ellis, Secretary. June 14, 1889.

June 14, 1889.

Meeting of the Commissioners held this day at the Office, 23, Nassau-street, Dublin.

Minutes of two preceding meetings read and confirmed.

Mr. James S. Macartney appointed to take a shorthand report of the sittings to be held at Baltinglass, Rathvilly, New Ross, Wexford, Carysfort, Arklow and Wicklow, from July 1 to July 6.

GERALD FITZGIBBON,

Wm. Edward Ellis, Secretary. June 19, 1889.

June 19, 1889.

Meeting of the Judicial Commissioners held this day at the Office, 23, Nassau-street, Dublin.

Minutes of preceding meeting read and confirmed.

Letter (June 17) read from Rev. D. Wilson, D.D., enclosing proposed amendments to the revised Scheme for the Villiers' Institution, Limerick, submitted to the Trustees.

A reply, as drafted, directed to be sent.

The Scheme for the Villiers' Charitable Institutions, Limerick, was further considered.

GERALD FITZGIBBON,

June 21, 1889.

Wm. Edward Ellis, Secretary.

June 21, 1889.

Meeting of the Judicial Commissioners held this day at the Office, 23, Nassau-street, Dublin.

Minutes of the preceding meeting read and confirmed.

Letter (June 20) read from the Right Rev. Dr. Gregg, Lord Bishop of Cork, returning the Revised Scheme for the Cork City Parochial Schools, with observations thereon.

The Scheme was considered, and finally approved.

GERALD FITZGIBBON,

June 28, 1889.

Wm. Edward Ellis, Secretary.

June 20, 1889.

Meeting of the Judicial Commissioners held this day at the Office, 23, Nassau-street, Dublin.

Minutes of preceding meeting read and confirmed.

Schemes framed by the Judicial Commissioners for the future government and management of the following Endowments were duly signed :—

No. 42.—The Villiers' Charitable Institutions, Limerick.
No. 47.—The Parochial Schools of the City of Cork ; The Green Coat Hospital, Cork ; The Cork Grammar School ; Brettridge's Charity, Cork ; and other Endowments in the City of Cork.
No. 53.—The Stephen-street School, Waterford.

The Secretary was directed to forward the above Schemes to the Chief Secretary to the Lord Lieutenant for His Excellency's approval, with the usual letter.

Gerald FitzGibbon.

Wm. Edward Ellis, Secretary. June 28, 1889.

June 28, 1889.

Meeting of the Commissioners held this day at the Office, 23, Nassau-street, Dublin.

Minutes of preceding meeting read and confirmed.

The Scheme framed by the Judicial Commissioners for the future government and management of the Endowments of the Ulster Royal Schools and for altering the constitution of the Commissioners of Education in Ireland was duly signed.

The Secretary was directed to forward the above Scheme to the Chief Secretary to the Lord Lieutenant for His Excellency's approval, with the usual letter.

Mr. Charles Ryan appointed to take a shorthand report of the sitting of the Commission to be held on Monday, July 8, and Thursday, July 11.

Gerald FitzGibbon,

Wm. Edward Ellis, Secretary. July 11, 1889.

July 11, 1889.

Meeting of the Judicial Commissioners held this day at the Office, 23, Nassau-street, Dublin.

Minutes of preceding meeting read and confirmed.

The Scheme for Hewetson's School, Clane, was considered and revised.

The Secretary was directed to send copies of the Revised Scheme to Mr. Cooke-Trench and Rev. Mr. Sherlock, and to request them to revise same carefully and to return them with their observations, also with a certificate of the correctness of the Schedules and the consent of the existing Trustees.

Gerald FitzGibbon,

Wm. Edward Ellis, Secretary. July 13, 1889.

July 13, 1889.

Meeting of the Judicial Commissioners held this day at the Office, 23, Nassau-street, Dublin.

Minutes of preceding meeting read and confirmed.

It was ordered :—

1. That the sittings of the Commission shall be adjourned from Saturday, August 11, to Tuesday, September 24.
2. That the offices of the Commission shall be open for the transaction of business on Tuesdays and Fridays during above period from eleven to one only.

Gerald FitzGibbon,

Wm. Edward Ellis, Secretary. July 19, 1889.

July 19, 1889.

Meeting of the Judicial Commissioners held this day at the Office, 23, Nassau-street, Dublin.

Minutes of preceding meeting read and confirmed.

Mr. John M'Bride appointed to take a shorthand report of the sitting of the Commission to be held at the Annahilt Endowed School, county Down, on Tuesday, July 23, 1889.

Gerald FitzGibbon,

Wm. Edward Ellis, Secretary. July 26, 1889.

July 26, 1889.

Meeting of the Judicial Commissioners held this day at the Office, 23, Nassau-street, Dublin.

Minutes of preceding meeting read and confirmed.

The Scheme for the Clonmel Grammar School was considered and revised.

Letter (July 23), read from Thomas Cooke-Trench, returning revised Scheme for Hewetson's School, Clane, with his observations thereon.

The Scheme was finally approved and ordered for signature by the Judicial Commissioners.

GERALD FITZGIBBON,
August 1, 1889.

Wm. Edward Ellis, Secretary.

August 2, 1889.

Meeting of the Judicial Commissioners held this day at the Office, 23, Nassau-street, Dublin.

Minutes of preceding meeting read and confirmed.

The Secretary was directed to send a letter, as drafted, to the Clerk of the Privy Council, with reference to the Scheme for the Drelincourt, Mall, and Callan-street Schools, Armagh, which was sent for observations of the Commissioners thereon.

The Scheme for the Clonmel Grammar School was considered and revised.

GERALD FITZGIBBON,
August 6, 1889.

Wm. Edward Ellis, Secretary.

August 6, 1889.

Meeting of the Judicial Commissioners held this day at the Office, 23, Nassau-street, Dublin.

Minutes of the preceding meeting read and confirmed.

The Schemes of the following Endowments were considered and finally approved:—

No. 27.—The Bertrand Female Orphan School.
No. 45.—The Clonmel Grammar School.

GERALD FITZGIBBON,
August 10, 1889.

Wm. Edward Ellis, Secretary.

August 10, 1889.

Meeting of the Judicial Commissioners held this day at the Office, 23, Nassau-street, Dublin.

Minutes of the preceding meeting read and confirmed.

Letter (Aug. 10), read from the Clerk of the Privy Council, remitting the Scheme for the Londonderry Academical Institution, with a declaration by the Lord Lieutenant in Council.

The Scheme was amended and the Secretary was directed to order four copies of the Scheme on thick paper for signature.

GERALD FITZGIBBON,
August 13, 1889.

Wm. Edward Ellis, Secretary.

August 13, 1889.

Meeting of the Judicial Commissioners held this day at the Office, 23, Nassau-street, Dublin.

Minutes of preceding meeting read and confirmed.

Schemes framed by the Judicial Commissioners for the future government and management of the following Endowments were duly signed:—

No. 27.—The Bertrand Female Orphan School.
No. 40.—The Londonderry Academical Institution. (Amended Scheme).
No. 45.—The Clonmel Grammar School.
No. 57.—Hewetson's School, Clane.

The Secretary was directed to forward the above Schemes to the Chief Secretary to the Lord Lieutenant for his Excellency's approval, with the usual letter.

GERALD FITZGIBBON,
October 11, 1889.

Wm. Edward Ellis, Secretary.

PART IV.

MINUTES OF THE ASSISTANT COMMISSIONERS.

October 4, 1888.

Meeting of the Assistant Commissioners held this day at the Office, 23, Nassau-street, Dublin.

Present:—Rev. Dr. MOLLOY, Professor DOUGHERTY.

Minutes of preceding meeting read and confirmed.

Letter read from Brother John P. Lynch, as to the Lombard-street National Schools, and St. Joseph's Seminary, Galway.

Letter from Rev. C. O. Wiley, Secretary, Diocesan Council of Killala and Achonry, was ordered to stand over for consideration by the full Commission.

Letter read from John C. Pounden, Secretary, Diocesan Council of Ferns.

An answer as drafted was ordered to be sent.

The distribution among the Commissioners of Schemes to be prepared for publication in December was considered.

A programme of Sittings to be held in the North of Ireland was prepared.

Adjourned,

J. B. DOUGHERTY,
October 16, 1888.

N. D. Murphy, Junr.,
Chief Clerk and Assistant Secretary.

October 16, 1888.

Meeting of the Assistant Commissioners held this day at the Office, 23, Nassau-street, Dublin.

Present:—Rev. Dr. MOLLOY, Dr. TRAILL, Professor DOUGHERTY.

Minutes of the preceding meeting read and confirmed.

The heads of a Scheme for the Central Corporation School Endowment were submitted and passed.

Adjourned.

ANTHONY TRAILL,
November 9, 1888.

N. D. Murphy, Junr.,
Chief Clerk and Assistant Secretary.

November 9, 1888.

Meeting of the Assistant Commissioners held this day at the Office, 23, Nassau-street, Dublin.

Present:—Rev. Dr. MOLLOY, Dr. TRAILL, Professor DOUGHERTY.

Minutes of preceding meeting read and confirmed.

The heads of a Scheme for the Munster Dairy School and Agricultural Institute were submitted and considered.

Adjourned.

GERALD MOLLOY,
November 16, 1888.

N. D. Murphy, Junr.,
Chief Clerk and Assistant Secretary.

November 16, 1888.

Meeting of the Assistant Commissioners held this day at the Office, 23, Nassau-street, Dublin.

Present:—Rev. Dr. MOLLOY, Dr. TRAILL, Professor DOUGHERTY.

Minutes of the preceding meeting read and confirmed.

The heads of a Scheme for the Munster Dairy School and Agricultural Institute were further considered and passed, certain points being reserved for the full Commission.

Adjourned.

J. B. DOUGHERTY,
November 23, 1888.

N. D. Murphy, Junr.,
Chief Clerk and Assistant Secretary.

November 23, 1888.

Meeting of the Assistant Commissioners held this day at the Office, 23, Nassau-street, Dublin.

Present:—Rev. Dr. Molloy, Dr. Traill, Professor Dougherty.

Minutes of the preceding meeting read and confirmed.

The Draft Scheme for the Stephen Street School, Waterford, was considered and reserved for the full Commission.

Adjourned.

Gerald Molloy,
November 30, 1888.

N. D. Murphy, Junr.,
Chief Clerk and Assistant Secretary.

November 30, 1888.

Meeting of the Assistant Commissioners held this day at the Office, 23, Nassau-street, Dublin.

Present:—Rev. Dr. Molloy, Dr. Traill, Professor Dougherty.

Minutes of the preceding meeting read and confirmed.

The Draft Scheme for the Stephen Street School, Waterford, was further considered.

Adjourned.

J. B. Dougherty,
December 7, 1888.

N. D. Murphy,
Chief Clerk and Assistant Secretary.

December 7, 1888.

Meeting of the Assistant Commissioners held this day at the Office, 23, Nassau-street, Dublin.

Present:—Rev. Dr. Molloy, Dr. Traill, Professor Dougherty.

Minutes of the preceding meeting read and confirmed.

The Draft Scheme for the Cashel Corporation School Endowment was considered, and the Assistant Secretary was directed to write a letter, as drafted, to the Town Clerk of Cashel, asking that the Corporation of Cashel should elect two persons as first representative Governors, whose names might be inserted in the Draft Scheme.

Adjourned.

Gerald Molloy,
December 14, 1888.

N. D. Murphy, Junr.,
Chief Clerk and Assistant Secretary.

December 14, 1888.

Meeting of the Assistant Commissioners held this day at the Office, 23, Nassau-street, Dublin.

Present:—Rev. Dr. Molloy, Dr. Traill, Professor Dougherty.

Minutes of the preceding meeting read and confirmed.

The Draft Scheme for the Gilson Schools, Oldcastle, was considered.

The heads of a Scheme for the Presbyterian Orphan Society were submitted and passed.

The Draft Scheme for the Incorporated Society was submitted by direction of Lord Justice FitzGibbon, and was ordered to be printed.

The Draft Scheme for the Parochial Schools of the Diocese of Meath and the Navan Endowed School was considered and passed.

Adjourned.

Anthony Traill,
March 1, 1889.

N. D. Murphy,
Chief Clerk and Assistant Secretary.

March 1, 1889.

Meeting of the Assistant Commissioners held this day at the Office, 23, Nassau-street, Dublin.

Present:—Dr. MOLLOY, Dr. TRAILL.

Minutes of preceding meeting read and confirmed.

The Draft Scheme for Hewetson's School, Clane, was considered, amended, and passed.

Adjourned.

GERALD MOLLOY,
March 8, 1889.

N. D. Murphy,
Chief Clerk and Assistant Secretary.

March 8, 1889.

Meeting of the Assistant Commissioners held this day at the Office, 23, Nassau-street, Dublin.

Present:—Dr. MOLLOY, Dr. TRAILL, Professor DOUGHERTY.

Minutes of the preceding meeting read and confirmed.

The Draft Scheme for the Cashel Parochial Deanery Schools was considered and passed.

The heads of a Scheme for Larne Grammar School were submitted and passed.

Adjourned.

J. B. DOUGHERTY,
March 15, 1889.

N. D. Murphy,
Chief Clerk and Assistant Secretary.

March 15, 1889.

Meeting of the Assistant Commissioners held this day at the Office, 23, Nassau-street, Dublin.

Present:—Rev. Dr. MOLLOY, Dr. TRAILL, Professor DOUGHERTY.

Minutes of previous meeting read and signed.

The Draft Scheme for the Presbyterian Orphan Society of Ireland was considered and passed.

Adjourned.

GERALD MOLLOY,
March 25, 1889

N. D. Murphy,
Chief Clerk and Assistant Secretary.

March 25, 1889.

Meeting of the Assistant Commissioners held this day at the Office, 23, Nassau-street, Dublin.

Present:—Rev. Dr. MOLLOY, Professor DOUGHERTY.

Minutes of preceding meeting read and confirmed.

The following Endowments were allocated among the Assistant Commissioners with a view to having six Schemes ready for publication in May:—

Kinsale Endowed School.
Mungret College, Limerick.
Leamy's Free School.
Shiel's Charity.
Midleton College.
Ballyroan School.

Downpatrick Blue School.
Mount Alexander School.
Admiral Leslie's Free School.
Dublin Diocesan Schools.
Dublin City Protestant Parochial Schools.
Bishop Hodson's Grammar School.
Cork Diocesan Schools.
Schools for the Belfast Presbytery.
Drogheda Blue School.
Ledley's Bequest.
Strabane Academy.
Cannus (Castlerea) Schools.
Masterson's Charity, Sligo.

The heads of a Scheme for the Southwell School Endowment, Kinsale, were submitted and discussed.

Adjourned.

J. B. Dougherty,
April 20, 1889.

N. D. Murphy,
Chief Clerk and Assistant Secretary.

March 23, 1889.

Meeting of the Assistant Commissioners held this day at the Office, 23, Nassau-street, Dublin.

Present:—Rev. Dr. Molloy, Professor Dougherty.

The heads of a Scheme for the Southwell School Endowment, Kinsale, were considered and approved.

The heads of a Scheme for the Ballyroan Endowed School were submitted and approved.

The heads of a Scheme for the Ledley School Endowments were submitted and approved.

The heads of a Scheme for the Larne Grammar School were considered and approved.

Adjourned.

J. B. Dougherty,
April 20, 1889.

N. D. Murphy,
Chief Clerk and Assistant Secretary.

April 24, 1889.

Meeting of the Assistant Commissioners held this day at the Office, 23, Nassau-street, Dublin.

Present:—Rev. Dr. Molloy, Professor Dougherty.

The following list of Endowments was prepared, for six of which it was arranged that Draft Schemes should be prepared for publication in the month of June:—

Shiel's Charity, Rochfortbridge.
Mungret College.
Strabane Academy.
Bandon Endowed School.
Youghal Endowed School.
Lismore Endowed School.
Brown's Endowment, Ballyhalbert.
Drogheda Blue School.
Bangor Endowed School.
The Irish Non-Subscribing Presbyterian Orphan Society.
Midleton College.
Dundalk Grammar School.
Cannus (Castlerea) School.

It was arranged that a Public Inquiry should be held on Tuesday, May 14, at Rochfortbridge, with regard to Shiel's Charity.

Adjourned.

J. B. Dougherty,
April 29, 1889.

N. D. Murphy,
Chief Clerk and Assistant Secretary.

April 26, 1889.

Meeting of the Assistant Commissioners held this day at the Office, 23, Nassau-street, Dublin.

Present:—Rev. Dr. MOLLOY, Professor DOUGHERTY.

Minutes of the last three meetings read and confirmed.

Letter read from the Very Rev. Canon Donnelly, Magherafelt, asking to have a Scheme settled for the new Convent Schools, Magherafelt.

A reply, as drafted, was ordered to be sent.

The heads of a Scheme for the Educational Endowments of the Presbytery of Dublin were submitted, approved, and ordered to be printed.

Adjourned.

ANTHONY TRAILL,
May 3, 1889.

N. D. Murphy,
Chief Clerk and Assistant Secretary.

May 3, 1889.

Meeting of the Assistant Commissioners held this day at the Office, 23, Nassau-street, Dublin.

Present:—Rev. Dr. MOLLOY, Dr. TRAILL, Professor DOUGHERTY.

Minutes of the preceding meeting read and confirmed.

The Assistant Secretary was directed to write for the Trust Deed of the Strabane Academy.

Letter from Dr. Laffan to Dr. Molloy was read, dealing with the Cashel Corporation Endowment Scheme, and asking for the return of certain documents.

The Assistant Secretary was directed to answer the part referring to the documents.

The heads of a Scheme for the Cork Diocesan Endowments were submitted and approved.

Adjourned.

J. B. DOUGHERTY,
May 10, 1889.

N. D. Murphy,
Chief Clerk and Assistant Secretary.

May 10, 1889.

Meeting of the Assistant Commissioners held this day at the Office, 23, Nassau-street, Dublin.

Present:—Rev. Dr. MOLLOY, Dr. TRAILL, Professor DOUGHERTY.

Minutes of the preceding meeting read and confirmed.

The heads of a Scheme for the Downpatrick Blue School were submitted.

The Draft Scheme for the Lelloy School Endowments was submitted, and approved.

The Draft Scheme for the Southwell School Endowments, Kinsale, was submitted and approved, subject to certain questions which were reserved for the full Commission.

Adjourned.

GERALD MOLLOY,
May 13, 1889.

N. D. Murphy,
Chief Clerk and Assistant Secretary.

May 13, 1889.

Meeting of the Assistant Commissioners held this day at the Office, 23, Nassau-street, Dublin.

Present:—Rev. Dr. MOLLOY, Dr. TRAILL, Professor DOUGHERTY.

Minutes of preceding meeting read and confirmed.

Letter read from the Rev. F. A. Sanders as to Tullyvin School.

Referred to the full Commission.

The Draft Scheme for the Endowments belonging to the Dublin Presbytery was considered and passed.

The Draft Scheme for the Crofton School, Macroom, and the Crofton School, Clondrohid, was considered and passed, certain questions being reserved for the full Commission.

The heads of a Scheme for the Strabane Academy were submitted and approved.

Adjourned.

ANTHONY TRAILL,
May 15, 1889.

N. D. Murphy,
Chief Clerk and Assistant Secretary.

May 16, 1889.

Meeting of the Assistant Commissioners held this day at the Office, 33, Nassau-street, Dublin.

Present:—Rev. Dr. MOLLOY, Dr. TRAILL, Professor DOUGHERTY.

Minutes of preceding meeting read and confirmed.

Letter, as drafted, was directed to be sent to the Trustees of the Will of Samuel Ledley, requesting information as to the present amount and particulars of the Ledley Endowment.

Adjourned.

J. B. DOUGHERTY,
May 23, 1889.

N. D. Murphy,
Chief Clerk and Assistant Secretary.

May 23, 1889.

Meeting of the Assistant Commissioners held this day at the Office, 33, Nassau-street, Dublin.

Present:—Rev. Dr. MOLLOY, Dr. TRAILL, Professor DOUGHERTY.

Minutes of preceding meeting read and confirmed.

Letter read from the Rev. D. O'Sullivan as to Macroom Parochial School.

Letter from Rev. J. Kennedy as to Lurgan Grammar School was ordered to be brought up for consideration by the full Commission on Friday.

The preparation of Schemes for the following Endowments was undertaken by the Assistant Commissioners with a view to publication at the end of June:—

The Shiel Charity.
Morgan's School.
Bishop Hodson's Grammar School.
Presbyterian Sabbath School Society.
The Strabane Academy.

Heads of Schemes for the following Endowments were submitted and approved:—

The Shiel Charity.
Bishop Hodson's Grammar School.
Presbyterian Sabbath School Society.

Adjourned.

GERALD MOLLOY,
June 1, 1889.

N. D. Murphy,
Chief Clerk and Assistant Secretary.

June 1, 1889.

Meeting of the Assistant Commissioners held this day at the Office, 33, Nassau-street, Dublin.

Present:—Rev. Dr. MOLLOY, Dr. TRAILL.

Minutes of the two preceding meetings read and confirmed.

The heads of a Scheme for the Irish Non-Subscribing Presbyterian Orphan Society were submitted and approved.

Adjourned.

ANTHONY TRAILL.

N. D. Murphy,
Chief Clerk and Assistant Secretary.

June 6, 1889.

Meeting of the Assistant Commissioners held this day at the Office, 33, Nassau-street, Dublin.

Present:—Rev. Dr. MOLLOY, Dr. TRAILL, Professor DOUGHERTY.

Minutes of preceding meeting read and confirmed.

The Draft Scheme for the Southwell Charity and the Parochial School Endowments, Downpatrick, was considered, amended, and passed.

The principles upon which a Scheme should be prepared for Brown's Endowments, Ballyhalbert, were discussed.

Adjourned.

J. B. DOUGHERTY,
June 7, 1889.

N. D. Murphy,
Chief Clerk and Assistant Secretary.

June 7, 1889.

Meeting of the Assistant Commissioners held this day at the Office, 23, Nassau-street, Dublin.

Present:—Dr. Traill, Professor Dougherty.

Minutes of preceding meeting read and confirmed.

The Draft Scheme for the Shiel Charity, Rochfort Bridge, was considered and passed.

Adjourned.

Anthony Traill,
June 13, 1889.

N. D. Murphy,
Chief Clerk and Assistant Secretary.

June 13, 1889.

Meeting of the Assistant Commissioners held this day at the Office, 23, Nassau-street, Dublin.

Present:—Rev. Dr. Molloy, Dr. Traill, Professor Dougherty.

Minutes of the preceding meeting read and confirmed.

The Draft Scheme for Bishop Hodson's Grammar School was considered and passed, certain questions having been reserved for the full Commission.

Adjourned.

J. B. Dougherty,
June 14, 1889.

N. D. Murphy,
Chief Clerk and Assistant Secretary.

June 14, 1889.

Meeting of the Assistant Commissioners held this day at the Office, 23, Nassau-street, Dublin.

Present:—Rev. Dr. Molloy, Dr. Traill, Professor Dougherty.

Minutes of the preceding meeting read and confirmed.

The heads of a Scheme for Brown's Endowments, Ballyhalbert, were submitted and approved.

Adjourned.

Anthony Traill,
June 17, 1889.

N. D. Murphy,
Chief Clerk and Assistant Secretary.

June 17, 1889.

Meeting of the Assistant Commissioners held this day at the Office, 23, Nassau-street, Dublin.

Present:—Rev. Dr. Molloy, Dr. Traill, Professor Dougherty.

Minutes of preceding meeting read and confirmed.

The Draft Scheme for the Presbyterian Sabbath School Society was considered and passed.

The heads of a Draft Scheme for Bangor Endowed School were submitted and it was agreed that a Draft Scheme should be prepared and brought up for consideration.

Adjourned.

Gerald Molloy.
June 19, 1889.

N. D. Murphy,
Chief Clerk and Assistant Secretary.

June 19, 1889.

Meeting of the Assistant Commissioners held this day at the Office, 23, Nassau-street, Dublin.

Present:—Rev. Dr. Molloy, Professor Dougherty.

Minutes of the preceding meeting read and confirmed.

The Draft Scheme for the Strabane Academy was considered and passed.

Adjourned.

J. B. Dougherty,
July 16, 1889.

N. D. Murphy,
Chief Clerk and Assistant Secretary.

July 19, 1889.

Meeting of the Assistant Commissioners held this day at the Office, 23, Nassau-street, Dublin.

Present :—Rev. Dr. Molloy, Professor Dougherty.

Minutes of preceding meeting read and confirmed.

The heads of a Scheme for the Banbridge Presbytery were submitted and passed.

Adjourned.

Gerald Molloy,
July 31, 1889.

N. D. Murphy,
Chief Clerk and Assistant Secretary.

July 31, 1889.

Meeting of the Assistant Commissioners held this day at the Office, 23, Nassau-street, Dublin.

Present :—Rev. Dr. Molloy, Dr. Traill, Professor Dougherty.

Minutes of preceding meeting read and confirmed.

The Draft Schemes for the Banbridge Presbytery and for the Leighlin Diocesan Endowments were considered and passed.

Adjourned.

Anthony Traill,
August 3, 1889.

N. D. Murphy,
Chief Clerk and Assistant Secretary.

August 3, 1889.

Meeting of the Assistant Commissioners held this day at the Office, 23, Nassau-street, Dublin.

Present :—Rev. Dr. Molloy, Dr. Traill, Professor Dougherty.

Minutes of the preceding meeting read and confirmed.

The Draft Scheme for Joseph Brown's Endowments, County Down, was considered and passed.

Adjourned.

J. B. Dougherty,
August 8, 1889.

N. D. Murphy,
Chief Clerk and Assistant Secretary.

August 8, 1889.

Meeting of the Assistant Commissioners held this day at the Office, 23, Nassau-street, Dublin.

Present :—Rev. Dr. Molloy, Professor Dougherty.

Minutes of the preceding meeting read and confirmed.

An alteration proposed by Professor Dougherty in the Governing Body to be constituted by the Draft Scheme for Joseph Brown's Endowments, Ballyhalbert, was adopted, subject to the approval of the Judicial Commissioners.

Adjourned.

Gerald Molloy,
September 25, 1889.

N. D. Murphy,
Chief Clerk and Assistant Secretary.

September 25, 1889.

Meeting of the Assistant Commissioners held this day at their Offices, 23, Nassau-street, Dublin.

Present:—Rev. Dr. Molloy, Professor Dougherty.

Minutes of preceding meeting read and confirmed.

It was agreed—

That Dr. Molloy should undertake the preparation of certain parts of the annual Report, and that Professor Dougherty should prepare a list of Endowments to be inquired into, with a view to arranging a Circuit list for the month of October.

The Assistant Commissioners were engaged during the day in carrying out the business allocated between them.

Adjourned.

Anthony Traill,
November 1, 1889.

N. D. Murphy,
Chief Clerk and Assistant Secretary.

September 27, 1889.

Meeting of the Assistant Commissioners held this day at their Offices, 23, Nassau-street, Dublin.

Present:—Rev. Dr. Molloy, Professor Dougherty.

Letter read from the Rev. A. Miller, Armagh, asking that certain corrections be made in his evidence.

The portions of the evidence referred to were considered and corrected by the Commissioners, and the Assistant Secretary was directed to send a copy of the corrected proof to Rev. Mr. Miller for his approval.

Adjourned.

Anthony Traill,
November 1, 1889.

N. D. Murphy,
Chief Clerk and Assistant Secretary.

EDUCATIONAL ENDOWMENTS (IRELAND) COMMISSION,

1888-89.

APPENDIX A.

MINUTES OF EVIDENCE.

PUBLIC SITTING—MONDAY, OCTOBER 8, 1888

Oct. 8, 1888.

At the Courthouse, Mullingar.

Present:—The Right Hon. Lord Justice FITZGIBBON and the Right Hon. Lord Justice NAISH, Judicial Commissioners; and the Rev. GERALD MOLLOY, D.D., D.SC., ANTHONY TRAILL, Esq., LL.D., M.D., F.T.C.D., and Professor DOUGHERTY, M.A., Assistant Commissioners.

The Assistant Secretary, N. D. MURPHY, Jun., was in attendance.

Lord Justice FITZGIBBON made an introductory statement.

HEVEY'S INSTITUTION, MULLINGAR.

The Most Rev. Dr. *Nulty*, Lord Bishop of Meath, sworn and examined.

The Most Rev. Dr. Nulty, Lord Bishop of Meath.

1. Lord Justice FITZGIBBON.—I believe, Dr. Nulty, you are, as Bishop of Meath, one of the trustees of Hevey's will?—Yes.

2. How long have you been bishop?—Since 1866. I was Coadjutor Bishop from 1864, and in 1866 I succeeded Dr. Cantwell, the late bishop of the diocese.

3. Before that, you had been connected with this locality, and with the charity?—Yes, I was curate of Mullingar for many years, and I was teaching in the Classical school from January, 1857, to October, 1863.

4. The original trustees were the Roman Catholic Bishop of Meath, the Roman Catholic Bishop of Ardagh, the Administrator of Mullingar, and two laymen—Sir Richard Nagle, and Mr. Gerald Dease?—Yes.

5. Are the Roman Catholic Bishops of Meath and Ardagh *ex-officio* trustees?—The Bishop of Meath is an *ex-officio* trustee; the Bishop of Ardagh is not. The bishop of any diocese in Ireland may become a trustee. After the death of the late Bishop of Ardagh, the late Cardinal Cullen became a trustee, and he continued a trustee from 1854 down to his death, and attended regularly.

6. Lord Justice NAISH.—What is the exact provision for the appointment of new trustees?—When any trustee dies, the surviving trustees have, under the will, the power of appointing his successor, it being always understood that the Bishop of Meath for the time being will be one. The Administrator of the parish of Mullingar is to be another; and then any other bishop in Ireland may be the third. The two laymen are co-opted.

7. Is it necessary that they should be Catholics?—Yes.

8. Have you a copy of the will?—We have the original.

[The witness handed in the document.]

9. Lord Justice FITZGIBBON.—(Reads). The probate bears date April 1, 1837. The will is dated December 17, 1833, and there is a codicil dated February 23, 1837.

Witness.—Mr. Hevey died in 1837.

10. Lord Justice FITZGIBBON.—Who is now the second episcopal trustee?—Dr. Donnelly, Bishop of Clogher.

11. Who is the present Administrator of Mullingar?—The Rev. P. Callery.

12. Who are the lay trustees?—Mr. Thomas Maher and Mr. Hugh O'Neill, both justices of the peace.

13. Are they resident in the neighbourhood?—Quite near.

14. Lord Justice FITZGIBBON.—The property is given, subject to the contingencies thereinafter mentioned, on trust, to apply the rents and profits of the lands of Bryanstown to the maintenance and education of as many of the poor children resident in the parish of Mullingar as the rents are sufficient to maintain; then to fully educate them in such branches of literature, science, and theology as the trustees, or the majority of them, shall think fit:—

"It being my intention that the majority of my trustees shall at all times have power to select and limit the individuals among the poor children of the said parish who are to obtain such maintenance and education, and to remove them without appeal, and to select others in their stead; provided that no difference of religion shall be a ground or reason for not selecting, excluding, or expelling any child from the benefit of this bequest."

The testator then declares a further trust, to erect and furnish a school or college, for the maintenance and education of these poor children, the great majority of whom, if not the whole, being Roman Catholics. He provides for inspection, and declares his intention to found a school or college for the maintenance and education of the poor children of the parish, to be freely selected from among the children of persons not in opulent circumstances—it is not to be an objection to the selection of any child that its parents may have some property—and then he empowers the trustees to make rules for the management of the college, and declares that the trustees are to have the full power of the visitors of any endowed school or college, and then he adds:—

"Having, with regard to the said lands of Bryanstown, no further or other charitable intention or purpose than the [illegible]

Oct. 8, 1888.

The Most Rev. Dr. Kelly, Lord Bishop of Ross.

which I have hereinbefore declared, and being decidedly opposed to any court or tribunal in this country, or within this realm, taking on itself to regulate, or make any alteration, or meddle with such, my intentions, I declare that if any court shall intermeddle, or if the Commissioners of Charitable Donations and Bequests shall intermeddle, or attempt to intermeddle, or file any bill or information for the purpose of being allowed to intermeddle, or if any person shall file any bill or information with the intent of bringing the said charity under the control or management of the said Commissioners, then, and in any such case, I revoke all and singular the bequests hereinbefore mentioned, and the trust and purpose hereinbefore expressed, and I give, devise, and bequeath the lands of Brynestown to the Right Reverend John Cantwell, Right Rev. William Higgins, Rev. Patrick Kelly, and the survivors and survivor of them, as joint tenants, and to the heirs of such survivor, for ever, absolutely discharged of every trust, bonus, or purpose."

15. I suppose these gentlemen are dead, and that your lordship has no idea who is the heir-at-law of the last survivor?—The Rev. Patrick Kelly survived the others, and I don't know who his heir-at-law is. I could make it out.

16. He would probably turn up if there were any chance of the lands of Brynestown going to him?—But the trust regularly and legally devolves from one set of trustees to another; each trustee is appointed by deed as the will directs; and the succession has been kept up legally and regularly from the death of the three original trustees.

17. Of what do the lands of Brynestown consist?—There are 376 acres, 2 roods, and 3 perches, Irish plantation measure.

18. What is the rent?—The rent varies very much. It began with considerably over £500 a year, and continued so for some time; but our tenants from the commencement were not very punctual in their payments. I found that in 1863 one of the tenants, named Richard Hanna, owed £1,224, and the other, Mrs. M'Cormack, owed £2,059, with the result that the trustees had to take action and evict them, and I believe lost a lot of money in consequence. New tenants were let in, and they paid their rents punctually for a considerable time, until 1879, when one of the tenants became a defaulter, and owed the trustees £900. Mr. James A. Dease, Sir Percy Nugent, Cardinal Cullen, and myself were then the trustees. We took proceedings against him, and evicted him; and after he had been evicted a considerable time he brought his case before us again, and asked an abatement of the rent, and a remission of the arrears due. I, myself, was personally opposed to giving him any such thing, but Mr. M'Evoy was then trustee with Mr. Dease, and I was overruled by both, and the arrears were remitted on the understanding that he resigned all rights and claim to any improvements that he might have made, and to any benefits that he could have derived under the Land Acts of 1870 and 1881, and he was re-admitted, as I said, against my will, in 1884, at an abated rent—something under the original letting, which I think, was £1 11s. an acre. His half year's rent used to be £265 up to that time. Then the rent was abated, not much, and he was re-admitted on the distinct understanding that he would be more punctual in his payment in future. He did not fulfil that promise; on the contrary he ceased to pay anything at all; and it ended in his owing us £700 13s. 7d. in addition to the £900. Then we took proceedings against him again, and evicted him finally and completely; and we had another tenant appointed in his place.

19. Dr. Traill.—In what year was the last eviction?—I think in 1888.

20. Lord Justice FitzGibbon.—The present tenant of this holding has only been in occupation since 1888?—That's all.

21. At what annual rent is he supposed to hold?—His rent is £396 5s. 6d. for the whole year.

22. Up to what date is it paid?—He is paying regularly according as it falls due. The other tenant is Mr. M'Cormack, whose rent is £291 6s.; but he is not at all satisfactory as a tenant. We had in 1884 to remit him half a year's rent, owing to the depression of the times. Then in 1885, we had to take his promissory note for another year's rent, the greater part of which still remains unpaid. Then the year before last we had to reduce his rent 20 per cent. We did that voluntarily in consequence of the depression of the times, seeing that it was very difficult to pay rent at all. But this year, which comes to a close in November, he is claiming 30 per cent., which we are not at all disposed to allow. It came before a cash meeting which we had the other day. We took no action; but all the trustees were of opinion that we should at once proceed to deal sternly and determinedly with him; and at a full meeting I think the resolution we will come to will be that we shall be obliged to get rid of him if he does not pay.

23. Then he owes you a very considerable sum?—He does not. All that he really owes is the residue of the promissory note, which, I believe, amounts to £172. This year's rent is paid, deducting thirty per cent.

24. He has paid you seventy per cent. of it?—Yes.

25. Dr. Traill.—Is he any relation of the Mrs. M'Cormack who owed you the £2,059?—He is her son.

26. What became of that sum that she owed?—We had to remit a lot of it.

27. Who was the tenant that took her place?—Her son, not the present man but his brother; and that tenant was most satisfactory and paid regularly and punctually while he lived. When he died he left his property to his brother, the present tenant; and the brother is not at all as satisfactory.

28. Who is the tenant of the other evicted farm?—His name is Casey. We have taken precautions against Mr. Casey. We have required him to lodge £500, on which we allow him five per cent.; and in case he becomes a defaulter we can draw on that £500, and also draw on it for legal expenses if we find it necessary to put him out.

29. Lord Justice FitzGibbon.—Then you have security to the amount of £500?—Yes.

30. How do you manage the lands?—One of the priests, who is Secretary to the Charity, receives the rents. We have only two tenants; and there was no trouble with them until they became defaulters. We had an agent, a Mr. Ford, for a great many years. He died, and since his death no one has been appointed in his place.

31. Then your actual income is about £500 a year?—Our actual income at present, if the rents were paid, amounts to £588 15s. 6d.

32. About £500 a year are your actual receipts?—I suppose so. It used to be something over £600 a year, clear. It is going down regularly.

33. Lord Justice Naish.—Before 1882 it was £685 a year?—Yes.

34. Dr. Traill.—You have not suffered very much?—We have, with this tenant. We have lost £1,600.

35. Still, if you get £588 per annum, you have not lost very much as things go?—We have not got it. One of the tenants stopped thirty per cent. of his rents last year, and we gave him twenty per cent. the year before.

36. Has the Plan of Campaign been tried here?—No, not yet.

37. Lord Justice FitzGibbon.—These lands of Brynestown are the only endowment you have?—The only lands. We have no accumulated money whatever; but we are clear, we owe nothing. But a large amount of money was expended in the building of the two houses that comprise the Kerry College. We have a house for the education of poor female children

It was built very early in the charity at an expense of £2,651.

38. Lord Justice Naish.—Where did that money come from?—From the rents of the estate.

39. Is there anything due for it now?—No. Then we built the College proper—a very large building, on which we expended about £8,000. The contract for the building alone was £5,000; and the furniture and other things amounted to £3,000 more. Our funds were exhausted, and we had to borrow; and we borrowed from the Presentation Nuns £1,200 at four per cent., with the obligation that we were to repay it in instalments of not less than £200. We went on paying and clearing it off, and we would have had it all cleared off long ago were it not for the deficiency of the tenants that I have alluded to. But we have cleared off a very large amount, and the only portion remaining is £450. We owe that to the Presentation Nuns, paying interest on it at four per cent. We used to pay them every year £35 for the education of poor female children of Mullingar, in conformity with Mr. Hevey's will, and we owe them £175 together with the £450, which is the total amount of our liabilities.

40. Lord Justice FitzGibbon.—Formerly there was a classical school; is there one still?—There was a classical school attached to the English school from the very commencement. I was the first person appointed classical teacher, with an assistant; and I continued teaching there for seven years. Another priest succeeded me when I left, and that continued till three years ago, when I found that owing to the extraordinary mortality of the priests of the diocese, the necessities of the mission required that I should withdraw that priest from the school. Then the trustees appointed a Christian Brother to teach classics in the school; and that classical teaching is carried on by another brother at present. The old English school remains under the control of the Christian Brothers.

41. How many children attend the Convent School?—The average is 400.

42. Is that school in connexion with the National Board?—It is.

43. Then the £35 a year that was formerly paid is the only advantage which that school has from the endowment?—The only advantage, with the exception of the house, which is ours.

44. Dr. Traill.—Are they 400 girls or 400 children?—400 girls.

45. Lord Justice FitzGibbon.—I believe all the teaching of the boys is done through the Christian Brothers?—At present. In 1857 the teaching was first done in the English school by the Christian Brothers, and they continue that teaching still. The classical teaching was done by a priest or two from 1857 to 1868. From 1868 to the present the teaching is done in both schools by the Christian Brothers, an additional brother having been obtained for the purpose of teaching in the classical school.

46. Are all the children attending the schools Roman Catholics?—Not all, there has been always a certain percentage—but a small one—of Protestants. Our attendance of Protestants at the present time amounts to 11—between the two schools.

47. Is there any other classical school in Mullingar?—No. There had been a classical school, and the trustees in those days before the erection of the College contributed to that classical school. They paid for the education of fifteen boys, £10 a year to a classical teacher before they were able to erect a school of their own. Of course when they got their own school furnished and completed they withdrew that, and the teacher left the town altogether.

48. I believe there never have been any boarders in the school?—Never.

49. So that the trust to "maintain" children of the town of Mullingar as well as educate them has not been carried out?—It has not been carried out because we have not been able to do so; but we have the house accommodation for their education, maintenance, and support as boarders, and as soon as our funds enable us to carry out that part of the will, we will do so.

50. Have you ever had any paying boarders?—No, we have had no boarders at all.

51. When you have any appointment of trustee to make, how is it done?—By deed. All the survivors execute the deed appointing the new trustee in the room of the deceased trustee.

52. Dr. Traill.—What does that cost you each time?—I should think about £3 or £4. It is an ordinary deed executed by the survivors. I don't know the cost exactly.

53. Rev. Dr. Molloy.—When the Administrator of the parish of Mullingar is promoted to another parish does he continue to be a trustee?—No, the succeeding Administrator is appointed in his place, because the will states distinctly that the third trustee after the two bishops is always to be the priest of Mullingar. The moment a priest ceases to be the Administrator of Mullingar his trust ceases, and a new trustee is appointed in his place.

54. Lord Justice FitzGibbon.—But you have to appoint him by deed?—We have.

55. Dr. Traill.—Does the Administrator of Mullingar often change?—Not often.

56. Every time that the Administrator changes have you to get a new deed?—We have a new deed, the number of the trustees is always to be five, namely, two bishops, and the Roman Catholic priest of Mullingar for the time being. The first Roman Catholic priest of Mullingar named in the will was Father Kelly, and he continued in because the trust was made to him personally. After his death the priest of Mullingar for the time being is trustee.

57. Have you filled the vacancies as fast as they occurred?—Within three months after the death of a trustee, we are bound to appoint a new trustee in his place, and we have done so at all times.

58. Who makes the selection of the children that come into the school?—They are all poor children, and we believe them all to be entitled to the bequest. We see no ground for making distinctions between them.

59. Lord Justice FitzGibbon.—Are there any school fees?—A penny a week.

60. Does the ordinary rule of the Christian Brothers apply of getting what fees they can?—The fees are limited to a penny a week, and they don't get them from all. I don't think they ever get more. They don't get that even except from a certain proportion.

61. Dr. Traill.—Practically there is no selection because they are not boarders?—Not boarders.

62. Every day child that comes is accepted?—Being a poor child and not merely the poor children, but if they are not considered to be in opulent circumstances. That is a very elastic term, and very hard to make distinctions under. We consider that nearly all the children that present themselves are entitled.

63. Do the Protestant children apply themselves to come in?—They apply themselves to come in.

64. Is there any provision for their religious instruction?—None.

65. What do they do at the times of religious instruction?—They go away. They are always excluded from the religious instruction. The instruction given to a certain extent is denominational, because theology—moral and dogmatic—and catechetical and elementary theology can be taught, and ought to be taught; but of course the branches of theology to be taught are determined by the trustees.

66. Are any of the Protestant children taught theology?—The Protestant children are not taught any religious teaching at the hours for it, and never have been. Their religious principles have been

Oct. 6, 1886.

The Most Rev. Dr. Nulty, Lord Bishop of Meath.

OCT. 6, 1888.

The Most Rev. Dr. Nulty, Lord Bishop of Meath.

always scrupulously attended to with this result that though Protestants have come from the commencement to the present time, when there are eleven in the school, not a single Protestant child has ever lost his faith.

67. But on the whole you consider it a Roman Catholic endowment?—Of course we do, because we have the power, under one of the provisions of the will, to teach theology, as well as literature and science. Theology is religious teaching.

68. And you would not consider it a reason for altering the governing body that the institution should be open to Protestant children?—We have no power to alter the governing body, because it has been fixed by the will, and defined to be the Catholic Bishop of Meath, for the time being, and another Bishop of Ireland, the Roman Catholic priest of Mullingar, for the time being, and two Catholic laymen.

69. You don't consider that the fact of the endowment being open to the children of other denominations would be a sufficient reason to change the governing body?—No, we do not. We could not change it. We would invalidate the will if we did, and the trust would then cease; because the will says that this property is to be administered by the five trustees as he chose them; and if there is any interference with their freedom and liberty, then the trust lapses, and it becomes the private property of the three trustees.

70. I suppose you would not object to apply the same principle to the Incorporated Society's property?—I am not acquainted with that society. I don't understand it sufficiently to be able to give any opinion.

71. Lord Justice FitzGibbon.—Mr. Hevey's will provides that an "Inspector shall visit and examine the pupils once a week, and weekly report, for the information of the trustees, and that he shall be entitled to be paid £30 a year, by two half-yearly payments;" is that payment still made?—It is not—on a principle of economy. Two of ourselves are there constantly, and we look at the schools and examine them, and look after them, not once, but several times in the week, while an inspector should be appointed at a salary of £30 a year.

72. I think the parish priest is to be the inspector?—Yes; the administrator is to be the inspector. As soon as the funds will enable us to pay an inspector we will appoint him, in the same way that we will have boarders as soon as the funds enable us to support and maintain them, for you see all the intentions of the testator are to be carried out as far as the rents and profits of the estate enable the trustees to do it, and they have done so.

73. I believe there is some tradition that this will was drawn by Mr. O'Connell?—It was certainly drawn by Mr. O'Connell.

74. Dr. Traill.—Were there ever any boarders?—Never. We have been always struggling. We have not got the charity clear yet. We have the new buildings perfect.

75. How many boarders would they accommodate?—The utmost that we ever expect to accommodate would be about fifteen.

76. Lord Justice FitzGibbon.—How is your £500 a year spent?—As to the expenditure the account book can be shown to you. We have a great many burdens on our property. We have tithe-rentcharge, county cess, and poor rate, and a lot of other things. We have to pay the rent of the ground on which the college stands. Then there is the £35 a year to the Nuns, and the remainder to the Christian Brothers, and there is the interest on that £150 that we owe.

77. Do you keep a separate account for Hevey's trust?—Oh, certainly.

78. In a former report it is stated that an account is kept of Hevey's charity along with other general charities having no connexion with the Hevey endowment. The will directed that separate account books should be kept?—There has been a separate account kept from the very commencement. The transactions of every meeting are recorded in one book, and the accounts kept in another ever since 1837. (Account books produced.)

79. You have got parchment books, I see?—Yes. The accounts are kept most accurately. The expenditure is examined carefully, and all the items and vouchers are compared; and after having been drawn up on a rough sheet and audited by the trustees they are transferred to that book.

80. The trustees do the auditing?—They always audit themselves.

81. How often do they meet?—At least once a year. Sometimes they meet twice. When we had trouble with our tenants they met three or four times.

82. Dr. Traill.—How much do you pay the Christian Brothers every year?—Our first engagement was that the Brothers were to be paid at the rate of £40 a year each. The last Brother who was appointed is paid £50 a year, because circumstances are changed and maintenance costs more now than at the time when we entered upon the trust.

83. There are four items for salary due to them up to the 1st May, 1887?—During the difficulties we could not afford to pay them anything.

84. This is a sort of arrear—£50, £40, and £120, making £210 for the half year?—Yes.

85. And £100 in November?—Yes. That is owing to the fact that a great lot of arrears is due to them. We lost £1,800.

86. They have got since the 1st of January in this year £100, then £100, and then £100, besides the four payments last year?—Yes—that was entirely owing to the clearing off of the debts that were due to them before.

87. Lord Justice FitzGibbon.—According to the minute book there was a meeting on July 8, 1883, at which the Most Rev. Dr. Nulty was chairman, and Dr. Donnelly and the Rev. Laurence Gaughran also attended. There was no meeting in 1884. A meeting on March 9, 1885, was attended by the same three trustees. Then the next meeting was on April 13, 1886, and was attended by Dr. Nulty, Dr. Donnelly, and Fr. Gaughran and the Rev. J. Nulty, secretary. He is not a trustee?—Not a trustee.

88. At a meeting on January 26, 1887, Dr. Nulty, Mr. Thomas Maher, J.P., and Mr. Hugh O'Neill, J.P., attended, and also Mr. Mooney, solicitor. The account books were produced, examined, and found to be correct; and some resolutions were passed about your tenants. The trustees met again, it appears, on February 14, 1887, when a deed appointing new trustees was executed; and Mrs. Casey and her sister attended and made proposals for a holding. On April 6, 1887, you met again, when there were in attendance Dr. Nulty, the Rev. Philip Callery, Mr. Thomas Maher, J.P., and Mr. Hugh O'Neill; and you had a communication with Mr. M'Cormack, one of your tenants. You next met on October 4, 1887. That is your last meeting. Do your meetings not held at any regular time?—The usual time for holding the meetings is in September or October every year; but sometimes we are before that date, and sometimes we are obliged to meet a little after.

89. Apart from their regular meetings, what opportunities are taken by the trustees of looking after the schools?—I am here constantly.

90. You see the schools from time to time?—Of course I do.

91. And the parish priest attends regularly?—He does, and goes through them several times during the week; and four or five other clergymen do the same.

92. Is the Presentation Nuns School entirely a primary school?—It is.

93. You have erected a convent here for the superior education of girls?—Yes, it is a branch of the school in Navan.

94. A girl from it got a medal in modern languages

last year?—Yes; and this year they got four exhibitions. It is an ordinary day school.

94. It has nothing to do with the Presentation Nuns School?—Nothing whatever. It has nothing whatever to do with the endowment.

95. Dr. Traill.—How many Christian Brothers are in your own school?—Five Christian Brothers and a lay teacher compose the ordinary staff.

96. What is the annual salary supposed to be paid to them?—Well, the annual salary was supposed to be £30 a year for the first five brothers, and £50 for the last who was appointed, making £200. Then we supply them with coal, candle light, and furniture.

97. I observe in the account, that in salaries alone you paid in fifteen months £4?0?—Yes, I believe we did; but that was entirely owing to the fact that in former years we were unable to pay them anything at all.

Oct. 4, 1888.

The Most Rev. Dr. Nulty, Lord Bishop of Meath.

99. Lord Justice Naish.—There were arrears due?—Yes; and we feared that we would have been obliged to close the schools. Only that they drew on resources of their own which carried them over that period they would have been obliged to close the schools.

100. Dr. Traill.—You don't appear to have received any arrears, looking to the credit side of the account for that year?—We had to surrender £1,300 altogether.

101. Lord Justice FitzGibbon.—Your experience goes to confirm that of other people, that charity trustees having lands don't profit much by them?—It is the most precarious, I think, of all incomes, especially for a school.

Rev. Br. Edward Vincent Geary sworn and examined.

Rev. Br. Edward Vincent Geary.

102. Lord Justice FitzGibbon.—How long have you been teaching in Hervy's School?—Since 1870.

103. You are the principal now?—Yes.

104. How many schools have you got?—Five at present, with a brother for each school.

105. How do you divide the five schools?—When the brothers first came to Mullingar in October, 1856, they were given in charge four schools. We call them the "general school." The first is the lowest; the second is more advanced; and the third and fourth are the senior schools.

106. Are these all primary schools?—All primary.

107. What numbers have you attending them?—We have 400 on the roll for the four; and the daily average attendance for the twelve months ending the 1st of July was 203.

108. What assistance do you get from the endowment for these four schools?—Nothing, excepting the salaries of the brothers and the repair of the schools.

109. How many of your pupils pay fees?—None in these schools, except a penny a week. That goes for slates, pencils, maps, and other school requisites.

110. Tell us about your upper school?—In the classical school we have at present eighty on the roll, and there has been a daily average attendance of fifty-nine for the twelve months ending the 1st of July last.

111. Lord Justice Naish.—Do any boys who are attending the ordinary schools attend the classical school at the same time?—No.

112. Lord Justice FitzGibbon.—Of the eighty boys on the roll how many are past pupils of the lower schools?—I suppose about forty.

113. And the remaining half are boys who joined first as pupils of the classical school?—Exactly.

114. What is your course of teaching in the classical school?—Greek, Latin, French, English, Mathematics, Natural Philosophy, Magnetism, Electricity, Chemistry, and Drawing.

115. Lord Justice FitzGibbon.—What provision do you make for the teaching of Greek?—We have a teacher in the school and a paid classical professor who teaches Latin and Greek.

116. Who pays him?—We pay him £80 a year from the income of the school.

117. What is the income from the school?—About £130 a year from fees.

118. Is the professor resident?—No.

119. What fees do you charge?—We have a scale of fees. We have junior boys who pay 10s. a quarter. The more advanced boys in the English course pay 15s.; and those studying classics £1 a quarter.

120. Is that the highest?—Yes.

121. Of what class are the boys?—Well, shopkeepers sons and farmers sons.

122. Are they preparing for professions?—Some of them are. Many of them go to the classical seminary in Navan.

123. What have you done in the Intermediate examinations?—In 1887 we presented 63 boys, and of them 33 passed, taking honours in various subjects, besides one junior grade exhibition of £15 and two book prizes. In 1888 we presented 29 boys, and gained 31 passes with honours in a good many subjects, also one £20 exhibition in the junior grade, and a £3 book prize.

124. Dr. Traill.—How do you manage the religious instruction?—At the time of the religious instruction the non-Catholic children leave the school in which it is held.

125. Have you a special hour for it?—Yes, twelve o'clock.

126. And then they leave?—They leave; and in fine weather they go out about the grounds, and in cold wet weather they retire into another room.

127. Lord Justice FitzGibbon.—How many non-Catholic pupils are there?—We have three in the general school and eight in the classical school.

128. Rev. Dr. Molloy.—There is a National School in the town besides the Christian Brothers School?—There is.

129. And I suppose most of the Protestant children go to the National School?—I suppose so.

130. But you receive any who present themselves?—Yes, that is the wish of the trustees.

131. Dr. Traill.—The will says that the trustees were to make a selection of children to be taught in the school; is everyone that comes admitted, or is there any selection made?—Those that present themselves and that the trustees consider eligible are admitted.

132. Are their names submitted to the trustees, or is every child admitted that comes to the school?—Well, if we have any doubt about a child——

133. What do you call "doubt"—is it that the parents are too rich or too poor?—Oh, no, but as to his moral character, for it might not be well to admit all sorts among the children.

134. How do you submit the children's character to the trustees?—The senior priest of the parish is one of the local trustees, and as such he has a better means of knowing the characters of the children than we have.

135. Do you ever ask the Protestant clergyman about the character of a Protestant child?—Oh, no, as he is not one of the trustees.

136. Lord Justice FitzGibbon.—Have you had any question about admitting any child?—Yes, we have, but very seldom. During the last seven years it only happened once or twice.

137. Was that a question of moral character?—Yes.

138. But no child was ever excluded because it was a Protestant?—Oh, no, never within my memory.

139. Lord Justice FitzGibbon.—This case of Hervy's Charity is very peculiar. The endowment is not exempt from our Act because, although exclusively

Oct. 8, 1886.

Rev. W. Edmund Vincent Casey.

under the jurisdiction of Roman Catholics, it is not exclusive as regards the objects of the charity, which include all poor children of Mullingar, irrespective of their religious belief. It is, however, a question always for the discretion of the Commissioners, whether the Act of Parliament is to be put in force or not with regard to any particular charity. Lest there should be any "intermeddling"—the word in the will—with his charitable intentions by any court or tribunal, the testator endeavoured to provide that in such case the property should go over altogether. If it became necessary to discuss the question, there is a great deal to be said against such a clause being legally effective, being an attempt to keep outside the law. On the other hand it might be held lawful for a man to provide that if anybody set about altering the intentions he himself had expressed, another intention should take effect for the purpose of preventing the original design from being defeated. The person really concerned here would be whoever is now the heir-at-law of the last survivor of the three original trustees. The person who occupies the position of heir-at-law of the last survivor of those three trustees, would be the object of the testator's bounty if this clause should take effect. If we were to set about settling a scheme for this charity, the result possibly might be to encourage somebody to come forward as heir-at-law of Patrick Kelly, and to bring an ejectment against the Harvey trustees, contending that the property was absolutely his. One of our objects is to avoid litigation—not to give occasion for it. We are satisfied that the endowment is being applied substantially as Harvey intended that it should. The poor of the parish of Mullingar are getting the benefit of it, and there is no reason whatever to suppose that any violation of trust is going on. If there were any violation of trust, this clause would never prevail to prevent its being set right; but a discretionary jurisdiction such as ours—I speak for my colleagues as well as for myself—we exercise most wisely in saying and ruling—as we do now—that although this charity is not exempt, under the circumstances we do not deem it expedient or necessary to undertake the settlement of a scheme for it. I am sorry the trustees have had trouble in the management of their land. The only thing we could do for them, if the difficulty I have referred to did not exist, would be to incorporate them so as to prevent the necessity for having a deed of conveyance on the appointment of each new trustee. But it would not be worth while to raise any question about their position for so small an object as that; and, therefore, I think we shall act most wisely in leaving it as it is.

140. Lord Justice Naish.—I concur in what Lord Justice Fitzgibbon has said. I don't think it would be expedient for us to frame any scheme for altering the management of this charity.

WILSON'S HOSPITAL, MULTYFARNHAM.

The Rev. *Hill Wilson White*, LL.D., M.A., sworn and examined.

The Rev. Hill Wilson White, LL.D., M.A.

141. Lord Justice Fitzgibbon. You were formerly Head Master of Navan Endowed School?—Yes.

142. And you removed thence to become Head Master of Wilson's Hospital?—My title is not head master; it is chaplain and superintendent. That is the title under the Act of Parliament and the wills.

143. The charity was founded under two wills—that of Andrew Wilson of 1724, and that of William Wilson of 1761?—Yes. The wills are incorporated in the Act passed in the second year of George III.—1761. The first report of the Endowed Schools Commission of 1807 incorporates the words of the will of 1724. The will states the hospital to be intended for a habitation for aged men, being Protestants and decayed housekeepers of Westmeath and other adjoining counties, not exceeding 40; and also for a habitation for Protestant men's children of the same counties not exceeding 150. There is also a provision for the erection of a schoolhouse adjoining the hospital; and it is provided that the aged men and the children are to be provided with diet, clothing, firing, and the other necessaries of subsistence. The trustees are to be the Primate of all Ireland, the Archbishops of Dublin and Tuam, and the Bishops of Meath and Kilmore. So under the 5th clause of the 7th section of the Act I submit it is one of the endowments to which the Act does not apply.

144. There is no longer any Archbishop of Tuam?—No; but the Bishop of Tuam succeeded him.

145. You still have five trustees—the Archbishops of Armagh and Dublin, and the Bishops of Tuam, Meath, and Kilmore?—Yes. The Act provides that they shall have continuance for ever, with the name of the trustees and guardians of Wilson's Hospital in the county of Westmeath, with perpetual succession, and to be capable of suing and being sued.

146. What provision is there for the appointment of the chaplain?—The hospital has clearly three objects—habitation for old men, educational establishment for boys, erection and maintenance of chaplaincy. There is the ecclesiastical foundation which is now a benefice in the diocese of Meath—the chaplaincy. One of the provisions was that the trustees should—

"Erect a chapel adjoining the hospital, and from time to time for ever appoint a chaplain to be resident, and to be accommodated with diet, lodging, and firing, and to be paid out of the rents and profits such salary as should appear to them proper, not exceeding £40 sterling; and such chaplain shall read prayers once a week according to the liturgy of the Established Church of Ireland."

The course of education is laid down plainly under the will also. The children are to be taught to read and write, and are to be carefully instructed in the grounds of the Protestant religion, and to be taught the Catechism, and to sing the Psalms. I carry out that provision by having daily service always in the chapel, with the Psalms chanted, both morning and evening.

147. Rev. Dr. Molloy.—Do you receive pupils of different Protestant denominations?—No, they are all members of the Church of Ireland, and all attend the daily services, and are instructed in the Catechism and the singing of the Psalms.

148. Professor Dougherty.—Which Catechism?—The Church Catechism.

149. Dr. Traill.—Not the Westminster Confession of Faith?—No; but then I must say that the education has been greatly improved since the Intermediate examinations came in.

150. Lord Justice Naish.—How many boys have you at present?—Sixty boys on the roll.

151. All boarders?—All boarders.

152. And free?—All free. There is no payment of any sort; and when the boys leave the hospital they are still looked after in the way of giving them guidance and situations.

153. Rev. Dr. Molloy.—Do you send up boys to the Intermediate examinations?—Yes, every year since they commenced.

154. Can you give us the results?—Yes, for every year since 1880. This year the boys obtained 2 honours. I sent up 11 and all passed—10 in the junior grade and 1 in the middle grade. My boys are all almost too young for the Intermediate, because they come to me between the ages of 8 and 11, and leave after being with me for five years. One little boy went in at between 12 and 13 and passed in honours in five subjects. I had altogether this year, with 11 candidates, 20 honours, and 60 passes.

making the total of 56 passes and honours. Five passed with honours in English; 7 in honours in arithmetic; 3 in book-keeping; 3 in Euclid; 3 in algebra; 1 in natural philosophy; 8 in drawing; 5 obtained honours in music; and there were 9 passes in [illegible]; 4 in natural philosophy; 7 in book-keeping. Only one boy failed in book-keeping.

155. Where do the boys generally go when they leave you?—The clever smart boys obtain positions in the Excise and in the Second Class Civil Service, and in business.

156. Do they obtain these direct from your school?—Directly. One passed directly for the Second Class Civil Service in 1884, and this year he has been appointed one of the inspectors of the Post Office over the heads of a great number. A question was asked about it in the House of Commons, and the answer given was that he was the best qualified for the appointment. He is a young man named Thompson. He had been in the hospital as a pupil and monitor for nine years.

157. Have you any limit of age for the boys?—From eight to eleven. There is no limit of age as to a boy remaining. Five years is the time that a boy is supposed to remain; but a discretion is left to me to retain clever boys as monitors with a view to getting them a better class of situations than if they were apprenticed to ordinary trades. One boy got a gold medal in ethics in Trinity College in 1883, and he is now a clergyman in London.

158. The general run of boys leave between thirteen and sixteen?—Between fourteen and sixteen. Boys rarely leave as young as thirteen. It is not legal to apprentice a boy before the age of fourteen.

159. And in special cases you keep them on to seventeen or eighteen?—To seventeen or eighteen.

160. Lord Justice FitzGibbon.—But only for assistance in teaching?—For assistance in teaching; but they still go on with their studies under the schoolmaster.

161. I see a great reduction in the numbers during the last ten years?—There has been a large reduction in the income. I cannot tell you the income, not being the agent of the estates, but I can tell you that I received in 1878 £3,440 2s. 8d.; in 1888 £2,850, and next year it will be £400 less than that.

162. Why is that?—By the reduction of the rents. There has been a large reduction. When I went to the hospital first I received from the agent £300 a month for carrying on the establishment. I now receive £200, so that the income is reduced nearly 33½ per cent.

163. Lord Justice Naish.—Where are your estates situated?—Principally in Westmeath. There is one large farm in the county of Kildare. There are some small properties in Longford held under leases for ever, hardly anything is got from them.

164. Rev. Dr. Molloy.—Has the reduction been made chiefly by the Land Commission or by voluntary arrangement?—Altogether by voluntary arrangement between the tenants and the agent, as far as I know.

165. Lord Justice FitzGibbon.—The Report of 1878, p. 806, says that the lands—

"Contain 4,464 acres, 3 roods, and 7 perches, statute measure, let to yearly tenants, and they comprise in addition a head rent of £36, and a rent-charge of £179 18s. 5d. per annum. The Rental of the lands amounts to £3,874, and the Poor Law Valuation, £3,718, excluding the buildings. If the valuation of the houses were added the rental would probably be found at least one per cent. below the valuation. The lands comprise a great variety of soil and appear generally let at very moderate rents. The tenantry appear comfortable, and many of the houses exceedingly good. The trustees have drained some portions of the estate and added the reclaimed land to the adjoining holdings; they allocate £300 per annum to the improvement of the estate, and many of the tenants have thus been induced to build their 'capital houses.' During the winter, 1879–80, a number of the tenants were kept in employment by the trustees in making improvements on their own lands."

At that time the rental was £3,800; do I understand you to say that it has been reduced to £2,800?—Not the rental but the amount paid to me to carry on the hospital. There are a number of expenses—agent's fees, law expenses, disbursements, and other things that I have nothing to say to. The agent and the trustees manage that between them.

166. When do the trustees meet?—According to the Act of Parliament there is a special date appointed for the meeting of the trustees, the last Monday in November of each year. The constitution of the trustees consists of the Bishops of Meath and Kilmore, and they meet any time they think fit; but the special meeting appointed by the statute is the time at which any alteration in the management must legally take place.

167. Dr. Traill.—Do they meet on that last Monday in November?—On every last Monday in November; and then I attend with all my accounts to be audited and vouched. My accounts are audited by the trustees.

168. Lord Justice FitzGibbon.—How is the management of the estate carried on?—The late Charles Hamilton, of Dominick-street, was agent till his death, and one of his sons is agent now. His management is greatly praised in a report of the Endowed School Commission, which says that the tenants are contented and happy, and that the estates are managed much on the English principle, the farm buildings having been erected by the trustees.

169. Dr. Traill.—I suppose we will get particulars from Mr. Hamilton about that?—The trustees were under the impression that Wilson's Hospital was totally exempt. When this Act first passed a notice was sent in claiming exemption, as required by public advertisement.

170. Lord Justice FitzGibbon.—Are the 40 old men still there?—There never were 40 old men. There are 11 old men there at present. I have been there since January 1, 1880, and the yearly average of boys since then has been 118.

171. Dr. Traill.—Could you give us the averages for each year?—I can. In 1880 there were 163 boys on the books and 21 old men. From 1880 to 1881, there were 142 boys and 21 old men. From 1881 to 1882, 131 boys and 18 old men; from 1882 to 1883, 96 boys and 20 old men, from 1883 to 1884, 103 boys and 19 old men; from 1884 to 1885, 103 boys and 21 old men; from 1885 to 1886, 100 boys and 21 old men; from 1886 to 1887, 87 boys and 20 old men; from 1887 to 1888, 79 boys and 18 old men; and at present there are 69 boys and 11 old men.

172. Lord Justice FitzGibbon.—Let me ask you to take the last completed year?—The last completed year was from August 1st, 1887, to July 31st, 1888.

173. What was the amount paid during that completed year for the maintenance of the institution?—£2,890.

174. How much is the salary of the chaplain and superintendent?—£400 a year. It was £500 a year in my predecessor's time. I was appointed since the last report at a salary of £400.

175. What staff have you?—My head master is paid £100 a year, and has also board, lodging, washing, and maintenance. Then I have an assistant master who receives £20 a year, and his board and maintenance in the house, and the steward receives £50.

176. Formerly there was a second master at a salary of £80?—He is now master in an endowed school at Clonmellon, and there being a much smaller number of boys the same staff is not required.

177. The salaries at present are about £570 a year?—Yes.

178. There should be still remaining £2,350, after payment of the salaries, towards the maintenance of the establishment?—There won't be next year.

179. I am speaking of last year?—Yes; for last year.

180. Do the old men get any money allowance?—

Oct. 4, 1888.

The Rev. [illegible] White, [illegible]

Oct. 6, [illegible]

The Rev. [illegible] Wilson Waite, LL.D., M.A.

They get a small trifle of pocket money—6d. a week. That is 26s. a year.

181. Then about £[illegible] altogether goes to these; that still leaves £2,810—how is that spent?—It is spent in apprenticeship fees for the boys partly; I can give you for each year what the apprenticing of the boys costs.

182. Kindly give me what it was for last year?—Last year £1[illegible] [illegible]s. 6d. was spent in apprentice fees.

183. How many boys were apprenticed?—The apprenticeship fee is paid two years after the boy goes out. The amount is £10, of which £5 is paid at the end of two years, and £5 at the end of the apprenticeship.

184. To what sort of trades can you get boys apprenticed for fees of that sort?—To firms such as Mitchell of Grafton-street, as cooks; Hodges of Westmoreland-street, as plumbers. A great number of those firms don't take fees at all, and the fees are used for the payment of the board and maintenance of the boys at the Working Boys' Home in Denzille-street.

185. Then you don't apprentice the boys for that amount?—I get them places in Dublin. I pay 5s. 6d. a week for them there till they can earn wages. Most of the tradesmen in Dublin give boys 3s. or 4s. a week to commence with. A great many of the boys go as apprentices to printers in Dublin. They are also bound to tradesmen in the country—carpenters, smiths, plumbers.

186. We have been told in Londonderry that a greater number of boys go to printing than to any other trade, because they can get a small subsistence quickest at it?—They get 3s. a week at starting. The difference between that and the 5s. a week which is the charge in the Home, is paid out of the apprenticeship fee.

187. That still leaves about £2,000 per annum to be accounted for; what are the other outlays?—There are the household expenses. I have not brought any synopsis of them.

188. Do you clothe the boys?—Yes. I clothe the boys and the men, and boys going out. Every boy gets an outfit costing between £4 and £5.

189. What does the maintenance cost?—The average for eight years I have totted up to £23 15s.

190. Do they get meat every day?—No, they do not. The old men get meat every day. The boys get meat twice a week, and eggs on another day, rice, vegetables, and new milk.

191. I suppose the men and boys are nominated by the trustees?—No person can be admitted without an order signed by the committee of the trustees, the Bishops of Meath and Kilmore. There is no examination for entrance. The hospital has been kept to what the founder intended it for, namely, for the benefit and support of poor people. The clergyman of the parish, and the churchwardens must testify that the parents of the boys, through poverty, are unable to support and maintain them.

192. Where do they come from as a rule?—I have made a synopsis with a view to this inquiry. Since the foundation of the hospital there have been 3,6[illegible] boys maintained, and 348 old men.

193. What date do you go back to?—1763—the hospital was opened in 1761. Two thousand two hundred and eighty-five boys have come from Westmeath—it is practically a charity for the Protestant children of Westmeath and the adjacent counties, Meath, Longford, and Cavan.

194. Have you boys from a wider area?—Very few, unless those that claim relationship with the founder, for he has provided that those of his own name and kin should be preferred before others; and so there have been 376 Wilson boys in the hospital, and 43 old men—Wilsons. The place has never been without Wilsons. Three hundred and nine boys were from Meath; 253 from Longford; 370 from Cavan; 55 from King's County; 26 from Roscommon; and 16 from Dublin, since 1761.

195. How many from Armagh?—There have been two from Armagh, non-Wilsons. Many Wilsons have come from Armagh.

196. The Archbishop of Armagh did not nominate many?—He had no power. For many years the Bishop of Meath claimed the exclusive right of nomination, and Bishop Stopford nominated all the boys. The Bishop of Kilmore asserted his right to nominate equally, and since then the Cavan boys came in.

197. Lord Justice NAISH.—Of the 60 boys you have now, how many are from Westmeath?—I should fancy about 25.

198. Lord Justice FITZGIBBON.—If the building originally accommodated such a large number of both old men and boys, how is it utilised at present?—The large dormitory is empty, because the income has gone down; but you will see the enormous size of the place that has to be kept in order, a sort of monument to the memory of Andrew Wilson.

199. Have you tried getting boys at a low rate of payment to come in?—I have made that suggestion to the trustees, but I don't know if they intend to act on it or not.

200. Surely you would be able with your staff and buildings to give very valuable education to boys at a low rate?—For £20 a year I would take as many boys as would be sent in to me, because the establishment charges would be very nearly the same, in fact the establishment charges are almost identical now with what they were at the time of my appointment. I could accommodate with ease 120 boys.

201. I believe there is a registrar in Dublin who gets £100 a year?—Not that I know of. I am the registrar. My office comprises almost everything. I have to keep the whole building in repair, and look after the expenses of the old men, the payment for medical attendance, and everything else of the kind incident to a large establishment.

202. Dr. TRAILL.—What is the average age of the old men?—I have at present an old man who is ninety years of age, and who attends chapel every morning and evening, and can walk two or three miles as an exercise. The average age is seventy-five. A few years ago the average age of eighteen old men in the institution was eighty-one years and three months.

203. Rev. Dr. MOLLOY.—About what age do they come to you?—I should say the average age for coming in is seventy-four. There have been some of them as young as sixty-four, but these were men permanently disabled from earning their bread. A form has to be sent to the trustees on the part of the recommenders of the old men testifying that they are unable any longer to earn their own bread, and that that arises not from misconduct or any cause within their own control. The youngest man I have is sixty-four years of age, and he is a cripple from rheumatism.

204. What do you consider an old man?—I suppose a man would be qualified at about sixty. As a matter of fact men are never admitted at such an age. The candidates are mostly men coming up to eighty, and generally the oldest and poorest are admitted.

205. Lord Justice FITZGIBBON.—What class do they belong to?—Reduced farmers, reduced gentlemen, and reduced tradesmen. The next person to be admitted as an old man, is a doctor of medicine. I had a scholar of Trinity College, formerly a Classical Master at Drogheda, as one of my old men. People who have been reduced by causes that they could not control are admissible.

206. Have they got separate apartments?—Some of them have, and some of them have not. Then the boys in the same way belong to all classes of society. Any boy is admissible whose parents are so poor that they are unable through poverty to maintain him. I have gentlemen's sons in the hospital at present and labourers' sons; poverty is the one qualification—poverty and religion.

207. Lord Justice FitzGibbon.—Wilson's Hospital seems clearly to come within the exemptions from the Act. The governing body are all dignitaries of the church as established at the time the statute regulating the institution was passed; therefore the only question is whether the objects of the charity are exclusively persons of the same religious denomination. Other denominations of Protestants might possibly have been included in the terms of the will. But when we read the whole document it appears pretty clearly that the term "Protestant" is used in the narrow sense, for they are to be taught the Catechism, and there are provisions for the maintenance of a chaplain, and for their attending Divine service according to the rites of the Church of Ireland as then established; therefore we have only to declare Wilson's Hospital exempt. Dr. White will communicate with the trustees, and if there be any modification of the trusts or any addition to their powers which they think it would be advantageous to look for while our Act is in force we have jurisdiction to do anything of that kind that they require with their express consent, but not otherwise; and even with their express consent it will be our duty to observe all the intentions of the founder, so far as is consistent with keeping up the usefulness of the charity. The trustees being all ecclesiastical dignitaries, might, perhaps, think of adding one or more laymen, to assist in the management of this large property.

Rev. Dr. White.—They manage it by their agent.

208. Lord Justice FitzGibbon.—There is an application pending from the diocese of Meath to incorporate a body of trustees representing the Church of Ireland to hold educational endowments and superintend them throughout the diocese; possibly Wilson's Hospital School might be made useful as a school for boys who could pay something towards their schooling. It might be an object to place Wilson's Hospital at the top of the diocesan system and to make it a good school to which the cleverer boys could be promoted from the elementary schools of the diocese. You have plenty of accommodation.

209. Dr. Traill.—How can you teach sixty boys with such a small staff?—A number of the boys are very young, and our hours for school are long, and some of the boys preparing for the Intermediate—the older and more advanced boys—act as teachers.

210. You say you have one head master?—I have one head master who was first of the first under the National Board, and was for eleven years and a half master in a model school. He teaches French.

211. Does he teach mathematics?—He teaches mathematics, and one of my boys last year got ninety per cent. in algebra out of a possible 600.

212. Do you teach classics?—No classics.

213. What do you teach yourself?—I am not supposed to teach anything except religious knowledge. I superintend and look after everything as chaplain and manager of the school.

214. As a matter of fact do you not give any assistance in the teaching?—As a matter of fact, I examine the boys occasionally to see how they are getting on.

215. Does this master teach drawing?—He does. A number of boys—as I mentioned before—passed the Intermediate examination in drawing.

216. Have you any workshops attached to the school?—There is a carpenter's shop, where some of the boys amuse themselves occasionally in working; but I find that it is not well to mix up school work and trade work together. They are apprenticed.

217. Would they not make better apprentices if they learned the use of their hands while they were at school?—They learn the use of their hands very much in keeping that large place tidy, and helping the steward in the farm and garden.

218. You would not call helping a steward in a farm or a garden learning the use of a boy's hands—I mean the learning of some sort of carpenter's work?—Most of my painting and simple work of that kind is done by the boys. The boys are very young, their average age being under thirteen. The cleverer and older boys are generally working for the Intermediate, and their time is occupied in that way.

Lord Justice FitzGibbon.—We can do nothing to extend the usefulness of this endowment without the written consent of the trustees.

Oct. 8, 1885.

The Rev. Hill Wilson White, LL.D., &c.

FARRA SCHOOL, BUNBROSNA (INCORPORATED SOCIETY).

Thomas G. Foster, M.A., sworn and examined.

219. Lord Justice FitzGibbon.—You are the head master at Farra?—I am. In June, 1873, I was appointed—a little over ten years ago.

220. How many boys have you at Farra now?—Fifty-four.

221. How many are foundation boys?—Twenty-five. The number on the foundation varies considerably; twenty-seven is about the regular number.

222. Are you paid for them according to the same system as in the other Incorporated schools?—Yes, 10d. a day for each day the boy is in the house.

223. Of the others how many are parlour boarders?—I have twenty-two boarders altogether, of whom five are parlour boarders.

224. Are the remainder half boarders?—Yes.

225. What do the parlour boarders pay you?—£33 a year, and the half boarders £25 a year.

226. From what schools do you get the foundation boys?—From various schools in the counties of Westmeath, Meath, Longford and Cavan.

227. Have you any list of the schools they come from?—Not of the schools, but I have a list of the counties.

228. Are they admitted by competition?—The foundation pupils are solely admitted by competition.

229. How often are examinations held?—Once a year. The Incorporated Society holds two examinations for foundation pupils in Farra—one at the school taking in four boys from certain counties in the neighbourhood, and one in Dublin taking in boys from Dublin and Kildare.

Thomas G. Foster, M.A.

230. Lord Justice Naish.—Who nominates the boys?—Nobody.

231. Can anyone enter in?—Anyone can come in, but they must have certificates of qualification signed by the clergyman of the parish testifying as to the fitness and eligibility of the candidate and also as to the circumstances of his parents.

232. Lord Justice FitzGibbon.—These come to you, I suppose, in the same way as to the other Incorporated Society's schools, certifying that the candidate is a fit object for the Society's endowment, that he has been resident in the parish for a year, and that his conduct has been good and satisfactory?—Yes. The boys must be between the ages of twelve and sixteen.

233. Rev. Dr. Molloy.—How many have you generally competing for the four places?—On an average about fourteen or fifteen at the examination in Farra. Of the competition in Dublin, I know nothing.

234. Lord Justice FitzGibbon.—You get the boys down from Dublin with an order to admit them?—Quite so.

235. Dr. Traill.—Is it not one of the terms that all the boys must be members of the Church of Ireland?—It is not expressly stated.

236. Are they not considered to be such ?—I receive them on the express understanding that they are members of the Church of Ireland and I treat them as such.

237. Dr. TRAILL.—How many day-boys have you ?—Seven. There is a list of the counties to which the boys belong (hands document). Of the foundation boys three have come from Westmeath, eight from Cavan, two from Dublin, one from Longford, three from Kildare, one from Queen's County, and one from Kerry.

238. Lord Justice FITZGIBBON.—The largest number is from Dublin—two ; do you know what schools they came from ?—From St. Mathias' School, St. Peter's School ; a good many from Swords Schools ; and occasionally boys from other places.

239. Cavan is the place with the next largest number ; where were they principally from ?—The majority from Tullyvin School.

240. How many came from Tullyvin School ?—I think about five.

241. Do you know where the other three are from ?—There is a boy from Derrylane, and I think another from Bailieborough.

242. Westmeath three—where are they from ?—two from Castlepollard. We used to have boys from Mullingar, but latterly we have not any.

243. Kildare three—where are they from ?—From Celbridge. They are sent down from Dublin.

244. Rev. Dr. MOLLOY.—Your examination at Farra is only for Westmeath, Cavan, and Longford ?—Yes.

245. And from these counties you have twelve boys ?—Yes.

246. How many years do they usually remain ?—They are limited to three years.

247. Lord Justice FITZGIBBON.—The subjects of examination are the Old Testament to Deuteronomy, and the New Testament ; the Church Formularies and the Church Catechism with Scripture references, showing its doctrines to be confirmed by the Word of God. The school subjects are reading, writing, the rudiments of grammar, and the geography of Europe, Palestine and Asia Minor. Arithmetic to the Rule of Three and Vulgar and Decimal Fractions. Do you know what proportion the religious examination bears to the school portion ?—More than one-half.

248. In order to get in, must a boy be specially prepared in these specified subjects ?—Specially prepared or he would have no chance.

249. Do you find that the necessary special preparation is only to be got in a small number of schools ?—Yes, I find it to be the case.

250. Has the effect of this examination been to confine these foundation scholarships to the pupils of a few specially prepared schools ?—It is so, and what is more, I think that those boys who are so prepared in Scripture are not intellectually the best boys. They are [illegible] up. The questions are nothing more than riddles and puzzles in my estimation.

251. Then specially acquired capacity of answering Scripture riddles and puzzles contributes over 50 per cent. towards getting the foundation scholarships ?—Yes.

252. Professor DOUGHERTY.—I suppose you would not like to enlarge this examination yourself ?—I had to do so.

253. Lord Justice FITZGIBBON.—In the secular subjects how far does the examination go—how far is it necessary for the candidate to be advanced ?—Their education in the school subjects is very elementary.

254. How many classes have you in the school ?—We usually divide them into classes so as to comply with the Intermediate courses.

255. Do you send them direct to the Intermediate Examinations from Farra ?—Yes, certainly, and have been successful.

256. Dr. TRAILL.—Just tell us who the examiners for the foundation scholarships are ?—Principal fellows and professors of Trinity College—Dr. [illegible], Canon M'Ilraugh, and Dr. Walsh. Mr. Poole has also come down, and the Rev. Morgan Jellett.

257. Who are the examiners in the secular subjects ?—The same examiners.

258. Do they examine in arithmetic ?—Yes.

259. Does the Rev. Morgan Jellett ?—I imagine he examines in arithmetic and geography.

260. Lord Justice FITZGIBBON.—Now, about the Intermediate examinations ?—Within the last few years I sent in sixty pupils in the various grades of the Intermediate examinations ; and out of these fifty-two passed, obtaining altogether 180 passes in honours, one gold medal (senior grade, in mathematics, in 1887), six special prizes of £10 in mathematics for special excellence, and several book prizes.

261. Did the boys who got the gold medal in mathematics and the other special prizes go up direct from Farra ?—Direct.

262. How is it that they were not promoted to Santry ?—The boy who got the gold medal got the first place in Santry before he left. He got the Intermediate distinctions before going to Santry.

263. Dr. TRAILL.—What is his status ?—[illegible]. He is at present in Santry reading for science [illegible].

264. Lord Justice FITZGIBBON.—What assistants have you ?—I have three.

265. What are the salaries ?—I have a salary of £100 a year myself, and an allowance of £10 a year towards the keep of the assistants.

266. They get no salary beyond that which they have from the Incorporated Society ?—Not from the Society.

267. What you get from the Society's endowment is £100 a year in money and 10d. a day for each foundation boy ; and you have the place kept in repair ?—I get a little more. I get an allowance of £10 a year for servants, and £10 a year for coal—in all I get £220 a year from the Society.

268. And you have the place maintained ?—Maintained by the Society.

269. You have nothing to do with that ?—Nothing at all.

270. To what class in life do the boys belong as ?—Those that come in on the foundation are the children of poor parents. They are generally the sons of small farmers.

271. Rev. Dr. MOLLOY.—And shopkeepers ?—Quite so.

272. Lord Justice FITZGIBBON.—Do you know any other school besides Tullyvin where they board for a year in order to be prepared to go to Farra ?—I am not aware of any other.

273. Dr. TRAILL.—What suggestions would you make for the improvement of the examination ?—I would moderate the quantity of Scripture required from the boys, but I should by all means have qualifying examinations in Scripture.

274. Professor DOUGHERTY.—Would you not diminish the requirements in regard to Church formularies ?—Certainly not ; I would like a boy to be grounded in the principles of religion.

275. Dr. TRAILL.—It is the total of Church formularies and Scripture being over 50 per cent. of the examination that you object to ?—Quite so ; I don't think the standard very high in the secular subjects.

276. At what age do they come in ?—Usually between fifteen and sixteen, so that they are not eligible to compete in the junior grade of the Intermediate system.

277. Rev. Dr. MOLLOY.—Do they continue their Scriptural education in Farra ?—They do.

278. And have they to pass a Scriptural examination before going into Santry ?—A most stringent one.

279. So that if they had not studied Scripture

before going into Farra they could hardly be prepared for the Sentry examination?—Quite so.

280. Professor Dougherty.—Do most of the boys become theologians?—A good many do. Not long ago two of my boys became ministers and were ordained a few days ago.

281. Lord Justice FitzGibbon.—Have you no boys younger than fifteen years of age in the school?—Yes, paying boarders.

282. How long does the foundation scholarship last?—For three years at Farra, and, if they succeed in getting another scholarship at Sentry, one year more, and sometimes two years.

283. That would bring them up to twenty?—Yes.

284. Are not these ages a little too advanced?—I think so. I would suggest that the age for a candidate getting into Farra should be reduced from a minimum of sixteen to one of fifteen, so as to enable them to compete in the junior grade of the Intermediate examinations.

285. What is the minimum at present?—They must be over twelve years of age on the 1st of June previous to the day of the examination. I would not alter that. I would have the age between twelve and fifteen instead of sixteen.

286. The course of teaching has been limited, in Farra, with respect to classics?—The Incorporated Society don't recognise the teaching of classics to foundation pupils.

287. Do you teach them?—Certainly; I have a classical teacher, but the classical teaching is restricted by the fees of pupils.

288. Do you think it would be an advantage for the foundation boys that they should get more classical teaching?—By all means.

289. Lord Justice Naish.—Are the foundation boys taught Latin and Greek?—They are, but they pay a small fee for it—half the fee that is charged to the boarders.

290. They are not taught them unless they pay a certain fee?—Certainly not.

291. Dr. Traill.—How many boys have you from Mullingar?—Three from the whole county of Westmeath.

292. Can you explain why they don't come?—I think the primary schools of Westmeath are very few.

293. Do they not come from the National schools?—No, because they are not prepared in Scripture there.

294. Lord Justice FitzGibbon.—As a matter of fact is not the cause this—that it requires special instruction and training to pass this Scripture examination which cannot be got in any ordinary National school?—Quite so; very special instruction.

295. Dr. Traill.—Are the examinations by paper or viva voce?—It is partly on paper and partly viva voce.

296. Do the questions strike you as being rather "tips"?—Certainly; the majority of them are "tips"—a great many puzzles.

297. What is that from?—I should say from having the same examiners so long. A man is bound to repeat himself if he continues to be an examiner.

Dr. Traill.—Don't advertise your examinations as being held by fellows and professors of Trinity College for they are neither the one nor the other. Dr. Biddle comes here from the Incorporated Society; and the others are fellows or professors of Trinity College.

298. Lord Justice FitzGibbon.—Kindly send us in writing the schools from which each of the twenty-four boys on the foundation have come. How have your boys been doing at Sentry?—They compare favourably with those of other schools.

299. They compete with Athlone, Primrose Grange, and Dundalk?—Yes.

300. Professor Dougherty.—Is the school in the best possible situation?—I would hardly say it is in the best possible situation so far as the needs of the locality are concerned.

301. Dr. Traill.—How far is it from this?—About eight miles.

302. Professor Dougherty.—You have forty-seven boys and only three boarders from the County of Westmeath?—At present.

303. Have the numbers diminished?—I should say not. They are at about the average. Mullingar is my nearest town.

304. Lord Justice FitzGibbon.—You are not in a situation where you could have many day boys?—Certainly not.

305. As to the boarders is it not a disadvantage to be a long way from a town?—No, it is rather an advantage.

306. I suppose the clergyman of the parish is the catechist?—Yes, the Rev. Mr. Campbell was so until this year.

307. When does he attend?—Weekly, or sometimes twice a week.

308. What does he do in the way of inspection?—I don't think he inspects in the way of looking over the boys' work, but he sees that the school is kept tidy and in order, and that no irregularity occurs. He imparts spiritual education. Mr. Campbell has been catechist for nine years.

309. Are there any local gentry who take an interest in the school?—Not at present, except Lord Greville who takes an interest in it.

310. Does he visit the school?—He has, once or twice.

311. You have no local committee of any kind?—No, apart from the catechist.

312. Do you think that gentlemen of the county being associated with the Incorporated Society would lead to getting the boys of Westmeath the benefit of this institution?—There was a former member of the Incorporated Society, Mr. Smythe of Barbavilla, who took a great interest in the school; but I really don't see what benefit would be derived from it.

313. Would it be a benefit to the boys of Westmeath to see that the form of examination was such as to enable them to compete fairly, and to see that boys from National schools were not practically excluded?—I think it is the business of the clergymen of the county to do that.

314. If you had some local clergymen at a committee, do you think they would exercise a controlling influence over these examinations?—I am not prepared to say that.

315. May I ask you to state the condition of the school when you took charge of it?—When I was appointed there were only eleven foundation pupils, and no boarders; the state of the premises was very bad. They had fallen into a great state of dilapidation for three or four years before I got there.

316. How long are you at Farra?—Ten years. Mr. Campbell was appointed catechist at the time I was appointed master.

317. Rev. Dr. Molloy.—Were you head master at the time of Lord Rosse's Commission?—Yes.

318. What was the success of the candidates from Farra at the Sentry examinations in 1887?—In 1887 I sent up six boys and five of them succeeded in getting foundation scholarships, taking 1st, 2nd, 3rd, and 5th places. There were only nine foundation scholarships given in that year and we obtained five of them.

319. And in the present year what has been the success of the boys competing in Sentry?—I sent 6 candidates and they all succeeded in obtaining places, namely 1st, 2nd, 3rd, and 5th class also, which was a coincidence. In the last five years I sent forward 33 candidates for Sentry scholarships, and 23 of these succeeded in obtaining places, including three first places.

320. Have you had to refuse boys as boarders as the school was full?—I refused three or four this year as paying boarders for want of accommodation.

321. Dr. Traill.—How is it that in 1886 there were only 11 boys here?—I cannot conceive the reason. A school fluctuates very much.

Oct. 4, 1886.

Thomas G. Power, B.A.

Oct. 4, 18[illegible]. — Thomas C. Foster, B.A.

322. How many does the house hold?—The present dormitory arrangements suffice for 35 or 36 without overcrowding. By giving up a room of my own I was enabled to take in 46 or 47.

323. Are these 54 boys you have mentioned all boarders?—No—47 boarders and seven day boys.

324. Isn't there direct railway communication from all parts of Ireland to Farra?—Yes.

325. What is the nearest station?—Mullyfarnham.

326. As to the situation of the school could it be better or more healthful than it is?—I don't think a healthier place could be found at the present time.

327. Lord Justice FitzGibbon.—Have you any means of getting additional buildings—did you apply to the Incorporated Society?—At the last meeting I sent up an application.

328. Dr. Traill.—Haven't they laid out a large sum of money on the school?—Not lately. Since I came they laid out a large sum of money, and it was all needed. More is needed still.

329. Rev. Dr. Molloy.—What is the average expenditure on Farra school by the Incorporated Society, everything included?—I could only give a rough approximation. I should say between £500 and £600 a year.

330. At the time of the last Commission it was about £1,000 a year?—Yes; but I can explain that by the fact that they were just after expending nearly £1,000 in improvements and repairs. Taking it every year, it costs about £600 a year.

331. Dr. Traill.—Have you any agricultural department in it?—None whatever.

332. It used formerly to be an agricultural school?—So I was told.

333. Lord Justice FitzGibbon.—What land is there?—I rent 12 statute acres, at a yearly rent of [illegible] an acre.

334. Besides this, was there any other land attached to the school?—When I was appointed I was told that the house was situated on 5 acres of land, free of rent. When I came I was told that the free land consisted of a garden and a yard.

The Rev. *John [illegible]*, B.A., sworn and examined.

Rev. John [illegible], B.A.

335. Lord Justice FitzGibbon.—You are the clergyman of the parish in which Farra school is situated?—Yes.

336. You hold the office of catechist?—Yes.

337. What is the salary of the catechist?—£20 a year.

338. Are you supposed to give religious instruction once a week, and to visit the school?—Yes; and to exercise a general supervision. The post of catechist is something like an inspectorship. There is constant communication between the catechist and the Secretary of the Society. In fact, if I don't send Mr. Hackett a weekly or a fortnightly letter, I have a letter from him to know what is going on.

339. You have heard the evidence about the entrance examination for the foundation scholarships; have you any suggestion to offer as to how the advantages of the school could be extended to a larger class of boys?—Well, I think, giving my own opinion, altogether apart from my position as catechist, that if the Scripture examinations were modified somewhat it would throw open the competition to a greater number of schools of the diocese and locality that are eligible for Farra. The competition at present is limited by the fact that there is an undue weight attached to Scripture and Church formularies. Most of the schools now in the diocese are in connexion with the National Board. There is not the same facility for grinding up boys in Scripture and Church formularies in connexion with the National Board as there was under the old Church Education Society's schools; and consequently the competition has got into the hands of a few schools where the masters who attend the examinations get the questions, and record them and keep them so as to be able to grind their pupils up in the required answers.

340. Dr. Traill.—Do you think that would be remedied by changing the examiner every year?—Yes, to some extent. We had down to Farra this year Dr. Lee, and he modified considerably the whole character of the Scripture examinations. I think the Scripture examinations this year were very good and very fair.

341. Lord Justice FitzGibbon.—Did any boy from a new school succeed?—The success of one school was not so great as was expected in consequence of the Scripture examiner being changed.

342. Would it not take some time before other schools could become aware that they had got a chance from the change in the examiners?—I think that if so many marks were not given to Scripture and Church formularies a greater number of schools would compete.

343. Then the special weight and peculiar character of the Scriptural examinations prevents a number of eligible schools from competing?—I think so. I think the National schools would compete if they were not handicapped.

344. Rev. Dr. Molloy.—Do you consider the education of the day pupils at Farra satisfactory?—Oh, nothing can be better.

345. I ask the question because at the time of the last Commission it was reported not to be so.

Mr. *Foster*.—Allow me to explain that circumstance. I was Head Master then. I was asked for my most elementary class, and produced three boys, two of whom did not know their letters. The report made was that they were the worst he had ever examined, and I think it was most unfair.

346. Rev. Dr. Molloy.—The report was made with respect to the boys examined, but it was a mistake to represent them as a type of the school I think so. There is a course of examination in the school little short of that for a sizarship, and yet he said that the answering of the day scholars was disgraceful. He was going away with altogether a wrong opinion about the day boys, but I asked him to examine my senior class. At the present time there are not more than seven day boys, but after a time I think there will be a greater number, in fact I know that after some time four or five boys will attend the school, who are not eligible now, in consequence of being too young.

Rev. Mr. [illegible].—There is a rising Protestant population in the district.

THE MEATH AND ARDAGH DIOCESAN FREE SCHOOL.

The Very Rev. *Francis Swift*, Dean of Clonmacnois, sworn and examined.

Very Rev. Francis Swift, Dean of Clonmacnois.

347. Lord Justice FitzGibbon.—You are the Rector of Mullingar?—Yes.

348. Do you remember when there was a Diocesan Free School here?—I do. There was a Diocesan Free School about a quarter of a mile outside the town. Mr. Geoghegan was the last master. He died I think about the year 1855 or 1856.

349. There was no Diocesan Free School in [illegible]

house at the time of the passing of the Church Act?—No.

349. Do you know what became of the land and premises?—I don't know whether the land belonged to any public board, or whether it was rented by the last master.

350. Lord Justice Naish.—What has become of the building?—It is inhabited. It is let by Colonel Cooper.

351. Is it private property?—I think so. I cannot tell you that. I don't think it was a diocesan school, so far as I know. I think the house was rented merely by the master.

352. Lord Justice FitzGibbon.—The matter stands thus:—The Commissioners of Education have now nearly £700 belonging to this Meath and Ardagh Diocesan School, and the money is at present used by them to meet divers debit balances or other accounts. It is lying idle, in fact, so far as the locality is concerned. We have put it into the notice of this sitting in order that the people of the neighbourhood might know that the money is in existence, and we will have to settle some scheme for the application of it. There is a similar but rather larger sum belonging to the Tuam Diocese, and £250 belonging to Leighlin and Ossory, which I have no doubt was the result of the sale of some land.

Very Rev. Francis Swift, Dean of Clonmacnois.

Dean Swift.—I never heard of any property belonging to the diocesan school here.

354. Lord Justice FitzGibbon.—You probably never would have heard of it until the end of time but for a Commission like this. The money has been accumulating for many years in the hands of the Commissioners. It is primâ facie open to all classes of the community, and should be distributed in some way for public education.

WESTMEATH PROTESTANT ORPHAN SOCIETY.

355. Lord Justice FitzGibbon.—This is a letter which we got on the 29th of November, 1887; it has been lying over because we could not come here until now:—

"Mullingar, 29th November, 1887.

"Re Westmeath Protestant Orphan Society.

"Dear Sir,—I have been instructed by the Committee of this Society to take the necessary steps to make an application with a view to having their powers increased as to the disposal of a legacy the interest of which is increasing owing to a failure of the class of persons for whom it was intended by the testator, will you kindly therefore inform me as to the procedure by which I shall bring the matter before your Commissioners.

"Yours truly, John Irwin.

"W. E. Ellis, Esq., Secretary,
"Educational Endowments Commission,
"23, Nassau-street, Dublin."

There is some difficulty about utilizing the legacy, but we have power to alter the trusts if necessary.

Rev. Richard Deane.—It has not been made available.

R. E. Meares, Esq., Solicitor, sworn and examined.

356. Lord Justice FitzGibbon.—Have you consulted Mr. Irwin, who wrote to us?—I have.

R. E. Meares, esq.

357. What do you know about this bequest?—I knew very little about it until this morning, when I was consulted on the subject. On looking over some papers in Mr. Irwin's office, I saw a kind of report in which it was stated that by the will of Mr. Kinsey in 1828, a sum of £2,000 was left to be invested in order to pay marriage portions to Protestant children reared in connexion with the society. The words are:—

"I bequeath the sum of £2,000 to the Governors of the Protestant Orphan Society, in the county of Westmeath, for the benefit of the institution, and I request that the same may be invested at interest by the Governors of the said money, the interest thereof to be from time to time expended, as far as the law will allow, in providing marriage portions of £30 each, on the marriage of any orphan, male or female, reared and brought up in the said Westmeath Orphanage Society, and who shall be a member of the Protestant Episcopal Church of England and Ireland."

358. Lord Justice Naish.—What are the [illegible] attending the bequest?—That the number of those who could claim the benefit of it seems to be diminishing.

359. What do the society propose should be done with any available surplus?—That they should widen it a little, so as to allow the terms to apply to any Protestant children that would be recommended by the committee.

360. Do they ask to have it applied to any educational purpose?—No, certainly not.

Rev. Richard Deane.—Mr. Irwin was instructed to take counsel's advice as to whether this money could not be applied in a retrospective way—that is, in giving portions to persons who had married in years gone by.

361. Lord Justice FitzGibbon.—Under our Act endowments for marriage portions may be deemed to be educational endowments. We have all the powers of the Act over money for marriage portions, but subject to the provisions of the Act. Any scheme that is to be settled must have the consent of the Governing Body, and must have due regard to the original intentions of the Governors. Who are the present trustees?

Rev. Richard Deane.—Mr. William Edward Smythe and Dr. White.

362. Lord Justice FitzGibbon.—Under a scheme, we can vest this stock, without any transfer, directly in a body incorporated to hold it, and get rid of all appointments of trustees in future; and the Bank of Ireland will act on our scheme, as if there had been a transfer. So, if the money has not yet been transferred, you need not go to any expense or trouble about it; but somebody ought to look after it. We should be glad if it were incorporated with the General Meath Diocesan Scheme for it is a fund for the benefit of that diocese.

Rev. Richard Deane.—The whole amount is in the hands of Messrs. Craig and Gardiner. The stock never was in my name.

363. Lord Justice FitzGibbon.—Who is the responsible secretary of the society?

The Rev. Richard Deane.—I am Honorary Secretary.

364. Lord Justice FitzGibbon.—Have you any other moneys invested belonging to your society?

Rev. Richard Deane.—There are some other funds. A Gentleman stated that there was £6,000 altogether, of which £4,000 belonged to the Orphan Society, and £2,000 formed the Kinsey bequest.

365. Lord Justice FitzGibbon.—This endowment is exempt from our jurisdiction except by consent, but it is one with respect to which you want further powers. We can vest the whole in trustees for you; and if you

don't like to make it a diocesan thing you can keep it yourselves.

Dean *Swift*.—We cannot make it diocesan because it is limited to Westmeath.

365. Lord Justice FitzGibbon.—We can, if you please, vest it in the Diocesan Body, limiting the benefits of it to Westmeath.

Dean *Swift*.—The greater part of our funds are supplied by voluntary contributions.

367. Lord Justice FitzGibbon.—It may be wiser for you to keep this fund in the county. We can limit the application of it in any way you think proper.

Dean *Swift*.—As far as the Kinsey bequest is concerned it might be limited; but it will injure us if you have anything to do with the Orphan Society as an orphan society.

368. Lord Justice FitzGibbon.—We don't want to meddle with your society, but we can incorporate trustees to hold the Kinsey money, and at the same time, or afterwards, the other moneys can be vested in the same trustees, if you like. But don't be limiting this Kinsey money to £30 marriage portions, that is a most useless way of applying it.

Rev. *R. Deane*.—In what other way should it be applied?

369. Lord Justice FitzGibbon.—I think it would be better spent in fees for binding apprentices, or enabling young people to advance themselves in life.

Lord Justice Naish.—You can bring a scheme before us. It is for you to consider it.

Rev. *R. Deane*.—I suppose it would be better for us to wait until after the next committee meeting.

370. Lord Justice FitzGibbon.—The practical thing would be to appoint a committee of one or two, and authorize them to communicate with our office.

Rev. *R. Deane*.—We would have done so before, but were informed that it could not come under your cognizance at all, and therefore did nothing.

371. Lord Justice FitzGibbon.—Understand that it comes under our cognizance only if you so consent; we can enable you to utilize the money in apprenticeship fees, marriage portions, or any other way for the children of your denomination. A scheme will cost you only about 30s., and settle the fund for ever, whereas any sort of proceeding in Chancery would cost you more than so many pounds, and you would have to go back there any time you wanted to appoint a new trustee.

Rev. *R. Deane*.—After our next committee meeting we will communicate with your secretary.

THE BELVEDERE ORPHAN SCHOOL, TYRRELLSPASS.

The Rev. *Richard Deane* sworn and examined.

372. Lord Justice FitzGibbon.—You are trustee of the Belvedere Endowment?—There should be three trustees—there are two actually now. The three trustees were myself, Mr. John R. Somers, of Dublin, and the late Mr. Rochfort-Boyd. On his death, his son, Captain Boyd, now Major Boyd-Rochfort, became his successor; and Mr. Somers' son now fills the place of his father, who wished to retire. In fact I have been the committee myself.

373. Have you got a copy of the will?—I have.

374. I believe the Countess of Belvedere died in 1836?—She did.

375. She bequeathed £6,000 for the use of a female school at Tyrrellspass, the interest of the £6,000 to pay all the expenses of the said school, where there must be thirty-six orphan girls, to be brought up in the Protestant religion; none of the children to be taken into the school under seven years of age or over twelve; the parents of the children must have been both dead; they are to be taught most carefully the Bible, and a competent schoolmistress must be obtained for that purpose; and then she says:—

"The children of my school in Tyrrellspass are to be dressed in purple camlet with green ribbons on their bonnets."

Is the school still in existence?—It is.

376. What is the present endowment?—£5,000 has been lent at 5 per cent. to the representative of the late Lord de Blaquiere, and nearly £1,000 is in 3 per cents. It is £5,000 still; but before Mr. de Blaquiere's death we reduced the interest on the £5,000 at 4½ per cent. The mortgage was to the late Lord de Blaquiere.

377. Who are the trustees?—The clergyman of the place—if he doesn't refuse—that is, myself, Major Boyd-Rochfort, and Mr. Samuel H. Somers.

378. How many orphans are there at present in the institution?—We have had an average of about twelve for several years. Our funds came very low at one time. There was a good deal of expense, so that we could not enlarge the number of orphans. At present we have eleven in the school, and we have vacancies for a few more.

379. Are they fed and clothed?—They are fed and clothed.

380. I see that the matron is to be a member of the Church of England?—Yes.

381. And that the children are to be educated in the knowledge of the Bible, and in the principles of the Church of England?—That was, of course, before disestablishment.

382. How are the trustees appointed?—By the surviving trustees.

383. Do you think you could make more of it if you had a larger number of trustees?—I don't think we could; it works very well.

384. Rev. Dr. Molloy.—You don't want any change?—No change.

385. Lord Justice FitzGibbon.—You have some school lands. There is a grant of four acres of land at a rent of £8 0s. 0d.; and there was expended by the trustees in building six cottages £2,311 0s. 11d.?—That was in my predecessor's time—in Mr. Eaton's time. The bequest lay by for a great number of years before any orphanage was built at all. Then the interest that had accumulated was all sunk in building accommodation for thirty-six orphans, whereas we cannot support more than thirteen or fourteen.

386. Rev. Dr. Molloy.—What is done with the six cottages?—Some are occupied by orphans, and the rest are untenanted.

387. Lord Justice FitzGibbon.—You don't let them?—We used one of them as a residence for a schoolmaster, but two of them are unoccupied.

388. Are you limited as to the denomination to which your trustees belong?—I should think we are. We never had any but of the one denomination.

389. I see that twelve Protestant ladies were to be appointed governesses of the institution?—That never has been done.

390. Dr. Traill.—Wouldn't that help you in the working of it?—Well, there are not many Protestant ladies in the neighbourhood; but my wife and other ladies do inspect the place and superintend it.

391. Lord Justice FitzGibbon.—As far as I can see, from reading this copy of the will hastily, the endowment appears to be exempt from the Act.

392. Rev. Dr. Molloy.—What is your annual income at present?—There is the interest of £5,000 at

4½ per cent., and the interest of nearly £1,000 at 3 per cent.

393. About £250 a year?—Yes.

394. Lord Justice FitzGibbon.—You feed, clothe, educate, and teach twelve children for that?—Yes.

395. How are the girls taken care of?—According to the original scheme they were all to be brought up in the one house. According to the scheme afterwards settled by Master Lyle these cottages were built, and there is a nurse with three children in each cottage, and a matron or superintendent also.

396. Wouldn't it be useful for you to affiliate this to the Westmeath County Orphan Society?—I don't think it would. It works very well at present. The girls have gone very well out of it. One is an assistant in the Model School of Kildare-place—Miss Havern. They are taught in the parochial school. It has been a Church school up to the present, but I think it will be under the National Board.

397. Have you attendance enough to keep up a National school?—Yes; we have an average of thirty. We have a very good school there.

398. How far is it from Mullingar?—About eight miles.

Oct. 8, 1888.

Rev. Richard Dunn.

PUBLIC SITTING—TUESDAY, OCTOBER 9, 1888.

Oct. 9, 1888.

At the Courthouse, Sligo.

Present:—The Right Hon. Lord Justice FitzGibbon and the Right Hon. Lord Justice Naish, Judicial Commissioners; and the Rev. Gerald Molloy, D.D., D.Sc., Anthony Traill, Esq., LL.D., M.D., F.T.C.D., and Professor Dougherty, M.A., Assistant Commissioners.

The Assistant Secretary, N. D. Murphy, Junr., was in attendance.

MANORHAMILTON NATIONAL SCHOOL.

The Rev. Isaac Coulter sworn and examined.

Rev. Isaac Coulter.

399. Lord Justice FitzGibbon.—You are the Incumbent of Manorhamilton?—Yes.

400. And the manager of the Manorhamilton National School?—Of the Masterson National School.

401. I believe there is a sum of Government Stock as an endowment for the school?—Yes.

402. Do you know who holds the stock?—It is in the Government 3 per Cents. The Commissioners of Charitable Donations and Bequests hand the dividends to myself as the Incumbent of Manorhamilton.

403. How much do you get from them?—£37 10s. yearly.

404. What school premises have you?—We have an ordinary National school. It is on the grounds held with the church.

405. What other resources have you?—Just private subscriptions. I have got three-quarters of an English acre on which to build a residence for the teacher, under a lease from Colonel Clements.

406. To whom was that lease made?—To me and my successors as trustees for the purposes of the school.

407. What attendance of children have you?—Of late we must have over thirty; and in one or two quarters since I came we had over forty in average attendance; the number on the roll is about seventy.

408. Then the school has improved during the last two years, for at the date of the last report the average attendance was only twenty-seven?—Yes.

409. Does anyone take an interest in the school except yourself?—The Select Vestry are interested very much, but they don't interfere in the management. Mr. Stewart, the agent of Colonel Clements, takes an interest, as regards inquiring after the welfare of the school, and gives £10 a year for a female assistant teacher.

410. Your numbers only enable you to have one teacher under the National Board?—Yes, we have a male teacher trained under the Church Education Society, and classed under the National Board.

411. What class does he hold?—Third, but he will soon qualify for second.

412. What age is he?—About twenty-seven.

413. You said you had a female teacher?—Yes, a young girl. She only gets £10 a year—a subscription from Colonel Clements. She is a monitress just to look after the little ones.

414. Are any school fees paid?—Yes, by the better classes.

415. Do you give any higher instruction than the National school programme?—No.

416. What are the terms of Masterson's will?—I have the will. (Hands in document.)

417. Lord Justice Naish.—The will of James John Masterson, of Royal-row, parish of St. Mary, Lambeth. How did he come to be connected with Manorhamilton?—I don't know.

418. Lord Justice FitzGibbon.—The will bears date April 1, 1808, proved on May 10, 1809. He gives his residuary property to be, as soon as possible after his death, invested in 3 per cent. Consols, to be added to the other stock standing in his name, and, within a year after his death, to be transferred to two or more persons to be named as trustees by and on behalf of the minister and churchwardens of the parish of Manorhamilton; he directs the dividends to be remitted by the trustees to the minister for the time being of the parish of Manorhamilton, to be applied by the minister and churchwardens in educating

"such poor children of the said parish as they shall deem proper objects of this my bounty; new trustees to be appointed by the minister and churchwardens; and he directs that the bequest be read in the vestry of the parish, once in every year, on the usual days of meeting of the Parish Vestry."

Do you go through that form still?—I have not read it.

419. You ought to do so, it might encourage other people. I find mention in your vestry book (permanent) of an annuity under the will of Patrick Cullen of Longford, do you receive that annuity still?—Yes.

420. "It is to be distributed, in case of public calamity amongst twenty of the poorest individuals of the parish and no more, by the minister for the time being, if then resident, or, in his absence, by the curate or seneschal of Manorhamilton, and three of the most reputable Protestant inhabitants then residing in the town."

By whom is that annuity paid?—It comes off the property of the Rev. Mr. Armstrong, and is paid by Mr. Templeman, his agent.

[illegible]

431. Lord Justice FitzGibbon.—(Reads). I find on Easter Monday, 1853, it was resolved that—

"An effort be made, by public subscription, to raise the funds necessary for building a parochial schoolhouse for the [illegible] School, and that application be made to the Earl of Leitrim for a site, and that the clergyman and churchwardens be appointed a committee to carry out the above object."

14th May, 1853:—

"Vote of thanks to the Earl of Leitrim for his kind promise of a site for the parochial school-house, and for his liberal donation towards the building of same."

Then a note dated 1854:—

"The schoolhouse has not been erected on the site above referred to."

When was the school built?—The school is only built twenty years. I think it was about 1860.

432. There is an entry of June 3, 1853:—

"That the repairs necessary to be done at the schoolhouse shall hereafter be executed by the Select Vestry out of the funds under their charge"?—

Yes, they took charge of it.

433. Dr. Traill.—The schoolhouse probably became vested in the Representative Church Body?—It is built on a corner of the graveyard round the church.

434. Is it a healthy site?—I think so.

435. Have they stopped burying there?—It is only comparatively recently that they began to bury there.

436. Is it a public burying-ground?—It is a new one, reserved for Church people only, and Dissenters.

437. How near to the schoolhouse are they going to bury?—Some of the graves, I think, are within a few yards of the back of the school.

438. Was there an old burying-ground there?—Not at the church; it was in the town. A very few old families bury in the old place; but recently they have been opening this new graveyard, and the oldest grave in it is of recent date. There are very few buried in the churchyard.

439. Is the old burying ground full?—It is.

430. Is there no public cemetery?—No.

431. Where do the people of the whole parish bury?—There is the old burying place in the town, some bury there still; and there is an old burying place called [illegible].

432. Lord Justice FitzGibbon.—About 1830 the parish of [illegible] seems to have been divided into three, and claims were made by the other two parts of the parish for portions of the Cullen bequest. On July 2, 1830, the Commissioners of Charitable Donations wrote saying that they considered themselves bound by the directions of the testator who bequeathed the annuity to the minister of [illegible] and his successors, and directed that the distribution should be made by him. I suppose you still receive the whole of the money?—Yes.

433. You had to pay £17 10s. for a lease; had that anything to do with the school?—It was in connection with the new glebe.

434. Lord Justice Naish.—Do you receive the income from the Commissioners of Charitable Bequests?—Yes.

435. Are you apprehensive that any inconvenience will result from allowing that state of things to continue?—I am not. The income is likely to be reduced.

436. Lord Justice FitzGibbon.—On October 11, 1838, the vestry appointed a schoolmaster, and ordered "that the schoolhouse be repaired at a cost not to exceed £10."

So that besides keeping the place in repair the vestry appears to have taken on them the appointment of the schoolmaster?—The clergyman thinks it wiser to consult them in these matters.

437. Dr. Traill.—Who, as a matter of fact, has the appointment of the schoolmaster?—I am both patron and manager.

438. Lord Justice FitzGibbon.—But the Select Vestry keep the school in repair, and maintain the schoolmaster, and if the manager did not take their nomination matters would come to a dead-lock?—Quite so.

439. I see a proposal in 1887, to start a school in [illegible], to be conducted by a lady who could teach English, French, and Music, and the Select Vestry were to consider the propriety of appointing her organist at a salary; and they appointed a committee, consisting of yourself and four others, to further the matter. Has anything been done since?—The school has been started, but independently of us. The Select Vestry have nothing to do with it, it is a private ladies school.

440. She is not the organist?—No, we are getting the playing in the church gratuitously done.

441. Was the school under the National Board before you became rector?—Yes.

442. Was the former clergyman manager?—Yes. The Commissioners wrote to me, when the Rev. Robert Grierson, my predecessor, resigned, saying that I would be appointed patron and manager.

443. Lord Justice FitzGibbon.—This endowment appears perfectly safe. The money is in the hands of the Commissioners of Charitable Donations and Bequests, and the site of the school in the Representative Church Body; but the repairs of the building and some contributions have come from your Select Vestry. All that we could do for you is to incorporate the minister and churchwardens, and any couple more, as a school committee, and secure your title to the building and money.

Witness.—I think that would be the safest thing to do, and the wisest.

444. Dr. Traill.—Who supplied the funds for the building besides Lord Leitrim's subscription?—I don't know, he gave a liberal subscription.

445. You don't know how much the school cost?—I think it would take over £100—perhaps £150.

446. Lord Justice FitzGibbon.—Would it stimulate subscriptions if you had a school committee?—In fact we have a school committee in our Select Vestry.

447. We might legally constitute them as such; we will send you one or two schemes already settled for other parishes; bring those before your Select Vestry, and if you desire it we can frame a similar scheme for you. It will cost you about £1.

Witness.—I think that would be a wise thing to do. I have not consulted the Select Vestry, and I would not like to act without consulting them, because they really are the paymasters. The clergyman generally gets up an entertainment and collects money in that way for prizes, and the repairs have been done by the Select Vestry, out of the church funds.

448. Lord Justice FitzGibbon.—They maintain the fabric of the school just as the church?—Quite so.

449. You think it would be better that they should have a legal trust to that effect, and should appoint two or three of themselves upon a committee?—Yes.

450. If you pass any resolution suggesting anything we will be glad to consider it. Is there any other National school competing with you?—There are four other National schools.

451. Under Protestant management?—The Methodists have a female National school.

452. Dr. Traill.—How do you spend that £27 10s.?—We give it to the master in lieu of school fees.

453. What salary does he get from the Board?—A third-class salary—I think £40.

Oct. 5, 1886.

BALLINCARLY NATIONAL SCHOOL, CALRY.

Mr. William Clarke sworn and examined. Mr. William Clarke.

454. Lord Justice FitzGibbon.—We had some letters from you about the Calry school?—You had. If you will allow me I will go a little farther back into the Calry school. I am a member of the select vestry of Calry Church, and a tenant of Erasmus Smith's land. When Erasmus Smith became the owner of property in the parish he built a charter school, and endowed it for fifty boys to be educated and taught trades. I was in that house when it was in full working order. The fifty boys were educated there in trades.

455. Rev. Dr. Molloy.—Were you a pupil there?—No, but I was a friend of the master. They were taught reading, writing, and arithmetic, and taught trades. Tailoring, shoemaking, carpentering, and everything were taught there up to the time when Parliament passed the Act for the National schools. The trustees of Erasmus Smith then turned the whole of them out, and shut up the school. The late Right Hon. Owen Wynne of Hazelwood gave four acres of land free to build the school on, and it was built and endowed by Erasmus Smith.

456. Were these boys boarders or day boys?—They were boarded in the house. Owen Wynne of Hazelwood was one of the Governors, and Colonel Irwin was another; and when a vacancy occurred the fact was brought before the Governors and they appointed a new pupil.

457. Dr. Traill.—Who paid for the board of the boys?—Erasmus Smith's revenues out of the parish of Calry—£130 a year. The boys were boarded out of that money. When the trustees withdrew the money from the Charter school, the late Right Hon. Owen Wynne built the Ballincarly school out of his own pocket for his tenants; and we of the church of Calry are interested in Ballincarly school and in Calry school, and out of our slender means we contribute a slender sum to pay a female teacher at Calry.

458. How far is Ballincarly from Erasmus Smith's school?—About a mile and a half.

459. What has become of Erasmus Smith's school?—It was given up with Mr. Wynne's four acres, and I got possession of it. Afterwards it was sold under the Court, and Mr. Eccles keeps a classical school in it now.

460. How far is Ballincarly school from the old Erasmus Smith's school?—Not two miles. We have a female school at Calry church which we maintain out of our church money.

461. Lord Justice FitzGibbon.—Is there any grant from Erasmus Smith's estate to the Ballincarly school?—Not a penny.

462. Is any grant paid by the Erasmus Smith Board to any school in Sligo now?—Not to my knowledge.

463. Were the old trade school and the four acres of land taken from Mr. Wynne?—Mr. Wynne lowered the ground.

464. When the National Schools were opened that school and land were surrendered?—Surrendered to Mr. Wynne.

465. Do you say that the school was afterwards sold as Mr. Wynne's private property, and bought by Mr. Eccles?—Exactly—and he keeps a school there.

466. It has now no connexion with Erasmus Smith's Board, and is Mr. Eccles' private property?—His private property, he gave £1,100 for the whole concern.

467. We find amongst Erasmus Smith's property 2,133 acres of land, with a poor law valuation of £880 a year, and a yearly rental of £130 2s. 6d., in the county of Sligo?—That's the money I mentioned. The lands are all in the parish of Calry. The names of the townlands are Cleavearagh, Ballincarly, and King's Mountain.

468. Are there many tenants on them?—I am one, Harper Campbell is another, and the present Mr. Owen Wynne is another.

469. When the school existed were any tenants' children attending it?—My children were at the school. When they shut up the school and turned the boys out, the late Mr. Owen Wynne, who was a governor, wrote to know why they did so. They said—"We will make it a day school"—and sent a man named Harvey, a very good scholar. My children were educated there. After a certain time they turned out Harvey too, and gave up the place to Mr. Wynne, and I got possession of it.

470. When?—About the year of the Famine. When the poorhouse was not able to contain all the poor, I allowed the Guardians to use the underground floor of the Charter school for the poor.

471. Was there any grant by Erasmus Smith's Board after that in aid of a school in Sligo?—By no means. We sent our rents to Mr. Sanders, of Sanders Park, Cork—it was all sent off to Cork, and we never saw a penny of it after.

472. Dr. Traill.—Are all the tenants Protestants?—I believe they are.

473. Rev. Dr. Molloy.—Have they all large holdings?—All large holdings.

474. Lord Justice Naish.—What is the size of your own holding?—I hold about twenty-seven acres, but in three different places.

475. Professor Dougherty.—What is the extent of Mr. Harper Campbell's holding?—About sixty acres.

476. Rev. Dr. Molloy.—What has Mr. Owen Wynne?—He has Cleavearagh. The land begins at Ballincarly and runs to Hazelwood demesne—more than 800 acres.

477. Dr. Traill.—What age are you?—I am over eighty.

478. Lord Justice FitzGibbon.—I want to ask you about another school to which the Erasmus Smith Board appear to be still making a grant—the school at Drumcliffe?—I don't know anything about it.

479. How far are you from Drumcliffe?—About two miles and a half. I never knew that they gave a penny.

480. What school is there besides the National school for the education of Protestant children?—There is none but Ballincarly, and a little girl can do very little in the way of teaching a boy.

481. Dr. Traill.—What rent do you pay for the twenty-seven acres?—£31, including county cess. We have a great many intelligent young men—Protestants of the parish of Calry—all tenants of Mr. Wynne.

482. On the lands that he holds under Erasmus Smith?—Not on the Erasmus Smith holding. Mr. Wynne's tenants are mostly all Protestants about Hazelwood. His estates are very extensive. We have young men growing up, and they have nothing to do to provide for themselves, except to go to America without a bit of learning in their heads.

483. Professor Dougherty.—Would you be in favour of reviving the teaching of trades if you got the school opened again?—Oh, yes. Our poor rising generation in the country are at a loss for many things.

484. But you said it was a grammar school that you wanted?—Yes; for poor young men to learn geometry and navigation before they go out into the world.

Oct. 9, 18[illegible].
Mr. William Clarke.

485. Would you prefer a grammar school to a school like the old charter school, where some attempt was made to give boys a technical education?—I would rather have a grammar school. Give me an educated boy—an educated man—and he is fit to go to any place. Learning makes the man.

486. Rev. Dr. Molloy.—What sort of education do you think would be best for the tenants of the property?—The young men ought to be educated in science, algebra, and Euclid, and all that sort of thing. Give me an educated boy and I will put him into a bank.

487. But would it not be better for them to stay at home?—If they can get openings at home, but it is not every day that they can get it.

488. Would it not be better to develop some new industry in Sligo?—If you could do it, but the idea of having a little girl teaching big boys!

489. Lord Justice Naish.—How do you know that Erasmus Smith built that school?—The late Right Hon. Owen Wynne gave the four acres of land free; and in proof of that, when the school was shut up, I got possession from Mr. Wynne.

490. Yes, but who built the school itself?—It was built out of Erasmus Smith's money. He derived £430 a year out of Calry.

491. Dr. Traill.—But it was not Erasmus Smith that built the school?—He got it built.

492. But he was dead long before that?—But it was his money.

493. Lord Justice Naish.—Of what religion were the pupils of the school you spoke of?—Protestants.

494. Were there any Catholic children in it?—None. No boy would be admitted but a grown boy, and the governors always, whenever there was a vacancy, elected a boy for it.

495. Lord Justice FitzGibbon.—He seems quite right in his recollection. The Report of 18[illegible] [illegible]:—

"Calry.—Erasmus Smith's School Endowment—[illegible] from the funds of Erasmus Smith. Authority—Select Committee of the House of Commons. Report for 18[illegible], Appendix 152."

That report stated that there was no endowment attached to the school other than the income from the Board of Erasmus Smith, which had been withdrawn, which is exactly what the witness says. They withdrew the income and the school was closed. We may conjecture how the landlord got it back, as many of Erasmus Smith's schools were built on sites granted on the condition that they were to revert if the schools were closed. So far as this building is concerned we have no more jurisdiction now than we have over any other private property in the country. But it is a question for Erasmus Smith's Board whether the tenants of their Sligo estate should not have some provision for education. They don't appear to have any. When we settle a scheme for the Erasmus Smith's Foundation, we may consider whether they should not make some grant for a school on their Sligo property.

496. Dr. Traill.—If they gave a grant, which of the schools would be the most important?—Unluckily it is the most important for it is in the centre of Mr. Wynne's estate.

497. Whose does it belong to?—Mr. Wynne holds it and he ought to be the owner of it.

498. Lord Justice FitzGibbon (to witness).—Thank you. You are the first tenant of Erasmus Smith's lands that has come before us to claim the benefits he intended for his tenantry.

The Rev. *James Berry* sworn and examined.

Rev. James Berry.

499. Lord Justice FitzGibbon.—You are Rector of Calry?—Yes.

500. What schools have you in the parish?—Two National schools—Calry school and Ballinurly school—I am patron and manager of both.

501. Are there any others?—A Model school which is not in connexion with our parish.

502. Do you know what number of children attend the Sligo Model school?—I should say 170 children altogether.

503. How many of these are Protestants?—I understand all but two.

504. Do they come from your parish or from St. John's?—I should say about half and half.

505. First take the Calry National school, how is it supported?—By a National Board grant, and a supplemental grant of £10 from the Select Vestry of Calry.

506. How many children are in attendance?—Forty-five are on the roll.

507. Is there any difference in the education from what is given in the Model school?—Practically not; except that it is entirely under my own control.

508. Rev. Dr. Molloy.—Is the Model school in the parish?—It is in the Mall. It is in the town of Sligo.

509. Ballinurly is in the country part of the parish?—Yes.

510. Lord Justice FitzGibbon.—What distance is there between the Calry and Ballinurly schools?—About three English miles.

511. How many children are attending Ballinurly?—Thirty-three on the roll.

512. Have you any means of supporting it?—None, except the results fees and the £10 grant.

513. Rev. Dr. Molloy.—What is the attendance at Ballinurly school?—At the examination last week there were twenty-seven children present.

514. Lord Justice FitzGibbon.—All Protestants?—Yes.

515. Have you got a grant?—Only a small capitation fee.

516. If you could get a few more pupils you could have a grant?—Yes.

517. What teachers have you?—A female teacher in each school.

518. They are both mixed schools?—Yes.

519. How are the teachers qualified?—The Calry teacher is first class; the Ballinurly teacher is third class, trained in Marlborough-street.

520. Is there any provision for Intermediate Education in Sligo for Protestants?—The school that Mr. Clarke was speaking of just now—the old Charter school—became afterwards a Diocesan school, and has since been purchased by Mr. Eades who was the Diocesan schoolmaster, and it is now entirely a private school.

521. I believe that Mr. Eades held the office, in 1858, of Diocesan schoolmaster of the diocese of Elphin?—I understand so.

522. He converted and compounded?—I do not think so.

523. But he purchased this property with his own money?—Yes, and now it is entirely in his own hands.

524. Dr. Traill.—How did it become a Diocesan school?—I don't know. It had been originally a Charter school.

525. Mr. Clarke's account of it is, that it became Mr. Wynne's private property?—It was called the Diocesan school.

Lord Justice FitzGibbon.—The only diocesan

inducement was the salary of the diocesan schoolmaster, who held his annuity as such.

526. Lord Justice Naish.—Mr. Eades was the late diocesan schoolmaster, and taught in that house?—Yes.

527. Lord Justice FitzGibbon.—Then that private school is the only Protestant intermediate school at present in Sligo?—The only one.

528. Is there any other in the neighbourhood?—Primrose Grange.

529. Do you agree with Mr. Clarke that there are any considerable number of Protestant inhabitants who want an intermediate school?—There is a large number of farmers on the property of Mr. Wynne. I don't know that they would avail themselves of an intermediate school.

530. Rev. Dr. Molloy.—Are these farmers on the estate of Erasmus Smith, or on the property of Mr. Wynne, outside of that estate?—They are on Mr. Wynne's own property, outside of the Erasmus Smith estate. The Erasmus Smith property is in the hands of three tenants—Mr. Wynne, Mr. Clarke, and Mr. Campbell. They don't sublet it.

531. But one of them, Mr. Wynne, has a large property in the immediate neighbourhood, and there are a large number of Protestant farmers on that property?—There are a large number, chiefly Protestants.

532. Dr. Traill.—I think you said you thought Mr. Eades never compounded?—I fancy he has his life annuity still, but it only lasts as long as he teaches.

533. If he wanted to wind it up he would have to compound?—Yes.

534. Lord Justice Naish.—Are there sub-tenants on the portion of the Erasmus Smith property held by Mr. Wynne?—No. It is in Mr. Wynne's own hands. It borders on his demesne. It runs up to the demesne gate.

535. He uses it as a home farm?—Yes.

536. Lord Justice FitzGibbon.—As far as we can make out, your only provision for intermediate education is dependent on Mr. Eades continuing to keep this private school?—That's all.

537. Do you know how many boys are attending it?—I fancy about twenty-five.

538. Lord Justice Naish.—Are they boarders or day boys?—He has one or two boarders.

Rev. James Berry.

PRIMROSE GRANGE SCHOOL (INCORPORATED SOCIETY).

Mr. W. A. Stubbings sworn and examined.

Mr. W. A. Stubbings.

539. Lord Justice FitzGibbon.—How long have you held the post of head master of Primrose Grange School?—Since January, 1878.

540. Where were you educated?—At Dundalk and Santry.

541. You were promoted by competitive examination to Santry?—Yes.

542. Had you got admission to Dundalk by competitive examination?—Yes.

543. You were one of the foundation scholars of the Incorporated Society—first at Dundalk, and afterwards at Santry?—Yes.

544. Did you take a University degree?—No; I have not matriculated.

545. I suppose you went through the full course of teaching given at Santry?—Yes.

546. When you went to Primrose Grange what number of pupils did you find there?—Nineteen foundation pupils; no pay boarders.

547. What was the condition at that time of the premises?—They were in very fair repair; not so good as at present.

548. Who was your predecessor?—The Rev. George M'Craughan, now incumbent of St. Peter's, Athlone.

549. How long had he been master before you came?—Fifteen years.

550. What is the present number of your pupils?—Thirty—twelve foundation pupils and eighteen pay boarders.

551. Is there any fixed number of foundationers?—Twelve is the usual number; occasionally the society take extras.

552. How many are you bound to take?—As many as they send to me.

553. Dr. Traill.—Why were there nineteen before and only twelve now?—Formerly the foundation pupils were elected for four years. When I came there were four for each year, which would be sixteen; and there were three extras, which made nineteen. About this time the Incorporated Society made a rule reducing the length of the scholarship from four years to three.

554. They did not increase the number of pupils admitted annually?—Four is the usual number; but occasionally they elect an additional one.

555. Where is the examination held?—Generally in St. John's Female School, Sligo.

556. How many half boarders have you?—Eight at present.

557. How many parlour boarders?—Ten.

558. Is thirty the full number that your building will accommodate?—The full number.

559. How long has your school been full?—I hand in a table showing the numbers for several years past:—

Year.	Foundation Boys.	Pay Boarders.	Day Boys.	Totals.
1878, . .	[illegible]	[illegible]	[illegible]	[illegible]
1879, . .	[illegible]	[illegible]	[illegible]	[illegible]
1880, . .	[illegible]	[illegible]	[illegible]	[illegible]
1881, . .	[illegible]	[illegible]	[illegible]	[illegible]
1882, . .	[illegible]	[illegible]	[illegible]	[illegible]
1883, . .	[illegible]	[illegible]	[illegible]	[illegible]
1884, . .	[illegible]	[illegible]	[illegible]	[illegible]
1885, . .	[illegible]	[illegible]	[illegible]	[illegible]
1886, . .	[illegible]	[illegible]	—	[illegible]
1887, . .	[illegible]	[illegible]	—	[illegible]
1888, . .	[illegible]	[illegible]	—	[illegible]

They have been steadily increasing since 1878, and if the premises were larger, and I advertised the school more, I am sure we would have more pupils.

560. What are the terms for half boarders?—Twenty guineas. There are a few extras. If they wish to learn Classics, French and Drawing they are charged extra.

561. Do you find that the boys learn Classics?—Nearly all. For Classics I charge the foundation pupils half the ordinary fees. They almost all learn Classics during the first two years. During the third year, when they are preparing for Santry Scholarships, owing to the severity of the examinations in Science and Religious Knowledge, they have to discontinue Classics.

562. Would it be an advantage if Classics were made a part of the examinations in Santry?—I think so; they want Classics afterwards. Some of my pupils who have gone to Santry matriculated in the Royal University and in Trinity College. One, at the Royal University, not long ago, took fifth Mathematical Honours. Another pupil took Mathematical Honours in Trinity College; and another, a year after leaving Primrose Grange, and after having spent a year at

Santry, took sixth place at the entrance examination in Trinity College. Another boy took a History prize, and not long ago another took a Catechetical premium; and this year a former pupil, who entered the Royal University from Santry, took Honours in French and a Junior Exhibition.

563. Dr. TRAILL.—Did any of them obtain Sizarship in Trinity College?—One got Sizarship a good many years ago, and eventually took a Studentship in Trinity College.

564. Who was that?—His name is Mackintosh.

565. He is a Fellow of Cambridge now?—Yes.

566. Lord Justice FITZGIBBON.—Did he begin his teaching under you in Primrose Grange?—He was a schoolfellow of mine in Santry. He was under my predecessor in Primrose Grange, and went to Santry.

567. What are your terms for parlour boarders?—Thirty guineas a year, with some extras, as in the case of the hall boarders.

568. What is the extra charge to them for Classics?—Four guineas.

569. Is it two for the foundationers?—Yes.

570. What is the extra charge for French?—Two guineas.

571. Is Drawing an extra?—For boarders it is; not for foundation pupils. The charge is two guineas for boarders—the same as for French.

572. I suppose you have, according to the ordinary arrangement, 10*d*. a day for each foundation boy that is with you?—The same as in the other schools.

573. Do your hall boarders get exactly the same feeding as the foundationers?—Exactly the same.

574. What is the difference between the treatment of the parlour boarders and of the others?—In every respect the same, except in dietary. The dietary of the parlour boarders is better; they dine at the master's table.

575. Is the master's table in the same room as the table for the other pupils?—Generally speaking it is in the same hall with the other boarders.

576. Are the dormitory arrangements and the recreation arrangements the same for both?—Identically. The only difference is, that I have one dormitory which I confine, as a rule, to the junior boys. It is sometimes occupied by foundation boys if they are very young; but there is no distinction made as to whether they are foundation boys or boarders.

577. Dr. TRAILL.—Is it not inexpedient that the parlour boarders who pay extra for extras that should take their meals in the same room with the other boys?—I don't think it makes any difference. They take the meals in the same hall, but not at the same hour.

578. Lord Justice FITZGIBBON.—What is the difference between the dietaries?—The dietary of the hall boarders, and of the foundation pupils, is according to the scale laid down by the Incorporated Society; and the dietary of the parlour boarders is of a better description.

579. In what respect is it better?—They get better, and they get meat every day. The hall boarders get meat on four days in the week for dinner, and they get soup on the other days. The parlour boarders get meat every day, and pudding, &c.

580. The difference is principally in the meat on every day in the week, and the better?—Yes; and better again in the evening for supper. There is a greater variety and the table arrangements are much better.

581. Do you find the hall dietary wholesome and sufficient?—It is plain, but substantial and healthful. I should like it to be better, and that the Incorporated Society would give the allowance of 10*d*. a day during the whole time that the boys are with us. We are not allowed it during the vacations.

582. Rev. Dr. MOLLOY.—About how many working days have you in the year?—About 300 working days.

583. Dr. TRAILL.—Is the 10*d*. a day enough?—According to the scale laid down the 10*d*. about covers the expense.

584. Would you not rather have an even allowance?—Most certainly.

585. Rev. Dr. MOLLOY.—It is about £12 10*s*. for a year of forty-three weeks?—Quite so.

586. Lord Justice FITZGIBBON.—Is your district such that you can't expect to have a considerable number of day boys?—Yes; we have not any number of day boys, being in a country district, and the children of the parish are educated with the National school. Occasionally we get a boy who has been at the National school.

587. We were at the National school this morning, and saw that the boys appeared all to belong to the class of farmers and labourers?—They are entirely from a country district.

588. Where do the foundationers come from?—Dioceses of the diocese of Derry and Raphoe; the portion of the diocese of Kilmore situated in the county of Leitrim; the portion of the diocese of Tuam situated in Sligo and Mayo; the portion of Ardagh situated in Leitrim, Sligo, and Roscommon; and from Killala and Achonry. During my experience as head master about 11 have come from Skreen, in the county of Sligo.

589. Were these 11 all educated in the same school?—Yes; 8 have come from Dromore West, a village between Sligo and Ballina; 7 have come from Ballymote; 7 from Collooney; 11 from Sligo; 3 from Foxford, in Mayo; 4 from Kilglass, a village in the county of Sligo; 8 from Ballysodare; 7 from Riverstown; 1 from Geevagh; 1 from Riverstown; 3 from Killala; 1 from Ballinamore; 1 from Lisadell; 3 from Mohill, in Leitrim; 1 from Strokestown; 1 from Mount Charles, in Donegal; 3 from the Kay School, in Manor Cunningham, a day school connected with the Incorporated Society; and 3 from Dublin.

590. To what do you attribute the large number of pupils from Skreen?—Formerly there was a school there where the boys were better prepared. It was a sort of training school maintained there by the late Rev. Mr. Nangle.

591. Is that still in existence?—Not on the same standing.

592. Has it sent any more boys to you lately?—Not lately.

593. Do you find that the boys require a special preparation for entrance into Primrose Grange?—They require special preparation in Scripture.

594. Professor DOUGHERTY.—Who conducts the examinations?—A deputation from the Incorporated Society.

595. Lord Justice FITZGIBBON.—The same who examine elsewhere?—Yes, they generally come from Athlone to Farra, and on to Primrose Grange.

596. Have you been present at these examinations?—Generally.

597. Dr. TRAILL.—Are they public?—A portion of the examination is public; but they get paper questions from which the public are excluded—generally in arithmetic, &c. In the public examination they are examined in Scripture, geography, and arithmetic, &c.

598. Do you know are the same questions given in the different places?—I don't know.

599. Did you ever hear that persons who have heard the examination in one place prepare boys for the examination in another place in advance?—I have not heard.

600. Lord Justice FITZGIBBON.—We have been informed that the boys require to be specially taught, and that a certain number of schoolmasters have got the questions that have been asked over and over again, and have succeeded in preparing boys and getting them in in that way?—There are some schoolmasters who are very familiar with these examinations, and who are able to "grind" boys in religious knowledge.

601. Professor DOUGHERTY.—Do you, from your experience, think that these examinations are a satisfactory test of the fitness of the candidates?—Most

[illegible]

definitely. I have had only one or two cases of very stupid boys who got in by being very well grounded in formularies.

602. Lord Justice FitzGibbon.—No doubt the examination is a test of intelligence, but have the best boys from other schools a fair chance against those who have been crammed with these special questions? I think, for instance, in the model school in Sligo they get an excellent secular education; but if a boy did not go elsewhere to get taught in religious knowledge there would be a possibility of his failing.

603. You have had eleven boys from Sligo, as against twelve from Screen, and eight from Inishcrone. These are very startling figures. How is a clever deserving model school boy, thoroughly taught in mathematical and arithmetical subjects, to get the special knowledge necessary to carry him into Primrose Grange in Scripture and the Formularies?—He must go to another school where more attention is paid to religious knowledge, or the Incumbent of the parish might take a special interest in him, and work him up.

604. Then in fact the best boy from a model school would have no chance whatever of getting into Primrose Grange unless he could get special instruction not obtainable in a National school?—Not unless he prepared his portion of Scripture knowledge properly himself, or got it taught to him.

605. Could any boy teach himself for this special religious examination?—Well, I think he should have had experience under a master acquainted with this particular examination. I think self-study would not always get him through.

606. Rev. Dr. Molloy.—Then in addition to an ordinary good elementary education, they must get coached up in religious subjects in order to have a fair chance of getting into your school?—They must have a certain amount of religious knowledge.

607. Dr. Traill.—Were the examiners from the same examiners coming year after year?—We have had a variety from time to time. We had the Rev. George [illegible], the Rev. Canon M'Donogh, the Rev. Dr. [illegible], Dr. Stubbs, Canon Jellett, Dr. Walsh, &c.

608. Lord Justice FitzGibbon.—For entrance at Sizary is there a special religious examination?—A much more extensive one.

609. How have your boys got on in the Sizary competition?—Very well.

610. Dr. Traill.—Who gives the religious instruction in your school?—The masters and catechist.

611. Who is the catechist?—The Rev. John Galbraith, Incumbent of [illegible].

612. Lord Justice FitzGibbon.—Give us your results at Sizary?—This year four candidates competed from Primrose Grange, and all were successful. In 1887, three were successful out of four. In 1886, two were successful, and in 1885, three.

613. Do you send up four every year?—Almost every year. Sometimes a boy may leave before this examination, and sometimes a boy is not promising enough to go to Sizary.

614. What are the limits of age for admission into Primrose Grange?—Twelve to sixteen.

615. Does not that prevent a good many boys from competing at the Intermediate Examinations?—Yes, I find it very inconvenient when boys come at sixteen. They have then to enter for the Middle Grade of the Intermediate Examinations, and they cannot be prepared so as to obtain honours at the end of their first year.

616. Do you think it would be an advantage if the limits of age were altered?—Most decidedly.

617. What alteration would you propose?—Twelve to fifteen.

618. Do you think the lower limit low enough?—Yes.

619. You don't want boys younger than twelve?—I think not. The limit would enable a boy to have four chances; and if he fails in the three, I don't think he is deserving of a fourth.

620. How have your boys got on at the Intermediate Examinations?—Very well. This year I had seventeen candidates, including foundation pupils and pay boarders. Eleven passed the examination generally. Including those who passed only in certain subjects, there were altogether fifty-seven passes with honours, and thirty-five passes without honours. Boys passed with honours in all the grades, and two obtained exhibitions—one in the Middle Grade and one in the Junior Grade; another pupil obtained a book prize, first class. One pupil secured full marks in English, Middle Grade; another full marks in arithmetic, Junior Grade; another took fourth place in trigonometry, Senior Grade.

621. Was the Middle Grade exhibition retained or gained?—It was gained. The pupil who obtained it this year obtained a Junior Grade exhibition last year, he was fifth in Ireland in the Junior Grade last year.

622. What place did he get this year?—Not so high, but a very good place in the Middle Grade.

623. Previous to that had you any exhibitioners?—Several foundation pupils qualified by their answering for exhibitions, but owing to their holding scholarships from another endowment were disqualified.

624. Dr. Traill.—What age was the boy who took fourth place in Trigonometry?—Eighteen. He afterwards obtained a Sizary scholarship; but boys in their third year are generally over age, others are not able to go in for many subjects in the Senior Grade, having to study the examination course for Sizary.

625. Do you find that it is not the boys that come to you at the age of sixteen who succeed?—Yes. The boys that come at a younger age, I find as a rule to be smarter boys.

626. If you were to lower your upper limit of age from sixteen to fifteen you would only exclude boys from coming in as foundationers?—Yes; as a foundation pupil of course he cannot benefit as well by the Intermediate Examinations, he cannot compete in the Junior Grade. A boy who comes at sixteen sometimes gets honours in mathematics, but not high marks, but if he came at fifteen or younger we would be able to prepare him for the Junior Grade, and he would probably win an Exhibition.

627. Have you had any boy who came to you at fifteen and got honours in the Junior Grade?—Oh, yes, a good many; and younger than fifteen. If they are able to enter the Junior Grade at the end of the first year they almost invariably get honours in mathematics after being with us one year.

628. Professor Dougherty.—I see that the [illegible] trustees reserve the right to nominate a certain number of boys; do they ever exercise that right?—I don't know.

629. The founders also provided for the establishment of an agricultural school connected with Primrose Grange. How much land do you hold?—About twelve acres.

630. Is any attempt made to instruct the boys in agriculture?—None.

631. There never was any appointment of an agricultural master in accordance with the terms of the deed of foundation?—Not during my time, or in the time of my predecessor. I have heard that it was an agricultural school at one time, but that it was not successful and had to be discontinued as such.

632. No attempt is made at present to instruct the boys on the foundation who desire it, in farming or gardening?—I don't think there is any desire for it. They prefer literary education.

633. You think that there is no demand for an agricultural school, such as was intended?—Not to my knowledge.

634. Lord Justice FitzGibbon.—How are the repairs of the buildings done?—The Incorporated Society pay the expense of repairs.

635. Have you anything to do with that expenditure?—I generally make suggestions, and the board

Oct. 4, 1886.

Mr. W. A. Shepherd.

or deputation, if they see that anything is necessary, they require it to be done.

636. The house has been improved lately?—It has during the past five or six years. Considerable additions were made about six years ago.

637. Would you have additional pupils if you had additional sleeping accommodation?—I think so.

638. In other respects is your accommodation sufficient?—Not quite for the master's family. It is not sufficiently large. There are only two bedrooms in the master's residence, and, if the master has a large family it is very inconvenient.

639. Dr. TRAILL.—Have you a large family?—Four.

640. Lord Justice FITZGIBBON.—You have no room into which a boy who is ailing can go?—None.

641. Is that a want?—A very great want.

642. You would rather have something in the nature of an observation room than a room to put a boy into for any serious illness?—Just a room in which he might be isolated.

643. Lord Justice NAISH.—What pursuits in life do your boys betake themselves to?—A great number have become tutors; a few have gone to the College of Surgeons. Last year I sent up two for the College of Surgeons. One of these tied for first place, the other got a high second. Some go into banks and Civil Service, some graduate in the universities, and afterwards enter the ministry.

644. Rev. Dr. MOLLOY.—Then, practically, your school prepares pupils for professional careers, for the banks, for official life, and for the teaching profession?—Yes.

645. Lord Justice NAISH.—None of them go back to their own homes again?—Very rarely.

646. Industries and useful arts have no share in your system of education?—Industries have not.

647. That was the special purpose for which the Incorporated Society was established?—I think Primrose Grange was established for the purpose, in addition to giving an agricultural education, of also providing a good English education.

648. Lord Justice NAISH.—Is your school the only Protestant school in Sligo that prepares young men for these pursuits?—There is the Diocesan School in the town of Sligo.

649. Are the wants of Sligo fully met by these two schools?—I don't know about the town, but boarders come to Primrose Grange from Sligo, Donegal, Leitrim, Fermanagh, and Mayo, and I have had some from Dublin.

650. Rev. Dr. MOLLOY.—Of course you are not in any way responsible for the character of the education that is given. You give the education which you were appointed to give, but it may be well to notice that the Society hold the endowment of Primrose Grange subject to a deed bearing date 1842, in which the following trusts are specified:—

"To establish in connexion with the English school an agricultural school, and appoint an agricultural master; to instruct all the boys on the foundation, and also such of the day scholars as wish to avail themselves of the opportunity, in farming and gardening by the agricultural master; to defray the expense of the reclamation and improvement of the land by draining and fencing the land; to supply lime and to have a regular rotation of green crops raised by the agriculturist."

WITNESS.—I think it is not a very suitable locality for a model farm, but it is a very good locality for lime, as there is plenty of limestone.

651. Dr. TRAILL.—I suppose the farmers think their boys would be just as well at home, as bestowing their labour on an agricultural school?—Quite so.

652. Professor DOUGHERTY.—In other countries the experience, as to agricultural schools, has been very different?—I have not any knowledge of them.

653. Lord Justice FITZGIBBON.—The grant of the house and lands of Primrose Grange was in 1721, and 1842 was the date at which the Incorporated Society became possessed of it?—I think so.

654. It is an old endowment, and it got into a great state of inefficiency. It passed from the hands of Commissioners who conveyed it, on the recommendation of the bishop, to the Incorporated Society. You farm part of the land?—Twelve acres.

655. What do you pay for it?—£13 16s. 8d.

656. How was that fixed?—By agreement.

657. Is there any local interest taken in the school?—There are some gentlemen who take an interest in the Science and Art examinations.

658. You are obliged to form a local committee for that purpose?—A local committee.

659. Whom have you got?—Rev. J. Galbraith, Mr. Walker, J.P., of Rathcarrick, a resident gentleman, and Mr. William Cochrane, a Civil Engineer, who lives close by; also Ven. Archdeacon Kearney, Rev. Canon Flood, Mr. A. Jackson, C.E., Mr. Brabazon, Bank of Ireland, all of Sligo.

660. Do you think it would be an advantage if some more of the gentlemen of the neighbourhood were on that committee?—It is rather difficult to get a committee to suit the requirements of the South Kensington Department, with the exception of the two gentlemen I have named, and our catechist, the Rev. Mr. Galbraith. I have to come to Sligo to get others.

661. Do you think representatives of the Diocesan Council, or the Incorporated Society would be able to form a local committee for you?—I think the gentlemen of the diocese could do so. I don't know if Colonel Cooper is a member of the Incorporated Society.

662. He is not a member of the committee of fifteen. I believe they are pretty nearly all residents in Dublin?—I think so. I don't know all the members of the committee.

663. Dr. TRAILL.—What results did you get out of South Kensington?—I had two classes in connexion with South Kensington—one in mathematics, and another in plane, and solid geometry. The boys did very well, and got Queen's prizes and certificates.

664. What amount of money did they earn for you?—Unfortunately the Science and Art Department don't pay for mathematics, except in the advanced stages. Certain endowed schools are not paid any results fees for subjects which are carried on in the ordinary working of the school.

665. Lord Justice FITZGIBBON.—Did you try anything in the way of art for South Kensington?—No. I think the multiplication of classes and examinations would be injurious.

666. You could hardly do it with your present staff?—Hardly.

667. Your staff consists of yourself and an assistant?—Myself and an assistant, and I utilize some of the senior boys occasionally.

668. Dr. TRAILL.—What salary have you?—£100 a year from the Incorporated Society, with a residence and certain allowances, and 10d. a day for the foundation pupils, and profits from pay boarders.

669. Lord Justice FITZGIBBON.—What have you for servants?—£36 a year for servants. Of course that doesn't cover all the expense. Also £40 a year for the assistant master; £37 a year for coal; £9 a year for light, and £6 a year for washing.

670. Dr. TRAILL.—What do you pay the assistant?—£40 a year. He is resident. I have to supplement the allowance given by the Incorporated Society.

671. Lord Justice FITZGIBBON.—Did they make any provision, in adding to the buildings, for baths for the boys?—There is a bath in my own part of the house which I got at my own expense, and a moveable bath for the smaller boys. This is not such a one as I would like, but I think the Incorporated Society will allow me to get one of a better kind.

672. At present you are confined to basins?—Not altogether. The juniors are sent weekly to the laundry, where they get washed in moveable baths.

673. Mr. Maberly was struck with that ten years ago?—And Mr. Moore. Oct. 6, 1885.

674. The Society is rather slow in getting you anything of that kind?—Well, I cannot complain of the help the Society have given me. They have made a great many improvements during my time. Mr. W. A. Shekleton.

675. Dr. Traill.—Is the Rev. Mr. Galbraith your catechist?—Yes.

676. Lord Justice FitzGibbon.—I suppose your boys attend his church?—They do. They are all members of the Church of Ireland.

677. Paying boarders and all?—Paying boarders and all at present. Of course I did not inquire what the foundation pupils were; but when they come to Primrose Grange they are required to learn the formularies of the Church of Ireland.

678. The system of admission is the same as elsewhere, the evidence of their fitness is a certificate from the clergyman of the parish?—Yes.

679. Dr. Traill.—They could not be with you except as members of the Church of Ireland?—Not except as members of the Church of Ireland. Our present catechist is not here; but there are two gentlemen here who were formerly catechists, namely, the Rev. Mr. Hamilton and the Rev. Mr. Coulter.

The Rev. *Frederick John Hamilton* sworn and examined.

680. Lord Justice FitzGibbon.—You were catechist of Primrose Grange?—Yes, for about two years—from November, 1881, to January, 1884—while I was incumbent of St. Anne's, Knocknarea. Rev. Frederick John Hamilton.

681. Is the incumbent of that church always the catechist of the school?—I don't think necessarily, but by custom he is.

682. What were your duties?—To attend at the school one day in the week for about an hour, and give religious instruction, and generally to supervise the school arrangements, to look into the school accounts and initial them, and sign my name to any returns made to the Incorporated Society.

683. Dr. Traill.—What pay did you get for that?—£20 a year.

684. Lord Justice FitzGibbon.—While you were catechist were there any gentry of the neighbourhood who took an interest in the school?—Yes; those whom Mr. Shekleton mentioned—Mr. Walker and Mr. Cochrane.

685. Do you think it would be any advantage to a school like this, if a local body such as the Diocesan Council, had a representation on the Incorporated Society?—I think it might, so far as Primrose Grange School is concerned; but I must say—although Mr. Shekleton is present—that under his management everything is so well done and efficiently worked that I think it is hardly required; but there might possibly be cases in which it would be required.

686. It is a great encouragement to a good master to have somebody to take an interest in his work?—Oh, yes.

687. And if there be anyone not so good, to keep him up to his work?—Yes.

688. Is there anything that you wish to say about the school or its arrangements?—I was present at several of these entrance examinations, and was allowed to be present at the private part of them in my capacity of catechist, and I think that on the whole they are very well conducted, and that the best boys are selected.

689. Dr. Traill.—You do not think that the Scripture examination is too hard or too catchy?—Well, yes; I think on some occasions it was. It depended very much on the examiner that came round.

690. Lord Justice FitzGibbon.—To what do you attribute the undoubted fact that two or three small localities have got the lion's share of this foundation?—The thoroughly good local schools under the Church of Ireland.

691. Thoroughly good at cramming for this particular examination?—I don't think so. I think they would be attended with good all round.

692. We have been told that the best boys from the Model School would not have a chance without this previous Scripture preparation?—The boys examined in the Scriptural examination would not have a chance unless they got such an education in the other branches as the Model School can give.

693. Dr. Traill.—Is not the examination in secular subjects more elementary than that in Scripture?—Yes; but the examiners have shown me papers which exhibited such bad spelling and were otherwise so badly worked out that no matter what the Scriptural knowledge of the boy was, I fancy that he never would have been taken in. Though it is elementary it must be a sound secular education.

694. Lord Justice FitzGibbon.—But if the Scripture examination is so peculiar as has been described, is there not a risk that the secular examination would be catchy also?—I don't think so. It is conducted first by dictation, and the examiner afterwards reads out the papers.

695. Of course in reading, writing, the elementary rules of arithmetic, and such things, there must be good teaching; but we have been told that the masters of particular schools had got the questions from year to year, and then crammed the boys in those special things, wouldn't that equally apply to one subject as to another?—It possibly might.

696. Dr. Traill.—Are there the same examiners in secular as in religious subjects?—Generally not. They generally brought round the papers—a few examination questions.

697. Are these papers let out of the room?—Never. They take up the papers along with the answers.

CASTLECONNOR AND KILGLASS SCHOOLS (VALENTINE ENDOWMENT).

The Very Rev. *William Skipton*, Dean of Killala, sworn and examined.

698. Lord Justice FitzGibbon.—Dean Skipton, I believe you are one of the trustees of the Valentine School Endowment?—Not under any appointment in the will. The bishop has been in the habit of appointing someone in the neighbourhood as his secretary; and when my predecessor, Dean Jackson—who was one of the trustees—died, the bishop asked me to take the management of it as secretary. Very Rev. William Skipton, Dean of Killala.

699. I find the foundation is under the will of Thomas Valentine, Vicar of Castleconnor, dated September 10, 1763. He gave £800 for the support of distressed widows of the clergy of the dioceses of Killala and Achonry; and £400 towards the foundation of a Protestant Charity School for the putting out of Protestant apprentices to trades, which school he ordered to be erected within the union of Frankfort, and he nominated the Lord Bishop of Killala, and the Vicar of Frankfort to be trustees of the same.—Yes.

700. Is there still a parish of Frankfort?—It is divided into two parishes of Castleconnor and Kilglass.

701. Was the school erected?—It was erected almost immediately after Mr. Valentine's death.

702. I understand that the money is divided now

Oct. [illegible]

Very Rev. William [illegible], Dean of Killala.

among several schools?—There are four schools in the parish—two in each division.

703. Lord Justice Naish.—Has not the £400 become much larger by accumulation?—It amounts now to £2,485 0s. 10d. in the hands of the Commissioners of Charitable Donations and Bequests, producing a yearly income of £74 11s.

704. Do you receive that direct from the Commissioners?—It is sent by the Commissioners to the bishop, and by him transmitted to me.

705. What do you do with it?—I divide it between the two parishes.

706. In equal shares?—In equal shares. There is one school at Kilglass that receives the whole portion that goes to Kilglass parish. It was the school built immediately after Mr. Valentine's death.

707. What style of school is it?—It is conducted on what used to be known as the Church Education plan; and the master increases his emoluments by taking in a number of pupils from the surrounding parishes to prepare them for Primrose Grange.

708. How many pupils has he?—About twenty-four.

709. He has not a sufficient number to get a National Board grant?—They have never tried for it so far as I know. He has been a long time there. He gets half the endowment. The other half goes to the parish of Castleconnor.

710. To whom do you pay it?—To the Incumbent of Castleconnor.

711. What schools has he?—One at Castleconnor, and one at Scurmore. They both receive capitation allowances under the National Board.

712. Do you know the numbers attending them?—In one there are at present fifteen pupils, and in the other twelve.

713. Are they both under female teachers?—Both.

714. Is the money applied directly as a subvention to the salary of the teachers?—I don't know, but I believe the Castleconnor school gets the greater part of it.

715. How has the accumulation gathered?—I have tried to trace that accumulation and I really cannot make it quite out. In the early days of the trust they paid the schoolmaster only £8 a year, at the time that they had fully £20 a year coming to them.

716. Dr. Traill.—Is the money vested in the Commissioners of Charitable Donations and Bequests now?—It is.

717. Lord Justice FitzGibbon.—Have they paid any money for putting out apprentices to trades?—They did. I have looked into the account, and I find that the last was in 1877.

718. Mr. Valentine seems to have been Vicar of Castleconnor, Kilglass, and Easkey?—I believe it was a sort of union; but he gave no money to Easkey. The will provided that it should go to Frankfort.

719. The Bishop seems to have appointed you as a kind of deputy?—His deputy simply, to look after it.

720. I think the best thing we could do would be to follow the will, and give the Bishop the power legally—which he at present exercises voluntarily—of nominating the clergy of these two parishes to act for him.

Witness.—These are two parishes that are very likely to change Incumbents very quickly, and it seems to me that it would be better to put some one in now, that would be likely to remain in the neighbourhood.

721. Dr. Traill.—They change very quickly, as the incomes are very small?—Just so.

722. Lord Justice FitzGibbon.—Do you think the Diocesan Council would be a good body to exercise a power of selection?—I don't know. I cannot give an opinion.

723. The Bishop at all events could nominate some one?—Yes.

724. Dr. Traill.—Is your diocese thinking of forming a body of Trustees to hold school property?—Yes, they are.

725. Lord Justice FitzGibbon.—If so it would be better to let this fund be vested in that body, and to declare the trust to apply it for the schools of the two parishes.

726. Dr. Traill.—Is your parish near?—My parish borders on Castleconnor.

727. It is only by accident that you are connected with the endowment?—The Dean might bring in some other part of the diocese.

728. Lord Justice FitzGibbon.—Is there an Archdeacon of Killala?—There is. He is resident at Killala.

729. Do you know anything of the buildings?—I know them quite well.

730. How is the Valentine school building held?—There are about three acres with the school that were given by the Bishop of the time—the lord—to allow the bequest to be carried out. The schoolmaster farms the land at present as part of his emoluments.

731. Has he a residence?—There is a schoolhouse and residence.

732. Is that all that is in the parish of Kilglass?—No, there is another school in the parish, which receives no money, but it was built by the Valentine endowment. At one time my predecessor, Dr. Jackson, had an accumulation of some £300 in his hands, and he built this school house in Enniscrone.

733. How is the site of the Castleconnor school held?—It was given by Mr. Orme, the landlord there. He gave it in exchange for a quarter of an acre of glebe land without boundaries. It was known to be there, and he simply gave off this in lieu of it.

734. It is a quarter of an acre?—I think it is.

735. And the building is on it?—Yes.

736. When was that?—Somewhere about 1866–1867.

737. Is there any schoolmaster's residence there too?—There is, in part of the same building. It is a small place. It is adjacent [illegible].

738. Dr. Traill.—How many children are there?—I think about a dozen.

739. How far is it from the other school?—About two miles.

740. Would the one school accommodate the two parishes?—No.

741. How was the master trained—is he a Church Education teacher?—I think so.

742. Lord Justice FitzGibbon.—Formerly it was stated that there was a subscription of £40 a year to the Scurmore school?—That was through the agency of Mr. Stratford. When he died his successor withdrew it from that to the Enniscrone school.

743. How is the Castleconnor school held?—The Castleconnor school was on a corner of an old glebe, and when the Church Act passed, it was vested in the Representative Body.

744. What land is there?—I don't know if there be as much as a quarter of an acre. There is a residence in the building.

745. The fourth school?—The fourth school at Enniscrone was built by Colonel Wingfield, who kept it in his own hands for a length of time, and then gave it up to the parish about 1867.

746. What premises are there?—Just what it stands on, and a little bit of ground between the house and the road. It has a residence.

747. Lord Justice FitzGibbon.—We had better let you see the scheme that we have prepared; and if you want a separate one for the Valentine Endowment you can have it.

Witness.—The only thing is that there should be some plan for having the money received and transmitted.

Lord Justice FitzGibbon.—The Incumbents of the parishes, and whoever are associated with them as trustees, should receive the money; and it will be for the Commissioners to look after the spending of it.

SLIGO DIOCESAN SCHOOL.

[illegible]

William Christopher Eades, M.A., sworn and examined.

William Christopher Eades, M.A.

748. Lord Justice FitzGibbon.—You are carrying on a school in the premises formerly called the Caby Endowed School?—Yes.

749. You also hold the position of diocesan schoolmaster of Elphin?—Yes.

750. When were you appointed?—At the end of 1868.

751. You held office at the passing of the Church Act?—Yes.

752. And you still hold an annuity as the diocesan schoolmaster under the Act of Elizabeth?—Yes.

753. When you were appointed were there any school buildings belonging to the diocesan school as such?—There were, I believe, at Elphin, because part of the annuity that I receive is derived from the worth of the buildings and land at Elphin.

754. Is that paid to you by the Commissioners?—Yes.

755. How much did they pay?—I could not say precisely, because it was all lumped in one sum under the Act, but I think it was between £40 and £50. The whole matter was settled in the time of my predecessor, Mr. Robinson. He applied to the Commissioners frequently from time to time, and at last succeeded in getting the value of this land and house at Elphin allowed to him. It had not previously been so.

756. You get your whole income as diocesan schoolmaster from the Land Commissioners as the successors of the Church Temporalities Commission?—Yes.

757. You have no premises belonging to any diocesan school?—None at all.

758. Do you know how the premises in which your present school is, were held?—They were held under a lease from the late Mr. Wynne to certain trustees in Sligo for the purposes of the school.

759. What is the term of that lease?—I believe thirty or thirty-one years; I know it expires in this year, 1888.

760. You have purchased the reversion of the lease?—I purchased the lease as it stood.

761. You have bought up your own rent?—Yes.

762. And you hold the premises now in fee simple?—Yes.

763. Was that purchased through the Landed Estates Court?—It was.

764. And the property is not now subject to any trust for education?—It is not.

765. Except so far as you are bound to continue to teach for the annuity?—Yes.

766. And you provide yourself with the premises and appliances?—Yes.

767. Dr. Traill.—What is the amount of the annuity?—£163 7s. is the total.

768. Lord Justice FitzGibbon.—Is there any other Intermediate school attended by Protestant pupils in the town of Sligo?—Not that I am aware of.

769. About how many pupils have you had in Sligo?—We have had at the utmost, I think, in my time, about thirty, including boarders and day boys. We have seventeen on the roll at present, all day boys belonging to the town.

770. You prepare them for the Intermediate examinations?—Yes.

771. And for Trinity College?—Yes; I sent up one last year.

772. You are free to commute your annuity still?—I think not now. There was a time limited within which I might commute or compound.

773. Then you are bound to perform the duties of diocesan schoolmaster as long as you are able?—As long as I am able; but I think the Act provides for an efficient substitute.

774. Rev. Dr. Molloy.—You would be free to use the present building as your private property?—Quite so.

775. And if you did that how would you fulfil the duties of schoolmaster?—I suppose I might rent any other place in the town if I did so.

776. Would you be bound to rent a place?—Well, I don't know how I could carry on without some premises; but I don't say that I am bound to these particular premises.

777. They could not compel you to keep a school in that particular house?—I think not.

778. Lord Justice Naish.—The whole arrangements in connection with diocesan schoolmasters are carried out, we know, under an Act of Parliament with which we have nothing to do.

Witness.—Is there no possibility of retaining that endowment of £163 for the purposes of education?

779. Lord Justice FitzGibbon.—The endowment at present consists entirely of your own life annuity.

Witness.—Why should it stop with my life?

780. Lord Justice FitzGibbon.—That is one of the most extraordinary provisions of the Irish Church Act. The diocesan schoolmasters allowances were a charge on the Church property for the purposes of education, and yet they were treated as if they were part of the Church property; since 1869 they expire with the lives of the holders, or on their commuting or compounding. I think there are now only three in existence—yours, one at Ballymena, and one at Tuam. Even the composition balance is not liable to any trust for education.

COLLEGE OF THE IMMACULATE CONCEPTION.

781. Lord Justice FitzGibbon.—This endowment is under the management of a Roman Catholic body, exclusively and is for Roman Catholic pupils; it is therefore exempt from our jurisdiction.

Oct. 13, 1886.

PUBLIC SITTING—WEDNESDAY, OCTOBER 13, 1886.

At the Courthouse, Boyle.

Present:—The Right Hon. Lord Justice FitzGibbon and the Right Hon. Lord Justice Naish, Judicial Commissioners; and the Rev. Gerald Molloy, D.D., D.SC., Anthony Traill, Esq., LL.D., M.D., F.T.C.D., and Professor Dougherty, M.A., Assistant Commissioners.

The Assistant Secretary, N. D. Murphy, jun., was in attendance.

BOYLE ACADEMICAL INSTITUTION.

Lord Justice FitzGibbon read the following memorial, received on April 12, 1886:—

To the Commissioners of Educational Endowments.

The Memorial of the undersigned respectfully showeth:

That the Boyle Academical Institution was established in 1880 to supply a want long felt in Boyle and its neighbourhood, and to take advantage of the Intermediate Education (Ireland) Act.

At a public meeting, convened for the purpose, a representative committee was appointed to solicit subscriptions, select a suitable Head Master, &c., &c. The Institution was opened on 1st August, 1880, under the patronage of the Right Honorable Colonel King-Harman, M.P. The present teaching staff consists of a Principal, a Lady-Principal, and a Mathematical and Science Master. The course of instruction embraces the following subjects:—English, Mathematics, Natural Philosophy, Latin, Greek, French, German, Botany, Music and Drawing. Pupils are thoroughly prepared for the Intermediate and South Kensington Examinations, for Pass and Honour Examinations at the Universities, and for the different branches of the Civil Service.

The Institution is open to both boys and girls, and is perfectly non-sectarian. The day-pupils are composed of Protestants of all denominations, and of Roman Catholics. The boarders are equally representative, and are drawn chiefly from the counties Roscommon, Sligo, Leitrim, and Mayo. From the first the Institution ranked high among the educational establishments of the country, as is manifest from the success of the pupils at the Intermediate and University Examinations. For example, last year (1885) seven pupils were successful in the different grades at the Intermediate Examinations. One obtained an exhibition (of £15 a year for three years) the eighth place in all Ireland, and three (two of them girls) obtained prizes in books. Each pupil passed with honours, two with honours in five subjects, and one with honours in nine, the total number in which he presented himself. At the Examinations in connexion with Trinity College, Dublin, the Royal University, and the College of Surgeons, our pupils have been equally successful during the year. One pupil obtained a first class certificate in the College of Surgeons; two girls matriculated in the Royal University, and one passed the examination for women at Trinity College, taking honours in several subjects; and two, a boy and a girl, passed the Second Examination in Arts in the Royal University, one of them winning an exhibition of £[illegible]. At the South Kensington May Examinations, twenty certificates, six of them First Class, were awarded to the pupils of the Boyle Academical Institution.

There are few schools in Ireland, certainly none of same standing and number of pupils, which have such a brilliant record of success for 1885, and the prospect for the present year (1886) is even more brilliant. Eleven pupils are being prepared for the coming Intermediate Examinations, [illegible] of them exhibitioners of last year. We anticipate fifty certificates from the South Kensington Department after the May Examinations. Two pupils are reading for the Royal University Matriculation, one for the Preliminary Examination of the Pharmaceutical Society, one for the College of Surgeons, and two for the Incorporated Law Society's Preliminary Examination.

The school has no endowments whatever, and the Managing Committee are responsible for the rent of house (£[illegible] and taxes) and the salaries of the teachers.

The Right Honorable Colonel King-Harman, M.P., the members of the Committee, and many others interested in higher education, have subscribed very liberally from the first to its maintenance; but owing to the depression in trade and other causes, this source of income is very precarious. The undersigned memorialists, members of the Managing Committee, would therefore respectfully ask the Commissioners of Educational Endowments to grant the school such an endowment as would enable them to carry on the Boyle Academical Institution with increased efficiency.

And your memorialists, as in duty bound, will ever pray—

William Lawrence, Chairman.
Francis Ed. Clarke, M.A., LL.D., [illegible], &c., Rector of Boyle and Rural Dean.
William J. Smith.
Robert Kane.
Alexander Dunlop.
Jas. Black.
Michl. M'Donagh.
Henry Mahon.
Robert [illegible].
James Wilson, [illegible].
Thos. Stuart.
John Watson, B.A., Hon. Sec.

The Rev. John Watson, B.A., sworn and examined.

Rev. John Watson, B.A.

782. Lord Justice FitzGibbon.—You are Honorary Secretary of the Boyle Academical Institution?—Yes.

783. What is the composition of your committee?—It consists of twelve gentlemen, of whom six are Presbyterians and six Episcopalians.

784. How were they appointed?—They were appointed at a public meeting convened at the Courthouse in 1880. It was a representative committee, appointed with power to add to its numbers. It consisted at first of eight gentlemen. In a year or so two others were added, and by and by two others; so that at present it consists of twelve.

785. Are these all subscribers to the Institution?—Yes, they have been all subscribers from the beginning.

786. Have you any fixed scale of subscriptions to qualify for membership of the committee?—No; the intention was that the school in a short time should become self-maintaining. For the first year the committee guaranteed the teacher £100, with school fees and results fees. We commenced with one teacher, but found he was unable to do the work of the school, and we had to appoint a mathematical master. When we opened the school for girls we had to appoint a lady principal; and the consequence was, that the school fees and subscriptions were unable to meet the salaries and the rent of the schoolhouse.

787. Was there a guarantee fund?—We guaranteed the head master £100 a year, and raised that money by subscriptions.

788. Lord Justice Naish.—What is the rent of the schoolhouse?—£50 and taxes. We opened the school in this room, as we had then no schoolhouse; the head

... afterwards took a suitable house and brought the school to it.

789. Lord Justice FitzGibbon.—Is he tenant of the house?—The present schoolhouse is a rented house. The committee rent the house from the owner, and the head master has the house rent free. The committee are responsible for the rent. The house is the committee's.

790. Dr. Traill.—If the head master were changed, he could not hold possession of the house against the committee?—Not at all.

791. Is it held under a written agreement?—Yes.

792. Who are the parties to that agreement?—I am one of the parties. We could be evicted at six months notice; we hold it from year to year.

793. Professor Dougherty.—Who signed the agreement?—The chairman and secretary as representing the committee.

794. Who is the chairman of the committee?—Mr. Lawrence has been chairman since 1881.

795. Dr. Traill.—What do you pay for the house?—Fifty pounds a year and taxes—it amounts to £54 a year altogether. There was some outlay for desks and furniture.

796. Lord Justice FitzGibbon.—Where were the funds got?—By public subscription. I can give you the report for 1881 and the list of subscriptions. (Handed in document.)

797. The guarantee fund of 1880 and 1881 amounted altogether to £103, of which £93 is stated to have been paid. There is a statement of accounts giving a year's salary to the schoolmaster, £100; 15s. for the use of the rooms; and 16s. 7d. for various expenses; leaving a balance due to the treasurer of £10 11s. 7d. on November 1, 1881. The subscriptions vary from £10 from Colonel King-Harman down to £1 each from a number of subscribers.

Witness.—This is the report for 1882, also giving a list of subscribers. (Hands document.)

798. Lord Justice FitzGibbon.—In 1882 the subscriptions were £83 1s. all paid; balance carried forward, due to the treasurer, £10 11s. 7d., two salaries, Mr. Hamilton £38, and another, £35; five desks, £3 3s. 6d., and sundry other expenses, leaving a balance of £4 0s. 11d. (To Witness.) Did you continue to receive subscriptions after that?—We publish a report every year; but we ceased after some time to collect annual subscriptions. It was the intention of the committee and of the people of the town that the school should be self-maintaining after three years. Then we had to increase our teaching staff and to add to our expenses. At the present time we are in debt over £50. For the last year there have been no subscriptions. The income was altogether obtained from school fees; and these for 1887 amounted to £184.

799. Lord Justice Naish.—How many pupils are there?—Twenty-seven at present; four girls and twenty-three boys.

800. How many of the boys are boarders?—Six.

801. What do the boarders pay?—Thirty-two pounds a year for education and board; and boys under fourteen pay £28. The boarding department is altogether in the hands of the head master; the committee don't interfere with the boarding arrangements.

802. Dr. Traill.—Are the boarding receipts included in the £184?—The head master pays the school fees of the boarders, and they are included in the £184.

803. Lord Justice FitzGibbon.—How much are the school fees?—For English, including Mathematics, Natural Philosophy, Chemistry, and Botany, £1 5s. a quarter; for Latin and Greek, 10s.; for Modern Languages, 10s.; for Music, £1 1s.; Singing, £1 1s.; and Drawing, 5s.

804. About £10 a year would be the average fee?—About £10 a year.

805. The same for boys and girls?—The same.

806. What has been your success since 1886?—At the Intermediate Examinations for 1886, 10 pupils passed, 2 obtained exhibitions in the middle grade—£25 for two years, and 1 twelfth place; 1 obtained a junior exhibition of £20 a year for three years; 1 girl a book prize, another pupil got a prize in the Pharmaceutical examination. At the Science and Art Examinations, South Kensington, 14 pupils obtained certificates in Mathematics; 7 in Physiography; and 1 in Natural Philosophy. In 1887, 1 pupil, a girl, matriculated in the London University; 1 girl matriculated in the Royal University; and 1 girl passed the First University examination.

807. Professor Dougherty.—Had she been in the school between the matriculation and the First University examination?—She had not attended regularly; she was taking lessons from the master.

808. But she had not received instruction anywhere else?—No. At the Intermediate examinations in 1887, 9 pupils passed, 1 taking third place in the senior grade with a prize of £40, a silver medal in Natural Philosophy, and a special prize of £4 in Latin composition.

809. Rev. Dr. Molloy.—What is his name?—Ashmore, he was a boarder.

810. Lord Justice Naish.—Where was he from?—From Crossdoney, in the county of Leitrim. In the middle grade 1 boy retained his exhibition and obtained a prize of £2. In the junior grade 2 exhibitions of £20 a year for three years were gained, and a first class book prize, besides silver medals in music and chemistry. In South Kensington 13 pupils passed in mathematics; 11 in physiography; 6 in mechanics; 3 in sound, light, and heat; 1 in magnetism and electricity; and 1 in agriculture; while 1 obtained Queen's prizes.

811. Rev. Dr. Molloy.—What was the total amount of your results fees from South Kensington in 1887?—About £32.

812. The numbers you gave overlap each other?—They all overlap each other.

813. I see that Ashmore passed the examination in South Kensington as well as the Intermediate examination?—Yes.

814. Do you find the Intermediate examinations satisfactory?—Yes.

815. What centre have you?—The boys go to Sligo and the girls to Dublin.

816. Lord Justice FitzGibbon.—You are a practical proof of the impossibility of relying on the evidence given to us, as to what schools cannot get on without. In several places we were told that they could not keep up a school because there was no Intermediate centre in the town. We have also had evidence that it is impossible to maintain a school doing this kind of work under £700 a year?—But we know what it is to meet with difficulties and overcome them.

817. Lord Justice Naish.—Do you think that if you had means to carry on a larger school you would have a larger number of pupils, or do your 27 pupils represent all the boys and girls that require this kind of education here?—I don't think so by any means.

818. Professor Dougherty.—Of the 27 pupils how many presented themselves at the Intermediate examinations?—In 1887, 10 presented themselves, and 9 passed.

819. What was the average attendance at the school in that year, 1887?—About the same as now. There may have been perhaps 30, but not more.

820. Lord Justice FitzGibbon.—Have you the results for 1888?—Yes, but this year has not been so brilliant, because Ashmore and some of the other best boys have passed through.

821. Rev. Dr. Molloy.—Where is Ashmore now?—Attending the Academical Institution, Belfast.

822. Is he reading for the Royal University?—Yes. He would have entered the Royal University before this, but he was ill.

Oct. 14, 1888.

Rev. John Watson, B.A.

823. Dr. Traill.—What age is he?—About nineteen. He passed the senior grade here in 1887. In 1888, at the Intermediate examinations, 9 passed—3 in the senior grade, 1 in the middle, and 5 in the junior grade. At South Kensington 6 passed in chemistry, 8 in physiography, and 10 in mathematics. At the Royal University I passed the second examination in arts, 1 the first examination in arts, and 3 matriculated, one taking third place in Ireland with a first class exhibition of £24, and first class honours in Latin, Greek, and English.

824. Lord Justice FitzGibbon.—How long had that pupil been out of the school at the time of his matriculation?—Never. He matriculated direct from us, and took third place in all Ireland. He took first class honours in Latin, Greek, and English.

825. Rev. Dr. Molloy.—What is his name?—John Mahon. His father lives here. Only for this school he would not have had an opportunity of getting his education. He has just been attending the examination in Dublin, and we hope he will take a classical scholarship.

826. Then he is distinguished in classics as Ashmore was in mathematics?—He is distinguished in both classics and mathematics.

827. You passed one pupil in the second examination in arts of the Royal University. Did he continue reading here till he went up for that examination?—He continued reading here till that time.

828. Lord Justice FitzGibbon.—I see that John Mahon got honours in South Kensington in 1887 in mathematics, and also in physics. There is another Mahon who seems to have passed in a greater number of subjects?—A brother of his—an older boy.

829. Professor Dougherty.—What did Mahon do at the Intermediate examinations?—He took an exhibition of £15 a year for three years in the junior grade—sixth place in all Ireland, and an exhibition in middle grade.

830. Dr. Traill.—You changed your head master more than once since you started the institution?—Our present head master is the fourth that we have had.

831. Lord Justice FitzGibbon.—What led to the changes?—On account of our not being able to retain them.

832. This sort of work is the best advertisement a young man can have?—Decidedly. Our late head master, Mr. Greer, is at present in charge of a school in Dublin—the Presbyterian Association Institution.

833. What is your present staff?—A head master, Mr. Stewart, who is a graduate of the Royal University, and a mathematical master, Mr. F. Smith, a graduate of the London University, an Englishman. We had a third teacher, a lady principal in Mr. Greer's time; but on account of the funds falling short we had to dispense with her. That is our great want at the present time. If we had funds to procure another teacher it would add very much to the efficiency of our school. It is impossible for two masters to overtake all the work of the school, there are so many classes.

834. Dr. Traill.—I suppose £50 a year would make you pretty strong?—It would make us strong.

835. Lord Justice FitzGibbon.—You have got a teacher in music?—Yes; Miss Hegarty has a number of music pupils. She comes on her own responsibility.

836. How is your principal paid?—We guarantee him a salary, and he gives us all the fees both of day boys and boarders.

837. I thought he did not give you the boarding money?—Not the boarding money, but he pays us school fees for the boarders, and charges them £33 a year.

838. He has to pay you £10 a year out of it?—It depends on the subjects they take; it is practically £10 a year.

839. Is he able to maintain the boarders for about £20 a year?—About that. I don't think he makes much out of it.

840. How much do you guarantee him?—Eighty pounds a year with the house rent free, and the results fees on the subjects that he teaches. The results fees from the Intermediate and South Kensington amount to £50 from both.

841. How is your second master paid?—His salary is £30 a year, with results fees on the subjects he teaches. We don't guarantee him a minimum, but he boards with the head master.

842. Do he and the head master settle that between them?—Yes. The head master charges him £20 a year for his board.

843. Then he has only £10 a year for himself and his results fees?—That is all.

844. No wonder that you can't keep your good men. Now, as to the music teacher?—During Mr. Greer's time we paid the music teacher £30 a year, and she taught not only music but French and some other things. Now Miss Hegarty comes as visiting governess, and gives lessons in the school. The mathematical master teaches French and German.

845. Have your pupils passed satisfactorily in these subjects?—They have.

846. Rev. Dr. Molloy.—Did two of your girls go from this school to the Royal University?—Yes.

847. Are they still reading here, or have they gone to another school?—They are not reading in connexion with this school at present. One of them is still in Boyle. One of the girls passed in the London University, and is in London. I think the girl who is here intends to graduate in the Royal University.

848. Is it not more difficult to prepare for the degree examination?—I think the second examination is quite as difficult as that for the degree, if not more so.

849. She has passed the second?—Yes.

850. Lord Justice FitzGibbon.—What religious denomination do your pupils belong to?—Protestants of all denominations and Roman Catholics.

851. Are all the Roman Catholics day pupils?—We have had Roman Catholic boarders.

852. You state in your prospectus that you give no religious training in the school, and that the boarders worship at the churches of their several religious denominations—is that still your rule?—Yes.

853. Lord Justice Naish.—How many Roman Catholics have you at present?—Two.

854. Lord Justice FitzGibbon.—Is there any other Intermediate school in Boyle or its neighbourhood?—None whatever of any denomination.

855. Dr. Traill.—What is the nearest school?—Elphin is the nearest endowed school.

856. Lord Justice FitzGibbon.—Is there any other Intermediate school, endowed or non-endowed, near you?—None in the counties of Roscommon or Leitrim. None nearer than Sligo.

857. Professor Dougherty.—Have you ever turned your eyes in the direction of the Elphin endowment?—We don't covet any particular endowment. What we want is an endowment.

858. I suppose you would see no objection to a redistribution of the Elphin endowment, and that the Boyle School should get a share?—None whatever. Of course Boyle is a much more important town than Elphin, which is only a village.

859. What is the population of Boyle?—3,000.

860. Rev. Dr. Molloy.—And of Elphin?—500 or 600.

861. Professor Dougherty.—You talked of opening a school for girls; do you mean taking the girls into the same classes as the boys and making a mixed school?—A mixed school. Our first intention was to have only a boys' school.

862. Have you found any difficulty in arranging for the boys and the girls being taught together?—None whatever.

563. You think it satisfactory from your experience? —From my experience perfectly satisfactory.

564. I suppose it is indispensable here that if the girls are to be taught at all they should be taught in the way?—Absolutely indispensable. There is no other school where they could get this higher education.

565. Do you find all the denominations working harmoniously?—From the beginning all the denominations have worked most harmoniously.

566. Lord Justice FitzGibbon.—What are the denominations of your teachers?—The head master is a Presbyterian and the assistant master an Episcopalian.

567. Was Mr. Greer also a Presbyterian?—He was.

568. If you had an endowment what do you consider the chief object to which it should be applied? —Certainly the great want is a building.

569. Rev. Dr. Molloy.—It would seem from this illustration on your prospectus that you have a pretty good building already?—It represents the school very fairly.

570. Dr. Traill.—Could you get that building permanently if you had money?—Certainly. The present owner would sell it to us if we had the money.

571. Lord Justice FitzGibbon.—Your prospectus says that—

"At the beginning of the present year"—apparently 1885—"the Committee resolved on the erection of a new schoolroom, which has been just finished, and has been furnished with all modern improvements. The Academy is situated on an eminence, amid some of the most beautiful scenery in the West of Ireland. It commands a view of the Boyle river, and is about ten minutes walk from the Boyle railway station."

I suppose, when you say you erected these premises, that they were built by the landlord who gets the £50 a year?—Yes.

572. Were they built for the purposes of your school?—Not altogether. I really don't know whether it was built with that view or not. We took the place while it was being built.

573. I find it stated that there are—

"Hot and cold water, and shower baths. Each boarder is provided with a separate bed, and the dormitory is large and well ventilated."

You have all these appliances in the house?—We have hot and cold water in the bath-room.

574. Rev. Dr. Molloy.—Is the building large enough for the purposes of your school?—If the numbers increased it would not be large enough; but it could be enlarged without any difficulty.

575. Lord Justice FitzGibbon.—Have you any suggestion to offer as to where funds could be obtained?—We don't like to claim any particular endowment. All we want is an endowment no matter where it comes from. All the members of the committee are present. Perhaps some of these gentlemen would give some suggestions.

576. If any member of the committee be present, we shall be happy to hear him. Give us the names of the committee as they stand. Who is the Chairman?—Mr. Lawson.

577. What is his position?—He is a resident of Boyle. He was the late Postmaster of Boyle, and is a very respectable inhabitant of the town.

578. And your Secretary?—I am the Secretary.

579. And you are also Minister of the Presbyterian Church of Boyle?—Yes. Mr. Sloan, Mr. Kane, Mr. M'Donald, and Mr. Mahon, are merchants of Boyle.

580. The last is the father of two distinguished pupils?—Yes. Mr. Stewart is a large farmer in the district, and Mr. Alexander Dickie was Steward to the late Colonel King-Harman.

581. Rev. Dr. Molloy.—Had he a son a pupil here? —Yes, and three daughters.

582. Who else have you got?—Mr. James Black, merchant, of Boyle; Mr. Joseph Gillespie, Clerk of Petty Sessions; Mr. James Watson, Veterinary Surgeon; also the Rev. Dr. Clarke, the Rector of the parish. Oct. 14, 1885. Rev. John [illegible]

583. You appear to have no funds, but a debit in the books of the Bank of Ireland?—That's all, I am sorry to say.

584. The Rev. Dr. Clarke.—I can endorse all that Mr. Watson has stated. He has given every information. The committee don't undertake any responsibility in connexion with the boarders. The pupils are almost all resident in Boyle. Rev. Dr. Clarke.

585. Lord Justice Naish.—Where are the boarders from?

Rev. Dr. Clarke.—Principally from a distance of from ten to fifteen miles round. Might I point out that this school in Boyle is open to people of all denominations, and there is a very considerable population in Boyle, while Elphin, is speaking but a village. Our school is conducted on the mixed undenominational principle; and though it has more largely supplied educational advantages to Protestants, it is equally open to our Roman Catholic fellow-countrymen. What we want is, in a centre like Boyle, to maintain a school supplying the best education that we can afford to give to all classes of people without any distinction either of creed or class; and if we had a small endowment given to us, no matter from what source derived, that would enable us not so frequently to be changing masters, which is at present a great drawback, and would also enable us to have a second master for the furtherance of mathematical study, and if possible to keep a third master for modern languages. It is exceedingly difficult to get a master for classics or mathematics who will combine with these efficient instruction in modern languages. If we had an endowment to enable us to supply these wants, we could give an education to young people of different religious denominations, which would supply a want in an important centre like Boyle. Of course anything that is done in Elphin, is, I am sure, very good work; but it amounts to giving advantages to boys and girls coming from a distance. This school, on the other hand, is to supply a want much needed amongst ourselves—amongst all creeds.

586. Lord Justice FitzGibbon.—Then in fact the school was established to supply the actual wants of the neighbourhood, and the inhabitants have joined in managing it themselves?—Decidedly.

587. Colonel ffolliott.—I have attended from time to time at the school by invitation of the committee, and was very much pleased with everything that I saw and heard there. Mr. Greer, the late head master, appeared to be very efficient, and was in every way exceedingly well conducted. All the members of the committee are well known to me, and I believe they have been very well satisfied with the management of the school; and I know that they would not be satisfied with anything short of a very good education—in fact I have been surprised to find how good it was in every branch—for the young men growing up in Boyle. I can certainly say it with perfect confidence and knowledge of the men who have their sons educated there, and of the young men themselves. Col. ffolliott.

588. Lord Justice FitzGibbon.—In Strabane also we found an institution started in this way and doing far more work than schools that had considerable endowments.

Colonel ffolliott.—I have been astonished at what has been done here.

589. Lord Justice FitzGibbon.—You know the Elphin School?

Colonel ffolliott.—Yes, I do.

590. It is doing, we have reason to believe, very good work indeed with one-half of an endowment the other half of which goes to the cathedral there?

Oct. 18, 1888.

Col. ffolliott.

Colonel *ffolliott*.—Yes, that is so.

891. Do you know the cathedral at Elphin?

Colonel *ffolliott*.—Yes, I do.

892. Do you think that the half of the endowment now devoted to the cathedral would be more usefully applied in education?

Colonel *ffolliott*.—Very much more so. I think the Dean certainly has used that money extremely well, and the church is more or less in want of it, and it has been restored, and the work has been exceedingly well done. But Elphin is not to be compared to Boyle. It is a very remote place, and not a place likely to get on very much; and I must say I do not think very much money is wanted for the cathedral there. The school appears to me to be doing very good work, but I think you will find that the pupils come from a considerable distance.

893. Lord Justice FitzGibbon.—It appears to supply a very great want, namely, a cheap good boarding school. I am now speaking subject to what we may hear when we go there, but we have no jurisdiction to divert—and we should be sorry to divert—any money whatever from education where it is doing good work. What I want to know is whether any of the money not going to education could be more usefully applied through a committee who would have power to manage it, and give some of it to Boyle?

Colonel *ffolliott*.—I am inclined to think so, but I don't wish to be understood as saying anything against the Elphin School. It appears to have done very good work, but it does not supply a local need in the way that Boyle school does.

Rev. Mr. Burke.

894. The Rev. Mr. *Burke*.—I am thoroughly acquainted with the Elphin School and its management, and with the almost incredible efforts of Dean Warburton, and, as a resident in Boyle, and also intimately acquainted with Elphin, I must, with the greatest respect, take a different view from Colonel ffolliott. I believe that Elphin wants every penny of its endowment in order to carry on the efficient work that it is now charged with. But if the question arises as to whether you would allocate the money that is given for the maintenance of the cathedral to the school, I would most cordially advocate that transfer to the Elphin School from the cathedral.

895. Professor Dougherty.—You would not like to see any of it coming to Boyle?

Rev. Mr. *Burke*.—I would not, although I am a resident in Boyle. One pupil of the Elphin School got an exhibition of £[illegible] this year. Twenty-two pupils have been brought forward to the South Kensington examinations, and every one of them has got distinctions.

896. Have you taken any interest in the Boyle Academy?

Rev. Mr. *Burke*.—No. Though I am a resident in Boyle, I am pastor of a neighbouring parish. Boyle is not in my parish.

897. Lord Justice FitzGibbon.—I believe you are aware, Mr. Burke, that in Sligo the only endowment for intermediate education is the annuity of the present diocesan schoolmaster, lasting for his life, and there is no provision subsequent to that, that we could discover, in Sligo for intermediate education. Do you think it would be possible to form any local body to look after the interests of the whole of this diocese of Elphin, with power to use whatever endowments they had, wherever they might be most needed?

Rev. Mr. *Burke*.—I believe it would. I think it would be better to have a committee on a broader basis than the Chapter of Elphin. As regards the representation of the whole diocese, it might be better to have a more representative committee, on which I would be glad to see Colonel ffolliott and some of the lay element, but I think the universal feeling, speaking from a denominational point of view—and I think Colonel ffolliott might agree with me if he looked into the whole case—is, that it would be better to strengthen what remains of Elphin so as to maintain a good school there, than to scatter and divide the resources throughout the diocese. We would certainly, I believe, rather have one strong school; and Elphin happens, though small and backward in one sense, to be otherwise in a historical point of view a place of importance. St. Patrick did not visit Boyle, but he did visit Elphin; and there are a great many traditions connected with Elphin that make it dear and precious to us.

898. Professor Dougherty.—I am afraid the people of Boyle prefer to consider the practical necessities of the present day.

Rev. Mr. *Burke*.—Yes; but Elphin is in the very centre of the county of Roscommon.

899. Is there a day school?

Rev. Mr. *Burke*.—A day school is being maintained in the greatest efficiency. There are 40 pupils in it at present. I am reckoning day pupils and boarders.

900. Lord Justice FitzGibbon.—This Boyle school is a most interesting and encouraging instance of what can be done in a town such as Boyle, where the people are determined to secure education for themselves. We had a similar case in Monaghan, where a local committee got up a school almost on the same lines. There we found a school building which had lain idle in the hands of the Commissioners of Education for several years. We were able to give that building, and the lands connected with it, to the local committee. I am sorry that in Boyle we don't find any premises similarly circumstanced. We will send a copy of the Monaghan scheme to the Secretary of the Boyle Committee, and if they should think it well to form themselves into a permanent body, as the Monaghan people have done with advantage, we could certainly do that for them, and it might strengthen the claim they have for any endowment that may become distributable. I am sorry the endowments in this part of the world are not larger, because the work done with them shows that you deserve to get a share of anything that is valuable. But you must all understand that the too common belief that we can hand over the endowments of one locality, or set of people, to another, is unfounded, and though you are in the unfortunate position of not having any endowment of your own, you must not expect us to give you other people's endowments without their consent. We must hear the Elphin case before we can say anything about it.

Rev. Dr. *Clarke*.—I wish to say that the committee are not anxious to covet the endowment of Elphin, or that Elphin should be handed over to us; but if an endowment could be got from any place where they are not doing as useful a work as could be done with it here, I believe we could utilize it faithfully and well.

Lord Justice FitzGibbon.—I am sure you could; and if we could turn the good opinions and wishes of the Commissioners into cash we should be most happy to do so for your benefit.

PUBLIC SITTING—WEDNESDAY, OCTOBER 10, 1888. Oct. 10, 1888.

At the Grammar School, Elphin.

Present:—The Right Hon. Lord Justice FitzGibbon and the Right Hon. Lord Justice Naish, Judicial Commissioners; and the Rev. Gerald Molloy, D.D., D.Sc., Anthony Traill, Esq., LL.D., M.D., F.T.C.D., and Professor Dougherty, M.A., Assistant Commissioners.

The Assistant Secretary, N. D. Murphy, jun., was in attendance.

BISHOP HODSON'S GRAMMAR SCHOOL.

Lord Justice FitzGibbon made an introductory statement, and read the following resolution of the Dean and Chapter of Elphin:—

"Resolved that the Chapter of Elphin Cathedral is of opinion that the large measure of success which has attended the operations of Bishop Hodson's Grammar School, managed under the rules and regulations sanctioned and approved of by the Court of Chancery, would appear to lead to the conclusion that no change in these rules is required. At the same time the Chapter is most willing to consider any suggestions which the Educational Endowments (Ireland) Commission may offer for their improvement, and for making the Institution more useful. The Chapter does not wish to abandon the trusts imposed upon them by the will and deed of the benevolent founder, 200 years ago, but desire to carry them out in a liberal and enlightened spirit, and this they hope they have heretofore done. They would be desirous of being relieved from the troublesome and expensive process of renewing the trustees, and they also think it desirable that they should have the power of selling the property to the tenants on equitable terms. They would also wish to have a legal sanction for the equitable course which they have heretofore pursued, in appropriating any balance which may remain of the moiety of the funds appropriated to Cathedral purposes, after providing for its wants, to the promotion of the Grammar School. They say 'the equitable course,' because by the books of the Cathedral it appears that up to the year 1812, the whole of the funds derived from Bishop Hodson's Endowment were expended in repairing and maintaining the Cathedral. Thus early the Chapter is of opinion, if not quite in accordance with the wishes of the testator, should have been armed with a view to carrying those wishes into effect; and had this been done there would have been in 1812, the very considerable savings of 177 years, available for the Grammar School. In view of this fact, the Chapter some years ago twenty years ago voted £300 of the Cathedral portion, in aid for the purpose of erecting those buildings which now belong to the Grammar School. The Chapter is further of opinion that Bishop Hodson, in making the grants referred to, in the strongest terms possible limited the benefits of his bounty to those who might reside in the locality; they therefore resisted and effectually the efforts of those who endeavoured to deprive the locality of the benefits bestowed on its inhabitants; the terms of the will and deed of the founder are for these purposes, and 'for no other purpose whatever.' No doubt, Bishop Hodson in creating these trusts had in view denominational education, and at this moment, a majority of the Chapter, only two of whose members are now living, refused to insert a conscience clause in these rules; but the Lord Chancellor of that period, the Right Hon. J. Napier, overruled the opinion of them, and sanctioned and approved of the rules now before the Educational Endowments (Ireland) Commission. The Chapter is of opinion that 'the results are very satisfactory.' Eighteen youths have passed through the Grammar School into the Civil Service; of them, 10 were members of the Church of Rome. Many of the persons holding, in the United Empire, and in the United States have, through its instrumentality, been appointed to situations of emolument and importance. Some of the pupils of the Grammar School have entered into and graduated in Trinity College Dublin. The Chapter is of opinion that the Institution supplies an urgent need. It is in the centre of a rich country. Many farmers desire to have their sons educated for professions. This they can accomplish through Bishop Hodson's Grammar School at a very moderate expense. The Institution was opened in 1879. In no single instance has there been any disturbance of that harmony and good will amongst the people which it is the earnest desire of the Chapter by all righteous means to promote. The Chapter would further state that the reason why more of the pupils have not attended the Intermediate Education Examinations is, that their parents cannot afford the expense, which is far greater than would be any advantages they could expect. The expense of their journey and of their board and lodging while absent amounts to about £3 for each youth. If the Educational Endowments (Ireland) Commission desire to remedy this difficulty by recommending an additional examination in Elphin, the Chapter will have pleasure in affording them the use, for the purpose, of Bishop Hodson's Grammar School. It is 40 feet by 22, and in every way suitable to the purpose.

William Warburton, Chairman.

The Very Rev. William Warburton, D.D., Dean of Elphin, sworn and examined.

Very Rev. William Warburton, D.D., Dean of Elphin.

901. Lord Justice FitzGibbon.—How long have you held the position of Dean of Elphin?—Forty years.

902. You have during that time been ex-officio a governor of Bishop Hodson's Grammar School?—Yes.

903. The origin of the foundation was a grant by Bishop Hodson, of June 30, 1683?—Yes.

904. He granted one moiety of the produce of certain lands for the maintenance of a Grammar School in the town of Elphin, that shall from time to time be approved of by the Bishop of Elphin, for instructing the children of the inhabitants of the town of Elphin, and for teaching such of the same children whose parents are poor, gratis, the same to be paid to the master of said Grammar School; and the other moiety of the same property to be laid out for repairing, maintaining, and adorning the Cathedral Church of Elphin in such manner as by the Bishop, for the time being, and the Dean and Chapter, shall be thought fit; and the honoured proceeds, in case one or more of the trustees shall die, the survivor or survivors shall, by direction of the Bishop of Elphin for the time being, and the Dean and Chapter of Elphin, assign their interest to such other person or persons and their heirs as the said Bishop, Dean, and Chapter shall think fit; and the oversight of the trusts shall be committed to the Bishop, Dean, and Chapter. There are also certain leasing powers. Under that will were the Bishop, Dean, and Chapter the original trustees?—Not trustees.

905. They had the oversight of the school?—The trustees were laymen, who had no power whatever. They were merely instruments to keep up the trusts.

906. Who are the present trustees of the lands?—I am one, and the Rev. Mr. Hamilton, who then lived five or six miles from here, was the other.

Oct. 14, 1885.

Very Rev. William Warburton, D.D., Dean of Elphin.

907. Lord Justice NAISH.—How was he appointed?—He was appointed by the Chapter, by deed, according to an opinion that we got as to the proper way of appointing.

908. Lord Justice FITZGIBBON.—Whenever a vacancy occurs in the trustees of the lands is it necessary for you to have a new deed?—Not every time. We wish to avoid expense. There were four trustees, and there are two living; when one of them dies it will be time enough to renew the trust, because the survivor can hand over the property to the new trustees.

909. I presume you are aware that if the last survivor failed to appoint you would have to go to his heir-at-law?—That case has happened before my time, the trust was lost, and there was a good deal of trouble in recovering it.

910. It is in our power to incorporate the Governors so as to enable them to hold the property for ever without any renewal?—That is what we wish.

911. If that should be done, would there be any advantage in having trustees of the lands different from the body having the oversight of the school?—I think not.

912. Lord Justice NAISH.—Who appoints the master?—The Chapter; but, practically, it devolves upon me. We have had uniform success not only since Bishop Hodson's school was established, but before that, because the Chapter allowed me this room to keep a National school in for eight or nine years, until we paid off the debt which we incurred in building this house. That was very expensive; but as I hoped that it would last for many generations I thought it better to do everything well, and I had the place built roomy and capable of holding a great number, because I don't at all think we are at the end of our success, or near it. I have not the slightest doubt that, in process of time, when the country recovers, houses will be built in the town to receive people who will come in to have their families taught.

913. Who at present constitute the Chapter of Elphin?—There are ten members of the Chapter. All the members of the Chapter, except the bishop, are incumbents of parishes.

914. In forming a corporate body to manage the school and property, is it your opinion that the Chapter would be the best body for that purpose, or that there should be any laymen added?—I would be very glad to see gentlemen of property in the country forming the governing body together with some of the clergy. I would put the bishop and one or two others on it.

915. We can easily select the clergy, but how do you think lay members could be selected?—I don't like to answer that question offhand, but I should be very glad to see the gentry of property around taking an interest in this institution.

916. In other cases we have given a nomination or two to the Diocesan Council, do you think that would do?—You could give them one or two. I think that would do very well.

917. And power to co-opt some more?—I would like to get people that would take an active interest in the school.

918. Have you had any subscribers?—We had subscribers to the building—a good many. We have one of our most liberal subscribers to the building here, Colonel Cooper, and I would be glad if you would prevail on him to be one of the committee of management. I might say any other gentlemen of the country that you thought fit. I would not at all object to some of my neighbours of other denominations. For instance, Mr. Grace, who is here, and Lord de Freyne. I have always found those gentlemen most anxious to promote the good of the people generally.

919. Is there any Intermediate school for Roman Catholics, or any other denomination in this neighbourhood?—None other to my knowledge; but I would like to remark on the clause in the will about teaching the poor "gratis;" that no child is now excluded from education by poverty, because the masters are paid by results, and no master will refuse any boy—on the contrary, they are very glad to get them.

920. Lord Justice NAISH.—You mean in the National schools?—In the National schools. Within three miles of where we are there are five National schools; all well officered. The teachers are intelligent well-conducted men, and it is their interest to have as many pupils as they can get. But I want to show that this clause of Bishop Hodson must necessarily be a nullity. We are always ready to take in any class. We have never refused any person that was poor. There was one family here of four sons, all of whom were educated in this school. Two are doing extremely well in England. The fourth by competitive examination got into the Excise. The father of those boys never paid a farthing. We would not exclude anybody, but I think it is right, wherever parents are able to pay, to let them pay something. There are members of the Roman Catholic Church, of whom I have asked four or five to come here, whose sons attended the school, and are doing well in the Excise and other branches. I have seen them myself. There is one man here—Mr. M'Cormack—whose son got into the Excise. I met him two years ago in London. He was educated here—a uncommonly nice-looking young man—and he was very glad to see me. Another neighbour of mine here—Mr. Byrne—has three sons that have been educated here, and they are all doing extremely well. One son went in for a competitive examination as an army teacher. He got in in London, and was the only Irishman that did get in. He has now £71 a year with £4 a year increase and his diet. Another young man has gone to the United States, and his father, who is here, told me that he has 16½ dollars a week. There are several others, some of whom are here, and I would be very glad that you would ask these questions as to what they think of the institution and how their sons were dealt with and taught.

921. Lord Justice FITZGIBBON.—What is the class of education you give?—Mr. Irwin will tell you that.

922. Of what does the endowment consist?—The estate consists of land in the county of Cavan. It was very valuable, but there has been a very great reduction upon it, and the very respectable man who manages it for me tells me that the Commissioners cut it down considerably more than the neighbouring properties. I suppose they thought it was no man's land, and that they might deal a little heavier with it. After that the recent Act took another slice off it—2s. 6d. in the pound. This has reduced it so much, and the rents have been so very badly paid that we are now in arrear with the officers and people that we pay.

923. Rev. Dr. MOLLOY.—What is the net annual income at present?—This year we received £260 13s. net.

924. Lord Justice FITZGIBBON.—Is that the entire year's receipts?—Yes, after taking out all the disbursements the amount is £260 13s. net for the purpose of the endowment. We ought to have got more.

925. Professor DOUGHERTY.—Did the amount include any arrears?—No; on the contrary there are increasing arrears.

926. Lord Justice FITZGIBBON.—How is the school society expended?—You will see that the cathedral is very nicely fitted up—not extravagantly, but still they are costly things. We have been latterly paying for the school out of the cathedral portion of the fund; and that is a matter that I would wish to have some instruction from the Commissioners upon. The property was ample for both, but it is impossible to say now what property can be depended upon. Therefore

how are we to do if we cannot pay up the salaries that we have engaged to pay?

927. Rev. Dr. Molloy.—Do you think that the cathedral, now that so much has been expended on it, is still in need each year of half the endowment?—No, not the whole of it. I would suggest to take into account the expenditure on the cathedral. I should say that the cathedral wants nothing at present, but hereafter we don't know what we may want. A storm might blow the roof off—things of that sort must be calculated on. I would be disposed to put a sinking fund by for the purpose of meeting any extraordinary expense. Let that sinking fund go to a certain amount—say £500—and let it be invested, and remain until it is wanted. If, in process of time, we should not want it at all, I would recommend that we should apply the saving to this institution. We are forbidden at present to apply the money to any other use, but if we should have a surplus from the cathedral account, I think we should appropriate it to the improvement of the grammar school—to the other branch of the charity. I wish to be guided in that. But, with regard to our present circumstances, I hope there are better prospects now; but, if there is not something better, we could not pay what we have been paying. There are very heavy charges of various kinds. In the first place we pay £10 a year for a National school, for the benefit of the property in the county of Cavan.

928. Lord Justice FitzGibbon.—There is a receiver's fee of £4 15s. a year—I suppose 2½ per cent. on the gross proceeds?—Exactly.

929. Is Mr. Parr your agent?—He has been for the last forty years.

930. I see there are four or five holdings on which there is a very great arrear of rent due?—A great arrear.

931. They don't appear to have paid anything during these last few years?—The fact of the matter is that they have an idea that it is Church property, and that they cannot be made to pay it.

932. Dr. Traill.—Are they Roman Catholic tenants?—Most of them. There are a few that are not.

933. You said—and very properly, I am sure, as regards your own feelings—that you would not object to certain Roman Catholic gentlemen being put on the governing body. Do you think that it would be consistent with Bishop Hodson's will and intentions that where the governing body was settled to be a Church of Ireland body, it should now be opened to Roman Catholic gentlemen, or gentlemen of any other denomination?—With regard to that I don't want to give any opinion; I merely say that it is my own opinion.

934. You would not object to certain gentlemen personally, but would you consider it in accordance with Bishop Hodson's will?—I don't think anything that you are doing is in exact accordance with Bishop Hodson's will; and I tell you candidly that the more you let us alone the better we will do.

935. We haven't threatened to do anything with you. Would your suggestion be consistent with Bishop Hodson's will?—I don't think, as I said before, that anything you are doing is exactly in accordance with Bishop Hodson's will.

936. Lord Justice FitzGibbon.—You asked us here to relieve you from the trouble and expense of renewing trustees. Is it in accordance with Bishop Hodson's will to do that?—It is not in accordance with it.

937. Lord Justice Naish.—Is it not against it?—It is not against it.

938. Lord Justice FitzGibbon.—You want to get a power to sell the property if you can get a good price for it?—That is merely a power, but we would not exercise it foolishly, or perhaps at all.

939. I think one of your own proposals is more against Bishop Hodson's intentions than any of those we have mentioned, namely that you should apply the portion of the money that was left for maintaining the cathedral to the school?—I would do it on the ground that necessity has no law. Supposing you had the money it is dead against Bishop Hodson's will to apply it to any other purpose whatever.

Dec. 18, 1888.

Very Rev. William Warburton, D.D., Dean of Elphin.

940. What was the condition of the school when you came first?—It was a wretched school, held down near the church. I did not take any active part to improve it, because I thought that with the old routine I could not get on very well with the master. I just was civil to him, and visited the school; but I took no active measures to keep him in. Then he went somewhere else; and I was very glad when, as I believed, he got a good appointment. Then I began on my own plan, and got the best masters that I could, without favour or affection of any kind; and from the very beginning we succeeded. Our boys got on extremely well; and this brought other boys to us. Then in 1881, I may tell you what first put the boarding house into my head. I saw Roman Catholic boys coming into the town, and living with a respectable tradesman who took them in at a very moderate rate. He only charged them for lodging and attendance 2s. a week. They provided their own food, and the people of the house cooked it for them. I thought that was very good, and it suggested to me—why should I not have a house to receive members of my own faith, many of whom I knew were very badly off for the means of education—and I did it. I set a subscription on foot. It was thought impracticable, utopian, and all that sort of thing. However, the people very kindly let me have my way; and it rapidly increased, so that everybody—even those who were most opposed to it—were greatly surprised and pleased.

941. I think you collected about £400?—I collected about £400.

942. And that enabled you to provide boarding accommodation for pupils getting instruction in the school?—Exactly.

943. From what parts of Ireland have they come?—From Kerry, Cork, Limerick, Waterford, Wexford, all the southern counties—Dublin, Belfast, Derry—in fact from all parts of Ireland.

944. What charge do you make?—We give them board and education for £18 a year; but we only give them meat three times a week.

945. I believe they can get meat on other days by paying something extra?—Yes; and some of the parents ask that their children shall be given a slice of bread and a cup of tea after their schoolhours in the morning. We do that at a certain price—just what covers the outlay—that and the meat they can get for £21 a year; but though many of these complained of the want of the meat, very few pay the difference—the £3 for it.

946. On the days that they don't get meat what do they get?—Potatoes and the best milk that can be got.

947. Who manages the domestic arrangements?—We have an excellent matron. Last year, while I was away, measles broke out, and nothing could exceed her kindness and attention.

948. Has she sole charge of the cooking and domestic arrangements?—The sole charge.

949. How do you manage about payments for food?—We make contracts and she sees that they are right.

950. Who looks after the payment of the accounts?—Mr. Irwin, chiefly; but I overlook them. He keeps them and gives them to me.

951. Rev. Dr. Molloy.—About what is the Protestant population of the parish of Elphin?—About 100; but there is a very common mistake about the Protestant population here. Many people think that formerly this was a great Protestant country. Now that's a perfect delusion. I have a copy of a paper which shows that the Protestant population of Elphin in the year 1704 was then only 172.

952. Dr. Traill.—There was a very small popu-

Oct. 10, 1885.

Very Rev. William Warburton, D.D., Dean of Elphin.

lation in the country altogether at that time?—Well, but I say it was then a very small population. People have thought that the bishop endowed this Grammar School for a large population; but it was not the case. In fact the bishop probably never anticipated that the school would grow to any size. He did it most likely for the wants of the time.

953. Rev. Dr. Molloy.—It would seem that when he left such a large endowment for the education of the poor he must have had the Catholics of Elphin in his mind as well as the Protestants?—I beg your pardon—it wasn't a large endowment, it was only £40 a year until about thirty years ago when I began this work.

954. How did it increase?—Originally he left a charge of £20 a year on it for a member of his family. That member afterwards assigned that charge to the trustees for the same uses and purposes as the original bequest. The estate was let to a middleman in those days. I have not been able to find much of it, but I am strongly of opinion that it was let at fines, and that the fines were applied to building the cathedral. It was let to a middleman who, I suppose, had a large interest in it, and that interest, having, in process of time, fallen in, the value of the land increased.

955. Dr. Traill.—The middleman disappeared after seventy or eighty years?—Exactly. The lease lasted about eighty years.

956. Lord Justice FitzGibbon.—What was the income before the recent depression in the times?—The gross income was between £300 and £400 a year, but there are very heavy deductions?—The net income this year is about £200.

957. Some years ago it was larger?—A good deal larger. I think probably it amounted to £360 a year.

The Rev. *Edward Irwin* sworn and examined.

Rev. Edward Irwin.

958. Lord Justice FitzGibbon.—You are the master of Elphin School?—Yes.

959. How long have you been master?—Almost twelve years and a half.

960. What is your emolument as master?—£110 per annum, paid by the trustees—a fixed salary. I had £110 a year from the time I came here. The Chapter wished to increase my salary to £120 a year some time ago, but they found they could not do it. They gave me a bonus in one year of £10 in addition to the £110.

961. What number of pupils have you at present?—On the roll at present there are forty-nine. We have actually forty in attendance to-day.

962. Of those how many are boarders?—Twenty-one here at present, one boy who is sick and not here, and another boy whose father, for reasons, cannot send him, but we have his entrance fee, which every boy pays, and his father, as soon as convenient, will send him back. Those two boys, with the twenty-one actually here, make twenty-three boarders. Two boarders who recently left are on the roll still.

963. Then you have twenty-four day boys and about the same number of boarders?—About that.

964. Have you anything to do with the boarding arrangements?—Yes, I receive them as if they were my own boarders. I look on them as such. I live in a house adjoining the school, and I continually go in and out and look after the arrangements.

965. What is the title to the site of the school buildings?

Dean Warburton.—It is a lease for ever, from Mr. Roper, who lives in Dublin, at a rent of £11 5s. a year.

966. Lord Justice FitzGibbon.—To whom is the lease made?

Dean Warburton.—I cannot tell; I think to the trustees, but I cannot say.

967. At all events it is school property that ought to be vested with the estates?

Dean Warburton.—Yes.

968. (To Witness.)—You have a free residence and a field?—Yes, two acres and a rood, Irish measure.

969. What are your arrangements as to the results fees and school fees?—Whatever they are, I have them.

970. What are your charges for day boys?—They vary from 1s. 6d. to £1 per quarter, according to the means of the boys. The amount has nothing at all to do with the instruction. A boy who pays 1s. 6d., or even a boy paying nothing might be learning classics, if he was not able to pay.

971. What steps do you take to ascertain what they can pay?—Originally, the Dean inquired into their circumstances, and as manager of the school arranged the matter; but after I had been here some years he said I might do so subject to his approval.

Dean Warburton.—When a parent came to me to get an order for his boy to attend the school, I would say—"The payment is so much." "Well," he might say—"I could not afford to pay that." Then I would ask him how many acres he had, and on his telling me I would say—"You can afford to pay such a sum."

Rev. Mr. Irwin.—Not unusually I have left it to the people themselves to say what they could pay. I have had boys who paid nothing.

972. Lord Justice FitzGibbon (to Witness).—What is your course of instruction?—Classics—such as would be required for the University—and mathematics. Eleven of my pupils were at some time or other, and some are at present, in Trinity College; 3 went to the Royal University; 2 to the Royal College of Surgeons; 17 succeeded by competitive examination in getting into the Civil Service; and within the last two years 8 succeeded in gaining exhibitions at the Intermediate Examinations in Greek, Latin, French, Algebra, Arithmetic, Natural Philosophy, Mechanics, Euclid, and Drawing.

973. What assistance have you in teaching?—Two pupil teachers.

974. Do they both live in the school?—No, one who was originally a day boy is attending as pupil teacher, and the other who was originally a boarder is a pupil teacher and boarder.

975. Have you any other engagement yourself besides the mastership of the school?—I act as Curate of the parish to the Dean.

976. What are the religious denominations of the boarders?—They are all of the Reformed faith.

977. Are they of various denominations of Protestants?—We have had Presbyterians. We had a Presbyterian minister's son here, and we have had Methodists. We take any member of the Reformed faith who wishes to come, as long as there is room.

978. As a matter of fact are they all, at present, members of your own Church?—I really could not say. But they all attend Church, for there is no other place of worship of the Reformed faith in the neighbourhood.

979. As to the day boys what are their denominations?—Protestants and Roman Catholics.

980. How many Roman Catholics have you?—This year we have had an attendance of 15 Roman Catholics.

981. The greater number of your day boys then are Roman Catholics?—The greater number.

982. The majority of the population here are Roman Catholics?—Yes.

983. To what class do your boys belong?—The day boys are respectable farmers' sons, who are working for the Civil Service and for professions; and sometimes they are the sons of shopkeepers in Elphin. For

boarders we have clergymen's sons, physicians' sons, and the sons of business men from Dublin.

984. Rev. Dr. Molloy.—How many years do they usually remain with you?—One left us the other day who was four and a half years with us.

985. Do they remain four years on the average?—I could not say. Some of them have been obliged to leave in consequence of not being able to pay the very small fee.

986. Do they come to you generally from the National schools?—The day boys—yes. Those who have been educated pretty well at the National schools and who wish for something better.

987. Lord Justice FitzGibbon.—Where were you educated yourself?—In Trinity College, Dublin.

988. You are a graduate?—Yes, I took a first silver medal in metaphysics and ethics.

989. Professor Dougherty.—Do you enter boys for the Intermediate Examinations?—Only those who are really anxious, and wish to go, on account of the expense.

990. Where is the examination held?—Athlone is the nearest centre. But some were Dublin boys and they preferred remaining in Dublin during the summer holidays.

991. Rev. Dr. Molloy.—Have you made any effort to get Elphin made a centre?—No.

992. Lord Justice FitzGibbon.—To-day at Boyle they told us that they send the boys to Sligo, and the girls to Dublin?—It is a great inconvenience that some of the boys here who would attend the Intermediate examinations cannot do so on account of the expense.

993. Rev. Dr. Molloy.—Would it be an advantage to you to have a centre at Boyle?—I don't think it would be of any use to us. It is not the travelling—it is the remaining at the centre. They must remain nine or ten days.

Dean Warburton.—You couldn't get a better centre, or a cheaper place than this.

994. Professor Dougherty (to Witness).—Have you any idea what it costs a boy to attend an Intermediate examination from here?—About £3. I know it from having myself given the boys the money, and they were very careful.

995. That includes the travelling expenses to Athlone, the nearest centre?—Yes.

996. Rev. Dr. Molloy.—Besides the expense there is considerable inconvenience in going there?—Yes. Some would send for it if it were held here.

997. Professor Dougherty.—Who experts send the Science and Art examinations?—Some members of our committee in the locality. Oct. 13, 1888.

998. Lord Justice FitzGibbon.—How is your committee for Science and Art constituted?—Some of the gentlemen around the country. Rev. Edward Irvin.

999. How do you get them together?—It is very difficult, on account of there not being many of that class in the country.

1000. Who were your committee?—Landed proprietors.

1001. Who were they?—The Dean is our Chairman; Mr. Lloyd, of Croghan, is our Secretary; Mr. Merrick Lloyd is also a member. Mrs. Warburton is on the committee, ladies being admitted, and there are also some landed proprietors, who live three or four miles from here, and some clergy. Some have come six miles to it.

1002. Then I suppose the persons that you mention as coming to this Kensington Committee would be the sort of persons that you would like to have on the managing committee of the school?—Some of them. If any arrangement like that should be made, it would be very suitable.

1003. Is there any provision for teaching girls?—No; it is distinctly excluded by the scheme drawn up under Chancery. The first rule says that a school for boys shall be established.

1004. Do you think it would be an advantage to extend the school to girls. We saw girls in the same class with boys, to-day, at Boyle?—I don't know about that.

1005. Professor Dougherty.—Is there any demand in Elphin for a higher class of education for girls than what they can get in ordinary National schools?—There is not.

1006. Dr. Traill.—Do you advertise for boarders from a distance?—Yes; we put advertisements into the *Irish Times*, *Express*, *General Advertiser*, the *Belfast News-letter*, and the *Northern Whig*.

1007. Lord Justice FitzGibbon.—I think the Dean does a great deal to make the existence of the school known for you?—The Dean writes a great deal.

1008. Rev. Dr. Molloy.—I suppose most of the day boys are from the town of Elphin?—From the town, and from within walking distance—three miles, or perhaps a little more.

1009. Lord Justice FitzGibbon.—If there is any gentleman here who has had a son at the school we would be glad to hear him. We need not examine him as a witness, but we should like to have his opinion as to whether the school is useful.

Mr. John Scott.—It has been always useful.

Mr. John Scott examined.

1010. Lord Justice FitzGibbon.—Had you one son in the school, or more?—One son. Mr. John Scott.

1011. What did he learn?—He learned everything that he wanted. He is in the Customs, at Peterhead, in Scotland.

1012. From the learning that he got here?—Certainly.

1013. Do you know more of your neighbours who have done the same?—Plenty.

1014. Had you ever any difficulty as to the management of the school?—I never could be better satisfied with anything.

1015. Your son attended as a day boy?—Yes. I live within three miles. He walked in from Mr. French's place. I am a tenant of Mr. French's.

1016. Lord Justice FitzGibbon.—Was it by competitive examination that he got into the Customs?—It was.

1017. He is provided for now?—He is, and he is well liked where he is.

1018. Rev. Dr. Molloy.—Does he find the Customs better than the farm?—It is five times better.

1019. Is there not very good land in this country?—Very good, but very little money to buy it with.

1020. Lord Justice FitzGibbon.—Have you any other son to look after the farm?—I have, but it would be better for him to be in the Customs, or some other place.

1021. Dr. Traill.—You would want somebody at home to help you on the farm?—Well I would.

Mr. Thomas Byrne examined.

1022. Lord Justice FitzGibbon.—Had you a son in this school?—I had two.

1023. What were they prepared for?—One of them went for the situation of Army teacher and took it; and the second stood an examination for the Customs but was not successful. He was tenth best.

1024. What has he done since?—He went to America. Mr. Thomas Byrne.

1025. How is he doing out there?—Very well, indeed; he is clerk in a railroad depot in Jersey State.

1026. Is it work for which his schooling seems useful?—It does, indeed.

Rev. Mr. *Irwin*.—With regard to the son who is the Army teacher, there were six vacancies for all England, Ireland, and Scotland, and he met, himself, at the examination in Dublin, nearly forty candidates. There were examinations in Scotland and England as well, and he was successful amongst the six from all the different centres. He was the only one from all Ireland, and there were first class National teachers amongst the candidates.

1027. Lord Justice FITZGIBBON (to *Witness*).—Do you consider that the school as it is managed at present is of use to the neighbourhood?—I am certain it is of the greatest use. A National teacher only goes to the sixth class with a boy, and is of no use to him if he wants to go higher. Before I sent my boy here he was two years learning from a National schoolmaster, and he got to the sixth class there.

1028. Was he a monitor?—He was.

1029. So that this school took him up when he had finished all that he could learn there?—It did.

1030. You are a Roman Catholic?—I am.

1031. And Mr. Scott?—He is a Roman Catholic too.

1032. Is there any Intermediate school under the management of your own people in the neighbourhood?—Not one.

1033. So that you have no choice except the National school or this one?—That's all; there was one started here by the Lord Bishop, but the people were not able to send their boys to it.

1034. Dr. TRAILL.—Did you ever find your boys' religious faith interfered with?—Never in my life.

1035. You had perfect confidence in the school?—Entire. It is not because the Dean is here I say so. He never meddled with it. He lived on the best of terms with us.

1036. The school is for secular and not for religious education?—Certainly; there was not a word about it.

1037. Rev. Dr. MOLLOY.—You are a farmer?—Yes.

1038. Have you any son at the farm?—I have four boys more going to school. God blessed me with seven. There are four of them going to the National school.

1039. Lord Justice FITZGIBBON.—And if they have a taste for books they will come here, and if for the plough they will stay at home?—Exactly.

1040. Or rather for sheep, for you don't seem to have many ploughs about here?—Well, it is hard for the plough if they were able, but generally they are not able. It is all prairie.

1041. Rev. Dr. MOLLOY.—Why don't you convert it into corn-fields?—It is not mine.

1042. Professor DOUGHERTY.—I suppose it pays better to feed sheep?—Well it does pay better to feed sheep and cattle. But generally it is the rich man that has it and not the poor man.

1043. Lord Justice FITZGIBBON.—We may take it as the general opinion then that this school is useful for those who want to get an education here and are certain it is.

1044. You would not like the school to be moved to Boyle?—I would not. I think the intention of the will of Bishop Hodson was that Catholic boys were not to be excluded from it.

Lord Justice FITZGIBBON.—They are not excluded, but the managers must all be of the other way of thinking. Sometimes Protestant bishops think about the Catholics as well as their own people.

Rev. Mr. *Irwin*.—There are two gentlemen here whose sons got into the Customs and Excise from the school.

Lord Justice FITZGIBBON.—You can make us out a written list of those results.

Colonel Cooper sworn and examined.

1045. Lord Justice FITZGIBBON.—Colonel Cooper, can you give us any suggestions as regards the management of this school?—I think the Council of the diocese are anxious to co-operate in forming a governing body for the school. I understand that the Church Act dissolved the Chapter of Elphin, so that it is not a corporation any longer; and I understand that it is necessary to form a governing body now. I was appointed as a member of the Council on the committee to watch this endowment when the Royal Commissioners should visit Elphin; and the opinion of the Council certainly was, that the governing body should be as nearly as possible in accordance with Bishop Hodson's will—that it should be a Church of Ireland governing body; but that probably some laymen should be introduced, who would take an interest in the management of the school; and, if it should be necessary to transfer the property to trustees, we formed a committee to take over any trusts.

1046. Dr. TRAILL.—You have formed a Diocesan Board to hold educational endowments?—Yes.

1047. You are a member of the Board yourself?—Yes.

1048. Lord Justice FITZGIBBON.—*Here is a provision of the Act*:—

"In framing schemes it shall be the duty of the Commissioners, with respect alike to the constitution of the governing body and to educational provisions, to have regard to the spirit of founder's intentions. And in every scheme which abolishes any educational advantages to which a particular class of persons is entitled, whether as inhabitants of a particular area or otherwise, they shall have regard to the educational interest of such class of persons, and where the founder has expressly provided for the education of children belonging to the poorer classes, either generally, or of a particular class, or within a particular area, the endowment shall continue, so far as requisite, to be applied for the benefit of such children."

That Act binds us, so that a general body—such as the Diocesan Council—would hardly satisfy its requirements. There should be a distinct local body for this Elphin endowment. If that be so, can you give us any suggestion as to where we could get one or two laymen?—The Diocesan Council is formed from the whole diocese. Mr. Lloyd, here, is a member of that council, and also of its committee to hold endowments. I think he would be a proper person. There is also Mr. French; and there are several from this neighbourhood who are members of the Council.

1049. Lord Justice NAISH.—Are you in favour of remaining it in Elphin?—Yes, from all I have heard it would be desirable to retain it here.

1050. It has been suggested in Boyle that some of the endowment should be given to Boyle?—I think it is hardly large enough to divide.

1051. Professor DOUGHERTY.—Would you see any objection to giving a discretionary power to the trustees, in the event of the educational requirements of Elphin being fully satisfied, to extend the benefits of the endowment to some other parts of the diocese?—So many would put in claims. I think it is too small a sum. I have no doubt that Sligo would put in a claim; it is in the diocese.

1052. But would there be any harm in giving a discretionary power?—There is no harm in having enlarged powers.

Dean *Warburton*.—It is not too large; it is insufficient as it is.

Witness.—It is more likely to be diminished than increased. I think that the property should be sold and the money invested in safe securities; but that would diminish the income very much, although it might make it more safe and the income less expensive to collect.

Rev. Mr. *Irwin*.—Our present difficulty is, that we have hardly enough for what we require.

1053. Lord Justice FitzGibbon.—For nearly 200 years this endowment was by no means efficient. Until the Dean took it up the school was not doing good work. So that if we judge of it entirely by its present condition we may be misled as to the future. We should try to put it on a permanent basis, so as to ensure its being carried on as it is; and it would be well to form a strong governing body with power to carry on the school as at present, so long as they can do so efficiently. If at any time they should fail to do so, we ought not to prevent them from keeping a grammar school elsewhere.

Dean Warburton.—I don't think you could carry on this school at less expense than we do.

1054. Lord Justice FitzGibbon.—Certainly not. It is so cheaply carried on as any of the Incorporated Society's schools, where they have larger endowments.

Dean Warburton.—If you look through the country you will not find any preparatory school in our position, and with our difficulties, that has produced better results.

Witness.—Have you power to deal with the moiety that goes to the Cathedral?

1055. Lord Justice FitzGibbon.—Certainly—with the consent of the governing body.

Witness.—What governing body?

1056. Lord Justice FitzGibbon.—The Dean and Chapter; because the trustees are merely trustees of the property. The oversight of the trusts, according to the deed is given to the Dean and Chapter. The Act provides, where any part of an endowment is applicable to non-educational purposes, the governing body may attend to the scheme departing from the existing provisions. If the Chapter followed the Dean's proposal, it would be in our power to provide a sinking fund and apply the surplus for the school; but if an accident should happen, and it should become necessary to repair the building, the primary trust might revive again.

Witness.—Could any part of the endowment for the repair of the Church be applied to the stipend of the clergyman?

1057. Lord Justice FitzGibbon.—Certainly not; the deed distinctly states that it is to be expended on the building.

Dean Warburton.—And for no other use or purpose whatever.

1058. Lord Justice FitzGibbon.—We have unlimited power over educational endowments; but we have no power to authorize money given for repairing the edifice to be turned into salary for a clergyman, because that would not be an educational trust. With the consent of the governing body it could be applied to any educational purpose.

Witness.—But not to any other?

Lord Justice FitzGibbon.—I don't think so. At all events I don't think we would do it.

1059. Dr. Traill.—It might meet the requirements of the case if, instead of having to divide the endowment into halves, the governing body could allocate the whole between the two objects in such proportions as they should find necessary in each year, at the same time providing a sinking fund to meet large repairs which might occasionally be required for the Cathedral.

Dean Warburton.—You would ruin the whole thing if you divided it. We might shut up shop.

Dr. Traill.—But you might be empowered to divide it between your own two objects in any proportion that you liked.

1060. Lord Justice FitzGibbon.—The Dean's proposal is free from all objection; if one half were to be accumulated for the Cathedral to form a "reserve fund" of a certain amount, and you were to apply the income of that to the Cathedral, you could fall back on that fund in any year in which it was wanted for the Cathedral, and in the mean time apply the rest of the income of the estate to the school.

Dean Warburton.—I think that would be very desirable.

1061. Lord Justice FitzGibbon.—We have got a number of applications from dioceses to incorporate bodies to hold small endowments; and there is nothing to prevent their holding large ones also. But here the trusts are so distinct that I think this endowment ought to have a scheme and foundation of its own. But we have had, in Sligo, evidence as to endowments—for example, in one parish, as to four schools, the titles to which are very doubtful; and no doubt there are a great number of other similar cases. We will ask your Diocesan Council to send us a list of any endowments in the diocese of Elphin which they may wish to vest in a central body of trustees. We have no power to form a body of trustees in the abstract. We can only form a body to hold existing property; but we can give them power, when incorporated, to take conveyances of further property. Therefore the first step is to give us a list—as they have done in the diocese of Meath and other places—of any school-houses, teachers residences, lands, or moneys that you may want to vest in a general body of trustees. We should then declare the trusts of such items of property, giving the general body of trustees some power of control over it. In that way you can set your diocesan scheme in motion. As regards this endowment, probably the better course will be to send Dean Warburton a draft of a scheme, and he can let the Chapter see it and give us their views on it. It is not an endowment with respect to which we would be likely to force anything on you against your wills. We can send Colonel Cooper a copy also, and would be glad to receive any suggestions before the scheme is published. But even after it is published there are two months to send in objections to it; and if we should overrule these objections, and you should not be satisfied with our decision, you can go to the Privy Council, so that there can be no harm done.

Dean Warburton.—I should be very glad, in this consolidated management, to include some of the landed gentry of the country. I think it is very important that they should take an interest in these things.

1062. Lord Justice FitzGibbon.—We could put in two representatives, or any other number, from the Diocesan Council. They seem ready at hand, as a good representative body to take laymen from; and we could give power to co-opt a couple more. We would provide that they should be resident within a certain distance of Elphin. We don't like appointing absentee trustees.

Colonel Cooper.—No, it would be very bad. I would only suggest that two of the governing body should be elected by the Diocesan Council.

1063. Lord Justice FitzGibbon.—Tullyvin School, in Cavan, is in some respects a similar foundation.

Rev. Mr. *Irwin*.—We had a son of the master of Tullyvin here. He was educated in one of the Incorporated Society's Schools and came to us to learn Classics, and entered College from us, and is now an assistant master. Another pupil of ours stood for sizarship and nearly got in. Would there not be some danger that under a new governing body, as proposed, members might get in who would not care to make Elphin School prosper?

Professor Dougherty.—Their primary trust would be to maintain a school of this character here.

1064. Lord Justice FitzGibbon.—We made the first trust at Tullyvin to maintain the school there; but if they should have money to spare they might use it to support a school at Cavan.

Rev. Mr. *Irwin*.—Would it not be possible to allow a portion of the Cathedral money to go to the school and a certain portion yearly towards the formation of a reserve fund?

1065. Lord Justice FitzGibbon.—That is matter for consideration in detail. We would make a pro-

Dec. 22, 1886.

Colonel Cooper.

vision that you should keep the Cathedral in repair each year at an expense not exceeding half the income of the endowment, and that you should pay £30 a year, if you had it, towards a reserve fund, and that any sum remaining after that should come down to the school.

The Rev. *Francis Burke* sworn and examined.

1066. Lord Justice FitzGibbon.—You are the Rector of Ardcarne?—Yes, I live within nine miles of here.

1067. You are a member of the Chapter of Elphin?—Yes.

1068. What is the opinion of the Chapter as regards spending a portion of the money now available for the Cathedral, on the school?—They are almost unanimously in favour of spending any surplus on the school that is not required for the Cathedral; they are all in favour of it.

1069. You are in favour of spending it on a school in Elphin rather than on a school anywhere else?—Most certainly. I say that without any personal motive or interest whatever.

1070. Professor Dougherty.—Would you be in favour of having a discretionary power to apply any part of your endowment elsewhere?—I think there is no occasion for it, because our present endowment is not sufficient for the objects of the school.

1071. Has the present endowment could be considerably increased if you were empowered to apply a portion of the Cathedral money to the school?

Dean *Warburton*.—I beg your pardon—we are doing that already.

1072. Lord Justice FitzGibbon.—For 137 years too much went to the Cathedral.

Dean *Warburton*.—At that time they applied the whole of it.

1073. Dr. Traill.—There is still a great deal due to the school.

Rev. Mr. *Burke*.—Calculated at compound interest it would be an enormous amount—nearly half a million of money.

Dean *Warburton*.—I have been extremely glad at meeting the Commissioners here to-day; and I have very great pleasure now in saying that we have the heir of Bishop Hodson here. He has come down to look what we are about. He has a right to demand our accounts every year whenever he pleases, and to look over them.

1074. Dr. Traill.—Would you like his name to be added to the governing body *ex-officio*?

Dean *Warburton*. I certainly would.

1075. Dr. Traill.—Would you object to that, Sir John Hodson?

Sir *John Hodson*.—No. I would have no objection, but I would not be able to attend.

1076. You could look over the accounts from year to year?—Yes.

1077. And you would like to come down occasionally?—Yes.

Dean *Warburton*.—Whether he can come or not we would be very glad to have his name.

Rev. Mr. *Burke*.—If the governing body is to be confined to a district, I would think that nine miles or so would be sufficient.

Dr. Traill.—That would just keep Doyle out.

PUBLIC SITTING—THURSDAY, OCTOBER 11, 1888.

At the Schoolhouse, Lisnaroe, Newtownbutler.

Present:—The Right Hon. Lord Justice FitzGibbon and the Right Hon. Lord Justice Naish, Judicial Commissioners; and the Rev. Gerald Molloy, D.D., D.Sc., Anthony Traill, Esq., LL.D., M.D., F.T.C.D., and Professor Dougherty, M.A., Assistant Commissioners.

The Assistant Secretary, N. D. Murphy, jun., was in attendance.

LISNAROE ENDOWED SCHOOL.

Lord Justice FitzGibbon made an opening statement.

Nathaniel Hone Dyas, Esq., J.P., sworn and examined.

1078. Lord Justice FitzGibbon.—What is the history of this endowment?—I have been a trustee of the school for twenty-five years. The deed of foundation bears date November 6, 1818. The Rev. James Mitchell was the founder. Mrs. Amelia Mitchell erected the school-house and teacher's residence on ground given by said James Mitchell. There are four joint trustees with myself. The founder granted a plot of four acres, Irish, as the site of the school. It is in the centre of a property of 4,000 acres, now the estate of Miss Mitchell, a lunatic, and her sister, Mrs. Douglas, wife of Captain Douglas. Captain Douglas is the committee of the lunatic, and manages the estate. An annuity or rent-charge of £30, Irish, was granted by the founder; it was charged on the townland of Carry, which is of ample value, and had always been paid by the agent, at present Mr. Henry Dyas. The master of the school was to be a member of the United Church of England and Ireland. If there should be girls at the school, the wife of the master, if a competent teacher, should be the schoolmistress. If the master should not be married, another schoolmistress should be appointed. A salary not exceeding £30, Irish, was to be paid between the master and the mistress, and was to be supplemented by the contributions of visitors received in a box which was to be fixed in a suitable place. The master and mistress were to educate—

"All such of the poor children of the inhabitants of the said parish of Lisnaroe, or of some of the adjacent parishes as shall apply for admission here and conform to the rules of the school, limited to such number as the trustees for the time being . . . . shall appoint, in the principles of the Christian religion, and in reading, writing, and casting religion and other proper and useful learning for poor children . . . . . without any reward, gratuity, or salary from the parents or friends of the poor children other than such as shall be from time to time ordered by the said trustees."

If the pious intentions of the founder should not be carried out, the annuity should cease. There were always to be five trustees. Mrs. Mitchell bequeathed for the boards of the school £1,000, now secured by mortgage, at 4 per cent. on lands in Westmeath. The present trustees are the Bishop of Kilmore, Ardagh, and Elphin, Captain Douglas, Mr. Nathaniel Rose Dyas, the Rev. Mr. Peyton, and the Rev. Mr. West, Rector of an adjoining parish. It is provided that the "trustees shall not be absent from Ireland." Captain Douglas is not permanently resident in Ireland. Mr. Peyton and myself are the acting trustees. The children are examined every year by an examiner selected by Rev. Mr. Peyton. The parish is Clongish, Lissanore being only a townland.

1079. Lord Justice FitzGibbon.—The instrument describes the objects as "the poor children of the parish of Lissanore, or of some of the adjacent parishes." Lissanore being in the parish of Clongish, what parishes touch it?

Rev. Mr. *Peyton*.—The adjoining parishes are, Killashee, Temple Michael, Mohill, and Killoe. Mohill is in Leitrim. Temple Michael and Killoe are in Longford. The nearest parish is Temple Michael. We have some young people from it.

1080. Dr. Traill.—How near is Temple Michael to the school?

Rev. Mr. *Peyton*.—About a mile and a half or two miles.

1081. Lord Justice FitzGibbon.—If we frame a scheme for the school, our duty to the governing body will be to have regard to the spirit of the founder's intentions; incorporating a governing body on the principles of the deed would get rid of all future deeds by the appointment of trustees, and would give a clear title to the property.

Witness.—It cost £16 to get the last deeds executed. It is a strain on our resources as we have only a small margin. My co-trustee thinks the endowment is exempt from the Act. The gift was made by a Protestant clergyman, the owner of the estate. He appointed two other Protestant clergymen and three Protestant gentlemen trustees. He made it a condition that the teacher should be a Protestant, and that he should give religious instruction. This estate was altogether peopled by Protestants, chiefly Scotch; it was called the Scotch Quarter, and is known to the present day as the Scotch Quarter. I received the rents for twenty years, and out of £3,000 a year there was not £300 a year paid by Roman Catholics. It has always been essentially a Protestant school and estate, and the governing power has been exclusively and always Protestant, and has within the last thirty years included the Bishop, the Archdeacon, and the Rector of the parish. The Bishop and the Rector have been always in it. We never refused to receive Roman Catholics into the school; but it was understood that they were required to conform to the rules, one of which was that there should be religious instruction given.

1082. Lord Justice Naish.—Are there any Roman Catholics in the school at present?—There were some about thirty years ago, but the parish priest took them away. A few have since come from time to time and remained a short time.

Lord Justice FitzGibbon.—In 1878 the pupils were all Church Protestants.

1083. Rev. Dr. Molloy.—When you were receiving Catholic children was it supposed that you were acting contrary to the intentions of the founder?—No; but that they came there to hear religious instruction that would be given, and which apparently their clergyman seemed to think was contrary to the strict exercise of their faith, so he took them away.

1084. Dr. Traill.—Were they all required to receive religious education when they came here?—Yes. Oct. 11, 1894. — Nathaniel Rose Dyas, J.P.

1085. Professor Dougherty.—The founder says nothing about the principles of his own Church, but merely speaks in a general way about the principles of the Christian religion.

Rev. Mr. *Peyton*.—The deed says that the teacher was always to be a Protestant, and was to instruct the children according to the rules and principles of the Christian faith. The attendants—except for a very short time—have been all Protestants, and hitherto the estate has been nearly peopled with Protestants.

1086. Professor Dougherty.—Are there Protestants of other denominations resident in the parish?

Witness.—There were Presbyterians. Some of the tenants were Presbyterians.

1087. Lord Justice FitzGibbon.—This is a matter that we have had to explain over and over again to gentlemen who seemed to think that we wanted to upset the arrangements of founders, which, on the contrary, we are bound to observe. The founder here provides that the master is to be of the Established Church of England and Ireland. That provision we would be bound to put into any scheme. The general constitution of the governing body must also remain as originally provided. But we have to decide whether this endowment was provided exclusively for the benefit of persons of a particular religious denomination. The school may be entirely under Protestant Church management, and under a Protestant master; but if the founder intended that people of other religious denominations should get the benefit of the school it would not come under the exemption in the Act, though in drafting a scheme we would be bound to observe all his provisions as regards the governing body and the teacher.

1088. Lord Justice Naish.—What are your wishes as to having in a scheme any alteration in the government of the school?

Witness.—My own personal wish would be to place it under the Diocesan Synod of Ardagh and Kilmore; but the representative of the family, who married the daughter of the gentleman who established it, does not like it to be taken from what it has been.

1089. Lord Justice FitzGibbon.—At present he has not got any right to be represented on this governing body. It is only by co-option of his co-trustees that he can be on it. But it would be open to us to provide—as we have done in other cases—that the founder's representative shall, in his own right, be a member of the governing body; and if he should find it inconvenient to act on the ground of non-residence, he might nominate one or more to represent him. In all matters of that kind, we shall be very glad to consult his wishes.

Witness.—But if you find that for so many years it has been a Protestant school——

1090. Lord Justice FitzGibbon.—So it must remain.

Witness.—Will it come under the Act at all?

1091. Lord Justice FitzGibbon.—Yes; unless Church Protestants only are entitled to benefit from it. It is one of those schools that we find now in good order, but which former reports showed to have been capable of great improvement?—The old master was aged and very deaf—and we all get old and infirm—and the endowment was not sufficient to give him a pension, so, as an act of kindness, we did not disturb him.

Lord Justice FitzGibbon.—To put it shortly, the interests of the school were sacrificed to the interests of the master.

1092. Dr. Traill.—Is he dead?—Yes, we gave him a small pension.

1093. Lord Justice FitzGibbon.—Do you think, Mr. Dyas, that the owner intended to benefit the Presbyterian tenantry?—Certainly; they were Protestants as well as the Church of England people and the Methodists.

1094. Rev. Dr. Molloy.—That brings the school under the Act. If the endowment was intended for different denominations of Protestants it is not exempt.

1095. Lord Justice Naish.—Are there Protestants of different denominations in the parish?

Rev. Mr. *Peyton*.—The Presbyterian tenants live in the neighbourhood of Longford.

1096. Lord Justice FitzGibbon.—Have you any Presbyterian children in the school at present?

Mr. *Livingstone*.—I have two to-day.

1097. How many are on the roll?—Only two at present.

1098. Are there any Methodists?—No.

1099. Are your two Presbyterians the only ones that don't belong to the Church?—That's all.

1100. Rev. Dr. Molloy.—Have you had Presbyterians from time to time?—We have had members of the same family, but now they are gone.

Lord Justice FitzGibbon.—You are not exempt; but still you are entitled to insist that the scheme shall be settled in accordance with the will.

1101. Dr. Traill.—What harm will a good scheme do you? It will save the expense of appointing trustees. Nobody proposes to confiscate your endowment, or to hand it over to Roman Catholics?—Unfortunately in Ireland if once the thin end of the wedge gets in you don't know where it will end.

Dr. Traill.—I am as anxious as you are to keep the wedge out.

1102. Lord Justice FitzGibbon (*to Witness*).—Do you take any part in the management of the school?—Very little, unless it is reported to me that anything is wrong, and then I attend to it.

1103. Do the trustees meet?—Whenever Captain Douglas comes over we have a sort of meeting—he, Mr. Peyton, and I. The others may attend if they wish. The Bishop is more or less ornamental, because he has too much to attend to. (*Accounts handed in.*)

1104. Dr. Traill.—You began the year with £50 to credit?—Last year we spent a little more.

1105. Lord Justice FitzGibbon.—This year you have received a year's annuity, £55 7s. 8d.; a year's interest, £40; total, £95 7s. 8d. from October 10, 1887, to October 10, 1888. Against that, there is one year's salary to the master, £80; extra allowance, £10; results fees, &c., £5; and poor rate, income tax, premium for the examiner, painting and repairs, which make a total of £96 8s. 5d. So that there is a balance this year against you, of about £1, and you have a balance in bank of over £100?—But against that there is the recurring salary.

1106. Who draws your cheques?—They are drawn and signed by two of the trustees, one of whom must be a layman, and the other a clergyman.

1107. In whose name is the bank account?—In the name of the five trustees.

1108. With power to two to sign?—Yes.

1109. Where is the account kept?—In the Bank of Ireland, Longford.

The Rev. *George B. Peyton* sworn and examined.

1110. Lord Justice FitzGibbon.—Are you the incumbent of the parish of Clongish?—I am.

1111. What is the Protestant population of the parish?—On this side about 182.

1112. Is this exclusively a day school?—Yes, we don't admit boarders except by consent of the trustees, and they have not consented except once or twice.

1113. You have not thought of such an arrangement as we found at Tullyvin and at Kilpike, of receiving boarders as well as day boys?—It was put before the trustees by the master, and they thought it better not to mind giving him the power of having boarders. However, Mr. Dyas, as one of the trustees, said that if it benefited the school he for one would not object.

1114. Dr. Traill.—What room is there for boarders?—At present the master has only his wife and son.

1115. Lord Justice FitzGibbon.—How long has the present master been with you?—Upwards of twenty years.

1116. Does his wife teach?—She teaches from time to time.

1117. Has he any assistant?—Not at present.

1118. It is a mixed school for boys and girls?—Yes.

1119. Is it entirely a primary school?—I cannot say that, because we have very advanced pupils who have been pushed on to the Civil Service. They took advantage of the capabilities of the teacher; but that did not interfere with the other teaching.

1120. Rev. Dr. Molloy.—You give primary education to the children that want it?—Yes.

1121. Lord Justice FitzGibbon.—Is the master qualified to give something better?—Fully.

1122. Are there any school fees?—I don't think there are any school fees; but sometimes if a person comes from outside, gets the benefit of his instructions, and chooses to give him a little benefit, we do not interfere.

1123. What are the arrangements as to the inspection of the school?—The trustees appoint a regular yearly inspector, who inspects the school once a year, and gives a report, a copy of which is sent to the trustees, and he is paid about 30s.

1124. Who is the inspector?—For the last two or three years it has been the incumbent of an adjoining parish, the Rev. Mr. Reilly, B.A., T.C.D., but we have had other incumbents as inspectors from time to time. We sometimes change in order that we may be the better able to judge.

1125. Rev. Dr. Molloy.—You are not connected with the National Board, I suppose?—No.

1126. Would it not be an advantage to you to receive salaries for your teachers from the National Board?—That's a matter, I consider, for the trustees.

1127. Dr. Traill.—Do you belong to the Church Education Society?—I do. The master might have been suggested to me at some time, but my present idea, I speak to [illegible] to think that we did not require the assistance of the National Board.

1128. Is your master qualified under the National Board?—I don't know about that, but he has shown capabilities, by the way in which he has brought on pupils.

Rev. Dr. Molloy.—If your school were connected with the National Board you would get inspection free, which would be one advantage, and at least a capitation grant for your teachers, and results fees.

Lord Justice FitzGibbon.—And the public aid would set free a portion of the endowment to pay the master for giving instruction in special subjects, and to pay an assistant.

1129. Rev. Dr. Molloy.—Is there not a good deal of practical inconvenience when the same master teaches some pupils the primary course and prepares others for the Bank of Ireland and the Intermediate Examinations?—The mistress attends to the junior boys. I don't know that we have found that there has been any detriment to the school by having those few with the master whom he pressed on for the Intermediate Examinations. I think they attended before school hours.

Mr. *Livingstone*.—My sister-in-law passed university examinations for women, and she took the junior pupils while I was engaged with the advanced pupils; and outside hours, I worked as I could, and charged [illegible]

1130. Rev. Dr. Molloy.—The numbers in attendance at the school have fallen off considerably in recent years?—They have fallen off within the last three or four years. In one year there was an epidemic of measles, so that they could not attend.

1131. In 1870 the number on the roll was 68, and in 1885 it is 31?—We have not had so many persons living round the school, and so they did not come.

1132. Dr. Traill.—Has emigration affected the school?—Emigration and death. Oct. 11, 1886.

1133. Rev. Dr. Molloy.—Do not the births compensate for the deaths?—There are six families within a radius of a mile and a half, or two miles of the school, in which there are from six to seven children each; and their parents told me that they are just waiting till their children are old enough to take advantage of the benefits of the teaching. That would make a difference of 40 or 50. Rev. George R. Payne.

Alexander Livingstone, Head Master, sworn and examined.

1134. Lord Justice FitzGibbon.—What was the date of your appointment as Master of [illegible] School?—1882. Alexander Livingstone.

1135. You were in the London University, I think?—Not at that time. I passed the Matriculation Examination of the London University since.

1136. You have not gone beyond that?—No, because I did not think it would be of any advantage, and I was much engaged.

1137. You were in one of the Queen's Colleges too?—I passed a local examination and got a first honour certificate.

1138. Had you any training as a teacher before you came here?—I was taught in a National Board school and in Church Education Society's schools.

1139. Were you a qualified teacher under the National Board?—I passed the Inspector, and then I left the school, but there was no disqualification.

1140. Were you afterwards in Church Education schools?—I was, before and since.

1141. What National school were you in?—In the county of Londonderry, near Coleraine, and I taught for two years in the Church Education school at [illegible], in the county of Down.

1142. Was it from [illegible] that you came here?—It was.

1143. What number of pupils did you find here?—There were but few, but they dropped in quickly.

1144. They came when there was an efficient master?—On the day I came there were but seven pupils.

1145. What classes have you got now?—Six classes, regulated according to the National Board system, the scale of proficiency being the same. But my own pupils I deal with.

1146. How do you manage about religious instruction?—The last half-hour of the day is devoted to it.

1147. What books do you use?—I use the National Board books.

1148. So that as regards books, curriculum, arrangement of hours and religious instruction, you have the National Board system, but without salary, results fees, or inspection?—Exactly.

1149. Dr. Traill.—Were you trained for employment under the National Board?—I qualified third class, that was all I could get.

1150. Lord Justice FitzGibbon.—What qualifications have you got in higher subjects?—I am qualified for the full curriculum of the London matriculation.

1151. What pupils have you requiring more than National Board instruction?—I have my own son, three other boys, and four or five who wish to get into the Civil Service as clerks.

1152. A considerable number of your pupils have obtained higher education, how were they prepared?—By dint of teaching.

1153. In school hours or out of them?—In and out. I have worked here night and day working up their papers.

1154. Has it all been done by yourself?—As long as my sister-in-law lived with me she taught.

1155. I presume it would be an advantage if you had paper assistance?—Most certainly it would, if we have the material.

1156. Have you any monitors or pupil teachers?—No.

1157. You have by yourself to teach the six classes under the National Board system?—Certainly; but I ask the advanced pupils to oblige me by taking the junior classes and working as monitors, but of course they are not paid.

1158. Dr. Traill.—Would you think it an advantage to be under the National Board?—Anything that is for the interest of the school of course is for my interest—anything that will give me fair value for fair work.

1159. Lord Justice FitzGibbon.—How old are you?—I am in my forty-fifth year.

1160. Of what class are the children who come here?—Generally they are the children of gentlemen farmers; also the children of the humbler classes. We have had children of the officers of the garrison from Longford, district inspectors sons, and so forth.

1161. Rev. Dr. Molloy.—Have you any pupils at present from the town of Longford?—I don't think so.

1162. Professor Dougherty.—Is there a Model school in Longford?—No.

1163. Is the education given in this school considered better than that of the ordinary National schools of the district?—It is not for me to say that. I have no way of bringing the pupils on but by dint of teaching.

1164. Lord Justice FitzGibbon.—Have you a better class of children than those who go to the ordinary National schools?—Those who come from a distance and have some particular end in view, would not come otherwise; it is not in human nature.

1165. It is plain from Mr. Livingstone's qualifications and position as a teacher that if there was a female teacher under the National Board here, who could take the younger pupils, a salary could be got for her, and Mr. Livingstone's time left free for what we saw well done at Elphin, where boys are getting good places in the Civil Service and elsewhere from being taught by a teacher qualified as Mr. Livingstone is.

Mr. *Dyas*.—Personally I would like that.

1166. Lord Justice FitzGibbon.—We saw Roman Catholic farmers yesterday at Elphin who send their children to the Bishop's school, and their boys have got on in the world through being taught in a school endowed as this is.

The Rev. Mr. *Payne*.—You mention the restrictions of the National Board. We are not under them. Any time that I or the curate of the parish come into the school we can, and have, at different times, taken up the Scriptures, and we are at perfect liberty to do so and examine any of the children.

1167. Lord Justice FitzGibbon.—The only practical difference is that, if you choose to come at a fixed hour of the day, you can do so under the National Board rules; but if you wish to preserve the liberty [illegible] to come in, say in the middle of arithmetic one day, and in the middle of spelling another day, you must sacrifice all the advantages of the other system.

1168. Professor DOUGHERTY.—How often have you exercised this privilege in the way you describe?—It all depends on circumstances. Sometimes I am taken up a good deal in the parish; sometimes there is illness in different parts of the parish. I don't say that I have been here as often as I might have been; but at the same time when I [illegible] my instruction to my assistant, the [illegible] of the parish, is that he is to come once a week.

1169. Dr. TRAILL.—Why could not he come at a definite hour?—Well, it would be well, as you say, not to interfere with the school lessons.

1170. You would not do it in your own [illegible]. I only wish to meet the objection, that [illegible] under the same restrictions as the National Board schools.

CLONTUMPHER SCHOOL.

Rev. George R. Peyton further examined.

Rev. George R. Peyton.

1171. Lord Justice FITZGIBBON.—You are one of the trustees of Clontumpher school?—Yes.

1172. You have there an annual rentcharge of £30?—Yes.

1173. Where is the school?—At the west end of this parish.

1174. What distance is it from this school?—Five miles.

1175. Is it entirely a primary school?—It is.

1176. What school buildings are there?—A school, a dwelling-house for the teacher, and some small offices.

1177. The provision in the instrument of foundation is, that the children are not only to be taught reading, writing, and accounts, but are all to be instructed in the Holy Scriptures, and such as are members of the United Church of England and Ireland are to be taught the Church catechism, and the principles of the Protestant religion as by law established. The Rev. William Digby and his successors, rectors and vicars, are to be among the five trustees, and are not to be subject to election; all the rest are co-opted?—Yes.

1178. And all are to be members of the United Church of England and Ireland as by law established, and there are to be five trustees for ever?—Yes.

1179. Lord Justice FITZGIBBON.—Who are the present trustees of Clontumpher school?—The Rev. [illegible] Edgeworth, Mr. Andrew Bole, and myself.

1180. There are two vacancies?—Yes.

1181. This seems to be a more exclusive school than the one we are in, for there is a provision that all the members of the governing body are necessarily to be members of the United Church. We will send you some schemes already framed for similar cases, and once for all you may relieve your minds of any notion that the powers we have are to be exercised to take away anything you have got. By extending your powers, and enabling yourselves to give fuller education in other subjects, you might make these schools more useful. Relief from law costs, too, will be an advantage to you.

The Rev. Dr. *Patterson*.—The Rev. Mr. Edgeworth requested me to attend. You mentioned that you would send down a few model schemes. Would it be optional with the trustees to make a selection from them?

1182. Lord Justice FITZGIBBON.—Not exactly a selection, for no two schemes are exactly alike. We endeavour in each case to draw a scheme suited to the requirements of the school, and we would send you schemes likely to be guides to you in suggesting what is best.

Rev. Dr. *Patterson*.—Would you afterwards receive from the trustees any remarks?

1183. Lord Justice FITZGIBBON.—Certainly; we would ask them first to give us their notions after the scheme is published; they could send us any suggestions or amendments they wish, and we would give them the best consideration. In such endowments as these—private endowments for purposes of particular religious denominations—we will carry out the wishes of the trustees appointed by the founder as far as we possibly can.

Mr. Andrew Burnett sworn and examined.

Mr. Andrew Burnett.

1184. Lord Justice FITZGIBBON.—Are you the teacher of Clontumpher?—I am. I was trained at the Church Education Society's school, Kildare-place. I spent two sessions there. I took second class at leaving.

1185. How long ago?—In 1864.

1186. What number of pupils have you at present?—Eighteen on the roll. The average attendance for the last two years has been over thirteen.

1187. Is it a school for both boys and girls?—Yes.

1188. What classes have you?—Six classes.

1189. How many are in the sixth class?—Only one.

1190. And in the fifth?—Three.

1191. Have you any pupils getting more than primary instruction?—No.

1192. You have no monitor?—No; the district is very poor, and as soon as the children grow up their parents take them away to work.

1193. What emoluments have you?—The endowment is £30, less income tax and poor rate. The teacher gets £41, with £3 for firing. The poor rate and county cess come to something about £1, and we have only about 10s. a year towards repairs.

1194. What sort of school buildings have you?—Very fair. They are kept in order by the trustees.

1195. Dr. TRAILL.—What religious instruction is given?—I give it myself.

1196. Does the clergyman come?—Yes, once a week.

1197. At any particular hour?—At no particular hour.

1198. Lord Justice FITZGIBBON.—What parish is Clontumpher in?

Rev. Dr. *Patterson*.—The union parish of Clonghill [illegible].

1199. Lord Justice FITZGIBBON.—Is there a permanent provision for the curacy under the Diocesan Scheme?—Under the Representative Body the curate gets so much a year independent of the rector altogether.

1200. (To Rev. Mr. *Peyton*.)—Were you the rector at the passing of the Church Act?—No, I came in just after the Act, in 1872.

The inquiry then closed.

PUBLIC SITTING—FRIDAY, OCTOBER 12, 1888.

At the Courthouse, Galway.

Present:—The Right Hon. Lord Justice FITZGIBBON and the Right Hon. Lord Justice NAISH, Judicial Commissioners; and the Rev. GERALD MOLLOY, D.D., D.SC., ANTHONY TRAILL, Esq., LL.D., M.D., F.T.C.D., and Professor DOUGHERTY, M.A., Assistant Commissioners.

The Assistant Secretary, N. D. MURPHY, Junr., was in attendance.

Lord Justice FITZGIBBON made an introductory statement.

COLLEGE OF ST. IGNATIUS.

The Rev. *Patrick Hughes*, S.J., sworn and examined.

1201. Lord Justice FITZGIBBON.—What position do you hold in the College of St. Ignatius?—I am Rector.

1202. Is it a diocesan college?—We have students for Maynooth, but it is not, strictly speaking, a diocesan college; it is a Jesuit college for general Intermediate education.

1203. What number of pupils have you at present?—Between fifty and sixty, all day scholars.

1204. Are they principally from the neighbourhood of Galway?—Principally; some are from a distance, and are lodging in the town for the purpose of getting education.

1205. What other Intermediate schools compete with you?—I think Erasmus Smith's school competes with us, and the school of the Patrician Brothers.

1206. Dr. TRAILL.—These schools compete with you in the general Intermediate examinations?—Yes.

1207. Are your pupils all Roman Catholics?—All.

1208. Erasmus Smith's school does not compete with you for pupils?—No.

1209. Lord Justice FITZGIBBON.—Is St. Jarlath's College, Tuam, the nearest Roman Catholic diocesan college?—I think so.

1210. Of what do the premises of your college consist?—We have school buildings. The boys simply come and attend the classes, and leave at a quarter to three o'clock every day. We only require schoolrooms.

1211. In whom is the property vested?—In the Jesuit Fathers as a body.

1212. Lord Justice NAISH.—A conveyance must have been taken?—It was taken in the names of some particular persons as trustees.

1213. Lord Justice FITZGIBBON.—Have you any invested funds?—There is a very small sum which is in the hands of one of the Fathers who invested it in three per cents.

1214. Have there been any bequests to the college?—None.

1215. Rev. Dr. MOLLOY.—Do you claim to be exempt from the compulsory jurisdiction of the Commissioners?—Certainly.

1216. On the ground that the college is exclusively denominational?—Yes; and on the ground of having no endowment.

1217. You have a building?—We have a building erected at our own expense.

1218. Is your governing body is entirely of one denomination?—Entirely of one denomination.

1219. And the institution is intended exclusively for the benefit of persons of one denomination?—Exclusively.

1220. Lord Justice FITZGIBBON.—Your college is exempt unless you consent to the exercise of our jurisdiction, in which case we could incorporate your trustees so as to save the expense of conveyances. It is entirely optional with you to give your consent; and if you should think it worth while, you can communicate with our office. May I ask does the number of your pupils represent the number of Roman Catholic boys belonging to Galway who require Intermediate education?—I would not say that. I think it represents the number of boys able to pay the pension we charge. There may be many other boys who desire a classical education but have not the means of paying for it.

1221. What is your pension?—We charge £6 per annum; the year is divided into three terms of £2 each.

1222. What teaching staff have you?—Six.

1223. Do they teach the whole of the Intermediate course?—We have not at present the senior grade course. Only one or two applied, and it is not worth my while to keep a master for two boys; it would not pay.

1224. Is there no Roman Catholic school in Galway where the boys go as far as the senior grade?—Not this year. We have had boys for the senior grade at other times.

1225. Have you any boys preparing for the Royal University?—No.

1226. Lord Justice NAISH.—Do any of your boys go on to Clongowes?—Sometimes, when their parents are well-to-do.

1227. As a rule, what positions in life do your boys go into after they leave you?—Some to the medical profession, some to the solicitor's, and some to the Civil Service. Of course many remain at occupations in the town.

1228. Lord Justice FITZGIBBON.—What is the average age at which boys come to you?—About ten or eleven.

1229. Up to what age do they remain?—Very often to twenty. Some of them, if they are going on for the ecclesiastical course, very often have to wait for vacancies, and they have to follow their ecclesiastical education still.

1230. Do they go direct from you to Maynooth?—Very often.

1231. Dr. TRAILL.—How many did you send last year?—There was no vacant place for this diocese last year; there is only a certain limited number for each diocese.

1232. Lord Justice FITZGIBBON.—How many did you send this year to the Intermediate examinations?—About 14.

1233. How did they get on?—Some passed and some did not. I don't think they got on very well.

1234. Had you any prizes or exhibitions this year?—Not any.

1235. To what do you attribute that—do the boys come to you too old?—I think that, partly, and it is also from the fact of their frequently not being able to supply themselves properly with the books.

1236. Is money so short in Galway that boys are prevented from going up to the Intermediate examinations by the want even of books?—It prevents them from going up with a chance of succeeding.

1237. Is there a centre here?—There is.

1238. So that they have no travelling expenses to meet?—No expenses of that sort.

1239. To what class do the boys belong?—Sons of shopkeepers and farmers of the neighbourhood.

1240. Where do the Roman Catholic gentry of the neighbourhood send their sons for education?—Some go to Clongowes.

1241. Do any of your boys go to the Queen's College?—I have not heard of any lately. Formerly some did go.

1242. Their going there is not approved by the authorities of your Church?—That is so.

1243. There is no other place to which they can go for more advanced education?—Not unless they join the Royal University.

1244. Are you able to give university instruction to boys who want it?—If we had a number of boys wanting it I would supply masters for them; but naturally I keep the staff of masters suited to the wants of the pupils.

1245. Are any of your staff paid masters?—No, they are all members of the order and live in the house.

1246. What is the division of work amongst the six teachers?—One takes the Latin and Greek class and prepares for the middle grade examination, another does the same for the junior grade. We have a preparatory school and a commercial class for boys who don't intend to study classics—these learn a little French, with Arithmetic, Algebra, and English. The other classes are divided. There is one teaching Natural Philosophy and the various extras that must be supplied. We find that the six have enough to do.

1247. Have you had any classes for South Kensington?—Never.

1248. Do you teach drawing?—We do not.

1249. Rev. Dr. Molloy.—Do you know of any endowment which you have a claim to share?—That's a leading question, I am afraid. I think it would be a great help to the Catholics of this county and neighbourhood if they had some endowment.

1250. Lord Justice Naish.—Is there a Model school in Galway?—There is.

1251. Lord Justice FitzGibbon.—We have no endowment to distribute that I am aware of; but if any money were available for Intermediate Education what is your greatest want?—I suppose free burses for eligible candidates.

1252. Rev. Dr. Molloy.—Would your pupils be more numerous if you were not obliged to charge such high fees?—I dare say. I think that of course has an effect on the number.

1253. If you were able to offer a certain number of free places, you would get a larger number of pupils?—I think so.

1254. Are there any elementary schools in the neighbourhood which prepare pupils for Intermediate education?—Yes, we have the Patrician Brothers school.

1255. I suppose they would be glad to get a free Intermediate education in your school for boys who had passed through theirs?—I am very sure they would.

1256. Lord Justice Naish.—Do they send any boys to the Intermediate examinations?—They did formerly. I don't think they sent in any last year.

1257. You mentioned books as one of the things that you found the boys wanted?—To have a good Greek lexicon and a good Latin dictionary is a very important thing, and they are very often not able to supply themselves. In the Intermediate courses the books are continually changing, and unless they get the modern authors they are handicapped.

1258. Then one of the purposes to which you would apply an endowment would be to supply books?—To get a supply of good books.

THE PATRICIAN BROTHERS' SCHOOL.

The Rev. Brother *John Patrick Lynch* sworn and examined.

1259. Lord Justice FitzGibbon.—You are the principal of the Patrician Brothers' school?—I am principal of St. Joseph's seminary, which is carried on by the Patrician Brothers.

1260. Where is your school?—At Nuns Island.

1261. How many pupils have you on the roll?—We had yesterday 105.

1262. And what is your average attendance?—Yesterday we had 93 attending.

1263. Are they all receiving primary education?—No; there are boys learning Greek, Latin, French, Irish, English, and mathematics.

1264. What proportion of your pupils are learning Latin?—Between 20 and 30.

1265. What fees do they pay?—There is a stated scale, but we are at liberty to reduce it. It is made very low in order to accommodate the wants of parents of the middle class in Galway—10s. a quarter, or £2 a year for classics is the normal fee.

1266. Do you find a considerable number of pupils not able to pay so much?—We do.

1267. Do you take what you can get, or admit poor pupils free?—Yes, if we find a boy of good disposition who is likely to go on in the ecclesiastical state, then at a sacrifice of the interests of the community, we admit him at a smaller fee. We have some that pay no fee at all.

1268. How is the school supported?—By the fees of the pupils and the funds of the community; and it has been also in connection lately with the National Board of Education.

1269. Is your class for Greek and Latin in connection with and conducted on the system of the National Board?—It is, and receiving result fees. We don't confine ourselves to that. We prepare pupils for the ecclesiastical state, and send them direct to the continental colleges.

1270. Lord Justice Naish.—Are there Christian Brothers in Galway?—There are. They are in charge of the Industrial school. They have no public school.

1271. Dr. Traill.—Are your boys day boys?—All.

1272. Lord Justice FitzGibbon.—How many of the community are engaged in teaching?—Five.

1273. How do you divide the work?—We just accommodate ourselves to the wants of the school. The Brother who teaches Greek in the morning may teach a low class of geography or grammar in the middle of the day. We require a larger staff, the classes are so varied. The pupils range in age from five to twenty or over, and necessarily there is a great variety of subjects to be taught, and we must try to do justice to the lowest as well as the highest.

1274. How do you hold your premises?—We have a lease to the present Archbishop of Tuam.

1275. Dr. Traill.—Who is the lease from?—The interest in the lease was purchased from Captain Thompson.

1276. Lord Justice FitzGibbon.—Do you pay rent?—Yes, to Mr. Staunford, a gentleman in Loughrea. He holds the property.

Oct. 13, 1888.

Rev. Brother John Patrick Lynch.

1277. Have you a long term?—We are secure for about twenty years.

1278. Lord Justice NAISH.—What is the rent?—We pay, after the allowance for taxes, between £10 and £11 a year.

1279. Lord Justice FITZGIBBON.—I suppose your governing body are all Roman Catholics?—The school is completely under the control of the members of the order, and of our ecclesiastical superior, the Bishop of the diocese.

1280. Are your boys all Roman Catholics?—At present they are, but we have received Protestant pupils.

1281. You take any pupils who pay the fees?—Yes. Protestants and Presbyterians have come to be taught navigation.

1282. What provision have you for teaching navigation?—I have some of the mathematical instruments and books necessary for the purpose.

1283. For great circle sailing and that kind of thing?—I don't know about great circle sailing, but Mercator's system and other systems.

1284. You have no means of teaching practical navigation?—No.

1285. Dr. TRAILL.—You are not on an island?—Like the Venetians.

1286. Lord Justice FITZGIBBON.—We saw a school building to-day called "The Piscatory school"; is any instruction in navigation or fishing given there?—That object is not carried out. The poor Claddagh men do not decide in that way, though in others they are. It has been turned into a National school, and is very efficiently taught. But the fishing part has been discontinued.

1287. Is it your experience that neither will fishermen leave fishing, nor agriculturalists agriculture?—Yes.

1288. Have you any bequests or funded property belonging to the school?—The community in charge of the institution are obliged to supplement from our own private funds the fees received from the National Board, otherwise the school would not be self-supporting. I don't covet what belongs to anybody else, but if there were a re-arrangement of any endowments, I think we would have a claim, because we educate children of every class. No person is excluded on account of his social position; if he be properly conducted and decently clothed, he is taken in, and paid as much attention to as the highest. Country gentlemen send their sons from the country to our school; and persons of the most respectable class in Galway send their children to us; but also, a very considerable portion of our pupils are the children of persons who reside on the lands of Erasmus Smith; and we teach those things that he wished to be taught in his schools.

1289. Rev. Dr. MOLLOY.—Could you say roughly how many of your pupils are the children of tenants of Erasmus Smith's estate?—I could not, but I could find out very readily.

1290. You might send us a return?—Yes, I can.

1291. Where is the property of Erasmus Smith in this neighbourhood?—A considerable portion of it is in the west of the city; there is a portion through the town.

1292. How far is it from your school?—Parts of it two miles, and parts of it less. Very good children come to us from there, some of whom are learning Latin, and aspiring to the ecclesiastical state.

1293. Dr. TRAILL.—Would you be content to take any of the funds of Erasmus Smith on the terms on which he left them?—I don't think we would.

1294. Lord Justice FITZGIBBON.—I suppose you would not like to teach Bishop Usher's catechism?—No.

1295. Professor DOUGHERTY.—Would you object to the catechism of the Assembly of Divines?—Oh, yes.

1296. Lord Justice NAISH.—What Latin is taught in your school?—We teach Virgil, Cicero, Livy, Cæsar; and we also teach Greek. I had a class—or at least a pupil—who was reading the Alcestis of Euripides.

1297. Lord Justice FITZGIBBON.—For the Intermediate Examinations?—Yes.

1298. Did you send any pupils this year to the Intermediate Examinations?—I did not send any lately. We found that we should be doing an injustice to the pupils that we had if we were to prepare them for the Intermediate course.

1299. Why?—Because I found that boys who passed creditably at the Intermediate examinations in the special subjects were nevertheless completely ignorant of other matters that were actually essential.

1300. Lord Justice NAISH.—Do you mean in subjects that it would not pay them to take up for the Intermediate course?—Yes. The portion, say of geography, prescribed for the junior grade, is attended to very carefully, and everything else connected with geography is neglected. The books of Euclid which are prescribed are very carefully attended to, but the far more practical and essential knowledge of mensuration is completely neglected. It is very rarely that questions are given in mensuration which is far more practical than the other parts of geometry for persons of the class I teach.

1301. Lord Justice FITZGIBBON.—According to your experience are the Intermediate courses not sufficiently practical?—They are not, and I also object to the frequent changes in the courses. If I prepare a class in the course for this year, a different course may be set out for the next session, and I think that is an injustice to the children.

1302. Rev. Dr. MOLLOY.—Yes; but the changes in the courses are rather changes in the books that are read in foreign languages; they are not changes in those things that are of a permanent character; they always have the same books of Euclid for the same grade, and the same portion of algebra?—Yes; the changes are principally in the languages.

1303. Is it not an advantage for the boys if they remain two years in the same grade that they have to read a different course in the second year?—The boys whom we have to educate have a difficulty in providing the books that are necessary.

1304. That difficulty is much less now than it used to be, because books are now published much cheaper, and better than formerly?—No doubt; at the same time there is a difficulty in providing them.

1305. Dr. TRAILL.—The difficulty of expense?—Yes.

1306. Lord Justice FITZGIBBON.—The Christian Brothers taught almost 60 per cent. of all the boys who passed the Intermediate examinations last year. How is it that you find this difficulty, when they don't?—I will tell you the reason. In Dublin, for example, they select from all their schools the pupils that are suited for a certain class. They have masters who pay special attention to that class, and prepare them, and take care of their passing. We have not that facility here, because our numbers are too limited to enable us to make a selection, and to have a teacher to teach such a class.

1307. That is so, no doubt, in places like Cork or Dublin. But we have seen a great number of Christian Brothers schools in places smaller than Galway, for example, in Dundalk they have seventy boys taught by two brothers. Have you ever tried to organise an Intermediate class?—I am trying it this year. I have a class for the Intermediate, and a class for the University. I am making that attempt this year. Last year we did better with the Science and Art Department, South Kensington. We sent in 15, of whom 12 passed very creditably in mathematics.

1308. I believe you get very small results fees for that?—Not much—about £16.

1309. Have you ever tried a class in Natural Philosophy?—Not yet, but we intend to do so. There is a

Sept. 12, 18[illegible]. Rev. Brother John Patrick Lynch.

difficulty there again—the necessary apparatus would be expensive.

1310. Rev. Dr. Molloy.—A little money would relieve you of a great deal of your difficulties?—It would.

1311. Dr. Traill.—Where do your own Order get the means of education?—They are educated in five native colleges, the novitiates of our Institute.

1312. Lord Justice Naish.—Is your Order an Irish Order exclusively?—We have houses in Australia, and a house in India, but it started from Ireland. It was founded by Dr. Delany, Bishop of Kildare, in 1808. It is Irish to the heart's core.

1313. How many houses have you in Ireland?—Five—in Tullow, Mountrath, Fethard, Mallow, and Galway. The mother house is Tullow, but the most important is in Mountrath.

1314. Dr. Traill.—When you prepare boys for Continental colleges do they go there with the view of coming back or of staying on the Continent?—For the ecclesiastical state they go for the most part to the Irish College in Paris and the Augustinian College in Rome.

1315. When they have been taught there do they stay abroad or come back to this country?—They come back.

1316. Would you say half of the boys of the school go into the ecclesiastical state?—No.

1317. Lord Justice FitzGibbon.—Of those who learn Latin what proportion become ecclesiastics?—I could scarcely give you an exact answer; a very small proportion.

1318. Lord Justice Naish.—How many of your boys are learning Latin at present?—Between twenty and thirty.

1319. Dr. Traill.—How many are learning Greek?—Not many.

1320. I suppose no one goes into the ecclesiastical order without learning Greek?—Lately, I am told, that some of the regular orders are not very particular about Greek; they require a good knowledge of Latin, but they rarely require Greek at the entrance examination.

1321. Lord Justice FitzGibbon.—When you speak of the ecclesiastical state you don't confine yourself to your own order?—No; we don't consider our order as ecclesiastical; we are not in orders.

1322. Rev. Dr. Molloy.—You send pupils to the Irish College in Paris?—We send them to the Irish College in Paris and to the Augustinian and Dominican Colleges in Rome. Several have also gone to the medical profession.

1323. Do you prepare for the Queen's College?—We don't prepare them for it, but they go there.

1324. Lord Justice Naish.—They are educated there?—Well, I dare say the laymen are some of them.

1325. Lord Justice FitzGibbon.—Assuming that there were any money available from the State for Intermediate Education, what is your great want?—I think books for the pupils, apparatus for the science classes, and the means of supporting an additional teacher. We don't want to make money. The object of our order is the education of the youth, and if we could get help I would be very glad.

1326. What are the largest result fees in any one year that you got from the Intermediate Board?—In one year thirteen of our pupils passed and we got about £16 or £19 for them. We discontinued for a while preparing pupils for the Intermediate, but we have a class in preparation this year.

1327. Do you find any additional expense in sending pupils up to the Intermediate examinations?—No expense on us, but the pupils incur expense in providing the necessary books.

1328. You were unable to supply them with books?—We supplied some, we could not supply all; our means would not allow us. Some of the children are so very poor that even the trifling expense of providing books would be an obstacle to them.

1329. Dr. Traill.—Would such children want Intermediate education if they were going to become farmers or labouring men?—I don't see what advantage it would be to them.

1330. I suppose you would confine Intermediate education to the clever boys of that class—you would not take a boy that was not very clever, give him an Intermediate education, and then let him go back to labour or the plough?—That was another of our reasons for discontinuing the class. We thought it would be an injustice to the boys to set them to work very hard on courses that never would be of any practical use to them in life.

1331. What proportion of the boys you educate from that class would you consider, on an average, to have sufficient talent to go forward to an Intermediate course?—As a rule the boys are talented. I can't say they are not so industrious as they [illegible] should be, but they are talented. I think almost all the boys when they come to a proper age would be capable of passing an Intermediate examination, if there were any reason for their not doing it.

1332. But they are not industrious?—Not so industrious, indeed, as we desire.

1333. How do you encourage them, do you apply corporal punishment?—I am very unwilling to make use of it at my age, after teaching for nearly half a century, but still I find it necessary; I cannot get on without it.

1334. Rev. Dr. Molloy.—We should wish you to send us a return of the number of your pupils for the last three years who were the children of tenants on the Erasmus Smith property. Also kindly draw up a return of the colleges to which your pupils who have received a higher education have gone, showing what work you are doing for the people of the locality, as well as for the young men going abroad for ecclesiastical training.

Witness.—I shall do that with pleasure. I shall send both documents to your office.

1335. Lord Justice FitzGibbon.—We can print your return along with the evidence. We want to present as fully and fairly as we can an account of the education in each locality. Your school is exempt from the operation of the Act, as having no endowment, as well as on the denominational ground.

LOMBARD STREET NATIONAL SCHOOL.

The Rev. *Peter Dooley* sworn and examined.

1336. Lord Justice FitzGibbon.—You are the manager of the Lombard street school?—I am.

1337. It is in connexion with the National Board?—It is.

1338. You are the parish priest?—I am; of St. Nicholas', East and North.

1339. What are the parishes in the town of Galway?—We had formerly St. Nicholas', South and West, also. There were four divisions formerly, but there are only two now.

1340. They were divisions of the old wardenship?—Yes.

1341. The town is now formed into two parishes, and you are the parish priest of both?—Yes.

1342. Is Lombard-street the principal primary school of your parish?—It is.

1343. What is the number of pupils?—The average for the last quarter was 257 in attendance. The number on the roll is over 300. They are principally the very poorest children of the town; and many of

Oct. 11, 1888.

Rev. Peter Dooley.

there are the children of fishermen, and almost themselves when they have no clothing, so that their attendance is very irregular.

1344. Does the school include boys and girls?—No—boys only.

1345. Where do the girls of the parish get their education?—At the Convent of Mercy principally, and a large proportion at the Presentation Convent.

1346. About how many girls are in those two schools?—There are about 1,000 pupils in both—or something over it—800 girls and 200 infant boys.

1347. What other primary schools for poor boys are there besides your school?—I have another school on the outskirts of the town, called the Bohermore National school, it is a mixed school. There was a large number of children who went through the town with milk, and who could not be at the Lombard-street school before the roll was called, and so I got the National Board to consent to Bohermore being a mixed school, so that they might turn in there. The principal dairies are in the locality.

1348. How many pupils are at Bohermore?—Sixty.

1349. What primary schools are there in the other part of the town?—There is that monastery school at the Claddagh, mentioned a while ago, which 100 boys are attending—it is a National school now—and there is a female school there at which about forty children are attending.

1350. Was there at any recent time any special instruction given in fishing industries here?—No.

1351. Is there any possibility of establishing it?—We would rather have it now in connexion with our Industrial school. We are waiting to see what will come. I think that the grand juries of both the county and the town would prefer that the boys should be sent to our own school under the Industrial Schools Act. It is within 200 or 300 yards of us.

1352. How many pupils are in the Industrial school?—Two hundred. It is the second largest in Ireland.

1353. Are many of these fishermen's children?—A large number of them are from Galway.

1354. Dr. Traill.—Are they all committed by the magistrates?—Yes.

1355. Could you not teach fishing industries to people who have not been committed under the Act of Parliament?—I dare say we would get the Claddagh boys to go into that. They have a taste for nothing else in the world. The most boy of fishermen's families here are altogether about two hundred.

1356. What is the nature of the fishing?—Herrings.

1357. The herring fishing only lasts a short time?—A short time; but then they go in for cod fishing, and also whiting, pollock, and mackerel fishing. They don't go outside the Islands of Arran.

1358. Your boats are not large?—Not very large.

1359. Rev. Dr. Molloy.—You might have a better class of boats?—At present the son does exactly what his father did, and no more.

1360. Is there any net making?—Very little. The wives of the Claddagh fishermen make nets, but nets are so cheap now that it is not worth their while to do so.

1361. But a good deal can be saved if they make their own nets and repair them?—A great deal.

1362. Lord Justice FitzGibbon.—Is there any boat-building?—All the small boats are built here. There are ship carpenters in town as well.

1363. Rev. Dr. Molloy.—New methods could be introduced?—Yes, if the learning were made compulsory.

1364. At present do they teach anything at the Industrial school in connexion with the special industries of Galway, such as boat building and net making?—No, nothing except the ordinary trades, as at Artane.

1365. Dr. Traill.—But these ordinary trades are of no use to fishermen?—No, but if we could have fishing taught like any other trade it would be useful. We have a large number of children from along the Connemara coast who would prefer that to any other trade—carpentering or anything else that they know nothing about.

1366. Lord Justice FitzGibbon.—To come back to your own school—in a former report it appears that this Lombard-street school has a site and school premises of the annual value of £30 10s., and bequests and donations invested, and producing altogether £100 a year?—Yes, it is more than that at present.

1367. How do you hold the site and school premises?—Free. It was the site of an artillery barrack formerly. Warden French, who was Bishop of Galway at the time—the last of the Wardens of Galway—purchased the site from the military authorities in 1822.

1368. In whom is it vested at present?—I really never could see the lease of it.

1369. Lord Justice Naish.—There is no rent?—No rent, it is a fee-simple property.

1370. What ground have you?—A small plot. Our house forms one side of the plot, and the school premises form two other sides.

1371. Lord Justice FitzGibbon.—I believe there was a further assignment in 18[illegible] of some additional ground?—There was, and of more ground since then.

1372. It is also stated in the report that you have two hundred acres of bog somewhere?—We have, near Tuam.

1373. How is it held?—In fee. The late Father Peter Daly purchased it with an accumulation of some donations that he had on hands.

1374. In whom is it vested?—In the present Archbishop of Tuam, the Bishop of Galway, and myself; but it is being transferred from the Archbishop of Tuam to the present Bishop of Galway.

1375. Whenever there are vacancies you must have a new deed?—A new deed.

1376. How much does each new assignment cost?—I don't know, it is in the solicitor's hands.

1377. You should consult your bishop and co-trustees and ascertain whether they desire to put an end to that sort of thing. You could incorporate the Bishop of Galway, the Bishop of Tuam, the Parish Priest, and any others you like to name as a corporate body if you please, to hold the property, so as to have no more deeds of conveyance?—I should be very glad.

1378. Dr. Traill.—Who manages the bog?—I collect the rents myself. It is reclaimed bog.

1379. Do you get money for the turf?—Nothing for the turf. The tenants have a right to cut as much turf as they like and sell it in Tuam. They cultivate and till the reclaimed portion.

1380. How do you mean a right?—The bog is their own property, and we let them cut as much as they like. They are supposed to pay us nothing for the turf but only for the reclaimed portion. The gross rent of it is £[illegible] 2s., but the amount I received last year was £[illegible] [illegible]s. [illegible]d.

1381. How was that?—Because the rents paid by the tenants are from £1 to £[illegible] a year each. Last summer twelvemonths was very dry, so that the bog and the corn got dried up, and they could get no one to buy it from them.

1382. Then you had to make a reduction in your rents?—I did not; but they paid as much as they could.

1383. Have you to collect the rents personally?—I do. They complained of bailiffs more than of the rent itself.

1384. Would you not be better off if you sold the property?—We would; but who would we get to buy it?

1385. The tenants?—We offered it to them.

1386. Are there any agricultural holdings or houses on your lands?—On the verge of the bog.

1387. How many acres of bog?—[illegible]. There are

100 acres on a solid basis. All the rest is like the bog of Allen.

1388. Why don't you get money for it?—How could we get it?—Who would buy it?

1389. Why don't you charge for the turf?—Who would buy it? The whole country is bog. You might as well ask me why don't we sell stones in Galway. Everybody has enough.

1390. Lord Justice FitzGibbon.—As I understand you, the whole surface of the 300 acres is in the hands of the tenants?—In the hands of the tenants.

1391. And those tenants, in order to clear the lands, cut the turf?—Yes.

1392. Surely there ought to be some profit out of that, enabling them to pay their rents?—They did pay until this last year.

1393. Dr. Traill.—Would it not be worth £1 an acre if they sell it?—It is not worth 4d., it is so abundant. They have no market for it. After the expense of cutting, drying, and carrying it they get 3s. 6d. a ton for it in Tuam.

1394. Turf is a drug in the Tuam market?—Of course.

1395. Rev. Dr. Molloy.—Why would not the tenants purchase under Lord Ashbourne's Act?—I made them an offer at fifteen years purchase.

1396. Lord Justice FitzGibbon.—If they only pay you £12 a year out of £25, and you sell to them for fifteen years purchase on that rental, you will do well?—I would do very well; but it was when I got double the amount that I made the offer of fifteen years purchase.

1397. I see that a Mr. Lynch, in 1834, gave £91, and that there were also donations, a mortgage, and bank shares belonging to the school?—Yes. The amount produced by the mortgage is £16 5s. a year.

1398. On what property is that secured?—The property of Mr. Donnellan, a gentleman near Woodlawn.

1399. Is your interest paid up?—Regularly.

1400. The money is well secured?—Well secured. We also have some shares in the London and Westminster Bank, and twenty-four shares in the National Bank.

1401. Who are the trustees of those securities?—For the London and Westminster Bank shares I am trustee myself. There are three trustees altogether, all ecclesiastics.

1402. What is your annual income altogether?—The gross income is £234 1s., including the landed property and some houses that we have.

1403. Where are the houses?—On Nun's Island. They are liable to £7 7s. 6d. ground rent. They are two old houses. We have very little interest in them.

1404. How do you apply the endowment?—We pay the Brothers of St. Patrick £185 for giving education to the poor boys of the town.

1405. In the Lombard-street school?—We pay it in lieu of school fees. They must admit any boys from the town.

1406. I suppose they also get capitation grants from the National Board?—They do.

1407. How do you dispose of the rest?—I don't get much. I debited myself with £50 last year, and I only got £18. Then there are quit rents and tithe-rentcharge to pay.

1408. There is a statement in the old report that 150 of the poorest boys got a free breakfast; do you continue that?—We do, but that is independent of the school. It has a fund of its own. There are donations.

1409. That is all the property you have got?—All that we have got.

1410. This is a case in which, if you wish, we can do something for you by giving you a scheme; we can save you expense if we cannot give you money. Under the Act every scheme must provide for inspection and annual audit. You are already under the National Board, and the inspection of the National Board is deemed sufficient in our schemes. The effect of a scheme would be to vest, without a deed, all your property in trustees of your own selection, not as individuals, but as members of an incorporated governing body. You can bring these matters before your bishop and co-trustees. We must declare your school exempt, except by consent. A good many people think that by giving consent they put themselves into our power to dispose of their property against their will. That is not so. In consent cases we prepare a draft scheme on getting an intimation that it is desired by the governing body, but we don't sign it until they have seen what it is, and are prepared to take it. We don't exercise the jurisdiction of the Act against the will of anyone who comes under it only by consent.

Witness.—I hope that we shall be able to be incorporated so as to have all our diocesan property under one management.

1411. Rev. Dr. Molloy.—We could do that for you.

Witness.—Including the breakfast institution and everything else?

1412. Lord Justice FitzGibbon.—Yes. Every time that you transfer your shares it costs you money, and there is also a risk. If you should omit to appoint trustees, forgetting that a change of office does not carry a change of trust property, you would have to go to the heir or personal representative of the last trustee to complete your title, and your tenants might give you a great deal of trouble, if you could not find the legal trustee. All these things our Act was intended to get rid of; but it is a voluntary matter for you entirely. For your encouragement I may tell you that the Presbyterians, who generally have their eyes open for anything that is good, are applying for the incorporation of a body to hold their funds, and so are the greater number of the dioceses of the Disestablished Church. If your bishops are considering about it, they had better not wait too long, for our powers will expire next March twelvemonths.

PARSONS PERSSE'S CHARITY (ILLERTON SCHOOL).

1413. Lord Justice FitzGibbon.—This case has been sent to us by the Commissioners of Charitable Donations and Bequests, as, in their opinion, the case is one which would be more satisfactorily dealt with by the present Commission. The endowment is under a will proved on September 21, 1812, by which Parsons Persse left an annuity of £25 a year charged on certain lands to pay the salary of a schoolmaster at Illerton, the school to be a free school for the children of the tenants on the testator's estate in the county of Galway. A scheme was framed on October 5, 1853—forty-one years afterwards—by which it was directed that a schoolhouse should be erected on the lands of Illerton, and that the arrears of the annuity should be applied in the purchase of school requisites and the erection of the necessary premises. The amount of the residue in the Commissioners' hands is £335 15s. 2d., with £16 [illegible] accumulated. In 1878 the school was discontinued, the Commissioners of National Education having reported that it was impracticable to re-establish it. An application was made to the Commissioners of Charitable Donations and Bequests by the representatives of the testator and others that the income should be transferred to a school at Kilchreest. The Commissioners resolved that as soon as a school

Oct. [illegible], 18[illegible].

at Kildrennt should be in operation they would consider favourably any application for making to transfer the endowment. Instructions were issued accordingly to carry out that object; but recently the Commissioners have been informed that the attempt to start the school at Kildrennt has failed. It is therefore necessary to frame a new scheme for the application of the property. It appears that there are five years of the rentcharge not paid. We put the event of the rentcharge in the list in order to ascertain if there were any persons from the localities of Riverton or Kildrennt who could tell us anything about it. If not, we will enter into a correspondence on the subject.

Mr. *Edward Townsend*, C.E.—I don't know where Riverton is, but Kildrennt is near Loughrea.

1414. Lord Justice FitzGibbon.—Can anyone tell us where Mr. Burton Persse's estate is which is charged with the endowment?

Mr. *Perry*, County Surveyor.—I know where it is.

1415. Do you know the extent of it?—No, I do not. The greater part of it is not in my district.

1416. Do you know if any school is in operation on the estate at all?—I do not.

1417. Lord Justice FitzGibbon.—We will report to the Commissioners that no person attended in Galway in reference to this school, but we will ascertain who the agent of the estate is, and will endeavour to summon him to Tuam.

ROCKFIELD INSTITUTION, CLIFDEN.

1418. Lord Justice FitzGibbon.—I have to state the facts connected with the Rockfield Institution. This is a case in which a mass of papers have been sent to us by the Commissioners of Charitable Donations and Bequests. I have tried to summarise the history of the endowment. The foundation was under the will of Colonel Daniel Lyons, proved in 1812. He was a colonel in the East India service, and left £12,000 to be invested, the interest to be spent in paying a number of charitable annuities to institutions chiefly situated in Dublin. There was to be an accumulated fund of £1,000 more to keep up the interest to the sum necessary to meet the annuities in case of the reduction of the interest on the Government funds, in which the £12,000 was to be invested. Therefore there should have been £13,000 altogether. The oversight of these charitable bequests was given to the magistrates of Loughrea, and the clergymen of the Established Church, and of the Roman Catholic religion. These bequests included a sum for distribution among the Loughrea poor. We have nothing to do with that portion of the will, and I don't know the funds are now forthcoming. I must read in full the portion of the will relating to Rockfield, which is as follows:—

"Should it please the Almighty to prolong my life a few years, I purpose expending the whole of my personal property, exclusive of the aforesaid donations, in the purchase of a small landed estate, which shall be entailed and inherited by my nephew, Thomas Bell, and his lawful heirs, on condition of assuming my surname and professing the Protestant religion, and conforming in every particular to the terms of this my will, together with his heirs in succession possessing my estate, and never, upon any pretence whatever, cutting off the entail, and in disobedience of which the aforesaid estate is to devolve to my nephew, Robert Bell, and his lawful heirs, who shall conform to the conditions of my will, or relinquish the aforesaid estate. In that event the estate is to devolve on my nephew, John McNevin, and his heirs, subject to all the conditions of my will. If the above-mentioned estate, in process of time, becomes a matter of dispute amongst remote relations, all claim thereto is to be finally settled by a clergyman of the Established Church, and four magistrates of the town of Loughrea (and its vicinity), and on their recommendation to a barrister, the claimants should forfeit the aforesaid estate. In failure of such male heirs, the aforesaid estate shall devolve to the next female branch of my relations conforming to all the conditions of my will. Having lately perused Mr. Brougham's letter to Sir [illegible] [illegible], Rendlg, describing an establishment in Switzerland (Canton of Berne), on Mr. Fellenberg's estate, the institution appears to me worthy of imitation, and I trust ere long very many gentlemen in Ireland will adopt Mr. Fellenberg's plan in all its branches. I therefore desire it to be considered a positive condition of my last will and testament that [illegible] Irish acres of the aforesaid estate shall always be appropriated in meadow, wheat, barley, hemp, potatoes, etc., etc., for the purpose of annually carrying into full effect every part of Mr. Fellenberg's institution, except the academy for young gentlemen. The agricultural institution and to consist of [illegible] or [illegible] boys, who are to be taught farming, and to conform in every particular to Mr. Fellenberg's institution. The seminary for poor children of the lowest order in the town of Loughrea, and vicinity of [illegible], never to exceed forty boys. This branch of Mr. Fellenberg's establishment is particularly deserving the most serious attention. It will therefore require constant vigilance, and unremitting care in the schoolmaster and usher to whom the boys are entrusted, on all occasions to bear in mind the system laid down by Mr. Fellenberg. On this subject an English translation (Rapport) from Fellenberg's de Hofwyl to remain at all times in the seminary, for the teachers' guidance, the principles of the system regarding the children never to be lost sight of, treating them with gentleness, kindness, and affection, and in all respects agreeable to Mr. Fellenberg's plan. The aforesaid boys are to be educated in reading, writing, arithmetic, and maintained on the produce of my estate, together with the aid of their labour. An intelligent schoolmaster and usher, to whom care the boys shall be entrusted, shall receive a salary of £[illegible] per annum—the usher £[illegible] per annum. A small house shall be erected for the schoolmaster, with an acre of ground annexed, near the seminary; he is also to have the grazing of two cows free of rent; the usher to reside in the seminary. Either the schoolmaster or usher shall at all times breakfast and dine with their pupils. Morning and evening prayers of the Established Church shall be read by the schoolmaster or usher before the boys set out for their daily labour, and in the evening, on retiring to bed, every boy maintained in the aforesaid institution shall be supplied with a Prayer Book of the Established Church, together with the Homilies of the Church of England. The schoolmaster and usher shall be members of the Church of England. The thirty-nine Articles of our Church shall be read to all the boys by the schoolmaster or usher on the first Monday in every month, and on the second Monday the Commandments and Catechism; every boy in the seminary shall get them by heart, and in failure of which he shall be discharged the seminary. Boys under nine years of age are not expected to fulfil the above conditions. The schoolmaster and usher shall each be supplied a Bible. Either the former or latter are enjoined to accompany the boys to and from Divine Service every Sunday or Holyday. The greater number of boys maintained and educated in the seminary are required to profess the Protestant religion, as by law established. Should, however, a difficulty arise in completing the required number, boys of the Roman Catholic religion to be admitted, but only one-third of the whole. Each boy's christian and surname, day of the month, and year, to be written in his Prayer Book and Homilies, Spelling, Arithmetic, and every book required in the seminary, and delivered over to each boy. The schoolmaster to remain in the seminary for the use of boys who are to succeed to them leaving the institution. Boys shall not be received under six years of age, nor discharged before the close of the fourteenth year, who they are to be made over to their parents or nearest relations, but if orphans, unless immediate employment can be procured, such individual should be apprenticed three or five years to a farmer. The ten boys is to be always completed to the number of [illegible]. The seminary is constantly to be supplied with abundance of writing paper, blank slates, pencils, quills, and ink, turf, candles, &c.; each boy to be furnished with good bed sheets and blankets, knife and fork, a hat, or leather cap, two pair of strong shoes annually, trowsers, waistcoat, milk pails, and cooking utensils, and servants to be supplied by my heirs when required. The boys of the seminary on all occasions to be maintained in a frugal and plentiful manner on potatoes, butter, skim [illegible] [illegible]

soft, and buttermilk, and abundance of vegetables, which they are to be taught to cultivate for their own use; a large piggery to be established, to prevent the necessity of purchasing in the market; three fat cows shall be slaughtered annually, for the use of the seminary. Mr. Fellenberg's plans on this head to be observed or improved upon. Should it be thought eligible, all the boys to dine at the same table. Small and large [illegible] to be [illegible] and to each boy with his name stamped on each. A few pair of scissors to cut for the use of the seminary. The manufactory of agricultural implements, similar to Mr. Fellenberg's in all its branches, to be established on a large or moderate scale, agreeable to the inclination and taste of my successors. And also a coarse cloth manufactory, called [illegible], and a coarse linen manufactory, shall be established on the aforesaid estate, for the purpose of having a sufficient annual supply of [illegible] and linen to make an annual suit of clothes and shirts, sheeting, tablecloths, and blankets, for every boy belonging to the seminary. Whenever leisure moments occur, some portion of time should be devoted in teaching the boys to knit yarn stockings for their own use. They should also learn to mend their clothes. A few old women should be constantly employed in spinning thread and yarn for the above manufactory. Wool and hemp to be regularly supplied by my heirs, sufficient for both manufactories. A piece of ground, consisting of a [illegible], enclosed with a strong wall of solid masonry, 8 feet high, to be appropriated for the use and instruction of the boys belonging to the seminary; fruit trees of all sorts, and vegetables planted therein. A careful intelligent gardener to be superintended by my heirs for this purpose, and his salary paid by them. Whatever unforeseen circumstances may have escaped my recollection, or through ignorance regarding the seminary, &c., &c., I desire it to be considered an essential condition of my last will and testament, that no sort of deficiency shall occur in amply supplying the boys of the seminary with every article heretofore stated, together with those now overlooked, when required, by the schoolmaster: spades, shovels, pitchforks, [illegible] and garden rakes, garden knives, &c., &c., to be supplied by my heirs. My successor to the aforesaid estate shall, within one month after taking possession, nominate his executors, not less than six gentlemen, in whom the management of the aforesaid estate shall devolve in the event of my successor's sudden death, or a long minority. This rule shall be constantly observed by my heirs; their names shall always be notified to the magistrates of Loughrea. Reserving the necessary cultivation and expected produce of 250 Irish acres of land very ample to support the seminary, and carry into effect the agricultural Institution, together with every expense of the [illegible] and stores from manufactory, and desirous of guarding against the neglect or wilful abuse of the aforesaid charitable institution by my successors, in that case I do hereby will and empower four magistrates of the town of Loughrea and its vicinity to prosecute and eject by regular course of law the possessor of the aforesaid estate. It is then to devolve to his lawful heir, or the next person in possession. Should an ejectment take place, the expenses incurred shall be defrayed by my successors. This mode of prosecution to be invariably pursued when absolutely necessary. The abovementioned magistrates are requested to visit and inspect minutely the aforesaid estate, institution, manufactory, &c., &c., twice a year; their travelling expenses shall be defrayed by the possessor of the aforesaid estate, and who it is hoped on such occasions will manifest Irish hospitality without holding the decanter, as formerly, to force the guests to drink."

I have read all these minute directions, to illustrate, by the history of this endowment, the futility of good intentions of the sort, and also that the intentions of the testator, the spirit of which it is our duty now to see carried out, are illusory. From 1819 until 1837 nothing appears to have been done. On August 24, 1837, the then Bishop of Tuam called the attention of the Board of Charitable Donations and Bequests to the will, and pointed out that no school was yet in operation. A correspondence took place during 1837 and 1838, which resulted in nothing; the matter appears to have been dropped until 1851. In 1851 the Commissioners of Charitable Donations and Bequests took it up again, and brought the matter into Chancery, to endeavour to carry out the wishes of the testator. There was a great deal of correspondence, and proceedings took place about that time, which resulted in showing that no estate had ever been bought; that the greater part of the testator's property had disappeared, but an estate, now known as Heathfield, was bought in 1863 with the sanction of the Court of Chancery, not in the vicinity of Loughrea, but in the farthest west of Connemara, within two miles of Letterfrack. The lands were bought for £3,316 13s. 11d. Consols, equal to £3,000 cash, apparently estimated as a sum sufficient to carry out the trusts of the will. The lands contain 540 acres statute measure, and were conveyed to Thomas Bell, his heirs and assigns, for ever, but on trust for the purposes of the charitable institution mentioned in an order of Master Litton, of January 12, 1863, made by the late Edward Litton, then one of the Masters in Chancery. That conveyance, therefore, amounted to a devoting of £3,000, part of Colonel Lynch's personalty to the purchase of a fee-simple estate, to be held upon the charitable trusts that I have read, as modified by a scheme settled in Chancery in 1863, some forty-four years after the death of the testator. The material provisions of the scheme are, that Thomas Bell was to carry out the trusts; that he was declared entitled to the residue of the testator's personal and real estate, after setting apart £3,000 for the purchase of these lands, and that the lands should be applied to maintain an educational establishment on the principles of the will, and that these lands were an equivalent to an endowment for that purpose. £500 more was applied from the funds for supplying stock and materials to start the institution, and directions were given authorising the purchase of this estate in Connemara, upon which to establish the industrial and agricultural, and self-supporting educational institution, which the testator wished to found. The conveyance was executed shortly after, and I greatly fear the subsequent correspondence shows that the testator's desire that wheat and other crops should be grown was as little regarded as his desire that the vicinity of Loughrea should be selected, for it appears that, with a very small exception, the lands for which £3,000 was paid consist of mountain and bog. Things went on somehow until 1870—seven years after the purchase—when an application was made on the part of Thomas Bell to appoint his own brother, Robert Bell, to be manager of the establishment. It was reported to the Commissioners of Charitable Donations and Bequests that this appointment would be the final destruction of the entire institution. They then sent Professor Baldwin down to see the place, and he reported that he found the institution alongside the public road between Clifden and Letterfrack; that it was a misapplication of terms to call it an agricultural school at all; that it had no attribute which he conceived should belong to an agricultural school; and that the pupils that were there did not appear to him to be fit subjects for a boarding agricultural school. He also said that a boy from the institution had come before him a few years before, along with a number of lads from other parts of Ireland, seeking admission as a free pupil into the Government Agricultural Training School at Glasnevin, but was unable to answer a single question that was put to him. He reported as to the land that no systematic course of management had been pursued with respect to it; that it was almost all in grass or waste; and that the grass, at the time of his visit, was eaten by graziers. He expressed his opinion in these words—

"I regard the school as calculated to create a distaste in the minds of those who would otherwise feel disposed to promote agricultural education; and viewing it in this light I would express my opinion that it ought to be discontinued forthwith or put on a proper footing."

That communication was addressed by Professor Baldwin to the Commissioners of Charitable Donations and Bequests on May 30, 1872, nine years after £3,000 had been spent by Chancery, with their concurrence, in buying this place. Nothing was done. The appointment of the manager seems to have been dropped, and from a body of correspondence of that period I send a letter of May 23, 1873, addressed by the Rev. Mr. Fleming, the chairman, and Mr. Ashman, a member of the then "Managing Committee" of it, to the Commissioners of Charitable Donations and Bequests, who are addressed as if they had never heard of the place before, and are given a melancholy but striking summary of its history—

"Rockfield Agricultural Institution,
"Ballinakill, Clifden, co. Galway.
"May 23rd, 1873.

"To the Commissioners of Charitable Donations
and Bequests for Ireland.

"Gentlemen,—We desire respectfully to bring under your notice the following particulars relative to the "Agricultural and Educational Institution of Galway," otherwise known as the Rockfield Agricultural Institution. The late Lieut.-Colonel Daniel Lyons left a certain sum of money to establish in the county Galway an institution for educating and training youths in agriculture. A good deal of litigation ensued which absorbed a large portion of the bequest before it could be made available. At length the present farm was purchased for the sum of £3,000, and an addition built to the house at the cost of £800, in order to make it suitable for the purposes for which it was intended. This almost exhausted the entire capital that was placed at the disposal of the committee, to whose management the institution was handed over by the Master in Chancery. The consequence has been that the institution, never having had a fair start for want of funds, has always been in a struggling condition. The house, which is an excellent one, capable of accommodating forty boys, stands on the farm, which contains nearly 600 acres, the greater portion of which is comparatively unproductive for want of proper drainage and cultivation, but most of it is capable of being made very fair land. There are abundance of turbary and limestone on the farm, also, close by, any quantity of good sea sand which is an excellent manure for reclaiming land. The house requires repairing. The farmyard, a large walled one, also needs some outlay. The Committee feel confident that if they could obtain a loan of £1,000 for the improvement of the farm, it would go a good way towards making the institution self-supporting, and they would be enabled to admit twenty boys at once. We therefore request that you will kindly authorise us to raise a loan of £1,000 on the security of the farm. This appears to us to be the only feasible way of carrying out the intention of the founder, as without funds, the institution cannot get on. The Committee will of course see that the funds are expended to the best possible advantage.

"We beg to remain, gentlemen,
"Your faithful and obedient servants,

"Thomas H. Fleming, Chairman of Committee.
"A. E. Ashman, Member of Committee."

During the year of 1875 there was a good deal of correspondence, which resulted in the Commissioners obtaining a census of the population of the town of Loughrea and of the county of Galway, and of their religious professions, apparently with some notion of making the place useful for Loughrea and its vicinity, but nothing was done. They did not apparently feel at liberty to allow the £1,000 to be borrowed; but Mr. Gernon, their Secretary, visited the place, and Mr. Baldwin was sent again, and encouraged them by the example of the then rather prosperous Agricultural School at Glasnevin, in the county of Westmeath, where, I may mention, agricultural teaching was afterwards abandoned. They also applied to some of the gentlemen of the neighbourhood for information; and on October 10, 1873, they got this report from Mr. Mitchell Henry:—

"I can tell you very little about the Rockfield Agricultural School, except that I have an impression that it is a very waste. A great portion of the lands are let, and some of them I rent for grazing; but I take no interest in the school and indeed have never visited it, because when it was brought here some years ago I said that it was an absurd thing to try in this locality. At the same time, several gentlemen do take an interest in it, and I have no doubt the Rector of the parish does also, and he (Mr. Fleming) is a very conscientious and competent man."

The correspondence then dropped until 1879, when it was taken up again by Mr. Fleming in the following letter to the Secretary of the Commissioners of Charitable Donations and Bequests:—

"Ballinakill Rectory, Clifden,
"Co. Galway, May 16th, 1879.

"My dear Sir,—You may recollect that some years ago you paid a visit to an Educational and Agricultural Institution in this parish which was purchased by a bequest of a Colonel Lyons. After the purchase of the farm and the building of the house there was a debt of over £900 on the place. You proposed that a portion of the property should be sold in order to pay the debt, and also to realise a sum of money to start the institution. However, the Committee did not like, if it could be avoided, to part with any of the property. We made an appeal to the public which brought in but a mere trifle. The Rev. Canon Cory, Rector of Clifden (one of the Committee) and myself raised on our own personal security as much money as was necessary (£300) in order that the institution might be started. Ever since it has maintained on an average from eighteen to twenty boys, and is now in full working order under the care of an excellent master and matron. The house has been furnished, the premises kept in thorough repair, the farm partially stocked, a good deal of the land cropped and improved, and at present there is about £800 worth of property on the place. The Committee now feel that it would be desirable to clear off all debt on the place without stopping the work, and have a few hundred pounds on hand to develop the resources of the farm and enable them to take in a larger number of boys. A sum of £600 would be required for that purpose, and there are but two ways of obtaining it—either by raising a loan on the security of the place, on which the interest merely would have to be paid, or, as you suggested, by disposing of a portion of the property. The Committee have therefore instructed Messrs. Webb, Scott, and Ferguson to look up the title deeds of the place and see what can be done. I feel sure from the kind interest you have already taken in the matter that you will do what you can to further the wishes of the Committee. The institution is much crippled for want of funds in order to carry out the intentions of the founder. Trusting you will excuse the trouble.

"Believe me, dear sir, yours very truly,
"Thomas H. Fleming, Rector of Ballinakill.

"Wm. Gernon, Esq."

Nothing was done, until amongst the papers I find the following letter, six years later, from the Rev. B. M'Andrew, P.P., of Letterfrack, to Mr. Gernon, Secretary of the Commissioners of Charitable Donations and Bequests:—

"Letterfrack, co. Galway,
"April 28, 1885.

"Sir,—Allow me to bring under your notice the Rockfield Institution, in the parish of Ballinakill, Connemara, which has been founded by a charitable bequest left for the benefit of the district, and which is under the control of your Board. This institution is situate in my parish, and I venture to think that my position entitles me to ask to be informed as to the conditions under which the bequest was given. Was it intended that the institution should be purely sectarian? Was it the wish of the donor that the institution founded by his bequest would be under the direction and management of proselytising agents? I shall thank you to give me the information at your earliest convenience. I have already heard quite sufficient to determine me to sift this matter to the bottom by means of the press and House of Commons, as it is not unlikely that an inquiry will unearth a huge scandal which has been tolerated too long.

"I remain your obedient servant,
"B. M'Andrew, P.P.

"To William Gernon, esq., Secretary,
Board of Charitable Bequests, Dublin."

He was then given the will and scheme; and writes—

"With sincere thanks I return your papers. It appears by its constitution to be sectarian, and I may inquire is it in your power to alter that character?"

Of course it was not in their power to alter the character of the institution; but they were bound to see that the institution was conducted in accordance with the trusts. And in July, 1884, inquiry was made of the Commissioners by Mr. Seymour, of Dublin—

"Whether Col. Daniel Lyons's charity had been handed over to the Managers of the Irish Church Missions?"

And one of the publications of that society was brought under the notice of the Commissioners, which enumerated among the schools of the Irish Church Missions this Bostfield Institution, as if it were their property. The Commissioners then wrote to Mr. Fleming to inquire who the present managers were, and received the following reply, which brings this long history down to modern times:—

"Ballinakill Rectory, Clifden, co. Galway.
"January 3rd, 1885.

"Daniel Lyons's Charity, Bostfield Agricultural Institution.

"Dear Sir,—Herewith I send you the information you ask for relative to the Agricultural Institution in this parish, and I will respectfully ask your Board, when considering it, to bear in mind that there are, and have been for over twelve years, practically no funds, except what were collected by the Committee to work the Institution. The Government valuation of the house and land is only £29 15s., and the whole thing, if let to-morrow, would not bring £160 per annum. That would not pay the salaries and maintenance of the master and matron, the taxes on the place, and keep the building in repair. We have an excellent master and matron, to whom we pay (and have done so for the past ten years) a salary of £40 per annum with rations and apartments. There is also an assistant (who was trained at the Institution) and who works on the farm, and has a general supervision of the place, who gets a salary of £10 per annum with clothing, rations, and lodging. It has therefore been only through the greatest exertions on the part of myself and a few friends that the place has been at all kept going. My predecessor have obtained permission from your Board to collect funds from the public, but this appears not to have been availed of to any extent, as I found the place in debt for over £300; no stock on the farm; no furniture in house; the building in dilapidation, and two boys in the Institution.

"In reply to your queries—First, names and addresses of present Committee.

"Rev. Canon Fleming, Ballinakill Rectory, Clifden, county Galway; Rev. G. Hodgson, the Paragon, Blackheath, S.E.; Rev. H. W. Townsend, 11, Vanbrugh Park road, Blackheath, S.E.; (Canon) Lowder, 88, Campden-hill Gardens, W.; Lieut.-Col. Wilmot Brooke, Dale Lodge, Kidbrook-grove, Blackheath, S.E.; J. Gibson Watson, Esq., 20, Clanricarde-gardens, W.; and W. Pasley, Esq., The Limes, Brixton, London. It would be a great help to us if some local gentlemen were on the committee; but there is not one in this part of the country except Mr. Gibson Brown, who resides within two miles of this. He was originally a member, but resigned some fourteen years ago. Some time before I came to this parish I asked him when I came here to allow his name to be put again on the committee, but he declined, saying that the responsibility was too great, as there were no funds to work the Institution. I may here mention that I was one of the members of the first committee which was formed. I was then incumbent of Renvyle, but after a short time I was appointed to another living twenty miles from here, and resigned my seat on the committee. In six years after I got my present living, and then it was I found the place in such a wretched condition. It is very difficult to get persons to act on the committee, besides it is very important to get well known persons (as the present members are) who will command the confidence of those who are likely to help the Institution.

"Secondly, the number of meetings held.

"In 1882—three—members present at two of them, Rev. Canon Cory and Rev. Canon Fleming (myself). At the other, present, Rev. H. W. Townsend, J. Watson, Esq., W. Pasley, Esq., and Rev. Canon Fleming.

"In 1883—three—present at two, Rev. Canon Cory and Rev. Canon Fleming; at the other, present Rev. H. W. Townsend and Rev. Canon Fleming.

"In 1884—three—at one, present Rev. Canon Cory and Rev. Canon Fleming; at two, present Rev. H. W. Townsend and Rev. Canon Fleming. Although there were not any more formal meetings, I have been in constant correspondence with the members of the committee. I visit the Institution, which is quite close, on an average twice a week, and make up accounts once a fortnight. About six months ago Canon Cory resigned his seat on the committee, stating that he had more than he could attend to in his own parish, seven miles from here, and he has since, owing to failing health, resigned a number of the duties of his parish.

"Thirdly, the average number of boys in the Institution for 1882 was twenty; 1883, twenty-one; 1884, twenty-two; and I may add that the average for the past ten years has been twenty-one. On a separate sheet I send the names, ages, &c., of the boys at present in the Institution.

"The committee never thought it necessary to inquire into the religion of the parents; but no boy was ever admitted into the Institution unless it was certified that he was a Protestant, and desired to be educated as such. During the past year (1884) two boys have been sent out into situations, and during the past ten years fifty-one boys have been sent out from the Institution to situations, and almost without an exception have done well. The boys are under no restraint except what is necessary for discipline. A boy can write whenever he chooses (the letters are not inspected) to his friends, who can and do freely visit him, and any parent or guardian may remove a boy at a moment's notice. However, this has never yet been availed of in a single instance since the Institution was opened. So popular is the Institution in the neighbourhood that during the whole of the disturbed times and agitation in this part of the country it never received the slightest annoyance. With regard to the words 'all denominations' in a recent appeal for the Institution, as I explained in my former letter to you, I did not see a copy of the appeal until it was printed off and some copies circulated, but the moment I did I corrected it so far as it concerned, and directed all future copies to be corrected before circulated. The gentleman who drew it up merely gave me in conversation an outline of it. We have not been able to get the place out of debt, and there is at present a debt of between £200 and £300 on it; but the stock on farm, crops, farm implements, furniture, &c., would bring about £300. When you visited the place (I think about two years ago) you may recollect that it was proposed to sell as much of the land as would clear the place of debt. Perhaps this would be a good plan. The public road intersects the land, the portion to the south of it being for the most part mountain, and least valuable for agriculture. If this was sold it would bring about £[illegible], and leave nine-tenths (about 200 acres) of the best portion of the land and on which the house and offices are built. There is a clause in the scheme saying that preference should be given to boys from Loughrea, but though advertisements have several times been put into the county Galway papers for boys, there never was a reply. I shall be happy to give any further information in the matter. I must be in Dublin on the 15th instant, and could have an interview with you, or appear before the Board if necessary.

"Believe me, yours truly,

"Wm. Garrett, Esq." "Thos. H. Fleming.

The list of boys attached shows that there were then in the Institution 1 boy from Cork, 9 from Dublin, . from Galway, 4 from Wicklow, 1 from Roscommon, and 1 from Athenry; and the writer states:—

"By the above return it will be seen that there are 22 boys in the Institution, 12 of whom are free; towards the support of the other 10 there is £6 per annum paid for each. It takes about £18 per annum to clothe and feed each boy."

Further communications were made to the Commissioners in 1885 by parties who appeared to desire that the Institution should be brought more nearly into conformity with the wishes of the testator, and ultimately Canon Fleming applied again for power through the Commissioners of Charitable Donations and Bequests to sell a portion of the land in order to discharge the debt. He says:—

"We can easily spare, without in the least crippling the institution, as much of the mountain land as will bring from £800 to £1,000,"

and he asks the Commissioners to give their authority for the sale of that land. That authority has not yet been given, and the whole case and correspondence has now been sent to us. It would be within the power of our Commission to allow a portion of the land to be sold if necessary, or to sell the whole concern and seek to carry out the intentions of the testator in some other place. It will be seen that communications upon this matter have been sent to us from persons having different interests in the matter. We have asked Canon Fleming to attend, and will take his evidence as to the present condition of the place, and as to how far it corresponds with the testator's directions, and we shall be glad to receive suggestions for promoting the usefulness of the endowment.

Oct. 22, 1886.

Rev. Canon Fleming.

The Rev. Canon *Fleming* sworn and examined.

1419. Lord Justice FitzGibbon.—You are the Rector of the parish of Ballinakill, and the Rockfield Institution is in your parish?—Yes.

1420. How long have you been rector of that parish?—Seventeen years.

1421. During the whole of that time have you been one of the managing committee of Rockfield?—Yes.

1422. How many of the present trustees are resident in Ireland?—Two—myself and the Rev. C. Graham.

1423. Where does he live?—At Clifden.

1424. In whom is the property vested that is on the place?—In the managing committee.

1425. What property is there upon it?—There is property worth £400 on it—9 milch cows, 6 head of one and a half year old cattle, 4 pigs, 1 horse, and 1 jennet.

1426. What does the land consist of?—The land is chiefly bog and mountain. The valuation is £53 15s. There are about twelve acres of really arable land in the whole place. The remainder is partially reclaimed and unreclaimed mountain.

1427. Could meadow, wheat, barley, turnip, or potatoes be grown on the place?—Not all; potatoes and a few acres of barley can be grown; also meadows.

1428. Have you any meadow?—Yes, about eight acres.

1429. Were you connected with the institution at the time of the purchase?—But a very short time. I was the incumbent of a parish about eight miles off, and when I left that part of the country I resigned my seat on the committee.

1430. Do you happen to know how it came that the purchase of this estate was made so far from Loughrea?—I never heard. The Rev. Robert Mullen, rector of Ballinakill, took the chief management.

1431. Lord Justice Naish.—How are the trustees now appointed?—When vacancies occur the committee fill them.

1432. The provision in the will respecting the intention of the testator has never been carried out?—No, because the scheme which was supplied to me by the Commissioners of Charitable Donations does not say anything about it. I never heard the terms of the will until I heard it read to-day.

1433. Lord Justice FitzGibbon.—Master Litton's order of March 12, 1864, is as follows:—

"Ordered, that an estimate be procured for the supply of iron bedsteads, beds, bedding, sheets and blankets, tables and forms, wooden chairs and forms for the dormitory and eating room, also for the necessary supply of table linen, towels and sponges, combs and brushes; also for a suitable supply of schoolbooks and other school requisites such as are used in National schools, together with a sufficient number of prayer books and Bibles of the Church of England in such quantities as the committee may direct. It is further ordered that the solicitor do insert advertisements for the hiring of a proper agriculturalist, schoolmaster, and matron; it is further ordered that the committee do give out of the sum to be placed to their credit £70 for the purchase of stock; with regard to the culture and course of husbandry, it is ordered that the same be not attempted at present until the institution is further developed, and that after the agriculturalist is appointed he do forthwith lay out a plan for the appropriation of a sufficient portion of the land for cultivation for the use of the institution, including therein a plan for the gradual reclamation annually of a sufficient portion of the land now unreclaimed, and also including in the present reclaimed portion what may be required for the growth of seed potatoes and of other seeds to be used for the present sowing."

What portion of the land has been reclaimed?—About thirty acres.

1434. Has that been done since the date of this order?—Yes, since I went there within the last fifteen years.

1435. How much of it was reclaimed at the time you went there?—I don't think there was any of it, except what was reclaimed before the purchase, and that was very little.

1436. Do you know at the time of the purchase in 1853 how much reclaimed land there was of the whole 400 acres?—There were about 160 acres partially reclaimed, but none of it was thoroughly reclaimed.

1437. Do the boys work on the land?—Yes.

1438. What agricultural employment have they?—The land is drained and cropped, and they are taught to look after the cattle.

1439. What kind of crops are on it at present?—The crops at present on it are worth about £140—turnips, mangold, potatoes, oats, and hay.

1440. What acreage is under crops?—Including hay and all, about twenty acres.

1441.

"It is further ordered that, when the said arrangements shall have been completed, and when the committee shall direct that the petitioner's solicitor do advertise for boys to be taken into the institution, a preference shall be given to boys from the town of Loughrea and its vicinity, and of the Protestant religion, commencing with ten boys for the first year, between the ages of ten and fourteen, and if necessary for the employment of a person to teach the said boys to make and mend their own clothes."

Have these provisions of the Chancery Order been observed?—Not lately. There were advertisements published several times, but there were no replies.

1442. How long is it since the last advertisements were published?—Twelve or fifteen years ago.

1443. Have you had any boys from Loughrea?—From Galway. I don't think we ever had a boy from Loughrea. I don't think there are any boys there that would be suitable. I know they never applied, and the Committee thought it would be a waste of money to be looking for them.

1444.

"It is ordered that the name of the institution be "The Agricultural Institution of Galway.""

Does it bear that name?—It is called Rockfield. That is the name by which the place was called when it was purchased, and it is called by that name in most of the papers.

1445. Who is the present representative of Thomas Bell, of Brooke Hill?—I could not tell you. We have heard nothing of him for the last twelve years.

1446. The provision for the appointment of new trustees is as follows:—

"It is further ordered that Thomas Bell, of Brooke Hill, in the county of Galway, and the following resident gentry, viz.:—Edward Browne, J.P.; Thomas Lopez Prior, J.P.; the Rev. Roland Mullen, Rector of Ballinakill, the Rev. Thomas H. Fleming, and Gilbert Browne, esq., be appointed the Managing Committee of the Institution, with power to them at a special meeting to fill up any vacancy that may arise in their number by death, incapacity, or unwillingness of or on the part of any of the said committee, or of the future members thereof, to act and from time to time to elect others to fill the places of such of the said committee as shall die, become incapable, or be unwilling to act."

When did each of these gentlemen cease to have anything to do with the place?—They are all dead except Mr. Gilbert Browne, and myself.

1447. How has it happened that those elected to fill the vacant places are all resident in England?—Because no one in the county could be found to take it up.

1448. Rev. Dr. Malloy.—How were the London gentlemen selected?—I knew some of them. They were men of position, and we hoped that through them we might be able to get some funds and work the place, as there were no funds available.

1449. Lord Justice FitzGibbon.—The power to

Oct. 13, 1885.

Rev. Canon Fleming.

effect is to be exercised at a special meeting; have there been any special meetings of the trustees?—Just the ordinary committee meetings.

1450. What do you call the "ordinary committee meetings"?—Two form a quorum, and at the ordinary committee meetings, when there were vacancies, others were elected.

1451. Each special meeting was to be summoned on notice to all?—On several occasions there were special meetings summoned.

1452. What was the largest attendance at any meeting?—Not more than two for the last three years. I recollect as many as five. They are not resident in the country.

1453. Rev. Dr. Molloy.—Are the minutes of the meetings kept?—They are.

1454. Could we see them?—Certainly. The minutes of the committee meetings that were held in Ireland I have; the minutes of those held in London I have not got.

[Minutes produced.]

1455. Lord Justice FitzGibbon.—The order further proceeds:—

"The said committee, or a sufficient number of them, not less than two, shall meet the second Monday in every month, to investigate the affairs of the institution."

Have you carried out that?—No, we have not; because it could not be done.

1456. I believe you have met about three times in the year?—Not so often lately. In fact there is very little to be done; there are no funds.

1457. Lord Justice Naish.—How many boys are in the establishment at present?—Only eleven. We sent out six this year to different situations. We have had about an average of twenty-two for the last sixteen years; I think the highest number we had was thirty-three.

1458. The testator's idea was that the institution was to be self-supporting?—The land is of no use unless there is money to work it, especially land of this kind. We have the mountain portion set at present, and it brings us £20 a year.

1459. How many acres are included in that letting?—About 200. It is poor mountain land; it is the worst portion: we set it for grazing.

1460. Dr. Traill.—Who pays the county cess?—The trustees.

1461. Lord Justice FitzGibbon—

"It is further ordered, that it shall be the duty of the agriculturalist to attend to all matters in relation to the management and cultivation of the land, and to the stock that may be on the land for the use of the institution."

Have you an agriculturalist?—We had an agriculturalist up to six months ago, when we had to discharge him from want of funds to pay him; but our master, who is a very good man, understands a good deal about agriculture—cropping, draining, and the management of stock.

1462. When you say you have no money, have you not stock on the land?—Yes; but there is a debt on the place.

1463. How much is the debt at present?—It is above £900, but against that we have to set nearly £400 worth of assets on the place. When I got the place there was a debt of nearly £400 on it.

1464. Dr. Traill.—To whom was the debt due?—To different persons; for instance, the master and matron were owed two years salary; money was due also to the persons who supplied the place with food. There were three executions out against the place, and it was going to be sold; but I thought it would be a pity to let it go, and I borrowed money and paid off the pressing debts, put the place in proper repair, furnished the house, and stocked the land.

1465. Lord Justice FitzGibbon.—You practically found the place derelict?—Quite so.

1466. Was that at the time the application was made to appoint the brother of the owner of the property to be manager?—Yes, just at that time.

1467. Rev. Dr. Molloy.—How many members generally attended the meetings of the committee?—Two.

1468. Who were those two?—Myself and the rector of Clifden, Canon Cory; and Canon Goodison has been appointed in Canon Cory's place, who is dead.

1469. Are the other members expected to attend the meetings?—No. Several meetings have been held in London, but the London members would hardly come from London.

1470. Then what is the use of having them?—With the hope of interesting friends, or getting money to work the place.

1471. They are not put on to attend the meetings of the committee?—Not in Connaught, they could not; but there have been meetings in London. I have been at two of them myself.

1472. How many meetings were held in London?—About four or five; perhaps half a dozen—not more.

1473. Was that for the management of the institution at Renkfield?—It was to make inquiries about what was going on, and also as a means of raising money.

1474. Then in fact the business of the London members was to try to raise money?—Yes.

1475. And the institution at Renkfield was managed by yourself and the rector of Clifden?—Yes, and if there was any resident gentleman who would join, we would be too happy to have him. The only one is Mr. Gibson Browne; and he said there was no use in trying to work the place without funds.

1476. Can you give us the dates of the appointment of the London members?—I could not give you the exact dates; within the last six or seven years.

1477. Were they appointed at meetings of the committee?—They were.

1478. At meetings held in London?—At meetings held in London.

1479. Who attended those meetings?—I was one of the persons there. There was another member there, the Rev. Mr. Townsend.

1480. What connection has the Rev. Mr. Townsend with the neighbourhood of Renkfield?—None.

1481. Why was he thought a useful person?—Because he knew a great many persons; and because he is a practical farmer.

1482. Has he any connection with the county of Galway?—Not practically; he has no property there.

1483. How are the boys nominated?—An application is sent into the committee to appoint them—practically to myself and Canon Goodison.

1484. From your letter of January 3, 1885, I find there were 9 boys from Dublin?—Yes.

1485. What schools did they come from?—Most of them came not from any school, but from the county of Wicklow.

1486. There were nine from Dublin, and three from Wicklow. The nine from Dublin—where did they come from?—I could not say. Some of them were sent down by persons residing in Dublin.

1487. What conditions do you require to be fulfilled in order to receive them?—The conditions are, that they are Protestants to be brought up according to the tenets of the United Church of England and Ireland according to the will.

1488. Are any of those entered in the list the children of Catholic parents?—No, there never was a child of Catholic parents admitted into the institution except one, and when I found it out I had the child withdrawn.

1489. In the list before me there is "John Holland," and in the column headed "religion of parents" I find the words "Roman Catholic"?—Yes, but Holland was the one who was withdrawn afterwards. The gentleman that recommended him said he was a Protestant, and that he had been for a good while educated at a Protestant school.

1490. At what Protestant school?—Some school in Dublin, or in Wicklow, I think. It was Mr. Spencer that recommended the boy, I think.

Lord Justice FitzGibbon.—There is a note opposite to the name, stating that he was educated as a Protestant, and entered as such, and you say that he was afterwards withdrawn.

1491. Rev. Dr. Molloy.—How long did he remain with you?—Within six months he was withdrawn.

1492. Lord Justice Naish.—Do you get boys from Galway?—Yes.

1493. What schools do they come from?—Not from any particular school.

1494. Is this school connected with the Irish Church Missions?—No, not at all—except that the boys are educated at my parochial school, the master of which is paid by the Church Missions.

1495. Does this school get any subvention from the Irish Church Missions?—No, not a shilling; but one of the agents of the society is allowed to assist in the management of the place.

1496. Are these gentlemen in London connected with the Irish Church Missions?—Some of them are, and some are not.

1497. Is General Lowder?—He is.

1498. Is Mr. Townsend?—He is the clerical superintendent of the Irish Church Missions.

1499. Did he hold that office when he was appointed on this committee?—Yes.

1500. Lord Justice FitzGibbon.—One of the documents which has been sent down to us is a copy of the *Irish Church Missions Magazine* of July 1, 1884, with the following statement in it marked—

"The Homes in Connemara. There are four of these occupying the East by the sea at Spiddal—Glenowen. The Girls' Orphanage; the Girls' Home at Clifden; Ballyconree, the Boys' Orphanage; and Rockfield Boys' Farm."

Quite unauthorized. The committee knew nothing whatever about that, and I was very much annoyed when I saw it.

1501. Rev. Dr. Molloy.—What committee knew nothing about it?—The committee at Rockfield.

1502. But isn't Mr. Townsend a member of that committee?—But I don't believe he ever saw that. If he saw it he would not have allowed it to pass.

1503. As Superintendent of the Church Missions, ought he not to have known something about this publication?—Yes, but he had nothing whatever to say to that publication. It was quite unauthorized; and I am happy that it has been brought out in order that I may give the statement a contradiction.

1504. Lord Justice FitzGibbon.—Would there be no possibility of applying this endowment to the purpose for which the founder intended it, namely, teaching agriculture to boys connected with the county?—The boys are being brought up as farm servants; last year we sent out an excellent young fellow whose education was completed at Glasnevin.

1505. But they are not boys from Loughrea or its vicinity, or even from Connaught?—It is not necessary. You see that boys may come from other places.

1506. Yes, but a preference was to be given to the boys of Loughrea and its vicinity?—And so we do give a preference to Galway.

1507. But in this return, dated January 8, 1885, there are only four from Galway?—In that year there may have been only that number; but we have had boys from almost every county in Ireland.

1508. What steps did you take to try to get local trustees?—I asked the only gentleman of the place. Mr. Henry would not act—I spoke to him years ago. Mr. Gibson Browne is the only gentleman who would, and he said he did not see that the institution could be carried out unless there were funds.

1509. There is a provision in the scheme that—

"The committee shall keep in the institution as many boys as the funds will support, and that the education to be given shall be according to the tenets and principles of the Church Establishment of England and Ireland, and that the boys to be admitted shall be of the religion of the said Established Church, if such can be procured, to be selected in the first instance from the town of Loughrea, and its vicinity, and next the locality of the institution. And thirdly, from any other portion of the county of Galway, or any other part of Ireland the said committee may think fit."

I don't see that you have any pupils from the own locality?—No.

1510. Have you a Diocesan Council here?—Yes.

1511. Could they not appoint some gentlemen who would look after this institution?—I should be very happy if they would. It would relieve me of a great responsibility.

1512. Dr. Traill.—I suppose there is a money difficulty in the way?—A money difficulty deters a great many.

1513. Rev. Dr. Molloy.—Have you got much money from the London members of the committee?—No, I am sorry to say.

1514. That speculation failed?—It failed.

1515. Might they not retire now as they have not been able to carry out the object for which they were appointed?—Most gladly would they retire. There is no object in their joining. Some of them only remain at my request. They would be only too happy to retire if any other persons could be found to assist.

1516. Lord Justice Naish.—At the present moment how much does the institution owe?—About £900.

1517. To a bank?—To different individuals.

1518. Who pays, or is responsible for payment?—The stock on the farm is responsible, and my credit is pledged for a large amount. The place would have been sold if I had not taken the responsibility on me. I did so reluctantly; but I thought it a pity to see the thing go, and I made myself responsible for £400.

1519. Rev. Dr. Molloy.—Are the members of the committee who live in London personally responsible?—No; the property of the institution is responsible.

1520. Lord Justice FitzGibbon.—Perhaps you can tell us what is the largest item due to any one person?—Four hundred and odd pounds.

1521. How was that lent?—Simply lent on my security by a private individual—a private loan. There is about £70 due to the bank.

1522. In whose name is the bank account kept?—In my name.

1523. Rev. Dr. Molloy.—Then the other members of the committee are not responsible?—No.

1524. Then the financial responsibility is no reason why gentlemen of the county of Galway should not act?—Certainly not. I would only be too happy if any gentlemen would join me.

1525. But I thought you said that gentlemen of the county were afraid to join on account of the liability?—Not on account of the liability—I don't think so. As long as there are assets they are quite safe; but they thought the institution could not be carried on unless there was money forthcoming to work it.

1526. Dr. Traill.—Agricultural schools have generally failed in this country?—I don't know.

1527. Lord Justice Naish.—Is the land near the sea?—It is.

1528. Is it fit to produce corn crops?—If it were reclaimed it would produce oats, but not wheat. It is boggy land.

1529. Had you anything to say in the selection of this place?—Nothing whatever.

1530. Lord Justice FitzGibbon.—Let me read this minute:—

"June, 1881. Meeting at Clifden Rectory. Canon Fleming in the chair. The accounts for 1880 were examined. Resolved—That on the bill for £400 at the National Bank, Clifden, becoming due, in the second week

Oct. 18, 1886.

Rev. Canon Fleming.

Oct. 14, 18[illegible].

Rev. Canon Fleming.

of June, £[illegible] to be paid on the bill being renewed for another six months, and then another appeal be at once issued to raise an interest for the institution and pay off the additional liabilities."

Was any money raised at that time to help you?—Very little.

1531. Did you get money from some private individuals to pay off the bank?—Since that—yes, and partly through collections, and partly by the sale of stock.

1532. Collections would have paid the debt off, but getting money from another person would leave it where it was, and you say the debt is now £[illegible]—

"[illegible] February, 18[illegible]. Clifton Rectory. Canon Fleming in the chair. The accounts were passed, and it was decided that unless some effort be speedily made to increase the funds of the Institution, it will be necessary to sell a portion of the property, in order to place the Institution in a secure position."

Was that the minute that led to the correspondence with the Commissioners of Charitable Donations and Bequests?—Yes.

1533. The next meeting was on October 5, 1885; there do not appear to have been any meetings in 1883 or 1884?—I think that was the year we were over in London.

1534. After careful consideration of the subject it was resolved that—

"For the purpose of clearing off the debts which press so heavily on Rockfield Institution, the Commissioners of Charitable Donations and Bequests be requested to consent to the sale of that portion of the lands lying to the north of the main road leading to Clifden, such portion being less valuable, and so situated that its sale would not hinder or affect the working of the Institution or impair its usefulness."

In one of your letters you stated that that portion of the lands was worth from £800 to £1,000?—Yes. It was stated to be worth that.

1535. Did you get any offer for it?—Yes; we were offered £700 about six months ago.

1536. You say in one of your letters that owing to the dulness some £300 had to be taken off the offer you got?—Yes; we could have got £900 for it—about 185[illegible]—before the depression.

1537. Dr. Traill.—How many acres are there in that part?—About 2[illegible] acres.

1538. Is that the portion for which you get £30 a year for grazing now?—Yes, partly; but the remainder is better land.

1539. Lord Justice FitzGibbon.—There was no minute from 1885 till 1888, and this is the last—

"[illegible] September, 1888. The attendance is not stated in any of the minutes, but you are stated to be in the chair. It was reported that during the past year three boys were sent to Canada as farm servants, and that two more are in good situations in Ireland. It is to be regretted that the sale of the lands referred to in the minutes of the previous meeting has not yet been effected owing to the depressed value of land at present, and that therefore the debt on the Institution remains unpaid. Resolved—That a special effort be made towards effecting the sale of those lands."

And then it is stated that the accounts for 1887 were submitted, examined, and passed. A proposal for this portion of the lands was received more than a year ago—an offer of £700; do you think you would get more?—It ought to be worth £800, at least.

1540. If you got £800 for this part, how much ought you to get for the whole?—The other is the best part. The whole ought to be worth £1,800.

1541. Is the place worth £1,800 altogether?—No.

1542. If you got that sum, would it be advisable to give the benefit of the endowment to the people of Loughrea?—I am only one member of the committee.

1543. Rev. Dr. Molloy.—You are the principal member?—I have done the work, I know, for the last fifteen or sixteen years.

1544. Do you think that the school is really doing any substantial good?—I do.

1545. To nine children from Dublin and three from Wicklow; don't you think you might leave Dublin to take care of itself?—We would be only too happy to take in boys from Galway.

1546. If you were to get, as the Lord Justice suggests, £1,800 for the property, would you not do something for Loughrea?—But will it benefit Loughrea to establish another institution there?

1547. You could give them some educational benefit that they are not getting at Rockfield?—Yes, I think they are.

1548. Lord Justice FitzGibbon.—Are there no poor boys of the Protestant Church in the whole county of Galway?—At all events they have not applied.

1549. Perhaps they don't like to go to Ballinakill?—It would be hard to deprive the parish of the benefit.

1550. Rev. Dr. Molloy.—But the parish gets no benefit from educating nine boys from Dublin and three from Wicklow?—We have none from the immediate locality, but we may at any moment have other boys.

1551. Dr. Traill.—What is the Church population of the parish?—About 300.

1552. Lord Justice FitzGibbon.—Do any number of that population get any benefit from the institution?—I think about three have done so, but not for some years.

1553. How long is it since any member of the Protestant population of the parish of Ballinakill gained any benefit from it?—Not for the last ten years.

1554. Rev. Dr. Molloy.—Would it not be more economical to send the endowment up to Dublin where the children are, than to be sending the children down from Dublin to Ballinakill?—We don't get them all from Dublin; we have had boys from Galway, Roscommon, Cork, Tipperary, Wicklow, and [illegible] County.

1555. Those places are very remote from Ballinakill. I should be sorry to do any harm to Ballinakill, but I cannot see what benefit the parish of Ballinakill is at present getting from this endowment?—At present the poor of Ballinakill are deriving no benefit from it, but bye and bye it may not be so. Besides, I don't like to have an educational institution of the kind removed from my parish. I take an interest in educating boys.

1556. The intentions of the founder to benefit the poor boys of Loughrea and its neighbourhood by teaching them agriculture are not carried out.—Several advertisements have been inserted and there never was a reply. Of course if it comes under the purview of the Commission, and if they direct advertisements to be inserted, we will be only too happy to do it.

1557. Lord Justice FitzGibbon.—I have looked through your minutes from 1876 to 1888, for the last twelve years, and the only appointment that I can see is that of Mr. Thomas Spencer, of 49, Wellington-place, Clyde-road, Dublin, as a member of the committee, on September 30, 1877. Is he still on it?—No.

1558. When did he leave it?—About four years ago.

1559. Have you any minutes of the appointments of the others?—Not in the locality. I could get them.

1560. Then the meetings at which all the rest were appointed must have been held in London?—In London.

1561. And all those who now hold office, except yourself, have been appointed in London?—They have, except Canon Cowdon.

1562. And not at any special meeting of the committee held in Rockfield, or its neighbourhood?—No, except when the meetings were there.

1563. Rev. Dr. Molloy.—When were the first appointments made at meetings held in London?—Five or six years ago.

1564. When was the last appointment made at a

meeting held in Ireland — since Mr. Spencer's appointment in 1877 no one was appointed at any meeting held in Ireland?—Not in Ireland.

1565. Lord Justice FitzGibbon.—You have asked in your correspondence for power to sell a portion of the lands; in your opinion is there anything further wanting for the sufficient working of the institution? —No, all we want is money to work it. We have got the land and nothing to work it with.

1566. Lord Justice Naish.—In what way could the land be worked if you had money—would you enter on a system of reclamation?—Yes; a great part of the land could be made valuable if it were drained and reclaimed.

1567. Lord Justice FitzGibbon.—Could you suggest where we can find anybody to cooperate with you a little nearer than London?—In the parish none, except the two I have mentioned.

1568. Have you any diocesan committee to look after education?—Yes.

1569. Are any of the members amongst your trustees?—Canon Goodison is one.

1570. Has your diocese made application to incorporate diocesan trustees for educational endowments? Ven. Archdeacon O'Sullivan.—We have appointed four trustees in Tuam.

1571. Lord Justice FitzGibbon.—Even at the worst you have got 400 acres, of which 300 are fair land and the rest mountain; you have buildings, furniture, and appliances, and you say you have £500 of stock; you have that much property subject to a debt of £900. Don't you think that a farm could be carried on at which the boys working the land could get their home and food, maintaining themselves, as the master intended, with the capital that you would have left if you sold the mountain land for enough to pay your debt?—Yes, I think so, certainly. The best part of the land is reserved.

1572. Are you paying interest on the debt?—Yes.

1573. Dr. Traill.—Your debt does not leave you any capital to work upon?—No, it does not.

1574. Has that debt been steadily increasing every year?—It has.

1575. It appears that you began with a debt of £500, that it went up to £700, and that it is now £900; how would selling a portion of the land enable you to work the rest more profitably than you were able to work the whole?—I am sure a great many persons would support the institution if it were not in debt. People don't like to embark in a sinking concern.

1576. Against the debt the property has been increasing a little on the other side of the account?—It has.

1577. And now there is stock on the farm which would reduce the debt if sold?—Quite so; and besides we have been reclaiming and teaching the boys.

1578. Lord Justice FitzGibbon.—Reclamation, according to modern ideas, is not a very profitable thing?—You must teach the boys. If you want to teach the boys agriculture you must reclaim the land.

1579. Would it not pay better to pay even £4 an acre for good land in Meath or Roscommon?—There are only twelve acres of really arable land; the remainder is reclaimed bog.

1580. Lord Justice Naish.—Mr. Mitchell Henry has reclaimed a quantity of land down there?—He has.

1581. Lord Justice FitzGibbon.—Is reclamation of land in that neighbourhood a thing that a practical farmer would like to put his money into?—Well, Mr. Henry told me a short time ago that it paid pretty well. Besides, it would be a training for the boys, although it might not pay as a speculation. The boys must be taught drainage if they are to know anything about agriculture.

1582. What is the education that the boys are getting?—They are taught reading and writing. They get a capital English education.

1583. They attend a primary school in the neighbourhood?—The parochial school, within a few yards of the place. Oct. 22, 1880. Rev. Canon Fleming.

1584. They get the ordinary primary education there?—They do.

1585. You are the manager of the school?—Yes.

1586. Then all they get from Rockfield is a residence, and whatever food grows on the place?—They are taught agriculture up to a certain point; they are taught drainage, and they work on the land when they are not in school.

1587. Rev. Dr. Molloy.—How many boys are in the school they attend besides themselves?—Very few.

1588. Not a dozen?—No.

1589. Are there any?—There are four.

1590. Lord Justice FitzGibbon.—Do they pay any fees for teaching?—None whatever; they get it free.

1591. How is the school maintained?—The funds for the schoolmaster are paid by the Society for the Irish Church Missions.

1592. What salaries are you paying at Rockfield? —We only pay out of the funds of the institution the matron's salary of £15 a year.

1593. Then it would appear, from the accumulation of this debt, that the farm as it stands, held in fee-simple and paying no rent, has, during the last twenty years, been making a loss every year?—It is making a loss for want of money to work it.

1594. It began at a level in 1860?—That was before I took it up. I am only speaking of the last sixteen years. There was a heavy debt on it when I took it up. It took £500 to set it right.

1595. Dr. Traill.—Are the other four boys converts from the Roman Catholic religion?—No.

1596. Then how is it that the Irish Church Missions consent to pay the schoolmaster?—They educate the Protestants.

1597. I thought their special business was to pay for the education of converts from Roman Catholicism? —Yes, so it is.

1598. Are there any of them at your school?—One.

1599. Lord Justice Naish.—Do you mean in the institution?—No, not in the institution.

1600. Dr. Traill.—What salary do the Irish Church Missions pay your master?—£30 a year.

1601. Lord Justice FitzGibbon.—Is he a qualified teacher?—He has been in their own training school.

1602. Where is that training school?—In Dublin.

1603. Where is it?—It is a private training school in [illegible]-street.

1604. How long has the present master been at Rockfield?—Not quite three years.

1605. Rev. Dr. Molloy.—Do the three Protestant boys in your school represent the whole Protestant population of the parish that require instruction?—No. I have two other schools in other parts of my parish.

1606. Lord Justice FitzGibbon.—How far are they from Rockfield?—One is three miles distant and the other nine.

1607. Rev. Dr. Molloy.—How many boys are in each of the other schools in your parish?—Of course I can give you the information if necessary.

1608. I ask it with the view of seeing whether there is material there to supply boys for the Rockfield Institution?—No; there are no boys in those schools who would go to the Rockfield Institution. If you wish I will give you the information.

1609. Lord Justice FitzGibbon.—What we want to see is whether there are any boys in your neighbourhood to whom this endowment can be made of use?—There are no boys who would go to it—no boys in the immediate neighbourhood who require to get the instruction.

1610. Why don't the boys in the primary schools—one of which is three miles off and the other nine—go to it?—Because they remain at home with their parents and work on their own farms.

[illegible]

Rev. [illegible]

1611. Rev. Dr. Molloy.—Would not education in agriculture be useful to them for that purpose?—I would be very glad if some of them would come, but they will not. They have plenty to do at home. It is not so easy to get boys to an institution of the kind.

1612. It is strange then that they should come from Dublin?—They come from all parts of Ireland.

1613. But none from Ballinakill?—Because they are not there.

1614. But you have three schools there?—Yes, but the boys won't go into the institution; they don't want to go. They go on very well at home on their own farms; and some of them are too small.

1615. Lord Justice FitzGibbon.—The evidence being that the boys of Loughrea and Ballinakill don't want to go to it, what is the nearest locality where there are boys that would derive benefit from this institution?—I could not exactly say.

1616. What do you think the whole concern, if it were sold, would bring?—I think £3,000 is as much as it would bring, including rents.

1617. And of that it owes at present, over the value of the stock, about £800?—Yes, it would owe £800 along with the rents. I suppose about £800 would clear it, and the profits would be between £400 and £500.

1618. We may take it that £800 and the stock on it would clear it?—Yes, and the crops; there is not value there for £3,000 over and above all liabilities, because I don't think more than £3,000 would be got for the whole place, including rents. I don't think it would fetch £3,500.

1619. Dr. Traill.—Then ought you not to accept the offer of £700 as soon as you can for the worst part of it?—It is very reclaimable land, and lies very well.

1620. But if reclaiming is only a loss why would a person give more than £700 for it?—I think that part of the land would pay. It could be made much more valuable than it is.

1621. Rev. Dr. Molloy.—Would the people at Ballinakill be glad to get some of the land?—They would.

1622. Perhaps they would buy it under Lord Ashbourne's Act?—That has been proposed.

1623. Lord Justice FitzGibbon.—The gentlemen of the committee, I suppose, are all members of the Church of England?—Yes.

1624. The will appears to provide that instruction shall be given to all the pupils in Church doctrines?—I thought the institution was exempt from the Act, inasmuch as it is strictly Protestant.

1625. Dr. Traill.—I wonder you did not make that claim up to this?—I thought that was understood all along.

1626. Do you ask that it should be formally declared exempt?—I do ask it.

1627. Rev. Dr. Molloy.—You said you never heard the will read until to-day?—Never.

1628. It provides that if you cannot get enough of Protestant children from the neighbourhood of Loughrea you may take in boys from other parts of Ireland, and if you cannot get Protestants enough you may take in Catholics to the extent of one-third?—From Loughrea?

1629. Lord Justice FitzGibbon.—Here is the provision in the will:—

"The greater number of the boys to be educated and maintained in the seminary are required to profess the Protestant religion as by law established. Should, however, any difficulty arise in completing the required number, boys of the Roman Catholic religion are to be admitted, but only to the number of one-third of the whole."

The required number is forty.

1630. Dr. Traill.—If he admitted one-third of Roman Catholic boys they also were to be taught the formularies and Catechism of the Church of England.

Witness.—So it would appear by the will.

1631. Lord Justice FitzGibbon.—There is some doubt about that, for he speaks of this one-third as being Roman Catholics to be admitted in case they did not get the required number. The clause says:—

"The greater number of the boys maintained and educated in the seminary are to be required to profess the Protestant religion."

From which it would seem as if the minority need not; and he goes on:—

"Should a difficulty be found in completing the required number, boys of the Roman Catholic religion are to be admitted, but only to the number of one-third of the whole."

Then he makes a number of provisions about books and prayer-books and the homilies, in which, apparently, all the pupils are to be instructed.

Dr. Traill.—They are each to get Bibles and prayer-books, and there are to be morning and evening prayers.

1632. Lord Justice FitzGibbon.—At all events, it is perfectly clear that this endowment was founded by a Protestant, with the intention of making it mainly, if not entirely, a Protestant institution. It is of little use at present, and of none to those whom the founder desired to benefit, and we ought to consider whether we cannot make something better of it.

1633. Dr. Traill (to witness).—Could you not suggest some scheme under the powers of this Commission by which the institution can be made more useful than it is at present?—There is no money attached to it except the value of the land.

1634. Lord Justice FitzGibbon.—There is property worth about £3,000 net?—I could not take it on myself without consulting the other trustees.

1635. Dr. Traill.—If you cleared off all your liabilities and found that even £1,000 was left, could you not suggest some plan within the Church of Ireland by which the money could be made useful to boys of the Church?—Of course; I shall think it over.

1636. Do you think it could be used in educating Protestant boys from this part of the country, to be sent up to some other institution?—Yes.

1637. Say clever boys from the National schools of Galway, to be sent to the Training College in Kildare-place, for instance?—Yes.

1638. Where their education could be paid for out of the interest of the money, and all further operations with it stopped?—Yes, if the others would consent.

1639. You are the acting member and you have all the responsibility?—I shall be happy to confer with them.

1640. I think you could do more for the Protestant boys of Galway by using the interest of whatever balance should remain out of this endowment, after a sale of it, by providing for their education somewhere else. There is no use in any scheme unless you have the money. It has been in a struggling position ever since it was started.

1641. Lord Justice FitzGibbon.—When you were appointed what was the total amount of the pecuniary liability?—Between £300 and £400.

1642. And at that time what was the total value of the stock?—Nought. Not a single beast was on the place.

1643. Then at that time, sixteen years ago, the lands were encumbered to the amount of £400?—Yes, fully that, because the buildings had to be put into repair—they were in a wretched state of repair—and there was no furniture in the house.

1644. Give us as nearly as you can the correct figures. When you had got through the expenditure necessary to make the institution fit for the boys what was your position?—We were about £500 in debt.

1645. What you have now is the same land and about £400 worth of stock, but you owe £800 instead of £500?—Yes.

1646. Therefore it has been exactly a [illegible] with you for the last sixteen years?—About that—yes.

1647. Dr. Traill.—And with the value of land going down in the meantime?—We have reclaimed about twenty-five acres of our land.

1648. Lord Justice FitzGibbon.—Practically you have been just with your head over the water all that time?—Quite so. Only that a great effort was made the place would have gone. Oct. 18, 1888

1649. Then after spending all that you could collect, your 400 acres and whole establishment has been able to maintain only from twelve to twenty boys without growing worse?—I suppose so. Rev. Canon Fleming.

The Venerable James O'Sullivan, Archdeacon of Tuam, examined.

1650. Lord Justice FitzGibbon.—You are one of the Tuam Diocesan Trustees?—Yes.

1651. You have heard Canon Fleming's evidence?—Yes.

1652. We should like to see the management of this endowment a little nearer than London, and would be glad to hear any suggestions in the matter, bearing in mind that the leading intention of the founder was to confer benefits on Church Protestants?—I will undertake to speak to the four trustees and they will lay some proposal before the Commissioners.

Rev. Dr. Molloy.—As far as possible in accordance with the intentions of the founder, which appear to have been inadequately carried out.

1653. Lord Justice FitzGibbon.—It is in our power to deal without limit with the landed property, that is to say, either the whole or part of it could be sold, and after Canon Fleming's liability is satisfied the balance could be handed over to be dealt with under the scheme. Once the question is settled that the intention of the founder was denominational, it will be our duty to carry out that intention. We cannot hand over any endowment from one denomination to another. But we have unlimited power to make the thing useful within the scope of the founder's intention.

O'Sullivan.—Shall I convey to the trustees that this institution is exempt from the compulsory powers of the Act?

1654. Lord Justice FitzGibbon.—That is a difficult question, and I have some doubt about it; but it would make practically no difference as to the provisions of the scheme, except that if we hold the endowment within our compulsory jurisdiction, we would prepare a scheme whether the existing committee concurred or not, and if they did not like our decision they could take the opinion of the Privy Council on it. But once you are informed, as we now tell you, that we are satisfied that the spirit of this founder's intention was to promote practical education amongst members of his own Church, you ought all to join in trying to make the thing more useful than it is, and should not raise any difficulty about jurisdiction. Ven. James O'Sullivan, Archdeacon of Tuam.

Dr. Traill.—Don't press the question of exemption to a decision when you have got that declaration.

1655. Rev. Dr. Molloy.—In order to prove a title to exemption it must be shown that the endowment was intended exclusively for the benefit of one denomination; and it would be very hard to do that here, where the founder expressly provides that one-third of the boys may be Catholics.

Archdeacon O'Sullivan.—I will undertake to speak to the other gentlemen of the Diocesan Committee.

1656. Lord Justice FitzGibbon.—You should also communicate with Canon Fleming and his committee. They are in possession and are doing the best they can, and the place would have gone to ruin altogether but for them some dozen years ago.

Archdeacon O'Sullivan.—I will do so within a reasonable time.

Dr. Traill.—It is for the advantage of the institution that it has been stated that it is not a proselytising institution.

The Rev. Canon Fleming.—That I emphatically deny. It was not intended to be such, and the money was not given for such a purpose.

Lord Justice FitzGibbon.—We will expect to hear from the Diocesan Trustees and from the existing committee, say before the end of January next; if they agree on any practical proposals we will carry them out if we can. If not we must try to draft a scheme ourselves. In the meantime, we say nothing on the question of exemption, which possibly may never be raised.

ERASMUS SMITH'S GRAMMAR SCHOOL.

Lord Justice FitzGibbon.—We took general evidence on former occasions as to Erasmus Smith's endowments. We propose now to examine the head master as to the present condition of the Galway Grammar School. Afterwards any persons interested in the endowment will be at liberty to ask him questions; and we shall be prepared to hear anything that any person interested wishes to say.

Richard Biggs, M.A., LL.D., sworn and examined.

1657. Lord Justice FitzGibbon.—When were you appointed head master of Erasmus Smith's Galway Grammar school?—In the summer of 1878. I have been here twelve years. I waited a year for alterations in the premises.

1658. What was the condition of the school premises when you were appointed?—Very bad indeed.

1659. Who was your predecessor?—The Rev. J. W. Kilgorell.

1660. I believe at one time he had a prosperous school here?—I don't remember, of course, I am told he was a good master when he came, but he let the school go down.

1661. Dr. Traill.—Did he die?—No, he resigned.

1662. Lord Justice FitzGibbon.—How many pupils did you find here when you came?—About 15 day boys. There had been no boarders for some time.

1663. After you came, what were the numbers?—I brought more than 40 boarders with me from Parsonstown, where I had a private school at Chesterfield, to which Lord Rosse gave a small endowment. I had 63 pupils altogether when I started—40 boarders and 23 day boys. Next year I had 73. The following year we went down to 39 boarders and 28 day boys, making 67. In 1878 and 1879 we went down to 21 boarders—our lowest number being 17, and 23 day boys. Richard Biggs, M.A., LL.D.

1664. I suppose the 40 that you brought with you left, and you did not immediately get others to take their places?—Exactly.

1665. How have the numbers been since?—There was a slight rise in 1879–80 to 28 boarders and 40 day boys. In 1880–81, 28 boarders and 30 day boys; in 1881–82, 27 boarders and 30 day boys; in 1882–83,

[illegible]

34 boarders and 41 day boys; in 1883–84, 41 boarders and 29 day boys—a considerable falling off, owing, I suppose, to some accident; in 1884–85, 36 boarders and 26 day boys; in 1885–86, 44 boarders and 30 day boys; in 1886–87, 44 boarders and 30 day boys; and in 1887–88, we have had 45 boarders and 34 day boys.

1666. Then for the last three years you have had a maximum of 44 or 45 boarders?—The maximum of boarders at any one time was 52.

1667. Is that the largest number you could accommodate?—Nearly.

1668. Your day boys have fluctuated a good deal, but they don't appear to have ever been less than 20?—They never were less than 20, nor more than 41.

1669. To what do you attribute the fluctuation in the number of day boys?—Entirely accidental causes—families coming and going.

1670. What fees do the boarders pay?—£48 to £54 a year. There is a difference of £3 for boys under thirteen. Payment in advance also reduces the fee—£48 is the lowest.

1671. Have you had difficulty in getting the fees regularly paid?—Very little; I have had only two or three serious bad debts. The depression of the times operated by boys being removed.

1672. You think you would have had more boys but for that?—Yes, certainly; boys have been removed avowedly on that ground. The parents could not afford it, and many others would have been sent if I had consented to reduce the fees.

1673. What fees are paid by the day boys?—The lowest is £8 a year, including English, mathematics, and one foreign language. For another language it is £3 more.

1674. What is your teaching staff?—Four besides myself regularly employed, and a music master; drawing is taken by one of the resident masters.

1675. What is the division of labour amongst your four assistants?—Mr. Hewson, the second officer—who is appointed by the Board and not by me—takes mathematics and some English literature.

1676. Dr. Traill.—Are all your assistants appointed by the Board?—No. Mr. Hewson only. He has now put in nearly thirty years service here. The first classical master takes the upper forms in classics. He is employed and paid by me entirely.

1677. What is his salary?—£250 a year. He is not resident.

1678. Who is he?—Mr. Hughes. He was a distinguished man in Trinity College.

1679. Lord Justice FitzGibbon.—Who is the third?—The junior master is resident and gets £75 a year and his board.

1680. Who is the fourth?—Mr. Dupre, who teaches French, German, and Italian. He has been here about thirty-two years.

1681. For what do you prepare your boys?—The universities, the Intermediate examinations, and the Civil Service.

1682. What proportion go in for a university education?—Not so large a proportion as I should like. We sent three for matriculation in Trinity College, Dublin, in 1880, three in 1881, four in 1882, one in 1883, three in 1884, none in 1885, two in 1886, and none since.

1683. Your school won three university studentships, the highest distinction attainable, in three years?—Yes.

1684. I suppose your boys have got a number of other honours in Trinity College too?—Yes, a great many. We have also gained altogether about twenty at the Royal University since 1881.

1685. What about the Queen's College?—We have sent in candidates for the entrance scholarships there nearly every year. In 1877 we got two scholarships; in 1878, one; in 1879, two; in 1880, one; in 1881, none; in 1882, two; in 1883, none; in 1884, five; in 1885, four; in 1886, three, and last year we got one.

1686. What is the number of scholarships each year?—About ten.

1687. And you got from three to four, in several years, out of ten?—Yes—as many as five.

1688. Rev. Dr. Molloy.—I suppose most of your pupils who matriculate in the Royal University go to the Queen's College?—Yes.

1689. Lord Justice FitzGibbon.—In the Intermediate examinations, how have you been getting on?—We have done fairly well. In 1885 we gained four exhibitions, three junior and one senior. There were two retained besides in the upper year. In that year, 1886, we passed twenty-seven. In 1887 we only gained one exhibition, and retained two; but we got several book prizes. We only passed sixteen. That was due to a great difference in the natural philosophy paper. The boys must pass in three subjects. We tried to teach them mathematics and English as well as we could, and rather let the natural philosophy take its chance. In 1886 there was a very favourable paper in natural philosophy, and they all passed in the three subjects. I took the same standard of instruction in 1887, and unfortunately it was below the mark.

1690. Rev. Dr. Molloy.—A new examiner came in, I suppose?—I suppose so. I can not says. The weak boys had only three subjects, so that their only chance of passing failed.

1691. Lord Justice FitzGibbon.—Then you send up a large number of boys who don't qualify in Latin and Greek?—Yes, a good many.

1692. Did the boys that failed, fail in everything?—No, they passed in Mathematics and English as a rule.

1693. What were your results this last year?—This current year we gained 4 exhibitions, and retained 1, and our passes were 17.

1694. What have you found to be the quality of the Intermediate Examinations as a test of education?—On the whole, good.

1695. The best boys get the best places?—Certainly.

1696. When boys distinguish themselves in the Intermediate examinations, do the same boys distinguish themselves afterwards in the Universities?—To a great extent.

1697. Do you send boys to the Civil Service Examinations?—Seldom direct. They go from us to a grinder for the Civil Service Examinations. A boy left us about eighteen months ago, who was admitted into the Indian Civil Service this year. He was specially prepared by Mr. Craig.

1698. To what class do your boys belong—first take the day boys?—Amongst the present day boys I have one son of a clergyman, one of a landlord, three sons of farmers, one of a doctor of medicine, one of a civil servant, one of a solicitor, one of an ex-constable of constabulary, two of merchants, three of shopkeepers, and one of a banker. These are all paying day pupils. Then the parents of the free day pupils are, two farmers, one solicitor, four shopkeepers, two scripture readers, one tailor, two soldiers, and one mechanic.

1699. How many free pupils have you?—Eighteen.

1700. How do they come in?—They come to me and I give them a printed form of application to the governors. The boy brings me the printed form filled up. I examine him and then send his application to the governors, with a report of any own as to his proficiency. The governors at their next meeting consider the case, and without assigning any reasons one way or the other, elect him or not.

1701. Rev. Dr. Molloy.—Is the number of free boys limited?—The number of tenants sons is unlimited. The number of free boys, whose parents are not tenants, is limited to 20.

1702. And you have never reached that limit?—Never.

1703. How many boys have you who are the sons of tenants?—I don't know. They never mention

Oct. 13, 1882.

Richard Biggs, M.A., LL.D.

that in their applications, or mistakes. I know I have one or three, but there may be more.

1704. Lord Justice FitzGibbon.—Do you find the system of admitting free boys a good one?—No, I should like to see it done on a much more regular plan. The Charity Commissioners in England who have been drawing up schemes, universally adopt the plan of exhibitions, or free scholarships, from the primary schools to the middle class schools, and from the middle class schools to the higher schools, whence of course they proceed to the scholarships of the universities. I should like something of that sort to be done—suppose the best pupil of a primary school, to be selected either by me or by the governors, and to be sent in here; I think that would be better than the present system. Since I came here I have had in all 53 free pupils. Of those 23 belonged to the Church of Ireland, 17 were Protestant Dissenters, and 13 were Roman Catholics.

1705. Professor Dougherty.—What do you mean by "Protestant Dissenters"?—Presbyterians chiefly; also Wesleyans.

1706. I thought there were no Dissenters in Ireland?—I beg pardon; I used the term under marks of quotation.

1707. How many of the seventeen were Presbyterians?—I should say about twelve.

1708. Lord Justice FitzGibbon.—Is there no limitation as regards religious denomination as a qualification for the free pupils?—Practically none.

1709. Were all these boys from the locality of Galway?—They came from as far as Athenry.

1710. They are all from this part of the county?—Yes.

1711. What education are they entitled to get as free boys?—Free education in English subjects, mathematics, natural science, and two languages. They have to pay extra for music, or for a third language—if they take French, Latin, and Greek.

1712. Are they taught with the other scholars?—There is no distinction. In fact, it is not known who they are; no one knows but myself. Of the fifty-five who have been with me only ten, so far as I can trace, have gone into the higher walks of life—namely, seven to learned professions, two into the Civil Service, and one into a bank. If a more intelligent system of election were adopted the endowment would be used to greater advantage. Personally I have been glad to teach those fifty-five boys, but it seems to me that more value could be got from a different system.

1713. The Incorporated Society have very stiff examinations at entrance, and their boys are promoted by further examinations to the higher school at Santry. Do you think something of that sort would be an improvement in connexion with your school?—I do.

1714. As a foundation for the superstructure is there any system of primary schools from which you could draw boys?—There is the model school. A large proportion, say three-fifths, of our free pupils have been previously at the Galway Model school.

1715. Your boys who want higher education come chiefly from the Model school?—Chiefly.

1716. Dr. Traill.—You think the governors prevent test is not ability but poverty?—I don't know that there is any test at all.

1717. Out of fifty-five free pupils only ten have gone forward to higher walks of life?—Possibly another ten of those with me now might go.

1718. Professor Dougherty.—You attribute the failure of the free pupils to go forward, not to their poverty, but to want of intelligence?—Yes, and to their want of industry.

1719. Lord Justice FitzGibbon.—Are there any other primary schools in Galway which lay the foundation for a boy's promotion to better instruction?—There is the school of the Patrician Brothers; I have had a few boys from that school. It is the only other I know of besides the Model school.

1720. Have you had three-fifths of your free pupils from the Model school and the remaining two-fifths from the Patrician school?—No; I have had only two or three from the latter.

1721. Where did the rest come from?—They were chiefly the children of strangers coming to the town.

1722. What did you find their condition to be when they came to you?—Those coming from the Model school knew their English subjects fairly well, English in a rather formal way, and arithmetic generally very well. They are also very good in writing. In fact, I am afraid they don't improve in writing much with us.

1723. Then you think that a modified competition among pupils of primary schools would be a very good thing for boys coming to you as free pupils?—I think it would be very desirable.

1724. Dr. Traill.—What are the ages at which they are admitted?—Between nine and fourteen.

1725. Do you think that boys should be subjected to competitive examinations before fourteen?—I think fourteen ought to be soon enough, but they should begin classics earlier than that.

1726. Would you take these boys upon a report of their general ability than by subjecting them to a competitive examination?—I should be willing to do so.

1727. Rev. Dr. Molloy.—What number of boys applying to be admitted as free pupils have been rejected by the Board?—Very few in my experience, not more than seven or eight.

1728. Then the only effect of competition would be to exclude pupils that are at present admitted?—A further effect would be that others might be attracted or stirred up.

1729. Lord Justice FitzGibbon.—In the Incorporated Society's schools the limits of age are from twelve to sixteen, and the masters told us that they thought a boy should not come to the school before twelve; but that the other limit was too high because it brought them too late for the Intermediate examinations. What do you think the best limits of age?—I dare say from twelve to fourteen. At present the limits are nine to fourteen; but as a matter of fact we have none so young as nine, and only one under twelve.

1730. What assistance do you get from the endowment?—I have a house and about twelve acres of land free. For the grazing of the land I get a rent of about £35 a year. The boys have the full use of the whole of it, and have cricket and football grounds and two ball alleys.

1731. Dr. Traill.—How do you get the rent of £35?—It is set for grazing.

1732. The same land that the boys play on?—Yes, that right is reserved. The field in front of the house is not used for any games.

1733. Do you allow cattle on it in the winter?—Yes, all the year round.

1734. Who pays the county cess for it?—I pay it.

1735. Are the graziers let in on it from May to November?—Yes.

1736. Lord Justice FitzGibbon.—How are the repairs done?—I am responsible for all the internal repairs, and I have done a good many of the external repairs. When I came I spent about £300 myself on various things about the place. In 1877 I spent £70; 1878 and 1879 were bad years and I only spent between them about £30; in 1880 I spent £54; in 1881, £40; in 1882, £30; in 1883, £60; in 1884, £116; in 1885, £34; in 1886, £61; and last year £64.

1737. Do these sums include improvements?—They do. I paid a large share of the cost of the play-shed in 1884. I whitewashed the large schoolroom; I paid a large share of the cost of the bathroom; and I keep the whole of the interior whitewashed and painted.

1738. You have no claim for your expenditure against the Governors?—No claim at all.

1739. Besides what you have expended what have the Governors done?—When I came they spent, I believe, something like £1,000, to put the place in

Oct. 13, 188[illegible]. — [illegible] [illegible], M.A., LL.D.

order. For several years after that they did not spend much. In 1880 they spent £14; in 1881, £55; in 1882, £25; in 1883, £65; in 1884, £116—exactly the same as I spent myself; in 1885, £27; in 1886, £112—in that year new sewerage was put in, and the whole of the external colouring was renewed; and last year they spent £45. These figures are approximate.

1740. Who inspects the place?—Mr. Symes, of Millar and Symes, comes about once a year.

1741. What are your pecuniary endowments?—£100 a year for myself. Mr. Rowan gets his salary of £120 direct from the Governors, and I get £30 a year for the payment of another master.

1742. Rev. Dr. Molloy.—There have been fifteen free pupils who were Catholics out of fifty-five admitted by the Board?—Yes.

1743. Then you have been authorised by the Board to receive them?—Certainly. The Board accepted them, not I.

1744. Are there any other Catholic pupils besides the free pupils?—Yes. At present we have seven Catholic day boys who pay fees and five free pupils.

1745. Lord Justice Naish.—How many day boys have you altogether?—Thirty-four.

1746. Rev. Dr. Molloy.—Then by the judgment of the Board Catholics are admitted to a share in the endowment?—They never ask the question as to whether the applicant is a Catholic or a Protestant.

1747. You are not required to teach them Archbishop Ussher's Catechism?—No. We work under the conscience clause of the Intermediate Board, to the effect that religious instruction is to be given at such a time and in such a way as that it shall not interfere with the secular instruction of any.

1748. Then the Board has sanctioned a departure to that extent from the intentions of the founder. He said he was anxious to found a school to propagate the Protestant faith according to the Scriptures, and, therefore, he directed that the master should catechise the children out of Primate Ussher's Catechism and expound the same to them, and that that should be done under penalty of the master forfeiting his place?—I don't do it, and I have not yet forfeited my place.

1749. I suppose the Board consider that there has been such a change in the circumstances of the case as to warrant this departure from the will of the founder, and that Catholics should be allowed to share in the endowment without prejudice to their religious convictions?—I should think so. I have never had the smallest trouble in any way.

1750. Professor Dougherty.—Did you tell us that you had an entrance examination in the case of boys seeking to be admitted on the foundation?—I examine them informally.

1751. Do you make a report to the Governors?—Yes—simply as to whether they are fit to join any class that we have in operation.

1752. The Governors do not send anyone to see the boys?—No.

1753. Lord Justice FitzGibbon.—Is there any inspection by the Governors?—Yes, twice annually.

1754. Who is the inspector?—Rev. Mr. Gray, F.T.C.D. He goes through all the classes, and examines every boy.

1755. Does he examine the fabric?—Yes, but I believe it is no part of his duty.

1756. Dr. Traill.—When you send up a report in reference to the admission of a boy do you put his religion opposite to his name?—No.

1757. So that in the selection by the Board in Dublin they do not know whether a boy is a Roman Catholic or not?—I think they do in some cases.

1758. How do they know if you do not give them the information?—It is sometimes stated by the parents.

1759. Professor Dougherty.—I suppose every boy must submit his baptismal certificate, or something equivalent to it?—Yes.

1760. And from that they might know?—The baptismal certificate has to be sent and they would know from it.

1761. Have the Governors ever refused admission to any pupil that you recommended?—Yes, they have.

1762. Did they acquaint you with the grounds of their refusal?—No, they don't give any grounds. In one or two instances boys whom I thought not quite fit were admitted.

1763. Against your recommendation?—Against my recommendation; and in at least one instance a boy who I thought was fit, was not admitted.

1764. Rev. Dr. Molloy.—Do many of the boys remain at home here in Galway when they have finished with you?—A good many. From the form I filled up for you in 1883 I find that twenty-four per cent. went to some university; about six per cent. ultimately went into the Civil Service; five into the Church; two to law; ten to the medical profession; twelve to mercantile pursuits, and twenty-five to other callings. That includes all those that I know, or about sixty per cent. of the whole.

1765. You have supplied a considerable number of doctors to the country?—Yes, in common with most educational places; it is a very favourite profession.

1766. Dr. Traill.—Where were you educated yourself?—In England.

1767. Were you not a scholar of Trinity College, Dublin?—Yes, and a medallist.

1768. Lord Justice FitzGibbon.—Is there any provision in Galway for the intermediate education of girls?—There is an attempt being made now to establish a ladies' school.

1769. A private school?—Yes.

1770. Have you ever thought of doing what they are doing so frequently in the North, giving intermediate education to girls in the same school with boys?—It never came within the range of practical politics to me, for I believe the Governors would not listen to it.

1771. What is your own idea on the subject?—My own opinion is, that it is the right idea to carry it. I would be a radical reformer in that way.

1772. Rev. Dr. Molloy.—What is the objection of the Governors?—I imagine they would think it quite outside their powers. I think the education was intended by Erasmus Smith for boys exclusively, but I may be wrong.

1773. I don't think girls are expressly excluded by him; but in the time of Erasmus Smith it was not supposed that girls were to be educated at all?—I should think not.

1774. Professor Dougherty.—You think the Governors share the sentiments of Erasmus Smith?—I don't know. Perhaps I should not have spoken of their feelings.

1775. Lord Justice FitzGibbon.—What is your own idea as to the expediency of giving intermediate education to girls in the same school with boys. Our Act of Parliament provides that we shall extend the endowments to both boys and girls?—My own opinion is that it would be the right thing to do, but there would be some difficulty in starting it.

1776. Where have your boarders come from?—At present I have eighteen from Leinster; three from Ulster; six from Munster; eleven from Connaught; five from the colonies, and two from Greece. Their parents are English living in Greece.

1777. Do you think a local committee in connexion with the school would be of advantage in attracting pupils?—In some ways it might do so.

1778. Do you think such a committee would be of advantage to the school?—If the committee consisted of capable men.

1779. Professor Dougherty.—Men who would leave the head master alone?—I think that would be the test of their good sense.

1780. Lord Justice FitzGibbon.—And if men of

good ones, would they be useful in keeping up an interest in the institution?—Yes.

1781. And occasionally, perhaps, in providing new inducements, as they do in the North, in the way of prizes?—Yes—anything of that kind I should welcome.

1782. If you were allowed to try the radical experiment of admitting young ladies, a local committee, to satisfy the inhabitants that they were properly looked after, would be an advantage?—Certainly.

1783. You would have no objection to working with a sensible local committee?—None at all.

Oct. 13, 1888. Richard Biggs, LL.D.

Hermann Dunn sworn and examined.

Hermann Dunn.

1784. Lord Justice FitzGibbon.—You have been a long time connected with the school?—Thirty-two years, nearly.

1785. What was the largest number of pupils in the school during Mr. Hallowell's time?—I think there never were more than about twenty; and we went down as low as six at one time.

1786. What was the condition of the school buildings in those days?—It was not very good.

1787. How were you originally appointed yourself?—By the governors—by competition. They advertised in the London *Times* for a teacher of modern languages; I was elected out of a very large number, but had still to submit to a special examination.

1788. You had some expectation of other employment here and did not succeed in realising it?—I did not.

1789. What was that?—Private tuitions.

1790. During what hours are you engaged at Erasmus Smith's school?—Now, from half-past nine to three; but originally I was only engaged for three hours in the day.

1791. Did you find it impossible to get pupils out of your school hours?—I found it very difficult. I had a few; but sometimes for two or three years I could not get any private tuitions.

1792. Dr. Traill.—Was there any original understanding about private tuitions when you were appointed?—A prospect was held out.

1793. Lord Justice FitzGibbon.—On what terms were you originally appointed by the Governors?—I was to get £50 a year for giving instruction in modern languages during five days for three hours each day.

1794. That engagement was put an end to, was it not?—Yes, about thirteen years ago.

1795. For the last thirteen years you have been, not under the Governors, but under Dr. Biggs?—Under Dr. Biggs, by private arrangement.

1796. Now, as I understand, you think you have a claim on the Governors for adequate employment?—Yes—or at least, as I stated in my paper (handed in), I came to Ireland, induced by the Governors, who held out very favourable prospects to me. These were not realised. I left all my prospects in London in order to come here.

1797. Lord Justice Naish.—In what year did you come?—In the beginning of 1857.

1798. And when did that engagement terminate which you held under the Governors?—In 1875.

1799. Since then you have continued to work with Dr. Biggs?—With Dr. Biggs.

1800. Lord Justice FitzGibbon.—Did you ever reside in the school?—I never did.

1801. Rev. Dr. Molloy.—Have you any document showing the prospects that the Governors held out to you at the time of your appointment?—No, not exactly.

1802. The advertisement, perhaps, would show it?—It was in the London *Times*; but it is so long ago. I might have some letters from Mr. Hallowell referring to the matter.

1803. In what way did they hold out these prospects to you?—Mr. Hallowell chiefly said that this was the capital of a province, and a watering place, and that there was not a single teacher of modern languages here.

1804. All that was true?—And that I would certainly have plenty of opportunities of making a very large income.

1805. You did not find these opportunities when you came here?—No; I did not.

1806. Lord Justice FitzGibbon.—Had you a large class in the school?—I had all the pupils who attended the school.

1807. You have been preparing the boys for the Intermediate examinations in modern languages?—Yes.

1808. You have now no arrangement for any retiring allowance?—No.

1809. We have no power to interfere with the engagement between you and Mr. Biggs, and you are for thirteen years no longer under the Governors.

Witness.—The governors induced me to give up all my prospects in England, and come here.

1810. Dr. Traill.—But you said it was Mr. Hallowell who wrote to you?—In the name of the governors.

1811. How could he write in the name of the governors?—He was head master.

1812. But he could not pledge the governors?—He only made statements.

1813. Were you engaged by the governors through Mr. Hallowell?—By the governors, through Mr. Hallowell.

Redmond M'Donogh, B.A., Solicitor.

Redmond M'Donogh, B.A.

1814. I appear on behalf of the Catholic inhabitants of Galway, and the Rev. Peter Dooley. I don't propose to discuss the bearings of the Act of Parliament, for that has been fully threshed out in Dublin, and it would not be my business to enter on it. I will only refer very briefly to the terms of the Act, and of the deeds, so far as they relate to Galway alone. It is stated that the income from the Galway estates was, in 1878—it appears at page 108 of the report—£2,680. I propose to confine my remarks to what particularly relates to Galway, and not to enter into the general question as to the scope and effect of Erasmus Smith's deeds, for your lordships have had sufficient discussion of that already.

Lord Justice Naish.—It was very fully argued before us in Dublin.

1815. Mr. M'Donogh.—Dr. Biggs has stated that there are only 11 boarders from Connaught; all the day boys are from Connaught, but only three of them are tenants sons, and, as I read the original deeds and settlement, the tenants children were the primary objects of the donor's bounty, and any scheme which does not succeed in ensuring to the tenants children the benefits intended for them by the testator will have failed in its purpose, and will require to be amended. Now, I need hardly call evidence that the children of those tenants of the lands in and around Galway, from which this large income is derived, are almost exclusively Catholics, and, whatever the reasons may be, this school, notwithstanding the excellent management of Dr. Biggs—a management which the evidence proves clearly is very much superior to any previous management—there are only three of the tenants children attending the school.

Oct. 13, [illegible]
Reverend M'Donogh, [illegible]

Dr. Biggs.—I only know there are two or three. There may be many more.

1816. Mr. M'Donogh.—If there are more Dr. Biggs can correct that afterwards. In the town of Galway the Catholics stand to the Protestants numerically in the relation of fifteen to one, and the part of Galway in which Erasmus Smith's estates are situated is much more Catholic than the town part of the town, the ratio there being about forty to one. The Catholics do not consider that under the present system they get as much benefit as they ought. Of course it will be for the Commission to decide whether the present system carries out the intentions of the testator. But the Catholics submit that it is a great grievance to them, being the ratepaying body, and the body from whom this £3,000 a year and upwards comes, that they should by the existing scheme be deprived of any benefit from the endowment. I am instructed to urge that inasmuch as Erasmus Smith in giving these lands originally had in view to a very great extent the children of the tenants upon his estates; and having regard to the fact that then, as now, those children were nearly exclusively Catholics, the Catholics should get directly some portion of that large endowment. I would ask that, having regard to the fact that Catholics are not altogether excluded from the benefits of this endowment, and having regard also to the letter that is referred to in one of the reports wherein Erasmus Smith himself directs that the head master of Galway school shall not be allowed to continue to refuse to allow Catholic children to go to the school. I would ask you, having regard to all these facts, to hold that the Catholics are entitled, qua Catholics at all events, to some portion of this endowment. One thing referred to by Mr. Carton in Dublin, I will strive to illustrate by an example taken from Galway. The argument is, that inasmuch as at the time when this foundation was instituted, no one but a Protestant could teach, any provisions as regards Protestant teachers should not be taken in the same strict sense in which they would now be taken, when it is open to all persons and to all religions to teach and be taught. I bring this forward as a local illustration of the system. In the following passage from Hardiman's History of Galway, page 176, with reference to a report made to the House of Lords in 1731 by the then Mayor of Galway, Walter Taylor:—

"That part of the report which related to the popish schools stated that the Mayor on the information of Mr. Garrett, master of the Free School, gave him his warrant against one Gregory French, whom he alleged to be a popish schoolmaster, and to keep a Latin school, and that having called upon Mr. Garrett to know what he had done under the warrant, he said that French had dropped his school, and being further examined he declared he knew of no other Latin school, and that he could give no account of any other, or of any English or writing schools except that some of his scholars went out of school daily to learn to write, but he could not tell from whom."

This, at all events, shows that at that time there were existing in Galway no schools but Protestant schools, and no schoolmasters excepting Protestant schoolmasters, unless those who taught surreptitiously, and were not recognised by law. I wish merely to urge these considerations briefly, and to record the protest of the Catholics of Galway against the continuance of the present system, and their demand that they shall derive some benefit from this endowment. There are about 2,000 Catholic pupils in Catholic schools in Galway which have no endowments, or practically none, and it is a hardship that these 2,000 pupils should be in receipt of no endowment, whilst about 60 pupils in all should be in receipt of £3,000 a year.

1817. Dr. Traill.—What is your practical proposition?

Mr. M'Donogh.—I understand that the proposition would be to divide the endowment.

1818. Dr. Traill.—If there was a Roman Catholic endowment left open to all denominations, but with Roman Catholic Managers, would you be prepared to propose in that case also that the endowment should be divided amongst Protestants and Roman Catholics?

Mr. M'Donogh.—I think if we got a share of Dr. Biggs' endowment we would be quite prepared to divide what we have ourselves.

1819. Dr. Traill.—Would you apply that to the Roman Catholic endowments that are open to all denominations, such as Harvey's Charity at Mullingar?

Mr. M'Donogh.—In Galway we would put the whole into hotch pot and take our chance.

1820. Professor Dougherty.—What principle of distribution would you adopt?

Mr. M'Donogh.—The principle of sharing numerically. The revenues should be divided into scholarships and bursaries.

1821. Dr. Traill.—Would you have the money given according to Erasmus Smith's conditions or not.

Mr. M'Donogh.—That depends on the construction you put on his conditions.

Dr. Traill.—Nobody could make any mistake about it. He wanted to proselytise the Roman Catholic community.

Mr. M'Donogh.—I deny that entirely.

Dr. Traill.—His letter shows what his intentions were.

1822. Lord Justice FitzGibbon.—This is substantially the same question that Mr. Carton argued in Dublin. According to our Act of Parliament, and also according to the principles of justice, it is our duty, in framing schemes, to have regard to the spirit of the founder's intentions. Therefore we cannot look at this case as if we had £3,000 a year of public money to be applied in the interests of education as matters stand at present. In such a case as that we should be bound, and we should be very glad, to deal with the endowment in such a way that all parties would get their fair share of benefit. We have done that in every case where we had public money to deal with. But where educational advantages were given by a private founder, and were intended for a particular class of persons, we are bound to have regard to their rights. It is important to bear in mind that this very question arose in Erasmus Smith's own lifetime. In the year 1682, after he had founded all his schools, he got a report giving a very poor account of their condition, and he wrote this letter to those who then had the government of the country in their hands:—

"London, June ye 6th, 1682.

"My Lords and Gentlemen,

"I have received your letter, dated May 23rd, with copy of the report concerning the present state of the schools of Drogheda, and am sorry you have been put to so much trouble: I give you my humble thanks for your careful inspection of the schools, and especially that of Drogheda. The letter following was written before the receipt of yours, which I now humbly present unto you, not doubting but it will be satisfactory to your honours as it will be to myself if followed.

"My end in founding the three schools was to propagate the Protestant faith according to the Scriptures, avoiding all superstition, as the Charter, and the bylaws, and rules established doe direct. Therefore, it is the [illegible] of His Majesty to consider the children out of Popish Ushers, and [illegible] the same unto them, which I [illegible] desire may be observed upon the penalty of forfeiting their places.

"Now, that the scholars educated in these foundations may be encouraged, I humbly request that it may be recommended to the Provost and Fellows of Trinity College, Dublin, to present to your honours six fitly qualified according to the Charter, laws, and Rules, to enter in the room of Mr. Scott, late schoolmaster at Drogheda, giving preference to those that have been educated in these schools, that others educated upon the same foundations may be encouraged to pursue [illegible] worthy of the [illegible] choice; if none among them be qualified, I leave it at large, and as I find their [illegible] I shall be encouraged to trust them for the future. I desire the Charter may be observed as to what doth concern the duly, and privileges both of master and scholars, and the laws and rules called Canons, and that a table may be fairly written thereof and hung up in the most publique place in every schoole, that neither master nor scholar may pretend ignorance.

"My Lords, my designe is not to reflect upon any, only I give my judgment why these schooles are so unacceptable, which are, and is, and will be (if not prevented) the many popish schooles, their neighbours, which at present draw the town. If parents will exclude their children because prayers, catechisme and exposition is commanded, I cannot help it, for [illegible] to remove that, were is to make them seminaries of Popery. Therefore, I beseech you to command that that shall be presented and approved by your honours, to observe them that deviate from duties and expell them, which will oblige, my Lords and Gentlemen,

"Your most humble servant,

"Erasmus Smith."

That letter shows that he then had this question brought up before him, and that he preferred that the schools should not be attended by Roman Catholic pupils, rather than that the Protestant character of the teaching should be taken away. We shall certainly not throw any additional difficulty in the way of education being given in these schools as at present to any who choose to accept it; but it has struck us that the founder has made it an essential condition that there shall be specifically Protestant government and Protestant teaching in the schools supported by his bounty, and we can hardly have a right to alter that because the law is more favourable to education now than it was a couple of hundred years ago.

Mr. M'Donagh.—But independently of that letter, would you construe the Act of Settlement and the deed itself as making these schools exclusively a Protestant foundation?

1822. Lord Justice Fitzgibbon.—Not in the sense that the Governors should refuse Roman Catholic pupils who were willing to come on the founder's terms. On the contrary, his object was that they should be admitted with a view to their getting instruction in the Protestant religion which he wanted to prevail; but the question is whether he intended that the Protestant instruction should give way to admit pupils who would not take it. That was the question raised and answered in his own letter.

Mr. M'Donagh.—I had not seen that letter before.

1823. Lord Justice Fitzgibbon.—You base your present claim on the further ground that he wished his bounty to be extended to the children of his tenants?

Mr. M'Donagh.—Yes—that it was his primary intention that the children of all his tenants should share as far as possible his endowments. Another argument is that he expressed his intentions by a deed which was confirmed by an Act of Settlement, and that that should override any other document such as this letter.

1824. Dr. Traill.—He attached conditions about which there can be no possibility of mistake. No Roman Catholic pupil is to be excluded if he chooses to comply with those conditions. Dr Biggs has gone very far already in introducing a conscience clause for the day boys. But to say that we are to confiscate the founder's property, because certain pupils will not agree to the conditions that he has prescribed, would be going too far.

1825. Rev. Dr. Molloy.—These conditions have been already set aside by the Board. They don't teach Primate Ussher's Catechism, as Erasmus Smith directed, nor do they expel Catholic pupils who refuse to attend Protestant worship. Therefore, the Board have practically abolished the conditions laid down by Erasmus Smith.

Mr. M'Donagh.—That would not a good many other conditions go overboard with them?

1826. Dr. Traill.—Then would you contend that the more liberal a man is in the administration of his property the more it is to be confiscated?

Mr. M'Donagh.—No; but I say that if you can break through a man's intentions in one respect you are at liberty to break through them in others.

1827. Dr. Traill.—That is, that if a man's intentions are broken through in the direction of liberality his property is to be transferred to another denomination. The only result of pressing that argument would be to get all the restrictions put on again.

Mr. M'Donagh.—As regards transferring property from one class to another you have a good many instances of that in recent years, and it is not considered at all such a great crime now. The Acts of 1869 and 1887 did it.

Dr. Traill.—That is not the function of our Commission; we are not Land Commissioners.

Lord Justice Naish.—Mr. M'Donagh, this was argued very fully in Dublin, and you have put forward your views very fairly, and of course, before we bring out any scheme, everything will be considered, but there is great difficulty in the question.

1828. Lord Justice Fitzgibbon.—Up to the present, where we were dealing with public money, as in the case of the Royal School endowments, we considered ourselves not only at liberty, but bound, to try to make the endowments available for education on conditions acceptable to all those who had a right to benefit. The same principle applies to Erasmus Smith's endowments. We have first to determine who are entitled to the benefit of that endowment; and it is difficult to say whether the founder's intentions were entirely in favour of his tenants, or entirely in favour of Protestantism, or were a mixture of both. If both, we have to determine which was the leading intention. He did not contemplate dividing the endowment, for he established schools to be conducted on defined principles. These schools have been left open to Roman Catholic pupils by the Governors, who have not strictly followed the provisions of Erasmus Smith's will. Mr. M'Donagh has put very forcibly an argument founded upon that; but if we found that the Governors were violating Erasmus Smith's intentions, it might be our duty to make them stop doing so, and the only effect would be to exclude Roman Catholic pupils from what Erasmus Smith's foundation is now pretty well understood to have been a private grant by one charitable individual.

Mr. M'Donagh.—I wish to point out that in the grant of December, 1667, to the original trustees, he provides for teaching the pupils in the original tongue, and gives the lands—

"To the intent that out of the annual profits of the premises the trustees and their successors shall erect five school-houses for the teaching of the grammar of the original tongue, and of spelling, writing, and accounts, to be built."

Lord Justice Fitzgibbon.—That was Hebrew. That, and not Irish, was "the original tongue" that he desired to be taught in his five schools in Ireland.

Oct. 19, 1888.

Professor M'Donagh, M.A.

The Rev. John C. Clarke.

1829. I am a Presbyterian minister, and I desire to offer these suggestions. I have the utmost confidence in the management of Dr. Biggs. If he were a member of my own Church I would not have more confidence in him than I have as head master of this school. So long as he is head master it does not matter very much what kind of board we have; but if the head master was not doing his duty, and was letting the school go down, then I think a local board would be of the utmost importance.

Rev. John C. Clarke.

* "Taxt is inscribed in the original Minute Book, but the context shows that it has been improperly inserted."—Rev. Dr. Q. [illegible], Endowed Schools Commission Report, 1858, Vol. II., p. 193.

Oct. 13, 1887.

Rev. John G. Clarke.

1831. Lord Justice Naish.—Do you not think that an efficient board in Dublin might also be very useful under such circumstances? Very often local boards are hampered by their personal acquaintance with the schoolmaster?—Under these central boards a good many schools go to wreck. If you have a competent local board the master would not be allowed to wreck the school. This very school was not in a good condition until Dr. Biggs got it. As to free pupils, I don't sympathise entirely with Dr. Biggs' views. I think we are getting too much into competitive examinations, and I don't think it would be well to have it altogether competitive for the class of pupils intended to be benefited.

1832. Dr. Traill.—But he said he would be satisfied to take the recommendation of the master of the school from which the candidate came, as to the candidate being a boy of promising tendencies, without subjecting him at too early an age to a competitive examination?—But pupils have come who were privately educated, and have claimed the benefit of the foundation, and have got it although they have not been at any school.

1833. Lord Justice FitzGibbon.—What are your suggestions about free pupils?—I acknowledge that it adds something to Dr. Biggs' position that he should have clever boys; but I don't see that because one boy is clever, another of a respectable family, who is slow in his early years should be shut out. I think that the foundation should rather take up those boys, for they are just the very ones that need to be helped, and that may prove the best pupils in the school.

1834. Whether do you think a committee of the Dublin governors, or a local committee, subject to the approval of the Dublin governors, would be the better tribunal to select free boys?—My opinion would be in favour of a local committee, and at the same time a central board, as a court of review. If we were all parties, I would say a local committee, and nothing but that.

1835. Dr. Traill.—With regard to forwarding in life boys that are less able to push themselves forward—non-clever boys—it appears from Dr. Biggs' evidence that, out of 55, only 10 have been pushed forward. Is it advisable to take boys out of their own class, unless they have got abilities? I don't speak of giving them an education that will fit them for the world, but of shoving them up into a superior class?—My experience is, that very often a boy who at twelve years of age is considered slow and backward, will—if he gets a fair chance—become the best afterwards.

1836. But Dr. Biggs has shown that out of 55 who got that fair chance, 45 were not able to go on?—I have had no opportunity of examining into the circumstances of those boys, so that I cannot answer you as to that.

1837. Lord Justice FitzGibbon.—What is your idea?—That a local committee should first select the pupils, and ascertain the capabilities of the boys; and I would like a court of review in Dublin, lest there should be any job, and of course the candidate should pass a fairly searching examination in each case. The next point to which I would refer is the education of girls. So far as I know the history of the foundation, girls have been educated in the lower schools, but not in the higher; but only because girls were not educated in any higher schools in the olden times. I think it is clearly within the limits of the endowment to apply some of it to the higher education of girls, and we need that very much in Galway.

1838. Is there any provision for girls education here?—We are just moving a little now, and we hope to have an Intermediate school open in about a month or so.

1839. Professor Dougherty.—What steps have you taken in that direction?—A local committee has been formed, and I have got a promise from a fund in connexion with our church, of £20 for a year or two, until the thing is fairly started.

1840. Are you promising the teacher any fixed salary?—No. A committee representing the various Protestant denominations, guarantee for the rent part of the rent of a house, £15 a year for a certain time.

1841. Are the £20 a year to go towards the rent?—Is not to be handed over at the rate of £5 a quarter.

1842. Lord Justice FitzGibbon.—Have you selected a teacher yet?—Yes. It has not come before the committee for full sanction, but they know that young ladies were being negotiated with, and that they have consented to come.

1843. Have these ladies been engaged in teaching elsewhere?—Their sisters have a large establishment in Belfast. One of these taught in their place; and the other is qualified in scholarship and has also had considerable experience in teaching. In Galway we would have been greatly benefited if we had had even a small endowment for the higher education of girls.

1844. Rev. Dr. Molloy.—Would it meet your views to have the classes of the present Grammar School opened to girls?—That would meet my views fully. Dr. Biggs knows that I asked him was that possible.

1845. That would be a much easier way of obtaining a share in the endowment than to press for money.

Rev. Mr. Clarke.—I don't know the feelings of the people of Galway generally on the subject, but my sympathies are with the course which has been taken in the Methodist College and in other places.

1846. Professor Dougherty.—Have you had any free boys from your congregation in the school?—Yes.

1847. There was no difficulty about their reception?—No. Dr. Biggs forwarded any claim that I on the part of my congregation made; and I have no reason to complain on that ground. If a new scheme were made out there are certain privileges I would like to have. I think I might give religious instruction in the school. I believe that has been recognised in the High School in Dublin, but I did not press it because I knew this matter would be coming up here, and because I had full confidence in Dr. Biggs.

1848. Lord Justice FitzGibbon.—The case made by the Governors in Dublin was, having regard to the provisions of the deed and charter as regards the approval of the bishops, the reading of Archbishop Ussher's Catechism, and the teachers subscribing certain of the Thirty-nine Articles, that these all taken together showed that he intended to limit the government of the schools to the hands of members of the Established Church.

Rev. Mr. Clarke.—That is the central question.

1849. Lord Justice FitzGibbon.—I know it is. I should point out that you and Mr. M'Donagh, in this respect, have very much the same difficulty to meet, except that, I believe, the Catechism of the Assembly of Divines would have suited you very well?—Quite well.

1850. Professor Dougherty.—You still use the catechism originally prescribed for the use of these schools?—That is quite true.

1851. Dr. Traill.—Do you use Archbishop Ussher's Catechism?—We do not.

1852. Professor Dougherty.—Have the Governors appointed a Presbyterian Catechist in the High School in Dublin?—Yes, that was done a short time ago, and I would have moved in the matter here also, but that I saw that the Commission was coming down, and I did not think it would be well to anticipate their action.

1853. I suppose you would like a local committee to represent the various religious denominations?—Most certainly.

1854. And you would like to see a central board constituted somewhat differently from the present one?—Quite so.

1855. Dr. Traill (to Dr. Biggs).—What provision do you make for religious instruction?

Oct. 12, 1888.

Rev. John C. Clarke.

Dr. Bigger.—The first half hour of the day—from half-past nine to ten.

1856. Is it given by a clergyman?—No—by ourselves.

1857. Has the Church of Ireland clergyman any particular rights?—I don't know about rights, but the Church clergyman takes an interest in the school.

1858. Does he attend?—Yes. In the evening.

1859. Is there any special arrangement with him?—There is no special arrangement, as nothing arises.

1860. Do you invite him in, or does he come as he likes?—We are quite agreed about it.

1861. Does he teach the Catechism?—No.

1862. He has not charge of the religious education of the school?—No.

1863. That is under your own control?—Yes.

1864. Professor Dougherty.—Does he instruct all the boys of the school or only those of his own denomination?—Only the boys of his own denomination.

Rev. Mr. Clarke.—There is this marked distinction, that we have not a master connected with our Church there.

1865. Lord Justice FitzGibbon.—There is a very strict provision in the deed about the masters.

Rev. Mr. Clarke.—I was satisfied that the matter was in good hands in Dublin, and therefore I did not think it necessary to attend.

Lord Justice FitzGibbon.—We are glad to have heard the views of the local gentlemen in this matter. In fact, it was largely for that purpose that we thought it our duty to come here before entering on the preparation of a scheme.

The inquiry then closed.

PUBLIC SITTING—SATURDAY, OCTOBER 13, 1888.

Oct. 13, 1888.

At the Courthouse, Tuam.

Present:—The Right Hon. Lord Justice FitzGibbon and the Right Hon. Lord Justice Naish, Judicial Commissioners; and the Rev. Gerald Molloy, D.D., D.Sc., Anthony Traill, Esq., LL.D., M.D., F.T.C.D., and Professor Dougherty, M.A., Assistant Commissioners.

The Assistant Secretary, N. D. Murphy, Junr., was in attendance.

TUAM DIOCESAN FREE SCHOOL.

The Very Rev. *William Chambers Townsend*, Dean of Tuam, sworn and examined.

Very Rev. William Chambers Townsend, Dean of Tuam.

1866. Lord Justice FitzGibbon.—How long have you been Dean of Tuam?—Nine years.

1867. The Diocesan School was in existence when you came here?—Yes.

1868. Who was the master?—The Rev. Dr. Henry Coote Murphy.

1869. When did he retire?—He left in 1880.

1870. He compounded?—Yes.

1871. Since that time no annuity has been payable for a diocesan school-master?—No.

1872. Where was the school?—In his own private premises—The Grove—with eight acres of land. He held under a lease, and holds the premises still.

1873. Lord Justice Naish.—Had they been used as a Diocesan School before he came?—I think he was the first that used them for the purpose.

1874. Was there any building that had been previously used as a Diocesan School?—There was an old building—now M'Donnell's shop in the town—but it was sold.

1875. Lord Justice FitzGibbon.—Then, so far as you are aware, the money now in the hands of the Commissioners of Education consists of the proceeds of the sale of the Diocesan School buildings and the accumulations since?—Yes.

1876. What provision is there in Tuam for intermediate education?—I don't know of any for Protestants.

1877. What number of pupils were in the Diocesan School when it was in existence?—From twenty-four to thirty boys.

1878. Why did Mr. Murphy give up?—He wanted to become a parochial clergyman. He has been appointed now to a parish in Kildare. I dare say he was getting tired of school work.

1879. As to the Diocesan School Fund, £750, have you considered what way it might be applied?

Witness.—Might the Diocesan Trustees frame a scheme?

1880. Lord Justice FitzGibbon.—We must see what was the origin of the fund. Some Diocesan schools were built by Grand Jury presentment; and where they were built with public money the trusts would be different from what they would be if the funds were originally given by a private person. Where the foundation was public property we are to utilise it, as far as we can, for the benefit of all denominations.

1881. Dr. Traill.—How much did Mr. Murphy leave behind when he compounded?—The interest is about £3 a year.

1882. What becomes of it?—It goes into the general funds of the diocese.

1883. Lord Justice FitzGibbon.—The Church Body have got it?—The Church Body have got it. A gentleman tried to keep on the school for a while, and we let him have the £3 a year, the interest on Mr. Murphy's composition balance, as long as he was here.

1884. The capital has not been applied to any specific purpose?—No, it goes into our diocesan funds.

1885. Then your Diocesan Synod would be able still to devote it to diocesan educational purposes, and to add anything else they could to it?—If they had any more, they would be glad to add the £3 to it.

1886. I suppose you have no other endowment in the neighbourhood?—I am sorry to say we have not, except the Blake Bequest.

Oct. 13, 1885.

Very Rev. [illegible], Dean of Tuam.

THE NETTERVILLE BLAKE BEQUEST FOR A PROTESTANT ORPHANAGE.

1887. What is the Blake Bequest?—About two English miles from Tuam there is a very good house and offices, and a good many acres of land, which are left to be made a Protestant orphanage in connection with the Protestant Orphan Society of Ireland after the death of the founder's widow and two sisters, one of whom is dead.

1888. The endowment is not available during her, Mrs. Blake's, life?—No.

1889. What age is she?—About forty. The sister is in delicate health.

1890. Lord Justice Naish.—What is the income?—About £170 a year.

1891. Lord Justice FitzGibbon.—Has any step been taken to form a governing body to look after the charity, and to manage it when it becomes available?—Mr. Blake left it to three trustees. Two of these, Mr. Cameron, and Mr. Denis Kirwan, of Castle Hackett, are dead; the third, Mr. Henry, of Toghes, is a very feeble old gentleman. We would be glad to have new trustees, and we ask you to appoint them.

1892. Have any steps been taken in your diocese to appoint diocesan trustees to hold educational property?—Yes. We have appointed four trustees; I am one of them.

1893. Would it be your view that this Blake Endowment should be held by the Central Diocesan Body or that there should be a special governing body for itself?—I would be better pleased that the Central Body should take it up.

1894. Is there any provision in the will for the appointment of new trustees?—No.

1895. Lord Justice Naish.—Is the object of the will to found a new orphanage or to work in connection with an orphan society at present in existence?—I think it is to found a new orphanage; but that would be very difficult because the income is very small for the purpose.

1896. It may be forty years before it is available?—Yes.

1897. So that it might be premature to make a scheme?—Except that it is necessary to appoint trustees to hold the property.

1898. Lord Justice FitzGibbon.—I suppose all that can practically be done now is to vest the property in the Diocesan Trustees, so that they will be there to utilise it when it falls in?—I suppose so.

1899. Lord Justice Naish.—The probability is that some person is named in the will who has power to appoint new trustees. Even though no power to do so is given by the will, under different Acts of Parliament the surviving trustee would have power.

1900. Lord Justice FitzGibbon.—Would it be satisfactory to leave the appointment of the trustees of a property which is ultimately to become educational in the hands of private individuals?

Witness.—We should prefer to have it in some other hands.

1901. Dr. Traill.—Is there any danger of waste or cutting of timber if it be not in the hands of proper trustees?—Yes.

1902. Lord Justice FitzGibbon.—Who is occupying the lands at present?—Mrs. Blake, the widow. It may be rather hard on her to keep the place in proper repair.

1903. We cannot do anything against her will, at least without consulting her. Is she friendly?—Yes, she is most anxious that this Commission should take the matter up and appoint new trustees.

1904. Then we will look at the will, communicate with Mrs. Blake and with the Diocesan Trustees, and see whom they suggest to hold the property. We could hardly settle a scheme for the management of the orphanage as we cannot tell what may be the state of affairs when the property comes into possession.

ST. JARLATH'S COLLEGE, TUAM.

The Very Rev. *Patrick [illegible]*, D.D., sworn and examined.

Very Rev. Patrick [illegible], D.D.

1905. Lord Justice FitzGibbon.—You were examined in Dublin. I believe you are President of this institution?—I was President up to February last. I appeared at Nenagh immediately after the meeting of the Catholic managers. Gentlemen appeared before you on that occasion to say that you should give a large amount to each school—not less than a minimum of £100 a year. That was not the feeling of some of the Catholic managers, who thought that even a small sum would be productive of great advantage, especially to poor schools, in parts of the country where money is not easily procurable.

1906. You thought that £50 would be of use?—Of great use. We saw a strong corroboration of your opinion at Boyle, where a most excellent school is doing good work, indeed, under a mixed committee; and they told us that £50 a year would be quite enough to keep them going, and £100 a year would make them always rich. St. Jarlath's was founded in 1817?—Yes, about that time.

1907. Who are the present managers?—The Archbishop has the direction, but the President is the Rev. Michael O'Connell, and there is a staff of professors. The Archbishop, of course, directs the institution very much by the opinion of the President and Professors.

1908. How many are the teaching staff?—Six—five priests, and one gentleman who is not a priest.

1909. How many pupils are there now?—The number of students during the last five years was as follows:—In 1884, 84; in 1885, 76; in 1886, 75; in 1887, 67; and at present about 54.

1910. Lord Justice Naish.—There is a decrease?—Yes.

1911. Lord Justice FitzGibbon.—How many of these are boarders?—Last year there were 67 boarders, and two or three day boys besides.

1912. Why have you so few day boys?—We do not encourage day boys, because we consider their presence interferes somewhat with discipline. It is entirely an ecclesiastical college.

1913. Lord Justice Naish.—You are near the town?—We are near the town, and we thought they were introducing matters that seriously interfered with discipline.

1914. Rev. Dr. Molloy.—Contraband of war?—Contraband of war.

1915. Lord Justice FitzGibbon.—Is it an ecclesiastical college?—It is generally ecclesiastical, but there are opportunities for a very good secular education.

1916. You send boys to the Intermediate Examinations?—Yes, but we are very much debarred from presenting the best students owing to the age limits. In this part of the country the people are very poor; and they think that the few years spent by their sons in preparing for the priesthood would be better spent for themselves, and that they can achieve the same results at a later age. Therefore they don't send them in until the last moment, until they are sixteen or seventeen years of age. It takes a year or two then to prepare for the Intermediate Examinations, and the consequence is that they are excluded.

1917. Rev. Dr. Molloy.—How are they occupied between the time when they finish their primary education and the time when they come to St. Jarlath's?—I could not say. They finish their primary education up to that time. They are going on in the country schools—moving along quietly.

1918. Do they continue on in country schools till they come to St. Jarlath's—till they are sixteen or seventeen years of age?—Yes. They have not very good opportunities for primary education.

Oct. 16, 1888.

Very Rev. Patrick Kilkenny, D.D.

1919. Are the country schools chiefly National schools?—Chiefly.

1920. And they continue reading the National school course up to seventeen?—Yes.

1921. Dr. Traill.—Do they not enter the National schools at the ordinary age, or is there a lack of students?—They are kept at labour.

1922. I suppose they begin at from five to eight years old, what are they doing from that until they are seventeen?—I can only state the facts for you. Their parents keep them at home and on their farms very often.

1923. Lord Justice FitzGibbon.—We were told the same thing in Galway, that the attendance is bad, even at a good school, because the children are kept at work or at home by their parents on market and fair days, and the school-teaching is interrupted, and takes a long time in consequence?—That is quite the fact; and, in addition, most of the country boys are taken to help their parents in farm work during the spring time.

1924. Are your young men at St. Jarlath's all from this diocese?—There are a few externs. Numbers used to come from America, the children of parents who had gone from this diocese to America.

1925. Lord Justice Naish.—Did they send their children back to school here?—They sent their children back to school here; and the friends of priests who had been educated here directed their brothers to come to St. Jarlath's to get their education. That happens at present. There is a boy from Gibraltar whose father belonged to the diocese, and there is another from Melbourne.

1926. Lord Justice FitzGibbon.—What is the stipend?—It varies from £22 to £16. Those who pay the additional amount are accommodated with better treatment—a special lunch, and so on.

1927. What is the fee for the day boys?—A pound a quarter, but, as I said, we don't encourage them.

1928. What premises have you?—Two splendid houses, and we have five acres of land immediately connected with the college.

1929. Have you other land also?—We have two farms near the town.

1930. Are you tenants or owners?—We are tenants.

1931. Rev. Dr. Molloy.—Have you any lease of land?—No. With regard to the Intermediate Examinations, we have not many to enter, owing to the age limits, but often younger boys come whose parents are pretty well off; and I think the proportion that we have sent in who have passed and obtained prizes is very fair.

1932. Lord Justice FitzGibbon.—Give us the figures?—In 1884, 15 entered, of whom 13 passed; in 1885, 10 entered and 7 passed; in 1886, 10 entered and 7 passed; and in 1888, 8 entered and 7 passed. Two years ago a boy got an exhibition, and last year another boy got a first-class exhibition in the Middle Grade. These have continued to retain their exhibitions.

1933. To what do you attribute the falling off in the numbers of late years?—To the depression in the country—no other reason.

1934. To the inability of parents to pay the stipend, or to the necessity for keeping their children at home? —I would say to the inability of the parents to pay the stipend; and therefore if we could obtain something that would enable the poorer boys to come at an earlier day, the college would be vastly more successful as an educational establishment.

1935. Supposing any money were granted for intermediate education, how would you think it most necessary to apply it?—By helping to diminish the pensions for some of the boys.

1936. You formerly had ninety pupils; at present you have over seventy. If you got a grant of £50 or even £100, how would you apply it so as appreciably to lower the fees?—Either lowering the fees or creating half a dozen free places. It would help to bring in good boys at an early age, so that they would have full advantage of the education for the Intermediate.

1937. Lord Justice Naish.—In Galway we were told that one of their necessities is money for books—have you felt that?—Not so much. The boys procure the books.

1938. They complained in Galway that to supply the books necessary to keep the boys up to the Intermediate course entailed great expense?—So it does.

1939. Dr. Traill.—I suppose books are a small item for a boy that is able to pay from £22 to £26?—Yes; they would be able to obtain the books at all events.

1940. Lord Justice FitzGibbon.—You don't encourage day boys; where do the Roman Catholic boys of Tuam get their education?—A great number of them get it under the Christian Brothers. Under the present management, I understand, there is a desire to get day boys, and very rightly, and to provide that they observe discipline, which is a very good thing. There is a very good Christian Brothers' school here in which primary education is given. But I may say that a little strictness of discipline would no doubt diminish any excesses, and, I dare say, increase the number of day boys.

1941. Had you any serious trouble in the way of discipline?—We thought there was a tendency amongst them to introduce things not permitted in the college.

The Rev. *Michael O'Connell* sworn and examined.

Rev. Michael O'Connell

1942. Lord Justice FitzGibbon.—You have been President of St. Jarlath's College since the retirement of the last witness?—Yes, since last February.

1943. What are your present numbers?—*Fifty-five boarders and nine day students; sixty-four pupils altogether.

1944. For how many have you accommodation?—We could accommodate between eighty and ninety boarders. We have any amount of accommodation for day boys.

1945. To what do you attribute the small number of day boys?—In addition to the reason Dr. Kilkenny has given, I attribute it to the fact that the pension is so small that it is almost as good for the boys that come from a distance to become pensioners as day boys.

1946. Are there no more boys in Tuam requiring the education you offer than the number you have?—No. These don't even represent Tuam; they are from other places, some of them.

1947. Are they boys that live in the town?—One of them is apprenticed to a chemist.

1948. The boys of Tuam get their education with the Christian Brothers?—As a rule; or they enter the college, or go to some other college. I believe the number of day students will increase. The pension for them is £8 at present. It was only £4 in Dr. Kilkenny's time.

1949. For the £8 pension what course of education do they get?—The whole Intermediate course.

1950. Do you prepare for all the three grades?—Yes.

1951. Have you any boys learning Greek?—Yes; I think about sixty.

1952. About what proportion are going to the ecclesiastical profession?—About two-thirds.

1953. The remainder go to ordinary colleges, the professions or the Civil Service?—As a rule, many of them.

1954. Dr. Traill.—Do the ecclesiastical students go to Maynooth or to foreign colleges?—To Maynooth, to the Irish College in Paris, to All Hallows' College, and others.

1955. Do they go to the Dominican College in Rome?—Not lately.

1956. Lord Justice FitzGibbon.—They go to May-

* At present (March, 1889), the number of boarders is fifty-nine.—Michael O'Connell.

Oct. 11, 1886.

Rev. Michael O'Connell.

enough for your own diocese, and to All Hallows for going abroad?—Yes.

1957. Have they to pass an entrance examination at those colleges?—Yes.

1958. What subjects does it include?—Greek and Latin, science and history. We sent twelve students to Maynooth last summer, and they all passed.

1959. This year, how did you get on at the Intermediate examination?—Eight students were entered, and seven passed. Two were exhibitioners and retained their exhibitions; and one of them got a first class prize of £3 in the middle grade. He failed to get honour marks in algebra this year, and in consequence of that he failed to get a new exhibition. The other gentleman got honours in most of the subjects.

1960. Rev. Dr. Molloy.—Have you a centre at St. Jarlath's?—We have.

1961. Lord Justice FitzGibbon.—What are your means of supporting the institution?—The pensions of the students; and a contribution from the clergy of the diocese of £3 from each parish priest, and £1 from each curate.

1962. Rev. Dr. Molloy.—Annually?—Yes.

1963. Lord Justice FitzGibbon.—How much does that amount to in the year?—About £150.

1964. That £150 is for your subsistence, in addition to the fees of the pupils?—It is. It principally accounts for the maintenance of the pensions of the ecclesiastical students.

1965. How much do the total fees of the students come to?—Perhaps, somewhat over £1,500 a year, taking £24 for the average.

1966. Do you make anything of your land?—No; but they are of advantage to the college, because we get potatoes, vegetables, and things of that kind for the college from them, and we have some cattle and sheep.

1967. I suppose the governing body and teachers are all Roman Catholics?—All.

1968. Are your students all of that denomination?—They are all of that denomination, but there is no exclusion.

1969. You are under the Intermediate rule as regards that?—Yes, and before the Intermediate system there was no objection whatever to Protestants.

1970. Are you in connexion with South Kensington?—Yes; this was the first year. We entered in elementary mathematics, sound, light, heat, and theoretical mechanics. Fifty presented themselves for examination in mathematics. Eleven got first class passes, twenty-six got second class passes, and thirteen failed. In all, seventy-four per cent. passed and twenty-six per cent. failed.

1971. What results fees have you got?—We have a claim for £56 but it has not yet been received. For seven of the boys who passed we don't claim, because there is a rule against allowing it in the case of a boy whose parents have an income of over £200 a year, and we considered that the cases of those seven boys come under that rule.

1972. Then you have got seven pupils whose parents have over £200 a year?—Yes, we believe that. I wish to bring under your notice the fact that we have in the college at the present moment boys from Westport, Castlebar, Ballyhaunis, Mayo, and Clifden, and that covers a total population of nearly 250,000 Catholics. That is the area from which we have a regular draw. I consider the Kensington examination a better test than the Intermediate of the teaching of the college, because it covers our general system, and so we have not so large a number going in for the Intermediate as for South Kensington, merely on account of the age limit.

1973. Professor Dougherty.—Are the examinations equally difficult?—Well, I think the South Kensington examination is a stiff examination. I believe our results are better than the general results of all the schools.

1974. Dr. Traill.—What do you earn in result fees at the Intermediate Examinations?—The average has been about £45 for the last five years. The average is about £5 a head. They passed very high. Sometimes four of our boys were in the Senior Grade. In South Kensington we now get £1 for each Second Class pass, and £2 for each First. There is a higher amount allowed in the Intermediate.

1975. Rev. Dr. Molloy.—Why do you think the examinations in South Kensington are a better test of general education than the examinations of the Intermediate Education Board?—Because it brings the working of our system more into evidence.

1976. Is it your opinion that the examinations at South Kensington are a better test of the efficiency of education?—Of our college. Not considering the system as better than the other, but because we have more boys put into one, and it shows the general teaching of our college.

1977. Professor Dougherty.—Did I understand you to say that you thought the system of South Kensington better adapted to your curriculum?—No, I did not intend to say that.

1978. Dr. Traill.—Why do you send a larger number of boys to the one than to the other?—Because there is no age limit in South Kensington, and we are debarred by the age limit of the Intermediate Board.

1979. Lord Justice FitzGibbon.—In the interests of education whether do you think it would be better to extend the age limits of the Intermediate Examinations, or, by providing funds, to induce boys to come at an earlier age to the college and keep the age limit as it is?—I could not answer that question, but it would be better for us to extend the age limit. I believe we could induce boys to come in at an earlier age. At present we have made more provision for younger boys.*

1980. Dr. Traill.—Would it not be very prejudicial to the interests of education if the rule for all Ireland allowed boys who ought to be in the universities to be competing with school boys?—Yes.

1981. And if the age limit were extended for the benefit of one or two places, would it not bring in men to compete with school-boys?—That's the reason why I could not answer the general question—because I really don't know. All I say is that it would be better for us.

1982. What do you argue from the statement as to 700,000 Roman Catholic inhabitants being in the area from which this college draws its pupils?—That the college which has practically given effective Intermediate education to that number would have a claim in any distribution of funds.

1983. Lord Justice Naish.—What are the dioceses?—The whole archdiocese of Tuam.

1984. Dr. Traill.—What has the population of 300,000 to do with the fifty-five boys here. Does it not show that they don't want Intermediate education, but that it is primary education they want?—There is a very large number of Catholics who would require it if they got the encouragement.

1985. You have only fifty-five boarders?—That is on account of inability to pay.

1986. Rev. Dr. Molloy.—I understand you to say that the area from which your pupils come would supply a far larger number of pupils, if you were able to assist the poorer boys to pay their pensions?—Exactly.

1987. Dr. Traill.—What class of society are the boys taken from?—From the humbler classes, and the merchants and farmers.

1988. Rev. Dr. Molloy.—I suppose they are chiefly the sons of farmers and shopkeepers?—Yes.

1989. Dr. Traill.—Do they come from the National schools to you?—Principally.

1990. Are they tested as the best boys?—Not always.

1991. Do you find them sufficiently educated, or have you got bad material to begin with?—Bad, is different, and good material. We generally keep back the boys who are not prepared.

* This year (1887), owing to encouragement we have been able to give, a large portion of the freshmen are young boys and are being prepared for the Intermediate examination of next year.—Michael O'Connell.

Rev. Bro. *Joseph Delany* sworn and examined.

1992. Lord Justice FitzGibbon.—Are you the head of the Christian Brothers in Tuam?—Yes.

1993. How many schools have you here?—Under our rules, three. We have three brothers teaching.

1994. Is that the whole community here?—Three teaching brothers, and one for domestic duty.

1995. What are your numbers?—270 on the roll, and an average attendance of 178.

1996. Have you sent boys to the Intermediate Examinations?—Yes.

1997. What number?—This year, 12. We generally have had a larger number.

1998. Are these boys who have been promoted from lower classes?—From class to class in our schools.

1999. Have you any boys of the better classes?—We have a good many of the better classes belonging to the town, and a few from the country.

2000. About how many day boys have you from the town of Tuam getting a better education than ordinary primary teaching?—Those for the Intermediate classes, say from 12 to 20. This year they have been smaller than at any period for a considerable time. Owing to the pressure and necessity of the times and emigration, the younger portion of the country boys were called on to do work that used formerly to be done by the adult classes.

2001. What provision is there for maintaining the community here?—A collection, and £20 from the Archbishop.

2002. That is an annual collection in the town?—An annual collection in the town. We get very little fees outside the town.

2003. What are your stipends?—We have no particular stipend. We simply get £20 from the Archbishop, and a supplementary collection which fluctuates from year to year.

2004. Have you to bear the fluctuation yourselves?—We have to abide by the times.

2005. Lord Justice Naish.—Are there any school fees?—There are. They go to keep the fabric standing.

2006. They do not go to support the community?—In no way.

2007. Lord Justice FitzGibbon.—The boys pay for their books?—They pay for the books.

2008. Dr. Traill.—Do you use your own books or those of the National Schools?—Our own.

2009. Do you use the National School books at all for the younger classes?—No. The National Schools don't allow any of our books into their schools.

2010. Rev. Dr. Molloy.—And you return the compliment?—We return the compliment.

2011. Dr. Traill.—We found that in the Christian Brothers Schools of Waterford they use the National School books?—I am not aware of that.

2012. Lord Justice FitzGibbon.—How do you hold your premises?—I am not aware. The Archbishop provides them.

2013. What provision is there in Tuam for teaching girls?

Very Rev. *P. Kilkenny.*—There are two Convent Schools, one of the Presentation Order and the other of the Sisters of Mercy.

2014. Do the Sisters of Mercy give an advanced education to the girls?—They do. Their programmes are according to the National System of Education, I think.

Lord Justice FitzGibbon.—These three schools that we have heard about now are exempt from the operation of our Act except by consent.

PUBLIC SITTING—FRIDAY, OCTOBER 19, 1888.

At the Courthouse, *Londonderry.*

Present:—The Right Hon. Lord Justice FitzGibbon and the Right Hon. Lord Justice Naish, Judicial Commissioners; and the Rev. Gerald Molloy, D.D., D.Sc., Anthony Traill, Esq., LL.D., M.D., F.T.C.D., Professor Dougherty, M.A., Assistant Commissioners.

The Assistant Secretary, N. D. Murphy, Junr., was in attendance.

Lord Justice FitzGibbon made an introductory statement.

THE ROBERTSON ENDOWMENT—OBJECTIONS TO THE DRAFT SCHEME.

1. Inspection.

2015. Rev. Dr. *Jagon.*—We apprehend that it may be the Inspector's interest if paid for the Robertson schools to prevent the few remaining Church Education schools from coming under the National Board.

2016. Lord Justice FitzGibbon.—I do not think there is any reason for your apprehension. The Lord Lieutenant has the appointment of the Inspector, who is bound by the Act to report whether the scheme is being carried out or not. The National Board Inspector will probably be appointed in all cases of primary schools, and his appointment will have the opposite effect to what you fear.

Rev. Dr. Molloy.—I cannot see that the Inspector would have any interest in preventing the school from being connected with the National Board.

Sir Samuel Hayes.—Where a Robertson grant is given to say an Erasmus Smith's school, which already has an Inspector, would there be another Inspector appointed?

2017. Lord Justice FitzGibbon.—In such a case the Governing Body should apply to the Lord Lieutenant to recognise the existing Inspector. We have reason to hope that the statutory Inspection will not cost any appreciable amount to the schools.

Oct. 24, 1885.

2. Stranorlar School.

2018. Lord Justice FitzGibbon.—There is some mistake about Stranorlar, where two schools are given.

Rev. *Henry F. Macdonald*.—The old school has been lost to the endowment. The son of the former school-master claimed a prescriptive right to the building and established it at Quarter Sessions. Unfortunately the clergyman was old and not able to attend to these matters, and his successor was not fit to do so, hence the Robertson Fund has lost it. The other school is the Erasmus Smith School which has the benefit of the Robertson grant.

2019. Dr. Traill.—Did you test the question regarding the other school by ejectment?—Yes, before the Quarter Sessions.

2020. Did you sue in the name of the Representative Church Body?—Yes, and failed.

3. [illegible] School.

2021. Lord Justice FitzGibbon.—Regarding the [illegible] Parochial School, [illegible], the Rector asks if the Commissioners propose any alteration in the management of his school?

Mr. *W. H. Porter*.—That school is in the schedule already. There are two schools which are aided, but the school-house in one case is not the property of the Governors.

Lord Justice FitzGibbon.—Whether the schools are the property of the Governors or not, every school that gets Robertson money should be mentioned in the schedule. We must ask you to give a complete list of all the schools and school-houses aided from the fund, and also a correct description of all the buildings and lands which you want to vest in the new Governing Body.

4. The Governing Body.

2022. Lord Justice FitzGibbon.—The next matter of consequence is the constitution of the Governing Body. The Draft Scheme proposes that there should be three *ex-officio* Governors, the Bishop, the Dean, and the Archdeacon, with two clerical members elected by the clerical members of the Diocesan Council, and five lay Governors elected by the lay members of the Diocesan Council. It has been suggested that a better representation would be got if the lay and clerical members of the Council voted together in electing the ten representatives on the Governing Body. We should like to hear what you say as to that.

Rev. Mr. *Macdonald*.—That is not one of our amendments, but I think it would be more satisfactory.

2023. Lord Justice FitzGibbon.—You would be likely to get a better selection of members by joint voting than by voting by orders?

Rev. Dr. *Jagoe*.—I would prefer that the election be by the Diocesan Synod. It is not the practice of our Church to give elections to the Diocesan Council except of its own Committees. A much greater interest would be taken in the matter if the election was made by the whole body of the Synod.

2024. Lord Justice FitzGibbon.—Do you propose that the vote should be by orders?

Rev. Dr. *Jagoe*.—No, by the whole body of the Synod.

2025. Dr. Traill.—Do you propose to issue voting papers to those not present?

Rev. Dr. *Jagoe*.—No. If they do not choose to come up they may fairly lose their votes.

Rev. Canon *R. Babington*.—In the Diocese of Derry and Raphoe, the Synod has handed over to the Council the election of all Committees. The Council elect at their first meeting all the committees for carrying on the business of the Diocese. The Synod thought it was too unwieldy a body.

2026. Lord Justice FitzGibbon.—We might give the power to the Synod, authorizing them to delegate it to the Council if they think fit. Would that satisfy you?

Rev. Canon *R. Babington*.—It would.

2027. Lord Justice FitzGibbon.—There should not be a vote by orders but the whole ten representatives should be elected by the whole body.

Dr. Traill.—Whether by the Synod or by the Council?

Rev. Mr. *Macdonald*.—We are quite satisfied to leave either.

Sir *Samuel Hayes*.—The constitution of the proposed Governing Body appears somewhat unequal. There is a preponderance of clergymen over the laity in the proportion of eight to five. I hope there will not be any difference between us but I think the two elements might be more equalised.

2028. Dr. Traill.—Would you be satisfied if the ten persons were elected irrespective of whether they were clergy or laity?

Sir *Samuel Hayes*.—I think not; why not make the numbers equal? The three *ex-officio* clergymen make the difference of course.

2029. Lord Justice FitzGibbon.—If we regard the intentions of Pounds Robertson, the founder, he gave the whole thing into the hands of the Bishop, Dean, Archdeacon and Clergy of the Diocese, so whatever the laity get now, they get for the first time.

Rev. Dr. *Jagoe*.—I strongly support Sir Samuel Hayes' proposition. The more the laity can be induced to take an interest in education, the better work we shall do. Besides, from their occupations, we cannot expect to have the same percentage of attendance from them, and therefore they should be the large body.

2030. Lord Justice FitzGibbon.—The three *ex-officio* Governors were appointed by the testator and we cannot interfere with them. Dividing the remainder equally seems fair. The next point is [illegible] of some moment. It is proposed to limit the power of election to the representatives of the Diocese of Raphoe only, and that the scheme should recognise only that portion of the Diocesan Council which comes from Raphoe. Do all work together as one Diocesan Council.

Rev. Canon *R. Babington*.—Any member has the power to require the Councils of Derry and Raphoe to sit and vote separately.

2031. Dr. Traill.—Do the Raphoe Council ever sit separately?

Rev. Canon *R. Babington*.—For years they have not.

2032. Dr. Traill.—Have they a different place of meeting?

Rev. Canon *R. Babington*.—We all meet together.

Rev. Dr. *Jagoe*.—The Derry Synod is a much larger body, and the place of meeting is more convenient for the attendance of the Derry men. I would be very much in favour of the Raphoe Synod sitting separately.

2033. Lord Justice FitzGibbon.—Is there a Raphoe Synod?

Rev. Dr. *Jagoe*.—They have never sat separately, but you should never have the whole Derry Synod voting. We should be swamped by the Derry men.

2034. Lord Justice FitzGibbon.—Then it is understood that whether the Synod or the Council is to elect, the Raphoe portion only is to vote. We give the election of these ten governors to the Diocesan Synodsmen of the Diocese of Raphoe, excluding Derry, with power to them to delegate it to the members of the Diocesan Council from Raphoe, if they see fit.

Rev. Canon *R. Babington*.—The election will take place at the annual meeting of the Diocesan Synod, which always takes place before the end of October. It might meet in September. The scheme should be altered accordingly.

Lord Justice FitzGibbon.—The scheme will be altered so that you need not call a special Synod.

3. Retiring Allowances.

2035. Rev. A. G. Cochrane, Ballyclough.—I object to any provision for retiring allowance for teachers on the ground that the funds are so small for such a number of schools, that if you give pensions or gratuities they would eat up the money, and injure the schools individually.

2036. Lord Justice Naish.—How many of the schools are in connexion with the National Board?

Rev. Dr. Jagoe.—Seventeen.

2037. And how many are not connected?

Rev. Dr. Jagoe.—Eleven or twelve.

Rev. Mr. Macdonald.—The Committee are in favour of power being given to the new governing body to apply some of the funds in the way of pensions, to get rid of incompetent teachers. There are one or two schools occupied by old men, who are quite useless, and we cannot get rid of them without turning them adrift, which we do not wish to do. If we had the power to give them a gratuity we might get them away, and have really good schools established.

2038. Lord Justice FitzGibbon.—The National Board will not take over a school if the master is above a certain age. In such cases it might be the cheapest thing for the school to pension the teacher, and bring it under the National Board, getting a good teacher, and a larger salary. It is only with the sanction of the Commissioners of Charitable Donations that pensions can be given. We feel it to be a dangerous power, but we probably would not apprehend any abuse of it in this case.

Rev. Mr. Cochrane.—If the old teacher wanted to stay on, a small gratuity would not be sufficient inducement to him to leave.

2039. Lord Justice FitzGibbon.—Then put him out.

Rev. Dr. Jagoe.—I think if you provide that no pension shall be given to those teachers who are in connexion with the National Board there would be no objection. That would get rid of seventeen at once, and probably in a short time the remaining schools will get into connexion with the National Board.

Rev. Mr. Cochrane.—I have only offered the objection that occurred to myself, and I have nothing more to say about it.

Dr. Traill.—It would affect your objection very largely if the pension system were not applied to National teachers.

2040. Lord Justice FitzGibbon.—We will limit the power of awarding pensions to teachers who are not entitled to a pension under the National Board.

Rev. Dr. Jagoe.—Can you do anything to facilitate getting the remaining schools under the National Board?

2041. Lord Justice FitzGibbon.—We cannot force them.

Rev. Dr. Jagoe.—Would it be possible to come to some arrangement, by which the Board would promise to take up the remaining schools.

2042. Lord Justice FitzGibbon.—The National Board will take them whenever they comply with its conditions.

Rev. Dr. Jagoe.—My teacher is too old there, and I wish to be in a position to give him a pension. It would be well if the Board would relax some of its conditions, and take up these schools as they stand.

2043. Lord Justice FitzGibbon.—We cannot force them to take schools over on special terms. The outstanding schools are joining very rapidly now, perhaps on discovering that the National Board is not so bad as was thought. We have been asked to provide that the incumbent should in each case be a consenting party, before any alteration is made in the management of a parish school. The same point was met in Dublin, in the case of St. Peter's Schools, by a provision that the incumbent shall in each case be the manager of the school.

Mr. Porter.—If he did not want to be manager there might be difficulties.

2044. Lord Justice FitzGibbon.—If he did not wish to be manager the Board would appoint someone else. It might be provided that where the school is not under the National Board it should not be placed under the National Board against the will of the incumbent. What do you say to that?

Rev. Dr. Jagoe.—You might use some pressure to bring them under the National Board.

2045. Lord Justice FitzGibbon.—But the incumbent might have a conscientious objection if his school was forced under the National Board in spite of him; the working of the school would probably not be very satisfactory. We shall provide that no incumbent in office at the date of the scheme shall have any school of which he is the manager put under the National Board against his will.

Rev. Mr. Carre.—I understand that the scheme was not to take away any of the rights of the incumbents under the old system.

Lord Justice FitzGibbon.—An incumbent cannot be permitted, by refusing to act, to prevent anything being done to improve an old school. The most we can give him is the right to have the management if he likes, with the additional protection that no school shall be placed for the first time under the National Board, without the consent of the incumbent, if he holds office at the date of the scheme, and is willing to act as manager. This is vital to the friendly working of the system.

4. Stated Meetings—Paid Officers.

2046. The next point is as to the number of stated meetings. You want two instead of four in the year. Then you want to except the secretary of the committee from the prohibition to have a paid officer on the governing body. We have a very strong objection to allow any one person to be both officer and master. If you appoint a paid secretary, he ought not to be a governor.

Mr. Porter.—The objection did not come from me, but we have a very valuable secretary whose services we have had for some time. When Dean Gwynn was here he was the acting secretary, and when he left he requested Mr. Macdonald to take up the work. At that time there was a suggestion that some remuneration should be given as it took up a good deal of Mr. Macdonald's time. He has very faithfully discharged his duties to the satisfaction of all the old governors, and you might possibly see your way to allow him to receive a salary.

2047. Lord Justice FitzGibbon.—As I understand, Mr. Macdonald at present is honorary secretary, and no salary is attached to his office?

Mr. Porter.—That is so, but when Dr. Gwynn requested Mr. Macdonald to take up the work, a hint was thrown out that there would be a salary.

2048. Dr. Traill.—The objection is to his remaining a governor at the same time.

Rev. Canon R. Babington.—It is very important to have him as a governor.

2049. Lord Justice FitzGibbon.—He may receive a salary provided it is not paid out of the endowment, or he may get it out of the endowment provided he ceases to be a governor. We object to having the endowment applied to pay a salary to a governor. We have refused to sanction that in any case where the original trust did not provide for it.

Rev. Dr. Jagoe.—The payment might be provided from another source.

2050. Lord Justice FitzGibbon.—There would be no difficulty were it provided from any other source than the endowment.

Rev. Dr. Jagoe.—The endowment is so small, that if we are to pay all these sums out of it there will be nothing left for the schools that require help.

Oct. 18, 1888.

7. Payment of Rent of Schools—Evidence of By-laws.

2031. Lord Justice FitzGibbon.—The next amendment proposes to give express power to the Governors to pay rent for school premises. The scheme already provides that you may spend the money for "the purposes of education," and renting a school-house would be included, but we may insert the amendment. The next point is that you wish to provide that the minutes and by-laws of the Governing Body, when duly certified, shall be accepted as legal evidence. My colleagues and I will consider whether we have power to alter the laws of evidence; there are similar provisions in some Acts of Parliament, and this is a very practical suggestion. Another amendment, relieving the Governors from liability for loss or depreciation of investments, is unnecessary, as a trustee is not by law liable for that.

8. Parishes.

2032. Mr. Porter.—I want the definition of parish widened to include branches, divisions of parishes or unions of parishes as they may be arranged from time to time by the Diocesan Synod.

Lord Justice FitzGibbon.—The will has it "one school in each parish."

Mr. Porter.—That would apply to the old ecclesiastical parishes, but the Diocesan Synod has made many alterations of boundaries. There are now forty-one parishes in the diocese, whereas there were only thirty-one when the endowment was left.

2033. Lord Justice FitzGibbon.—Your object is to provide for one school in each parish as existing from time to time?

Mr. Porter.—Precisely.

9. Funds—Investments.

2034. Lord Justice FitzGibbon.—With reference to the £14,364 12s. 0d. standing to the account of the committee in the Bank of Ireland, Mr. Porter calls attention to the fact that the five shillings bonus on the conversion of the stock may have been added to the sum. We must be informed of the precise particulars of the stock now existing. Mr. Porter wants to limit the power of investment to "investments of trustees sanctioned by Act of Parliament." Trustees are not allowed, except in special cases, to take debenture stock. We have invariably refused to allow trust money to be put into shares, as trustees have no right to become shareholders or members of a trading company. We may safely extend the power of investment to bonds and debentures.

2035. Mr. Porter.—Section 8, sub-section 7, as the draft scheme stands, would not embrace the case of a school where an incumbent declines to act, and where a layman might be appointed manager.

Lord Justice FitzGibbon.—The schools must be conducted in all cases in accordance with the provisions of the scheme.

2036. Mr. Porter.—We think the power proposed to be given to the General Synod to alter the scheme is rather arbitrary.

Lord Justice FitzGibbon.—They have no power to alter it; but they may apply to the Commissioners of Charitable Donations and Bequests to do so. The Diocesan Synods and Councils might be altered, and the supreme authority of the Church ought, in such a case, to possess authority to alter the constitution of this Governing Body.

Mr. Porter.—We thought that this being a purely diocesan endowment, the Diocesan Synod would be the body most directly interested, and having the best facilities for knowing what was required.

Lord Justice FitzGibbon.—It would be extremely difficult to pass an Act of the General Synod that was opposed by the diocese.

Mr. Porter.—It leaves it open to the General Synod to make a lay board or a clerical board, or whatever they like.

2037. Lord Justice FitzGibbon.—Perhaps the best course would be to give the Diocesan Synod or the General Synod power to apply to the Commissioners of Charitable Donations and Bequests for an alternative.

Rev. Canon R. Babington.—There ought to be some powers, because we do not know what the course of time may bring forth.

Mr. Porter.—The General Synod should do it on the motion of the Diocesan Synod.

2038. Lord Justice FitzGibbon.—Supposing the Diocesan Synod became extinct, the General Synod is the chief body.

Rev. Canon R. Babington.—I do not apprehend any difficulty.

Lord Justice FitzGibbon.—It is a Church endowment, and we ought to recognise the supreme authority of the Church.

THE LONDONDERRY ACADEMICAL INSTITUTION—OBJECTIONS AND AMENDMENTS TO THE DRAFT SCHEME.

2039. Professor Leebody, M.A., D.SC.—I appear on behalf of the Board. Our objections are merely verbal, except a slight change in the constitution of the Governing Body.

2040. Lord Justice FitzGibbon.—Why do you propose to increase the amount of the subscription qualifying for membership from £10 to £20?

Professor Leebody.—It was felt to be unfair to those who had paid their £20 subscription in the past to have new men get the same privileges for £10.

2041. Professor Dougherty.—What are the privileges?

Professor Leebody.—The right of voting in the election of Governors. £20 was fixed, because a subscriber of £60 has a free nomination for three years, which means £30 of his money back again, leaving his subscription £30.

2042. Lord Justice FitzGibbon.—In the Belfast Academical Institution, £10, I think, is the qualification. The point is, which is most likely to bring in money?

Professor Leebody.—I objected to the change, but did not urge my personal opinion against the feeling of those who had contributed most largely to the Institution.

2043. Lord Justice FitzGibbon.—£20 is a very high qualification, and I don't think you will get half as many to give you £20 as you would get to give you £10.

Professor Leebody.—You are expressing my opinion.

Mr. Alexander M'Fadden.—Numbers of those who had subscribed largely thought that it was lowering the franchise much more than was necessary to make it £10, especially when there were other ways by which people could become members at less expense.

2044. Dr. Traill.—How many subscribers of £20 have you?

Mr. M'Fadden.—A considerable number.

2045. Lord Justice FitzGibbon.—The only right got for the £10 is to attend a meeting once a year and vote for Governors. The £60 franchise, on the other hand, is valuable, because it includes free nominations.

Professor Leebody.—I do not defend the objection, because I opposed it.

2046. Lord Justice FitzGibbon.—The fact that the gentlemen who established the Institution paid more ought not, I think, to affect the question. You propose to strike out the franchise for those who have paid for people.

Rev. Dr. Molloy.—I thought this provision would be an encouragement to people to send boys to the Institution.

3067. Dr. Traill.—You think perhaps that a man who has paid for the education of his boys has got sufficient value for his money already.

Professor *Leebody*.—That is so.

3068. Rev. Dr. Molloy.—It would attach to the Institution persons who had sent their boys there, and form a connection for the school.

Professor *Leebody*.—My own opinion is, that your four sections are very much better than the substituted ones.

3069. Rev. Dr. Molloy.—We thought it would be important to keep up the connection of the old boys with the Institution.

Professor *Leebody*.—These amendments embody the opinions of some of the largest subscribers; my own opinion is that your proposals are the best.

3070. Rev. Dr. Molloy.—Then you are personally in favour of sub-sections (*a*), (*b*), (*c*), and (*d*), as they stand?

Professor *Leebody*.—I am personally in favour of them.

Lord Justice FitzGibbon.—What we want to secure is public support for the school, and the wider the basis the more support will it get.

Rev. Dr. Molloy.—We have adopted similar provisions in the scheme for the Royal Belfast Academical Institution, and they have not been objected to.

3071. Lord Justice FitzGibbon.—You ought not to impose a higher franchise than the Belfast Institution. We shall see that Belfast and Londonderry are put on the same basis in this respect. Now, as to the governing body?

Professor *Leebody*.—The scheme contemplated no marked change in the governing body. We had a pretty fair mixture of the lay and clerical elements. We had a considerable number of laymen, *ex-officio*. Then we had some of the Non-conformist clergy of Derry, *ex-officio*—five Presbyterians, two Covenanters, one Independent, and one Methodist. Then there were two *ex-officio* from Magee College. As the scheme at present stands, there is no provision for more University men on the Board than the two from Magee College, and the great majority of the subscribers being business men it is presumed that they would select business men in preference to clergymen. We have found in the working of the school that the presence of the clerical or professional element was of the greatest importance, and we think it better to provide for a stronger representation of it than the scheme proposes. We suggest that the Presbytery of Derry should appoint two of its members as members of the Governing Body, and that the Diocesan Council of the Protestant Episcopal Church should have the same power. The majority of our subscribers are Presbyterians, but the Episcopalians have shown a very large measure of confidence in the school. More than half our boarders are Episcopalians, and more than thirty per cent. of the day boys.

3072. Lord Justice FitzGibbon.—Have you only one boarding house for the two denominations?

Professor *Leebody*.—Yes.

3073. Lord Justice FitzGibbon.—Do you find that satisfactory?

Professor *Leebody*.—It must be, because they are coming in increasing numbers. The Dean of Derry presided at our last public meeting, so we are getting along very amicably with our Episcopalian brethren in educational matters, and we therefore wish to have them represented on the Board.

3074. Lord Justice FitzGibbon.—What about the other denominations?

Professor *Leebody*.—We are afraid we cannot take any more than the leading denominations.

3075. Lord Justice FitzGibbon.—The Methodists complain if they are left out?

Professor *Leebody*.—They are not a numerous body. If we took in the Methodists, we would be bound to take in the others.

3076. Dr. Traill.—You have two Methodists already.

Professor *Leebody*.—They may be so, but not as elected representatives.

3077. Dr. Traill.—What is the proportion of Methodists in Derry to all other denominations?

Professor *Leebody*.—Very small.

3078. Dr. Traill.—But they are a very highly educational body.

Professor *Leebody*.—Yes, they are.

3079. Dr. Traill.—Are the non-subscribing Presbyterians an influential body in Derry?

Professor *Leebody*.—They are non-existent. The Covenanters who are a section of the Presbyterians have two congregations. The head master is a Covenanter. There is a Methodist boarder at the school.

3080. Lord Justice FitzGibbon.—Is there an Independent Congregation in Derry?

Professor *Leebody*.—There is.

3081. Lord Justice FitzGibbon.—It is right to remember that some of the smaller bodies are remarkably active in educational matters. Could we not give power to co-opt certain clergymen and university men instead of giving the Diocesan Council and Presbytery the exclusive privilege of election.

Professor *Leebody*.—You might give power to co-opt four clergymen officiating in Derry or its neighbourhood.

3082. Lord Justice FitzGibbon.—The other denominations ought to have some chance of being represented on the Board.

Professor *Leebody*.—That would meet the views of the Board, to get on the clerical element.

Professor Dougherty.—There might be a compulsory provision requiring the co-option of four clergymen.

3083. Dr. Traill.—You should make a fair distribution of the four, so as not to have the power of co-opting entirely in the hands of one denomination.

Professor *Leebody*.—That is so. There is likely to be always a working majority of Presbyterians on the board. Our strongest supporters are Presbyterians. It is very hard to get others.

3084. Dr. Traill.—Your majority is all right, but if you want money make your basis as wide as possible. This institution was supposed to be founded on an absolutely non-sectarian basis?

Professor *Leebody*.—It was.

3085. Dr. Traill.—If any arrangement were made by which the Academy and Foyle College could be joined, how would that work?

Professor *Leebody*.—It would require a very clever man to work Foyle College after Dr. Hime left the position. The school has been maintained more by the personal energy of Dr. Hime than by any public support it has received.

3086. Lord Justice FitzGibbon.—We quite agree with you that some provision to secure the continuance of the clerical and literary element is desirable. We will see whether we can devise something better than your proposal to give representation only to the Church and Presbyterians. It would never do to offend the Independents, Methodists, Covenanters, and Baptists.

Mr. M'Fieler.—We see no possibility of bringing them in without encumbering the Board, but it might be made compulsory to co-opt from those outside.

3087. Lord Justice FitzGibbon.—If Foyle College became distinctively a Church school it would be the interest of the Church people to keep it up, and then the two representatives of the Diocesan Council might really become a hostile element.

Dr. Traill.—They would be in such a minority that they could do no harm. But suppose Foyle College were to fall off and become vacant, and your master went there, how would that work?

Professor *Leebody*.—We would expect them to come to us.

2088. Lord Justice FitzGibbon.—You wish to have it left optional with yourselves whether you are to have one head master or two?

Professor *Leebody*.—Yes. We have found two head masters very satisfactory, but it might be found desirable hereafter to have only one.

2089. Lord Justice FitzGibbon.—You want to strike out the beginning of clause 20.

Professor *Leebody*.—The head masters pay their assistants and appoint or remove them, and we do not want to alter the present state of affairs.

2090. Lord Justice FitzGibbon.—Would it not be better that all the fees should be paid to the Governing Body who could then arrange with the head masters to pay assistants?

Professor *Leebody*.—The Governing Body have a veto on anything the head masters may do. We were afraid that the head master might be hampered, and obliged to say he could not appoint until after a conference with the Board.

2091. Lord Justice FitzGibbon.—Clause 20 provides that—

"After conference with the head masters the Governing Body shall determine the number of lecturers, assistant masters, and other teachers."

But the head masters appoint them. The object of the clause is to prevent a head master from starving his school by not appointing a sufficient staff. You should have power to compel your head masters to employ a sufficient number of qualified assistants.

PUBLIC SITTING—SATURDAY, OCTOBER 20, 1888.

At the Town Hall, Coleraine.

Present:—The Right Hon. Lord Justice FitzGibbon and the Right Hon. Lord Justice Naish, Judicial Commissioners; and the Rev. Gerald Molloy, D.D., D.Sc., Anthony Traill, Esq., LL.D., M.D., F.T.C.D., and Professor Dougherty, M.A., Assistant Commissioners.

The Assistant Secretary, N. D. Murphy, Junr., was in attendance.

Lord Justice FitzGibbon made an introductory statement.

THE IRISH SOCIETY'S FREE SCHOOLS, COLERAINE.

Campbell M. Loughridge sworn and examined.

2092. Lord Justice FitzGibbon.—You are the head master of the Irish Society's Boys School here?—I am.

2093. How long have you held that office?—Since 1873—fifteen years. I was first assistant for the previous seven years.

2094. Rev. Dr. Molloy.—What is the exact title of your school?—We have two names—the Honourable Irish Society's Schools and the Coleraine (No. 2) National Schools.

2095. Professor Dougherty.—The popular name is the Irish Society's Schools?—Yes.

2096. Lord Justice FitzGibbon.—We saw no name outside the building indicating that it was a National school; how is that?—Our board is at present under repair.

2097. When it is repaired what is on it?—We have both names—"Honourable Irish Society's Schools" and "Coleraine (No. 2) National Schools," on the board.

2098. Is it a mixed school?—Yes, the whole building, with the three schools, boys, girls, and infants, is on the roll of the National Board as one school, No. 2, Coleraine.

2099. What is the number on the boys roll and the average attendance?—The number on the roll is from two hundred and thirty to two hundred and forty, and the average attendance one hundred and ninety-five. Last year the numbers were lower, the roll being two hundred and ten, and the average attendance one hundred and seventy-five.

2100. To what do you attribute the falling off?—It came from our not getting our usual supply from the infant school. According to a rule of our committee we take children at seven, and as for a year or so we had no committee, the head mistress of the infant school kept the little people a year longer, and we have not yet recovered.

2101. Can you tell the number on the roll of the girls school?—About the same as the boys.

2102. And the infant school?—About the same. The three schools keep pretty close together.

2103. There would be a total of about seven hundred and fifty on the rolls, with an average attendance of about six hundred?—Yes.

2104. Lord Justice Naish.—Who is the manager?—Mr. Montgomery, the agent of the Irish Society.

2105. Lord Justice FitzGibbon.—Have you a school committee?—We have.

2106. I believe you are in connection with South Kensington?—Yes.

2107. Who form your school committee in connection with that?—We have a science committee, of course. They are the agent and the school committee who care to act.

2108. Who constitute the school committee?—You will get a copy of the scheme from Mr. Bailey.

2109. What teaching staff have you in the boys school?—Three assistants and four monitors.

2110. Are you a classified teacher?—I am, first of the first class—highest under National Board.

2111. How long have you held that qualification?—Four years.

2112. When you were appointed what class did you hold?—I had second, but took first about the same year.

2113. How long has the school been connected with the National Board?—Since 1834.

2114. What are the qualifications of your assistants?—My first and second assistants are first of second, and my third assistant has been in training for the last year at Kildare-place under the Irish Church.

2115. Rev. Dr. Molloy.—He has just been up for his examination, and has not yet got his classification?—Yes. Has since received his class—second.

2116. Lord Justice FitzGibbon.—You get class salaries from the National Board, and results fees?—Yes.

2117. How are the results fees distributed?—I get two shares, and each of the assistants one.

2118. Your results fees are divided into five, and you get two-fifths?—Yes.

2119. About how much would the results fees amount to in the year on the average?—About £150. One year we had £120, another year £80, and another

£12—from one to twelve shillings a head on the average attendance.

3120. What assistance do you get from South Kensington?—We get fees for pupils. The pupil who takes a first class gets £2, and the one who gets a second, £1, and for those who fail we get nothing.

3121. About how much on an average from that source?—About £30 a year. I had £33 last year.

3122. In addition to the ordinary daily National School programme, have you any extra instruction?—Yes, Drawing, Algebra, and Euclid, not later than four o'clock, and evening classes in connection with the Science and Art Department.

3123. About how many attend those evening classes?—We started with thirty-eight, but they fall away towards the examinations.

3124. Those who are not likely to pass the examination do not continue?—They do not.

3125. What are the ages of the boys who attend your Science and Art classes?—The average would be about fifteen.

3126. Do any of your pupils go up to the Intermediate Examinations?—I have a little class this year, but we have a great deal of trouble with it. There is so little time, but this year I expect to send six or eight, if the boys remain at school.

3127. When do you prepare them?—Before or after school hours. Mathematics we teach sometimes in the school, and sometimes from three to four, and experimental and mechanical physics, and so on, usually outside school hours.

3128. What is the teaching staff of the girls school?—The same as in the boys, a head mistress, three assistants, and four monitresses.

3129. Do you know the classification of the head mistress?—Second of first.

3130. Are her three assistants all trained and classified?—They are all trained and classified.

3131. What is the staff of the infant school?—They have the same staff.

3132. Have you any school fees?—None whatever.

3133. Are any fees charged for the Science and Art classes?—According to the rule of the department, it being a free school, elementary pupils from the school are free, and outsiders pay, their fees being returned as prizes if they pass. If they pass, the small fees are supposed to pay the teacher for their education.

3134. Do any girls attend the Science and Art classes?—Very few this year; other years we have had eight or ten. We had only two girls, one from the girls school, and one from outside.

3135. Do you get any payment from the Society?—I have a supplemental salary from the Society.

3136. Is that a fixed sum?—It is fixed in one sense, and not in another. I began with sixty pounds, and recently they kindly increased my salary to eighty pounds. It is subject to increase for long service.

3137. Rev. Dr. Molloy.—It is never subject to decrease?—No. They never do anything of that kind.

3138. Lord Justice Naish.—Have you a residence?—I have, but I am likely to lose it.

3139. Lord Justice FitzGibbon.—What salary have you from the National Board?—About seventy pounds.

3140. Dr. Traill.—Why are you likely to lose your residence?—The Society contemplate putting it into the school which is too small.

3141. Lord Justice FitzGibbon.—The building is fully occupied by the school?—Fully. We need more space.

3142. Where were you educated?—In a National school.

3143. Had you gone through a course of training before you came here?—I came here in 1865, and the same year I went to the training college, Marlborough-street, Dublin, for a half-year course. I went in August, and came back in December.

3144. Rev. Dr. Molloy.—Would it not be an advantage for your Science and Art classes if you could spend a year at South Kensington?—Certainly, but I could not spare it from the school. The South Kensington people have special classes of one month in the summer that I should be glad to attend. I have offered on several occasions, but they did not accept me.

Oct. 16, 1888.

Mr. Campbell M. Longbridge.

3145. You cannot go without a certificate?—No.

3146. Would not a recommendation from the manager be sufficient to get you accepted?—I am not aware that it would be of any service. They send a circular to the teachers asking if they wish to attend, and giving a selection of subjects. I selected subjects year by year and have not been called.

3147. What were the subjects you selected?—Agriculture, chemistry, and so on.

3148. Did you tell them the importance of your school and the large attendance you had?—They would not consider that important.

3149. Professor Dougherty.—Some neighbouring teachers, perhaps, have been recommended, and that has militated against your application?—Yes.

3150. Lord Justice FitzGibbon.—It is a wonder that the Irish Society, being on the spot, could not get them to accept you.

3151. Dr. Traill.—Perhaps they think you are fully occupied otherwise?—They don't consider that at all.

3152. Lord Justice FitzGibbon.—We saw a teacher at Skibbereen who went to South Kensington, and, as the result, got grants and results fees for a school much smaller than yours. There were not seventy boys in the whole school. Are boys who attend these science and art classes generally engaged at work during the day?—Yes; a good many of our boys last year were boys in shops.

3153. Do you find it possible to get a large number of boys who are working during the day to attend to education in the evening?—It is very difficult.

3154. What is the effect, according to your experience, on the attendance, of the school being entirely free?—I hardly know. Our average attendance is sometimes from eighty-four to eighty-six per cent. of the number on rolls, which is considered very good, and usually shows that the education given is prized.

3155. The school is fully taken advantage of?—We have the name of giving a good education.

3156. Do you teach classics?—I have a class in Latin this year, this is my first year. I am teaching it simply that the boys may have a little knowledge of it.

3157. Professor Dougherty.—Is it an Intermediate class?—No.

3158. You have got Latin under the National Board programme for results?—No; we are quite fully occupied without that.

3159. Is there any industrial teaching in the girls school beyond the National Board needle-work teaching?—Not that I know of.

3160. You have no class learning agriculture?—We taught agriculture for many years, but the inspector frowned on it a little. He thought we were teaching too many things, and we have given it up in school, but we teach Agricultural Chemistry under the Science and Art Department.

3161. How many pupils had you?—Between eighty and a hundred.

3162. Was the instruction of a practical character?—No; we have no garden or land, simply theoretical agriculture from Baldwin's book.

3163. Dr. Traill.—Have you any workshops for teaching the use of tools?—No.

3164. Would that not be a desirable thing?—It might if our secular programme were not so extensive.

3165. Have you a certificate in handicraft?—I never thought it would come to anything or be of any service. I believe I could take one, for I possess handicrafts myself.

Oct. 28, 1886.

Mr. Campbell H. Loughridge.

2166. You would get results fees of five shillings per boy?—That is in soldering, &c., for which we cannot spare time with the present programme.

2167. Mr. *Daniel Taylor*.—What would be the average age of the boys attending the school?—About eleven years.

2168. Mr. *Taylor*.—There is a very large proportion in the fifth and sixth classes; what would be their average age?—The highest boy is fifteen.

2169. Lord Justice FitzGibbon.—Do these boys when they leave school generally go straight out into trades or to business?—Straight out, except one or two occasionally who go to the Model School.

2170. Do they go to the Model Schools as being higher class pupils?—No; if there is any dissatisfaction regarding the school, they just shift from one to another.

2171. Professor Dougherty.—Do children of all classes attend your school?—Nearly all classes.

2172. Are your pupils of the same class as those that attend the Model School?—The majority of the children attending the Model School would be of the same class as ours—children able to pay one shilling and one penny per quarter. Children that would pay a pound a quarter our committee would not receive. Every child received into school must have an application for admission.

2173. Lord Justice FitzGibbon.—A certificate that he requires free education?—Not that it requires, but simply that it is to receive free education.

2174. Rev. Dr. Molloy.—A nomination, I suppose?—Yes.

2175. Professor Dougherty.—Is that by individual members of the committee?—Yes.

2176. Dr. Traill.—If any child presented itself at the school could you refuse it?—Yes, if it had not a line.

2177. How could you do that in a National school?—The Commissioners of National Education do not interfere with the manager unless he breaks their rules badly.

2178. One of the rules that no manager can diverge from is that he must take every child who applies?—In that case there would be no refusal. A case requiring refusal has never occurred so far as I know.

2179. Every statement was that the committee would not give a line to anyone who could pay £1 a quarter. Such people never apply.

2180. Lord Justice FitzGibbon.—Do any of your boys go in for higher education at Intermediate schools?—Yes, we have some who go to the Institution. Not a great many.

2181. Rev. Dr. Molloy.—On the whole is the education you give of the same character as that given in the Model School?—Exactly the same.

2182. What is it, in your opinion, that determines some to select the Model School and some to select yours—is it that the Model School requires payment and yours is free?—That is very much the way. The children at the Model School are children whose parents are able to pay, and I find that as our boys grow older and their people perhaps get into better circumstances, they get ashamed of free education and are withdrawn.

2183. Mr. *Daniel Taylor*.—Did one of your boys leave and go to the Institution and afterwards go to Trinity and take the highest place in all Ireland?—He did.

2184. Lord Justice FitzGibbon.—Coleraine Academical Institution took the first three places at Trinity College Entrance in October, 1885, and three out of the first four this month?—One of these boys was educated at this school.

2185. Lord Justice Naish.—What are the denominations attending your school?—Different denominations. Presbyterians are in the majority, and we have Episcopalians, Wesleyans, Baptists, Independents, and two or three Roman Catholics. There would not be ten Baptists and Wesleyans altogether. The two largest denominations vary a good deal. At one time the Irish Church boys and Presbyterians were about equal. Within the last few years the Presbyterians have been in the majority. The numbers may be equal again.

2186. Professor Dougherty.—Can you account for the diminution in the attendance of the Irish Church boys?—There has been some little agitation recently regarding that.

2187. Lord Justice FitzGibbon.—Are there National schools in Coleraine under Irish Church management, or is it that they have gone to the Model School?—I do not think they have gone anywhere. The circumstances are so altered that there are none of those children to go.

2188. Rev. Dr. Molloy.—Is the change in the attendance the result of the natural diminution of the population?—Yes.

2189. Lord Justice FitzGibbon.—What are the other National schools in the Coleraine district besides the Model School?—There is a school in Killowen under the management of Rev. Mr. Stewart, the Rector of the parish of Killowen, on the other side of the river.

2190. Professor Dougherty.—You would not be likely to get any pupils from Killowen?—We have a good many from Killowen.

Rev. Mr. *Stewart*.—I am taken by surprise. There are, I know, three or four.

2191. Rev. Dr. Molloy.—You don't take more than that?

Rev. Mr. *Stewart*.—No.

2192. Lord Justice FitzGibbon (to witness).—What other schools are there?—Father Carroll's—Coleraine No. 1. He is the parish priest.

2193. How many pupils has it got?—I think the school is small. These are all the National schools in town.

2194. There are a number of schools mentioned in the report of the Commission of 1880 which got grants from the Society—three in Killowen—two girls' schools, and a boys' school.

Rev. Mr. *Stewart*.—I have two of these schools, and Professor O'Brien has another.

2195. Then the second Presbyterian Coleraine school?—That is exclusively a Sunday school.

2196. "Newmarket, Coleraine, Evening Ragged School"?—It is not under the National Board—it is supported by subscriptions.

2197. Rev. Dr. Molloy.—You get the lion's share of the endowment?—We do.

2198. Professor Dougherty.—Your schools are the property of the Irish Society, and they support their own schools?—Yes.

2199. Lord Justice FitzGibbon.—Have you anything to do with the expenditure?—Nothing. I pay no money, except the prizes, and they are given to me by the treasurer.

William Bailey, junior, sworn and examined.

William Bailey, jun.

2200. Lord Justice FitzGibbon.—You are clerk to the Irish Society?—Yes.

2201. Are you in Mr. Montgomery's office?—Yes.

2202. I believe he is not able to attend to-day?—Yes. He is confined to bed.

2203. What amount of grants has the Society made during the past three years to the Irish Society schools in Beresford-place?—The amounts during the past three years I am not in a position to give, but for the year 1887, the sum was £637 towards teacher's salaries, awards, and incidentals.

2204. Who pays for repairing the building?—The Society alone.

2205. Is a grant specially made when anything of the sort is wanted?—It goes under the head of incidentals.

2206. Who looks after the repairs?—The committee.

2207. How is the committee constituted?—I hand in the scheme laid down by the Society in 1887.

2208. This is a scheme adopted on the report of a special committee of the court. It is entitled an "Amended scheme for the management of the Honourable the Irish Society's Schools, Coleraine;" it provides that the general agent is to be manager; that the home government of the boys, girls, and infants schools is to be in the hands of a committee consisting of the general agent, and the clergymen of all denominations officially connected with the Town of Coleraine. Does that include rectors, curates, ministers, assistant ministers, and all clergy of all denominations and degrees?

Mr. Taylor.—All who have official work in Coleraine.

2209. Associated with these are twelve gentlemen, resident in the parishes of Coleraine or Killowen, or any part of the Society's estate in the Coleraine district, to be appointed as follows:—The Town Commissioners, four; the Harbour Commissioners, four; the Irish Society, four; the elected members of the committee to continue in office for three years, on the expiration of their term of office to be eligible for re-election; vacancies, as they occur on the committee, to be filled up by the Town Commissioners, Harbour Commissioners, or the Honourable Irish Society, as the case may be; elected members absenting themselves from meetings for twelve months, or ceasing to reside within the qualifying area, to be superseded; five members to form a quorum, and religious instruction to be given three quarters of an hour each school day; the appointment of teachers "to remain as at present." Do you know how that is?

Witness.—The Society appoints all teachers.

Mr. Taylor.—They generally ask the committee to select three, and out of these they appoint one.

2210. Lord Justice FitzGibbon.—The Society would be called the patrons of the school?

Mr. Taylor.—They make Mr. Montgomery the patron and manager.

2211. Lord Justice FitzGibbon.—The scheme provides for a visiting committee of twelve ladies to visit the schools at least weekly. Have you got a visiting committee of ladies?

Mr. Taylor.—Yes, and they have been doing remarkably well.

2212. Rev. Dr. Molloy.—Where does the committee meet?

Mr. Taylor.—At the schools. There is a special room for that purpose.

2213. How often do they meet?

Mr. Taylor.—Quarterly, unless specially called together.

2214. Do the clergy of all denominations go there?

Mr. Taylor.—They generally do. Sometimes we have not Father Carroll. He has been there once or twice. Dr. O'Brien has not been with us.

2215. Dr. Traill.—Who are the officials of the committee?—We have a secretary paid for by the Society, Mr. Reston, who is laid up also to-day.

2216. Lord Justice FitzGibbon.—The committee distribute the money?

Witness.—Yes. At the end of the year the committee forwards the accounts, and the court looks into the whole.

2217. Professor Dougherty.—At the annual visitation, the deputation visits this school?—Yes.

2218. Rev. Dr. Molloy.—You get salaries for all your teachers from the National Board?

Mr. Taylor.—For all that are classed.

2219. Rev. Dr. Molloy.—The fees from the National Board and South Kensington you do not interfere with?

Mr. Taylor.—We look upon that as outside our management altogether.

2220. Rev. Dr. Molloy.—Practically the income from all sources would appear to be something like £1,600 a year?

Mr. Taylor.—Rather more than that.

2221. Lord Justice FitzGibbon.—Now about the buildings?

Witness.—The buildings were erected by the Society, and are held by them as their own property.

In fee?—Under charter.

2222. Lord Justice Naish.—They don't pay rent to anyone?—No.

2223. Lord Justice FitzGibbon.—The site is in the possession of the Society as a corporation?—Yes.

2224. It is not vested in trustees?—It is vested in the Society. It is not held under any trust for education.

2225. Does the court determine each year how much money is to be given?—It is reported upon every year by the agent who considers the matter. His estimate is upon the amount previously paid. It rarely changes much.

2226. Supposing the expenditure in the previous half year was more than they had voted, would they give an extra vote?

Mr. Taylor.—They vote so much for each purpose, for the different teachers, awards, and so on.

Rev. Canon O'Hara handed in a newspaper of 14th May, 1887.

2227. Lord Justice FitzGibbon.—This is an abstract of the receipts and expenditure of the Honourable the Irish Society, for the year 1886. It gives the particulars of all the educational grants, including Coleraine, £3,656 5s. 5½d. The particulars of payments for Coleraine are all set forth, including donations to the schools (date of the grant, 1818); to the Society's school for boys, £60, an allowance for pupil teachers, an allowance for fuel, salaries of the masters and mistresses in the different departments, £30 for premiums, £10 for rewards, £36 to the secretary to the committee, and other items. Who distributes the premiums and rewards?

Mr. Bailey.—They are generally given away during the Society's visitation to the town.

Rev. Canon O'Hara.—The committee severally distribute them.

2228. Lord Justice FitzGibbon.—Then follows a list of schools getting from £5 up to £15. They pay the caretaker of their own schools, besides £50 for incidental expenses.

Rev. Canon O'Hara.—Every expense is paid by the Society.

2229. Lord Justice FitzGibbon.—Even £10 for a lending library. We shall now be glad to hear any evidence regarding the general state of education in the locality, what provision there is, and any suggestions for the improvement of the local educational facilities.

Oct. 26, 1888.
Coleraine.
Taylor, jun.

The Rev. Henry O'Hara, Incumbent of Coleraine, sworn and examined.

2230. Lord Justice FitzGibbon.—I believe the town of Coleraine stands partly in the parish of Coleraine and partly in Killowen?—Yes.

2231. You are rector of the Coleraine part of it?—Yes.

2232. These schools are in your parish?—They are. Rev. Henry O'Hara.

2233. What do you wish to say about them?—I am a member of the managing committee, and when appointed rector of the parish, I was specially requested by the Society to look after the schools, and take an

[illegible]

Rev. Henry O'Hara.

much interest in them as I possibly could. This I have always endeavoured to do. My chief interest has of course been with the religious part of the education. That has been a fruitful source of difficulty from time to time; but recently a change has been made which I think is a great measure mitigates the difficulty. The rules in force in vested schools are in force here as if this was a vested school. Clergymen of every denomination have easy access at fixed times to the children of their own persuasion to impart religious instruction.

2734. Professor DOUGHERTY.—What was the original arrangement?—Everything was done in a hap-hazard sort of way, and a difficulty arose some years ago. Now, Biblical instruction is given on four days in the week, and on one day in the week separate instruction is given in the denominational formulæ of each Church by the clergyman or his teacher. My difficulty is, that in having to deal with something like half the entire school, I have not been able to get a sufficient proportion of the teaching staff to give my portion of the scholars instruction in the principles of our Church, and this has caused a good deal of discontent among my people—that the religious instruction has not been so satisfactory as it might have been. It has caused some of the children to be withdrawn from the school.

2735. Probably the Irish Society in appointing these teachers had regard simply to their qualification to give instruction in secular subjects?—The Society try to do fairly by everybody, but I am afraid the fact of the applicant being a member of a certain denomination would prevent him being appointed.

2736. What is the religious distribution of the teachers at present?—In the boys school I have one teacher—the most junior of all.

2737. Rev. Dr. MOLLOY.—Begin with the head master?—He is a Presbyterian.

2738. The three assistant masters?—Two Presbyterians and one Irish Church.

2739. Professor DOUGHERTY.—These appointments have been made by the Irish Society?—On the recommendation of the committee.

2740. Rev. Dr. MOLLOY.—Now take the girls school. The head mistress?—A Presbyterian.

2741. Her three assistants?—One belongs to the Irish Church, one is a Presbyterian, and one an Independent.

2742. And in the infants school?—The two senior teachers were not appointed by the Society. It was a separate school taken over by the Society who retained the teachers. The head mistress is a member of the Irish Church, and of the assistants one is a Presbyterian, one a Wesleyan, and one a member of the Irish Church.

2743. Among the teachers altogether there are four of your Church, of whom one is a head teacher?—Yes. I am not satisfied with the present arrangement. I fear when appointments are to be made hereafter, unless there is some guarantee of a reasonable proportion of the teaching staff between the different bodies, an injustice will be done.

2744. Professor DOUGHERTY.—Have you not sufficiently qualified candidates?—I have always sufficiently qualified candidates, but they have no chance of being elected.

2745. You do not wish to impute partiality?—All I wish is to have a sufficient proportion of the teaching staff to give denominational instruction.

2746. Lord Justice FITZGIBBON.—The head master told us one of his teachers had recently returned from Kildare-place training college. Is he the junior assistant?—Yes.

2747. Is he the only representative of the Irish Church in the boys school?—Yes. I pointed out this to the Society, and represented the great difficulty I had in instructing three classes of children with one teacher, and they kindly allowed me £10 a year temporarily for this purpose. I have therefore got a lad who gives instruction. He is a monitor.

2748. Then all the religious instruction laid down in the scheme is conducted, so far as your denomination is concerned, by one monitor and an assistant teacher only just trained?—Yes.

2749. Dr. TRAILL.—On the other days of the week, when you are not there for the catechism, why should not the Presbyterian and Irish Church boys be all taught the scriptures together?—That was where the friction arose. We have got a special course of instruction laid down by the Diocesan Board of Education, and the Presbyterians have got a different course.

2750. I should like to see a Scriptural course common to both Churches.

Canon O'HARA.—I would like to see it, but then it is not practicable. The education of the town on the whole would be more efficiently carried out without the association. The association has been a source of a great deal of irritation, friction, and trouble from time to time, and the Society felt this so much that they re-organized the whole thing. Whether it is an improvement or not I shall leave you to judge.

2751. How was the old committee constituted?—They appointed themselves, which led to continue the [illegible]. This new committee has only been formed a year. I may now hand in a memorial which we recently sent to the governor of the Irish Society. It is signed by all the clergy of this parish, and of Killowen, and representatives of our Church, church-wardens, and members of the select vestry. It represents lay as well as clerical opinion, and is the almost unanimous opinion of our Church people in Coleraine and neighbourhood.

2752. Lord Justice FITZGIBBON.—The memorial[*] sets forth that the members of the Church of Ireland in Coleraine are more numerous than any other denomination, but have never had a fair share of influence on the committee of the Irish Society schools, and that, in consequence the interests of Church teachers and children have been ignored; that the Church children have been leaving the school in large numbers, and that there has been much friction between members of different denominations on the committee. You also say that the committee is not recognised by the National Board, and that in no other case in Ireland is a large primary National school managed in the same way. You therefore pray that the committee may be abolished, and that a share of the present grant for primary education be given for local National schools, to be managed by the local clergy, such share to be equal to the proportion which the members of each denomination bear to the entire population. You also say that this would be about thirty-five per cent. to the Church of Ireland, thirty-five per cent. to the Presbyterian Church, and twenty per cent. to the Roman Catholics, the condition being that each school should be free to the poor, be conducted in accordance with the principles of the National Board, and be called one of the Honourable the Irish Society schools. You would also provide that all accounts and reports be annually submitted to the court of the Society. You claim that this would greatly extend the benefits of the present institution, put all denominations in a position of perfect equality, and remove a source of much friction and discord?—That is our belief.

2753. Professor DOUGHERTY.—Your proposal is to break up the present establishment in Brookdale-place and distribute the funds denominationally?—Yes.

2754. How do you provide for the smaller denominations?—If they are sufficiently numerous they can get their own proportion, and if they are not sufficiently large they can go to some of the larger schools.

2755. Would not that involve the very injustice you complain of as existing in the Irish Society's school?—If they were not sufficiently large they could not get a school of their own; in any case they are protected by the conscience clause.

[*] Appendix B, No. I., p. 793.

2256. You would split up these schools and funds into three, giving one share to your own Church, one to Roman Catholics, and one to Presbyterians?—Yes, if they wished.

2257. And you would propose to allocate the endowments in proportion to the numbers of these denominations in attendance, leaving out of account the smaller denominations that are not worth considering?—Yes, practically. I have very excellent school premises of my own which I should use in case the scheme were carried out. I should have girls and infants in them, and boys in one of the Hereford-place schools.

2258. Lord Justice FitzGibbon.—Are those schools of yours in connection with the National Board?—There is no day school there, only a Sunday school.

2259. What accommodation have you got?—For about 400.

2260. Rev. Dr. Molloy.—You consider that every poor child in Coleraine has an equal claim upon the Irish Society's funds?—Yes.

2261. And you propose that the funds should be made available for all?—Yes.

2262. At present is that the case?—No.

2263. Mr. Taylor.—Is there any rule, or anything in the government of this school that prevents children of any class or creed attending its classes?—There is not, but practically they don't attend.

2264. Mr. Leech, Solicitor.—You propose that Killowen should be separately recognised?—I think it is very important that it should be so. It is a very poor district. Within the municipal boundary, Coleraine proper represents about two thirds, and Killowen one third. I should like to see Killowen get an equal share.

2265. Professor Dougherty.—Is Killowen on the Irish Society's estate.

Mr. Hodge.—They own nothing in Killowen but the river.

Canon O'Hara.—A large number of the poorer class who work in Coleraine reside in Killowen. They are the very class for whom free education should be provided.

2266. Is there not a large factory in Killowen?—There is, and some of the workers live in Coleraine. The very poorest live in Killowen.

2267. Mr. Taylor.—Are there not double the number living on this (Coleraine) side of the river?—There are. Killowen is to Coleraine as about one to two.

2268. Mr. Leech.—Does the Killowen school imitate the example of the Irish Society in providing education free?—Yes.

2269. Professor Dougherty.—The Killowen schools provide free education under denominational management?—Yes.

Mr. Leech.—The Presbyterians are well provided for and recognised.

2270. Rev. Dr. Molloy.—Can you give us the amount of the grants to the other schools in Coleraine?—The only other grant I am aware of is one to the Roman Catholic school of £20.

2271. That is hardly in proportion to the Catholic population?—No.

2272. What about Killowen?—It gets £17 a year from the Society.

2273. The total contribution of the Society towards the education of the poor in Coleraine is then about £300 a year?

Rev. Canon O'Hara.—It is, roughly speaking, about £700, because they give a grant to the Model School for prizes.

2274. Professor Dougherty.—Would you propose to carry out this principle of yours in connection with intermediate schools as well as primary schools?—It is not so necessary in that case.

2275. The Academical Institution gets a grant from the Society and is managed by a mixed committee that worked very satisfactorily?—Very satisfactorily.

2276. Can you tell us why the primary school committee has worked less satisfactorily than the other?—Because the parents of children taking advantage of intermediate education are quite able to look after their religious training, while the poorer classes are not.

2277. Has there been any attempt to interfere with the religious convictions of the children in the Hereford-place Schools?—No.

2278. Your complaint is that the religious teaching has been insufficient?—Yes, and the cause of perpetual dissatisfaction.

2279. Would you like this three-quarters of an hour of religious instruction on four days of the week, to be of a distinctly denominational character?—I would.

2280. You wish to have the Diocesan Board's course given to your children, and the Presbyterians to have something of the same kind?—Yes.

2281. Dr. Traill.—In the daily teaching of the Scriptures what plan is followed?—I or my curates go when we can, and superintend and assist the teachers of our own denomination.

2282. Are the children separated into the different denominations every day?—We teach the Scriptures only on four days out of the five, and the catechisms on one. Some years ago, when the whole thing was in confusion and at haphazard, an arrangement was made by which we should give united Biblical instruction on four days of the week and separate catechetical instruction on one. When that arrangement was changed last year we separated every day, and the practice of the Model School was carried out.

2283. Would it not be quite sufficient if they got the special instruction of their denomination on one day, and on every other day read the Bible together?—It is only loyal to my Church to see that its young are thoroughly instructed in its principles.

Rev. Dr. Wylie, Presbyterian Minister, Coleraine.—We had a common programme for some years and everybody was satisfied except Canon O'Hara.

2284. Lord Justice FitzGibbon.—What function is fulfilled in Coleraine educational work by the Model School?

2285. Rev. Canon O'Hara.—The Model School takes an intermediate place between the Society's Free School and the Academical Institution. They get, as a rule, farmers' children and the shop-keeping and well-to-do classes.

2286. It is supposed to be superior to a primary school?—Yes.

2287. Professor Dougherty.—What religious instruction is given in the Model School?—The children are instructed every day by the teachers; and the authorities at Marlborough-street are always prepared to give a fair proportion of teachers corresponding with the religious denominations of the people.

2288. They are bound by their rules to do so, but do they act on their rules?—There was no Church teacher in the Model School when I came here, and on representing that to the authorities at Marlborough-street, they very kindly remedied it, and now there is a teacher for the boys and one for the girls.

2289. Lord Justice FitzGibbon.—How many children attend the Model School?—I think there are about 300 on the roll.

2290. About what proportion of these are Protestants?—The vast majority.

2291. And what is the proportion of Church children?

Rev. Dr. Wylie.—The figures are:—Presbyterians, 206; Episcopalians, 35; all other denominations, 35.

2292. How is the Ragged School supported?

Mr. Taylor.—By voluntary subscriptions and a grant of £10 from the Irish Society.

2293. Who manages it?

Mr. Taylor.—A benevolent gentleman in town, assisted by a few committee men.

2294. Dr. Traill.—How is it that the Presbyterian population, being 900 less than the Church population, have 160 more children at school than the Church people?

Oct. 26, 1888.

Rev. Canon O'Hara.

Dec. 11, 1888.

Rev. Canon O'Hara.—They are a wealthier class.

Dr. Traill.—The poor have always most children.

Mr. Taylor.—The reason probably is that a large number of children come from beyond the borough of Coleraine, and those country children are generally Presbyterians.

2295. Professor Dougherty.—Was there any reply from the Society to your memorial?

Canon O'Hara.—They replied that as the schools had only been recently put in operation, and had not got a fair trial, it would be premature to reopen the question.

2296. Do you think the Society will regard favourably your proposal to allocate the money according to numbers?—I have reason to think they are favourably disposed to it.

The Rev. James Stewart, Rector of Killowen, sworn and examined.

Rev. James Stewart.

2297. Lord Justice FitzGibbon.—You are manager of the Killowen schools?—I am manager of the Killowen No. 2 National Schools.

2298. What number of children attend your school?—In 1885, there were 216; 1886, 277; and 1887, 274.

2299. What is the average attendance?—In 1885, 128·0; in 1886, 110·7; and in 1887, 101·4. There were on the rolls on 12th October last 168—of whom 114 are Church children, 41 Presbyterians, no Roman Catholics, and 13 other denominations.

2300. Professor Dougherty.—What is the number of free scholars?—All. We have no school fees whatever.

2301. Lord Justice FitzGibbon.—How are the schools supported?—By payments from the National Board, £12 from the Irish Society; £10 from Sir Harvey Bruce.

2302. How did you get the building erected?—I begged from Church people the world over to enlarge and repair the old building which we used at first. But it was insufficient and we had to build a new school. For that purpose we held a bazaar, which was very largely supported by all denominations in town. By that means we raised £300, and the National Board gave a grant of £600. The total cost of the schools was £857.

2303. The £600 was a free grant from the National Board?—Yes. It is a vested National school now.

2304. Who are the trustees?—The Bishop of Derry, Sir Harvey Bruce, and James Blair Stirling.

2305. Have you any school committee?—The trustees compose the committee. I am not formally appointed manager but I have been acting as such.

2306. Mr. Lamb, Solicitor.—What class attend the school?—All very poor.

2307. Do you find a willingness among the people of Coleraine to subscribe for the free education of the inhabitants of Killowen?—The inhabitants of Coleraine have always manifested the greatest sympathy with the poor of Killowen. The labouring classes of Coleraine largely live in Killowen.

2308. Professor Dougherty.—Have you not a large factory in Killowen, and do not the factory hands live there?—There is no hard and fast line. Some of them live in Killowen and a good many on this side of the river.

2309. The impression is being conveyed that the artisan population live on the other side of the river. Is that so?—Largely.

2310. Rev. Dr. Molloy.—Should you be in favour of the Irish Society giving to each school a grant according to the number of its pupils?—That is the very thing I want.

2311. Do you think that mode of distributing the grant would do the greatest amount of good to the greatest number of children?—That is the principle they, no doubt, try to carry out, but a great wrong has, no doubt unwittingly, been done by the Society towards the children in my part of the town.

2312. Would it be easy to estimate, on this principle, the claim of each school, and to divide the endowments according to the average attendance at each?—Nothing could be easier.

2313. You would be content with your share of the £760 calculated on that basis?—I want a fair field and no favour.

2314. You think that would be an equitable arrangement?—Most certainly.

2315. What teaching staff have you?—We have a master, an assistant mistress, an assistant master, and two monitors.

2316. Lord Justice FitzGibbon.—Is it a mixed school?—No, but it is under one principal teacher.

2317. Your attendance would be enough to give you two principal teachers?—Yes, but I would not then be able to have two assistants.

2318. Rev. Dr. Molloy.—What is the classification of your principal teacher?—First of second.

2319. Where was he trained?—Kildare-place.

2320. Are all your teachers members of your own denomination?—The three teachers are, and the monitor and monitress are Presbyterians.

2321. Are they appointed by competition?—One was appointed by competition before the inspector as being the best boy in school. The girl was got from the other school, and is acknowledged to be one of the cleverest girls in the town.

2322. Would it promote a healthy competition between the schools if the grants were made in proportion to the attendance?—A most healthy competition, and give everybody encouragement. It would secure the greatest amount of good for the greatest number of people.

2323. Dr. Traill.—Would they compete better in different schools than in the same school?—It would set up a healthy competition trying to get each school better.

2324. Would the people not compete better if all were together in one school?—They do not into the understanding.

2325. How would separating them give them the understanding?—I do not mean the boys but the managers and teachers. It would give them greater [illegible].

2326. Lord Justice FitzGibbon.—The greater number of children would go to the school that had the best reputation?—Precisely.

2327. Dr. Traill.—I understand you proposed to divide these grants amongst National Schools which would be under denominational management. You were asking practically for denominational education. —That did not apply to Killowen.

2328. You want to take your share of the Irish Society's grants on the same principle as Canon O'Hara. Instead of having all denominations taught together, you want the grants split up amongst schools managed denominationally?—I joined Canon O'Hara in that memorial because we found it was impossible for the committee to work harmoniously, and I want to secure some fair play for the school in Killowen. Canon O'Hara's object would be carried out on a wider basis. Mine is simpler. I do not want to interfere with the management of these schools over here. What I want is, that a school in Killowen with a trained teacher in connection with the National Board, giving a free primary education to any child who desires it, being named an Irish Society's school, and being reported upon every year by the inspector both as to numbers and efficiency, should get a grant.

2329. Rev. Dr. Molloy.—Your scheme would allow every child in Coleraine to go to whatever National school he pleased?—Yes.

2330. Dr. Traill.—Would you attach to that a condition that these should be called Irish Society's schools?—I would have no objection.

Oct. 25, 188[illegible]. Rev. James [illegible].

2331. Professor Dougherty.—Supposing the Society asked a little share in the management of your school what would you say?—I cannot speak for the Board of Management, but I do not see any difficulty in making the agent of the Society a joint trustee.

2332. Would you give a voice to the Society in the appointment of teachers?—I do not think so.

2333. They might object to pay the piper while you chose the tune?—I do not think it would be a reasonable objection.

2334. How long is it since you adopted the principle of free education in Killowen?—I have established it for the last fourteen years. It was always free in schools not in connection with the National Board.

2335. Have you any provision for free education beyond your own school?—There is a free school at Laurel Hill.

2336. Does that provide for the wants of the poorer class in that neighbourhood?—To no appreciable extent.

2337. Do you agree with Canon O'Hara as to the allocation of the school buildings and endowments in Beresford-place amongst the three principal denominations?—I do not want to interfere in the local management of this side at all. I merely want an extension of the Irish Society's area.

2338. Are you a member of the committee of the Beresford-place Schools?—I am.

2339. Lord Justice FitzGibbon.—How are the buildings of your school held?—On a nine hundred and ninety-nine years lease to the three trustees.

2340. We could incorporate your trustees if you will fix the mode in which they are to be appointed from time to time?—I simply want to get a part of the Society's grant.

2341. But the grants are given annually and voluntarily and the Society could stop them altogether if they liked?—The Irish Society, as trustees, are morally bound to give equal shares.

2342. Dr. Traill.—How can you expect the Irish Society to spend large sums in subsidies to other schools in opposition to their own schools?—My scheme would not operate in that direction at all. The children now attending the Killowen school were on the street, and in gross ignorance, and never went to the Irish Society's schools.

Lord Justice FitzGibbon.—The Irish Society's schools are too full.

2343. Professor Dougherty.—Would it be inconvenient for the children of Killowen to attend at Beresford-place?—It would.

2344. Rev. Dr. Molloy.—The principle on which the Society professes to act is to do the greatest amount of good to the greatest number. Would they obtain this end by distributing their grants amongst all the schools according to the attendance?—Yes.

The Rev. *Robert Wallace*, Presbyterian Minister, Coleraine, sworn and examined.

Rev. Robert Wallace.

2345. Lord Justice FitzGibbon.—What position do you hold in Coleraine?—I am a Presbyterian Minister.

2346. Is there more than one congregation?—Three.

2347. Which congregation is yours?—The second—New row.

2348. What is the provision for primary education of Presbyterians in Coleraine?—Our children attend the Irish Society school, the Model school, and a good many of them go to the Academical Institution.

2349. The Institution is managed successfully by a mixed Committee?—Yes.

2350. As regards the primary schools is there anything you can tell us?—I would have liked very much, on account of what has been stated here to-day, that the Committee had been more largely represented. We did not know of this sitting.

2351. Do you not look at your newspapers? We advertised these sittings, and also sent notice to your teacher and manager?—I only heard of the visit this morning. I saw it in the papers last night. The Committee has been misrepresented to-day, and I should have liked an opportunity of conferring and appointing representatives to appear here to-day.

2352. Dr. Traill.—Are you on the Committee?—I am. In the Presbytery of Coleraine Church, we arrange that certain members of Presbytery shall superintend all religious instruction of our denomination in the different schools to which we have access. I have had charge of that department for a number of years in the Irish Society's schools. I never saw the slightest misunderstanding among the Committee until 1878, and the Committee was appointed thirty years ago. In 1878, Canon O'Hara thought an injustice was done him in regard to the appointment of teachers, and complained very much. We have had occasional misunderstandings since in regard to the appointment of teachers, and in consequence the Irish Society took the power of appointing teachers out of the hands of the Committee. The head teacher and the assistants were appointed by the Committee up to 1878. There was then a difference of opinion. The Committee made an appointment by a very large majority. Exception was taken to it by Canon O'Hara who appealed to the Society through the agent, and since then we have differed occasionally.

2353. Was that majority composed exclusively of members of one denomination?—I do not remember the numbers.

2354. What about religious instruction?—During the last two years Canon O'Hara and I both superintended religious instruction in the schools, perfectly agreed as to a common Scripture programme for the boys school, and it was understood that the two denominations were to read this programme day after day, with the exception of one day in the week, when there would be a separation for denominational subjects. As for the complaint of a want of a sufficient staff for teaching religious subjects, on the part of Canon O'Hara, I may say we had a far greater ground of complaint, though we were not disposed to make it. For example, in the infant school, while we have 168 children on the roll, and according to the last census of the school the children of all other denominations numbered only 123, we have only one teacher, while Canon O'Hara has the principal and an assistant.

2355. Rev. Dr. Molloy.—You have ground of complaint as well as Canon O'Hara?—Precisely.

2356. And you are also dissatisfied?—No.

2357. Is the denominational difference greater in the boys school than in the girls?—There is nearly the same proportion.

2358. Lord Justice FitzGibbon.—Canon O'Hara has said that the two teachers of his denomination in the infant school were taken over with the school?—The principal teacher in the infant school was the teacher from the beginning, and when the school was taken over by the Society she remained the teacher still.

2359. Dr. Traill.—Does Canon O'Hara's complaint of the want of a teacher for special religious instruction make so much difference in the infant school as with boys and girls of maturer age?—I do not think so. I think it would be infinitely better for the community and for the children, that Protestant children of all denominations should read the Scriptures together without any separation, except on one day in the week for denominational teaching. If you divide that class of children it leads to irritation and bitter feeling, and that will be engendered and increased as they grow up to be men and women.

2360. The clergymen of all denominations should

Oct. 25, 1886.

Rev. Robert Wallace.

agree upon a common religious programme for the children?—Decidedly, and I am most willing to do that. During the last two years Canon O'Hara and I agreed about a religious programme for the boys school, and in order to show a thoroughly conciliatory spirit, I accepted his programme of Scripture. I asked him to come to an understanding in the girls school this year, but I am sorry to say we have not. The present committee are in charge of the girls school for the first time this year. Formerly it was in charge of ladies. We make no complaint. We have an idea that if we want denominational instruction, if we have a larger number in one school we can ask one of the other teachers in during the time of religious instruction.

2361. In your Church are these matters managed by each Presbytery, or is your programme recommended by the General Assembly?—We have a programme recommended by the General Assembly, but we are not bound to accept it.

Rev. Dr. Wylie.—I think a wrong impression was conveyed unwittingly by the teacher, and confirmed unwittingly by the Rev. Canon O'Hara, that the Presbyterians and Episcopalians were practically equal. The case really stands in this way—Presbyterians on the roll, boys school, 134; all other denominations, 83. Presbyterians in the girls school, 128; all other denominations, 102. Presbyterians in infant school, 143; all others, 125. Total, Presbyterians, 401; all other denominations, 310. We have the largest number of children in the schools. Last year it was still more in our favour, there being in the boys school Presbyterians, 100; all other denominations, 73.

2362. Dr. Traill.—Canon O'Hara's point was that this falling off had taken place in recent years owing to the friction about the committee and the religious teaching.

Rev. Dr. Wylie.—The totals this year are—Presbyterians, 401; all other denominations, 310. Last year, Presbyterians, 406; all other denominations, 301. In 1884, Presbyterians, 413; all others, 301. 1885, Presbyterians, 437; all others, 331. 1884, Presbyterians, 410; all others, 316. 1883, Presbyterians, 400; all other denominations, 414. That is the highest figure.

Dr. Traill.—That is his point.

2363. Rev. Dr. Molloy.—There is one consideration which seems to have been overlooked. The Presbyterians and Episcopalians are about equal in the borough of Coleraine; but the school draws children from outside the borough, and the majority of these are Presbyterians?—This school is largely attended from outside the borough and that changes the nature of the religious population altogether.

2364. Lord Justice FitzGibbon.—The Census for the Parliamentary borough appears to be Episcopalians, 2,373; Presbyterians, 2,351; a difference of two.

2365. Professor Dougherty.—The Presbyterians have no elementary school under Presbyterian management in the town of Coleraine?—No.

2366. Whereas there is one at least under the management of the Irish Church?—Yes.

2367. Lord Justice FitzGibbon.—Do you attend to religious instruction in any of the schools?—The Model School.

Mr. Lumbridge.—I think I made a slight mistake in conveying the impression that the schools were already full. They are not full; we have space for 720. We could take in Mr. Stewart's school quite well. There is also another misapprehension that may have been left on your minds that there was anything haphazard in the religious instruction in the school. I had special charge of it for years. I have been here for a quarter of a century and I know the facts. I had the senior division, my first assistant had the next division and so on. The instruction was thoroughly organized, and we were able to give education to the various grades, the boys of all denominations receiving Scriptural instruction from the same teacher. My idea always was that the teachers should be selected from the best candidates no matter what religious denomination they belonged to.

2368. Mr. Lock.—Have you applied for additional school room to the committee?—We have applied in this way, that we have a very large schoolroom and very small classrooms—mere boxes. The society contemplate converting my residence into additional classrooms.

2369. Mr. Taylor.—Is that on account of the division with regard to religious instruction?—Yes; we want a room for the Baptist children; but there is not the slightest necessity for taking my house. Our schoolroom proper is a very large one—sixty feet by twenty-four—and our classrooms are extremely small. I have applied to the Irish Society to give me a larger classroom and to put the two into one.

2370. Professor Dougherty.—You would be quite ready to incorporate Mr. Stewart's school?—Yes.

The Rev. *John Carroll* sworn and examined.

Rev. John Carroll.

2371. Lord Justice FitzGibbon.—What is your parish?—It is called the parish of Coleraine.

2372. Are the Roman Catholic parishes divided in the same way as the Protestant parishes?—Yes. We are in the diocese of Down and Connor; Killowen is in the diocese of Derry.

2373. What provision have you for the education of Roman Catholic children in your parish?—I have schools under the National Board—a male and female school.

2374. How are they supported?—The Society have given £20 a year for the support of the two schools up till 1882.

2375. Do you speak to each or both?—Both.

2376. What is the number of your pupils?—At the present 164 in the two schools—ninety in one and seventy-four in the other.

2377. What is the average attendance?—It varies from 110 to 122.

2378. What teachers have you?—A male and a female teacher—second class teachers.

2379. How are they paid?—They are depending on their class salaries received from the Board, the results fees, and whatever little school fees the children are able to give.

2380. Lord Justice Naish.—The school is not free?—Practically they may pay or not. The system adopted in the Irish Society schools of giving a free education interferes considerably with the payment of school fees. The parents look upon it as hard to have to pay fees where they see children in a better position in life getting free education.

2381. Rev. Dr. Molloy.—Consequently the grant of the Society handicaps your school by making it very difficult to get school fees?—Yes.

2382. Lord Justice FitzGibbon.—What school buildings have you?—Two school buildings—male and female. They are on a site leased by the Irish Society.

2383. Who keeps the buildings in repair?—I have to keep them myself.

2384. Lord Justice Naish.—Who erected the buildings?—It was done by voluntary contributions.

2385. How long ago?—About fifty years. They have been forty-four years under the National Board. It is No. 1 Coleraine on the National Board roll.

2386. Rev. Dr. Molloy.—Do you consider your school to be as well entitled to share in the grant of the Irish Society as the other schools?—I should think

Oct. 18, 1888.

Rev. John Carroll.

so. All the children attending the schools are living on the property of the Society. I have to pay school fees for children unable to pay.

2387. I suppose you pay out of money you collect?—Yes.

2388. How much per annum are you obliged to raise from voluntary sources to keep your school going?—I guarantee the teacher £12 a year above his class salary and the female teacher £10.

2389. What did the buildings cost?—£600. That was raised by subscriptions.

2390. How much did the Society give?—Nothing.

2391. What do the annual repairs cost?—I suppose £10.

2392. Have you any outlay for school requisites?—The school requisites are paid for by the teachers and given to the children. I guarantee the teacher what they lose by it regarding books or materials. That comes to about £3 more.

2393. Then your contributions over and above the National Board grant would be more than £25 a year?—Yes, for the two schools. At the present time I am building new schools.

2394. By voluntary contributions?—The Irish Society gave a hundred guineas, and last year they raised their annual contribution from £5 to £20.

2395. Professor Dougherty.—On which side of the river is the larger Catholic population, Killowen or Coleraine?—On Coleraine side.

2396. Your new school building is required for the wants of your parishioners?—Yes, one of the present schoolrooms is rather small.

2397. If this plan of Canon O'Hara were adopted, would it be acceptable to you?—All I want is that my teachers be placed on an equal footing with the teachers of the Society's schools.

2398. Rev. Dr. Molloy.—You have one-fifth of the average attendance of the Irish Society schools. I suppose you would be content if you got a fifth of the grant?—Yes.

2399. Dr. Traill.—Would you be content to take one of the rooms of the Irish Society school buildings in Brookford place?—I do not think so.

2400. One of the proposals of Canon O'Hara was that each denomination should get one room, and provide for their girls and infants elsewhere?—I could not surrender what I have.

2401. Rev. Dr. Molloy.—You are content with your own buildings?—Yes.

2402. How much are you going to spend on these schools?—£600, of which I get two-thirds from the National Board.

2403. You are more easily contented than Canon O'Hara. You only ask for a share of the money grant, and you do not want any part of the buildings.

Canon O'Hara.—I have laid out £1,600 on a school house where I am prepared to take my children in.

2404. Rev. Dr. Molloy.—Then do you agree with Father Carroll. Are you content to get a share of the grant in proportion to your attendance, and do you withdraw your claim to a share of the buildings?

Canon O'Hara.—I would prefer to have one share of the buildings. I do not care what is done with the others.

2405. The present distribution, Father Carroll, does not give you a portion of the grant proportionate to your attendance?—(Witness).—Not at all. They only contributed £5 until last year and gave nothing whatever to the erection of the previous schools.

2406. Dr. Traill.—They did not want to support schools in opposition to their own until it was proved that there was no room in their own?—I suppose so.

Canon O'Hara.—It is not a necessary part of our scheme that we should get part of the present premises though it would be convenient to get a share.

2407. Lord Justice Naish.—Do you understand the £20 a year is to be continued by the Society?—I expect so.

2408. Rev. Dr. Molloy.—Is it the general opinion in Coleraine that these contributions of the Irish Society are entirely voluntary, or that they are bound by their trust to make these contributions to education?

Mr. M'Laughlin, Solicitor.—They are trustees for public purposes.

2409. Rev. Dr. Molloy.—Do any of the Catholic children attend the Society's schools?—There may be two or three.

2410. Professor Dougherty.—I suppose they have a conscientious objection to accept the education in the form in which it is provided there?—They do not go.

2411. Have you attended the Committee?—Occasionally I have.

2412. Do you find the proceedings harmonious or otherwise?—Very fair. I was not present on the stormy occasion.

2413. Dr. Traill.—But you have exercised your privilege to attend?—Yes.

Very Rev. Edward O'Brien, P.P., Killowen.—I get £3 from the Irish Society towards my school.

2414. Lord Justice FitzGibbon.—What are the numbers?—90 on the roll, and an average attendance of 65.

2415. You have no means beyond the £3, except what you get from voluntary contributions?—No.

Daniel Taylor, esq., J.P., sworn and examined.

Daniel Taylor, esq., J.P.

2416. Lord Justice FitzGibbon.—You are a member of the committee?—Yes, the oldest one.

2417. Whom do you represent at present?—I was nominated by the Irish Society. I was one of their four. The old committee always appeared to me to work harmoniously with regard to religious teaching. The committee were almost unanimously against separating the children. It was a difficulty as to the appointment of a teacher that led the Society to make this new arrangement. After some consultation it was thought best to constitute the committee on a public basis, and to leave the election to the Town Commissioners and Harbour Commissioners, who are undenominational in every sense, and of course elective. The committee have not very much power. Mr. Montgomery is practically the party through whom the Board communicates everything, and though the Society generally does what we recommend, we have virtually no power to do anything directly.

2418. What is your relation to the National Board?—We have no connection with that Board whatever.

2419. They do not recognise you?—No.

2420. Dr. Traill.—You are a consulting committee for the Irish Society?—Yes.

2421. Lord Justice Naish.—You have no power except to make suggestions?—We really do things, and they are always agreed to when pointed out. In connection with the appointment of a teacher, for instance, we make a selection and return them to the Society, who choose one from our short list. I think it is only fair to say that their wish is to do the most good to the children of the town.

2422. Professor Dougherty.—Their object is to conduct their schools on principles that any child, no matter what his religion is, would be free to go there and receive education?—That is so, and there never has been since ever I recollect any interference with the religion of any child in these schools. During the whole time I have been on the committee, and that is forty years, the object has been always that that committee should consist of such individuals as would deal with the schools in that form. If it has not been carried out thoroughly it has been from no wish of the committee to do anything that would hinder any child in Coleraine from taking advantage of the

Oct. 29, 1886. Daniel Taylor, Esq., J.P. here. I know there are difficulties in regard to the Catholic population, not having a teacher of their persuasion, but that arose from no fault of the committee. If there had been a number sufficient to justify the appointment of a Catholic teacher one would have been appointed. I would have supported that, and I supported Canon O'Hara in getting an additional teacher for denominational education.

3423. Rev. Dr. Molloy.—The Catholics do not want to attend the school?—They do not.

3424. Because it is contrary to their principles to go to a school under a system of that kind?—That is their difficulty. The Society wish to do everything in their power to enable all children who require a free education to attend, and we fear that our schools would be ruined if they are divided or deprived of any part of the funds. I have no doubt if the Society was properly approached, and if their means would allow it, they would assist other schools as far as they could, but to split up these schools would, in my opinion, ruin them. Their character stands exceedingly high, and they would suffer by division. A good many children go to these schools and get a very good education they would not otherwise get.

3425. Professor Dougherty.—Do the parents of the Church of Ireland school children in Coleraine share the views of their clergy?—I have heard they do not, but I would not say so. I have heard that they do not at all share their views. It is a matter I would not give evidence about.

3426. We have had evidence that their representatives signed a memorial to the Irish Society on the subject?—I do not know if it would have been signed by the people. One reason why the Presbyterian element is greater in these schools as regards attendance is that there is no National school under Presbyterian management.

3427. Lord Justice FitzGibbon.—The Presbyterians are satisfied with the Irish Society's schools, the Roman Catholics have schools of their own, and want a share of the grant, and the Church Protestants want schools of their own and another share of the grant. We have taken this evidence to learn the condition of education here. I may now state our own position in the matter. The grants of the Irish Society for educational purposes are only part of the money given for the purposes of their trust. The evidence we have got up to the present is, that the Irish Society, as now constituted, can withhold, increase, or diminish any of these grants for any particular purpose; but whether there is a general trust attaching to their estates under which they are required to distribute their property for public purposes, whether there is any earmarked and determinate part of their property applicable to educational purposes, or bound by an educational trust, is another question. That being so, we have no power to settle a scheme for the administration of property which might be withdrawn. One of the exemptions from our Act is "voluntary contributions." It would be manifestly impracticable to settle a scheme for a mere annual grant. If the Society thought proper to alienate any specific portion of their funds for the purposes of their own or of any other schools it would be within our jurisdiction to settle a scheme by which the present committee would get a legal status and definite powers, but we could not entertain that unless upon the application of the committee backed by the Society. It would not be sufficient if the committee [illegible] applied without the consent of the Society, for if they were created a corporation, being without aid or countenance, as is proverbial with such bodies, they might also find themselves without any property. They are better off as they are with money at their back than they would be as a legal corporation without money. We therefore find that the funds derived from the Society do not constitute an endowment that we can deal with, unless the Society themselves enable us to do so. The Rev. Mr. Stewart's school is in the position of a great number of schools. We can incorporate his trustees if he wishes, but we would not force a scheme upon him. He is managing his school excellently.

CAMUS (CASTLEROE) SCHOOL ENDOWMENT.

3428. Lord Justice FitzGibbon.—In this case an Endowment was left by Francis Bennet by will dated June 28, 1836, by which he devised to Stephen Bennet the lands of Mount Sandel in the parish of Coleraine, and charged him to pay five pounds every Christmas Day for premiums and clothing to children attending Camus and Castleroe School. He also provided that in the event of his son dying without lawful issue, which event has taken place, I believe, certain lands should go to another son of the testator, Thomas Bennet, to pay the following legacies and donations:—£5 a year to the schoolmaster of Camus; £5 to a minister of the Presbyterian Church for preaching not less than five sermons in the year in the Camus School; and £5 for a mistress to teach sewing. And he also provided for erecting a gallery in the school. We shall now hear the evidence of the present manager of the school.

Rev. *F. A. Gardiner* sworn and examined.

Rev. F. A. Gardiner. 3429. Lord Justice FitzGibbon.—I believe you are Minister of the First Presbyterian Church, Coleraine?—Yes.

3430. Are you now the Manager of the Camus and Castleroe School?—I am.

3431. How far is it from Coleraine?—About a mile and a half.

3432. Is it in a district over which you have charge?—There are some of my people living in that direction.

3433. What are the school premises?—One large room and a gallery, erected as mentioned in the will. It is a detached building.

3434. Is there a separate plot of ground with the schoolhouse upon it?—Yes.

3435. There is no teacher's residence?—No.

3436. How is the land held?—There is no security or instrument of any kind.

3437. Was this land part of the Bennet Estate?—I understand it is.

3438. It has been exclusively occupied for school purposes for a number of years?—It has.

3439. There is no claim for rent upon the school premises?—No.

3440. Is the £5 yearly paid on every Christmas Day for premiums as laid down in the will?—It is being paid, but one of the difficulties we have is the method of distribution.

3441. Where does the money come from?—It is paid by Mr. James [illegible], of [illegible].

3442. Who is the owner of the property?—Rev. Edmund Bennet, son of Thomas Bennet, and a grandson of the testator.

3443. To whom does he pay the £5?—Formerly the whole sum of £20 was paid to the manager who distributed it. Formerly the manager of the school was also the minister who conducted the five services annually.

3444. Is the school in connection with the National Board?—It is.

3445. Are you the manager?—I am.

3446. Is it a vested or non-vested school?—A non-vested school. Almost immediately after I came a change took place. I had been paid one sum of £5 for conducting the services, and I had handed another sum of £5 to the teacher for the premiums. I was doing my duty in the matter when Mr. Sinclair arbitrarily, as I think, took the money out of my hands. He himself sent the money to the master, and transferred the £5 which I formerly held as conducting these services to another gentleman, and also transferred the distribution of the £5 for premiums and clothing which was formerly under the control of the manager and teacher, to a farmer in the neighbourhood, Mr. Crown, who now distributes it. He is here.

3447. There are two payments for the schoolmaster and schoolmistress?—Mr. Sinclair pays these direct.

3448. Who appoints the schoolmaster and mistress?—I do. It was the invariable rule previously that the gentleman who conducted the five services was the manager of the school. I had been conducting these services regularly, and, without any warning or explanation from Mr. Sinclair, he suddenly transferred the payment to the Rev. Mr. Torrens, of Macosquin. Part of the reason was that he lived out more in that direction. Oct. 24, 1888. Rev. E. S. Gardiner.

3449. Who, in your opinion, would be the proper body to take charge of these payments?—One way might be to appoint the Session of First Coleraine as governing body. Another way would be to appoint a board in connection with the Presbytery.

3450. Does the Presbytery of Coleraine extend its jurisdiction to the school?—Yes; the Presbytery would have direct supervision.

3451. Is the school exclusively attended by your children?—I could not say so. There are farmers' sons and daughters and labourers' children.

James Sinclair sworn and examined.

James Sinclair.

3452. Lord Justice FitzGibbon.—You are agent of the Bennet estate, and pay this money?—Yes.

3453. How are the schoolmasters and schoolmistresses appointed?—I could not say. It is under the National Board.

3454. The owner of the estate does not interfere?—No.

3455. Five pounds is payable every Christmas day for premiums and clothing for poor children. How do you pay that?—It was paid for several years to the schoolmaster.

3456. To whom is it paid now?—It is paid lately to a farmer in the neighbourhood, Mr. Crown.

3457. How was he selected to receive it?—I selected him myself. There was a complaint made to me that this money was not distributed among the children of the two townlands of Gamus and Castleroe. He is a tenant of Mr. Bennet's, and a most respectable man.

3458. How does he ascertain whether the children are deserving of premiums or not?—It is given to Mr. Crown to dispose of in the way he thought best.

3459. Did you get any account of it?—He gives me an account.

3460. About the £5 for preaching?—It was paid up till within a few years to a gentleman who was a tenant on the property, Rev. Mr. Martin. It was then paid to Mr. Fleming, who also held a lease under Mr. Bennet. After Mr. Fleming's death, I thought it was the proper thing that the Presbyterian clergyman of the parish should get it, that is Mr. Torrens of Macosquin.

3461. Who selects the minister?—I selected him.

3462. But you are only the person charged with paying the money?—I thought the person in charge of the parish was the person entitled to it.

3463. Who is the owner of the estate now?—Rev. Edmund Bennet.

3464. Is he resident in Ireland?—No. He is resident in England.

3465. Has he a parish in England?—I think it is a curacy.

3466. Is he a clergyman of the Established Church in England?—He is.

3467. He is not of the same way of thinking as the testator?—I do not know what his private opinions are.

Rev. Mr. *Gardiner*.—The testator was a Presbyterian.

3468. Mr. *Leech*.—What Church was Mr. Martin connected with?—The Presbyterian Church of Macosquin.

3469. Professor Dougherty.—Mr. Fleming was Mr. Gardiner's predecessor. How many years had he enjoyed that grant?—I do not know. He lived quite close to the schoolhouse.

3470. When Dr. Martin got this money was he manager of the school?—He was.

Rev. Mr. *Torrens*.—I am the minister interested in that money at the present time. There is a sabbath school held there every sabbath. I receive that money because I am minister of the parish. It was handed over to me by Mr. Sinclair.

3471. Lord Justice FitzGibbon.—Who attends these occasional services?—The people of the neighbourhood, the sabbath school children and so on.

3472. Who teaches the sabbath school?—Mr. Crown, the teacher, is superintendent.

3473. Is the school attended by a large number of children living in your district?—Yes. I do not see that Coleraine has anything to do with it at all.

3474. *Professor* Dougherty.—How is it that you are not manager of the school?—By right I should be manager.

3475. Lord Justice FitzGibbon.—It is clear there must be some authority created now which will both appoint a manager, and also select a clergyman to conduct the services. We cannot divert the money from the purposes for which the testator gave it, but we can ensure that it shall be properly applied.

Rev. Mr. *Torrens*.—I have no objections to the Governing Body being appointed, but I would suggest that its members should be persons living in the district.

3476. Professor Dougherty.—Do you object to the representation of Mr. Gardiner's session on that body?—They have got nothing to do with that district.

Rev. Mr. *Gardiner*.—Mr. Crown is one of my session, a local man.

3477. Lord Justice FitzGibbon.—Is there any boundary by which we could identify the section?

Rev. Mr. *Torrens*.—There is no definite line drawn in the form of parishes. The Governing Body might consist of two members of Presbytery and two gentlemen living in the district.

Mr. *Leech*.—It strikes me that the intention was that the proprietor should regulate these matters, but he did not provide for it. Rev. Mr. Gardiner ought, however, to be fully represented on the new body.

Mr. *Sinclair*.—Would you see your way to allow this £5 to revert to the estate?—It would save difficulty.

3478. Lord Justice FitzGibbon.—That remark shows that we should look after these funds.

Mr. *Sinclair*.—I am sure Mr. Bennet does not care

Oct. 18, 1886. — James Sinclair.

whether he is represented or not, and I don't care either.

3479. Lord Justice FitzGibbon.—The Presbytery might nominate two ministers of congregations in the neighbourhood, and two laymen living within a fixed distance of the school. These four, with a representative of the owner of the estate, might direct a simple [illegible]. How many pupils are there on the roll?

Rev. Mr. Gardiner.—Sixty. Forty Presbyterians, ten Irish Church, and ten Roman Catholics.

Daniel Crean, farmer, Cranna, sworn and examined.

Daniel Crean.

3480. Lord Justice FitzGibbon.—You have been for some time distributing the £5?—Yes. We have given the premiums for good attendance.

3481. How do you distribute the money?—Mr. Sinclair allows me to give it every Christmas Day to the poor children. I gave it as near Christmas as possible, and I thought the best premiums I could give them at that season was to cover their bare feet. I excluded farmers' sons and daughters, and parties who have to get them from the dispensary were the ones I considered eligible.

3482. Your system was in accordance with the principles by which red tickets go?—Dispensary tickets.

3483. Did you give it in money?—I gave no money whatever. I thought orders for boots and shoes was the wisest distribution I could make at Christmas.

3484. Professor Dougherty.—Have you been in the habit of consulting the teacher and manager as to the allocation of the money?—The manager never consulted me and I never went to him. That was his own fault, not mine. I made it a point that each child must have attended on one hundred days in order to be entitled to a share of the money.

3485. Rev. Dr. Molloy.—Might there not be a better distribution of some part of the money than in boots and shoes?—Not about Christmas Day. The farmers about my neighbourhood are mostly Presbyterians, more than three to one of all other denominations.

3486. Professor Dougherty.—Had you any regard to educational attainments in this distribution of the [illegible]—None. It was given partly as a reward for attendance.

3487. Lord Justice FitzGibbon.—I suppose there were many children without boots who had made 100 attendances?—We gave boots to every child who had made 100 attendances and was poor.

3488. I suppose you have had your own trouble with it?—I did not get much thanks but I did what was right.

Rev. Mr. Wallace.—There might be two clerical members and two lay members of Presbytery within a certain district appointed on this Board. It would save much trouble and irritation.

3489. Lord Justice FitzGibbon.—We will have to get assistance in selecting means and settling a scheme for the regulation and preservation of these endowments in accordance with the wishes of the founder. We must provide for the representation of the owner, and we must also recognise the position of those who have the management of the school. Mr. Crean has had so much trouble and taken it so kindly that he ought to have a vote as long as he is willing to act.

Alexander Given, teacher of the school, sworn and examined.

Alexander Given.

3490. Lord Justice FitzGibbon.—How long have you been teacher of this school?—Eighteen years.

3491. Are you a classified teacher under the Board?—First of third.

3492. How many children are there in your school?—Sixty.

3493. What average attendance?—Somewhere about forty.

3494. It is a mixed school?—There is but one teacher, and a workmistress who claims the money for teaching to sew.

3495. Who looks after the school?—The teacher in conjunction with the manager.

3496. Do any local people take an interest in the school?—Yes; we raise funds there for keeping the school in repair.

3497. How are these raised?—By my own efforts in connection with concerts—assisted by friends from Coleraine and neighbourhood.

3498. Professor Dougherty.—Beyond the endowment the owner of the estate has taken no interest in maintaining the school?—Not for some time. The former owner lived in the neighbourhood. An accusation has been brought that this £5 was not properly distributed. In my recollection it was given to all children who came to the school without reference to townlands. Part of it was given in premiums and part in clothing. A certain number of prizes was given to the different classes upon marks obtained during the year.

3499. Was that more advantageous than giving it in boots?—Yes.

3500. Mr. Lamb.—Did you ever get it in these days?—No, the manager had the entire control of the grant.

3501. Lord Justice FitzGibbon.—The intention was that part of it should be given in premiums to the best scholars and part in clothing to the poor children?—Yes. The late Thomas Bennett, Esq., who resided in Cranbrook, took a very great interest in the matter, and attended the school at the distribution of clothing and premiums.

3502. Rev. Dr. Molloy.—The child that has been of his own gone on benefit from the charity at present?—No. About five years ago it was restricted to the two townlands, and whereas formerly about forty would get clothing and sixteen money premiums, now only eight or ten get anything.

3503. Mr. Crean.—I understand the will limits the distribution to the two townlands on the estate.

3504. Mr. Sinclair.—I was under the same impression.

3505. Rev. Mr. Stevens.—That was my impression.

3506. Mr. Given.—It has operated seriously against my school.

3507. Lord Justice FitzGibbon.—There is no such restriction in the will. It says "to the poor children of Cranna and Gortherne School."

3508. Rev. Dr. Wylie.—The townlands changed are on the other side of the river from the school.

3509. Lord Justice FitzGibbon.—We shall have no difficulty in drawing up a scheme for the future administration of this endowment.

PUBLIC SITTING—MONDAY, OCTOBER 29, 1888.

At the Courthouse, Magherafelt.

PRESENT:—The Right Hon. Lord Justice FITZGIBBON and the Right Hon. Lord Justice NAISH, Judicial Commissioners; and the Rev. GERALD MOLLOY, D.D., D.SC., ANTHONY TRAILL, Esq., LL.D., M.D., F.T.C.D., and Professor DOUGHERTY, M.A., Assistant Commissioners.

The Assistant Secretary, N. D. MURPHY, Jun., was in attendance.

---

*RAINEY'S SCHOOL, MAGHERAFELT—†OBJECTIONS TO DRAFT SCHEME. PROPOSED EDUCATIONAL GRANTS OF THE SALTERS COMPANY.

See also Evidence, infra pp. 262–274.

2310. Lord Justice FITZGIBBON made an introductory statement, and read the objections to the Draft Scheme for the consideration of which the sitting was held. He referred to the correspondence between the Commissioners and the Salters Company, and said that since the publication of the ‡Draft Scheme the Company had executed a Deed of Declaration of Trust relating to certain property, but had accompanied it by §a letter, in which they declared it to be an escrow, to take effect only on certain conditions attached to the Endowment being carried out by a Scheme. Therefore, at present that deed did not operate to create any endowment, except conditionally. The endowment created by the will of Hugh Rainey was one with respect to which the Commissioners were bound by Act of Parliament to have regard to the founder's intentions and, as to the proposal of the Salters Company, to make up to Rainey's School what it would lose by the sale of the Salters estate, and the withdrawal of the company's former contributions, it must be understood that the proposed endowment was one of which the Commissioners had the disposal or regulation in no sense whatever. It was offered by the Salters Company on certain conditions, which the Commissioners could not accept if they did not fall in with Rainey's will. Rainey's foundation was Protestant in character. Under his will the Governing Body was Presbyterian. Under the subsequent Act of Parliament the Protestant Primate was made sole trustee of the property, and under the existing Chancery Scheme he obtained the exclusive management of the school. The Salters Company, on the other hand, in their correspondence, declared their desire to be that the benefits of their endowment should be open to all religious denominations; but by the deed which they had executed as an escrow on September 27, 1888, they purported to declare a trust of certain property, apparently consisting of some vacant places in Magherafelt, and some neighbouring buildings, for the purposes of Rainey's School "in connexion." By a letter they had called upon the Commissioners to provide that the body to hold and administer that property should be the Governing Body named in the Draft Scheme, which consisted partly of Presbyterians and partly of members of the late Established Church, and was exclusively Protestant. The Salters Company, therefore, made it a condition of their grant, first that the Governing Body of Rainey's School should be partly Presbyterian and partly Episcopalian; and, on the other hand, that the school should be open to all denominations. Before accepting such conditions, or dealing with the proposed endowment by the Scheme, the Commissioners should be satisfied that the proposal was fair to the Roman Catholics on the one hand, and consistent with Rainey's intentions on the other. The Lord Primate had objected to any interference with his existing powers, and on that point the Commissioners should be glad to hear any arguments to show that an exclusive management by the Archbishop was in accordance with the intentions of the testator, who desired that the Presbytery of Ulster should select those to take charge of the pupils. On the other hand they should also have regard to the advantages which the inhabitants had derived from the endowment in recent years. An objection had also been received from the Roman Catholic inhabitants claiming to have their interests recognised. They should be called upon to point out the grounds on which they contended that they had any claim upon Rainey's Foundation. The Commissioners were not at liberty to extend the benefits of the endowment to any class of the community for which it was not originally intended. In all cases of schools open to denominations, but under an exclusive governing body, the Commissioners adopted the principle of inserting a conscience clause. There was also an objection by the present head master (Mr. Kincaid) with respect to the provision for his retirement. There was no provision in Rainey's will, or in the Act of Parliament or Chancery Scheme, for a retiring allowance, and as Mr. Kincaid had hitherto been paid by the Salters Company, it might appear that the proper quarter in which to look for his pension would be the Company, and not the new trustees of Rainey's fund. The Commissioners had also received communications from the representatives of the Presbyterian Church, claiming a considerable, but not an exclusive, representation on the Governing Body.

Mr. F. Campbell Gaussen appeared for Mr. Kincaid.

Mr. D. S. Henry (instructed by Mr. Hartidown, solicitor) appeared for the Roman Catholics of Magherafelt.

Rev. Dr. Jordan appeared to represent the Primate.

Mr. Andrew Brown and Mr. Glover appeared in support of their own objections.

Rev. Dr. H. B. Wilson (Cookstown), represented the Educational Committee of the General Assembly.

2311. Lord Justice FITZGIBBON.—Does anyone appear for the Representative Church Body.

Rev. Dr. Jordan.—On Saturday I had a communication from the solicitor of the Representative Church Body, stating that they would not send any lawyer down, but that I in understanding the views of the Primate should submit them to you.

2312. Lord Justice FITZGIBBON.—We have had a letter from the Salters Company, dated the 17th inst., withdrawing their proposed [illegible] the [illegible] receipt of certain [illegible] belonging to the charity, and [illegible] their claims to certain arrears.

[Lord Justice FITZGIBBON also read the letter of the Company, dated October 8, 1888, to Messrs. John Maxwell and Son, Solicitors of the Representative Church Body, containing the following statement of the conditions upon which the deed of October, 1888, was executed]:—

"Herewith we hand you Deed of Declaration of Trust executed by the Salters Company in duplicate, together with memorial thereof, which please have stamped at your early convenience. The Salters Company have executed this deed on the condition that the property comprised therein should be vested by the Scheme of the Schools Endowment Commission in the Governors about to [illegible]

*See, generally, Appendix B, No. II. (a) to No. II. (m), pp. 851–858. See also Report and Evidence, 1886–87, pp. [illegible].
†Appendix B, No. II. (m) to No. II. (t), pp. [illegible].
‡Appendix B, No. II. (a) and No. II. (l), p. [illegible].
§Appendix B, No. II. (l), p. 857.
‖Appendix B, No. II. (t), p. [illegible].

Oct. 22, 1886.

appointed for the school. The deed, consequently, is an escrow, and we must request you to hold it as such on behalf of the Company until we learn that the Commission accept the Company's conditions, and the deed should not be registered at present."

2513. Mr. *Campbell Graham*, J.P.—As a lineal descendant of Hugh Rainey, the testator, if any movement is made to interfere with his endowment I should like to be heard.

Lord Justice FitzGibbon.—The difficulty is that his intentions were interfered with long ago.

2514. Lord Justice Naish.—Do you inherit any portion of the estate?

Mr. *Graham*.—No; the estates have passed away from the family.

2515. Lord Justice FitzGibbon (to Dr. *Jordan*).—Are you willing to accept the governing body proposed by the Draft Scheme?

Rev. *Thomas Jordan*, D.D.—After consideration with the Primate we thought we would make a sacrifice of our feelings and accept that body on the understanding that the position of the Primate, which he has held so long, would be continued. The position we took was, that if we conceded so much, our Presbyterian friends should go with us in maintaining our position. The Primate writes:—

"I never heard of a trust formed by Act of Parliament, and ratified by the Court of Chancery, being cancelled when no charge of violation of that trust was made. I consider it, if carried out, an exercise of power which the Privy Council on appeal would not sanction. We have made a concession with a view to a settlement, and if I am deprived of my position in the Rainey School, no endowment for a sacred trust will be free from desecration."

2516. Lord Justice FitzGibbon.—I understand you to say that you were prepared to sacrifice your feelings if your Presbyterian friends were willing to accept the proposed Governing Body?

Rev. Dr. *Jordan*.—In reference to the objections made to the Draft Scheme by the Primate and myself, I consider our proposal extremely moderate. We felt that it was giving up a very great deal on our part to accept a mixed Board, half Church and half Presbyterian. The Primates had been the sole trustees of the charity for 160 years, and under their direction the school had been administered in a liberal spirit, extending the advantages of the charity to all Protestant denominations, while each was protected by a stringent conscience clause.

2517. Lord Justice FitzGibbon.—That seems to be a mistake. Down to 1852 the Primate was merely trustee of the estate under the Act of Parliament, and this school was to be governed in accordance with Rainey's will.

Professor Dougherty.—The government of the school did not pass to the Primate under the Act of Parliament, nor until the Chancery scheme.

Rev. Dr. *Jordan*.—Well, the Primate was the sole trustee for 150 years under Church Trusteeship. We know that our Presbyterian neighbours and friends urged a claim on the charity on the ground of Mr. Rainey having been a Presbyterian. But Mr. Rainey desired in his will that an Act of Parliament should be procured for the administration of the trust, and it was at the instance of his representatives that the Act was procured which made Primate Boulter the sole trustee.

2518. Professor Dougherty.—But the whole thing was a fraud.

Rev. Dr. *Jordan*.—I won't answer that. If people now blame anyone for the Act of Parliament procured so long ago it is only fair to remember at whose instance it was procured. While accepting the proposal of a mixed Board, we desire that the trusteeship of the Primate should be preserved for the following reasons:—(*a*.) The trusteeship originated in an Act of Parliament procured by direction of the will, and at the instance of representatives of the testator. (*b*.) In the records of the School I find that an opinion was had on April 14, 1848, from Serjeant Warren, in which he stated among other things—"The entire management of the Charity has devolved upon the Primate," and the schoolhouse was surrendered to the Primate on April 25, 1848. (*c*.) The trusteeship was confirmed by the Court of Chancery to which an application was made by the Primate of the day, and a scheme was framed adapting the School to the wants of the times, and placing its entire direction under the Archbishop of Armagh. The Salters Company concurred in this Act, and the consequence of their concurrence was the building by them of the present house in 1864. (*d*.) The trusteeship gives the school the advantage of the experience, wisdom, and character of the Primate, and is therefore a protection to it. (*e*.) The preservation of the trusteeship will not mar the present scheme, as the Primate would pay over through his agent, as in times past, the proceeds of the Rainey Trust to the proposed governors of the school. (*f*.) The trust has been discharged faithfully, and always keeping in view the requirements of the time as to education. When I came here ten years ago and became a visitor of the school, it was placed, with the concurrence of the late Primate, under the provisions of the Intermediate Education Act, and the pupils have appeared each year at the Intermediate examinations, with credit to themselves. For these and other reasons we earnestly ask the trusteeship to be preserved. I cannot but think if the Moderator of the General Assembly had been trustee of this Charity for 160 years there would be a very strong feeling manifested if it were contemplated to remove him from it. We trust that in equity and out of a fair respect for the historical and legal position this will not be done. Having given up so much, we very earnestly ask that this may be preserved. As to the officials of the school, we feel that the Primate ought to have the appointment of the head master as heretofore, and that the other officials should be appointed by the Board, with the concurrence of the head master. As the Primate is a permanent official, and has always been sole trustee, it is most natural and reasonable that he should be chairman of the meetings of the governors with a casting vote.

2519. Professor Dougherty.—Do you ask that this right should be reserved to the present Primate during his life or that it should be reserved to the Primate for all time to come?

Rev. Dr. *Jordan*.—Yes; giving it to the present Primate as a personal favour would not be the thing at all. The population of the town of Magherafelt, according to the Census of 1881, is: Roman Catholics, 631; Church, 441; Presbyterians, 939; Methodists, 22; others, 42; total, 1,614. The population of the Salters estate, as I learned it from their offices, is: Roman Catholics, 3,791; Church, 3,373; Presbyterians, 2,972; Methodists, 116; others, 140; total, 10,312. The Commission will see from these figures that the Church people, as compared with the Presbyterians, have a considerable majority, both in the town, and also on the Salters estate.

2520. Lord Justice FitzGibbon.—We went this morning through the three primary schools in the town—the school of which you are manager, the school of which the parish priest is manager, and the school of which the Presbyterian minister is manager—can you give us any information as to the relative number of children attending these schools? How many have you got at your own school?

Rev. Dr. *Jordan*.—At the boys school, under the National Board, we have about forty and at the girls school thirty-five. I cannot speak for the other schools.

2521. Lord Justice FitzGibbon.—Your numbers are much smaller than the others. At the Roman Catholic school we found an attendance of between eighty-eight at the boys school and ninety at the girls, and in the Presbyterian girls school we found the largest attendance of all, while the attendance of boys was small. How do you explain the small proportion of Church children attending your schools?

Oct. 22, 1886.

—It may be possible that some Church children are attending the Presbyterian schools.

Dr. Traill.—I found fifteen girls and four boys, Church children, attending those schools.

2322. Lord Justice FitzGibbon.—We don't regard evidence of population so much as the number of the school going population. You propose that the Archbishop of Armagh shall for ever have the appointment of the master. What do you say about Rainey's request that the Presbytery of Ulster should be consulted?

Rev. Dr. Jordan.—The will has been set aside in a great many respects, and I was going on the Acts of Parliament and the Chancery Scheme. In the practical working of the National school, if a Church man is appointed master an effort is made to get a Presbyterian for second teacher, and if a Presbyterian master is appointed, conversely we try to put a Church person in as second teacher. On that principle we thought of an arrangement with regard to the head-master being appointed in future by the Primate, and then the other man might be appointed by the Board, and to prevent any unpleasantness the head master would have a voice in the appointment.

2323. Professor Dougherty.—By your proposal the Primate would control the Board as well as appoint the head master?

Rev. Dr. Jordan.—The arrangement that the Primate should be chairman is in the draft scheme.

2324. Lord Justice FitzGibbon.—In his will, Rainey suggested that if either of the two old men, who were to have the care of the boys, should become defective or unable to perform his duties, "he should be eased and another wrote for to the Presbytery of Ulster, who should be found very capable and fit to be an instructor of youth."

Mr. Campbell Gunning.—Hugh Rainey was a Presbyterian, who left his property to his son-in-law, Colonel Thomas Ash, who was to carry out the arrangement as to the school. The Ash family were Episcopalians, and in that way it slipped from the Presbyterian body to the Episcopalian body.

2325. Dr. Traill.—When did the Ash family become Episcopalians?

Mr. Gunning.—They were always so.

2326. Professor Dougherty.—Whatever they were, they had assuredly no power to set aside the trusts of Rainey's will.

Mr. Gunning.—Colonel Ash was a very extravagant fellow, and his guardian was the Rector of Magherafelt. But they were Episcopalians at all times.

Rev. Dr. Jordan.—It is a very common arrangement to have a local board under a manager; the local board is often most useful in adapting a school to the requirements of the neighbourhood, but the appointment of the teacher rests with the manager.

Mr. Gunning.—As representing the Rainey Endowment, I would have no hesitation in having the Presbyterians have their full share in the management, and no objection to Roman Catholic children attending the school, but I object most decidedly to Roman Catholics having anything to do with the management.

2327. Lord Justice FitzGibbon.—What would be your view as to the appointment of the schoolmaster?

Mr. Gunning.—Seeing that the original founder was a Presbyterian, I find that in all fairness the Moderator should have a share in it.

2328. Dr. Traill.—Would you give the power of selecting the master to the new body to be constituted by this scheme?

Mr. Gunning.—Yes, I think it is a very fair arrangement.

Rev. Dr. Jordan.—If we are to have a school of any value, it must be supported both by the Rainey Trust and the Grant of the Salters Company. It is hopeless to have a school for any purpose except by union of the two endowments. It would be very important for us to have the board which has been sketched out by the Commission, and as visitors of the school, acting under the approval of His Grace the Primate, we would be disposed to enter into the board and work with sincerity and honest intentions on the trusteeship being preserved on the points I mentioned. I think the true plan is what is put forward in the draft scheme, and that the Primate should be chairman. With regard to the appointment of the head master I was honoured with a question from Professor Dougherty as to the interest which the Primate had shown in the school. There is no doubt the Primate took a very deep and true interest in the school. It has been contended fairly enough that Mr. Kincaid, the head master, was appointed by the Salters Company. It must have been with the concurrence of the Primate he was appointed, but the very fact of the Salters Company having encouraged Mr. Kincaid to come over as they did—for if he had not belonged to our Church he would have been a more prosperous man—shows that you could not have the head-mastership of the school in better hands than those of the Primate. If the Primate of that day had been allowed to have his way, his opinion as to the poor would have been carried out, and I do not think that appointment would have been made. It was by the Salters Company Mr. Kincaid was appointed, and the Primate allowed his own opinion to be overruled. The Primate was deeply anxious for the poor, and when it was pressed upon him that it was to be a school for the better classes, he was steady in his views and in his efforts on behalf of the poor. In the position of Primate you have a guarantee for the carrying out of your scheme, a security that everything will be done to secure the best man for the head-mastership. If these points be conceded to us—that the Primate shall be chairman and shall have the appointment of the head master, we will do our best in an earnest active manner for carrying on the school, with a governing body consisting one-half of Churchmen and one-half of Presbyterians.

2329. Rev. Alexander Minnis (Saltersland).—I appear with Mr. Andrew Brown on behalf of the Magherafelt Presbytery, and I wish to say a few words in relation to the will of Hugh Rainey, and the efforts to set aside the solemn disposition of his property. Mr. Gunning has today admitted that Rainey was a Presbyterian. He was a ruling elder in Castledawson Congregation. The Presbytery of Ulster were to select the two old men who were to act as teachers to the boys, and he gave a bequest of £5 yearly to the Presbyterian Minister of Magherafelt. It is a sad fact, however, that by legislation that will was subsequently set aside. There is no doubt that if Rainey had been living he would have considered it a terrible violation of trust that this money should have been taken from the Presbyterians, and placed in the hands of the Primate, no matter how distinguished the position of that gentleman. It is a fearful violation of the trust, that his endowment should be placed under the management of one in whose divine right he did not believe. However that has been done, and we do not wish to say more about it. But we delight in seeing that you have given us something like a shadow of justice in this scheme. We are not inclined to object to the scheme in toto.

2330. Lord Justice Naish.—Do you object to representatives of the late Established Church being placed on the governing body?

Rev. Mr. Minnis.—No; in these days of religious equality we do not wish to raise objections, and for the sake of that peace and harmony which Dr. Jordan so much desired, we are willing to overlook the serious injustice that has been done. Frequently I have been addressed as to the monstrous injustice of taking this property given by the will of the deceased, good Presbyterian, and putting it into the hands of the Primate of all Ireland.

2331. Lord Justice Naish.—This was done under Act of Parliament.

Rev. Mr. Minnis.—Again and again I have been

Oct. 22, 1886.

spoken to about the awful state of the times, when such a thing would take place.

2532. Lord Justice FitzGibbon.—You are using strong language, and I must remind you that under the Act of Parliament the Primate simply became trustee of the property, but the trust to carry on the school in accordance with Rainey's will was not thus affected.

Rev. Mr. Minnis.—The thing having been done we will say no more about it. We wish, as I have said, to live in harmony with our brethren of the late Established Church of Ireland and with all denominations, but certainly we object to that part of the scheme which gives the Primate the chairmanship of the Governors and allows him two votes. If that dual voting is kept up with regard to the chairmanship, we think the office should be occupied alternately by representatives of the Episcopal Church and the Presbyterian Church.

2533. Lord Justice FitzGibbon.—We must make a scheme that will work. The proposed board is half and half, and if there is no provision for a casting vote, etc. we will bring matters to a dead lock. It is necessary to have some means of deciding every question.

Rev. Mr. Minnis.—Supposing that at one meeting a Presbyterian presides, and that at the next there is an Episcopalian chairman, we could hold our own.

Lord Justice FitzGibbon.—The result would be that at one meeting there would be a majority one way, and at the next meeting there would be a majority the other way, and the result would be worse than having a perpetual tie.

2534. Dr. Traill.—Do you not think there is a difference in having for chairman the Primate who holds office permanently, and the Moderator of the General Assembly who changes from year to year?

Rev. Mr. Minnis.—We have always a Moderator, just as there is always a Primate.

2535. Dr. Traill.—But the gentleman himself would not have the same feeling about it as one who is in office permanently?

Rev. Mr. Minnis.—But we would take him more into our confidence and entrust it to him more.

2536. Dr. Traill.—Would you be content if we left it to the present Primate, who is now a governor, for his lifetime only, and then remove both Primate and Moderator from the future Governing Body?

Rev. Mr. Minnis.—I would most seriously object to such an arrangement as that; I consider that it would put the power altogether in the hands of the governors who represent the Episcopal Church.

Mr. Andrew Brown.—Under the scheme proxy voting is admitted, and I am afraid we Presbyterians would always be in the minority.

2537. Lord Justice FitzGibbon.—There is no proxy voting for governors. The Primate cannot vote unless he comes to the meeting. Subscribers may vote by proxy if they like, but that is to encourage people to subscribe.

Mr. Andrew Brown.—The casting vote would take the power away from us altogether.

2538. Lord Justice FitzGibbon.—Although the Primate and the Moderator are to be governors, I do not think either of them would attend the meetings frequently, and we must provide some means of having matters decided. We cannot go back to the ancient method of tossing up.

Mr. Brown.—There is another question, as to the balance of power in the governors the Salters Company may appoint.

2539. Lord Justice FitzGibbon.—They won't appoint anybody.

Rev. Mr. Minnis.—We object to the Primate appointing the head master, as that would give the other party complete control.

2540. Lord Justice FitzGibbon.—We have many most successful schools throughout Ulster under mixed boards, and where it would be hard to say whether the Episcopalians or the Presbyterians were in the majority. We find that the head masters have been appointed by such boards for their qualifications and not because of their denominations.

Rev. Dr. Molloy.—Under our scheme it is the governors who have the power to appoint the head master.

2541. Professor Dougherty.—Would you allow the governors present at each meeting to appoint their own chairman?

Lord Justice FitzGibbon.—Then if they sit man down, or if even numbers voted, how would you make a majority to elect a chairman?

Mr. Campbell Graham.—We think the present Primate should be chairman.

2542. Professor Dougherty.—How does that comply with Rainey's will that two Presbyterians should be appointed to take care of the boys? The Act of Parliament gave the Primate no control whatever over the school.

Mr. Graham.—From the position the Primate would always occupy, and that he would not be changed annually like the Moderator, I think our Presbyterian friends would not be wrong in electing him.

2543. Professor Dougherty.—I should like to ask Dr. Jordan how often during his incumbency the Primate has visited the school?

Rev. Dr. Jordan.—If I thought Professor Dougherty would have honoured me by asking that question, I could have had here a bundle of letters regarding the school which I received from the Primate during the short time he has held that office.

2544. Professor Dougherty.—How long has he been Primate?

Rev. Dr. Jordan.—Two or three years.

2545. Professor Dougherty.—Has he ever visited the school?

Mr. H. S. Kinnaird.—The last Primate visited the school once, but the present Primate never visited it.

Professor Dougherty.—Which shows that the Primate takes very little interest in it.

Dr. Traill.—It also shows that the question of Chairman is one of very little importance if the Primate never attends.

2546. Rev. H. B. Wilson, B.A. (Cookstown).—I wish to take stronger exception than Mr. Minnis to the relative number of Episcopalians and Presbyterians on the Governing Body. I was somewhat agreed at the Rev. Dr. Jordan pointing to the sacrifice of his feelings and conceding so much, when he is only giving up a portion of what he has wrongfully held. The Rainey Endowment is purely Presbyterian, and we have a right to ask this Commission to hand that endowment over to the Presbyterian Church in connection with Magherafelt. It will be said that the Act of Parliament is against us, but the Act of Parliament simply invested the Primate as a matter of official arrangement with the trusteeship, because, in the time of George II., Dissenters were not in the habit of getting any property assigned to them by Act of Parliament. There is a Chancery decree in the case, but I presume this Commission is appointed, in the matter of educational endowments, to look at the equity and justice of a case, and to settle it in accordance with those principles. I am only asking what is right when I ask you to restore the Rainey Endowment to the Presbyterian Church. Then as regards the Salters Company, I think they are entitled to apply their endowment to the benefit of all denominations of their tenantry.

2547. Lord Justice Naish.—As regards the Salters Endowment, I may state that it is not the Commissioners who have the power of giving it, or of stating how it is to be applied or divided. It is not subject to our control unless we are asked to frame a scheme, or called upon to administer it as we think fit, and the Salters Company have taken very good care not to do that.

Mr. Andrew Brown.—The Salters Company are giving property to be dealt with under the scheme and unless they are satisfied with the scheme they won't give the property.

Rev. Dr. Wilson.—I am aware of that, and I know they are prepared to make a liberal endowment, and willing to have it extended to every denomination.

Lord Justice Naish.—We have really to settle the scheme for Rainey's School first, and they say when we have done that in a particular manner, they will give this other endowment. That prevents us from settling their endowment in the way we would do if it were a free endowment.

2548. Lord Justice FitzGibbon.—The Rainey School is not now able to maintain itself on its own endowment alone. We might adopt Solomon's judgment, and cut the child in two. But if we cut off Rainey's endowment from the one offered by the Salters Company, the school will be killed. Won't it be for your interest in Magherafelt to keep both endowments for this institution, and to do that you must give a good representation to both denominations?

Rev. Dr. Wilson.—Out of the eight governors four are clerical and four are elected, and the scheme, as it stands, gives superiority in voting power to the Episcopalians, and yet the fund comes half from the Presbyterians and half from the Salters Company. You are giving to the Episcopalians more than they are entitled to. If it was robbery to take this money at first, it was robbery all through the years which have since passed, and therefore I maintain that we as Presbyterians are not getting our right if you do not hand us back this Rainey Endowment.

2549. Dr. Traill.—Do you hold the same doctrine with regard to the lands of Ulster generally?

Professor Dougherty.—We are not discussing the question of the lands of Ulster at present.

Rev. Dr. Wilson.—I would like to get back twelve acres that belong to this Rainey Endowment. I propose, however, that you either give us a superiority of voting power on the mixed board, or else make an arrangement for giving us a separate board to ourselves.

2550. Lord Justice Naish.—That means giving the Rainey Endowment to your body?

Rev. Dr. Wilson.—Yes; we want it in the Presbyterians of Magherafelt.

[Lord Justice FitzGibbon referred to the letter of Sir Henry Cartwright, agent of the Salters Company, dated March 8, 1887, suggesting as a Governing Body for the Rainey School the following:—

"The Rector of the Parish of Magherafelt, and one other Protestant Episcopal member to be nominated by him or elected by the Vestry; two members of the Presbyterian Church, appointed or elected by that body; two members to be nominated under seal of the Worshipful Salters Company, and one member to be co-opted by the above, in addition to the Primate as Chairman."]

2551. Dr. Traill.—You couldn't ask to get the Rainey Endowment and the half of the Salters money as well?

Rev. Dr. Wilson.—We could ask it very well—give us a trial!

2552. Dr. Traill.—No, we will not give you a trial of that.

Lord Justice FitzGibbon.—If we did, I do not think we should be extending its usefulness.

Rev. Dr. Wilson.—If you unite the two endowments, I think it would be but fair that you should take into account all the facts connected with Rainey's Endowment, and give a larger proportion of Presbyterians on the Governing Body.

2553. Dr. Traill.—Do you come forward with any mandate from the Presbyterians?

Rev. Dr. Wilson.—No.

2554. Dr. Traill.—I understood you to say that you represented the Presbyterians here to-day?

Rev. Dr. Wilson.—I am Convener of one of the Education Committees of the General Assembly (Elementary Education Committee).

2555. Dr. Traill.—I now find you are not authorized by the Presbyterian Church to appear here.

Professor Dougherty.—Dr. Wilson says he is Convener of the Committee. Oct. 25, 1888.

2556. Dr. Traill.—Yes; but he is only speaking his own opinion.

Rev. Dr. Wilson.—I am Convener of that Committee, and I have in my pocket a telegram from Dr. Todd-Martin saying he cannot attend here, and I have been asked to do so. Dr. Martin is the Convener of the Intermediate Education Committee.

2557. Dr. Traill.—I don't think it is fair that you should make a statement that you appear here as a representative of the Presbyterians, and now, when asked on that point, it seems that you are only expressing your personal opinion on the matter.

Professor Dougherty.—Anyone who knows Dr. Wilson's position in the Presbyterian Church knows that he is at liberty to speak on this subject. He is Convener of the Elementary Education Committee, and he has a telegram from Dr. Todd-Martin, Convener of the Intermediate Education of the Presbyterian Church, saying that he cannot attend here, and Dr. Wilson takes his place.

2558. Lord Justice FitzGibbon.—We have received the objections from Dr. W. Todd-Martin. In your proposal for separating the two endowments you are expressing your own opinion?

Rev. Dr. Wilson.—Yes.

2559. Lord Justice FitzGibbon.—Dr. Todd-Martin says:

"(1.) The Salters Company having 'proposed to make permanent provision in connection with said school,' it is in their power, under par. 4, to qualify subscribers, and so give undue preponderance to one denomination on the Governing Body. It is therefore proposed, that the paragraph in question shall be so amended as to provide against such use of the moneys to be received from the Salters Company.

"(2.) Exception is taken to the arrangement (par. 22) constituting the Archbishop of Armagh Chairman of the Governors, and the Moderator of the General Assembly Vice-Chairman. It is proposed that the scheme be amended by providing that the Archbishop and Moderator shall fill the office of Chairman alternately, or that the selection of Chairman and Vice-Chairman be left to the Board of Governors."

There are grave objections to separating the two endowments. If the Salters Endowment is placed by the Company under the management of a joint body with Rainey's Endowment, have you any suggestion to make as to how we could best work the two together?

Mr. *Andrew Brown*.—Dr. Todd-Martin sent a telegram to the Rev. Mr. Montgomery, who is one of the Governors under the scheme, and he recommends we should adopt the scheme, having equal powers of voting.

2560. Rev. Dr. Molloy.—Our scheme does not deal with the Salters Endowment; it deals only with the Rainey Endowment. The Salters Company then comes in, and seeing our scheme, they say they will, under certain conditions, give to the Governing Body an additional endowment.

2561. Lord Justice FitzGibbon.—Knowing your opinion to be of great weight, we should be glad, Dr. Wilson, to have your views on this subject. I do not think we should take that alternative of separating Rainey's Endowment from the Salters unless forced to it, but we should be glad to have any suggestions from you as to the working of the joint endowments.

Rev. Dr. Wilson.—I think, all things considered, you should not separate the Rainey Fund from the Salters Endowment, but should give us the larger representation, to which we, as Presbyterians, are entitled. What we want is stop to the Episcopal Propaganda. We hold that money left by Presbyterians has been employed to turn Presbyterians into Episcopalians. We want to stop that with you, and to stop it also with the Salters Company. If you put the two together, and appoint the Primate Chairman with a casting vote, you have the Episcopalians [illegible] still higher in office than in the past, and you have done us no good by the change.

2562. Professor Dougherty.—If you cannot get a majority on this Governing Body, can you suggest any means of securing equality for the Presbyterians?

Rev. Dr. Wilson.—I do not agree with the Rev. Mr. Minnis as to having an alternative chairman. I quite agree with Lord Justice FitzGibbon that we should not have that, because the chairman of to-day would not be the chairman next day, and you will have interminable confusion. I want for the Presbyterians a majority of voting power—that is all we want.

2563. Rev. Dr. Molloy.—You think that the Presbyterians have a better right to a preponderating voice on the Governing Body than the Episcopalians?

Rev. Dr. Wilson.—Yes, because we contribute one-half through the Rainey Endowment, and have a right to our portion of the endowment coming from the Salters Company. One important item of statistics Dr. Jordan did not give, namely, that the rental of the Presbyterians is by far the greater part of the Protestant rental of the Salters Company.

2564. Dr. Traill.—It was not for rich people the school was founded.

Rev. Dr. Jordan.—I am anxious to state, with regard to the remark of Dr. Wilson, for whom I have very great respect, that I never used any influence in connexion with this school to bring people over to my own Church. I would ask the head master, Mr. Kincaid, were not the boys brought in and the examination made, and I never asked them a question as to their religion?

Mr. Kincaid.—That was so.

Rev. *Thomas Fisher* examined.

Rev. Thomas Fisher.

2565. I am Incumbent of a neighbouring parish. There are Presbyterian boys in the school, and I used my best efforts to get them into it.

2566. Professor Dougherty.—Are you one of the examiners appointed by Dr. Jordan?—I was.

2567. And I suppose the Presbyterians won on their merits?—They did. I merely wish to say that an Episcopal propaganda does not exist.

Rev. Dr. Wilson.—During the last forty or fifty years the population on the Salters estates is marvellously changed as regards Episcopalians and Presbyterians. At one time the Episcopalians were only one fifth. The Salters Company always sent an Episcopalian agent here, and every man below him was the same, and Rainey's School has produced results which show there is a propaganda.

2568. Mr. *Henry*.—I appear for the Roman Catholics, and my remarks may unite the Presbyterians and Episcopalians once more. I submit that the Roman Catholics are entitled to certain privileges. The scheme deals with two matters. Although you do not deal directly with the Salters Endowment, you indirectly you do so by dealing with the Rainey Endowment. As regards the Rainey Endowment, I would submit that it was perfectly undenominational, and that we also are entitled to the benefit of it.

2569. Lord Justice Naish.—When the pupils are to be instructed in religion, and when the right of nominating the persons to instruct them was vested in the Presbytery of Ulster, do you not think that gives to the school a sectarian character?

Mr. *Henry*.—If you examine Rainey's will, you will see that there is nothing sectarian there. I would give every weight to the intentions of the founder; but he has shown no sectarian spirit as regards the management of the school. He provided that "two old grave and good men, who should read the Scriptures, sing psalms, and pray both morning and evening, should be maintained, and that they should also take pains to instruct the boys and make them also pray apart both morning and evening." They were to be of a certain religious body, but the appointment of these two old men to take care of the boys showed in no respect that they were to take charge of the school. There was nothing to show that Roman Catholics were not to be admitted to the general benefits of the school, and taught by the other teachers, if there were any. In many respects the will of the testator has been set aside, and it is a serious matter, taking the figures quoted by the Rev. Dr. Jordan, which show that the Roman Catholics are largely in excess of any other denomination on the Salters estates, if they are to be altogether left out of consideration. As to the Salters Endowment, I think we are on a perfectly equal footing. Speaking on behalf of the Catholics of the district, they have very little confidence in a school where they have no voice in its management.

2570. Rev. Dr. Molloy.—Do you understand exactly what the scheme does? It deals only with the Rainey Endowment; and in accordance with Rainey's will it provides a Protestant governing body, but the Roman Catholic children who go to the school are protected by a conscience clause.

Mr. *Henry*.—But the Roman Catholics have no share of the management.

2571. Rev. Dr. Molloy.—The scheme was framed with the view of carrying out Rainey's intention, which was that the governing body of his endowment should be Protestant.

Mr. *Henry*.—But there is no necessity that it should be an exclusive governing body.

2572. Lord Justice FitzGibbon.—I think you will find that under Rainey's will it should be an exclusive body, and when the Salters Company were asked for their views on that matter, they said they desired to remain neutral. In a previous letter regarding their proposed endowment, they had proposed that the governing body should consist of:—

"The Rector of Magherafelt Parish, and one other Episcopal member to be nominated by him or elected by the Vestry; two members of the Presbyterian Church, appointed or elected by that body; two members to be nominated under the seal of the Worshipful Salters Company, and two members to be co-opted by the eleven, in addition to the Primate as chairman."

There was a conscience clause to be enforced, so as to prevent the exclusion of any children of Baptists, Roman Catholics, or other persuasions. We pressed them to say whether it was that the board to be constituted for the administration of their endowment should be exclusively Protestant, and asked them to give effect to their proposal by telling us whom they wished to nominate. They first said they would remain neutral, and then they said they would not nominate any person. In short, the Salters Company have only said "We are willing to give a sum of money to be added to Rainey's Endowment, and to be administered by the same body, provided the present scheme is carried out." At the same time, while professing to desire to open their endowment to all denominations, they know that, according to Rainey's Foundation, the governing body is to be exclusively Protestant.

Mr. *Henry*.—But I apprehend you will take into consideration the large number of Roman Catholics who are tenants on the Salters estate, and it would be a hard thing on them neither to have any representation on the board nor to get anything out of the endowment. What we would prefer would be this: We would be quite willing to abandon all claim to Rainey's School, provided that from this endowment of the Salters Company, you hand over to us an annual sum or share—proportional to our claims—for the purpose of supporting a better school for girls in Magherafelt. The Rainey School could be managed with the Rainey Endowment and the remainder of the Salters Endowment.

2573. Lord Justice Naish.—Do you think we have power to do that?

Mr. Henry.—We could bring our views before the Salters Company, and let them consider those views.

2574. Dr. Traill.—Have they ever given any money to your schools?

Rev. Joseph J. Quinn, c.c. (Secretary to the Roman Catholic School Committee).—They have been giving gratuities to the teachers of the various schools, but I do not say they will continue that.

2575. Lord Justice FitzGibbon.—Sir Henry Cartwright, in a letter to the Primate, of December 1, 1881, said:—

"The Commissioners, will, I believe, be disposed to favour a scheme by which the advantages of the Intermediate Education may continue to children of all denominations, with a Board of Management on which the Church will be fairly represented, in the ducal interest it has, without excluding the Presbyterians or Roman Catholics, though in practice the latter will take no part in the management, and I have just given over to them (Roman Catholics) schools, male and female, of their own. On these principles I shall propose to my Company to meet the wishes of the Commissioners, and endow the school with the entire buildings, and a subsidy to maintain its [illegible] [illegible]."

Mr. Henry.—The Salters Company have markets for which there is no patent, and it is from those markets and some flax stores that the proposed endowment comes. Nearly twelve out of every thirteen of those who keep up the markets are Catholics, and if they have no voice in governing the markets, a large body might leave and set up other markets.

2576. Professor Dougherty.—Does not that show that this endowment is of a precarious character?

Mr. Henry.—It does, and the governing body of the school would really be the governing body of the markets.

Dr. Traill.—But if a man wants to get a good price for his potatoes he will go into the market.

2577. Lord Justice FitzGibbon.—We have been a year and a half in correspondence with the Salters Company on this very point. We asked them to nominate a Roman Catholic representative on the governing body, and although they would not say they would not, yet they did not.

Mr. Henry.—I do not think this representation as to the markets was ever placed before the Salters Company.

Lord Justice FitzGibbon.—We had no opportunity of bringing it before them since September 27, when it came for the first time under our notice.

2578. Professor Dougherty.—How much did the Company take out of the estate when they sold it?

Mr. Henry.—£340,000.

2579. Dr. Traill.—Why would you not go to the Salters Company and ask them for money for your own schools? Why would you cut down the endowment of Rainey's School and make it more helpless than before?

Lord Justice FitzGibbon.—There are the two alternatives—the one offered by the Company of adding their endowment to Rainey's, placing both under the governing body proposed in the scheme; the other, that suggested by Dr. Wilson of settling the scheme for the Rainey Endowment by itself, letting the Salters dispose of their own property as they please. You might try to get an additional grant from them; but now that they have sold their property, you are looking a gift horse in the mouth if you object to take the market premises. Oct. 18, 1888.

2580. Dr. Traill.—What do you ask for?

Mr. Henry.—We ask for two-fifths of the Salters grant.

Mr. P. C. Gamson, B.L.—The receipts of the Salters Company at present from the markets are £160, and the Markets Committee, after paying rent, necessary expenses, and the salary of the manager, have had a clear balance during the past two years, of nearly £150, and the present receipts from the markets can be enormously increased.

Mr. Samuel Porter (Joint-Lessee of the Markets).—I beg to contradict what Mr. Gamson says. We merely pay £70 a year. We borrowed £400, for which we pay £16. We have spent our time and money in improving the markets; we have spent £500 on new buildings, which we do not intend to hand over to the Governing Body. There are also flax stores and grain stores with which we, the trustees, have nothing to do; the company can let them from year to year. They are an additional source of revenue to the Salters Company.

2581. Dr. Traill.—What tenure have you?

Mr. Porter.—About 10 years; but we are not going to give the present rents if any conflict of opinion should arise. There is a scheme at present being set forth that new markets will be opened, and the consequence will be that the money for the Rainey fund won't be £30 a year, instead of £150. For the last three years the revenue of the Salters Company from the markets has not been anything like £150. The markets are at present managed by a committee, and a Roman Catholic and a Protestant are joint lessees.

Mr. Henry.—We do not think this difficulty has been brought home to the Salters Company. If any change is made, we would put in a claim on separate school buildings. The Roman Catholics of Magherafelt, who deserve encouragement for what they are doing for education, have a sum of £1,000, with which they propose to found an Intermediate School for girls, and they propose that two-fifths of the Salters' grant, which is clearly for the good of all denominations, should be devoted to that. The Protestants and Presbyterians have Rainey's School, from which the Roman Catholics are practically excluded.

2582. Rev. Dr. Kelly.—You say that the endowment of the Salters Company is intended for the benefit of their tenants of all denominations, and that if it goes to the Rainey School it will not be available for the benefit of Catholics.

Mr. Henry.—Yes; at present the endowment they are giving is no endowment at all to the Roman Catholics.

2583. Lord Justice FitzGibbon.—Let us now find out the particulars and value of the several pieces of ground, the markets and stores which are included in the deed executed by the Company. We should satisfy ourselves that it is property which it would be prudent to vest in the Governing Body of Rainey's School.

Samuel Porter sworn and examined.

2584. Lord Justice FitzGibbon.—As one of the market trustees, can you give us information as to the premises included in the Salters deed?—The old grain stores we have no claim on at present, but the new stores we built ourselves. We have an unexpired term of 20 years in them, and for that we pay £16 a year. Mr. Harbison and I manage the markets for the benefit of the town. We are trustees of the markets and stores.

2585. How was the Market Committee appointed? Mr. Samuel Porter.—At a public meeting, and we were appointed lessees by the Committee.

2586. Have you a tenure still to run of 20 years?—Yes; we borrowed money from the Salters Company, and when each year's accounts were made up if we had any surplus we repaid it to the Company.

2587. Dr. Traill.—How much have you repaid?—I should say £300 or £400.

Oct. 22, 18[illegible]

Mr. Samuel Porter.

2588. You spent this at your own money?—We borrowed it, on interest, from them, and we repaid the interest and the principal.

2589. Lord Justice FitzGibbon.—But you paid interest on it from the time that you got it?—Yes.

2590. Are the old stores let now?—They are let for storing grain.

2591. Lord Justice Naish.—Who holds them at present?—The Salters Company; the receipts from them would be whatever was got for storing grain; originally they were let at £25, but now they are in the hands of the Company, and they are worth about £15 a year.

2592. How much are the new stores worth?—£16 a year, the present rent.

2593. How do you hold the markets?—From year to year; we are supposed to pay £96 for the flax markets and £4 for the butter market, making £100, but each year we have had returned to us £30 for repairs, which leaves a net rental of £70.

2594. Then as to the old flax stores?—They are used by flax buyers on market days.

2595. What becomes of the profits of the markets?—It is paid back to the Salters Company. We are willing to take the whole markets, and pay the rents to the governing body.

2596. If you got the premises at their full letting value, what would they be worth?—After the working expenses——

2597. Don't mind the working expenses. If a man lets premises to a tenant the working expenses must be paid by the tenant; the school people cannot manage markets, they can only let them out, and I ask what the school people would be likely to get as rent from all this property if fairly let to a solvent tenant?—Taking into consideration the dilapidated state of the markets at present, I believe £120 would be the full letting value of the markets and stores; we had an offer from the Salters Company to hand them over to us at £130 a year, and we declined the offer.

2598. Rev. Dr. Molloy.—Did that offer include the flax stores?—Yes.

2599. And does your estimate of £120 include the flax stores?—Yes.

Mr. Henry.—There are all denominations in the market committee?—Yes, and there are two Quakers.

2600. Mr. P. O. Gorman.—Your accounts are audited?—Yes, by Mr. Brenan, who is the representative of the Salters Company.

2601. What has been the average balance in hand over and above the working expenses?—About £40 a year.

2602. Professor Dougherty.—Did that include the £30 annually allowed for repairs?—Yes.

2603. Lord Justice FitzGibbon.—There has not been any very great expense gone to in painting or glazing?—No; that is the reason I allow £120 as the full letting value of the premises in their present state.

2604. How much would it cost to keep these structures in repair?—About £50 a year; some of them are at present in a dilapidated state.

2605. We saw a high wall that will soon come down if you don't look after it?—Yes; we have £100 on hands at present, which we intend to lay out for the benefit of the markets.

2606. Mr. P. O. Gorman.—Do you object to the markets being handed over to the Governing Body of the school?—We have no objection to pay the same rent as we have been paying heretofore, or we will leave it to arbitration what the proper rent should be; we will manage the markets as heretofore, and pay a reasonable amount for them in the same way as we have done to the Salters Company. There is a deputation going to London to press on the Company that if they persist in handing the markets over to a Governing Body, composed entirely of Presbyterians and Episcopalians, they will create bad feeling among the Roman Catholics. Besides, we object to the Archbishop of Armagh being manager of our markets.

2607. Dr. Traill.—You may rest assured that he does not want to be that.

Witness.—It is better to watch him than trust him; and we will take very good care to keep ourselves out.

2608. Mr. P. O. Gorman.—How much does the borrowed money amount to now?—About £400.

2609. And how much was it originally?—About £700.

Arthur Brenan sworn and examined.

Mr. Arthur Brenan.

2610. Lord Justice FitzGibbon.—You act now as agent for the Salters Company at Magherafelt?—Yes.

2611. You heard the evidence of the last witness as regards the market premises?—Yes, and that is correct.

2612. How much do you receive out of the markets?—The markets are let at £96 a year. There are then the new grain stores let at £16 a year to the market lessees. The old stores are let to whoever may apply for them from time to time. At present they are all unlet. The last letting up to November was at £22.

2613. Rev. Dr. Molloy.—Do you anticipate that the next letting will be the same?—Yes.

2614. Have you had any offers for them?—Not at £22; two are let at £12, and two at £10 per annum. That is the fixed rent for them, and I have no power to let them for less. The butter market is let at £4, and the rental of the flax stores is £44, if all were let; I have taken an average for five years, and as some of them are always vacant, the amount is £35 annually.

2615. Lord Justice Naish.—Do you allow anything for caretakers or repairs?—No; the repairs are done by the landlord. The rental, if the flax stores were all let, would produce £56. Every year the Company expended a certain amount on repairs and improvements all over the property.

2616. Lord Justice FitzGibbon.—But for the fairs that is all gone?—Yes.

2617. Lord Justice Naish.—Off the £96 and £4 agreed to be paid by the lessees, there was an allowance of £30 by the Company?—Yes; the market lessees paid the whole amount, and the Company then gave back £30 as a donation.

2618. Dr. Traill.—Was that to compensate them for repairs?—That may have been the object.

Mr. Arthur Brenan.—It was given to provide for tear and wear.

2619. Mr. P. O. Gorman.—Can you give us your opinion as to the possibility of these premises being let at a higher rate now?—No; I could give no opinion.

2620. Mr. Porter has told us that the accounts were audited by you?—Yes, for the last two years.

2621. What were the gross profits?—I could not tell the gross profits, and I would not be justified in giving any information on the matter.

2622. Lord Justice FitzGibbon.—These are the accounts of the tenants' profits with which we have nothing to do.

Mr. P. O. Gorman.—It is important in connection with the income of the School, and also for the purpose of seeing how much the markets could contribute towards the retiring allowance of the head master.

(To Mr. Porter).—You have no objection to Mr. Brenan's giving us the information?

Mr. *Porter*.—I object to his giving you any further evidence about our accounts.

2623. Mr. *Andrew Brown*.—Does not the £100 represent the tolls?

Mr. *Porter*.—No. The £86 does.

2624. Lord Justice FITZGIBBON.—The £86 is the rent for the market yard, and the £1 for the butter market. These represent the tolls, but £30 of that £100 is given back for repairs. Then there is £35 estimated rental for the old grain stores, none of which are now occupied. The letting value according to the last witness is £35. The new grain stores are held under lease at £14, while the flax stores are estimated at a rental of £54, but some of these are always vacant, and the average actual receipts amount only to £30 per annum. According to these figures the actual annual value of the proposed endowment would be in all £139, less by deductions for landlord's taxes, agency fees, and other outgoings.

Oct. 12, 1888. Mr. Arthur Brown.

Mr. *Porter*.—The Trustees and the Committee have given day after day of their own time for the benefit of the markets, and by that means the profits for the last three or four years have been about £40 a year, but £20 of that we received from the Salters Company.

2625. Lord Justice FITZGIBBON.—No School Committee personally could work the markets, and they would be obliged to let them to the best advantage. If that were done, how much do you think they would get for them?

Mr. *Andrew Brown*.—I cannot name any price.

Mr. *Porter*.—We are not antagonistic to the interests of the Schools; we are willing to pay to the Governing Body any reasonable rent which might be fixed by the Salters Company.

Alexander Johnston sworn and examined.

Mr. Alexander Johnston.

2626. Lord Justice FITZGIBBON.—You can give us some information regarding these markets?—I think they should be held under an incorporated body.

2627. If that were done how much do you think the town would be able to get out of them?—We were trying to get the markets under the Towns Improvement Act, and I for one would think were a bargain at £150 a year if we got them under the Towns Improvement Act, but I would not give £20 for them unless they were in the hands of a public body holding them for the town.

2628. Dr. TRAILL.—There would be certainty then, and there is uncertainty at present?—Yes.

2629. Rev. Dr. MALLOY.—Unless they were under the Towns Improvement Act they would not be worth £150?—They would not be worth more than £20.

2630. How much do you think they would be worth to the new Governing Body of Rainey's School? —The Governing Body of Rainey's School would find them worth very little if given to them against the wish of the people.

2631. Dr. TRAILL.—But if you got them under Town Commissioners they would be worth £150?—They would.

2632. Lord Justice FITZGIBBON.—Under the Towns Improvement Act would you have authority to establish them as public markets?—Yes, that is what we are asking for, so as to have them properly managed.

2633. Mr. *Hawys*.—You are a Presbyterian?—Yes.

2634. And you believe that if they were managed by one denomination entirely it would be a wrong thing?—I do; I would go in for them at £150 if they fell in with the wishes of the people.

Mr. *Andrew Brown*.—We are opposed to the management of the markets as it has been, and no private board, so long as I am alive and can lift my voice, shall have it.

Mr. P. C. Gannon.

2635. Mr. *P. C. Gannon*.—Representing Mr. Kincaid, the head master, and representing also the interests of the school, I say that anything done to widen the basis of the school would tend towards its success. I object to clause 37 of the scheme, as Mr. Kincaid's interests would not be properly protected. His position as teacher is considerably altered since the draft scheme was proposed. The Salters Company have now offered to give certain property and to transfer certain rights and liabilities with it. One of these liabilities is Mr. Kincaid, whose claims and services should be generously considered. Mr. Kincaid, before his appointment to this school, twenty-four years ago, had a school in London, from which he was drawing an income of about £1,000 a year, and he had also some private pupils. An advertisement appeared for a master for Rainey's Foundation School, to which he responded. On February 21, 1865, he received a letter from the secretary of the Salters Company. It stated:—

"In August last, in consequence of an advertisement by the Salters Company respecting the appointment of master to Rainey's Foundation School at Magherafelt, in Ireland, you made an application respecting it, and you were one of the candidates selected from the list of ninety-two. If you are still desirous of the appointment I have to inform you that from an unexpected occurrence the appointment is not yet made, and should you still be willing to apply on the subject, I beg to inform you that the Committee of the Court of Assistants of the Salters Company will meet on Monday next, the 27th inst., and if it should be convenient to you to be at the hall about three o'clock, they would like to see you on the subject. In your letter of 25th August last you mentioned that you have testimonials, which you will be happy to show, but none were forwarded with your letter. Should it be convenient for you to attend on Monday next, perhaps you will be so good as to bring them with you."

One of the requirements was that Mr. Kincaid should be a member of the Church of England. Mr. Kincaid visited Ireland after he decided to take the school, and he was sent to have an interview with the Primate, who first inquired whether he was a member of the Church of England, and ultimately he was appointed, with a fixed salary of £130 a year, and the fees to be derived from the pupils. One thing which caused Mr. Kincaid to accept the appointment was his knowledge of the Salters Company, and his conviction that so long as he performed his services to their satisfaction there would be no difficulty with respect to superannuation. Another thing was the possibility of developing the school. The Salters Company stated they were trying to develop the school, and that they wanted a school on intermediate education lines for the respectable middle classes. Here is a letter from them as to how that experiment was to be carried out. The Primate wished it to be carried on as an elementary school of the lowest class, and the Salters Company, writing to Mr. Kincaid on May 24th, 1865, say:—

"The Committee of the Salters Company have now arranged with Mr. [illegible] that he is to be in London on the 31st inst., and to meet with the Committee at five o'clock, and I am to request that you will meet him on the occasion. I have had a letter from the Lord Primate, not altogether of a very satisfactory nature as regards his views as to the object and expectations of Rainey's School. In adverting to your undertaking the school for twelve months he kindly adds:—'In doing this he shall have every aid I can afford, to make his effort to form a good and useful school there successful.' He afterwards adds that he hopes you are fully impressed with the idea that the school is a charitable institution intended for the benefit of the lower orders, and that the permission to have boarders is a concession foreign to the intent and object of the school, and that the Rainey School is not an institution to educate gentlemen's sons, but to aid the middle and lower classes, especially the latter, and that whoever is educated there as a boarder must receive his education in the public school

Aug. 25, 1886.

along with the rest of the scholars, and it would be out of any man's power to do justice to a school and instruct private pupils also, and if such double duty were attempted the school would be a failure. The boarders are not to be private pupils, but scholars; the school should be carried out on much the same principles as English Mercantile Schools. I have thus given the Lord Primate's ideas of the school, although I have before written to His Grace that you were quite aware that there can be no distinction made in the treatment of the scholars, except such as the difference of their attainments requires. With the assent of the Company, I have mentioned to the Primate that the Company regret to observe the low standard in which he would keep Rainey's School, and that they hope by the efficiency of the Master to raise its character, so as to benefit youths of a respectable grade, as well as the lower orders, and indeed they consider it probable that the two classes may mutually benefit by the spur of rivalry. In the town of Rainey the neighbourhood of Magherafelt would not yield any number here of an ordinary class, but there is no good reason for supposing that he would have objected to benefit the more respectable class of children, if willing to avail themselves of the facilities offered by the school."

The Commissioners will observe that Mr. Kincaid is told:—

"If you develop the school you get a fixed salary, and the fees, and if you make it a successful school it will be more profitable to you."

You see the dispute between the Primate and the Salters Company. Mr. Hogan was the Rector of Magherafelt, and stood in the position which the Rev. Dr. Jordan now occupies. The Scheme settled by the Court of Chancery practically left the matter with the Lord Primate. Mr. Hogan and Dr. Jordan recruited the boys generally from the lowest class of the community. They could not go to school for a long enough period to be really developed into anything, and Mr. Kincaid found that although respectable boys attended at first, they fell off, and he was unable to carry on the work which he had set before himself.

2636. Lord Justice Naish.—The Scheme settled in Chancery gave the general direction and control of the school to the Archbishop, with power to discontinue the schoolmaster and other teachers.

Lord Justice FitzGibbon.—Mr. Kincaid's actual appointment must have been by the Primate.

2637. Professor Dougherty.—Who paid Mr. Kincaid?

Mr. Gunson.—The Salters Company.

2638. Lord Justice FitzGibbon.—What is your contention with regard to the position of the Salters Company now? The Salters Endowment was a voluntary payment, and we cannot transfer to the Rainey Endowment any merely voluntary payment by the Company.

Mr. Gunson.—The whole course of conduct of the Salters Company, as I will prove, amounted to this—That Mr. Kincaid's services should be retained by them so long as he performed his duties to their satisfaction.

2639. Lord Justice FitzGibbon.—Has he any interest unless so long as he satisfied the Lord Primate beyond that? Was there ever any actual provision by the Company for Mr. Kincaid's retirement.

Mr. Gunson.—No actual provision—nothing except the express promise of Sir Henry Cartwright.

2640. Lord Justice FitzGibbon.—But that is like the expression of a man who tells you that he will make a will in your favour. We can only deal with what Sir Henry Cartwright has actually done.

Mr. Gunson.—Mr Kincaid went to see Sir Henry Cartwright on this matter, and Sir Henry said to him:—"You will have your salary for life, rest assured of that," but the Salters Company nevertheless have actually refused to pay the expenses of the school for the current quarter.

2641. Lord Justice Naish.—If the Primate had the power of removing the master nothing said by Sir Henry Cartwright could interfere with that.

Mr. Gunson.—The Salters Company say—"We give you the management of this endowment, and you are to take the position we have been occupying."

Rev. Dr. Molloy.—They state nothing about the position.

2642. Lord Justice FitzGibbon.—They wrote to the Rev. Dr. Jordan warning him that they would not be responsible for the salaries of the current quarter.

Rev. Dr. Jordan.—I was warned by them more than once. They wrote that they would not pay the expenses for the quarter ending 30th June last, nor the expenses then coming due, and then we got funds through Messrs. Mommoll and Son which were the accumulations of many years ago.

2643. Dr. Traill.—Do you want us to put a charge into the Scheme for compensation to the Head Master and also to name the figure.

Mr. Gunson.—Yes. Mr. Kincaid's emoluments have diminished from £400 when he was appointed to £240 at present.

2644. Lord Justice FitzGibbon.—We can feel for Mr. Kincaid's position, but what money is there to provide for his superannuation?

Mr. Gunson.—This property is taken from the Salters Company on the condition that the governing body take over all the Company's rights and liabilities—

2645. Lord Justice FitzGibbon.—Upon what legal grounds can we put a prior charge of this kind upon either Rainey's endowment or the Salters endowment?

Mr. Gunson.—Mr. Kincaid's position is that the claims which he had on the Salters Company, and which their conduct showed they always recognised, should now be recognised by the governing body that takes their place. Mr. Kincaid was brought over by the Company to take charge of this school. He had no knowledge of any religious friction existing here; if he had he would not have come to the position in which he was placed by the Company, and in which he found himself in antagonism to so many persons in Magherafelt.

2646. Dr. Traill.—If the words were, "Dismissal with the Primate's consent," would that be satisfactory? Does he ask for the Lord Primate's vote against the new governing body?

Mr. Gunson.—I say that he cannot be dismissed except by the Salters Company.

Lord Justice FitzGibbon.—He can be dismissed by the Lord Primate at any time. He at present has no security for his salary. Rainey's endowment is insufficient to pay it, and for the last half year he has been paid out of money saved some twenty-five years ago.

2647. Rev. Dr. Molloy.—If there be any claim against whom would it be?

Mr. Gunson.—He would still be in touch with the Salters Company, and in perfect sympathy with them; they always have paid him.

2648. Dr. Traill.—Then why do you not go to them for compensation? Have they not compensated Sir Henry Cartwright?

Mr. Gunson.—I am sure they have.

2649. Dr. Traill.—Then why did Mr. Kincaid not go to them, too? Why does he not retire and go to them for compensation? (To Mr. Kincaid.)—Have you ever applied to the Salters Company?

Mr. Kincaid.—No, I have not.

2650. Lord Justice FitzGibbon.—If no scheme passed at all, and the Lord Primate gave him notice to discontinue his services, what claim has Mr. Kincaid under the original arrangement?

Mr. Gunson.—We would have our moral claim on the Salters Company.

2651. Lord Justice FitzGibbon.—That moral claim you have still, but you are trying to establish a vested interest against the endowment, which has no legal existence. The Primate has no money to pay any superannuation. He has only Rainey's endowment, which is not sufficient even to keep the school open, and there is as yet no existing Salters endowment.

I suppose the Salters Company have given something to the teachers of their primary schools? Oct. 29, 1888.

Rev. Dr. Jordan.—They are paying some money to the master of my boys' school.

2652. Dr. Traill.—Are they going to continue doing that?

Dr. Jordan.—Yes, while the present master holds the office.

Mr. Gerrard.—Some members of this new governing body will, no doubt, be wanting to bring new blood into the school, and Mr. Kincaid does not want to be left in a position of uncertainty. We say that this new body should give him now what the Salters Company would have given him. We wish to ascertain what provision Mr. Kincaid will be entitled to as a matter of right, in case his services should at any time be dispensed with by the new governing body from any circumstances not arising from his personal default.

Lord Justice FitzGibbon.—We should be glad to receive his evidence as to his exact position.

Mr. H. S. Kincaid sworn and examined.

Mr. H. E. Kincaid.

2653. Mr. P. C. Gerrard, B.L.—You are the head master of the Rainey Foundation School?—I am.

2654. When were you appointed?—In 1865.

2655. Was the letter of February 21, 1865, which I read, the first that you received in connexion with the appointment?—That was the first letter.

2656. What was your salary?—I received £150.

2657. What permission was given to you with reference to boarders?—To take out boarders.

2658. Had you boarders?—I had two; one paid £40 a year, another paid £40.

2659. Were you brought over here to be the principal of a Church School?—Yes, certainly.

2660. Before being appointed had you an interview with the Primate?—Yes.

2661. Was it a sine qua non that you should be a member of the Church of England?—Certainly.

2662. Had you any idea of the conflicting interests in Magherafelt?—Certainly not.

2663. Dr. Traill.—Do you mean by a Church school that all the boys were to be Church boys?—No.

2664. That it was to be open to boys of all denominations?—Yes.

2665. Mr. Gerrard.—The management was to be Church?—Yes.

2666. You thought it could be developed into a good school?—Yes.

2667. You were allowed the school fees to increase your income?—Yes.

2668. Dr. Traill.—What were the school fees?—They were 10s., 15s., and 20s. a quarter.

2669. Lord Justice FitzGibbon.—What is the present number of pupils attending your school?—About thirty-eight.

2670. How many of these are free?—Twenty-four.

2671. Can you state the fees of the remaining boys for 1887?—About £40 altogether. My emoluments has been about £240—viz., salary, £150, house and grounds, £20, fees, £40, allowances, £15, and results fees, £5.

2672. Mr. Gerrard.—Has the school been the success that you were ready to make it?—It has not.

2673. Why has that success not been attained?—For several reasons. There was an element opposed to me, of which I had no idea whatever when I accepted the office, and it has been a most unfortunate thing that they did appoint me. If they had appointed a Presbyterian the school would have been a very great success.

2674. What was the system of nomination in operation when you came?—By the rector of the parish, the late Mr. Hogan, and the Salters Company, in equal numbers.

2675. What class of boys were nominated?—A very low class of boys.

2676. Rev. Dr. Mahaffy.—Do you mean low in point of education?—I mean low socially; I mean labourers and labourers' sons; a very low class; and I could get no boarders. It was a class that prevented the better class of boys from attending.

2677. Professor Dougherty.—The idea was to use this as a sort of parochial school?—Yes.

2678. Mr. Gerrard.—When you came did the children of the respectable people attend your school?—At first they did.

2679. Did you find it necessary to apply a different system of education?—Yes.

2680. Dr. Traill.—Did you find that the foundation boys were deficient in intellect?—I did not say that at all.

2681. Mr. Gerrard.—Was the result that the better class of boys fell off?—Yes; I do not mean to say that that was the reason altogether, but this element also operated against me.

2682. It was an important factor; what is the system of nominating now?—By competition since Dr. Jordan came.

2683. Was that in consequence of representations you made?—Well, my representations helped.

2684. Lord Justice FitzGibbon.—What is the education given now to the Foundation boys?—English generally, to about the fourth class of the National schools.

2685. Mr. Gerrard.—Is there any room for a higher class of boys?—Certainly.

2686. Professor Dougherty.—Are some of those poor boys taking Intermediate education?—Yes.

2687. Would you like to see a school here for the Intermediate education of boys?—Yes; I think some of those Foundation boys would make very good Intermediate boys.

2688. You would not deprive them because of their poverty?—Oh, not at all.

2689. You would wish the poor boys to remain long enough to take full advantage of the Intermediate Education system?—Yes; but generally the Foundation boys do not remain long enough for training for Intermediate education.

2690. Lord Justice FitzGibbon.—You saw the Primate on the occasion of your appointment to the school?—Yes.

2691. By whom did you consider the appointment was made?—By the Salters Company.

2692. Lord Justice Naish.—You knew you were to be appointed with the sanction of the Primate?—Yes.

2693. Lord Justice FitzGibbon.—Have you recently had any difficulty about the payment of your salary?—Yes; but I understood from Mr. Scott, the clerk of the Company, that it was owing to some payments not having been made to the Company by the trustees of the late Primate.

2694. As regards your future emoluments have you had any correspondence with the Salters Company latterly?—I wrote to know who would now pay the salaries, and Mr. Scott stated that they had refused to pay any more money after a certain date.

2695. Mr. Gerrard.—Had you any communication with Sir Henry Cartwright as to the change, and also as to your position?—Yes; about a month before he left I went into his office and said to him: "As the Salters Company are now parting with their estate, what will be my position?" "Oh," he said, "you will be all right; you will have your salary as long as you live."

2696. Dr. Traill.—He did not say from whom?—He did not.

5697. Mr. *Gemmell*.—Did you ever look to the Primate at any time as your master?—Never.

5698. You always dealt with the Company?—Yes.

5699. Mr. *Gemmell*.—Was your knowledge of the Salters Company one of the things that led you to accept the position of headmaster?—Oh, yes; for I had always known of the London Companies, and believed that their conduct would be most generous. I have at all times received from the Salters Company the greatest personal kindness and consideration.

5700. Dr. TRAILL.—Is there any reason why they should not be applied to by you now?—Well, I do not know what course to adopt.

5701. Lord Justice FITZGIBBON.—Any claim must be addressed to the Salters Company. Sir Henry Cartwright is one old servant of the Company, Mr. Kinnaird is another, and both should be treated alike; and they have sold out here, and left Mr. Kinnaird behind. The Primate has absolute power to remove him, but no power to grant him superannuation.

Mr. *Andrew Brown*.—You will remember that I have an objection to the superannuation clause in the draft scheme, as it would be virtually throwing the charge on us.

5702. Lord Justice FITZGIBBON.—We must try to make fair arrangements for those in the existing institutions.

Mr. *Brown*.—This is paying for the services of a man brought here five-and-twenty years ago by the Company who have now gone away.

Lord Justice FITZGIBBON (to Mr. Gemmell).—You should lay your case before the Salters Company before we revise our scheme. We can send them a report of the evidence, and they will see that no compensation can be charged on Rainey's Endowment.

John Glover (Solicitor).

5703. I sent a letter to the Secretary of the Commission, stating that there are two congregations of Presbyterians here in different Presbyteries.

Lord Justice FITZGIBBON.—Apparently the General Assembly should decide. Both should be represented on the Governing Body, and if only one, which of them?

5704. Dr. TRAILL.—Is the town of Magherafelt divided between two Presbyteries?

Mr. *Glover*.—Yes.

5705. Dr. TRAILL.—In what proportion?

Mr. *Glover*.—About half and half.

5706. Lord Justice FITZGIBBON.—How have you got two congregations in different Presbyteries in one town?

Mr. *Andrew Brown*.—Because we could not agree; but I have strong hope that we will yet be united.

Mr. *Glover*.—It would be greatly in the interest of education that the strength of the Presbyterian body should be thrown into the government of the school.

5707. Professor DOUGHERTY.—Is there any large country congregation connected with the Tyrone Presbytery, near Magherafelt?

Mr. *Glover*.—There is Lecumpher.

5708. Lord Justice FITZGIBBON.—We might add another Church representative for Dr. Jordan, and another from your congregation. I suppose the General Assembly has power to distribute the congregations between the Presbyteries, or to place them under the same Presbytery at any time.

Mr. *Glover*.—Yes.

5709. Lord Justice FITZGIBBON.—Would it satisfy you if we gave two representatives to the Presbytery of Magherafelt and one to the Tyrone Presbytery, with power to the General Assembly afterwards to distribute them as they thought proper?

Mr. *Glover*.—Yes; or leave the whole matter to the Assembly. I think representatives selected by the General Assembly would have more weight than those locally selected.

Rev. *H. B. Wilson*, B.A.—There is evidently some local feeling on the matter. Mr. Glover is connected with Union-road Congregation, which is in the Tyrone Presbytery, and while we would be glad to have that congregation represented, we do not care to interfere.

Mr. *Andrew Brown*.—Mr. Mناis and I have been appointed to represent the Magherafelt Presbytery.

Mr. *Henry*.—If we had an opportunity of bringing the evidence taken today before the Salters Company, along with our memorial, we are confident we would get another endowment for the Roman Catholics.

5710. Lord Justice FITZGIBBON.—Then try for it by all means. We are really very anxious about Mr. Kinnaird also; and it would be better for him also to have an opportunity of laying his case before the Company, with the support of this sitting.

Mr. *Henry*.—We will support Mr. Kinnaird in the matter.

Rev. *Joseph J. Quinn*, C.C., Magherafelt.

5711. The various religious denominations here live on the most amicable terms, and I should be sorry to see any conflict of interests disturbing that good feeling; but I fear if the present scheme be adopted as it stands, it will lead to that peace and good feeling being destroyed. No matter in what way we consider the statistics of the district we see that the Roman Catholics predominate. The Salters Company built schools for the late Established Church and for the Presbyterians, but the Roman Catholics have now to build their own primary schools.

5712. Lord Justice FITZGIBBON.—What then is the meaning of this statement in Sir Henry Cartwright's letter of December 14, 1884, "I have just given over to them (Roman Catholics) schools, male and female, of their own."

Rev. Mr. *Quinn*.—I do not know; we have then been about to build larger National schools, and I suppose he means the old schools.

5713. Professor DOUGHERTY.—But I understand you to say that the old schools were built by your own money?

Mr. *Henry*.—The Presbyterian and Roman Catholic schools were, at all events, built at much less expense.

Rev. Mr. *Quinn*.—The present new schools are to be built by the Roman Catholics themselves, but as regards the old schools, I have been making inquiries, and have been told that they were built substantially by the Salters Company. The Roman Catholics have been making great efforts to promote primary and intermediate education in the district, and they have bought the late manor house and grounds of Salters Company for that purpose, costing about £2,500.

Professor Dougherty.—Have they paid for it?

Rev. Mr. Quinn.—Yes. Moreover our people show the practical interest they take in the promotion of education, for within the last year, they have realised £2,000 by a bazaar, and they have guaranteed £1,200, of which they have already paid a fourth. Besides they have two other handsome donations, so as to be able to carry on a successful primary and intermediate school for girls. But while doing so much themselves, they would like to get some assistance from the Salters Company, and obtain a share of their donations or endowments for education.

3714. Dr. Traill.—Would it not be better to try to get an extra endowment?

Rev. Mr. Quinn.—No. I would like, that the various religious denominations should each receive something out of the grant that the Company has proposed to make, not only because it would be fairer, but also because it would bring on a conflict of interests if the markets were handed over to one denomination. In that case the Roman Catholics would have no interest in the markets, the profits of which would always go to the Rainey Schools. Besides the Roman Catholics are in a great majority in the markets. Of the merchants and buyers of the various dealers (?) who support the markets more than nine-tenths are Catholics; and in the population of a ten mile radius of Magherafelt, they are more than all others put together. On the Salters estate they number about 58 per cent. In the Roman Catholic parish of Magherafelt, and in the town of Magherafelt (according to my statistics) they are 47 per cent. Therefore nearly half of the people would be excluded from participating in the profits of the markets if given to Rainey's School.

3715. Dr. Traill.—I thought one of the trustees of the markets at present is a Roman Catholic?

Rev. Mr. Quinn.—Yes, at present, but then the markets would be handed over to the Governing Body.

3716. Rev. Dr. Molloy.—Would it be open for the Catholics to establish a market of their own?

Rev. Mr. Quinn.—Yes.

3717. Dr. Traill.—And would there be Protestant purchasers sold in it?

Rev. Dr. Molloy.—And the profits realised from the other market would be thereby diminished?

Rev. Mr. Quinn.—Yes; and the Roman Catholics, considering their numbers, and the part they take in the support of the markets of the town, should not be altogether left out of consideration.

3718. Rev. Dr. Molloy.—What I understand from you is this: that the Catholics of Magherafelt contribute largely to the prosperity of the markets, and therefore it is reasonable they should get a share in the endowment given by the Salters Company, which is derived from the markets. If they don't get a share in the grant, they can establish markets of their own, which would be made a source of revenue for their own schools.

Rev. Mr. Quinn.—Yes; I would be sorry to see the markets in the hands of one or two denominations. Oct. 22, 1888. Rev. Joseph J. Quinn, P.P.

3719. Lord Justice FitzGibbon.—Is there any immediate prospect of there being Town Commissioners established in Magherafelt?

Rev. Mr. Quinn.—I have heard something of it.

3720. Dr. Traill.—If the town were incorporated, and markets put under the Town Commissioners, would you object to that?

Rev. Mr. Quinn.—Yes, I would, if the profits of the markets, or rather the rents derived from them, were to go to the sole benefit of one or two denominations to the exclusion of any other denomination. I would wish to give all an interest in the markets and in the town's welfare by extending to all a share in the management and profits thereof. By leaving the Rainey School in the hands of the present proposed Governing Body, with the Rainey grant and three-fifths of the revenues of the markets—which would be increased by all taking an interest in them—and by giving the Roman Catholics two-fifths of the proceeds of the markets, all would be satisfied and work harmoniously, and education would be better attended to. Moreover, provision would be thus made for boys and girls of all creeds and classes. Of course I see the difficulty your Commission is in in dealing with the Salters grant, and what we ask you to do is not to finally frame your scheme until we have time to approach the Company and ask them to reconsider the matter.

3721. Lord Justice FitzGibbon.—We will send* a report of to-day's proceedings to the Salters Company as soon as we can get it printed. At present we cannot deal with the Salters Endowment in consequence of their having granted it only upon a condition which cannot take effect until after the scheme has come into force, and also in consequence of the inconsistency of the conditions that the school shall be under exclusively Protestant government, and shall be available for all denominations. When we send the report to the Company, and mention the difficulties of the case, and the claims put forward here, we shall have done all we can to secure you the necessary help. We must settle the scheme in accordance as far as possible with the views of Hugh Rainey, the founder. The Protestants evidently do not want to place the school exclusively under the government of one denomination, and they seem to admit that the value of the school depends on its being placed under a governing body fairly representing both Episcopalians and Presbyterians. But the proposal to endow such a school with the public markets of the whole community seems open to grave observation. With reference to the representation of the two Presbyteries, we will try to meet your wishes, but if we have to add a Presbyterian representative, we must add one at the other side also.

This concluded the proceedings.

* See Appendix B., No. II. (y) No. II. (m), pp. 486–502.

PUBLIC SITTING—TUESDAY, OCTOBER 23, 1888.

At the Courthouse, Ballymena.

Present:—The Right Hon. Lord Justice FITZGIBBON and the Right Hon. Lord Justice NAISH, Judicial Commissioners; and the Rev. GERALD MOLLOY, D.D., D.SC., ANTHONY TRAILL, ESQ., LL.D., M.D., F.T.C.D., and Professor DOUGHERTY, M.A., Assistant Commissioners.

The Assistant Secretary, N. D. MURPHY, JUN., was in attendance.

GUY'S FREE SCHOOL—OBJECTIONS TO THE DRAFT SCHEME.

Lord Justice FITZGIBBON made an introductory statement.

John Alexander sworn and examined.

3722. Lord Justice FITZGIBBON.—How long have you been master of Guy's Free School?—Since November, 1858—almost thirty years.

3723. What are your qualifications?—I am classed second of first under the National Board. I have been several sessions at South Kensington, and I have been studying sound, light, heat, electricity and magnetism, animal physiology, and agriculture.

3724. Besides conducting Guy's day schools, you have evening classes?—Yes.

3725. How many attend your evening classes?—We have at present thirty attending the science classes. The other evening classes are attended by about twenty-five at present.

3726. Do those who attend these evening classes pay fees?—Yes; those who attend the science classes pay a small fee; the Department requires that they should pay a fee. Those who attend the evening school also pay.

3727. Dr. TRAILL.—What is the difference between the two?—The evening school is under the National Board, and is on much the same lines as the day school.

3728. Rev. Dr. MOLLOY.—Are the pupils who attend the science and art classes distinct from those who attend the evening classes under the National Board?—Yes; we have seldom the same persons attending both.

3729. Lord Justice FITZGIBBON.—Who constitute your committee for the science and art classes?—Some of the trustees. The Rev. Mr. Davey, who is a trustee, as chairman; Dr. Kidd as secretary, Mr. William Orr Wilson, one of the trustees, Mr. Samuel R. Young, Mr. Andrew Simpson, Mr. William J. Craig, Mr. Alexander Patterson, and Dr. Mullen.

3730. Rev. Dr. MOLLOY.—What classes did you attend at South Kensington?—The summer classes, which are given chiefly for teachers. I have gone there also at times, and have a collection of apparatus. I paid half the price of all non-breakable articles. I paid for my present collection about £30 altogether, and of that I got about £10 from South Kensington.

3731. What courses did you attend?—The courses on sound, light, heat; electricity and magnetism, animal physiology, agriculture, and chemistry.

3732. Do you find that pupils take an interest in these subjects here?—Grown up people do; but there is not sufficient interest taken in them; still we manage to have fair classes.

3733. Are these subjects useful to them in their subsequent career in life?—I believe they are.

3734. What do the pupils of your science and art classes go to after they leave you?—Some become clerks, others shopmen, some farmers, others tradesmen of various handicrafts.

3735. Are the examinations held here?—Yes.

3736. You get the results fees?—Yes.

3737. How much?—The amount differs very much. Last year I got £22, the previous year £25; one year I got £75, and another I received £58.

3738. A good deal depends upon the pupils of each particular year?—Just so.

3739. Lord Justice FITZGIBBON.—Have they reduced the scale since you got £75?—No; the classes were larger then.

3740. What is the teaching staff in the boys day school?—Besides myself, two assistants and two monitors.

3741. And the girls school?—Beside the head mistress, two assistants, and I believe two monitresses.

3742. In the infant school?—The head mistress, two assistants, and three monitresses.

3743. Give me the numbers on the rolls of each school to-night present there are on the roll of the boys school, 184; of the girls school, 178; and of the infant school, 237. That makes a total of 599.

3744. What is the attendance?—For the last quarter, the average attendance was:—boys, 121·3; girls, 97·1; infants, 177·4; total 395·8 for quarter ended September 30th.

3745. Professor DOUGHERTY.—Have you any half-timers?—None in my school. Some of the half-timers have been taken away from the girls' school.

3746. Lord Justice FITZGIBBON.—Compare the religious denominations of the pupils in 1881 with the present time?—In the last quarter of 1881, the total number of boys on the rolls was 243. Of these 91 belonged to the Irish Church, and all others amounted to 152, of whom I should say all were Presbyterians but 13 or 14. In the girls' school during the last quarter of 1881, the number on the roll was 230; of these 47 belonged to the Irish Church, and 183 to all others. In the infant school there were 204 on the roll; of these 31 belonged to the Irish Church, and 173 to all others. The 129 Irish Church pupils who then attended the three schools formed 19 per cent of the total. At present the pupils of the Irish Church are only 6·3 per cent. We have now on the rolls 184 boys, of whom 24 belong to the Irish Church, and 160 to all others. That is a percentage of 13 now as against 37 in 1881. In the girls school we have 178 on the rolls; 14 belong to the Irish Church, and 164 to all others, giving a percentage of 7·8 now as against 20·4 in 1881; of the infants there are now 237 on the roll, of whom 4 belong to the Irish Church, and 233 to all others, giving a percentage of 1·6 now as against 15·1 in 1881.

3747. Professor DOUGHERTY.—Can you assign any reason for this diminution of Church children in attendance?—Greater exertions have of late been made by the Irish Church clergymen to have their children in attendance at their own school, the Ballymacarrett National school.

9748. How long is it in connexion with the National Board?—Only a few years.

9749. There is a large proportion of Presbyterians there also?—Yes.

9750. Lord Justice FitzGibbon.—What are the denominations of your teaching staff?—In the boys' school we are all Presbyterians but one monitor whose time has just expired, and he is at present occupied as a substitute for a teacher in training.

9751. What emolument do you get directly from the endowment?—The trustees pay me a yearly salary of £33 17s. 6d.

9752. You have first class salary and results fees under the National Board?—Yes.

9753. Have you any school fees?—Yes. For the one year the fees were—boys' school, £9 15s. 6d.; girls' school, £9 18s. 11d.; infants' school, £5 17s. 1d., making a total of £25 5s. 4d.

9754. Dr. Traill.—Yet they are called free schools?—They are free to all; what they give is contributed voluntarily; no child is obliged to contribute; they are asked to do so for the purpose of paying incidental expenses, but they are not charged.

9755. About 90 per cent. are Presbyterians?—Undoubtedly there are that many.

9756. Rev. Dr. Molloy.—Roughly it would be 90 per cent. of Presbyterians, 6·9 of Episcopalians, and 3·1 of other denominations?—Yes.

9757. Lord Justice FitzGibbon.—Have you a residence?—Yes, under the same roof with the school; there are two dwellings in one house adjoining the school for the principals of the girls' and infant schools.

9758. Dr. Traill.—Do you know how much your results fees under the National Board amount to?—My results fees have varied of course; last year they were about £53.

9759. How is the religious education arranged?—We have half an hour each morning for religious instruction, and on Tuesday the Presbyterians are brought into one room and the Irish Church children into another room, and there they are catechised. On other days we simply read the Scriptures, and in doing so all join.

9760. Are the Scriptures read according to any particular programme?—We have a programme drawn up by the education committee of the General Assembly.

9761. Is that the Scriptural programme read every day?—Yes.

9762. You do not read the programme of the Church of Ireland Diocesan Board?—Not every day; the Church children are instructed in their own programme on Tuesdays.

9763. I thought that day was for the Catechism?—Yes, and the Scriptures too.

9764. Do you, in the General Assembly's programme, read right through the Scriptures?—There is a portion selected, and the reading of that is continued for one year.

9765. Lord Justice FitzGibbon.—It is similar to the programme used by the Church, only that the portions of Scripture used are not the same?—Yes.

The Rev. *Charles Davey* sworn and examined.

9766. Lord Justice FitzGibbon.—You are manager of Guy's Free School?—Yes.

9767. How often do the trustees meet?—I think during the year we have had four meetings, but we have no fixed time for holding them.

9768. Who are the present trustees?—Sir Hugh Adair, Mr. John Patrick, J.P., Mr. William Gihon, Mr. William Orr Wilson, and myself.

9769. You occupy an *ex-officio* place as minister of the First Presbyterian Church, Ballymena?—Yes.

9770. Of what denomination is Sir Hugh Adair?—An Episcopalian.

9771. Do you happen to know what the William Adair of 1818 was?—No.

9772. What is William Gihon?—An Episcopalian.

9773. Is he any relative of Mrs. Mary Gihon who gave the bequest to the school?—Yes, he is her son.

9774. What is Mr. John Patrick?—An Episcopalian.

9775. And Mr. Wilson?—A Presbyterian.

9776. Under your present arrangements for religious instruction, all clergymen who have pupils at the school instruct them for half an hour on one day in the week?—Yes; the arrangement is not a recent one.

9777. Does it work satisfactorily?—Very.

9778. Dean Murray, in his letter, by way of objection, asks that provision should be made in the scheme for the continuance of this catechising as heretofore?—I can see no objection to that.

9779. He next says—

"As the Governing Body of the school now stands there are two members of it who are members of the Church of Ireland, but as it will be constituted in future, it is certain to become wholly Presbyterian. The school was established for the education of all denominations of Protestants, and as a matter of fact, a large number of those attending are members of the Church of Ireland. It is not, therefore, too much to ask that one of the Governing Body should be appointed by the Select Vestry of the Church of St. Patrick, Ballymena."

Have you any suggestion to offer on that?—Considering the will and the facts that have been elicited as to the percentage of Episcopalian children that attend the school, I think that the two trustees who are Episcopalians, and who will continue to occupy places, ought to fairly represent the Episcopalian Church.

9780. Professor Dougherty.—What was the denomination of the four original trustees?—With the exception of William Adair, who seems to have been doubtful, they were all members of First Ballymena Presbyterian Church at the time they were appointed.

9781. Dr. Traill.—Do you know that of your own knowledge?—I have seen it stated in the will that they were all members of the First Presbyterian Church.

9782. Lord Justice FitzGibbon.—Dean Murray's proposal is not to increase the number of Church representatives proposed in the draft scheme, but to make provision that the Governing Body shall not become wholly Presbyterian?—I do not quite see the risk to which he refers.

9783. Rev. Dr. Molloy.—Have you any objection to the Episcopalian Protestants always having one representative on the governing body?—If you appoint one Episcopalian they would be almost equal.

9784. Lord Justice FitzGibbon.—At present you have a majority of Church representatives, but nobody considers that that should be the case in the future, and the Dean wants to secure one Church representative?—He has three already.

9785. Rev. Dr. Molloy.—The Dean is anxious to secure at least one representative of his Church on the governing body; that is the point?—I cannot see that he is entitled to it.

9786. He has got almost 7 per cent. of the children attending the schools, as the head teacher tells us?—Yes. I have no objection whatever to offer to the draft scheme.

9787. Professor Dougherty.—Is there any proposal whatever to turn out the present members of the Governing Body who belong to the Episcopal Church?—No.

Oct. 22, 1886. — The Rev. Charles Seaver.

2788. Dr. Traill.—Is not the proposal of the scheme to replace them by Presbyterians?—No.

2789. Lord Justice FitzGibbon.—The three original trustees, William O'Hara, John Patrick, and William Orr Wilson, are to remain until they die, resign, or become bankrupt, cease to act, or cease to reside within ten miles of Ballymena, or for one year fail to attend any meeting of the governors. In any such case there must be a vacancy, and do you think it reasonable or unreasonable that one at least of the Governing Body to fill these vacancies should be appointed by the Church?—I see no reason why the Episcopal Church should not have one representative on the Governing Body, provided that a certain percentage of the children attending are Episcopalian.

2790. Professor Dougherty.—I gather from your hesitation that you think the Protestant Episcopalian Church, as such, has no right to representation on the Governing Body of an endowment founded by a Presbyterian?—Yes.

John Patrick, J.P., further examined.

John Patrick, J.P.

2791. Lord Justice FitzGibbon.—You are one of the present Governing Body of Guy's Free School?—Yes.

2792. How often have you attended the meetings of the trustees?—I always attend when I can; I think on an average twice a year.

2793. Do you also visit the school?—Yes, occasionally.

2794. The question now is whether it would be better to have a Governing body exclusively of one denomination, or one with some Episcopalians on it?—My opinion is that whether the Board is of Presbyterians or Episcopalians it should be kept a non-sectarian institution. I have heard my father's views on that point, and I think the object was to make it a non-sectarian school from beginning to end.

2795. Professor Dougherty.—Are not the Presbyterians great supporters of non-sectarian education?—Yes.

2796. Are they the only people in this country who stand up for it?—I won't agree with you on that matter at all.

2797. One proposal of Dean Murray's is to put on one representative from the select vestry of the Church of St. Patrick?—I think that would be very reasonable. I would have no objection that the increase should be made from other denominations.

2798. Are the present trustees descendants of the original trustees?—Yes.

2799. Your grandfather was one of the original trustees?—Yes.

2800. What was he?—A Presbyterian.

2801. He was an elder of First Ballymena Presbyterian Church?—Yes.

2802. The original trustees, with the exception of Mr. Adair, were all Presbyterians and members of First Ballymena Presbyterian Church?—They were.

2803. Lord Justice Naish.—What was Mr. Adair?—I could give no opinion about Mr. Adair. The others were Presbyterians at that time.

2804. Professor Dougherty.—You told me when we were here before that you regarded this as a Presbyterian endowment?—I scarcely meant to say that.

2805. You said that it was "practically regarded as a Presbyterian endowment"?—I meant to say that this is a Presbyterian school.

2806. I presume you would not think it reasonable or fair to ask for a representative of the Protestant Episcopal Church on an endowment which is practically Presbyterian?—As far as I gathered from my father the intention was to have it a non-sectarian school from beginning to end, and if you make the Board sectarian, you make it a sectarian school.

2807. How can that be with a conscience clause?—I don't know about the conscience clause.

2808. Lord Justice FitzGibbon.—Who appoints the teachers?—The trustees.

2809. The teachers are all of one denomination; how has that come about while there were three Episcopalian trustees as against two Presbyterians?—We appointed the best teachers we could get for the school. We never thought of this sectarian question.

2810. We should like to hear your own suggestions as to any amendment which you may think desirable in the constitution of the Governing Body?—It has worked very well as it is, and I think the Ballymena Presbytery are fighting over the spoil already. If I were forming the Board according to my own inclination I would give the Methodists a voice.

2811. Professor Dougherty.—How many Methodists have you in Ballymena?—I do not know.

2812. Are they the most numerous denomination of dissenters?—No.

2813. Then why did you select them—why did you not name the Plymouth Brethren?—Well, I have no objection; I would give the Roman Catholics a voice if they sent their children to the school.

2814. Lord Justice FitzGibbon.—We asked this morning, and there is not a single Roman Catholic pupil there.

2815. Rev. Dr. Molloy.—Did you ever hear to what denomination Mr. Guy belonged?—No, I heard the last time you were around here that he was a Moravian.

2816. Dr. Traill.—How do you account for his leaving so much to the Moravian widows?—He must have been very fond of the widows.

2817. Lord Justice FitzGibbon.—You think it would be reasonable to allow a representative on the Governing Body of any denomination that had a certain proportion of children in the school, but you do not propose to have representatives of denominations that have no children in the school?—Yes.

2818. Professor Dougherty.—Would you like to see that principle carried out all round and applied to Protestant Episcopalian endowments?—I am only giving my ideas on the matter.

2819. As to the Church school, do you think the Presbyterians should claim representation there because they have a large proportion of children at the school?—That is a different thing. My view is that the parochial school was never intended for a non-sectarian school and the other was. I think it a great pity that we cannot get Presbyterians and all denominations into the school.

2820. Have you not heard that your ministers have been trying to withdraw some of their children from this school?—I was not aware of that.

2821. Mr. Alex. Carson (Solicitor).—Do you not know that the Adairs were Presbyterians?—I believe they were.

2822. Was not William Adair understood to be a Presbyterian?—I believe he was.

2823. And that he occupied a pew in the First Presbyterian Church, and that the Adairs still have a pew in that church?—I do not know that, but I will take it for granted.

2824. Mr. Carson.—This scheme has raised this question of denominations; people were all getting on fairly before.

Rev. Thomas Eaton.—I heard a statement that the Episcopal members were in the majority and could carry a vote against the Presbyterians in the Governing Body.

2825. Lord Justice FitzGibbon.—My colleague, Lord Justice Naish, and I were not here at the previous inquiry. The school is now managed in harmony by five trustees, of whom three are members of the Church of Ireland, and two are Presbyterians. Under the proposed scheme, one Governor is to be minister of the First

Oct. 31, 1888.

John Pounds, J.P.

Presbyterian Church, and three are to be selected by the trustees, and necessarily they will be Presbyterians. There remain four others, three of whom will represent the existing trustees and will be co-opted by a body of whom when the vacancy occurs the majority will be Presbyterians, the only remaining governor will be the proprietor of the Ballymoney estate. I understand the Dean asks for but one representative. I think it was a Presbyterian endowment in this sense, that it was given by a Presbyterian to trustees of whom the majority were Presbyterians. Since then matters have changed in this respect, that the majority of the trustees are no longer Presbyterians. We think Presbyterians should form the majority of the governing body, but the question is whether other denominations which have a large number of children in the schools, should have a representation on the governing body.

The Very Rev. J. W. Murray, D.D., Dean of Connor, further examined.

The Very Rev. J. W. Murray, D.D., Dean of Connor.

2826. Lord Justice FitzGibbon.—What is the present arrangement with regard to the religious teaching of your children at Guy's School?—I, or one of my curates—generally one of my curates—attend every Tuesday for half an hour in the morning, and instruct them in Scripture and catechism. We received permission from the trustees some years ago to do that.

2827. Do you think that arrangement ought to continue?—I think it should. From the central position of the school it is almost certain that there will always be a considerable number of Church children attending it; it is more convenient for them to attend it than the school in Ballymoney-street which is under my management.

2828. How was the Ballymoney-street School established?—It was built by subscription about 1865 or 1866. It was then put under the Board of Erasmus Smith, and continued so until a few years ago, when the Board of Erasmus Smith withdrew, and we then placed it under the National Board. I am the manager of the school.

2829. What local aid is there for it?—We get a considerable subscription from Sir Hugh Adair; we have also the ground rent of a field which formerly belonged to the school, but which was surrendered to Lord Waveney, and he allowed us £15 a year for it.

2830. Lord Justice Naish.—How was the school built?—Entirely by public subscription. It cost £1,000.

2831. There was no grant from the National Board?—No; it was put under the Board then.

2832. Dr. Traill.—How do you account for the great falling off in the Church children attending Guy's school?—We were anxious to get them as much as possible to the parochial school.

2833. Owing to the distribution of the population the Presbyterian children attend your school?—Yes.

2834. Lord Justice FitzGibbon.—How many children at your school are Presbyterians?—About a third.

2835. Professor Dougherty.—When we come to your school will you object to a Presbyterian being on the governing body?—One of the governing body is a Presbyterian.

2836. Would you like to have a Presbyterian always on the governing body of that school?—Certainly not; it is a National school, and the "governing body" is another name for the Trustees of the building.

2837. You have a large proportion of Presbyterian scholars, and you have a Presbyterian member of committee; that appears to constitute a very strong case for having Presbyterians on the governing body of your school?—No; it is a National school and there is no endowment.

2838. The building and site and your ground rent constitute an endowment?—But the building was raised by Church people, by their subscriptions, and it is simply the building we have to do with.

2839. Dr. Traill.—And the endowment is a voluntary endowment on the part of Sir Hugh Adair?—Yes.

2840. Lord Justice FitzGibbon.—What is your proposal with regard to Guy's School?—It is this, that as a great majority of Presbyterian children attend there, they should have a great majority of the trustees, and I simply ask for one representative for my Church. If we had no children there I would not ask for this. I think a representative should always have something to represent.

2841. Professor Dougherty.—Then it is because there is a proportion of Church children at the school that you ask the representative, not because you have any claim on the endowment?—Yes. I may also state, with regard to the representative we look for, that I would not make it a point that he should be nominated by the Select Vestry. He could be selected in any other way. I merely suggested that as a sort of machinery.

2842. Lord Justice FitzGibbon.—Would you be satisfied that, so long as there is an appreciable percentage of Church children there, a member of your Church should be co-opted?—Yes; provided that there shall be at least one.

2843. Dr. Traill.—You do not ask that your representative should be a clergyman?—I do not; in fact, I would prefer a layman. I have no ambition to be upon the Board.

2844. Are you satisfied that the majority of the Board shall remain as proposed in the scheme, provided you receive one representative thereon?—Yes.

William Orr Wilson further examined.

William Orr Wilson.

2845. Lord Justice FitzGibbon.—You were examined on the former occasion?—I was. I am in a position to say that all the members of the original lease were Presbyterians.

2846. Lord Justice Naish.—How do you know that?—From the records of the Church; I find the names of all the trustees recorded there. Mr. Adair was not at that time a member of the Presbyterian Church, but all the others were.

2847. Lord Justice FitzGibbon.—There was no question about any but Mr. Adair. Have you any information about him?—No; I only know that his brothers were Presbyterians. His name appears as a pew-holder. Lord Waveney was very proud of his descent from the Rev. Patrick Adair, who was a Presbyterian minister here, and he has exhibited in the Castle the texts from which he preached. There is no doubt that there will always be a representative of the Episcopal Church on the proposed governing body in the person of the lord of the soil.

2848. I thought you said the lord of the soil was a Presbyterian?—But he is not so at present. Hitherto there has been amongst us no question of religious denomination; no feeling on that matter at all; the practice has been to elect successors in the families of the original trustees, no matter whether they were Episcopalians or Presbyterians. That there are some now Episcopalians who were originally Presbyterians

Oct. 24, 1884.

William Orr, Witness.

has not had any effect on the elections. I believe the successors of the present trustees will likely be elected in their father's places. I would be willing to elect Mr. Patrick's son, in the event of his death.

2849. Do you think the co-opting of the trustees should be left to themselves?—They are the descendants of the original trustees.

2850. Professor Dougherty.—Would you confine the co-opting to the descendants?—Yes. The original idea of the founder was to have a governing body which would be *Presbyterian*; I know that to be a fact.

2851. Dr. Traill.—How do you know that?—He selected the original trustees from the Presbyterian body; he had an opportunity at that time of putting Episcopalians upon it if he had wished to do so, but he didn't do it. William Adair was connected with the estate.

2852. He has another claim, for he gave the site of the building?—Yes, but that was after the death of John Guy.

2853. Lord Justice FitzGibbon.—The school was to be built on a certain site which it is quite evident Adair was then going to give for it?—He was lord of the soil, and the only man to give it.

2854. What about the proposal to bring in representatives of the three other Presbyterian congregations?—We have no objection to the proposals of the Commissioners; our only objection was a financial one which you have done away with.

2855. Then do you wish the school to remain as it was?—I am perfectly willing to let it remain as it was.

2856. Lord Justice Naish.—Has it worked well?—It has.

2857. Dr. Traill.—You have not found that the Episcopalian element on the governing body has militated against the Presbyterians?—Not in the slightest.

Rev. *John Gibson* (Clerk of the Ballymena Presbytery) examined.

Rev. John Gibson.

2858. Lord Justice FitzGibbon.—The Ballymena Presbytery in their resolution say:—

"The Ministers of the Presbyterian Churches in Ballymena shall be *ex-officio* governors, and instead of three elected governors representing one session, each session of the separate congregations should elect one governor, the three co-opted governors and the *ex-officio* governor to remain as in the scheme."

On what grounds do you advocate that?—In his will John Guy spoke of "the Dissenting clergyman of the congregation of Ballymena." We had only one Presbyterian Church at that time in Ballymena, but now we have four—First Ballymena Church, West Church, Wellington-street Church, and the High Kirk. Wellington-street Church was erected in 1828, and the West Church was opened in 1863. The High Kirk was placed where it is long subsequent to the will of John Guy. Our position is that all these congregations have poor, and that their ministers who all take an interest in the poor of their congregations should be *ex-officio* members of the governing body. In some of these congregations, as a matter of fact, there are more poor members than in the Church of First Ballymena.

2859. Professor Dougherty.—Is admission to the school restricted to the children of people connected with First Ballymena Church?—No.

2860. Have there been any complaints?—We do not know.

2861. Dr. Traill.—These four Presbyterian Churches embrace the district connected with Guy's school?—Yes; we have no parishes or districts in our Church.

2862. You may each go through the other's congregations?—Yes.

2863. Lord Justice FitzGibbon.—Your proposal would place four clerical governors on the governing body, and Guy only named one?—But there was only one congregation at that time; we hold there might have been four.

2864. Dr. Traill.—He might have put on four laymen as well as clergymen, what you propose would make a very large body?—Not much larger than what is proposed in the draft scheme. All we wish to touch on is with reference to the Presbyterian management; we do not wish to interfere with the other part at all; our position is, that, in addition to the minister of First Ballymena, the ministers of the other three congregations should be *ex-officio* governors, and the Sessions of the four Presbyterian congregations should each elect one Governor.

2865. Which of these ministers do you propose as manager of the school?—I think the Governors should have a right to nominate their own manager.

2866. Would you leave it to the whole Board?—I would.

2867. Mr. *Carroll*.—Would that not upset the arrangement of the testator?—I don't think it would, there are four ministers now instead of one.

2868. Lord Justice FitzGibbon.—Is not the minister of the First Presbyterian Church the direct successor of the minister mentioned in the will?

Lord Justice Naish.—I presume there was no question ever raised about that.

Mr. Carroll.—His ministry is the only one that was then in existence; I do not see the necessity of bringing so many ministers in; there will be more friction if more are brought in. As to the Church children, it appears from the evidence of Dean Murray that he does not encourage the children of his people to go to Guy's school; on the contrary he has established a rival school, and if you take the view of giving them representation in proportion to the numbers attending, having regard to the limited interest they take in Guy's school, I would propose that if the Episcopalians have twenty per cent. of the children in attendance there should be a representative of the Episcopal Church on the governing body.

2869. Lord Justice Naish.—Would you say 15 per cent.?

Dr. Traill.—If the children are there they should be looked after.

Mr. *Carroll*.—But it is admitted that the Dean takes no interest in this school, and tries to get as many to go to the other school as he can.

Dean *Murray*.—I do take a deep interest in Guy's school, and have done so for many years. Every Tuesday morning my curate attends there and catechises the Church children.

2870. Rev. Dr. Molloy.—I understand that you prefer that the children should go to your own school, but as a considerable number do go to the other school you would like to look after them there?—Quite so, and we take an interest in the school.

The Rev. *Thomas Eaton* (Presbyterian Minister), Kells, Ballymena.

Rev. Thomas Eaton.

2871. You should clearly understand the position which the Ballymena Presbytery takes up with regard to Guy's school. The Presbytery believe that the original intention of John Guy was to leave the management of the school in the hands of the Dissenters, not restricting the benefits to any denomination. We believe as a Presbytery, that there being only one Dissenting Congregation at that time, the congregation became too large for one minister, and that three other Congregations now in Ballymena are simply hives off the old Congregation, and have the same interest in this endowment as the old Congregation. It will be better, therefore, for the school if these Congregations have each a representative on the governing body.

2372. Professor DOUGHERTY.—Do any of the existing Congregations in Ballymena represent the old seceding Synod?—One does.

2373. How do you call that a hive?—We may be wrong, but as a Presbytery we thought that the other Congregations have the same rights as the old Congregation, and that is the reason why we ask that the sessions of the other three Congregations should each select a governor, and by being all represented on the governing body, we think we would be best carrying out the intentions of John Guy in that matter. Oct. 10, 1888. Rev. Thomas Lyle.

Rev. *David M'Meekin* (Presbyterian Minister), Second Ballymena.

2374. In our corporate capacity as a Presbytery, we believe that the basis of this school should be broadened in one way or another. What interest can a man take in this school who is resident eight miles away, or another who is resident in Suffolk? We would like the poor of all denominations to be brought into the school and to receive the benefits of it.

2375. Lord Justice FITZGIBBON.—How do you think that could be best done?—That is a matter for the Commission, in the light of what they have heard here to-day.

2376. Professor DOUGHERTY.—Would you like to see it broadened on the lines indicated by Mr. Patrick or Dean Murray?—Dean Murray wanted it widened on the basis that there should be a representative of his Church there.

Dean *Murray*.—No, but on the basis that a considerable number of my children were attending the school.

2377. Lord Justice FITZGIBBON.—(To Rev. Mr. *M'Meekin*.)—You spoke of broadening the basis so as to bring children of all denominations into the school; —how do you think could that best be done?—If this Commission would not grant a representative to the Presbyterians outside the *First* Ballymena Congregation, the school would evidently diminish in consequence. Dean Murray wants a representative because he has children of his Church there. If he must have a permanent representative of his Church, then I think by a parity of reasoning we, the Presbyterians, must have representation on the other school in Ballymoney-street, which was certainly built by public subscription, and if I am rightly informed, was built largely by Presbyterian subscriptions. I have attended at the Ballymoney-street school for the purpose of catechising the Presbyterian children, and it appeared to me that the great body of the children there were Presbyterians. Rev. David M'Meekin.

2378. Dr. TRAILL.—Were you here when that school was built?—No.

2379. Can you give us the names of the subscribers to the building?—They can be found out. I was present at the last sitting of this Commission here, and the Ballymoney-street school was then inquired into, and if Dean Murray gets a representative on Guy's School, we should have a representative on Ballymoney-street school.

2380. Which would you propose—that there be a representative in both cases or in neither?—I would give it in neither.

2381. Lord Justice FITZGIBBON.—That could scarcely be called broadening the basis of Guy's school. The Judicial Commissioners will consider this matter carefully; possibly we may come to the conclusion that the existing Governing Body, which is working so harmoniously, might go on as it is. We certainly should not like to disturb the good relations which have existed up to the present time. There should no doubt be a distinct provision giving all clergymen a right to attend in Guy's Schools and to catechise the children of their own denominations in accordance with the rules of the National Board.

BALLYMENA COLLEGIATE SCHOOL.—OBJECTIONS TO THE DRAFT SCHEME.

Lord Justice FITZGIBBON made an introductory statement.

[Mr. Orr produced the minute books connected with this school since 1878, with a list of subscribers.]

2382. Lord Justice FITZGIBBON.—If you make out a full list of all gentlemen who have paid sums of not less than ten guineas each, we will place them on the qualified list of subscribers in the scheme.

Rev. *John Wilson* (Clerk of Ballymena Presbytery).—According to the draft scheme the Town Commissioners have the right to three representatives on the Board; the Diocesan Council, three; and the Presbytery, three. In not accepting the three gentlemen mentioned in the draft scheme, we have no personal objection to any of them, but we did think it strange that the Town Commissioners of Ballymena had the right to select their three representatives; they held a meeting and chose their own three, but we received no communication on the matter at all. We are a constituted body, we meet monthly, and we think we are just as competent as the Town Commissioners to return our three members of the Governing Body. The gentlemen mentioned in the draft scheme we honour very highly, and most of them subscribe to the school, but I am able to prove that some of the gentlemen whose names have now been sent forward by us, have also subscribed according to their ability, and we think that when the Town Commissioners got their will in the selection of names we should have had the same privilege.

2383. Dr. TRAILL.—When the Presbytery met how many laymen were present?—I cannot state; there should be a layman from each congregation.

2384. There is no layman on your proposed list of Governors?—While we believe in our laymen very much, it was understood that the ministers would take the leading part in this matter. They have more time at their disposal, and are better able to help.

2385. Do you not think laymen should be on the governing body?—I think laymen should be on it.

2386. Mr. William Young, whose name we have put on, appears to be a very proper person to have on?—We have no objection to him.

2387. You have put his name out?—We only want to assert our right.

2388. Lord Justice FITZGIBBON.—A certain number of gentlemen had been engaged in working the school, and subscribing to it, who appeared to us likely to carry on the work, and we wished to place them on the new governing body. I believe we got a non-official communication that all those whose names we selected were members of the Presbytery.

Rev. *Thomas Evans*.—I think it would do harm if we overlooked the ministers who according to their means have subscribed as liberally as the others. The Episcopal Church has two ministers on the Board, and we do not object to them if they put them there, but the clerk of the Ballymena Presbytery is a very well known official, and we thought we should have had

Oct. 12, 1886. the liberty of electing our own representatives. To the persons elected we have not the slightest personal objection, quite the reverse.

2889. Dr. Traill.—Those named as your representatives will only hold office for one year; it is only a provisional list of governors.

Rev. *Thomas Eaton.*—We believe the year of the start of the school is by far the most important year, and we therefore think it should be started as efficiently as possible.

2890. Professor Dougherty.—Are not these names mentioned in the scheme, the names of gentlemen who have taken a practical interest in the matter?

Rev. *Thomas Eaton.*—I do not think the merits of any of the gentlemen should come into the question at all.

2891. Lord Justice FitzGibbon.—It is impossible to have a regular election before the scheme comes into force. We have always tried to find out good representatives of the various interests and put them on the governing body by the scheme; at the first election the franchise would come into operation.

2892. Rev. Dr. Molloy.—Is your suggestion that the three persons selected to represent the Presbyterians should be selected by the Presbytery.

Rev. *Thomas Eaton.*—Yes.

2893. Lord Justice Naish.—At the meeting of the Presbytery at which the three names brought forward by you were selected, was there a full attendance of the entire Presbytery?

Rev. *Thomas Eaton.*—As full as we could have.

2894. Professor Dougherty.—Was there any intimation that this business was to be taken up at the meeting of Presbytery on that day?

Rev. *Thomas Eaton.*—There was.

Rev. *David M'Meekin.*—I attended that Presbytery meeting, and the point before us was the exercise of our right of nominating three Presbyterian members of the governing body; we thought that we as a Presbytery should exercise our right in suggesting three names.

2895. Lord Justice FitzGibbon.—We really want to satisfy the Presbytery that they were in no way slighted in the matter. The Town Commissioners received no more formal communication than the Presbytery, but they proceeded more publicly, and held an election which we never asked them to hold. We had merely invited a suggestion of good names, and we invited a similar suggestion from some leading Presbyterians, as we did also from Dean Murray. When will the next meeting of the Presbytery be held?

Rev. *John Gibson.*—On the first Tuesday of November.

Professor Dougherty.—There was no intention to overlook the Presbytery, and I think you might very well withdraw the objection.

2896. Lord Justice FitzGibbon.—You also ask the Commissioners "to delete the portion of paragraph five, referring to the co-option of three additional Governors"?

Rev. *John Gibson.*—Yes, the Presbytery objected to that. If the Board happened to be divided, the majority would be able to co-opt three additional members to assist them, and that might lead to grave difficulties. If political or religious matters happened to come up for discussion, and a question was carried by one of a majority, that majority then would co-opt those three additional members.

Rev. *Thomas Eaton.*—We are in a minority on the Board, and at no time could possess the majority; if the co-opting clause remains, the majority could strengthen their position by co-opting three additional members. Two-thirds of the Governors in that case might represent one denomination while nine-tenths of the inhabitants of the town and district hold different religious opinions.

2897. Mr. *Caruth* (solicitor for Sir Hugh Adair).—Sir Hugh Adair has sent me a copy of his English solicitors' letter, and having read it over, I will not trouble you with any remarks as to the first point raised, viz., as to a reverting trust in favour of the owner of the Ballymena estate, if the school ceased to be a diocesan school, inasmuch as your lordship in your opening remarks gave your opinion on that point. The other point, that a right of pre-emption should be given to the owner of the Ballymena estate seems reasonable, and in such a case the amount to be paid by the owner of the estate should be confined to the then value of the buildings, not of the ground on which they stand, as it was given free of rent by William Adair, a former owner of the estate.

Lord Justice FitzGibbon.—The land was given once and for all; it is not Sir Hugh Adair's any longer, and I doubt whether we could make any change in the matter. I do not know to whom we could refer the fixing of the price, unless we go to the Commissioners of Charitable Donations and Bequests.

2898. Dr. Traill.—Have you any instructions as to giving Sir Hugh Adair power of nominating his agent to act as a governor in his absence?

Mr. *Caruth.*—Sir Hugh Adair never instructed me with reference to that.

2899. Professor Dougherty (to Captain Perry, J.P.)—Have you any information upon that point?

Captain *Perry.*—I know that is his wish.

2900. Dr. Traill.—Have you consulted him on the matter?

Captain *Perry.*—Yes. He spoke to me about it.

Rev. *Thomas Eaton.*—But is not this a public and not a private school; it is a school in which all the community is largely interested, and not a private foundation like Gray's school. Whoever gets a place on the governing body should come to the meetings. Sir Hugh Adair could do a great deal more by his appearance here than he could by deputy.

2901. Dr. Traill.—But if he appears by deputy is he not likely to subscribe?

Professor Dougherty.—I suppose you would like to get the money before you gave the right of representation?

Rev. *Thomas Eaton.*—I do not think that it is a wise thing for him to appear by deputy.

2902. Dr. Traill.—I think if you want to get money from a gentleman like him, the plan is to give him the most liberal representation.

Mr. *Caruth.*—I expect that he will be a large subscriber.

Captain *Perry.*—Although Mr. Caruth does not remember the incident, Sir Hugh Adair discussed the point in Mr. Caruth's own office.

Rev. *Robert King*, B.A., Principal of Ballymena Diocesan School, further examined.

Rev. Robert King, B.A. 2903. Lord Justice FitzGibbon.—You want us to preserve your annuity for you in case of your being incapacitated?—Yes.

2904. In that case would you not be retiring on your annuity?—If I were laid up, I can now appoint a competent person to act for me.

2905. Rev. Dr. Molloy.—If you were permanently incapacitated?—Yes. If I were to resign the place I would lose the buildings, which I consider to be worth £50 per annum.

2906. Lord Justice FitzGibbon.—You built part of the house?—Yes. I spent close on £1,100 upon it.

2907. What would you consider your life interest in that to be worth now?—I have never made a calculation of that.

2908. Dr. Traill.—Would you not like to have a clause in the scheme giving power to the new governing body to deal with you on a figure to be agreed upon between them and you for the purchase of your life interest in case you retired?—I can see no objection to such a clause provided it is not compulsory.

9909. Without naming the figure?—Without naming the figure.

9910. Do you claim the right of appointing a deputy?—Yes, according to the Church Act.

9911. Rev. Dr. MOLLOY.—Do you claim a right to provide a deputy permanently?—No, merely during temporary incapacity. Has it been kept in view in considering the position of the school, that it is the Diocesan school of Armagh and Connor?

9912. Lord Justice FITZGIBBON.—Yes, there is no Diocesan Endowment now remaining except your salary; the county Antrim Grand Jury built the house; we are bound to save your vested interest. What name do you think would be the best to give the school?

Rev. Mr. King.—The Ballymena Grammar School, or some such name. It is not Collegiate.

9913. Lord Justice NAISH.—Is there another "Collegiate school" in the town?

Rev. Samuel Megaw (Galgorm-road, Ballymena.)—Yes, I am manager of the Ballymena Collegiate and Intermediate School, the name of which has been on a plate on the school door for the past six years or more.

Some gentlemen present suggested the title of "The Ballymena Academy," and others "The Ballymena Academical Institution."

The inquiry then terminated.

Oct. 23, 1888.

Rev. Robert King, D.D.

PUBLIC SITTING—WEDNESDAY, OCTOBER 24, 1888.

Oct. 24, 1888.

At the Town Hall, Holywood.

Present:—The Right Hon. Lord Justice FITZGIBBON and the Right Hon. Lord Justice NAISH, Judicial Commissioners; and the Rev. GERALD MOLLOY, D.D., D.SC., ANTHONY TRAILL, Esq., LL.D., M.D., F.T.C.D., and Professor DOUGHERTY, M.A., Assistant Commissioners.

The Assistant Secretary, N. D. MURPHY, Junr., was in attendance.

SULLIVAN'S SCHOOLS, HOLYWOOD—OBJECTIONS TO THE DRAFT SCHEME.

9914. Lord Justice FITZGIBBON.—The Draft Scheme for the Sullivan Schools was published on August 15, last. We were glad to find nothing to indicate that it has in any substantial matter failed to satisfy those interested in the schools. We have, however, received some objections as to matters of detail which, being in this part of Ireland, we thought it well to come here and discuss. We received a communication this morning from the Rector of Holywood, the Rev. Mr. Crozier, who says he has no desire to appear before us as he is very well pleased with the scheme. On October 1, 1888, the Rev. G. J. M'Alister, Secretary of the Trustees, writes on behalf of the Committee, to inform us that they have carefully considered the scheme, and that with its main provisions they entirely and cordially agree; but they submit for consideration the following suggestions:—

(1.) In section 4 the substitution of 'townships' for "parish" of Holywood. That is a matter of local geography as to which we will ask the gentlemen present to inform us. The testator wanted the school to benefit Holywood as his native place, and whatever area closely corresponds to that object should be the district for the scheme.

(2.) In section 6 they think that a 'triennial' would be preferable to an 'annual' election of governors. The question of the period of these elections has been very frequently brought before us. No doubt there is some additional trouble if you have an election annually instead of every three years; but if you only have an election every three years, people get so that take very little interest; if you have the election every year, you can re-elect those members of the Governing Body who are doing good work, and, without offence, substitute others for those who through press of business, or sickness, or other circumstances, are not found efficient governors. While glad to consult your wishes, we would ask you to consider whether it would not be better on the whole to have an election annually.

(3.) The trustees would wish to add at the end of section 7, 'unless prevented by sickness or absence abroad.' We might fairly make the alteration in many cases where a governor for a variety of reasons might not have been able for a time to attend, it might be advantageous to elect him again. I think we might even go further than your proposal.

(4.) "In section 22 they strongly recommend the introduction of a clause restricting admission of pupils of National schools to the Upper School at reduced rates to those whose parents are not assessed for income tax. The object was to afford children of parents in humble circumstances the means of obtaining a higher education should their tastes or talents so incline them. At present some children of parents possessed of good means are receiving their education in the Upper School at one-third of the ordinary rates. They further suggest that no pupils should be admitted at the reduced rate who had not attended two years at a National school in the parish."

There is a great deal of difficulty about this. Under the Chancery Scheme, no doubt, the trustees were to fix the fees, and it was never intended that children of those who could pay a higher rate should come in, but we must take care that any restriction we make can be worked, and will not be unjust. The returns of income tax are privileged, and the assessments for taxes often afford no criteria of the worldly circumstances of the person assessed. We have put it upon the Governing Body to determine what applicants are deserving. They might prescribe a form of application and certificate from those acquainted with the people as to whether they were really poor. I think something of that kind would turn out more practical than this proposal as to the income tax. However, we will hear what you have to say about it, and also as to the suggestion that no pupils should be admitted at the reduced rate who had not attended two years at a National school in the parish. We will have the benefit of the experience of Mr. Spears, who has been in both the lower and upper schools, and who ranks as one of the highest National teachers at any time in the service of the Board. Two years might exclude a promising student, and the desire to limit the pupils to *bona fide* residents in the parish might be met by one year instead of two.

(5.) "In section 23 they think that two scholarships annually, would be preferable to four."

The scheme suggests that the governors may establish four free scholarships tenable for three years. You feel that twelve would be a larger number of free pupils than [illegible] would be desirable, and it is suggested by the committee, and also by Mr. Spence, that the number should be reduced from four to two annually, giving a maximum of six. Having regard to the large amount of the endowment, we would like to have a fairly large number of free places available. These free pupils would only represent a loss of half the ordinary fees, £1 or £1 10s. per quarter. They also would prefer the sixth class as the standard for examination for Foundation Scholarships, but Mr. Spence thinks that the competition for the free scholarships should be in the final stage of sixth class; that for admission to scholarships at reduced rates the fifth class standard should remain the qualification. Our only object is to get the children most likely to do credit to the school, and to get advantage from the endowment. We adopted the lower standard in the Sewards School and it has been found satisfactory.

(8.) "In section 82 they suggest 'five shillings' as a quarter."

Mr. Spence, the head master, has suggested with respect to the qualification for Free Scholarships and Scholarships at reduced rates that—

"To prevent the abuse of a privilege evidently intended to benefit the industrial classes only, a provision should be added, restricting the privilege to the children of parents who are not assessed to income tax; or, at least, who are in the receipt of income not exceeding £300 per annum."

All such rules are difficult to apply. Mr. Spence again says:—

"To prevent pupils that have received intermediate education in the Upper School at the lower rates or free, from going to another school, when their education is so advanced that they may pass the Intermediate Examination, or win prizes or exhibitions; thus to deprive the Upper School of the credit of their education, and of the results fees accruing therefrom, it should be provided that at the admission of any pupil to the privilege of a scholarship the parents shall sign an agreement that such pupil shall sit the Intermediate and other examinations for which he has been prepared in the Upper School."

I am afraid you would find it difficult to get parents to sign an agreement of that kind. The best security that any teacher can have is the success of the children attending the school, and I think Mr. Spence in that respect offers assurances that no other school can surpass. Mr. Spence, with regard to the Foundation Scholarships, believes that two new ones each year would be sufficient to meet the ordinary requirements of the case. Being each tenable for three years there would always be at one time in the Upper School a total of six free students. The concluding paragraph of Mr. Spence's letter is as follows:—

"I think that at least two years attendance at a National school in the parish should be part of the qualification for either a Free Scholarship or one at reduced rates."

On all these matters we will be happy to hear what statements are to be made.

Rev. C. J. M'Alester (Holywood), Honorary Secretary of the Sullivan Schools, further examined.

Rev. C. J. M'Alester.

2915. Lord Justice FitzGibbon.—Are there Town Commissioners in Holywood?—Yes.

2916. Lord Justice Naish.—Are there children coming to the schools from portions of the parish of Holywood not within the township?—Yes; several children come from Sydenham, near Belfast, and also from Rockport, beyond Craigavad.

2917. Dr. Traill.—Is there any place of worship there to which they belong?—There is an Episcopal church at Craigavad, of which the Rev. Dr. Duke is the clergyman.

2918. How far is that from Holywood?—About two and a half miles.

2919. How many children are coming from that district?—Probably a dozen.

Mr. Spence (Head Master).—About a dozen.

2920. Dr. Traill.—Are there any other places of worship in that direction?

Witness.—There is a Presbyterian church at Ballygilbert, in which the Rev. Mr. Quarry preaches.

2921. How far is that outside the township?—Some three miles.

Mr. John Anderson, J.P.—The township has a small boundary, but the parish boundary extends for miles.

2922. Professor Dougherty.—Is Ballymacarrett inside the township boundary?

Mr. Anderson.—No. There are Strandtown, Belmont, and other churches in the direction of Belfast, but they have no connection with the town of Holywood. The clergy there are totally distinct from those here. It was proposed that that district should be formed into a township separate from Belfast.

2923. Professor Dougherty.—It is not likely that you have any pupils from any of those places outside the township?

Mr. Anderson.—No; all the churches connected with Holywood are within the township.

2924. Lord Justice FitzGibbon.—Could we fix the limit by distance?—Three miles would leave Belfast out. I understand one of your objections was that a portion of the borough of Belfast was inside the parish boundary—say a limit of two miles.

2925. Rev. Dr. Molloy.—What would you think of a radius of three miles?—I would prefer two, because it places the matter beyond all doubt.

Lord Justice Naish.—You would get near to the boundaries of Belfast with three.

2926. Rev. Dr. Molloy.—You would take in the whole of the township?—Oh, much more; perhaps it would be better to say one mile.

Mr. Robert L. Patterson.—I think a mile and a half would cover all the ground necessary.

Witness.—I think a mile and a half would be better.

(Here the witness and Mr. Anderson pointed out the township and parish boundaries on the map.)

2927. Dr. Traill.—Except the outlying portion towards Belfast a radius of two miles would cover the parish.

Mr. Anderson.—Have a mile and a half radius.

2928. Lord Justice FitzGibbon.—Fractions are inconvenient; what about two English miles as the radius?

Rev. Dr. Molloy.—It is doubtful whether that would not bring in Craigavad.

2929. Lord Justice FitzGibbon.—We will get the boundaries laid down on the map, and ask you to mark all the places of worship to be represented; but the children may come to compete from any place in the whole parish?

Mr. Anderson.—Certainly.

2930. Why do you prefer a triennial to an annual election?

Witness.—It is quite possible that in some Presbyterian places of worship there might be some excitement over the matter.

2931. Dr. Traill.—Are they more excitable than other people?—No; but I think a triennial election would be preferable.

2932. Lord Justice FitzGibbon.—In my church annual elections go over very quietly. It is only at the triennial elections that we get up any excitement.

Mr. Anderson.—At present the members of committee are elected for as long a period as they remain in the parish. I think an annual election would give a vast amount of trouble. Our town commissioners are elected for three years. I do not see if you get the consent of the people on a Government and that they are willing to act, why they should be put to the trouble of an annual election.

2933. Lord Justice FitzGibbon.—If you get good men on who are attentive to the school, no parents will disturb them; but if you have an election only every three years, and have a man on the board who takes no interest in the school, you must keep him on the board until the triennial election comes round. The clergymen are *ex-officio* who have the people in attendance at the school. This question only relates to the laity.

Mr. Andrews.—It is not a serious point; but though with an annual election there would be a good deal of trouble, yet if there was a paid secretary, it would not matter so much. I think it might be better to have an election annually. Congregations would then have to choose members at a certain time, otherwise not choose them at all. If congregations would not elect members, could there not be a clause to the effect that the Governors in office should then remain on.

2934. Lord Justice FitzGibbon.—There might be a congregation that did not desire to elect anybody, although they had a right to do so if they chose. In that case we might not be able to give to others the power to fill the places thus left vacant; but as regards the period, if we extend it to three years we ought to provide that the office of any governor who does not attend for a whole year shall become vacant.

Mr. Andrews.—Quite right.

2935. What about the income tax?—That should be left to the governors.

2936. Rev. Dr. Molloy.—If parents send their children to a National school is that not taken as indicating that they are in humble circumstances?

Mr. Speers.—Not in all cases.

Witness.—The object was that children in humble circumstances who had been attending National schools should come up here for a higher education, but the children of parents in better circumstances, who had not been attending National schools, were to pay an increased rate. At the time of the Chancery Decree no children of parents in good circumstances ever attended National schools, but we have now children of parents in very good circumstances attending National schools, and these pupils can have these (Sullivan) schools at a cheaper rate. I think every man who pays income tax should pay the fees.

2937. Lord Justice FitzGibbon.—You might have a clerk in receipt of £150 a year paying his income tax, with a family of, say, ten children, and an artisan with one child, receiving £3 a week, and really far better off than the other. The determination of the question is altogether for the governing body. You might require a certain form to be filled up by the parents declaring their inability to pay.

Mr. Andrews.—We have no other upper school here, and consequently we have known people here worth £1,000 a year whose children were educated at this school.

Oct. 20, 1880.

Rev. G. R. Wilson.

Adam Speers, B.SC., Head Master of Upper Sullivan School, further examined.

Adam Speers, B.SC.

2938. The parents of such children used to pay. I know that well to do people who sent their children to us when I was at the head of the lower school paid me handsomely for extra branches.

2939. Rev. Dr. Molloy.—What proportion of your pupils are on the lower fees?—About forty-five per cent.

2940. How has it been determined hitherto?—By the pupils having previously attended a National school in the parish, in consequence of which they claim admission at reduced rates as a right. I think it would be more satisfactory if people who pay income tax and are in good circumstances, should not be able to claim it as a right, or that it should be left to the Governors to determine who shall be admitted at reduced fees, and how much the fees should be reduced in each particular case; it is a very great privilege surely for people in good circumstances to get their children educated in a High school such as this where the fees are low at the best—half a guinea a term for the various subjects.

2941. Lord Justice FitzGibbon.—We consider it would answer the purpose to have a form drawn up which should be signed by the parents, declaring their inability to pay the full fees.

Rev. Mr. M'Alister.—Your suggestion is very satisfactory.

2942. Lord Justice FitzGibbon.—I think you will find that a better check than the taxes. (To witness): You think "at least two years attendance at a National school should be part of the qualification for either a free scholarship, or one at reduced rates"; it is one year under the Chancery Scheme?—The reason why I mentioned two years was with the view, in the first place, to benefit the National school, and, in the second place, that the children might be better prepared for entering the Upper school. Instances have occurred of people in good circumstances sending their children only one year to a National school in the parish, in order to claim a higher education in the Upper school at reduced rates.

2943. The rule as to two years attendance would be a great difficulty with parents who came to reside in Holywood with a child say thirteen years old; if that child was compelled to attend for two years he would be thrown out. I think a form such as we have suggested removes many of the difficulties on the other point also?—That alters the circumstances entirely.

2944. Then you think that the competition for the free scholarships should be in the first stage sixth class programme of National schools; but for admission to scholarships, at reduced rates, the fifth class standard should remain the qualification?—I would draw the distinction between free scholarships where the pupils had nothing to pay, and the scholarships at reduced rates, and I would make the scholars feel that the privilege is worth competing for; therefore I have suggested that the examination should be held on the programme of first stage sixth class of National schools.

2945. Why not let the examination be held on the fifth class programme and then those able to answer in the sixth class programme could compete along with them?—If we examined on the fifth class programme, pupils who had studied that programme only, might beat those who were more advanced, if fresh from the study of that particular programme.

Rev. Mr. M'Alister.—It might be arranged that the standard should not be below that of the sixth class.

2946. Lord Justice FitzGibbon (to witness).—You wish to reduce the number of free scholarships; have you any at present free in the Upper school?—We have two.

2947. How were they admitted?—One was admitted free because he was a distinguished scholar in the National school, at the time I entered the Upper school over two years ago, and I therefore admitted him free. There is another pupil I do not charge for; but there is a large number getting their education at reduced fees.

2948. Rev. Dr. Molloy.—What are the full fees?—10s. 6d. a term per subject.

2949. How many terms are in the year?—Four; and if a pupil takes four subjects, which most do, it would be two guineas per quarter.

2950. That would be about the average?—Yes.

2951. That would be eight guineas a year?—Yes. I allow pupils who take four subjects to get a fifth subject free. Our ordinary subjects are English, Latin, Greek, French, German, Mathematics, Modern Science, and, as an extra subject, Drawing.

7951. Lord Justice FitzGibbon.—Would it not be better to give the whole programme?—We would do the whole for one guinea a quarter, with the exception of Drawing.

7952. Why not give it?—Because to get Drawing at all costs us nearly £60 a year.

7953. What proportion of the children learn drawing?—About one-third of those who attend the High school, and some others besides.

7954. And how many in the National school below?—They all learn drawing, but not from an art master; it is rudimentary drawing from the head master of the National school.

7955. What does the art master cost?—£40 per annum paid as a fixed salary, and in addition the results fees from the Intermediate Board and the Science and Art Department.

7956. And cannot the endowment afford that?—It cannot; Mr. M'Alister will tell you that the endowment is entirely used up.

7957. Drawing is a very great attraction, and we are told everywhere that it is necessary to have it. Now, as to the number of scholarships, suppose that we allow two free and two at half fees?—There is no limit to the number that may be admitted at one-third fees, therefore there is no reason for admitting two scholarships at half fees.

Professor Dougherty.—There will be now.

7958. Lord Justice FitzGibbon.—At present you have only two free scholarships?—Yes.

7959. Of the forty-five per cent., could you roughly estimate how many could not qualify on the ground of poverty?—Perhaps a third; fifteen per cent. of the whole.

7960. Professor Dougherty.—Do you think these free scholarships will attract boys from other schools?—I do, but the number of free scholarships proposed in the new scheme, I am convinced, exceeds very much the requirements of the neighbourhood.

7961. Rev. Dr. Molloy.—You propose that in all cases there should be six free scholarships, provided there are pupils whose answering qualifies them, and an entrance of two each year?—Quite so, and that we might, if the answering was very excellent, have three some years.

7962. Lord Justice FitzGibbon.—Mr. Anderson, what is your opinion about the demands of the district for free scholarships?

Mr. Anderson.—There has been a good demand, but I think six free pupils would be quite enough.

7963. I think we may leave the trustees to increase the number should they consider it desirable. The next matter is with regard to quorum, you suggest three instead of five?

Mr. Anderson.—There is difficulty sometimes to get a quorum.

Dr. Traill.—I think three are enough for a quorum—you might require a quorum of five if you have important business to be transacted, and of only three if it is a mere meeting of routine business.

7964. Rev. Dr. Molloy (to Mr. Spears).—You propose that the parents of such pupils as are admitted free, or at reduced rates, should be required to sign an agreement that such pupils shall sit Intermediate and other examinations for which they have been prepared in the upper school?—Yes; take for example a boy who has attended the upper school for two or three years, who is well qualified to pass the Intermediate examination, and has been trained specially on the programme of the Intermediate Board, and who, when the time comes, will not go into the examination. Perhaps his father orders him not to go into it; that boy deprives the school of £4, £5, or probably £8 of a grant. It has cost us a great deal to educate him, because we have to employ a large staff of teachers in consequence of working the school on Intermediate lines. What that boy does, two or ten might do. That boy might not only deprive the school of results fees by refusing to be examined under the Intermediate Board, but might also, after having received his training in Holywood, go off to the Royal Academical Institution, or the Methodist College, or any Intermediate school in Belfast, and give that school the credit of having educated him, and the results fees accruing from his success at such Intermediate examinations.

7965. You propose that boys prepared in the upper school, at low rates or free, should be required to present themselves for these examinations?—Yes, unless there is sufficient cause to the contrary.

7966. And the consequence is that you prevent his going to another school?—Only until after he has discharged his obligation for that year by sitting the examination.

7967. Lord Justice FitzGibbon.—No pupil can ever carry results fees at the Intermediate examination, unless he has made one hundred attendances at his school. You mean to prevent a boy from going to another school after he has been partly educated by you, but is there not a give and take all over Ireland?—What I mean is this—suppose that a boy having attended our school for a few years is eligible for examination under the Intermediate Education Board, and that he has got his education with us free or at reduced rates; I would like both the boy and his parents to feel that he is under a moral obligation to go in for that examination in connection with our school.

7968. Are there many cases of that kind?—Only one; but if this thing was permitted to occur I consider a great deal of evil would result. If a boy possesses the ability to sit an examination he should be required to do so both for his own advantage and that of the school.

7969. You suggest that each boy obtaining a free scholarship, or a scholarship at reduced rates, should present himself for examination if required?—That is all I want.

Rev. C. J. M'Alister.—There is a note as to change of names—

"I am further instructed to inform the Commissioners that our committee at a late meeting, in order to complete the representation of the several churches, nominated the following as members of committee:—Mr. David M'Cutcheon, Craigavad, and Mr. James Moore, Holywood, representing the First Congregation in connection with the General Assembly; Mr. Alexander Finlay, Willesden, Holywood, representing the Second Congregation in connection with the General Assembly; the Rev. Samuel Hollingsworth, and Mr. John M'Afee, representing the Congregation of Wesleyan Methodism."

Lord Justice FitzGibbon.—We have no objection to that.

Rev. C. J. M'Alister.—Now that the inquiry has terminated, I beg on behalf of those connected with the Sullivan Schools to thank the Commissioners for their great kindness and courtesy here to-day.

7970. Lord Justice FitzGibbon.—I assure you it is really a pleasure to us to deal with a case where we find everybody willing to get it settled.

Mr. John Anderson.—This scheme of yours is very highly approved of; in fact we are all delighted with it.

This concluded the proceedings.

PUBLIC SITTING—WEDNESDAY, OCTOBER 24, 1888.

Oct. 24, 1888.

At the Courthouse, Bangor.

Present:—The Right Hon. Lord Justice FitzGibbon, Judicial Commissioner; and the Rev. Gerald Molloy, D.D., D.Sc., Anthony Traill, Esq., LL.D., M.D., F.T.C.D., and Professor Dougherty, M.A., Assistant Commissioners.

The Assistant Secretary, N. D. Murphy, Jun., was in attendance.

Lord Justice FitzGibbon made an introductory statement.

BANGOR ENDOWED SCHOOL.

Hon. Somerset Ward, J.P., sworn and examined.

Hon. Somerset Ward, J.P.

2972. You are the agent for Viscount Bangor and Robert Edward Ward?—Yes.

2973. Lord Justice FitzGibbon.—You produce the deed under which the Bangor Endowed School is founded and carried on?—Yes.

2974. It purports to have been executed by Lord Viscount Bangor and Robert Edward Ward?—Yes.

2975. The building has since been used for the purpose of a school?—It has.

2976. Are both these parties still living?—Viscount Bangor is dead but Robert Edward Ward is alive.

2977. Who is the present heir of that Lord Bangor?—Henry Viscount Bangor, his brother.

2978. Are the trustees living?—Both Mr. Crawford and Mr. Kennedy are dead.

2979. Has there been any appointment of new trustees?—Not that I am aware of.

2980. The management of the school was vested in Viscount Bangor and Mr. Ward?—Yes.

2981. Did they appoint the present master?—They did.

2982. Do you know whether Robert Stewart Kennedy or William Crawford was the latest survivor?

Robert Edward Ward, D.L.—Robert Stewart Kennedy died first.

2983. I believe this is not now carried on as a Navigation School?—No.

2984. Why was the teaching of navigation given up?—So long as I have known the school it has not been used for navigation, and I do not know anything that caused it to cease to be so used.

2985. It is now an Intermediate school?—It is for both boys and girls.

2986. Can you give us any suggestion as to how it should be worked?—I would say that the management should be continued by Lord Bangor and Mr. Ward. As a matter of fact the fees paid by the pupils have been given to the master in their entirety, and the whole of the repairs connected with the school have been carried out by Lord Bangor and Mr. Ward out of their own pockets.

2987. Do you know anything as to the present invested funds?—No; we receive the interest from the Commissioners of Charitable Donations and Bequests. They pay it to me, and did not seek to have other trustees appointed. I do not know what the amount is that is invested.

2988. £3,972 3s. 6d. Consols is the amount they return to us. We saw the school today and it seems to be overcrowded; would there be any likelihood of getting assistance to enlarge the school in the neighbourhood?—I do not know.

2989. Do any of the local clergy look after it in any way?—The local clergy have no connection with it.

2990. About what expenditure has there been on the buildings one year with another?—I suppose it would cost £10 a year.

2991. No account has ever been opened for the repairs fund?—No.

2992. You have no endowment but the ground on which the house stands, and the Government stock, producing £50 a year which is paid to the master?—Yes, paid by me to him.

2993. Rev. Dr. Molloy.—Since what time have the girls been introduced?—Since the present master was appointed; before that the school had dwindled down to six boys; after Mr. Rainey was appointed the school rapidly rose in numbers.

2994. Has the system of having boys and girls together worked satisfactorily?—Yes.

2995. Lord Justice FitzGibbon.—You are the actual managers of the school?—Yes.

2996. At present you seem to have no legal status?—No.

2997. Would it be possible to preserve the rights of Lord Bangor and Mr. Ward in the matter of appointing and removing the master, and yet to form a committee of people in the neighbourhood, who would possibly take an interest in the school, collect funds for it, and place it in connection with South Kensington?—I do not see any objection at all; I think myself it would be a very great advantage.

2998. The school seems to be dependent now on the voluntary support of Lord Bangor and Mr. Ward for repairs and matters of that kind?—Yes.

2999. How would you propose to get a local committee together?—I don't see why you should not be able to get up a committee.

3000. There appear to be two leading denominations here; would the Dean of Down, and the minister of the Presbyterian congregation be proper members of the school committee?—Very. There are two ministers of the Church of Ireland and two Presbyterian ministers.

3001. Are there two Presbyterian congregations and also two Episcopal churches?—No.

3002. How is that?—There is but one church, and two Presbyterian congregations.

3003. The Church clergymen are the Dean of Down and his curate?—Yes.

James H. Rainey (Head Master), sworn and examined.

James H. Rainey.

3004. Lord Justice FitzGibbon.—When were you appointed head master here?—Nine years ago.

3005. In what condition did you find the school premises?—Satisfactory enough.

3006. What was the attendance then at the school?—It had dwindled down, and was very small when I was appointed.

3007. Who had been your predecessor?—Dr. Maloney.

3008. The school was not in a satisfactory state when you joined it?—No.

3009. Have you got a collegiate training?—Yes; I am an undergraduate of the Queen's University, and was so at that time.

Oct. 24, 1888.

James B. Bailey.

3010. What has been the state of the school since then?—It has steadily progressed. I introduced girls a year and a half or two years after I was appointed.

3011. Had you boarders?—We had, but we never have had room for more than three.

3012. Have you any boarders now?—One.

3013. What are the terms on which you receive boarders?—Boys under twelve, thirty guineas per annum, and over that forty guineas.

3014. What are your terms for day boys?—The terms are in the preparatory school, boys and girls under eleven, 10s. 6d. per term; upper school, English, one guinea per term; English, mathematics, and natural philosophy, one and a half guineas; Latin, one guinea; French, a half guinea; music (piano), one guinea; music (theory in class), 5s.

3015. What number of pupils have you at present on your rolls?—Seventy-seven.

3016. How are they divided?—In the upper school the numbers are, boys nineteen; girls twenty, and the remaining number are in the lower school.

3017. How are the upper and lower schools divided?—By the age of the scholars.

3018. What is the course of instruction in the lower school?—Simply reading, writing, and rudimentary training for upper school.

3019. Elementary education is given in the lower school?—Yes.

3020. Is it different from a National school?—It is different in so far that it is arranged to direct them into Intermediate study.

3021. Are your children of a different and higher class from those who attend the National school?—Yes, I think so.

3022. Is there any difference in the teaching?—I follow the curriculum of the Intermediate Education Board.

3023. What assistants have you?—We have three assistants in the lower school.

3024. And in the upper how many?—One lady assistant and Mrs. Bailey, who teaches music and domestic economy.

3025. You are the only male teacher?—Yes.

3026. Rev. Dr. Molloy.—How much would people pay in following the course for the Intermediate examinations and taking six or seven subjects?—About a guinea and a half in the term.

3027. How many terms in the year?—Four terms in the year.

3028. In the preparatory school what would be the average of the fees paid?—10s. 6d. a term, two guineas a year.

3029. You appear to have an extremely good attendance in the upper school; on the roll you have 39 and you have an average attendance of 33?—Yes, I took that for September.

3030. Lord Justice FitzGibbon.—But in the preparatory school the average attendance seems deficient. You have 38 on the roll, and an attendance of 19·8?—They are very much younger children, and on inclement days they would not come out.

3031. We find, generally, that in National schools it is the reverse?—That arises from the class of their parents; those people want their children out of the way, but that does not exist among people of a high class.

3032. Is there any distinction between the summer and winter attendance?—Yes; there is an falling in the summer.

3033. Rev. Dr. Molloy.—When Mr. Mahaffy visited the school you had just been appointed head master?—Yes.

3034. Lord Justice FitzGibbon.—What is your minimum attendance in the months of December and January?—It is just as it is now.

3035. None of your children at present are summer attendants?—No.

3036. It is a *bona fide* attendance at present?—Yes.

3037. What class of children are they?—The children of merchants and commercial men, going up daily to Belfast, but who reside here.

3038. Have you made navigation a special subject?—No, I never had any applications regarding it, and I never knew that study to be pursued there, although I enrolled in the school myself.

3039. Rev. Dr. Molloy.—About what number of pupils were in attendance when you were a pupil here?—It never exceeded thirty.

3040. The present number exceeds the number at any previous time?—Yes.

3041. Lord Justice FitzGibbon.—The first year you sent pupils to the Intermediate examinations they all passed. That was in 1880. In 1881, 6 passed with honours in the junior grade; in 1882, out of 8 who entered, 6 passed, one in the middle grade securing honours, and 5 in the junior grade, 3 of whom gained honour certificates. In 1883 out of 10 pupils who entered 7 passed, 3 in the middle and 4 in the junior grade, and in these grades honour certificates were obtained. What have you been doing since that time?—I have not made out a full report, but last year we took a junior grade exhibition, and the year before we did the same. This year one girl won a junior grade exhibition, £15, tenable for three years, and three passed with honours in several subjects. Last year two of my boys had full marks in algebra. One boy, who had failed the year previously, passed in the junior grade this year, and two also passed with honours.

3042. Rev. Dr. Molloy.—Have you any apparatus for teaching natural philosophy?—I have not, and it is a great drawback.

3043. Lord Justice FitzGibbon.—Have you ever put yourself in communication with South Kensington?—No.

3044. You can get apparatus there at half price?—I was not aware of that. Mr. Ward offered me a subscription of £5 in order to secure apparatus.

3045. Rev. Dr. Molloy.—If you had a committee formed in connexion with the school you would soon get, in subscriptions, half the actual cost of the apparatus, and South Kensington would give the other half, and then you would be able to get results fees?—An effort was made some years since to get Science and Art classes in Bangor, but it proved a failure.

3046. Lord Justice FitzGibbon.—Why?—I do not know, but the people did not attend the classes.

3047. One of the best schemes we have seen of that kind is in the Sullivan schools in Holywood, and would you not think that something of the same kind might be done here?

3048. A French teacher is mentioned in your prospectus—is he still with you?—No; Miss Allen has charge of the French school now, and under her control the French department has been much more successful than under a French master.

3049. Your school is entirely secular?—Entirely.

3050. Have you any religious instruction in the school?—No.

3051. What are the religious denominations of the children that attend?—All members of the various Protestant denominations.

3052. No Roman Catholics at any time?—Yes; some of my most successful pupils are Roman Catholics.

3053. Is there any Roman Catholic school in Bangor?—No.

3054. Professor Dougherty.—How are the Protestant denominations divided?—About half Church and half Presbyterians—perhaps more than a half Presbyterian. I am an Episcopalian myself.

3055. Lord Justice FitzGibbon.—You receive the £80 and the fees of the pupils?—Yes.

3056. Are you engaged under any written agreement?—Yes, by Viscount Bangor and Mr. Ward.

3057. Professor Dougherty.—Do the clergymen show any interest in the school?—The Dean of Down and the Rev. Mr. Clarke have shown some interest.

Rev. William Clarke, Second Presbyterian Church, Bangor, sworn and examined :—

Rev. William Clarke.

3058. I think a committee of management would be preferable to the present state of things, and the sympathies of the neighbourhood would, I believe, lead to an increase in the attendance.

3059. Lord Justice FITZGIBBON.—What would be the best way, in your opinion, of securing those sympathies ?—The school has been largely in the hands of Lord Bangor and Mr. Ward, and their wishes would have to be consulted in the matter, but I think an amicable arrangement could be made that would be satisfactory to all parties.

3060. Dr. TRAILL.—Would that bring in money ?—I think it would. I think it would be better to have a joint management, and by that means funds could be more easily procured.

3061. Would you give a franchise to subscribers to elect a certain number to act on the board of management ?—No, I would not go in that way.

3062. How would you expect to get money ?—I think when the wants of the school were placed before the public they would do their best to raise the money.

3063. How is the board of management to be chosen ?—I do not know as to that.

3064. Is there a second Presbyterian congregation in Bangor in connexion with the General Assembly ?—Yes.

3065. Is there any other Protestant denomination here ?—Yes, the Methodists.

3066. What are the relative numbers of the Presbyterians and Methodists ?—The large majority is Presbyterian.

3067. How do the Church people stand in numbers ?—In numbers they are below the Presbyterians. This is not only a Presbyterian town, but the immediate neighbourhood is the most Presbyterian part of Ireland.

3068. Rev. Dr. MOLLOY.—What would be the proportion of the Presbyterians to all others—would they be three-fourths ?—I should say so.

3069. What is the size of the Methodist congregation ?—I understand it is very small.

3070. Professor DOUGHERTY.—You say the Presbyterians are three-fourths of the population—do you mean in the district or in the town ?—Perhaps that would hardly hold good as to the town, but it will hold good as to the neighbourhood around.

3071. Dr. TRAILL.—Are the visitors who come to this town during the summer chiefly Presbyterians ?—We have all denominations.

3072. Mr. *Rainey*.—It is only fair to say that the higher class of Presbyterians have a school provided for their education at Upper Clifton, and it has been in operation for seven or eight years.

3073. It is an Intermediate school ?—Yes.

3074. Has it been successful at the Intermediate examinations ?—It has.

3075. Lord Justice FITZGIBBON (to *Witness*).—Would you see any objection to meeting the Dean and Mr. Ward, and writing to us as to what might be done ?—No ; I think that might be a very useful course to adopt.

3076. We ought to look to the position of the school in case the present supervision was withdrawn. We should try to make the school permanent, and the best way to do that is to get a committee. The nomination of the head master seems to rest with the two founders ?—Yes.

3077. Rev. Dr. MOLLOY.—It appeared to me today that there would be an advantage in a certain outlay on the schools themselves ?—Certainly.

3078. The school seems to have prospered far beyond what was originally intended ?—Yes.

3079. Lord Justice FITZGIBBON.—We would be glad to do anything we can to assist you. Our only object is to make the school permanent and efficient.

The *Dean of Down*.—Would that local committee interfere with the patronage as to the head master ?

3080. Lord Justice FITZGIBBON.—At present the patronage is vested in Lord Bangor and Mr. Ward, the founders, and they ought to retain it unless they desire to give it up to the managing committee. Speaking for myself, I would hardly think it desirable to take it from them. If there was an efficient committee it would possibly be better that the appointment should be made by them, reserving a veto to Lord Bangor and Mr. Ward ; but without their consent we ought not to take it from them. That is a delicate subject to be dealt with ; it would be better for you to confer amongst yourselves about all these matters.

Mr. *Rainey*.—Will I have liberty to meet with them in order to protect my own interests.

3081. Lord Justice FITZGIBBON.—We are bound to protect your interests, and if you meet with the committee, your opinion might be of use to them.

The Hon. *Somerset Ward*.—I think from the state in which Mr. Rainey found the school, and the state which it is in now, that you want something more permanent.

BANGOR—CLANBRASSIL ENDOWMENT.

3082. Lord Justice FITZGIBBON (to the *Dean of Down*).—Mr. Dean, can you give us any information about the Clanbrassil Endowment ?—No.

3083. (To the Hon. *Somerset Ward*).—It appears in some of our papers as in operation ?—In none of the papers can I find any trace of the £18, mentioned in the Parliamentary Reports as a separate sum. But Mr. Ward subscribes a much larger sum to this school, and it may be that some years back it got merged in the larger subscription.

3084. I suppose the Dean's school on the opposite side of the street gets some of it ?

The *Dean of Down*.—I receive some money from Mr. Ward as an addition to the teachers salaries.

3085. But you take it as a subscription ?—I don't know from what source it comes.

3086. Professor DOUGHERTY.—Does he subscribe to any other schools in Bangor ?

Rev. William Clarke, (Presbyterian).—I would like to know if the donation to the Ward school comes from Mr. Ward directly, or from charitable money held in trust by him. There is a strong feeling in the place that it comes from church lands intended for the benefit of all denominations.

3087. Lord Justice FITZGIBBON (to the Hon. *Somerset Ward*).—Do you know whether the money given by Mr. Ward to the Ward School comes from the income of church lands ?—There are certain lands called church lands, the income of which is paid to Mr. Ward, but to what purpose it is to be applied I do not know. There are two lots of church lands here ; the income of one lot is payable on Lord Bangor's estate, and the income of the other on Mr. Ward's estate. The income from Lord Bangor's church lands is applied to charities in another part of the county which have nothing to do with Bangor, but to what purpose the income of the church lands on Mr. Ward's estate is devoted I cannot tell.

3088. Dr. TRAILL.—What is the amount of that income ?—£34.

3089. Lord Justice FITZGIBBON.—You have no document dealing with this trust ?—No, I have never seen any.

3090. Professor DOUGHERTY.—Who gave those lands ?

The Hon. *Somerset Ward*.—Judge Ward.

3091. Under a will, I suppose ?—Yes, under a will ; I think it is dated about 1760.

Oct. 25, 1886.

BALLYMACONNELL NATIONAL SCHOOL; BALLYMULLEN (CRAWFORDSBURN) NATIONAL SCHOOL; BALLYRALLAGH NATIONAL SCHOOL.

3091. Lord Justice FitzGibbon.—This is John M'Gowan's Endowment, the trustees of which are Lord Dufferin, Mr. Mortimer Thomson, and the Very Rev. Edward Maguire.

The Very Rev. Edward Maguire, Dean of Down, sworn and examined.

Very Rev. Edward Maguire, Dean of Down.

3092. You are one of the trustees of John M'Gowan's Endowment?—I am. When I came to this parish I received a letter from Mr. Mortimer Thomson, then agent for Lord Dufferin. It is dated March 15, 1878, and is as follows:—

"Dear Sir,—

"M'Gowan's Trusts.

"Major Crawford has, I understand, explained to you that there are two charities existing for the benefit of certain schools in Bangor parish, and for the poor of the parish respectively, known as M'Gowan's Trusts. There were three trustees of these charities, in whose names the funds are invested, namely, the present Earl of Dufferin, the late Rev. Dr. Binney, and the late Mr. Thomas S. M'Cullough.

"Lord Dufferin, the only surviving trustee, being absent in Canada, it is advisable that two gentlemen should be at once appointed in the place of the two deceased.

"Under the deeds of establishment of the Trusts, the appointment of the Trustees for the 'Schools of Bangor Charity' rests with the Resident Church Clergyman of Bangor Parish and the land agent for the time being of the Earl of Dufferin.

"The appointment of the trustees for the second charity, namely, for the poor of Bangor Parish, rests with Lord Dufferin alone. At the last appointment, however, the same gentlemen were nominated in each.

"It has been proposed by Major Crawford that it would be advisable that yourself, as Vicar of the Parish, and myself, as Lord Dufferin's agent, should be appointed in the place of Dr. Binney and Mr. M'Cullough, and if this suggestion meets with your approval, I propose to submit it to Lord Dufferin for his concurrence.

"In the meantime it will be necessary for Lord Dufferin to authorize someone to receive the dividends of the Trusts which have hitherto been paid to Dr. Binney. If you have no objection to receive the money in the same way, I propose to request Lord Dufferin to give the necessary authority to pay the dividends to you.

"Before, however, this can be effected a certificate of the burial of Dr. Binney must be produced, and as this, I believe, can be furnished by yourself, perhaps I may ask you to send it me at your convenience.

"I beg to enclose, for your perusal, a copy of the will of the late Mr. M'Gowan, founding these charities, and a letter from Messrs. Crawford and Lockhart, solicitors, who executed the last deeds of appointment of the trustees. I shall feel obliged, however, by your kindly returning me these two documents.

"Believe me, dear sir,

"Yours faithfully,

"Mortimer Thomson."

Witness (continuing).—M'Gowan left money for the three schools—Ballymullen, Ballyrallagh, and Ballymaconnell—and the amount is £760 16s. 6d.

3094. In whose name is the stock standing now?—I think Lord Dufferin's.

3095. Professor Dougherty.—Are those schools mentioned in M'Gowan's will as the objects of his bequest?—Yes; for the payment of free pupils who were not able to pay. There is, as I have stated, £760 16s. 6d. at New Three per Cent., and, less commission, that sum yields £22 6s. per annum. Ballymullen school gets £11 13s.; Ballyrallagh school gets £5 16s. 6d.; and Ballymaconnell school gets £5 16s. 6d. The schools are all in this parish.

3096. Lord Justice FitzGibbon.—Do you know how the schoolhouses are held?—No, I am not officially connected with the schools; they are chiefly Presbyterian.

3097. Professor Dougherty.—You are not manager of any of them?—No: I am only a trustee under the will.

3098. Lord Justice FitzGibbon.—As rector of the parish you were appointed trustee under the will?—Yes.

3099. Professor Dougherty.—Who is Lord Dufferin's present agent?—Mr. Howe, who is manager of two of the schools, and Mr. Clarke is manager of the Ballymaconnell school.

3100. Lord Justice FitzGibbon (to Rev. Mr. Clarke).—How is that schoolhouse held?—I think it is a free grant. That part of Lord Dufferin's property passed into Mr. Houston's hands.

3101. Ballymullen and Ballyrallagh are still on Lord Dufferin's property?—Yes.

Witness.—Every time the teachers come to me for payment I ask them "Have you any free pupils, and if they paid you would it amount to that sum," and they say "It would amount to a great deal more."

Rev. *William Clarke.*—I am manager of Ballymaconnell school. I could not say how many are on the roll, but I think the attendance is about forty or forty-two.

3102. How many of them are free?—I could not say; I take nothing to do with the administration of the funds. That duty belongs to the Dean of Down.

3103. Dr. Traill.—Would it not be better for you, Mr. Clarke, to discharge that duty—that the one who pays the money should be connected with the school?

Witness.—I have no objection to that.*

3104. Professor Dougherty.—The great majority of those children are Presbyterians?—They are; I have nothing to do with the schools except to get the money and give it away. The teachers come a long way to my house to get the money.

3105. Lord Justice FitzGibbon.—Is there any connexion between the three schools?

Rev. Mr. *Clarke*.—None whatever; they are in different localities entirely; they are in a triangle of about three miles by two miles.

Witness.—Mr. Howe, Lord Dufferin's agent, who is manager of two of the schools, does not reside in this locality.

3106. Where does he reside?—At Hillsborough.

3107. Professor Dougherty.—Is it the rule of the Dufferin estate that the management of the schools should be kept in the agent's hands?

Rev. Mr. *Clarke*.—Lord Dufferin keeps the management in his own hands. Any repairs made on the school of which I have the management were made at the expense of Mr. Houston and myself. I refer to the Ballymaconnell school.

3108. Lord Justice FitzGibbon.—Now, as to the other two?

Rev. Mr. *Quartz* (Ballygilbert).—They are in connexion with the National Board, and Lord Dufferin makes the repairs; his lordship has hitherto done so. Lord Dufferin is really the manager of the schools, but Mr. Howe acts in his place.

3109. Lord Justice FitzGibbon (to the Dean of Down).—With regard to these endowments, might not an arrangement be made whereby the payments might be made by some of the people connected with the schools, instead of by a minister of another denomination who has nothing to do with them? They are, however, in your parish, these schools?—Yes.

3110. As to the Episcopalian children at those schools, you should see that they have all the rights recognised under the National Board, and that they are looked after.

* The M'Gowan Trust Money, for poor, as well as for the three schools above named, is sent to me quarterly in one sum by Messrs. [illegible], stock brokers, 97, [illegible], Dublin. If the Rev. Mr. Clarke becomes the paymaster to Ballymaconnell school, [illegible] should be sent to the stock brokers to pay Mr. Clarke his share directly from their office, but it seems quite simple enough to let all pass through me as heretofore.—Edward Maguire, D.D., Dean of Down.

Rev. Mr. Clarke.—As to Ballymacarrett school, it is open to the Dean at all times; I have no desire to take the duties of this office out of the Dean's hands—none whatever.

3111. It is all right when you have the Dean, but another person might hold the office who would not take the trouble at all. Oct. 24, 1888.

PUBLIC SITTING—THURSDAY, OCTOBER 25, 1888. Oct. 25, 1888.

At the Courthouse, Donaghadee.

Present:—The Right Hon. Lord Justice FitzGibbon, Judicial Commissioner; and the Rev. Gerald Molloy, D.D., D.Sc., Anthony Traill, Esq., LL.D., M.D., F.T.C.D., and Professor Dougherty, M.A., Assistant Commissioners.

The Assistant Secretary, N. D. Murphy, jun., was in attendance.

Lord Justice FitzGibbon made an introductory statement.

THE COUNTESS OF MOUNT ALEXANDER (MALE) SCHOOL, DONAGHADEE.

Daniel Delacherois, D.L., sworn and examined.

Daniel Delacherois, D.L.

3112. You act as manager under the National Board of the Mount Alexander Male School on behalf of the trustees?—Yes.

3113. Give particulars of instrument of foundation—the school is endowed under the will of Mary Angelica, Countess of Mount Alexander, dated May 30, 1764?—Yes (document produced).

3114. Lord Justice FitzGibbon (reads)—

"I leave to the Lord Bishop of Down and Connor, his Vicar-General of the diocese of Down, or his officiating surrogate of the same diocese, all for the time being, and their successors for ever the sum of £120 a year, to be paid out of my real estate in the parishes of Comber and Donaghadee for ever, in trust for the several purposes following:—£30 a year, part of said £120 a year, to be paid to a licensed English schoolmaster who shall be of the Protestant religion, as by law established, and who shall instruct thirty poor children yearly in reading, writing, and the four common rules of arithmetic, without any other fee or reward save the £30 a year above mentioned; which said schoolmaster shall be appointed by the said Bishop of Down, his Vicar-General or officiating surrogate and subject to their visitation, and I do hereby empower and authorize the said Bishop, his Vicar-General, or officiating surrogate to remove said schoolmaster as often as on these shall seem just cause, and to appoint another qualified as above set forth, in his stead, or when a vacancy shall happen by death or otherwise; also £30 a year, a further part of said £120 a year, to be laid out in clothing said thirty poor children; also £25 a year, a further part of said £120, to be divided into apprentice fees for such of said children as shall be apprenticed out to Protestant tradesmen; also £20 a year, a further part of said £120, to be at every Christmas divided equally, share and share alike, by my trustees hereinafter named, to twenty-five poor housekeepers, who have been at least seven years resident in the town of Donaghadee, or on my estate in the parish of Donaghadee, before they shall be entitled to any distribution above named, and I do hereby empower and authorize the Vicar of Donaghadee for the time being, and his successors, or his or their curates to nominate and apprentice out said poor children, and that the said vicar or his resident curate shall, on or before the 20th day of December in every year, [illegible] to my trustees hereinafter named, the twenty-five poor reduced house-keepers who shall be entitled to a [illegible] share of said £20; and it is my will that widows shall always have the preference, and also that £10 a year, the remaining part of said £120, be paid yearly to the officiating clergyman of Donaghadee, for reading morning prayers on every Wednesday and Friday throughout the year in the parish church of Donaghadee, and that my trustees shall account yearly at the annual visitation held for said diocese of Down, before the Bishop, his Rector, Vicar-General, or officiating surrogate for said sum of £120 a year."

(To Witness)—Is there at present any Vicar-General of Down?—No, since the Church Act that office has been done away with. The Chancellor of Down takes the place of the Vicar-General.

3115. Is £120 a year still paid?—Yes, on the certificate of the clergyman.

3116. It is only £120 Irish money?—That is all.

3117. On whose estate is it charged?—One part on mine, and the other part on the estate of Mr. Crommelin, of Carrowdore; they are separate estates but the charity is a charge upon both equally.

3118. To whom is the money paid?—Every Christmas the Incumbent sends in a list of the twenty-five poor house-keepers, and of the pupils, and my agent pays the amount as he does the other charities. Then there is a certificate that the schoolmaster has done his duty and he gets his money. Mr. Crommelin pays one-half and I pay the other half. The clothing is paid for when the Incumbent certifies that it has been provided, and when the Incumbent sends in a certificate that a certain number of boys are eligible for receiving the apprentice fees and are going to trades, the amount is granted. I may say I do not think it has been done in a *bona fide* way for some time past, because the boys take the money and do not go to the trades, and it is rather a bogus sort of business. It seems practically rather useless in the way it has been given of late.

3119. The Incumbent nominates the house-keepers and the children who are to receive fees?—Yes, he looks after the thirty five boys in the school, and knows when the time has arrived for them to go to a trade.

3120. Is there any provision for girls in the school?—It has always been treated, since February, 1856, when it became connected with the National Board, as a male school. Under the Erasmus Smith arrangement there were girls.

3121. You had a grant from Erasmus Smith's Board?—Yes, until 1856, when they discontinued the school for want of funds. I then told the present Primate that if they did not put it under some board the school would drop to pieces, and he got it put under the National Board.

3122. Rev. Dr. Molloy.—Since 1856 you have got nothing from Erasmus Smith's endowment?—No.

3123. Professor Dougherty.—Have your boys still the privilege of competing for places in the Blue Coat Hospital?—I do not think any have gone there.

3124. Rev. Dr. Molloy.—It is now practically an ordinary National school?—It is.

3125. Lord Justice FitzGibbon.—How is the building kept in order?—Under the will there is no fund for keeping the schoolhouse in order. There was an old schoolhouse, and in 1842 my uncle, Daniel Delacherois, when giving the present schoolhouse in exchange, arranged to pay £3 a year towards keeping it in repair. I have here an extract from the indenture which was made on February 10, 1842.

3126. Lord Justice FitzGibbon (reads)—It was made between Daniel Delacherois of the one part, and the Lord Bishop of Down and Connor and the Rev. Edward Carpdan, Vicar General of the diocese, of the other part. It recites that it would be for the advantage of the Charity School in Donaghadee to have a change in the house in which the school was held, and that the change having been made, the trustees are to pay one peppercorn for ever as a nominal rent to said Daniel Delacherois, and the said Daniel Delacherois to pay for ever to said trustees and their successors, or to any person authorised by them to receive same, on the 1st day of November in every year, the sum of 10s., to be applied by the trustees for keeping the demised premises in repair, so far as the said sum will enable them to do so?—I pay that 10s. every year; but £3 would never keep up a building of that kind; it would require £40 to put a slate roof on it at the present time. I have laid out a good deal of money on the schoolhouse from time to time.

3127. Those were all voluntary contributions on your part?—Yes; there is nobody else to do this.

3128. Did the Bishop appoint the present master?—No. Erasmus Smith's Board appointed him, but by the approval of the present Primate, and when Erasmus Smith's Board gave up the school it was taken up by the National Board on February 1, 1884, and he has continued ever since as master.

3129. Besides the 10s. a year, what have you paid for the school?—I have had to supplement the £3 with about £20 for keeping it in repair, and also to expend £34 in building out offices for the school. There is no provision whatever for fuel, requisites, &c., and I have been paying every expense since the school was given up by Erasmus Smith's Board up to the present time. There should be a separate fund for that purpose. There is no fund now to pay for those things.

3130. Dr. Traill.—Has there been any accumulation of the £10 a year apprenticeship fund?—Yes, the Cromwellian part of the Bequests was not paid for some years, and accumulated over, and then the Bishop, through the Commissioners of Charitable Donations and Bequests, arranged that it should be spent in providing the present schoolhouse.

3131. Lord Justice FitzGibbon.—There is no similar fund available now?—Not that I know of. I wish to mention that the prayers prescribed by the will have not been read for some time past.

3132. Has the £10 been paid?—Not latterly, for the prayers were not read.

3133. What has been done with the £10?—It has not been paid by either Mr. Cromwell or me; it is a matter for the lawyers to say whether the prayers not having been read, the money is to be paid for that purpose.

3134. Can you tell us how long back it has not been paid?—No, I cannot.

3135. Rev. Dr. Molloy.—Your motto is, No Pater noster, no penny?—We did not get the Pater noster, and accordingly we did not pay the penny.

James W. Clarke, Head Master, sworn and examined.

3136. Lord Justice FitzGibbon.—When were you appointed to take charge of this school?—On September 1, 1878; I was appointed by Erasmus Smith's Board, subject to the approval of the Bishop of the diocese, and the rector of the parish.

3137. Where were you engaged before that?—In England, in the Academy in Derby, and also in Stafford. I was educated in the Ranelagh Institution at Athlone.

3138. When you came here what number of children were in the school?—The school was in a very low state, and the children only attended half time; there were about 18.

3139. At that time it was not under either Erasmus Smith's or the National Board?—No; it was under neither.

3140. When you came it was put under Erasmus Smith?—Yes, and it so remained until January 31, 1884.

3141. How much did you get from them?—I got from them £33 a year altogether.

3142. How much have you got since you came under the Board?—I had £35 salary from the Board last year, and the results fees were £16 5s. 6d. I went in provisionally under the Board, and want to go up and get classed higher; I applied to get up for training last year and was not called.

3143. Your classification on joining would be third class?—Yes.

3144. What number of pupils have you now?—I have sixty-two on the roll, and an average attendance of forty-five at present; it is sometimes up to fifty, and I have had sixty, but in the summer time the children who are poor run messages for the visitors who are stopping here for the benefit of the sea.

3145. The children are principally resident in Donaghadee?—Yes.

3146. What are their religious denominations?—Fifty-six belong to the Episcopal Church, four are Presbyterians, and two Methodists. The school is also open to Roman Catholics, but none attend. There are thirty-five free pupils, and twenty-seven paying pupils.

3147. Are there any Roman Catholic schools in Donaghadee?—No.

3148. Have you any monitor?—No, my number is more than enough; I applied in June, but the National Board are not appointing monitors of late.

3149. Have you children at your school of all classes?—Yes, from the first to the sixth class; there is only a very small sixth class.

3150. How do you account for that?—The people are poor, and as soon as the children grow up they are sent off to work.

3151. Are there any more advanced schools in Donaghadee than yours?—No.

3152. What fees are paid?—I have thirty-five scholars nominated by the rector; the remainder pay from a penny up to fivepence a week; I have some paying fivepence.

3153. Have you any free scholars besides those nominated by the vicar?—Some whose parents are so poor that I take them on free myself.

3154. Are those who are nominated by the vicar Church children?—Yes, he gives a preference to Church children.

3155. £30 is the amount annually allowed for clothes?—Yes, £30 Irish, which is £27 13s. 9d.

3156. Dr. Traill.—Who supplies the clothes?—A tailor, subject to the approval of the rector.

3157. Are they got through you?—I look after them.

3158. Are the children who get that clothing all poor children?—Yes, very poor.

3159. Lord Justice FitzGibbon.—Do you feel

the distribution of clothes useful?—Very useful; the children come to the school more for the clothes than the education. The attendance of these children is under the average of the paying children, but I will have an attendance of from fifty-five to sixty from this to Christmas.

3160. Rev. Dr. Molloy.—Qualifying for the clothes?—Yes.

3161. Lord Justice FitzGibbon.—What is done with the £10 for apprentice fees?—That is for the boys who have been at school for the proper length of time. It amounts to £9 4s. 7d. (English), and is paid half by Mr. Crommelin and half by Mr. Delacherois.

3162. Do you know how the boys work for those fees?—This indenture (produced) was filled up in this way before I came here, and we continue to fill it up.

3163. What fee is paid with each boy?—£1 16s. 11d.

3164. What value do they get in return?—None at all if they do not go.

3165. Dr. Traill.—To whom is the money paid?—To the boys themselves.

3166. Not to the master that they go to learn their trade with?—No.

3167. Lord Justice FitzGibbon.—Would not that money be better spent on the school?—It would, as at present it is not serviceable to the boys; they get the money and go to be labourers, or something like that, afterwards. Really the thing is, as Mr. Delacherois has said, a bogus affair.

3168. It is a premium paid to the boys who have remained in the school five years?—That is practically what it amounts to. Oct. 16, 1882. James W. Charnock.

3169. Rev. Dr. Molloy.—It is rather demoralizing to have things carried on in that way?—I should say so.

[Lord Justice FitzGibbon here read the indenture of Thomas Morrison, who was to serve an apprenticeship of five years as a tailor.]

3170. Rev. Dr. Molloy.—Where is that boy at present?—He is fishing with his father.

3171. He did not go to tailoring?—The tailor would not have him, and knew from the beginning that he wouldn't go to the trade.

3172. Thomas Nelson is another boy apprenticed to a tailor; where is he?—He did not go as an apprentice to the tailor mentioned in his indenture, but went to another. He did not go to M'Kibben because the thing was simply arranged to get the fee. He went to a man named Davidson, who really wanted an apprentice, and so he got his fee, and M'Kibben did not take him.

3173. Dr. Traill.—That money would be better spent on the repairs of the school?—I think so. The school fees that I receive are very small.

3174. Lord Justice FitzGibbon.—What do they amount to?—Last year they amounted to £5 11s. 0d.

3175. What do you receive from the endowment?—£18 9s. 3d.—that is £20 Irish.

3176. What is the average age of the pupils?—Nine years.

Rev. *Richard H. Coote*, B.A., Rector of Donaghadee, sworn and examined.

3177. Lord Justice FitzGibbon.—How long have you been Rector of Donaghadee?—Since July, 1877—three years.

3178. How are the children selected for receiving clothes?—They are chosen from the free boys. We try to encourage them to attend well, and out of these Mr. Clarke (the schoolmaster) gives me a list of the poorest and of the best attenders.

3179. You select the poorest, and give the clothes as a reward for the best attendance at the school?—Yes.

3180. As to the Apprentice Fund, how do you dispose of it?—As my predecessor did for forty-seven years, with the consent of Mr. Delacherois and that of Mr. Crommelin.

3181. What qualification do you require for a boy before you say he is entitled to the money?—As a matter of fact five boys come out every year, having attended five years, and they get the money with the intention that they should be enabled to procure some clothes, so as to continue their attendance at church. That was the idea always.

3182. The money is not enough to pay apprentice fees?—No, nor never was, even in Lady Mount Alexander's time. I think that money should be put to the clothing fund, and that the boys going out should get their suit of clothes to continue their attendance at church. This school was a sort of feeder to the church.

3183. Rev. Dr. Molloy.—Would it not be a good plan to give it in the form of prizes?—Yes; but failing that, I think the best plan would be to give them a suit of clothes.

3184. Might not a suit of clothes be given as a prize, not to every boy who had finished his career at school, but to those who had distinguished themselves by attendance, assiduity, or answers?—Yes, I think so; I think that would be a very good way.

3185. Professor Dougherty.—Do you find any difficulty with regard to maintaining a fund for paying the expense of repairs?—Well, Mr. Delacherois is more interested in that. Any man who wants to benefit the community could not adopt a better plan.

3186. Lord Justice FitzGibbon.—Then you propose that he should continue doing this?—That is for him.

3187. It might be as well for you to have some other fund for keeping the school in repair in case voluntary assistance failed?—In that case we would have to appeal to the public, and meet the expenses by public subscription, as is done in many other schools. Rev. Richard H. Coote, B.A.

3188. But Mr. Delacherois is a mere voluntary acting for the Bishop in the management of the school?—Yes, but he is also manager for the National Board.

3189. But, legally speaking, he is appointed by the Bishop. Is there no Vicar-General now?—No; the Chancellor is the nearest thing to it.

3190. Who is the Chancellor?—Mr. Lefroy.

3191. Would you not be better off if some local people were connected with the management of the school?—I think we would.

3192. Admiral Leslie's school for girls corresponds with this one for boys?—Yes.

3193. What about the £10 set apart for prayers?—Unfortunately, it was never paid in my time. It was paid, as I understand, in Mr. Hill's time, not with any degree of regularity, but still it was paid.

3194. Dr. Traill.—I suppose he had morning prayers regularly on Wednesdays and Fridays?—I find the evening services better, and then for the best part of the year you get the working classes to attend. For the last part of the year I have an evening service and a sermon once a week, and that service is well attended. I have from 90 to 120 present, whereas if we had morning prayers there would be no persons present.

3195. On what day of the week have you that service?—On Tuesday. I found, after going round a number of the days, that, curiously enough, that evening answered the people best.

3196. Lord Justice FitzGibbon.—It would be quite within our power to alter this trust if we had the consent of the officiating clergyman, and also of the other two persons interested—namely, Mr. Crommelin and Mr. Delacherois. What is not educational cannot be altered without the consent of those interested?—If that could be altered, the evening service is more conducive to the good of the place.

3197. Would it not be better either to substitute the evening service or to transfer the endowment for

Oct. 30, 1886.
Rev. Edward H. Coote, M.A.

the school?—I think it would not be right to transfer it from the church, for though I may not fulfil the conditions, my successor might do so, and I am his trustee. At present the money is not paid at all.

3298. Dr. TRAILL (to Mr. Delacherois).—Would you rather that the money should be paid for educational work in the school, or for the prayers.

Mr. *Delacherois*.—I do not see why the prayers should not go on in the church without extra pay for it, and I think the £10 would be better spent on the school.

3299. Lord Justice FITZGIBBON.—But Lady Maria Alexander gave her money for the church?

Mr. *Delacherois*.—Yes, but for morning prayers.

3300. Dr. TRAILL.—Do you not think that an evening service, with a sermon, is better than two morning services, when people won't attend?

Mr. *Delacherois*.—No, I do not think that, and Mr. Crommelin has a voice in this matter, as he pays half.

3301. Rev. Dr. MOLLOY.—It has not been paid for some years?

Mr. *Delacherois*.—No; it was simply withheld because the work was not done, and no application for the money was made.

3302. Dr. TRAILL.—Do you think it advisable to have the morning services in an empty church?

Mr. *Delacherois*.—But why should it be empty?

3303. Because the people cannot go?—But no effort has been made to get them to go, and a bell has not been rung. Mr. Hill was not able to attend to the work in recent years.

3304. Was this duty not performed by Mr. Hill in recent years?

Mr. *Delacherois*.—No; and I don't think he was in the school very much. He did not go in for more services than he could help, on account of his advanced age.

WITNESS.—Mr. Delacherois, some years since, told me, during the life of Mr. Crommelin's father, that if Mr. Crommelin would pay the money he would pay his share, and I did make an application through the bishop to Mr. Crommelin, hoping that if he paid the money Mr. Delacherois would fulfil his promise. Mr. Crommelin said what Mr. Delacherois said, that after consultation with lawyers and so forth, unless the prayers were said in the way mentioned in the will they would not pay the money. I do not think the services would be attended in the morning by more than three or four persons at the outside.

3305. At what hour would you have them?—It does not mention that, but I don't think it would be conducive to any good to have them in the morning. I have from 90 to 130 of an attendance at my week-day evening service.

3306. Lord Justice FITZGIBBON.—You ought to consult together as to whether you should leave this as it is, or make a change, and whatever you agree to do with the money we can carry out for you.

3307. Dr. TRAILL.—Would it not be better to let the money go to the school?—No, because I think I have no right to do that.

3308. Would you let it go for prizes to the Sunday School scholars?—I don't know whether my successor might not fulfil the conditions mentioned.

3309. But you don't care about your successor?—Yes; I think we ought to care about our successors.

3310. You cannot get this money by the present arrangement?—But by some other plan we may.

3311. Lord Justice FITZGIBBON.—How many registered vestrymen are there?—I think 91.

3312. You have churchwardens?—Yes.

3313. There is no curate?—I have no curate. There is not enough of work for one at present.

3314. There is little doubt that the Act only applies to this endowment with the consent of the governing body. The only persons who have any control are the Bishop, the Vicar-General, and Surrogate. The master of the school must be a member "of the Protestant religion as by law established." The children who are to receive benefits are to be nominated by the Vicar. Except with the consent of the governing body we cannot deal with it. The better plan would be to vest the endowment in a local governing body, and give them power to raise and apply the funds necessary for carrying on the school, which at present depends on Mr. Delacherois' benevolence. If he failed them, the governing body would naturally have to fall back on the parishioners, for this endowment is quite too small to keep the school going. As to the £10 to "be paid yearly to the clergyman for reading morning prayers on every Wednesday and Friday throughout the year," very possibly his attendance at the school catechising the children would be useful work, and we could make his doing that the conditions of receiving the grant, but that is for the clergyman himself and Messrs. Delacherois and Crommelin to consider. All schools must be dealt with according to their respective circumstances, but if you decide to move in this matter you need not be frightened about the expense, which will be trifling, and as to inspection you are already under the National Board.

ADMIRAL LESLIE'S FEMALE NATIONAL SCHOOL.

Daniel Delacherois, D.L., further examined.

Daniel Delacherois, D.L.

3315. Lord Justice FITZGIBBON.—You are one of the trustees of Admiral Leslie's school?—Yes.

3316. How was the trust created?—By the will of the late Mrs. Martha Leslie, dated August 15, 1839. The testatrix died on August 13, 1843. She devised to her nephew, Edmond Francis Leslie, and to the person who, at the time of her decease, should be rector of this parish, and to their heirs and assigns, always provided they are Protestants, a plot of ground purchased by her late husband, subject to a rent of £3 0s. 8d., and also the sum of £1,300, and she declared her will to be that the said trustees for the time being, being Protestants, should stand possessed, of the said plot of ground and money upon trust, to expend the sum of £200 sterling, part of the sum of £1,300 in building upon the said plot of ground such schoolhouse as they should think suitable for the scriptural education of eighteen little girls as day scholars, in the admission and selection of whom the orphans and children of sailors should be preferred; and she further declared her will to be that such scholars should be instructed daily in the Holy Scriptures, and should be taught useful needlework, and should be provided each (every Christmas) with a blue stuff gown and cape, and two white linen collars; also a straw bonnet with dark blue ribbon, and that the said school should be called "Admiral Leslie's Free School." The trustees were also to expend the sum of £100 sterling, part of the said sum of £1,300, in erecting such memorial to the memory of her husband as they should think fit in the ground belonging to the schoolhouse; and she further declared her will to be that the trustees should stand possessed of the sum of £1,000, the residue of the said sum of £1,300, upon trust, to invest the same in lands, rents, or Parliamentary stocks, or public funds, or upon Government securities, upon trust, in the first place, out of the dividends to pay the rent (£3 0s. 8d.) and taxes and other outgoings of the said plot of ground, and to defray the expenses of keeping the schoolhouse in repair, and the ground about the same in proper condition, and in the next place to apply the residue of the said dividends towards the payment of the person, being a Protestant, who shall be appointed mistress or teacher of the said school, and the defraying of the cost of the annual clothing of the scholars as thereinbefore directed, and other expenses incidental to the proper maintenance of the said school. And she declared that upon the occurrence of any vacancy among the trustees, if it should occur, by reason of the death of the said Edmund Francis Leslie or of any new trustee appointed in his place, in every such case the new trustee to be appointed, being a Protestant, shall be the heir-at-law of the said Edmund Francis Leslie, a male of the full age of twenty-one years, if he shall consent; thereto, otherwise shall be such person either of the family of the said Edmund Francis Leslie, or otherwise, as the then continuing trustee or trustees shall think fit; and if such vacancy shall arise by reason of the death or removal of the then rector or incumbent of the parish of Donaghadee, in such case the new trustee to be appointed shall be the next succeeding, or the then actual incumbent (being a Protestant) of the parish of Donaghadee, if he shall consent, otherwise shall be the incumbent (being a Protestant) of such adjoining or neighbouring parish, as the then continuing trustee or trustees shall in their absolute discretion think fit. By a codicil dated March 19, 1860, she appointed Daniel Delacherois of Donaghadee, esq., to be a trustee in place of Edmund Francis Leslie, and along with the person who at her death should be the rector or incumbent of the parish of Donaghadee, and bequeathed a further sum of £700, to be applied in addition to the sum of £300, part of the said sum of £1,300, in building the school-house.

3217. You are the Mr. Delacherois mentioned here?—Yes.

3218. Who was incumbent of Donaghadee at the death of the testatrix?—The Rev. John Hill. He is still living in Donaghadee.

3219. Dr. Traill.—But Mr. Crate is incumbent now?—Yes.

3220. Mr. Hill has resigned the incumbency, and Mr. Crate is incumbent now?—Yes.

3221. What aged man is Mr. Hill?—He told me that he will be ninety next January.

3222. Is he still capable of doing business?—Yes, perfectly; he has very little business to do, but he does it.

3223. Lord Justice FitzGibbon.—How does the school get on?—Very well; it is under the National Board.

3224. What is the endowment?—The plot of ground is held under a fee-farm grant, subject to £3 5s. 6d. She left £1,000, which was invested in Midland Railway debentures of 4½ per cent., and they were paid off. I consulted Chief Justice May, as a personal friend, as to what I should do, and he told me to put the money into 4 per cent. Indian Stock. Afterwards there was a great loss of interest, and last October it was converted to the 3½ per cent. Indian Stock at £106 per cent.

3225. Did you not convert the 4 per cent. into 3½ per cent. Stock?—We never got any notice of the matter.

3226. Public notice was given in all the papers. What was the amount of your 4 per cent. India Stock?—£934 10s. 1d. for the £1,000.

3227. I presume, having omitted to convert it, you will only get par value for it?—We have been negotiating with Mr. Cunningham, a stockbroker in Belfast, as to what we should do with it. The amount of the yearly endowment up to October last was £35 3s. 6d., and out of that the teacher received £24 a year. The remainder was paid for rent, free books, fire insurance, repairs, painting, &c.

3228. Did that exceed your funds?—Very nearly so, but so long as we got the large interest we could follow out the wishes of the testatrix as regards clothing, however, each girl's clothing, as described in the will, would cost about 16s. 6d., and there was absolutely no money left for that purpose.

3229. Have you been giving no clothing of late?—Not since about 1882. We had a communication with a solicitor about the matter, and were told it would be better to get an agreement signed by the parents that they were willing to forego the clothing. We thought it prudent to save ourselves, and took that step. (Document produced.)

3230. The parents signed this paper, agreeing to your discontinuing to provide stuff gowns and caps, linen collars, and so forth?—Yes, the parents signed that; we had not the money, and we will have less now. The school teacher will also lose a certain part of her salary.

3231. Who nominates the children?—Mr. Hill and I.

3232. How are they selected?—We always get the teacher to inquire what children are orphans and are desirous of being taken into the school.

3233. This school would be open for the sisters of the boys at the Mount Alexander School?—Very much so.

3234. Professor Dougherty.—Do you give a preference to the children of fishermen, as required by the will?—We do, always.

3235. Lord Justice FitzGibbon.—Have you any considerable number of sailors about here?—No, not many.

3236. Is it not a good fishing place?—Not very good; it has failed very much in recent years, except for codfish in winter.

3237. Dr. Traill.—Would you like one governing body for both these schools?—No, I can scarcely say that.

3238. Are not the objects very much alike, and would it not be well to have these schools under one governing body?—I would be glad to see any good scheme for the working of the schools in an efficient manner. I applied to the Bishop to get the National Board to take them over.

3239. Only for that they never would have been kept alive?—Never.

3240. You are trustee for one of these schools and not for the other—would it not be better for you to be on the governing body of both?—Could that be done and Mrs. Leslie's trust be carried out?

3241. Certainly; if you give your consent. No scheme can be forced on you without your own consent?—But you would have to keep the funds and accounts separate.

3242. Lord Justice FitzGibbon.—Yes, we could not possibly mix them up. This lady manifestly intended that the incumbent of the parish for the time being should be manager of the girls' school?—Yes. But supposing the present incumbent were to go away or die, the new clergyman might come and say "I want to be appointed," then there would be a difficulty here on account of the frequent want of these new appointments.

3243. The scheme would get rid of that, as the incumbent would be a governor by virtue of his office; this lady appointed her relatives, and I suppose whoever is resident here would take that office by right?—If I died, would my eldest son succeed to the office?

3244. Not under the codicil; by the original will Edmund Francis Leslie's heir-at-law was made trustee, but by the codicil you were selected in his place.

3245. Dr. Traill.—Could not General Leslie's name be added to this governing body as well as yours?—Yes, and he has two sons.

3246. Would it not be well to have a representative of the Leslie family as well as one of the Delacherois family?—I think it would.

3247. Lord Justice FitzGibbon.—I think we should have a joint governing body for both schools, the trusts being kept quite separate. There would be a representative of the Delacherois family, and one of the Leslie family, if willing to let their names be added. The local residents will no doubt be led to take an interest in the schools.

Oct. 25, 1888.

Daniel Delacherois, J.P.

Georgiana [illegible], sworn and examined.

3248. Lord Justice FitzGibbon.—You are mistress of the Admiral Leslie Free School?—Yes, since February, 1877.

3249. You are classed under the National Board?—Yes, a third class teacher.

3250. Have you been trained?—I was under training, but had to leave through illness.

3251. How many pupils are on the roll?—Sixty-five, including infants.

3252. How many infants are there?—Eighteen on the roll at present.

3253. Rev. Dr. Molloy.—What is the average attendance?—Last year it was forty-nine.

3254. Lord Justice FitzGibbon.—How many of the children pay fees?—All except eighteen free children who are nominated by the trustees.

3255. What fees do they pay?—A penny a week.

3256. What are your results fees?—Last year they were £15 7s. 6d.

3257. And the salary, £27 10s.

3258. Have you a residence?—Yes, a free residence.

3259. That is not in connexion with the school?—No.

3260. (To Mr. Delacherois).—I suppose that the residence is supplied by yourself?

Mr. *Delacherois*.—Yes.

3261. It is not school property?—No.

3262. (To Witness).—How many of your children are in the fifth and sixth classes?—Eleven in the fifth and no sixth class.

3263. What about needlework?—There is half an hour every day at needlework.

3264. Do you teach that yourself?—Yes, I have no other teacher.

3265. You have no monitress?—No, the Company has not appointed one as yet.

3266. Then you have to do all the teaching yourself?—Yes.

3267. Professor Dougherty.—Have you a return of the denominations of your pupils?—Yes; fifty-seven Irish Church, and eight Presbyterians.

3268. How many of these eight Presbyterians are free scholars?—None of them, I believe.

3269. Have you ever had any Presbyterian free scholars?—Not in my time.

3270. Rev. Dr. Molloy.—Where were you trained?—In Marlborough-street.

NO. 1 NATIONAL SCHOOL, DONAGHADEE.

John [illegible], sworn and examined.

3271. Lord Justice FitzGibbon.—You are teacher of the school of which the Rev. Mr. [illegible] is manager?—Yes.

3272. He is one of the Presbyterian ministers of Donaghadee?—Yes, the First Presbyterian Church.

3273. Your school is a vested National School?—Yes, we have no endowment; the buildings are vested in the Commissioners themselves.

3274. What is the attendance?—The average attendance in the male school for the year ending December last was forty-three, and 45 in the female school.

3275. Are they under separate teachers?—Yes.

3276. What are the denominations?—In the male school there are at present on the rolls twenty-nine Presbyterians, thirteen Episcopalians, and eleven Roman Catholics.

3277. And in the female school?—There are thirty-seven Presbyterians, twenty-six Episcopalians, and ten Roman Catholics.

3278. I suppose the greater number of the Roman Catholics attend your schools?—Yes, I believe so.

3279. What are the other schools in Donaghadee except those we have heard of?—There is a school under Methodist management, and one in connexion with the Second Presbyterian Church.

3280. Rev. Dr. Molloy.—What is your classification as a teacher?—First class.

Lord Justice FitzGibbon.—What is the classification of the lady who looks after the girls' school?—The same class.

CARROWDORE, WOBURN, NATIONAL SCHOOL.

Rev. *R. A. Cooper, Rector of Carrowdore*, sworn and examined.

3281. Lord Justice FitzGibbon.—We want to obtain information from you about the Carrowdore, Woburn, School. Sarah Dunbar Pilkington, by her will, dated September 17, 1874, bequeathed to trustees sums of £250 and £100 respectively, upon trust to pay the interest of said sum of £250 to the Incumbent for the time being of the parish of Carrowdore, near Donaghadee, to be applied by such Incumbent towards the salary of the schoolmaster for the time being of the Woburn School, in the county of Down, on the property of her uncle, George Dunbar, and to pay the interest of said sum of £100 to such Incumbent, for providing premiums either in clothes or books, for the children attending such school. She speaks of this school as being erected on the property of her uncle, George Dunbar?—The school is on the property of Miss Dunbar, who lives at Woburn.

3282. It was stated in 1879 that the school premises belonged to Captain Dunbar; you say they are Miss Dunbar's now?—Yes, Miss Dunbar is the only representative there, and she resides there now.

3283. What do you receive under the will?—We receive the interest of those two sums; the interest of the one goes to the teacher's salary, and the interest of the other goes in prizes of clothing and books at the end of the year.

3284. What are the numbers of pupils attending the school?—The average at present is forty.

3285. What are their denominations?—Chiefly members of the Church of Ireland; there are a few Presbyterians—not more than half a dozen—and there are at present five Roman Catholics, but that is entirely because there are now two Roman Catholics at the coast guard station.

3286. What is the total number on the roll at present?—About sixty.

3287. How many of these belong to the Church?—Very nearly fifty.

3288. Have the Presbyterians established a school in the locality?—There is a Presbyterian school.

3289. The Presbyterians used to attend the Woburn school in considerable numbers; is there any reason why they have ceased? In the report in 1879 it is stated that there were in attendance twenty pupils belonging to the Church of Ireland and seventy Presbyterians, no Roman Catholics?—There is a school about three quarters of a mile on one side under Presbyterian management, and another about a mile off; and any Presbyterians that do attend this school are those whose parents are working on Miss Dunbar's estate.

3290. How long has your present teacher held office?—I have been rector of the parish for over five years, and the present teacher was there when I came, and I think for two years previously.

3291. Are these Presbyterian schools in the neighbourhood taught by a master or mistress?—One is taught by a master and the other by a mistress.

3292. Do you get any subscriptions?—No, the teacher is very well off.

3293. Do you know how this money is invested?—It is invested with the Commissioners of Charitable Donations and Bequests, and the interest is sent to me regularly by them.

3294. There is nothing we can do for you to make your school better than it is. You ask that things may be allowed to go on as they are. The school premises appear to be private property. If they had belonged to the school we might have secured them for you. The money is safe, and I may declare the matter outside our jurisdiction.

The inquiry concluded.

PUBLIC SITTING—THURSDAY, OCTOBER 25, 1888.

At Ballywalter National School.

Present:—The Right Hon. Lord Justice FITZGIBBON, Judicial Commissioner; and the Rev. GERALD MOLLOY, D.D., D.SC., ANTHONY TRAILL, Esq., LL.D., M.D., F.T.C.D., and Professor DOUGHERTY, M.A., Assistant Commissioners.

The Assistant Secretary, N. D. MURPHY, Junr., was in attendance.

BROWN'S ENDOWMENT, BALLYHALBERT.

3295. Lord Justice FITZGIBBON read the following statement as to the endowment:—

"By will, dated November [illegible], 18[illegible], Joseph Brown of Portaferry, in the County of Down, devised and bequeathed all his real and personal estate to certain trustees upon trust, amongst other things, out of the annual income to pay yearly to a committee of all the clergymen, of every religious sect or denomination, who should for the time being be officiating in or for the parishes of [illegible] [illegible], Ballyhalbert, Inishargy, and Ardkeen, in the County of Down, and should notify their consent to act on such committee, a sum of £100—[illegible], yearly, to be expended in the purchase of suitable and warm clothing to be distributed in the month of [illegible] in every year amongst such children of the poor as should during the preceding year have been regular attenders, equal to the average of the rest of the scholars in any of the schools in operation in the aforesaid townlands, such distribution to be made equally without reference to religious creed or opinion, and in such manner that each donation should be sufficiently large to be useful and beneficial to the object of such donation. And, also, upon trust to set apart a further sum of £100 and apply the same in every year as follows, viz.:—That the said trustees should in the month of December in each year ascertain and ascertain how many schools should be in operation in the aforesaid townlands, on the principle of imparting secular education to children of all creeds and denominations, and so conducted that no pupil should be required to be present at any religious instruction of which he or his parents or guardians would not approve. The said sum of £100 to be divided between the patrons or managers of such schools, in proportion to the average number of pupils in attendance in each school during the preceding year, and to be distributed by the patrons or managers as prizes in books or money as they should think fit. The said yearly sum of £100 to cease to be payable and merge into the residue of the estate in case there should cease to be a non-sectarian school in the aforesaid townlands."

The Testator also provided—

"That in case there should in any year be any surplus remaining of the income of his real estate and the residue of his personal estate after answering the previous trusts of his will, that his trustees should out of such surplus retain a sum of £[illegible], and should distribute the remainder amongst and for the benefit and support of such then existing charitable or educational institutions in the County of Down, conducted and managed on principles which his trustees should consider the testator would have approved of if living as his trustees should think proper. The testator died on the [illegible] June, 18[illegible]. Each year since his death there was a surplus of about £[illegible] available for the purposes of the trust, the accumulations of which were represented at the date of the last published account of the trustees ([illegible] January, 18[illegible]), by a sum of £[illegible] cash invested in Government Stock, and a sum of £[illegible] [illegible]s. [illegible]d. lying on deposit receipt in the Belfast Bank. The yearly rental of the testator's real estate amounted to about £[illegible], and the personal estate was represented by a sum of £[illegible] [illegible]s. [illegible]d. Government Three per Cent. Stock. A scheme for the application of the surplus was settled by the Court of Chancery on December [illegible], 18[illegible]. By this scheme it is provided that the surplus income shall be applied each year by the trustees for the support and benefit of such non-sectarian schools in the County of Down as the trustees shall think fit; the same to be distributed in prizes awarded at public examinations held at each school by an examiner appointed by the trustees."

Frederick Saunderson sworn and examined.

3296. Lord Justice FITZGIBBON.—Are you one of the trustees of the Brown Endowment?—I am; my father was previously a trustee.

3297. How many trustees are there at present?—Only two; one died within the last few months.

3298. Have you power to make a new appointment under the will?—We have.

3299. Dr. TRAILL.—Was your father one of the original trustees?—He was one of the original trustees. He died and I was appointed by the others.

3300. Your father was William Saunderson of Newtownards, who was by a codicil appointed to be an executor of Joseph Brown's will, in lieu of John Welsh?—Yes.

3301. Lord Justice FITZGIBBON.—You have not increased the number of trustees?—No, but one has recently died, leaving two surviving, and we are about to appoint another in place of the deceased.

3302. Of what does the property consist?—The accounts are published every year in the newspapers according to the directions given, and I have here an epitome of the whole thing.

3303. What is the value of the real estate in County Clare?—That has been reduced; the income originally

[illegible]

was £449, and by the operations of the Land Courts it has been reduced to £320; there are arrears £212 we have not recovered; we have not taken out evictions as there is no good in forcing the tenants in the matter. There are 270 acres in County Clare part of townland of Upper Ayle, 367 acres part of townland of Lower Ayle in the same county; also 18 acres part of the townland of Derryabbert, making 615 acres altogether purchased by the late Mr. Brown in the Encumbered Estates Court by deed dated June 8, 1850, for £5,550, and then let to fifteen tenants at a gross rental of £465 7s. 6d. This estate is now let to twelve tenants at a net rental of £321. The average rental from Mr. Brown's death in 1848 to 1878 was, net £480; from 1878 to 1887, net average £301; present gross rental £391; charges, £70; leaving a balance of £311; arrears due by tenants at November, 1887, £77 7s. 9d., and at May, 1888, £135 1s.; the total arrears due being £212 8s. 9d. I have here the accounts as published in the *Belfast Morning News* on February 1, 1888.

3304. Do you publish them every year?—Yes. We are directed by the testator to publish the accounts in detail in three newspapers in Belfast—twice in each. That has been invariably complied with.

3305. He also allowed the trustees to appoint agents, accountants, and other persons to assist them?—At the first there was a good deal of work to be done; the agent used to get £40, and then we reduced it to £30; last half year it amounted to £15.

3306. What other property have you?—The proceeds of some American property. It consisted of two houses situated in South Williamstreet, New York, subject to a mortgage for 14,000 dollars effected during Mr. Brown's lifetime. By his will he empowered his trustees to sell this property. The amounts which they received out of the American property were as follows:—In 1869, £233 18s. 10d.; in 1870, £258 19s. 1d.; in 1871, £254 18s. 6d.; in 1872, £280 7s. 3d.; in 1873, £273 16s. 11d.; in 1874, £264 8s. 9d.; in 1875, £273 8s. 9d.; in 1876, £347 10s. 11d.; in 1877, £273 14s. 10d. In 1878 and 1879, there were extensive repairs effected, new roofing, &c. In 1878, the amount received was £31 7s. 10d.; in 1879, it was £3 16s. 7d.; and in 1880, nothing. Then in 1881, £73 9s. 9d. was received, and in 1882, up to May, the sum was £117 3s. 10d. The total amount received during the fourteen years was £2,681 8s. 4d. making an average net rental for that period of £187. The late Mr. Brown not being a citizen of the United States it was considered advisable to sell the property, and bring the proceeds to this country. This was effected in 1882. There was considerable difficulty in carrying out the sale, giving a title, &c., as Mr. Brown had no want of kin or heir, and a doubt arose as to whether the will and probate would be sufficient to convey the property to the trustees. An application had to be made to the American Legislature on the matter, which was finally settled as follows:—the property was sold for a gross sum of 25,000 dollars, less charges. These charges were:—mortgages 14,000 dollars; interest on same 203 dollars; proportion of accruing rent 141 dollars, and costs attending the sale 924 dollars, making in all 15,269 dollars. That left the net proceeds to be 9,730 dollars which was the sum remitted to and received by the trustees. It amounted to £1,986 16s. 3d., and this sum now forms part of the surplus invested in Government Stock. In addition to this £1,986 16s. 3d., we had £360 13s. of a balance of personal estate left by the deceased after the payment of legacies, debts, duties, costs and expenses. That made £2,347 9s. 3d. Then there was a balance of accumulated surplus income from the death of Mr. Brown up to 1879, when it was capitalised and invested in Government Stock by the Order of the *Master of the Rolls*, on December 9, 1879, and a scheme was settled for the disposal of the future annual surplus income. That balance was £2,209 9s. 3d., and added to the £2,347 9s. 3d. made a total cash capital of £4,556 2s. 6d. We have £1,827 9s. invested in Indian Stock, and £2,167 5s. 1d. in Consols; they both produced in 1887, £135 12s. 4d.

3307. What Indian Stock do you hold?—Four per cent. Government Stock; it has been reduced lately to £3 15s.

3308. To £3 10s. I think?—I think it is to £3 15s.

3309. You did not convert it?—No, we let it stand.

3310. It is curious that both here and in Donaghadee, the trustees of educational endowments had India Stock, but did not convert it as they might have advantageously done?—We did not get long enough notice.

3311. In your account published in the newspapers in February, 1888, in the Balance of Revenue Account, we have £3,000 in Consols, £709 0s. 3d. in India Stock, and £16 7s. 11d. in Belfast Bank. Does that balance of Revenue Account represent the accumulation during the time the endowment was not applied?—It does.

3312. Your gross income appears to be about £371 a year?—Yes, I have that brought out in the general statement I have here.

3313. There are four annuities mentioned here as fixed charges payable out of this income; who receive them?—They are all old people living in the neighbourhood; their names are Mary Bellis, £15; Hugh Johnston, £10; William Clint, £10, and Hugh M'Manus, £10.

3314. Then there are £75 as trustees remuneration?—They get £75 a year for managing the property.

3315. The next thing you mention is the cost of carrying on the trust, including law costs, publishing accounts, &c., average £60 a year. Of law costs how much have you incurred?—In connection with the Clare estate there have been pretty heavy costs.

3316. Dr. Traill.—Have you had much expense in the Land Courts?—Yes; one of our tenants got his rent reduced from £400 a year to £220 in the Land Courts. We were advised to appeal against that and we did, and the sub-commission was confirmed; it was confirmed without the cost of the Sub-Commission cost against us, but we had to pay for the rehearing.

3317. You obtained from the Court of Chancery in 1879 a scheme for the future application of the annual surplus income?—Yes.

3318. Have you a copy of that?—No, not here; but a copy of that is hung up in each of the schools. There was an annual surplus after providing for everything in the will, and we had to work out a scheme to apply that surplus. It was £140 for one year, but the reduction of the rents came in, and there has been since a deficiency.

3319. What powers did you get to apply that surplus?—There was a long scheme settled upon, to apply to the whole of County Down, and there was then a very complicated arrangement for dividing it amongst the different schools.

3320. Lord Justice FitzGibbon.—After the charges I have mentioned amounting to £180, I next find "Clerical Commission, £100"; is that money paid to all the clergymen?—It is.

3321. You have nothing to do with the distribution of it?—No; it goes for food and clothing for the poor during the year.

3322. Then the next item is "school premiums, £100"?—Yes, we are ordered to pay in proportion to the pupils that are in attendance.

3323. There is £30 also for Ballykeenagh Church?—Yes, that is to provide twelve free sittings for the poor.

3324. These make up £380, so that there appears to be an estimated annual deficiency of £76, assuming the reduced Clare rents are regularly paid?—That is so, and we were not able to pay in full last year; if there is not enough to pay £100 in full, they are all to be paid in proportion.

3325. Does that apply to the £75 paid to the trustees

also?—No, we take care of the trustees, and pay them in full as directed by the will.

3326. Your present receipts you say will enable you to pay a sum of 11s. in the pound to the charitable annuitants, and when the private annuities fall in, you believe the funds will then pay 17s. in the pound?—I think we will be able to reduce the working expenses; we might save £10 out of that.

3327. Have you tried to sell to the tenants under Lord Ashbourne's Act?—No, but I would be very glad to do that, and to get the money invested in funds.

3328. Have you got an agent in Clare?—Yes, Mr. Watson, the same agent as when Mr. Brown was alive. We reduced his salary from £30 to £20. He lived on the ground, near the estate, but he has had to go to Dublin to live on account of threatening letters.

3329. Dr. Traill.—Who are your law agents?—Messrs. Wallace and Co., Downpatrick.

3330. What are your legal difficulties?—I cannot explain them, but we could not do without a solicitor as many legal questions arise. The Master of the Rolls when we were getting the scheme settled, said we could get a paid secretary.

3331. Rev. Dr. Molloy.—Would two trustees be able to do all the work?—Oh, they would, but we will appoint a third; we want to keep up the number mentioned in the will.

3332. The will provides that you are not to reduce them?—We have a person in our mind for the position vacant.

3333. Professor Dougherty.—What are the denominations of the present trustees?—One is a Unitarian as the testator was, and as for myself I am liberal minded in matters of religion; I never go to any church, and I think for the third we will have a Presbyterian. I don't think we should take the sectarian matter into consideration at all.

3334. Do you know any of the schools that get the benefit of this endowment?—Not further than to see that this scheme is stuck upon the walls. The patrons and managers of the National schools have charge of the distribution of the premiums. The teacher in one school awards the prizes in another. The managers get their share of the £100 in proportion to the number of scholars in attendance, and then they divide it according to the will amongst the scholars.

3335. Dr. Traill.—If the rents are falling in this way, would it not save money if you did not fill up the place of the third trustee at the present time. You are reducing a good many items, but would it not be well to make provision for reducing the number of trustees. It would be a great pity to create a new interest when rents are falling.

Lord Justice FitzGibbon.—It might be worth considering whether money might not be saved by a body being incorporated; the cost would not be more than £3 for the scheme.

Witness.—When you speak of a scheme do you refer merely to the distribution of the surplus?

3336. Lord Justice FitzGibbon.—To the distribution of the educational endowments, and the management of the property generally.

Witness.—There is £100 to the Clerical Committee; £50 of that is for fuel and warm clothing amongst the labouring and industrious poor, and the other half is for warm and comfortable clothing amongst the children attending the schools. Of the £100 first mentioned £50 goes for fuel and warm clothing amongst the poor of the district, and the other £50 for clothing to the children at the schools—in warm clothing also. Oct. 26, 1888. Frederick [illegible].

Lord Justice FitzGibbon.—There is money given here for clothing, both for the poor people themselves and for the children attending the school, and then there is also the money for educational purposes.

3337. Rev. Dr. Molloy (to Witness).—About how much was spent last year on these two purposes—clothing for the poor, and clothing for the children attending the schools?—We can only tell the amount we gave to the Clerical Committee; we cannot tell what they did with it. Here is a copy of the last balance sheet; they got £75.

3338. Did the trustees leave to the Clerical Committee the selection of the schools who shared in the benefit?—No; they are mentioned in Mr. Brown's will.

3339. Professor Dougherty.—Did he name particular schools, or did he name a particular district?—Nonsectarian schools in a certain district, namely, the parishes of Ballyhalbert, Inishargy, and Ardkeen.

3340. Then I suppose all the schools in those three parishes participate in the benefit of the fund?—All non-sectarian schools in those three parishes. There is a notice just now of a new school, which the promoter wishes to participate in the fund. It was formerly a denominational school, the Rev. Mr. M'Evoy's; it was a Roman Catholic school at first.

3341. Rev. Dr. Molloy.—Does every other National school in the district get a share?—Yes.

3342. Is Father M'Evoy's school at present under Roman Catholic management?—Yes; the Rev. Mr. M'Evoy is the parish priest.

3343. It is a National school?—He is about to convert it into a National school.

3344. Lord Justice FitzGibbon.—As every National school in the district is sharing in the fund, apparently this new school has a right to a share in the money. You and your co-trustee at present, and your new co-trustee when he comes in, will have a vested interest in this to the extent of £75 a year. It is money payable to you personally, so you will understand that if a scheme be settled under our Act that money is your right; so long as the three trustees continue to do their duty under the will they shall be paid their £75, but when they fall out in the course of time we can arrange that the governing body will apply that £75 to the cost of management, or in some other way?—We would then have no duties to perform.

3345. You must perform your duties as long as you receive the money?—I thought you wanted to take the whole fund over and manage it.

3346. We could not do that without your consent. It would appear that the £75 could be made available for the purposes of the charity, subject to the vested interests of those who are paid now?—Yes; I think so.

Rev. R. A. Lyle, M.A., Incumbent of Kircubbin, sworn and examined.

3347. Lord Justice FitzGibbon.—Do you know the bequests mentioned by Mr. Brown in his will?—Yes.

3348. We are told there are five schools in the district?—There were five until recently, and a new one, making six altogether, has been opened within the last few months.

3349. You hold the office of secretary to the Clerical Committee?—Yes: the Clerical Committee's part is only to distribute the money after they get it; we made a scheme for the distribution.

3350. What is your present scheme?—The plan of distribution is according to the will—that every manager of a school furnishes to the Clerical Committee the number of children in attendance, and then the money is distributed in proportion to the numbers attending the several schools. This plan gives only 3s. 7½d. per child for clothing, a wholly insufficient sum; however, after a good deal of difficulty we arrived at this scale. The will of the testator says that it should be sufficiently large to be useful and beneficial. We have adopted a scheme giving a certain number of clothing allowances to each school. Rev. R. A. Lyle, M.A.

3351. Professor Dougherty.—Is it on the ground

Oct. 23, 1885.

Rev. E. A. Lyle, M.A.

of poverty that the children receiving clothing allowances are selected?—We do not find any ground specially stated; the children attending most of the schools are poor, and a large proportion of the children gladly accept of clothing.

3352. Dr. Traill.—Are well-to-do pupils counted in the administration of the fund or not?—That rests with the managers of the schools.

3353. Do you not investigate that in committee?—No, each manager looks after his own district. It has been disputed from the first, how far the clerical committee should investigate particular cases. The managers are not necessarily on the committee; all the members of the clerical committee are not managers of schools.

3354. Lord Justice FitzGibbon.—Who constitute the clerical committee now?—The Rev. Samuel Hawthorne, Presbyterian Clergyman, Kirkcubbin; the Rev. Peter M'Evoy, the Roman Catholic Manager of the new school; the Rev. George Grey, Rector of Ballyhalbert; the Rev. Mr. Douglas, Methodist Clergyman, who has no school; the Rev. Robert Workman, Presbyterian Clergyman, Glastry; the Rev. Mr. M'Ferran, Unitarian Clergyman, Ballyhalbert; the Rev. W. A. Whiteley, Presbyterian Minister, Clough, two miles from Portaferry, who has no school; the Rev. Hugh Boswell, Incumbent of Ardkeen, who has no school; Rev. E. G. File, curate of Kirkcubbin; Rev. J. J. Sullivan, Roman Catholic curate. That is the whole number.

3355. Rev. Dr. Molloy.—When the Clerical Committee are distributing the fund they give to each manager what he is entitled to receive under the scheme agreed on?—Yes. The committee meet and give all the money to the clergymen. Each clergyman takes his own share home and makes provision for the distribution. The children who receive grants all get equal shares exactly.

3356. Lord Justice FitzGibbon.—I see last year the distribution was as follows:—The Rev. Samuel Hawthorne, patron and manager of Kirkcubbin National School, £17 10s. 1d.; the Rev. Robert Workman, patron and manager of Ballyeasboro' National School, £18 19s. 1d.; the Rev. G. Grey, patron and manager of Portavogie National School, £15 13s. 6d.; the Rev. E. A. Lyle, patron and manager of Tubber-na-Carrig National School, £13 14s. 11d.; and the Rev. J. M'Ferran, patron and manager of Ballyhalbert National School, £10 13s. 2d. —in all £75; that is all for premiums?—Yes; these sums are paid to the managers of the schools for the premiums. We appoint examiners for the schools, and the money is distributed in money amongst the scholars entirely for proficiency and regularity of attendance, irrespective of poverty; that is in accordance with the will.

3357. Dr. Traill.—Why do you get examiners besides those of the National Board?—The Board examinations would not fit in at all; they are in summer, whereas these other examinations are in December.

3358. Lord Justice FitzGibbon.—Have you any suggestions to make whereby you think the money might be made more useful?—I think the scheme as devised by the testator is a very complicated and difficult one to work. I think we have done about the best we could, and I think the Clerical Committee are doing their best to utilize their money also, and the result has been a very much increased regular attendance at the schools, as the children are encouraged to be in regular attendance so as to secure the money and the clothing. It has had a very good effect in this respect, though a lowering effect in another.

3359. Do you think these doles of money are useful?—I think they have a lowering tendency.

3360. Dr. Traill.—Would it not be better to give book prizes than to have the children looking for 2s. 7½d. in money; do you not think a book value 2s. 6d. might be considered a more honourable distinction?—I think it would.

3361. Rev. Dr. Molloy.—But if instead of giving this amount indiscriminately to all, you gave it for good answering at the examinations, would it not be better?—I think it would be better that the premium money should be so distributed; the 2s. 7½d. is practically not given in money; we give a line to a shopkeeper that the 2s. 7½d. must be given in clothing.

3362. The money given for clothing could be given to all children who were poor and attended regularly, irrespective of their intellectual powers, and the money left for prizes could be given for good answering?—Yes.

3363. Lord Justice FitzGibbon.—As the manager of each school gets a share in proportion to the number of children at his school, I understand that you feel bound to give an equal share to each child?—We are bound by the will, but I do not think all the children poor enough to receive a share.

3364. Rev. Dr. Molloy.—Would it not remove all difficulty if the amount was distributed among the schools in proportion to the attendance recorded in the books?—That is done with regard to the £100 for prizes.

3365. Dr. Traill.—But it could not be done with the £50 for which you have to take an average of the poor children excluding those who are well to do?—That is the difficulty, and it has been met by taking a certain number as representing the poor children attending each school.

3366. Professor Dougherty.—Is Clough a very poor district?—Yes, very poor.

3367. Kirkcubbin is a richer district I understand?—There are a great many poor there.

3368. Rev. Dr. Molloy.—Might not the new [illegible] increase?—They will fall off this year in consequence of the new school being added; the amounts will accordingly be reduced.

3369. Is this school list revised every year?—We have had no alterations for years.

3370. Dr. Traill.—If you had another school or an increasing number of those who are to receive a share it would reduce the amount of each grant?—Yes: this new school is situated just between two other schools. We thought it a hardship at the time it was first established.

3371. Did the Roman Catholics attend those other schools previously?—Yes, and the result is to reduce the number now attending those schools, which was reported by the Inspector to be about the best school in the county. Mr. M'Evoy has another school about two miles distant from the present school, beside the Roman Catholic chapel. I think the suggestion, that the money now given for clothing should be given as rewards for attendance, is a good one, and that it would lead to a better application of the money.

3372. Lord Justice FitzGibbon.—Do you not think the committee might manage the whole affair, and thus save £75 a year in the course of time?—Things are working pretty well, but the saving of £75 a year would be important, because we do not at present receive the original bequests. We were reduced last year from £100 to £80, and are quite in a fix by the reductions that have taken place.

3373. Professor Dougherty.—How do you think the present trustees manage the Clare estate?—I am sure they do the best they can.

INISHARGY TURBER-NA-CARRIG, NATIONAL SCHOOL.

Rev. E. A. Lyle, M.A., Incumbent of Kirkcubbin, further examined.

3374. Lord Justice FITZGIBBON.—This school has an endowment of £1,000 invested?—Yes; it is invested in 4 per cent. preference shares of the Great Southern and Western Railway. That is derived under the will of the late Mrs. Ward.

3375. By whom is the money paid to you?—The dividend warrants are sent to me, and by me forwarded to London for signature by Mrs. Kennedy, 6, Onslow Crescent, London, who is the executrix. She sends them back to me to be cashed.

3376. How is the school site held?—This school is built on the property of Mr. Ward of Bangor. It was built at a cost of £240, which came from Mrs. Ward and other private sources. Whether there was a transfer of the land or not I cannot tell, but there was a transfer of the ground on which the teacher's residence stands to three trustees; the Board of Works advanced £250 for which they receive £4 5s. 0d. a year; the other half of the interest is payable by the National Board. There were three trustees for repayment; Mr. William Percival, the late Mr. John Boyd and myself.

3377. Would it not be as well to get a body incorporated to hold this money?—The intention as stated in the will—of which I have a copy here—is, that this money should be managed by the Incumbent of the parish, and so far as I know, it is as well managed as it could be. The capital sum ought to be in the keeping of some permanent body. Supposing that I were dead and gone, and Mrs. Kennedy were gone also, there is no record more than the will of the deceased. We both are aware of the circumstances connected with the case, and now there is no confusion.

3378. She could transfer it to official trustees, and they could be incorporated with representatives of the person who gave the money, and one or two others?—I do not know who could be mentioned as representatives of the deceased.

3379. Dr. TRAILL.—Would it not be better to lodge the money in the hands of the diocesan trustees?—I don't know. Mrs. Ward left £25 annually for the benefit of the school, and £15 annually for a coal fund. She was in the habit of distributing coal amongst the poor of all denominations. I adopt the system which she herself had practised, so that Roman Catholics, Presbyterians, Episcopalians, all share in this coal fund. I consulted Mrs. Kennedy, the executrix, and she thought I should do as I have been doing. It is a considerable advantage, for the poor people get a ton of coal each, and I think it would be a hardship to take it away from any of them. It is a very great benefit to the neighbourhood.

3380. Are you patron of the school also?—I am practically, but I requested Mr. Ward to become patron and to make me manager.

3381. The school endowment is one of which you are really manager and to which one denomination is entitled; it is therefore exempt from our jurisdiction unless you want it altered; would you like to have larger powers of investment or any alteration in the trusts?—I would like to consult Mrs. Kennedy before I answer that. If she would like to put it into a permanent trust what shall I do?

Write to our office and we will send you the schemes in some similar cases that we have already dealt with.

GREYABBEY, TULLYCAVY, NATIONAL SCHOOL.

George Allen, sworn and examined.

3382. Lord Justice FITZGIBBON.—You are a relative of the founder of this school?—Yes.

3383. I understand it was endowed in 1821?—Yes, I succeeded to my father's property in 1878. My uncle, Mr. Marland of Downpatrick, was my agent and is my agent still. He has sent his manager here to-day to explain to you anything you want to know, and I have also the schoolmaster here.

3384. Do you know anything of the working of the school; what do you pay towards it?—I pay £10 a year; I also give a supply of coal and keep the school in repair.

John Moran, Mr. Marland's manager, stated:—

3385. Alexander Allen bequeathed £400 for the school. The building was not to exceed £100, and the school was to be maintained for the education of orphans and the children of poor people belonging to the neighbourhood. Mr. Marland received on May 13, 1822, £276 18s. 5d., equivalent to £300 Irish, that was the residue of the £400 Irish after £100 had been spent on the building. I cannot say what security was given by Mr. John R. Allen, the predecessor of Mr. George Allen. The latter gentleman has paid £10 a year to Mr. Boyd, the schoolmaster, and in addition he has supplied it with one and a half tons of coal, and has also kept the school in repair.

3386. Lord Justice FITZGIBBON (to *Mr. Allen*).—You understand this to be a charge upon your estate?—Yes.

3387. And you have been making payments by way of interest on that amount?—Yes; I have been giving more than the interest.

3388. Is the schoolhouse on your estate?—It is; my father gave the grant for the school; I do not claim any title to the school as long as it is used as it is.

3389. Who are the trustees of the testator's will?—Mr. Alexander Allen is the surviving trustee.

3390. Who is manager of the school?—I am; Alexander Allen, the trustee, is patron.

Thomas Boyd, sworn and examined.

3391. Lord Justice FITZGIBBON.—How long have you been master of the school?—For eighteen years past.

3392. Who appointed you?—The late Mr. Allen, brother of the present gentleman.

3393. You are under the National Board?—Yes.

3394. How are you classed?—First of first.

3395. What is your attendance at present?—About fifty-four; the season accounts for that.

3396. What is the number on your rolls?—Eighty-one.

3397. The number seems to have diminished during the past ten years?—Only during the past year. This summer has interfered a good deal. It was a very wet summer, and then the harvest came in all at once.

3398. Rev. Dr. MOLLOY.—Will the winter attendance be better?—Yes; in the winter there would be on the rolls about ninety-five or ninety-six.

3399. Lord Justice FitzGibbon.—In the previous report the number on the roll was one hundred and five—fifty-one boys and fifty-four girls; eighty-nine Presbyterians, twelve Episcopalians, and four Roman Catholics?—We have no Roman Catholics now.

3400. Rev. Dr. Molloy.—Where do they go now?—There was only one Roman Catholic family and they have gone away to England.

3401. Lord Justice FitzGibbon.—How many Episcopalian children have you now?—About fifteen out of the eighty-one on the roll.

3402. What is your own denomination?—Presbyterian.

3403. This is a Presbyterian locality?—It is.

3404. All is going on very well now, but there is no legal settlement of the money or the schoolhouse, and it would be well to get a scheme settled by the Commission while in [illegible].

Mr. George Allen.—If you wish I will pay the money off.

3405. Dr. Traill.—Would you pay four per cent. if a Governing Body was appointed?—I would rather pay it off.

3406. Lord Justice FitzGibbon.—With regard to the governing body in this matter, it would be better to have a proposal reduced to writing. I would suggest now that you should get all this put into the shape of a scheme under which Mr. Allen and his estate would be responsible for this sum at four per cent. until he paid off the principal.

Mr. Allen.—I am willing to clear it off at any time.

GREYABBEY, MOUNTSTEWART, ERASMUS SMITH'S SCHOOL.

3407. Lord Justice FitzGibbon.—Can we receive any information regarding this school?

Mr. M'Cluggage (Ballywalter).—Lord Londonderry has an interest in the school, and I understand he is going to appoint the Rev. Mr. Goldsmith of Greyabbey as patron of the school.

No other evidence was received.

BALLYWALTER NATIONAL SCHOOL.

Mr. M'Cluggage, sworn and examined.

3408. Lord Justice FitzGibbon.—You are master of this school?—Yes.

3409. How long have you held that office?—For four and a half years.

3410. By whom were you appointed?—By Mr. Mulholland.

3411. What is the average attendance of scholars?—There is an average attendance of seventy.

3412. What are the denominations of the children?—Fifty-six Presbyterians, thirty-four Church of Ireland, and three Roman Catholics, making a total of ninety-three on the roll. There are about thirty children each in the girls' school and infant school.

3413. This is a mixed school?—Yes.

3414. Where do the funds come from for maintaining this school?—There are the Board's salaries and the results fees, with an endowment of £20 to me and £5 each to the other two teachers.

3415. How is the building held?—It is on Mr. Mulholland's own property.

PUBLIC SITTING—FRIDAY, OCTOBER 26, 1888.

At the Courthouse, Belfast.

Present:—The Right Hon. Lord Justice FitzGibbon, Judicial Commissioner; and the Rev. Gerald Molloy, D.D., D.SC., Anthony Traill, Esq., LL.D., M.D., F.T.C.D., and Professor Dougherty, M.A., Assistant Commissioners.

The Assistant Secretary, N. D. Murphy, Jun., was in attendance.

Lord Justice FitzGibbon made an introductory statement.

APPLICATION FROM THE DIOCESAN COUNCIL OF DOWN AND CONNOR AND DROMORE FOR THE INCORPORATION OF A DIOCESAN GOVERNING BODY FOR EDUCATIONAL ENDOWMENTS OF "THE CHURCH OF IRELAND."

The following deputation from the Diocesan Council of Down and Connor and Dromore appeared before the Commissioners in support of the application:—The Very Rev. Theophilus Campbell, D.D., Dean of Dromore; the Venerable Charles Seaver, D.D., Archdeacon of Connor; the Rev. Precentor Hartrick; Mr. Alexander Tate, C.E.; Mr. Joseph John Murphy (Hon. Secretary), and Mr. David Morrow (Assistant Secretary) to the Synod.

3416. Lord Justice FitzGibbon.—We have received from the Diocesan Council the following Memorial:—

"To the Right Honourable the Commissioners of Educational Endowments (Ireland).

"The Diocesan Council of Down and Connor and Dromore, learning that your Commissioners are willing to grant a charter to trustees to be named by the Council, enabling them to hold such school property as may be transferred to them by the present owners or trustees thereof, without prejudice to the rights of the present patrons or [illegible], have appointed the following as trustees for the purpose:—

"The Right Rev. William Reeves, D.D., Lord Bishop of Down and Connor and Dromore, and his successors.

"The Very Rev. Edward Maghera, D.D., Dean of Down, and his successors.

"The Very Rev. John Walton Murray, LL.D., Dean of Connor, and his successors.

"The Very Rev. Theophilus Campbell, D.D., Dean of Dromore, and his successors.
"Robert H. [illegible], Esq., J.P., [illegible], Donaghcloney, Co. Armagh.
"Sir William Ewart, Bart., M.P., Glenmachan House, Strandtown, Co. Down.
"Robert Jay, Esq., J.P., Millmount, Banbridge, Co. Down;

with power to the Diocesan Council to fill up vacancies occurring among the lay trustees.

"The Diocesan Council have appointed a committee to consider, and to correspond upon this business. The committee find as the result of inquiries made by all the incumbents of the dioceses, that there is scarcely any property in the form of endowments for schools, and the objects of the trust must, for the most part, be confined to school buildings, with, in some cases, a teacher's residence attached. Of these, many are vested in the Representative Church Body, and others are the property of private owners, who are not disposed at present to part with the ownership of the property.

"The Committee, however, acting for the Diocesan Council, respectfully request that the Commissioners will issue a charter to the above-named, as trustees, enabling them to hold in trust, without prejudice to the rights of the present patrons or managers, the school buildings, whereof a list is annexed, the owners or trustees of which have signified their willingness to transfer them to Diocesan Trustees, and granting them further power similarly to hold in trust any other school buildings or endowments in the united Dioceses of Down and Connor and Dromore, which from time to time may be transferred to them by the owners or persons thereof.

Theophilus Campbell, D.D., Dean, | Hon.
Joseph John Murphy. | Secretaries.

"Schedule of School Buildings referred to in the foregoing Report.

"Diocese of Down.—Dromara, Ballykeel schoolhouse and teacher's residence.

"Diocese of Connor.—Aghalee, schoolhouse, with teacher's residence; Portaferry, Ardoy, schoolhouse, with teacher's residence over the schoolroom; Culfeightrin, parochial schoolhouse; Connor Crumkill, National school.

"Diocese of Dromore.—Garvaghy, National school—the site of the school is supposed to have been part of the glebe lands; Newry, Ballykeel schoolhouse, with teacher's residence; Seapatrick, schoolhouse, the property of John Temple Reilly, Esq., J.P., Scarvagh House; Shankill or Lurgan, Kilmore National Schoolhouse, with teacher's residence at Kilmore, Co. Down."

3417. Lord Justice FitzGibbon (to the *Dean of Dromore*).—You are one of the Secretaries of the Diocesan Synod?—Yes.

3418. Are all the buildings mentioned in the schedule now used as schools?—Every one of them.

3419. Are they all under the management of the clergyman of the parish?—Yes. The school in Kilmore is under Colonel Waring, Mr. George Brush, and myself; it is a school in connexion with our Church. Colonel Waring is patron; the clergy have the thorough management of it.

3420. The number of schools scheduled is very small; would it not be well to have all your Church schools vested at the same time?—We have communicated with every clergyman in the dioceses on the subject, and we give you the result of the replies we have received.

3421. This presents a great contrast to the Diocese of Meath, where arrangements have been made for vesting a large number of schools?—Many of the owners of property are unwilling to allow the property to pass out of their hands, and I believe that is the reason we have got such unfavourable replies.

Mr. *J. J. Murphy*.—Most of the schools are on church premises; those schools which are not on the premises of a church are not vested in the Church Body.

3422. Lord Justice FitzGibbon.—What are you going to do with those vested in the Representative Church Body; we have been told that they disclaim all educational trusts? Oct. [illegible]

Mr. *Murphy*.—I believe they have got the opinion that they cannot hold educational trusts.

The *Dean of Dromore*.—I presume in the case of schools vested in the Representative Body they will continue under the charge of the rector of the parish.

3423. Dr. Traill.—The Church Temporalities Commissioners never named any schoolhouses in their vesting orders, and they refused to give any list of the schools.

Mr. *David Murray* (Secretary to the Diocesan Council).—We have a list of the churches in this diocese vested in the Representative Body, and also number of the schools connected with those churches.

3424. Rev. Dr. Mulloy.—What would be the annual value of those schools in the schedule?

The *Dean of Dromore*.—There are very few schools there, but we thought the number scheduled would be sufficient to justify us in asking the Commissioners to frame a scheme. When the scheme is framed, and when landlords and others know that there is a Governing Body in existence, and are convinced that they would not be confiscating their property in handing it over to this body, I am confident that the schedule will be largely increased.

3425. Lord Justice FitzGibbon.—You should remember that the advantage we can offer to you is not so much in the incorporation of a body capable of holding property, as in the vesting of the property, without expense, in that body.

The *Dean of Dromore*.—There are four schools on Lord Lurgan's property which I would like to have scheduled, but I could not touch them without his lordship's permission.

3426. There are no leases?—None.

Dr. Traill.—A great many schools in this district have reverted to their owners in this way.

3427. Lord Justice FitzGibbon.—The powers of our Act have been extended until March, 1890, but we must conclude all our preliminary business within the coming year. When does your Synod meet?

The *Dean of Dromore*.—On Tuesday next.

3428. Lord Justice FitzGibbon.—We might prepare and publish a draft scheme but not sign it, and let it lie over as long as possible in order to enable you to include any additional property.

The *Dean of Dromore*.—That would be a very satisfactory arrangement.

3429. Lord Justice FitzGibbon.—The real advantage we can give you is in the vesting of the property. As to the expenses of the scheme, I may say that for the Methodist College the whole cost was, I believe, under £1, and for Magee College, Londonderry, the cost was less than £1.

The *Dean of Dromore*.—I see the advantage of having the scheme, and I have been pressing the importance of it upon others, who are unwilling to part with their property. We have no doubt that if I could go to Lord Lurgan, and say—"Your property is being sold, would you have any objection to transfer your schools to us," he would do so. All we have are the schoolhouses and teachers' residences.

3430. Rev. Dr. Mulloy.—They do not represent a large amount of property.

Rev. *Precentor Harrick*.—A great many of these school-houses were merely built on a plot of ground given by the proprietor to the clergyman, and the clergyman carried on his school in that house from that period up to the present time. They were altogether in his possession, and under his control and management. How are we to get the possession that will satisfy you as Commissioners?

3431. Lord Justice FitzGibbon.—That is a natural question, and I will endeavour to answer it. Possession is evidence of title, and anyone whom we find in possession of property applicable to educational purposes we are willing to trust as [illegible] in it for the purpose of our scheme. We cannot, like the Landed Estates Court, give you any title, but we can vest in the new Governing Body whatever title those now in possession have. This would make you defendants instead of plaintiffs in case of any dispute. Our scheme will be evidence that those persons named therein were in possession at the date of the scheme, and so will be *prima facie* evidence of title. I may add that the present patrons of schools would not be interfered with by the proposed scheme. They would have the same powers as before.

CHARITABLE BEQUEST OF SAMUEL LEDLEY, FOR THE PURPOSE OF ERECTING A SCHOOL IN BALLYMACARRETT.

3432. Lord Justice FITZGIBBON.—The case of the Ledley Bequest has been sent to us by the Commissioners of Charitable Donations and Bequests with the following statement from the trustees of the endowment:—

"(1.) Samuel Ledley, late of *Belfast*, in the county of Antrim, died on or about the 19th day of April, 1884, having previously made and published his last will and testament in writing bearing date the 27th day of April, 1874, probate whereof was granted forth of the Principal Registry of the Probate and Matrimonial Division of the High Court of Justice in Ireland to his trustees and executors, Edward Ross, James Watson, and Edward Gribbon on the [illegible] day of June, 1883.

"(2.) That by his said will the testator left and bequeathed to his said trustees and executors in his said will named, in conjunction with the incumbent for the time being of Ballymacarrett Church, the sum of £1,000 to be expended in the erection of a schoolhouse in connection with the Church of Ireland in Ballymacarrett.

"(3.) That the amount of said Charity is at present invested upon deposit receipt in the Northern Banking Company (Limited), in the joint names of your petitioners.

"(4.) That the Rev. Thomas W. Ros, M.A., was at the date of the death of the said testator, and still is, the incumbent of Ballymacarrett Church, and he along with the said Edward Ross, James Watson, and Edward Gribbon are the present holders of the fund.

"5. That there is no provision made in the will of the said testator whereby the petitioners are authorised either to take, purchase, or take a lease of ground upon which to build the said schoolhouse; nor has the testator by his will made provision by his said will for the preparation of plans, specifications, or advertising for same, nor for the furnishing of said schoolhouse, so as to make it available for the purpose intended by the testator.

"Under the foregoing circumstances the undersigned make application to the Board for their direction on the following points, that is to say:—

"(1.) May your petitioners purchase or take a grant in fee, subject to a fee or otherwise, of a piece or parcel of ground upon which to build the said schoolhouse and pay the purchase-money out of the said legacy or bequest of £1,000.

"(2.) May your petitioners apply a reasonable amount of the said legacy of £1,000 towards furnishing the said schoolhouse for educational purposes, and in obtaining plans and specifications and advertising for same.

"(3.) That your petitioners may be directed and authorised to charge the said legacy of £1,000, with the costs of the opinion of counsel already incurred, and all costs as between solicitor and client incidental to this petition, and the costs of the preparation of conveyance or grant of the ground to be purchased or taken against the said bequest, and any other costs incidental to the carrying of the charitable bequest."

The Commissioners of Charitable Donations and Bequests gave this answer to the trustees on November 19, 1886. Their secretary wrote—

"I am directed to inform you that after a careful consideration of the facts of the case, my Commissioners are of opinion that the case is one which could be more satisfactorily dealt with by the Educational Endowments Commissioners. They have arrived at this conclusion from observing that although £1,000 is left for the erection of a schoolhouse there is no endowment whatever for the future maintenance of the school. It would appear to them, therefore, to be a matter of more than doubtful expediency to direct the trustees to purchase a site and to build and furnish a school which might never come into operation. Under the Educational Endowments (Ireland) Act, 1885, the Commissioners have power to alter the conditions and provisions of the endowments, to amalgamate or combine it with other kindred endowments, &c., and it appears to my Commissioners that the present is a case in which the exercise of such powers would benefit the endowment."

3433. Mr. *J. M'Ildowie*, B.L. (instructed by Messrs. George M'Ildowie and Sons).—I appear on behalf of the Rev. Dr. Ros, Vicar of Ballymacarrett. There are already twenty-three schoolhouses in Ballymacarrett, and no additional schoolhouse is required near the Ballymacarrett parish church. The facts are set forth in the following letter of the Rev. Dr. Ros to the Commissioners of October 20, 1886—

"An additional schoolhouse is not only not required near the parish church of Ballymacarrett, the parochial schoolhouse, situated on the church grounds, having been recently enlarged at a considerable expense, and made capable of accommodating, with a large class-room attached, over 400 children. The whole district adjacent to the church is at present well supplied with schools, belonging to different denominations. Indeed, I may say it is overcrowded. The expenditure, therefore, of the Ledley Bequest in that quarter would be decidedly a wasting of the funds. There is, however, a part of the parish (at Bridge End, near the Queen's-bridge and the river) where a schoolhouse is required, a district swarming with children, totally neglected and running almost wild, and where no educational provision whatsoever has been made up to the present by any denomination. There is a continual cry from the people in that quarter for a school for their children, particularly as it has been always understood that the Ledley Bequest had been intended for that district. Indeed, the testator told me so himself, as I had several conversations with him on the subject. This district is fully half an Irish mile from Ballymacarrett church, and is so situated and so distant from other schools, that young children are unable to attend. As a congregation, we have no funds whatever to supplement the bequest with regard to site, furniture, or any other expenses. But I believe this bequest is fully ample for every purpose, and I have no doubt the testator was of the same opinion. I may add, there is a site that may be had in the locality itself which would suit our means very well, and be quite convenient to all the families residing in that important and populous locality."

3434. Professor DOUGHERTY.—Is the district to which Dr. Ros refers that which is half a mile from the parish church and on which so much building is going on at present?

Mr. *M'Ildowie*.—Yes; from the Queen's-bridge to the river on one side, and on the other side back to the railway. There is no school there at present. There are some members of the Select Vestry present who would give their opinion on the matter. There are already two schools connected with the church; one immediately beside the church and another on the Short Strand. The schools are marked on the map (produced).

3435. Professor DOUGHERTY.—Are these all the elementary schools in Ballymacarrett?

Mr. *C. H. Field* (teacher of Ballymacarrett [illegible] National School).—Yes.

3436. Not alone those under Episcopal Church management?—No.

3437. Have you any Church Education Society's schools?—No.

The *Archdeacon of Connor* (Ven. Charles Seaver).—I think what Dr. Ros says is quite right. A school is no doubt very much required in the thickly populated district to which he refers.

Mr. C. H. Todd.—I am teacher of the school on the church grounds, and also Secretary of the Select Vestry for the last ten years, and a deputation to here from the Vestry to oppose this proposal for building a new school. The Select Vestry are £1,500 in debt, and cannot go into debt any further. A new school would cost us about £30 a year more, for fire, cleaning, &c. and as the present schools are not large enough, we think it would be much better to enlarge them. Oct. 31, 1889.

3438. Professor Dougherty.—Were the existing schools built by public subscription?—I have heard so, but I have no official knowledge.

The Archdeacon of Connor.—The Short Strand School was built by public subscription.

Charles H. Todd sworn and examined.

3439. There are three schools connected with the church; No. 5, on the map, is close to the church. There is an attendance of about 350 and sometimes of 370; the average attendance this year will be 340. Charles H. Todd.

3440. Lord Justice FitzGibbon.—What is the number of Vestrymen?—About fifty.

3441. That seems rather a small number?—There is perhaps a reason for that; Dr. Roe had an objection to any person signing the register unless at a public meeting of the Vestry, and it is difficult to get the members of the congregation to do so. On Sundays the congregation amounts to between 200 and 300.

3442. There are twenty-three schools in the Ballymacarrett district?—Yes.

3443. The Vestry object to have any more schools?—They are entirely opposed to it. We met yesterday in Dr. Roe's house, and every one there was opposed to it; they appointed a deputation to attend.

3444. How long have you been Secretary to the Select Vestry?—Some ten years.

3445. What is the view of the Vestry as to utilizing the £1,500?—They want to enlarge the present schools and make them equal to the requirements of the parish. Mr. [illegible], the Inspector of National Schools, said we have only accommodation for 283. We have an average attendance of 330. Last year the attendance went up to 350 and 370. The school would not have been enlarged only that the order came from the National Board either to turn out some of the children or enlarge the school. I expect a similar order next again. It is round about the church that the building of houses is going on. Ground has been taken for about 1,000 houses. The proposed site of Dr. Roe's is on slob land.

3446. Rev. Dr. Molloy.—How far is the Church from the place mentioned by Dr. Roe?—About half a mile; then there is the other school within a quarter of a mile of the place.

3447. Who wants the school built at this place?—The only person that I know of is Dr. Roe himself.

Mr. M'Aldowie.—Dr. Roe thinks it was the wish of the testator that the school should be placed in that locality.

3448. Lord Justice FitzGibbon.—The endowment is £1,600 "to be expended in the erection of a school-house, in connexion with the Church of Ireland, in Ballymacarrett."

Witness.—The present school is a large building with walls fourteen inches thick; they would support another story, and we have a lot of ground around the church free in perpetuity; another story might be added and also an infant department.

3449. Have you no infant department?—No; I have one classroom; it is hard to work the school up with such limited space.

3450. Dr. Traill.—Is there room round the church?—Yes, the church and school stand in the centre of a square of about 250 yards.

3451. Lord Justice FitzGibbon.—Have you space for a playground?—We have space for the best playground in Belfast.

3452. Is it a burying ground?—There never was any person buried there.

The Dean of Dromore.—Ballymacarrett was not originally the parish church; it was a chapel of ease to Knockbreda.

3453. Lord Justice FitzGibbon (to Witness).—How is the Short Strand School held?—It is vested in Mr. William Q. Ewart, the Rev. Dr. Roe, and Mr. Smith, who was at one time churchwarden of the parish. It was a school in connexion with the Erasmus Smith Board, and they handed it over to Dr. Roe on the terms that it would be always held as a school, and it is held in trust for school purposes.

3454. Is there any ground there?—Very little; really none at all.

Mr. David Morrow.—The other two trustees consent and Dr. Roe objects to handing it over to the Diocesan Board.

Witness.—What the parishioners would like to see carried out is the enlargement of the school beside the church. They and teachers would contribute to the proposed enlargement of the school, and paying off the debt on the church. Mr. Moore, the teacher of the Short Strand School, has a dwelling-house attached, and it was proposed to throw that dwelling-house into the school, and enlarge it in that way.

3455. Dr. Traill.—Is the roof of the schoolhouse near the church in good order?—It has a low ceiling, although the school has been greatly enlarged.

Mr. M'Aldowie.—There is a very good report from the teacher of the Short Strand School; I saw him yesterday.

The Archdeacon of Connor.—I think it would be a greater benefit to the parishioners, and that the wishes of the testator would be best carried out by following Dr. Roe's suggestion, and erecting a school in that thickly populated district, where, there is no doubt about it, a school is much required. Of course there is the difficulty of supporting it.

3456. Lord Justice FitzGibbon.—Is it not a bad thing to build a school-house without having any funds for the maintenance of the school?

Dr. Traill.—This other school is not more than a quarter of a mile off it.

The Archdeacon of Connor.—But a quarter of a mile in town means a good deal.

3457. Lord Justice FitzGibbon.—We have received a letter from "T. Gayton," dated October 29th, 1889, as follows:—

"The Ledley Schools, as the above term runs, [illegible] the wish of the donor of the bequest, as to how the money was to be appropriated, and as one of the representatives of the body to whom that money was bequeathed, I would strongly object to it going any other way. I have lived in the district for the last twenty-five years, and have watched the growth of the district, together with the formation of educational establishments [illegible] to the number of thirteen, all of which are actively engaged. While in the large district called the Bridge End (which no doubt the donor saw when he bequeathed the money), no such establishment exists. I fully concur in the sentiments made by both Messrs. Moore and Todd, which I trust may be met by kind and interested friends extending, but in all faith to the friends of the deceased, as also to the trustees I consider we are bound to carry out the donor's wishes. While to anybody kindly disposed to bequeath, they may rest with confidence in the assurance that their bequest will be carried out to the letter in every particular. With reference to the establishment of this school being an injury to existing establishments, and I would beg to remark that the whole district is but in its infancy, that as street by street is springing up, doubtless additional accommodation will be required. If any other course is taken with the money than the one bequeathed, I should feel rather nervous, that steps might be taken against us for a breach of trust or something of that nature, which legal gentlemen might make out of it. I therefore pray your high Commissioners will carry out the terms of the bequest."

Oct. 22, 1886.

Charles H. Todd.

The Archdeacon of Connor.—I have no doubt the Rev. Dr. Roe will be able to raise money enough to put the school in working order, and the National Commissioners would then take charge of it. I think there need be no difficulty as to putting it in order and having it worked when connected with it you would have a man of Dr. Roe's great ability.

Witness.—We had a bazaar for the purpose of paying off debts on the school. The people of the parish were scarcely able to raise anything, it was the teachers who had to raise it. We believe if we were put in a proper position we could assist in paying off the debts, otherwise we cannot. There is a debt of £439 on the schools, in consequence of the recent enlargement.

3458. Professor Dougherty.—The debts on the church can hardly be connected with debts on the schools?—One member of the congregation, Mr. Craft, said he was prepared to do all the repairs to the church if we allowed him to let the [illegible] and pay him five per cent. Dr. Roe wished to have a vicarage and in order to pay the Board of Works he got one-third of the cost from the bazaar. The vicarage was to cost £650, but it cost between £1,100 and £1,300, and therefore the teachers were just left as if they had no bazaar at all.

3459. Does that debt of £439 bear interest?—Yes, Mr. Craft died and we had to pay the executors. Dr. Roe lodged securities in bank and we had to pay interest and will have to pay the principal to Dr. Roe.

The Dean of Dromore.—You might spend out of the Ledley Bequest £500 on building a school and £200 in furnishing it.

3460. Lord Justice FitzGibbon.—Then how is it to be supported?—The National Board always insist upon an assurance of local aid, for repairs, &c.

The Dean of Dromore.—They will pay the teachers' salaries, and that with the fees of the children, and the result fees, are quite sufficient to maintain the teachers.

3461. Lord Justice FitzGibbon.—There must be an assurance that the buildings will be kept in repair and provided with requisites.

The Dean of Dromore.—I am not sure of that; I have known them to take new schools without such an assurance.

Witness.—There was a written agreement with Dr. Roe as regards the requisites. Dr. Roe was to provide all the requisites, and he is unable to do so. I have paid nearly £1 a year for the water that the children drink, and the [illegible] of the [illegible]. I am only allowed one ton of coals for the Sunday School.

3462. How much would it cost to keep a school supplied with coal, light, gas, water, &c.?—I believe it would cost between £40 and £50 a year at the very least, and there is no contribution towards it, except in a Model School, or in a school vested in the National Board.

The Archdeacon of Connor.—The expenses of my school do not amount to half the sum just mentioned; my extra expenses are certainly under £10.

3463. *Witness.*—Is it a National School?—No, I have nothing to say to National Schools.

Witness.—That is the explanation.

The Dean of Dromore.—I have built a school-house in Lurgan that will hold 800 children, and it did not cost £800; there is no necessity for spending £1,000 in building a school; £700 would build it.

3464. Dr. Traill.—To hold how many?

The Dean of Dromore.—800.

3465. Professor Dougherty (to *Witness*).—I suppose you go in for necessaries in education before going in for what might be termed luxuries?—I teach algebra, geometry, drawing, book-keeping, or other advanced subjects. I have a science class in connexion with my school, and teach sound, light, heat, and the steam engine, and while I am teaching that, another teacher is teaching magnetism and electricity, and these classes interfere with each other in the same room.

3466. How many boys are running about the streets of Ballymacarrett not going to school at all?—I do not know. We cannot help it if the children will not attend, and the parents seem to have no interest in their attendance; since the results system was introduced they think that it is for the teachers' benefit. Even in Clonallon [illegible] adjoining my school they will not attend.

3467. Do you think Ballymacarrett is sufficiently well provided with schools for its present population?—There are a sufficient number of schools, but those which should be enlarged, because the larger the school, as Mr. Gordon, National School Inspector, says, in his report, the greater is the efficiency.

3468. But you must place the schools at convenient distances and I understand there is a rapid growth of population away from some of the schoolhouses?—There are streets running all over the district.

3469. Rev. Dr. Molloy.—You say that the great bulk of the building is going on round about your school and the church?—Yes.

Mr. M'Elderry.—There is a great deal of building going on in that whole district; it is an important place, as it is near the great ship-building works of Messrs. Harland and Wolff.

3470. Lord Justice FitzGibbon.—The Short Strand School appears to be in a wide street.

Witness.—It is on the Woodstock Road, near the corner.

Mr. M'Elderry.—Dr. Roe's opinion on the matter still is, that the school should be built at a place where there is none at present.

3471. Rev. *Provost Hartrick*.—What distance is that from the church and Mr. Todd's school.

Mr. M'Elderry.—Half an Irish mile. That is the place where Dr. Roe wishes it to be erected, and Mr. Ledley wanted the school built wherever it was most needed. The map also shows the distance it is away from the Short Strand School and it cannot be enlarged.

Witness.—It is a mistake to say that school cannot be enlarged; the teachers' residence could be easily thrown into the school.

3472. Lord Justice FitzGibbon.—I will read the report of William Moore, Principal Teacher of the Beltaire School, Short Strand, regarding those schools:—

"These schools consist of a lower room for infant pupils and an upper room for seniors. The rooms were built about fifty years ago by the Governors of the Erasmus Smith's Board, and the Board paid the ground rent of £2 10s. 0d. till 1878, when they handed over the deed of the place to the Select Vestry of Ballymacarrett, on their appointing trustees and guaranteeing that the place should be used for educational purposes. For many years the schools were merely church schools, but in 1872 they were opened in connexion with the Board of National Education, and were opened on the 1st of January of that year, with an attendance of sixty-eight pupils. From that day have steadily improved, and at the present time there is an average of over 150 children, with a staff of two principal teachers, eight assistants, and [illegible] teachers. The schools have always got good reports from the Board's Inspectors. When these schools were placed in connexion with the National Board, there were but [illegible] National schools in Ballymacarrett, with a population of 18,000; now there are twenty-two schools and a population of about 33,000 in this part of the city. Many of the old schoolhouses have recently been enlarged to double of their original dimensions, and at the present time there is a large school about to be built in connexion with Mount Pottinger Presbyterian Church, and as this room will not be far from us it will be very hard for us to hold our ground unless our rooms are made equal or almost equal to them. The National Board's Inspector urged Dr. Roe to enlarge these schools in 1878, which was then done, and a classroom was added to each again in 1884, but while additional floor space was given, the head room remained the same, and no additional space added to the yards. The ceiling in the lower room is not quite ten feet high, and the upper room about eleven, thus keeping the cubic space very small. At a cost of about £400 or £500 the principal rooms could be increased to nearly double their present dimensions, the ceiling in each one raised to fourteen or fifteen feet, and an additional yard space of 200 square feet added. At present there are only 280 square feet of yard space. I beg to state that it is absolutely necessary for the health of the pupils, the health of the teachers, and the improvement of education, that these schools should be made in keeping with the requirements of the rules of health and the advancement of education. The larger they are, and the better equipped, the better will they be able to do the work, and the higher the character of the schools, the better for Ballymacarrett church and parish."

The *Archdeacon of Connor*.—The Rev. Dr. Hanna is here, and besides being a Commissioner of National Education, he knows a great deal as to the educational requirements of Belfast.

3473. Lord Justice FitzGibbon.—We could form a governing body on which the Diocesan authority and the Parochial authorities would be represented; and power could be given to this body to invest the money, and not spend the principal until they wanted it for building purposes. Power could also be given to them to lay it out upon one school, or two schools, or in what way they thought might suit best.

The *Dean of Dromore*.—We would be quite satisfied with that ourselves.

3474. Lord Justice FitzGibbon.—Do you think the Select Vestry would be ready to take part in this?

Witness.—The Select Vestry are anxious to have the schools enlarged. We will be getting an order to our school at the church, either to turn out scholars or enlarge the school, and I think it very hard after I have worked up the school, and worked so hard also to pay off the debt, as the other teachers have also done. If a new school be built we will have to pay the rest of it, I suppose.

3475. Lord Justice FitzGibbon.—What do you think would be the cost of maintaining a school of the kind mentioned?

Rev. Dr. *Hanna*.—£20 a year.

3476. Lord Justice FitzGibbon.—For what purpose would this be applied?

Rev. Dr. *Hanna*.—For lighting, cleaning and occasional repairs. I suppose there would be rent also but, I think £20 a small sum to pay for lighting, cleaning and general purposes, money is wanted for the maintenance of a school.

Dr. Traill.—Leaving out the ground rent there would be £12 or £15 at any rate, you think, for other purposes.

3477. Lord Justice FitzGibbon.—Is it not desirable to have some little fund for prizes and matters of that kind.

Rev. Dr. *Hanna*.—Certainly, I am taking that into consideration. As to the proposal to build a school near the Queen's Bridge I may say that I have for years felt that there was no place where a school was more required than at the Bridge End there, and if I had got the money I would have had a district school there long ago. There is no doubt to me that a site could be got. I quite agree as to the extension of the other school; the population out there is increasing enormously.

3478. Lord Justice FitzGibbon.—Would it be a healthy place to build a school?

Rev. Dr. *Hanna*.—Well, perhaps, not the healthiest, but a school is required there.

3479. Lord Justice FitzGibbon (to Witness).—To what schools do the children of that district go at present?—They go to other schools in Ballymacarrett and some of them go over the Queen's Bridge to St. George's School.

Rev. Dr. *Hanna*.—I have not the slightest doubt that is quite accurate. If you had an infant school established there you would have an attendance of say 300.

3480. Lord Justice FitzGibbon.—If you do what I have suggested to you, the money could be invested and power given to the local governing body and the clergy to apply the interest to educational purposes until they want the principal for building. It is much more prudent that the building should only be undertaken when all parties are agreed. On the schools there is a debt of £400, on the Church the entire amount of liability is £1,750; this, then, is not the time to undertake another liability. The testator left £1,000 "to be expended in the erection of a school-house in connection with the Church of Ireland in Ballymacarrett." It is with regard to the building of that school-house that the Trustees applied to the Commissioners of Charitable Donations and Bequests. I do not say that an infant school would be the sort of school to erect in Ballymacarrett but those in charge may fall in with the Rev. Dr. Hanna's suggestion.

The *Dean of Dromore*.—For myself I would say that we would be quite willing to comply with that. I think we would settle it very easily if once left in our hands.

3481. Lord Justice FitzGibbon.—How is the money invested at present?

Mr. *M'Ildowie*.—In Government Three per Cents. Some of that will be required for the purchase of a site. We will certainly require a school sooner or later and unless the site be bought soon, the ground will all be bought up. Mr. Ewart has considered that part of Ballymacarrett and perhaps you would examine him on the matter.

William Quartus Ewart examined.

3482. Lord Justice FitzGibbon.—There are not many open spaces at present in the district mentioned?—No, there are very few sites, and I think if we wish to secure the site something must be done very soon. It is a very growing neighbourhood. I agree with Dr. Hanna as to the place for the school.

3483. Dr. Traill.—Then you agree with the Rev. Dr. Ree's suggestion?—I do, and with regard to the enlargement of the existing school they could be enlarged by special efforts.

3484. Do you think it could be done at once, with a debt of £1,100 on the parish, and I think £600 on the parsonage, which is being paid off yearly, and £400 on the schools, for which Dr. Ree is personally responsible?—I don't look upon that as a serious weight on that parish. Crowds of little children are running about, at the place referred to, in danger of being run over by tramcars.

The *Dean of Dromore*.—If you vested the money with the Diocesan Trustees, they would exercise a due discretion as to the expending of it.

Rev. *Professor Herrick*.—Ballymacarrett is a very popular as well as populous district, and it has strong claims on those who live in and around Belfast. If an appeal was made to the public, the amount required for the schools would be obtained before long. The Rev. Dr. Ree would have no difficulty in obtaining it.

Mr. *Ewart*.—I am sure the scheme you propose will be quite satisfactory to Dr. Ree.

James Major (People's Churchwarden), examined.

3485. The population is increasing very much in the neighbourhood of Mr. Todd's school, which is just beside the parish church. In that portion of Ballymacarrett, there have been no less than 1,000 houses recently built, and what is to become of the additional children when you have not accommodation in the present school. The Short Strand School is both unhealthy and overcrowded, and this place where it is

Oct. 22, 1888. Charles R. Todd.

William Quartus Ewart.

James Major.

[illegible]

proposed to build a new school, is a very good place for the manure heaps of the Town Council. When the bequest was left, Dr. Ross took the initiative and is to see this place. I said they had no right to buy any ground, and that it would be foolish to do so, when they had so much ground at the church fron. What they should do with the money of the Ledley Bequest, would be to enlarge that school at the church, and these afterwards call it the Ledley School if they liked. Mr. Moore of the Short Strand School was willing to give up his house in order to have that school enlarged, and in the making of additions to these two schools, the money would be well laid out.

3466. Dr. Traill.—I suppose Mr. Moore would get a residence there?—Oh, yes, and he is ready to do what I have stated.

3467. Do you think that site would be an unwholesome place?—I do.

3468. Professor Dougherty.—I remember when the other parts of Ballymacarrett were not considered particularly salubrious?—Yes, but the Corporation made roads, sewers, &c., and it is not an unhealthy district of the town now at all.

APPLICATION FROM THE ELEMENTARY EDUCATION COMMITTEE OF THE GENERAL ASSEMBLY FOR THE INCORPORATION OF GOVERNING BODIES FOR EDUCATIONAL ENDOWMENTS CONNECTED WITH THE PRESBYTERIAN CHURCH IN IRELAND.

3489. Rev. *H. B. Wilson*, D.D., of Cookstown (Convener of the Elementary Education Committee of the Irish General Assembly).—When I received from the secretary your communication to say that you would receive us to-day, I convened the Elementary Education Committee, and they appointed a small deputation, consisting, amongst others, of the Rev. William Johnston, D.D., the Rev. Hugh Hanna, D.D., and myself. We three are here as part of that deputation. Our schools may be divided into three classes as regards title. One class consists of those that are called vested schools. They are vested in the National Board of Education, and we have nothing to do with them. Another section of our schools may be called church schools—that is to say, the school is of the same standing as the church and manse, and with these congregational schools we do not wish to part. Then there is another large number of schools scattered over the country, built by subscriptions, and supposing the present men were to die off, and this generation passed away with no security, there would be no record of any title to them; and we want to know what counsel you would give us in the matter. The General Assembly embraces five synods and thirty-six presbyteries, and we think it would be a cumbrous thing to have a corporate board for each presbytery. The Belfast Presbytery is large, and some of our western presbyteries are very small. My idea would not be to have thirty-six corporate bodies for our presbyteries. If you advise thirty-six, your advice would be fixed with us.

3490. Lord Justice FitzGibbon.—What do the synods consist of?

Rev. Dr. *Wilson*.—The presbytery consists of the local congregations of the district, and then the synod groups them together.

Lord Justice FitzGibbon.—We had some difficulty the other day where two presbyteries overlapped.

3491. Professor Dougherty.—That never occurs with synods?—No; the synod groups the presbyteries; there are five synods—the Synod of Belfast, the Synod of Dublin, the Synod of Derry and Omagh, the Synod of Armagh and Monaghan, the Synod of Ballymena and Coleraine.

3492. Lord Justice FitzGibbon.—If it so happened that two presbyteries belonged to different synods you would still have two congregations from the same locality in different synods?—I don't think that ever occurs.

Lord Justice FitzGibbon.—No, but it might occur.

3493. Rev. Dr. Molloy (to witness).—The Assembly consists of five synods?—It does.

3494. Is every minister belonging to the General Assembly a member of that Assembly?—Yes; the Assembly consists of every clergyman in the Assembly, and also a layman from every congregation in it.

3495. Lord Justice FitzGibbon.—Each of your bodies is a subdivision of the General Assembly?—Yes, for local convenience. In some cases, where there have been disputes between congregations, they have been put in different presbyteries; but what I wish to point out is, that the Rev. Dr. Johnston, for instance, has a number of schools under his control, and as regards title they are somewhat in danger. What we want is to get some grip of them, in order that they may be made all right in the future.

3496. I do not see what you could do by means of a general body representing the General Assembly; the Assembly does not seem to be connected with the management of property?—The General Assembly would appoint a committee to carry out the details. We have what we call our sustentation capital. I merely give you this as an illustration, and the trustees for it are drawn from each of the five synods of the Assembly. There are clergymen and laymen there from each synod, and a few general trustees besides.

3497. Professor Dougherty.—That is under an Act of Parliament?—Yes, and we would take that as our model here, and not have a large collection of trustees.

3498. Lord Justice FitzGibbon.—We have the power under our Act to incorporate a body. I suppose when one of your trustees dies you have to appoint another one in his place?—We simply ask the synod to which he belonged to nominate another man. It is a mere matter of record by the clerk.

3499. Professor Dougherty.—It is questionable whether a body of that kind would be so vigilant or active as a number of bodies scattered over the country?—If it were not too cumbrous.

Lord Justice FitzGibbon.—There is nothing cumbrous about it at all.

3500. Rev. *William Johnston*, D.D.—Our deputation is very much in the position of people coming to learn, and we have much to learn in this matter. We have a large number of schools, some of which are held by lease, some bought out, some vested in trustees, others vested in the ministers themselves. When I die who is to appoint my successors in these trusts. There are eleven schools in Belfast that would be in that position, as in Belfast there are eleven schools of which I am trustee. As to some of these I may add that I bought the ground out, and built the schools at a cost of £1,800.

3501. Lord Justice FitzGibbon.—Were they conveyed to yourself?—I have them in my own power.

3502. The power is one thing and the legal title is another; supposing you had to sell them who is lessee?—In some cases I am trustee, and in some other cases one of my deacons.

3503. You cannot make a deacon or even a minister a corporation; you may make over property to your deacons or your successors, but instead of going to them it will go to your heir-at-law, or next of kin, or to your executors if you have made a will?—We lost an immense amount of property in Derry, and I think with that experience before us that it would be exceedingly desirable we should get some protection.

3504. The Roman Catholic Church suffered in the same way; some £700 had to be paid to clear up a question of title on the death of one dignitary?—We have suffered in the same way regarding titles; there are a number of cases all over the country which should be attended to, and we want to know what course you would recommend in order to secure our school property to the General Assembly for the purpose for which it was bought and built. In your opening remarks you said something, as I understood, to the effect that you could not act unless you had an endowment to administer; do you recognise school property as an endowment?

Yes; a simple site and the building of a school constitute an endowment.

3505. Rev. Dr. *Johnston*.—How far would this general corporation interfere with the legal rights of the sessions and deacons' courts of our different congregations; would they have power to transfer their rights to that commission so far as our school property is concerned?

Lord Justice FitzGibbon.—We are obliged to define the trusts in the schemes. If you make out a list of the actual endowments you want put into the scheme, we can prepare a draft and correspond with you as to whether you are satisfied with it. You could show that draft to the General Assembly. The same course was adopted in the case of the Methodist College. We prepared a draft, it was afterwards submitted to the Methodist Conference and was agreed to.

3506. Rev. Dr. *Johnston*.—Will you reserve the rights of the deacons' courts and of the minister to make appointments?

Lord Justice FitzGibbon.—Whatever you state what your trusts are, we will define them for you, we won't force anything upon denominational bodies that they are not willing to accept. There are two regulations which every scheme must provide for, namely, that the school accounts shall be publicly audited, as to which we have made arrangements whereby the expense will be merely nominal; and that the school shall be under the inspection of an Inspector appointed by the Lord Lieutenant.

Rev. Dr. *Johnston*.—There is a school we have, and it has been stated that we should take steps to secure our title to it, on the ground that it was not good.

3507. How long have you had it?—Twenty years.

3508. Well twelve years are enough?—The Synod was saying we should get it done, but these attorneys like would frighten anybody.

3509. Nobody can turn you out without proving better title; if you are there for twelve years it is quite enough?—As to the proposed corporate body, our friends here of the dioceses of Down, Connor and Dromore want a scheme for the sphere in which they work; now we as a General Assembly are one family, and if the Assembly adopt this principle, I would like to take the Elementary Education Committee, which has special charge of the Elementary Education question in all its developments, and all communications with the landlords, on the one side and the Mission Board on the other, and I think that would form a fairly impartial tribunal, representing the rights of our Assembly.

3510. How is that Committee appointed?—By the General Assembly.

3511. Is it representative of all the Synods?—It has representatives from almost all the Presbyteries of the Church. We had a very fine old gentleman here in Belfast called John Gray, and on his death he left a large amount for various matters connected with the Presbyterian Church, but he required that those in charge of his bequests should present a report each year to the General Assembly, and that Committee is appointed from year to year to administer the funds left by him. I think it would be an endless thing to appoint a Corporation for every Presbytery in the Assembly; I think one for the whole Church should do.

Dr. Traill.—Or perhaps one for the North of Ireland with a centre in Belfast, and another for the South with a centre in Dublin.

3512. Lord Justice FitzGibbon.—Suppose you had an incorporated general body such as you speak of, it would have charge of these schools all over Ireland, that is wherever you had such schools as we refer to, and suppose a caretaker got into one of them, and refused going out, your large general body would not know so much about the case as a smaller one for the district?—Every one has just to look out for himself.

Rev. Dr. *Hanna*.—I have one school vested in local trustees, and others vested in the National Commissioners. I do not know whether I am bound to submit this matter to your acquaintance or not.

3513. Lord Justice FitzGibbon.—We have no power to meddle with a school where the governing body belongs to one denomination, and the children are of the same denomination.

Rev. Dr. *Hanna*.—The trustees in this case are members of my own congregation, and no difficulty is likely to arise. My Committee have control of it, and I do not know whether this Commission has anything to do with it. We have no difficulty about it, and we don't anticipate any difficulty; I have it clearly, as the Church property does.

3514. Dr. Traill (to Dr. *Johnston*).—You say that you have a good many schools under your control in Belfast?—Yes.

3515. Are they scattered all over the town?—They are.

3516. In the future would the same minister of the same congregation be the only person to hold these same schools scattered all over the town?—No, that remains to be settled.

3517. Your Church does not adopt the parochial system; for instance you might have schools in Dr. Hanna's district, and he might have schools in yours?—Yes, he might.

3518. What I am thinking of is that corporate bodies might overlap under such an agreement.

Rev. Dr. *Hanna*.—That will not occur in Belfast so as to cause any difficulty; there may be some advantages in this, in the country, but I do not see that we require separate corporations. I do not think that in Belfast we are likely to trouble. I don't anticipate any difficulty with regard to my schools.

3519. Rev. Dr. Molloy.—Then are you in favour of leaving things as they are and doing nothing?

Rev. Dr. *Hanna*.—No, I think, we should have a corporate body to take cognisance of our schools, and to which appeal might be made in a case of difficulty.

3520. Lord Justice FitzGibbon.—The only thing we can do is to provide for the future management of this property. If at present, for instance, somebody put up a factory near the school, and sent people into the school-room, who is to sue them, and make them stop it?

Rev. Dr. *Johnston*.—Yes, or build next door to you; some of my brethren have defied the whole Presbytery of Belfast.

Rev. Dr. *Wilson*.—The practical result of this interview I suppose will be, that we as a committee, should gather up all the statistics we can as to our endowments, school-sites and school-houses, and lay them before you.

3521. Lord Justice FitzGibbon.—And if you collect the statistics of any specified locality, we would prepare a draft scheme for that locality for you, and if it met your approval you could have others prepared. If you wait to get information from all over Ireland you will never have it ready.

Rev. Dr. *Wilson*.—By this arrangement which you propose, the property will still be held by the Presbyterian Church subject to the existing trusts?

THE PRESBYTERIAN ORPHAN SOCIETY.

3522. Lord Justice FitzGibbon (to Rev. Dr. Johnston).—In the case of the Presbyterian Orphan Society, you have got securities of all kinds, and as regards some of them, it is doubtful whether you are justified in holding them in the way you do. We could vest all these securities in the existing committee of that Society, making that committee a corporate body.

Rev. Dr. Johnston.—We have about £23,000 invested for our Presbyterian Orphan Society. Our income last year was £11,400. One of our rules is that bequests become regular capital. If we get £1,000 we invest that, and put it into our general fund. Every investment is made by the committee. We have a financial committee and every investment is made with their full knowledge and approval.

3524. I only mention that, as an instance of the powers we have. We could by our act make your Presbyterian Orphan Society identical with the Representative Church Body, that is as regards legal position. Your investments could then be made right once and for all, and you never would have to appoint any more trustees.

Rev. Dr. Johnston.—Your information is most valuable and I will report it to the directors. We administered above £10,000 during the past year, and regarding these orphans, we go into their cases with all care.

BROWN-STREET SCHOOLS, BELFAST.

Rev. Wm. Johnston, D.D., sworn and examined.

Rev. William Johnston, D.D.

3525. Lord Justice FitzGibbon.—You are Secretary of the Brown-street schools?—Yes, and have been for forty years.

3526. How is the committee appointed?—At the annual meeting, every year.

3527. The schools are maintained largely by public subscription?—Yes.

3528. How are the buildings held?—The Brown-street Sunday and Daily Schools Society was formed in 1812. In 1836 the Rev. Mr. Brown and his brother, who were proprietors of the soil, made an order giving them over to Wm. Clarke, Robert Magee, and James Blair, three trustees, to hold them for educational purposes. That continued up to 1853, when Mr. Brown's property went into the Incumbered Estates Court, and we went in, and bought our interest out. It was only a nominal sum we had to pay, and now we hold by Incumbered Estates Court title.

3529. To whom did the Incumbered Estates grant the property?—To John Clarke, Robert Magee, and John Getty—all dead.

3530. It was given to them—

"for the use, benefit, and advantage of the committee for the time being of the Brown-street Sunday School, and subject to an indenture of demise, bearing date the 8th day of March, in the year 1836, made by the Rev. John Brown, and Alex. Gordon Brown, to William Clarke, Robert Magee, and James Blair,"—

for certain lives?—Yes. There is a transfer of the property from the original trustees to the present gentlemen. That was on the 7th of January, 1864, and the trustees now are Robert Lindsay Wilson, and William M'Neill. The only thing I have is a duplicate of the conveyance.

3531. Is there any invested money belonging to the schools?—No.

3532. What is the qualification of subscribers?—It is 5s. 6d. Here are our report for last year, and our rules—

"Any person who, at one or more payments, shall have subscribed £10 to this Society, shall be a guardian. The executors of any person bequeathing a legacy of £10 to the Society, shall be guardians. Every person giving a [illegible] of ten guineas shall be a member for life. Every person subscribing 5s. 6d. annually shall be a member during the continuance of such subscription."

The affairs of the Society are managed by a committee consisting of thirty members (subscribers of at least 5s. each), five of whom shall be a quorum. They are unendowed schools, and I have already stated the last trustees were appointed in 1864. We have spent £116 there on repairs.

3533. Dr. Traill.—What corporate body would you suggest for these schools?—Oh, no corporate body at all. We take in Presbyterians and Episcopalians, and we will, on the ground of charity, take in Methodists also. The schools are prosperous. According to the rules:—

"(1) The Sunday school shall be exclusively devoted to the reading and study of the Holy Scriptures, and such other means of religious instruction as the directors, managers, and teachers may be able to advise and employ. (2) The object of the Daily Schools shall be to furnish such instruction in reading, writing, and arithmetic, and other branches of education as may prepare the pupils for usefulness in life; to train them up in the habits of cleanliness and regularity, and to afford to all a free and unrestricted access to the reading and study of the Holy Scriptures."

We put no man on the committee, or in any office, who does not pay his way, and support the charity.

3534. The Rev. Dr. Donald (Methodist).—As the Brown-street schools have been undenominational from the beginning, and the committee are agreed to continue them as such, I think it is only right that the word undenominational should be inserted.

3535. Dr. Traill.—By undenominational you mean as regards Protestants?—Certainly.

3536. Professor Dougherty.—There are no Roman Catholics connected with the schools?—No.

Rev. Dr. Johnston.—The schools are conducted so as to secure perfect liberty of conscience to all who go there.

This concluded the inquiry.

PUBLIC SITTING—SATURDAY, OCTOBER 27, 1888.

At the Courthouse, Carrickfergus.

Present:—The Right Hon. Lord Justice FitzGibbon, Judicial Commissioner; and the Rev. Gerald Molloy, D.D., D.SC., Anthony Traill, Esq., LL.D., M.D., F.T.C.D., and Professor Dougherty, M.A., Assistant Commissioners.

The Assistant Secretary, N. D. Murphy, jun., was in attendance.

Lord Justice FitzGibbon made an introductory statement.

CARRICKFERGUS PAROCHIAL SCHOOL.

Rev. *George Chamberlain*, Incumbent of Carrickfergus, sworn and examined.

3537. Lord Justice FitzGibbon.—Is Carrickfergus Parochial School under your management?—Yes.

3538. What is the endowment of the school?—Here is an extract from the will of Ezekiel D. Wilson, dated November 3, 1818—

"I give and devise to the rector of the parish and his successors for ever, one annuity or yearly rentcharge of forty guineas, to be issuing and payable out of all my estates and property, and to be paid by him as a salary for a schoolmaster to instruct forty poor boys and twenty girls of the parish of Carrickfergus. I devise that the Lord Bishop of Down and Connor, and the Dean of Connor for the time being, shall have the nomination, appointment, and power of removing such schoolmaster; and it is my wish that the person to be appointed by them should engage to take the children, who shall be entrusted to his care, to church every Sunday, and that he shall be qualified to instruct them in psalmody."

3539. Is the school in operation?—It is in operation.

3540. You are in possession of it?—I am.

3541. It appears from the Report of 1858 that the school house was erected in 1819 on a free site granted by Lord [illegible]?—I am a comparative stranger in the parish; I have been here only about two years.

3542. But you have not paid any rent during that period?—No.

3543. What do the premises consist of?—Of a boys' school and a girls' school; the boys' school is below, and the girls' school upstairs.

3544. Are there any outoffices or playground?—No; there is a little yard in front and another little yard in the rere.

3545. Is the school in connexion with the National Board?—Yes; that I think was effected in 1884.

3546. Originally the school got a grant from Erasmus Smith's Board?—Yes.

3547. What is the average attendance?—The average attendance in the boys' school is about forty-nine.

3548. How is the Wilson rentcharge applied?—We keep the bulk of it for the master; of course the schoolmaster does not teach the girls. I found an arrangement here when I came, that the mistress gets a proportion for teaching the girls. There are two mistresses, one for the infants and the other for the girls, and they get a fair proportion of it.

3549. Are there many girls educated free?—There are a good many who do not pay and some who pay the fees.

3550. Do you make any distinction between the free pupils and the others?—No.

3551. What class is the male teacher?—First of second class, and I think the mistress in the girls' school is second of first.

3552. What is the average attendance in the girls' school?—About forty-nine or fifty, probably forty-nine.

3553. And what is it in the infant school?—I think this year it is forty-five.

3554. What are the numbers on the rolls?—The numbers on the rolls are sixty-two boys; girls, sixty-nine, and infants, sixty four.

3555. Did the Bishop and the Dean of Connor appoint the present teacher?—They concurred in the appointment on my recommendation; I have their approval.

3556. Have you any local committee helping you?—No; it is all in my own hands.

3557. Do you think it would be an advantage to have such a committee?—No, I do not think it would.

3558. You would rather have the management in your own hands?—Yes.

3559. Dr. Traill.—Would it not be better to have a few persons associated with you in the management of the school?—No, it is a very simple matter.

3560. Lord Justice FitzGibbon.—What are the religious denominations of the children attending the school?—Episcopalians, Presbyterians, Independents, Methodists, and Baptists. In the girls' school there are forty-two Church, sixteen Presbyterians, six Independents, three Methodists, and two Baptists. In the boys' school, forty-nine Irish Church, six Presbyterians, five Independents, and two Methodists; and in the infants' school, fifty-seven Irish Church, four Independents, and three Presbyterians.

3561. Professor Dougherty.—Have you any free Presbyterian pupils?—We have.

3562. Lord Justice FitzGibbon.—What other National schools are there in Carrickfergus?—There are the Model school, a Methodist school, a Roman Catholic school, a Mill school, and two Presbyterian schools. The Mill school is connected with Messrs. Taylors mill.

3563. What is the attendance at the Model schools?—I do not know.

3564. Do you not visit there?—I do visit there, but I do not know the numbers.

3565. How many Church children are there?—More than thirty.

3566. Professor Dougherty.—I suppose you have not the means of teaching extra subjects here?—We have not the appliances for some subjects, but the teacher is competent to give such instruction, and does so.

3567. In a previous report regarding the school it was mentioned that reading, writing, arithmetic, geography, grammar, mensuration, Euclid, algebra, Scripture, drawing, and music were taught?—They are all taught still; I am not sure about drawing in the boys' school, but in the girls' school it is.

3568. Lord Justice FitzGibbon.—Are you connected with South Kensington?—No.

Oct. 26, 1888.

Rev. George Chamberlain.

3569. Are your teachers qualified to give education in the Science and Art classes?—The master is, but the mistress not.

3570. The Report of 1880 states that the Christian Knowledge Society, in return for an annual subscription of £5, gave books and other prizes to the value of £10. Do you still get that £10 worth of books and other prizes from the Christian Knowledge Society?—No, we do not.

3571. What is the master's salary?—At present he gets £33 6s. 8d. I should explain that in consequence of the female teacher having a number of small boys, relatives of the girls attending her school, I raised her portion a little, and she gets £10 a year now. The endowment is apportioned to supplement the salary of the three teachers—one male and two females—but the master receives the largest share.

3572. What does the teacher of the infant school get?—She gets £6 13s. 4d. a year.

3573. Who built the school?—It was built by Dean Chaine.

3574. But it appears also to have had a grant of £300 from the Governors of Erasmus Smith's schools, and £300 from public subscriptions; do you know who keeps the title deed of the site or where it is?—I never discovered that.

3575. Was Dean Chaine Rector of Carrickfergus?—He was.

3576. Who are the governing body of the school now?—The Bishop, the Dean, and myself. I believe the Bishop would have been here today had he been well.

3577. Dr. Traill.—Would it not be a benefit to you to have a scheme and to have these questions of title settled; if the deeds are not forthcoming about this site you might have considerable difficulty in the matter?—I have made no particular inquiries about them.

3578. Who are the representatives of Dean Chaine?—I do not know.

3579. Who pays you this salary?—Mr. O. A. W. Stewart, m.a., the agent for the Wilson estate.

3580. Rev. Dr. Molloy.—You think you are getting on very well?—Yes.

3581. The persons to have control of this school were to be the Lord Bishop of Down and Connor, the Dean of Connor, and the Incumbent of Carrickfergus; the children were all to be of one denomination, and it was directed that they were to be taken to church every Sunday; is that done?—Well, he does not actually take them by the hand, but he encourages them to go.

3582. We have it here that he was to take the children to church on Sundays, and teach them singing; does he do that?—He does, and so does the mistress, but it is utterly impossible that he could take forty children to church; he encourages them to attend church.

3583. Lord Justice FitzGerald.—This does not come within our jurisdiction; but if the governing body consents we might arrange for associating some members of the select vestry with you as a committee to look after the school and get subscriptions for its maintenance and improvement?—I feel I could do nothing without consulting the Bishop and Dean.

3584. You might consult with the Bishop and Dean, and you could also tell them that the expense of a scheme, should they decide upon having one, would be something about one pound or thirty shillings?—I could consult them on the subject.

3585. There is a sum of £300 of Miss Lee's; how is that invested?—Oh, that is for the poor. I get the money from Mr. White, the Presbyterian minister; it is divided between the ministers of the Established and Dissenting Churches in Carrickfergus; I do not know where the money comes from.

3586. There is nothing of an educational character in it?—No.

3587. If you thought of forming a corporate body for your parish they could hold property for other purposes, and you could get a number of gentlemen on your select vestry to act?—Yes.

[Oct. 27, 1888.

PUBLIC SITTING—SATURDAY, OCTOBER 27, 1888.

At the Grammar School, Larne.

Present:—The Rev. Gerald Molloy, d.d., d.sc., Anthony Traill, Esq., ll.d., m.d., f.t.c.d., and Professor Dougherty, m.a., Assistant Commissioners.

The Assistant Secretary, N. D. Murphy, Junr., was in attendance.

LARNE GRAMMAR SCHOOL.

Professor Dougherty made an introductory statement.

Rev. James Kennedy sworn, and examined.

Rev. James Kennedy.

3588. Professor Dougherty.—You are secretary to the trustees of the Larne Grammar School?—Yes; and a trustee also.

3589. What is the date of the foundation?—The 9th of March, 1886 (original deed produced).

3590. Can you tell us the source from which the endowment is derived?—There were £2,000 given by Mr. John Crawford, of Larne, and subsequently he gave £250 more for the erection of the wall in front, and the erection of a gatekeeper's house, railing, &c. There were also £1,000 received from Sir Edward Coey together with this site which consists of 1 acre 3 roods and 18 perches, at a shilling a year for 1,000 years.

3591. How much was expended on the building?—The contract for the building was £2,080, but there were some few extras. The cost of building the school was £2,230 approximately. The estimate was £1,980.

3592. What has been done with the balance?—£1,000 of Mr. Crawford's money is a permanent investment to pay the salary of the head master, and there are £400 more to keep up the school buildings.

3593. Have you additional endowments from any other source?—No, but we live in hope; the present endowment is the site, the buildings, and £1,400 invested. I believe the money is lent to the Harbour Commissioners under bond at 4½ per cent.

3594. What is the character of the school?—It is

to be strictly non-sectarian, to give a good liberal English and Classical education, and the principles of Christianity are to be taught.

3595. The trust deed states—

"The instruction afforded in the school shall be the fundamental principles of the Christian religion, the Greek and Latin languages, mathematics, algebra, arithmetic, a modern Continental language, general English literature and composition, sacred and profane history, geography, reading, and writing, and also such other languages, arts, and sciences, as the trustees may from time to time think expedient, so as to give the scholars a sound moral, religious, and liberal education."

(To Witness.)—The school is intended for boys only?—Yes, but under certain circumstances we can admit girls.

3596. But it requires the unanimous vote of the trustees to do so?—Yes.

3597. As regards investment you have tolerably wide powers?

Mr. M'Neill (Solicitor to the School).—They are rather wider than the ordinary powers.

3598. Professor Dougherty (to Witness).—Who are the trustees?—The Rev. John Lyle Donaghy, Rev. James Kennedy, Malcolm M'Neill, Edward Coey, David Nelson, Charles Hewitt, and Hugh Smiley.

3599. Rev. Dr. Molloy.—What provision is there for the continuance of the trustees?—The trust deed fully explains that—

"The number of the trustees shall not be increased beyond seven, and shall not be reduced below four, and where a trustee of these presents either original or substituted and whether appointed by a court or otherwise is dead or remains out of the United Kingdom for more than twelve months, or desires to be discharged from the trusts or powers hereby reposed in, or conferred on him, or refuses or becomes unfit to act in the trusts and powers hereof, or is incapable of acting therein, or ceases to reside within twenty miles of the town of Larne, afterwards then the said John Crawford and Sir Edward Coey, and the survivor of them, and after the death of such survivor then the surviving or continuing or retiring trustee or trustees for the time being of these presents, or the personal representatives of the last surviving or continuing trustee, may, by writing, appoint another person or other persons to be a trustee or trustees in the place of the trustee dead or remaining out of the United Kingdom, desiring to be discharged, refusing, or being unfit, or being incapable, or ceasing to reside as aforesaid. Provided always that if at any time after the death of the survivor of the said John Crawford and Sir Edward Coey, the minister for the time being of the First Presbyterian Church of Larne, and the minister for the time being of the Old Presbyterian Church of Larne, shall not both be trustees of these presents, then the person to be selected to fill any vacancy therein existing, and the number of the trustees of these presents shall be the minister for the time being of the said First Presbyterian Church of Larne, or the minister of the said Old Presbyterian Church of Larne, if such minister is not then a trustee of these presents, and is willing and fit to act, and capable of acting as such trustee, and resides within five miles of the said town of Larne."

3600. Professor Dougherty.—Is Mr. Crawford a member of your congregation?—Yes.

3601. Sir Edward Coey was a Presbyterian?

Mr. Hendren.—Yes, and worshipped in the First Presbyterian Church.

3602. Rev. Dr Molloy.—You have no Catholic on the board of trustees?

Witness.—No.

3603. And the trust deed is drawn up in such a way as to ensure that none shall ever be on it?—No, I don't say that, and I would be glad if we had one. We can select whom we will.

3604. A board composed entirely of Protestants is not likely to elect Catholics?—I have not sufficient experience to allow me to speak.

3605. Who nominated the first trustees?—The donors.

3606. They have excluded Roman Catholics?—Practically they have not done so.

3607. Dr. Traill.—Is there any denominational clause required for a trustee?—I don't believe there is.

3608. Rev. Dr. Molloy.—At all events there is little probability of a Catholic being elected now?—If you get me a man of social position who is able and ready to act, I venture to say that the first vacancy which occurs he will get it.

3609. And why did you not put him on at first?—Well, generally speaking, the Roman Catholics separate themselves from us on all educational questions.

3610. Dr. Traill.—Have you had any Roman Catholic pupils at the school?—No, none.

3611. Professor Dougherty.—Do you wish to have a governing body incorporated? Naturally I would like to do anything for the future prosperity of the school.

3612. If a draft scheme were framed would you wish to make provision for having a representation of subscribers on the governing body?—I am not prepared to answer any questions of that kind.

3613. Rev. Dr. Molloy.—In whom are the school and land vested?—In the trustees, but we would consider it invidious to do anything regarding the school contrary to Mr. Crawford's wishes.

3614. Dr. Traill.—Is Mr. Crawford here to-day?—No, he cannot be here. He is very frail.

R. M. Jones (Head Master), sworn and examined.

3615. Rev. Dr. Molloy.—You are head master of the school?—Yes.

3616. When did you commence your duties here?—On the 10th of April.

3617. Who appointed you?—The governing body; the trustees.

3618. You were appointed in accordance with this deed of trust?—Yes; I know what I was appointed to do.

3619. How many pupils have you?—I have forty-three; twenty from the town itself, and twenty-three from the surrounding districts. I have nine boarders.

3620. To what denominations do the pupils belong?—There are twenty-five Presbyterians, eight Non-Subscribing Presbyterians, ten Episcopalians, and no others.

3621. Are your boarders of different denominations?—Of the nine boarders, four are Presbyterians and five Episcopalians.

3622. And you do not find any practical inconvenience in this arrangement?—None whatever.

3623. Have you any assistant teachers?—I have two at present; one for the whole period of the day, and the other for four hours.

3624. What are their qualifications?—One was a teacher of the Intermediate School that existed here before this school was commenced, but does not exist now; that is the permanent master, and the other one is an undergraduate in the Royal University, reading for his degree this year. He has not gone in for his examination yet, but is preparing for it.

3625. Professor Dougherty.—Where were you before you came here?—I was with Mr. Dick in the Academical Institution, Londonderry.

3626. How long were you there?—About two years.

3627. And prior to that?—In the Royal Academical Institution, Belfast.

3628. Where did you graduate?—In the Royal University.

3629. In what subjects did you take your degree?—Classics.

3630. I suppose you take charge of the classical department here?—Yes, and the English.

Oct. 17, 1888.

Rev. James Kennedy.

R. M. Jones.

Oct. 27, 1886.

R. H. Jones.

3631. And your assistants take mathematics?—Yes, and French also, in which I share.

3632. You had a distinguished career at the Royal University?—I was an Exhibitioner at the Royal University, first class.

3633. You aim at carrying out the idea of giving a non-sectarian education, with instruction in the non-sectarian principles of the Christian religion?—Yes; I do not teach religion at all; I have no set time for it.

3634. Rev. Dr. Molloy.—Is it not taught in your school?—No.

3635. What about the boarders?—I carry out the wishes of their parents, and they go to the churches which their parents select.

3636. Do they get any religious instruction?—I read the Scriptures every day.

3637. Dr. Traill.—You consider the Scriptures a fair basis for the Christian religion?—Yes.

3638. Are they not read every day in school?—No, not for the day boys; they are for the boarders.

3639. Professor Dougherty.—I suppose there is no wish expressed by the parents in the matter?—No; the school is conducted on the same principle as the Academical Institution in Belfast.

3640. And Dr. Steen, there has boarders of different denominations?—Yes.

3641. Have you drawing classes?—No.

3642. Have you French and German taught?—Yes.

3643. How do you provide for the teaching of these subjects?—It is hard enough; I take the German myself; one boy wants German.

3644. Is there any demand for drawing?—There would be if I had a teacher for it, but the fees would not nearly come up to the amount I should have to pay him.

3645. Does your proximity to Belfast not enable you to obtain teachers for special subjects?—There is no difficulty in getting the teachers if you pay the salary, but if you cannot pay the salary you do not get the proper class of men; you get birds of passage.

3646. What is your salary?—I have £35 a year.

3647. That is the interest of the £1,000 invested for the payment of the master's salary?—I presume so, and then I have the fees.

3648. Dr. Traill.—How many terms have you in the year?—Four.

3649. Do most of these boys take all these courses or only the first or the prospectus?—I have twenty-three boys who take only the English and mathematical course.

3650. That is course No. 3?—I have twenty boys who take course No. 1; they take English, mathematics, and some other subjects, such as classics or French. That makes up the forty-three boys.

3651. Your boarders, I see, pay eight guineas a term?—Yes, unless they are under thirteen years, or unless there are brothers.

3652. If over thirteen years of age are your terms raised?—If a boy comes to me as a boarder under the age of thirteen, it is not raised on him till he is fourteen; that is to encourage early attendance. I have had boarders since the 3rd of September.

3653. I thought you were appointed in April?—Yes, but I lived in lodgings until recently.

3654. Rev. Dr. Molloy.—You have no connexion with South Kensington at present?—No.

3655. Dr. Traill (to Rev. Mr. Kennedy).—I would like to ask you as to your interpretation of part of the trust deed. We are told that the pupils are to receive "a sound, moral, religious, and liberal education," and also that "the instruction afforded in the school shall be the non-sectarian principles of the Christian religion"; did you understand that this subject was to be taught in the school or only to the boarders?

Rev. *James Kennedy*.—Oh, no, I thought it was not to be taught to all.

3656. Dr. Traill.—Do you think the reading of the Scriptures would be a carrying out of the principle or a violation of it?

Mr. *Kennedy*.—I think it would be a carrying of it out.

3657. Dr. Traill.—Did your trustees instruct you in that effect?

Mr. *Kennedy*.—No.

3658. Professor Dougherty.—Is there any other trustee who would like to be examined?

Mr. *David Nelson*, J.P.—I am a trustee, and I think we have nothing to add to what has been already said.

Rev. *John Lyle Dunlop* (First Larne Presbyterian Church).—I have nothing to say.

3659. Dr. Traill.—Does Mr. M'Neill take any interest in the school? How often do your trustees meet?

Rev. Mr. *Kennedy*.—As often as we consider it necessary we call a meeting.

3660. Has Mr. M'Neill attended?—I do not remember him coming last year.

3661. Do the trustees attend fairly well?—(Mr. *Jones*, head master.)—Yes, they have come up sufficiently well.

Rev. F. P. Morgan, Rector of Larne, sworn and examined.

Rev. F. P. Morgan.

3662. Dr. Traill.—Is there any evidence you would like to give or suggestion you would like to make?—I observed in the evidence, it was stated that there were twenty-five Presbyterians, eight non-subscribing Presbyterians, and I know, as a fact, that there are ten members of the Church of Ireland.

3663. Yes, it was stated that there were ten members of your Church. Of these ten, five are boarders and five day boys.

Witness.—But it is not made quite clear what is meant by a non-sectarian Christian religion.

3664. Professor Dougherty.—There is no doubt the principle laid down in the trust deed is the non-sectarian principle.

Rev. Mr. *Kennedy*.—Quite right.

3665. Dr. Traill.—This money was given by a Non-Subscribing Presbyterian, and a Presbyterian, and they have a perfect right as donors to select their own governing body, and in selecting Mr. M'Neill, they do not profess to take him as a member of the Church of Ireland, but they were anxious to have him on the Board of Trustees.

Witness.—I think I heard one of the gentlemen say that the Roman Catholics would be represented if there was any one to claim the office.

3666. Rev. Dr. Molloy.—I think it is quite evident that the founders of this institution did not wish to put Roman Catholics on the Board, and yet they call it undenominational.

Rev. Mr. *Kennedy*.—I think your language is rather hard in saying that they did not wish to put Roman Catholics on the Board. Had there been a Catholic able and willing, and in a proper social position they would have put him on.

3667. Rev. Dr. Molloy.—In the existing state of things they did not put a Catholic on.

Rev. Mr. *Kennedy*.—I object to the expression that they did not wish. I am sure that nobody was consulted who refused to act.

3668. Rev. Dr. Molloy.—We know nothing of their intentions; but the fact is, that there is no Catholic on the Board.

Mr. *Jones* (Head Master).—There is no member of the Wesleyan Church on it either.

Witness.—If it is made clear that the non-sectarian principles of the Christian religion are not obligatory.

3669. Dr. Traill.—But that is not made clear at all.

Rev. Mr. *Kennedy*.—The teacher must give religious instruction.

Mr. Nolan, A.B.—That is meant by the donors.

Rev. J. L. Donaghy.—The two ministers on the board cannot give this religious instruction.

3670. Dr. Traill.—No, that must be left to the master.

Rev. Mr. Donaghy.—Yes.

3671. And he does not give any at present except to his boarders?—Yes, and he may regard it as obligatory on him to teach the non-sectarian "principles of the Christian religion" to every pupil.

Witness.—As long as Mr. James is here it is perfectly satisfactory, but I do not know who Mr. James's successor may be.

3672. Dr. Traill.—According to the terms of the trust, "The instruction afforded in the school shall be the non-sectarian principles of the Christian religion." I cannot see any other non-sectarian basis for the Christian religion than to read the Bible without note or comment.

Professor Dougherty.—It is a question for the trustees.

3673. Rev. Dr. Molloy.—Of course the founders have full power to define the principles on which the school is to be conducted; but I want to ask you whether you consider the system of giving instruction in the non-sectarian principles of religious belief satisfactory to the members of your Church?—No.

3674. Professor Dougherty.—If there was the reading of the Scripture without note or comment, would that be acceptable to you?—Oh, perfectly acceptable.

3675. When you said to Dr. Molloy that this principle was not acceptable to the members of your Church, you meant where the reading of the Bible was omitted?—No, I meant when the reading of the Scriptures is accompanied with the instruction specified in the clause.

3676. I should be glad to hear from you what you consider a satisfactory method of religious education under the terms of this deed of trust?—To have the Scriptures read without note or comment.

3677. Dr. Traill.—You think if the Bible were read without note or comment it would be a fair interpretation of the words that the scholars should receive "a sound moral, religious, and liberal education"?—I think it would be.

3678. If that were done you would be inclined to support the school as purely undenominational?—I would. But I believe at the same time that the right solution of the difficulty is to strike out the clause altogether.

John A. Bowman examined.

3679. The question which arises in my mind with regard to the discussion on this subject is simply this—it seems to me by the trust deed that the trustees are to see that instruction in the non-sectarian principles of religion is to be carried out, and so far as my mind is concerned I see a great difference between a sincere and simple reading of the Scriptures.

3680. Dr. Traill.—How would you propose to get out of the difficulty?—My view would be to give more than a mere reading of the Scriptures. There is a difficulty, but it states that instruction of this kind should be given. The education is to be "religious" as well as "liberal."

3681. Do you not think the best plan on the whole is to read the Bible without note or comment?—Well, really, I do not know.

Rev. Mr. Morgan.—I think the phrase in the deed a very unhappy one.

3682. Dr. Traill.—Will you give us your opinion as to how you think we can carry out the terms of the deed except by reading the Scriptures without note or comment?—It is difficult, but I think we should get out of the difficulty best by reading it without note or comment.

Professor Dougherty.—I am afraid we are drifting into a discussion on theological questions, and we had better avoid that.

3683. Dr. Traill.—Does anyone know of any other way of carrying out the words stated in the deed. There appears to be no other method except the one I have suggested. I have asked every one in the room, and I have got no other suggestion. Mr. Morgan himself admits there is no other way if the clause must be retained, and every one else seems to be of the same opinion.

Rev. John Nolan, Roman Catholic Curate, sworn and examined.

3684. Professor Dougherty.—You wish to make a statement?—I have not much to state for I have learned all I know about this institution since I came here today. I have been in Larne since 22nd April, 1887, and so far as I know no member of our community was consulted regarding it.

3685. Dr. Traill.—Were you curate all that time, or parish priest?—Curate.

3686. Do you know the founders of the endowment?—I have seen Mr. Crawford and the other gentlemen. I have no personal acquaintance with them.

3687. Professor Dougherty.—Have any pupils of your community attended the school?—No.

3688. Is there a large Roman Catholic community in Larne?—I cannot say exactly. We have two National schools, exclusively Catholic, in Larne. In the boys school there are 180. In the girls school there are 130.

3689. Are these both National schools?—Yes.

3690. Among the boys attending your National school is there a considerable demand for higher education?—I think there is a fair proportion for higher education if it were afforded.

3691. How do you judge of that?—Well, from the social position of their parents, and the abilities of the pupils.

3692. Is there any provision in the town of Larne for giving education in a way that would be satisfactory to them?—No provision.

3693. What is the nearest Intermediate school under Roman Catholic management?—The nearest school of a higher grade is St. Malachy's College, the Diocesan College at Belfast.

3694. Have you any boys in attendance at that school?—We have had one boy going to it.

3695. A day boy?—Yes.

3696. Have you had boarders?—Yes, formerly, but not for some time past. In my time there were two of our boys at the Ballymena College. There is another boy at Highgate.

3697. Are the boys who attend St. Malachy's College preparing for professions?—For mercantile life.

3698. Dr. Traill.—What proportion of your boys would you consider likely to require an Intermediate education, taking into account their abilities and the social position of their parents?—I have never considered the question.

3699. Would you say one-fourth, one-fifth, one-third, or one-half?—I have never considered the question.

3700. How many boys in your National school have you in the fifth and sixth classes?—Over thirty. In reference to sending boys to Belfast by train, we would discourage them, as we consider it demoralising to have them daily travelling up and down by train.

3701. Professor Dougherty.—Would you take advantage of a school in Larne?—Yes.

3702. And this Larne Grammar School is not satisfactory to you as now conducted?—By no means.

Oct. 24, 1888.

Rev. John Kelso.

3703. Could you indicate any way that it could be made satisfactory and advantageous to your people?—Well there are so many conflicting parties to make it agreeable to—so many communities to be satisfied, that it would be difficult to devise to make this school acceptable to our congregation.

3704. Would representation on the governing body diminish the difficulties of your people with regard to the school?—Well so long as religious instruction will be carried out in the way mentioned here to-day I am afraid that we could not be satisfied.

3705. Dr. TRAILL.—That is taking it as carried out as now, when there is no religious instruction given at all. Would your boys attend provided they got religious instruction?—I am afraid they would not. We object to religious instruction apart from secular education.

3706. But under the National Board don't you separate religious and secular education? Must you not do so according to the rules of the National Board?—But we have there a time set apart for religious instruction, and we have a guarantee there that the boys are placed under the proper kind of teachers—that they are placed under teachers of a moral and virtuous character.

3707. Rev. Dr. MOLLOY.—They do not profess to teach religion, but they inculcate the moral principles of the Christian religion?—They profess to teach the "unsectarian principles of the Christian religion," or, in other words, a negative religion, with which Catholics, whose belief is based upon *positive* principles, can have no part.

3708. Dr. TRAILL.—But during four hours they do not teach any negative religion?—No; not during those four hours.

3709. Your difficulty then is that the teacher must be a Roman Catholic?—No, it is not that.

3710. Your difficulty is that the children must be taught by a Roman Catholic in secular as well as in religious matters?—Well, I do not think that is a fair interpretation.

3711. I do not want to take any advantage of you, but you state that in your National school, even in secular matters they are under Roman Catholic teachers, and you think that they must be taught in secular matters by Roman Catholics?—I have made no statement to justify you in saying that.

3712. But didn't you make that statement, that the difference between this school and the National Board school was that the teacher must be a Roman Catholic in one case, and it is not so here?—We have power to enter the National schools and teach religious instruction for half-an-hour, and our children are under Catholic teachers, and our schools are under Catholic management.

3713. Professor DOUGHERTY.—The great difficulty with you is that the principle upon which this school is founded is at variance with what you consider the true principles of education?—Yes. With reference to the words of the secretary I wish to draw attention. He said, regarding the appointment of trustees, that there was no Catholic gentleman in the community who was in a social position suitable to be appointed. The secretary and the Board of Trustees know well that there is a Catholic gentleman in the community who is thoroughly qualified to take his position on any Board, and that gentleman is my parish priest.

3714. Dr. TRAILL.—But would he be willing to act on this Board?—As far as I know he has not been asked.

3715. Would he be willing to act from what you now know—would he be willing to act now?—(No answer.)

Rev. Mr. *Kennedy* (secretary of the Larne Grammar School).—I may say that I had not the slightest idea when I made the remark of intending it as an insult to any person.

Witness.—But I am not taking it in that way.

3716. Rev. *John Lyle Dunlop* (Presbyterian Minister).—If you were appointed on the Board would that satisfy you?

3717. Dr. TRAILL.—I think he has proved that neither he nor the parish priest could sit on the Board.

Witness.—I have learned since I came here that this institution is for the people of Larne of all denominations. We are part of the people of Larne, and if that endowment is given to the people of Larne, we have a claim to some portion of it—that is if it was given for the benefit of all denominations.

3718. Dr. TRAILL.—But the endowment was not given on any such terms for all denominations. It was only given under specific directions, which you repudiate in this room. How can you have a claim on the endowment?—If the endowment has been given for the education of the people of Larne of all denominations, then why as a part of that people have we not a right to some of it?

3719. But it was not given on those terms; it was given on terms that you repudiate. How do you say it was given to Roman Catholics if you repudiate the terms upon which it was given?—If this institution is founded, not for the entire community, but for a section of the community, then of course the thing is different, and we freely waive all claim.

3720. It is for the whole community, if you will accept the terms of the donors, but you repudiate those terms and yet you claim a share of it. It was not given for any special section of the community: it is open to all sections of the community on certain conditions. Can a man not make his will as he likes? And if men leave an endowment on certain conditions, you cannot come forward and ask us to remove those conditions in order that you may get a share of the property?

3721. Rev. Dr. MOLLOY.—I understand you to say that although it was the intention of the founders to make the endowment available to all denominations, it is not so in fact, because the conditions are such as practically to exclude Catholics. That is my view of the question.

3722. Dr. TRAILL.—Having heard the whole evidence of the intention of the founders, would you not consider that you had no claim against it?—I wrote to the Commissioners for information about the school some time ago, but they were unable to give me any; consequently I am labouring under a disadvantage here to-day, because I have only learned the state of the institution and the terms of the Deed of Trust since I came into the room.

3723. We are all in that position. Do you mean that you want to take a share of the money and set up a separate school?—It would require some time to study that, but I believe it was the intention of the founders of the institution to give every member of the community an opportunity of receiving a higher education here at home, and, as far as I can at present form an opinion, I believe they did not intend to exclude the Catholics.

3724. Nobody said they did; but I understand you to claim not to be admitted along with the Protestants, but separate from the Protestants—is not that what you want?—If they intended to give us a share in the endowment we have a right to a share in it.

3725. As I said, do you mean that you wish to take a share of the money and set up a separate school with it—do you mean to get a separate portion of the money and hand it over to the Roman Catholic community?—I mean the Roman Catholic community should not be deprived of the benefits it has a right to. I think our children have a right to a separate share.

3726. A separate share of this money?—Yes.

3727. Do you really think that was the intention of the founders?—Yes. It has been distinctly shown in evidence that they did not intend to exclude us.

3728. They say the school is to be strictly undenominational, and yet you think that part of the money should be given to a strictly denominational school in a community to which they themselves did not belong?—I think the intention of the donors should be carried out with reference to our community, and that it should get a share of the endowment.

3729. You think, although they meant it was to be a strictly non-sectarian institution, that portion of the money should be taken and handed over for a mixed to a denomination to which they themselves did not belong?—I am sure they did not want to exclude our congregation.

3730. Mr. *David Nelson*, J.P.—One of the donors, Mr. Crawford, who has been my partner for thirty years, intended that it was to be a school for all denominations who were willing to avail themselves of it.

3731. Dr. Traill.—You do not think it was his intention to make it a denominational school?

Mr. *Nelson*.—No, certainly not; he has given £100 to every Church in Larne, including the Roman Catholic Church. The trust deed was drawn up very carefully, and was read over to Mr. Crawford frequently in my own house, and the schools are being conducted in accordance with his wishes.

Witness.—But this gift of £100 was for the poor, and not for the purposes of education. Do you think it was his wish to found a school and to exclude the Roman Catholics?

Mr. *Nelson*.—No, and the school is open to Roman Catholics at the present moment.

3732. Professor Dougherty (to witness).—Is there anything you wish to add? We are bound to respect the intentions of the founders; if both founders were dead the only means we should have of arriving at their intentions would be the terms of the trust deed. But in this case one of the founders is still alive.

Rev. Dr. Molloy.—If all religious instruction were excluded from the school, would the Catholics be able to avail themselves of the advantages of this endowment?—My answer is, that the Catholic religion objects to the exclusion of the name of God from secular instruction, or of separate religious and secular instruction entirely.

3733. Therefore it would still be open to objection if no religious instruction were given?—It would.

3734. But it would not be so objectionable as when religious instruction is given?—Scarcely.

3735. To a certain extent you do avail yourselves of the National Schools, although religious instruction is excluded during the greater part of the day?—Yes.

3736. Professor Dougherty.—At present religious instruction is excluded from this school?

Rev. Dr. Molloy.—No, there is the reading of the Bible.

Mr. Jones (Head Master).—That is only in my own family and with the boarders, but not with the day boys.

3737. Professor Dougherty.—If religion were wholly excluded would that be satisfactory to you?—Then I think it would be impossible to carry out the principles of the donors and to give a sound, moral, and religious education. We have no representation among the teachers in the school, or on the board of trustees; we have no right I suppose to go into the school at any time; we have not been consulted as to the management of the school, and yet my opinion is that the founders did not wish to exclude our community from the benefits of the institution, but at the same time our share of the endowment was overlooked, and if they had considered our case, or our position in the matter, they would not have excluded us as they have practically done, from our share in the endowment. Oct. [illegible], 18[illegible]. Rev. John [illegible].

3738. Dr. Traill.—If there were four hours of secular instruction here, would you consider it a difficulty if the Roman Catholics could get their religious instruction elsewhere?—It would still be open to objection.

3739. Then you could not accept it at all on the terms given here?—We cannot countenance the principle of non-sectarian education, nor the system which excludes the teaching of the Christian religion from secular instruction.

Dr. Traill.—Then you cannot accept the advantages of this school at all.

3740. Professor Dougherty.—Then I suppose what you desire is a separate school for yourselves?—That is what we want.

3741. Dr. Traill.—But you did not ask that?—I do not think the donors wished to exclude our community.

Dr. Traill.—But you say they have done so.

3742. Professor Dougherty.—Is not one of the donors still in existence and in possession of all his faculties?—Yes.

Mr. *Nelson*. And he is perfectly satisfied with the manner in which this school is being carried on.

3743. Professor Dougherty.—A man has a perfect right to do what he likes with his own?—He has, and I do not question his right to do what he likes with his own, but I wish to explain our views on the question.

3744. You are perfectly justified in coming here to explain that you could not accept the education at this school on the terms the founders have associated with it, and we are obliged to you for having done so?—I believe when the matter has been brought before Mr. Crawford, who has been such a generous donor in this matter, then he will reconsider our case.

John A. Bowman further examined.

3745. Professor Dougherty.—You are a resident in Larne?—Yes.

3746. You have taken an interest in the foundation of this school?—I have taken as much interest as I could.

3747. You are not one of the trustees?—No, and I wish to make a very simple statement indeed, that while the Methodists are not represented on the Board of Trustees, I do not consider that as a grievance.

3748. Are you a member of that community?—I am. We all understood that this Grammar School was to be strictly undenominational and non-sectarian, and with that I was perfectly satisfied. With those terms I was perfectly satisfied, and so I think was nearly everyone else. With those terms I did not make any effort to be represented on the Board. I had a personal claim for being on the Board, because Sir Edward Grey's nephew, who is now his heir, is a nephew of mine, and I should say that if any one in the town had a claim it was myself, but I felt no grievance in not being put on. I may just say this in case the school is in any shape or form changed while one of the donors is still alive, that if all the denominations of the town are to be represented on it, I would claim a representation of the Wesleyan body on the Board as well as any other denomination. John A. Bowman.

3749. Dr. Traill.—Would you prefer it remaining as it is, or having it denominationally represented?—I would prefer it remaining as it is. I have the utmost confidence in all connected with the school. I certainly must say with regard to the late Sir Edward Grey and the present Mr. Crawford, that I believe they had no desire to exclude the Roman Catholics from all the benefits of the school. I simply make this statement to the trustees and all concerned, that in case the school is placed on any other foundation different from that which it now is on, our body should be represented on it.

3750. Professor Dougherty.—What is the size of your denomination in Larne?—We have a body of about 300 persons.

3751. One congregation?—Yes, one congregation.

3752. You are not so numerous as the Presbyterians?

Oct. 27, 1888.

John A. Dunnan.

—No, the Presbyterians predominate very largely in this town and neighbourhood.

Rev. Mr. *Morgan*, Rector of Larne.—I hope I am not intruding, but our numbers in the last census numbered between 700 and 800.

Witness.—The Presbyterians largely predominate.

Rev. Mr. *Nolan*, C.C.—The Catholic people of Larne number about 1,600 persons.

3753. Rev. Dr. Molloy.—What would be the average number of each family?—About five in each family. In connection with our Church there are people who attend to our Church which is a centre of 5,000 persons.

3754. Professor Dougherty.—The absence of Methodist children is not because of any difficulties in connexion with the character of the education?

3755. Mr. [illegible].—No.

3756. Your Church has always had an interest in the advancement of education?—Yes.

3757. Rev. Dr. Molloy.—There is nothing in your present deed that we could not introduce into the new scheme. We must always have regard to the wishes of the founders, and in this case you have the advantage of having one of the founders still living.

The inquiry then concluded.

Oct. 29, 1888.

PUBLIC SITTING—MONDAY, OCTOBER 29, 1888.

At the Courthouse, Downpatrick.

Present:—The Rev. Gerald Molloy, D.D., D.SC., Anthony Traill, Esq., LL.D., M.D., F.T.C.D., and Professor Dougherty, M.A., Assistant Commissioners.

The Assistant Secretary, N. D. Murphy, jun., was in attendance.

DOWNPATRICK BLUE COAT SCHOOL.

Dr. Traill made an introductory statement.

Col. *Forde*, D.L., and R. *Nevland*, Esq., solicitor, attended on behalf of the Trustees of the School.

3758. Dr. Traill.—Has any document been obtained from the Court appointing the present trustees?

Mr. *Nevland*.—I think there was.

Mr. *Wallace*.—There is attached to the schools a grove, which was open from time immemorial to the public; I understand that Mr. Mulholland claims ownership over it.

3759. Dr. Traill.—From whom did Mr. Ker purchase the property?

Mr. *Wallace*.—He purchased from the heirs of Lord de Clifford.

Mr. *Nevland*.—This grove was part of what was conveyed by the Landed Estates Court.

3760. Dr. Traill.—This question of the grove is between the public and Mr. Mulholland. Our present business is to ascertain the present condition of the schools, and of the endowment.

Colonel *Forde*.—It has been said that the trustees were consenting parties to the deed in 1874, when the property was handed over from Mr. Ker to Mr. Mulholland. It was quite the contrary. Very soon after that I tendered my resignation. What I want now is to be relieved of the trusteeship.

John R. M'Connell sworn and examined.

John R. M'Connell.

3761. Dr. Traill.—What position do you hold with regard to this endowment?—I am steward to the charity. The funds all pass through my hands. Up to May, 1887, Mr. Mulholland paid a larger sum than was mentioned in the codicil to the will, viz.:—an average of £204 per annum.

3762. Could you give us the sum he was bound to pay?—£[illegible] 18s. for the entire charity, of which £67 7s. was to be applied to the male school, and £65 11s. 7d. to the female school.

3763. Dr. Traill.—In whose hands is the grove now?

Mr. *M'Connell*.—In Mr. Mulholland's.

Mr. *Wallace* here handed in a copy of the Landed Estates Court map.

Mr. *M'Connell*.—I dispute that map; it is not a copy of the Landed Estates Court map.

3764. Professor Dougherty.—You say this grove is conveyed to Mr. Mulholland?

Mr. *M'Connell*.—So far as I know. I quite dispute what Mr. Wallace says.

Mr. *Wallace*.—If it is in the Landed Estates Court map there is an end of it.

3765. Professor Dougherty.—Why was the girls' school closed?

Mr. *M'Connell*.—In May 1, 1887, the former mistress, having received notice that their salaries would not be paid, the mistress resigned. I saw the Rev. Mr. Price and we thought it better, as a temporary measure, to put the girls under the tuition of the master, and pay him the united salaries. Of course, it is entirely a temporary measure.

Mr. *Wallace*.—It was discontinued because the funds were not forthcoming.

Mr. *M'Connell*.—She was only entitled to £11 [illegible] and we could get no person for that salary. The [illegible] consented to circulars, pending future arrangements. Not only that, but the mistress's house was vacant also, and I felt, as a man of business, it would be a mistake to have that house vacant, and accordingly I let it.

3766. Dr. Traill.—You were appointed by Mr. Mulholland?

Mr. *M'Connell*.—Yes. I have been acting since 1873. According to the foundation there was a sum of £36 8s. allowed to the old people. Mr. Mulholland, following Mr. Ker's footsteps, paid an average sum of £[illegible] instead.

3767. Mr. *Wallace*.—Has that ceased also?

Mr. *M'Connell*.—It has ceased during the last twelve months.

Colonel *William Brownlow Forde*, D.L., sworn and examined.

Colonel William Brownlow Forde, D.L.

3768. Dr. TRAILL.—What governing body would you suggest we should form for this school?—I think that parties resident in the town, who are here interested in the charity, would be the proper parties. Rev. Mr. Price, the rector, should be on the governing body.

3769. Is there any layman who might be associated with him?—I would say Mr. Mulholland himself, as having a great interest in the matter—that is, the owner of the estate for the time being.

3770. Would the select vestry be likely to elect a representative?—I don't know.

3771. Is there any possibility of subscribers coming in and helping the school?—I think not; there are so many schools in the town.

3772. Would there be any objection to putting this school under the National Board?—So far as I am concerned I see no objection.

3773. Would it not add to the teachers salaries?—I should think so.

3774. Professor DOUGHERTY.—Would Mr. Mulholland be likely to take any interest in the school?—I think he would ask his agent to do so.

3775. Rev. Dr. MOLLOY.—Do you suggest that the children should go to the National Schools?—Yes.

3776. What purpose could the present buildings be applied to?—I don't know.

3777. Is there sufficient room in the present parochial schools for the children attending the Blue Schools?—I don't know that.

Rev. Dr. MOLLOY.—It would not be a good thing to sacrifice the existing school buildings.

Robert Stuart, Head Master, sworn and examined.

Robert Stuart.

3778. Dr. TRAILL.—How long have you been head master?—I have been head-master twenty-one years. I am a Church Education teacher. I have not been trained at all, nor have I ever been under the National Board.

3779. What attendance has there been in the school?—While the boys were alone in the school we kept it at about twenty. Ten Blue boys were named in the will to be educated, &c., but there are a number of free children. I received £40 a year and had a house and garden up till May, 1857. My salary amounts, with the rents of the houses, and my own house, to about £44. There is a surgeon of militia living with me.

Mr. *M'Connell*.—Mr. Stuart is a single man, and has one room and one bedroom, and it was thought fair enough that he should be at liberty to let the apartments. The number of boys now is sixteen, and of girls ten.

3780. How are the free boys selected?

Mr. *Stuart*.—They are selected by Mr. Price, who has been acting for Mr. Mulholland and the trustees. The Blue boys receive 1s. 10d. each per quarter. I get no school fees.

3781. Do you require them to belong to any particular denomination?—Yes; Episcopalian.

3782. What subjects do you teach?—The ordinary subjects of reading, writing, mensuration, a little algebra, book-keeping, and such things.

3783. Rev. Dr. MOLLOY.—Is the school ever inspected?—Every year.

3784. Professor DOUGHERTY.—Is it inspected in religious or secular knowledge?—Both.

3785. Dr. TRAILL.—Could you qualify for the National Board if these schools were placed under it?—I am beyond the age. The schoolroom is not adapted for a National school. It would not accommodate more than thirty.

3786. How far are you from the other school?—The Parochial school is down the street. Another objection is that the children are all Episcopalians, and if it were a National school, we would have to admit all that came.

3787. It would not hurt you to have a female assistant who would be paid by the State?—It would not. I would differ from Mr. M'Connell. He seemed to imply that my position as teacher came to a termination. I was engaged by Mr. Ker, and the only notice I got from Mr. Mulholland was that he would not be responsible for my salary, but I am not removed or dismissed.

3788. All you are granted is the school salary?—I have given faithful services, and the salary amounted this year to £14. The house and garden are worth £10. I am worth about £30 a year. I forgot to mention that I am paying a sewing mistress, who teaches the girls.

3789. What do you pay her?—It is a small sum of £2, but she is a competent sewer.

3790. Professor DOUGHERTY.—How long have you been connected with the Church Education Society?—I am twenty-nine years teaching elsewhere, but not continuously, in connection with Church Education Society.

3791. Dr. TRAILL.—What school books have you?—There is a sum of £2 Irish set apart for each school. By putting the two schools together we have effected a saving. I have a great many maps, more than I want at present.

3792. The Church Education Society does not provide you with books?—We get some at a reduced rate. Their inspector offered to take the school under their management, and give salary, and it would suit very well.

3793. Rev. Dr. MOLLOY.—By whom were you appointed?—By Mr. Ker and the trustees.

3794. Have you the letter of appointment?—No, I have not.

Mr. *M'Connell*.—So far as the appointment is concerned, he was appointed regularly by the trustees.

3795. Professor DOUGHERTY.—You have no document from Mr. Mulholland, promising you £40 a year?—I have not.

Mr. *M'Connell*.—According to the foundation the amount of money was £13 16s. 11d. British, and after that he was paid to teach ten free boys, as Mr. Ker then thought it was better to increase the salary of the master, and give him a little more to do.

Rev. *T. Blackwood Price* sworn and examined.

Rev. T. Blackwood Price.

3796. Dr. TRAILL.—You have been acting on behalf of Mr. Mulholland in the management of his school?—Yes, in the way that has been described.

3797. Had you any authority from the trustees?—I had not. I only came here after Mr. Mulholland became owner of the property. Mr. Mulholland was allowed to take charge of this matter so long as he paid the same figures.

3798. He acted through you as his deputy?—Exactly, as has been described.

3799. Have you any suggestion to make as to placing the school under a new governing body?—I quite agree with what has been already said with regard to the future governing body. I think the rector should be one, and, under all the circumstances, any one nominated by him should be the second. With regard to what was said as to the select vestry, I think it would be well that some officer connected with the church besides the rector should be appointed—perhaps one of the churchwardens. The vestry might select a couple of names.

3800. Do you think there are a sufficient number of

Oct. 22, 1887.

Rev. T. [illegible] Price.

persons who would subscribe to the school if they got a voice in the control of it; would not more money become available?—That is uncertain. I don't think any large subscriptions could be got. The present parochial school is very largely attended. There are upwards of eighty at the boys, and somewhere about one hundred at the girls school.

3801. Are your own schools under the National Board?—They are. I confess my sympathy is not strong with the National Board.

3802. Have your teachers got residences?—No.

3803. Where do they live?—They live in lodgings.

3804. Would it not be an important matter if one of these residences could be used; supposing one of these residences was found necessary for the schools, would it not be much better that your teacher should live in it?—I suppose it would.

3805. Colonel *Forde*.—What is the difference between the management of the schools since 1857 and before that?

Canon *Price*.—The simple difference is that the girls are now taught as well as the boys by one master.

3806. Professor DOUGHERTY.—Do you think it is better for girls to be taught in ordinary subjects by a master than by a mistress?—I do think in many cases it is.

3807. Have you thought of trying amalgamation?—I have not complete control over these schools. The control of the Parochial Schools is vested in the trustees, the rector and his curate, the minor canon of Down Cathedral, the two church wardens, and persons who subscribed £50 towards these schools, and their heirs.

3808. Dr. TRAILL.—You have only one voice?—Yes.

3809. Rev. Dr. MOLLOY.—Do you think it would be advisable to amalgamate the Blue School and the National School?—I would prefer they should be kept distinct.

3810. Dr. TRAILL.—Why so?—They are quite in a different position. They have different privileges.

3811. Are the buildings of your schools vested in trustees?—I am not sure.

Mr. *Wallace*.—There is a lease made.

Mr. *M'Connell*.—This is the lease made out. There are five trustees—Mr. Johnston, J.P.; Mr. Boyd, Mr. Kerr, Mr. Hastings, and Mr. Filson.

3812. Dr. TRAILL.—How many survive?

Mr. *M'Connell*.—Mr. Johnston.

3813. Dr. TRAILL.—Could you give us any information about the old Diocesan school?

Mr. *Murland*.—I could not.

3814. Dr. TRAILL.—I understand the house reverted to Mr. Mulholland?

Mr. *Murland*.—It belongs to Mr. Mulholland. It ceased to be used as a Diocesan school.

Mr. *M'Connell*.—At its ceasing to be a Diocesan school the Grand Jury took possession of the building.

3815. Dr. TRAILL.—Under what powers; did they subscribe to it originally?

Mr. *M'Connell*.—It was handed over to them.

3816. Dr. TRAILL (to Mr. *Murland*).—You will supply us with all the papers?

Mr. *M'Connell*.—I have none of these deeds; I never saw any.

Mr. *Murland*.—I will have the information sent to you.

3817. Professor DOUGHERTY.—How long is it since the Diocesan school was discontinued?

Mr. *Murland*.—About ten or twelve years.

KILLOUGH SCHOOL.

Hugh Finlay sworn and examined.

Hugh Finlay.

3818. Dr. TRAILL.—Who are you?—At one time my wife and I taught in the school. The patron was Lord Bangor, and the manager was the Rev. Mr. O'Flaherty. When I was appointed to the school it was not under the National Board, my wife and I received £20 a year, and then it was increased to £30. The School was placed under the National Board in 1877, and in 1880 I ceased to be Principal; my wife then became Principal, and has since continued as such. There is an endowment of £30.

3819. Were you a certified teacher under the National Board?—No.

3820. Or your wife?—She was. When we came first it was a male and female school. Then we made it a mixed school.

3821. What is the attendance now?—The average attendance is about fifty.

3822. Rev. Dr. MOLLOY.—Including boys and girls?—Yes. In addition to the £30, we get a free house and garden, and firing for ourselves and school.

3823. Dr. TRAILL.—Lord Bangor must have supplemented the endowment?—He did. My wife gets £30 per annum in addition to the Board's salary. Before this school was erected, I understand there was always a school, but not the same school.

3824. Rev. Dr. MOLLOY.—When was the present school erected?—I could not say. I find since it was in 1835.

3825. Do you teach in the school now?—I do not. I have another situation.

3826. Professor DOUGHERTY.—Do the children attending these schools belong to the late Established Church?—Yes.

3827. Have you any Presbyterians?—We have none. They have no school of their own.

3828. Rev. Mr. *Brennan*.—Are there any Catholics at it?—No, sir.

3829. Do you know of a woman named Kerr—are not her children at the school?—I don't call her a Catholic.

3830. Was the school created by the endowment?—I cannot say that.

3831. You are aware the boys school has ceased to exist?—It is a mixed school.

3832. Dr. TRAILL (to Rev. Mr. *Brennan*).—Have you any claim on this school?

Rev. Mr. *Brennan*.—I thought the endowment might be going to both. There was an agent of the estate took it from the Catholics.

Dr. TRAILL.—You can have access to the will of Judge Ward.

SHIRGLEY SCHOOL.

Lachlan MacLaine, J.P., examined.

Lachlan MacLaine, J.P.

3833. Dr. TRAILL.—What is the endowment of this school?—These schools have an endowment of 150 paid up shares in John Martin & Co., Limited, vested in myself and another as trustees for the benefit of the National School in connection with the works. We have large works, and the National School was part and parcel of the place. Mr. John Martin was formerly proprietor of the place. Some six months before he died he settled these shares on the school.

3834. What is the governing body?—It is under the National Board.

3835. Who is the manager?—I am.

3836. Who is the patron?—I presume it is the directors. I am managing director. The directors don't live there at all.

3837. Is it a private affair in connection with your works?—Yes.

3838. Is it open to all denominations?—It is.

3839. Do you wish to avail yourself of the present

of the Commission for the purpose of getting the governing body altered?—No; I came here just to give you information.

3640. What is the annual available income of the endowment?—About £45 a year. It is a National Board school, attended by all denominations.

3641. Is there any provision for religious instruction?—We have had a Sunday school for years. The Presbyterian clergyman comes once a month.

3642. Does the parish priest attend?—He does, and the clergyman of the Church of Ireland also attends. There is a mixed school, and one infant school. We have a master and mistress and two monitors.

3643. I suppose you would like to keep these schools in your own hands?—Yes.

This concluded the inquiry.

PUBLIC SITTING—SATURDAY, NOVEMBER 10, 1888.

Nov. 10, 1888.

At Hewetson's School, Clane.

Present:—The Right Hon. Lord Justice FitzGibbon and the Right Hon. Lord Justice Naish, Judicial Commissioners; and the Rev. Gerald Molloy, D.D., D.Sc., Anthony Traill, Esq., LL.D., M.D., F.T.C.D., and Professor Dougherty, M.A., Assistant Commissioners.

The Assistant Secretary, N. D. Murphy, Junr., was in attendance.

HEWETSON'S ENDOWMENT.

See Evidence infra, pp. 188–195, and Appendix B, 842–48.

Thomas Cooke-Trench, J.P., and the Rev. William Sherlock were present on behalf of the Trustees.

Thomas Cooke-Trench, J.P., sworn and examined.

3644. Lord Justice FitzGibbon (reads the Chancery Scheme, dated June 21, 1880).—The Report of the last Commission brings the history of this school down to the year 1879, when it was proposed that the school should be moved from Betaghstown to Clane, and I see the Court of Chancery, in 1880, gave you permission to carry out this. When was the school actually moved to Clane?—The new school was opened about six years ago, in 1882.

3645. You gave the site for the new school?—Yes; the Chancery Scheme provides for that; and on June 8, 1881, I executed a deed of grant of two acres of the lands of Millicent to the trustees for a site.

3646. What did the new school-house cost?—About £1,384. Of this the Chancery Scheme sanctioned the expenditure of £900. I gave £200 myself, and the remainder was raised by the leave of the Commissioners of Charitable Donations and Bequests.

3647. Where did all this money come from?—From accumulations of the income of the endowment which had accrued before the old school was opened in 1836. The accumulations, in 1838, amounted to £2,048 1s. 11d. stock.

3648. What is the amount of the accumulations at present—is it invested?—We now have £462 6s. 0d. stock to the credit of the school.

3649. What is the accommodation of the present schoolhouse?—It is built to accommodate fifteen day boys and twenty-five boarders.

3650. What has been done with the dwelling-house and demesne of Betaghstown since the school was removed to this place?—The house and twenty acres of land were let on a yearly tenancy to a man named Hemingway at a rent of £50.

3651. Is that rent still paid?—No; the tenant says he cannot pay this rent now, that the tenancy was created before the bad times came on, and that the place is not suited for an agricultural holding, but only for a residence.

3652. Is Hemingway still in possession?—Yes.

3653. Why don't you turn him out?—I do not think we would get any person to take the place at £50 a year.

3654. Coming now to the Charity estate belonging to the school, have you got the rental?—No; there is no recent rental. Leonard Dobbin & Co. were the agents. Lately, however, a member of the firm who acted as agent, having gathered in all the rents he could, absconded.

3655. Do you know how much he carried off?—I cannot tell. On reference to the minute book of the trustees, which I now produce, I find that the nominal or gross rental of the estate is £468, valuation, £370. I have no statement of the net rental, but I find that in 1883 £311 were lodged by the agent; in 1884, £282; in 1885, £267; in 1886, £177; in 1887, £190; and in the present year, up to March 25, £100 were lodged as against £300 due from the tenants. For the past six years, therefore, the average net rental would be about £250.

3656. Have you tried to sell the estate under Lord Ashbourne's Act?—We have. In 1884 we offered the estate for sale to the tenants at twenty years purchase of the rental; and I find a minute that this sale, less deductions, would have realised £8,500 for the charity. The trustees offer was, however, refused by the tenants. No further step has been taken in this direction.

3657. I see the Chancery Scheme provides for a payment of £30 by the Select Vestry of Clane, in consideration for the right of nominating twenty-five day boys. How does this stand?

Mr. Lowe, Head Master.—At present there are only twenty day boys. The £30 is paid.

3658. Lord Justice FitzGibbon (to Mr. Cooke-Trench).—Therefore the present annual income of the school is about £250 from the estate, £30 from the Select Vestry, the dividend on the stock, and whatever you can get out of the letting of the Betaghstown house and the twenty acres attached to it?—We also get £10 for the shooting of part of the property, let to Mr. Fleetwood Rynd.

3659. Mr. Hewetson's will provides that the school should be open to both sexes, but I see that the Chancery Scheme limits the school to male pupils—why was this change made?—In times gone by the old school at Betaghstown was worked by a former Bishop of Kildare; the school was managed according to the terms of the founder's will, boys and girls being boarded together in the house; this led to great immorality between them, and, as a result, the old school was broken up, and the rents of the estate accumulated, and were subsequently invested in Government stock.

3660. I observe that under the Chancery Scheme of 1880 you have five trustees—do all these regularly attend at the meetings of your Board?—No, the Archbishop of Armagh takes little or no interest in the School, and does not attend; the Archbishop of Dublin, being Bishop of Kildare, has been down here two or three times. Mr. Sherlock, myself, and Archdeacon Dulleagh do most of the work.

3661. Then you have a difficulty in forming a quorum of the trustees?—Yes, I think it would be an advantage if we had a larger governing body.

3662. Would you have the two Archbishops, the Incumbent of Clane, and the Archdeacon of Kildare ex-officio governors?—The first three certainly, but I

Dec. 10, 1888. Thomas Cavin-French, Esq.

do you think it would do to have the Archdeacon as manager; the Archdeacon of the diocese would not always be constantly holding a [illegible] near the school.

3862. Do you think you could get in the neighbourhood any subscribers who would contribute to the funds of the schools?—I do not think there is much chance of that.

William Lemon, Head Master, examined.

Wm. Lemon.

3864. Lord Justice FitzGibbon. How long have you been teaching?—I have been for thirty-three years a teacher; I was reared in the Queen's County, and prepared to go to the Kildare-place Society, but I never went there, and I have never been trained; I was fifteen years with the Rev. Mr. [illegible] as a teacher under the Church Education Society.

3865. The school has been built to accommodate twenty-five day boys. How many have you at present?—Twenty.

3866. Do these pay school fees?—Yes, they pay £3 10s. per annum.

3867. What salary are you paid?—Up to the time of the agent's defalcations I was paid £1 [illegible]—since that time I only receive £[illegible]. Mr. French, however, has guaranteed to me the school fees of two boys, and Archdeacon [illegible] has guaranteed the pay of another—a fourth is also guaranteed to me.

3868. Rev. Dr. Molloy.—What class of boys attend as day boys?—Boys of the National school class.

3869. Lord Justice FitzGibbon.—Do you take in none but your boys?

Mr. Cavin-French.—As a temporary expedient the trustees have resolved to take in some of [illegible] gentlemen as boarders at £18 per annum each.

3870. Lord Justice FitzGibbon (to witness).—Have any of your boarders ever run away?—This happened occasionally—one bad boy will lead others wrong; in a case I remember one boy enticed another to run away with him.

3871. Are any boys apprenticed now?—No, there is no money available.

May 4, 1889.

SATURDAY, MAY 4, 1889.

At the Office, 23, Nassau-street.

Present:—The Right Hon. Lord Justice FitzGibbon and the Right Hon. Lord Justice Naish, Judicial Commissioners; and the Rev. Gerald Molloy, D.D., D.SC., Anthony Traill, Esq., LL.D., M.D., F.T.C.D., and Professor Dougherty, M.A., Assistant Commissioners.

The Secretary, Wm. Edward Ellis, LL.B., and the Assistant Secretary, N. D. Murphy, were in attendance.

*ULSTER ROYAL SCHOOL ENDOWMENTS.

The following deputation attended, to express the views of the General Synod of the Church of Ireland with regard to the Revised Draft Scheme for the Ulster Royal Schools Endowments, viz.:—

His Grace the Lord Primate, Right Rev. the Lord Bishop of Derry, Right Rev. the Lord Bishop of Clogher, Right Rev. the Lord Bishop of Kilmore, Venerable the Archdeacon of Clogher, Very Rev. the Dean of Armagh, Rev. Precentor Ovenden, Rev. W. A. Hutchinson, B.D., Rev. Canon [illegible], Rev. William Moore Morgan, LL.D., and Colonel Ffolliott.

3872. The Lord Primate.—I have to thank you for giving us an opportunity of laying before you some of the objections which the General Synod thought it desirable that we should express by deputation rather than by correspondence; and, in saying so, I wish to guard ourselves against your considering that they are the only objections we have to the scheme. We put forward these objections without prejudice to such other objections as we may think it desirable to put in on behalf of the different Diocesan Councils of Derry, Armagh, Clogher, and so on. The objections now presented are some of the salient objections that the General Synod think it desirable to bring before you: I will ask Colonel Ffolliott to state our first ground of objection, which I will read, as it is in the resolution adopted in the Synod:—

"That this Synod protests against the Revised Draft Scheme for the Ulster Royal Schools Endowments, and among other reasons for so doing, specifies the following objections:—

"(1.) That it gives the Roman Catholic Church a share of the endowments which the statistics of Intermediate Education prove to be most excessive."

That is our impression, and I will ask Colonel Ffolliott to state the grounds of it.

3873. Colonel Ffolliott.—I am instructed by the Synod to put forward the chief ground on which we think we have not got sufficient consideration in dealing with the endowments for Intermediate Education. I have taken the figures which I found in your report; and to begin with the question of Intermediate Education, we find that of the number of pupils who passed the Intermediate Examination in 1886 67½ per cent. were Protestants; and in 1887 77 per cent. were Protestants. That struck the Synod as a very important reason why they should receive greater consideration as regards the endowments.

3874. Rev. Dr. Molloy.—Do you mean 77 per cent. of all who passed from the six counties?

Colonel Ffolliott.—From five counties.

3875. Rev. Dr. Molloy.—That is leaving out Monaghan?

Colonel Ffolliott.—Yes.

3876. Rev. Dr. Molloy.—Do you mean by Protestants, the members of your Church?

Colonel Ffolliott.—No; all non-Catholics. That includes a few of whom we are not quite certain. Of course it is true that the population, in some places, of Roman Catholics is larger; but we have to deal with those capable of receiving education. The Roman Catholics have received, and very properly so, a much larger advantage from primary schools under the National Board than those who are non-Catholics; and, for different reasons, they avail themselves very much more of them, and a great number of the poor classes, who avail themselves of the primary schools only, are Roman Catholics. In the five counties, of the illiterate population, that is, of those who can read and write, we find the Roman Catholics 67·63 per cent.; and of those receiving instruction in primary schools the Roman Catholics were 66 per cent., whereas those receiving instruction in the superior schools were only 25 per cent. We also find that of the persons rated for a large sum in respect of large holdings, the larger proportion are Protestants; and, as we go down to a lower figure, the proportion becomes even more. I have only got the figures from two counties, but they are sufficient to illustrate what I mean. In Fermanagh and Monaghan the numbers of those rated over £[illegible] were—Protestants, 1,0[illegible]; Roman Catholics, [illegible]. Of those rated at £[illegible]—Protestants, 1,044; Roman Catholics, 479. Of those rated at £[illegible]—Protestants, 3,[illegible];

* See Appendix B, Nos. XII. (r.) and XIII. (a.), pp. [illegible].

and Roman Catholics, 1,235. It is, I think, very properly noted on behalf of the advocates of the Roman Catholic claims, that while hitherto the members of their Church have not received the same benefits from intermediate education that other denominations have, that will not be so in the future. And I have no doubt the Commission had that in their view when they gave three years for the purpose of giving both parties a fair start, which we think a fair and reasonable thing. But it is still the opinion of the Synod that the Protestants ought to have greater consideration than the Roman Catholics in the matter of these endowments. As regards the progress of the proportion of Roman Catholics who will pass and distinguish themselves in the Intermediate Examinations increasing, of course we would be glad to see that they were increasing, and I have no doubt they will increase; and we don't consider them in any sense inferior to us, nor have we any wish to treat them with any disrespect; but, at the same time, I cannot help saying for myself, that I do not think that the principles of the Roman Catholic Church, as we have them all over the world, are so favourable to the advance of education. I do not say it as a matter of reproach to them, but it is their principle to control the matter as they think right to a greater degree than we do, and I distinctly consider that the result does not make us think that they, starting fair in the race with the Protestants, will be able, in this matter of education, to hold a more advantageous position than we. It is within your recollection, that when you were in Sligo you were very much struck by the extraordinary efforts made by a few Protestants in that place, entirely on their own resources, and the immense results they had achieved in this matter. I believe there are some grounds for the contention of the Synod in this matter, and I am sure it will receive your usual careful and full consideration.

3377. The *Lord Primate*.—The next point to which we direct attention is:—

(2.) "That it assigns to the Church of Ireland a wholly inadequate representation on the proposed Local Board which will deal with Protestant endowments."

This is a question relating solely to the Protestant Churches, and I would ask Canon Babington to explain it.

3378. Rev. Canon *Babington*.—It has been assigned to me to bring forward the views of the Synod on the resolution which relates to the representation given to the different Protestant denominations on these boards. We think as we before contended before this Commission, that on some of these Boards we are not properly represented, and we wish the Commission to take that matter into their consideration, and to draw up such a plan even if they do not increase the numbers, as will at least put us into a more favourable position in dealing with these endowments.

3379. Lord Justice Naish.—Is it your objection that the representation is inadequate as compared with the other Protestant bodies?

Rev. Canon *Babington*.—"That it assigns to the Church of Ireland a wholly inadequate representation." Now I guard myself carefully that what we say here to-day is without prejudice to what we may be obliged to bring before the Commission hereafter. We wish to-day to state some objections, but not in such a formal manner as may be necessary hereafter, and as I may have counsel hereafter who would have to deal with other matters, I do not wish it to be stated when we go into the broader question afterwards, that I put these forward as the only ground on which we object. A great deal has been made out of the point that before the Commission we all differed, but looking at the scheme as printed, and looking to the different interests in the different localities, you will see that the Commissioners recognised that there were conflicting interests, and that it was utterly impossible not to have differences at first, but so far as the Church of Ireland is concerned, the different Diocesan Councils are now perfectly agreed as to what we wish the Commissioners to do, and they have asked me to state that the protest of the Synod does not purport to convey altogether what the Councils desire; but it is easy for me in connection with this to put it before the Commissioners, and I trust they will give it due consideration. First, we have already placed before them the figures on which we protest against the representation which in some of the dioceses we have got. I believe the Commissioners have corrected those figures. We have taken them as far as possible from the Census, and we stand by them. I don't know where the Commissioners have got their figures on which they rely, but the Census figures are fairly open to all, and they are not open to the observation that they are drawn up by people who might give way to their imagination in drawing them up. They are there in print, and we rely on them. We say we have not got a fair representation in those districts in which we have been placed in a decided minority. We wish to state that there is a way by which the Commissioners might modify their plan and satisfy all parties. In their present plan they have drawn a settlement, and they have married us under compulsion; we have no power to make any agreement with the parties with whom we are joined, and who in some instances will have conflicting interests and conflicting opinions to us on educational points. What I propose is that they should make a settlement if they like; but don't marry us; give us an opportunity of joining. I believe that will be for the interest in every district, in every diocese, in every county of Ireland of the class who will be in the minority there.

3380. Lord Justice Naish.—Do you apply that to every district?

Rev. Canon *Babington*.—Yes; in every district the minority will be induced to join, for they cannot carry on efficient education without joining the stronger body, but the weaker body can make its own terms, and say, "We will agree with you on these terms," no party will be placed at a disadvantage. You have just done the reverse of that; you have joined us and given us power to divide; we want you not to divide us, but to give us power to join; that is just simply our ground. This was brought before the Commission on a former occasion. Lord Justice FitzGibbon said: "We must carefully "consider the opinions of the Standing Committee on "the general question. We understand you to sup"port Mr. Bewley's contention on these two points, "but you have put your argument in a way that was "not put to us before; and it will require considera"tion whether a separate Board with power to unite, "would not be preferable to the proposal of the "scheme—united Boards, with power to divide."

3381. Lord Justice FitzGibbon.—That was the view which the Archbishop of Dublin put forward?

Rev. Canon *Babington*.—Yes, and I believe if you give us that it will do away with a great deal of the difference of opinion.

3382. Lord Justice FitzGibbon.—We will be very glad if you can tell us how to carry it out.

The *Dean of Armagh*.—Do exactly as you have done for the Catholics; give us separate boards with power to unite; all we ask is just the reverse of what you have given us. At present the boards are united, and we want them separated; give us separate boards with power to unite, and not united boards with power to separate.

Rev. Canon *Babington*.—As far as we are concerned in the one particular instance in which I am interested, we would join and join without difficulty.

3383. Rev. Dr. Molloy.—How many separate boards do you propose?

Rev. Canon *Babington*.—One board in each district.

3384. Rev. Dr. Molloy.—There are Methodists, Presbyterians—what would you do with them?

The *Lord Primate*.—Only two boards—Protestant and Catholic.

3585. Lord Justice FitzGibbon.—I ask you to give attention to the question how this is to be done, for we quite agree that your mode of putting the objection is exceedingly enticing. You ask a separate board for yourselves; are the other Protestant denominations to be left to take care of themselves?

The *Lord Primate*.—We only ask that the Church of Ireland should have a Board for itself.

3586. Lord Justice FitzGibbon.—You told us, Canon Babington, that the representation of the Church on the Protestant boards was inadequate.

Rev. Canon *Babington*.—Certainly.

3587. Lord Justice FitzGibbon.—On what do you base that? There was a difference of figures between us last August, and we have tried to find out how it arose, and the only way in which we could find any approximation to your figures was by deducting the illiterate population over five years old from the whole population, treating the whole population under five years of age as potentially literate. That was the principle on which Roman Catholics claimed to count the whole population as having a potential claim on these endowments, but we want to know whether you have added every child under five years of age to the literate population.

The *Dean of Armagh*.—We have our census returns with us to show how the matter stands.

3588. Lord Justice FitzGibbon.—We have them here too, and the only district where there is any difference in result between your figures and ours is in Tyrone. Remember each board consists of only nine members, and if any denomination has less than a ninth, but is entitled to a representative, we cannot give it less than one man. Therefore we cannot divide the representation mathematically, but we have tried to give a working majority in each case to the body which is in a majority of the literate population. Bearing these principles in mind, we have given the majority accurately in every district according to the figures we have, and the only place where your figures change the majority is in Tyrone.

The *Lord Primate*.—We have more than 6 to 3 in other districts.

3589. Lord Justice FitzGibbon.—Perhaps a nearer proportion would be 6 to 2 in Cavan or Fermanagh, but 3 is a more efficient representation than 2, whereas there is no practical difference between a majority of 6 to 3 and 6 to 2. In Tyrone we cannot make your figures agree with ours, and we have only guessed at two solutions of your calculations; one was that you treat all children under five as if they were literate, and the other that possibly you have omitted the portion of the Archdiocese of Armagh which is in county Derry, where there is a considerable preponderance of Presbyterians. We would like you to look into this matter, it is a mere matter of figures, and if we are wrong we are ready to be corrected.

Rev. Dr. *Morgan*.—I was partly responsible for that matter, and the first solution is the correct one.

3590. Lord Justice FitzGibbon.—Then we must ask your reasons for counting all children under five as literate. We don't think it is right to do so for the purpose of giving any denomination an apparent majority of the literate population.

Rev. Dr. *Morgan*.—On the principle that the education of all the people is to be improved.

3591. Rev. Dr. Molloy.—But on your principle a child is literate up to five, and after five it becomes illiterate.

Lord Justice FitzGibbon.—We don't think that is a right principle.

3592. The *Lord Primate*.—The third objection is—

(3.) "That of the gross endowments it proposes to distribute the greater part as so called result fees in the allocation of which results will be entirely out-weighed by mere numbers."

The Dean of Armagh will bring forward this objection.

3593. The *Dean of Armagh*.—In the Draft Scheme of last year there was a scheme of results to which we objected very strongly, and we have to thank you for having considered our objections and given effect to them. Unfortunately we have as strong objections to this scheme which has taken its place, and I think we are likely to be dissatisfied with any system of results fees. In the memorandum accompanying the Draft Scheme of last year we found something which startled us very much. On page 3 you admitted the principle of localisation, but on page 6 we found you had thrown the larger portion of the Endowment into a sort of caldron of result fees, and you justify that by the statute 3rd Geo. 4th, cap. 79; but it occurred to us to look at that statute, and we found you had acted on a principle which, if I may say what I think frankly, is the very opposite to what the statute lays down. The clause in question is recited on page [illegible], appendix B, in your report of last year. The principle in the statute is to spend the money first in buildings, then on masters, and then if there is a residue from the locality, pass that away for use elsewhere. Under the Act 53 Geo. 3, cap. 107, the residue shall be applied in providing scholarships. The nearest approach you have made to the scholarship is the results fees, and the use you have made of that statute is to give them a preference instead of putting them last, as is laid down in the statute. It seems to me that principle is very nearly the reverse of what is laid down in the statute. Apart from that we have no objection to the principle as now laid down in section 44 of the scheme. "The whole amount of such residue after providing for the [illegible] places hereinafter required to be provided by the Commissioners shall be divided by the Commissioners among the several local boards for the benefit of the qualified schools for which such claim shall have been made or established to the satisfaction of the Commissioners in proportions to be calculated by results in accordance with the provisions contained in the first schedule hereto." That is precisely what we say is not done, and we ask for the abolition of all these heavy tests, and we ask that the division shall be finally made so that there shall not be a scramble in the end for the biggest share of what remains. We say that the principle does not work satisfactorily, and distribution by results according to our contention breaks down, for in this matter of Intermediate Education we agree that although persons who might deserve results might not pass that test, yet on the whole one school with another will ultimately get a fair share—we don't object to that—but we say to give a mere pass without regard to honours, which was the principle you admitted last year, and which we did not challenge, for there was a preference for the higher grades over the lower grades, to give one mark and one only to pupils passing the Intermediate examination we do not think sufficient; we also complain, and this is the gravamen of the complaint, that one additional mark shall be allowed for every pupil who at any time during the year for half as long has been under education in the prescribed subjects. If you are really trying results, why not enumerate them. It does not say the pupil shall have been 100 days under instruction in those subjects, or that he shall have been throughout the year in receipt of this instruction.

Lord Justice Naish.—I think it implies that.

3594. Lord Justice FitzGibbon.—You may take it for granted not only that we agree, but that we are anxious to make this really a test of genuine Intermediate education throughout the year. That was our intention in departing from the proposal of last year. I will refer presently to where the alteration came from, and by whom it was supported. We are now dealing only with the details, and we want to secure a share of the endowments for each genuine Intermediate scholar, and any recommendation you

May 1, 1888.

can make, or any assistance you can give to test whether each participating school is really an efficient Intermediate school or not, will be of great use. The other question is one of principle, whether we can decide by results at all; but if we are to decide by results our intention and desire is to ensure that genuine Intermediate pupils only shall count. You may take it for granted that each of these one hundred attendances must be an attendance for real teaching at an efficient Intermediate school. The definition you object to in the schedule is taken from the Intermediate Education Act, and is in the form of the conditions under which they pay results fees. I am far from saying that you are not quite right in thinking it open to objection, and any amendment to make the test more strict we shall be happy to consider.

The Dean of Armagh.—Our contention is that it does not say he has worked during the year.

3895. Lord Justice FitzGibbon.—We are anxious to remove all ground for doubt on that point, but we should wish to know how you propose to overcome the claims on this fund, assuming it to be a fund for Intermediate as distinguished from primary education. How are we to divide it fairly?

The Dean of Armagh.—The Inspectors should examine the children in Intermediate subjects. The difference between your Inspector and the National Board Inspector is that one examines the pupils and the other does not.

3896. Lord Justice FitzGibbon.—The Intermediate Commissioners have no inspectors. A child might come up to the Intermediate examination from a school in which he had been taught nothing.

The Dean of Armagh.—It is only by passing his examination he gets any results. You are not paid pass with the Intermediate, but you are paid pass with the National Board; but the National Board Inspector examines the children. Your Inspector examines the building, and such like, and does not ascertain whether the instruction is genuine. My contention is that schedule 1, clause 1, will work this way—A large school, which ought to be treated for the most part as a primary school, the greater part of whose pupils are under primary instruction, may give a very superficial amount indeed of instruction in the required subjects to pass the necessary seven pupils; if they pass the necessary seven pupils, they may secure, under the name of results, for a vast number of children to whom education a mere veneer has been given in these required subjects, but that is no result at all. The Lord Justice has done me the honour of saying he would like to see what we would submit as a real test; I say, abolish No. 1, and keep No. 2. Give each school a share of the endowment in proportion to the number it can pass at the Intermediate Examinations.

3897. Lord Justice FitzGibbon.—The Armagh Royal School was one of the foremost in objecting to that.

The Dean of Armagh.—I don't care what Armagh objected to.

3898. Rev. Dr. Molloy.—We have been going through the country fighting the battle of the Intermediate Examinations, and we have been opposed by the schoolmasters, who refused to accept the Intermediate Examinations as a proper test for the distribution of endowments. We have been trying to satisfy them that, though not a perfect test, they are, nevertheless, a fairly good test, and practically the only test we have.

Lord Justice FitzGibbon.—Dr. Morgan was one of those who gave us evidence as to the satisfactory character of the Intermediate Examinations, yet he gave us the strongest evidence that parents had prevented him from sending in their children from Armagh Royal School, and therefore that the results obtained at the Intermediate Examinations were not a fair test of the work done at Armagh Royal School, because the parents would not allow the pupils to go up.

3899. Lord Justice Naish.—Are you satisfied to accept the Intermediate test?

The Lord Primate.—Certainly.

3900. Lord Justice FitzGibbon.—We must get a return from the six counties showing the numbers who have passed the Intermediate examinations. You have given us percentages of 61 and 77 per cent.; but the total number is so small that a single boy passing the Intermediate Examinations, if we take that as the sole basis of division, might mean an endowment of £100 a year to the school. We don't think that is practicable—the dividend is too small and uncertain, and the divisor is too large. If you take the Intermediate Examination test alone the results would be startling in the extreme. No matter how energetic and efficient the teaching may be, unless a school is very large it can not keep up a constant stream of boys of sufficient capacity, or sufficiently advanced to pass the Intermediate Examinations in anything like equal numbers in successive years. The boys one year will be older and another year more clever, and if you have a small number it will work curiously.

The Dean of Armagh.—Our point is that there is no other test. We disliked extremely the test of last year. You may say that the test of the Intermediate Examinations will work unequally; but we say on the whole it will equalise itself, and the average will assert itself over a number of years, and in the meantime you have no other, and perhaps no better test. You propose to count attendance, and every person who has been under instruction, be that instruction good, bad, or indifferent, during the year, that is not a right way of reaching a result test.

3901. Rev. Dr. Molloy.—Your proposition gives us considerable help in a very difficult matter. You have put forward a definite proposal, namely, to accept the passing of the Intermediate Examinations as the test by which the residue should be divided; and I would say for myself that this test seems to afford the simplest and best solution of the difficulty, if on full discussion it be accepted generally as satisfactory by the parties interested.

The Dean of Armagh.—The Lord Justice said that when you went to the different localities you found differences existing on various points, but there was no difference on the point which we are now presenting to the Commission.

* 3902. Lord Justice FitzGibbon.—This is a vital matter, and you had better not be hasty about it. We have got * returns which show how a division according to the Intermediate examinations would have worked in 1886, which you will be wise to consider. I find in Armagh there passed altogether forty-four pupils in 1886—five came from St. Patrick's College, Armagh; three from the College-street National School, Armagh; six from the Christian School, Armagh; one from the Cathedral School, Armagh; twenty from the College, Lurgan; two from the Academy, Portadown; and seven from private addresses. If you had taken the Intermediate test, the Armagh Royal School would have got nothing whatever, because the parents did not allow their boys to go up. The Christian Schools would have got six shares, and the Lurgan College twenty shares. In Cavan only ten passed—eight from the Christian Schools, Cavan; one from the National School, Cavan, and one from a private address; so that the Protestants would have got nothing at all, and the National School would have got one-tenth, and the Christian Schools eight-tenths. The Roman Catholic share is said to be exclusive under our scheme, but you would have given eight-tenths of the Cavan Royal School endowment to the Christian Brothers. Fifteen passed in Donegal; of these three came from the Diocesan Seminary, Letterkenny; seven from Prior Endowed School, Lifford; three from the Royal School, Raphoe; and two from the Intermediate School, Stranorlar. From the whole county of Fermanagh, although it has an endowment of £1,300 a year, only four passed—of

* See Appendix B., No. III (w.) p. [illegible].

May 5, 1890.

these three were from Portora Royal School, and one from the Kesh National School, Irvinestown. So that each boy would have been worth some £320 per annum to his school.

Rev. Dr. Molloy.—It is only right to say, in favour of the Dean of Armagh's proposition, that if it were adopted the figures would be very different in future years; for the education of these six counties would be conducted under quite a new system. If, however, we adopted the proposition, we should attach to it a rider that only those pupils who came from bona fide intermediate schools should be allowed to count.

3903. Lord Justice FitzGibbon.—You had better not object to this scheme without more information than you possess.

The Lord Primate.—You do not put forward these figures as a test?

3904. Lord Justice FitzGibbon.—No; but I put them forward to show the mode in which the exclusive use of the Intermediate Examination test, which you now propose, would have worked in 1888, and if it would have worked that way in 1890 it is strong evidence that in that year it would not have been satisfactory. In Tyrone forty-five boys passed—a larger number than in any other county, but see where they came from—six from the Intermediate School, Castlederg; four from the Intermediate School, Omagh; six from the Academy, Cookstown; ten from the Christian Schools, Omagh; two from the Intermediate School, Newtownstewart; and seventeen from the Academy, Strabane. There is no definition of a school entitled to share these endowments that would not necessarily include Strabane Academy and in that year it would have got seventeen shares, Dungannon being altogether excluded. You are now stating a new principle suddenly, but I should require to know how it would work before I would take the Intermediate results as a test; and I recognise the importance to a school of its endowment being a reliable source of income: £50 this year and £250 next year is not nearly so useful as a steady income of less amount, say £100 a year, and these figures demonstrate the fluctuating character of the Intermediate Examination test.

The Dean of Armagh.—These figures are destructive of your own proposal.

3905. Lord Justice FitzGibbon.—I don't think you do justice to our proposal as we intend it should work, and we shall be glad, indeed, to get any help that would secure its working as we intend. We don't propose that a boy shall be counted unless he gets genuine intermediate education throughout each year for which he is counted; and if he has got such education his schoolmaster should be paid for him even if he does not go up for the Intermediate Examinations.

The Dean of Armagh.—Although you say these figures don't represent what our number would be, yet they show that in Armagh the only school that would have got any results fees would be the College in Lurgan, no other school passed seven. In Cavan there is only one school that would get results fees.

3906. Lord Justice FitzGibbon.—Yes, the Christian Brothers. There is no doubt that although they have had all these Royal School Endowments, these six counties, except perhaps Armagh, are far behind the average of the rest of Ireland in regard to passing the Intermediate Examinations: our object in giving the three years is to let them work up.

Rev. Dr. Morgan.—No doubt the smallness of figures is very unsatisfactory, but smallness of figures is a different matter from the proportion.

3907. Rev. Dr. Molloy.—But percentages founded on small figures are constantly misleading.

The Dean of Armagh.—However unsatisfactory it may be it would be more satisfactory than the very same result from plan counting the heads however bad the education would be.

Lord Justice FitzGibbon.—We have told you we want to provide that [illegible] heads only shall be counted.

3908. Rev. Dr. Molloy.—With reference to the point of counting heads—what we have found practically, in the case of the Royal Schools, is that having been provided with very large endowments they have some of them dwindled away and for some years have been giving education to very few pupils. We want to secure, under our scheme, that the endowments shall be distributed in future amongst those schools only that are really giving education to a substantial number of pupils, and shall be distributed, roughly speaking, in proportion to the number taught. There is sufficient encouragement, from other sources, for pushing on the best boys; but these endowments should be applied, I think, towards extending the benefits of intermediate education as widely as possible.

The Bishop of Clogher.—A difficulty arose in this matter which I happen to know. A good many parents object to the Intermediate Examinations; they say we want to put our boys into the university and the courses are different—that is one of the reasons, as I know, why schools do not send boys forward to the examinations—the parents objected "you must give our boys work to fit them for the course of education intended for them." It has been suggested that you should take into consideration the entrance examination for the university for example and no doubt competitions might be added—suppose it is shown that any number of boys went to the university, that should be counted.

3909. Lord Justice FitzGibbon.—That was also we proposed last year. We proposed the test of examinations, not merely the Intermediate but also the examinations for boys leaving school and going to professions: we proposed to give graduated values to the university and higher grade examinations, and the objection was made that we could not give a complete catalogue of all the examinations for which a boy ought to be entitled to gain credit for his school; we were met further with objections to weighing the relative merits of the senior grade in the Intermediate, the entrance examination of Trinity College, the matriculations at the Royal University and at Maynooth, the examinations for the Royal College of Surgeons, for the Civil Service, &c.; everybody objected to give power to the Commissioners to take these different examinations into account, and so we were thrown back to try to find a test of what we may call the daily work of the school. I repeat that any assistance we can obtain in endeavouring to ascertain the relative amount of bona fide intermediate education given in each year in each school will be a welcome help to a satisfactory solution of this part of the question.

3910. The Lord Primate.—The fourth ground of objection is—

(4.) "That while the scheme recognises a right to compensation created by the expenditure of private money upon school premises, this compensation is nevertheless merged in the General revenue of the Financial Lord Board instead of going to the denomination to which the donor belonged."

Take the case of Armagh. It is stated and the name of my predecessors gave £4,000 or £5,000 of their own money as Educational Endowment: it is proposed to divide these under the present plan: A man has a sum of money and he proposes to give each of his four sons a fourth of the property, but he has absolutely given one of them a sum of £4,000. The man dies and his executors come to pay the sons the one fourth each which was left them, but they say to the son who has got the £4,000 we will not give you your fourth unless the £4,000 also is divided, although the sum of £4,000 had been given to him absolutely; would it be right to exclude him from his share of one fourth except upon that condition? I am quoting the very words of the Lord Justice himself: that the endowments which were exclusive endowments for any particular denomination must go to that denomination. There is only one more matter —in reference to the position of our bishops on these boards. The Catholic bishops are put on *ex-officio*, while our bishops are elected by the Diocesan Council. No doubt that was very kind to us, and I don't mean to say for a moment that the Commissioners meant the slightest slur on us, but all the same it had the effect of more or less handicapping us on our boards; no doubt the object of the Commissioners was that where the bishop was decrepid or from old age or other circumstances was unable to act, it should be in the power of the Council to elect a representative where they would require all their members. We don't see why you should not have given us the same power as you have given the Archbishop of Armagh in the case of the Hewetson school—that is the Bishops of the Church of Ireland should be *ex-officio* members with power, when from old age or infirmity they were unable to attend themselves, to appoint a commissary.

3911. Lord Justice NAISH.—You think it would be more satisfactory than to have them as representatives of the Church on these boards?

The Lord Primate.—That the bishops should be *ex-officio* the same as the Roman Catholic bishops are.

3912. Dr. TRAILL.—That instead of leaving power to the Diocesan Council to elect the bishop as one of the members the bishop should be *ex-officio* a member when he chose to substitute another person in his place.

The Lord Primate.—Yes.

3913. Rev. Dr. MOLLOY.—We thought it would be in the interest of your Church that the Diocesan Council should have the power to elect persons who would be able to attend.

The Lord Primate.—I fully recognise the kindness of the Commissioners to us, but I think we should rather have all the bishops as *ex-officio* members the same as in *Hewetson's* case.

The Bishop of Clogher.—We have a great deal to say with regard to Portora which is to reserve, and we have not committed ourselves in being silent here; I wish it to be understood, that what we have said is without prejudice to what we may say afterwards in regard to Portora.

3914. Lord Justice FITZGIBBON.—Your Grace was careful, when you commenced, to state that you reserved your right to put forward any other objections you thought proper at any future stage of the proceedings, and in what I am now going to say I am obliged to make a somewhat similar reservation; my brother Lord Justice and myself regard ourselves in all our work upon this Commission as fulfilling a judicial duty, which we are obliged to discharge in the presence of the parties, where all interested have full opportunity of being heard; and therefore on an *ex parte* occasion like the present we cannot commit ourselves finally to views which other persons interested might afterwards claim the right to modify. Therefore in what I am going to say, with the concurrence of my learned colleagues, you will understand that I am only attempting to state as plainly as I can, the principles on which the scheme is at present framed and the views which have induced us to—which is as a revised draft still open to further modification, but going so far as we have hitherto seen our way towards a just proposal for the settlement of this most difficult and complicated matter, I ought to say on to our three colleagues that while we seek their assistance in all our work here, in which I am happy to say we have been in many instances successful in unravelling things that looked rather stormy, the responsibility for the scheme in the present stage rests with my brother Lord Justice and myself. Let me first dispose of the last two points brought before us—parenthetically I may observe one of them seems to have been made the subject of very sever and the other of very strong language in your Synod. The proposal with respect to the bishops was in the scheme published last year, in identically the same terms in which it appears now, and not merely in the whole of the printed and written objections which we received, but in the whole course of the four days discussion that took place in August last, we never heard more than a passing reference to the point that the Roman Catholic Bishops were appointed *ex-officio* while the Protestant Bishops were included among the representatives of their Diocesan Councils. Therefore when the Commission is exposed to criticism, it should be borne in mind that the accredited representatives of the Church never made the slightest objection or even called our attention to what has been so vehemently denounced, but by their silence induced us to believe that it was satisfactory. The reason for the distinction is very simple—the Roman Catholic body is a homogeneous one. In fact your great objection is that you have not got a homogeneous body as they have. Having that, it makes very little difference to them whether they have eight efficient representatives or nine, but where there is a mixed Protestant board with proportionate representation, the introduction of any *ex-officio* representative would be contrary to the principle on which we proceeded unless we assured that the holder of the office was an efficient representative. We may have been wrong in assuming that in every case the first representative of a Diocesan Council would be the Bishop, unless there was some solid reason for passing him over; and if the Diocesan Council did pass their Bishop over it would be because the interests of the Church required it, and I certainly took it for granted that it would be with his own concurrence that the Council would ever substitute another person in their Bishop's place.

The *Lord Primate.*—I never brought it as a charge.

3915. Lord Justice FITZGIBBON.—But others did, and I am explaining why the provision is as it is—my brother Lord Justice and myself think that this is a question of the efficient representation of the Church, and if the members of the Church through their representatives tell us that they would rather have their Bishops *ex-officio* as their representatives their views would have very great weight with us. On the other hand, as has been already referred to, we have such precedents as Hewetson's school for giving the Bishop power to nominate some one to act in his place. I can say no more on that point now because our Presbyterian friends might say that recognising a Bishop *ex-officio* gave them cause of complaint—but on the other hand we are prepared to consider whether we may not treat the Bishop as a representative of his own denomination, and in that case it would not be a matter in which the Presbyterians would be interested or they possibly might not object.

The next point was the proposal to add to the Protestant share of the Endowments the value of gifts from former Dignitaries of the Church. That provision also was in the old scheme and not only did no Protestant object to it, but no Roman Catholic objected to it, and we thought it was accepted by everybody as a fair proposal.

Lord Primate.—This is a fresh proposal, taking our share and giving it to others.

3916. Lord Justice FITZGIBBON.—Pardon me, the clause in the original draft was in the very terms in which it is now, but it is only now, when the proposition is urged upon us of a further sub-division of the Protestant share, that this becomes material, and, beyond all doubt, if there is to be a further sub-division, it will necessarily carry with it an allocation of private benefactions to the particular denomination to which the donor belonged. If the thing was overlooked before, it is not too late to mend it now, and I do not entertain any doubt that the principle of the proposal is that the denomination to which each private benefactor belonged shall get the benefit of his benefaction.

The Lord Primate.—Before you divide it.

[illegible]

2917. Lord Justice FitzGibbon.—Certainly, but in the scheme, as it stands, there is no division beyond that between Protestant and Catholic, and any further division could take place only by agreement. We took it for granted that such agreements would provide for this matter, but, if it was an oversight, it was one to which only a passing reference was made, and it was not pressed at the hearing in August. It is, however, not too late to amend it.

Let us come to the broader questions. I will state exactly the mode in which we arrived at the present scheme. You cannot leave out of account what the property is. There are five separate estates or endowments, and the income from land applicable for education was £3,830 a year, on the average of the last three years, for all the schools. Some of these have debts, others have credits, but in addition to the £3,830 the endowments include £12,060 cash. These amounts are most unequally divided. From land Armagh has £944, and Cavan only £774, but Armagh has a debt of £1,180, whereas Cavan has over £6,000 in actual cash. Dungannon has a yearly average of £880, and about £800 cash to the good, while Enniskillen has £1,293 a year, and in addition £6,330, greatly the largest endowment—far beyond any of the others. The condition of the Raphoe endowment, on the other hand, to which Canon Babington is looking with anxious eyes for the future, is so deplorable that unless we do something for him in the direction of a subvention from the others, to which you have been objecting, Donegal will get nothing at all—the Raphoe net income is only £138 a year, and instead of having any money the estate owes £1,077 to the other endowments. It is also burdened with the vested interest of the head master, who has £100 a year, and two assistants claim £30 a year each. When members of the Church complain of their inadequate representation, they do not keep in mind that the three endowments of Armagh, Cavan, and Enniskillen, in the government of which they have a majority, produce £3,011 out of £3,830 per annum, and represent the whole of the £12,000 cash, and £399 besides, while the two Boards on which they are not in a majority, Dungannon and Raphoe, have to deal with endowments with an income of only £1,119, no cash, and £399 to the bad. The three Boards on which the members of the Church have a working majority are the boards administering the Protestant share of £3,011 a year, and £12,468 cash, whereas the two boards on which the Presbyterians are in a majority, have an income of £1,119—two-sevenths against five-sevenths—and they owe a debt of £460 instead of having an interest in £12,300. Now that is a calculation far more material than totting up the representatives on a number of distinct boards, which can never meet or vote together on any subject whatever.

Then what are the terms attaching to this property? From their foundation we believe them to be local endowments, and our Act binds us in every case where we modify educational advantages possessed by the inhabitants of any particular area, to have regard to the privileges which they previously possessed. Rightly or wrongly, my brother Lord Justice and myself, upon a full review of the whole history of these endowments, have arrived at the conclusion that they are local endowments, each in the first instance intended to benefit its own locality; but this is qualified by the clause to which my astute friend, the Dean of Armagh, has attached an application, which I do not think correct. The provision is that after providing the expenses of the school buildings and masters in each district, any residue left over may go to provide school buildings and masters in other districts, and when this is done, then to exhibitions. We believe that clause, fairly and not narrowly put, means that after providing for the present necessities of the intermediate school or schools of each district, the rest of the money should first be applied to similar purposes in other districts, and that is what the Scheme aims at. The distribution of the residue by results is to pay for schools and schoolmasters, and not for exhibitions, as the Dean said. This power is acted on now. Raphoe would have been shut up long ago if large sums of Cavan money had not been diverted from Cavan to Raphoe. Raphoe has been for the past six years carried on by incurring a debt of over £1,000, drawn from the funds of Cavan and Enniskillen. Therefore, not as a matter of theory, but in fact, the funds of each district not required for immediate expenditure within its own area are applicable and are now applied to maintain schools in the other districts, and that is all our scheme does. Where the intermediate education is given, it will, after paying the minimum grants, be paid for. As to the area, you must remember that ours is not the only scheme that will go before the Lord Lieutenant. The Commissioners of Education have prepared a scheme which it will be our duty to send forward to the Lord Lieutenant for comparison with ours. They, the present owners of the endowments, propose to establish one new school under a Roman Catholic head master in Munster, and another in Leinster, to make Dungannon a Presbyterian school, and Armagh a Church school.

The Lord *Primate*.—Three divisions, and we are to have one.

2918. Lord Justice FitzGibbon.—Pardon me. Nothing of the kind. Four schools, one of which is to be under a Church master; but the money is not to be spent in any fixed proportion whatever, and the three schools of Cavan, Enniskillen, and Raphoe are to be shut up. Dr. Traill brought forward another proposal, namely, to extend the area to Antrim and Down; but we could not see why Antrim and Down should come in when Derry, Louth, or indeed any other part of Ireland was left out; and having regard to the very large provision for education already existing in Belfast, bringing in Antrim and Down would have swamped the claims of the districts to which the endowments belong, and except that it might work to the advantage of one party and the disadvantage of the others, we could see nothing to recommend Dr. Traill's proposal. We considered that the area over which we should distribute this money was the old area fixed by the King's Charter and other ancient documents—a curious combination of dioceses and counties—and while each district should have a first charge for its own necessities, if it did not usefully employ the whole of the money, we thought the next charge was not for all Ireland, but for the other districts in the scheme.

The next question was—Who were the people within that area entitled to share this money? I think the idea lies at the bottom of a good deal of criticism directed against the scheme, that the Roman Catholics have no claim, or an inferior claim to the Protestants, on the endowments. If that question is to be argued, Lord Justice Naish and I agree that it must be argued elsewhere, for looking at the history of the Royal Schools, seeing that at this moment a Roman Catholic is head master of Banagher Royal School, a similar foundation, that the Commissioners of Education propose to establish two schools under Roman Catholic masters, and that every inquiry and report goes to show that these funds ought to be made available for every denomination, we have come to the conclusion, and I don't hesitate to say that I concur in it, that when the principle was introduced of no longer recognising any religious denomination as established by law, it went with it that public endowments for education, originally provided out of public funds, should be equally thrown open. Having come to that conclusion, I for one go further, and say that I will be no party to proposing a scheme purporting to admit the members of any religious denomination entitled to its advantages on terms which I know they cannot conscientiously accept. I will not "open" schools to Roman Catholics in the same sense in which Protestant places of worship are open to members of every denomination. Therefore, if the Roman Catholics of these dioceses were entitled to a share of the endowments, it follows that they must get that share for themselves, and accordingly they have got it under our Scheme. They are a homogeneous body, and just now ask the same advantages for your Church. That looks very fair, and it is a proposal we are quite willing to consider, and, what is more, you will permit me to remark that the Scheme gives you an opportunity, in every place where a sufficient majority so agree, of carrying out the object for yourselves. But we cannot force the Protestants of any district to split up their endowment, and to separate bona waste against their will. We believe in the existence of an united Protestant community. Before proposing mixed Protestant Boards we first went to the localities, and I must read you what occurred. At Cavan the proceedings were opened by the Bishop of Kilmore, who read a memorial signed by 677 persons of various classes in the county belonging to all Protestant denominations, and a committee actually appeared before us as representing all these denominations—the Bishop was the head of it; the secretary was, I believe, a Presbyterian minister, and the Methodists supported the demand that the Protestant share of the Cavan money should not be divided. When we went to Enniskillen the proceedings were opened by Mr. Mitchell, a Presbyterian minister, stating (5714):—

"I represent the whole Protestant community and what I am about to read states fairly our views."

Canon Ovenden was examined, and we again had a representative body of all the Protestant denominations claiming to act together in endeavouring to revive Portora. In Raphoe we found a local committee already appointed to work the Royal School if they could get it. Here they are:—Colonel Montgomery, D.L.; Captain Stoney, J.P.; Rev. Dr. Weir; Rev. R. T. Donaldson, M.A.; Rev. Wm. Berkeley, M.A.; Rev. J. A. Bain, M.A.; Thomas Ratcliffe, Raphoe; Wm. Wilson, Raphoe; Wm. Craig, Drumban, farmer. The Hon. Secretary when asked if that committee represented the Protestant and Presbyterian inhabitants of the district answered (6211):—

"Notice was given general notice there was a meeting to be held, and the result was a very large meeting held in the courthouse."

When asked did any Roman Catholics come, he said no, and that the Protestants were sorry for it. When we got to Dungannon the representative Protestant witness was Mr. Robert Stevenson; he was asked (6462):—

"You are chairman of the local committee that took up this question?"

He answered:—

"The chairman of a public meeting; the chairman of the Commissioners, Lord Ranfurly, was requested to call a public meeting and he did do so. I presided."

It was attended by the three Protestant bodies in the town.

"It was well attended by all."

"6463. What are you yourself?—An Episcopalian."

"6464. Were the Presbyterians who were members of the committee satisfied with the representation that you proposed to give them in the governing body?—Quite."

In Armagh, Mr. Elliott, Presbyterian minister, put forward in the strongest manner the Presbyterian desire to have a joint body, but it is just to say that the clerical members of the Church did not join as they had done elsewhere. The Dean of Armagh proposed separate instead of mixed boards. You must, therefore, see how our duties are modified by the fact that the Protestants in four out of the five districts having a first claim on the endowments desire to administer their share jointly.

Rev. Mr. Ovenden.—In Enniskillen we wanted a joint body of Protestants, Presbyterians, and Roman Catholics.

5919. Lord Justice FitzGibbon.—Yes; you wanted to offer the Roman Catholics what you knew they would not take, and this Commission is not prepared to adopt that as a proper solution of the difficulty. The principal if not the only objections to the mixed Protestant board have come from Armagh district and the Diocesan Councils, which we could only treat as representing some members of one Protestant denomination. I need not enter into the details of the differences of opinion among even the members of the Church last August on this point, but you all remember how the Bishop of Clogher was made the subject of a contest between his own Diocesan Council and the Fermanagh local committee. The Council claimed him as its head. The mixed Committee claimed him as their chairman. The Bishop of Kilmore avowed his confidence in a mixed Board for Cavan. Under these circumstances we had to consider what on the whole was the best proposal to make. It was not a case of marrying people under compulsion at all. We had four couples at the altar steps demanding to be married, and you want now to forbid their banns, and of the fifth couple, all you tell us is that one of the parties has not quite made up his mind. Under these circumstances we should only be making mischief if we sent all these denominations to wrangle over details and expose them to the danger of reopening the whole question. But there is a very important matter which we have seen with our own eyes in this part of Ireland, and which has weighed much with us. Wherever we went we found Intermediate schools that were prospering under mixed committees, and we found none such under exclusively Church management. The Bishop of Derry, the Moderator of the General Assembly, and the Mayor of Derry are the Governors of Foyle College. The Londonderry Academical Institution has actually asked us to alter their Scheme, so as to secure increased representation of the Church on their governing body, on which the Presbyterians have hitherto been in a large majority. In Monaghan the ruins of an old diocesan school were taken over from the Commissioners of Education by a mixed local committee, who have made it a good school. Strabane, Coleraine, and Lurgan are all prospering.

Rev. Canon *Babington*.—The Prior School, Lifford, is a good school under Church management.

5920. Lord Justice FitzGibbon.—Yes; I did not mention it, because it is chiefly a primary school, and a private foundation; but if you look at that class of endowment, I should also refer to Tullyvin school, which was under an exclusive Church board, but has been, under a scheme settled by us, placed under a mixed Board, with the concurrence of everybody.

Rev. Canon *Babington*.—You forget that Professor Witherow was examined.

5921. Lord Justice FitzGibbon.—Professor Witherow was the only Presbyterian witness who gave evidence against mixed education. He stood very much in the same position towards all the other members of his own denomination that the Armagh Church witnesses occupied with regard to all the other Protestants of Ulster who appeared before us.

The Lord Bishop of *Kilmore*.—So far as we have gone our joint board has worked well in Cavan.

Colonel *Saunderson*.—The Synod has not brought forward any resolution against your principle of mixed boards.

5922. Lord Justice FitzGibbon.—Then what is the meaning of the inadequate representation of the Church on the Protestant boards? If we accept your principle of separating the Protestants how are we to divide the money? If you once go beyond a single Protestant board how can you stop? It is all very well for you Church people to talk of Protestant Christianity as divided into Church and non-Church, as Colonel Nugent spoke of Catholic and non-Catholic, but what will you do with such figures as we have to deal with, where, for example, in Fermanagh the Methodists are 6,681, and the Presbyterians only 1,936. In Donegal the Presbyterians are 15,000 and the Methodists only 1,810; in Cavan the Presbyterians are 3,260, and the Methodists only 1,000, yet they are just as distinct from the Presbyterians as you are, and they protest against being either ignored or merged with the Presbyterians. The next point is as regards the principle of division, and with all respect, the principle of the scheme is not what the objections state. You complain that the Roman Catholics get a share otherwise according to statistics; we have hitherto deliberately refused to divide the money according to any numerical proportion. Our principle is to give to each distinct body which is entitled to a share the smallest sum which ought to be sufficient to enable them to maintain one good school. The reason why we have divided the Raphoe Endowment equally between the Catholics and the Protestants is not because the statistical proportion of Catholics and Protestants was equal, but because the Endowment is so small that nothing less than half would be of the slightest use to any body. We believed the localities had a right to get a somewhat larger local grant where their endowment is large than where it is small, and for that reason we gave twenty-five per cent. in certain cases, and in Cavan raised it to thirty per cent., but in every case we tried to give the local board a sum of money which would afford substantial assistance to them. We endeavoured to distribute all the rest of the fund in proportion to the actual Intermediate work done, not by way of reward for results, but because we believed the results to be the very best evidence of the true demand for Intermediate education of each denomination in each locality. Many Roman Catholic witnesses urged us to divide in proportion to the numbers of the population. We rejected that because we regard these endowments as devoted to superior schools. We rejected the literate population as the test, because it brought in the absentee rich who have taken their sons away from Irish schools, and would compel them to bring money into the district from which they had sent away their own sons, and, on the other hand, it would have left out those members of the uneducated poor by whom the argument might fairly be used that if they had more means they would get more education. No statistical test has been proposed which offered any prospect of acceptance. I admit every test is open to difficulty. We are not satisfied yet with the test we have got, but in adopting it and discarding the previous one, we were supported by the evidence of Dr. Moore Morgan and Archbishop Walsh, and in fact everybody agreed that our original test by public examinations was unsatisfactory, and that the single test was more likely to lead to a fair result. Mr. Bewley, counsel for the Armagh Board, said that it would be better to have one standard, and that it would be impossible to compare different standards. Mr. Shaw, for the Presbyterians, was of the same opinion, and in the end all seemed to agree to a single test; and the test of the single inspector to be appointed by the Lord Lieutenant appeared to be approved. Dr. Moore Morgan said, in August last (10080):—

"If we could get a broad, fair, and uniform test, we are all of opinion that it would be more satisfactory. I am sure that a diversity of standard would never give satisfaction all round. *Lord Justice FitzGibbon*.—What would you think of having but one inspector? *Rev. Dr. Morgan*.—That is far better—the inspector proposed in the schedule."

Mr. Drummond, who represented the Roman Catholics of Clogher, said—

"My clients would be satisfied to have one inspector appointed by the Commissioners."

And before that Archbishop Walsh had said—

"It may not be necessary to have more than one examiner. It is not a competitive examination."

With that evidence before us we have proposed to give each intermediate school of the prescribed size and efficiency an equal sum of money for every boy who passes the Intermediate Examinations in grammar school subjects, but also to give it as a main and regular source of income, an allowance for every boy to whom is given *bona fide* grammar school education during the year. I would direct your attention, with the view to making them more efficient, not merely to the schedule to which the Dean of Armagh has referred, but to the clauses of the Scheme which define what a qualified intermediate school is to be. Clause 43 prescribes the conditions which must be fulfilled by a school before it receives any share of the Royal School endowments. The list of subjects to be taught include a very substantial intermediate education, far higher than the test of merely passing the Intermediate Examinations, which can now be done without Latin, Greek, or even English. A boy could pass in a far smaller number of subjects than we require to be taught. Then we provide that the school shall afford intermediate education to not less than twenty pupils, each of whom shall have made 100 attendances in the year. The Scheme is much more precise than the schedule to which the Dean referred. There it goes on—

"The Inspector appointed by the Lord Lieutenant shall [illegible] the schools, and shall report and certify that during each school year for which a payment is claimed the buildings, premises, and appliances of the school have been sufficient and suitable for an efficient intermediate school, and have been in good order, that a competent staff for the efficient teaching of the required subjects has been employed in the school and that intermediate education has been afforded therein to the required number of pupils of the prescribed age."

If you can give us any words by which you can make these provisions more stringent we shall be glad to consider them, but we have framed these clauses with the intention of excluding from any money grant whatever a school that is not a large school, with an efficient staff, and a considerable number of pupils receiving *bona fide* intermediate or grammar school education, and we count such pupils only. If you can give us a test by which the school master will get a grant for every pupil to whom he really gives genuine intermediate education you will have solved the difficulty. That is the view with which we put these clauses forward.

The Dean of *Armagh*.—Your Inspector does not examine?

3922. Lord Justice FitzGibbon.—He must certify. We cannot insist that he shall examine every pupil separately, that might lead to very considerable expense. On the other hand the Lord Lieutenant is responsible for the appointment of a competent inspector, and I don't see how a gentleman of capacity could certify that intermediate education had been given to a definite number of pupils unless he had satisfied himself of its reality. Remember too the schedule imposes the duty on the Commissioners if there should be any doubt about the inspector's report. Then as to the seven pupils who are to pass the Intermediate Examinations, you did not say so here, but elsewhere you have attacked the smallness of this number as intended to tell in favour of the Roman Catholics and against the Protestants. In fact the pressure upon us to reduce the number to seven all came from the other side. The Roman Catholics have in nearly every district one large school—Cavan, Monaghan, Armagh, Letterkenny—for which they urgently want all the money they can get. The pressure came from the Protestants to lower the standard in order to let in smaller schools. We have been struggling hard against frittering the money away, and we believe the number of schools which will be able to qualify under the Scheme will be very small. The best proof of this is the figures I have given you for 1888. There are not more than three schools under Protestant management in the whole six counties that could now fulfil the prescribed conditions, and during the first three years they must work up to our standard of good schools. You must remember too that there is a provision in this scheme after that period, that if even four out of the five districts failed to put up any school to the required standard, the whole of the money would run to even a single school reaching the standard in the remaining district. I have now given you an outline of the real grounds on which this scheme has been framed, but do not misunderstand what I have said. I am not dogmatically insisting on our present opinion in a matter which we have yet judicially to decide. The problem is a very difficult one. We do not expect to prepare a scheme that will not be objected to, but all parties will see the great advantages of coming as near as possible to an agreement amongst yourselves before the matter passes from us to the Privy Council. I will only throw out one suggestion. There are great advantages in having any large boarding school under the management of persons of one denomination. You have two schools close together which have never succeeded at the same time—Dungannon and Armagh. They are competing schools in every sense. If our figures are right, the Presbyterians are entitled to a majority in Tyrone, and the Church people are certainly in a majority, though not a large one, in Armagh. If the Protestants of these two districts can come to an agreement before the scheme passes away from us, we can do by the scheme what we have left open to be done afterwards.* We could treat Tyrone and Armagh, for Protestant purposes, as one endowment, give you two Protestant Boards, and let each be denominational, each taking a school; but this can only be done if the local bodies will agree, as has occurred in other places, notably with reference to the Dungannon School buildings, between the Protestants and Catholics. As the Bishop of Clogher has mentioned that he reserved his objections with respect to Portora, I should like him to know that our action as to Portora has been entirely guided by the opinion which we hold as jurors, having no personal interest in the matter, that we could not inflict a greater injury on the Fermanagh Protestant Board than imposing on them the burden of keeping up with something like half the endowment a school which the whole of the endowment has failed to support.

The Lord Bishop of *Clogher*.—But the difficulty arises in meeting the conditions in three years for want of the buildings.

3724. Lord Justice FitzGibbon.—But within six months after the scheme comes into force you can have £1,500 in cash, which the scheme allows you to expend in buying or building a suitable school.

The Lord Bishop of *Clogher*.—You must give us fair play for three years.

3725. Lord Justice FitzGibbon.—During the first three years it is extremely unlikely that any district will have all the endowment, because the vested interests of the local masters takes precedence of everything else. In the case of Armagh, while Dr. Morgan's annuity is in existence, the amount divisible will be very much less than half the endowment. But if you sell Portora, you will get £3,500 for your share at once.

The Dean of *Armagh*.—I would not presume to enter into any sort of discussion on the judicial statement just made, but I will say we do not object to the small number of seven, but we object that the small number of seven is opening the door. It is a matter of counting heads; it is not to the number seven we object.

3726. Rev. Dr. Molloy.—Is it too small or too large?

The Dean of *Armagh*.—I did not express any opinion on that point. I did not object to the number seven at all.

3727. Lord Justice FitzGibbon.—It is introduced as a fair number to secure that the school is a good one. Any school passing seven at the Intermediate Examinations in the prescribed subjects would probably have twenty pupils. The ordinary scale is about a third.

The Dean of *Armagh*.—I express no opinion upon that. I object to clause 1 in the schedule as coming into operation as soon as clause 2 had taken effect. Clause 2 is a prize for the school that has passed seven, and I don't understand our deputation as objecting to clause 2; but it is to clause 1 the objection is taken.

3728. Lord Justice FitzGibbon.—Clause 1 does not count heads indiscriminately. It counts only those heads that fulfil the conditions of the scheme, and we beg you to help us in making those conditions so stringent that no boy shall be counted who has not throughout the year got genuine intermediate education in grammar school subjects. No one can fairly say, for example, that under our scheme if a Christian Brothers School, for instance, had an intermediate class at the head of it from which seven boys passed, all the other pupils could be counted for results.

The Dean of *Armagh*.—I did not intend to raise an objection to the seven at all.

3729. Rev. Dr. Molloy.—This clause to which you are now objecting seems to be the very provision which answers the first objection of the Synod. The objection is that the proportion given to Roman Catholics is excessive. Our idea was that each denomination had a right to some substantial aid towards at least one school; such aid is afforded by the minimum grant, which, in the three largest endowments, is fixed at 23 per cent. of the net income. After thus providing for each denomination the means necessary to maintain at least one school in each locality, we propose to distribute the residue between the several schools, according to the number of pupils receiving in each a *bonâ fide* intermediate education. This plan cannot be said to give an excessive proportion of the endowments to any one denomination; it gives to each first a necessary minimum, and distributes the remainder according to the number of pupils taught. If Colonel Plunkett is right in his estimate that the number of Protestants receiving intermediate education in the six counties will far exceed the number of Catholics, it follows that, under our scheme the Protestant schools will receive by far the largest part of the endowments.

Rev. Canon *Babington*.—We calculate that seven would not bring in a large number.

3730. Lord Justice FitzGibbon.—Seven is only one condition of the test. No school shall be regarded as efficient unless it passes seven boys, but that is over and above the condition that it shall also throughout the year give intermediate education to at least twenty boys. The whole difficulty, and I don't deny it, is to make sure that every boy of the twenty gets *bonâ fide* intermediate education. You all appear agreed that you would be satisfied with the Lord Lieutenant's inspectors if they examined the boys separately. We don't know who the Lord Lieutenant's inspector may be; but we will not take it for granted that somebody will be appointed who will certify what he has not ascertained. We provide "the Commissioners may accept the certificate of the inspector appointed by the Lord Lieutenant as sufficient evidence in the case of any pupil or pupils that the prescribed conditions have been fulfilled, or they may require such further or other evidence as they may think necessary." Therefore we do not bind you to any superficial certificate, and we have left it open to you to say that the Lord Lieutenant's inspector did not examine properly, and that any school ought not to get the endowment.

The Dean of *Armagh*.—He must only be satisfied that the conditions are fulfilled.

Lord Justice FitzGibbon.—As to each and every [illegible] whom he certifies.

3731. Rev. Dr. *Morgan*.—I would like to correct what would appear to be a misapprehension on page 450 of the last report of the Commissioners. Archbishop Walsh was examined very fully on the subject of the test as far as I remember; and as far as I understand Archbishop Walsh, he said—"Such a system" (as he proposed, that is, inspector's) "is worked by the National Board without difficulty in the thousands of schools

* [illegible] Appendix B., No. III. (m), et seq., p. 335–343.

[illegible]

they have under their direction. Probably there would not be more than forty or fifty schools altogether concerned in this matter." I understand that the Archbishop proposed that the examiner should attend as the National Board inspector attends.

3932. Lord Justice FITZGIBBON.—Certainly. And I made the objection that the cost of any sufficient inspection would be great, and the schoolmasters would never be satisfied with an examination that did not enable the inspector to report that each boy was being properly taught in all the required subjects, to which Archbishop Walsh said that perhaps the cost of the inspection might be paid out of the Consolidated Fund, as the expenses of the Commissioners of Education are now. I fear he might as well expect to get it from the next world. As the result of the whole discussion, we put into the scheme that the report of the inspector of the Lord Lieutenant might be taken as sufficient, with an appeal to the Commissioners.

Rev. Dr. MOLLOY.—The inspector must report not only that a certain number of pupils have received intermediate education, but that the staff is sufficient to give such education efficiently.

Rev. Dr. *Morgan*.—I think Mr. Fearon, who was one of the Assistant Commissioners, and is, I think, an authority, says in his work on school inspection—"No test of results can be considered satisfactory which is not accompanied by examination."

3933. Rev. Dr. MOLLOY.—Certainly; but the word "result" is very ambiguous. The "result" we look to is the number of boys getting *bona fide* intermediate education.

Lord Justice FITZGIBBON.—We have got weighted more or less by the unfavourable opinions expressed against what is known as "payment by results" under the Intermediate and National systems for example; but as put by Archbishop Walsh, our scheme proposes not a competition between pupils, but between schools. We want to ascertain the amount of teaching done during the whole year by the participating schools, and we do not want to expose ourselves to the observation that if a schoolmaster hammers away at stupid boys all the year and teaches them what they can learn, he is to get less than the master who has the good luck to get a clever pupil who passes the Intermediate Examinations.

Rev. Provost *Crozier*.—We Enniskilleners are firmly convinced that great care must be taken if you take Portora from us compulsorily that we should have a fair start, because the Roman Catholics have their school premises and all complete in Monaghan. They get their *bona fide* share for the first previous three years, and they will start all right; but if we are turned out in spite of our protests, and left homeless and houseless, and we have to spend those previous three years in finding a site and building a school, we will commence our three years when the whole opportunity has passed. We say that Portora, so far from being a burden on us—it is not like an isolated building—it is surrounded by an admirable piece of land, the rent of which is paid by people in the town to whom it is let, and is amply ample to keep the premises in repair—we could have in Portora a place for our head master and a residence for our assistant masters, accommodation for our boys, good room in the dormitories for ventilation; in fact, I would say every inch of Portora is an endowment to us for the purposes of education. We have to thank you for your kindly care.

3934. Lord Justice FITZGIBBON.—The more valuable you make out Portora to be, the more you increase its value as part of the local endowment, and if you take Portora, with its lands and buildings, you must give a *quid pro quo* to the Roman Catholic share. I am not expressing a judicial opinion at all, but simply telling you that, looking at Portora, we all thought £3,500 in cash would supply a much more suitable school for the wants of the Protestants of Fermanagh. If you take Portora you must debit yourselves with some £7,000 as its value, and you must diminish your funds available for its support. It is perfectly open to us to make an arrangement for any short period while you are looking out for a house. We might let you have some temporary school accommodation in Portora, of course charging a rent for it against your revenue; but you cannot permanently have Portora as a whole without giving to the other side a corresponding amount of value. It is a matter of common sense and prudence, and you must allow me to keep my opinion that £3,500 is better than taking Portora on the chance of making money to maintain it by letting the grazing land to a butcher in the town.

3935. Dr. TRAILL.—I don't want to go into any controversy, but as the Lord Justice referred to the fact that I proposed to bring in Antrim and Down, I would wish to state in a very few words, in the words of my report to the Lord Lieutenant, the reasons why I think it should be done. These words were as follows:

"As the original founders of the endowments by Royal Charter obviously intended them to be used for the benefit of the Protestant settlers, as part of the scheme for the Plantation of Ulster, it would seem only reasonable that when these benefits are being extended to Roman Catholics, they should be further extended to the large Protestant population of Ulster, by including the Counties of Antrim and Down and the remaining portion of Londonderry not at present included in the Scheme."

I thought if it was right to extend the endowment to other counties such as Monaghan it should be further extended to that part of Ulster which contained a large Protestant population. I don't think that unreasonable. The effect of my proposition would be to divide the fund into three equal parts between the three principal denominations—the Church of Ireland, the Presbyterians, and the Roman Catholics. I think it is only right to explain why I proposed to bring in Antrim and Down.

3936. Lord Justice FITZGIBBON.—The reason of our inability to follow that explanation was that we saw no more reason to extend the endowments to the Protestant population of that part of Ulster than to the Protestant population of the rest of Ireland. Besides, it would have brought the great schools of Belfast in on these small endowments, though they do not need them.

Dr. TRAILL.—These endowments were part of the Plantation of Ulster for the benefit of the Protestant settlers.

3937. Lord Justice FITZGIBBON.—Including Antrim and Down in the Plantation of Ulster is a historical inaccuracy. The Plantation no more extended to Antrim and Down than to Cork and Kerry.

Dr. TRAILL.—We all know that. I never said that Antrim and Down were part of the Plantation; neither was Monaghan.

3938. Lord Justice FITZGIBBON.—And no reason has been given for Dr. Traill's exclusion of the Plantation County of Londonderry, except that the Presbyterian majority there would have upset his calculations.

The Dean of *Armagh*.—We objected most specifically to the private educational endowments being divided.

3939. Lord Justice FITZGIBBON.—There was no discussion about that point except so far as it was involved in the question whether there should be mixed Protestant boards or not. We don't question that if there is to be any further subdivision of the Protestant share, the private endowments should follow the share of the founder's denomination. Under the scheme there could only be sub-division by agreement, and we took it for granted that in any agreement these private endowments would follow the denomination to which the donors belonged.

The Dean of *Armagh*.—If there is a mixed board the endowment should go to some Church of Ireland school under that board, and in support of that we claim your own definite assertion that the private endowments should go to the denomination to which the donor belonged.

3940. Lord Justice FITZGIBBON.—This money is in bricks and mortar, and so long as the schools are used by a school board, or by people of various denominations, I don't see how you can subdivide the endowments that are made to them; but if you sell them we will provide for giving the proceeds to the donor's denomination. Kindly send us all your proposals in writing, in the nature of definite objections or amendments, without unnecessary adjectives or adverbs, and we will be happy to consider them. The date up to which we can receive objections to the revised scheme has been extended to the 16th of May. Immediately after that day all the objections will be printed, and as soon as possible a day will be appointed for the final discussion.

The Dean of *Armagh*.—The only thing we want to do is to put our objections before you in black and white, and to get rid of the adjective "animal."

The Lord Bishop of *Derry*.—I think it is our duty, and we would be sadly wanting in our duty, if we did not thank you for the great courtesy and kindness, and, I take the liberty of adding, the clearness with which your remarks have been made.

The proceedings terminated.

PUBLIC SITTING—TUESDAY, MAY 14, 1889.

At the Convent National Schools, Rochfort Bridge.

Present:—The Very Rev. GERALD MOLLOY, D.D., D.SC., ANTHONY TRAILL, Esq., LL.D., M.D., F.T.C.D., and Professor DOUGHERTY, M.A., Assistant Commissioners.

The Assistant Secretary, N. D. MURPHY, was in attendance.

SHIEL'S ENDOWMENT, ROCHFORT BRIDGE, CO. WESTMEATH.

Mr. Wm. *Murray*, Solicitor, Mullingar, attended on behalf of the Trustees of Miss Shiel's will.

There were also present—Rev. *P. Fagan*, P.P., and *James King*, Esq.

Rev. Dr. MOLLOY made an introductory statement.

The Rev. *Peter Fagan*, P.P., sworn and examined.

3941. Rev. Dr. MOLLOY.—You are the Parish Priest of Rochfort Bridge?—Yes.

3942. When were you appointed?—In June, 1875.

3943. And are you also trustee of Miss Shiel's Charity?—I am.

3944. When were you appointed trustee?—Immediately after Miss Shiel's death; I think it should be about last September two years she died.

Mr. *Murray*.—I will send you up the deed appointing new trustees.

3945. Rev. Dr. MOLLOY—(To witness).—Are any of the original trustees now living?—No.

3946. Who were they?

Mr. *Murray*.—The original trustees were Father Robinson, Bernard W. Delany, and the Rev. William Hope.

3947. Rev. Dr. MOLLOY—(To witness)—They are all dead?—Yes.

3948. Who are the present trustees?—Mr. James King, myself, and the Rev. Michael Hughes; he is a native of this place, and he is curate of Castlepollard, but all his people live here, and I suppose it was thought that he would have an interest in the place, and that was the reason he was appointed.

3949. Dr. TRAILL.—Were the present trustees appointed during Miss Shiel's lifetime?—They were not.

Mr. *Murray*.—The last trustee was the Rev. William Hope, and the present trustees were appointed by Father Hope's executors.

3950. Rev. Dr. MOLLOY—(To witness).—From the deed it appears that it was the object of Miss Shiel to found and maintain a convent at Gortamloe House?—Yes.

3951. But since the deed was made, a convent has been established here at Rochfort Bridge?—Yes; the convent was here before the deed was executed at all, but I think it was opened here with the expectation that the premises at Gortamloe would go to the parish priest as a help to support the nuns.

3952. At present the residence of the nuns is adjacent to the schools?—Yes.

3953. When was the new convent built?—About sixteen years ago; the present buildings, where the school is now carried on, were originally the convent.

3954. But the new convent, you say, was built about sixteen years ago?—It was built about sixteen years ago.

3955. And the schools here now are quite sufficient to afford accommodation to the children of the neighbourhood?—Quite sufficient.

3956. Is it the opinion of the present trustees that the endowment would be better applied in maintaining the convent and schools at Rochfort Bridge than in founding a new convent and new schools at Gortamloe House?—That is the opinion of the trustees.

3957. Have the children from the neighbourhood of Gortamloe House easy access to the schools in Rochfort Bridge?—Oh, yes; if you had the schools at Gortamloe House the children would have to go a great deal farther—about half a mile or so—and the weight of the population is on this side of Gortamloe House.

3958. Then it is your opinion that the intention of Miss Shiel would be better carried out if the endowment was applied to the convent here than if a new convent were founded at Gortamloe House?—It is; besides I don't think the proceeds of the property would enable us to do that—then we should have to go to very large expenditure to convert that house into a convent.

3959. Dr. TRAILL.—Did she leave you money besides?—Only a small piece of land.

3960. Rev. Dr. MOLLOY.—You think that it would not be practicable to establish a convent at Gortamloe House?—I do. I don't think we could do it unless we spent a number of years setting the land—say twenty or thirty years—and even then, after the expenses would be deducted, there would be very little saving effected.

3961. And further, a convent founded there would not be as efficient for the purpose she intended as the convent here is?—No; this is the community which Miss Shiel intended to benefit.

3962. Dr. TRAILL.—What would you like to do with the property—would you sell it or let it?—Sell it if we could, and get the money and invest it.

3963. What do you suppose it would realise if sold?—Well, I was telling Mr. Murray that I thought it

May 14, 1886.

Rev. Peter Fegan, P.P.

would realise something like £2,000, but he does not agree with me in that.

3964. He thinks that too much?—Yes, he seems to think that £1,300 would be as much as we would get for it.

3965. I suppose that there is so much property in the market that this would not bring so much as you expect?—I don't know; it is a pretty thing, and is suited nicely for a hunting lodge.

3966. Rev. Dr. Molloy.—Can you tell us approximately the distance from Gortmaloe House to the present Convent Schools?—It is a mile exactly.

3967. When did Miss Shiel die?—September, I think, two years—that would be September, 1883.

3968. And during her lifetime the present convent and schools were erected?—Yes.

3969. Do you know whether she expressed any opinion as to what, in respect to this matter, during her life?—Oh, I think she did; she certainly wrote a letter before she died, which was to be handed to the nuns here—to the Rev. Mother—but it was not to be given to them until after her death, and this letter requested the nuns to discharge some little duties for her.

3970. Dr. Traill.—Is that letter forthcoming?—I think so. It was to this effect:—"I trust you will do this much for me as you are going to gain a great deal by me." Beside that, it was all along, during her lifetime, understood that the property would go to these nuns, and she exacted a good deal from them on account of this. When she was ill they had to go and get special permission from the Bishop to go and nurse her. She was ill for a good while and suffered a great deal, and the Bishop gave his consent to the nuns. There is no mistake about it, it was fully intended the property was to go to the nuns, and should go to the nuns for the purpose of a convent here. She told me herself, in the only conversation I ever had with her in connexion with this endowment, she gave Gortmaloe to the nuns in pursuance of a promise made to her own mother.

3971. Rev. Dr. Molloy.—Was this convent here when the bequest was made?—Yes.

3972. Professor Dougherty.—But I understand that the new buildings were erected since the execution of the deed?—They have been; the nuns were here in the house we are now sitting in, the schoolhouse first; but it was expected that they would come and move down to the Gortmaloe House after her death. The place they were in, however, was unhealthy and unsuited for them, and the nuns began to lose health and some of them died, and as it was seen that there was no immediate prospect of Gortmaloe House coming to them the nuns could not continue living here, and the new convent was built twelve or thirteen years before her death.

3973. Rev. Dr. Molloy.—Now, coming to the existing school buildings, in which we are sitting, in whom are they vested?—I think by deed they are vested in the Bishop of the diocese, the late parish priest, and Mr. R. Coffey, of Newcastle.

3974. How are the trustees continued?—The Bishop and Mr. Coffey are still surviving.

3975. Is there any provision in the deed by which a new trustee is appointed when a vacancy occurs?—I don't think there is. I am not aware. The schools are held by lease, and the lease is drawn in favour of these trustees, and there may be some clause in the lease to perpetuate one by another; I think the lease is for 999 years.

3976. Have you got the lease?—I think it is lodged in the Diocesan Archives at Navan.

3977. Dr. Traill.—To whom do you pay the rent?—Mr. Fitzmaurice, the land agent.

3978. Rev. Dr. Molloy.—Would there be any objection to letting us see the lease of these school buildings?—Certainly not.

3979. Dr. Traill.—And the letter that was written by Miss Shiel also?—Certainly.

3980. Rev. Dr. Molloy.—Who is the manager of the school?—I am.

3981. You are the manager recognised by the National Board?—Yes.

3982. And it would be your desire, I suppose, that the income derived from Miss Shiel's endowment should be applied in maintaining the schools and in paying the teachers?—Yes, that is what we wish.

3983. How many nuns are at present engaged in teaching in the schools?—At present there are seven.

3984. From the return handed in I see that the average attendance for 1883 was 163, for 1884, 16[illegible], for 1885, two quarters, 155; the present number on the roll, 155. It is not remarkable that the average attendance is equal to the number on the roll?—That is for the last two quarters.

3985. Dr. Traill.—How do you account for the falling off in attendance?—I cannot account for it.

3986. When was the number on the roll taken?—Yesterday; I asked the Rev. Mother to get it for me.

3987. Professor Dougherty.—The average attendance is taken for the first two quarters of the year?—We are on another quarter that is not yet ended; we are in the third quarter.

3988. Rev. Dr. Molloy.—I see that the number who pay from 1d. to 2d. per week is eighty-five, and that the number of free pupils is seventy-two?—Yes.

3989. Dr. Traill.—Is it a mixed boys and girls school?—Yes, there are forty boys.

3990. Rev. Dr. Molloy.—I heard from the Rev. Mother that the boys come here to the age of about—Yes.

3991. And then they pass over to the boys school?—Yes.

3992. Should you think it desirable that we should prepare a scheme constituting a body of trustees for the management of the property, and vest the property in them in trust for the maintenance of the school and the payment of the nuns engaged in teaching?—We have got that already by the present trustees, if only we had power to apply the proceeds of the property.

3993. Yes, but you have got trustees who will die, and cannot be replaced without expense?—Trustees for the present school here?

3994. I was speaking of the trustees of the Gortmaloe property; but perhaps what I said may be also true of the trustees of your present school premises?—I am not sure of that; there may be some clause in the lease enabling the appointment of trustees.

3995. Do you think the present trustees of the school premises are a satisfactory body for the management of the schools?—I think they would do very well.

3996. You are not one of them?—I pay the rent in their absence. Father Robbins is dead, and the other gentleman, Mr. Coffey, is the local man, but I suppose the lease that was taken to them would contain a clause that will provide for their successors.

3997. Dr. Traill.—Is not the parish priest an ex-officio trustee?—Not in that lease at all events.

3998. Rev. Dr. Molloy.—Would it not be better that you should be one of the trustees?—I suppose it would be better.

3999. Was your predecessor one?—Yes, he was one of them, and the lease was granted to the bishop, and Father Robbins, and Mr. Coffey; but if there is not any provision in that lease for the succession of trustees, I think it would be very desirable if you would make provision for it.

4000. I may tell you, Father Fegan, that what we find in many of these cases is that school buildings and endowments are vested in trustees, and it frequently happens that the trustees die, and no others having been appointed in their place, the legal ownership of the buildings and endowments passes to the representatives of the trustees that are dead. That has happened here yet, but it may happen?—No, it has not happened yet; but it would be a great matter if you could provide against anything like that.

4001. Dr. Traill.—Would you wish to have the same trustees for the school buildings as for Miss Sheil's endowment?—Yes.

4002. But they are not the same at present?—No.

4003. Rev. Dr. Molloy.—Do you see any difficulty in having a body of trustees who would manage the property at Gortanalee, and in whom the school buildings and premises should be also vested?—I don't understand you. My house and grounds are all in one lease with the school buildings, and this lease was granted by the landlord, Captain Rochfort, and I don't know how that will be; how could you do that? Abolish the rights of leases?

4004. Dr. Traill.—A new governing body incorporated by us might hold both endowments?—The difficulty is that the property would pass into other hands, the leasehold not being an endowment.

4005. It won't if we give you a governing body. What is the term of the lease?—99 years.

4006. Professor Dougherty.—Are the convent grounds included in the lease?—They are.

4007. Would there be any difficulty in placing the convent itself in the hands of a body of trustees created for the purpose of managing the rest of the property in Gortanalee?—I don't think there would, except that I already referred to.

4008. Rev. Dr. Molloy.—What is your own wish in the matter?—Well, just to let it stand as it is. As long as there is a convent here educating the poor children, we wish that this endowment may be applied to the same for that purpose, and then if, on the expiry of the lease, the convent grounds should pass to other hands, the Gortanalee property still remains for the education of the poor.

4009. If you wish we can constitute a corporate body of trustees for the management of the Gortanalee property, and also for the management of the school, or we can constitute a corporate body simply to manage the property, and pay over the income to the manager of the school. Which of these two courses would you prefer?—What we would desire would be to have the property managed for the benefit of the nuns, and to pay the proceeds of it to them so long as they continue educating the children.

4010. Professor Dougherty.—You are manager of the schools at present?—Yes.

4011. Would you like to have the present trustees connected in the management of the property?—Yes.

4012. Rev. Dr. Molloy.—And how would you propose to perpetuate that body. In our scheme we might provide that the parish priest should be always a member, *ex officio*?—Yes, and the bishop.

4013. You would have the bishop also *ex officio*?—Yes.

4014. And we might give them power to apply all the money received from Gortanalee for the support of the nuns and the maintenance of the schools?—I think that would do very well.

4015. Professor Dougherty.—Who is Father Hughes?—Well, his people all live about here, and he was born here himself.

4016. Where does he live now?—He is curate of Castlepollard.

4017. Is that within easy reach of the schools?—It is about twenty miles from them.

4018. Dr. Traill.—It is better that the trustees should reside in the place?—The parish priest and the bishop could always be got, and Mr. King lives convenient here.

4019. Rev. Dr. Molloy.—At present how is the property managed?—We only got it since June last, and when we got up possession we put a caretaker to mind there as we hoped to have a scheme from your board, and then we let the land in grazing, which realised within a few shillings of £30. That was all we did since.

4020. What is the extent of the land?—It is about fifty acres, Irish.

4021. Dr. Traill.—Is not the land worth £4 an acre?—It is not.

4022. Rev. Dr. Molloy.—And all you have realised since you got the land in June last is £30?—Yes.

4023. What do you calculate it would be likely to realise under a scheme which would enable you to let or sell the house and land?—I cannot possibly guess as to what it would be worth.

4024. I think you said you expected by selling it to get £2,000?—I said that to Mr. Mooney, and he said I was foolish to expect any such thing.

4025. If you were to let it from year to year what would it yield?—I think it would be uncertain; we might set the thing for two years and we might have it waste for a long time.

4026. Dr. Traill.—Would it not be worth £2 an acre?—It is not; there are many acres not worth 10s.

4027. That is where the whins are?—Yes; I don't think it would be worth 30s. an acre on an average all round.

4028. Rev. Dr. Molloy.—That would be £75 a year?—It is not worth that, the land alone.

4029. Is it subject to any rent?—None whatever, but the taxes, county cess, and poor rates.

4030. Then the income, practically available, would be whatever you can make out of the house and fifty Irish acres of land?—That is it.

4031. And you estimate that at possibly £70 a year?—It could not do that with certainty.

4032. Less than £70?—Yes, the land would not be worth it.

4033. Would you say £50 for the land?—It might bring that.

4034. Dr. Traill.—The house might be sold for a hunting lodge?—Yes, it would be sold for that.

4035. Are you satisfied, Mr. Mooney, about the appointment of the trustees?

Mr. *Mooney*.—Oh, yes.

4036. Were they appointed through the court?—They were not; they were appointed outside the court by the executors of the surviving trustee.

4037. Rev. Dr. Molloy.—Were there any costs in connection with the appointment of the new trustees?—Oh, yes, the costs of the preparation of the deeds.

4038. What would they come to?—Possibly £7 or £8, I think.

4039. So that the death of a trustee is rather an expensive affair?—Yes. What Father Fegan refers to, so far as the buildings are concerned, is it clear they would not appoint trustees at all; they don't require them to deal with the property except in a Deed of Trust of this kind. But if this place is sold and the money funded, it would be absolutely necessary that you should constitute a corporate body so that there should be new trustees appointed.

4040. Dr. Traill.—Did the court sanction the appointment of the present trustees?—Yes.

4041. Rev. Dr. Molloy.—The principal object of our scheme will be to constitute a corporate body, and to secure the application of the income according to the intentions of the founder?—It would be better to have a corporate body appointed. I am quite sure the bishop will be glad to have that.

4042. Rev. Dr. Molloy.—Do you know anything about the lease of the present school?—I don't know anything about it, but I am aware that Miss Shiel, during her lifetime, wished the benefit of this fund to go to this community of nuns.

4043. But is there any evidence that she intended the income to be expended on the convent here, and not on a new convent to be established at Gortanalee House?—I think not, but it was always her intention that the nuns should derive the benefit of the gift.

4044. What I understood from Father Fegan's evidence was, that the spirit and intention of the

May 15, 1889.

Rev. Peter Fagan, P.P.

founder would be more efficiently carried out by applying the income to the schools here than by establishing a new convent and school at Gortnamona House?—Certainly, it would be waste of money to do it at Gortnamona.

4045. Mr. King, do you wish to offer any evidence in the matter?

Mr. King.—I am perfectly satisfied with the evidence given by Father Fagan.

4046. How long have you been a trustee?—The same time as the others.

4047. Were the three trustees appointed together? Yes.

4048. Dr. Traill.—Were they appointed at the time of the suit in Chancery?

Mr. Hawley.—They were appointed for the purpose of that suit. At the death of Miss Shiel all the trustees were dead, and it was necessary to appoint new trustees. There was an ejectment brought in the names of the trustees, and a defence was entered to that by Mr. Hawley. The suit was heard in the Chancery Division and judgment was given in favour of the trustees.

4049. Rev. Dr. Molloy.—That shows the advantage of having a corporate body, for when the trustees died, as in this particular case, there was no new appointment until it became necessary for the purposes of a law suit?

Mr. Hawley.—That is so.

(The inquiry terminated).

May 31, 1889.

PUBLIC SITTING—FRIDAY, MAY 31, 1889.

At the Four Courts, Dublin.

*ULSTER ROYAL SCHOOLS ENDOWMENTS. †OBJECTIONS AND AMENDMENTS TO THE ‡REVISED DRAFT SCHEME.

Present:—The Right Hon. Lord Justice FitzGibbon and the Right Hon. Lord Justice Naish, Judicial Commissioners; and the Rev. Gerald Molloy, D.D., D.Sc., Anthony Traill, Esq., LL.D., M.D., F.T.C.D., and Professor Dougherty, M.A., Assistant Commissioners.

The Secretary, Wm. Edward Ellis, LL.B., and the Assistant Secretary, N. D. Murphy, were in attendance.

Lord Justice FitzGibbon.—We propose to take the objections received in the order in which they appear in the printed list. The first objection is from the Commissioners of Education, for whom Mr. M'Dowell, their Secretary, appears. The first objection is quite right; they wish power to appoint a deputy for the Secretary in his temporary absence. A provision to that effect will be introduced. The second objection is that it should be more clearly stated in section 40 that the power of removal of a pupil is, like all other powers of a similar character, to be given to the Local Board. That also is an amendment which will be introduced.

II. and III.—THE GENERAL SYNOD OF THE CHURCH OF IRELAND AND THE DIOCESAN COUNCILS OF ARMAGH, DERRY AND RAPHOE, KILMORE, AND CLOGHER.

4050. Mr. Bewley, Q.C. (instructed by Messrs. H. T. Ellis and Sons).—I represent these two bodies, and my instructions on behalf of the Standing Committee of the General Synod are to support the objections of the Diocesan Councils. Practically the objections may be considered as the same.

The first and principal objection which I bring forward is:—

"We submit that the Church of Ireland ought to have a separate and independent board of management, and we object strongly to mixed boards. We see no reason in principle why the Church of Ireland should not have its separate share of the endowments, and a separate board, in the same way as the scheme proposes for the Roman Catholic Church. We insist that whatever share of the endowment is allocated to the Church of Ireland should be given to a separate and not a mixed board, and that they should have the administration of it, and they alone."

The principle on which the distribution of the endowment may take place is a different matter, and might be considered afterwards. The principle might be ascertained approximately, not merely by taking the literate census, but by other means, by which you could ascertain in these different localities the population likely to require intermediate education. This approximation might be made by reference to a return which I understand can be obtained in the Registrar-General's office. You could obtain the numbers of the different classes, for instance, of landed gentry, of shopkeeping, mercantile, and farming classes, agricultural labourers, mechanics, and so forth, and it will not be difficult to estimate which of these classes will be likely to require intermediate education, and then to divide the endowment accordingly. However, that is a matter of detail. The first thing, I respectfully urge, is that the Church of Ireland should have a separate share of the endowments, and a separate board for the purpose of administering its endowments, and we also ask power for the different Church of Ireland Boards, in the different localities, to combine, and also power to the Church of Ireland to join with non-Episcopalian Protestant Boards, either in the same or in different localities, and we think there is no difficulty whatever in that.

4051. Lord Justice Naish.—Has the question been considered as to the proportion in which the remaining Protestant share of the endowment should be divided amongst the various denominations, after giving you what you claim as your share?

Mr. Bewley, Q.C.—We have made a rough calculation, founded on the census, of persons who can read and write, excluding, of course, children under five years of age, for we could not include them in the literate population, but I must say that I hold that division would not be fair to the Church of Ireland, and that they are entitled to a larger proportion than

* See Appendix B., No. III., pp. 300–348. † See Appendix B., No. III. (a), p. 352. ‡ See Appendix B., No. III. (b), p. 353.

that calculation would give. I will send in a calculation founded on that basis; it has been framed on the assumption that what is to be divided would be £3,480 per annum, and I will show you how we think it will work out between the different bodies. I hold, however, as I have said, that that is putting it too low in the interest of my clients, and that they are entitled to a larger amount than that calculation brings out.

4031. Lord Justice FitzGibbon.—We are anxious that everyone should know at the start what your claim is, and what figures you put forward, even provisionally.

Mr. Bewley, Q.C.—I have assumed the figure £3,480 per annum as being the income to be divided, and taking the population that can read and write in the counties of Armagh, Fermanagh, Tyrone, Cavan, and Donegal. In Armagh the figures would be: Roman Catholic £397 a year, Church of Ireland £363 a year, and all other denominations £296 a year.

Professor Dougherty.—Have you ascertained the proportion to be given to each of the various non-Episcopalian Protestant denominations?

Mr. Bewley, Q.C.—Practically it will turn out that there are only Presbyterians and Methodists. In Fermanagh the Roman Catholic would receive £463, Church of Ireland £404, all others £103; in Tyrone, Roman Catholics £583, Church of Ireland £511, all others £354; in Cavan, Roman Catholics £268, Church of Ireland £75, all others £25; Donegal, Roman Catholics £173, Church of Ireland £36, all others £41. The total would be as follows:—£1,649 would represent the Roman Catholic endowment, £1,404 the Church of Ireland endowment, and £794 the endowment of all others.

4033. Dr. Traill.—This calculation is not based on the number of Intermediate boys, but simply on the literate population?

Mr. Bewley, Q.C.—No, and it is, I think, putting it too low for my clients, but even according to the very lowest method of computing, that is what our rights would be. The £296 in Armagh represents £221 for Presbyterians, and £75 for all others; in Fermanagh, £26 for Presbyterians and £77 for all others; in Tyrone, £221 for Presbyterians and £83 for all others; in Cavan, £18 for Presbyterians, £7 for all others; and Donegal, £36 for Presbyterians, and £5 for all others. The general net would be that the Presbyterians would receive £522 as against £194 going to the other non-Episcopalian denominations.

4034. Professor Dougherty.—You don't take Monaghan into the calculation?

Mr. Bewley, Q.C.—No, but if necessary I could have a calculation made including it.

4035. Dr. Traill.—You don't consider Monaghan within the limit of the area entitled to the endowment?

Mr. Bewley, Q.C.—No. Now as I have said, those I represent think that is putting our case far too low, and we do not assent to that as a proper principle on which to make this calculation, but we think the Commission could ascertain who are the persons in each locality requiring Intermediate education, and that the division should not be merely according to the literate population, but according to the numbers of the different denominations requiring Intermediate education. A number of the literate population always will have their education in the National schools; and on the other hand, those requiring Intermediate education will come in for a large proportion from certain classes in society.

4036. Lord Justice Naish.—Would not the results test ascertain that proportion?

Mr. Bewley, Q.C.—No, not on the plan proposed in the scheme.

4037. Lord Justice FitzGibbon.—There are two totally distinct questions involved in what you are now presenting to us, first—whether the Church of Ireland should have a separate governing body for whatever share of the endowment it gets—and, secondly—whether what it gets should be a definite share. It is very important that these two matters should be kept distinct.

Mr. Bewley, Q.C.—Yes. We first say that the Church of Ireland should have a separate representation and a separate board with power to unite, not merely with the other Protestant board or boards in the same district, but also to unite, either with the Church board in any other district, or with any other Protestant board in another district where they thought it advisable to do so in order to secure an efficient school.

4038. Lord Justice FitzGibbon.—Allowing each denomination to have a separate management or representation for itself is not a violation of any principle of the scheme, but is merely an extension to one more denomination of the principle already adopted with regard to the Roman Catholics. The other point, however, that of giving a definite share to any denomination, Catholic or Protestant, finds place in the scheme only during the first three years, to which nobody seemed to object—when we want to get all into working order—afterwards the buildings and minimum grants are divided, and each denomination gets what it earns of the residue, and no more.

Mr. Bewley, Q.C.—In August last, evidence was produced, not merely on behalf of the Church I represent, but of the other Protestant bodies, in which they were all apparently of the opinion that it would be of the utmost importance that their share of the endowment should be defined now once and for ever and given over to their management. We object to this payment by results, first on the broad principle that it would be much more satisfactory for all parties now to let us have our share; let us know what it is and then we can consider whether having a certain endowment, we want to unite with the other Protestant bodies in any particular district, and make such arrangements among ourselves as will be encouraged by the then Commissioners of Education, and, as we think, for the interests of education. For instance, if the endowment is divided according to the literate amount I have mentioned: in Cavan the proportion coming to the Church of Ireland would be exceedingly small, and it would be quite impossible to support a school with it; but one of the adjoining counties might unite and contribute to it, and they might agree to establish a school somewhere on the confines of the two counties, and come to some arrangement by which the small contribution from Cavan could be utilised for the benefit of Intermediate education. We think it would be for the benefit of education generally that the amount should be ascertained once and for all, and that a distribution should be made now and not left open to change from time to time in a way that cannot but be detrimental to the general interests of education. Of course the scheme will require complete recasting if that is done. The persons I represent object, as they have objected all along, to this arrangement by results; they think there ought to be a final division now. But they also point that the provisions in the scheme with reference to results are manifestly unsatisfactory. As an illustration of that: if a school has a number of boys receiving Intermediate education, and sends up say forty boys to the Intermediate examination, and that all but seven are plucked and answer exceedingly badly, still seven pass; another school sends up boys who answer very well and pass in the senior grade, yet the boy who gets an exhibition only receives two marks, while all that came up from the other school and were plucked score one mark each for the school which succeeded in barely passing only seven out of the number. Of course that is a matter of detail, but we point it out to show that even as a system this is eminently unsatisfactory. If there be any results, we would oppose any one uniform standard of marks, let the whole work of the school

May 11, 1886.

May 26, 1886.

be tested, and let those who pass get marks in the different grades according to the nature of the examination in which they pass; but I am not here to discuss that, for my principal object in coming here is first to ask for this separate board for the Church of Ireland, and, also, to ask for this final division now of the endowment, leaving nothing to be ascertained in future by way of distribution according to results.

4058. Rev. Dr. Molloy.—Have you considered that if there was to be a final distribution now between the denominations, there should be four distinct boards for each district, or at least three?

Mr. Bewley, Q.C.—Yes, I have considered that, and it is quite possible that there should be three boards. I have no business to make any suggestion as a body with whom I am not concerned; all I say is let the Roman Catholics have their share, let the Church of Ireland have their share, and as for the other denominations—they are practically only two—let them unite and have one board, but I have no right to make any suggestion on their behalf as I do not represent them.

4060. Rev. Dr. Molloy.—Then have you considered the state of things that might arise in that case? If the schools connected with any one of these boards were inefficient and worthless for the purposes of education, that board would go on receiving its endowment and doing no educational work, whereas under our scheme the endowments will be applied only to those schools which are really efficient?

Mr. Bewley, Q.C.—We don't think that system would work.

Lord Justice FitzGibbon.—On the other hand, has your system ever worked? This endowment has been practically denominationally administered up to the present—I say practically—with the results you see before you.

4061. Rev. Dr. Molloy.—And while the whole of this endowment was being expended for an exceedingly small educational work in particular districts, a number of remarkably efficient schools have sprung up all over the North of Ireland which got no help from the endowment, the greater part of which was expended on schools that were doing practically nothing.

Mr. Bewley, Q.C.—But is not the mischief due to the management?

Lord Justice FitzGibbon.—And you want to stereotype a certain income, irrespective of the result of the future management, so that whether they manage well or ill no denomination can either forfeit or gain a penny.

4062. Dr. Traill.—Do you think that the denomination you represent now have ever had a bit more voice in the management of these endowments than any other denomination?

Mr. Bewley, Q.C.—No; I don't think they had.

4063. Lord Justice FitzGibbon.—Don't take that as the result of the evidence.

Mr. Bewley, Q.C.—I don't think that, because the school of a denomination has failed, ergo it was because it was the school of a denomination that it failed.

4064. Dr. Traill.—In some of these schools it appeared that the schoolmaster was left to himself, and there was no other management—that is what the evidence showed.

Mr. Bewley, Q.C.—There were certain views and abuses in connection with the management and in the constitution of the board in the past which it is not necessary to go into now. I represent a very large and comprehensive body. Last August it was represented that I only represented certain individuals, but since then this matter has been considered by the Diocesan Councils in these several dioceses; those Diocesan Councils were substantially representative of the persons in each diocese who were likely to require Intermediate education, and it is the unanimous opinion, first of the Diocesan Councils, and afterwards of the General Synod, that the Church should have a separate board, and that there should be this distribution of the endowment now and for ever.

4065. Dr. Traill.—It is not hostile to your proposal to give separate boards, that all the Protestants of Fermanagh should join afterwards to have a school for themselves?

Mr. Bewley, Q.C.—No; it would be entirely in accordance with what we propose.

4066. Lord Justice FitzGibbon.—When you speak of all the Protestants of Fermanagh, you [illegible] remember that there you have a large Church majority and two small minorities of other denominations, [illegible] if they wish to join, is the majority to have a vote [illegible] preponderating influence in dictating the terms [illegible] which the minority is to come in?

Mr. Bewley, Q.C.—As the scheme is at present framed, in places where we have a preponderating influence, that preponderating influence is taken from us in the constitution of the board.

4067. Lord Justice FitzGibbon.—In what way?

Mr. Bewley, Q.C.—In these mixed boards we [illegible] not the influence we ought to have at all in a degree corresponding to the number of persons belonging [illegible] the Church of Ireland in the districts as compared with the number of others, bearing in mind [illegible] requirements of particular classes, over others, [illegible] Intermediate education.

4068. Lord Justice FitzGibbon.—In what [illegible] have you been deprived of a preponderating influence in any place where your position or numbers entitle you to it?

Mr. Bewley, Q.C.—Take the numbers on the [illegible] as compared with the number of non-Episcopalians.

4069. Lord Justice FitzGibbon.—The only question raised before us was whether we ought to have put you [illegible] a minority in the Tyrone district, and your own figures to-day place you in a minority there, for you allow £384 for the share of the non-Episcopalians, as against £311 for the Church of Ireland. In Tyrone you [illegible] three representatives, the Presbyterians four, and [illegible] Methodists one. You must always remember [illegible] nine is the total number with which we have to [illegible]. If we had given the Church four representatives, [illegible] the Presbyterians four, we would have left [illegible] Methodists to turn the scale, though you yourself say the figures are against you as £311 to £[illegible]. Therefore, when the Synod tell us that the scheme assigns to the Church of Ireland "a wholly inadequate representation," and you say we have taken away "preponderating influence" to which you were entitled, the statistics show that we were right, in the case of Tyrone, the only board as to which there was [illegible] any question.

Mr. Bewley, Q.C.—Yes; but on other boards [illegible] have only given us a majority of one where we [illegible] in the proportion of two to one.

4070. Lord Justice FitzGibbon.—You must look at it reasonably. We had to deal with nine members, and we gave you a substantial working majority; [illegible] had to give some representation to each of the other denominations, and if you can in any instance suggest a better subdivision of the number nine than we have given you, we will be happy to take it. Besides, your majority can co-opt additional members.

Mr. Bewley.—Well, I am not going to discuss that, for I want to take my stand on question number [illegible] that there should be a separate board for the Church of Ireland.

4071. Lord Justice FitzGibbon.—Then do you withdraw the objection that we have given you inadequate representation on our plan? Your own figures are the clearest proof that you have a majority [illegible] ever you are entitled to it.

Mr. Bewley, Q.C.—Where we are in a majority [illegible] two to one, to give us a majority of one out of nine is hardly a fair proportion.

Dr. Traill.—I think you might be satisfied if [illegible]

have a majority on the board—a majority of one is all you want.

4072. Rev. Dr. Molloy.—If we were to contemplate three or four local boards in each district, have you considered how you would apply the principle of the minimum grant to each of those boards.

Mr. *Bewley*, Q.C.—No; for I go in for a final division.

4073. Rev. Dr. Molloy.—Then you propose that there should be no minimum grant at all?

Mr. *Bewley*, Q.C.—No, I want to have a definite and final settlement now.

The next objection is on the question of having the supreme controlling body situated in Ulster.

4074. Lord Justice FitzGibbon.—Before you go to that, we must dispose of the objections from the General Synod, in the order in which they have been printed.

The first objection of the Synod is that the scheme gives the Roman Catholic Church a share of the endowments which the statistics of Intermediate education prove to be "most excessive." Your own figures give £1,842 to the Roman Catholics and £1,948 to the Protestants. Is the share you describe as "most excessive," the difference between £1,842 and £1,948?

Mr. *Bewley*, Q.C.—You are not to take me as putting forward these as the proper figures at all on which to make a calculation. I do not put forward the literate population as the proper standard; if you adopt the Intermediate figures as the standard, the result will be very different; but I am not prepared to argue in detail these objections of the General Synod, the instructions I got were simply and solely to support the objections of the diocesan councils.

4075. Lord Justice FitzGibbon.—But these objections have been sent in by the General Synod whom you represent, and we must dispose of them as we go along, that the Privy Council may see how we dealt with each objection which the Act requires us to consider. If you can not tell us the foundation of the objection that the scheme gives the Roman Catholic Church "a share of the endowments which the statistics of Intermediate education prove to be most excessive," I suppose we may take it as disproved, especially as the scheme gives no fixed share beyond half the buildings and the minimum grants, and your own figures give the Roman Catholics nearly half the endowments.

The next objection of the Synod is "that the scheme assigns to the Church of Ireland a wholly inadequate representation on the proposed local boards which will deal with Protestant endowments." Do you admit that you have got a majority in each case where you are entitled to it?

Mr. *Bewley*, Q.C.—But we have not an adequate representation, and where the figures are five to four, in the absence of one of our members we might come to a dead lock.

4076. Lord Justice FitzGibbon.—And in the absence of a member of the minority you would have five to three, the proportion you claim.

Mr. *Bewley*, Q.C.—The Commissioners were good enough to allow a deputation from the General Synod to argue these objections, and now the attitude taken by the Standing Committee of the Synod is simply to support the objections put forward by the Diocesan Councils.

4077. Lord Justice FitzGibbon.—I only ask you to bear in mind that we are only a court of first instance, and we must send the matter in proper order before the Privy Council, and therefore must consider each objection unless it is withdrawn.

The third objection of the General Synod is "that of the gross endowments, the scheme proposes to distribute the greater part in so-called 'results fees,' in the allocation of which results will be entirely outweighed by mere numbers." The distribution by results is a matter of principle on which we will gladly hear you, but as regards the outweighing of results by mere numbers, we have already assented to the deputation our desire that no pupil should be counted for results unless he has got a real Intermediate education. We will amend the scheme in any way tending to test the results thoroughly.

The last objection of the General Synod—"that the compensation for the expenditure of private moneys upon school premises is merged in the general revenues of the Protestant local boards instead of going to the denomination to which the donors belonged," is one about which we need not trouble you, for we have stated that if the Protestant boards divide—whether under the scheme as you propose, or by agreement—it would be manifestly right that any private endowments included in the division should be treated as belonging to the denomination of the donor.

Mr. *Bewley*, Q.C.—But having regard to the provisions of the Act that the intentions of the founders shall be respected, is it in accordance with the Act to hand over what is essentially a denominational endowment to a mixed *Protestant* board?

Lord Justice FitzGibbon.—If the Protestants all work together, the buildings are not "handed over" to any sect in particular.

Now, we will pass to the objections of the diocesan councils. The first and second are substantially the same as the objections of the General Synod.

4078. Lord Justice Naish.—In case of the mixed boards being adhered to, would you claim that the bishops should continue to be members.

Mr. *Bewley*, Q.C.—I don't think I could make that claim if the board is to remain a mixed board; it is only if we should have our own board that we claim that he should be one of those representing the Church.

4079. Lord Justice Naish.—And if you are to have a separate board he should be chairman *ex officio*?

Mr. *Bewley*, Q.C.—Yes.

4080. Dr. Traill.—You also want power for the bishop to have some one to take his place if he is not able to attend?

Mr. *Bewley*, Q.C.—Yes.

4081. Professor Dougherty.—If we adhere to our scheme as regards the minimum grant and distribution by results would you still claim a separate board for the Church of Ireland?

Mr. *Bewley*, Q.C.—Yes, we claim a separate board in any case.

4082. Professor Dougherty.—Then Dr. Molloy's question is very much to the point. What do you propose as to the minimum grant for the separate Protestant boards.

Mr. *Bewley*, Q.C.—We claim first to have a separate board, and then to have an immediate division now and for ever.

4083. Professor Dougherty.—But I understand you to say that if the Commission does not see its way to amend the scheme as regards the minimum grant and the distribution by results, you still claim to have a separate board?

Mr. *Bewley*, Q.C.—Yes, I still claim that.

4084. Dr. Traill.—You still consider that you are entitled to have a separate board on the same ground as the Roman Catholics have claimed it, since they have been accorded a separate board?

Mr. *Bewley*, Q.C.—Yes.

4085. Professor Dougherty.—Then, in that case, what is to be done as to the minimum grant? What do you take it to mean?

Mr. *Bewley*, Q.C.—If there is to be a certain minimum given to each denomination, then the rest is to be distributed by results; the amount to be given to each denomination is not necessarily to be the same. However, that is not part of my objections at all, and I am not binding my clients in any way to it.

4086. Lord Justice FitzGibbon.—What is the foundation for the objection that, in some of the districts in question in the Church of Ireland in a numerical majority, yet in the boards of Tyrone and Donegal she is outweighed in the proportion of two to one? What is the evidence on which you base that statement?

May [illegible], 1886.

Mr. *Bewley*, Q.C.—As between them and the other Protestant denominations I believe that is so.

4067. Lord Justice FitzGibbon.—Then why do you give the figures as £264 for the other denominations, and only £111 for the Church of Ireland in Tyrone, and £[illegible] for the Church against £48 in Donegal?

Mr. *Bewley*, Q.C.—Because that is taken from the literate census.

4068. Lord Justice FitzGibbon.—But your ground of objection is, that in some of the dioceses the Church of Ireland is in a "numerical minority." That is not true of the literate population, and are we to understand that your objection rests on counting the whole population, literate and illiterate?

Mr. *Bewley*, Q.C.—The only place in which, on the illiterate census, the Church would be in a minority would be in Tyrone.

4069. Dr. Traill.—I suppose Dr. Morgan is ready to admit that the statement that there was a numerical majority for the Church in Tyrone, was not the fact, excluding children under five.

Rev. Dr. *Morgan*.—It left out the illiterate over five years of age.

4070. Dr. Traill.—Therefore it included all children under five as being literate.

Mr. *Bewley*, Q.C.—Objection No. 3 deals with the question of giving marks to those who if they came up would probably fail to pass the examination; No. 4 is a suggestion that the general Board of Management should be in Ulster. Now that all, except the Ulster Schools, are out of this Scheme, we think the Board of Management should have their head quarters in Ulster.

4071. Lord Justice FitzGibbon.—It may be a bad reason or a good reason, but our main reason for not altering the name or removing the place of the Board was to keep up the claim to have the administration paid for out of public funds. We can hardly ask the Treasury to pay for a new Ulster Board.

Mr. *Bewley*, Q.C.—The governing body of the Ulster Royal Schools should meet, and the supreme control should be situated in Ulster.

4072. Lord Justice FitzGibbon.—The Local Boards will meet in Ulster, but if you wish to press that the Commission shall also be an Ulster Board, the result may be the loss of the Treasury contribution to the expenses of the Commissioners of Education of £700 a year.

Mr. *Bewley*, Q.C.—If they would lose £700 a year by the change I think they will be likely to reconsider that point.

4073. Dr. Traill.—Have you any apprehension that if the Board is kept up in Dublin permanently, the proportion of representatives might possibly be changed; and that therefore the Ulster Endowments would come under the operation of a Board that is not half and half, Protestants and Roman Catholics?

Mr. *Bewley*, Q.C.—This objection was considered by the parties I represent, and there is nobody here who can bind them to withdraw or modify it; so I put it forward for whatever it is worth. The next objection deals with the representation of universities and other colleges. We made our objections last year and I have to reiterate them now.

4074. Lord Justice FitzGibbon.—Last year one set of objectors wished to have no Commissioners except those appointed by the Lord Lieutenant; the others wanted only those who had an educational qualification, and were nominated by the learned constituencies.

Mr. *Bewley*, Q.C.—Those whom I represent think that the representation of universities and other educational bodies can be sufficiently obtained by the Lord Lieutenant's appointments, and they also object to the exclusion of representatives of Maynooth and Magee Colleges, while—

"The only provision for the Church of Ireland is that the Lord Lieutenant shall nominate one chairman among his ten Commissioners, of whom five must be Roman Catholics, one a Presbyterian, and even the Methodists are put upon an equality with us, although we outnumber them in Ulster but twice over."

The sixth objection is practically the same as the first. It also refers to the evidence given in Dublin, which was practically unanimous in desiring a local distribution of the endowments.

In section 50 they object to the equal distribution of the endowments between the two Local Boards as being unjust to the Protestant population, especially in the County Armagh.

Then No. 8 corresponds with No. 4 of the objections of the General Synod.

4075. Lord Justice FitzGibbon.—We will do what we can to make that matter right. It was never intended to do anything unjust, and it will be perfectly immaterial wherever there is only one Protestant Board. As regards ascertaining the value of the private gifts, we did our best to ascertain their value, but we could not do impossibilities, and the value for practical purposes can only be ascertained when possession of the premises falls in to the Local Boards.

Mr. *Bewley*, Q.C.—It would be very important to have the value ascertained now.

4076. Lord Justice FitzGibbon.—It would be almost impossible; we got a report from the Commissioners of Education, and we saw the buildings ourselves. The claim practically comes to one wing of the building at Dungannon, and a defined portion of the building at Armagh, which an architect can value when you get possession.

Mr. *Bewley*, Q.C.—This Commission could ascertain as a fact what are the private endowments. All parties agree that it would be better to ascertain it now.

4097. Dr. Traill.—Would you be satisfied to have it stated in the schedule what amount originally was given by private donors, whether in cash or buildings, or represented by improvements to buildings?

Mr. *Bewley*, Q.C.—That would be better than leaving the thing as at present.

Lord Justice FitzGibbon.—But that is not what is wanted. The claim is for the relative value to the whole of the school buildings of such defined parts of them as were private gifts, and that proportion must be calculated at the time the Local Board gets the buildings.

4098. Dr. Traill.—The Roman Catholic Archbishop of Armagh seemed to consider that a fair way of ascertaining it.

Lord Justice FitzGibbon.—It is really a question for an architect in the future. Some of the buildings are much newer than others.

Mr. *Bewley*, Q.C.—But the thing is to ascertain the existence and nature of these private endowments, where made, and so forth.

4099. Dr. Traill.—You think if it was left to the future Boards there might be disputes?

Mr. *Bewley*, Q.C.—Not only as to form, but as to the value, and it ought to be set at rest now.

No. 9 is an objection to the provision for the alteration of the Scheme on the mere motion of the Attorney-General, and not upon the motion of the Commissioners or of any parties interested.

4100. Lord Justice FitzGibbon.—I should tell you why this change was made. The Attorney-General for Ireland can at any time proceed by information in Chancery, and we thought by enabling him to apply to the Commissioners of Charitable Donations, we were giving a cheaper remedy. I think the objection is put forward by gentlemen who don't know that, *ex officio*, the Attorney-General can bring the whole Scheme into Chancery at any time.

Mr. *Bewley*, Q.C.—But that is only in case of the abuse of the charitable trust, but if there is a beneficial change required, and the Attorney-General says that does not affect him, there is no means of moving him in the matter. In the former Scheme a certain number of the Commissioners had the power, and we think that they ought to have a voice in any application for a change in the Scheme.

Lord Justice Naish.—They can still apply if there is a sufficient majority in favour of a change.

Lord Justice FitzGibbon.—But one of the present

difficulties about the Commissioners is that their constitution is quite different on paper from what it really is. A great number of places have not been filled, no bishop has been appointed for many years, and our object was to give an independent power to apply for an alteration if the Commissioners themselves had become insufficient or unsatisfactory.

Mr. *Bewley*, Q.C.—But the Act of Parliament contemplated that the persons interested should have an opportunity of applying from time to time for alterations in the schemes. The Attorney-General never interferes except in cases of abuse of charitable trusts, and it would be in the interest of all parties to enable a majority of the Commissioners from time to time to set the law in motion.

4101. Rev. Dr. MOLLOY.—But that power is contained in the scheme, which provides that a change may be made on the application of the Commissioners.

Lord Justice FITZGIBBON.—And we require two-thirds of the Commissioners to concur, because we don't want to empower a mere majority in an evenly balanced board to ask for a change which might be more for the interest of one side than the other. We want this body to work away as they are until there is a preponderating opinion shared by both parties that a change is required.

Dr. TRAILL.—Your objection to the Attorney-General might be fairly supposed to mean that the Attorney-General is a politician, and that politicians might put pressure on him to effect a change in their own interest.

4102. Lord Justice FITZGIBBON.—The Judicial Commissioners could not take that view of the Attorney-General's position—he is the representative of the Crown, bound to see that all charities are properly conducted.

Mr. *Bewley*, Q.C.—But the Attorney-General is generally set in motion by some relator; if there is an abuse he may proceed of his own motion; but he will not interfere for the purpose of merely improving the administration of a charitable trust.

4103. Rev. Dr. MOLLOY.—Your objection is that the power of interference will have no injurious influence, and yet you seem to think that the Attorney-General won't interfere unless there is abuse.

Mr. *Bewley*, Q.C.—On the other hand it is suggested that he may for political reasons decline to make a change in the scheme.

4104. Lord Justice NAISH.—One of the earliest objections to any form of power to modify the scheme was made by the Commissioners of Donations and Bequests, who insisted that it should be left open to any one of the public to apply for a change in the provisions of the scheme.

Mr. *Bewley*, Q.C.—Yes, and the Privy Council decided against that view.

4105. Lord Justice FITZGIBBON.—On that occasion there was a point blank difference of opinion between us and the Commissioners of Charitable Bequests as to our powers. They said it must be left open to anybody having an interest to move to have the scheme altered. Our contention was that we had a discretion to limit the power. We put forward what we thought very strong reasons against leaving our schemes to be upset by every dissatisfied person, and we were very glad that the Privy Council took our view of it. But we gave an assurance then that we would in each case provide that an effete or inefficient or corrupt governing body should not be left the sole arbiter, but that we would give some outside body power to intervene. We have generally in denominational cases given this power to a recognised authority of the Church immediately concerned, and in other cases we have tried to find some independent authority. Here we thought the Attorney-General a suitable authority, but we should be glad of any better suggestion. It would be a pity to drive the Attorney-General to file an information in Chancery for the purpose of effecting a change which might be made on his application without expense through the Commissioners. That was our sole object.

Mr. *Bewley*, Q.C.—I am sure that is the entire object, but still I think the present provision is not so satisfactory as it might be.

4106. Lord Justice FITZGIBBON.—What improvement do you suggest, for we are very open-minded?

Rev. Dr. MOLLOY.—We thought it necessary to put in two authorities—one is the governing body. The Commissioners and we did not see any outside authority better than the Attorney-General. Can you suggest any better?

Mr. *Bewley*, Q.C.—I don't know enough about it to suggest, but perhaps in schemes affecting different denominational some person connected with those denominations—the heads of the Church perhaps.

4107. Lord Justice FITZGIBBON.—We would not like to give power to any one denomination or any one local authority to apply for a change, except in a matter concerning themselves only. The concurrence of two-thirds was to prevent applications in favour of one side only, but if you could suggest any representative bodies that might jointly apply we should be very glad.

Mr. *Bewley*, Q.C.—If you allow me to consider it, I may be able to suggest some body.

4108. Lord Justice FITZGIBBON.—You can send us any suggestion in writing; but you understand that the present proposal is to give the power to the Attorney-General as the official representing the Crown in charity matters.

Mr. *Bewley*, Q.C.—The next objection is as to the quorum.

4109. Lord Justice FITZGIBBON.—We fixed five on the practice of the Commissioners. A great part of their business is routine, matters of account, and a number of them are not living in Dublin, and we thought a small quorum might carry on the ordinary business.

Mr. *Bewley*, Q.C.—Could not matters of routine be transacted by a smaller number?

4110. Dr. TRAILL.—Would you be satisfied with a small quorum for routine work, and a larger quorum for matters of which notice had been given?

Lord Justice FITZGIBBON.—The small quorum might always treat any matters brought before them as routine work.

Mr. *Bewley*, Q.C.—The final objection is to the mixed Local Board delegating its functions to a committee. If these mixed Local Boards are to exist, gross injury might be done by a local board that had a preponderance of one or two delegating its powers to a committee all of one side, which committee would practically carry on all the work of the Board.

4111. Lord Justice FITZGIBBON.—I think in this objection you can hardly have understood Clause 53. "Committee" may be a bad name, but what we meant was to enable such Local Board to do what you are aiming at, that is, to separate itself into divisions, each representing one denomination, who could take charge of any particular schools and administer any part of the endowments committed to them.

Mr. *Bewley*, Q.C.—The language of Clause 53 is general, and according to it a mixed board might appoint a committee, and if the Commissioners sanctioned that committee it might consist all of one denomination and could allocate the endowments among their own schools.

4112. Lord Justice NAISH.—But under Clause 53, two-thirds of the Board must vote in the appointment of the committee, which practically means that the committee must have the sanction of the whole Board.

Mr. *Bewley*, Q.C.—If it was the intention that a denominational committee might be formed to distribute a share of the fund amongst schools of that denomination, that might be right, but I don't think that was the object of the section; we think that if the committee consisted all of one denomination they

May 21, 1889.

May 21, 1886.

might not take a right view of the proper proportion to be distributed amongst the different denominations that would be for the entire Board.

Rev. Dr. Molloy.—The committee can only be constituted by a resolution passed at a meeting specially convened for the purpose, and supported by not less than two-thirds of the full number of members of such local board convened—is not that a sufficient security that nothing unfair will be done?

Mr. *Bewley*, Q.C.—But in mixed boards in which there is a preponderance of one denomination they may proceed in the absence of the others.

Rev. Dr. Molloy.—No, they must have two-thirds of the whole Board supporting the resolution.

4113. Mr. *Bewley*, Q.C.—Two-thirds of course would mean six out of nine.

4114. Lord Justice FitzGibbon.—No one denomination has two-thirds of any board, so that it would require the co-operation of two denominations, including the one which is in a majority on the Board to do this.

Mr. *Bewley*, Q.C.—On the Tyrone Board there are six non-Episcopalians and they might carry a motion that a committee be appointed consisting exclusively of their own members.

4115. Lord Justice Naish.—But the resolution is also subject to the sanction of the Commissioners.

Mr. *Bewley*, Q.C.—The Commissioners might see no objection to it, or there might be a majority of non-Episcopalians among the Commissioners at that time—we don't know what the Lord Lieutenant's nominations may be.

4116. Dr. Traill.—Would you be satisfied if there were four Churchmen on the Tyrone Board?

Lord Justice FitzGibbon.—The Presbyterians are in an equal minority on three of the Boards.

Mr. *Bewley*, Q.C.—This but illustrates the friction that might arise if we have these mixed Boards, instead of handing over to the Church its portion of the endowment, therefore we come back to the first objection, and I ask the Commissioners to re-consider the scheme, and to hand over to the Church of Ireland whatever portion it is entitled to once and for all.

4117. Lord Justice FitzGibbon.—If we do not see our way to that, would you prefer that the power to divide should be subject to a unanimous vote, or if you like to a majority of seven out of nine?

Mr. *Bewley*, Q.C.—That would appear to be less objectionable.

IV.—THE INTERMEDIATE EDUCATION COMMITTEE OF THE GENERAL ASSEMBLY.

4118. Mr. *J. J. Shaw* (instructed by Mr. *James Henry*).—On behalf of the Intermediate Education Committee of the General Assembly, I am instructed to offer the most strenuous opposition to the proposal that there should be separate boards for each Protestant denomination. Considering the history of education in the north of Ireland, and the relative position of the various Protestant denominations, it is of the utmost importance for the educational efficiency of these schools, that they should be administered by mixed boards. With reference to what Mr. Bewley has said, I first ask your attention to the extraordinary statement that in framing this scheme you have paid no attention to the evidence given in Dublin by the authorised representatives of all the Protestant denominations, whom he described as claiming to have the same independent control in the education of their own children, which was claimed by the Roman Catholics. I have been at every meeting of the Commissioners where this matter was discussed, and I am not aware that any Protestant denomination except, perhaps, the one which Mr. Bewley represents, ever gave any evidence in favour of separate boards, as distinguished from mixed boards. No expression of such an opinion ever came from any of the Presbyterians as far as I am aware. Mr. M'Mullen, who represents the Methodists, will tell you whether they ever put forward such a representation. No such representation as far as I am aware was ever made by any Protestant body, except those Mr. Bewley now represents. Further than that, you have held meetings at which this question has been thoroughly discussed in every leading town in the north of Ireland. I was present myself in Dungannon, Derry, Coleraine, and Monaghan. You have also been at Cavan, Enniskillen, Raphoe, and Armagh, and I am within the mark when I say that, except in Armagh, at every town the representatives of every Protestant denomination were unanimous in pressing upon you that it was of the utmost importance for the educational efficiency of the schools that the various Protestant denominations should be united.

4119. Dr. Traill.—Would there be any objection to their uniting if they had each their share in their pockets separately—why cannot they all meet together afterwards, and make a joint scheme?

Mr. *J. J. Shaw*.—We think it would be better that you should unite the money. Mr. Bewley's clients want to have complete and separate control to themselves.

4120. Dr. Traill.—I don't think that is his contention at all—his contention is that each body should have control in the first instance, but there was nothing to prevent them joining together afterwards.

Mr. *J. J. Shaw*.—His claim is not merely to have independent control of the money, it is a claim to have independent control of the education, as the Roman Catholics have claimed for themselves. To the Roman Catholics this necessarily was conceded, because as Lord Justice FitzGibbon said, there is no use in offering people what they won't accept. The Roman Catholics won't have any education that is not under the control of their own Church. No such proposition has ever been put forward on behalf of any Protestant denomination in the north of Ireland. Mr. Bewley has for the first time appeared to claim for the body he represents the same independent control as is given to the Roman Catholics, that is to say, exclusive control, as a religious body, of the education of their children—an exclusive denominational control which is entirely unknown in the history of Protestant education in the north of Ireland. Every successful school, that has sprung up spontaneously in the north of Ireland has been a school in which the various Protestant denominations have been represented. The first great school in the north of Ireland—the Belfast Academy, a very great and flourishing school, where Sir James Emerson Tennent, Lord Cairns, and many other eminent men were educated—was from the first under the control of a mixed body. There was never any limitation such as that the masters should belong to this or that denomination; the governing body was always mixed. The next in order of time was the Belfast Academical Institution, in which Lord O'Hagan was educated, that was always a mixed school, and you heard the evidence given in Belfast, and saw how they resisted at the point of the bayonet the attempt of the Presbyterians to claim a larger representation on the governing body than they had got.

4121. Dr Traill.—Are either of these schools you mention boarding schools?

Mr. *J. J. Shaw*.—Both of them are and always have been boarding schools. When I was at school in Belfast there was a boarding house at one end of the Royal Academical Institution under a Committee master, and another at the other end under a Trinitarian master; there was no limitation; Protestants of all denominations were there, a very large number were Episcopalians, and a very large number Presbyterians. The same has been the history of education in the North of Ireland throughout. Wherever you find a successful school you find a mixed school—Coleraine, Foyle College, Londonderry Academical Institution, Lurgan, Monaghan, are all mixed schools and mixed boarding schools. The school at Monaghan, for which you have framed a Scheme, seems one of the strongest proofs that could be put before you that what the people in the north require and desire are mixed schools, because there you have now a mixed successful school: it was left derelict until it was taken up by the people on their own resources, and worked by a committee composed of the various Protestant denominations—the Bishop of Clogher and the Rev. Mr. Allison, the Presbyterian Minister, were representative members on the mixed board, and it has been made a most successful school under a mixed board.

4182. Lord Justice FitzGibbon.—We have got the statistics of the Intermediate Examinations in the six counties for the last three years: in Armagh the largest numbers are—Lurgan College, 1886, 19 passed; 1887, 21 passed; 1888, 23 passed; that school is under a mixed board, and under a scheme settled by this Commission. In Tyrone, from Strabane Academy, under a mixed board, for which we are now settling a scheme, 17 passed in 1886, 20 in 1887, and 15 in 1888; in Fermanagh, the Collegiate School, Monaghan, under the scheme you mention, passed 8 in 1887, and 9 in 1888—those are the largest numbers from Protestant Schools in the six counties.

Mr. J. J. Shaw.—Surely every district ought to have a scheme adapted to the opinions and ascertained wants of the people, and to the system of education which has been most successful. The best test of what is suited to a district is what springs up spontaneously amongst the people when working for themselves, and seeking to satisfy their own needs; where you have the schools established by the people themselves, and working successfully, all founded on the principle of mixed boards, where Protestants of all denominations work together in every instance harmoniously. Before that system, which suits the wants of the people, is altered, there should be some very strong reasons shown.

Dr. Traill.—Don't take me as objecting to your principles. I agree with them, but that is not inconsistent with the proposal that each denomination should approach the other with their own money in their pockets.

4183. Lord Justice FitzGibbon.—I have often asked to have a practical mode of working that proposal written down. How, for instance, are the Presbyterians and Methodists of Cavan with £25 in their joint pocket to approach the Episcopalians with £25 in their pocket, or how are the non-Episcopalians in Fermanagh, consisting chiefly of Methodists, with £[illegible] to approach the Churchmen who have £[illegible]. I can understand where a minority and a majority are joined together requiring them to agree on fair terms before they separate, but I don't see how any minority that is left outside at the start can be secured fair terms of admission afterwards.

Mr. J. J. Shaw.—They may get in, in the manner in which the lamb gets inside the wolf, but I don't see any other terms on which they could get in.

4184. Lord Justice FitzGibbon.—In two cases your "wolf" is Presbyterian, in three he is Episcopalian, and the same principle must be applied to all cases. Besides, under the divided system, in the localities such as Cavan where the Protestants are few they would get little or nothing.

Mr. J. J. Shaw.—Mr. Bewley argued as if this were a question between Episcopalian and non-Episcopalian, and he seems to think that an adequate division of the Protestant population of the North of Ireland. He should know that in the North of Ireland there are a great many Protestant denominations outside the denomination he represents, who differ doctrinally and historically quite as much from each other as from the Church of Ireland.

4185. Lord Justice FitzGibbon.—Substantially speaking, there are only three. There are some bodies who are quite different like the Jewish persuasion. There are others, like some Presbyterian denominations, which are almost alike—we can deal only with those which are distinct, and appreciably large, and practically these are Church Protestants, Presbyterians, and Methodists.

Mr. J. J. Shaw.—Historically, doctrinally, and in matters of discipline, the Methodist body is as close to the Episcopalians as to the Presbyterians.

4186. Lord Justice FitzGibbon.—The Methodist body is everywhere important in educational matters; it is much larger than the Presbyterians in Fermanagh, and the Fermanagh endowment is much the largest of all.

Mr. J. J. Shaw.—There are other matters to which Mr. Bewley referred with which I shall not deal, because the constitution of the local boards, and whether the Protestant board of each district is to be a mixed board or several separate boards, is the vital matter. If that is decided against Mr. Bewley's contention a great number of his other points become absolutely immaterial. The question of diverting the property created by Episcopal donations arises only in case you yield to his objection. Therefore I don't refer to it, at present. I content myself with saying that I am instructed to protest in the strongest manner against breaking with the whole history and tradition of education in the north of Ireland. The genius and tendency of the people of the north of Ireland are against this subdivision of the Protestant denominations, setting one Protestant denomination against all the rest, and creating divisions where no division has ever existed before; breaking the Protestant people into separate camps where they are all ready to work in one camp. Armagh is the only place where any objection has been made to the mixed boards. At the present moment you have here before you the very people who will be on the mixed board if it be constituted in Enniskillen; they come here united and unanimous asking for a certain thing which they want, but they make no suggestion whatever that in Enniskillen they want or intend to separate from one another. I don't know that any suggestion has come from any quarter except this one, and that a clerical one, in Armagh, therefore I think you should continue to hold the position you have taken up and continue these boards as they are sanctioned by the scheme.

XII.—THE LOCAL PROTESTANT COMMITTEE OF COUNTY FERMANAGH.

4187. *Mr. R. M. Dane* (instructed by Mr. J. Whiteside Dane.)—I represent the Local Committee representing the various Protestant denominations of the county Fermanagh; that committee adhere to the objections which they made on a former occasion, and consider that the original intention of the founders of these schools should be acted on.

4188. Lord Justice FitzGibbon.—At present we are dealing with Mr. Bewley's objections—what are the views of the Enniskillen people as to the two Protestant boards.

Mr. Dane.—Their views remain as they originally put them forward, that these endowments were originally granted for the use of the Protestant religion.

4189. Lord Justice FitzGibbon.—You claim the

* See Appendix B, No. III. (b), p. [illegible].

[illegible]

whole of the Royal School Endowments for exclusively Protestant purposes?

Mr. Dane.—Yes; but if the Commissioners adhere to what they have done, then we say that the amount to which each of these bodies—Episcopalian, Presbyterian, Methodist, and Roman Catholic—are entitled should be calculated first.

4130. Lord Justice FITZGIBBON.—That I understand, but what do you say to separate Protestant Boards?

Mr. Dane.—So far as Enniskillen and Fermanagh are concerned, we are all united; we have got a common mixed board and we are perfectly content to have it; we are content too that the amount coming to each of these bodies, Episcopalian, Presbyterian, and Methodist, should be put into a common fund; but Mr. Shaw goes too far when he says Mr. Bewley's argument is wholly inconsistent with the contention of the Enniskillen Committee. We are united, and we intend to remain so; but we conceive there may be other instances where these boards might not be willing to coalesce, and possibly where those three bodies don't wish to have a common board, they may have independent boards. But my committee think that the proportion of each body should be allocated in separate shares—amongst the Roman Catholics, if they are to have a share, the Methodists, the Presbyterians, and the Protestant Episcopalians.

4131. Rev. Dr. MOLLOY.—In your printed objections it is stated that the school in Portora has hitherto been under Protestant management—is that correct?

Mr. Dane.—Practically so.

4132. Rev Dr. MOLLOY.—The Commissioners in Dublin are not an exclusively Protestant body, and the management has been under them?

Mr. Dane.—Rather the mismanagement.

4133. Rev. Dr. MOLLOY.—Do you withdraw this argument—"we therefore maintain that, as a matter of equity, they belong exclusively to us"?

Mr. Dane.—My committee think that the endowment was originally intended for the Protestant population.

4134. Rev. Dr. MOLLOY.—They say that this £2,000, now belonging to Enniskillen, has been accumulated when the school was under Protestant management.

Mr. Dane.—Certainly.

4135. Rev. Dr. MOLLOY.—But it has not been under Protestant management—but under a mixed board on which Protestants had a majority.

Mr. Dane.—That may be, but it was Protestant management.

4136. Rev. Dr. MOLLOY.—Do you give up the argument—"We therefore maintain that, as a matter of equity, they belong exclusively to us"?

Mr. Dane.—No.

4137. Rev. Dr. MOLLOY.—The majority of the board being Protestant, you say the endowment belongs exclusively to you?

Mr. Dane.—We think that there has been no management in this school at all.

4138. Rev. Dr. MOLLOY.—But you say it has been under Protestant management, and that therefore, as a matter of equity, the endowments belong exclusively to Protestants.

Mr. Dane.—We may not eventually be able to maintain that argument, but at present I don't give it up. So far as it has been a boarding school, it has been exclusively Protestant. So far as the school has been managed at all, it has been managed by the resident Protestant masters; there never has been any other management.

4139. Rev. Dr. MOLLOY.—I suppose you don't press that objection?

Mr. Dane.—I don't press it and I don't withdraw it.

4140. Lord Justice FITZGIBBON.—We may be quite candid with you about this matter. We mentioned it to the deputation also. Lord Justice Naish and I are alone responsible for the law of this Commission, and we have come to the conclusion, looking to the history of the endowments, the words of our Act, the reports of previous Commissions, and all the facts and circumstances, that these endowments being derived from public sources, and being State foundations for educational purposes, should be regarded as intended for the benefit of all the inhabitants, according to the religious principles of the State, for the time being. The founder being the State, the principle involved in the Irish Church Act of treating all denominations as equal, seems to us to carry with it the principle that the State endowments for education should be open equally to all. We don't want to prejudice you in putting forward your argument elsewhere, but we practically have ruled it against you here. We consider ourselves bound to extend the enjoyment of this endowment to all denominations on fair terms, and we believe no terms can be fair which do not enable those entitled to benefit, to take and use their own fair share without violation of conscience. Supposing we rule so far against you, do you want one, or two, or three Protestant boards in Enniskillen?

Mr. Dane.—In Enniskillen we are united already. The only separation we want is as regards the funds.

4141. Professor DOUGHERTY.—What do you mean by separation as regards the funds?

Mr. Dane.—We are quite at one with Mr. Bewley that the distribution ought to be final now. We don't use the word "division," for we don't want to divide at all.

4142. Professor DOUGHERTY.—You don't want a division amongst the Protestant denominations?

Mr. Dane.—Yes, we do.

4143. *Lord Justice* FITZGIBBON.—You have made up your mind that as soon as you get your separate sums, you will administer them all as one, but you take up a position in order to support the others, which as regards yourselves you mean never to accept.

Mr. Dane.—Otherwise we know we could not maintain Portora in an efficient condition. We are all agreed about that. The printed objection is based on the lines that you have already decided, that the Roman Catholic Church is entitled to a share.

4144. Rev. Dr. MOLLOY.—But you still claim that the endowments are exclusively yours?

Mr. Dane.—I don't withdraw that claim, but the 83½ per cent. which we claim as a minimum grant is on the assumption that the Commissioners will not make a final distribution of the fund now.

4145. Lord Justice FITZGIBBON.—As no person appears now to represent the Protestants of any other locality besides Fermanagh, we should point out that when the deputation from the Synod was before us, the Bishop of Kilmore said (*supra* p. 168)—

"So far as we have gone our joint board has worked well in Cavan";

and Colonel Phillips, the lay member of the deputation, said—

"The Synod has not brought forward any resolution against your principle of mixed boards."

What do you say for the Methodists, Mr. M'Mullen?

4146. Rev. F. *M'Mullen.*—Mr. Shaw has said nearly all I intended to say. We have not used in any objection to the revised scheme, not that it might not be improved a little in our particular direction, but we thought it would not be much use. We still believe you have not dealt very generously with us in the matter of the Fermanagh board, seeing that we preponderate so very largely over our friends represented by Mr. Shaw in Fermanagh.

4147. Professor DOUGHERTY.—You must remember that Monaghan comes into the *Fermanagh* district?

Rev. Mr. *M'Mullen.*—But I don't think it is fair to us, for you accomplish your object by bringing in Monaghan where we are comparatively very weak. Still we think you ought to have given us a second representative on the Fermanagh Protestant Board.

on the whole, however, we are satisfied with the scheme as it is. If Monaghan is not removed of course we will claim three on the Fermanagh Board: as to the mixed boards we go in for Mr. Shaw's views—we object entirely to the separate boards.

4148. The *Dean of Armagh*.—With regard to the united boards it affects us more than other Protestants, because we are an Episcopal body and the others are not, and also because we claim to be the national Church and the others are not. The line of cleavage in the Protestant board will probably be deeper between us and the other communions than between the other communions amongst themselves. We ask for a separate board, because in nine cases out of ten—and these the only cases in which representation is necessary—the division will be between us and the other Protestants, and therefore we don't say whether there should be two or three Local Protestant Boards, but we wish to have the protection of a separate board for ourselves. One palpable injustice which will be done if we do not get it [illegible] the general position —namely, with regard to the private money which absolutely belongs to us and has gone into buildings. It was said to our deputation, that beyond all doubt that money should go to us if we had a separate board, but there is no means of preventing that money from being merged in the general property of the Presbyterians and Methodists unless we get a separate board; therefore, by the hard cash argument, that money which belongs to us cannot be given to us (and there an injustice must be done to us), unless we get a separate board. It was said there was no case in Ulster of a prosperous school which has not been non-denominational. The Wesleyan College in Belfast is probably the most successful denominational establishment in Ireland. The Wesley College in Dublin is also remarkably successful. The Coleraine Academy is a case in which there is an overwhelming preponderance of one denomination in the Governing Body. If communions see their way to work together, as I hope we and others may do voluntarily, with the protection that as they enter together voluntarily, so they can [illegible] if necessary—I do not deny but that this is likely to work successfully as in the case of the Coleraine Academy; but we should be left the power to join and work together. The difference between our application, "allow us to unite if we are willing," and your theory, "we will allow you to separate if you wish," appears to be this:—you say if you can make an harmonious understanding first we will allow you to divide, and we say unless we can make an harmonious settlement first, allow us to remain separate. But surely the absence of harmony is not favourable to union. As to the question of figures, I wish to show how the Commissioners own figures, which were quoted against us in August last—the "read and write" figures—which are very much under our legal claim—really affect us. At present the Roman Catholics have 54 per cent. of the whole population, and of higher education they have 33 per cent.; of the total Protestant literate population we have 56 per cent.; and of the higher education in the five counties we have 50 per cent.; and yet while they are given half of the representation, we are given only 21 members on the Local Boards out of 43. That is a [illegible] test of the way in which we have been dealt with as compared with the Roman Catholics. In Armagh we don't complain of our representation on the Protestant Board; we are as 68 to 33, and we are given 5 members to 4; but in other places there is more due to us. In Fermanagh we are as 43 to 11 of the Protestant community.

4149. Professor Dougherty.—Are you including Monaghan in the Fermanagh district?

The *Dean of Armagh*.—We protest against that. First, I take Fermanagh alone, and there we are as 43 to 11. Even in Fermanagh and Monaghan together we are as 29 to 13, and our representation is only 5 to 4; but in Tyrone our people are not as 20 to 18 but as 18 to 20, and yet we are only given 1 representative to the other 6. We are only given one-third where we are as 18 to 20, and when the proportion is lying the other way, the treatment is very different. It is so also in Donegal.

4150. Professor Dougherty.—But the circumstances of the Raphoe School are very peculiar; it is situated in a very Presbyterian district.

The *Dean of Armagh*.—Raphoe is not the district.

4151. Lord Justice FitzGibbon.—Practically it is. The great bulk of Donegal is as different from Raphoe as it is from Connemara.

The *Dean of Armagh*.—If that principle is to be applied let it be applied impartially, and if the district about Armagh is where our figures are precisely 6 to 8.

4152. Professor Dougherty.—Armagh is a railway centre with access from every part of the county, but there is no probability of people living in Donegal and Inishowen taking advantage of the Raphoe school.

The *Dean of Armagh*.—Passing from Armagh and Fermanagh, take Donegal and Cavan. In Cavan our proportion is as 80 to 6, and our representation as 5 to 4, but in Donegal, where it is 18 to 20, the proportion is 3 to 8.

4153. Dr. Traill.—But there is no money there.

The *Dean of Armagh*.—In the six counties we are as 119,640 to 107,480—on these figures—which we don't admit.

4154. Lord Justice FitzGibbon.—You have never shown us that they are wrong. We are anxious to be right about our figures, whatever else may be wrong.

The *Dean of Armagh*.—Don't take me as admitting them.

4155. Lord Justice FitzGibbon.—Do you mean to convey that they are wrong?

The *Dean of Armagh*.—I do not say they are wrong, but they are figures we don't admit.

4156. Lord Justice FitzGibbon.—That is hardly fair to us. They are Dr. Traill's figures; you have had them since August, and we are ready to accept any correction of them.

Dr. Traill.—They are my figures, and I stand to them.

The *Dean of Armagh*.—These figures being used against us in August last, we should have one save out of them now. In the six counties we are as 119,616 to 107,480 of the Protestants, and our representation is 21 out of 43. I maintain that is unfair.

4157. Lord Justice FitzGibbon.—It is quite immaterial, for it arises from the majority in Donegal and Tyrone being 6 to 1, and the local boards can never vote together. You have the majority in three of the five districts, and one of the two districts where you are in a minority has really no endowment.

The *Dean of Armagh*.—I call attention to section 24:—

"Each local board may from time to time appoint committees, each consisting of two or more of their number, to manage such business as the board may deem it expedient to depute to such committees. Any two or more local boards may in like manner appoint joint committees, each consisting of equal numbers of their members, for the transaction of any business in which the board may be jointly interested. The board or boards appointing such committee may fix the quorum, define the duties and regulate the proceedings of the committee as they may think fit."

We read that as meaning that these committees may become absolutely despotic and take into their own hands all the powers of the board. In our objections we point out that, even supposing the two-thirds majority applies—we are not lawyers enough to know whether it does or not—we are out-proportioned in the number of 3 to 1 in two boards, and we have no such protection in any place where we are entitled to it. I want also to point out how the Presbyterians are treated in proportion to numbers. In Fermanagh we are to them as 21,300 to 1,300—we are given 5 to 1. In Fer-

[illegible] Armagh and Monaghan taken together we are as 31,100 to 11,300. Taking in Monaghan, we are still nearly three times as many, yet the proportion given to us is 5 to 3. In Cavan we have 5 members to 4, while the proportion of the others is less than 1 to 4. It is all very well to say we have a working majority, but we have not a majority at all in proportion to our figures. Then we ask you to double the value of the private endowments instead of leaving it to the future Commissioners, who will have a direct monetary interest in the matter. With your recognised legal training you should protect the legal rights of every one—be a safeguard against that loss which we all are subject to.

4158. Lord Justice FitzGibbon.—What is the source of the figures you give as regards higher education?

The Dean of Armagh.—The census of superior schools.

*4159. Lord Justice FitzGibbon.—In these percentages the smallness of the figures dealt with makes the results very curious. In 1886 the * passes at the Intermediate Examinations in the six counties were Protestants, 521, Roman Catholics, 479; say 48 to 52—nearly half and half. In 1888 the Protestants were 656, and the Roman Catholics 334—two-thirds and one-third. But when we look to see what has made this great change, we find it due to three figures only. In 1888 a new school appearing at Armagh passed 15 boys; and 8 girls passed in Monaghan. These two figures are the only substantial additions to the Protestants between 1886 and 1888. On the other hand, there was a falling off in the number that passed from one Roman Catholic school, namely St. Macartan's, Monaghan, which passed in 1886 16 boys, but in 1888 passed only 3. Literally these three changes have altered the percentages of Protestant and Roman Catholic Intermediate passes from half and half to two-thirds and one-third in the six counties. We have therefore the greatest difficulty in dealing with percentages which are founded on such small figures.

The Dean of Armagh.—That entirely corroborates our contention that the test of higher education given at a larger amount than we receive under this scheme.

4160. Rev. Dr. Molloy.—But under the scheme your share of the endowment will be proportional to the amount of intermediate education you give.

Lord Justice FitzGibbon.—I don't want unfairly to press the argument, but if we were to take 1886 as the basis of the final decision you call for, the Protestants, on the Intermediate results, would get only half the endowments; whereas if we took 1888 as the basis, they would get two-thirds. What basis have we to divide this £3,500 per annum once for all and for ever, when in three years the fluctuations would have been so great?

Dr. Traill.—You want to count the population that is capable of receiving Intermediate education.

4161. Lord Justice FitzGibbon.—We all agree that we want to allocate the fund in proportion to the numbers requiring aid for Intermediate education. If you could foretell the number of boys who year by year will require Intermediate education, that would give the result we want. We have never yet been told how that is to be ascertained, and we propose to ascertain it experimentally, as soon as [illegible].

The Dean of Armagh.—I went into the point as to the result fees at some length on the deputation. Instead of taking, as at present, the Intermediate Examination result, plus the numbers in the schools, we would be willing to take the Intermediate Examinations as the only test. But we never counted the mere passes at the Intermediate Examination; we count passes in the prescribed subjects—the number who passed in the higher standard.

4162. Lord Justice FitzGibbon.—We threw out a suggestion to the deputation that as Dungannon and Armagh were competing schools, and the two endowments were substantially of the same amount, some arrangement might be made, in furtherance of your desire for separate boards, by which the Presbyterians should take the school at Dungannon, and the Episcopalians the one at Armagh. You told us you only wanted the opportunity of acting voluntarily, and we gave you this as the most promising opportunity of doing so.

The Dean of Armagh.—Nothing has been done.

4163. Lord Justice FitzGibbon.—There is a proposal, made nearly a month ago, under which you could try what you say you are anxious to do, and if ever now you could put your professions into practice we will give you a Presbyterian board and school at Dungannon and a Church board and school at Armagh, with power to work denominationally over the two counties. If you can deal with one another fairly, then we can leave the Cavan and Enniskillen people alone, as they want to be united, and we need not attempt to divide the miserable endowment of Raphoe. If you can't avail yourselves of the very best opportunity of doing what you propose, it will show your proposal not to be practicable. Will you try it even now?

The Dean of Armagh.—We shall open negotiations now without the loss of a day.

IV.—THE INTERMEDIATE EDUCATION COMMITTEE OF THE GENERAL ASSEMBLY.

4164. Mr. J. J. Shaw.—The first objection I have to make on behalf of the Intermediate Education Committee of the General Assembly is with reference to the Raphoe Head Master's retiring allowance, which they think should be paid out of the General Endowment and not out of the Raphoe Estate.

4165. Lord Justice FitzGibbon.—We are very unhappy about Raphoe: the figures are now worse than ever. In 1888 the income of the Raphoe Estate did not pay the expenses of collecting it, even without paying the master anything. There is no Raphoe endowment strictly speaking—that is to say, no Raphoe endowment of which anything can be made for education, except the school buildings. The Commissioners have for many years paid money out of the other endowments to keep Raphoe School open, and they have reported to Parliament in 1886, and again in 1888, that they continued to do so only because they were waiting to see what this Commission could do, and now more than £1,300 is due by Raphoe—or rather is entered by the Commissioners as a debt against Raphoe. The Act of Geo. IV. says that whenever any residue remains of the funds of any of the Royal Schools after defraying the expenses of the masters, &c., "it shall be lawful for the Commissioners, if they think fit, to apply such residue to the maintenance of any other school whose funds stand in need of such aid." That application has really been already made of the residue not spent on Cavan and Enniskillen to pay the Raphoe masters and keep the school open, and we think it a serious question whether it is not better to write that off as a bad debt, and leave the Raphoe endowment for the future to pay what it can.

Mr. J. J. Shaw.—The £1,300 already spent would clearly come within the section of the Act of Geo. IV.

4166. Lord Justice FitzGibbon.—I am glad to hear you say so, but the only way we can pay it is out of cash entered by the Commissioners as belonging to Cavan and Enniskillen. The sums which appear in their books to the credit of these schools have really been spent on Raphoe, and there is nothing now to represent them but an apparently irrecoverable debt.

Mr. J. J. Shaw.—The two Donegal Local Boards are unanimous on this point.

4167. Lord Justice FitzGibbon.—Of course they are; they want their debt wiped out.

Mr. J. J. Shaw.—A meeting was held, Dr. O'Do-

* See Appendix B., No. III. (w.), p. [illegible].

Nov. 21, 1888.

sell, the Roman Catholic Bishop, presiding; all the members of the Catholic and Protestant Boards were present, and they all ask you to do what you can in the way of providing an endowment for Raphoe. It is perfectly clear that if Mr. Weir's retiring allowance is paid out of the Raphoe endowment there will be nothing at all left for education.

4168. Lord Justice NAISH.—Will there be anything even for Mr. Weir?

Mr. J. J. Shaw.—I suppose there will be something.

Rev. Dr. MOLLOY.—The gross receipts of the estate last year were £53, and the cost of collecting the £53 was £56, leaving a net loss of £3.

4169. Lord Justice FITZGIBBON.—£53 out of the £53 were actually spent on law costs. In their report of July, 1887, the Commissioners say that the financial position of Raphoe is very bad; they repeat the same thing in their last report, and yet they have gone on paying the head master and assistants until the estate now owes over £1,200.

Mr. J. J. Shaw.—Under these circumstances I don't think there is much use in pressing this question, but under the Act of George IV. the residue remaining from any of the schools—and there has been a surplus in several—is applicable to this purpose.

4170. Lord Justice FITZGIBBON.—We are satisfied that the Commissioners had power to apply the past surplus to pay the Raphoe masters, but we are not clear that if the other districts require all their own money in future Mr. Weir can have any claim on the other endowments for his salary or retiring allowance. It is very hard to see what can be done.

Mr. Carton, Q.C.—The Fermanagh Roman Catholic Board would object to have any of the Raphoe expense thrown on their district; and it seems inconsistent with clause 50 of the scheme.

4171. Lord Justice FITZGIBBON.—Yes. The scheme as it stands will leave Raphoe altogether to its own resources. But we had no idea things were so bad as they appear now.

Lord Justice NAISH.—This £1,200 is only a bad debt. Raphoe owes it to the other schools, and has nothing to pay it.

Lord Justice FITZGIBBON.—It would be better to write it off; but let there be no misunderstanding about it. The Commissioners have treated it as cash in their accounts, and it must be written off by a *pro rata* deduction from the cash balances belonging to Cavan and Fermanagh.

Mr. Carton, Q.C.—What you require to do is to write off the present debt once and for all, but not to make Raphoe a charge for the *future* on the other endowments.

4172. Rev. Dr. MOLLOY.—There are two questions to be considered separately. First, there is the present debt of £1,200 due by Raphoe; what is to be done with it? Next, how will you provide for the vested interest of the present head master, and for the minimum grant for Raphoe in future?

Mr. Carton, Q.C.—This vested interest can only be a vested interest in the Raphoe endowment; and if there is no endowment, there is no vested interest.

4173. Lord Justice FITZGIBBON.—Mr. Weir's vested interest is the position which he would have if the scheme never passed. The power existed under the Act of George IV., where money is not wanted in other districts at the time, to spend it on Raphoe, and that has been done. The money not wanted year by year in Enniskillen is at present spent in paying the Raphoe salaries.

Mr. Dane.—Our contention is that it was very much wanted in Enniskillen, but we could not get it from the Commissioners. The Commissioners would not give it; they disobeyed the English master.

4174. Lord Justice FITZGIBBON.—After defraying the expenses mentioned in the Act, it was lawful for the Commissioners, if they thought fit, to spend the residue in aid of any other school. That is the law now; and each year, if the scheme did not pass, the same thing would go on; there would be a surplus in Cavan and Enniskillen, and they would apply it for Raphoe.

Mr. Dane.—The existence of that surplus is owing entirely to the mismanagement of Cavan and Enniskillen schools.

4175. Lord Justice FITZGIBBON.—But if the scheme never passed the mismanagement would go on; and so long as it goes on the surplus will go on too.

Mr. Dane.—But you are not to assume that it will go on; that is one of our grievances. The existence of that surplus is due to mismanagement. We say there would be no surplus if the school was properly managed.

4176. Lord Justice FITZGIBBON.—But there is the Act, which says that whenever in any year a residue remains of the funds of any of the schools, another school that wants it may get it. There has been that residue in Enniskillen for nearly twenty years, and in Cavan for nearly forty years; and if this scheme does not pass, that state of things will continue, and the head master of Raphoe will be paid. Besides, let us not cast aside all human feeling. What an awful state of affairs it would be if Mr. Weir, now at the age of sixty-two years, finds his life annuity to be charged only upon a hopelessly insolvent fund.

Mr. Dane.—There has been a serious diminution in the Enniskillen estate, and the school itself has been destroyed by threatened legislation and other matters. You cannot take last year as a test of the school's work or position.

Mr. Carton, Q.C.—I submit there is really no vested interest in the funds of other schools conferred by the Act of George IV., which leaves it entirely optional to apply any residue in aid of other schools. Therefore, in applying the residue by way of compensation or retiring allowance, you would not be applying it in accordance with the Act.

4177. Lord Justice FITZGIBBON.—There is a case in the Privy Council which says that in ascertaining a vested interest you are not to take legal rights merely, but also chances of emolument.

Mr. Carton, Q.C.—To apply the statute of George IV. by way of analogy, it ought to be applied to the schools as existing under the scheme; and the Fermanagh funds under the scheme will only be sufficient to support the Fermanagh schools; so there will be nothing for Mr. Weir, or any other master similarly placed. While it is a misfortune that a gentleman in Mr. Weir's position should have his vested interest charged on a deficit, that is no reason why Fermanagh should have a burden cast on it to which it is not rightly liable.

Mr. J. J. Shaw.—I am not instructed to appear on behalf of Mr. Weir, but only for those interested in the Raphoe school. Mr. Weir has a vested interest in the existing state of things, and that must be provided for before the new state of things is brought into existence.

The objection No. 2 of the Committee of the General Assembly refers to the qualification for schools in section 43. They consider the number 7 required to pass in each year from the qualified school at the Intermediate Examinations is too large, and they propose to substitute 5. I am instructed that of all the schools in the district in which this scheme has operation, only 3 schools—Dungannon and Lurgan, have passed seven pupils in the Intermediate Examinations in each year.

4178. Lord Justice FITZGIBBON.—We reduced the number already from 10 to 7 on the Presbyterian objection. We were charged somewhere with having done it to bring in the Christian Brothers schools, but that was quite a mistake. The Roman Catholics have one large school at least in each district, for which they probably want all the money they can get. If this money is to be of any use for grammar school education, it must not be frittered

[May 21, 1888.

away among too many schools. There is in each district at least one school that could comply within this restriction. In 1886, in Armagh, Mr. Gibson's school passed 11; Lurgan passed 21; the Intermediate School passed 6, and there is no school in that district that would be brought in by reducing the number to 5. Portadown and Newry girls schools passed 10 and 8. In Tyrone district, Cookstown and Dungannon Royal School passed 8 each, and it would not be too much to expect them to pass one more, particularly as Cookstown passed 9 in 1887. Strabane passed 15, 20, and 17 in 1886-7-8. In Cavan no school passed any. Monaghan passed 9 each year. In Donegal the Prior school passed 9, 14 and 11, and several girls schools are all well over 7.

Mr. J. J. Shaw.—Would it not be practicable where a school fell under the number in one year by an accident, any accident, to take an average of three years?

4179. Lord Justice FitzGibbon.—The scheme provides for any accidental reduction for one year. Whether it would be better in all cases after the thing gets started to take the average of three years is a question, but we do not like to go below 7.

Rev. Dr. Molloy.—A school with any pretensions to an Intermediate school would pass 7.

4180. Lord Justice FitzGibbon.—The proposal to fix a proportion between the numbers who pass the Intermediate Examinations and the others attending the school for whom marks are allowed seems a valuable one. We want to see that our test is a strict one, before any boy is paid for as receiving intermediate education. Boys who were never coming on to be anything might be counted.

Mr. J. J. Shaw.—If 7 passed out of 40 it would seem disproportionate that the passing of the 7 should secure marks for themselves and the 33 others.

4181. Lord Justice FitzGibbon.—But they must all be receiving genuine intermediate education.

Mr. J. J. Shaw.—We say that in case they pass only 7 they should only be allowed marks for 28 as getting genuine intermediate education. To pass one out of every 4, receiving genuine intermediate education is not too large a proportion to ask.

Rev. Dr. Molloy.—I think it is a very reasonable proposition.

4182. Lord Justice FitzGibbon.—This strikes us as a very valuable and to some extent an original suggestion, and we should like to hear some experts as to the proportions that usually pass.

Rev. Dr. Morgan.—Mr. Wilkins, who represents the Schoolmasters Association, wishes to speak to* that point.

4183. Rev. Dr. Molloy.—If it was merely passing the Intermediate Examination, three there would be sufficient, but for passing in those subjects which we specify, I think four times is reasonable; what do the head masters say?

Rev. Dr. Morgan.—I am not prepared to speak on behalf of the head masters.

4184. Lord Justice FitzGibbon.—Can you help us as an expert in an Intermediate school in thorough working order—of the pupils receiving genuine intermediate education, the business of the school also including the preparation of boys for professions and other things—what proportion should pass the Intermediate Examination in each year?

Rev. Dr. Morgan.—I would say about 30 per cent.

4185. Lord Justice FitzGibbon.—If it was a school preparing boys exclusively for the Intermediate Examinations, of course the boys would take a couple of years to prepare, and though they would count in the subsequent years when they actually passed, it struck us as fair that the school should be paid something for the years of preparation too.

Rev. Dr. Molloy.—Bear in mind they have to do more than to get a pass under the Intermediate Board; they have to pass in the specified subjects.

Lord Justice FitzGibbon.—Perhaps Archbishop Walsh can help us about this. We want to admit competent schools only, to provide against any school that is not really an efficient Intermediate school counting boys by the head, and to allow credit only for boys passing or preparing in the specified grammar school subjects.

4186. Archbishop Walsh.—According to my original proposal no result should be counted except a result ascertained by examination; not necessarily by the Intermediate Examinations, which are competitive, but by passing an examination to be conducted by a competent examiner.

Dr. Traill.—Like the National Board Inspector.

Archbishop Walsh.—Precisely so.

4187. Lord Justice FitzGibbon.—We were all agreed that we should like a test of that kind, but the expense and inconvenience of a special examination were the great difficulty. The scheme has been always in the direction of providing, without a special examination, that the school shall be paid for the boys receiving preparatory or other special grammar school instruction, as well as for those who pass the Intermediate Examinations.

Archbishop Walsh.—I think the suggestion of Mr. Shaw is an admirable one.

4188. Dr. Traill.—Don't you think 4 to 1 too high? Take for instance Mr. Gibson's school, where 11 passed.

Archbishop Walsh.—There may be a mistake about this; a boy may "pass" the Intermediate Examinations by passing in three subjects, but there is something more required here. On that account you must allow a larger margin. What do you mean by passing the examination?

4189. Dr. Traill.—If a schoolmaster passes 15 boys he is to be allowed for 60, but suppose 60 is more than there is in the whole school, what then?

Mr. Shaw.—He cannot get marks for more than he has in the school. He will get marks for as many as he has over the 15 up to 60.

Most Rev. Dr. Donnelly, Bishop of Clogher.—Why not have an examination, in writing, of the whole school by an inspector appointed by the Lord Lieutenant? That would be a very satisfactory test, and it would not be open to any grumbling about partiality or difference of treatment. An examination like the Science and Art examination.

Lord Justice FitzGibbon.—The difficulty is the machinery, the introduction of a new set of examinations, and the expense. Besides, we have no power to prescribe the duties of the inspectors appointed by the Lord Lieutenant. We want, if possible, to get a rough test that will not be too expensive.

4190. Rev. Dr. Molloy.—Have you considered, my lord, that these schools would like to share in the results fees of the Intermediate Education Board, and if we establish a special examination for the results of the Royal School endowments, the pupils would have to pass two examinations?

Archbishop Walsh.—You could take the passing of the Intermediate Examinations as a sufficient test.

Bishop Donnelly.—In order to ascertain whether a school deserves to share in these results, why not have the whole school examined in writing, to test its efficiency? Why may there not be an examination such as now occurs in the case of the Science and Art examinations?

Dr. Traill.—The schoolmasters say they are altogether overcrowded with examinations at present.

4191. Lord Justice FitzGibbon.—A Science and Art examination, an Intermediate Examination, and a new set of examinations would probably lead to confusion, and the masters would have to prepare a different set of pupils for each.

Lord Justice Naish.—We specially provide that before a mark is allowed for any pupil the Commissioners are to be satisfied that the pupil has been receiving intermediate education or has passed the examinations in the necessary subjects, and also that

* See Appendix B., No. III. (a.), p. 609.

the school has been certified as qualified by the Lord Lieutenant's inspector.

Bishop *Donnelly*.—That would be ascertained by an examination of the whole school.

4192. Lord Justice FitzGibbon.—Is that necessary? The inspector, instead of holding a special examination of the whole school after previous announcement and preparation, would go there at any time, see the teaching and the mode of carrying on the school, examine the pupils sufficiently to satisfy himself that they were receiving the prescribed instruction, and then on his responsibility as a Government officer he would certify how many of them were receiving genuine intermediate education. Then, to prevent any excessive proportion being allowed for, there could be the further extrinsic test of passing the Intermediate Examinations by a fair proportion of the school. Such a limit would be a very practical test of the somewhat wholesale verdict of the inspector that the others were receiving an efficient intermediate education; but to fix the proportion we should know about what proportion, in a large and mixed school, ought to be borne by the passes at the Intermediate Examinations to the whole number of pupils receiving education, counting, in both cases, pupils in grammar school subjects only.

Mr. *Wilkins*.—The Schoolmasters' Association would be for allowing no mark at all except after examination. They believe that in an efficient school the number of boys passing would be in proportion to the number of boys in the school; and if no mark is given except to those who do actually pass it would make a very fair test.

4193. Rev. Dr. Molloy.—Is it your proposition that the residue should be distributed amongst the various schools according to the number actually passing the Intermediate Examinations?

Mr. *Wilkins*.—Yes.

4194. Rev. Dr. Molloy.—That is the same as the proposal of the deputation from the General Synod—have you considered that, Mr. Shaw?

Mr. *J. J. Shaw*.—Yes, and I think it is objectionable, because it gives nothing for the pupils who are receiving intermediate education, and who are at an age or in a stage of progress such that they cannot go in for the Intermediate.

4195. Rev. Dr. Molloy.—But that would affect all schools in pretty nearly the same proportion, and each school would get a share practically in proportion to the number it was teaching.

4196. Lord Justice FitzGibbon.—I am not sure of that. The preparatory schools, and the schools working up backward pupils would get nothing, and all would go to the schools that crammed the pupils during the actual years in which they went up for the examinations.

Mr. *J. J. Shaw*.—We have got a school presumably efficient, and we have the inspector's report that it is an efficient school, giving grammar school teaching to a certain number of pupils. If out of the total number receiving education in that school, they pass one out of every four we consider that is an adequate test of the education actually given to all, because we think one out of four is a very fair share to pass these particular examinations. There will be a number of boys preparing for the University, or the Civil Service, who cannot go in for the Intermediate at all, others will be only preparing for it. We also take into consideration, that the scheme requires the pupils to pass in a larger number of subjects than the Intermediate Board require, and we think it would be better on the whole, to give a mark for each boy really receiving intermediate education, subject to the test of inspection, and to passing the proportion of one out of four. That we think would be sufficient and adequate.

4197. Rev. Dr. Molloy.—Do you think the result as regards the actual distribution, would be substantially different in the two cases, because if the result was the same, there would be an advantage in taking the Intermediate Examination alone, that being recognised universally as an impartial test?

Mr. *J. J. Shaw*.—Take the Armagh Royal School—a boy studying for a scholarship in the University, is getting an efficient intermediate education, and he would be counted on our plan, if the school proves itself efficient by passing one out of four.

4198. Lord Justice FitzGibbon.—The fluctuations of the Intermediate Examinations test alone, would be most injurious. In Armagh, for example, Gibson's school increased up from three to fifteen in one year, and in Monaghan, St. Macartan's went down from fifteen to three in three years, and in another case the fluctuation would be from eleven to twenty, and I mentioned already, that in the six counties in three years the Protestant and Catholic proportions of passes varied from half and half to two to one. That must necessarily arise where you have a limited number of pupils, coming on year after year, and the master's work in preparing them ought to be paid for as well as the work of passing them.

Archbishop *Walsh*.—In order to avoid fluctuation it would be necessary to make an arrangement to take the average of, say, three years. This would prevent any sudden transition in the amount, either as a sudden increase or a sudden falling off.

4199. Rev. Dr. Molloy.—What does your Grace think of these two propositions, one being to allow so much for each pupil getting intermediate education, and so much more for every pupil who passes; the other, to distribute the residue entirely in proportion to the passes at the Intermediate?

Archbishop *Walsh*.—I think it would be found impossible or very undesirable to have distinct examinations, and then Mr. Shaw's proposition is more desirable. It might be found inconvenient to have a separate examination, and if so, then Mr. Shaw's proposition would seem to be the best.

4200. Rev. Dr. Molloy.—Do you think four times the number of passes would be reasonable, as the maximum number of pupils that can be counted?

Archbishop *Walsh*.—I think the returns of the Intermediate Board ought to be looked into very carefully before any proportion is fixed.

4201. Lord Justice FitzGibbon.—It would be very important indeed, where we have conflicting evidence, if we had a return of the actual proportion of the passes to the number of pupils in some leading schools.

Archbishop *Walsh*.—It is not a question of mere passes, but of passes in a definite number of subjects.

Mr. *Wilkins*.—One in four would be, in my experience, about right.

4202. Lord Justice FitzGibbon.—Then you think Mr. Shaw's proposal about right.

Rev. Dr. Molloy.—Look at the subjects in which they are required to pass: English, Latin, Greek or French or German, Arithmetic, Euclid, Algebra or Drawing—five in all. And with this before you, will you be good enough to send to us a statement whether you think four times the number of passes in these subjects would be a reasonable allowance?

4203. Lord Justice FitzGibbon.—There is no restriction upon the number of pupils who may be taught in the school; but the money is to be given only for those learning the specified subjects, and only for a fixed proportion of such pupils above the number who pass the Intermediate Examinations in the same subjects. The school must teach these subjects to each pupil before they get one mark for him; and seven, at least, must pass the Intermediate before they get even that mark, but one additional mark will then be given for every pupil who passes the examinations in the specified subjects.

Mr. *J. J. Shaw*.—You dropped an observation that you might take the average of three years. Did you mean to require that the number should in no year fall below the minimum?

4204. Lord Justice FitzGibbon.—Yes.

Mr. *J. J. Shaw*.—I think that is objectionable.

[illegible] Suppose a school passed 19 this year, and an epidemic arose, and they passed none next year?

4305. Lord Justice FitzGibbon.—That is provided for already in the scheme. There is power to let you off for one year for accidental reasons.

Mr. J. J. Shaw.—But there is no provision that in each year they shall attain the minimum. Suppose a school passes 19 this year, and only 5 next year, is it not entitled to take the average, and thus reach the minimum?

4306. Lord Justice FitzGibbon.—I think not. Any school passing 19 this year and only 5 next year must have something wrong with it.

Rev. Dr. Morgan.—Mr. Shaw's proposal, as far as I understand it, is to fix the proportion of 1 to 4 of the pupils who in the same year shall have passed one of the Intermediate examinations, but he does not say in the subjects prescribed in the scheme.

4307. Lord Justice FitzGibbon.—We have said, and we stand to it, that no boy is to get any money out of this grammar school endowment, unless he is being taught or passes in what we call grammar school subjects.

Rev. Dr. Morgan.—In the subjects prescribed in the scheme?

Mr. J. J. Shaw.—That is what I mean.

* Archbishop Walsh.—In that view of the case, which I think is the correct one, it would be necessary to make very careful examination of the returns of the Intermediate Board, to see whether 1 in 4 is the proper proportion. It may be 1 in 3, or 1 in 5; and I think the two associations of the Protestant and Catholic head masters would willingly undertake that work for the Commissioners. I could get it done for the * Catholic schools. It is simply a question of figures.

4308. Lord Justice FitzGibbon.—We shall be very thankful for any such information, if we get it before tomorrow week, but we must not delay this scheme much longer.

Mr. J. J. Shaw.—The third proposition is that there should be an additional mark given for every pupil who shall have passed the junior grade; two additional marks for the middle grade, and three additional marks for the senior grade. This proposition is supported by the Schoolmasters' Association.

4309. Lord Justice FitzGibbon.—This is a matter we considered very carefully in revising the scheme. It appeared to us that if we gave increased credit for senior and middle grade passes, we could hardly refuse to bring in professional examinations, and all those others which, owing to the impossibility of classifying them, we have now left out. The pupil who passes in the senior grade will bring his school 2 marks for each of 3 years in succession; and, remember, the amount represented by each mark will be very considerable—we expect about £1,500 a year will go in this way. On your proposal a boy who passes the junior grade this year would get one mark as a boy receiving intermediate education, and another for passing the examination—2 marks. Next year he passes in the middle grade, and gets, in all, 3 marks. In the following year he will have one for receiving education, and 3 for passing the senior—4 in all; 9 marks in 3 years; 6 marks for his Intermediate performance, and 3 as a subsidiary besides. Under our rule he will get 6 marks in all. In other words, you give three times, and we give twice as much for a pupil passing the three grades as for a pupil merely receiving three years' education.

Mr. J. J. Shaw.—But this applies only to the schools that keep boys sufficiently long to pass the senior grade.

Mr. Wilkins.—A school might restrict itself to educating boys in the junior grade. A boy might be unable to get further education in that school, and might have to go to another school to get senior education. The other school ought to get some extra credit for that.

4310. Dr. Traill.—Besides, the teachers for the senior grade would be of a higher class, and would require higher salaries than the teachers for the junior grade boys.

4311. Professor Dougherty.—It is more expensive to provide teaching for the higher grades than for the junior grade?

Mr. Wilkins.—Undoubtedly.

Mr. J. J. Shaw.—The number is much smaller, and the proportion of expenses would be therefore greater still. It is a greater test of the efficiency of a school that a larger number go on to the higher grade; for it cannot retain its boys in the higher grades unless it is doing much good educational work.

4312. Lord Justice FitzGibbon.—If we have done 2 marks for the middle and 3 for the senior, is there any anticipation of our re-opening the old controversy about bringing in other examinations?

Mr. J. J. Shaw.—I don't propose to do it.

4313. Rev. Dr. Molloy.—Would you come and ask us to give special marks for those who pass the Indian Civil Service?

Mr. Wilkins.—No; because the boy who would pass the Indian would pass the Intermediate.

4314. Lord Justice FitzGibbon.—If you will all be satisfied with the Intermediate, I should be glad to pay you more for the higher grades.

Rev. Dr. Molloy.—If you stop at this proposal and don't ask us to introduce other examinations, I would have no objection; but I would rather make the proportion 2, 3, and 4 for the several grades than 1, 2, and 3.

Mr. Wilkins.—I don't much care about the proportions.

4315. Dr. Traill.—But don't you think that the proportion of senior and junior should be 4 to 2, or 2 to 1. If each boy is to get a mark in the first place, and then is to get this additional mark, if you add his one mark to each of the additional marks 2, 3, 4, they become 3, 4, and 5, which makes the ratio 1 to 3 instead of 2 to 1 between the senior and junior grade.

Mr. Wilkins.—The Commissioners seem in the schedule to have overlooked that there is no addition in the senior grade, except as bracketed with algebra.

4316. Rev. Dr. Molloy.—That is a flaw, and we will make it right.

4317. Rev. Dr. Molloy.—Do you think these Intermediate subjects are not too exacting—are they fairly within the competence of a good school?

Mr. Wilkins.—It is possible they might be too exacting. I don't think you should be more exacting than the Intermediate Commissioners for a test.

4318. Lord Justice FitzGibbon.—We cannot accept that test. The Intermediate rules this year make it possible to pass the examinations without knowing one single subject of a grammar school education. A pupil can now pass in any one language, say Celtic, not passing in Latin, Greek, French, or even English. It is very curious, but these mathematical subjects with Irish may now pass the Intermediate Examinations. That test is not high enough for the Royal School Endowments.

Mr. J. J. Shaw.—The fourth suggestion is that "No mark shall be allowed for any pupil whose parents (if alive) do not reside or (if dead) did not at the time of their death reside within one or other of the dioceses to which this scheme applies."

4319. Lord Justice FitzGibbon.—If there ever were boarding school endowments according to their history, are not these?

Mr. J. J. Shaw.—Yes; but that was not the intention of the founders.

4320. Lord Justice FitzGibbon.—The end of this would be to make it perfectly hopeless to use these buildings.

* See Appendix B, No. XXI (b.), p. [illegible].

4221. Lord Justice NAISH.—Is it not a great advantage to the locality to have a boarding-school in it?

Mr. *J. J. Shaw.*—It is subject to great abuse. A great number might be drafted into a school who did not belong to the district and for whom the endowment was not intended, and they might swamp a school that was really educating the people of the district.

4222. Dr. TRAILL.—A boarding school is a great help to the day boys in supplying larger funds for the payment of better masters—would you be satisfied if a certain proportion of the boys were required to belong to the district?

Mr. *J. J. Shaw.*—We don't care how many boarders they educate from other districts, provided they don't get paid by results for it.

VI.—THE MOST REV. DR. LOGUE, LORD ARCHBISHOP OF ARMAGH.

4223. Rev. *F. M'Keon.*—His Grace was unable to attend to-day owing to Confirmation which he had arranged before he knew of this sitting.

4224. Lord Justice FITZGIBBON.—Do you represent him?

Rev. Mr. *M'Keon.*—Yes. Until this draft scheme came out he did not know there was £40 rent to be paid for part of the land belonging to the Armagh Royal School. That would make a difference in the capital sum of £1,000 or £800 a year he thinks, in the value, although the property was valued at £7,500. As to the allowance to be made for private benefactions, the evidence, so far as I remember, was only of belief or hearsay. That matter should be carefully calculated and evidence given how much was expended. He also asked me to enter his strongest protest against any alteration that would allow the Catholics a less proportion than what is laid down in the draft scheme at present. He approves both of the general provisions of the scheme, and the system of results proposed. If results were abandoned it would be merely a scramble for a share instead of earning it by working for it as at present. He also protests against any conclusions adverse to the Catholic claims that might be drawn from the arguments and figures quoted by the General Synod. As regards the education of the* farmers in certain districts, the figures in the past show that these prove nothing, for in those very districts of Fermanagh and Monaghan, the schools in the past, when they had abundant money for intermediate education, were allowed to be unused. If there is a desire for intermediate education among these farmers, it must be recently created, because it did not exist in the past. The facts on the other side show that the poorer Catholic population have a strong desire and will make great efforts to secure this education for their children. This is proved by the colleges they have built and have to a considerable extent endowed. In Armagh, for instance, there is a diocesan collection for promoting higher education, and during the time of the late Primate, Dr. M'Gettigan, all the students belonging to the diocese going into certain classes were allowed £10 a year abatement off their pension, and in addition certain sums were given to pupils who gained prizes. The present Primate last year altered the conditions on which these prizes are given. I have here a circular he sent to the clergy with regard to the exhibitions that were established by him. There are four exhibitions of £20 each, tenable for two years, and seven exhibitions of £10 each, tenable for three years, or in case of boys of thirteen years or under, for four years. I quote this to show that these people manifest a strong desire to secure intermediate education for their children, and even make sacrifices to secure it. Then as to the Intermediate passes, he does not consider that a fair test to apply to us, because, as appeared from the evidence of the several head masters, Protestant pupils are attracted to Ulster from Dublin and from the centre and South of Ireland, and in fact far more than half the pupils of the Protestant schools in some places were not residents in the Royal School area, but from other counties.

4225. Lord Justice FITZGIBBON.—We are now getting into the old complaints about the proportion. We have in the scheme gone upon a principle of minimum grants and division of the residue by results, to which these observations do not apply. As regards the mode of valuing the private benefactions, we have adopted the principle for which Archbishop Logue contends, that the allowance is to be based on the proportionate value of the parts built with private money to the whole present value of the buildings, at the time when the buildings are handed over to the Local Boards; but I am afraid we cannot do what he wants us to do, namely, to ascertain and declare now what the value of those benefactions will be when the vested interests expire. When that time comes the Commissioners can do all that we could do now, namely, send a competent surveyor to make the valuation, and leave it to those who claim the allowance to prove their claim. As regards the other matter of the relative claims of Protestants and Catholics, we cannot open it again, when the scheme is so framed as to render it immaterial.

Rev. Mr. *M'Keon.*—His Grace wishes to give this reply to the objections of the General Synod as to the Intermediate Examinations in the past. For instance, the Catholic girls' schools did not go in for the Intermediate Examinations generally.

4226. Lord Justice FITZGIBBON.—A great many of them are on the lists now, and in these districts too.

Rev. Mr. *M'Keon.*—In the Armagh schools, three-fourths of the pupils were boarders, and objected to going in for the examinations.

4227. Lord Justice FITZGIBBON.—You have now a large number of girls passing in Armagh and Fermanagh. Two of the largest Catholic schools in the six counties are girls' schools. One school has 13 and 18, and another 13, 20, and 22.

Rev. Mr. *M'Keon.*—If the Intermediate Examinations are to be taken as the test, the only passes allowed for results should be those of pupils from the Royal school area. They should not be handicapped by the introduction of pupils from other parts.

4228. Lord Justice FITZGIBBON.—We cannot exclude boarding schools; and if we admit them we can make no difference between the pupils on the score of where they come from.

Rev. Mr. *M'Keon.*—We object that the test of the Intermediate Examinations in the past should be quoted against us. One school in Armagh sent in boys to those Examinations who were credited to the County Armagh when three-fourths of them did not belong to it.

4229. Dr. TRAILL.—The Royal schools have passed hardly any for the last few years. Those on the list are from other Protestant schools.

Rev. Mr. *M'Keon.*—In every Protestant school in Ulster a large number of the pupils came in from other parts of Ireland.

4230. Rev. Dr. *MOLLOY.*—Are you content to take your share of the residue in accordance with the educational work done in your schools?

Rev. Mr. *M'Keon.*—Quite content.

4231. Lord Justice FITZGIBBON.—That is the principle of the scheme as it stands; and in your educational work we think you are entitled to count work done for boarders. It is really amusing to find both sides—Mr. M'Keon and Mr. Shaw—equally apprehensive of a new plantation of Ulster to carry off the lion's share of these Royal School Endowments. If we found this part of the country occupied by large boarding schools, giving education also to all the day-pupils of the locality, it would be the crowning proof of the success of our scheme in extending the usefulness of these endowments.

* See Appendix B, No. III. (a), p. [illegible]

RAPHOE ESTATE.—TOWNAWILLY TENANTRY SCHOOL.—MR. FOX'S VESTED INTEREST.

4232. Mr. *Fox*.—I wish to direct the attention of the Commissioners to my position. More than £400 has been contributed within the last two months towards the Townawilly School, in the form of rents. I am the master of the school, and I have a primary claim that my salary should be paid. The school has been in receipt of the endowment for more than forty years; from time immemorial there has been a free school there, and the Commissioners have paid it to me for the last nine-and-a-half years.

4233. Lord Justice FITZGIBBON.—Is your school under the National Board?

Mr. *Fox*.—Yes.

4234. Lord Justice FITZGIBBON.—Have you got a class salary?

Mr. *Fox*.—Yes.

4235. Lord Justice FITZGIBBON.—What did you get last year from the Commissioners?

Mr. *Fox*.—I received no salary as yet for last year. The Commissioners at present owe me fifteen months salary.

4236. Lord Justice FITZGIBBON.—What is your present title to the office?

Mr. *Fox*.—I was appointed by the Commissioners, and I have continued in the service of the National Board for nine-and-a-half years.

4237. Lord Justice FITZGIBBON.—Who is the manager of the school?

Mr. *Fox*.—The Rev. H. M'Fadden, P.P., of Donegal, is the manager.

4238. Lord Justice FITZGIBBON.—Have you any document showing the terms on which you hold your office? We have nothing to do with your past salary. We can only deal with any vested interest you have now.

Mr. *Fox*.—I have an agreement with Mr. Stewart, the representative of the Commissioners of Education, and their former agent. I was receiving £30 a year, and a free house and place from them. It is not signed by the Commissioners, but by their agent—the person they appointed to manage—the local manager of the school.

4239. Lord Justice FITZGIBBON.—They have no power that I know of to give you £30, unless they have got the money from the estate.

Mr. *Fox*.—The endowment has been given from time immemorial.

4240. Lord Justice FITZGIBBON.—Have they given you any intimation whether they are willing to continue to pay or not?

Mr. *Fox*.—I have a communication which is entirely contradictory of the statements your lordship had read from their reports—that pending the action of your Commission no change would be made.

4241. Lord Justice FITZGIBBON.—What is the communication you have got?

Mr. *Fox*.—It is extinguishing my rights altogether, and stating that at a meeting of the Board I was dismissed from the 20th March last. [Handed in.]

4242. Lord Justice FITZGIBBON.—I am afraid we cannot go behind this:—

"21st March, 189[illegible].

"SIR,—I am instructed to inform you that by resolution of the 20th March last, the Commissioners have dismissed you from the position of master of the Townawilly School, and deprived you of the emoluments connected therewith.

"JEFFREY MCDERMOTT, for R. McDonnell, Secretary to the Commissioners of Education."

Mr. *Fox*.—But I claim that that is a perfectly illegal action.

4243. Lord Justice FITZGIBBON.—We cannot determine whether it is or not. You have no vested interest that we can recognise.

VII.—THE MOST REV. DR. DONNELLY, LORD BISHOP OF CLOGHER.

4244. Lord Justice FITZGIBBON.—Dr. Donnelly has two small points that he wishes to bring forward. The first is to substitute the name of the Rev. James Morgan, P.P., Tempo, for that of the Very Rev. James Canon M'Quaid, P.P., Clonelish, on the Fermanagh Board. The other is about enabling each Local Board to pay a secretary. Now, we have deliberately tried to prevent these Local Boards from applying the endowments to pay secretaries. If we put in a provision, apparently harmless in itself, enabling the boards to give some small salary to one of their members, we would risk all the unpleasantness which has arisen in other places. The evidence is all against salaries being paid out of the endowments. If the Local Boards want to pay secretaries let them apply their own funds to the purpose.

Mr. R. P. Carton, Q.C. (instructed by Mr. Wray).—I appear on behalf of Dr. Donnelly, and so long as the scheme remains as it is he is quite prepared to accept it and the principle on which it is proposed to divide the endowments; but if there is any yielding on the part of the Commissioners to the objections made by Mr. Bewley, on behalf of Dr. Donnelly I respectfully ask you not to depart from the principle or details of the scheme.

4245. Professor DOUGHERTY.—I suppose you wish Monaghan to be retained in the Fermanagh District?

Mr. *Carton*, Q.C.—Yes. I referred you on the last day to the statutory authority that the district was to be regulated by the diocese, and we think Monaghan ought to be included, being in the Diocese of Clogher. There is one small matter of detail: If the Protestant Bishops are given power to nominate substitutes we would ask the same privilege for the Roman Catholic Bishops. There seems to be some conflict between Section 45 and Section 50 as to whether the value of the school premises is to go into the "common fund," under Section 45, or "to be applied exclusively for the benefit of the district," under Section 50. It would seem to me that if there were inserted before the words "shall be treated as a common fund" in Section 45 some such words as "subject to the provisions of Section 50," it would make it clear.

4246. Lord Justice FITZGIBBON.—There is no doubt we meant to give the value of the buildings in addition to the minimum grant in each locality.

*Mr. *Carton*.—In Section 50 there is a kind of upset price—a "sum of £7,000—at which the Enniskillen premises are to be sold to either Her Majesty's Secretary of State for War or to any other purchaser. I don't know what data you went on, for Mr. Hagan, a very experienced architect, has valued the buildings and land at £9,100.

4247. Lord Justice FITZGIBBON.—We would be very glad if you can get £9,100 for them.

Mr. *Carton*, Q.C.—But the scheme as it stands would compel the Commissioners to sell them for £7,000.

4248. Lord Justice FITZGIBBON.—No, but we wanted to compel them to sell rather than keep them if they can get £7,000 or upwards for them. We tried to get an offer of £8,000, but failed. The War Office have made a proposal to buy for £7,000. The Enniskillen people want to keep the premises for a school.

Rev. Dr. MOLLOY.—Have you a purchaser for a higher sum?

* See Appendix B., Nos. III. (d) to III. (l), p. 3[illegible].

Mr. *Carson*, Q.C.—I am not aware we have, but it appears rather injudicious to tie the Commissioners down to £7,000.

6249. Lord Justice FitzGibbon.—We do not tie them down to take £7,000 if they can get more, but the War Office say they are willing to give £7,000, and the object of the clause was to prevent the Enniskillen Protestant Local Board from insisting on keeping what we thought was a "white elephant," if £7,000 cash could be got for it.

Mr. *Carson*, Q.C.—I may have misconceived the effect of the clause. All I want is that the Commissioners shall not be bound to sell for £7,000 if they can get more.

6250. Professor Dougherty.—The clause will not require them to sell to the Secretary for War for £7,000 if anybody else gives £8,000.

Lord Justice FitzGibbon.—We have yet to hear a very strong protest from the Enniskillen people against selling Portora at all.

Mr. *Carson*, Q.C.—Provided we are not compelled to take £7,000 if we can get more, I am content that the clause should remain as it is.

6251. Dr. Traill.—Is Dr. Donnelly prepared to offer more than £7,000?

Mr. *Carson*, Q.C.—He has got a valuation of £9,100.

6252. Lord Justice FitzGibbon.—If you offered £9,000 possibly the Fermanagh Protestant Board would offer something more, and there is no knowing where the competition between you would stop. We thought it far better for the Enniskillen people on both sides to have £3,500 each in cash with which to establish and work schools of suitable size, and the object of the clause was to prevent them from keeping Portora at a ruinous valuation.

Mr. *Dane*.—It is only right to say that a very representative committee, presided over by the Bishop, with the Methodist and Presbyterian ministers and the rectors, are * unanimously of opinion that the buildings are not a "white elephant," and that they can be perfectly well suited to the Protestants.

6253. Rev. Dr. Molloy.—Are they prepared to give £3,500 for them?

Mr. *Dane*.—Yes; they are prepared to allow the Roman Catholics £3,500 for them. They have got a very strong idea that the people of that locality have a very strong claim on the endowment of Portora, and they also have a very strong idea that they ought, in strict equity, to get the buildings free, but they are willing that £3,500, half the value of the property, should be handed over to the Roman Catholics out of the accumulated fund belonging to Portora.

6254. Rev. Dr. Molloy.—You want to take the buildings worth £7,000 for your side, and to give £3,500 out of the endowment to the other side—that is, half as much as you are getting?

Mr. *Dane*.—Yes, and having regard to the fact that we think it is our own I think it is a very fair and generous offer, having regard to the provisions of the 13th section that you are to have regard to the intentions of the founders, and this endowment was for the benefit of the Protestants of Fermanagh.

6255. Lord Justice FitzGibbon.—If you are right in that the Roman Catholics have no right to get anything.

Mr. *Carson*, Q.C.—With regard to the first objection made by Mr. *Bewley*, that the scheme gives the Roman Catholic Church a share of the endowments which statistics of intermediate education prove to be most excessive; no proof is brought forward in justification of that charge, and I ask the Commissioners to retain the provisions under which they propose to distribute the endowment as provided in the scheme.

VIII.—THE MOST REV. DR. M'GENNIS, LORD BISHOP OF KILMORE.

6256. Mr. *Drummond*, (instructed by Mr. Hugh T. Kennedy).—I appear on behalf of the Roman Catholic Bishop of Kilmore. I withdraw the first of his objections, but I ask attention to the amount to be given as a minimum out of the Cavan Endowment, considering what a small net income it has.

6257. Lord Justice FitzGibbon.—I think the Bishop of Kilmore is under a misapprehension about this. In the original draft we allowed only 25 per cent. of the net rental as a minimum grant to each Local Board in Cavan, but the whole of your money and stock was hypothecated to pay the compensation for vested interests. I don't know that the Bishop understands that we now propose that the stock shall remain as part of the Cavan Endowment—you have £3,300 each—and that each board shall get 30 per cent. of the dividends as well as of the rents.

Mr. *Drummond*.—Taking that view of the matter I would not be disposed to press that point very much, but taking the interest in the £3,300, and adding it to the £274 net rental, I think, considering the position of the two boards in Cavan, it would not be unreasonable to ask 40 per cent. In Cavan the Roman Catholic Board is very much in need of funds. The Cavan College has no private income or endowment, and there is a debt of £5,000 against the building at present.

6258. Lord Justice FitzGibbon.—Do you happen to know what rate of interest that debt bears?

Mr. *Drummond*.—I think 5 per cent., and that is a very large deduction out of any income they could derive from pupils or otherwise. Consequently the effect of keeping up this college is very severe, and considering that no such debt will be attached to the schools being started in the other counties. Even if they had the £274 and the interest on the £5,000, 40 per cent. would not be too much to ask. It would leave less for the real maintenance of the school than they have in any of the other counties under the scheme. Then comes another question, the value to be put upon the premises of the present Royal School. That is capitalised at £4,000 in the scheme. Dr. M'Gennis has no desire to ask that the very utmost value of these premises should be put on by the Commissioners; he is anxious that the matter should be treated reasonably and fairly. He has got a civil engineer and a valuator to go over the premises and land, and they have no doubt that the value is far in excess of £3,000 and very close on £4,000. The land alone, which is over sixteen acres, can be let at £4 or £5 an acre. On the other side of the town the land attached to St. Patrick's College is let at £4 an acre, and being so close to Cavan it will sell for at least twenty years' purchase. Dr. M'Gennis has got it valued at more than £1,600.

Dr. Traill.—He puts down the fair capital value at £4,800, and he fixes the fair rent at £120; so that he takes forty years purchase of the fair rent as the fair capital value.

6259. Lord Justice FitzGibbon.—We saw this place, and there are a great many drawbacks to it as land. In the first place, the school buildings occupy a large space in the centre of it, there is a great deal of waste about the house and offices, a great deal of ground under trees, and the only way into the place is through the private property of the head master. The tenement valuation of the buildings is £70, and of the land £26 10s., in all £96 10s. for the whole concern; I think the Bishop can hardly expect any one—though the tenement valuation is only a rough test—to accept his valuation of £4,800 as likely to be realised, nearly fifty years purchase of "Griffith's Valuation."

Mr. *Drummond*.—In a great many cases the tenement valuation is no test at all.

* Report 1887-88, p. [illegible].

Lord Justice FitzGibbon.—Whatever it can be used against anybody it is no test at all.

4360. Rev. Dr. Molloy.—At how many years purchase do you estimate it?

Mr. Drummond.—Taking the land by itself, it is worth over £1,000.

4361. Lord Justice FitzGibbon.—There are not ten Irish acres in the place; the buildings, yards, and waste have to come off that; it is not agricultural land. How would you make such a sum of money of it?

Mr. Drummond.—I am only looking at the value of it as land.

4362. Lord Justice FitzGibbon.—We consider ourselves bound to keep these buildings as a school. The Protestants of Cavan want a school, and this is a very suitable place for them. It is not too big; it is close to the town, and altogether it is just a handy, useful set of school premises. You don't want it, for you have a large college already. We ought not to sell it or let it out as a market garden, looking to its value as a school, and we think £100 a year is about the outside value school people would be asked to put upon it. We found you owing a heavy debt to the bank, and taking you as paying five per cent. on it, we gave you £2,000 to spend in reducing the charge on your own buildings. We therefore relieved you to the extent of £100 a year, in a way we allowed nowhere else.

Mr. Drummond.—We are not looking merely to the value of the premises to be handed over to the Protestant Board, but the Bishop is looking to his own position, because you give him a corresponding sum; in proportion as you lower the value of the premises, you lower the sum you are giving him.

4363. Lord Justice FitzGibbon.—What you want to raise is not the price on the Protestant Board, but the amount we are to give you towards your debt.

Mr. Drummond.—We want the amount given to be fixed at a reasonable amount.

Lord Justice FitzGibbon.—And we think £100 a year is the fair value, and twenty years purchase of that is £2,000.

4364. Dr. Traill.—Why do you value it at £120, and then place forty years purchase on it? Is there a landlord in Ireland who would get that number of years purchase, if he sold his property?

Mr. Drummond.—The land is valued at £1,000, and the value put on the premises by a competent valuator was £3,800.

4365. Lord Justice FitzGibbon.—I suppose a competent valuator on the other side might be found who would say that the buildings are not worth the expense of keeping them in repair.

Mr. Drummond.—We suggest that the Commissioners should send a valuer to value these premises, or that it be left to the Local Boards to come to an agreement about them. We think £2,000 is hardly fair.

4366. Lord Justice FitzGibbon.—We tried to value this place on the materials we had, and we all agreed that £2,000 was a fair price. We also agreed to give you the £2,000, not to be invested in Government stock, but to pay off part of your interest-bearing debt. I arrived at the £2,000 as twenty years purchase on £100 a year.

Rev. Dr. Molloy.—I took a slightly different view, but with the same result. I took the Bishop's own figure—£120 a year—and allowed seventeen years purchase on that.

Mr. Drummond.—But land so close to the town will go far higher.

4367. Rev. Dr. Molloy.—Do buildings and land in the neighbourhood of Cavan sell for more than seventeen years purchase of the fair value?

Mr. Drummond.—I am sure it would, when you remember that on the other side of the town they are giving £5 an acre.

4368. Rev. Dr. Molloy.—I am not speaking of the annual value. Will a dwelling-house and land sell for more than seventeen years purchase of the fair rent?

Mr. Drummond.—I think a house of that kind with good land attached to it would. I am instructed we will undertake to get £3,800 for it.

4369. Lord Justice FitzGibbon.—This building is very large compared with the size of the holding. We really could not have gone more carefully into the matter than we did in trying to find the fair price to allow for it.

Mr. Drummond.—I am instructed that we will guarantee more than £3,000 will be given for it.

4370. Dr. Traill.—Can you give us the name of any person who will take it at £3,800? A higher offer was made in the case of Enniskillen.

Mr. Drummond.—If you allow the point to remain open, I will undertake that an offer will be made for considerably more than £2,000.

4371. Lord Justice FitzGibbon.—That is only speculation. Remember it is only the reversion on the head master's vested interest that we can deal with, and the Cavan Protestants want it for a school. The real question is this, how much is a fair equivalent to allow the Roman Catholics for these premises, which we consider we are bound to use for the educational purposes for which they are wanted.

Mr. Drummond.—I adhere to the statement I made before, that we don't wish to put any unreasonable price on this property.

4372. Lord Justice FitzGibbon.—Then why did you put down £4,800 as the value?

Mr. Drummond.—We put that down as the possible value, to show the reasonableness of our objection to the £2,000. To alienate at £2,000 out of the £4,000 belonging to Cavan, in return for the school, is too little.

4373. Lord Justice FitzGibbon.—If we sold the schools for £2,500, only half the additional £500 would come to you. Therefore you would only be the interest on £250 the richer, and the Protestants will be only so much the poorer if we value the school premises at £2,500. Will you undertake to say no more about it, if we give you £2,500 out of the endowment?

Mr. Drummond.—Yes, I would be justified in doing that. We thought, considering the enormous debt we have, and considering that the £2,000 comes out of the £6,000 that was allowed to accumulate, it was too small; and we ask you to stretch a point and make the amount a little more than £2,000, which the Bishop considers too low under the circumstances of his case.

4374. Lord Justice FitzGibbon.—I think we ought to say that if we increase this sum, it is not so much because we think the strict value of the school premises is more, but because we think we may be somewhat liberal in appropriating a portion of the Cavan money in the very legitimate use of clearing your buildings from part of the cost of erecting them, for which you are at present paying interest, especially as we regard the fund as half your own.

Mr. Drummond.—And in doing that, although you nominally increase the value of the buildings £500, it is in reality only giving us £250 more.

4375. Dr. Traill.—Would you be better satisfied if you got £3,000 out of the £6,000?

Mr. Drummond.—The figure already mentioned, £2,500, is not an exorbitant figure.

4376. Dr. Traill.—Would you like to capitalize any portion of your unbillowance grant at twenty years purchase?

Mr. Drummond.—I wouldn't like to answer that question.

Dr. Traill.—If you want to pay your debt, it would be a very good way to do it.

4377. Lord Justice FitzGibbon.—We are going very near the wind in applying the endowment at all to pay off your debt, and it is only under the special circumstances of the case, and having regard to the nature of your buildings, that we do it, but I can be no party

May 15, 1888.

to capitalising any part of the minimum grant, which is provided for the permanent maintenance of an efficient school for the Catholics of Cavan. Your next question is, where the salary of Mr. P. J. Anderson was fixed at £200 a year. We got the date of Mr. Anderson's appointment from the Commissioners of Education.

Mr. Drummond.—I don't press that point.

4278. Lord Justice FitzGibbon.—Clause 50 of the scheme answers the last of your objections, in which you ask, what is to be done with the money that has accumulated out of the income of Cavan School, and which is now beyond £3,000, is answered by Clause 50 of the scheme:—

"Every balance to credit, so far as it consists of income for the current year, shall be treated as accruing income, and so far as it consists of accumulations shall be treated as part of the capital of the endowment to which it belongs."

Mr. Drummond.—Would you think it unreasonable that the whole £6,000 should be allocated to the Cavan Boards?

4279. Lord Justice FitzGibbon.—I will tell you at once why it would be unreasonable. We have allocated you 60 per cent. of the rental of £274, and if we allocated you all the stock and cash besides, the Cavan Endowment would be contributing nothing to the common residue fund except 40 per cent. on £274—say £110 a year; and it would not be reasonable to let your schools compete for a residue to which they did not contribute. Besides, we want these Cavan schools to be under some temptation, and the same pressure, to work efficiently. Why should Dr. Dowdall's College at Monaghan contribute 50 per cent. of the large Fermanagh rental to the residue—getting only 25 per cent. maximum grant—while your schools in Cavan kept all their own stock and cash, and 60 per cent. of the rents too, and were allowed, besides, to participate in the residue from the other districts.

Mr. Drummond.—This is simply an accumulated fund that was intended for Cavan, under the Acts of Geo. III. and Geo. IV. I submit that the Commissioners, in whose name you stated, would have no authority to hand over this accumulated fund, as it will be handed over under this scheme. Under the Act of Geo. III., the property of each district was to be used for its own purposes; but under the Act of Geo. IV., for the first time power was given to take the surplus, if any, and use it for certain defined purposes only.

4280. Lord Justice FitzGibbon.—That is going back to a very wide question that we heard before. If you make out that we must keep the whole Cavan endowment for the Cavan district, the same argument must prevail in all the other districts, and the result will be to upset the scheme altogether—giving £1,800 a year to Fermanagh and confining Cavan to its own small endowment, though all the Fermanagh schools put together passed only 4 pupils at the Intermediate examinations in 1887, 2 in 1888, and none at all in 1889. The whole object of this scheme is to compel every school to work before it gets money, and when it works, to give it a claim on part of the funds of the whole area. You want to neutralise all this, in order that you may make sure of 60 per cent. of the Cavan Endowment, and vegetate in Cavan without any obligation or inducement to work for good results.

Mr. Drummond.—But considering the position of this college in Cavan, and the debt they have to pay, if they are to start on terms of equality with other schools, they must start as a self-supporting institution; and assuming you give them £1,500, they will have the rest of that debt over them, so that they will be unable to start in the same position as the schools in Monaghan and Armagh. I submit that considering the Roman Catholics in Cavan have endeavoured to support this school under very difficult circumstances, that the £6,000 is Cavan money, and that it will be almost impossible to keep up this school properly with the endowment proposed. It is not unreasonable that while a proportion of the income of the property will go to the common fund, the whole of the £6,000 ought to be allocated to Cavan. The Roman Catholic school, which is far the more important of the two, has a large number of pupils, and would have sent in a large number of pupils to these examinations, if it was not that they were throwing away their money on this large debt.

4281. Professor Dougherty.—If you have built a school that is too expensive for you, it would not be fair now to throw it on the endowment.

Mr. Drummond.—They wanted to build a school for a certain number of pupils with no money.

4282. Dr. Traill.—Surely the buildings are four times as valuable as those of the other school?

Mr. Drummond.—And there would be twice four times as many pupils to-morrow if they were free of debt.

4283. Lord Justice FitzGibbon.—I don't think we could do you a worse service than to hand you this capital to pay your debt, leaving you with nothing to carry on your school in future. We allow you to pay off part of the debt, not to spend money on new buildings, but to pay for those you already have, being satisfied they are well built, and suitable, though perhaps too extensive for your needs.

Lord Justice Naish.—You get a quid pro quo towards the maintenance of your school, in being admitted to compete for the general fund.

Mr. Drummond.—They are allowed to compete nominally, but they won't really be in a position to compete. Cavan is the most backward place probably in the whole of Ulster in this respect. The efforts of the gentlemen at the head of that institution will be paralysed by the fact that their funds must go to liquidate a debt.

4284. Dr. Traill.—Would you be satisfied to get half of this fund and not have the right to compete for the money derived from the residue of the other school endowments.

Mr. Drummond.—No; but I propose to give a reasonable return for the permission to compete.

4285. Lord Justice FitzGibbon.—What is it?

Mr. Drummond.—Forty per cent. on £274 a year, contributed to the common fund.

4286. Lord Justice FitzGibbon.—For liberty to compete for a residue of about £1,500 a year?

Mr. Drummond.—But it will be some time before they will earn it.

Lord Justice FitzGibbon.—That is the extent of what they may earn.

IX.—THE VERY REV. R. M'NAMEE, P.P., V.F., OMAGH.

4287. Lord Justice FitzGibbon.—Father M'Namee, you still object to the scheme, because the Tyrone district includes portion of Derry, and because the Derry diocese has only three representatives on the Tyrone board?

4288. Very Rev. R. M'Namee.—Yes, and I am sorry you are not of the same mind as when you promised me four representatives.

Lord Justice FitzGibbon.—But the Archbishop came next day to complain that you had left a large portion of his diocese out of the calculations on which you got us to admit your claim.

Very Rev. R. M'Namee.—I answered the question I was asked. I am still strongly of opinion that you should give me four representatives. The county Derry is provided for by other means.

4289. Professor Dougherty.—What are they?

May 31, 1889.

Very Rev. R. M'Namee.—The Irish Society and the London Companies.

4290. Professor Dougherty.—The provisions the Irish Society and London Companies have made in Derry for education are becoming small by degrees.

Very Rev. R. M'Namee.—I see in the last return £3,800 given by the Irish Society alone. Besides, since I addressed you last, one of the London Companies has sold its property at Magherafelt, and persons of their fund has been set apart for educational purposes.

4291. Lord Justice FitzGibbon.—Do you know how much?

Very Rev. R. M'Namee.—I believe the Roman Catholic portion is £51 a year.

4292. Professor Dougherty.—They have given as an educational endowment a lot of property they could not sell?

Very Rev. R. M'Namee.—If every parish belonging to Tyrone had £51 allotted to it, you would have very little to divide. This is brought in because it belongs to the archdiocese of Armagh, and that archdiocese has a board of its own, and a separate and good endowment as well. If charity extends to the whole diocese, I suggest see the consistency of leaving out Louth, which belongs to Armagh Diocese, and taking in this portion of Derry.

4293. Professor Dougherty.—I suppose you are aware that this part of Derry was originally part of county Tyrone?

Very Rev. R. M'Namee.—If you follow that argument why not take in the remainder of the diocese of Derry. The result is to destroy the equilibrium altogether in the management of this fund for the county Tyrone. In other cases you have consulted for the bishops, but the position of the Bishop of Derry is not at all equal to that of any of the other bishops. In the first place he is outnumbered; in the second, it would be impossible for him to attend the ordinary meetings of the Tyrone local board. Of course, if the majority of the board are in the archdiocese of Armagh they will fix the hours of the meetings, and they will be held in Dungannon. How is the Bishop of Derry to attend them? It would require two days, most of it occupied in travelling, for unless he starts from his own place at six in the morning, he cannot reach Dungannon before twenty minutes to four o'clock, and he could transact no business at that hour. The next point is that if you establish a school in Dungannon, and one in Armagh they will be two competing schools. We have some experience as regards schools in Dungannon, and it is not a matter of speculation at all. There were two schools there, and not one of them was able to appear on the Intermediate list. They both died of inanition, but that is not the case in Omagh, where schools are established spontaneously without extraneous aid; when they are established by people living there, and they are in active operation at the present time, and likely to succeed, it shows that the schools were wanted there. I say, with all respect, that these are the schools you are to encourage, and not endeavour to classify the remains of dead ones.

4294. Lord Justice FitzGibbon.—Under the scheme, as it stands, on the results of the last three years, the whole Tyrone endowments would have gone to the girls and boys schools in Omagh. What more can you want? The arrangement of the board was made the subject of communication with the Bishops of Clogher and Derry and the Archbishop of Armagh, who wished the Bishop of Derry to be put in his place, as he had his own board. We cannot give you four members unless we put Dungannon in a minority or leave Clogher out altogether.

Very Rev. R. M'Namee.—I only ask four, and that will leave four to Armagh and one to Clogher.

4295. Dr. Traill.—Would you be satisfied if the Bishop of Derry was able to nominate a person to take his place?

Very Rev. R. M'Namee.—No; for you practically give four for Armagh, which, I really think, must have been an oversight.

4296. Lord Justice FitzGibbon.—That is because you call that part of Tyrone which is in the archdiocese "Armagh," and you call your own diocese "Tyrone," though the Magherafelt part of county Derry is "Armagh" too.

Very Rev. R. M'Namee.—If you are so anxious about furnishing that part of county Derry, why not attach it to Armagh. The population of Tyrone is 197,719—of these 109,793 are Catholics, and to this large number in the county Tyrone you make an addition of 8,000, whereas, if you added that number to the county Armagh the whole population would be 177,000 against 197,719. I cannot understand how you can make this arrangement and expect the Bishop of Derry to have guidance or interest in it. It is all very well to say he will go occasionally, but my experience is that those who go occasionally do more harm than good.

4297. Lord Justice FitzGibbon.—You have fought very hard for your corner, and I think we must make some provision to enable your bishop to have an efficient representative in his absence; but we cannot give you four representatives.

Very Rev. R. M'Namee.—Then you don't give what you agreed to give before, and I would like to have it recorded on what principle you do this.

4298. Lord Justice FitzGibbon.—I will not go over the figures again, but we have satisfied everybody but yourself that we were right in correcting the figures you first gave us.

Very Rev. R. M'Namee.—You must consider the whole district.

4299. Lord Justice FitzGibbon.—And you will get the whole endowment if your schools go on as at present.

Professor Dougherty.—Recollect that the school in Derry which educates a large part of the population of Tyrone will not get any share of this endowment.

Very Rev. R. M'Namee.—Yes; but Tyrone was always pointed to as the district to which this endowment is applicable. It is not a good reward for having, through good report and evil report, established and maintained two schools in Omagh. The Roman Catholic population of that part of the county Tyrone, which is in Derry diocese, is nearly 48,000, and of that part which is in the archdiocese of Armagh is about 50,000, and you add this portion of the county Derry by which you get 8,000 more; that is what I object to, and I don't see why you do that except to throw the whole control into the hands of Dungannon.

4300. Lord Justice FitzGibbon.—The endowment was for the archdiocese of Armagh, and the school might have been in Magherafelt, and we felt that Magherafelt had the same right as Omagh.

Very Rev. R. M'Namee.—Yet you put out part of the diocese of Derry, and make a most invidious distinction.

4301. Lord Justice FitzGibbon.—That is the fault of those who laid down the boundaries of the dioceses. Now with reference to Dean Byrne's objection, the intention is that each representative shall either hold ecclesiastical office as a clergyman, or be resident as a layman, in the portion of the district which he represents. Is Dean Byrne satisfied with the scheme as it stands in other respects?

Very Rev. Dean Byrne.—Yes.

XV., XVI., and XIX.—DR. MORGAN, DR. RINGWOOD, AND DR. MOORE.

4302. Right Hon. S. Walker, Q.C. (instructed by Messrs. Kisby and Lloyd).—On behalf of Dr. Ringwood and Dr. Moore Morgan, the head masters for whom I appear—we don't intend at present to say more than to renew our former objections. Dr. Ringwood is perfectly willing to retire at the earliest date the scheme will permit, and to accept the terms stated, provided you increase the £200 you offer him to £300. If not, he will stand on any rights he has. Dr. Morgan is placed in such a position that he feels himself bound to contest the matter, and it would not be reasonable that I should enter into all the objections I made before. He is offered £266 a year, and £160 for his vested interest, but he feels so dissatisfied with the scheme that he cannot accept those terms.

4303. Mr. Bewley, Q.C.—On behalf of Mr. Prior Moore, Master of Cavan, I renew my objections. I submit that the scheme does not preserve his vested interest; and he certainly cannot accept it as it now stands.

Mr. Drummond.—With regard to section 44, Dr. M'Comb wishes to know exactly how he stands. I understand that the £2,500 will come out of the accumulated sum of £5,000, but that 60 per cent. of the interest on the balance and of the net rental of £374 will be given to each of the Cavan schools.

4304. Lord Justice FitzGibbon.—Yes; the present sum of £2,000 will be raised to £2,500, which you may take, on the completion of the scheme, towards your building debt. It will be paid out of the Cavan stock or cash, and 60 per cent. of the interest of the remainder (subject to striking off the Raphoe debt) will go to the Cavan schools, and the remaining 40 per cent. to the general fund.

XII.—THE LOCAL COMMITTEE OF PROTESTANT DENOMINATIONS IN THE COUNTY OF FERMANAGH.

4305. Mr. Dane.—I appear on behalf of a committee of the county Fermanagh, representing the various Protestant denominations of the people there. In the first place the Committee wish to stand by their original protest and objection, which were fully gone into at the sitting in August, by Mr. Atkinson. Assuming that the Commissioners do not see their way to granting what the Committee think they are entitled to, they have lodged further objections concerning which I will say a few words in detail, but first I have to say that my Committee feel entirely with the views put forward by Mr. Bewley, that the division of this fund amongst the four sects entitled to the same, should now be made and should be final, and therefore no necessity should exist for the provisions contained in the Scheme with reference to the three years or the minimum grants, or the results, say with a final division made now.

4306. Lord Justice FitzGibbon.—That raises a subquestion which you should answer plainly. Do you mean that each of the five endowments should be separately divided into four parts, in proportion to the claims of the denominations in its own district, whether calculated on the literate population or the Intermediate results, or in any other way you please, or that all the five endowments shall be put together and then divided into four shares according to the proportion of the claims from the whole area.

Mr. Dane.—You are allocating the fund among five sects, and I say the fund to be divided in which I am interested is the fund of the Enniskillen estate only, and its accumulations.

4307. Lord Justice FitzGibbon.—Then I suppose the Presbyterian and Methodist gentlemen whom you represent are aware that they will only get the sums mentioned by Mr. Bewley, £[illegible] and £50 a year.

Mr. Dane.—It is wholly immaterial what they get, they are all united.

4308. Professor Dougherty.—Are they satisfied to take £[illegible] as their share?

Mr. Dane.—They have not worked it out, because we don't want to divide it, we merely want the division made as a matter of calculation.

4309. Lord Justice FitzGibbon.—Then you are going to make it merely a matter of book-keeping, but you must say whether you support Mr. Bewley's contention, which is that all the five endowments are to be added together, and then divided amongst the different denominations?

Mr. Dane.—I don't; I say you are to divide the Enniskillen estate separately.

4310. Lord Justice FitzGibbon.—If we do that, the Fermanagh Protestants, who have the largest share of the largest endowment, will keep it to themselves, and Armagh, Tyrone, Donegal, and Cavan must content themselves, each with their own share of their own small fund.

Mr. Dane.—That is what I intended to argue.

4311. Dr. Traill.—It makes no difference to the Presbyterians of Fermanagh, for they are all joined.

Mr. Dane.—It makes no difference, for they are quite united and quite willing to trust their co-religionists.

4312. Lord Justice FitzGibbon.—I think it is only necessary to refer to Mr. Bewley's figures to show how utterly destructive of the interests of the Protestants of the other districts the acceptance of your help would be on the principle on which you offer it. In Cavan, for example, the whole Protestant share would be £160 a year, and the Presbyterians and Methodists would get scarcely anything. The Fermanagh Presbyterians would get £[illegible].

Mr. Dane.—With reference to the proposal to bring in Monaghan, I have got further statistics which I would commend very strongly to the attention of the Commissioners. You are aware of the provisions of the 13th section of the Act. I say in framing this scheme and annexing Monaghan, you are ignoring entirely the intentions of the founder, because you are bringing in and annexing to Fermanagh which is essentially a Protestant county, Monaghan, which is essentially a Catholic county, and was never in the original settlement.

4313. Lord Justice FitzGibbon.—We have explained over and over again that we don't take one penny from the Protestants by doing that; on the contrary it gives them a claim for their schools in Monaghan, which, during the last three years, would have earned far more money than all the Fermanagh schools put together.

Mr. Dane.—But annexing Monaghan to Fermanagh will deprive the Protestants of Fermanagh of a very large proportion of this fund which they believe was intended by the founder for the benefit of the Protestant people there.

4314. Lord Justice FitzGibbon.—It does not take anything from them. The minimum grants and value of the buildings are not reduced one farthing.

Mr. Dane.—It has been, so to speak, the Maynooth's College, to compete and take money away from the place to which this endowment was given by King James I.

Lord Justice FitzGibbon.—Under the law existing since the reign of Charles II., the Royal School might be removed from Enniskillen to Monaghan, which is in the same diocese. I might remind you that under the Act of George IV. Enniskillen money has been applied by the Commissioners for the schools at Raphoe and even at Banagher.

Mr. Dane.—But the founder never intended Monaghan to be benefited.

May 12, 1886.

4315. Professor DOUGHERTY.—Do you mean that Monaghan never was planted?

Mr. Dane.—It never was within the settlement.

4316. Professor DOUGHERTY.—That is a mistake.

*Mr. Dane.—What are the figures? You have four bodies in Fermanagh—the Church of Ireland, the Methodist body, the Presbyterians, and the Roman Catholics—who are entitled to this fund, and how are you to distribute it between them? The scheme proposes to give 50 per cent. for the first three years to the Protestants of all denominations, and 50 per cent. to the Roman Catholics. The statistics as regards the persons rated in Fermanagh certainly disclose very curious facts. Since the last sitting we have got the *statistics of the £20 rating, and what is the result? In Fermanagh the Protestants rated over £20 a year are 1,726, the Catholics only 612, but according to your scheme the corporation which represents one-fourth of the population gets 50 per cent. of the endowment.

4317. Lord Justice FITZGIBBON.—Almost the entire population of the country towns is left out by taking a £20 rating, which brings in nearly all the farmers. The people in the towns, and especially in Enniskillen, are those most likely to want intermediate education.

Mr. Dane.—From my own local knowledge, I would say bringing in the towns would increase the proportion.

4318. Lord Justice FITZGIBBON.—But this rating test of educational wants is open to all sorts of observation. We think the test of being able to read and write is a great deal better, and the actual work done by the schools from year to year the best of all.

Mr. Dane.—The return for Fermanagh alone shows a majority of 1,114 Protestant rated occupiers. In Monaghan there are 1,103 Protestants rated over £20, and only 773 Catholics, and these figures added together for the joint counties give 3,028 Protestants and 1,285 Catholics.

4319. Rev. Dr. MOLLOY.—What your argument proves is that the Protestants will receive the greater part of the endowment under our scheme, because they are a large majority of the class receiving intermediate education. Under our scheme they will, according to your figures, receive more than twice as much as the Catholics. The only equal division that takes place, according to our scheme, is the equal division of the minimum, which we give merely as a substantial sum towards the support of one school for each denomination.

Mr. Dane.—They may, if they are able to send in their boys to gain it in result fees.

4320. Rev. Dr. MOLLOY.—They will have a greater number of boys receiving intermediate education, and they will get credit for them in the division of the endowment. If you are right in your figures, by far the greater part of the endowment, under our scheme, must go to Protestant schools.

4321. Dr. TRAILL.—But if the endowment is not restricted to Fermanagh, it is competed for by all the other five counties.

Mr. Dane.—Yes, and that is no advantage to us.

4322. Lord Justice FITZGIBBON.—The bringing in of Monaghan seems to frighten you, and you all seem to be under a misapprehension about it, and to think that we have given the Roman Catholics some unfair advantage by it. The numbers at present in Fermanagh alone who can read and write are 23,349 Catholics and 25,763 Protestants of all denominations—nearly half and half. In Monaghan there are 37,706 Roman Catholics who can read and write, and only 20,144 Protestants; so that in the two counties you have 61,000 literate Roman Catholics, against 47,000 literate Protestants. In Cavan the Protestants are in a much smaller minority; in the other districts the proportions vary; but we did not take into account those returns for any purpose except roughly to see that for the first three years, while the new arrangements were getting under way, it would be fair to say half and half. After that the division will be proportionate to the actual education.

Mr. Dane.—At the same time, these literate returns are not a true test.

4323. Lord Justice FITZGIBBON.—They are, at least, a truer test than rating, but neither of these tests has any effect either on the frame or on the results of the scheme. All such tests, and the objections to them, would become material if we attempted to frame such a scheme as you and Mr. Bewley are asking for, one involving a final division on some principle, and no principle has yet been suggested that would be just or could be permanent.

Mr. Dane.—We are all agreed that the money should be divided once and for all.

4324. Lord Justice FITZGIBBON.—Of course the Fermanagh Protestants are so agreed, because you are resolved to make all you get, and because the Fermanagh Endowment is really twice as large as any other; but we cannot forget, when you claim it for ever for yourselves, that while you have had the whole of it spent on your own school, you have been doing less educational work than any other county in Ulster, or probably in all Ireland. From the whole Fermanagh District 17 pupils passed in 1886, 9 in 1887, and 4 in 1888. Nearly all of these passed from the Monaghan Collegiate school. In 1888 the only Protestant pupils who passed in the two counties were 9 boys from Monaghan Collegiate, and 8 girls from two Model Schools in the same county. Therefore, you want to keep £1,300 a year for ever as an endowment for a county which has not shown at all in the Intermediate returns for last year.

Mr. Dane.—We rely on these figures as showing the position in which the county has been placed by the past mismanagement of the school.

4325. Lord Justice FITZGIBBON.—But the past mismanagement of Portora will not explain no boys at all passing the Intermediate Examinations. You are lower than Cavan or than many counties which have no endowments at all. How do we know that you will ever do work adequate to this large public endowment—the finest in Ireland.

Mr. Dane.—I am not aware of any place more provided, except Cavan, and the headmaster said he did not intend to send up boys to the examinations.

4326. Lord Justice FITZGIBBON.—He passed two boys in 1884.

Mr. Dane.—And the circumstances under which those two boys were sent forward are what has made those unite in Enniskillen, to try to reconstruct Portora. If Monaghan, which was never intended by the founder of this endowment to benefit by it, is to be annexed to Fermanagh, surely the Fermanagh people who have got no school at all should be allowed a quid pro quo. You have a Protestant majority in Fermanagh of 1,114, and in Monaghan of 330, with 1,743 persons rated over £20 a year, who would be likely to make use of this system of education. If we are to be saddled with Monaghan we ought to get some quid pro quo. The Roman Catholics have their own schools already there.

Lord Justice FITZGIBBON.—If things go on as they are you will get a very substantial quid pro quo—in 1887 and 1888 you would have got a large sum out of the residue, all earned in Monaghan and not a penny earned in Fermanagh.

4327. Dr. TRAILL.—I suppose you think if Portora was re-organised you would be able to earn it?

Mr. Dane.—Yes; we believe it would be one of the best schools in Ireland.

Lord Justice FITZGIBBON.—And in that case you would not only have your minimum grant, but your share of the residue besides, and if the school became anything like the success you anticipate, your share of the residue would be proportionately large.

4328. Dr. TRAILL.—Haven't you some objection about the compulsory sale of the Enniskillen school premises?

* See Appendix B., No. XII. (a.) p. [illegible].

Mr. Dane.—Yes, we strongly object to clause 30, so far as it relates to the compulsory sale of Enniskillen school premises to any purchaser except the Fermanagh Protestant board, which has already proposed, and still intends to take them as part of its endowment. If you are to have any regard to the intention of the founder, surely one of the first things you ought to do is to give the local board possession of these buildings. It is admitted by Mr. Carton and those he represents that they don't want these buildings, for they have a very ample building of their own. Those I represent do want them, and they think they would be able to occupy them. I don't think the proposal they make is unfair—give us the buildings—you have already valued them for Government purchase at £7,000; let us have them at £7,000, and give the Catholics £3,500 out of the accumulated savings.

Mr. Carton, Q.C.—That is not giving us anything at all.

Mr. Dane.—You get £3,500 out of the savings that have taken place while the school was under Protestant management, and we believe the school to be a matter of equity our property.

4329. Rev. Dr. Molloy.—Do you think that in your proposition you are treating the school premises as equally the property of the Catholic and Protestant denominations?

Mr. Dane.—I don't want to go into that at all, the persons I represent think that in equity they are entitled to claim the school premises as exclusively theirs.

4330. Rev. Dr. Molloy.—You think that by offering £3,500 out of the savings you are dealing generously with the Catholics?

Mr. Dane.—Yes.

4331. Rev. Dr. Molloy.—Does the proposal you are now making, according to your own understanding of it, deal with the school premises as equally the property of Catholics and Protestants?

Mr. Dane.—No; we don't think that. The Protestants in Fermanagh requiring these schools are four to one, and if you assume Monaghan where the Protestants are in a minority, the Roman Catholics can come in for a substantial share of the endowment that was never intended for their benefit.

4332. Rev. Dr. Molloy.—You think it is a matter of gift.

Mr. Dane.—We think we are treating them most generously.

4333. Rev. Dr. Molloy.—Assuming that each denomination has an equal right in these buildings your proposition could not be entertained?

Mr. Dane.—I presume in that case you would not yield to my proposition.

4334. Lord Justice Naish.—Would the Protestants of Fermanagh be prepared to buy the buildings?

Mr. Dane.—I don't think that would be feasible.

4335. Lord Justice FitzGibbon.—I may mention as an instance of what can be done by a small community where they are united and determined in a matter of this sort. Maryborough and Abbeyleix are competing for an endowment at Ballyroan, and in a few days the Maryborough people made up more than £800 to build a school in order to obtain part of the endowment, and Abbeyleix has since subscribed more.

Lord Justice Naish.—Suppose the view we take is that these premises are part of the general endowment, and the property of both denominations, the position you would stand in is that if you got the schools the value you put upon them is at least £7,000. Have you thought of that?

Mr. Dane.—But there is another question that arises. It is admitted that on these school buildings over £4,000 has been laid out by the present master.

4336. Lord Justice Naish.—The accounts between Dr. Steele and the Commissioners were all settled, and it would be absolutely impossible for us to set up Dr. Steele's claim again, and still less possible to set up as standing in Dr. Steele's shoes the body you represent.

Mr. Dane.—Surely if the previous master invested £4,000 in the school some account must be taken of it?

Lord Justice FitzGibbon.—If there were any equity at all to such an account, it would be Dr. Steele's, but twice or three times there have been payments of money to close the matter. Furthermore, instead of Dr. Steele's expenditure, so far as not repaid, having added to the present value of the buildings, it is the other way.

4337. Lord Justice Naish.—The view we take is that these premises are portion of the common endowment belonging to both sides; if you get the school you would be getting a thing of which the value is £7,000. We then would have to give an equal amount to the Catholics; but the entire amount of the accumulation is only £6,000, and you would still want at least, £500 to equip the school after you got it. There is no way of giving you over the buildings as part of your endowment, except you are prepared to pay £7,000 for them.

Mr. Dane.—But in any case £3,500 of that would be our own money.

4338. Lord Justice Naish.—I think there is a fallacy about that—you assume that you get the money out of your own fund.

Mr. Dane.—Whatever is the value of the buildings we are entitled to half of it.

4339. Lord Justice FitzGibbon.—Under the scheme what will happen? I don't want to argue the question of preference. If the place was sold to-morrow for £7,000 to the War Office, it would be the duty of the Commissioners, under the scheme, to draw two cheques, each for £3,500, to provide school premises, if required. We all thought that with that sum you could have acquired, equipped, and started in Enniskillen, or the immediate neighbourhood, an infinitely more suitable school than Portora would be. However you differ with us, you are entitled to your opinion, and we cannot force our view upon you; but if you get the buildings, for which there is an offer of £7,000, you must give an equivalent to the other Board.

Dr. Traill.—Don't take it for granted that we are agreed as to what £3,500 would do for you in the way of providing a school. I don't think suitable premises could be got about Fermanagh for £3,500. I take Mr. Dane's proposition that the buildings should not be taken as half the property of each side; but even taking the proposition the Commissioners themselves lay down, the proportion of who will want this school will be at least three to one of the people Mr. Dane represents, and if you consider the buildings to be property of the different denominations there, one-fourth of the buildings would represent the Roman Catholic claim under the scheme.

Mr. Dane.—That is the view our Board took—that they are acting generously in agreeing to hand over £3,500 to the Catholics.

4340. Dr. Traill.—You don't consider that each side should have half, but that the division ought to be in proportion to the people who require education, or are likely to send their children there for education?

Mr. Dane.—Yes, and we think we are acting liberally in saying half and half. The 30th paragraph does not give the persons I represent the right of pre-emption even at the sum of £7,000; and having regard to the strong majority of the Protestant element, and that Monaghan was outside the old settlement, that the Roman Catholics have a splendid building at Monaghan, I don't think it is at all unreasonable that the Commissioners should put in a provision giving the Fermanagh Board the right of pre-emption.

4341. Professor Dougherty.—There is an offer of

May [illegible]

£7,000, and you don't propose that your committee should have the right of pre-emption at less than that amount?

Mr. *Dane*.—No.

4312. Lord Justice Naish.—Do you think if the right was put in there would be any chance of its being acted on?

Mr. *Dane*.—It will do no harm.

4313. Dr. Traill.—If you want the buildings for educational purposes you have a claim before the War Office.

Mr. *Dane*.—If you decide against us on the contention we have taken it would do us no harm, but it might do us good to have a clause giving us the right of pre-emption.

4314. Rev. Dr. Molloy.—You will start with a great load about your necks in the Fermanagh district.

Mr. *Dane*.—They don't feel that; they feel that above all things they must get the buildings. There is a great history attached to Portora and its school.

4315. Rev. Dr. Molloy.—The history would be very dear at £7,000.

Mr. *Dane*.—Another matter that weighs with those I represent is that a great portion of the existing buildings are actually built out of £4,000 of Dr. Steele's money. Is that to be divided too?

4316. Lord Justice FitzGibbon.—All the buildings which the Commissioners considered suitable have been paid for by them, but I don't understand how you can put forward a claim to Dr. Steele's expenditure.

Mr. *Dane*.—It is a benefaction.

4317. Lord Justice FitzGibbon.—Except as to a sum of, I think, £1,[illegible], which you will see referred to in the Reports, he has been paid; but as to anything still unpaid, he puts forward a claim for himself.

Mr. *Dane*.—But you won't give it to him, and when you won't give it to him you ought not to grab it. We say it is a private benefaction.

4318. Rev. Dr. Molloy.—Why say you to "grab" it?

Lord Justice FitzGibbon.—If anybody has any right to it it is Dr. Steele. If we pay anybody, we must pay Dr. Steele, and pay him out of the Enniskillen Endowment. He wants the money himself badly, and if it is anybody's money it is his.

4319. Dr. Traill.—I suppose what you say is that if it is not paid back to Dr. Steele it is a benefaction for his own people, and if he does not get it you ought to get it, as representing the people for whom he intended it.

Rev. Dr. Molloy.—If Dr. Steele is entitled to it he ought to get it; and if he is not, what claim have you to it?

Mr. *Dane*.—The Commissioners say he is not to get it.

4320. Rev. Dr. Molloy.—Then what title have you to get it?

Mr. *Dane*.—It is a private benefaction in equity.

Mr. *Conway*.—There is no doubt that Enniskillen is a very important centre. I am living there for the last twenty-five years, and I believe it is the natural centre for a school. In Dr. Graham's time the school was not so good; he became old and retired with a fortune, and then Dr. Steele got it, and brought it up to a very high pitch and had great success.

4321. Professor Dougherty.—In Dr. Graham's time was the school educating the people of Fermanagh?

Mr. *Conway*.—Yes, if you call the shopkeepers and others of Enniskillen the people of Fermanagh. The work Portora did in that part is marvellous. I could give you the names of men all over the world who were educated there, and who occupy magnificent positions. There was one shopkeeper who had a large family, and he could not have educated them in any other way. One of them is now a commissioner in India, in receipt of £4,000 a year, and the whole family are occupying fine positions. Hundreds of other cases could be given.

4322. Professor Dougherty.—I have no doubt there are exceptional cases of that kind, but it is the first time I have heard that the Royal Schools educated the people of the locality.

Mr. *Conway*.—Hundreds of people in that locality, but of course they had boys attending from other places also.

4323. Lord Justice FitzGibbon.—We have the best evidence that £7,000, and no more, is the market value of these buildings. We tried to get an advance on the price from the War Office, and failed. If the Protestant Committee think they can work this place as a school, and are willing to allow £7,000 to the account for it—whether it is wise or not it is not for us to say—are we to refuse them the right of pre-emption?

Mr. *Carton*, Q.C.—My instructions are, first, to take care that no portion of the £7,000 comes out of the £8,200 accumulated fund; and next, that if there is to be a right of pre-emption, we also should have it, if we desire to purchase.

Dr. Traill.—You don't want it and St. Macartan's in the same diocese. You could not keep up two such establishments in the same diocese.

4324. Lord Justice FitzGibbon.—£7,000 really represents the market value. You have got St. Macartan's, and they should get this if they wish it, at the price of £7,000. We can't give both of you a right of pre-emption.

Mr. *Carton*, Q.C.—Surely there is no necessity for altering clause 30, if they produce the £7,000.

4325. Lord Justice FitzGibbon.—Yes, for under the clause as it is, if they put down £7,000, and the War Office said guineas, it should go to the War Office. The clause was intended to prevent the Protestant Board from insisting on keeping Portora if anything over £7,000 could be got for it, and they would not pay the full price for it. We thought it would be a bad bargain for education. However, they don't agree with us.

Lord Justice Naish.—They are to pay £7,000 if they want the place, and there is no favour shown to one side more than another.

Mr. *Carton*, Q.C.—We have no objection to a clause of pre-emption at £7,000, provided it does not touch on the corpus of £8,200. In other words, they are to provide from some outside source £3,500.

4326. Rev. Dr. Molloy.—I take it that Mr. Carton's clients would receive £3,500 in cash under this arrangement.

Mr. *Carton*, Q.C.—Leaving the £8,200 to be dealt with as portion of the corpus of the endowment, the fund is to be supplemented, so far as the Catholics are concerned, by an additional £3,500, or half the value of the buildings, to be provided by the Protestants out of a fund of their own.

4327. Rev. Dr. Molloy.—The only difference would be that instead of receiving the £3,500 from the War Office, you would receive it from your friends in Enniskillen.

Mr. *Carton*, Q.C.—Quite so.

4328. Lord Justice FitzGibbon.—Are you satisfied that the price is a fair one. We can show you the correspondence with the War Office if you wish to satisfy yourselves that we could get no more.

Mr. *Carton*, Q.C.—Having regard to what you have told us about the £7,000, and the way it was arrived at, I would not press the matter further.

4329. Mr. *Dane*.—As I understand, you will insert our right of pre-emption in clause 30?

4330. Lord Justice FitzGibbon.—We will give you the right of pre-emption at £7,000.

Mr. *Carton*, Q.C.—As the War Office has offered £7,000 there ought to be some limit of time in which the right should be exercised, lest the offer of the War Office should be lost.

4331. Lord Justice FitzGibbon.—Of course; but

it will be a time limited from the date of the scheme coming into operation in Enniskillen.

Mr. Dane.—You see, the present head master may not resign.

Mr. Carton, Q.C.—The worst of that will be that the offer of the War Office will be lost.

4560. Lord Justice FitzGibbon.—We cannot put Dr. Steele out, except at a price which would be ruinous to the whole business.

4561. Dr. Traill.—Do you press the point about the open public examinations?

Mr. Dane.—No, we have made an arrangement there. We wish to call attention to clause 59. Assuming that you make no final division of the fund, and that the result system will come into operation on the present wording of clause 59, "the first three years" might be only two years and a day, and my clients think there ought to be at least three full years.

4562. Lord Justice FitzGibbon.—We cannot make it a fixed number of years, because the machinery of the scheme, when it is at work in the five districts, will require each year's accounts to be kept separate, and we cannot have them beginning at different periods in the different districts.

Mr. Dane.—We want three full years; if we get this building we will have to equip it, and get it into working order, or we may have to get a new school.

Mr. Carton, Q.C.—I would support Mr. Dane in that, because it might happen that half the income would be applicable to each board only for two years, and a fraction over.

4563. Lord Justice FitzGibbon.—It might turn out on the other hand, that it might be applicable for three years all but a day.

Rev. Dr. Mahaffy.—It is a question of two years and a fraction or three years and a fraction.

Mr. Carton, Q.C.—I would suggest that we should necessarily have three full years at least.

4564. Lord Justice FitzGibbon.—We will think over that; it might result in almost four years.

Mr. Dane.—We would press very strongly for 33⅓ per cent. instead of the 25 per cent. minimum grant which the scheme gives.

4567. Lord Justice FitzGibbon.—That would be securing £1,000 a year for ever to the Fermanagh Board in face of the returns for the last three years.

Mr. Dane.—But we object to your counting that against us, for we rely upon that as the strength of our position.

4568. Lord Justice FitzGibbon.—If we give you 33⅓ we must give it to Armagh and Tyrone as well.

Rev. Dr. Mahaffy.—See the injustice you will be doing yourselves; you say you will have an immense number of pupils, and the larger the number the larger the share you will get.

Mr. Dane.—We would sooner have the bird in the hand. We would like to have the minimum grant extended to 33⅓.

Lord Justice FitzGibbon.—You would like to have the whole of the Fermanagh endowment confined to Fermanagh, and then we should have to give the scheme up altogether.

4569. Dr. Traill.—I suppose you would be satisfied if the three years in the 57th clause were to be extended for ever?

Mr. Dane.—We would not object to that at all. The only other matter is as regards the annual election. We don't think the members should be subject to re-election every year.

4570. Lord Justice FitzGibbon.—The alternative is that if you give a term of years and they become incompetent, you can't get rid of them. As long as they are efficient they will be re-elected as a matter of course.

Mr. Dane.—While the Roman Catholics are appointed for life the lay members of the Protestant Board have to seek re-election every year.

4571. Lord Justice Naish.—It appeared to be wished for amongst the Protestants that they should be subject to re-election.

Mr. Dane.—Mr. Conway who knows, says that is not so.

4572. Dr. Traill.—Would three years be better?

Mr. Dane.—It would be better. I don't think one year would work properly.

4573. Lord Justice FitzGibbon.—The Roman Catholic members must not get it into their heads that they are to remain on for life, whether they discharge their duties or not; if they don't attend one-third of the meetings in any one year they will be put out.

Mr. Dane.—It would be better to have it for five years or triennial elections.

4574. Lord Justice FitzGibbon.—There is no objection from the electing people—the only objectors are the elected.

Mr. Dane.—The opinion of the Board I represent is the result of a meeting of all classes in the county and they forward the opinion of their people.

4575. Dr. Traill.—Are Mr. Bewley's clients satisfied with a triennial election so far as Armagh and Tyrone are concerned?

Mr. Bewley, Q.C.—I cannot say.

Mr. Dane.—I am asked to press this point very strongly, for when a gentleman was invited to become a member of this board, it is rather hard that he should be subject to election every year.

4576. Lord Justice FitzGibbon.—The General Assembly meets every year, and the diocesan councils as a rule meet every month.

Mr. Dane.—That is so; but the members of that council are elected by the General Synod for three years.

4577. Lord Justice FitzGibbon.—No; at least, in Dublin the council is elected every year, and speaking for myself, I think it only right that if any one neglects his duty for a year, he should be put out without waiting for a triennial election.

Mr. Carton, Q.C.—As to the £6,750 at page 37, it is stated that the capital and corpus, including the £6,200, which are accumulations to the credit of Fermanagh, are to be treated as portion of the endowment for three years, and afterwards to bear the minimum grant, and to be thrown into the common fund. Is the income to be applied permanently for the purposes of the district?

4578. Lord Justice FitzGibbon.—Up to the present the Commissioners have been keeping a joint investment, and have been paying for Raphoe and Armagh out of a common fund. This is to be stopped, and each account is to be separate from the date of the scheme. After the scheme coming into force in each district, the income and the stock and cash will go with the rents, and after the three years each board would get its percentage of the income of whatever is not spent, and the rest would go into the residue. We cannot see any way out of paying this Raphoe debt of £1,750 out of the money in the Commissioners' hands—it can never be recovered, it has been spent—and you will have to bear more than half the loss.

Mr. Carton, Q.C.—My clients object to have the Raphoe debt saddled on them.

4579. Lord Justice FitzGibbon.—It really has been saddled on them already; the cash entered by the Commissioners to the credit of Fermanagh and Cavan is not there—£1,750 of it has been spent on Raphoe, which is bankrupt.

Rev. Dr. Mahaffy.—There is credited to the Enniskillen school £2,692 stock; that exists. There is also credited to it £3,200 represented as cash; but that does not exist—it is a debt partly due by Raphoe and partly by Armagh.

4580. Mr. Dane.—What is the real available surplus?

Mr. Carton, Q.C.—There is £2,692 in three per cents.

4581. Lord Justice FitzGibbon.—The Raphoe debt is now £1,717, and will probably be £1,800 before the end of the year. There is nothing to pay it but the sum which appears to the credit of the schools which en[illegible] the money.

Dr. TRAILL.—If the £1,277 were wiped out your proportion of the debt would be £797, and you would have £1,[illegible] in cash left to Enniskillen.

4382. Bishop *Donnelly*.—What is the net accumulation of Enniskillen?

Mr. *Carton*, Q.C.—The net accumulation would be £[illegible], but that is treated like the other endowments leaving the minimum grant after three years, and the rest going into the general fund.

Mr. *Dane*.—We strongly protest against your paying any more out of the Enniskillen fund towards Raphoe; if we have to bear our share of the £1,277 debt already, it is quite enough without making us pay further for Raphoe.

4383. Lord Justice *FitzGibbon*.—What are we to do? Is Mr. Weir to starve?

Professor DOUGHERTY.—Part of your assets is a bad debt—how is it to be realised?

Mr. *Dane*.—We want to stop the leakage.

XIII.—THOMAS GORDON, M.A., ASSISTANT MASTER, ROYAL SCHOOL, ARMAGH.

4384. Mr. *Stanley*.—I would not feel justified in trespassing on your time in repeating the arguments which I have already addressed to you on behalf of Mr. Gordon. He has sent in a very elaborate objection, and he desires to protest against the result of the amended scheme.

XIV.—THE SCHOOLMASTERS' ASSOCIATION.

4385. Mr. *Wilkins*.—You have dealt with all the matters referred to by the Association except the second paragraph of section 37 of the scheme. The Association expressed its view already on this matter in a communication sent last June to the Secretary. They believe that if section 37 stands it will work injuriously for education, as it gives power to the local board to interfere with every detail of the school. Of course it is perfectly right that the board should have every control and authority possible, but that power would be best exercised by deputing certain of their powers to the head master. I have before me a typical English scheme—that for the Sedbergh Grammar School in Yorkshire, of which the 44th section is something similar to your 37th section:—

"37. Within the limits fixed by this scheme the governors shall prescribe the general subjects of instruction, the relative prominence and value to be assigned to each group of subjects, the division of the year into terms and vacations, the payments of the day scholars, the number and the payments of the boarders, and the number of holidays to be given in term. They shall take general supervision of the sanitary condition of the school buildings and arrangements. They shall determine what number of assistant masters shall be employed. They shall every year assign the amount which they think proper to be paid out of the income of the trust for the purpose of maintaining assistant masters and of maintaining a proper plant or apparatus for carrying on the instruction given in the school."

That is qualified by the 46th and 47th clauses.

"46. Before making or altering any regulations under the last preceding clause the governors shall consult the head master in such a manner as to give him full opportunity for the expression of his views."

"47. Subject to the rules prescribed by or under the authority of this scheme, the head master shall have under his control the choice of books, the methods of teaching, the arrangement of classes and school-hours, and generally the whole internal organisation, management, and discipline of the school. Provided that if he expels a boy from the school he shall forthwith make a full report in writing of the case to the governors."

In fact the head master is placed in a position of despotism tempered by dismissal. If he goes wrong an appeal is made to the governors. The 48th section says:—

"The head master shall have the sole power of appointing and, subject to appeal to the governors, of dismissing all assistant masters, and shall determine, subject to the approval of the governors, in what proportion the sum assigned by the governors for the maintenance of assistant masters and of plant or apparatus shall be divided among the various persons and objects for the aggregate of which it is assigned, and the governors shall pay the same accordingly either through the hands of the head master or directly, as they think best."

So that the governors don't interfere unless the master is acting wrongly. I believe you have no experience of local boards such as you think of starting, whereas I could furnish you with precedents of how such boards have worked. I think everyone will feel that education will be very fortunate if you can get a board as good as the Board of Erasmus Smith's Schools. That Board pays some of the assistant masters—the chief assistant masters—in each of the four provincial schools. They used to appoint these gentlemen, but their experience of that system caused them to drop it, and now each of these assistant masters is appointed by the head master and dismissed by the head master, although he is paid by the governors. Another example is the school of Erasmus Smith in Dublin, of which I am head master. In it the governors tried appointing the assistant masters, but have now given it up.

4386. Lord Justice FITZGIBBON.—There are a great many different forms in which this clause might be put. Though we have not your experience, a good many of our schemes are at work for a good while in such places as the Methodist College, the Belfast Academy and Institution, and the Coleraine Academical Institution.

Mr. *Wilkins*.—At Coleraine the head master appoints all the assistant masters.

4387. Lord Justice FITZGIBBON.—Yes, under our scheme. In several instances we have provided that the assistants shall be appointed by the head master, but in all cases the body having supreme control has power to dismiss the assistant masters as well as the head master.

Mr. *Wilkins*.—I don't believe the head master should have power to put in an assistant of whom the Board disapproved, or to keep an assistant master against the will of the superior body.

4388. Dr. TRAILL.—You surely don't think that each should have a voice in the appointment, but that the power of dismissal should vest in the head master alone?

Mr. *Wilkins*.—I don't argue that the head master should have power of keeping any official in the place of whom the Board does not approve.

4389. Rev. Dr. MOLLOY.—Do you propose that the local Board should appoint the head master?

Mr. *Wilkins*.—Yes.

4390. Rev. Dr. MOLLOY.—And that the head master should have power to appoint the assistants and all the domestic staff?

Mr. *Wilkins*.—Yes.

4391. Rev. Dr. MOLLOY.—Then as to determining the various branches of education to be taught, the regulation of the fees, the fixing of the terms and vacations, would it meet your views that, after consultation with the head master, these things should be done by the local Board?

Mr. *Wilkins*.—That would be an improvement, but it would not meet our views.

4392. Lord Justice FITZGIBBON.—But surely the Local Board ought, as in the English scheme you quote, to be the body to decide what subjects of education should be taught? It has been a subject of complaint that the Royal Schools give a class of education that the people did not want.

Mr. Wilkins.—The course is to a great extent laid down for the head masters—for instance, he must push boys for the Intermediate Examination. There is no fear of the head master ruining the school by his crotchets, for if he was found at that the Governors would dismiss him.

4393. Rev. Dr. Molloy.—Would it not be better to provide against these crotchets by giving him a voice in the matter referred to, but leaving the supreme control with the Local Board?

Mr. Wilkins.—What we are afraid of is the crotchets of the Local Board. You will have clergymen and country squires and men who have no experience of education, and there is the greatest possible danger of these gentlemen having crotchets of their own. Every schoolmaster has experience of crotchety amateurs who forget the terrible problem of the conflict of studies—for example, you may have one Governor who wants elocution taught, and no doubt it is a very good thing, but elocution will crowd out a subject more important.

4394. Rev. Dr. Molloy.—The nine Governors are not likely to have the same crotchets.

Professor Dougherty.—We must take the law of averages as applying to these crotchets.

4395. Rev. Dr. Molloy.—And there is more danger of crotchets from an individual than from a body.

Dr. Traill.—In Coleraine the Governors leave it almost entirely to the head master to do as he likes.

Mr. Wilkins.—I have known a head master to have the greatest possible difficulty until he carried the very point I am making now.

4396. Lord Justice FitzGibbon.—By the rules of the Sedbergh School which you have quoted, the Governors have the power of prescribing the general subjects of instruction, the relative prominence and value to be assigned to each group, the division of the year, and so on; but they are to consult the head master. In several of our schemes we have inserted such a clause, and in several of our schemes we have even made him more independent; but that is quite different from giving him the power of laying down the general scale of instruction.

Mr. Wilkins.—Look at the clause which follows that, clause 41:—

"Subject to the rules prescribed by or under the authority of this scheme, the head master shall have under his control the choice of books, the method of teaching, the arrangement of classes and school hours, and generally the whole internal organization, management, and discipline of the school."

Nobody is going to dispute that these powers should be within the scope of the Governors' authority, but there is a definite rule that they should be deputed to the head master, and there is no such suggestion in your scheme. We believe that your plan will lead to such terrible friction that the school cannot possibly prosper.

4397. Lord Justice FitzGibbon.—The institution where the head master is under the most "terrible" despotism in Ireland is perhaps the most prosperous. In the Methodist College, Belfast, the head master and everybody else goes out of office once a year, without any compensation or retiring provision.

Mr. Wilkins.—Has he the power of appointing assistants?

Lord Justice FitzGibbon.—No; and they too are appointed once a year.

4398. Rev. Dr. Molloy.—I should be inclined to go with you as regards the assistant masters and the dismissal; but I think it would be desirable to reserve to the Local Board the supreme authority.

Mr. Wilkins.—I am not disputing their authority at all.

4399. Dr. Traill.—You agree that they shall have the authority of dismissal, but you do not wish that they should interfere in every matter of detail.

Mr. Wilkins.—Our plan is the only one to ensure promptness—the action of the Board would be almost always too slow in certain circumstances.

4400. Dr. Traill.—If the head master does not pay his assistants sufficiently he will have very inferior teaching in the school, and it is very important that the Governors shall have power to see that the salary paid by him is sufficient to secure good assistant masters?

Mr. Wilkins.—Certainly.

4401. Professor Dougherty.—Would you be willing to give the parents the right of appeal to the Governors from the decision of the head master to retain the services of the assistants?

Mr. Wilkins.—Yes. I don't object to an appeal on anybody's part. The head master would not be such a fool as to run against the Governors on such a point. As to the fixing of the vacation, it would be very inconvenient to have the Governors deciding that question—there might be an examination at the time they fixed or some other engagement of the school might be upset.

4402. Lord Justice FitzGibbon.—The Sedbergh scheme puts that expressly into the hands of the Governors.

Mr. Wilkins.—But the 47th section says the master shall have generally the whole internal organization, management, and discipline of the school.

4403. Lord Justice FitzGibbon.—We are much obliged to you for calling attention to that matter, and for your reference to the English scheme. There is no doubt we should put in some further provisions to secure the position and powers of the head masters of the schools sharing in the Royal Endowments, for the form adopted in this scheme is about the least favourable to their position to be found in any of our schemes.

THE MOST REV. DR. WALSH, LORD ARCHBISHOP OF DUBLIN

4404. Archbishop Walsh.—As to the Carysfort Endowment, I fear that in this scheme some power has been left to the reconstituted Commissioners to transfer it elsewhere.

4405. Lord Justice FitzGibbon.—No. We thought we could deal more comprehensively and intelligibly with the Ulster endowments alone, and therefore this scheme leaves the Carysfort and Banagher endowments in the hands of the Commissioners on the old trusts. It was not our intention for a moment to forget Carysfort, and we intend, as soon as possible, to bring out a separate scheme for Carysfort and Banagher.

Archbishop Walsh.—The sooner the scheme is framed the better.

4406. Lord Justice FitzGibbon.—The money is accumulating, and I don't think anything will be gained by finally settling the scheme until we see what the Privy Council will do with this one.

*Archbishop Walsh.—As to the "constitution of the Board, you understand me as still pressing the objection which I put before you in the name of the Catholic Bishops at your last meeting—that we cannot regard as sufficient protection for Catholic interests that the Lord Lieutenant should have unrestricted power to nominate the Commissioners. We think the persons nominated as Catholics ought to be persons having the confidence of the Catholic body.

4407. Lord Justice FitzGibbon.—We gave the greatest possible consideration to your suggestion, but found it very difficult to give any definite meaning to the expression, "persons having the confidence of the Catholic body," and for that reason we did not insert it.

Archbishop Walsh.—I wish it to be understood that the interests of the Catholics are not sufficiently protected by the scheme as it stands. I admit it may be hard to secure the object expressed in the words

* See Appendix B., No. LXI. (v) p. [illegible]

[illegible]

"persons having the confidence of the Catholic body," but, at the same time, Catholic interests are not sufficiently protected.

4408. Lord Justice FitzGibbon.—We should be very glad to consider any other suggestion for attaining an end we all desire.

Archbishop Walsh.—My suggestion was to have names sent up to the Lord Lieutenant by the local boards, and that the Lord Lieutenant should appoint from the number so sent up. That would insure that the appointments would be from a number of persons having the confidence of the persons concerned, both Catholic and Protestant—but, of course, I am only speaking for the Catholics.

4409. Dr. Traill.—Are you still in favour of having persons nominated by the various learned bodies?

Archbishop Walsh.—Yes, otherwise it will degenerate into mere local representation.

4410. Lord Justice FitzGibbon.—If the local bodies are to send up names, they are likely to be local people?

Archbishop Walsh.—Whether they are local or otherwise, they will have the confidence of the persons whose interests they are to represent. We have experience of the other system of nomination, and it is altogether unsatisfactory. It is difficult, I admit, to devise an effective amendment of the scheme.

4411. Lord Justice FitzGibbon.—If you allow the local bodies the power to nominate the Lord Lieutenant's Commissioners, it will give them a preponderating voice over the educational representation by two to one.

Archbishop Walsh.—It is a great difficulty, I see.

4412. Lord Justice FitzGibbon.—The Commissioners are supported by a large public vote, the endowments are of public origin, and I think we must have a large portion of the representation with the Executive.

Archbishop Walsh.—That is a matter for your consideration as Commissioners.

4413. Lord Justice FitzGibbon.—We think we should leave at least a third of the new body to be appointed as at present, so as to maintain the continuity of the body. Remember, under our scheme two-thirds of the body will be nominated by bodies in whom those interested will have confidence.

Archbishop Walsh.—Once the question of Catholic and Protestant members comes in, it becomes essential that the persons to be appointed can be looked upon as representative of the Catholic and Protestant interests: I speak only for the Catholics; but it is, of course, equally important to both Catholic and Protestant, and this system of nomination by the Lord Lieutenant is very unsatisfactory.

4414. Lord Justice FitzGibbon.—If your Grace between this and to-morrow week can give us any practical proposal that would make the scheme more satisfactory, we will carefully consider it.

Archbishop Walsh.—I don't see that it would be possible if you retain the principle of having nominations by the Lord Lieutenant.

4415. Lord Justice FitzGibbon.—I am afraid you must have nominations by the Lord Lieutenant.

Archbishop Walsh.—Then you must have an unsatisfactory scheme.

4416. Dr. Traill.—When it comes to spending public money you must give the State a share in the management.

Archbishop Walsh.—You should have names sent up by the local bodies in the first instance.

4417. Lord Justice FitzGibbon.—That objection is at the principle of having any one appointed by the Lord Lieutenant.

Archbishop Walsh.—Suppose it was thought to leave them—retain the representation of the local bodies, giving those power to send up a certain number of names to the Lord Lieutenant, and leave the direct representation to the local boards. Give the learned bodies power to send up a large number of names, and then let the Lord Lieutenant select from them.

Dr. Traill.—Between them the local boards and the learned bodies have two-thirds of the representation under the scheme.

4418. Lord Justice FitzGibbon.—Our idea was that there should be one-third of the Commissioners to represent the State, and that in the selection of those representatives the State should be bound to consider the religious denominations; that the local boards should have a third, and the learned bodies a third; from their formation the Commissioners are probably certain to be half and half Protestant and Catholic, and the election of two out of every three members of the board will be in the hands of people possessing the fullest confidence of the denominations they represent. At present you have no voice at all in the selection of any one.

Archbishop Walsh.—What will happen if the Lord Lieutenancy is abolished?

4419. Lord Justice FitzGibbon.—That, like a great many other things that people who talk lightly on the subject don't understand, will have to be provided for by statute before the abolition is accomplished.

XXII. & XXI.—W. T. VALENTINE, ESQ., M.A., AND CURT HENNIG, ESQ., ASSISTANT MASTERS, ENNISKILLEN.

4420. Mr. Dane.—I also appear for Mr. Valentine, of Enniskillen, who has a claim.

Mr. Carton, Q.C.—I am instructed that Mr. Valentine has no right to a residence. He never had any residence at the school until he went, as a kind of caretaker when Dr. Steele left.

Mr. Dane.—That is not so. He has a residence, and has never left it. But that is not the only point. He has a vested interest which ought to be saved, and it has not been saved.

4421. Lord Justice FitzGibbon.—We could not save it. We could not defer bringing the scheme into force until the last assistant master has disappeared.

Mr. Dane.—His appointment was approved by the Lord Lieutenant in writing, and he produced it in Court, but this scheme does not save his interest.

4422. Lord Justice FitzGibbon.—We cannot save it. At first we tried to buy up the interests of everybody, but we found the claims made would leave nothing at all. Now we have saved the interests of the head masters, but we cannot save the interests of the assistant masters. We can only make them due compensation when their offices come to an end on the head master's retirement.

4423. Mr. Dane.—I also appear for Mr. Hennig, another assistant master, who would retire on an annuity of about £[illegible] at present, while Mr. Valentine has £[illegible]. Assuming that they are thrown out of employment, it is exceedingly unfair that their vested interests are not saved by this scheme.

4424. Lord Justice FitzGibbon.—We give you the choice of taking a certain sum or retaining a life annuity.

Mr. Dane.—You only gave us three years.

4425. Lord Justice FitzGibbon.—We offer a lump sum, and if you won't take it we leave you the annuity. We will consider whether we cannot give all the assistants somewhat better terms.

Mr. Dane.—We think you should make some more liberal allowance to us.

4426. Lord Justice FitzGibbon.—We thought it was more for the interest of the endowment to pay annuities during their lives than to allow them to compound.

Mr. Dane.—I don't see how you distinguish between Mr. Valentine's case and that of the head master.

4427. Lord Justice FitzGibbon.—We don't allow the head masters to compound at all. We did so in the original scheme, but found they demanded nearly the whole fund.

Mr. *Dane*.—But you put a premium on their retiring, and you have saved their whole salary; but you retire Mr. Valentine with less than half his salary and emoluments. You give him an annuity of £50, and the most he could get is £200 if he wants to be equated. That is too little, having regard to the fact that under the Act of George he is one of the persons having a claim on the rents.

I have also to draw your attention to the memorial of John McLoughlin, who lived in the gatehouse of the [illegible] for 35 years. He looked after the gas and water [illegible] prepared for the house, and in consideration of that he was left at the gatehouse, and his rent of £5 a year has been paid for him by the Commissioners of Education.

4428. Lord Justice FitzGibbon.—The Commissioners gave us a return of everybody they paid, and he is not included.

Mr. *Dane*.—This was before you in August last. I happen to know the man myself, and I said I would appear for him.

[Memorial read.]

Dr. Traill.—There is no rent payable for the gate lodge.

4429. Lord Justice FitzGibbon.—The only question is whether he is paid out of the endowment. If so, we must see to his compensation. The last application we have had is from the widow of an old man who died at Dungannon, and she asks compensation from the Royal Schools Endowment.

Mr. *Dane*.—I would ask you to communicate with the Commissioners and see what can be done for this man.

Lord Justice FitzGibbon.—We will do so.

Lord Justice Naish.—We must see what his rights are.

The sitting closed.

PUBLIC SITTING—MONDAY, JULY 1, 1889.

At the Courthouse, Baltinglass.

Present:—The Right Hon. Lord Justice FitzGibbon and the Right Hon. Lord Justice Naish, Judicial Commissioners; and the Rev. Gerald Molloy, D.D., D.Sc.; Anthony Traill, Esq., LL.D., M.D., F.T.C.D., and Professor Dougherty, M.A., Assistant Commissioners.

The Assistant Secretary, N. D. Murphy, was in attendance.

STRATFORD LODGE SCHOOLS.

Mands G. Dennis, Esq., sworn and examined.

4430. Lord Justice FitzGibbon.—Mr. Dennis, I believe you have a copy of the will of Lady Stratford, under which the *Stratford Lodge Schools* were endowed?—Yes. [Produced.]

4431. Lord Justice FitzGibbon. [Reads.]—The will is that of Lady Elizabeth A. Stratford, dated August 22, 1819. She gives all her lands in the County of Wicklow to Charles Doyne and the Rev. Henry Scott, of Baltinglass, and their heirs and assigns for ever, in trust, for the use of Lord Amborn for life, after his death to his issue in tail male, and in default to his daughters and their heirs; and the will proceeds:—

"It is my desire that my said trustees shall also pay all expenses and uphold for ever the Stratford Lodge Schools as are established out of the issues or profits of my freehold estates so hereby devised."

In the event of Lord Amborn dying without issue, she leaves her freehold estates to her valued friend, the Rev. Henry Scott and his heirs for ever:—

"Subject, however, to the upholding of the Stratford Lodge Schools under the same arrangements as are at present established."

I believe that is the provision for the schools?—That is the whole provision.

4432. What position do you hold with regard to [illegible] held under the will of the Rev. Henry Scott. There was a failure of issue of Lord Aldborough, and the property came to Mr. Scott, who left it to me as the nearest relation of Lady Elizabeth Stratford, believing that I would carry out the trust.

4433. You are both beneficial owner and trustee?—Yes.

4434. What were these Stratford Lodge Schools at the time of the will?—They were Protestant schools. I see in Lewis's Topographical Dictionary that there were two other schools in Baltinglass, having some large number of scholars; and Lady Elizabeth Stratford got up these schools, I believe, for the Protestant children entirely.

4435. Where are they?—They are not in existence at present; they have been pulled down. The schools are in existence, but the schoolhouses have been pulled down; the railway ran right through them.

4436. Where were they?—Close to the edge of the town. The school is at present held in the [illegible]. I am keeping it up until I can build a new schoolhouse.

4437. Dr. Traill.—What did the railway company pay for the schoolhouses?—I don't know exactly—I cannot recollect. They paid sufficient to enable me to build new ones.

4438. Lord Justice Naish.—Where is the money?—It is in my possession. I must build the schools. I made an agreement with the late Mr. Anderson for a plot of ground close to the church, but they have not been able to make title. The trustees of the late Lord Aldborough are willing, and they agreed to sell this particular piece of land to me for the schools. I have the agreement for the purchase of it.

4439. Dr. Traill.—Who is Mr. Anderson?—He is dead. He was Lord Aldborough's agent.

4440. Lord Justice FitzGibbon.—I see by the report of 1879 that there was an acre and a half of land in the site of the old schoolhouses. Was that all taken by the Railway Company?—Not all; there is a piece left at the top, but it is not of any use—it is not available for anything. There may be a rood or perhaps not so much. That land was not of any value to the school except as a playground. There was a little garden at the back. It was in the [illegible] and was fenced off from it. I fenced it since myself with wire fencing.

4441. Lord Justice Naish.—About how much did the railway company pay for the school premises they purchased?—I could not tell you. They took a lot of land down the whole way.

4442. Did they pay one sum for all that they took?—No, they paid two lump sums on the award of the arbitrator.

4443. Was there a separate number in the award representing the premises belonging to the school?—There may have been; I don't know. I was in Germany at the time the award was made. I think they paid £1,760 for the whole.

4444. For the freehold of other lands besides the school lands?—Yes.

4445. Was the whole amount of the award paid to you?—All paid to me as the owner of the estate.

4446. No part was set apart by you as representing the school property?—None whatever.

4447. What is the present condition of the schools?—There are two teachers—a master and a mistress.

4448. In 1879 they are put down as under the National Board?—I think it was in 1879 that I put them under the National Board for the sake of the inspection and the other advantages.

4449. How long had they been under the National Board before they were taken by the railway?—For perhaps a couple of years. They are under the National Board still.

4450. What does the master get at present?—I think £65 a year, made up of the National Board allowances, and my allowance.

4451. The National Board salary is included, I suppose?—Yes.

4452. Is there a mistress also?—Yes.

4453. Are there two National schools or only one mixed school for boys and girls?—A mixed school.

4454. What are the numbers in attendance?—They vary very much according to the weather. I think generally there are about fifty.

4455. Forty-nine was the number in 1879. I think there are considerably less now. I have another school of my own at Port Granite.

4456. Lord Justice Naish.—What salary does the mistress get?—£30 a year.

4457. And the master £65?—Yes.

4458. How much of that is contributed by the National Board?—Nothing for the mistress. I think £40 for the master. I only got that as a temporary thing. The Board can take it away at any moment.

4459. Lord Justice Fitzgibbon.—How long do you know the schools?—All my life—since they were built.

4460. Down to the time that they were taken by the railway company were they always conducted in the same way?—Always.

4461. First under the private management of Lady Elizabeth Stratford, and afterwards under the trustees of her will?—Yes.

4462. Who were your predecessors in trust?—The person who preceded me was late Lord Aldborough—except I may say the Rev. Mr. Scott for a few months, but he had not time to do anything.

4463. Lord Justice Naish.—Was the school established by Lady Elizabeth Stratford?—Yes.

4464. Did she build the schoolhouse?—Yes.

4465. Was she in the habit of giving anything to keep it going?—Certainly, but I don't know how much. She kept them up as best she could.

4466. Did she manage it as a Protestant school?—Entirely. There were two other schools, as stated in Lewis—for I don't know of them myself—in existence here, which were not Protestant schools, so she built this school for the purpose of having it a Protestant school; and it was not only a Protestant school but a Church of England school, for the late Lord Aldborough had to dismiss a master from here because he was a member of the Plymouth Brethren. Mr. Anderson, the agent, was a Plymouth Brother, and he appointed him while Lord Aldborough was absent, and he had to dismiss him.

4467. Lord Justice Fitzgibbon.—Do I understand you to say that the school is being but temporarily carried on in this building pending the building of a new schoolhouse to take the place of the one removed by the railway?—Yes.

4468. Two schoolrooms, teachers' apartments, out-offices, garden, and playground, are mentioned in the former report—have those all been swept away by the railway?—Yes.

4469. So that the old school premises are no longer available, and are represented by whatever proportion of the £1,760 represents the school property?—Yes, but my simple duty is to maintain the school as then established. I don't allow at all that I am bound to every single farthing that was paid for these premises. All I am bound to do is to keep the school up as established by Lady Elizabeth Stratford; and if I could keep the school up efficiently and properly for sixpence a year I am informed that I can do it.

4470. But I am afraid that is not likely to occur?—No; but I think the school is far better now than it was.

4471. Professor Dougherty.—Do you consider that you are bound to replace the teacher's residence?—Certainly.

4472. Rev. Dr. Molloy.—Have you got a site?—I have got a site, and I have the materials drawn to it, but I cannot make a title.

4473. Is the new site as large as the old one?—No, but there will be more ground available.

4474. Mr. Dagg (Clerk of the Union).—Was not the greater part of the £1,760 that you got in respect of compensation for the school?—Certainly it was, but I don't know how you are interested.

4475. Lord Justice Fitzgibbon.—Everybody that may have children to send to the school is interested.

Witness.—He is only married about a week, and I don't know that I am bound to have it a free school.

4476. Lord Justice Fitzgibbon.—That will depend entirely on what the Stratford Lodge Schools were, and the arrangements under which they were established in 1846; and I understand from you that they were established at that time for the Protestant children of the parish?—Not of the parish alone; all the children of the country used to go there.

4477. Lord Justice Naish.—Were they admitted free, or were they subject to the payment of school fees?—I don't know.

4478. Professor Dougherty.—In the former report it is stated that £80 a year was the amount expended?—That was my return.

4479. At present do the master and mistress get you £95 a year?—I did not state that they cost me £95. The salaries are £95 a year.

4480. And of that the National Board pay £44, which leaves £51?—Yes.

4481. And you have also the interest of the compensation money as well as the lands?—I have got the estate certainly; and if I could do the thing for a shilling a year I don't think anyone has any power whatever over me—at least so I am advised. I must keep up the school, and endeavour to keep it up efficiently and correctly, as well as I can; and it will be better when I get the new schoolhouse. But I won't answer to anybody. I am bound under that will to keep up the school, as Lady Elizabeth Stratford had it entirely under her control for the benefit of the Protestant children, and that I intend to do.

4482. Lord Justice Fitzgibbon.—How long is it since the old schoolhouse was taken possession of by the railway company?—Some of the gentlemen present, I suppose, will be able to tell.

Some one present said about five years.

4483. Mr. Dagg.—Have the trustees of the Earl of Aldborough been able to give title to the railway company?

Lord Justice Fitzgibbon.—The railway company could get title at once under their Act of Parliament.

4484. Mr. Dagg (to witness).—This building that you are going to put up—are you going to erect it yourself or by the aid of a Public Works grant?

Witness.—As I choose—in the cheapest way I can and the most efficient way.

4485. Will it be built by the time I have children?

—No, it will not. Very likely I will forbid your children to go there at all, because I have the power of doing it.

4486. Rev. Dr. Molloy.—How many people are at present going to the school?—I said I thought over fifty, but I can ascertain.

4487. Lord Justice Naish.—Are they all Protestant children?—All Protestant children.

4488. Dr. Traill.—When you say "Protestant," do you mean "Church of Ireland" Protestants?—Church of Ireland.

4489. Are there any Presbyterians or Methodists?—I don't think there are. There may be. I don't know.

4490. Lord Justice FitzGibbon.—Is there a Methodist congregation here?—I don't know.

[Some person present said there was a Methodist Church in the town.]

4491. Professor Dougherty.—You do not object to extend the benefits of the school to all Protestants?—Not at all. I would be very glad they came. I don't consider that I should debar Roman Catholics from it either.

4492. Lord Justice FitzGibbon.—Was the school in Lady Stratford's time a National school?—No, it was placed under the National Board first by myself.

4493. Mr. Patrick Byrne.—There are people in the town—Catholics—who went to that school; and there was no difference or distinction made from 1840 to 1852. It was a free school, and there was no hindrance to any one attending it.

Witness.—Nor would there be now.

4494. Lord Justice FitzGibbon.—What other schools are there now in Baltinglass?—There is a National school under the Roman Catholic priest.

4495. Has the Rev. Mr. Usher, the Rector, any school but this one?—Mr. Usher has nothing to say to this school.

4496. Then there is no school under Mr. Usher?—No.

4497. Mr. Dopp.—Was not this school for the inhabitants of Baltinglass generally without regard to religious denomination?—I dare say it was. I don't believe any Roman Catholic would have been refused; but they have no right in the matter.

4498. As a matter of fact did Roman Catholics attend?—I really don't know anything about that. I could not answer that. But the Scriptures were to be read; and that was a matter so stringently insisted on, that I would not have put the school under the National Board, but that the manager of a National school has a right to prescribe what religious instruction, if any, is to be given.

4499. Professor Dougherty.—Did Lady Elizabeth Stratford prescribe the Church Formularies?—Yes, and I don't think any objection was made to them by anyone.

Aug. 1, 1888. Maurice C. Dennis, Esq.

4500. Lord Justice Naish.—Do you know if there was any religious teaching in the school in the time of Lady Stratford?

Mr. Byrne.—I heard not. I can produce a witness who was at the school.

Lord Justice FitzGibbon.—We shall be glad to hear any witness who can tell us how the school was conducted in 1852.

4501. Rev. Dr. Molloy (to witness).—At present the school is under the National Board, and all pupils who come to it must be admitted?—Yes, certainly.

4502. Dr. Traill.—With a conscience clause?—Yes.

4503. Mr. Byrne (to witness).—You are the proprietor of the school at present?—I don't know what you mean.

4504. Is it not held in the old jail at the back of this courthouse?

Witness.—I have taken the place temporarily.

4505. Lord Justice Naish.—Do you pay rent for it?—I do. I did not conceive myself at liberty to leave the school for one day out of work.

4506. Is there anything done towards getting the new school premises?—There is everything that I can do. The materials have been drawn to the place for the last three or four years. I had a good deal of communication with Mr. Anderson on the subject; and he assured me that all he was waiting for was the purchase of that land from the executors of the late Lord Aldborough.

4507. Dr. Traill.—Lady Stratford refers to keeping up the school "as now established"; and in another place she says "under the same arrangements as at present established." Is there any document in existence which will show how the school was established at the time she made this will?—I don't think so.

4508. Mr. Dopp.—Has the schoolmaster got an increase of salary from the National Board since you appointed him?—I don't know.

4509. What is his classification?—Oh, you will have that from himself. If you want to know if the schoolmaster has got an increase of salary since he was classed, he has of course—he has got the benefit of all the increases of salary. But that's on account of being able to keep up the average attendance above thirty. If the average were below that he could have no advantage, for the Board could give none. I have got a second class teacher at Fort Granite, and she has not got it, because the average is not kept up.

Mr. Claude Henry Sweeney sworn and examined.

4510. Lord Justice FitzGibbon.—You are the master of the Stratford Lodge Schools?—Yes.

4511. How long have you been in office?—It will be two years on August 1, next.

4512. Are you classified under the National Board?—Yes, second class.

4513. Was the school under the National Board when you were appointed?—No, not for about two months afterwards; since then it has been under the Board.

4514. Lord Justice FitzGibbon.—At the time you were appointed you were not classified?—No. I never was under the National Board previously.

4515. Are you first or second of the second class?—First of the second. The salary is £44 a year. I was never a third class teacher. When I was first appointed I was allowed third class salary; but the Inspector gave me second class papers, and I got the second class grade when I passed the examination, which I did satisfactorily.

4516. Mr. Byrne.—How much did the National Board allow you at first?—I think £35 a year.

Mr. Claude Henry Sweeney.

4517. Did you get the balance of £30 from Mr. Dennis?—Yes.

4518. When you were classified as a second class teacher at £44 a year, you were still only paid a balance of £25?—That's all.

4519. Lord Justice FitzGibbon.—Then you receive £65 a year, and Mr. Dennis credits against that your salary from the National Board?—Yes.

4520. The more the National Board pays the smaller is the balance he pays?—Yes. I think the salary Mr. Dennis agreed with me for was £55; and when I passed the examination Mr. Dennis raised my full salary to £65.

Mr. Dennis.—I don't know what you are going into this for. I knew perfectly well that I would not get a teacher at all without giving him a certain salary, which was about £50—I won't state the sum accurately for I forget. But I agreed with him that as soon as

July 1, 1886.

Mr. Claude Hagy Sweeney.

he passed the examination I would secure him a salary of £65.

4521. Lord Justice FitzGibbon (to witness).—Do you get results fees over and above the £65?—Decidedly.

4522. Rev. Dr. Molloy.—Do you get all the school fees?—Yes. I think last year they amounted to something over £10.

4523. Dr. Traill.—And how much did the results fees amount to?—For fourteen months to something over £15.

4524. Rev. Dr. Molloy.—Your emoluments amounted in all to about £90?—£96.

4525. Lord Justice FitzGibbon.—Have you a residence?—Yes, a free residence.

4526. Where is it?—In the building behind the courthouse.

4527. What accommodation had you in the old building?—There were four rooms in the house.

4528. What have you where you are now?—About the same number of rooms.

4529. What assistance have you in teaching the school?—Mr. Dennis has appointed a female assistant who is also a workmistress recognised by the National Board.

4530. She gets a salary from Mr. Dennis of £30 a year, but no salary from the National Board?—No, because the attendance does not warrant it.

4531. Does she get an allowance as workmistress?—She does not get any separate allowance as workmistress; she gets results fees.

4532. I thought they make an allowance to workmistresses?—Only where the average attendance amounts to twenty, and it does not here.

4533. What are your numbers?—Thirty-four boys and twenty-one girls on the roll, making a total of fifty-five, with an average attendance of forty-two and three-tenths.

4534. What denominations attend the school?—Irish Church; no Roman Catholics; one child of one of the Plymouth Brethren.

4535. Professor Dougherty.—Have you had any Presbyterian children during your term of office?—There are three children at present classified as Irish Church. Their father had been a Presbyterian, but he always attends service in the church.

4536. How did you arrive at their present classification? Did you ask their father before you registered them?—I didn't ask him. I thought that since they were allowed to attend the Sunday school of the church and all the services they might as well be classed in the same way.

4537. As a matter of fact they are Presbyterian children?—Only in so far as their father is a Presbyterian; but their mother is an Irish Church woman. At least my belief is that their father is a Presbyterian, but I could not say positively.

4538. Lord Justice FitzGibbon.—What religious instruction is given in the school?—Prayer, the reading of the Scriptures, and the Church catechism.

4539. Is the school visited by any clergyman?—Occasionally by Mr. Usher, but not very frequently.

4540. Does he pay any regular visits?—He does not.

4541. Dr. Traill.—Did Mr. Usher ever complain of the time for religious instruction being fixed at an inconvenient hour?—No, he did not.

4542. What is the hour for religious instruction?—From half-past ten to ten minutes past eleven.

4543. At what time does the school open?—At ten o'clock, but I am there at half-past nine.

4544. You don't have the religious instruction first?—I don't, because I consider it best to have all the children present.

4545. What subjects come on first?—Writing I begin with, because the people consider that writing is an important thing, and I thought they would have their children at school for it.

4546. You think they attach more importance to writing than to religious instruction?—Yes, that was my idea.

4547. Professor Dougherty.—What is the character of the religious instruction you give?—The reading of the Scriptures, and the Church Catechism on one day of the week, accompanying the reading by any moral lesson that I consider appropriate.

4548. Do you teach the Church Catechism to all the children?—Yes, to all. I don't think there is any exemption made.

4549. Has there ever been any exemption made?—No, never.

4550. Dr. Traill.—Does the child of the Plymouth Brother learn the Church Catechism?—I don't think so.

4551. Professor Dougherty.—Have the parents of the children objected to it at all?—Never.

4552. Rev. Dr. Molloy.—You provide religious education practically for all the Protestant children of the neighbourhood of Balbriggan?—Yes.

4553. And the others don't come to you?—No, it is practically a Protestant school.

4554. Is there any other Protestant school?—Not nearer than Port Granite.

4555. Professor Dougherty.—Then any Protestant children in Balbriggan must be sent to you, if they are to go to school at all?—If they have anything to object to in my teaching, and they are sufficiently well off, they are sent to Bough school, three or four miles distant.

4556. Lord Justice FitzGibbon.—I find three boys and a girl in the sixth class, and three boys and three girls in the fifth class, second stage, and two children in the fifth class, first stage; so that fifteen out of your roll are in the fifth and sixth classes?—Yes.

4557. Have you any monitor?—No, the Inspector objected to appointing a monitor after the last one I had until we had a regular schoolhouse built.

4558. Rev. Dr. Molloy.—What is the school accommodation that you have at present?—We have one good large room.

4559. For boys and girls together?—Yes, it is a mixed school.

Mr. Dennis.—It is not at all sufficient or desirable.

4560. Dr. Traill.—Was it a mixed school in the time of the former building, or were the boys and girls separated?—I heard they were separated.

4561. Were there separate rooms for the boys and girls in the old schoolhouse?—I believe there were.

4562. Did you not teach there yourself before the railway ran through it?—Yes.

4563. Were there two sets of rooms?—No, it was a mixed school, and we only used the one room though there were two.

Mr. Dennis.—In the old building there were two schoolrooms—one for the boys and one for the girls; and an infant school was held in the same house.

4564. Lord Justice Naish.—Was there a distinct room for it?—No.

4565. Lord Justice FitzGibbon.—We have it reported in 1879, that there were two schoolrooms, besides teachers' apartments in fair repair, excellent, a garden and a playground.

Mr. Dennis.—I must explain that. There was a room which was built as a "pay shop," but it was not used for that purpose, and for convenience sake the infant school was put into it.

4566. Dr. Traill (to witness).—Have you any class for infants below eight years of age at present?—They are included under the head of "infants" in the first class.

4567. Lord Justice FitzGibbon.—There are eight "infants" on the roll of the boys, and four on that of the girls. The first class is practically an infant class—there are four boys in it and six girls. That makes twenty-two infants. The next two classes are very small. The bulk of the school is in the fourth class; but there are very substantial fifth and sixth classes.

(To witness).—Did you go through a course of training?—I was trained in the Church Education Society's Institution, Kildare-place, in 1852.

4568. Rev. Dr. Molloy.—I suppose there are hardly any Protestant children in the neighbourhood who don't come to your school?—Very few, indeed.

4569. Mr. Edward O'Kelly.—Mr. Sweeny, do you consider that the school at present is in a sanitary condition for a school?—So far as the usual sanitary condition is concerned it is right enough, but the accommodation for the children I don't think is sufficient at all.

4570. Lord Justice FitzGibbon.—It is perfectly plain that under this will Mr. Dennis is bound to provide a schoolhouse instead of the one taken by the railway. He tells us that the present is only a temporary arrangement, and that there is some delay about this; but his duty will be to get that temporary arrangement wound up as soon as he reasonably can. It seems to be rather slow.

Mr. O'Kelly.—I would ask you to admit evidence with regard to the attendance of Catholics at this school.

4571. Lord Justice FitzGibbon.—We will take any evidence you can give us.

Mr. O'Kelly.—In case of any division, the Catholics might have a claim.

Lord Justice FitzGibbon.—There is no question of a division. The schools must be kept up as Lady Stratford founded them.

[illegible]. Mr. Claude Haley Sweeny.

Mrs. Rebecca Kavanagh sworn and examined.

Mrs. Rebecca Kavanagh.

4572. Lord Justice FitzGibbon.—You were a pupil in Lady Stratford's old school?—I was.

4573. May I ask you how long ago?—I left off at eleven—I am seventy-six now.

4574. So that you left off in the year 1826, sixty-five years ago?—Yes.

4575. Was Lady Stratford living here then?—She was. I spoke to her when I was giving up my books. She lived in a place above the old ruins, over the railway.

4576. When did you go to school first?—When I was very little—just a child able to walk. I went there five or six years altogether.

4577. At the time you were there where was the school held?—Up on the hill where the railway went through.

4578. What sort of school was it?—There was a place for the master next the boys schoolroom, and there was a room for the mistress next the girls school—two rooms below stairs and two rooms above stairs.

4579. At that time how many pupils were in the school?—I don't remember. There was a good large number in it. They used to come in from Stratford—them sides—as near as I can recollect, there were up to a hundred or so.

4580. At that time were there any other schools in Baltinglass?—Not many, but they were beginning to get up.

4581. Was there any school at that time under the priest?—I don't remember. There might have been.

4582. At the time you speak of what teachers were in the Stratford schools?—A Miss Doyle was mistress. There was one master and one mistress.

4583. Did Lady Stratford ever teach herself?—I think she did. I am not certain.

4584. What denominations were there at the schools in those times?—There were Catholics and Protestants. Any Catholic children that wished to go might go there.

4585. Do you remember when the first school was established here under the priest?—About the time that I left off school the Catholic clergy were beginning to object to Catholics going to a Protestant school.

4586. When you left that school did you go to another?—No, I left off going to school any more.

4587. About that time was there a separate school established for the Roman Catholics?—Yes—the Catholic clergy were objecting at that time to Catholics going to a Protestant school and they withdrew them.

4588. Dr. Traill.—What do you call a Protestant school—were the Scriptures taught there?—Yes.

4589. Were you taught the Scriptures there?—I read a lot of Scripture.

4590. And it didn't do you any harm?—Not harm, but a great deal of good. I could tell you a good deal of it.

4591. Lord Justice FitzGibbon.—Was there Scripture teaching in the school every day?—There was, and for all the pupils.

4592. And the Roman Catholic clergy objected to that?—They did not object to it. They objected to the children going to the school at all. They wanted them to go to a separate school where they would be taught their own religion.

4593. Was that how the separation came?—I dare say it was. I cannot say. I did not know much about it at that time.

4594. Who managed the school in those days?—Lady Elizabeth herself. She visited it every other day.

4595. Rev. Dr. Molloy.—Was there an infant school there?—There was.

4596. Lord Justice FitzGibbon.—Was it a separate school?—Yes.

4597. Who kept it up?—Lady Elizabeth too.

4598. Do you remember how many children were there?—I could not say.

4599. Was it under a separate teacher?—Yes, there was a teacher in that school designed for the infant children.

4600. Then there must have been three teachers—a woman for the infants, a woman for the girls, and a man for the boys?—Yes.

4601. Rev. Dr. Molloy.—Were you ever in the infants school yourself?—I often went into it, but I was not there as a pupil.

4602. Dr. Traill.—Were the boys and the girls taught in separate rooms?—Yes, there were separate rooms—one for the boys and one for the girls.

4603. Lord Justice FitzGibbon.—Do you remember whether the teachers were always Protestants?—Yes, they were, certainly.

4604. Both male and female?—Both male and female.

4605. Dr. Traill.—And that was what the priests objected to?—Yes, that was what the priests objected to.

4606. Did it make any great difference in the size of the school when the children were withdrawn by the priests?—Not a great deal.

4607. What was the proportion of Roman Catholics—were they half?—Oh, no.

4608. Rev. Dr. Molloy.—At the time you went to the school it was the only school in the town?—I dare say when I went at the commencement it was the only school; but before I left there were others.

4609. You say there were about one hundred pupils?—I think there were.

4610. Do you mean one hundred girls?—I think there were one hundred girls.

4611. Lord Justice Naish.—How many boys were there?—Very nearly the same, for they came from all parts of the country.

[illegible]

4612. Do you mean that there were two hundred children attending the schools?—As nearly as I can say.

4613. Was there room for them?—There were two very large rooms.

4614. Was there some ground round the school?—There was a very nice place before the door with shrubs on it, and also fields.

4615. Was there a garden?—No garden.

4616. Had the teachers anything except the house?—No; they had a way of sewing something.

4617. I heard you say that there were two storeys to the house?—There were two rooms below and two rooms above for the master and mistress. The house where the teachers lived separated the boys school from the girls.

4618. Lord Justice FitzGibbon.—Can anyone tell us how many pupils are in the National school of which the priest is manager?

Mr. Sweeny.—I think Mr. Browne, the master, told me he had an average of about a hundred or a hundred and ten.

4619. How many pupils are attending the Kane school?—There are one hundred and thirty. There is another Catholic school under the management of the priest about two miles outside the town.

4620. Mr. Sweeny.—The old schools were so pretty that Mr. Watkins of the Irish Academy thought them worth painting. In some of the old National Education books there are pictures of the school. There was a two-storied house with wings at the ends.

4621. Lord Justice Naish.—Is the one that was painted by Watkins the same that the railway ran through?—Yes.

4622. Mr. Dennis.—I could not get anything from the National Board that was at all like it. I was obliged to go to an architect to draw a plan for me which would in some way carry out the design of the old establishment. I could not get a decent plan from the Board of Works. I would like to ask this old lady a question. In Lewis's Topographical Dictionary there is a statement that "at Stratford Lodge there are two schools, one an infants' school, both of which are supported by Lady Elizabeth Stratford; and there are two other schools, altogether affording instruction to about 260 boys and 190 girls." Can you tell me what schools are alluded to by the words, "two other schools"?—(Witness)—No.

4623. Dr. Traill.—What is the date of that?—1837.

4624. Lord Justice FitzGibbon.—Lewis is not very accurate, but he generally has a foundation for what he says; and what this lady says fits in with it. Sixty years ago brings you to 1828, and she says that just about that time there were other schools being established under the priest, who objected to his children going to Lady Stratford's school.

Mr. Dennis.—I believe it was on account of Lady Stratford working the Protestant school that the other was built, and after it the National school.

Lord Justice FitzGibbon.—The National Board was not established until 1832, but the dates nearly fit in with what she says.

4625. Professor Dougherty.—Is it long since the Roman Catholic National school was built, does anyone know?

[Some persons present said it was upwards of forty years.]

4626. Rev. Dr. Molloy.—Do you remember the National school for forty years?

Mr. Kelly.—I remember it for thirty-five years.

4627. Lord Justice FitzGibbon (to witness).—I suppose the Roman Catholics have not gone to Lady Stratford's school since you left?—No.

Mr. Dennis.—When the National school was in Baltinglass a good many Protestant children went to it.

Lord Justice FitzGibbon.—That would depend on the efficiency of the teacher.

Dr. Traill.—And if there were not a good Protestant school here a great many Protestants would be driven to the National school.

4628. Rev. Dr. Molloy.—Are there any Protestants going to the National School at present?—I don't think there are.

4629. But is not your school a National school?—Yes, but of late my school has been going down.

4630. Lord Justice FitzGibbon.—Everywhere we have found that if the Protestant school is not under the National Board, a large proportion of the Protestants go to the nearest National school, because the inspection, classification, and other things in it are better.

Mr. Dennis.—That is my great object.

4631. Lord Justice FitzGibbon.—The thing to do is to hurry on this new building, Mr. Dennis.

Mr. Dennis.—If you ask information it is a different thing; but I am not bound to give information to the public as to my arrangements.

4632. Lord Justice FitzGibbon.—You should understand that the old school, with its site, land and buildings, appears from the former reports to have been contributed to by public funds. A trust attaches to the purchase money for providing an equally good building to that which has been taken away, and that will also impress that building upon you and your estate.

Mr. Dennis.—I hope to do that. I have been in communication, not only with Mr. Anderson before his death, but also with Mrs. Anderson, and I have been informed that there is a likelihood of this being made in a short time. You may depend upon it I am anxious to get it.

4633. Lord Justice Naish.—You should bear in mind that as regards the school buildings, the grounds, and all belonging to the school, it would be very hard to say that the money that represents that should not go entirely for school purposes.

Mr. Dennis.—I do not know that. That money is dissipated. I intend to build the school whenever I can get the money; and I will get the money whenever I can; and I will carry on the school according to Lady Stratford's directions.

4634. Lord Justice FitzGibbon.—Apparently it would be a school for which a Board of Works grant of two-thirds could be got. As regards denominations you have all heard this old lady's statement of the school. Lady Stratford founded the school, kept the management of it in her own hands, obliged all the children to receive religious instruction in the school, and always appointed teachers of her own denomination. The clergy of the opposite persuasion, of course preferred to have that sort of thing in their own hands, and they set up another school; but the school was open to everyone who chose to go to it.

Mr. Kelly.—Mr. Dennis said he did not wish to let every one know his arrangements about this school. I think the public have a right to know them. The building in which the school is now held belongs to the Grand Jury. We are paying £20 a year for a police-barrack, and there is a splendid barrack outside here that could be got for nothing. I think as a matter of taxation we are entitled to have the school taken out of this place as quickly as possible.

4635. Dr. Traill.—Did the police live here before?

Mr. Kelly.—They did.

4636. Lord Justice FitzGibbon.—We have nothing to do with the police; but you are quite right that the schools ought to be taken out of this place as soon as possible. They are entitled to have buildings and premises of their own.

Mr. Dennis.—And I tell you more, that the present buildings are badly suited for a school. They are the best that I could get, and if Mr. Kelly will give me better I will take them.

KILTEGAN (ERASMUS SMITH'S) SCHOOL.

4637. Lord Justice FitzGibbon.—Can you tell us anything about Kiltegan School?

Mr. Dennis.—The Board of Erasmus Smith have withdrawn the grant and given up the school to Mr. Dick.

4638. Lord Justice Naish.—Is it used for a school still?

Mr. Kelly.—Yes.

4639. Dr. Traill.—And the schoolmaster from there still?

Mr. Kelly.—Yes.

This terminated the inquiry.

PUBLIC SITTING—TUESDAY, JULY 9, 1889.

At the Schoolhouse, Bough.

Present:—The Right Hon. Lord Justice FitzGibbon, and the Right Hon. Lord Justice Naish, Judicial Commissioners; and the Rev. Gerald Molloy, D.D., D.Sc.; Anthony Traill, Esq., LL.D., M.D., F.T.C.D., and Professor Dougherty, M.A., Assistant Commissioners.

The Assistant Secretary, N. D. Murphy, was in attendance.

D'ISRAELI'S SCHOOL, BOUGH, RATHVILLY.

4640. Lord Justice FitzGibbon.—We find by the reports of former Commissions that this school possesses an endowment, dating from 1816, of a schoolhouse and residence, five plantation acres of land, and a capital sum in the hands of the Commissioners of Charitable Donations and Bequests amounting to over £3,000. The founder, Benjamin D'Israeli, directed that this endowment should be applied for the purpose of a school to be conducted "on the most enlightened and liberal principles." It is reported to be under the care of the Bishop of Leighlin and Ferns, and the founder's heir-at-law, and to have had in it, in 1857, 14 boys and 11 girls. In 1879 the numbers had greatly increased, being at that time 41 boys and 35 girls; and it was reported by the Inspector that the present master conducted it usefully and successfully, and that the premises were in good condition, but that a portion of the expense had been borne by the master.

The Right Rev. William Pakenham Walsh, D.D., Bishop of Ossory, Ferns, and Leighlin, sworn and examined.

4641. Lord Justice FitzGibbon.—As Bishop of Leighlin and Ferns you are one of the trustees under the will of Benjamin D'Israeli for the management of this school?—Yes.

4642. Is anyone now acting as a trustee representing the heir of the founder?—I discovered about three years ago that there was a Major Cumming, of Craven Hall, near Cavan, an elderly gentleman, who was entitled to act as heir of Hugh Cumming. I asked him could he attend, but he said it was impossible. He had taken no practical interest in the school, and he could scarcely be expected to attend at his time of life.

4643. Has Major Cumming any property here?—No; his family have parted with their property here.

4644. Has he any connexion with the school, or with the neighbourhood?—I think none.

4645. How long have you been Bishop of the diocese?—Between ten and eleven years.

4646. During that time has any part been taken in the management of the school by the heir of the founder?—None. I did not know that there was any representative of the founder until a few years ago, when I found this old gentleman who could not attend.

4647. On former occasions it was reported that the Bishop claimed sole and entire authority over the school. Is there no record of the heir of the founder having in recent times taken any part in the management?—I think not. I may mention how the heir of the founder came to appear at all. In the original will the trustees were the Bishop of Leighlin, the Incumbent of Rathvilly, and the two churchwardens. Owing to some dispute the matter went into Chancery after Benjamin D'Israeli's death. He died in 1816. The matter was referred in 1816 to Master Howe, who reported on July 21, 1819, that in future the Bishop of Ossory for the time being and Hugh Cumming should be the sole trustees.

4648. Under what circumstances was that report made?—I don't think it was disputed. I think the clergyman of the day did not wish to take any responsibility.

4649. Lord Justice FitzGibbon.—The will is as follows:—

"I, Benjamin D'Israeli, of the City of Dublin, devise and bequeath to the minister and churchwardens of the Parish of Rathvilly, in the County of Carlow, £[illegible], to be invested in Government Securities or Bank, and the interest to be applied every Christmas Eve in the purchase of provisions, to be distributed every Christmas Day to the poor of the parish. I bequeath to the Lord Bishop of Leighlin and Ferns, and the minister and churchwardens of the Parish of Rathvilly, £1,000, to be expended in building a good and substantial house as near to the Town of Rathvilly as may be, for the purpose of a free school for the education of the poor children, and the accommodation of a schoolmaster; and to the said Bishop of Leighlin and Ferns, and the minister and churchwardens of the Parish of Rathvilly, £3,000, as a fund to defray the expenses of the said school, for ever, to be invested in the purchase of lands, and to be invested in the public funds until such purchase; the interest to be applied—first, in the payment of the rent of the ground, and of five Plantation acres, for the use of the master of the school; next, in the payment of a salary of £[illegible] a year to the master, in half-yearly payments; and the residue to be applied to the uses and purposes of the said school, which, it is my wish and desire, shall be conducted on the most enlightened and liberal principles, under the care and superintendence of the said Bishop, minister, and churchwardens, or such person or persons as they may think proper to appoint for the purpose."

you were appointed by the Bishop, and he had control over you in the discharge of your duties?—Yes.

4692. When you came what pupils were in the school?—Before I came there were very few. When I arrived there were under ten. I had taught in the neighbourhood before, and the children of my old pupils and their connexions came back to me.

4693. What had been your previous experience as a teacher?—I was trained by the Church Education Society. I got a certificate from the Committee of Council, and I obtained a first class matriculation in the London University, but the bishop put his foot on my completing my course there.

4694. Rev. Dr. Molloy.—In what year did you matriculate?—In 1863. Eleven or twelve years before that I had a situation in Norwich. I was also in Cheltenham engaged in teaching under Dr. Boyd.

4695. What was your previous connexion with this neighbourhood?—I had a Church School in Tullow just forty years ago.

4696. Lord Justice FitzGibbon.—How old are you?—Over sixty.

4697. How did you get your pupils together here?—The Church Education Society's rules seemed very stringent for the kind of school that I wanted to establish; however, the Inspectors approved of my work, and I was not interfered with. I had to step beyond the scheme of the Church Education Society.

4698. Rev. Dr. Molloy.—In what respect?—I had boarders; and I had to give them a more liberal and extensive education—Classics, French, and everything that I could teach.

4699. Lord Justice FitzGibbon.—What was the largest number of boarders you ever had?—I had sixteen.

4700. Did they live in this building?—We stowed them away. I had eight children of my own.

4701. Rev. Dr. Molloy.—In addition to the sixteen?—Yes.

4702. Lord Justice Naish.—Where did the boarders come from?—Chiefly from Carlow, Wicklow, and all the neighbourhood—the sons of well-to-do farmers.

4703. Lord Justice FitzGibbon.—What were your terms for boarders?—£30 a year for boys up to fifteen, and £35 for boys of over fifteen.

4704. What was your course of teaching?—Anything that they wanted to learn. I never refused to teach the poorest child in the school anything that I knew.

4705. Dr. Traill.—What help had you?—I had a family of eight children.

4706. That would not be a help?—I had no official help; only my own ingenuity, if I might pride myself on having such a thing. I had great working power.

4707. Rev. Dr. Molloy.—As your family grew up I suppose you got some assistance from them?—Yes—help to cut bread, and in doing anything; and hearing lessons.

4708. Then, as a boarding school, this appears to have been very successful?—Very successful.

4709. What led you to abandon the boarding school?—My family all began to do for themselves, and my wife and I began to grow older. I was sorry to give it up, but the domestic arrangements were very heavy on my wife.

4710. Lord Justice FitzGibbon.—How long have you given up the boarders?—They began to die out. I did not take any new ones from about 1883.

4711. When did the last leave you?—More than two years ago.

4712. What was your largest number of day pupils?—I had over sixty on the books.

4713. What is your number now?—Thirty-two on the books.

4714. What was the cause of the falling off?—Families left the parish. The population moves in cycles or waves. All the farmsteads the children came from are there, but there are no children.

4715. I suppose there will be at some future time?—I hope so.

4716. What are the fees paid by the day pupils?—I got sorry for coming here, and a gentleman who is behind me guaranteed £16 from four residents. At one time I suppose it was £40. At present I don't get a shilling from the parish.

4717. Do you mean that no fees are paid?—I get them from some outsiders from Baltinglass and from a distance; but I don't get a shilling at present from parish pupils, nor have had for two or three years. I don't ask it.

4718. Is there any scale of fees?—Five shillings a quarter is the highest; and where there are a number who balk at paying I get £1 a year from some.

4719. Are you under any regulations as to the fixing of fees, or is that left to yourself?—At the time of my appointment the Bishop agreed that I should get fees from children that were able to pay, but that no child should be excluded by reason of inability to pay.

4720. I have seen the school in the Intermediate returns; what have you done in that way?—The Bishop asked me to write out a list of the distinctions obtained from the school. (Handed in.) There are seven in succession who went to the Bank of Ireland.

4721. Did they go direct from you?—Some did, and some went to business first.

4722. I see one named Earl, a B.A. and Bachelor of Medicine, Trinity College?—That is my son. He is now assistant to Dr. Power for Trinity College.

4723. J. B. Jackson, M.D., assistant, Cornwall, and William Langran, medical practitioner, Devonshire?—Jackson was a native of this parish.

4724. Thomas Kidd, Licentiate of the Royal College of Surgeons, Rathvilly dispensary?—He was a boarder here.

4725. John Kenny, M.D.?—He is over a lunatic asylum in Scotland.

4726. William Murphy, L.R.C.S., of Coolgreany dispensary; a medical practitioner in the United States; another member of the Royal College of Surgeons; another Mr. Earl, a medical student in Trinity College—that is another son of yours?—Yes.

4727. I see also surgeons in the United States and in Australia; and medical students in Leeds and Edinburgh; Dr. Doherty, practising in Dublin; two medical students in Dublin; two gentlemen who have passed the preliminary examination for the College of Surgeons; a civil engineer, deceased; another Mr. Earl, M.A., T.C.D., Vicar of Sherburne, in Yorkshire—is that a third son of yours?—Yes; he is a vicar at £400 a year.

A curate in Belfast, a missionary in Central Africa; a junior exhibitioner, Trinity College; an attorney's apprentice; four gentlemen in the Civil Service; four veterinary surgeons in Edinburgh; an assistant county surveyor; three engineers in Australia, and two in the United States; Mathew Crowe, B.A., Cambridge, head master of the Hindoo College, Tinnevelly.

Witness.—He has eleven assistants.

4728. Lord Justice FitzGibbon.—A dentist; a clerk in an agent's office, and three gentlemen in business. Amongst the girls we have Fanny Young, Queen's scholar, nineteenth on a list of 400, and now schoolmistress in Selby; another pupil passed the Senior Intermediate examination and obtained the Bishop's silver medal; Miss Lizzie Earl, B.Sc.(?), and of Cambridge, mistress in a High school, Birmingham; Miss Ada Earl, Governess Scholarship, R.C.S., and undergraduate, London, mistress in King Edward's High School, Birmingham; Margaret Earl, R.U.I., certificated Kindergarten teacher; Susan Bergin, Intermediate with honours, now a teacher in Australia; and Maude Earl, Intermediate Exhibitioner, Scholarship in King Edward's School, and first class

July 8, 1858.

Mr. James Earl.

London. Then you said that the number on the books of the school at present is thirty-two; the average for the past half-year twenty-three; the number on the roll in 1858, sixty-one; and the average forty-six. A very remarkable and varied list of disciplines. Is there anybody in the neighbourhood who has ever taken an interest in the school?—The late Mr. Hume and his family took a great interest in it, and Lord Rathdowne has contributed £110 during my time.

4729. How has that been applied?—Ten pounds a year to my salary. It was given on a promise made by his father when I came, which has been carried out faithfully since.

4730. Your emoluments are £30 a year from the endowment, and £10 a year from Lord Rathdowne?—Yes.

4731. Have you the land in your own hands?—Yes.

4732. Is it liable to any rent?—No.

4733. Do you know in whom the property is vested?—I think in the Commissioners of Charitable Bequests. There is one thing that has not cropped up in evidence yet. The late Mr. Hume told me that a girls school was to have been built in Dublin. I conclude that it was in order to bring that girls school here that Mr. Hugh Cumming was substituted for the local governors.

4734. We can get copies of the Chancery Scheme and of the Will and see how that stands.

Witness.—There is a sum of £1,000 or £2,000 in question; an additional endowment for a girls school.

4735. There was £1,000 to be spent on the five acres and the building, and the £2,000 held by the Commissioners of Charitable Donations and Bequests consists of the original bequest of £2,000, with accumulations.

Witness.—But there has not been a word in all the evidence about a girls school.

The *Bishop of Ossory.*—I suppose that they found they had more income each year than paid the £30 a year to the master, and they thought it desirable that there should be a female teacher.

4736. Lord Justice FITZGIBBON.—There is nothing in the will limiting this school to boys. It is for "poor children."

Rev. Dr. MOLLOY.—I don't think there is any part of the endowment missing. It consisted of £1,000, which is now represented by the buildings and land, and £2,000 for the maintenance of the school, which is represented by the £2,373 Government stock.

4737. Professor DOUGHERTY (to Witness).—Do I understand you to say you are under the impression that in addition to these moneys there was an endowment under the will of Mr. D'Israeli for a girls school?—For a girls school to be built in Dublin.

4738. How did you get that impression?—The late rector of the parish, the Rev. Quintin Hume, brother of Mr. Dick, told me.

4739. Lord Justice FITZGIBBON.—That will turn out to be a misapprehension—there is a legacy of £500 for the Female Orphan House in Dublin. (To the Witness)—Can you give any suggestion with a view to making this place more useful and permanent than it is—such, for example, as having a local governing body?—Of course, as a schoolmaster, I set myself before either the minister or the churchwardens as regards experience in teaching. But I will do what I am told. My idea is that it cannot be maintained with the present salary. If I were a policeman I should have a better salary than I have as schoolmaster.

4740. But £30 a year often keeps a school going?—If it is a free school it won't.

4741. Dr. TRAILL.—How is the £90 spent?—I and my wife get £30 each, and there is £10 for fuel.

4742. Rev. Dr. MOLLOY.—When you had sixteen boarders paying £20 and £25 each you made a good income?—I had a large family. I had plenty of ways of spending it.

4743. Still the endowment enabled you to maintain the school and to receive boarders; and the income from them helped to maintain you and your family?—It gave me standing ground.

4744. Dr. TRAILL.—What became of the other £20?

The *Bishop of Ossory.*—There are insurance and repairs of the building.

4745. Did they come on an average to £10 a year?—I think so.

4746. Have the Charitable Bequests Commissioners bound themselves to hold the £130 as a reserve fund as capital or will they only give you the interest of it?—I think they would give me a larger sum if I wanted it.

4747. Have you drawn any of it as capital?—I only ask for £30 at a time. It is partly capital and partly interest.

4748. Lord Justice FITZGIBBON.—Is there no provision for the retirement of the master?—No, there is not.

4749. For that is a thing that should be provided when a man gets old.

Witness.—Since I became a schoolmaster I pride myself on having done good in my generation. If I had been a policeman, I should have been better paid, and have a pension besides.

4750. Mr. *Paul A. Browne, Solicitor.*—I appear for the Rev. Father Phelan, P.P., the Manager of the National School.

To Witness.—I understand you to say, Mr. Earl, that £30 a year is what you receive from the endowment?—Yes.

4751. Is that the entire sum?—That is my entire salary.

4752. Are there any other sums that you receive?—I receive £10 for fuel. I have to keep the school in good.

4753. How much for stationery?—Nothing, except what comes for the school.

4754. Isn't there a certain sum allotted for stationery?—Not for my stationery. For school requisites there may be.

4755. You send in an account for stationery?—I do, certainly.

The *Bishop of Ossory.*—No certain sum is allotted. Mr. Earl makes his return, and I carry it out.

Witness.—The repairs and stationery amount to about £5 a year.

4756. What is the actual sum that you have been allowed for stationery on an average for the last ten years?—Just what turns up. I make out the account, and send it to his lordship; the amount may be £1 for stationery, ink, pens, and some reading books.

4757. As a matter of fact hasn't it been £5 a year. I am instructed that there is a certain sum allowed.

The *Bishop of Ossory.*—There is no certain sum allowed. Mr. Earl sends me his account—it may be £1 13s. for one half-year, £2 5s. for another, and so on. There is also an allowance for materials for the girls sewing. Whatever it is, if it be reasonable, I recommend the Commissioners to pay it.

4758. They pay it directly. The income does not pass through your lordship's hands?—I never receive a halfpenny.

4759. Would it not be better for the amount to go through the hands of the governing body?—I don't think it would be less pleasant to me.

4760. Dr. TRAILL.—If it is paid on your certificate is not that all that you want?—That is all I want. If I thought the things were unreasonable I would say so.

4761. Mr. *Browne* (to Witness).—Isn't there an allowance for keeping the clock?—I know nothing about it.

4762. Mr. *Browne.*—What I have been instructed is, that there was £5 a year allowed to the master of the school for keeping the clock, and that for twenty-five years the clock has not been going. That is £125.

July 6, 1886.

Mr. James Earl.

Witness.—The clock was stopped before I came. I made an effort to get it into repair. Mr. Donaldson sent a man to examine it; but he said the clock was so out of repair, and the works so ill assorted, some of the works being so large, and some so small that he would not undertake it.

4763. Lord Justice FitzGibbon.—The clock has never gone for twenty-five years?—Never.

4764. The Bishop of Ossory.—And you never received a penny for it?—No.

4765. Dr. Traill (to Mr. Brown).—How does the clock concern you, and those who instructed you?

Mr. Brown.—I was instructed that £3 a year was allowed for the maintenance of the clock.

4766. Dr. Traill.—This is a Church school, you know, under the Bishop. How does the school clock concern you and your clients?

Mr. Brown.—I don't know what the terms of the endowments are.

4767. Lord Justice FitzGibbon.—He is quite at liberty, if he has been under the impression that £3 a year was being thus applied, to call attention to it.

Mr. Brown.—As the clock has not been going for twenty-five years it would be a misapplication of funds to allow £3 a year for it.

4768. Rev. Dr. Molloy.—I understand that no money has been spent on the clock, and that the clock has not been going.

The Bishop of Ossory.—There has been no money spent on anything except what passed through my hands, and no money for that purpose was ever ordered by me.

Mr. Brown.—I was merely asked to make these inquiries.

4769. (To Mr. Earl).—Of what religious denominations are your pupils?—They are all supposed to be Irish Church.

4770. At any time had you pupils of other denominations?—I had pupils that didn't learn the Catechism. I think they were Plymouth Brethren. They came from Balinaglera.

4771. Lord Justice Naish.—Had you ever a Roman Catholic?—Never.

4772. Lord Justice FitzGibbon.—What are the rules of the school about religious instruction?—I was under the Church Education Society up to a certain time. When we went under the Intermediate system I applied to the Bishop for a conscience clause, and his lordship granted it.

4773. Then you have worked the school as an intermediate school, open to children of all denominations, no child being excluded from secular instruction by reason of non-attendance during religious instruction?—Something like that.

4774. Lord Justice Naish.—Is that hung up in the school?—Not hung up, but signed, and honestly carried out.

4775. Lord Justice FitzGibbon.—Your list is not a list of children instructed in the ordinary curriculum of the Church Education Society, but of pupils who got much higher instruction?—We were under the Church Education Society, and that was my difficulty, I had to do double work.

4776. Rev. Dr. Molloy.—You applied the principle of the will, and gave education according to the "most liberal and enlightened principles"?—It cannot be made much more than an elementary school, except by double energy on the part of the teachers.

4777. Lord Justice FitzGibbon.—Very few intermediate schools in Ireland show a better record than yours, in proportion to your numbers. At the Intermediate Examinations in 1879 you had 11 passes; in 1880, 7; in 1881, 6, including a prize and an exhibition; in 1882, 8; and in 1883, 6.

4778. Rev. Dr. Molloy.—I understand that you would not have been able to give this education except for the assistance that you got from members of your own family in teaching?—Not so efficiently.

4779. Consequently for the future this higher kind of education cannot be carried on without additional teaching power?—We cannot make bricks without straw. We haven't the class of children at present that would go forward. The financial circumstances of the surrounding farmers hardly give them heart to go forward. They are not as good as they were when I came. Bad times have occurred since, and the farmers have not been able to put their children to school.

4780. Were your successful students mostly from the farming classes?—With one or two exceptions they are all from the farming classes. I only throw it out as my private opinion—as you asked me—that the school would be better under the National Board. We would have regular inspectors; we would have books; and some result fees, perhaps very little.

4781. You would not be able now to qualify as a teacher under the National system now?—I am over age.

4782. Lord Justice FitzGibbon.—You could get over that by keeping the intermediate teaching in your own hands and having an assistant under the National Board.

Witness.—I could get nothing from the Intermediate Board for a National School. A small school has no chance in the Intermediate system. I had to send children of twelve to compete with children of sixteen. That would be easy in a big school; but I would have no chance of money or credit for it here.

4783. Mr. Brown.—Are there thirty-two in regular attendance at the school?—Yes.

4784. I have been instructed that the number is five. Are you quite sure that the number you have given is correct?—They are registered.

4785. Do they regularly attend?—Sometimes a child is absent. There must be a great many absent in the fall of the year.

4786. What are the times during which they are supposed to attend the school?—Five days in the week.

4787. Lord Justice FitzGibbon.—The average attendance for the half year is twenty-three. That is seventy per cent. of those on the roll, which is the average in an ordinary National school.

4788. Mr. Brown.—As I am instructed the roll-call does not represent the average attendance, for it is managed in such a way that persons attend on behalf of others. What I want to understand is, how many of the thirty-two attend regularly on five days of the week?—I cannot tell you off-hand. If you let me look at the register I will tell you.

4789. Lord Justice FitzGibbon.—The register is before us; it is kept in the ordinary form of the Church Education Society, and substantially in the same form as the registers of the National Board.

Witness.—On a wet day children do not come until eleven o'clock perhaps, and I cannot object to that.

4790. Is your average attendance calculated for any fixed hour, or do you count every child present at any time during the day?—At any time. When they come they stay.

Lord Justice FitzGibbon.—One of the advantages of being under the National Board would be that the roll would be called regularly at the same hour every morning.

4791. Mr. Brown.—My instructions are that the average attendance is five, and I want to see that the roll-call is accurate.

Witness.—I am on my oath, and I said it to the best of my opinion fairly.

The Rev. *Samuel Quinton* sworn and examined.

July 5, 1889. Rev. Samuel Quinton.

4792. Lord Justice FITZGIBBON.—You are Incumbent of the parish of Rathvilly?—Yes, since 1878.

4793. The testator directed that the Minister and Churchwardens should be governors of the school?—I was under that impression till lately.

4794. Have you or the churchwardens taken any part in the management of the school?—None whatever.

4795. Do you think it would be an advantage that they should be restored to the place the testator gave them?—Decidedly.

4796. What is the present number of registered vestrymen in your parish?—About forty-five.

4797. What is the extent of the parish?—It is a large parish, but there are no Protestants living in a great part of it.

4798. What is the Protestant population of your parish?—It is one hundred and ninety-two at present.

4799. Besides those from the parish of Rathvilly, do you know from what distances pupils come to this school?—I have not come to the school, but I know they come from all the parishes about—Baltinglass, Kiltegan, and Minnanagh.

4800. What schools under the management of members of your Church are there in the neighbourhood—what is the nearest to this school?—Only Lady Rathdonnell's school, for small children.

4801. Is it in connexion with the National Board or the Church Education Society?—It is under the Board of Religious Education of the diocese. It is not connected with any society.

4802. What is the nearest National school under Protestant management?—The one at Baltinglass and one at Kiltegan, about four miles off. There is a National school in this parish about two miles off.

4803. Who is the manager?—Father Phelan.

4804. I suppose it is chiefly attended by Roman Catholic pupils?—Altogether, I should say.

4805. What are the wants of the neighbourhood in the way of education?—I think the place is very well off for schools for both denominations, Roman Catholics and Protestants. We have two schools, one at each end of the parish, for our own people. They have a National school at Rathvilly; another outside the parish, about two miles off; and a third on the opposite side of the parish.

4806. Do you think there would be any chance of getting people to subscribe to maintain an Intermediate school here?—I don't think there would.

4807. Is there any possibility of getting the parents of children who want better education to pay something in the way of school fees?—I don't think any one wishes to do that. There might be some.

Mr. *Earl.*—They have done so, and will do so.

4808. Lord Justice FITZGIBBON (to Witness).—Do you think any of the parents of the pupils would take some interest in the management of the schools?—I am sure some of them would be glad to have a part in the management.

4809. If they had some representation on the governing body would it bring in any funds?—If they had the churchwardens, for the time being, to represent the parishioners it would be a very good thing. It is the arrangement that Mr. [illegible] intended.

Mr. *James Earl* re-examined.

Mr. James Earl.

4810. Rev. Dr. MOLLOY.—On looking over this roll, Mr. Earl, I see that some of the pupils have not attended from January 1, 1889, down to the present date. There is William Corrigan?—He is my pupil. He got typhoid fever, and has not been in a fit state to come; and it would not be fair to strike him off.

4811. You have entered him as absent. John Corrigan?—He is ill.

4812. Jane Corrigan?—She is his sister.

4813. Lizzie Jackson has not been here since January 1, 1889?—She may come; her brothers and sisters come. We have not struck her off.

4814. Martha Neill?—She led me to suppose that she would return. She has not been in good health.

4815. Lord Justice FITZGIBBON.—What is the rule as to writing out the school roll?—It is a quarterly roll; I usually mark it daily. This roll is from January 1 to March 31, as the book shows. In a National school, if only five children come on a wet day, the National Board would not include that in the attendance. I act on the same principle, and I shut out that day from the calculation of the average.

4816. Dr. TRAILL.—Then, in the average of twenty-three, those days that have been left out in that way are not counted?—No.

4817. Lord Justice FITZGIBBON.—Up to what date is your average of twenty-three for the past half year made up?—To last Friday.

4818. Mr. *Brown* (to Witness).—When were those three names of new pupils written down that appear there?—As they came. On the 14th January I wrote out the roll, and those three came in the early days of March. "A" is "absent." They are not entered until March. They are not marked until then.

4819. Is this the actual roll that is kept from day to day?—This is the veritable roll, kept from day to day.

4820. This particular document before us now?—This particular document. The children marked there today are all out in the playground.

4821. Lord Justice FITZGIBBON.—I see in your list a special prize given by Mr. Burgess and a prize given by Mr. and Mrs. Adair?—Mr. Burgess has given it for many years.

4822. He resides in the neighbourhood?—Yes, and his family taught here.

4823. He would be the class of gentleman who would appear as churchwarden undoubtedly?—No better man.

4824. Who are Mr. and Mrs. Adair?—Resident gentry, the successors of Hugh Cumming.

4825. Then you have resident gentlemen who take an interest in the place?—They take great interest in it. Mrs. Adair comes and hears a class in dictation, and carries away the marks and awards the prizes herself. Mrs. Adair is present.

4826. Rev. Dr. MOLLOY.—I think, Mr. Earl, that the principal improvements you suggest would be to put the school in connexion with the National Board to obtain the advantages of inspection, result fees, and if possible, a salary for the master?—If possible, I think so. If we have an annual inspection, we ought to have result fees.

4827. Lord Justice NAISH.—Mr. Brown, do you want to say anything to us?

Mr. *Brown.*—No, my lord, I have no observations to make; the parish priest is unfortunately absent, he was anxious to give evidence; but his curate, Father Byrne, is in attendance.

4828. Lord Justice FITZGIBBON.—We will be glad to hear anything he has to say.

Rev. Father *Byrne.*—The only thing I wish to ask Mr. Earl is this. I have been told that up to 1857 there were a good many Catholic children attending the school, but that since that time Catholic children have not been attending. I would ask what was the reason of that?

Mr. *Earl.*—I was only appointed in 1865.

4829. Lord Justice NAISH.—When was the Catholic school established at Rathvilly?

Rev. Father *Byrne.*—In 1861.

4830. Lord Justice NAISH.—(To Mr. Earl)—Do you know anything of the falling off of the attendance of Catholic children from 1859?—I do not.

4831. Lord Justice FITZGIBBON.—It was reported in 1857:—

"Our Assistant Commissioner found only twenty pupils present, seven in the boys' school and thirteen in the girls, the numbers on the roll being seventeen and fifteen respectively. This attendance contrasts strongly with that shown in the return to Parliament in 1851, when the number was [illegible], and with the returns of several subsequent years when it was nearly as large. With regard to the course of instruction which is very elementary, the boys, in general, proved backward, but the answering of the girls was more satisfactory. It is to be observed that the schools are gratuitously supplied with books by the Church Education Society, and are at present under its inspection. There is nothing in the terms of the will to make these schools exclusive; yet we find that the pupils, with the exception of one Roman Catholic in the boys' school, are members of the United Church. We think that the placing of non-exclusive schools under the inspection of an exclusive society is an objectionable proceeding on the part of the Commissioners."

It is quite plain that since the National School was established under Roman Catholic management, the Roman Catholic people have attended their own school.

Rev. Father *Byrne*.—Up to 1852 I heard that there were a number of Catholic children attending here.

4832. Dr. TRAILL.—Do you want them to come back, Father Byrne?

Rev. Father *Byrne*.—No; I want to know why they fell off.

4833. Lord Justice NAISH.—Did you hear any special cause assigned?

Rev. Father *Byrne*.—I did not.

4834. Dr. TRAILL.—Do the authorities of your Church allow the children to come to a Protestant school?

Rev. Father *Byrne*.—Not if they had schools of their own; but for a higher class of education, and if the children were secure, they might come.

4835. Mr. *Dease*.—Is it your idea that the establishment of a classical school here would be a benefit?

Rev. Father *Byrne*.—Yes, that is my idea.

4836. Rev. Dr. MOLLOY.—The last report was in 1860, and in that year the attendance was forty-one, of whom thirty-seven were Protestant Episcopalians, one was a Presbyterian, and there were three others, but no Roman Catholics.

Rev. Father *Byrne*.—There have been no Roman Catholics here since 1852, except one. I don't know whether you wish to hear evidence as to the National School.

4837. Lord Justice FITZGIBBON.—Certainly; is it a vested or a non-vested school?

Rev. Father *Byrne*.—Non-vested.

4838. Lord Justice NAISH.—What is the average attendance.

Rev. Father *Byrne*.—Sixty-eight boys and about fifty-five girls.

4839. Lord Justice FITZGIBBON.—We were there this morning, and the schoolmaster said that there were seventy boys and fifty girls.

4840. Lord Justice NAISH.—What is the amount of the grant that you get from the National Board?

Rev. Father *Byrne*.—The Master is classed as a second of first class teacher, and has £85 a year salary.

4841. Lord Justice FITZGIBBON.—We have now heard the evidence as to this foundation, and we are all quite agreed about it. The school was placed by the founder under Protestant management. That was the leading intention of the testator. He did not desire to exclude children of any denomination, but he left it in the hands of a Protestant body to manage the school on what he called liberal and enlightened principles, as a free school—that is, as a school open to everybody—not necessarily that the pupils were to pay nothing, but that the school should be open to everyone. We are required to pay attention rather to the intentions of founders than to Decrees of Chancery or other subsequent documents. The school must be open to all denominations, and for that purpose there must be a conscience clause suitable to the circumstances of the school. The Intermediate Education conscience clause has been in force here for several years, and has worked apparently well—that is, the children are not debarred from secular instruction by declining to receive religious instruction. At the same time, religious instruction should be provided for those of their own faith to whom the governing body desire to impart it. The testator was more practical in his ideas than the Court of Chancery, for he associated the Incumbent and Churchwardens, persons resident on the spot, with the Bishop, in the government of the school. We should like to restore them, and also to see on the governing body some representative of the founder. Lord Rathdonnell is a subscriber and friend to the school, and others have been mentioned who take a practical interest in it. If we could get one or two gentlemen of the neighbourhood to join the governing body we might hope to make the school more useful than it would otherwise be. Apparently the endowment could be usefully employed in supplementing public funds by giving a better education than could otherwise be provided.

4842. Rev. Dr. MOLLOY (to the Bishop).—Perhaps your lordship would not object to our giving power to the governing body to put the school in connexion with the National Board if they should think proper?

The Bishop of *Ossory*.—I have not any personal objection to that.

4843. Lord Justice FITZGIBBON.—You could have a National school in one room, and the Board would have an Intermediate school or class in another part of the house, with power to take boarding pupils.

Mr. *Earl*.—I have had that idea for many years.

4844. Lord Justice FITZGIBBON.—We will get the copies of the will and Chancery documents, and prepare a draft scheme which will be published, and sent to every person interested; we will consider any suggestions we can get. Afterwards we will sign the scheme, and send it to the Privy Council, if it does not give satisfaction it can be objected to there. We cannot publish it before October.

The inquiry then closed.

PUBLIC SITTING—WEDNESDAY, JULY 3, 1889.

July 3, 1889.

At the Courthouse, New Ross.

Present:—The Right Hon. Lord Justice FitzGibbon, and the Right Hon. Lord Justice Naish, Judicial Commissioners; and the Rev. Gerald Molloy, D.D., D.Sc., Anthony Traill, Esq., LL.D., M.D., F.T.C.D., and Professor Dougherty, M.A., Assistant Commissioners.

The Assistant Secretary, N. D. Murphy, was in attendance.

Lord Justice FitzGibbon made an introductory statement.

NEW ROSS ENDOWED SCHOOL.

H. G. Hinson, Esq., Solicitor, appeared for the Trustees.

H. G. Hinson, Esq.

4845. Mr. *Hinson*.—We are prepared to give you every information as to Ivory's school, and the trusts of its endowment, but the trustees submit that their school comes under the exception in your Act of Parliament, and is not within your jurisdiction, being a school the endowments of which are provided exclusively for the benefit of persons of one particular religious denomination. Sir John Ivory, being at that time head of the Corporation of New Ross, was desirous to make a grant for educational purposes, and he vested the endowment in three trustees, John Giffe, William Napper, and Henry Napper, and the survivors or survivor of them, and their heirs.

4846. Lord Justice FitzGibbon.—I thought the Corporation and the Vicar were governors?

Mr. *Hinson*.—No; they only had a power of appointing the schoolmaster, and the nomination of four free boys.

4847. Lord Justice Naish.—Protestant boys?

Mr. *Hinson*.—Yes. The grant was for the purpose of establishing a free school in the town of New Ross, for ever, and it vested the endowment in the three gentlemen I have mentioned, and their heirs, for the maintenance and continuance of a free school, and for a schoolmaster for the time being, for ever. I am reading the original grant of 1713, made by Sir John Ivory, by deed. I have a copy of it from the Rolls Office. I will give it to you.

4848. Rev. Dr. Molloy.—What meaning do you attach to the words "free school"?

Mr. *Hinson*.—I think the deed puts a construction on that. The words are:—

"The schoolmaster shall be obliged yearly, without fee or reward, to teach four poor scholars recommended to him by the Sovereign, the Recorder, and the Vicar, or the major part of them, provided the said scholars shall be of the Protestant religion, as by law established."

Sir John Ivory was a Protestant, and the trustees were Protestants. The school was conducted in that manner without dispute up to 1837. From time to time very respectable gentlemen were appointed as schoolmasters. The Rev. Mr. Banks and the father of the late Dr. O'Brien, Bishop of Ferns, were schoolmasters here in old times. In fact it was represented by very learned men. But in 1840 Mr. Henry Martin, the then schoolmaster, resigned, and Mrs. Neville was then the heiress at law of Mr. William Napper, the last surviving trustee, and it fell into her hands.

4849. Lord Justice FitzGibbon.—What "fell into her hands"? You did not tell us what the school is.

Mr. *Hinson*.—It is purely a classical school.

4850. Lord Justice FitzGibbon.—What are the premises?

Mr. *Hinson*.—There is a large amount of premises which have been very well cut under lease since the scheme framed by the Court of Chancery. The yearly rent is now £88. I have prepared a rental for you. Then there is the schoolhouse, with a residence for the master, and a small playground and garden attached. In 1864 Mrs. Neville was repairing the premises, which had got into a state of great dilapidation during the time Mr. Martin was schoolmaster, when the Town Commissioners took upon themselves the authority to appoint a schoolmaster, and appointed a man named Green, a Roman Catholic, in the very teeth of the grant. This man remained in possession for a considerable time, teaching in the school. Eventually he died suddenly. Then a representation was made to the Attorney-General, who directed an information to be filed in the Court of Chancery, and a scheme was prepared and settled by the Court of Chancery.

4851. Rev. Dr. Molloy.—What was the date of the scheme?

Mr. *Hinson*.—February 16, 1877. The school was practically in abeyance. The Town Commissioners had seized on the school and appointed Mr. Green; they would not recognise the right of appointment in Mrs. Neville and the vicar of the parish. The right of appointment of the schoolmaster was vested by the grant in the Vicar, the Sovereign, and the Recorder of the old Corporation of New Ross; but by the scheme that right of appointment is now vested in the Vicar of the parish, two trustees, and the Chairman of the Town Commissioners, subject to the approval of the Commissioners of Charitable Donations and Bequests.

4852. Lord Justice FitzGibbon.—Here it is:—

"The trustees, or the majority of them, shall have power from time to time to appoint and remove the said schoolmaster; and should the trustees not appoint, within six months after the vacancy, the Bishop of Ferns, and his successors, may appoint to the vacancy."

Mr. *Hinson*.—Following the words of the original grant you will find by the scheme that the Chairman of the Town Commissioners is excluded from having any control over the property.

4853. Lord Justice FitzGibbon:—

"All the property shall be vested in the said trustees other than the Chairman of the Town Commissioners."

Mr. *Hinson*.—As soon as this scheme was prepared the trustees went into possession; they set to work with a public subscription, and collected over £800 from Protestants, and Protestants only, not a single person belonging to any other denomination subscribed a penny. That £800 was expended on the permanent buildings. You will see the dwelling that has been erected, and how the place has been improved. The Rev. Mr. Hunt, the curate of the parish, was appointed schoolmaster. He remained for several years, and when he got a parish in the North of Ireland the present curate, Mr. Green, was appointed, and he has been schoolmaster since the year 1884. We propose to submit Mr. Green for examination, and he will be-

July 1, 1885.

R. G. Hinson, esq.

form you how the school has progressed, and you will find that since the school fell into the hands of the present trustees it has been very successfully carried on. Four Protestant boys are educated gratuitously if they can be found in the town, and then Mr. Greene charges seven guineas for the other boys attending the school. The school is open to the whole world. Any person can send his child to it, to be educated in Greek, Latin, or any other subject included in the present system of education.

4854. Lord Justice FitzGibbon.—Do I understand you to say that according to the original deed the schoolmaster was to be a Protestant?

Mr. Hinson.—No; the four poor scholars are to be "of the Protestant religion as by law established."

4855. Lord Justice FitzGibbon.—According to the scheme there are four trustees, of whom two are elected, and the two others are the Vicar of St. Mary's, and the Chairman of the Town Commissioners. The property is vested in the trustees, other than the Chairman of the Town Commissioners, but all the trustees for the time being are to collect the rents, and to see that the school is properly carried on; the decision of the majority is to bind the others; all the trustees may join in appointing the schoolmaster, and if they fail to do so the Bishop is to appoint him. The schoolmaster is to teach Greek, Latin, and such other subjects of education as may be directed by the trustees, or the majority of them; and he shall also, without fee or reward, teach four poor scholars, members of the Protestant Church of Ireland, who shall be recommended by the trustees for the time being, or the majority of them. The trustees also have the power of leasing. With reference to the question of exemption our course has been to determine that question first, and you should understand that even if the school comes within the Act, we are nevertheless bound, in settling a scheme, to have due regard to the intentions of the founder in every way.

Lord Justice Naish.—There is no qualification in the original deed of foundation, or in the Chancery scheme, providing that the fourth trustee, the old "Sovereign" and present Chairman, is to be of any particular religious denomination.

Mr. Hinson.—He may be of any religion according to the scheme; but at the time of the original grant all the parties whose names were mentioned in it were Protestants.

4856. Lord Justice FitzGibbon.—But our Act only exempts endowments that are provided exclusively for the benefit of persons of a particular religious denomination, and are also under the exclusive control of persons of the same denomination. We have had a good many cases in which trustees of other denominations have come in, and in such cases it has been our duty to put the governing body back again to its original denominational form, when the endowment is exclusive.

Mr. Hinson.—We contend that the endowment is still under the exclusive control of Protestants.

4857. Rev. Dr. Molloy.—The school is open to persons of all religious denominations?

Mr. Hinson.—We open it to all because we are very liberal.

4858. Rev. Dr. Molloy.—But in doing that you are not acting against the original trust?

Mr. Hinson.—Certainly not.

4859. Rev. Dr. Molloy.—How then can you say that the original trust was one for the exclusive benefit of a particular denomination?

Mr. Hinson.—We think it was.

4860. Dr. Traill.—It was given for one denomination, but you are very liberal and have opened it to all denominations if they choose to pay.

Mr. Hinson.—That is it.

4861. Dr. Traill.—If they do not choose to pay I don't think they should get the benefit of the endowment.

Mr. Hinson.—No, except the poor scholars.

The Rev. Francis Le Louw sworn and examined.

Rev. Francis Le Louw.

4862. Lord Justice FitzGibbon.—You are vicar of New Ross?—I am, for about seventeen years.

4863. During that time you have been an ex-officio trustee of the New Ross Endowed School?—I have.

4864. Up to the time of the Chancery scheme how was the school managed?—It was in a very bad state when I came here. Mr. Greene had been placed in it long before I came, and there was really no school—only three or four boys. According to the opinion of the Master of the Rolls, Mr. Green had been illegally appointed, and when this matter came out he was discharged. Then the scheme was settled and possession was given to the trustees under the scheme.

4865. Have they since had possession of the property?—We have.

4866. Who is now the Chairman of the Town Commissioners?—Mr. Patrick Tierney.

4867. Who are the two co-opted trustees?—Colonel Tottenham and Mr. Neville.

4868. There has been no vacancy since the date of the scheme?—There has not.

4869. Is the Chairman of the Town Commissioners changed annually?—I believe so. There have been frequent changes.

4870. Have the trustees any fixed times of meeting?—We have not; but whenever it is necessary to appoint here we give notice.

4871. Has the Chairman of the Town Commissioners at any time acted under the scheme?—Never.

4872. Is the management substantially in the hands of the other three?—Entirely.

4873. What was done with the school premises?—They were in a very bad state—they could not have been much worse. We collected money, and rebuilt the house, and put it into a fair condition; but a good deal might still be done. We have no funds; still it is in a very good condition and the school is carried on.

4874. What amount did you collect?—I don't remember the exact amount—about £600 I think.

4875. How was it laid out?—In rebuilding the house.

4876. What did you do as regards letting the property?—We made leases to different parties and improved the income very much.

4877. Do you manage it yourselves personally, or have you an agent?—An agent—Mr. Hinson.

Mr. Hinson.—The rents are all paid up to last September.

4878. Lord Justice FitzGibbon.—But we should like to see last year's accounts.

Witness.—I have copies of them—they are audited.

4879. Lord Justice FitzGibbon.—Who audits them?—Well, we ourselves. Colonel Tottenham is very accurate about auditing. He always comes down.

4880. Your yearly rental amounts to £35?—Yes.

4881. Of that £25 is under a lease for 250 years of August 22, 1884, with a covenant to spend £1,000 within six years?—Yes.

4882. Has there been any expenditure on these premises yet?—There has not.

4883. The term is running out; do you expect that the tenant will carry out the covenant?—I am afraid not. There is a very great change in circumstances since 1881.

4884. What are the premises likely to fetch if the expenditure be not made on them?—Well, I could not say. The lessee was willing to take them and to build stores. We had other offers at the time, and this was the best.

4885. I suppose the lease contains a clause of re-future if the expenditure be not made at the end of six years?—It does.

4886. Lord Justice Naish.—If those premises were taken up now as they stand, would you get £25 a year for them?—It is very hard to say. We expect that we should.

4887. Lord Justice FitzGibbon.—There was no schoolmaster when the trustees came into possession?—None.

4888. Who was their first schoolmaster?—Mr. Hunt. He was a very excellent schoolmaster—a clever man, and very distinguished in natural science especially.

4889. Was he a graduate of any University?—Yes, of Trinity College, Dublin.

4890. He was also curate of the parish?—Yes.

4891. What arrangements had you with him as to his emoluments as schoolmaster?—At that time we were obliged to keep the rents to pay off a portion of the money due for repairs, and I don't think he got anything. But now, I am happy to say, we have paid them off and the present schoolmaster gets the entire, except about £10 a year retained for repairs.

4892. Then, subject to the deductions for repairs, the schoolmaster now gets the proceeds of the endowment? He does.

4893. And also occupies the school buildings?—He does; he lives in the school.

4894. What was the number of scholars when Mr. Hunt opened?—I could not say exactly. The numbers were about twenty more than there are now. There are not a great many to come.

4895. Do you continue to nominate four free scholars?—We do.

4896. How are they selected?—We exercise our judgment as to whether they are objects of it in the way of poverty—that is, as to the means of their parents—and likely to benefit by the education.

4897. Dr. Traill.—And are they children of poor parents?—Of parents in poor circumstances. We advertise that a vacancy is to be filled up. The parents send in applications. We consider those applications; and if we consider the candidates eligible they go through an examination, and those who answer best are elected.

4898. Lord Justice FitzGibbon.—Then you don't make the appointments without public notice?—No.

4899. Rev. Dr. Molloy.—Are there generally more candidates than vacancies?—There have been, generally.

4900. It is entirely a day school?—At present it is.

4901. Then the only available candidates are from the town and immediate neighbourhood of New Ross?—I think we are limited to the neighbourhood of New Ross.

4902. Lord Justice Naish.—They are not limited to the neighbourhood.

Lord Justice FitzGibbon.—As long as there are eligible candidates from the neighbourhood they would get a preference.

Witness.—It was extended to Old Ross. We appointed some from Old Ross, which is five or six miles off.

4903. Lord Justice Naish.—Are you satisfied with the way in which the school is working at present?—I am quite satisfied. I think we are all satisfied.

4904. Rev. Dr. Molloy.—Do you think the Chancery scheme gives you all the powers that you desire to have?—I do. The decree of the court declared the appointment of Patrick Green to the office of schoolmaster to be illegal and void.

4905. Lord Justice FitzGibbon.—I suppose there was a good deal of expense in connection with these Chancery proceedings?

Mr. *Hinson*.—Mr. Lane Joynt took £125.

Witness.—The costs of suit were paid out of accumulated rents, and £60 were received for stones quarried from the premises by one of the town commissioners.

Mr. *Hinson*.—Only for that we should never have tided over the difficulty.

Witness.—It exhausted everything we had.

July 5, 1888.

Rev. Francis Le Bas.

The Rev. *Godfrey G. Greene*, Head Master, sworn and examined.

Rev. Godfrey G. Greene.

4906. Lord Justice FitzGibbon.—How long have you held the office of Master of New Ross Endowed School?—Since January, 1884.

4907. Under what terms were you appointed?—I was appointed by the Bishop under a writing.

Mr. *Hinson*.—The time had lapsed. The circumstances were peculiar, and the Bishop made the appointment.

4908. Lord Justice FitzGibbon.—What are your emoluments?—I have the house free. At the time I was appointed I understood that there was a debt standing against the endowment, for improvements and repairs, which had to be paid off, and when that debt was paid off I was to get the balance of the money coming from the endowment after any expenses incurred by the trustees.

4909. Do you understand your rights to be still subject to the payment to the trustees of the necessary expenses of maintaining the place?—Yes.

4910. How many pupils were there when you came?—I opened the school with six.

4911. How many have you now?—I have ten at present. At one time I had as many as fourteen.

4912. What are the terms on which they are received?—There are four free boys according to the endowment; and for the others I have a scale of charges the same as that drawn up by my predecessor.

Lord Justice FitzGibbon.—

"For boys under ten—seven guineas for a general English and commercial education. Senior boys—English, classics, and commercial education, £7 10s.; classical education—nine guineas. Extras—Modern Languages and Drawing."

4913. Dr. Traill.—Then all your boys are day boys?—All are day boys.

4914. Lord Justice FitzGibbon.—You are yourself a graduate of Trinity College?—Yes.

4915. Do you teach classics—Latin and Greek—in accordance with the will?—Yes.

4916. What inspection of the school is there?—No inspection.

4917. Do the trustees at any time visit the school?—I don't think they do.

4918. There is no official visiting.

Rev. Mr. *Le Bas*.—No.

4919. Then practically, it is in your own hands?—In my own hands.

4920. Are all your day pupils from New Ross and its neighbourhood?—They are.

4921. Have you ever had any boarders?—No.

4922. Is there any room for boarders in the premises?—I suppose I could take a very few boarders.

4923. You never thought of doing that?—Never.

4924. Dr. Traill.—Are you married?—I am.

4925. Rev. Dr. Molloy.—What are the religious denominations of your pupils?—At present, all members of the Church of Ireland.

4926. Have they been always so since you became master?—To the best of my belief they have.

4927. Lord Justice FitzGibbon.—Have you sent any boys up to the Intermediate Examination?—The first year I was in the school I sent in three boys, one of whom passed with honours, and the other two did not pass. This is not a centre, and I found that the expense of sending boys to Waterford was too heavy on the parents, except in the case of an exemp-

July 5, 1886.

H. G. Hinson, Esq.

form you how the school has progressed, and you will find that since the school fell into the hands of the present trustees it has been very successfully carried on. Four Protestant boys are educated gratuitously if they can be found in the town, and then Mr. Green charges seven guineas for the other boys attending the school. The school is open to the whole world. Any parent can send his child to it, to be educated in Greek, Latin, or any other subject included in the present system of education.

4654. Lord Justice FitzGibbon.—Do I understand you to say that according to the original deed the schoolmaster was to be a Protestant?

Mr. Hinson.—No; the four poor scholars are to be "of the Protestant religion as by law established."

4655. Lord Justice FitzGibbon.—According to the scheme there are four trustees, of whom two are elected, and the two others are the Vicar of St. Mary's, and the Chairman of the Town Commissioners. The property is vested in the trustees, other than the Chairman of the Town Commissioners, but all the trustees for the time being are to collect the rents, and to see that the school is properly carried on; the decision of the majority is to bind the others; all the trustees may join in appointing the schoolmaster, and if they fail to do so the Bishop is to appoint him. The schoolmaster is to teach Greek, Latin, and such other subjects of education as may be directed by the trustees, or the majority of them; and he shall also, without fee or reward, teach four poor scholars, members of the Protestant Church of Ireland, who shall be recommended by the trustees for the time being, or the majority of them. The trustees also have the power of leasing. With reference to the question of exemption our course has been to determine that question first, and you should understand that even if the school comes within the Act, we are nevertheless bound, in settling a scheme, to have due regard to the intentions of the founder in every case.

Lord Justice Naish.—There is no qualification in the original deed of foundation, or in the Chancery scheme, providing that the fourth trustee, the old "Sovereign," and present Chairman, is to be of any particular religious denomination.

Mr. Hinson.—He may be of any religion according to the scheme; but at the time of the original grant all the parties whose names were mentioned in it were Protestants.

4656. Lord Justice FitzGibbon.—But our Act only exempts endowments that are provided exclusively for the benefit of persons of a particular religious denomination, and are also under the exclusive control of persons of the same denomination. We have had a good many cases in which trustees of other denominations have come in, and in such cases it has been our duty to put the governing body back again to its original denominational form, when the endowment is exclusive.

Mr. Hinson.—We contend that the endowment is still under the exclusive control of Protestants.

4657. Rev. Dr. Molloy.—The school is open to persons of all religious denominations?

Mr. Hinson.—We open it to all because we are very liberal.

4658. Rev. Dr. Molloy.—But in doing that you are not acting against the original trust?

Mr. Hinson.—Certainly not.

4659. Rev. Dr. Molloy.—How then can you say that the original trust was one for the exclusive benefit of a particular denomination?

Mr. Hinson.—We think it was.

4660. Dr. Traill.—It was given for one denomination, but you are very liberal and have opened it to all denominations if they choose to pay.

Mr. Hinson.—That is it.

4661. Dr. Traill.—If they do not choose to pay I don't think they should get the benefit of the endowment.

Mr. Hinson.—No, except the poor scholars.

The Rev. Francis Le Hunte sworn and examined.

Rev. Francis Le Hunte.

4662. Lord Justice FitzGibbon.—You are vicar of New Ross?—I am, for about seventeen years.

4663. During that time you have been an ex-officio trustee of the New Ross Endowed School?—I have.

4664. Up to the time of the Chancery Scheme how was the school managed?—It was in a very bad state when I came here. Mr. Green had been placed in it long before I came, and there was really no school—only three or four boys. According to the opinion of the Master of the Rolls, Mr. Green had been illegally appointed, and when this matter came out he discovered. Then the scheme was settled and possession was given to the trustees under the scheme.

4665. Have they since had possession of the property?—We have.

4666. Who is now the Chairman of the Town Commissioners?—Mr. Patrick Tierney.

4667. Who are the two co-opted trustees?—Colonel Tottenham and Mr. Neville.

4668. There has been no vacancy since the date of the scheme?—There has not.

4669. Is the Chairman of the Town Commissioners changed annually?—I believe so. There have been frequent changes.

4670. Have the trustees any fixed times of meeting?—We have not; but whenever it is necessary to appoint boys we give notice.

4671. Has the Chairman of the Town Commissioners at any time acted under the scheme?—Never.

4672. Is the management substantially in the hands of the other three?—Entirely.

4673. What was done with the school premises?—They were in a very bad state—they could not have been much worse. We collected money, and rebuilt the house, and put it into a fair condition; but a good deal might still be done. We have not funds; still it is in a very good condition and the school is carried on.

4674. What amount did you collect?—I don't remember the exact amount—about £200 I think.

4675. How was it laid out?—In rebuilding the house.

4676. What did you do as regards leasing the property?—We made leases to different parties and improved the income very much.

4677. Do you manage it yourselves personally, or have you an agent?—An agent—Mr. Hinson.

Mr. Hinson.—The rents are all paid up to last September.

4678. Lord Justice FitzGibbon.—But we should like to see last year's accounts.

Witness.—I have copies of them—they are audited.

4679. Lord Justice FitzGibbon.—Who audits them?—Well, we ourselves. Colonel Tottenham is very accurate about auditing. He always comes down.

4680. Your yearly rental amounts to £351?—Yes.

4681. Of that £50 is under a lease for 200 years of August 23, 1884, with a covenant to spend £1,000 within six years?—Yes.

4682. Has there been any expenditure on those premises yet?—There has not.

4683. The term is running out; do you expect that the tenant will carry out the covenant?—I am afraid not. There is a very great change in circumstances since 1884.

4684. What are the premises likely to fetch if the expenditure be not made on them?—Well, I could not say. The lessee was willing to take them and to build stores. We had other offers at the time, and this was the best.

4685. I suppose the lease contains a clause of re-

July 1, 1885.

Rev. Francis Le Hunte.

lieu of the expenditure be not made at the end of the year?—It does.

4886. Lord Justice Naish.—If these premises were taken up now as they stand, would you get £35 a year for them?—It is very hard to say. We expect that we should.

4887. Lord Justice FitzGibbon.—There was no schoolmaster when the trustees came into possession?—None.

4888. Who was their first schoolmaster?—Mr. Bent. He was a very excellent schoolmaster—a clever man, and very distinguished in natural science especially.

4889. Was he a graduate of any University?—Yes, of Trinity College, Dublin.

4890. He was also curate of the parish?—Yes.

4891. What arrangements had you with him as to his emoluments as schoolmaster?—At that time we were obliged to keep the rents to pay off a portion of the money due for repairs, and I don't think he got anything. But now, I am happy to say, we have paid them off and the present schoolmaster gets the entire, except about £10 a year retained for repairs.

4892. Then, subject to the deductions for repairs, the schoolmaster now gets the proceeds of the endowment?—He does.

4893. And also occupies the school buildings?—He does; he lives in the school.

4894. What was the number of scholars when Mr. Bent opened?—I could not say exactly. The numbers were about twenty more than there are now. There are not a great many to come.

4895. Do you continue to nominate four free scholars?—We do.

4896. How are they selected?—We exercise our judgment as to whether they are objects of it in the way of poverty—that is, as to the means of their parents—and likely to benefit by the education.

4897. Dr. Traill.—And are they children of poor persons?—Of parents in poor circumstances. We advertise that a vacancy is to be filled up. The parents send in applications. We consider these applications; and if we consider the candidates eligible they go through an examination, and those who answer best are elected.

4898. Lord Justice FitzGibbon.—Then you don't make the appointments without public notice?—No.

4899. Rev. Dr. Molloy.—Are there generally more candidates than vacancies?—There have been, generally.

4900. Is it entirely a day school?—At present it is.

4901. Then the only available candidates are from the town and immediate neighbourhood of New Ross?—I think we are limited to the neighbourhood of New Ross.

4902. Lord Justice Naish.—They are not limited to the neighbourhood.

Lord Justice FitzGibbon.—As long as there are eligible candidates from the neighbourhood they would get a preference.

Witness.—It was extended to Old Ross. We appointed some from Old Ross, which is five or six miles off.

4903. Lord Justice Naish.—Are you satisfied with the way in which the school is working at present?—I am quite satisfied. I think we are all satisfied.

4904. Rev. Dr. Molloy.—Do you think the Chancery scheme gives you all the powers that you desire to have?—I do. The decree of the court declared the appointment of Patrick Green to the office of schoolmaster to be illegal and void.

4905. Lord Justice FitzGibbon.—I suppose there was a good deal of expense in connection with those Chancery proceedings?

Mr. Hanna.—Mr. Lane Joynt took £125.

Witness.—The costs of suit were paid out of accumulated rents, and £48 were received for stones quarried from the premises by one of the town commissioners.

Mr. Hanna.—Only for that we should never have tided over the difficulty.

Witness.—It exhausted everything we had.

The Rev. *Godfrey G. Greene*, Head Master, sworn and examined.

Rev. Godfrey G. Greene.

4906. Lord Justice FitzGibbon.—How long have you held the office of Master of New Ross Endowed School?—Since January, 1884.

4907. Under what terms were you appointed?—I was appointed by the Bishop under a writing.

Mr. Hanna.—The time had lapsed. The circumstances were peculiar, and the Bishop made the appointment.

4908. Lord Justice FitzGibbon.—What are your emoluments?—I have the house free. At the time I was appointed I understood that there was a debt standing against the endowment, for improvements and repairs, which had to be paid off; and when that debt was paid off I was to get the balance of the money coming from the endowment after any expenses incurred by the trustees.

4909. Do you understand your rights to be still subject to the payment to the trustees of the necessary expenses of maintaining the place?—Yes.

4910. How many pupils were there when you came?—I opened the school with six.

4911. How many have you now?—I have ten at present. At one time I had as many as fourteen.

4912. What are the terms on which they are received?—There are four free boys according to the endowment; and for the others I have a scale of charges the same as that drawn up by my predecessors.

Lord Justice FitzGibbon.—

"For boys under ten—seven guineas for a general English and commercial education. Senior boys—English, tuition, and commercial education, £7 15s.; classical education—nine guineas. Extras—Modern Languages and Drawing."

4913. Dr. Traill.—Then all your boys are day boys?—All are day boys.

4914. Lord Justice FitzGibbon.—You are yourself a graduate of Trinity College?—Yes.

4915. Do you teach classics—Latin and Greek—in accordance with the will?—Yes.

4916. What inspection of the school is there?—No inspection.

4917. Do the trustees at any time visit the school?—I don't think they do.

4918. There is no school visiting.

Rev. Mr. Le Hunte.—No.

4919. Then, practically, it is in your own hands?—In my own hands.

4920. Are all your day pupils from New Ross and its neighbourhood?—They are.

4921. Have you ever had any boarders?—No.

4922. Is there any room for boarders in the premises?—I suppose I could take a very few boarders.

4923. You never thought of doing that?—Never.

4924. Dr. Traill.—Are you married?—I am.

4925. Rev. Dr. Molloy.—What are the religious denominations of your pupils?—At present, all members of the Church of Ireland.

4926. Have they been always so since you became master?—To the best of my belief they have.

4927. Lord Justice FitzGibbon.—Have you sent any boys up to the Intermediate Examinations?—The first year I was in the school I sent in three boys, one of whom passed with honours, and the other two did not pass. This is not a county, and I found that the expense of sending boys to Wexford was too heavy on the parents, except in the case of an excep-

July 1, 1886.

Rev. Godfrey G. Owen.

tionally clever boy. So I did not send any boys again to the Intermediate Examinations until last year, when I sent in a boy who passed in six subjects, and got honours in three in the Junior Grade. I sent up two this year.

4928. Is there no centre nearer than Waterford or Kilkenny?—No.

4929. Is there any Roman Catholic Intermediate school in New Ross or its neighbourhood?—No. I wrote to the Superior of the Christian Brothers—Brother Synnott, who is since dead—of New Ross, but he said that their staff was not sufficient to have a special class for the Intermediate Examinations.

4930. Then they don't send boys to the Intermediate Examinations?—Not as a rule. They may send one or two to other centres.

4931. Dr. Traill.—Then there are not enough boys for a centre here?—Not enough.

4932. Lord Justice FitzGibbon.—You are aware that different denominations can join for the purpose of making up the number required for a centre?—Yes. I was very anxious to have got New Ross as a centre. I could send in five or six every year but for the expense of sending them away.

4933. Rev. Dr. Molloy.—Supposing there were a centre at New Ross, how many do you think would be available?—I cannot say how many would come from the Christian Brothers. I believe they have got a very large school there. For my part I would send in five or six each year.

4934. The number required for a centre is thirty-five?—I think it was thirty, and that two years ago they raised it to forty.

4935. The number at present attending your school is considerably less than the number that used to attend it in former times?—Yes.

4936. Can you account for the number not being greater than it is?—I don't think there are so many Protestants in the neighbourhood.

4937. Dr. Traill.—What accommodation have you?—The school-room would hold over forty boys comfortably.

4938. Lord Justice FitzGibbon.—The report of 1879 states that the school had been closed since 1875. At that time the new scheme was coming into force. Formerly there had been fourteen pupils of whom two were boarders; so that—without boarders—you have practically the same number now?—I had fourteen at one time.

4939. The school seems always to have been very small?—Except in old times. I believe about thirty years ago there was a very good boarding school at one time. The house was a great deal larger than the present one; part of it was pulled down.

4940. Rev. Dr. Molloy.—What is the character of the education that you give?—One of my boys passed for the Bank of Ireland, and I sent two to Trinity College last year, one of whom obtained a high place at the October entrance, and first honours in mathematics.

4941. Then you give an education which is intermediate between that of a primary school, and that which is preparatory for the Universities?—Yes.

4942. You don't give any elementary teaching?—Yes, some boys are in that class.

4943. Have the boys who come to you generally received an elementary education in some other school?—They have.

4944. What school do they come from?—The parochial school. The free boys generally come from the parochial school, which is one of the schools that you are to inquire into.

4945. Lord Justice FitzGibbon.—What elementary schools are there under Protestant management within reach of New Ross?—The parochial school of New Ross; and a parochial school at Old Ross, about five miles distant.

Rev. Mr. Le Hunte.—The present number in attendance at the parochial school is thirty-three, and there are sixty-two on the roll—boys and girls.

4946. Dr. Traill.—Have you had any other Protestant boys at the school, besides members of the Church of Ireland?—To the best of my belief I have not.

4947. You consider yourself quite free to take them if they pay the fees?—Yes.

4948. Do you consider the endowment applicable to them, over and above what you are bound to do for the others?—The endowment is not applicable to them in any way further than the use of the school-room.

4949. Did you understand by a "free" school an open school, or a school to give free education to certain boys?—A school to give free education to certain boys and to charge for any others.

4950. Lord Justice FitzGibbon.—That is not the legal meaning of it here. In the old deed the provision is for the maintenance and continuance of a free school and of a schoolmaster for all time, with another provision that the schoolmaster is to teach four poor scholars without fee or reward. You could not shut up the school and teach only those four poor scholars.

4951. Rev. Dr. Molloy.—You have sent some pupils to the Intermediate Examinations?—Yes.

4952. Did you sign any paper in connexion with those examinations?—No. This was the first year that I expected to be entitled to results fees. On the 1st of October I sent up a copy of the school roll.

4953. The Intermediate Education Board require a paper to be signed before they pay results fees?—That paper I never got.

4954. Then you got no results fees?—No results fees.

4955. Professor Dougherty.—You must have a conscience clause in operation, otherwise you would not be able to sign the paper?—I don't know what it is. I have never seen it.

Lord Justice FitzGibbon.—It is that no boy is excluded from the advantages of secular education by reason of declining to receive religious education.

4956. Dr. Traill.—You would not have any objection to sign that?—None whatever. There is religious education in the school from half-past nine o'clock until ten; and then the work of the school begins, and there is no religious education after that.

4957. Rev. Dr. Molloy.—Do you think that your school is attended by all the Protestant boys of the neighbourhood who require that kind of education?—No; some of the boys of the neighbourhood have been sent to schools in England.

4958. Dr. Traill.—Do you mean boys of the better class?—Yes; they have been sent to boarding schools.

4959. Professor Dougherty.—Have you any Protestants in New Ross who do not belong to your Church?—The Church population is about four hundred.

4960. Is there any considerable population of other denominations?—Not a considerable number; there are a few Methodists.

4961. Are there any boys belonging to the Methodists who might avail themselves of the education given in your school?—No; they are not at present availing themselves of it.

4962. Dr. Traill.—Is there any Presbyterian minister here?—No.

4963. Is there a Methodist minister here?—Yes.

4964. Rev. Dr. Molloy.—From what class do your pupils come?—Gentry, shopkeepers, respectable farmers.

4965. Would there not be among a population of four hundred—which would represent about eighty families—a larger number of boys anxious to obtain a superior education than is represented by the number of pupils you have?—I cannot say.

4966. Lord Justice FitzGibbon.—We cannot hold this school exempt from the Act, because the endowment and control are vested in the four trustees; and I presume that the Chairman of the Town Commissioners may be of any religious denomination, and probably is a Roman Catholic.

Mr. Hinson.—For a long time.

July 8, 1889.

Rev. Galfrey G. Greene.

4967. Lord Justice FitzGibbon.—Therefore the question arises whether we should undertake the settlement of a scheme. We are not bound to settle a scheme for every institution that comes under our Act; but whenever we do settle a scheme we must have regard to the intentions of the founder, and carry out the trusts of the endowment, as originally intended, as nearly as we can. We are quite satisfied that the school was founded by a Protestant, that it was placed under what was then exclusively Protestant management, as is evident not only from the denomination of the four free boys, but from the gift of the appointment of schoolmaster to the bishop whenever the trustees failed to appoint; also from the fact that the vicar of the parish is one of the trustees. At the time the deed was executed all the other trustees were required to be members of the then Established Church as corporate officers. Therefore in any scheme for this endowment regard should be had to these facts, and was had by the Master of the Rolls in the settlement of the present scheme, by which he placed the management of the school in the hands of a body of which three at least, in all probability, would remain members of the same denomination, and by which he preserved the right of nominating the schoolmaster in case of lapse to the bishop. We can incorporate the governing body, which the Court of Chancery has no jurisdiction to do. There is thus a saving of expense, and also of the risk of the property becoming vested legally in the last survivor of a body of trustees, or in his representative, or heir-at-law, whom it might be hard to find, in which case the only resource is to Chancery. There are some things in which improvements might be made. For example, it ought to be the duty of the trustees to inspect the school. Our scheme would provide for an inspection by the governing body and by an Inspector appointed by the Lord Lieutenant. Up to the present no such Inspector has been appointed; but once a year he should see that the provisions of the scheme were being carried out. He would not have any power of meddling with the school so long as its provisions were observed the scheme would have the force of an Act of Parliament. As regards the property, the powers of leasing contained in the existing scheme are limited; and it might be advantageous that sales should take place, or that unencumbered dealings should be possible. These powers we can give; but in the case of a small endowment like this, we should place them under the check of approval by the Commissioners of Charitable Donations and Bequests. The only remaining matter is the constitution of the governing body. As now constituted it includes the Chairman of the Town Commissioners, who represents the inhabitants. We could provide that he should nominate some Protestant to represent him, if he himself did not belong to that denomination. We could also institute a franchise for subscribers to the funds, who would represent any real interest taken by the inhabitants in the school. We have in some instances given a franchise to the parents of children who paid a certain amount of school-fees, or to past pupils who were supporters of it. The school is at present prosperous so far as your means allow, and though the number of scholars is small, it is important for the Protestant people of New Ross that the school should be a good one; the trustees should consider whether any of these matters to which I have called your attention would be worth the alteration of the Chancery scheme. In expense, our schemes contrast favourably with Chancery schemes, for they have varied in cost from £1 to a maximum of under £5. The only other expense is that of audit. Every endowment under a scheme framed by us must have its accounts annually audited by the Local Government Board, or by an authority approved by them. We are very glad to say that they have made arrangements by which the expense of their audit is extremely small; in such cases as this only about £1. We should think that money well spent. We must declare that the school is not exempt. We shall reserve the consideration of the question of the settlement of a scheme. Our secretary can furnish precedents for institutions like this, and you can communicate with him. We would not publish a scheme in this case without communicating with you, and your wishes will receive every attention from us.

4968. Mr. Neville.—May I mention, as one of the trustees, that though we have never had a regular inspection, there has always been a half-yearly inspection by some clergyman of the neighbourhood, and prizes have been distributed to the boys. My son has been attending the school every day, so that I know how the work is going on. I am constantly in the school; there is hardly a week that I don't go through the school-room.

4969. Lord Justice FitzGibbon.—We are quite satisfied that the school is well managed now, but generally it is well to have your rules in black and white. There might not always be as good trustees as there are now. As a rule, we don't like to have governors less than seven persons for a school of this kind. We have in many cases incorporated five, and allowed them to co-opt two more from the locality—persons of experience in education, an Inspector of National schools, or anybody that they thought would be useful.

Mr. James Colfer.

4970. The Very Rev. Dr. Kavanagh, the parish priest, asked me to state here to the Commissioners the desire that he and the other clergy of his parish entertain that there should be, if possible, a lay master of this school, instead of a clerical master, as under the present system. I should feel a considerable difficulty in putting forward any claim, for the premises have been restored, and a considerable sum of money expended which consists of subscriptions exclusively of Protestants. But the Rev. Mr. Kavanagh suggested that he and his flock did not desire that there should be any change made in the religion of the master, but merely that the master should not be a clergyman.

4971. Dr. Traill.—Does he mean that he would advise the children of his own flock to go to the school if the master were a layman?

Mr. Colfer.—Certainly, if the master were a layman. Of my own knowledge I can say that there is a considerable number of Catholic children of people of the better class who would be very likely to avail themselves of the school in such a case.

4972. Dr. Traill.—Is there no intermediate school in New Ross?

Mr. James Colfer.

Mr. Colfer.—There is not; none except the Christian Brothers school and the National school. There is no classical school whatever. I think a great many Catholics would avail themselves of the school if something of the kind were done.

4973. Lord Justice FitzGibbon.—As you candidly and fairly admit, the foundation is a Protestant one; therefore, it rests very much in the discretion of the governing body whether they will appoint a clergyman or not. The endowment is very small; the number of Protestant pupils is very small; and it possibly has never occurred to them that they could increase the number by such a course as you propose. The salary is more or less, as we understand, a supplementing of the curacy, and we could hardly prohibit them from appointing a clergyman.

Mr. Colfer.—There is no desire to press it so far as prohibition; but if anything could be done to facilitate the education of Catholics in the town it would be a very great advantage, and I have no doubt that at present a considerable number of people would pay a fairly good sum for the education.

4974. Rev. Dr. Molloy.—The number of pupils would be considerably increased?

Mr. Calder.—I think a considerable number would go to the school.

4975. Dr. Traill.—Is it the custom of the Roman Catholic Church to appoint laymen to be teachers in their schools?

Mr. Calder.—Generally religious bodies teach in them, such as the Jesuits and others, and I think the teachers are generally clerics in those schools intended exclusively for Roman Catholics. I believe that the terms of this trust do not in any way exclude Catholic children from going to the school. The only thing is, that there must be four children free pupils, who are limited to Protestant children.

4976. Rev. Dr. Molloy.—It would seem to be rather a matter for consideration for the governors whether they would improve the school by making such an appointment; but I don't think we could provide for it in a scheme.

Mr. Calder.—I don't say that you could. I have only brought it forward.

4977. Dr. Traill.—At Youghal we found that Canon Keller would not hear of such a thing as a layman for a schoolmaster.

Mr. Calder.—Well, this difference of views is somewhat healthy, surely.

4978. Lord Justice FitzGibbon.—Circumstances alter cases. In Elphin we found a school where the Protestant curate was master, and a considerable number of Roman Catholic pupils were attending there, because they had no school of their own. We would all like schools of our own.

Rev. Mr. Greene.—I will receive any number of pupils that they like to send to me, and I promise that their religious principles won't be interfered with during school hours. The religious instruction is given from half-past nine o'clock until ten in the morning, and there is none after that.

4979. Lord Justice Naish.—Mr. Calder, you have done quite right in presenting these views.

Mr. Hanna.—If Dr. Kavanagh agrees to send ten scholars in addition to the present number I think we might meet his views.

4980. Lord Justice FitzGibbon.—It would be a matter for the trustees to consider if they saw that there would be more pupils.

Mr. Hanna.—Perhaps he would be able to give them a guarantee.

Lord Justice FitzGibbon.—It is altogether a matter for the trustees. We would frame such a board of trustees as would give a somewhat larger representation of the people of the immediate neighbourhood, and they might think a lay teacher would be better for the school.

BALLYANNE SCHOOL (BOLGER'S ENDOWMENT).

4981. Lord Justice FitzGibbon.—The Parish Priest of Ballyanne ought to receive £18 9s. 1d. granted under the will of Mr. Houghton Bolger, as an annual rentcharge for the Ballyanne National School. Our duty is to see whether he gets it or not. There were seventy-nine Roman Catholic boys, eighty-nine girls, and one Church Protestant at the school in 1880. As no one appears we may take it that they do not want any help from us.

HILL SCHOOL (TOTTENHAM'S ENDOWMENT).

4982. Rev. Mr. Le Hunte.—I am manager of this school.

Mr. Boyd, Solicitor.—I represent Colonel Tottenham.

4983. Lord Justice FitzGibbon.—Mr. Tottenham granted a site in 1790, and Mrs. Paul granted an annuity of £3 Irish for the school. Is that still paid.

Rev. Mr. Le Hunte.—It is.

4984. What are your relations to the school?—I have the management of it.

4985. What is the nature of the foundation?—I cannot make out.

4986. Where is the school?—It is in the town.

4987. Lord Justice FitzGibbon.—Is it in connection with the National Board or the Church Education Society?

Rev. Mr. Le Hunte.—The Church Education Society.

4988. What number of pupils has it?—An average attendance of thirty-three boys and girls.

4989. Rev. Dr. Molloy.—It is called a "parochial" school?—It is. There are forty-two children on the roll.

4990. Lord Justice FitzGibbon.—There are some apprentice fees for the pupils under Mrs. Paul's will; do you get them?

Rev. Mr. Le Hunte.—We do.

4991. Lord Justice FitzGibbon.—Under our Act apprentice fees which have become useless from the smallness of the amounts or other circumstances, may be turned to other educational purposes.

Mr. William Gibb sworn and examined.

4992. Lord Justice FitzGibbon.—You are the Master of the Hill School?—Yes.

4993. It is a mixed school for boys and girls?—Yes, it is, at present.

4994. What assistance had you in teaching?—My wife assists. The elder girls come to me. The number of boys is at present small.

4995. How long have you been master?—I commenced teaching on January 10, 1876.

4996. What number of pupils had you when you came first?—I see by the roll that the previous master closed with twelve or fourteen. I opened with sixteen or eighteen.

4997. How many have you had since?—The school improved considerably for many years. I have had about forty-one or forty-two pupils in some years, and an average in some years of about thirty-three boys.

4998. Besides that was there an equal number of girls?—About the same number.

4999. In 1879 there were thirty boys on the roll and thirty-two girls, with an average attendance of twenty-two and twenty of each?—Yes.

5000. How many are at present in attendance?—Only thirteen boys and twenty-nine girls.

5001. What do you attribute the large falling off of the boys to?—Two causes operated very much in the falling off. At one time there was no endowed school open here; and there was a large factory which employed a number of English skilled workmen who had large families. These children were invariably Protestants, and they attended my school. The factory was closed some years ago, and those families returned to England.

5002. You seem to have as many girls as ever?—That may be accounted for by the fact that the girls come now at a younger age than they did.

5003. Rev. Dr. Molloy.—In the usual population there is not such a preponderance of girls over boys?—I find that the Protestant families of New Ross have at least three girls to one boy.

5004. Lord Justice FitzGibbon.—Perhaps the average will be pulled up at a later period?—Some of the boys go to Mr. Greene's school, but the girls don't go there.

5005. What was your training as a teacher?—I never was trained.

5006. Is your wife a trained teacher?—She is.

5007. Where was she trained?—Under the old Kildare Place System.

5008. What emoluments have you?—My salary is £40, hers is £15, and we are allowed £5 to keep a servant to clean the school.

5009. Lord Justice Naish.—That is £60 altogether?—Yes, and a residence.

5010. How is the school kept up?

Rev. Mr. *Le Hunte.*—By voluntary contributions, and the £3 Irish from Mrs. Paul. That is the only endowment. We are assisted also to the apprentice fees.

5011. Rev. Dr. Molloy.—Do any of your boys go to Mr. Greene's school after they leave you?—They are induced to go from my school to his, but not after they leave me.

5012. Dr. Traill.—At what age would that be?—It varies from about thirteen to my fifteen. Those that go to Mr. Greene from me are about fourteen years of age.

5013. That would not account for the falling off to thirteen boys in the school?—Five or six of Mr. Greene's scholars—some of whom went from me—left to go elsewhere; also two of my pupils left for the National school.

5014. Rev. Dr. Molloy.—Mr. Greene, have you any limit of age in your school?

Rev. Mr. *Greene.*—No.

5015. What is the youngest age at which they came to you?—I have not had any boys under ten.

5016. They come at ten?—Yes, between ten and eleven.

5017. Those that come at ten must get a primary education from you, whilst you are giving an advanced education to another set of boys?—Yes. I don't take any boy into the school until he is able to read and write and do simple sums in arithmetic.

5018. You don't require them to get as far as they can reach in an ordinary parochial school?—No.

5019. Wouldn't it be an improvement to let the parochial school prepare them in the elements and for you to finish them in the more advanced subjects?—I take the boys as they come to me.

5020. Professor Dougherty.—Do the boys that come to you at an early age belong to a different class from the others?—Yes.

5021. Dr. Traill.—What is the age at which the free boys are taken?—There is a limit imposed by the trustees of between eleven and fourteen.

5022. Lord Justice FitzGibbon.—Mr. Le Hunte, I understand the site was granted in 1788?

Rev. Mr. *Le Hunte.*—I know nothing about it.

5023. Do you pay any rent?—No.

5024. Has any rent been paid for the last twenty years, so far as you know?—No.

5025. Therefore we may take it that you hold the site and buildings in fee-simple?—I think so.

5026. Do you know the extent of the buildings?—There is a large house containing three rooms. We divide the upper and middle floor into two schoolrooms at present. The lower room we have as a meeting room, and there is one room and yard.

5027. That is all held free?—All held free. On either side there are wings forming the master's and mistress's apartments.

5028. Is the building all occupied for school purposes?—The master and mistress are husband and wife, and occupy one side. We let two rooms on the other side to a policeman and his family.

5029. Does the rent of that go to keep up the school?—Yes, half a crown a week.

5030. Who pays Mrs. Paul's annuity?—Mr. Dames Drake's agent, Mr. Ormond.

5031. Who is the owner of the estate?—Mr. Dames Drake.

5032. Is it a charge on the land?—Yes.

5033. Do you know the value of the land?—It is considerable.

5034. Ample to secure the charge?—Certainly.

5035. Is it regularly paid?—Yes.

5036. What are the apprentice fees?—When there are not Protestant children in the school at Stokestown our school comes in; and the boys and girls get £10 spread over two years—£5 for the first year, and £5 for the second.

5037. What arrangement is made about those apprenticeships?—I recommend the children to Mrs. Dames Drake—Mr. Dames Drake's mother—to find suitable persons to apprentice them to. We must apprentice them to Protestants by the deed. We sometimes offer to get them into an advanced school. Children have gone into the Training College in Dublin.

5038. Dr. Traill.—In whom are the school premises vested?—I don't know.

5039. Is it in the Representative Church Body?—It is not; but I think it ought to be.

5040. Supposing a diocesan scheme for the educational endowments of the diocese of Ferns were framed, would you be satisfied to allow the diocesan authorities to be the trustees to hold the property of this school?—I would if they don't put restrictions on us that I would not agree to.

5041. But suppose the management of the school were left to you?—Entirely. I would. I have reported to our Secretary, Mr. Pounden, about it.

5042. Lord Justice FitzGibbon.—How often do you get the apprentice fees?—Whenever I ask for them. I am continually asked have I more children; but we have not. There are some limitations.

5043. Assuming the funds to be accumulating, to what purpose could it best be applied in connexion with education?—I would say to keep our school. We find it very difficult to keep up the school.

5044. Dr. Traill.—Is Stokestown far away?—Two miles and a half distant.

5045. Professor Dougherty.—How do you propose to apply any additional endowment coming to the school?—I am out of pocket every year by keeping up the school. To help us to pay for it.

5046. Would it not enable you to improve the quality of the education?—If we got a sufficient sum it would.

5047. Rev. Dr. Molloy.—Could you not get an endowment under the National Board?—If we chose to put it under it we could; but I should object.

5048. Dr. Traill.—Have you sufficient numbers to get a grant if you applied for it?—I think we have.

5049. Why do you object?—Well, they would put restrictions on us as to the Scriptures.

5050. Are you not free to teach the Scriptures every day under the National Board?—Yes, but I would be bound to shut out the Scriptures for a great many hours, which I would never listen to under any circumstances.

5051. If you were teaching secular subjects in your own family, you would not put religious instruction into matters of secular education?—No, nor would I in any other teaching; but I would not bind myself under any circumstances to shut the Bible. I might have occasion to speak to my children of my own family—and I frequently have occasion to speak to the children of the school—out of the Bible. The free education we are giving would enable us to point out what the Scriptures say on those subjects.

5052. Lord Justice FitzGibbon.—You agree with the Christian Brothers in not excluding religion from any part of the school day?—I do, entirely.

If we could get grants for both of you from Parliament, it would be an improvement; but we have no jurisdiction about that.

July 5, 1886.

WHITECHURCH, STOKESTOWN (PAUL'S ENDOWMENT).

Mr. Joseph Wm. Deane sworn and examined.

Mr. Joseph Wm. Deane.

5053. Lord Justice FitzGibbon.—You are one of the trustees of Mrs. Paul's Endowment?—I was appointed about 1846.

5054. Have you any copy of the scheme under which the school is managed now?—I have not. All I find is, that the endowment was £1,400 under Mrs. Paul's will, half the interest of which was to be applied in the payment of a Protestant schoolmaster and schoolmistress. I have a copy of the will.

5055. The trustees mentioned in the last report are yourself and Mr. William Glascott?—I have a letter from him stating that he is not able to attend.

5056. Were you both appointed under the Court of Chancery?—Yes. My sister-in-law, Mr. Deane Drake's mother, was appointed at the same time.

5057. Here is the provision of the will:—She bequeaths to four trustees £1,400, the interest of which is to be applied to the following purposes:—Keeping in repair and finishing the schoolhouse built on her estate of Stokestown. Two acres are given for a garden for the master of the school for the time being. She devises half the interest of the £1,400 as salaries for a Protestant master and a Protestant mistress to instruct the boys and girls in reading, writing, arithmetic, and needlework, knitting and spinning, and correct and good morals, without interfering in their mode of religious worship further than that the Holy Scriptures be read and taught in the school. Neither the master nor the mistress is to receive more for the tuition of each child than a shilling a month. The representatives of the Drake family for ever, are to have the privilege of nominating twelve children, who shall be exempt from any payment; and then she nominates John A. Glascott, the Rev. William Maher, and Miss Sarah Drake the guardians of the institution. She appropriates the other moiety of the interest of the £1,400 for the purpose of yearly annuities to four aged men and four aged women, of good character, reduced circumstances, and infirm health, of the Protestant religion; those known to her brother as belonging to the parish of Whitechurch, to be preferred to others. These annuities are to be forfeited for misconduct; and the annuitants are to be elected by ballot, with black and white beans. There is a provision that the first moiety shall be expended either in the more complete finishing of the school house, or in binding out the Protestant children to Protestant masters and mistresses.

Witness.—That is all that has anything to do with the school. There is an additional fund for annuitants and apprenticing—£1,700.

5058. Lord Justice FitzGibbon.—She says that all her yearly subscriptions to the New Ross and Waterford charities are to be continued. The guardians of the Stokestown school are to see that the schoolhouse and premises are well kept, and that her intentions are carried into effect. The Stokestown Poor School was for a lasting memorial to John Drake. Then there is a bequest of £3 sterling for paralytic persons.

Witness.—There are thirteen persons now receiving that stipend. It is £9 Irish a year.

5059. Lord Justice FitzGibbon.—Then she appoints the balance subject to annuities, for apprenticing Protestant children out of the poor school at Stokestown to Protestant masters and mistresses, and if such deserving children were not in that school, for Protestant children from the Rosscarre school, and if there were no deserving objects there, for deserving Protestant children from any other Protestant school to Protestant masters and mistresses; and she entrusts the guardians to nominate by their wills or during their lifetime others to act after them as their representatives, and see that her intentions were carried into effect.

5060. Is Stokestown School in existence?—It is. The master and mistress are there.

5061. I find in the Report of 1858 that Whitechurch parochial school has a grant of an acre and a half to the Rev. William Glascott and another; but it is stated that there is no parochial school there owing to the circumstances of the neighbourhood. Mrs. Paul's school at Stokestown is separate from the parochial school?—Totally. It is two miles from the other.

5062. What funds are available for these charitable legacies?—There is money which we get from the Commissioners of Charitable Donations and Bequests.

5063. The whole funds are in the hands of the Charitable Commissioners?—Yes; it was invested in five per cent. stock.

5064. Lord Justice Naish.—What is the total amount of the fund?—£183 5s. 10d. yearly is what we have been getting. They have paid it free of income tax.

5065. How is that appropriated?—There are thirteen annuitants who get £8 6s. 2d.—equal to £9 Irish a year—each. That is £108 0s. 2d. The schoolmaster and schoolmistress have £20 a year each. Then there are the school and the apprentice fees; and there is a balance remaining of £35 5s. 8d. It provides coal and lighting and everything for the school; and the balance goes to the apprentice fees. Formerly we had more demands for apprentice fees than we could supply money for; but Mr. Le Hunte is not able to supply us with any apprentices now. We have no pupils in the school. We have a master and mistress, but not a single pupil except the mistress's son.

5066. What money would be available every year for apprentice fees if there were pupils to be apprenticed?—About £30 a year, I suppose. The £5 5s. 8d. would provide coals and lighting.

5067. Dr. Traill.—What do you do with the fund now?—It is accumulating.

5068. Lord Justice FitzGibbon.—Is it in your hands?—It is in the hands of Mr. Drake's mother, as treasurer, who has it in the bank at New Ross.

5069. The Commissioners of Charitable Donations pay the money to you?—Each half-year.

5070. Do you furnish any account to them of how it is spent?—No, never. They never demanded one.

5071. Is there no provision in the Chancery scheme for accounting?—I have never been able to see any Chancery scheme. There was a decree of the Court of Chancery about the year 1832. It is a most voluminous document, repeating Mrs. Paul's will verbatim without giving any explanations. That is what we have acted on hitherto with the exception of this, that the stipend of the master and mistress was to have been half the interest on the £1,400 Irish. We have paid it as of British at five per cent.

5072. Who nominates the objects of the charity—the old people?—We—the trustees. My sister-in-law, Mr. W. Glascott, and I are the surviving trustees.

5073. Rev. Dr. Molloy.—Do you say that there is only one pupil in the school?—Only one. I believe the schoolmaster is here.

5074. Lord Justice FitzGibbon.—Is Stokestown in the parish of Whitechurch?—It is just on the borders.

5075. Are there no Protestant children in the neighbourhood?—There have been some. The schoolmaster will tell you about it.

5076. Professor Dougherty.—Has this provision for apprentice fees ceased, in fact, to be used?—Mr. Le Hunte used to provide us, but he says there are not children of sufficient age in the school to be apprenticed.

Rev. Mr. Le Fanu.—Every year we apprentice about one or two.

Witness.—There would be enough for three every year. For years there were none at all.

5077. Do you think it would be a more advantageous disposal of the money to apply some of it to industrial education, in connexion with, say a school in New Ross?—We might have a school at Stokestown hereafter. There is nothing to prevent it. There could be no complaint like what Mr. Geffor made here with regard to the New Ross Endowed School, for our schoolmaster is not a clergyman. Our schoolmaster is a layman; and yet the Roman Catholic clergy won't allow their children to go to our school, because the Scriptures must be read in it.

5078. Rev. Dr. Molloy.—I suppose the Roman Catholic clergyman has a school under his own management?—He established a school within a few fields of our school. It is shut up now.

5079. Professor Dougherty.—Has he no children in the parish?—Plenty of them. There is a very large National school at Ballykelly, but it is three miles away.

5080. Lord Justice FitzGibbon.—The National Board rule is quite consistent with this will, for the school is to be carried on "without interfering with their mode of religious worship further than that the Holy Scriptures are to be read and taught in the school." A scheme of ours was approved the other day for a school in which the free and unrestricted use of the Holy Scriptures must be provided for every child during the hours set apart for religious instruction.

Lord Justice Naish.—Provided the child wished it.

Witness.—We tried to conciliate them by making use of the educational books of the National Board, but that didn't suit.

5081. Lord Justice FitzGibbon.—The last report, made ten years ago, states that the teacher had then been upwards of fifty years in office. Has anyone been appointed since?

Witness.—No. The same master is there still. He walked in here three miles to-day and is ready to walk back again.

Bryan Todd sworn and examined.

5082. Lord Justice FitzGibbon.—How long have you been master of Stokestown school?—Sixty-one years last month.

5083. How many pupils are there now?—Only one.

5084. When were there any others last?—About half a year ago.

5085. How many were there then?—From four to eight, between half a year ago and twelve months ago.

5086. What became of them?—Some of them were removed; some of them were servants children.

5087. Have you a school still?—I have.

5088. Where is it?—It is at home.

Mr. Deane.—I think he is alluding to a night school for the convenience of grown-up people, which is out of the endowment altogether. Adults come and learn at that night school; no man who cannot read and write, or who is under thirty years of age, comes there.

5089. Lord Justice FitzGibbon (to *Witness*).—How long is it since you had any children pupils in the day school?—Not, I suppose, these seven or eight years. I had a good school previous to that.

5090. How long is it since you had a good school in the day time?—Years before that. I am sixty-one years now in it.

5091. How long is it since the school dried up?—Fourteen or fifteen years.

5092. Have you had no day school for fourteen or fifteen years?—I had, about four or five years ago.

5093. Where do the children go now that used to go to you?—To a parochial school at Ballykelly, about two miles and a half from Stokestown.

5094. Who is the manager of Ballykelly?—I don't know. It is a National school.

5095. Is it under the priest?—Of course.

5096. What pay do you get?—£30. My wife had £30 more while she was alive. She is dead twenty-six or twenty-seven years.

5097. Who gets the other £30 now?—The schoolmistress.

5098. Is there a schoolmistress as well as you?—Yes.

5099. Has she any pupils?—No.

5100. How long is it since she had any?—I suppose something about twelve months.

5101. Who appointed you?—Counsellor Deane's father.

Mr. Deane.—My grandfather.

5102. Are you entitled to draw your salary whether you have any pupils or not?—I don't know; only Mr. Deane agreed to give me £30 for myself and £30 for my wife for keeping school.

5103. But you have no school?—I had then; I had 104.

Mr. Deane.—He had a good school, but the children were driven out of it by force.

5104. Lord Justice FitzGibbon.—How much accumulated money is in the hands of the trustees?

Mr. Deane.—About £160, or more.

5105. Where is it?—In the Bank of Ireland, in the name of my sister-in-law, as treasurer.

5106. Alone?—In her passbook.

5107. That the whole amount is in the hands of one person, on a private pass-book?—It is, of course, a separate account. It is perfectly safe. I am responsible.

5108. Lord Justice FitzGibbon.—It is not a legal position for it to be in?—I am responsible if anything goes astray.

5109. Does it consist of accumulations of unpaid apprentice fees?—Not altogether. At one time, after Mr. Todd's wife died, there was no schoolmistress.

5110. (To the *Witness*.)—How many years after your wife's death was Mrs. Bagg appointed?—I suppose twenty years.

5111. How many pupils had Mrs. Bagg when she was appointed?—About ten.

5112. Who appointed her?

Mr. Deane.—I did, with Mrs. Deane Drake.

5113. What were her qualifications?—It is a long time ago; I forget.

5114. (To *Witness*.)—Where was Mrs. Bagg trained?

Witness.—I could not tell that.

Mr. Deane.—She was recommended as a very highly accomplished teacher. My co-trustee, Mrs. Deane Drake, has the whole correspondence. She is trustee and treasurer, but she resides in London and we could not get her over.

5115. Lord Justice FitzGibbon.—What is the present title to the site and three acres of land?

Witness.—I have it; it is two and a half Irish acres.

5116. How is it used?—For tillage; barley, potatoes, and turnips. I don't till it; I am not able.

5117. What are the school buildings?—A splendid building, with fine out-offices, cow-house, and stable.

5118. Does Mrs. Bagg live in the building along with you?—She does.

5119. You have separate residences?—Yes.

Mr. Deane.—She occupies one of the schoolrooms?—Yes.

5120. And there is a schoolroom 30 feet by 20 feet?—30 feet by 16.

5121. One of the rooms is occupied by the schoolmistress, who has a sum; and the other one is occupied by the master?—Yes.

5121. Rev. Dr. Molloy.—Is there any prospect of pupils coming?

Mr. Doran.—A short time ago a Protestant farmer in the neighbourhood sent his children there, but he was induced to withdraw them for the sake of popularity, or something of the kind.

5122. Lord Justice FitzGibbon.—It would be hard to expect him to send them to be taught by this old gentleman.

Mr. Doran.—Well, I don't know. I dare say if you try him you will find him a good scholar.

5124. Lord Justice FitzGibbon.—After sixty-one years service, and being almost deaf, it is time for him to retire.

5125. Rev. Dr. Molloy.—I think you said that pupils were driven away; what did you mean by that?

Mr. Doran.—A long time before he was appointed a man named Fitzgerald was teacher.

5126. That was sixty years ago?—Upwards of sixty years ago. I recollect as a child Fitzgerald saying that the priest had been to the school and had horsewhipped the children out of it. Since this man was there he had a good school; and he will tell you that the horsewhip was not used, but that the clergyman came and turned the children out.

5127. The priest did not wish the Catholic children to go to the school?—Yes.

5128. Is there any Protestant population in the neighbourhood?

Mr. Doran.—There is; but as I told you, they have withdrawn their children for the sake of popularity.

5129. The school has no popularity with any denomination?

Rev. M. F. Pallisser.—There are no Protestant children there.

Mr. Doran.—A long time ago people used to come from the neighbourhood of Ross because they were certain of being apprenticed. We were thinking of offering a larger apprentice fee, say £15. That might be an inducement to children to attend Stakestown school primarily, and failing that, the school in Ross.

Professor Dougherty.—I think it is very doubtful if it would induce parents to send their children to a school managed as Stakestown school is.

5130. Lord Justice FitzGibbon.—Does anybody look after it at all?

Mr. Doran.—There is nothing to look after.

Rev. M. F. Pallisser.—I used to visit the school.

Mr. Doran.—The accumulations during the twenty years that no schoolmistress was appointed would be £400.

WHITECHURCH PAROCHIAL SCHOOL (GLASCOTT'S ENDOWMENT).

The Rev. M. F. *Pallisser* sworn and examined.

5131. Lord Justice FitzGibbon.—You are incumbent of the parish in which Stakestown school is?—Yes, since 1872.

5132. What schools, under Protestant management, are in it?—Whitechurch school is the only one.

5133. By "Whitechurch" school do you mean the parochial school?—Yes; what was the parochial school.

5134. Lord Justice FitzGibbon.—It is reported in 1880 that—

"Whitechurch parochial school is held under a grant from William Glascott, junior, and that the land comprises an acre and a half, but the rector states that there is no parochial school in the parish owing to the circumstances of the neighbourhood"?

—Yes, exactly.

5135. Has that school been opened since?—Occasionally. The family of a steward or a coachman may have attended; but there is no regular teacher. We have not been able to pay a trained teacher for it.

5136. Who holds the premises?—The clerk and sexton of the parish.

5137. Is it on Church ground?—No, it is on a field Mr. Glascott gave, only on condition that it was required for school purposes, and if not, that it was to revert to the proprietor of the Glascott estate.

5138. Have you any copy of the deed under which it is held?—I have not.

5139. Do you know anyone who has?—I don't know. When the Endowed Schools Commission was first started nobody knew that the school was endowed. I consulted the agent of the property, who had never heard of it. I sent up word to Dublin Castle stating that nobody knew that the school was endowed. They sent me a copy of a deed showing that a former Lord Powerscourt had endowed it. That was not this school, but it shows the way things are registered. I suppose the grant to this school is to be had too.

5140. What is the Ballykelly school?—A Roman Catholic National school connected with the chapel.

5141. Since 1872, what is the largest number of pupils that you knew to attend Stakestown?—I think a dozen, at the outside, all under the schoolmistress.

5142. Rev. Dr. Molloy.—Was that the present schoolmistress?—Yes.

5143. Lord Justice FitzGibbon.—What was the cause of the falling off?—They nearly all left. Some of them went to another school.

5144. Were they the Protestant population that you speak of?—Yes.

5145. Professor Dougherty.—What was the other school to which the pupils went?—Two of them went to Horeswood school.

5146. Lord Justice FitzGibbon.—Is there any possibility of making this endowment of Stakestown school useful?—I cannot conceive it. There is no possibility of getting Protestant children, or any children that I know of, to attend it. A different plan must be adopted with regard to a school.

5147. It is a very handsome endowment, and it is a pity to have it going astray?—It is,—there is no question about that.

5148. What suggestion do you make as regards making it useful?—I could not say. It is almost on the very edge of my parish.

5149. We have been told that at one time the children went from Ross to this school, looking for apprentice fees?—I dare say.

5150. Could the children from that neighbourhood come to the New Ross school?—I don't see why they should not. They go farther. I know children who go four miles to school.

5151. Rev. Dr. Molloy.—Is there at present any school in your parish under Protestant management that is largely attended?—Not one. There are no young children to attend school.

5152. Lord Justice Naish.—What is the nearest Protestant school to your parish?—Dunganstown, six miles from my parish.

5153. Lord Justice FitzGibbon.—Ross is nearer than that?—Of course.

5154. Professor Dougherty.—Is there any school in this neighbourhood in connexion with the National Board under Protestant management?—Not that I am aware of.

Mr. Doran.—According to the will the endowment is to keep up the school for ever.

5155. Lord Justice FitzGibbon.—Yes, but it is not keeping up a school to pay £40 a year to two people without pupils.

Mr. *Deane*.—There is the night school.

5156. Rev. Dr. MOLLOY.—You keep up a master and mistress and school buildings and no pupils. That is not a school in the ordinary acceptation of the word.

Mr. *Deane*.—If so the endowment ought to revert to the property out of which it comes.

5157. Rev. Dr. MOLLOY.—Would it be possible to apply the fund in New Ross so as to be available for any Protestant families that might hereafter come to Whitechurch?

Mr. *Deane*.—It is too far.

5158. Rev. Dr. MOLLOY.—If there were a good school at New Ross it would be cheaper to provide a conveyance for the children than to spend the £40 a year as it is spent now.

5159. *Lord Justice* FITZGIBBON.—If the Commissioners of Charitable Donations and Bequests had known what was going on they would not have paid the money to you at all. They paid it believing that it was going for a school, while in reality it was going into the bank.

Mr. *Deane*.—That was only during the time that there was no mistress.

5160. Lord Justice FITZGIBBON.—Quite so; and the accumulations ought to have amounted to £100. Mr. Pullen, do you think that *New Ross* would be the nearest place where pupils can now be found to avail themselves of this endowment to Slicketown?—Yes.

5161. Professor DOUGHERTY.—Is there any demand for industrial education in *New Ross*?

Rev. Mr. *Le Hunte*.—I don't think there is. It would require a considerable outlay to establish. I forgot to mention to you, in connection with the [illegible] school, we were left a bequest of £50 by a lady who died recently. So that the three guineas from Mrs. Paul is not the only endowment to that school. I thought I understood you to read out that the New Ross school was entitled to £10.

5162. Lord Justice FITZGIBBON.—Who is at present in possession of the demesne at Slicketown?

Mr. *Deane Drake*.—I am, my lord.

5163. Lord Justice FITZGIBBON.—(Reads)—The will provides:—

"Should there be at any time a surplus of interest from proper objects not being chosen, the said interest is to be appropriated to the binding out of Protestant children from Slicketown to Protestant masters and mistresses, or to trades." "In addition to the former part of my last will, I desire that all my yearly subscriptions to the Ross and Wexford charities be for ever continued. The Ross charities, with the addition of £10 every year, to be expended on the schoolhouse and garden, to be paid out of my demesne at Slicketown, so that the said schoolhouse and garden be well kept."

That would not be payable out of the fund the Commissioners have. It is a rentcharge on the estate, whatever school it goes to.

Mr. *Deane*.—I think that can be read in this way, that the estate is liable to the extent of £10 to keep the schoolhouse in repair.

5164. Professor DOUGHERTY.—You mean the Slicketown school?—Yes.

5165. Lord Justice FITZGIBBON.—Is the estate in the habit of paying the repairs of the Slicketown school?

Mr. *Deane Drake*.—I pay them out of my own pocket.

Mr. *Deane*.—If the schoolhouse should be kept in sufficient repair, I think you would find that that would satisfy the meaning of it.

5166. Lord Justice FITZGIBBON.—There is certainly £10 a year to be paid to some school.—I think it means the Slicketown school. That would be a rentcharge of £10 a year for the Slicketown building over and above the trust money.

Rev. Mr. *Pullen*.—I have heard that it is considered that the Slicketown school is under my jurisdiction.

5167. Rev. Dr. MOLLOY.—I know many parts of the country where people would consider themselves well off if they had such an endowment.

Rev. Mr. *Le Hunte*.—The New Ross schoolhouse was very much in the contemplation of the testator, and therefore it should come next, to share in any benefits left by the will.

5168. Rev. Dr. MOLLOY.—Do you mean the endowed or the parochial schoolhouse?

Rev. Mr. *Le Hunte*.—The parochial schoolhouse.

Rev. Mr. *Pullen*. It is proposed that the parish of Whitechurch should be ultimately joined to that of New Ross. It has been recommended already by the Diocesan Council.

Rev. Dr. MOLLOY.—That would facilitate matters.

5169. Lord Justice FITZGIBBON.—The first matter to be done is to send us an account of the money in hand, showing how much it is, where it was lodged, and bringing the account down to the present date. It is quite clear that this neighbourhood has an interest in this endowment. It is very large, and is not being usefully applied; it is our duty to settle a scheme by which it shall be usefully applied, as nearly as possible in accordance with the intentions of the lady who left the money. The parishes of New Ross and Whitechurch are both interested; and we shall be glad to receive suggestions either from the lady who has the money in her hands, or from the Incumbents of the two parishes. Children of all denominations were intended to be admissible to the school; but the teachers, both master and mistress, must be Protestants, and there must be religious instruction—not denominational but Scriptural instruction—given in the school each day. That does not mean, necessarily, that it should be given throughout the day, but that it should be provided for all the children attending it. We know that a provision of that kind is objected to by Roman Catholic people and by their clergy; and, therefore, they may stay away from the school, but they cannot insist on altering the conditions on which the lady gave the money. Accordingly the money is substantially available for Protestant education; but it is far more important that it is available, and not merely for maintaining teachers and a building with no pupils. As regards the application fund, the Act of Parliament contains an express provision enabling us to deal with the money as if it was an educational endowment. The section was put into the Act because very often these funds—as in the case here—have become, from changes in the circumstances of tenders and localities, very far from useful.

5170. Mr. *R. Carr*, Solicitor.—As a resident in the near neighbourhood for fifty years I know that the greatest good is being done by the children of the poor people of the neighbourhood, both boys and girls receiving instruction in the night school, which is held there. I have known of servants and clerks getting the only education that they could obtain from Mr. Todd and from Mrs. Bragg there. The school has been doing more good than anyone would suppose, and it has been always open for people to go and attend it.

5171. Lord Justice FITZGIBBON.—Everybody agrees that a day school is impossible under present circumstances; but there is no reason why there should not be an evening school under a teacher who could go the two miles from New Ross. We can make provision that a night school shall be kept up, if it is really wanted.

Mr. *Deane*.—We cannot bring that under the endowment.

5172. Lord Justice FITZGIBBON.—We can.

The inquiry then terminated.

July 2, 1888.

Rev. H. W. Pullen.

July 4, 1889.

PUBLIC SITTING.—THURSDAY, JULY 4, 1889.

At the Courthouse, Wexford.

Present :—The Right Hon. Lord Justice FitzGibbon, and the Right Hon. Lord Justice Naish, Judicial Commissioners; and the Rev. Gerald Molloy, D.D., D.Sc., Anthony Traill, Esq., LL.D., M.D., F.T.C.D., and Professor Dougherty, M.A., Assistant Commissioners.

The Assistant Secretary, N. D. Murphy, was in attendance.

THE TATE SCHOOL, WEXFORD.

Mr. *Elgee* appeared for the Trustees of the School.

Mr. *O'Connor* appeared for the Most Rev. Dr. Browne, Lord Bishop of Ferns.

Lord Justice FitzGibbon made an introductory statement.

5173. Mr. *Elgee*.—I am solicitor for the trustees, acting under the present Chancery scheme, namely, the Archdeacon of Ferns, the Mayor of Wexford, the two Churchwardens, and the Rector of Wexford. The will of William Tate, who lived in Jamaica, but formerly in the parish of Tredawary, in the County of Cornwall, was made on the 13th May, 1793, and by a codicil thereto of the 10th July, 1794, after sundry bequests therein mentioned, the testator nominated and appointed his friend, Captain Arthur Murphy trustee, in conjunction with the mayor, rector, sheriffs, and churchwardens, for the time being, of the town of Wexford, for the sum or sums of money which he bequeathed towards the erection and completion of the Charity school, and he bequeathed all the rest of his estate and effects, real and personal, whatsoever and wheresoever situate, unto the said mayor, rector, sheriffs, and churchwardens, to be by them laid out in laying the foundation, erecting, and completing of a Charity school in the town of Wexford, and to support as many children as the same would admit of, such children to be approved of by the mayor, rector, and other trustees before mentioned.

5174. Lord Justice Naish.—Is there not a reference to the school in his will?

Mr. *Elgee*.—I can't find anything about it in the will. There seems to have been some mistake, as if he thought he had mentioned it in his will. He died soon after the making of the will and codicil, and the thing appears to have lain over until 1854.

5175. Lord Justice Naish.—What became of the money?

Mr. *Elgee*.—It is now in the Court of Chancery, standing to the separate credit of William Tate's Charity. In the year 1856 an information was filed by the Rev. Richard Waddy Elgee, the then rector of Wexford, to have the trusts of the will carried into effect. That suit came on before the Master of the Rolls, and in 1857 the Master of the Rolls made a decretal order of the 7th of June, by which it was declared that the several moneys, by the will and codicil of William Tate directed to be applied in the erecting and supporting the Charity school, were well bequeathed for the charitable purposes of the said school, and it was referred to Master Litton to inquire and report what was the amount of the funds applicable to the charitable purposes mentioned in the codicil, and to approve of and settle a scheme for the application of such funds in laying the foundation of, erecting, and completing a Charity school in the town of Wexford, and supporting as many children as the same would admit of. Master Litton made a report in the month of July, 1858, by which he found that the Commissioners of Charitable Donations and Bequests had in hands at that time applicable to the purposes of the charity a sum of £7,517 18s. 4d., Government 3 per cent. consols, and £1,346 18s. 7d., Government new 3 per cent. stock. He settled a scheme for the carrying out of the trust, in 1858. Captain Arthur Murphy, who was mentioned in the codicil as one of the trustees, was then dead; and Master Litton reported that the Archdeacon of Ferns was a fit and proper person to act with the mayor, the rector, and the two churchwardens as trustees.

5176. Professor Dougherty.—Was Captain Murphy resident in Wexford?

Mr. *Elgee*.—I am not quite sure. He is described in the codicil as Captain Arthur Murphy. The master, by the scheme which he settled, proposed that the trustees should expend a sum not exceeding £[illegible] in the purchase of buildings, or of a piece of ground, and the erection of a schoolhouse thereon, such house and ground to be conveyed to the trustees either in fee-simple or fee-farm, or for a term of not less than 500 years, and the house to contain suitable apartments for the master and pupils, and such purchase or buildings to be approved of by the Commissioners of Charitable Donations and Bequests. The school was to be called Tate's School; and the residue of the funds was to be invested on trust to pay the rent, if any, of the house and ground, the expense of repairing and maintaining the house, and the annual salary of the schoolmaster, who was to reside in the house, and was to be a person of good moral character and fully competent to give a sound English, commercial, and mathematical education. The school was to be a boarding and day school for males; and the trustees were authorised to make such rules and orders for the internal management of the school, and for the clothing of the children who should be boarded as they thought fit; and they were required to account yearly to the Commissioners of Charitable Donations and Bequests. The Master of the Rolls, by an order of the 25th January, 1859, approved of that scheme.

5177. Lord Justice Naish.—What is the provision in the scheme for the appointment of the schoolmaster?

Mr. *Elgee*.—Here it is :—

"It shall be lawful for the said trustees to appoint such schoolmaster, and to remove him for any cause that may seem fit to them: but no such schoolmaster shall be removed except by the consent of a majority of the trustees."

In the year 1862 the trustees purchased from the Corporation of Wexford the piece of ground on which the schoolhouse was to be built; and immediately afterwards—or about the end of 1863—they erected the schoolhouse at an expense of £1,4[illegible].

5178. Lord Justice FitzGibbon.—Have there ever been since that time any appointments of new trustees, or conveyances to new trustees.

Mr. *Elgee*.—There never has been any conveyance but the one of the 10th April, 1862, to John [illegible] Johnson, Archdeacon of Ferns; the Rev. R. W. Elgee, Rector; John Green, Mayor; and Messrs. James M. Vinery, and Lett. S. Jefferes, Churchwardens, as

[illegible]

trustees for the time being, and to their successors. There never has been any other deed since that. The money never was paid to the trustees.

5179. Lord Justice FitzGibbon.—Did the Commissioners of Charitable Donations and Bequests transfer the money into the Court of Chancery?

Mr. Elgee.—As soon as the trustees got the deed they proceeded to carry out the trusts, and applied to the Lord Chancellor to have the money, under the finding of Master Litton's report, transferred to the trustees. The Commissioners of Charitable Donations and Bequests said that the trustees were a changeable body, and that they did not think it right to transfer the money to their names, as there would be no one who would be a continuing trustee; and accordingly the Lord Chancellor made an order that it should be brought into the Court of Chancery to the credit of the matter and the separate credit of Dean's School, and there it has been ever since.

5180. Lord Justice Naish.—What is the amount of it now?

Mr. Elgee.—The amount is now, I think, exactly £7,197 8s. Government Stock, and there is also a small sum of £90 11s. 6d. Consols.

Rev. Dr. Molloy.—The income is a little more than £210 a year.

5181. Lord Justice FitzGibbon.—I see that in 1879 the amount was reported to be £8,197 7s. 6d. Government Stock.

Mr. Elgee.—The exact amount then ought to have been £8,197 16s. 4d.

5182. Lord Justice FitzGibbon.—How did it get reduced?

Mr Elgee.—In the year 1877, two gentlemen of the town of Wexford, one being a bootmaker and the other a dentist, filed a petition in Chancery under Lord Romilly's Act, against the trustees for a breach of trust in connection with the way in which they were carrying out the school. That petition came before the Vice-Chancellor, and by an order of the 10th February, 1879, was dismissed as regards the breach of trust; but an amended scheme, which I shall bring before you, was then settled. By reason of the cost of that petition the fund was reduced; the costs came to no less a sum than £770.

5183. Dr. Traill.—I thought the losing side would have had to pay these?

Mr. Elgee.—It all came out of the trust fund,—the costs of the trustees, and of the Attorney-General, and of the Commissioners of Charitable Donations and Bequests, while the petitioners on their side got part of their costs.

5184. Lord Justice FitzGibbon.—Although it was dismissed; there must have been some foundation for the petition.

Mr. Elgee.—The desire was to make the scheme more extensive—to allow more boys to be taken in, and some paying pupils, which had not been done before.

5185. Lord Justice FitzGibbon.—Up to the present the sums of some of our schemes have been over £5. In that respect the contrast is to the advantage of this Commission.

Mr. Elgee.—In 1867, I think, the school had been opened, and it had continued on down to this. On the 11th of January, 1879, the new scheme, under which the school is at present carried on, was settled by the Vice-Chancellor. The trust clause under that scheme is that the Archdeacon of Ferns and the Rector of the parish of Wexford being clergymen of the Church of Ireland, the churchwardens being members of the Church of Ireland, and the mayor of Wexford for the time being, shall continue to be trustees of the funds belonging to the school. Paragraph 3 of the scheme is the same as in the old scheme, namely, that the trustees are to stand possessed of the funds for the maintenance of the school and the payment of the salary of the schoolmaster. Paragraph 6 provides, as in the old scheme, that the schoolmaster shall reside in the house, be a person of good moral character, and be fully competent to give a sound English, commercial, and mathematical education; and that it shall be lawful for the trustees to appoint and remove the schoolmaster, but that he shall not be removed except by the consent of a majority of them. Paragraph 7 is that all the pupils shall be entitled to receive a sound English, commercial, and mathematical education. Paragraph 8 provides that the school shall continue to be a boarding and day school for boys, that there shall be no paying boarders resident therein, and that the trustees shall have power to admit to the school both free day pupils and paying day pupils.

5186. Lord Justice FitzGibbon.—I suppose the meaning of "no paying boarders" is that all the boarders are to be free boys?

Mr. Elgee.—Yes; as many as the fund would admit of. They are to be maintained out of the trust funds. Paragraph 10 says that, in addition to the English, commercial, and mathematical education, there may also be given instruction in French and elementary classics, for which a further fee not exceeding £2 a year shall be charged to paying pupils, and the trustees may have the same instruction given to such of the free pupils as they shall consider deserving thereof, free of charge. Paragraph 11 gives the trustees power to dismiss or remove boarders or day boys for adequate cause, such cause to be specified in the order, and the sufficiency thereof to be in the sole discretion of the trustees. Paragraph 12 says the trustees shall meet at the schoolhouse of the charity or at such other place as they shall appoint for the transaction of the business of the charity, such meetings to be held at least twelve times in every year. Paragraph 13 enables any two or more of the trustees to summon a special meeting. Paragraph 14 provides that all meetings of the trustees, whether ordinary or special, shall be constituted of three trustees, and that all questions shall be determined by a majority, the chairman to have a second or casting vote. Paragraph 15 enacts that at all meetings of the trustees the Archdeacon of Ferns shall, if present, be chairman, and that if he is absent the Mayor of Wexford shall, if present, take the chair. It is further provided by the scheme that the trustees shall be at liberty, from time to time, to make such rules and orders for the internal management of the school, and for the clothing of the boarders as shall to them seem fit; and that they shall keep accounts of the receipts and disbursements, which shall be furnished every year to the Commissioners of Charitable Donations and Bequests,—which has always been done. That is the position in which the charity stands now.

5187. Lord Justice FitzGibbon.—Have you any suggestion to make in reference to it, Mr. Elgee?

Mr. Elgee.—No, I don't think so.

The Venerable J. C. Archdall, Archdeacon of Ferns, sworn and examined.

The Ven. J. C. Archdall.

5188. Lord Justice FitzGibbon.—How long have you held the office of Archdeacon of Ferns?—I think since 1875.

5189. Is the Archdeaconry attached to any particular parish?—No, it is not—not since the disestablishment of the Church.

5190. What parish was it attached to till disestablishment?—Adamstown.

5191. How far is that from Wexford?—I should think about twelve miles.

5192. It is not a parish connected with Wexford?—No.

July 1, 1886.

The Ven. J. G. Archdeacon

5193. As Archdeacon you have been Chairman of the Trustees of Tate's School?—I have.

5194. What was the deficiency in the working of the older scheme which lead to the new one being adopted?—I think the application arose from the fact that a very superior master, an Englishman, and a Fellow of Oxford—Mr. Aldhouse—had been appointed, and he made it very much a classical school. He had a very flourishing school, but it was not exactly of the kind that was intended, and the people of Wexford applied to the Lord Chancellor to have an alteration made.

5195. Is that it had been converted into a classical school for pupils in a good position of life?—I think that was the case; it was not having any but paying boarders there, and limiting the number of boarders too.

5196. When do the trustees meet?—On the first Tuesday in every month at the school.

5197. As a rule have you a quorum in attendance?—Yes; our quorum is three out of five; we generally have it. We are never deficient, I think.

5198. Does the mayor take part in the management of the Charity?—The present mayor has not been with us, but we have had the mayor occasionally, though not often. I think last year we had the mayor but once. When Mr. Green was mayor before that he used to attend very constantly.

5199. I suppose the mayors of Wexford have been of different religious denominations?—Yes.

5200. And is it when the mayor is a Catholic that he doesn't attend?—I don't know any reason why he doesn't, because we have always been on the best of terms.

5201. As a rule the four members who attend are the rector, the archdeacon, and the two churchwardens?—Yes, as a rule.

5202. Who is the present master?—Mr. Caldwell.

5203. How long has he been master?—I don't know.

5204. Was he appointed in 1879, after the new scheme?—It was after that new scheme came into operation that we appointed him.

5205. Does he still maintain the four free boarders?—Yes. For some time we were not able to maintain four, because the funds were diminished by the demands made on them in consequence of that application. We had to pay expenses, the £370 costs.

5206. Have you now got four boarders?—Yes.

5207. Besides the four boarding pupils, how many day pupils are there?—I don't exactly know. The master is here.

5208. To Witness.—How are the free boarders selected?—By the trustees. Their parents make applications; and we take in those that we think most necessitous, confining ourselves to the parish of Wexford for which we think the trust was intended.

5209. Rev. Dr. Molloy.—Are the number of applications generally in excess of the number of free places?—Yes, we generally have an excess of applications.

5210. Lord Justice FitzGibbon.—Do you give any notice when the vacancies occur?—Oh, we are obliged to give public notice by advertisement a considerable time beforehand in the public papers. We have a fixed time for the appointments.

5211. Do you appoint half-yearly or yearly?—When there is a vacancy we fix a time for the election.

5212. Have you free day pupils?—We have.

5213. How are they admitted?—By the trustees according to their judgment of the necessity of the case. We have a scale of payments for the others according to what we think to be the necessities of the parents.

5214. Then you take the circumstances of the parents into account in admitting the day boys?—Most rigidly. We take everything of that kind into consideration.

5215. What other qualifications do you require in the pupils?—They must be educated up to a certain point. You will see by the scheme, I think. We don't take them under nine years of age, or over thirteen. We examine them to see if they can read and write before we take them in.

5216. Rev. Dr. Molloy.—Do you receive pupils of all denominations?—No, we do not.

5217. Lord Justice FitzGibbon.—What denominations do you receive?—Only Protestant denominations.

5218. Do you receive all denominations of Protestants?—I think so. I have never known an objection to be made.

5219. Lord Justice Naish.—Has an application ever been made to receive a Roman Catholic?—Never. We have never had such an application that I am aware of. Not in my time.

5220. Rev. Dr. Molloy.—Would such an application be entertained?—Well, I think it would not.

5221. On what grounds?—Because I have always understood that it was so limited by Tate's will.

5222. Is there anything in the present Chancery scheme to exclude Roman Catholics?—Well, I don't see that there is.

Mr. Hore.—Nothing whatever.

5223. Dr. Traill.—I suppose you think that when the governing body, except the mayor, belongs entirely to the Church of Ireland, and that the appointments are left to your own discretion, you have a right to exercise it?

(Witness).—Yes. It never occurred to me that the school was available for anyone else.

5224. It would not be likely to occur to the governing bodies of other denominations either?—No, it did not occur to me in any way.

5225. Rev. Dr. Molloy.—Is it known to what denomination Captain Arthur Murphy belonged?—Oh, yes—Church of Ireland. He was the father of a Mr. Murphy who is now connected with a bank in Dublin. He was, perhaps, the oldest person in this town who held his property by prescription.

5226. There is nothing in the will, so far as I am aware, restricting the benefit of the Charity to Protestant children?—I have never heard the will read before; and, therefore, I do not know anything about it.

Rev. Dr. Molloy.—It simply provides for the foundation of a Charity school in the town of Wexford.

5227. Lord Justice FitzGibbon.—It is very short. The testator leaves all the rest of his property to the mayor, rector, sheriffs, and churchwardens for the time being, to be by them laid out in the founding, erecting, and completing of a Charity school in the town of Wexford, and the supporting of as many children as the same will admit of, such children to be approved of by the mayor, rector, and other trustees.

5228. Dr. Traill.—The mayor at that time was necessarily a Protestant?—Yes.

5229. Lord Justice FitzGibbon.—Do you know how many pupils there are there now?—I don't know.

5230. Is the school working satisfactorily from your point of view?—It is working satisfactorily. We have an excellent master, a very well educated young man, from Bantry. The education is good, and our boys have been very prosperous for their positions in life. It has been very successful so far.

5231. Is there any other intermediate school in Wexford?—Not that I know of.

5232. Then, I presume, yours is the only school at present open to the children of people who want intermediate education for their sons?—I think so.

5233. Dr. Traill.—You don't suppose the testator intended this to be a proselytising institution?—Oh, no, I should think not. I think he never thought of any but his own persuasion at the time he made his will.

5234. Lord Justice FitzGibbon.—I see in the will

another provision by which he gives a certain sum of money as a gift for bread, which it is specified shall be open to all denominations?—Oh, yes.

5235. Who administers that fund now?—It is done, I think, by the clergy.

Mr. Elgee.—The rector.

5236. Lord Justice FitzGibbon.—It is given apparently to the same trustees as the residue for the school.

Mr. Elgee.—The rector, I think, receives the dividends on it.

5237. Dr. Traill (to Witness).—Would you not infer from the fact that he said that that donation was to be open to all denominations, while he did not say that his school was to be open to all denominations, that he might perhaps have had a difference between them in his own mind?—I think so.

5238. Professor Dougherty (to Witness).—You said, Mr. Archdall, that the school was open, as regards free pupils, to pupils of other Protestant denominations besides those of your church?—Yes.

5239. Do you happen to know whether pupils belonging to other Protestant denominations have been admitted in recent years?—I could not say.

5240. Rev. Dr. Molloy.—Can you tell us any reason for doubting what the religion of the founder was at the time of his death?—I never heard any reason.

Mr. Elgee.—There can be no doubt about it, for it was found by Master Litton's report that he was a member of the then Established Church.

5241. Professor Dougherty.—Have you the evidence upon which Master Litton arrived at this finding?

Mr. Elgee.—Well, it is a long time ago, but I might be able to find the affidavits.

5242. Rev. Dr. Molloy.—Was it disputed?

Witness.—I never heard it questioned.

Dr. Traill.—Is it stated in the finding?

Mr. Elgee.—It is in his judgment.

5243. Dr. Traill.—Then he must have investigated the evidence at that time?

Mr. Elgee.—Here is what he says:—He finds that the testator was himself a Church of England man, and that three of the trustees whom he named as persons holding office were more distinctly identified with the Church Establishment than the other.

5244. Lord Justice FitzGibbon.—How did the archdeacon come into it?

Witness.—I cannot tell. It was before my time.

Mr. Elgee.—I can tell you how. It was the Bishop who was proposed first, but as he lived in Kilkenny it was thought that it would be very inconvenient for him to be having to come down here, and then the Archdeacon of Ferns was put in.

5245. Lord Justice FitzGibbon.—In fact as the resident working Church clergyman of the place?

Witness.—Just as I am now.

5246. Dr. Traill (to Witness).—You don't live at Adamstown now?—No; I live at Newtown Barry, which is a great deal further.

5247. How long did you take to get here?—I left home at nine o'clock, and I was here with you.

5248. In what year was Archdeacon Johnson connected with the trust?

Mr. Elgee.—In 1848.

5249. Dr. Traill (to Witness).—Would it not conduce to the improvement of the school if, saving your vested interest, your successor should be a person more directly connected with this place?—I don't think it would, because I think that the archdeacon as an official man would have more interest in the school than anyone else.

5250. He might live at the far end of the diocese?—I don't think so.

Lord Justice FitzGibbon.—Besides he would have to perform functions all over the diocese.

5251. Mr. O'Connor (to Witness).—Does not the fact of the archdeacon, who is not living in Wexford, being made a trustee, show that the scheme was intended for the whole diocese, and was not limited to Wexford?

Lord Justice Naish.—That is a mere matter of argument.

5252. Mr. O'Connor (to Witness).—Are the four free boys always taken from the parish of Wexford, and are the free day boys always taken from the parish of Wexford, or are they not also taken from parishes outside Wexford?

Lord Justice FitzGibbon (to Witness).—Where do your day boys and boarders come from?—The boarders from the parish of Wexford; the day boys either from that parish or from outside it.

5253. Rev. Dr. Molloy.—When you say "from outside it" you mean from the immediate neighbourhood of Wexford?—Oh, yes.

5254. Lord Justice FitzGibbon.—Is it a matter of inquiry when you are holding the election where the boys come from?—We do, always.

5255. Therefore you make it a qualification of the boarders that they shall have come from the parish of Wexford, but you don't make that a qualification of the day boys?—Exactly.

5256. Dr. Traill.—Or is it a qualification in this sense, that you give them a preference, but if you can't find four suitable boys in the parish of Wexford you feel justified in going outside it?—Certainly.

5257. Is that the only preference?—Yes.

5258. Lord Justice Naish.—There is nothing in the scheme to confine the free boys to Wexford?—There is not. It has been a matter of practice.

5259. Mr. Elgee.—Supposing there were a vacancy, and that no boy from Wexford applied, and that a boy, say from your parish, applied?

Witness.—We would take him. There is no rule to prevent us. Of course we would not leave the vacancy unfilled.

5260. Professor Dougherty.—Have you any form of application for boys who wish to be taken as free pupils?—I don't think we have any regularly printed form, or anything of that kind, but there is no difficulty about it.

5261. Rev. Dr. Molloy.—But as a matter of fact the free places have been hitherto awarded to boys from Wexford?—I think so.

5262. Mr. Elgee.—Weren't there two boys, brothers, from your own parish?—No, they were not from my parish. Their mother happens now to be my parishioner, but at the time they were admitted—not at all. She was a Waterford woman.

5263. As a matter of fact, have not boys been received from other parts of the diocese,—from the most distant parts of it?—No. At the time the boy was admitted she was not my parishioner, but she became so since.

5264. Lord Justice FitzGibbon.—Where did she live at the time of the election?—I think at Killaloe. We would take a pupil from any part of the diocese if we could not find one in Wexford; but we think we are limited to Wexford from the mention in his will of the mayor, sheriffs, and churchwardens of Wexford.

5265. In fact you are limited by the good old rule that charity begins at home, and you apply it as regards religious denominations as well as localities?—We do, certainly.

5266. Mr. O'Connor.—Do you say, Mr. Archdall, that there is no Intermediate school in Wexford but Tate's?—I don't know.

5267. Are you aware of the existence of St. Peter's College?—No. I don't know anything about it.

5268. You never heard of it before?—I heard of the college.

5269. Do you ever make any distinction, as regards their position in life, between the boys who are candidates for the position of pupils?—Never.

5270. Did you ever hear of its being done?—I did hear of the distinction being made, but it was not by me

Jan. 6, 1881.

The Ven. J. C. Archdall.

5271. Did you not know that that was one of the reasons why the petition was presented in 1877?—I think I did, but I am not quite certain. I heard some one say that the father of the boy objected to was a tailor or smith.

5272. Did you hear that that was the reason why he was objected to?—Well, no; nor would it be an objection in my mind.

5273. Do you know by what right the bread left by the will is distributed by the rector in the Protestant church although it was left for all denominations?—Under the will he does it.

5274. Lord Justice FitzGerald.—I will read what the will says:—He gives £1,000, payable in six equal payments within six years after his decease, in trust to the mayor, rector, sheriffs, and churchwardens of Wexford, to lodge the same in some good and sufficient fund at the most productive interest, and to apply the interest weekly, every week through the year, in the purchase of bread, to be impartially distributed amongst the indigent housekeepers of Wexford, without any distinction of religion, every Sabbath day, immediately after Divine service, for ever."

Mr. O'Conor.—That doesn't say where it is to be distributed.

Dr. Traill.—But they were all Protestants at that time, and he assumes that "after Divine service" meant in the Established Church. The Established Church was open to everybody.

5275. Lord Justice FitzGerald.—The Commissioners of Charitable Donations and Bequests hold the fund for the bread money. It is not in the hands of these trustees at all.

Mr. Elgee.—They simply remit the dividends each half-year.

5276. Lord Justice Naish.—If there is any suggestion of a complaint about it the Commissioners would interfere.

5277. Mr. Elgee. We don't make any. (To the Witness).—How often has the Mayor of Wexford attended your meetings,—does he attend any of them in the year?—I don't think the Mayor attended this year at all.

5278. How many Mayors have you known to attend these meetings?—First, there was Mr. Green, then Mr. Thompson.

5279. Did Mr. Harper attend?—No.

5280. Or Mr. Devereux?—I think he attended.

5281. These were the only three?—That I know.

5282. Dr. Traill.—Were they Protestants or Roman Catholics?—One was a Protestant, Mr. Thompson.

5283. Lord Justice FitzGerald.—Last year I find that on the 11th of January, 1888, a meeting of the trustees was held at which there were present the Rector, Mr. Latham, Mr. Wynne, and another. There was no meeting from January until May.

Witness.—I think there was illness.

5284. Lord Justice FitzGerald.—At the meeting on the 2nd of May, 1888, there were present the Archdeacon, the Mayor of Wexford, General Doran, Mr. Browne, and Mr. Latham. The whole body of trustees attended at that May meeting. Who was that Mayor of Wexford?

Mr. Elgee.—Mr. Harper.

5285. Lord Justice Naish.—What was he?

Mr. Elgee.—A Catholic.

5286. Lord Justice FitzGerald.—On the 6th of June a meeting was summoned and General Doran and Mr. Browne only attending, there was no quorum; but a cheque was drawn for the master's salary. On the 3rd of July the Archdeacon and Mr. Latham attended—no quorum, but cheques were drawn. At the August meeting Mr. Latham, General Doran, and Mr. Browne attended; the minutes were read, the accounts were reported, and three boys were admitted. On the 4th September Mr. Latham, General Doran, and Mr. Browne attended. On the 2nd October the Archdeacon, General Doran, Mr. Browne, and Mr. Latham attended. November meeting—the Archdeacon, General Doran, and Mr. Latham. December meeting—the Archdeacon, General Doran, Mr. Browne, and Mr. Latham. There was no meeting in January. On the 5th of February the Archdeacon, General Doran, Mr. Browne, and Mr. Latham attended. In March the attendance was Mr. Latham and Mr. Browne—no quorum. In April the attendance was the Archdeacon, General Doran, Mr. Browne, and Mr. Latham. There was no meeting in May. At the June meeting the Archdeacon, General Doran, Mr. Browne, and Mr. Latham attended. On the 2nd July there was a meeting, attended by Mr. Latham, General Doran, and Mr. Browne. So that the attendance seems to have been good.

Mr. Elgee.—If you turn back to earlier meetings you will see large attendances.

Mr. Richard Francis Caldwell, Head Master of Tate's School, sworn and examined.

5287. Lord Justice FitzGerald.—How long have you occupied the position of schoolmaster of Tate's school?—Since 1884.

5288. What position had you before you came here?—Master of St. Mary's Boarding and Day school, Dublin—20, Lower Dominick-street.

5289. Where were you trained as a teacher?—In Kildare-place.

5290. How long is it since you left Kildare-place?—In July, 1884.

5291. Have you been engaged in teaching since?—Yes.

5292. When you came, how many pupils were there in the school?—I don't think more than five or six for the first month. Another school had been established some time before I came.

5293. Lord Justice Naish.—What was the other school?—I think the Diocesan school.

5294. Dr. Traill.—A Protestant school?—A Protestant school, convenient to the town of Wexford.

5295. Lord Justice FitzGerald.—Is it still in existence?—No; as I heard it decreased, and the master left.

5296. How has Tate's school fared under you?—I have jotted down some figures, going as far back as 1884. In 1884 there were 40; in 1885, 37; in 1886, 39; in 1887, 37; in 1888, 35; and in 1889, 32.

5297. Lord Justice Naish.—Were these the numbers actually in attendance or the numbers on the roll?—On the roll.

5298. The average attendance is not, of course, up to that?—Not quite. The average attendance which we have, when compared to the number on the roll, is much better than it was in Dublin.

5299. Lord Justice FitzGerald.—Do the figures you have given represent the largest number of boys that were on the roll on any particular day in each year? The number for this year, you say, is thirty-two. Had you thirty-two boys there on one particular day of the year?—I just got the same date for each year—I forget what it was—and took down the number on the roll.

5300. Is there any cause that you know for the numbers being less now than in the previous years?—It may be more at the end of the year. The train from Wexford to Ballygeary ceased to run; by that I lost two boys.

5301. Of the thirty-two I believe four are free foundation boys who are fed and clothed and taught in the school?—And maintained in every respect.

5302. What arrangements are made about the boarding?—The trustees pay for each boy £23 10s. a year, and £1 for books and stationery.

5303. Does that include food and clothing?—Only food and teaching.

5304. Then the clothing is provided in addition?—By the trustees.

5305. Lord Justice Naish.—Do you know how much is allowed in the Incorporated Society's schools for free boys?—I do not, but they have good regulations.

5306. I suppose the clothing of your boys costs £5 or £6 for each. Have you anything to do with the providing of the clothing?—Except that I ask for them, and the trustees give me liberty and permission to buy them for them as cheap as I can, and good.

5307. Do you know about how much they cost per annum?—I don't.

5308. Dr. Traill.—You send the bill to the trustees?—Yes.

5309. Lord Justice FitzGibbon.—What is the dietary of the free boys?—They board with my own family.

5310. What family have you got living in the place?—I have eight children and two servants.

5311. Are any of your children amongst the pupils of the school?—There are two.

5312. Then the four boys and your own family all live together?—The boarders board with part of my family. I have daughters. We make two tables, but there is the same fare at each table.

5313. Have the four boys a separate table?—With my own sons and the assistant.

5314. Rev. Dr. Molloy.—Your own sons are not free boys?—Not at all.

5315. Lord Justice FitzGibbon.—What assistance have you in teaching?—I have a young man, a student of Trinity College.

5316. What does he teach?—Chiefly the classics.

5317. Are you yourself qualified to teach classics?—The junior classics—the elementary class, as they are called in the scheme.

5318. Who teaches French?—The assistant.

5319. What portion of the education do you give yourself?—Well, part of all.

5320. What are your emoluments?—The net salary is £60 a year, besides a house and coal.

5321. Have you any collars?—No.

5322. Lord Justice Naish.—Do you get any fees?—The trustees charge so much, according to the ability of the pupils to pay.

5323. Lord Justice FitzGibbon.—Do you get any share of the fees?—One-half.

5324. Lord Justice Naish.—And your assistant is paid by the trustees?—They give me £20 a year towards it.

5325. Lord Justice FitzGibbon.—How much do you add?—Sometimes £10; sometimes £5. I get the present man for £25.

5326. You make the supplement to him out of the fees of the pupils?—I never looked at it in that way. It is out of my own pocket.

5327. How much is your share of the school-fees for the year?—That I cannot tell you exactly. Perhaps the school book would.

5328. Rev. Dr. Molloy.—Have you a prospectus of your school?—No.

5329. Lord Justice FitzGibbon.—Have you sent any boys to the Intermediate Examinations?—I have.

5330. How did they get on?—Some got on very well.

5331. How many did you send this year?—I think three.

5332. Dr. Traill.—Is there a centre at Wexford?—There is; the examinations are held at St. Peter's College.

5333. Last year, do you remember, how many did you send?—I do not.

5334. When you say that some of them did very well, what were the highest distinctions that your boys got?—The list I hand in will show.

5335. Lord Justice FitzGibbon.—Here is the list:—

"Results of the Intermediate Examinations for 1887:—Boys from Wexford. Four from St. Peter's College all with exhibitions in the Senior Grade. In the Middle Grade six boys from St. Peter's College, of whom three had exhibitions, and one got a £3 prize. In the Junior Grade the first boy of the list is from Mr. Coldwell's [Tighe's] school, a £1 prize; and there are three others who passed."

5336. Mr. O'Conor.—I don't think the four boys from St. Peter's College all got exhibitions.

Rev. Dr. Molloy.—They got exhibitions in the Junior Grade, and retained them after having passed into the Senior Grade.

5337. Lord Justice FitzGibbon (to witness).—You have got four boys in the Junior Grade who passed in 1887?—Yes.

5338. Why have you not been able to send up more?—Well, I find that the boys don't care to work unless they think they will get prizes. They think that by working for the last year they will get a prize.

5339. Rev. Mr. Latham.—Hadn't you some boys for a school of the Incorporated Society this year?—Yes.

5340. How many of them went up?—Three.

5341. Were they able to read for the Intermediate examinations?—I forgot to mention that.

5342. Isn't it a fact that your boys, for the most part, are from a class who cannot go to the Intermediate examinations?—They are.

5343. Lord Justice Naish.—For what reason cannot they go?—The three boys that Dr. Latham refers to were three of the smartest boys that I had. They are reading for another examination in Kilkenny.

5344. Lord Justice FitzGibbon.—You say that they were preparing for an Incorporated Society's school; what school do you refer to?—The Pococke College.

5345. These boys would be younger than those who would go in for the Intermediate Examinations?—They would be the same age. They were three of my best boys.

5346. Dr. Traill.—Why were they excluded from the Intermediate Examinations?—They could not prepare for the two.

5347. They were not excluded by the rules of the Intermediate Examinations?—Oh, not at all.

5348. Lord Justice FitzGibbon.—The preparation for the Incorporated Society's school was enough for them?—Yes.

5349. Rev. Dr. Latham.—Of the attendance, on an average, since you began teaching, what percentage from Tighe's School passed the Intermediate Examinations?—I don't know.

5350. Rev. Dr. Molloy.—The number that went in was so small that any percentage founded on it would be delusive.

5351. Lord Justice FitzGibbon (to witness).—To what callings in life do your boys, as a rule, go?—Some to the medical profession and some to business.

5352. Have you prepared any boys for the Civil Service?—None.

5353. Rev. Mr. Latham.—Are you not preparing one at present?—Yes, but I don't know the result.

5354. Weren't the L'Ancies pupils of yours?—Yes, they passed for the Civil Service. It was for the Excise they passed.

5355. Lord Justice FitzGibbon.—So far as your experience goes, can you suggest any improvements in the management of the school, either as regards the course or method of education, or generally?—I don't think so.

5356. Lord Justice Naish.—I see by the scheme that the course of instruction, so far as classics are concerned, is restricted to an elementary course. Do you teach more than elementary classics?—Well, I had a pupil preparing for Trinity College, and I brought him through the Little-go and the Degree Examinations as a private pupil.

July 4, 1888. Mr. [illegible] Tighe examined.

[illegible]

6357. Dr. Traill.—Who is he?—A medical man of Dublin, named Poland.

6358. Lord Justice Naish.—You were not teaching in the school when it was started under the new scheme?—I was appointed immediately after that.

6359. Wasn't the objection to the previous working of the school that it gave too high a class of education?—I don't know.

6360. The provision in the scheme as to teaching is:—

"That in addition to the English, commercial, and mathematical education given in the said school, there may also be given instruction in French and elementary classics;"

which would seem to show an intention that the education was to be confined to elementary classics, and that the higher classics were not to be taught in the school.

6361. Dr. Traill.—

"For which a further fee not exceeding £2 a year extra may be charged."

How many out of the thirty-two are paying that?—I don't think we have any at present.

6362. Is French taught in the school at all?—It is.

6363. How many boys learn it?—Five, I think.

6364. Then they must pay the £2 apiece?—But they are free boys.

6365. Rev. Dr. Molloy.—What are the fees paid by the paying boys?—From £3 a year down to 1s. 3d. a quarter.

6366. Professor Dougherty.—Are boys entering from your parochial school received at a lower fee than those entering from other schools?—I don't think that has anything to do with it.

6367. There is a resolution on the minute book that they shall be received at a lower fee?—I did not know that that was the case.

6368. How many boarders can you accommodate in your building?—I think about twenty.

6369. But you are restricted to four by a resolution of the trustees?—No, we have had six.

6370. Would it be a disadvantage to the foundation if you were permitted to receive paying boarders in addition to the free boys?—I don't think it would.

6371. You said that because you were restricted to four boys, the cost of maintaining a free boy was greater than it might otherwise be?—I don't think I was restricted to four boys. We have had six.

6372. Dr. Traill.—Are you restricted at all?—I think not. It depends on the funds.

6373. Lord Justice FitzGibbon.—What happened was this. The paying boarders in Mr. Aldhouse's time appeared to have overshadowed the original intentions of the founder. When that was done the local people complained, and the Court of Chancery made a rule in the other direction altogether, that there should be no paying boarders at all. The circumstances, of course, in different localities vary. We have seen an excellent school at Tullyvin, in the county of Cavan, where they prepare boys in a course for the Incorporated Society; the boys board together, and are cheaply fed and well kept.

The Archdeacon of Ferns.—During Mr. Aldhouse's time the boys all boarded together, and the foundation boys never suffered in the least degree from having a large number of boarders.

6374. Dr. Traill.—How many boarders had he?—I think up to twenty-five. It was a very respectable and a very fine school. They all boarded together, and I have seen them at dinner together. The foundation boys never suffered in the least from it. I think it would be an advantage if we were allowed to have more boarders.

Lord Justice FitzGibbon.—But unfortunately the local people seem to have objected when Mr. Aldhouse made it a high class school, which was not what the founder intended.

6375. Lord Justice Naish.—Was the question fought out before the Vice-Chancellor as to whether there should be only free boarders?

Mr. Flynn.—It was all fought out, and he decided the point.

6376. Did the inhabitants of the town pray that there should be no boarders?—They did.

6377. Rev. Dr. Molloy (to Witness).—Who fixes the fees that the day boys are to pay?—The trustees.

6378. Dr. Traill.—Do you know, Mr. Archdeacon, how many day boys there were when exception was taken to the management of the school by Mr. Aldhouse?

The Archdeacon of Ferns.—I think over twenty.

6379. Did there appear to have been a falling off in the number of day boys owing to the fact of there being so many other boys to be taught?

Rev. John G. Jacob.—I was secretary to the trustees at that time, and I remember the circumstances perfectly. Mr. Aldhouse had a large number of paying day boys as well as free day boys, and he used to pay a certain amount of the fees to the trustees, which went to increase the number of foundation boys, in fact.

6380. Dr. Traill.—What was the exception taken by the inhabitants—how did the day boys suffer from the boarding school?

Rev. Mr. Jacob.—I believe the day boys did not suffer in the least from the boarding school.

6381. But the Vice-Chancellor must have had some case put before him?

Rev. Mr. Jacob.—The case put forward was that the trustees were going beyond their powers.

6382. And that somebody was suffering for it, I suppose?

Rev. Mr. Jacob.—Well, that was a matter of opinion; but in point of fact the two petitioners to the Court of Chancery had no children to go to the school, nor never had.

6383. Professor Dougherty (to Witness).—Have you any entrance examination in connection with the admission of boys to the school?—There is an examination—the trustees examine the boys.

6384. Is it a competitive examination?—I don't think it is.

6385. What are the religious denominations of the boys at present in attendance at the school?—They are all Episcopalians, I think, at present.

6386. You have had pupils of other Protestant denominations from time to time?—I have had.

6387. Presbyterian boys?—Methodists. I don't remember Presbyterians. Yes, I had.

6388. What religious instruction do you give in the school?—I don't well know how to answer that question. I only say the Bible.

6389. Is there any other religious instruction in addition to the reading of the Bible?—There is; in the principles of our Church.

6390. And is that religious instruction given to all the children without exception?—It is. Suppose that a Methodist comes we ask him has he any objection to say our catechism; and if he brings a note from his father to say that he does, I don't press it. But to the Bible there is no exception.

6391. Then you teach the catechism to all the boys unless their parents object?—Yes, but they have never done it.

6392. You have no conscience clause in operation?—Such a clause was not in the scheme.

6393. You receive results fees from the Intermediate Education Board?—Oh, yes, of course.

6394. Then before receiving the fees did you ever sign a paper saying that a conscience clause was in operation in your school?—I don't understand.

6395. Dr. Traill.—You seem to carry out a conscience clause, for you don't teach the catechism to any boy whose parents object to it. Professor Dougherty asks you if you ever signed the conscience clause of the Intermediate Education Board?—Yes.

5396. You signed a document without knowing what it was?—I don't know.

5397. Lord Justice FitzGibbon.—It is signed by all the schoolmasters of denominational schools. It is a declaration that no boy is excluded from secular education by reason of his objection to religious instruction; but unless a boy objects to the religious instruction, and is thereby excluded from the secular instruction, the clause doesn't attach.

Witness.—That declaration I sign every year.

5398. Lord Justice FitzGibbon.—Is it the case that you never excluded a boy from secular instruction by reason of his objecting to religious instruction?—Never.

5399. Rev. Dr. Molloy.—Under the scheme you receive children from the age of nine; at what age do they generally come?—Most of them are waiting till they are nine; that's about the age at which they come.

5400. Then you have to give them an elementary education as well as a superior education?—According as they are able to receive it.

5401. Children of nine will be in want of an elementary education?—Of course.

5402. Do you find much practical inconvenience in having to teach one set of your children a superior course and the other set an elementary course?—Not the slightest, because we arrange them in classes.

5403. Do you require from all the pupils coming to you a certain elementary knowledge before you admit them?—We do.

5404. How much?—The trustees examine them.

5405. What knowledge do you require from the pupils before they are admitted?—They must write a fair hand, know the fundamental rules of arithmetic, and be able to read and spell.

Rev. Dr. Latham.—In reference to the Intermediate Examinations, the question I asked was what proportion does the number of boys who passed these examinations bear to the number in the whole school?

5406. Lord Justice FitzGibbon (to witness).—Was that the largest number that you ever sent up to these examinations in any one year?—I am not sure.

5407. Rev. Dr. Molloy.—Can you tell us how many from your school passed last year in the Intermediate Examinations?—I think either three or four.

5408. And in the year before?—About the same.

5409. Lord Justice FitzGibbon.—That would be about one in ten?—About that.

5410. How many out of the thirty-two in your school would be of an age to compete?—There would not be more than ten. From twelve to sixteen is the age for the junior grade. They leave me about that age.

5411. And out of these ten you passed four?—Yes.

5412. Mr O'Conor.—How many of the four that you passed last year were your own sons?—Not one.

5413. Did any of your sons pass at all?—Oh, yes.

Lord Justice FitzGibbon.—I see that there passed in 1887 Charles W. Caldwell who got a £1 prize; also Richard Creed, James Jeffers, and a pupil named Arthur Rowe.

5414. Dr. Traill.—Was your son taught by yourself?—He was.

5415. There was no reason why he should not pass as well as any other boy in the school?—He passed better.

5416. Mr. O'Conor.—How many years have you been sending boys up to the Intermediate Examinations?—Since I came, in 1879, and I think in 1880.

5417. Did you ever get an exhibition in all that time?—The boys didn't; but two of my daughters did, one the fourth in Ireland.

5418. How many prizes did the boys get?—Only one.

5419. A prize of how much?—£1.

5420. Only one prize in nine years?—That's all.

5421. And the others passed in certain subjects?—Yes.

5422. In how many subjects, usually—what was the largest number of subjects, and what were the subjects?—They passed in English, French, Latin, arithmetic, Euclid, algebra, natural philosophy, and drawing.

5423. Did any one boy pass in all these?—No.

5424. Rev. Dr. Molloy.—I find that in 1887, Richard Creed passed in Latin; got honour marks in English; passed in French; got honour marks in arithmetic; passed in Euclid; got honour marks in algebra; and passed in natural philosophy, drawing, and the theory of music. That is a fair return. Was he a pupil of yours?—Yes.

Dr. Traill.—What became of him?—He is in the bank.

Rev. Dr. Molloy.—I understand Mr. Caldwell to say that his school is to a large extent an elementary school, but that he prepares for the Incorporated Society's schools, and also for the Intermediate Examinations.

5425. Dr. Traill.—How many of your boys passed at Kilkenny?—I sent candidates on two occasions, and on the first occasion they got the first and second places out of thirty-seven boys.

5426. Lord Justice FitzGibbon.—It is right to say that Mr. Caldwell could hardly be expected to pass any large proportion of boys, for the scheme under which the school is managed is manifestly framed to keep it down below the level of an intermediate school. It may have been that Mr. Alderman got it up too high; and that it was put down too low afterwards by way of reaction. All that is stated here is, that the pupils are to receive a sound English, commercial, and mathematical education. No doubt it is possible, but it is extremely difficult, to pass in the Intermediate Examinations without a second language besides English.

Witness.—Impossible.

5427. Lord Justice FitzGibbon.—It is now impossible, but only this year. The other instruction to be given is limited to instruction in French and elementary classics, for which a further fee of £2 a year is charged. So that at present the scheme makes it rather a superior primary school.

Mr. O'Conor.—But the Archdeacon said that this was the only Intermediate school in Wexford.

Rev. Dr. Molloy.—Mr. Caldwell has a distinct knowledge of St. Peter's College.

5428. Rev. Mr. Latham.—Has not Mr. Bonthey a school in Wexford?—Yes.

5429. Is it not chiefly for the class of boys who would go to St. Peter's College?—Yes.

5430. Lord Justice Naish.—Is that a Catholic or a Protestant school?

Mr. O'Conor.—It is a Protestant school.

5431. Lord Justice FitzGibbon (to Witness).—Then, your school is not supplying the wants of Wexford as regards intermediate education. You say yourself that it is a superior primary school?—You may call it that.

5432. Rev. Dr. Molloy.—It is plain that you passed your pupils very satisfactorily, for the means you had?—Thank you.

Dr. Traill.—And having regard to the restrictions under which you labour by the Chancery scheme.

5433. Mr. O'Conor.—How long was the school in existence that it had but four free boarders, I mean, since you came?—I don't think more than about six months.

Dr. Traill.—The Archdeacon said it was during the time of the lawsuit.

5434. Mr. O'Conor.—How long was that—how long did it take you to pay the costs?—I don't know.

5435. What is the lowest number of day boys that you have had?—The lowest number is in the present year.

5436. Did it ever go down as low as ten?—Oh, no—not since the time I speak of. I began with about eight.

June 4, 1888.

Mr. Richard Ferguson Caldwell.

July 1, 1886.

Mr. Richard Francis Colclough.

5437. Lord Justice FitzGibbon. — Substantially you have had between thirty and forty boys every year since?—We never had below thirty.

5438. Mr. O'Conor.—You said that some of your boys passed for the Civil Service. Did they pass direct from you, or go to a grinder in Dublin after they left you?—I am not sure.

Rev. Mr. Latham.—They did not go to a grinder. I am quite certain they did not.

5439. Mr. O'Conor.—Did you teach them specially for the Civil Service?—Oh, yes. They went in for it.

5440. How many of them passed?—Two, I think.

5441. Were these the only two that ever went in for that examination?—Yes.

5442. Dr. Traill.—For the Excise, was it?—For the Excise.

The Rev. James Latham sworn and examined.

Rev. James Latham.

5443. Lord Justice FitzGibbon.—How long have you been Rector of Wexford?—Eleven years and a half.

5444. During that time you have been an ex-officio trustee of Tate's School?—Yes.

5445. We have heard evidence leading to the conclusion that it is substantially a superior primary school with some intermediate teaching. Do you think the education given in it such as is most needed in the place?—Yes.

5446. What is the provision for intermediate education over and above Tate's School—you mentioned another school?—That is a private school. There have been two efforts since I came to get up special intermediate schools. One was called the Diocesan school—it was not a Diocesan school, but was held in a building which had been occupied by a Diocesan school. It was got up by a meeting of the parishioners, and Mr. King, from Ennis College, was master of it. He had the school here for a couple of years, and then gave it up, and went to Rathmines-square, in Dublin. He gave it up after our school was started.

5447. Lord Justice Naish.—What was the date of that?—I am not quite certain—about 1879 or 1880.

5448. Lord Justice FitzGibbon.—What was the cause of it?—I don't like mentioning private affairs, but I think the cause partly was that Mr. King did not get on well with the parents of some of the boys.

5449. Do you think there are a sufficient number of boys in Wexford to maintain an intermediate school?—I am afraid not. There are not more than from twelve to eighteen.

5450. Do you think this large and considerable endowment could be utilised for the support of an intermediate school as part of the work of the endowment?—So long as it is carried out according to the Chancery scheme I don't think the people would go to it if they had the chance of a private school. It is looked upon as a poor school in the place.

5451. Rev. Dr. Molloy.—The very fact of its being a charity school is an impediment in the way of its getting such pupils?—Yes.

5452. Lord Justice FitzGibbon.—What provision for elementary teaching is there in Wexford?—Tate's school for the boys, and a school under the National Board for the girls.

5453. Is there no National school for boys?—Only for small boys under nine.

5454. Rev. Dr. Molloy.—And they go to the girls' school?—They go to the girls' school.

5455. Lord Justice FitzGibbon. — What are the numbers in that school?—From thirty-eight to forty-two.

5456. You are the manager of it?—Yes.

5457. I suppose those numbers entitle you to a class salary for your teacher?—Yes.

5458. Then there would not be boys enough to get a class salary for a master for a boys' school?—We broke up the Parochial school when Tate's school was re-established. We found the numbers to be getting so small that the Erasmus Smith's Board would probably withdraw their grant, and we anticipated them.

5459. There is no Erasmus Smith's grant now to Wexford?—No.

5460. Would it be possible to establish an elementary department in Tate's school with assistance from the National Board, and utilising the endowment to give higher education?—I think it would.

5461. We should be glad to hear what you have to say regarding the restrictions under your Chancery scheme?—I think it would be a great advantage to have boarders in Tate's school. It would be a great help to the boys at present on the foundation, and would enable the trustees to put an increased number of boys on the foundation. Before Rankin's private school was got up we had boys attending who paid from £3 to £7 a year in fees, and we were able to board two extra boys. For several years we had six boarders in the school.

5462. Your paying boarders contributed to the support of the school?—Our paying day boys contributed to the support of the others.

5463. I find, in looking at the minute book, that on the 20th of February, 1878, Mr. Elgee presented a draft scheme, when it was ordered that a clause should be inserted in it that in addition to the free boys, day boys, whose parents could afford it, should be admitted on payment of certain fees?—That was carried out.

5464. It was then proposed that paying boarders should be admitted, and there voted for the motion Mr. Tronson and Mr. Latham ——

Witness.—I have changed my mind.

5465. Lord Justice FitzGibbon.—You voted for it; you have not changed your mind; and there voted against it Mr. King and the chairman. Motion lost by the chairman's casting vote. Mr. Tronson handed in a protest. Ordered that no clause should be inserted binding the trustees to the admission of any definite number of either boarders or day boys. Ordered that an application should be made to increase the number of the trustees or to limit the [illegible] selection for free boys; and the board was then adjourned to receive the Attorney-General's sanction of the petition. Mr. Tronson entered on the minutes a protest against the scheme resolution now prepared by the other trustees, whereby they withdrew from the amended scheme put forward by the three trustees whose signatures are attached thereto the clause allowing paying pupils as boarders.

5466. Lord Justice Naish.—The chairman is represented as having given his opinion in favour of the clause.

Witness.—I was only in Wexford a short time then, and I rather think I did not go in for boarders; but I certainly think that boarders now would be a very great advantage.

Professor Dougherty.—You are put down as having voted for the proposition then.

5467. Lord Justice FitzGibbon.—If you had been for it and the archdeacon for it ten years ago, it would be the law now; but the archdeacon having been against it, his casting vote decided it the other way.

Witness.—I think you are making a mistake. I think the archdeacon was for the boarders.

5468. Lord Justice FitzGibbon.—There is no doubt about what is here.

Witness.—If that be correct I have not changed my mind. I am still for the boarders.

5469. After your experience what is your view now?—I think it would be of great advantage to take boarders. I think there ought to be some means of providing that the foundation boys should not suffer, and, so far as I understand, they never did suffer from having boarders.

5470. Then you would be for admitting them on the same terms as in the Incorporated Society's schools—all taught together and all treated alike, but one set of boys free and the other set paying a reasonable sum?—Most decidedly. Those who would object to having the son of a navvy in the school would not come.

5471. Lord Justice NAISH.—If the son of a navvy was entitled to be taken into the school, why was he driven out?—I don't think he was. If there are five candidates and only four vacancies, you must reject somebody.

5472. Lord Justice FITZGIBBON.—Is the quality of the education what you think it ought to be?—I don't think it is.

5473. Lord Justice NAISH.—What do you think it ought to be?—The scheme says a sound commercial education and elementary classics.

5474. Would you confine it to elementary classics?—No, decidedly not.

5475. There you differ from the scheme in that respect?—Yes; but you cannot have advanced classics unless you take paying boarders. You will not have the means of paying a master. So that if the school continues as it is at present it cannot do better than it is doing.

5476. Lord Justice FITZGIBBON.—Then the changes you suggest are the introduction of a power to take paying boarders to be taught along with the other boys, and of a power to give a better class of education to those boys who want it?—Yes.

5477. Dr. TRAILL.—The parties had not the experience of the Intermediate Education Board before them at the time of the Chancery scheme?—No.

5478. And do you think that where all the schools in Ireland are giving facilities for that kind of education it ought to be extended to this school?—I am not quite sure whether the Intermediate Education system is the very best or not.

5479. Rev. Dr. MOLLOY.—Are you satisfied with the work done by your present head-master under the present circumstances of the place?—Yes, under the present circumstances.

5480. Do you think is possible to extend the benefits of the endowment to a larger number of the children of Wexford; the number actually receiving education under this large endowment is extremely small?—Well, unless you go to the higher classes you cannot go to the lower, because we take in every boy in the place, from the parish and from outside it. The numbers from which we have to draw are limited.

5481. Lord Justice FITZGIBBON.—What is the number of your Church population?—Between nine hundred and a thousand.

5482. Lord Justice NAISH.—About how many families?—About two hundred and forty, but a number of these are families without children.

5483. Rev. Dr. MOLLOY.—The numbers from which you can draw are limited by the action of the trustees who have excluded all but Protestants?—Well, I don't know that there is any rule excluding Roman Catholics.

5484. I think the Archdeacon told us that an application from a Roman Catholic would not be entertained?—It has never been made.

5485. Dr. TRAILL.—That is, for a free place?—The case has never occurred.

5486. Does your board refuse Roman Catholics if they apply to you?—They have never refused. They have never been asked.

5487. Mr. Elger.—As a matter of fact, since you came has there ever been an application from a Roman Catholic?—No.

5488. Mr. O'Connor.—How many boys do you say would go to higher schools if we had these boys?—I don't know.

5489. How many in Tate's school would go?—They all would go.

5490. How many would be fit to go?—I think any child is fit to go into any kind of school.

5491. Weren't you on the board of trustees yourself when the navvy's son was objected to?—No; I don't think it is correct to say that he was objected to. It is utterly false.

Mr. Elger.—It is utterly wrong. It is not out in the petition, but it was disproved. The Vice-Chancellor had it all before him. It is very unfair to make the charge now.

5492. Mr. O'Connor.—That is the reason why I asked it.

Mr. Elger.—As a matter of fact, the thing never happened.

5493. Lord Justice FITZGIBBON.—Here is the charge in the petition:—

"On the 11th of April, 1878, an application was made for the admission to the school of seven boys, one of whom, named Sprott, was rejected simply because he was a railway machinery's son. The said William Thompson, a trustee who did not attend on the occasion, said that afterwards he made inquiry as to why the said Sprott was not admitted, and was informed by some other trustees, who were present on the occasion, that if the boy Sprott had been admitted gentlemen's sons would not attend the school. There was no objection to the boy's character; he was the child of respectable parents; was fairly educated, and had passed the necessary preliminary examination; and he was rejected for the sole reason that his father was a mechanic, and that if a mechanic's son were admitted to the school gentlemen's sons would cease to go there. Your petitioners were informed by some one on behalf of the trustees that that was not the reason of his rejection, but that there were only five vacancies while there were six candidates, and that therefore the trustees only exercised their right of selection in rejecting the said boy Sprott. In reply, your petitioners allege that of the five boys who were selected for admission, one was not admitted because he was disqualified by being over age; yet the trustees did not admit Sprott."

Then it charges—

"That the trustees who were present and acted on the occasion were the Archdeacon, Rev. J. Peed, and Mr. W. J. Freeman; and that the said incident attracted public attention."

Then they inquired into the matter, and addressed the Commissioners of Charitable Donations and Bequests on the subject; and it ended in the petition.

5494. Dr. TRAILL (to witness).—Who was the head-master at that time?—Mr. Addison. When the scheme was drawn up one of the old boarders was connected with the railway—his name was Bell—so that he had been elected by the trustees, although his people were traders.

5495. Mr. O'Connor (to witness).—If a strictly Protestant Intermediate school were established, how many Protestant boys would you have going to it?—Well, I cannot prophesy anything about it.

5496. You know how many Protestants you have?—I know that all would go.

5497. Mr. Elger.—Dr. Latham, supposing that this were such a school as you suggest, do you think that all the boys now going to Boulter's school would have gone to this very school?—I think some of them would.

5498. How many has he?—About sixteen. I cannot be certain.

5499. Mr. O'Connor.—Would the boys who are now going to Tate's go to such a school?—If Tate's were an Intermediate school, not only would all the boys who are there at present remain, but I think a large number of others would go.

5500. Do you think they would leave Boulter's school?—Mr. Boulter is a capital master, and they are all fond of him, and I don't think any of them would leave him.

5501. Are there not some Protestants going to the college?—There are some, because the college fees are very low.

July 4, 1880.

Rev. James Latham.

July 8, 1886.

Rev. James Latham.

5502. Is that the only reason?—That is the only reason as far as I know.

5503. Are not the fees low at Boulter's also?—No.

5504. What are the charges there?—Nearly three times those of St. Peter's College. I think Mr. Boulter charges nothing less than £10, while at St. Peter's College it is only £4. It was stated to me that the boys would rather go to Boulter's than to the college on account of the fees.

5505. Rev. Dr. Molloy.—Is there any foundation for the allegation that a preference is given to gentlemen's sons in the admitting of free pupils?—Not the slightest.

Mr. Benjamin Hughes sworn and examined.

Mr. Benjamin Hughes.

5506. Mr. O'Conor.—You are an old inhabitant of Wexford?—Yes.

5507. Are you the editor of the *Independent* newspaper?—I am the manager and reporter of the *Wexford Independent*.

5508. Do you remember the first Commission that was here in 1855?—Yes—I was present at the first Commission under the Marquis of Kildare.

5509. You are aware of the scheme under which the school is now managed?—I have read it.

5510. You have read the will and codicil?—I did—the codicil.

5511. You published it?—Yes.

5512. What suggestions have you to make in reference to a new scheme?—I consider that the intention of Mr. Tate in establishing the school was, that it was never intended to be confined to one class of persons.

5513. You mean one denomination?—I do. I am aware that when I was a youngster——

5514. How long is that ago?—About 1834. I remember some of Tate's relatives in Wexford getting money left to them under Tate's will, and they were Roman Catholics.

Lord Justice Fitzgibbon.—There is a provision in the will for payments to his relations.

5515. Mr. O'Conor (to Witness).—Did you know Captain Arthur Murphy?—No.

5516. What would you suggest about the scheme?—That Tate's intentions be carried out.

5517. The first trustees were the mayor, the sheriffs, and the churchwardens?—The corporation always appointed the two sheriffs, who were known at that time by the name of bailiffs. In 1835 there were no sheriffs—the sheriffs had been abolished.

5518. Dr. Traill.—Were there sheriffs in 1794?—Yes. There were two called bailiffs.

5519. Lord Justice Fitzgibbon.—The original trustees were the mayor, the rector, the sheriffs, and the churchwardens.

Witness.—It was sheriffs that were spoken of at the different meetings of the Corporation.

5520. Dr. Traill.—These were necessarily all Protestants?—They were.

5521. So that he left his money all for Protestants?—No; my impression is, that taking the first part of the will right, he left it to persons without religious distinction. The will was made in a foreign country.

5522. Didn't he know that the mayor and the sheriffs were then all necessarily Protestants by law?—I could not say that.

5523. And he appoints with them the rector and the churchwardens of the Established Church?—Yes.

5524. How do you say that Mr. Tate's intentions were to open it to all denominations as regards the charity school?—Taking it with regard to the bread.

5525. It is specially mentioned that the bread was to be given to all denominations?—Well, in the other he didn't say that.

5526. Exactly; and when he leaves out any reference to all denominations in connexion with the other part of the bequest, wouldn't you naturally infer that it was not so intended?—I believe it was intended to be so given in consequence of the first part of the will.

5527. What part?—The part about the bread.

5528. Don't you think there is a difference?—I do not.

5529. Mr. O'Conor.—What is your proposal?—I would give it back to the Corporation.

5530. Dr. Traill.—He never gave it to the Corporation, but to the mayor, the rector, the churchwardens, and the sheriffs?—To the bailiffs.

5531. Mr. O'Conor.—Were the "bailiffs" and the "sheriffs" the same?—They were.

5532. Dr. Traill.—Do you mean that you would substitute for those two "sheriffs" two members of the Corporation now?—Yes.

5533. Mr. O'Conor (to Witness).—Who else would you appoint along with the two members of the Corporation?—Some person belonging to the town—an inhabitant.

5534. Would you give him a money qualification?—I say only a person belonging to the town.

5535. Dr. Traill.—What do you call a person "belonging to the town"?—A native of the town.

5536. Would the parish priest be a proper person?—I won't say any particular person.

5537. How many inhabitants are there in the town?—About twelve thousand.

5538. Lord Justice Fitzgibbon.—The mayor of Wexford is one of the trustees at present under the Chancery Scheme. Is the town under the Town Improvement Act?—It is.

5539. And "Mayor of Wexford" is the title held by the chairman of the Town Commissioners?—The same. I don't know whether this comes under your Commission or not; but in 1813 the present Lord Carbery's father left a large number of pictures to form a picture gallery for the town of Wexford.

5540. Dr. Traill.—Where are they?—No one can tell.

5541. Rev. Dr. Molloy.—Have you any document referring to it?—I have not.

5542. Professor Dougherty.—How did you obtain this information?—I read it when I was serving my time.

5543. Where did you read it?—In the *Independent*.

5544. Lord Justice FitzGibbon.—If he left anything for a school of art we could look into it. But unless it is educational we could not.

5545. Mr. *Elgee* (to Witness).—Are you aware that the Corporation actually tried to appoint two of their body to be bailiffs and thus trustees?—They did get Mr. O'Hara's opinion about it.

5546. And by a deed-poll of February, 1836, they appointed Richard Walsh and Robert Stafford to be trustees of this fund?—They did.

5547. Are you aware that when proceedings were taken in Chancery by the Rev. Mr. Elgee, the rector, and the other trustees of the will, that deed-poll was set aside as inoperative?—It was.

5548. Mr. *Elgee*.—And here is the finding:—

"I further find that William Tate, by his will and codicil, appointed the said trustees, that is to say:—The mayor, rector, sheriffs, and churchwardens, and Captain Arthur Murphy, since deceased, to be trustees; that Captain Arthur Murphy is long since dead; that there never was such an office as that of sheriff of the town of Wexford;

that no evidence was laid before me that the persons filling the office of bailiffs of the said town ever acted as trustees of the said will; and I further find that the deed-poll bearing date the [illegible] of February, 18[illegible], did not operate as an appointment of the respondents, Richard Walsh and Robert Bulford, as trustees, and that it is invalid."

Are you aware of all that happening?—I am.

[illegible]. Dr. Traill.—How can you say, after that legal decision, that it was in accordance with Mr. Tate's will for the Corporation to appoint these persons?—It is changed since.

[illegible]. Mr. Hynes.—He finds that there were no bailiffs?—Not at the time the scheme was framed; but at the time the will was made there was such an office.

[illegible]. And that there never was such an office as bailiff of the town?—Oh, we must admit that the bailiffs were sheriffs.

[illegible]. Dr. Traill.—Were the sheriffs called bailiffs?—They were—that is what they were called.

[illegible]. Rev. Mr. Ledlow (to Witness).—Was one English the name of Tate's relatives that got this money?—I cannot tell.

[illegible]. Was their grandmother a Protestant, through whom Tate was related to them?—I cannot tell, but I remember the persons being sent for.

[illegible]. Lord Justice Naish.—Was Tate a native of Wexford?—He was.

[illegible]. Lord Justice FitzGibbon.—Is any of the money for the relatives forthcoming, Mr. Hughes?—I don't know.

[illegible]. Mr. Hynes.—I recollect my father, who was mayor of Wexford, getting some of this money and distributing it.

[illegible]. Rev. Dr. Molloy (to Witness).—Did he die in Jamaica?—I think so.

[illegible]. Lord Justice FitzGibbon.—This case is singularly like one which we heard yesterday, namely, Ivory's Endowed School, New Ross. Twenty years ago Tate's School was made the subject of inquiry for a Chancery scheme, when it was found that the testator was a Protestant and a member of the then Established Church. He established a governing body for the charity, constituted of the mayor and two officers of the Corporation, with the rector and the two churchwardens, who were parish officers. At the time of the testator's will, in 1792, no person could be a member of a Corporation, either municipal or connected with a parish, unless he was a Protestant. Therefore, as the law stood at that time, the body which he established for the management of his charity would have been all necessarily Protestant. From that time forward there have been variations in the offices referred to. The sheriffs have been abolished, the mayor has become the chairman of the Town Commissioners ex-officio, and there have been changes also arising from the disestablishment of the Church. There still are the minister and two persons taking the title of churchwardens, although these are elected in a different way from that in which the old churchwardens were appointed. With the concurrence of my colleagues, I say that we believe the terms of the will do not show any intention on the part of the testator to exclude children of any religious denomination from the school—that is to say, every child was apparently entitled to come to the school and tender himself as a pupil, and there would be no breach of trust, or going beyond the intention of the testator, in taking pupils of any religious denomination, if they chose to come. But then the testator had a right to place the management of his property in the hands of any persons that he thought proper; and he gave it to a body which was of the Protestant character I have mentioned. Furthermore, it appears that these trustees, from time to time, have been in the Court of Chancery, and that their constitution has been modified to this extent, that the minister and the churchwardens still remain in, as they did under the will; the Archdeacon has been added to the body; and the mayor is still left in, but the sheriffs have disappeared. In other words, the two sheriffs have been exchanged for one archdeacon. Our duty is defined by the 15th section of our Act which says that in framing schemes it shall be the duty of the Commissioners with regard alike to the constitution of the governing body and to the educational provisions, to have regard to the spirit of the founder's intentions, and further that, in every scheme to maintain any educational advantage that was given to any particular class of persons, we must have regard to the educational interests of that class, and where money is provided for the education of children belonging to a particular class, either generally, or within a particular area, we must keep that money to be applied for the benefit of those children. Now, in the present case, Mr. Tate, a Protestant, has established a Protestant governing body for the management of the school, and, so far as the majority are concerned, it is so still. But, like many other men, he did not intend or desire that the benefit of the school should be refused to anybody that chose to take it. Great provisions have been made by our Roman Catholic fellow-countrymen for the education of those belonging to their own Church, in schools under the management of their own people; and to a large extent pupils who formerly attended schools under Protestant management, when they were the only ones available to them, have been withdrawn to schools under their own management. That creates no claim on the part of those who are conscientiously unwilling to accept the education given in this school; but it does give a right to those who choose to attend the school, and to take the benefit of the education to be got there, that they shall be able to get it without any violation of their conscience being imposed on them by the managers of the school. The same course has been taken at the other side, at St. Peter's College, where we hear that some Protestants are attending, who cannot get the class of education that they want elsewhere, and who prefer getting it at St. Peter's College to not getting it at all, though, no doubt, they would prefer to have it in a school under their own management if they could get it. There are several other matters to be considered. First, as regards the governing body, we could not, consistently with Mr. Tate's ideas, constitute any governing body but one which would be in its majority and in its general character Protestant; it always has been so, both under the Court of Chancery and also under the original will. But, subject to that, the question is, whether the body as now constituted, is the best that could be. It is small in number—five in all—of whom a member of the corporation is one, and the quorum is three. It is manifest that five persons with a quorum of three cannot always transact their business. We have in many cases introduced a provision that subscribers to a school, or the parents of children who pay fees to a certain amount, shall have a voice in electing one or two on the governing body, and this provision might be made use of here to increase the number of the governors. As to the character of the education given in this school there has been a little swing of the pendulum. At one time it became too good a school for the poor people of Wexford, and those who had the interests of those people at heart naturally objected; but in getting rid of that objection, they seem to have provided that the school should not be so good as they would now like to see it. The remedy would be to lay down that the education given in the school shall be such as the trustees approve of, and shall include an elementary education, or superior primary education, free for those who are entitled to it, giving the governing body a power of introducing a higher education if they think proper. If the gentlemen who are now trustees, or the majority of them, hold a meeting, and go fully into these questions, and send us in writing to our office on or before the 1st of October, any sug-

July 6, 1888.

Mr. Benjamin Hughes.

July 5, 1886. — Ven. Benjamin Hughes.

questions that they wish to put forward, we shall consider them carefully.

The Archdeacon of Ferns.—On behalf of my trustees, I have to thank the Commissioners for their patience and care in investigating the matter; for they have brought out matters of which I was not aware myself. We shall act on your suggestion of having a meeting, in order to see what we would recommend, and I will send the result to you.

ERASMUS SMITH'S SCHOOL, WEXFORD.

The Rev. *James Latham* re-examined.

Rev. James Latham.

5540. Lord Justice NAISH.—The grant to this school has been discontinued?—It was, some years ago, and the school itself is now under the Board of Education.

5541. Lord Justice FITZGIBBON.—The site was derived apparently from the Archdeacon of Ferns?—I have the original deed; it is dated June 28, 1821.

5542. Who are the trustees?

Mr. Elgee.—A new deed was executed in 1870 which I cannot find. We have only the draft of it. It was executed in that year by the Rev. James Peed, rector of Wexford, and the Rev. G. Richards, surviving trustees; and it appointed as new trustees Messrs. Bradish, Johnson, and another.

5543. Lord Justice FITZGIBBON.—This is a school vested in parochial authorities.

5544. Lord Justice NAISH.—Was any money paid for this grant, or was it a gift?

Mr. Elgee.—A gift from the Rev. John Elgee, then rector of Wexford.

Lord Justice FITZGIBBON.—There was a Lord Lieutenant's grant towards building the school.

5545. Dr. TRAILL.—Is there any provision in the deed for appointing successors to the trustees?—There is a provision in it for appointing new trustees. It is provided that at all times whenever any one or more of the trustees before appointed, or to be appointed, shall die or resign, the said Rev. John Elgee and his successors, with the consent of the surviving and remaining trustee or trustees, shall appoint by deed.

FERNS DIOCESAN FREE SCHOOL.

5546. Lord Justice FITZGIBBON.—Mr. Elgee, do you know anything about the Ferns Diocesan Free School. We have no information as to what has become of it, but it had an acre and a half of land?

Mr. Elgee.—Mr. Barrington was the master of that school. It is about half a mile outside the town. People named Geary claimed to be the owners of the schoolhouse and grounds, and somehow they got Mr. Barrington to take a lease for his own life.

5547. Lord Justice NAISH.—About what time was that lease made?—I should think twenty-five years ago.

5548. How long is it since he died?—He left the school shortly before he died. He is dead two years. The Geary family then brought an ejectment and sold in the Landed Estates Court, and it is all gone.

ST. PETER'S COLLEGE, WEXFORD.

The Rev. *Luke Doyle* sworn and examined.

Rev. Luke Doyle.

5569. Lord Justice FITZGIBBON.—You are the President of St. Peter's College?—I am. I am representing the Bishop for the whole county, and will answer anything your lordship wishes to ask me.

5570. How long have you held that office of President?—One year.

5571. Where is the college situated?—Inside the town.

5572. What quantity of land have you connected with it?—About forty-three acres.

5573. How is the land held?—By lease to the bishop and trustees. It is not all from one landlord; there are different leases.

5574. Do you know the terms of the leases?—I don't know.

5575. Who manages your business affairs for you?—Mr. O'Flaherty. I can get you all the leases.

5576. It is not necessary; do you know what the rent is?—It is subject to £163 rent.

5577. For forty acres?—For forty-three acres. The interest in a portion of the land was bought out—the landlord's interest. The rent was over £200, but it was reduced by £40.

5578. What buildings are there on it?—We have rather extensive buildings.

5579. It is stated to have been founded in 1819?—It succeeded an older establishment founded in 1811. The present portion of the buildings was opened in 1819.

5580. How were the funds provided for the building of the college?—By public collections, gifts, and donations from the people of the diocese.

5581. Were these diocesan collections made through the Roman Catholic Church?—Yes—altogether.

5582. Lord Justice NAISH.—Exclusively?—Exclusively.

5583. Lord Justice FITZGIBBON.—And applied entirely under the government of the bishop and the trustees?—Completely.

5584. Who appoints the trustees?—The bishop himself.

5585. It is a diocesan college?—It is a diocesan college.

5586. What is the present number of your pupils?—The number at present on the rolls is about eighty-nine.

5587. Lord Justice NAISH.—Are there both boarders and day pupils?—Both boarders and day pupils. The number is a little lower at present than usual, on account of the depression of the times. The average is over one hundred.

5588. What accommodation is there for boarders?—For seventy. There have been sixty-six in some years.

5589. Dr. TRAILL.—How many have you now?—Forty-two. In the earlier portion of the year it was less—only thirty-four. We have increased since Christmas.

5590. Lord Justice FITZGIBBON.—What is the largest number of boarders that you have had in recent years?—Sixty-six. I am speaking from memory.

5591. To what do you attribute the falling off?—To the depression in the times.

5592. What are your fees?—For boarders, £30 a year, and for day boys, £8.

5593. What course of education do you give?—The full course for the three grades of the Intermediate Examinations. We also prepare them for the Civil Service. Of course they are fit to pass the College of Surgeons.

5594. Dr. TRAILL.—How many is there accommodation for?—About seventy.

5595. Lord Justice FITZGIBBON.—Speaking roughly, what proportion of your boys are intended for the Church?—I should say seventy per cent.

5596. And the remaining thirty, I presume, get intermediate education for the secular professions?—Yes.

5597. Have you any theological department?—None at present. It is merely preparatory for Maynooth and the Irish colleges in Rome and Paris, and in Spain.

5598. Lord Justice NAISH.—Is there an Irish college in Spain?—Yes, one at Salamanca connected with the old university.

5599. Lord Justice FITZGIBBON.—Have you any invested funds on property of that character?—We have, for ecclesiastical students—bursaries.

5600. Are all the funds in your possession devoted for the purpose of educating pupils intended for the ministry of the Roman Catholic Church?—Yes.

5601. Have you any endowments for the education of lay pupils?—None whatever.

5602. They have the advantage of the school which, so far as its endowments are concerned, is intended for ecclesiastical students?—For ecclesiastical students.

5603. What success had you at the Intermediate Examinations?—I have a list here from the opening of the Intermediate Examinations up to the present day, and continued in manuscript up to last year. If you wish, I will read it.

5604. Lord Justice NAISH.—Give us a summary of it?—Beginning with 1884, in the senior grade one gentleman held his exhibition from the previous year, and won, in addition, a prize of £2; and a second gentleman held his exhibition from 1883, and won, in addition, a prize of £3. In the middle grade, Thomas Ryan won a new exhibition of £20, tenable for two years; Michael A. Hickey won a prize of £3; and John J. Meagher held his exhibition from 1883, and won an additional prize of £1—the total value being £2. I may mention that Thomas Ryan was fourteenth of all the pupils from Catholic colleges in Latin, and eighth of all Ireland in French, while in English he was third of all Ireland, and second of all Catholics. In the junior grade for the same year Thomas A. Washington won, in that year an exhibition of £15, tenable for three years; Edward J. Doyle won a prize of £3; and John J. Callaghan and Thomas Quigley won each a prize of £1. Thomas A. Washington held the sixth place in French of all Catholic colleges, and the second in algebra. In 1884 we also entered pupils for the Science and Art Department, South Kensington, and the result is given for two years.

5605. Lord Justice FITZGIBBON.—There was an Elementary School Scholarship of £10 for the best answering in junior grade mathematics and natural philosophy, and a Science and Art Scholarship of £15 in middle grade mathematics; who competed with you for them?—I think it was confined to students of the college itself. For the year 1885 Thomas M. Ryan retains his exhibition of £20 from the previous year, and won a £1 prize in books, and John J. Meagher holds his exhibition of £15 from 1883. In the middle grade for that year seven candidates passed. Thomas A. Washington retains his exhibition from 1884, and William H. Thompson wins a prize of £1 in books. In the examination in middle grade French, William H. Newport scored 511 marks out of a possible 700. In the junior grade for 1885, Edward J. Doyle won an exhibition of £15, tenable for three years; John J. Callaghan, an exhibition of £15, tenable for three years; Patrick King, an exhibition of £15, tenable for three years; James O'Hanlon, an exhibition of £15, tenable for three years; William J. Harper, a first class prize of £2 in books; Thomas Quinlivan, a first class prize of £2 in books; John J. Furlong, a second class prize of £2 in books; and Michael J. Butler, a third class prize of £1 in books. John J. Callaghan holds the twentieth place of all Ireland, and the sixteenth of all Catholics, in natural philosophy; Edward J. Doyle is seventeenth of all Ireland in Greek, ninth of all Catholics in English, and second in Latin; and Patrick King is first of all Ireland in algebra, having obtained the maximum number of marks in that subject.

5606. Lord Justice FITZGIBBON.—Did your college win any Burke Memorial Prizes?

WITNESS. John J. Callaghan won one. In 1886 none were entered in the middle grade. In the senior grade John Callaghan won a silver medal in French, a first class prize, and retained his exhibition of 1884; John Furlong won a first class prize; Edward Doyle won a second class prize and retained his exhibition of 1885; and Patrick King won a third class prize and retained his exhibition of 1885. Six others passed. In the junior grade for 1886, Thomas Quinlivan won a £20 exhibition, and got second place in English and ninth place in Latin for all Ireland. William Harper won a £20 exhibition; and Thomas O'Connor won a £15 exhibition; Michael Ryan won a second class prize; Michael Butler won a second class prize; and five others passed.

5607. Dr. TRAILL.—Are the pupils examined in Christian Doctrine and Sacred History by the Intermediate examiners?—No, but they are examined on the principle of the Intermediate Examinations.

5608. Rev. Dr. MOLLOY.—This return gives us the results of your Intermediate Examinations, but all the examinations were not held by the Intermediate Board?—Quite right.

5609. You have an Intermediate Examination in Christian Doctrine to supplement the examinations of the Intermediate Board?—It is carried out on the same principle. The papers are set by an examiner appointed by the bishop of the diocese. The young men put numbers on the papers only, and the examiners don't know whose they are reporting on. The papers are then sent to the bishop. In the year 1887 in the senior grade, John Callaghan won a third class prize and retained his exhibition, and Edward Doyle retained his exhibition.

5610. Lord Justice FITZGIBBON.—There were four exhibitions retained and a £1 prize gained. Were these four boys who retained their exhibitions the only boys who went up in the senior grade in that year from you had content any.

5611. Are they the only ones you have returned as passing?—The only ones I have returned here.

5612. I suppose the boys who remained, as those four boys did, for the senior grade, were kept on by reason of the exhibitions they had got?—No; they would not be qualified to enter Maynooth until they had passed the senior grade course. Their classical course is supposed to be complete when they enter Maynooth. The number of students in the senior grade is very small, and the greater number of the class are over age.

5613. Dr. TRAILL.—How do you account for those coming up late in life to you?—Well, it is the neglect of the parents, and perhaps also want of means.

5614. Do they go to the National schools first?—To the National schools first.

5615. Are they taken away from school for agricultural purposes?—I could not say that, but they are not sent up to us till they are perhaps fourteen or fifteen years of age, and then it is too late for the Intermediate.

5616. Professor DOUGHERTY.—Where do the boys receive their elementary classical teaching?—The elementary classical teaching is given with us—all the classical teaching is.

5617. Lord Justice FitzGibbon.—What is the youngest age at which you take boys?—About ten.

5618. Dr. Traill.—What is the oldest age at which you take them in?—At any age, so long as they are fit to qualify for the Church, and become priests.

5619. Lord Justice FitzGibbon.—I see that in the middle grade you have three exhibitions, and two passes?—Yes. In the junior grade for the year 1883 we have nine passes. In the senior grade William Harper wins a third class prize, and retains his exhibition; Thomas O'Connor retains his Exhibition of the previous year, and passes; and one other passes. In the middle grade James O'Connor wins an exhibition of £25, and four others pass.

5620. James O'Connor was not amongst those that passed in the previous year?—He went in twice in the middle grade, and three others passed in that grade. In the junior grade we have James M'Millan obtaining an exhibition of £15, a £3 prize in Latin composition, and a £3 prize in Greek composition, and he is also fourth in Classics in all Ireland. He was the second in Greek. There is one second class prize in the junior grade—William Quinlivan and six others passed.

5621. What is your teaching staff?—There are five and myself.

5622. Lord Justice Naish.—Are they all clergymen?—We have one lay teacher—a trained teacher, who teaches mathematics and science. He was trained in St. Patrick's Training College, and attended for six years in South Kensington.

5623. Rev. Dr. Molloy.—Did he go from St. Patrick's Training College to South Kensington?—No; he was a school assistant in Sh[illegible].

5624. And then he came to you?—He has been here again last September. His name is MacCarthy.

5625. Lord Justice FitzGibbon.—Was Mr. Hogan the principal of the school from which he came?—Yes, and this gentleman had charge of the other department. He was for six years attending the lectures in South Kensington during the vacations in each summer.

5626. He is your sole lay assistant?—Yes.

5627. You all reside in the College?—All but the lay teacher. He does not.

5628. What is his stipend?—£100 a year, and 50 per cent. of the results.

5629. Dr. Traill.—Do you find much difficulty in the matter of teaching Greek?—Yes.

5630. Because I observe that in some years you have had very good answering in the junior grade Greek, and in some years no answering at all in the junior grade?—Oh, yes; there is a difficulty. A great number of boys do not go in in Greek the first year. They go in in Latin. The number of those entering in Greek varies.

5631. How do you account for that?—By the difficulty of learning Greek.

5632. Do they pull up afterwards?—They learn Latin more easily, and we don't put them into all the subjects each year.

5633. I suppose all your students going into ecclesiastical life eventually must know Greek?—Yes; they cannot enter an ecclesiastical college without knowing Greek, it is essential at the examinations.

5634. Mr. O'Conor.—How many Protestants are in the school?—I think we have nine.

5635. Is James M'Millan a Protestant?—He is.

5636. Professor Dougherty.—What denomination does he belong to?—He is a Presbyterian, I think. I am not sure. He is the son of an Inspector of National schools.

5637. Mr. O'Conor.—Do you think he would send his son to St. Peter's College for the sake of saving £4 a year?—I do not think he would.

5638. Mr. [illegible].—Hasn't Mr. M'Millan a very large family?—I believe he has.

5639. Lord Justice Naish.—Didn't his son get an exhibition?—Last year he got £15, and he won prizes in Greek composition and Latin composition, and he is the fourth in classics in all Ireland.

5640. Dr. Traill.—I suppose you don't require him to pass in Christian doctrine?—No, we do not.

5641. Mr. O'Conor.—I suppose there is no interference with the Protestants as regards religious teaching?—None whatever.

5642. They are not let in to the religious instruction at all?—Never.

5643. Rev. Mr. Latham.—Does St. Peter's College take no pupils in under £10 a year?—We take some in for nothing if we find they are of respectable parents.

5644. It is not necessary that a boy going into St. Peter's College should pay £10 a year?—Not absolutely necessary. We make exceptions for particular individuals.

5645. Have you any knowledge of boys paying only £4 a year?—Yes.

5646. Then if a boy be not able to pay £10 a year he might be able to get into St. Peter's College for £4 a year, or even for less?—It is not usual.

5647. But he might be able?—We sometimes take boys in completely free.

5648. Mr. O'Conor.—How much does M'Millan pay?—£8.

5649. There is no special reduction made because they are Protestants?—None.

5650. Rev. Dr. Molloy.—I suppose if you had Tate's endowment you could receive a larger number of free pupils?—Yes.

5651. Lord Justice FitzGibbon.—What provision is there in Wexford for the elementary teaching of Roman Catholics?—There are convent schools and Christian Brothers schools for boys.

5652. Lord Justice Naish.—How many Christian Brothers schools are there in the county of Wexford?—There are four—Wexford, New Ross, Enniscorthy, and Gorey.

5653. Are there National schools also?—There is a National school in Wexford and a National school in New Ross.

5654. What difference, if any, is there between the two?—The books for the National schools are cheaper.

5655. Why should there be both Christian Brothers schools and National schools?—One reason is that we are not able to maintain a sufficient number of Christian Brothers by voluntary contribution. There are six here.

5656. How are they paid?—They get a collection every year and live on it as well as they can.

5657. Rev. Dr. Molloy.—Is there a Model school in Wexford?—There is in Enniscorthy.

5658. Do the Catholics get any substantial benefit from the Model school?—None whatever. The bishop of the diocese forbade Catholics to attend it. It was opened about twenty-seven years ago; and since then his two successors have also forbidden Catholics to go there. There may have been one or two Catholics attending it from time to time.

5659. How is the Model school in Enniscorthy attended?—I cannot speak very much as to the number of children there. Some years ago it was about thirty.

5660. Dr. Traill.—Is the head master a Protestant or a Roman Catholic?—I cannot say. At present I think he is a Protestant. There was a Catholic master there for a short time.

5661. Lord Justice FitzGibbon.—But that made no difference as regards approval or disapproval of the school?—No; it was done against the wishes of the bishop.

5662. Dr. Traill.—What is the exception that they take to the model school?—That it is godless—that there is no religion taught in it.

5663. Mr. O'Conor.—Would the Lord Bishop allow Catholics to go to Tate's school under the present scheme?—Under the present scheme I should say not, unless there was some conscience clause.

5664. Lord Justice FitzGibbon.—But even if there were a conscience clause?—I should think he would not, where there is a school already.

5665. Dr. Traill.—Wouldn't the conscience clause make it a godless school—if Roman Catholics were to a Protestant school with a conscience clause, wouldn't it be a godless school for them?—Unless there were some provision made for the training of the children.

5666. Wouldn't the Protestant school be a godless school for them?—If it were a Protestant school the bishop would not allow them to go there under any circumstances.

5667. Therefore there would be no object in making provision for them in Tate's school?—None whatever.

5668. Lord Justice Naish.—Is St. Peter's the only diocesan college in the diocese?—That's all.

5669. Lord Justice FitzGibbon.—What is the nearest intermediate school?—There is a school in Enniscorthy that sometimes sends in boys to the Intermediate Examinations. It is a Catholic school, without an endowment, and was formerly taught by a clergyman. At present it is in the hands of a layman.

5670. Are there any of the teaching orders at that intermediate school?—None.

5671. Does the Enniscorthy school send boys to the Intermediate Examinations?—Yes, to Wexford. They have no Intermediate class in Wexford.

5672. Lord Justice Naish.—Is there any endowment in the diocese of Ferns for any Catholic school except those bursaries in Wexford?—None. The great necessity in Enniscorthy is school buildings. They are very badly off for school buildings. There is a convent school for the intermediate education of girls.

5673. The convents generally have some small endowment?—Well, the one in Enniscorthy has no endowment.

5674. Dr. Traill.—Is the convent school here for girls under the National Board?—We have three convent schools under the Board, and one higher class school. In number one convent school there is an attendance of seven hundred.

5675. Lord Justice FitzGibbon.—Give us the attendance?—In the Presentation Convent school there is an attendance of about seven hundred daily. It is a poor school. In the Sisters of Mercy school there is an average attendance of four hundred, I should say.

5676. Is there any difference in the class of people attending the two schools?—No, they are both poor schools; there is no pay there. In the St. John of God Convent they have a school with over four hundred of a daily attendance. It is also a poor school.

5677. You said that there was an upper class school?—There is an upper class school under the Loretto Nuns with an attendance of about one hundred.

5678. Of them, how many are boarders?—Forty, I think, at present. July 4, 1888.

5679. Do they send pupils to the Intermediate Examinations?—Yes. Rev. Luke Doyle.

5680. How have they got on?—I have a general return from the nuns from the year 1882. They won three medals in music and one in drawing and English during that time; also eight exhibitions and twenty-five prizes, and they got seventy-seven passes. A great many pupils are sent in over age. A good many parents don't care for having their girls in the Intermediate Examinations.

5681. Rev. Dr. Molloy.—But the exhibitions and prizes gained were very numerous in proportion to the number of pupils sent in?—During the same period it got five medals, eight exhibitions, ten prizes, and thirty passes. At the Loretto Convent school in Enniscorthy, which is a day school, the average attendance is about eighty, but the children are very young; it is more or less an infant school. They also went in the Intermediate Examinations and won five prizes and twenty passes. They have no centre in Enniscorthy, which is very inconvenient, so that they have to send them here, and the same way from Gorey. More would have entered if they had had a centre in Gorey.

5682. Rev. Dr. Molloy.—I suppose they would be all glad to get an endowment?—They would be all glad; and particularly in Enniscorthy if we could get some buildings.

5683. Dr. Traill.—What help for all those children do they get from the State?—None.

5684. Don't they get State money in the National schools?—Those that are for the Intermediate Examinations do not, but the poor ones do.

5685. In the Enniscorthy schools do they get help from the State?—No; they have the Presentation Convent school with three hundred children and the Sisters of Mercy with two hundred and upwards.

5686. If you got more money from the State you would not want the Protestant endowment?—No.

5687. Lord Justice FitzGibbon.—As regards this particular endowment of St. Peter's College, it comes under subclause (b) of section 7 of our Act, which prevents the Act from applying to any endowment provided exclusively for the benefit of persons of any particular religious denomination, or under the exclusive control of persons of that denomination, unless the governing body of that endowment signify their wish in writing to have a scheme framed under the Act. That is a matter which I believe has been under your consideration. You should understand that the main advantage that we could confer on you would be to vest your property in an incorporated body which could hold it without a deed. It is for yourselves to consider whether you will apply for that or not.

5688. Lord Justice Naish.—Is it under consideration in your diocese?

Witness.—The Bishop has been taken more or less by surprise. He has not had time to consider a scheme.

DUNCORMACK SCHOOL (RICHARDS GRANT).

The Rev. Robert H. Dowse sworn and examined.

5689. Lord Justice FitzGibbon.—You are the rector of the parish of Duncormack?—Yes. Rev. Robert W. Dowse.

5690. Is there any parochial school in Duncormack parish now?—Not belonging to our Church.

5691. Do you know what has become of the old one?—It is there.

5692. Who is in possession of the land?—I am. There is three-quarters of an acre.

5693. How is it used?—For grazing.

5694. Is there any building on it?—There is a small house.

5695. It is stated here that there was a grant from a gentleman of the name of Richards, on the 12th of March, 1828, of one acre, two roods, and nineteen perches; do you know by what title the land is held?—Five shillings a year.

5696. Is it under any trust for a school?—It is under me.

5697. Have you got the grant?—I have.

5698. Dr. Traill.—To whom do you pay the 5s. a year?—I have not paid it.

5699. Lord Justice FitzGibbon (Reads)—"It is a

July 4, 1889.

Rev. Robert R. Dunne.

grant to the Right Rev. Thomas, Lord Bishop of Ferns, and the Rev. R. Bentley, to enable the minister to establish a school in pursuance of Act of Parliament, the grant being of part of the lands of Ballygriff, one acre plantation measure, to hold for ever, in trust for the use of a resident schoolmaster to be appointed by the resident minister for the time being, and for no other purpose, paying on the 1st May in each year a rent of 5s. The master shall be not only appointed by the minister but removable by him at all times by writing under his hand, and he shall teach and instruct all such children as shall be named to him by the written directions of the minister, in reading, writing, the English language, and arithmetic, and such of them as shall be the children of parents of the Established Church, in the Church Catechism, in such mode and according to such plan of education, and such regulations as shall be from time to time ordered by the minister. No person is to be allowed into that position unless he shall have signed an agreement to yield it up on the request of the minister." (To Witness).—How long is it since there has been a school there?—Eight or nine years.

5700. I suppose there is neither schoolmaster now nor scholars now?—No.

5701. Where is the nearest elementary school to this site at Duncormick?—About a hundred yards off there is a National school.

5702. Under whom is it?—Under the priest.

5703. Was it established since the Duncormick school, or is it there as long as you have known the parish?—As long as I have known the parish.

5704. Are there any grown Protestant children in the neighbourhood?—None.

5705. Is there any possibility of making this site available for educational purposes there?—I think not.

5706. What do you think ought to be done with it?—I don't know.

5707. Lord Justice FitzGibbon.—How far is this place from Rathaspeck?—Six or eight miles.

5708. Because there is a sum of money belonging to Rathaspeck school,—do you know anything of it?—No.

5709. Lord Justice FitzGibbon (to Mr. J. G. Pounden).—Who understands the position of this matter now.

Mr. Pounden.—This parish of Duncormick is united, subject to Mr. Dunne's life interest, to the parish of Bannow. There is a school at Bannow under the National Board, and if this endowment is to be transferred to any other school the natural place for it would be Bannow.

5710. Dr. Traill.—How can we transfer the building to any other site?

Mr. Pounden.—Not the building but the value of it.

5711. Lord Justice FitzGibbon (to Witness).—What sort of a building is on the land?—A two-storey house.

5712. Do you remember the school being attended by pupils at any time?—Oh, yes.

5713. What was the largest number?—Fifteen.

5714. Were there any others besides Protestant children?—Yes there were some Roman Catholics.

5715. But the Protestants have left the neighbourhood?—Oh, yes, they are gone away. Some of them are dead. When the Church was disestablished we lost £60 a year.

5716. What was that?—The Clerk to the Church had it. He was schoolmaster too.

5717. Mr. O'Conor.—Do you remember the other school being built by the Catholics ten years ago?—I don't know anything about the Catholic school at all.

5718. But you remember Catholics attending your school?—A few.

5719. And they attended up to the time it was stopped?—Oh, they left off before it was stopped.

5720. Rev. Mr. Latham.—Mr. Dunne, do you consider that Protestant children are Catholics?—No.

Rev. Mr. Latham.—Well, I do.

The Rev. Thomas Roche sworn and examined.

Rev. Thomas Roche.

5721. Mr. O'Conor.—You are the Roman Catholic curate of Duncormick?—Yes, of the district.

5722. Have you made any inquiries about this school?—I have.

5723. Tell the Commissioners the result of them?—With your permission I will read a few brief notes embodying the little information I was able to make out. (1) The Mr. Richards who made this grant in aid of the Duncormick school was a Protestant gentleman and a small land owner in the parish of Duncormick. (2) I have not seen a copy of the deed by which the grant was made, so that I am unable to say what exactly the extent of the grant was, nor am I able to give the exact date; but it seems certain that an acre of land, free of rent, was given for ever by Mr. Richards about sixty years ago, by way of endowment for a free school at Duncormick. (3) As I am informed, the Protestant clergyman and the churchwardens for the time being of the Duncormick church were constituted to manage the grant; and since the grant was made they have always had, and still have, the management. (4) I am informed, moreover, that the Duncormick school, built upon this acre of free land, was built by the committee of management with money borrowed from some charitable or benevolent society. (5) For many years after this school was opened all the Protestant and Catholic children of the district attended and received instruction there without any distinction whatever of religion. (6) The Catholic clergyman, after some time, had a school built out of private funds, which is now a National school; and after that school was built the Protestant children only of the district attended the free school. I should say that it is nearly fifty years since this Catholic school was built.

5724. Lord Justice FitzGibbon.—Then it must have been one of the first National schools?

Witness.—It was not under the National Board at first, but it is now under the National Board. (7) The Duncormick Free School is now closed, and has been closed for the last ten or nine years. At the time it was closed there were, I believe, but six Protestant children attending for instruction. (8) At present there are but six Protestant families in the Duncormick district, and, I believe, but four Protestant school children. (9) The Protestant children of the district have been attending the National school of Duncormick since the free school was closed. There are at present four Protestant children on the roll of the National school. (10) The present National school of Duncormick is one of the most successful in the county, and the master of it is a most efficient teacher. It is, however, a bad and ill-ventilated building not suited for the requirements of the place. There are over 100 children on the school roll at present. (11) The master of the Duncormick National school has no residence, and in fine and foul weather has to walk two miles to his work, and two miles to his lodgings in the evening. (12) I am of opinion that the acre of free land given by Mr. Richards to the people of Duncormick by way of endowment for the education of their children, should be given over to trustees, one of whom should be the parish priest of the place, and that these trustees should see to the building of a new National school with a teacher's residence thereto, and that the free ground remaining should be given to the schoolmaster, for the time being, for his use and

July 4, [illegible]. — *Rev. Thomas Roche.*

hands. I think in this way we should be consulting for the interests of both the Protestant and the Catholic children alike, as the Protestant inhabitants of the district have no place to send their children for instruction to but the National School.

8725. Lord Justice FitzGibbon.—What area is served by the National school?—The nearest National school is within two miles of it, at Baldwinstown. The number of children attending is about the same.

8726. What number of children are at the Duncormuck National school?—There are over one hundred on the roll and an average attendance of about sixty-five.

8727. Are the three or four Protestant children in the Duncormuck National school the only Protestant children in the neighbourhood?—I don't think there are more Protestant children in the district.

8728. Dr. Traill.—Do they attend the school regularly?—Yes.

8729. Rev. Dr. Molloy.—If there were any other Protestant children is there any other school that they could go to?—There is no other school available.

8730. Dr. Traill.—What is the size of your school—is there accommodation for the hundred children?—No, very poor accommodation; it was built about fifty years ago.

8731. Rev. Mr. Jellett.—Is it vested or non-vested?—It is a non-vested school.

8732. Therefore the clergyman of the parish could not interfere to give religious instruction?—I am not very well up in the matter. Whatever the rules of the National Board allow is permitted there.

8733. Lord Justice FitzGibbon.—What is the distance between the National school and the free school?—About 150 yards.

8734. Is it near enough to enable the clergyman teaching his own children during the hours for religious instruction to take them from one school to the other and back again?—That's about the distance I should say.

8735. Dr. Traill.—Is the accommodation for the free school larger than the accommodation for your school?—I don't think it could be converted into a new school. It might be into a teacher's residence, which is wanted very badly.

8736. Supposing that the building was let to you for a teacher's residence, what rent would you be inclined to pay for the house and acre and a half of land?—I could not undertake to answer that question. I suppose the teacher should pay a reasonable rent. I suppose it would be worth £5 a year. We could have a new house for £6 a year from the Board.

8737. Have you got a site for a new house?—It is impossible to get a site.

8738. How much land have you round your school?—None, it was built in a small hole.

8739. Is there no land round about for a teacher's residence?—None.

8740. Would the house require much changing?—It could be converted for a few pounds into a residence for a teacher, but there should be a new school built.

8741. You spoke of it as a school erected originally as a free school for all denominations?—I say that I did not see the will.

8742. But did you hear it read out now that it was left in trust for a residence for a schoolmaster, and that the children to be sent to it were to be named in writing by the rector of the parish?—Yes, I heard it for the first time.

8743. Lord Justice FitzGibbon.—This case is similar to a considerable number of others, and you will see at once the problem to be settled. This house and plot of land were intended for educational purposes, and were in the hands of the clergyman of the parish under the supervision of the bishop. It is not quite the case that only those of the Church to which the grantor belonged were contemplated to attend the school, because although there is a provision that the scholars were to be nominated by the clergyman, there is also an express provision that only those children that belonged to the Established Church should be instructed in the Church catechism; that provision apparently contemplated that the children of other denominations should be entitled to attend there until they had provided a school for themselves. The difficulty we have is this, whether the endowment should be turned into money—either rent or purchase money—and applied in the nearest Protestant school; or whether we can make the school available for the Protestants of the immediate locality, and for the Roman Catholics as well. It depends very much on the numbers. If there is any substantial number of Protestants likely to be permanently there, they have the first claim on an endowment of this kind, which was intended, generally speaking, by the grantor for some purpose connected with his own estate. The provision we make in some cases of this kind is, that so long as there is a very great majority of Roman Catholics in the neighbourhood, the management should be mainly Roman Catholic, but that the school should be put in the same position as a vested school under the National Board, namely, that the clergyman of the Protestant denomination should have a right to come in and teach their own children, but so as not to interfere with the secular work of the school; and we also provide in such cases that if the numbers of the denominations which are in the minority ever reach a certain proportion, the assistant teacher shall be a Protestant if the minority are Protestants, so as to have somebody to look after the Protestant children's religious instruction during the time that the others are engaged in their own religious instruction. We shall also have to deal with Mr. Fowler's proposal to include a number of schools similar to this in a different arrangement. Whether we shall make a separate scheme for such a small property as that of this Duncormuck School is a question; but in any case if we should do so, the Roman Catholics of the district will have an opportunity of looking at the scheme and forwarding their views about it, and any objections they may have to it to our office. I think myself that where the number of Protestants attending the National school already in existence is so very small—only three or four—the most convenient way of dealing with this piece of land and house, would be to make it available, either as a house or as land for the educational benefit of the school in the immediate neighbourhood, which is overcrowded, and which wants an outlet of the kind, and that some pecuniary compensation should be given, representing what the thing is fairly worth.

The Rev. *John Alexander* sworn and examined.

Rev. John Alexander.

8744. I am the Incumbent of the next parish. The Rev. Mr. Roche, stated that there are but four Protestants in the Duncormuck district to which he referred. (To Mr. Roche). Do you know their names?

Rev. Mr. *Roche*.—I don't think there is anyone from your parish.

8745. Lord Justice FitzGibbon.—What number have you attending your school? (*Witness*).—Twenty.

8746. Are you in connexion with the National Board?—My teacher is too old for it, I am sorry to say. I cannot get result fees or anything, unless I dismiss my teacher. If I teach the children, or get them taught, I don't see that it matters whether the man who teaches them is a hundred years old or not.

ESMONDE ENDOWMENT, RATHASPECK.

6747. Lord Justice FitzGibbon.—By an order of the Master of the Rolls, March 12, 1868, a payment was directed to be made of £1,644 4s. 6d. in respect of a legacy of £3,000, under the will of Lady Esmonde, for the support of the school of Rathaspeck. Can anyone tell us anything about that school?

6748. Mr. Elyn.—I have a copy of the will made by Lady Esmonde in 1867, while living at Johnstown Castle, adjoining Rathaspeck church. It directed that £3,000 should be invested in Government Stock, and that the annual income of that sum should be applied to the support of the school at Rathaspeck, which was to be under the superintendence of the Ferns Diocesan Church Education Society of Ireland.

6749. Lord Justice FitzGibbon.—What has been done with the money?

Mr. Elyn.—Nothing, since the allocation order of the Master of the Rolls was made. The whole amount of the legacy is £1,644 4s. 6d.

6750. Lord Justice Naish.—Is there a school actually existing at Rathaspeck?

Mr. Elyn.—There is. There was a piece of glebe land immediately opposite the church, and in 1870, after Church Disestablishment, some of the parishioners subscribed some money and purchased the field; and a small school has been built on it which children are attending.

The Rev. *James Lothere* re-examined.

6751. Lord Justice FitzGibbon.—Is the Rathaspeck school in your parish?—Yes. The parishes of Wexford and Rathaspeck are joined.

6752. What distance is the school from Wexford?—Not quite three miles.

6753. What school accommodation is in the building?—About thirty pupils could be fairly well accommodated in it.

6754. How many are attending?—The average is about twenty.

6755. Is it in connexion with the National Board?—Yes, the teacher receives capitation fees and result fees.

6756. Who holds the land on which the school is built?—The Diocesan Trustees. It was bought by the parish seven years ago. At the time the Church Act passed, the then rector, Mr. Ford, bought it; and the Select Vestry bought it from Mr. Ford for £120.

6757. Lord Justice Naish.—What quantity of land is there?—Four acres.

6758. With what money was the school built?—Voluntary contributions.

6759. Rev. Dr. Molloy.—Is it close to Johnstown Castle?—Opposite to the nearest gate of the castle.

6760. Lord Justice FitzGibbon.—Was there a school in 1867?—Yes, but it was owned by the family of Lord Granard.

6761. That school has ceased to be used for educational purposes?—We could not get hold of it without paying more for it than it was worth, so we gave it up and built one for ourselves. The Diocesan Trustees merely hold the property for the parish.

6762. Lord Justice Naish.—Have you considered what is best to be done with this money?—I have seen some of the schemes which have been drawn up, and I think the scheme of the Central Protestant Diocesan Schools would answer this, except that in that scheme there is a conscience clause, whereas Lady Esmonde wished this school, as her will states, to be carried out on Church Education principles.

6763. You have the school as a National school, and you are under a conscience clause?—We are at present, and I have no difficulty about it; but some of my predecessors had, and some of my successors might have. Personally, I would be glad if the exact wishes of Lady Esmonde could be carried out.

6764. Lady Esmonde was a strong Protestant, but I don't think she wished to found a proselytising school?—It need not be a proselytising school.

6765. Lord Justice FitzGibbon.—National schools are open to every one who chooses to come, and the schoolmaster cannot refuse any pupil. In these cases the conscience clause is imposed by the National Board that every child has a right to demand secular education without receiving any religious instruction that has not been sanctioned by the parents or guardians of the child. Then there are schools where the manager is under no compulsion to accept any pupil, and can lay down his own rules and oblige every child who comes to conform to them. This is the case of the Church Education Society's schools. If Church children only are admitted, no conscience clause at all is necessary. But if the manager chooses to accept children of another denomination, we ask that they shall not be given any religious instruction to which their parents or guardians object. I cannot understand how any case could arise in which that form of conscience clause could work in any way wrongly. If the parent objects to religious education being given to his child, and if the manager chooses to take the child, he must either respect the objection, which is all that the clause requires, or he must give the instruction against the parents will, which could only be done either by breaking faith with the parent, or unlawfully.

Witness.—Personally, I would have something of the kind myself; but I think that Lady Esmonde desired to have her school carried out on Church principles.

6766. Lord Justice FitzGibbon.—What is there in those principles inconsistent with what I have said?—I think the clause might read:—

"The governors may make such provisions for the religious instruction of those attending the school as shall be approved of by the Ferns Diocesan Board of Education, and as shall be in accordance with the principles of the Church Education Society; provided that, if the school be in connexion with the Commissioners of National Education, such instruction shall be given in accordance with the rules and regulations of the Commissioners."

6767. Rev. Dr. Molloy.—That would allow them to receive children of all denominations, and teach them according to the principles of the Church Education Society?—As long as the school was not under the National Board it would.

6768. Rev. Dr. Molloy.—We will give you liberty to give religious instruction according to your own principles, without restriction, so long as you receive children of your own denomination only. But if you choose to receive children of more than one religious denomination, we consider that you should not require the children to be present at any religious instruction to which their parents object.

Witness.—I would personally think that quite right; but Lady Esmonde has given the money under certain conditions, and I am merely suggesting them for your consideration.

Dr. Traill.—Mrs. Nicholson, of [illegible], left money on similar conditions, and we have framed a scheme under which the school is to be worked under the National Board.

6769. Lord Justice FitzGibbon.—But this school is already under the National Board.

Witness.—It is; but the question is, what her intentions were. A member of the clergy of the Church of Ireland objects to the National Board, and if one of these were appointed to the parish it would

Jan. 2, 1886.

Rev. James Latham.

be very unfair to compel him to work the school as a National school.

5770. Rev. Dr. Molloy.—All that he would be compelled to do would be to receive children of his own denomination only, if he insisted on their receiving religious instruction from him.

Mr. J. G. Pounden.—Mr. Latham is at present acting in contravention to Lady Kennedy's will.

Witness.—I beg your pardon.

5771. Lord Justice FitzGibbon.—It is a mistake to suppose that you cannot give any religious instruction you please in a National school. The only restriction is that it must not be mixed up with the other instruction, nor given without parents' sanction. All that we ask is that if you take children of different denominations you shall not give them religious instruction to which their parents have objected. We don't even require you to obtain the previous sanction of the parents. I never could understand the difficulty about our conscience clause, because it does not operate at all unless the parent has made an objection to his child's receiving the religious instruction. If the objection is made, unless the child is accepted as a pupil, the clause does not operate. If the child is received into the school, either the instruction is given in defiance of the objection, which is unlawful, or it is given without the parents knowledge, which is immoral, or the objection is respected as it ought to be, which is the only case in which the conscience clause takes effect.

Mr. Pounden.—I think the clause a fair and reasonable one.

Rev. Mr. Latham.—It is not a question between me and the National Board. It is simply a question as to the desire of Lady Kennedy as expressed in her will. Mr. Pounden makes quite a mistake. He says we have been going against Lady Kennedy's instructions up to the present. We have not got one penny for Lady Kennedy's bequest up to the present, either for the Church Education Society or the Ferns Diocesan Board.

5772. Lord Justice FitzGibbon.—If the diocesan trustees, who have now the ownership of this school and schoolhouse, desire to have it included in the scheme, we can attach the endowment of Lady Kennedy to it, placing it under the superintendence of the Diocesan Board of Education. But we will add the conscience clause I have mentioned, and if the strictest Church Education clergyman, on examining that clause, can say that there is anything in it which offends his conscience, we will consider his objection. But we have never yet got any rational reason for objecting to the clause we have adopted.

Mr. J. G. Pounden.—I asked this morning to have the Ferns scheme brought on in order to clear the way for this discussion.

Rev. Mr. Latham.—Before Mr. Pounden begins I wish to add that the school at Rathnagreck is now carried on under the National Board, I am the manager of it, and we have not got a penny of Lady Kennedy's money.

5773. Lord Justice FitzGibbon.—Has this £1,844 been paid out of Chancery to anybody?

Mr. Eyre.—No.

5774. Lord Justice FitzGibbon.—Is it invested?

Mr. Eyre.—I think so.

5775. Then it is accumulating?—I think so.

FERNS DIOCESAN SCHEME.

5776. Mr. J. G. Pounden.—This scheme has been brought forward by the Board of Education of the Diocese of Ferns. It is framed on the lines of the Meath scheme. The Board of Education of the Diocese of Ferns was formed by the Diocesan Synod of Ferns, in succession to the Church Education Society of Ferns. The Board of Education has certain rules. It gives grants to Church Education schools, and also to National schools, but only for religious education. The Board found from time to time that certain endowments were very likely to lapse; and certain endowments have gone. They accordingly appointed a committee who met and altered the Meath scheme into the one now brought forward. The report of the committee went before the Board of Education; and the only point of discord was this conscience clause, which was clause 11 in the Meath scheme. I think there can be no objection to it; and after a very hot discussion, only two members of the Board of Education were for Dr. Latham's proposition, which I don't exactly understand—nor do I know what words he intended to leave out?

5777. Lord Justice FitzGibbon.—It is clause 17 in your draft, and is as follows:—

"The Board and the local school authorities shall provide such religious instruction as they shall think fit for the pupils belonging to the said Church who may attend the elementary schools, provided that in any of the schools which may be in connexion with the Commissioners of National Education such instruction and education shall be given in accordance with the rules and regulations of the said Commissioners, and that in any elementary school to which pupils not belonging to the said Church are admitted, no child shall at any time be compelled or persuaded to receive or to be present at any religious instruction to which his or her parents or guardians object, and the time for, and the mode of, giving religious instruction shall be so fixed that such pupil shall not be in effect excluded, directly or indirectly, from any of the other advantages afforded by such school."

Does that satisfy you?

Mr. Pounden.—That satisfies the views of the majority of the Board of Education; but the Board wish to have the power of helping other schools which might not be in connexion with them. And, accordingly, they have taken, from the Enniscorthy Scheme, clause 31 enabling the Board to take transfers of property held in trust for schools or institutions in the Diocese of Ferns under the exclusive management of members of the Church; and also clause 32, enabling the Board to undertake duties, by way of inspection and otherwise, for the promotion of education among the members of the Church in the diocese which the Diocesan Synod may intrust to them. This clause ought to satisfy the gentlemen who feel with Canon Le Hunte and Canon Latham.

5778. Lord Justice FitzGibbon.—It is our desire in dealing with every denominational endowment to have the management perfectly free as regard religious instruction. The only difficulty arises where the school is intended for more denominations than one. There it is impossible to have it perfectly free, but we leave it as free as justice and fair dealing allow. There is no objection to the insertion of the clauses you mention, they are in other schemes.

Mr. Pounden.—Am I right in assuming that clause 17 relates to all schools of which the Board of Education would be the owners, but that the other clauses enable the Board to help schools of which they would not be the owners themselves.

5779. Lord Justice FitzGibbon.—The object of those clauses is to enable the body incorporated under the scheme to take conveyances of property connected with the Church, and to undertake educational functions intrusted to them by the Church authorities. They must administer any property so taken in the same way as any other trustees of it.

5780. Dr. Traill.—Have you a schedule prepared?

Mr. Pounden.—I have. In clause 3 we wish to continue the practice in this diocese that the Archdeacon in Church matters takes precedence of the Dean. We have inserted a clause that a clergyman qualified to sit as a layman in the Diocesan Synod shall be considered a layman. We strongly object to the limitation to members of the Board of Education resident in the diocese. One of our best men, Colonel Tottenham, lives in the county of Wicklow, and it is just as easy for him to attend as it is for me. We also think that the words in clause 5:—

"Who shall for the space of one year fail to attend any meeting of the Board,"

should be left out.

Lord Justice FitzGibbon.—If you are going to let in persons who are non-resident, you should have the power of putting them out if they don't attend.

5781. Dr. Traill.—Why should you keep a person on year after year who never attends? According to that draft scheme you can put him on again at the end of two years.

Mr. *Pounden*.—In bringing forward these matters I have been taking the place of Mr. Alexander, who is the secretary; the Diocesan Council asked me to act, but I would ask you to hear Mr. Alexander.

Rev. *John Alexander*.—I have nothing to add.

5782. Lord Justice FitzGibbon (to Mr. Alexander).—Do you think the conscience clause satisfactory?—I quite agree to it.

5783. You have had the advantage of seeing the Meath scheme before your own has been printed or published. After the scheme for this diocese has been published you will have two months to bring forward objections.

Rev. Mr. *Latham*.—The Diocesan Synod meets in the first week in August, and possibly this scheme may be thrown out altogether there. I don't think we understand all about this scheme. One question that several are anxious to have answered is, what title will this scheme give to the property it deals with. Will it act as a Landed Estates Court deed?

5784. Lord Justice Naish.—If the title at present is a bad one, and the persons in possession of the property are not entitled to hold it, this will not give them a parliamentary title, but it will transfer to the new governing body all the title that is in the present holders.

Rev. Mr. *Latham*.—Then the only advantage is, that it will incorporate the body holding the property?

5785. Lord Justice FitzGibbon.—It has also this great advantage, that it transfers to the incorporated body all the lawful title existing at the time. We cannot confer title, but we can transfer it, and with the title the actual possession will pass wherever it is held for the schools; the incorporated body would thereby have the advantage of being defendants instead of plaintiffs in an ejectment, in any case where they got possession.

Rev. Mr. *Latham*.—Another question some of us are anxious to have answered is, will a school included in this scheme, when it shall have been approved of, be afterwards able to withdraw?

5786. Lord Justice Naish.—That is a matter of arrangement.

Rev. Mr. *Latham*.—If the parish of Wexford joins the scheme for Lady Ranelagh's endowment, could the governing body afterwards withdraw from the scheme?

Lord Justice Naish.—That would have to be provided for in the scheme.

5787. Lord Justice FitzGibbon.—It would be necessary to make special provision securing Lady Ranelagh's endowment for the particular school to which it was left. We could vest Lady Ranelagh's endowment in the incorporated body, making them trustees to spend it on the [illegible] School. As to withdrawing from the scheme once you are in it, the scheme might so provide; but there would be no advantage in doing so, and the scheme should bind the incorporated body to carry out the trust.

Rev. Mr. *Latham*.—There is one thing more which I wish to ask, and I hope it will not be a question offensive to anybody. It would help one very much towards coming to a decision to know what the Roman Catholic dioceses in Ireland have done with reference to this Endowments Commission. Have any of them gone in for schemes?

Lord Justice FitzGibbon.—Not yet.

Rev. Mr. *Latham*.—I would be glad to know their practice.

5788. Lord Justice FitzGibbon.—I will give you an instance of their past experience which may show the wisdom of taking advantage of our powers. On the occasion of a succession of a bishop in one diocese, we were told that it cost £720 to trace the title and transfer the Church property to trustees under the new bishop. We cannot exercise any power over a denominational endowment without the written consent of the parties interested, and we have no desire to frame schemes for you against your will. If you like to know what others are doing, the Presbyterians, who are as hardheaded as anybody, are applying for several schemes, and the Methodists have got one for their Belfast College. If you choose, you can stay outside; but you must make up your minds soon, for our time is nearly up. As to expense, no scheme costs £5, and some have cost less than £1. We can undertake to let you have a printed copy of the draft scheme by the end of this month; but we have no power to put any denominational school into it, small or large, without a written consent from the present owners or managers. In the Cork diocesan scheme, 110 schools have been provisionally put into the schedule, but for each one of these schools, if it be an exclusive case, we must get a written consent before we sign the scheme, and we must strike the school out if we don't get the consent.

Dr. Traill.—That protects you. Putting the school into the schedule provisionally does not commit you finally.

Lord Justice FitzGibbon.—You have two months after the publication of the scheme to put forward objections, and to bring in the necessary consents or to withdraw altogether.

The inquiry then terminated.

PUBLIC SITTING—FRIDAY, JULY 5, 1889.

July 5, 1889.

At the Royal School, Carysfort.

Present:—The Right Hon. Lord Justice FitzGibbon, and the Right Hon. Lord Justice Naish, Judicial Commissioners; and the Rev. Gerald Molloy, D.D., D.Sc., Anthony Traill, Esq., LL.D., M.D., F.T.C.D., and Professor Dougherty, M.A., Assistant Commissioners.

The Assistant Secretary, N. D. Murphy, was in attendance.

CARYSFORT ROYAL SCHOOL ENDOWMENT.

5789. Lord Justice FitzGibbon made an introductory statement. He mentioned that two of the Assistant Commissioners had visited the Carysfort Royal School in 1887, when they found that the schoolmaster had become much more of a farmer than a schoolmaster; that no regular school was kept by him, and he had only five or six scholars attending occasionally. He had since died; on his death the school was discontinued. The Commissioners had this morning (July 5, 1889), visited the Macreddin National school, under the management of the parish priest, within about half a mile of the Royal school. Nearly all the children of school-going age in the immediate neighbourhood, Roman Catholics and Protestants, were stated to be going to the Macreddin school, being the only school in the neighbourhood. There were about fifty children on the roll, and the average was a little over thirty. There were eight Protestant children on the roll who had formerly been pupils of the Royal School; and five of them were in attendance. The result was that they have been able to save up money; and when we last heard from them they had about £1,000 invested in Government Stock, representing accumulated surplus income from the estate. They had about £100 in cash; so that altogether at the present time they have between Government Stock and cash about £1,200 of capital, put by from the savings of the estate from year to year. That produces about £30 a year, and, added to the £130 from the other sources would make altogether about £160 a year. The Royal School Endowment was now represented by a capital sum of cash and stock of about £1,200, and a rental of about £150 a year, subject to charges and deductions, leaving a net income of about £100 a year.

The Very Rev. John O'Brien, P.P., sworn and examined.

Very Rev. John O'Brien, P.P.

5790. Lord Justice FitzGibbon.—You are the parish priest of Aughrim?—Yes.

5791. What are the boundaries of your parish?—It extends from the foot of Lugnaquilla to near the Wooden Bridge.

5792. Is Macreddin in the parish of Aughrim?—It is. I live in Aughrim.

5793. Then, the parish is Aughrim?—The parish is Aughrim.

5794. What schools are under your management?—Macreddin, the National school, is the nearest; then Aughrim National school. Aughrim has a large population, and there is an average attendance of about seventy-five at the school. Macreddin school has an average attendance of a little over thirty. There is another school at Kirikee where there is an average attendance of over forty. There is also Muckilagh school in this parish with an average attendance of something over thirty there. Those are the four Catholic schools in the parish.

5795. What are the distances of those four from the Royal School?—Macreddin is not more than a mile, Aughrim two miles, Muckilagh might be four miles, and Kirikee about four miles.

5796. Are Kirikee and Muckilagh schools accessible to children from this neighbourhood?—Not exactly. There are several mountains around.

5797. From what distance do the children come to Macreddin?—Some of them come up from within half a mile from Aughrim.

5798. If there were any improvements made in the school are there any children that could be expected to come to it beyond what are there now?—Probably very few.

5799. Dr. Traill.—But there are fifty on the roll?—You might see thirty-five or forty in attendance, but never fifty together. The average is about thirty.

5800. Rev. Dr. Molloy.—We heard from the schoolmistress of Macreddin that the attendance at her school represented all the school-going population of an area of from two to two and a half miles Irish round the school?—I think it does.

5801. Lord Justice Naish.—Does it get all the children from up here?—Yes, all round here.

5802. Dr. Traill.—Are there any more children at this end of the parish who would attend here if this school were under Roman Catholic management?—I don't think there are many more than those who at present go to Macreddin. I don't think you would have more than six or seven to come here.

5803. Even if it were under your own management?—Well, if it were under my management, perhaps there might be some more.

5804. Supposing that this school were put under Roman Catholic management, would more children attend here; it is a very much finer building than the schoolhouse at Macreddin?—Some few might, but not a great many.

5805. Lord Justice Naish.—Is Macreddin or this the more convenient place for a school?—Macreddin is more convenient for people coming from the off side.

5806. Lord Justice FitzGibbon.—In disposing of this building as part of the endowment for the benefit of education in the locality, whether would it be better in your opinion to move the Macreddin school into it, or to sell or let it?—I think it would be better to have Macreddin school than this school for the neighbourhood.

5807. But this is the better building of the two?—If a few pounds were expended on the other building it would do very well. It is a good solid house.

5808. Lord Justice Naish.—Did you get a grant from the National Board for Macreddin?—Not for the building; but the school is under the Board at present.

5809. Did you ever try to get a building grant?—I never asked for it.

5810. Dr. Traill.—Or a grant for a residence for your teacher?—I never asked for it.

5811. Professor Dougherty.—Which of the build-

July [illegible]

Very Rev. John O'Brien, P.P.

longs in sense to the Royal School Estate?—This is on the estate, but Macreddin is a mile from it.

5612. Dr. Traill.—Are there many children on the estate?—I could not say—perhaps ten.

5613. Rev. Dr. Molloy.—Do you know whether the Royal School was ever at Macreddin or has it always existed here?—I could not say. I know that the schoolhouse at Macreddin was built some forty or fifty years ago by one of the priests.

5614. Lord Justice FitzGibbon.—How is the land held on which the Macreddin schoolhouse stands?—In fee-simple. It belongs to the parish. It was part of the Carysfort commons. We do not pay a halfpenny for it.

5615. Having regard to the fact that this building would give you a residence for a teacher, or even for two, as well as a good school, and that the buildings are in good repair, whether would it be more useful to improve your school-house and build a teacher's residence there, or to move your school up here?—I am certain it would be better to have it below.

5616. Have you any suggestion to make as to how the endowment would be best spent?—The school at Aughrim is a very large school, and it would be very useful if it got a part.

5617. How would you propose to apply it?—I suppose to give prizes and encourage the teachers.

5618. Lord Justice Naish.—Would you propose to supplement their salaries, or do you consider the salaries they receive from the National Board sufficient?—The children pay a penny a week, and it is very hard on the poor people to make up that money.

5619. Then you wish to provide free education?—Yes.

5620. Lord Justice FitzGibbon.—We are told everywhere that education is more valued when the people have to pay the penny a week for it?—But it is very hard to get it sometimes.

5621. Rev. Dr. Molloy.—Is there any industry suitable to the neighbourhood that could be promoted by a special teacher?—The Board is inclined to encourage dressmaking, and stocking manufacture also might be encouraged. Wool is very plentiful. It is a great sheep country here, and these things if encouraged amongst the people would be useful.

5622. Dr. Traill.—Do you think that this building could be used for that purpose, or that it should be let to a tenant as a farmstead?—It would be just as well, perhaps, to let it as a farmstead.

5623. What do you think you would get for it annually if it were let?—The land and house are pretty fair. At present it is let pretty fairly. The tenant is here, and says it is let rather high.

5624. Lord Justice FitzGibbon.—Is there anything else that you would wish to say?—The other two schools at Mucklagh and Kirikee would be very glad if they could get a portion of anything in the industrial or prize way.

5625. Lord Justice Naish.—In what way do you think industrial education could be forwarded?—I don't know, unless by teaching sewing and knitting, and things of that kind.

5626. Lord Justice FitzGibbon.—Needlework is already taught in the National schools?—Yes, in a certain way.

5627. I may give you another idea, which has been carried out pretty successfully at Bessbrook, and which offers a chance to the clever pupils of advancing themselves in the world, and that is competition for scholarships, say of £10 or even £20 each?—I think it would be very useful. Some would certainly work for it. It would supply a motive to encourage them in their school course.

5628. Professor Dougherty.—What is the classification of your teacher at Aughrim?—There are two, a head teacher and an assistant; both are first of the second class.

5629. Do you teach any of the extra subjects in the programme of the National Board?—Sewing machine is taught.

5630. If you got a portion of the endowment would you be able to improve the quality of the education at Aughrim?—I am almost certain I would.

5631. In what way?—You would have a number of our highest class engaged in making dresses and other things, and perhaps in making stockings. It would be useful in that way.

Lord Justice FitzGibbon.—We have heard that at some schools where they established stocking-making they could not afterwards get rid of the stockings the competition was so great.

5632. Lord Justice Naish.—What salaries do your teachers get from the National Board?—At Aughrim the head teacher gets £34 10s., and the second gets £27 10s. The head teacher also gets about £23 in results fees, and the second teacher about £11.

5633. What does the teacher at Macreddin get?—She gets £24 10s. salary, and she got £13 results fees last year.

5634. Has she a residence?—No.

5635. Dr. Traill.—Has the Aughrim teacher a free residence?—No; she has to pay for it.

5636. Lord Justice Naish.—Do you consider that the salaries paid by the National Board are sufficient without being supplemented by the endowment?—If they got extra work I think it would be very well to give them something more.

5637. Lord Justice FitzGibbon.—But if they had extra work they would get more results fees. Apparently the first want of your teacher at Macreddin is a residence?—There is a residence required at the other place too—the Aughrim residence is very bad.

5638. Dr. Traill.—Have you ground for a residence at Macreddin, or could you get it?—I don't think we could get it. There is not more room for a residence at present.

5639. Is there any land available at the other side of the road?—No.

5640. Not even if you were to buy it?—I could not say whether the landlord would give it or not. The tenant might give it, but you should have the approbation of the landlord.

5641. Who is the landlord?—Mr. Acton.

The Rev. G. J. [illegible] sworn and examined.

Rev. G. J. [illegible]

5642. Lord Justice FitzGibbon.—You are the incumbent of this parish?—Yes.

5643. What is your parish?—It is called Ballinaclash, but it corresponds in extent with the ancient parish of Ballykine which is in the Roman Catholic division called Aughrim.

5644. Your boundaries are the same as those of Father O'Brien?—Practically the same. The Glenmalure river bounds the parish on this side, and it extends to Aughavannagh bridge.

5645. What churches are in your parish?—I have two, one at Ballinaclash, on the road from the Meeting of the Waters to Glenmalure, between Greenane and Ballinaclash, and the other at Macreddin.

5646. Is Aughrim in your parish?—Part of Aughrim is. The river is the boundary.

5647. Rev. Dr. Molloy.—Has the Macreddin church been recently built?—It was built in 18[illegible]. There was a little building here in the village of [illegible] that was erected by public subscription, and this church was an improvement that took its place.

5648. Was Macreddin considered a better situation?—I don't think it was a better site, but there were

July 2, 1888.

Rev. C. J. Hickson.

some difficulties about getting a permanent site here, and Mr. Acton gave the present site to the Archbishop of Dublin, on condition that it should be used for a church only, and that if the church should ever be abolished for any reason, the land should revert to him. It is not consecrated—it is simply licensed.

5849. Lord Justice Naish.—What is the Protestant population of your parish?—About two hundred.

5850. How many families?—I would say fifty.

5851. Lord Justice FitzGibbon.—How many of these families worship at Macreddin church?—I should say a congregation of thirty to forty.

5852. Rev. Dr. Molloy.—Representing, I suppose, about eight families?—There are more than eight families in this district, there are twelve or thirteen.

5853. Lord Justice FitzGibbon.—From what distance do they come to church at Macreddin?—Some come from Aughavannagh—eight miles.

5854. Farther than children would come to school?—Yes.

5855. Did you know this school when it was in operation?—I have known it these ten years.

5856. What number of children of your denomination are there in this neighbourhood of school-going age?—I think there are about twelve in this immediate neighbourhood, and a few in the neighbourhood of Aughrim.

5857. About how many are there at Aughrim?—There is a family not actually in the parish, but just outside it, at a place called Killacloran, who come to Macreddin church.

5858. Where do the Protestant children of this neighbourhood get their schooling—we were told that they were all going to Macreddin school?—All except one family, I believe.

5859. Where do they go?—I don't think they go anywhere at present. I advised their parents to send them to Macreddin, or that they should get a donkey cart, and go to our school at Ballinacarrig.

5860. Dr. Traill.—You did not take care to have them entered as of your own denomination at Macreddin, for I found all the Church of Ireland children entered there as "P. D.," which means Protestant Dissenters?—Perhaps the schoolmistress made a mistake.

5861. Rev. Dr. Molloy.—How many schools have you under your own management?—The Parochial school at Ballinacarrig.

5862. What is the attendance there?—Thirty, and sometimes forty.

5863. Lord Justice Naish.—What is the distance to Ballinacarrig from here?—About four Irish miles. Greenane is not really in my parish; it is at the other side of the river. On this side, near where the chapel is at Ballinacor House is where my church is at Ballinaclash.

5864. Lord Justice FitzGibbon.—Are there in this neighbourhood Protestant children enough to maintain a Protestant school?—The population fluctuates very much. Some years ago when I came first it was very much larger than it is. One reason was that the Protestant Orphan Society sent a great many children down here to be nursed, and sent to school; but owing to the reports that were sent up of the state of the school, and of its being practically in abeyance, these children were, I think, very properly removed and sent to a more efficient school. The schoolmaster was always more or less of a farmer. I don't think he could have lived without farming. I had no control over this school whatever—not even to the extent of making a suggestion to the master. He told me he held his appointment from the Lord Lieutenant.

5865. Professor Dougherty.—Did you ever make a representation to the Commissioners of Education on the subject?—No, I did not like to do so. He was a very old man.

5866. Lord Justice FitzGibbon.—What number of Protestant children are there now in this district?—In the immediate neighbourhood of this school about twelve to fifteen, but there are a good many infants that would make up the number possibly to twenty.

5867. Rev. Dr. Molloy.—But as the infants grow up to be children, the children grow to be men and women?—Yes, and not having much to induce them to stay at home, they go away.

5868. Has there been much emigration from this neighbourhood?—Very much. Even in my time the population has declined very perceptibly.

5869. Lord Justice FitzGibbon.—What suggestions have you to make for utilising this foundation?—I should say benefiting the existing schools, and promoting something in the way of technical industries—something that would employ the farmers' daughters in their own homes.

5870. What existing schools would you regard as having a claim on the fund?—The parish school at Ballinacarrig, and those schools which Father O'Brien has mentioned.

5871. Rev. Dr. Molloy.—That is five schools in all?—Five schools. I don't think there are any schools outside that would have claims.

Lord Justice FitzGibbon.—Ballinacarrig, Macreddin, Kirikee, Aughrim, and Muckla[illegible].

5872. Dr. Traill.—Is there a Roman Catholic school near yours at Ballinacarrig?—There is between two Roman Catholic schools one and a half and two miles distant.

5873. Rev. Dr. Molloy.—Will you give us your opinion as to the possibility of introducing home industries or technical education?—Special teachers should be provided to go round the schools and give instruction in such industries as spinning, carding, home weaving, and the working of those knitting frames that have turned out more or less of a success in other parts of Ireland. I don't see any reason why they should not be a success here. They would tend to the improvement of the condition of the people.

5874. Professor Dougherty.—Is there any district in Ireland where spinning by hand is remunerative at present?—I think in Donegal. I saw some work the other day at the Irish Home Industries Depository.

5875. Lord Justice FitzGibbon.—They look very nice in glass cases, but when you come to count their cost it is another matter?—I think it most important that some home industries should be started to enable the farmers' daughters to stay at home.

5876. Professor Dougherty.—What would you think of teaching agriculture?—I am not an authority on agriculture. I think it quite possible that an improved dairy system might be useful.

5877. Rev. Dr. Molloy.—With this endowment you could get special teachers in different subjects, and if one industry did not succeed another might be tried?—Yes.

5878. Should you be in favour of having a drawing-master to give instruction in the schools?—I am not sure that drawing would be very useful. Land surveying might be.

5879. Drawing would be a good foundation for land surveying and for many other useful pursuits?—Yes.

5880. Professor Dougherty.—Do the boys of the locality ever become carpenters or masons?—Very few.

5881. Would not drawing be useful for those pursuits?—Yes, I think drawing should be taught in all elementary schools—free hand drawing and geometrical drawing, when they have any talent for it. It is very necessary for many pursuits.

5882. Rev. Dr. Molloy.—What would you say to carpenter's work and the use of tools?—I think they would be very useful, especially if they have to emigrate as many of them have.

5883. Lord Justice FitzGibbon.—Do any boys emigrate from this to Arklow, or any other industrial centre in the neighbourhood?—I don't know a single instance of it. They go to shops, but not generally to handicrafts.

5884. Is there any connexion between this locality and Arklow that would be likely to make an industrial

July 4, 1888.

Rev. G. J. [illegible]

school there of use to any of your children?—I don't think there is any immediate connexion between them.

5885. Professor Dougherty.—Is there any prejudice amongst the boys of the locality against being taught handicrafts?—No, I think not; but the demand is very small for carpenters in this place.

5886. Dr. Traill.—Did you ever try the experiment with boys?—No.

5887. I have tried it, and I found that nine boys out of every ten were delighted to get the chance of learning to use tools?—I think it would be very useful.

5888. Lord Justice FitzGibbon.—Is there any probability of getting any clever boys or girls from the five schools to compete for prizes of £10 or £20 which would enable them to go out into the world—which would be a sort of apprenticeship fee for them?—I think it would be beneficial. It would promote healthy rivalry to have something like that open to the children of this parish.

5889. Dr. Traill.—What class of teacher have you in your school?—She is a Church Education Society teacher. If we had more money we might provide a more efficient teacher. I would suggest that the money should not be given unless the teacher were trained and classed under the National Board.

5890. Lord Justice FitzGibbon.—Are there any schools in the district that are not under the National Board?—Mine is the only one.

5891. What is the reason of that?—It is due to an old prejudice, I suppose. I have been here only ten years and I found it in existence when I came. We had not sufficient numbers at that time to get a grant from the National Board, and when the number increased, not wishing to disturb the teacher that was in it was the principal difficulty. That teacher is still there.

5892. Dr. Traill.—Is she too old to qualify under the National Board?—She is beyond the age for qualifying now.

5893. Rev. Dr. Molloy.—Is there any netmaking industry in this neighbourhood?—I have not seen anything of that kind except in Arklow.

5894. Would not the establishment of a school of netmaking here be useful to the people of Arklow, by supplying them with nets?—Such a thing might be useful, but I have not sufficient knowledge to give a definite answer.

5895. Dr. Traill.—Would not nets be under made in Arklow?—I don't know.

5896. Professor Dougherty.—If part of the endowment were utilized in providing travelling teachers to visit the different schools and give instruction in special subjects, do you know whether such an arrangement could be carried out between the Protestant and Catholic schools?—I know that instruction in the use of hand-knitting machines could be obtained, because the people that sell the machines have agents for giving instruction in the use of them, and when one of the machines is purchased they provide instruction in the use of it.

Dr. Traill.—They do, but it is very difficult to teach the use of the machine unless you get the teacher for a considerable time.

5897. Professor Dougherty.—What I wish to find out is—if a teacher were appointed to give special instruction would he have freedom of access to all the schools?—Yes.

5898. If a Catholic teacher were appointed would he have free access to your school?—Yes, so far as I am concerned.

5899. Have you the control of your own school?—It is supposed to be under my control, and the ground on which it stands forms part of the same site as the church.

5900. Then a Catholic travelling teacher would be admitted to give special instruction in your school?—I should have to ascertain one or two points before giving an answer to that.

5901. Dr. Traill.—In a purely secular matter it would not make much difference?—No. Certainly not.

5902. Lord Justice FitzGibbon.—Do you think it would tend to a solution of the matter if you got a sum of money from the endowment on condition of admitting the teacher?—Of course it would.

5903. You spoke of your boys emigrating; do any of them go to trades in Ireland?—Very few go to trades. They generally go into shops as assistants.

5904. For that sort of employment a year at a better school would be an advantage?—It would.

William Carter sworn and examined.

William Carter.

5905. Lord Justice FitzGibbon.—I believe you are now the occupier of this schoolhouse and of the land connected with it?—Yes.

5906. How much land have you?—Belonging to the school—three acres and the schoolhouse.

5907. When did you get possession?—I got the land on November 1, 1887. I got the house in June, 1888.

5908. How do you hold it?—I am yearly tenant.

5909. Have you a written agreement?—I have a copy of a written agreement. I have not got it here.

5910. Lord Justice Naish.—Who let it to you?—The agent, Mr. Gubbins.

5911. Lord Justice FitzGibbon.—What rent do you pay?—£13 a year for the whole thing.

5912. Dr. Traill.—Are you living in the house?—No. I got it for my own son who is living in it. I have another farm.

5913. Lord Justice FitzGibbon.—Are you a tenant on the Commissioners estate?—I am.

5914. Do you know how many tenants are on the estate altogether?—Nine.

5915. How many of them are Protestants and how many Roman Catholics?—Five are Protestants and four Roman Catholics.

5916. Do you all send your children to Macreddin school now?—They don't all send there. There are six children in one house that don't go anywhere.

5917. Are they all of age to go to school?—They are.

5918. Did they all go to this school when it was open?—They did. Henry Langrell has three now and none of them go to school.

5919. Dr. Traill.—Why don't they go?—I don't know.

5920. Lord Justice FitzGibbon.—They are getting no schooling at present?—No. I have a good many children, and two of the smallest of them are going to Macreddin. There are a good deal more to go. The elder girls went at first to Macreddin, but they are not going there now. I have ten children.

5921. Professor Dougherty.—Then your family must have been the main support of this school for a good many years?—No; there were a good many children, but the master got old and neglected it. He was a farmer, and there was no one to look after him. It was altogether the master's fault. If that master had minded the school there would have been plenty of children. I think there are up to twenty-six Protestant children here now.

5922. How near is this school to the youngest children?—They are all within a mile of it. There are some of them too small, but they are coming on.

5923. Rev. Dr. Molloy.—About how many Protestant children of school-going age are there on the estate now?—I think there are up to twenty.

5924. Of these only eight are going to Macreddin?—There could be a great deal more.

5925. Are there twelve children of school-going age on the estate who are going to no school?—There are, and more.

5926. Lord Justice FitzGibbon.—What have you to say as to how the school could be made useful?—I think if a good school were opened here it would be well, provided a schoolmistress could be got that would come cheap. The Protestants don't like to send their children to a Roman Catholic school, and they would wish to have a good school, and a schoolmistress that would pay attention.

5927. Dr. Traill.—What do you mean by "coming cheap"?—A schoolmistress would teach cheaper than a master.

5928. But there is plenty of money?—Well, the school was neglected, and no one looked after it.

5929. Lord Justice Naish.—Was the school never inspected?—Never.

5930. Lord Justice FitzGibbon.—We have a record that it never was inspected between 1859 and 1879, when two successive Commissions inquired about it?—They never examined the children.

5931. Lord Justice FitzGibbon.—I understand there are five Protestant families?—There are three families more on the next townland, about half a mile or a mile off.

5932. Professor Dougherty.—Did not the schoolmaster hold more land in addition to the three acres attached to the school?—He did.

5933. Who got it?—My brother bought some from his widow, and a man named Stevenson got some.

5934. Dr. Traill.—What did you pay for the tenant-right?—I did not buy it; my brother bought it. I could not tell what he gave.

5935. Rev. Dr. Molloy.—Your children came to the school when it was open?—Yes.

5936. Did they come regularly?—[illegible]

5937. They are getting a better education now at the National school than they were getting here?—They are not getting any, except the two little ones.

5938. Well, the two little ones are getting a better education than they were getting before?—I cannot say that. I would rather have the education they got here.

5939. The National school is open every day for them, and the other was not?—It is.

5940. Dr. Traill.—Do you belong to Mr. Hindson's congregation?—I do.

5941. Do you know that your children are all entered on the books at Macreddin as Protestant Dissenters?—I don't know how that is. We sent a couple of the little ones sooner than have them without any school.

5942. Rev. Dr. Molloy.—Have you children yourself of school-going age that are not going to any school at present?—Yes, two girls, from thirteen to fifteen.

Lord Justice FitzGibbon.—The Macreddin schoolmistress told us that these two girls did go to Macreddin, and were examined and found to be only able to pass in the third class, and they were so big that they did not care to be in the third class, and stopped going.

5943. Rev. Dr. Molloy.—Why do you not send them to school?—I don't care to send them.

5944. Are they too grown?—No, they are not.

5945. You send the two younger ones?—Yes; I would send more than the two girls if there was a school. I have ten children.

5946. Dr. Traill.—You would like to have a school under Protestant management?—Yes, I would.

5947. Have you any objection to the management of the other school except that it is under the priest instead of the clergyman?—That's my objection.

5948. Lord Justice Naish.—Have you any other objection to it; has anything been done to interfere with the children's religion?—I cannot say. I don't think there is, because I only send the two little ones.

5949. Lord Justice FitzGibbon.—At present you have only the choice—not a very pleasant one—of sending them to a school that you would rather have under other management, or not sending them to school at all?—Yes.

[illegible] (margin)

Mr. Thomas Acton sworn and examined.

5950. Lord Justice FitzGibbon.—Where do you reside?—At Kilmastury.

5951. How far is it from this?—Nine miles.

5952. Have you got property in this neighbourhood?—Yes.

5953. Are there any resident gentry near enough to take any interest in a school here?—I think not. Colonel Kennedy is the nearest, except Mr. Littledale, of Whaley Abbey, something like four miles from this.

5954. How near does his property come to this?—In a straight line, about three miles. Mr. Kennedy's place is about four miles distant, by the road. He is very seldom there.

5955. Are you ever brought by business or pleasure to Aughrim or hereabouts?—I have been in Aughrim occasionally.

5956. Can you give us any idea how this endowment could be made useful to the people who have claims on it?—I think by keeping a school here in this house.

5957. That was tried for a great many years without much success?—I am quite aware of that; but with good management it might be different.

5958. What sort of management would you suggest?—Of course the National Board.

5959. Rev. Dr. Molloy.—But if you had a National school here, with a grant from the Board, a large amount of the endowment would be available for other purposes—how would you propose to apply it?—I could not tell.

5960. There is a thousand pounds and a hundred a year—you would not spend the whole of that on a National school?—I would not spend the whole of it on one National school, but there are three or four others. There are Macreddin and Aughrim.

5961. You would make it available for all the five schools of the parish?—For all five.

5962. Lord Justice Naish.—Would you found a National school here in addition to the five?—Not an additional one. I would change the Macreddin school to this place.

5963. And leave it under the management of the parish priest?—I understand the National Board give two managers, but I don't know anything about the National Board. I won't have anything to do with the National Board if I can help it.

5964. Dr. Traill.—What is your objection to the National Board?—I think the National Board is in the hands of the Roman Catholic clergy.

5965. Indeed it is no such thing. I have a very good school vested in the National Board?—Well, I have a school in my own hands altogether. The children of my school passed best in the examinations at Rathdrum.

5966. By whom were they examined?—Some of the Church Education people.

5967. Professor Dougherty.—Do you advocate a division of the surplus endowment of this school amongst all the National schools of the neighbourhood?—Yes, I would like Ballinatone to get some of it.

5968. How would you allocate it?—In proportion to the numbers attending the schools.

5969. Lord Justice Naish.—Where is your own school?—At a place called Kilcandra, two and a half miles from Rathdrum.

5970. It is not in this parish?—No.

5971. Professor Dougherty.—How would you

propose that the efficiency of the schools sharing in the endowment and not under the National Board should be tested?—That is, Ballinascreen?

5972. Take your own school—if it shared in the endowment, how would you propose that its efficiency should be tested?—I am not asking anything for my school.

5973. But if Ballinascreen school shared in the endowment, would you allow an independent inspection?—Yes.

5974. By an inspector of the National Board?—I would.

5975. Dr. Traill.—Do you own the land along Macreddin?—Yes.

5976. Have you any objection to give ground for a teacher's residence there if he were paid out of the endowment?—I have.

5977. You would rather the teacher was brought up here?—Yes.

Rev. C. J. [illegible] re-examined.

5978. Rev. Mr. Hindson.—I wish to add something to what I said. I was under the impression that it had been fully decided to abolish this concern as a school, and to divide the endowment amongst the existing schools. But if that be not the case, it might simplify some of the difficulties very much if this place could be maintained and used as a school, under any management, on the National system. A great many children are growing up, and their numbers will, I have no doubt, increase, and you cannot blame people very much if they object to mixed education. They like to have their children mixing with others of the same denomination and the same class as themselves; and it would simplify matters very much if we could have a slice out of this endowment—which is larger than I thought it was—kept for this place.

5979. Dr. Traill.—You are satisfied that a share of it, as public money, should be distributed amongst the other schools?—Of course, certainly; but make six divisions of it instead of five, and let the sixth share be for the benefit of this place. I think this place, being the centre from which the income is derived, should have a sixth towards an elementary school here.

5980. Professor Dougherty.—Would you have any regard to numbers?—I think not. The numbers are small at present, and less than a sixth would not be of any use.

5981. Would you take into account the efficiency of the teaching?—I would leave the rest to be divided amongst the five schools according to their efficiency—according to the results of inspection.

5982. Lord Justice FitzGibbon.—I fear you are reckoning without your host in thinking of establishing another National school here. As the numbers stand, the withdrawal of the Protestant people would bring the Macreddin school below the average required for a salary. The school could not obtain connection with the National Board unless it showed a fair prospect of an average attendance of thirty-five, without interfering with the existing school, which is within a mile. If the attendance were between fifteen and thirty-five, the school could only get a capitation grant, and the National Board gives nothing under an average attendance of fifteen, which would mean twenty, at least, on the roll. There is no evidence that you could maintain that average here.

5983. Rev. Dr. Molloy.—On what grounds do you expect that the population of this neighbourhood will increase?—Those who are at present infants will become of school-going age.

5984. But as that process goes on, the children who are now of school-going age will pass beyond it. Have you any other reason to believe that the school-going population will increase?—If anything like home industries were promoted amongst the people that would enable the farmers' daughters to stay at home until they were married, instead of emigrating as they do now, as soon as they are of any use, or going into service; but what is the endowment, I want to know?

Lord Justice FitzGibbon.—About £100 a year and £1,000.

Rev. Mr. Hindson.—Less than £20 a year would hardly be of much use towards keeping up a school in this locality.

Lord Justice FitzGibbon.—I don't think you could establish a second National school here.

Mr James Just sworn and examined.

5985. Lord Justice FitzGibbon.—Where do you live?—About half a mile from this.

5986. Are you one of the tenants on the school estate?—No, I am a tenant of Baron de Robeck.

5987. You have known this school a good while?—I have known it before it was built.

5988. Do you remember the old school?—I do, it was at a little bye spot here above. I went to school there myself. It was up at Carysfort.

5989. Are there any remains of the old school?—No, it is all gone.

5990. When was this school-house built?—I can't say the date, but I was as good a man when this place was built as ever I was since.

5991. How old are you?—I am eighty-three.

5992. Then it is about sixty years since this school-house was built?—About sixty years or beyond it.

5993. Rev. Dr. Molloy.—Do you remember when any part of the old castle of Carysfort was standing?—I do not.

5994. Lord Justice FitzGibbon.—What is the largest number of scholars that you ever remember attending the school?—The largest number that I remember was something about twelve; but there were four or five more that I often saw coming and going from the school—destitute children that were maintained here by the Protestant people.

5995. The orphans that Mr. Hindson spoke about?—Orphan children.

5996. Do you remember the school being attended by Roman Catholics as well as Protestants?—I do not, in this school. There never were. Some Catholics came to this school when there was no school in Macreddin or Aughrim. They should go to some place, and they came here. There was a big school in the old school-house, somewhere about fifty or sixty. I was in it when there were sixty, but the population of all kinds has been very much reduced indeed here since then.

5997. What do you think would be the best thing to do with the money belonging to the school?—I would say to lay out the money for the good of the children, by improving the school that is in being, to advance the poor children whose parents have no means to pay the teacher the penny a week for instruction in the first Book of Lessons. I know five parents having children from two to four years old that have no means to pay the teacher. The child that has not a penny to give to the teacher won't go to school; if it had the penny it would go to school freely, and would be saved from the ignorance it labours under. The schools that are in being should be put into repair. I heard you say you were at Macreddin school and you saw the dilapidated state it

July 1, 1889. Mr. James Jess.

was in—the windows falling in, and so forth. Mach-[illegible] school might also be seen to be the same. Kilrea school is in the same way. There are all in this district. If this school could be kept for the Protestant people to send their children to, that are sending them at present to Macosquin, it would be a great boon.

5998. Dr. TRAILL.—Would you keep up this school just besides Macosquin?—That's the question; there should be a certain number to keep up a school under the National Board.

5999. Do you think there are enough to keep up a school here under the National Board?—I do not.

6000. Lord Justice NAISH.—Would you give anything to Ballinamore Protestant school?—Ballinamore school might be kept up, for it extends a good way down in the place populated by Protestants.

6001. Lord Justice FITZGIBBON.—All the people in this neighbourhood don't want school pence for their children?—No, they do not.

6002. It would take very little to pay the school pence for the poor children?—I know that.

6003. Tell me the feeling of the people. In the case of a very farmer, is it better to give him schooling for his children for nothing, than to make him pay some little thing to the teacher?—The teachers in the National schools get their yearly money from the Board, and they make the scholars pay a certain amount to them, besides.

6004. What I want to know is whether you want to have any free teaching for the children, who can pay something every Monday morning, or only for the poor children?—Well, I do not. The patron of the school attends frequently, but I won't say on oath whether he pays for the poor children or not.

6005. Would it satisfy you if the patron got money to pay for the poor children?—It would.

6006. You don't want to let everybody off to be taught for nothing, whether he can afford to pay or not?—The man that is able to pay has a right to pay for his child.

THOMAS STEVENSON sworn and examined.

Thomas Stevenson.

6007. Lord Justice FITZGIBBON.—Are you one of the tenants on the school estate?—I was born and reared on the estate, and educated in this school, and my children were educated in it, and they ought to be educated here still.

6008. About what size are the holdings on the estate?—They vary—some are small and some large.

6009. Have you one of the large holdings?—No, just middling; thirty acres two roods and twenty-eight perches. The valuation is £14, and the rent between £13 and £14.

6010. There is something allowed off that for lime?—Yes.

6011. Rev. Dr. MOLLOY.—What is the allowance for lime?—Three shillings an acre, or three shillings in the pound—I forget which.

6012. Lord Justice FITZGIBBON.—You got some additional land from the schoolmaster's widow?—Yes, about three and a half acres.

6013. What rent is it liable to?—£3 6s. There is a small holding, the rent of which is divided between us and another man who bought a part.

6014. You occupy it at the same rent that the widow paid for it?—Yes.

6015. What did you pay her for the four acres that you got from her?—I gave her more than it is worth—£30. It is not worth it.

6016. Dr. TRAILL.—You gave £10 an acre tenant-right?—That's what I gave, at least nearly £30, for three and a half acres is about £8 10s. an acre.

6017. Lord Justice FITZGIBBON.—What do you say about making use of the money and the land for schooling?—I would like some of it to be given to this school and part to the other schools.

6018. Could you keep one school here and another at Macosquin?—We could help the school ourselves so as to have it convenient for the children.

6019. Had you to pay in the old days, or was the school free?—I had not to pay Mr. Wheeler.

6020. How did the school fall away so much?—He fell away himself, and neglected the school.

6021. Did none of you represent that he ought to have an assistant?—Not to my knowledge. The man got old, and he was a good neighbour and we did not complain. If one did not complain another would not, and the school was falling away. We had not good encouragement to send the children, and he neglected teaching them when they would come.

6022. Do you think the tenants on the estate could appoint one of themselves to help to look after the school in case it was re-opened?—We would look after it. Everyone that is concerned would look after it.

6023. You don't seem to have looked after it since you were at school yourself?—Yes, I have looked after it. Mr. Wheeler's salary was £50, and if you leave us the house and land we would help the master's salary. We asked the Commissioners for £25—half the late master's salary—and also the house and field.

6024. If you got that how would you propose to get a master?—As cheap as we could, or even a mistress.

6025. Professor DOUGHERTY.—Have you anybody in your eye for the post?—No. It would be time enough when we got the grant.

6026. Do you know anyone that would take the situation on those terms?—There would be people to take it.

6027. Dr. TRAILL.—Do you consider that being tenants on the estate you have a right to have a school here as you pay the rents which keep up the endowment?—I do.

6028. Do you consider that this school was primarily intended for the benefit of this estate?—I do, and I was born and reared on this townland. I consider that it would be a hardship to take it from us.

6029. Lord Justice NAISH.—Is Ballinamore too far from this to send children to school there?—It is.

6030. Professor DOUGHERTY.—Are the rents on the school estate higher or lower than on the adjoining estates?—I don't know. I would be very glad the rents were smaller, anyhow.

6031. You don't consider it a disadvantage to live on this particular estate?—Not a bit of disadvantage.

6032. Dr. TRAILL.—As long as the money was spent on education you would not grudge it?—No.

6033. You would not like to see it wasted?—No; I would like to see it go for education, and to the other schools as well.

6034. Who has the shooting on the estate now?—Mr. Bennett. A gentleman named Lovell had it before.

6035. Is there any shooting on it?—Yes—grouse, hares, and snipe.

6036. Do you pay for the schooling of your children at present?—Yes. The tenants have to work very hard, and it would be a hardship on them to lose the school.

6037. How much do you pay?—I have two little girls—one was going to Macosquin school, and the other went on Monday morning. One pays three halfpence a week and the other a penny.

6038. You think they are entitled to education free here?—I do—I claim education free for them.

6039. Do you belong to Mr. Hisbury's congregation?—I do.

6040. Do you know that your children are entered as "Protestant Dissenters" in the Macosquin school?—I mentioned the name, "Irish Church." I think the schoolmistress made a mistake.

July 6, 1886. Thomas ——, the same.

6041. Lord Justice FitzGibbon.—Suppose a school was established here and a good teacher got, how many children would go?—I can't not exactly say. If we ever got something to help this school, we could help ourselves. There are days that our children cannot go to Moyvaddin.

6042. About how many children are there on the estate?—I think there ought to be twelve or fifteen children. There are several infants now, not many of whom would be able to go.

6043. Dr. Traill.—You think that if the school were here there would be plenty more children grown in the country?—There are small children that are not able to go to Moyvaddin.

6044. How many have you?—Only two that are going to Moyvaddin now. Some of my elder children were educated in this school.

6045. Lord Justice FitzGibbon.—I suppose they are suffering now from the want of a better education?—They are. I have no fault to find with the Moyvaddin teacher. I believe she attends to the teaching of my children; but I would rather have the school here.

Patrick Clancy sworn and examined.

Patrick Clancy.

6046. Lord Justice FitzGibbon.—Are you one of the tenants on this estate?—I am a tenant's son.

6047. Are you a Protestant or a Roman Catholic?—A Roman Catholic.

6048. What holding has your father?—Something over forty acres.

6049. What is his rent?—£29 a year is the full rent.

6050. His is one of the larger holdings?—Yes.

6051. Do you know how the endowment could be made useful?—I think the best purpose to which it could be put would be to divide it amongst the schools of the parish.

6052. Rev. Dr. Molloy.—Were you a pupil of this school yourself?—I came only, I think, once to it.

6053. Where did you go to school?—To Moyvaddin all through.

6054. Is there any chance of teaching trades, or anything of that sort here?—If there was something started like a trade it would be useful.

6055. Have you brothers or sisters?—I have.

6056. Are they all here still?—All, except one sister that's in Dublin. She has served her time to a milliner.

6057. Did she learn needlework at Moyvaddin?—She did.

6058. So that there would be some use in teaching it there?—There would.

6059. Lord Justice FitzGibbon.—Is the estate high rented or low rented?—Some of it is high rented—higher than anything around it. There is some of it adjoining the hill let at £1 an acre that is not worth it.

6060. Has there been any talk of the tenants buying their holdings?—There was some little talk. Two Commissioners—I think those gentlemen were—spoke of it when they came.

6061. Rev. Dr. Molloy.—What did the tenants think of it?—I think it would be a good idea for the tenants to buy their holdings, if they got them at a fair value.

6062. Professor Dougherty.—What would you think a fair price for your holding?—I suppose about twelve years purchase.

6063. Dr. Traill.—If you got the purchase money on a loan from Government at 4 per cent. to be repaid in forty-nine years, and gave eighteen years purchase, would you not prefer that to paying the present rent?—I would not be contented to pay the present rent. I think the present rent is too high.

6064. Lord Justice FitzGibbon.—If you got it at twelve years purchase, the instalments would be £11 10s. instead of £29.

6065. Professor Dougherty.—Do you think the tenants would advance on that offer?—I think they would not advance very much.

6066. If you can live paying £29 a year, could you not live paying £20?—Yes, in a sort of a way; struggling—not to say half starving.

6067. Dr. Traill.—If you bought at twenty years purchase of £29, and borrowed the money under Lord Ashbourne's Act, you would pay £23 4s. for forty-nine years, and then you would be free of rent for ever. Would not that be a good bargain—instead of £29 a year for ever, £23 4s. for forty-nine years?—I expect there will be some better Act passed that will give it to me cheaper than that.

6068. But you are paying the full rent while you are waiting?

Witness.—Perhaps we won't have to pay it always.

6069. Lord Justice FitzGibbon (to His Grace Archbishop Walsh).—Does your Grace desire to say anything?

Archbishop Walsh.—I think not. I have no special information to give.

6070. Lord Justice FitzGibbon.—We must consider the matter. There are some points on which we might receive further assistance. It is quite plain that there are not scholars here for two schools under the National Board. The present attendance at Moyvaddin barely reaches the necessary average; and the largest number that the most enthusiastic witness suggests as likely to come to a school here is twenty. Therefore, apparently neither denomination alone has a sufficient number to secure a National School salary. But both denominations together appear to have the requisite number. Then there is the problem what to do with that building. If Moyvaddin school remains where it is, and exclusively under Father O'Brien's management, the objection will remain that others have to send their children there. On the other hand, we might put this school under the management of the parish priest as representing the largest denomination, but with a provision for the appointment of a Protestant assistant teacher—subject of course to the ordinary rules as regards religious instruction of the National Board. Then this building would manifestly supply both a better schoolhouse, and also a teacher's residence. Whether that proposal under the circumstances of this locality, would be acceptable to Father O'Brien or not it would be for himself and his ecclesiastical authorities to say. If that proposal did not commend itself, then we might divide the endowment among the neighbouring schools, where it would be very much broken up, and it may be doubtful if the result would be good. Ballinalee, the only school attended by a substantial number of Protestants, is a long way off. Aughrim also is a considerable distance, and the Protestants of the estate would gain little or nothing unless they got a share in the management of some school here. But the allowance to each school on a division among all the schools in the parish would not exceed £30 a year.

6071. Archbishop Walsh.—Are any of these schools not under the National Board?

Rev. Mr. *Hickson*.—Ours is not.

6072. Dr. Traill.—You said you would put it under the National Board if you got a grant.

Rev. Mr. *Hickson*.—That is, if I could have the control of it. The local landlord, I believe, also claims that. It has been always a Church Education school.

6073. Dr. Traill.—But the conditions of joining the National Board could be attended to a grant of public money.

Rev. Mr. *Hickson*.—Of course.

Archbishop Walsh.—You attended that condition to the Swords schools.

6074. Dr. Traill.—Would there be any objection, your Grace, in case a grant were given to Macreddin, and the schoolhouse enlarged by an outlay of capital, that it should be treated as a vested school—that is, and at a certain hour of the day the Protestant clergyman should be at liberty to enter for the purpose of giving religious instruction to the children of his own denomination?

Archbishop Walsh.—I see no objection to that at all; it would be a most reasonable arrangement.

Rev. Mr. *Hickson*.—I think it would mitigate very much the opposition, in case the last suggestion were acted on, if the numbers were sufficient, that the second teacher should be nominated by me, and should be a member of the Church of Ireland, of course being at the same time a trained teacher.

6075. Dr. Traill.—What does your Grace think of that?

Archbishop Walsh.—I think it would be better for them to have separate schools. They all seem to prefer it.

6076. Dr. Traill.—But that would take up a large portion of the endowment. The school at Macreddin is very badly off for want of some capital expenditure.

Archbishop Walsh.—We all assent to that. No capital expenditure is required anywhere else.

Lord Justice Naish.—As I understand, the proposal of the Protestant population here is, that if they get £30 a year with this building and the ground attached to it, from the endowment, they would pay for the teacher themselves.

6077. Lord Justice FitzGibbon.—Where a poor teacher struggles on in a small school upon £20 or £30 a year, the school is never good. As a rule, the schools are very bad where they are not National schools, and there is only a small endowment. We have seen a great many of them, and I should be sorry to set up such a school here.

Archbishop Walsh.—You could make a distribution of the income proportionate to the numbers passing the results examinations in each school, not merely proportionate to the attendance.

6078. Lord Justice Naish.—I suppose the feeling is that the money ought to be kept for the district?

Rev. Mr. *Hickson*.—I think we are all agreed on that point.

6079. Lord Justice FitzGibbon.—Mr. Stevenson, if we gave you twelve months or even two years to start a school here, and made it afterwards depend on your keeping it up efficiently, do you think you would try it?

Mr. *Stevenson*.—I think we would if we got some help, and a good master or mistress.

6080. Archbishop Walsh.—It occurs to me to make one suggestion in the matter of asking fees or school pence. The plan we have adopted at Swords is to give a restitution of school fees as a prize for regularity of attendance. The poorer children there have nothing to complain of, and it is a means of inducing them to attend. To any child who attends one hundred and fifty times in the year we give a restitution of the school fees as a prize.

6081. Dr. Traill.—It is not confined to cases of poverty?

Archbishop Walsh.—Not at all. It is given as a reward, and the poor children earn it by attending regularly.

6082. Lord Justice FitzGibbon.—At Swords the inhabitants claimed the right to free admission there.

Archbishop Walsh.—That was one of the difficulties and we got over it in that way.

6083. Dr. Traill.—If the second teacher in Macreddin school were a Protestant and the patron were a priest it would give rise to difficulty.

Archbishop Walsh.—It would cause a great deal of friction. I don't think either side would be satisfied.

6084. Dr. Traill.—But there is no objection to the proposition that at certain hours the clergyman should be at liberty to enter to give religious instruction to his own denomination?

Archbishop Walsh.—That would be a matter of course.

6085. Lord Justice Naish (to Mr. *Stevenson*).—Would it remove the difficulty if you had your own clergyman to teach religion in Macreddin school?

Mr. *Stevenson*.—If the second teacher was a Protestant we would be satisfied.

6086. Lord Justice FitzGibbon.—Father O'Brien and Mr. Hickson, we should be glad if you would consider the matter and write to us. You have heard the evidence. Give us, each of you, your views in writing. You have heard the proposals. One is to enlarge and improve Macreddin school, another is to use this building instead of Macreddin schoolhouse, there being but one school in the locality. The alternative is, two separate schools, and Mr. Stevenson has mentioned the amount of money which he thinks would enable the local people to maintain a school here. That might seriously affect the Macreddin school.

Father O'Brien.—My view would be in favour of keeping up Macreddin.

6087. Rev. Dr. Molloy.—Of spending as much money on it as would put it into a thoroughly efficient condition as a school for the whole neighbourhood?—Yes.

6088. Dr. Traill.—You would not move up here even though you were made patron of this school yourself?—No.

6089. Rev. Dr. Molloy.—How far was the old school of thirty years ago from the present schoolhouse of Macreddin?

Mr. *Jago*.—About three quarters of an Irish mile, it was at the top of the hill, close above here.

6090. How far from this school?—Not more than 200 yards.

The inquiry then closed.

PUBLIC SITTING—FRIDAY, JULY 5, 1889.

At the Courthouse, Arklow.

Present:—The Right Hon. Lord Justice FITZGIBBON, and the Right Hon. Lord Justice NAISH, Judicial Commissioners; and the Rev. GERALD MOLLOY, D.D., D.SC., ANTHONY TRAILL, Esq., LL.D., M.D., F.T.C.D., and Professor DOUGHERTY, M.A., Assistant Commissioners.

The Assistant Secretary, N. D. MURPHY, was in attendance.

CARYSFORT ROYAL SCHOOL ENDOWMENT.

APPLICATION FOR TRANSFER TO ARKLOW FOR INDUSTRIAL EDUCATION.

6091. Lord Justice FITZGIBBON made an introductory statement, and read the following resolutions:—

1. Resolution of the Town Commissioners of Arklow—

"That we, the Town Commissioners of Arklow, beg to submit to Her Majesty's Royal Commissioners, before disposing of the Carysfort Endowment Fund, the great necessity for establishing a technical school in the town of Arklow, there being a very large population of poor people almost entirely belonging to the fishing interest, so that where that fails, great distress is sure to follow, inasmuch as they have no other occupation to fall back on."

2. Resolution of public meeting held in the town of Arklow—

"Proposed by Mr. R. Philpott, seconded by Mr. J. Hanagan, and resolved—That if Her Majesty's Royal Endowment Commissioners, taking into consideration the great necessity of establishing a fishery school in the town of Arklow, kindly transfer the Carysfort Endowment to our town, we, the clergy, merchants, and traders of the town hereby pledge ourselves to supplement the fund by an annual subscription; and that the following gentlemen be appointed as a deputation to present the foregoing resolution to the Commissioners:—Rev. J. Dunphy, P.P., Rev. Mr. Harper, Mr. Philpott, Mr. Hanagan, Mr J. Lynch, and Mr. J. Doyle. Chairman, Rev. J. Dunphy, P.P."

6092. Mr. *Philpott*.—I attended the public meeting here last evening, and the general feeling was that in the town our young people are in great want of instruction in industrial pursuits. At present the families of the fishing population are not taught any branch of skilled labour, and are comparatively unable to help themselves and their parents. In addition, the fishermen only having opportunities of taking fish at intervals throughout the year are, during a large portion of their time, idle. It would be very desirable if the boys and girls were able to contribute to the earnings of the town and the support of their families and themselves by making fishing appliances; and great improvement could be made in the mode of taking fish if the people were taught the use of more approved and scientific means of pursuing that avocation. The idea was, that if an industrial school could be established, with the primary object of imparting instruction in the manufacture of fishing tackle and in the art of taking and curing fish, it would be a very great advantage to the town. The resolution which has been read was brought forward at that meeting.

6093. Lord Justice FITZGIBBON.—Was the meeting held on public notice?

Mr. *Philpott*.—On public notice. I understand it was held by the instruction of the Town Commissioners, who held their meeting on Monday.

6094. Lord Justice FITZGIBBON.—Should the school you want to establish be in connexion with any existing school?

Mr. *Philpott*.—The feeling was that it should be distinct and separate.

6095. Lord Justice FITZGIBBON.—I do not know any instance of a school which is entirely a trade school. Technical instruction is generally joined with other education. What schools have you here?

Mr. *Philpott*.—Two National schools, one of which is in connexion with the Roman Catholic Church, comprising a male, a female, and an infant boys school, and the other is in connexion with the Methodist Church, and two parochial schools, one under the direction of the Rev. Mr. Hallowes, the rector, and the other maintained by Lady Carysfort.

6096. Lord Justice FITZGIBBON.—I don't know that you could establish a school for the manufacture of fishing nets, or such things, and not in connexion with a school for reading, writing, and other elementary instruction. The Baltimore Fishery School is an industrial school, meeting the purposes you want, but the boys there receive an elementary education as well as industrial training.

Mr. *Philpott*.—The meeting thought that adequate provision for literary instruction was already made by the National and the parochial schools, and that what is wanted is instruction in industrial pursuits, to enable these people to contribute to their own support.

6097. Rev. Dr. MOLLOY.—Do you contemplate having that industrial teaching in a building distinct from the schools already existing?

Mr. *Philpott*.—In a distinct building, so far as I could gather.

Rev. *Father Dunphy*, P.P.—A building could be obtained at a moderate cost.

Rev. *Mr. Hallowes*.—I heard casually that there was to be a meeting, and I took for granted that if my attendance had been required I would have heard of it before. Even if I had heard of the meeting I could not have attended last evening—that is the reason why I was not present.

6098. Lord Justice FITZGIBBON.—We will now be glad to receive evidence of the existing provision for education here, and the views of those interested as to the best way of applying any money that may be available.

The Rev. J. Dunphy, P.P., sworn and examined.

6099. Lord Justice FITZGIBBON.—How long have you been parish priest of Arklow?—Eleven years.

6100. I suppose you are well acquainted with the educational wants of the neighbourhood?—Very well.

6101. What schools are there under Roman Catholic management?—A boys school, a girls school, and an infants boys school.

6102. Are all these under the National Board?—Yes. They are separate schools, with separate numbers. I am manager of the three schools.

6103. What are the numbers?—The number on the roll in the boys school is two hundred and thirty, in the female school two hundred and thirty, and in the infant boys school one hundred and twenty; total on the rolls five hundred and eighty.

6104. I suppose the attendance is about four hundred and fifty?—More. Generally in the summer time I have the whole attendance. I think there are over 800 attending the schools for the Catholics in the town of Arklow.

6105. You have no Christian Brothers schools?—No. The girls school is conducted by the Sisters of Mercy, in connexion with the Board, and the other two are under class-teachers.

6106. What teachers have you?—In the boys school a principal teacher, four assistants and monitors. The infants school is conducted by a lady and a assistant. There are monitors, of course, in the female school.

6107. What are the classes of your teachers?—The principal teacher in the boys school is second of the first, and in the infants school, first of the second.

6108. Is there any instruction in the "extra subjects"?—Yes. In the female school knitting, sewing, drawing, and music, I think.

6109. Have you any teaching of drawing in the boys school?—No.

6110. Have you any technical instruction?—No. The boys are taught extra subjects, including book agriculture.

6111. What is your idea as to industrial education in this place?—There are a large number of young men and young women in this town. A year or two ago, after the Sisters had been established about five years, I had occasion to get together a number of grown-up girls belonging to the town; and on that occasion 150 grown up girls attended the first instruction. The subject they were instructed in was knitting. I understand from the Reverend Mother they had a course of instruction in knitting guernseys, Gaelic dresses, and other articles; but in consequence of not having a place for these persons to come together in, the class was reduced to ninety. There was no place to accommodate the girls; and the Sisters had to bring them to the hall of the convent, for want of a place to meet them and give them special training in. Out of that class, I understand, there were ninety excellent workers. The articles which they knitted were sold in some shops of Arklow; these shops had agents in London; and the guernseys were sold in London, and were, as I understand, first rate.

6112. Why has that experiment been discontinued?—In consequence of not having a place to keep the girls together. There was not a sufficient demand for the Gaelic dresses, and I believe a good deal of the manufactured material remained in the Sisters hands.

6113. Rev. Dr. Molloy.—It has been suspended partly on account of the difficulty of finding a room, and partly on account of the difficulty of selling the material?—Certainly; and, I think, I could state on my oath, that 150 girls could be found to work any day in the week in Arklow—girls of from sixteen to twenty five.

6114. Lord Justice FitzGibbon.—That is, if you had a market for the proceeds of their industry?—Yes.

6115. Did they work in the convent?—No. The class-rooms were not used. The nuns had some little shed round their own building; and they brought them into the hall of the building.

6116. I understand it was a "home" industry—the workers used to take the stuff home and work it at home. Yes; take it home and come weekly with it to the convent.

6117. Is there anything for the boys to do at Arklow?—Nothing at all beyond the school education.

6118. Your resolution proposes to establish something if you had an endowment to help; had you in contemplation any particular building, or to carry on industrial training in the existing schools?—We could not carry it on in the existing schools for we have not room. The existing school premises are not adequate at all to the attendance. There are five hundred children going to these schools, and they are not made to accommodate more than four hundred.

6119. It is your idea that this industrial education should be confined to partly grown-up lads and young women?—Certainly.

6120. To those who have passed what we call their school-going years?—Certainly.

6121. Has any industry of that kind been attempted?—Some time ago I started an industry of making straw covers for bottles, and got a large number of girls, and hired an unused house in the town for the purpose. I continued it for five or six months, and got the principal houses in Dublin to take the materials. But the house was taken from me, and I had no other place where I could assemble the girls under supervision.

6122. Rev. Dr. Molloy.—Otherwise it would have been a success?—It would; and if I got the place to-morrow it would be, for I got an outlet for all that were made.

6123. Lord Justice FitzGibbon.—Were you not able to get any other house?—No.

6124. Professor Dougherty.—What were the financial results?—Of course they were on the wrong side for the time.

6125. Did you look forward to making it pay?—I did. I got encouragement from all the traders in Dublin, who took the material, for it was very good.

6126. According to your resolution, the clergy, merchants, and traders, are to supplement the fund by an annual subscription; what sort of local governing body do you contemplate?—The traders of the town—the boat owners, the vessel owners, and the clergymen.

6127. Lord Justice Naish.—What is the population of the town?—There are nearly six thousand in the township of Arklow. There are nearly five thousand in the town proper.

6128. How many families are engaged in the fishing business?—Nearly all except the traders, and I believe they are engaged as well.

6129. Lord Justice FitzGibbon.—What fishing, except during the herring season, is there in Arklow?—There is no permanent fishing, only the herring and oyster fishing.

6130. How long in the year does the herring fishery last?—There is the summer, the autumn, and the winter fishing. The summer herring fishing begins in June. The mackerel fishing begins in March, when a large body of fishermen go from here to the west coast—to Kinsale, Baltimore, and Castletown Bere.

6131. Does the summer herring fishing last more than three weeks or a month?—They would stay longer if the herrings remained here. The men don't lose time. The moment the mackerel season is over they go either to Howth, Dunmore, Ardglass, or the Isle of Man; and in several years they went to Scotland—to Aberdeen, and even as far as the Shetland Isles.

6132. Their families live in Arklow?—Certainly. The families remain behind—boys and girls. The men are away.

6133. How many boats are registered in Arklow?

Mr. Story.—One hundred and fifty.

6134. Rev. Dr. Molloy.—About what size are these boats?

Mr. Story.—Any of those that are fishing carry six or seven men. The mackerel boats carry eight.

6135. Lord Justice Naish.—Are there one hundred and fifty boats of that class?—One hundred and fifty boats carrying six or seven men each.

6136. What oyster fishing is there in Arklow?

Witness.—There was a great fishery in times gone by. There are now from twelve to twenty boats fishing during four or five weeks. If the weather is bad it prevents their continuing at it.

6137. Lord Justice FitzGibbon.—Where is the market?—Dublin buyers. French buyers used to come.

July ..., 1885.

Rev. J. Dunphy.

6138. To buy seedling oysters?

Mr. Story.—To put them on artificial beds.

6139. Is that trade going on still?

Mr. Story.—In a small degree. The place was run out a few years ago. They used to have only about one hundred dredges, but they imitated the Germany men and increased the number to seven hundred and then ran out the beds. There has been a cessation of oyster fishing for some time, but it is reviving again.

6140. Lord Justice Naish (to the Witness).—Do you know anything, Father Dunphy, of the working of any fishery school such as you propose?—I saw Father Davis's school on the occasion of its opening. Of course here, as things exist at present, it would be impossible for me to think of building an industrial school on that principle. It could not be thought of.

6141. Lord Justice FitzGibbon.—Why not?—You would want a good deal of local aid.

6142. Rev. Dr. Molloy.—He got £1,000 from the Grand Jury. Could you not find a Baroness?

Witness.—I think we will have somebody in the locality who will emulate the Baroness; for on the whole coast there is not a larger fishing population or a better class of boats than in the town of Arklow.

6143. But the fishing here is not to compare with that at Baltimore?—The fishing is considerable here for herrings and oysters, but there is very little trawling.

6144. Would it be possible to establish the artificial culture of oysters here?—I don't know, I suppose the oysters are there. I understand from the fishermen that they are growing. The beds were overdredged twelve years ago. They are reviving, I believe. If we had a large concern with sheds round about it for repairing and net-making, and whatever else you like, so as to let the boys and girls live in their own homes, it would be very desirable.

6145. Lord Justice Naish.—Is there any boat-building going on?—Not at present. Everybody used to do it in times gone by.

6146. Rev. Dr. Molloy.—Supposing a special teacher were provided to give instruction in industries suitable to Arklow, would it be possible for him to give instruction in the several schools have out of school hours, or in the evening?—I think so.

6147. In that way the teaching could be made available for all denominations, and for all the schools without the expense of a new building?—The buildings I contemplate would be merely sheds. I would not contemplate a college like Father Davis's.

6148. Lord Justice FitzGibbon.—Could you expect or hope to make money by making nets or ropes—you would have to compete with machinery and many other advantages?

Witness.—Some gentlemen will tell you by-and-by of the quantity of money laid out here every year in nets and ropes. But I am answering you as to how the growing population may be utilised. There is very little use in training boys here to sail a boat. They know how to do that—they have been bred to it all their lives. In times gone by they used to make their own nets.

6149. Rev. Dr. Molloy.—Could that industry be revived?—Certainly it could. We have a great many old men in this place who know how to make nets. The boys can get employment at any time up to sixteen years of age, for they can go to sea; but the girls are badly off after the time that they leave school.

6150. You think it desirable to have for them a hall where they could carry on suitable industries?—Certainly—knitting industries.

The Rev. Richard C. Hallowes sworn and examined.

6151. Lord Justice FitzGibbon.—How long have you been Rector of Arklow?—Four years.

6152. What schools have you under your charge?—Four schools altogether, and two hundred and five pupils on the rolls.

6153. What are the four?—Lady Carysfort's girls school, with seventy-eight on the roll; a mixed infants school, with fifty-two on the roll, at Tinnahask, which is part of Arklow; a boys' school at Tinnahask, with forty on the roll; and a country school at Coolroe, with thirty-five on the roll.

6154. How far is Coolroe from Arklow?—About three miles. The instruction there is not advanced, and when they get too old they come to the other school. The girls school that Lady Carysfort maintains has eighty on the roll. It is quite close to the railway station.

6155. Are any of these schools in connexion with the National Board?—At present none are, but we are building a boys' school which will be placed under the National Board.

6156. How are these schools maintained?—For the infants school and the Coolroe school there is an endowment of £1,000, divided between them. It is vested in trustees, of whom I am one, and the rector of the adjoining parish is another.

6157. That would only give you £16 a year apiece for them?—Yes.

6158. How is the rest of the expense made up?—The parish makes it by subscriptions. The boys school is partly maintained by a grant from the Incorporated Society of £40 a year.

6159. How is Lady Carysfort's school maintained?—Entirely by herself.

6160. What buildings has it?—A schoolhouse and teacher's residence. It is entirely in Lady Carysfort's hands.

6161. What other buildings have your schools?—The schoolhouse at Tinnahask belongs to the endowment.

6162. What is the title to the buildings?—I have never been able to find out. I never saw any title deed.

6163. Rev. Dr. Molloy.—Do you pay rent?—We pay no rent.

6164. Lord Justice FitzGibbon.—Is any industrial training given in any of those schools?—No. At the boys' school they are taught navigation and English, and the master teaches it well.

6165. Have you thought how industrial training in Arklow could be carried out?—I have not. It struck me when the resolution was read that one matter was omitted, namely, the constitution of the school itself. I would be as willing as any one else to subscribe annually, but before making a promise I would like to know the constitution of the board that would manage the school. With regard to the observations of Archbishop Walsh as to the Carysfort endowment being transferred to some of the existing schools here for the purpose of a new department of education, I did not think that would tend to bring subscriptions in. I rather thought that if we had a board independent of the existing schools there would be a greater likelihood of receiving help from outside.

6166. Rev. Dr. Molloy.—How would you propose that the Board should be constituted?—I would not myself ask to be on the Board; but if the thing were put before me, I would say that the Parish Priest and the Rector should be on the Board. Religion is looked after in all our schools sufficiently, and I think we need not fix on . . technical education to any of the schools where religion is taught. I think if it is kept separate it would be better. Father Dunphy suggested that the Commissioners should take the management; but I don't know how long they intend to exist.

6167. Lord Justice FitzGibbon.—Possibly [illegible]

July 4, 1888. Rev. Richard G. Hodson.

ing of industries would be separated from religious teaching; I say possibly, because difficulties arise where you don't expect them; but if industrial training is to be given in the existing schools it could only be given in the way Dr. Molloy has pointed out, namely, by sending a teacher round to teach in the different schools, and possibly with a night school for grown people. All that we could do would be to incorporate some body representing all parties in the town who would manage the industrial teaching, and distribute any available fund. The fund would have, to a great extent, to be a local fund.

Witness.—Very little time has been given to us to think over the matter, and we are really unprepared.

6168. Lord Justice FitzGibbon.—It takes a long time to start your thinking in Arklow, for we published our proposal about the Carysfort Endowment last May twelvemonths; and the proposal of Archbishop Walsh, which I read, is dated July 10, 1886.

Witness.—We don't see the newspapers. I wrote a letter to the Freeman last year in which I called attention to the evidence of Archbishop Walsh.

6169. Lord Justice FitzGibbon.—I understand the numbers in all the Protestant schools counting Godyns would be about two hundred?—There are one hundred and two and twenty who should be added. There are one hundred and two attending the Methodist National School, and twenty attending the higher class school of the Rector of Kilbride. These numbers bring up the children attending our schools in Arklow to 357.

6170. Do you know the Church population of your own parish?—Yes—we put down the subscribing members of the Church of Ireland roughly at one thousand.

6171. Rev. Dr. Molloy.—Which of the two plans would you prefer? One would be to establish one common industrial school for all denominations in Arklow, partly by means of this endowment, and partly by means of local subscriptions. The other would be not to establish an industrial school but to provide special teachers of particular industries who would teach in turn at all the schools?—I would suggest to the Commissioners to give us a certain time within which we could come forward and see whether we can procure a certain sum of money to supplement whatever you give us.

6172. Lord Justice FitzGibbon.—We could do nothing on a mere resolution passed at a public meeting. It is easy to carry a resolution at a meeting, but when the meeting is over the gentlemen committed to the resolution separate also. Father Dowd first collected a large sum of money and built a school; and then got a scheme framed under our Act incorporating a governing body to manage the school and its funds. His school is maintained under the Industrial Schools Act; and the money that he collected represents capital expenditure. If in the course of the next month or two you Arklow people are able to do the same thing, to put down a certain list of responsible names, and above all to get an actual building or site, or to show that you have any fund with which to build a school, it would be a very different matter, we would then know with whom and with what we were dealing, and could incorporate a governing body to give permanence to the undertaking.

Witness.—In order to have the thing taken up it will be essential to arrange about the governing body to the school. I believe that larger subscriptions would be obtained if it were known what body was to regulate it.

Lord Justice FitzGibbon.—If the people themselves form a body spontaneously, it will be the best proof that its constitution will work satisfactorily.

6173. Rev. Dr. Molloy.—I think you may assume that if you hold a meeting here and agree among yourselves about the subscriptions, you would get a corporate body which would correspond to the character of the meeting and of the subscribers; but what we don't know—and we cannot see until we know it—is whether you will agree or not amongst yourselves to have a mixed governing body.

Witness.—I don't think we ought to anticipate any difficulty of that kind.

The Rev. William Burgess sworn and examined.

Rev. William Burgess.

6174. Lord Justice FitzGibbon.—You attended the meeting last night?—Yes.

6175. You are the clergyman of the Methodist congregation here?—Yes.

6176. What is the number of your congregation?—About one hundred and fifty in actual membership.

6177. What school have you under your charge?—A school under the National Board, with * one hundred and two children on the roll.

6178. To what denominations do these children belong?—They are all Methodists and Episcopalians, in about equal proportions.

6179. There is no National school under Protestant management to compete with you?—No.

6180. What teachers have you got?—A female teacher and an assistant.

6181. What is the class of the head teacher?—First of the second class.

6182. Do your children get any industrial instruction?—None, except needlework, cutting-out, and dressmaking.

6183. What is your idea as to an industrial school?—My coming to the meeting was simply to get information concerning the endowment; and so far as I could gather from all that was expressed in the meeting, the idea was the establishment of an industrial school separate from the existing schools.

6184. Father Dunphy appeared to contemplate rather a school for grown-up pupils than one where younger pupils would also learn reading and writing; which do you think preferable?—I think, with Father Dunphy, that the idea before the meeting was a school for grown-up young people more than for children.

6185. Could not instruction be given to pupils of that class in the existing school buildings in the evening or afternoon?—Not always in my own school. It is frequently used for other purposes in the evening. I could not speak for the other schools.

6186. Have you in your mind any particular place for an industrial school?—I have not.

6187. Rev. Dr. Molloy.—Have you considered what number of pupils you would be likely to have in the proposed school?—I have not given it much consideration.

6188. Father Dunphy spoke of a school of one hundred and fifty girls, and of grown-up boys of equal number—that would give three hundred of his denomination alone. The other denominations would be probably represented by one hundred; that would make an industrial school of four hundred?—There would be quite that number, I believe.

6189. What would a building suitable for such a school cost?—I have no idea. It was stated at the meeting last evening that buildings could be had for a much smaller sum than would be needed to build new schools.

6190. You think it would be more desirable to have a separate industrial school available for all denominations than to get teachers who would go round and teach in the existing school buildings?—I believe it would.

6191. Dr. Traill.—Are the Church of Ireland children that go to your school mostly boys or girls?—Both boys and girls—in about equal proportions.

6192. Is your school more favourably situated, as regards its position, for them than the Church school?—No.

* The present actual number is one hundred and three.—Wm. Burgess, 9. 8. 88.

6193. They came to you merely for the improved education that they get relatively under the National Board teacher?—Yes.

6194. How does Mr. Hallowes account for the fact that fifty of his children are in your school?

Rev. Mr. *Hallowes*.—Mr. Harper's school is not in my parish. It is in the adjoining parish of Kilbride. If I had that parish I should try to get them.

6195. Lord Justice FitzGibbon.—I understand there is a higher school at Kilbride at which there are about twenty pupils.

Rev. Mr. *Hallowes*.—Mr. Harper has a higher class school under his own control.

6196. Lord Justice Naish (to the *Witness*).—What is the total amount of the grants that you get in the year from the National Board for education, including teachers' salaries?—£80 in round numbers, with books and inspection.

6197. Dr. Traill.—Are both your teachers Methodists?—One is a Methodist; the assistant is an Episcopalian.

6198. They ought to be very much obliged to you for looking after the education of their children so well, when their own clergyman doesn't seem to do it?—I don't think it would be for the advantage of the neighbourhood to have another National School to compete with mine. I believe that a school with one hundred pupils is better worked than two schools with fifty pupils each could be.

Rev. Mr. *Hallowes*.—I am very much obliged to him. The National School we are going to have now will be a boys school only.

6199. Lord Justice FitzGibbon.—Lady Carysfort provides for the girls?—Yes.

6200. Is she opposed to the National Board?—I think not.

Mr. John Story sworn and examined.

6201. Lord Justice FitzGibbon.—Were you at the meeting?—Yes.

6202. You are a Town Commissioner?—Yes.

6203. How long have you held that office?—Two years.

6204. Can you give us any suggestions?—If the foundation would allow of it, I believe that a separate school in which net-making, rope-making, and scientific fishing would be taught, would be much the better plan; but failing that from want of funds, the question is, would it be right to attach a class of that description to the present schools or not.

6205. Would you expect a separate school to be attended by older pupils who have passed the ordinary school time?—Yes, pupils of from fourteen to eighteen.

6206. Could pupils of that kind be got to attend during working hours—in other words, could it be anything but an evening or night school?—If there were profits, and the profits could be divided so as to give them some little interest in it, there would be a great number of pupils.

6207. Is there any school in which the earnings of the school pay its expenses?—Even in the prisons they are paid a small sum for their work.

6208. But they are kept and fed there for nothing?—I don't mean to feed them in the school.

6209. Then they would have to feed themselves?—But if they are idle at home they have to be fed too.

6210. What employment have young people at present in Arklow?—The boys go out fishing at the age of fourteen, and get half a share. They would be at home nine months out of the twelve. They might get a berth for mackerel fishing and herring fishing for a month or two.

6211. Do they remain idle the rest of their time?—They have nothing to do.

6212. What employment have the girls?—They have not a great deal. They sew, and a good many go to service. There is a good deal of surplus population that have no remunerative employment at all.

6213. Then your plan is to have a school to carry on a remunerative industry that would support itself by the sale of its products?—That was to meet the objection that they could not live if they were to attend school.

6214. Dr. Traill.—Where would they get a market for the things that would be made in the school?—There would be no use in teaching them if there were no market. There is one gentleman here who buys £200 or £300 worth of nets every year in the Isle of Man and Scotland. Perhaps a couple of thousand pounds worth of nets come into Arklow every year. If those nets were made locally there would be some return.

6215. But are they not made by machinery extraordinarily cheap?—But we should want to get machinery too. That is where the capital would be wanted.

6216. Lord Justice FitzGibbon.—Some years ago a net making and mending company was got up in Howth, somewhat similar to what you propose for Arklow; but it was soon wound up, and all the money was lost.

6217. Rev. Dr. Molloy.—I don't think there is any example of a school teaching an industry, and at the same time making a profit. The most it could hope to do would be to contribute towards paying its expenses.

Witness.—If you teach them to make nets and ropes in a school, there must be a market found for them. If the teacher were paid out of the endowment there would then be the local subscriptions.

6218. Lord Justice FitzGibbon.—If all the capital were supplied from outside, would it pay its own working expenses?—I believe it would.

6219. Are you connected with the sea?—I am, largely.

6220. Are any hand-made ropes used now?—I don't speak of hand-made ropes. Hand-made ropes cannot compete with those made by machinery—that is out of the question. I mean spinning ropes by machinery for long lines and nets.

6221. You would require very considerable capital?—There would be a good deal of machinery wanted.

6222. Have you thought how much would be available from local sources to start a thing of the kind?—We discussed that question last night and this morning again; and if the Commissioners would give an endowment to pay a teacher, and allow a limited liability company to be formed amongst the business people at £1 to £5 a share, a sufficient capital would be got, with the hope of saving themselves if there were a profit; whereas if they gave subscriptions only it would be sunk money.

6223. Dr. Traill.—Do you expect that these boys of eighteen, when they grow to be young men would continue to work in the factory?—If there are employment for them; if not they would be in a position to go off elsewhere.

6224. As long as the boys were learning the trade would they not be apt to destroy the material?—Not with a skilled teacher. He would not put a boy to skilled work where he would waste. You would let a boy learning carpentering begin on a rough piece of board.

6225. Would it require much training for the boys before they could begin the manufacture you have been contemplating?—I don't think it should.

6226. The machinery used for making nets is so simple that they would not require much practice?—They make nets by hand here. It would be a great deal cheaper to make them by machinery.

6227. Rev. Dr. Molloy.—Do you think that if competent teachers were provided out of the endow-

July 1, 1888.

Mr. John [illegible].

ment the people of Arklow would do the rest?—That was the idea amongst the business people. They went further, for they said that if there was a profit beyond 5 or 5½ per cent. they would give the surplus back again to the school to develope the industry.

6228. Professor Dougherty.—You spoke of scientific fishing. What exactly do you mean by that phrase?—We have only the old-fashioned plan of fishing here, and for that reason we are several months idle. The winter fishing ends in December. The mackerel fishing begins in March, and the people have nothing to do in the interval. The herring fishing lasts till July, and they have nothing to do from July till October or November.

6229. How would what you call scientific fishing help you to fill up that interval?—They might take to long line fishing, or they might trawl. We have only two or three boats trawling.

6230. There used to be an objection on the part of the ordinary fishermen to trawling?—I don't think there would be here.

6231. Dr. Traill.—Don't the trawlers go out some distance to fish?—Yes, we want a market for the produce of the trawl fishing to encourage that industry.

6232. What sized boats have you here?—We have boats here that would carry fifty-five tons or better. Another thing would be fish curing. I believe the Board of Works would lend money on security to establish a curing-house here.

6233. Lord Justice Naish.—At present are any of the fish taken off Arklow cured?—In small quantities.

6234. Professor Dougherty.—I thought you had only short seasons during which you can fish for herrings and mackerel?—They don't confine themselves to local fishing.

6235. They would not return to Arklow to cure fish caught elsewhere?—If they get a large take of herrings, and there is no market for them, they must sell them at a sacrifice, if there are no means of curing.

6236. Lord Justice FitzGibbon.—Can they cure herrings at this time of the year?—I believe they can. We can cure them in winter, and they cure mackerel now.

6237. Dr. Traill.—What fish do you catch in December?—Herrings and oysters. Mackerel in March.

6238. Lord Justice Naish.—Do you mean off Arklow?—Yes, mackerel excepted.

6239. Lord Justice FitzGibbon.—At what times of the year are any fish caught off Arklow, or so near Arklow as to be brought in here?—From July to September—two months at all events they fish. Then they go out for the fall fishing in October, and the winter fishing would be up to Christmas, or six weeks prior to Christmas.

6240. That is two seasons of six weeks or two months each?—I would say there would be better than three months of local employment.

6241. Have you had of late years a mackerel season of six weeks?—We have had a scattered season of two months.

6242. Can you say that the "scattered season" has been more than a fortnight or three weeks of good fishing?—Possibly not more without interruption. They would hardly have a month's continuous fishing round the coast of Great Britain. One shoal is broken up by the fishermen, and goes, and another shoal comes in its place.

6243. Your idea is rather to have a factory for young people than a school for children?—In reality it would be a school. The moment they should leave the educational establishments they would be just fit to enter it. It would be to teach them their business after they had learned to read and write.

6244. Dr. Traill.—What is your own occupation?—I was originally an Examining Officer of the Customs, but have been superannuated, and I have now an interest in a good many vessels.

6245. Lord Justice FitzGibbon.—Is there any boat-building here?—A good deal. We had forty-five class fishing boats built by a Government loan here last year. During the last five or six years the Arklow fishermen have got a lot of fine deep sea fishing boats, and they go to the Shetland Islands, Aberdeen, &c.

6246. Were they built in Arklow?—Yes, and equipped.

6247. Would boat-building be a suitable industry here?—It would; but we have carpenters enough for the amount of trade that we have at present. If you taught boat-building you would turn out the men that are now at it, unless we could get a market in other places.

6248. Professor Dougherty.—Would the existing carpenters object to the establishment of a technical school for boat-building?—I am afraid they would. I am afraid it would interfere with the local trade. If there is work for ten boat builders, and you supply twenty, the rate of wages must come down.

Rev. Father Dunphy.—A large number of our boys go ship sailing.

Witness.—We have had some boys out of the National school that qualified themselves to be masters of ships. We have one vessel in Arklow that carries seven hundred and twenty tons.

6249. A foreign-going vessel, sailing for freight?—Yes. She went to Monte Video from London, and is back in Antwerp now. There are also one or two Arklow vessels discharging at Wexford from Canada at present.

6250. Built here?—No; registered from Dublin, but owned in Arklow exclusively.

6251. Rev. Dr. Molloy.—Could you develop the boat-building industry?—One great difficulty would be the want of water sufficient to enable vessels of large size to come in to be repaired. We have not sufficient water over the bar for them to come in. We have a sand bar.

6252. Lord Justice Naish.—How many ships belong to Arklow?—I think there are one hundred registered vessels.

6253. That could cross the Atlantic?—I think they could if a tempting offer were made them.

6254. Are there any registered shipowners here?—Yes; there is the firm of Kearon and Tyrrell, registered shipowners, and several individual owners.

Mr. Daniel Condren sworn and examined.

Mr. Daniel Condren.

6255. Lord Justice FitzGibbon.—You are chairman of the Town Commissioners?—Yes.

6256. You speak in your resolution of establishing a technical school in the town of Arklow: what sort of school do you contemplate?—A commencing industrial school under local management, to be subject to the control of your board.

6257. But our board is only temporary?—Well, subject to the sanction of your board.

6258. How would you set about constituting such a body?—I don't know, unless a meeting of the traders and general representatives of the town selected a body, and submitted their names to your board for approval.

6259. What prospect would you have of getting premises?—I think the parties should get a short time to consider where suitable premises could be obtained, the amount of money likely to be realised, and the class of industry most suitable to be established before they could explain to your board what they require from them. I can add nothing to the evidence that has been given, except the fact that there are two hundred and fifty boys and girls who are past the time of receiving instruction in the schools, and who could be employed in an industrial school before they come to an age to go out into the world, so as to get proper training to enable them to earn their living elsewhere.

6260. If you had an industrial school with two hundred partly grown-up people in it, where would you expect to get a market for what they made?—It would be necessary to employ them in the manufacture of goods that would be useful for general trade.

6261. Would there be any danger of the people who are already in general trade objecting to have industrial school manufactures brought into competition with theirs?—I don't know how they could object to the youth of the country being trained to an industry. There is no net manufacture carried on in Ireland, and thousands of pounds go from this town alone to Scotland for nets.

6262. Do you know how or where the nets are made that are sold at present?—I do not. I believe that net manufacturing should be an after consideration because it is a very heavy business to launch in. There would be the putting up of the looms, &c., and it could not be considered at first. What they want is the nucleus of some fund to start industrial schools that could be enlarged by degrees as they were seen to take in the town.

6263. Rev. Dr. Molloy.—What would you start with?—With local fishery industries. That would be for a public meeting to consider; and it would require some time to mature their views as to the works that would be remunerative without a large expenditure or plant. I believe that net making might be a future consideration.

6264. Are repairs of nets executed in Arklow?—They are executed by the people who are engaged in the fishing industry and their wives and the other members of their families.

6265. Is that a branch that would be capable of being improved by an industrial school?—Yes, more of the girls and the boys of the town could be trained to net-making, so that when they had started the fishing industry they would be competent to look after their own gear.

6266. Dr. Traill.—What preliminary industries do you think they should start?—That would be very difficult to say. It would be important for a body of people to consider.

6267. But a body of people could not invent the thing unless there were some people who had a general idea of it?—I believe they should be trained to different classes of trades—that it should not be confined to any single branch of trade: there should be carpenters, shipcarpenters, joiners, and all the minor trades.

6268. Rev. Dr. Molloy.—Do you mean that they should be taught all trades, or rather the use of their hands and the management of tools?—Boys could be selected, according as they had different tastes, and taught to pursue different crafts; the whole body should not be confined to one industry. The industrial school should embrace various trades, so as to put some to joining, others to shipcarpentering.

6269. That is a fine conception, but is it practicable? Teachers of each trade would be very expensive. To carry out your idea it would be necessary first to select two or three definite things which you would teach, in the hope that in the course of time you would be able to add others?—Two or three things should be taken up at the start, and afterwards they could increase the sphere of operations. The girls should be taught two or three different branches; for if the whole body of them were confined to knitting alone, it would become practically useless, for they would not be able to get sale for the produce. Some might be taught dressmaking, and others a better style of cooking, so as to be competent to take high-class situations as servants.

6270. Lord Justice FitzGibbon.—The National Board are going to put the girls in the fifth and sixth classes to spend the greater part of their time at industrial subjects—cooking, dressmaking and the rest; so that from this time forward, you will have those subjects taught in your own National Schools. Do you propose a new school for teaching industries in, or to teach classes in the existing schools special industrial subjects?

Witness.—For one particular school you would receive more generous support if it were established as a non-sectarian school for the benefit of the general public.

6271. Are you in a position to put a figure on the amount of support you would be likely to get?—No; but if you give the people of the town a fortnight to consider the best school for them, they could canvass the parties around and ask them to put down a figure.

6272. Dr. Traill.—Do you think that at a public meeting they would be prepared to elect persons on a board irrespective of all religious and political considerations?—I believe they would. All such considerations would be thrown overboard for the public good.

6273. Rev. Dr. Molloy.—Is there any existing building available for such a school?—I could not say without consideration.

6274. It would be very expensive to build such a school?—It would be very expensive; it would be almost impossible.

6275. How much money do you think could be raised in Arklow—a thousand pounds?—I would not like to say.

6276. You would not like to commit the Town Commissioners?—They can do very little.

6277. Lord Justice FitzGibbon.—What is their revenue?—The valuation is £4,000 on house property and £1,000 on land. They can only levy 3d. in the pound on land, and 1s. in the pound, at the highest, on house property. The maximum rate is about £1 [illegible]. It is levied at present.

6278. Is that required for cleaning?—No, the sanitary arrangements are under the Poor Law Guardians. The Commissioners are not the Urban Sanitary Authority; lighting the town is their principal duty.

6279. Have you gas light?—No, paraffin.

6280. Dr. Traill.—Are you incorporated as Town Commissioners?—Incorporated under the Towns Improvement (Ireland) Act.

6281. Lord Justice FitzGibbon.—Do the Public Libraries Acts apply to you? Can you raise a rate of 1d. in the pound for teaching purposes?—No, we could not.

6282. Rev. Father Dunphy.—Does any inhabitant wish to make any statement?

There was no response.

Mr. James Tyrrell sworn and examined.

6283. Lord Justice FitzGibbon.—Are you a partner in the firm of Kearns and Tyrrell?—Yes.

6284. You have heard the evidence as to establishing an industrial school here. Can you tell what local support it would be likely to have?—From the feeling expressed both outside the meeting and inside of it, I believe it would be supported by all the traders and work people, by the shopkeepers, merchants, traders, and vessel owners of the town.

6285. What sort of school would suit best?—I believe the school that is most wanting in the town is a net factory or rope factory. We are pretty well supplied with other things so far as [illegible], but we have nothing in that shape. A great lot of money goes out of Arklow every year for ropes and nets.

6286. Rev. Dr. Molloy.—Give us an idea as to the amount?—I would be safe in saying that not less than £2,000 or even £2,500 leaves Arklow every year for ropes and nets. We ourselves pay from £1,000 to £1,500 a year for ropes, and we are only one buyer.

6287. Where do you get them from?—Liverpool, Belfast, Glasgow, and Dublin.

6288. Lord Justice FitzGerald.—Do you think that you could with any chance of success enter into competition with the Belfast rope makers?—I believe that if we had a factory we could—if we had machinery in a small way.

6289. But if you only manufactured in a small way, would you be able to compete with Belfast?—I think we could. It would do away with the expense of carriage.

6290. How do the ropes and nets come here?—By sea from Scotland to Belfast and Dublin; and by rail from thence here.

6291. What are the rates per ton?—From Dublin the charge for nets is about 15s. a ton, and sometimes up to £1 and 25s. a ton. Heavier and rougher goods come at from 7s. 6d. to 8s. a ton.

6292. How much value would there be in a ton of nets?—A ton of nets would be worth I dare say £315.

6293. Then 25s. a ton carriage on £3,000 worth of nets would only represent £20 a year. Have you ever seen the Belfast rope works?—I have seen drawings of them.

6294. I am afraid they would be too many for the people of Arklow?—I don't know. We are able to get as good ropes from England as from there yet.

6295. Where are the nets made?—In Scotland and the Isle of Man.

6296. Are they machine made?—All.

6297. Are there any hand-made nets in use in the trade now?—I believe not. They are not able to make them fine enough.

6298. Rev. Dr. Molloy.—Have you any idea of the cost of the machinery necessary for net-making?—I have not. It is wonderful the amount of rope and yarn that is used. There is a large fishing fleet in the town, and every day they are consuming nets and ropes, that is they are buying them every day to keep the supply up; and while they are away working during the season in Kinsale or in the North, they are preparing for the next season.

Rev. Father Dunphy.—And also sail-making?

Witness.—Also sail-making. We use a great deal of canvas. The boys and girls could be employed in spinning flax and working at home.

6299. Lord Justice FitzGerald.—There is no hand-spinning now?

Witness.—Some of the yarn that is supplied is not suitable. They get it from Russia, but it is too coarse, and very few use it. As a rule, we prefer the home-spun yarn for rope-making.

6300. Rev. Dr. Molloy.—By "home-spun," you don't mean "hand spun"?—I mean spun by machinery, but the machinery fed by hand.

6301. Lord Justice FitzGerald.—What sail-making is there?—Our firm have a sail loft one hundred and seventy feet long.

6302. How many people are employed there?—Sometimes four, sometimes three, sometimes two. Paid by the day.

6303. Do you ever fit out ships?—Yes, we have fitted out several. Other people employ sail-makers as well as we.

6304. In making new sails or mending old ones?—Making new sails and repairing others.

6305. What coasting vessels come in here?—About a dozen, on and off; but the great proportion of our fleet don't come here at all unless to be repaired. We look for persons to bring them here to be repaired, so as to leave the money in the town. They leave from £400 to £500 in repairs.

6306. How are the repairs done without slips?—We go down to the water's edge, by stages and ladders; and the smaller vessels are hove down on one side, and turned bottom right up, according to the old system.

6307. Dr. Traill.—How do you keep the bar down?—It is pretty fair since the new harbour was made.

6308. What height of water have you over it at high tide?—From nine to ten feet; but during the time of the improving it silted up a good deal.

6309. Lord Justice FitzGerald.—Is the pier all right?—The pier is all right.

6310. Rev. Dr. Molloy.—Is it finished?—One is. We should have two. We want another.

6311. You heard Mr. Henry's plan of a joint stock company for establishing and carrying on an industrial school: do you think it would be likely to be successful in Arklow?—I think it is the only thing that would be successful, for the people would be used to it, and they would have an interest in it.

Mr. *Alexander Taylor* sworn and examined.

6312. Lord Justice FitzGerald.—You are Lord Carysfort's agent?—Yes.

6313. Is Arklow on Lord Carysfort's property?—Yes.

6314. How far does the property extend?—Down to the boundaries of the county of Wexford.

6315. Inland, how far does it extend?—It goes up to the back of the mountains.

6316. It doesn't go beyond Aughrim in the direction of Macreddin?—No, it does not, the river is the boundary. It goes up to Wooden-bridge.

6317. Can you tell us your ideas as to the wants of the town in the way of industrial teaching?—I think that if any feasible plan could be adopted it would be a very good thing. I am not expressing any opinion as Lord Carysfort's agent, for no scheme has been laid before him. My own idea is that it would be very difficult to get the thing to pay financially.

6318. Do you think that the people of the town with the help of those interested in the property would be likely to support the school?—I think they would; if they were serious, it would be good for the town and also a success.

6319. In what form do you think it would be most likely to turn out successful?—I really have not considered the point.

6320. Is there any land or building available for a site in the town?—I don't think there would be any difficulty whatever about a site.

6321. Is there any disused public building that could be made available?—No. We have a large sawmill which we work about three months in the year.

6322. Are there any disused mills?—No, but there is plenty of available spare land near the harbour.

6323. Rev. Dr. Molloy.—Is the sawmill worked by water power?—No, steam power. Nothing is worked by water power. I think if we could get the whole of the endowment there would be some chance, but I understand you to say, we would only get a very small portion of it.

6324. Lord Justice Naish.—We had another inquiry this morning at which a strong case was made by the people of the neighbourhood of the estate in favour of its application there. So long as there are local people for a local endowment we cannot ignore it.

Witness.—That would leave us very little to get here.

July 5, 1886. — Mr. Alexander Taylor

6325. Rev. Dr. Molloy.—You could do better with the whole of it than with the half of it?—That would give us some chance here.

6326. Lord Justice FitzGibbon.—We have heard fully the views of the representative people here. There is no immediate hurry about the matter, for we shall not be able to publish a draft scheme for the Carysfort Endowment sooner than October. If in the meantime the people of Arklow can suggest any feasible plan we shall be very glad to consider it, and to give it any assistance that the available funds will enable us to do. But there are other claims on this particular endowment. At the same time there are other public funds available for industrial education. Also, you should see how much money will be available from the locality. We shall be glad to receive any communications, say up to the 1st of October. But it will be necessary to look at the matter much more in detail than you have done, to count the cost and to see how to lay out the money, and through whom; and it will be absolutely necessary for you to agree amongst yourselves as to the body that will have the managing of it. You appear to aim more at a factory than a school, and at some advantage to be carried on by young people rather than by school boys and girls. You will have to meet many difficulties, especially with the people already in the trades, who have made difficulties elsewhere where an artificial system of production has been brought into competition with them. Also, you would be in competition with large people who are making nets and ropes for profit on a very large scale and with every possible advantage. On the other hand, there is the much less ambitious scheme of allowing each of the existing schools to add classes for senior pupils who would get from [illegible] industrial instruction, and also the result fees offered by the National Board. We have separately to consider the claims of the [illegible] school and the old Carysfort school, and three or four other schools in the same parish; and we have to regret that the money is not sufficient to meet all the demands upon it.

THE INCORPORATED SOCIETY'S SCHOOL, ARKLOW.

6327. Lord Justice FitzGibbon (to Rev. Mr. Halloran).—Mary Boland, on March 20, 1807, granted to the Incorporated Society some property for the benefit of the Charter School near Arklow. What money you have got from that source, and how it has been applied?

Rev. Mr. *Halloran*.—I have often heard of the "Charter School," but I know nothing about it.

Mr. *Alexander Taylor*.—The Charter School has no buildings now.

6328. Lord Justice Naish.—Who gets the rent of the old premises?—We get the rent from a tenant who has the grass.

6329. Lord Justice FitzGibbon.—It is not held on any educational trust?—Certainly not.

6330. What does Incorporated Society give you?

Rev. Mr. *Halloran*.—At present they give us £40 a year. I believe that formerly they not only gave that, but there used to be a certain number of boys free at [illegible]. At present we have three girls at Celbridge.

6331. Did they get in by competition?—Yes.

6332. Dr. Traill.—What is the £40 given for?—To supplement the schoolmaster's salary.

6333. That keeps you from the National Board?—It has kept us up to the present from going to the National Board.

6334. Lord Justice FitzGibbon.—I see in the report of 1880 that the salary of the master was £[illegible] a year, of which the Incorporated Society paid £[illegible], and the rector and subscriptions provided £[illegible].

Rev. Mr. *Halloran*.—The master's salary now is £60, made up of £40 and £20.

6335. Lord Justice FitzGibbon.—At that time there were fifty-five pupils on the roll, with an attendance of forty-two, all members of the Church. I understand from you that the attendance now is ninety-two?—Yes; the endowment under the Incorporated Society is exclusively given to the boys' school.

6336. You never looked into the terms of the Boland trust?—No; I never could get any information.

6337. Lord Justice FitzGibbon.—The Incorporated Society have got a number of endowments given by private people for special purposes, besides, they have a good deal of property available for the general purposes of the society. We are at present preparing a draft scheme for the management of the whole of them; and it will be our duty to see that any local trusts are carried out.

Mr. *John Redmond* sworn and examined.

Mr. John Redmond.

6338. Lord Justice FitzGibbon.—You remember the Charter School?—Yes.

6339. Who was the master of it?—A man named Harris.

6340. What pupils do you remember attending?—He had a fine school; some came from England and Scotland, and from Dublin; they were all gentlemen's sons. It was a boarding school.

6341. Were they all Protestants?—No; there were some Catholics—day boys from Arklow; the boarders, generally they came from England.

6342. What became of it?—It fell.

6343. What brought about its fall?—The man died, and shortly after his death it all dwindled away and fell down.

6344. The building fell down?—Yes.

6345. What became of the scholars?—They generally went home to their own houses.

6346. About how many Arklow boys were going to it?—About a score; and there were boarders besides.

Rev. Mr. *Halloran*.—I am informed that is not the property out of which the Incorporated Society get the money.

6347. Rev. Dr. Molloy (to the Witness).—How long is it since Harris died?—About sixty years.

6348. Dr. Traill.—How old are you?—Seventy-four.

6349. Who got possession of the land after Harris died?—The Earl of Carysfort.

6350. Lord Justice FitzGibbon.—The Incorporated Society hold land let at a rental of £70 [illegible], and there is a sum of £[illegible] [illegible] Government Stock, representing some land taken by the Railway Company, producing £3 [illegible] 10d. a year, making a total of £73 [illegible] 10d. a year. We are making a scheme for the management of the endowments of the Incorporated Society, and one of our duties is to look after local trusts. This endowment was originally given "for the support of the Charter School near Arklow." The Charter Schools were at one time handed over to the Incorporated Society.

Mr. *Sharp*.—It is out of houses in Arklow that the Incorporated Society get their money. There are a number of tenants.

6351. Lord Justice FitzGibbon.—The old Charter School is gone; but they have been giving £40 a year to the nearest Church school. We will see the trusts of Mary Boland's will, and when our scheme for the Incorporated Society's endowments comes out you had better look at it.

The inquiry then terminated.

PUBLIC SITTING—SATURDAY, JULY 6, 1889.

At the Courthouse, Wicklow.

Present:—The Right Hon. *Lord Justice* FITZGIBBON, and the Right Hon. *Lord Justice* NAISH, Judicial Commissioners; and the Rev. GERALD MOLLOY, D.D., D.SC., ANTHONY TRAILL, Esq., LL.D., M.D., F.T.C.D., and Professor DOUGHERTY, M.A., Assistant Commissioners.

The Assistant Secretary, N. D. MURPHY, was in attendance.

July 6, 1889.

CROFTON SCHOOL, ASHFORD. WICKLOW DIOCESAN SCHOOL. WICKLOW FREE SCHOOL.

The Rev. *Henry Banks*, M.A. examined.

Rev. Henry Banks, M.A.

6351. *Lord Justice* FITZGIBBON.—Mr. Banks, we are anxious to try to get information as to the property of these endowments which don't seem to be in question, and in case any of the property is remaining we want to see whether we can get anything done to secure it. As to the Crofton School we are anxious to know how it has been working under the scheme that was settled by the Court of Chancery.

Witness.—I believe the Crofton endowment is now given to the present parochial school at Kilbride, which is a National school under the Rev. Mr. [illegible].

6353. The Diocesan Free School ceased to exist at the time of the Church Act. Do you remember where it was held?—There has not been a schoolmaster in it since 1839. The last was the Rev. James Cochrane, who lived at the foot of Church Hill.

6354. Was that house a school-house in any sense?—I think not. It is private property. It belongs to the [illegible] family.

6355. Was there no diocesan school since then?—Not since 1839. In 1857 the Lord Lieutenant appointed the Rev. Elrington M'Kee to the school, but it was afterwards found, that the former had not the right of appointment, and that it was in Archbishop Whately. He investigated the case, but neither confirmed Mr. M'Kee's appointment nor appointed another. He said he did not want to make the clergy. The appointment has dropped since then. In Archbishop Trench's time some of the churchwardens sent a memorial bringing the matter before him, but he declined to act on the same grounds; he said he did not think the clergy would benefit much by it, that they had enough to spend, and that he did not see the necessity for it, so no appointment was made.

6356. The old diocesan tax was not imposed since 1839?—No. I should mention that there is property near Black Castle, about twelve acres, the rent of which Mr. Cochrane, the master of the diocesan school was allowed to receive. Since then the Government held it and sold some of it and there are eight acres or more in the hands of the Government. There was no regular diocesan school built. It was held in a house.

6357. By the augmentees who took the diocesan tax until 1839?—Yes.

6358. And from 1839 no schoolmaster has been appointed, and the whole thing is in abeyance?—Yes.

6359. Then in very much as is reported, namely, that the endowment was in abeyance in 1857, and that at the time of the passing of the Church Act it had ceased to exist. You had no schoolmaster that had any capacity at the time of the passing of the Church Act?—No.

6360. There is no property belonging to the diocesan school at all?—None whatever. The *Earl* of Chesterfield was Lord Lieutenant in 1746. He is mentioned in one of the old papers that I have.

6361. The report speaks of twelve acres three roods thirty-three perches, from which there was a net annual income of £40 a year. No appointment was made, it is stated, since the death of the last master in 1834; and part of the land was sold by the Government?—Yes.

6362. Can you tell us anything about that?—Well as regards the selling I cannot; but I have an agreement here by which you will see that the Rev. Jacob Bryan was the first appointment made. [Hands in document.]

"This is to certify that I am content that Mr. William [illegible] shall hold the whole concern belonging to the Black Castle of Wicklow, as Governor, during the time of my tenure of office, at the yearly rent of £[illegible] a year, to be paid quarterly on the conditions usual between landlord and tenant, the first quarter to be payable on the 25th December, 1755;"

and it is signed Jacob Bryan.

6363. What is the meaning of that?—He was the diocesan schoolmaster at that time. It is mentioned in one of these papers. These papers were drawn up at the time of making the appeal to Archbishop Trench, by Dr. Andrew Nolan, who, I think, was churchwarden then. [Hands in documents.]

6364. *Lord Justice* FITZGIBBON read the "Case of the Wicklow Endowed School," in which it was stated that the endowment was granted in 1746, and that the first schoolmaster was appointed in 1748, and held the lands until 1780. About the year 1810 the Rev. James Cochrane was appointed master and held the lands until his death in 1837. His family were allowed to hold possession until the end of the year in order to enable them to get the crops. No further appointment was made to the school until 1857, when His Excellency appointed the Rev. E. M'Kee to the diocesan school; which appointment, it was much to be regretted, was set aside, at the instance of the Archbishop, who had since refused to make any further appointment to the diocesan school.—(*To Witness.*)—Do you consider that this free school for which Lord Chesterfield gave the land was the same as the diocesan school?—I don't think it was—I don't believe it was.

6365. Is there any record of any school existing since 1837 as a free school?—Not that I am aware of; and I think I should have known if there was.

6366. When you say that the Government sold part of this land, who is in possession of it?—Well, that's the very point I am looking for. It is not mentioned in any of these papers. I think it is *Sir* Thomas Esmonde, as well as I can make out, that is indicated here. He has part of that Black Castle land now.

I hand in a copy of a memorial on the subject.

6367. *Lord Justice* FITZGIBBON.—(*Reads*). "This is a copy of a second letter addressed to Archdeacon West, Archdeacon of Dublin, dated Wicklow, 18th November, 1859:—

"I should have sooner replied to your favour of the [illegible] October, but that I awaited the result of a meeting about to be held here, the memorial from which I beg to forward, together with a copy of one forwarded to the Lord Lieutenant. I beg to say, that in asking for the re-establishment of the diocesan school in Wicklow, we don't assume that Wicklow has any exclusive right to its being established here, but inasmuch as it was the place chosen by a former Archbishop, and was recommended by more than one Board of Education Commissioners, who considered it the most fitting place, more particularly now that railway communication places it within easy reach of all parts of the diocese, and from its healthy situation and the advantages of one building, &c., we deem that it possesses many pluses in its [illegible]. That the experiment made twenty years ago should have failed to confer any permanent benefit on the neighbourhood was to be expected from the appointment there made, which was only intended to benefit an individual, the object being to provide for a person of forty years standing, who, though a respectable and able man was, from his time of life, incapable of establishing the school on a permanent basis. The school, therefore, lingered on during his life, and did not offer any inducement to repeat the experiment, to the present time."

Who was referred to in that, do you know —that would be about 1837?—That would be Mr. Cochrane.

6368.

"But you are aware that in some instances endowments for education have tended to produce slackness, but only where the endowment is so large as to render personal exertion unnecessary; but when—as in this contemplated endowment, it is so small as to offer only an inducement to the good scholar who is often without pecuniary means there is no risk of failure, and one whose competition runs so high in educational establishments have no fears for the result. The endowment made by Lord Chesterfield, we know, has no connexion with the Diocesan school; but as the Lord Lieutenant allowed Mr. Cochrane, when master of the Diocesan school, to receive the rent of the land, we have little doubt that our present Viceroy will permit the payment of the rent, or the sale of the land to be applied for the purpose for which they were appropriated, and then the objection of the Archbishop that the Grand Jury did not build or aid the Diocesan school, will be obviated; and if he will accede to the prayer of the memorialists and co-operate with His Excellency, we hope to see a school established in Wicklow, which will be greatly for the advantage both of the gentry and of the clergy of the diocese."

How is the land used that was given by Lord Chesterfield originally?—Well, I don't know exactly about the extent of the land; but of late years there has been a sort of Government fort built there, and they have militia there for six months in the year and target practice.

6369. On the land near the castle?—Quite close to the castle. This is the document that was drawn up for Archbishop Trench:—

"With respect to the land granted by Lord Chesterfield which is now reduced to eight acres by the sale of the Government in 1862."

6370. Dr. Traill.—When did they sell it to?—There is a name in one of these papers that I cannot very clearly make out; but he says—I may mention that the rent is now paid to the Rector.

6371. Lord Justice Naish.—Was it a grant of Lord Chesterfield's private property, or of public property?—I don't know that, for it was in 1744.

6372. Has he an estate here?—Not that I am aware of. Lord Chesterfield was Lord Lieutenant at that time.

6373. Lord Justice FitzGibbon.—In 1862 the lands were advertised for sale, and two acres were sold to Sir Thomas Esmonde; and eight and a-half acres remained unsold, the rent of which was paid to the Rector.

To Witness.—You don't happen to know who is in possession of the eight acres?—Yes; I have always understood it to be in the possession of the Government. I don't know of any payment being made from the town at all in connexion with it.

6374. What school accommodation is there in Wicklow at present—first, is there any intermediate school, Protestant or Roman Catholic?—No, there is no intermediate school now.

6375. Was there at any recent time?—Well, there was a school in the town which was chiefly under the management of the Roman Catholics, and I really can't say anything about it. I think it was some public school.

6376. Under a teaching Order, do you mean?—No, I think it was the Canon or Priest here that had something to do with it. I think it was a public school. I don't know whether it was an intermediate school or not.

6377. What elementary schools are there?—There are our parochial school which is supported by the parishioners; a National school at the convent; and a boys school near the chapel.

6378. Is your school, which is supported by the congregation, in connexion with the National Board?—No, not at all.

6379. About how many children have you attending it?—From eighty to one hundred.

6380. Dr. Traill.—Is it in connexion with the Church Education Society?—No.

6381. Who inspects it?—We have a Diocesan Inspector.

6382. Lord Justice FitzGibbon.—Is there any particular reason for its not being in connexion with the National Board?—Well, I never joined the National Board; and the school is used by a great number of respectable people in the town—not only tradespeople but shopkeepers. I sent my own children to the school at one time; and we felt that if we threw it open as a National school we could not object to any one. There is a great number of the humbler classes; and if they attended the school the respectable ones would have all gone, and there are no other school for them to go to. Therefore, we have striven to keep the school, in fact, under my control as far as we could.

6383. Dr. Traill.—Where do the humbler classes get their education if they don't get it there?—They all go to the Roman Catholic National School.

6384. The Protestant children?—They all come to us.

6385. I thought you said that if the children of the humbler classes came to the school the respectable ones would be driven out?—Well ours are of a better class. It got out in the town at one time that the school had been changed to a National school, and some children from a very dirty locality came up to it, but the master said—"I am not under the National Board and I cannot receive you."

6386. Lord Justice FitzGibbon.—You have not thought of doing as they have done at Holywood, namely, to have a better class of school in connexion with a National school, so as to get a National Board grant, and also give an education of a better kind?—We have not done that. The master has some boarders of his own—several very respectable boys—and in that way he is enabled to derive a better income from the school.

6387. What income do you pay him?—The select vestry, as well as I remember, only pay him £30 a year; but he is allowed all the fees from the children, and there are gradations of fees.

6388. Who appoints him?—The select vestry now.

6389. How long has the present master been there?—About four years. We were under Erasmus Smith's Board, who endowed the school; but when they made reductions they took away the grant from our school.

6390. They withdrew the grants in all cases where the numbers were sufficient to entitle the school to aid from the National Board. What buildings have you for your school?—We have land that was given for an English school, under a very old document. We hold it independently. It was given by the Rev. John Wall, D.D., in the time of His Grace Archbishop Magee—Archbishop of Dublin.

6391. Lord Justice FitzGibbon.—The document is an indenture of the 30th September, 17[illegible], between the Rev. John Wall, D.D., of the first part, Richard Lord Archbishop of Dublin, of the second part, and Edward Bury and Samuel Edge, churchwardens, of the third part. It recites the Act of 1731, providing that for the better encouragement of English schools it should be lawful to grant land; and by virtue of that Act he grants to Messrs. Bury and Edge, churchwardens, the field or plot known by the name of Hannah Byrne's field, lately in the possession of Thomas Ryder, containing one acre, which is part of the glebe land of the parish, bounded, &c.—to hold to Messrs. Bury and Edge, the churchwardens, and their successors the churchwardens, for ever, to and for such use as by the recited Act is intended and for no other use whatever.

6392. Lord Justice Naish.—There was a schoolhouse built on it?—Yes.

6393. Lord Justice FitzGibbon.—Was there any schoolhouse referred to as existing at the time of the grant, or is the schoolhouse a new building?—I think it is a new building.

6394. How was your present building erected?—When Dr. De Burgh was curate he collected funds and built the schoolhouse.

6395. Is there a schoolmaster's residence?—Yes, in connection with the school.

6396. Is it there he keeps his boarders?—Yes.

6397. How many has he?—I think about four.

6398. Where was he trained?—He was one of Erasmus Smith's best masters, and had the highest recommendations from the Inspector, Mr. Rodgie. He came in under the Erasmus Smith Board, and remained with us.

6399. Lord Justice Naish.—How long has the Erasmus Smith grant been withdrawn?—Four or five years. This master was under them when they took away the grant and he remained on.

6400. How is your school maintained now?—By the collection of a special fund every year. The parishioners collect it and the Select Vestry pay it out. There are also fees from the children.

6401. Dr. Traill.—Could your schoolmaster qualify under the National Board?—No, he is too old.

6402. Lord Justice Naish.—What number of boys have you attending the school?—There are about forty girls and nearly the same number of boys—nearly a hundred altogether.

6403. Is that the attendance?—The number on the roll.

6404. What is the attendance?—As a rough guess, I would say up to something about fifty-five.

6405. Lord Justice FitzGibbon.—Do you know what is the Protestant population of the parish?—Well, my charge is supposed to be between nine hundred and a thousand.

6406. How far does your parish extend?—A long way.

6407. Is the whole town in it?—Oh, yes, and it goes out half way to Ashford.

6408. Does it include Rathnew and Newrath bridge?—Yes. We have another school at Rathnew, which has a grant from the Glendalough branch of the Church Education Society.

6409. You are in the diocese of Glendalough here?—Quite so.

6410. Lord Justice FitzGibbon.—As regard this school, there is nothing that we could do for it except this; We have had a great many cases in which property has been left to churchwardens, and has passed to persons who are no longer legally churchwardens; we could cure for all, if you thought well of it, vest your property in an incorporated body, containing representatives of the select vestry, and also the clergyman of the parish. One of our schemes would cost you less than a deed, and you would have no more trouble about it. It is for yourselves to consider about that; but as long as things are going on well at a school, we do not like to interfere. Of course we would be bound to preserve the character of the school as it is now.

6411. Dr. Traill.—It would be a common scheme of course. Is there any talk in your diocese of diocesan trustees to hold the Church property?

Witness.—I never heard the question raised.

6412. Dr. Traill.—We have published them for a number of other dioceses?

Witness.—I have heard nothing of it in this part of the diocese.

6413. Dr. Traill.—In many cases scattered properties are taken possession of by people who cannot be got out. If your property is vested in an incorporated body, anyone who takes hold of it afterwards would have to prove his title; otherwise you would have to prove your title as against the trespasser. No scheme will be forced on you. We will send you models of schemes.

Witness.—I would like to consult the select vestry.

6414. Lord Justice FitzGibbon.—I suppose you have no invested funds?—No.

6415. You have not got any legacies?—We had between £30 and £40 a year from a house in Dublin, a good many years ago, but the lease expired, and we lost it.

WICKLOW TERESIAN ORPHAN SCHOOL (WALDRON'S BEQUEST).

6416. Lord Justice FitzGibbon.—There is another endowment that appears to be Roman Catholic, and that was formerly applied for the benefit of children in this county. In the year 1823 a Mr. Waldron bequeathed £311 10s. 3d. Government Stock, for the founding of an orphan poor school in Wicklow, of which a Mr. Edward Allen, of Liffey-street, Dublin, was to be president. At the time when he was [illegible], they used to send the orphans to some district in the country where they were boarded and lodged in farmers' houses, while they received their education in the National schools of the locality. Children thus supported, were located at Clondalkin, in the county of Dublin. None of you, Wicklow people, seem to be curious about this property.

Rev. Mr. Eade.—It never was mentioned in any bequest connected with the parish.

6417. Lord Justice FitzGibbon.—We know from former Reports that it was a Roman Catholic bequest; but what the orphan poor school in the county of Wicklow was, does not appear, nor do we know who the present patron of it is. It was called the Teresian school.

Rev. Mr. Eade.—I never heard of it at all. The old documents that my rector gave me do not mention it in any way.

6418. Lord Justice FitzGibbon.—You would not have got it at all events. It was for people of another way of thinking. We thought the priest might be able to tell us something about it; but Wicklow doesn't seem to have got it.

Rev. Mr. Eade.—There never was any orphan school here for either side since I came here.

6419. Lord Justice FitzGibbon.—The date of the will was 1823, and the charity was in existence in 1867.

Mr. *Joseph Smith*, of Abbey Hill, sworn and examined.

6420. Do you know anything about this endowment?—I was born in Wicklow. I remember eight acres of land being sold by the Commissioners of Education to Mrs. Kavanagh, twenty-five years ago. Sir Thomas Esmonde had four acres, but he sold them to the Government as training ground for the militia. The nuns of the convent bought the eight acres from Mrs. Kavanagh, who was a farmer's daughter. The four acres include the site of Black Castle. Witness never heard how Sir Thomas

July 4, 1888.

Rev. Henry Eade, M.A.

Mr. Joseph Smith.

July 8, 1889.

Mr. Joseph Smith.

Esmonde got the four acres. They were in Sir Thomas Esmonde's possession ten years ago. They were in his family's hands. The Harbour Commissioners paid compensation seven years ago for the use of them to Sir Thomas Esmonde. The nuns have been in possession for four years; the Esmondes still hold the Black Castle. I remember Mr. Corcoran, head master, having eight acres in 1842. They were usurped before his time. Mrs. Kavanagh worked the lands as a farmer. I was at school with Mr. Corcoran in 1833 and 1835. Mr. Corcoran rented a house for the school.

Mr. *Joseph M'Carroll* sworn and examined.

Mr. Joseph M'Carroll.

6421. I am a Town Commissioner. Mr. Patrick Waldron, father of the chairman of the Dublin, Wicklow, and Wexford Railway Company, gave money in trust for a Roman Catholic Orphan Society, in the county of Wicklow. Mr. Lawrence Coffey, of Liffey-street, was chairman. It was a Teresian Orphan Society.

6422. Lord Justice FITZGIBBON.—£411 Government Stock was in the hands of the patron of the charity. There is no school; and the money has been used for orphans sent to Clondalkin.

Witness.—I will ascertain where the money is, and who the trustees of the stock are. It was there in 1857. They organized an infant school seven years ago, but it fell off from want of funds two years ago; it was a Roman Catholic school but was open to all Protestants; it had twenty-four pupils. It was once flourishing but collapsed. Canon Dillon, P.P., and the Town Commissioners formed the corporation, two or three Protestants came to it, and four of my own boys went to it; one of them went to Maynooth, some go now to St. Malachy's; one of my sons went there. I think every town should have a good preparatory school at which boys could be prepared for larger schools.

The inquiry then terminated.

July 8, 1889.

PUBLIC SITTING—MONDAY, JULY 8, 1889.

At the Offices, 23, Nassau-street, Dublin.

Present:—The Right Hon. Lord Justice FITZGIBBON, and the Right Hon. Lord Justice NAISH, Judicial Commissioners; and the Rev. GERALD MOLLOY, D.D., D.SC., and Professor DOUGHERTY, M.A., Assistant Commissioners.

The Secretary, Mr. WM. EDWARD ELLIS, LL.B., and the Assistant Secretary, N. D. MURPHY, were in attendance.

HEWETSON'S SCHOOL, CLANE.—* OBJECTIONS TO DRAFT SCHEME.

The Rev. *William Sherlock*, Incumbent of Clane, and *Thomas Cooke-Trench*, Esq., J.P., represented the Trustees of the School. Rev. *S. G. Cotton*, Rector of Carogh, appeared to object to the Draft Scheme.

* Lord Justice FITZGIBBON read the objections of (1), The Rev. S. G. Cotton, Rector of Carogh; (2), The Trustees.

6423. Rev. Mr. *Cotton*.—The Rectors of three adjoining parishes, Hill, Ballynafagh, and Carogh are invited, whenever a vacancy occurs, to nominate a candidate.

6424. Lord Justice FITZGIBBON.—The testator did not mention any parishes.

Rev. Mr. *Cotton*.—I have sent notice by registered letter to the Rev. Wm. Sherlock to produce all papers and minutes to show of what three parishes the incumbents are served with notice every time a vacancy occurs, with the privilege of nominating a candidate.

6425. Lord Justice FITZGIBBON.—What do you mean by the privilege of nominating a candidate?

Rev. Mr. *Cotton*.—I am Rector of Carogh; every time a vacancy occurs I receive a notice stating that a vacancy has occurred, and sending me a printed form to nominate a candidate. There are two parishes with a similar privilege, and I have applied to the Governors to tell me what parishes are entitled.

6426. Lord Justice FITZGIBBON.—Is there any rule to that effect?

Mr. *Cooke-Trench*.—No, it is a mere matter of courtesy on the part of the Governors; they have given instructions to the teacher whenever a vacancy occurs to send notice to the rectors of the adjoining parishes in case they should wish to put forward any candidate.

6427. Lord Justice FITZGIBBON.—What are the adjoining parishes?

Mr. *Cooke-Trench*.—I really am not quite prepared to say—Carogh is one, Naas is another, Ballynafagh is another, Celbridge is another, and I think Kill is another.

6428. Lord Justice NAISH.—But is the recommendation a mere recommendation which does not bind you?

Mr. *Cooke-Trench*.—It is merely a matter of courtesy on our part; there is neither a recommendation nor a rule.

6429. Lord Justice FITZGIBBON.—It is an application to the rectors of the adjoining parishes for information as to suitable candidates?

Mr. *Cooke-Trench*.—It is an invitation to put forward a candidate—an intimation that there is a vacancy.

Rev. Mr. *Cotton*.—A printed form is sent.

6430. Lord Justice FITZGIBBON.—That is an excellent way of ascertaining who are the suitable objects of charity in the neighbourhood; but it gives no right or privilege either to the rector or to the parish. There is no limitation in the will that the people are to be nominated by anybody.

Mr. *Cooke-Trench*.—In the original draft scheme there was no notice of that practice. At my own instigation words have been introduced giving a preference to the parish of Clane and the adjoining parishes. I see now that it might have an effect very different from what was intended, and I will ask the Commissioners to strike those words out, and restore the scheme to its original shape.

* See Appendix B, No. IV. (a) and IV. (b), pp. [illegible].

Rev. Mr. *Sheriock*.—The Archdeacon of Kildare was not able to attend, but he asked me to say that he would prefer a clause giving a preference to Clane and the three parishes to remain.

6431. Lord Justice FitzGibbon.—It is usual in the case of a local endowment to give a preference to those from the locality.

Mr. *Cooke-Trench*.—A question might arise as to what a preference means.

6432. Lord Justice Naish.—There is nothing in the original foundation giving any right of this kind?

Mr. *Cooke-Trench*.—Nothing whatever.

Rev. Mr. *Cotton*.—I have given notice to the trustees to produce the minute books, and would it not be satisfactory to ascertain the minute or rule on the subject?

Mr. *Cooke-Trench*.—We don't acknowledge Mr. Cotton's right to command us to produce any document here.

6433. Lord Justice FitzGibbon.—We have the right to ask for the production of any document.

Mr. *Cooke-Trench*.—Certainly.

6434. Lord Justice FitzGibbon.—Perhaps you can tell us what the minute is.

Mr. *Cooke-Trench*.—There is no minute; it is a practice of the governors.

Rev. Mr. *Cotton*.—In the inquiry ten years ago the matter was alluded to, and since that inquiry a notice was sent to me on a printed form whenever a vacancy occurred, which had not been done previously.

6435. Lord Justice FitzGibbon.—Now you understand how it is done, and it is a very proper thing to do. This being a charity school intended for children to be instructed in the principles of the Protestant religion, the trustees send to the Protestant clergymen of the adjoining parishes notice when there is a vacancy; they are official persons to whom people would like to go when they want to learn what children of that denomination are available for the charity, but it gives no right to anybody.

Rev. Mr. *Cotton*.—My impression is strong that there were three parishes that had the privilege of having such notice, and only three.

6436. Lord Justice FitzGibbon.—That appears to be a mistake. We had better go through the clauses in order. The first question is on Mr. Cotton's objection to the removal of the school from Betaghstown to Millicent. That has been done by the Court of Chancery, and we cannot undo it now.

Rev. Mr. *Cotton*.—I thought your powers were absolute, even as regards the Court of Chancery.

6437. Lord Justice Naish.—It would require some very strong ground to lead us to undo it.

Rev. Mr. *Cotton*.—It is interfering with the bequest of the late Mr. Hewetson, when he expressly mentioned Betaghstown, to remove the school without strong reasons. The Rev. Mr. Cooke—before the former Commission—complained that Betaghstown was three miles distant from his residence. I measured the distance and it is only two English miles and a small bit, about one and a-half Irish miles, so the distance would not interfere with the removal of the present school back to Betaghstown, where both boys and girls could be accommodated on the income of £300 a year; it is a locality separated from houses or a village, and peculiarly, in my opinion, adapted for a boarding school.

6438. Lord Justice Naish.—The Court of Chancery sanctioned, in 1873, this removal to Millicent.

Rev. Mr. *Cotton*.—They did, but under a misapprehension as I conceive. I, as one of the rectors of the three adjoining parishes that had a certain privilege extended to them, appealed, and it was Lord Justice FitzGibbon, I think, who ruled I had no locus standi.

6439. Lord Justice FitzGibbon.—They have spent £3,300 of the endowment in building the existing school, and to that extent, under the authority of the Court of Chancery, the endowment is now invested in the present school at Clane. Mr. Trench paid £300 more as a donation from himself. We saw the school; it is a very nice building and suitable to the subject, and we would not throw away all that property to go back to a place where, from 1763 to 1818, there were more or less unsuccessful attempts to keep up the school.

Rev. Mr. *Cotton*.—That was in consequence of the teaching. The £1,300 if invested would realise, at four per cent., £48 a year, and the income which the trustees receive from the old house is £20, so the charity is at a dead loss of £28 a year.

6440. Lord Justice FitzGibbon.—We have to deal with the endowment as it existed at the date of the passing of the Act in 1885; at that time the school was at Clane, and we cannot move it back to Betaghstown.

Rev. Mr. *Cotton*.—Then, my lord, as regards the education of the girls?

6441. Lord Justice FitzGibbon.—The next matter is the formation of the governing body; you desire to enlarge the number.

Mr. *Cooke-Trench*.—I propose to meet that difficulty by introducing "may" for "shall" on page 8, not to make it imperative to co-opt in case there are not suitable persons. If there were suitable persons we always would fill the vacancies, but there is no use putting in dummies to be turned out at the end of the year for non-attendance.

Rev. Mr. *Cotton*.—My amendment would add the incumbents of the three adjoining parishes, making the number seven.

6442. Lord Justice FitzGibbon.—Why should we bring in the incumbents of the three adjoining parishes?

Rev. Mr. *Cotton*.—Because, in the first place, they have hitherto been recognised as recommending people to the consideration of the trustees; and next, being the incumbents of the three adjoining parishes, they would be the most suitable persons to sit on the board; and thirdly, being always in the neighbourhood, they would be on the spot and taking a part in education.

6443. Lord Justice FitzGibbon.—If suitable, the trustees can co-opt them. They can select any three qualified persons resident within fifteen miles of Clane.

Rev. Mr. *Cotton*.—The governing body at present hold peculiar views which are not acceptable to the majority of the Protestants in Kildare. The majority of the Protestants who would send children there hold views in accordance with the principles of the Reformation. I regret to urge that the majority of the gentlemen at present comprising the governing body, hold views which I think are antagonistic to those principles.

6444. Lord Justice FitzGibbon.—The present governing body are the Archbishop of Armagh, the Archbishop of Dublin, the Incumbent of Clane for the time being, Thomas Cooke-Trench, and the Ven. Archdeacon de Burgh.

Rev. Mr. *Cotton*.—The gentlemen who for the most part act would be the three last named. They are highly respected gentlemen who show a great deal of liberality; but it cannot be denied that they hold views which, from my standpoint, are antagonistic to the views of the Reformation, and the views of the laity.

6445. Lord Justice FitzGibbon.—We are not learned in distinctions of that kind, but where the Archbishop of Armagh, the Archbishop of Dublin, the Incumbent of Clane, and the Archdeacon of the diocese are on the governing body, I am afraid we cannot recognise your standpoint as the only one to be regarded.

Rev. Mr. *Cotton*.—But as a matter of justice to the poor Protestants educated there, would it not be fair play to let there be a makeweight on the governing body, and not have there altogether gentlemen in the locality who are certainly tainted with peculiar views, which are not acceptable to the majority of the Protestants?

6446. Lord Justice FitzGibbon.—We have arranged that they shall appoint one member of the select vestry at least, that is, a body elected by all the registered vestrymen of the parish.

Rev. Mr. *Cotton*.—But we know what sort of gentlemen they will select.

6447. Lord Justice FitzGibbon.—No one can be on the select vestry unless by the votes of the majority of the parishioners.

Rev. Mr. *Cotton*.—Are the majority of the Clane vestrymen to regulate the religious views of the parishes adjoining?

6448. Lord Justice FitzGibbon.—No, but this is now the parochial school, and the select vestry made a large contribution towards it, we wished that there should at all events be one representative of the select vestry; I think we should require you to co-opt at least one member of the select vestry, and we may leave it optional to co-opt others.

6449. Lord Justice Naish.—Outside the five members you need not be bound to co-opt others.

Rev. Mr. *Sherlock*.—I thought the cooption of one might be made imperative.

6450. Lord Justice FitzGibbon.—Our intention was, that there should be always one member of the select vestry. You did not like that he should be directly elected by the select vestry, and therefore we put in this provision that he should be selected from the select vestry by the trustees. You don't object to that remaining?

Mr. *Cooke-Trench*.—I should like to change "shall" into "may," putting in a proviso at the end that there should be always one from the parish.

6451. Lord Justice FitzGibbon.—That is, that we should retain it as "shall" with regard to the one from the select vestry, and "may" as regards the two others.

Rev. Mr. *Cotton*.—Might I again urge that if it should seem objectionable to the Commissioners to put on the three rectors, at least one in addition to the Archdeacon of Kildare, who is rector of one of the parishes, should be put on; I don't urge myself, but say the rector of Ballynafagh.

Rev. Mr. *Sherlock*.—I think it is better to leave it so, that the trustees can choose either a layman or a clergyman.

6452. Lord Justice FitzGibbon.—As a rule, the boards work best on which there are some laymen.

Rev. Mr. *Cotton*.—Will that question be taken into consideration, or do you finally decide it now?

6453. Lord Justice FitzGibbon.—Speaking for myself, I don't see that we could impose on this board the incumbents of the three adjoining parishes.

Rev. Mr. *Cotton*.—Then say one of them, the incumbent of Ballynafagh.

6454. Lord Justice Naish.—There is nothing in the will giving any right to the incumbents of these parishes.

Rev. Mr. *Cotton*.—Would it not be a fair thing that a clergyman of some adjoining parish, taking an interest in the education of the Protestant youth, and to whom reference is made whenever a vacancy occurs, should be on the board?

Rev. Mr. *Sherlock*.—I should like to know how long that supposed privilege has existed; my opinion is the intimation was given merely by direction of one of the trustees who happened to be resident in the place.

Mr *Cooke-Trench*.—Who happened to be rector of an adjoining parish.

Rev. Mr. *Sherlock*.—It was on his motion, and not the act of the trustees generally.

6455. Lord Justice FitzGibbon.—But it is a very proper thing to do.

Rev. Mr. *Sherlock*.—No doubt, but I don't think it should give them a right.

Lord Justice FitzGibbon.—I don't think it does.

6456. Lord Justice Naish.—Bodenstown is in the parish of Clane?

Mr. *Cooke-Trench*.—Yes.

6457. Lord Justice Naish.—Mr. Hewetson lived in the parish of Clane?

Mr. *Cooke-Trench*.—Yes, his whole will was with reference to the parish of Clane. The governors would object very strongly to putting on any more *ex-officio* governors.

6458. Lord Justice Naish.—Or to compelling you to nominate a particular incumbent, or one of two incumbents.

Mr. *Cooke-Trench*.—We should object very strongly to that; we don't know what locus should they have in the matter, beyond our, perhaps, misguided courtesy in sending them notice of vacancies.

Rev. Mr. *Cotton*.—Does it not appear strange that Mr. Cooke-Trench should object to even one of the three clergymen to whom notices are sent now by courtesy.

6459. Lord Justice Naish.—Sending notice of a vacancy is a very different thing from putting on a member of the governing body.

Mr. *Cooke-Trench*.—The Archbishop has power to appoint a member of the chapter; the first such governor is to be the Archdeacon of Kildare, who is the incumbent of an adjoining parish.

6460. Lord Justice FitzGibbon.—The scheme provides for even more than has been done already. Under the 13th clause public notice must be given of each election, and of the manner and form in which application for admission may be made. It is in only very few instances, and these are to be regretted, where vacancies are filled without letting people have a chance. The Incorporated Society send out notices, and every well-managed society does the same, but that does not give a right to interfere in the management. The incumbent of Clane has a special connection with the school, not only on account of its being in the parish, but from its having been amalgamated with the parochial school. The compulsory introduction of an incumbent from outside might lead to differences of opinion that would not be for the advantage of the school, but if there is an eligible incumbent the trustees have power to co-opt him. I am not altogether satisfied to leave it purely optional to make any addition to the number; it is a very small body, and there is some risk if the vacancies are not filled. We have had many cases where, from the number of governors being very small, the efficiency of the school fell away. Would it be possible to give the Archbishop of Dublin the same power as the Archbishop of Armagh, of nominating an additional governor?

Rev. Mr. *Cotton*.—But from its being merely a school for the benefit of Clane you are extending the benefits generally through Ireland.

6461. Lord Justice FitzGibbon.—We are not extending it; the testator gave his money to maintain a school for as many poor boys and girls as the trustees thought fit, and beyond the fact that they were to be instructed in the principles of the Protestant religion, and apprenticed to Protestant masters and mistresses, he left all Ireland open for their selection.

Rev. Mr. *Sherlock* handed in the printed form of application for admission.

6462. Lord Justice FitzGibbon (reading).—This answers Mr. Cotton's inquiry. The form states:—

"The following rules previous to the admission of a boy are to be strictly observed by the schoolmaster. Whenever a vacancy occurs he shall immediately communicate such to the trustees. He shall give immediate notice of such vacancy to the minister of the parish of Clane, and to the ministers of the three adjoining parishes. And he shall at all times furnish them with copies of form of admission, the vacancy not to be filled up until one month subsequent to the date of notice [illegible] to be given as above."

Rev. Mr. *Cotton*.—I asked for the names of those three parishes.

6463. Lord Justice FITZGIBBON.—That is a geographical question that you ought to be able to answer yourself.

Mr. *Cooke-Trench*.—I will give the answer. I believe it was drawn up by the Rev. Mr. Aylmer, who was commissary of the Bishop of Kildare—he was evidently ignorant of his geography—there are six adjoining parishes, and he only knew of three—Clane, Mainham [illegible], Ballynafagh, Donadea, Naas, and Caragh, that is six.

Rev. Mr. *Cotton*.—After that printed notice, I do pray the Commissioners to consider whether it would not be fair to nominate one of the clergymen of those adjoining parishes on the board; it can do no possible harm, and may be of great advantage on one point which all Protestants have at heart, namely, the proper superintendence and supervision of the Protestant children of the school.

6464. Lord Justice FITZGIBBON.—No incumbent was appointed by the testator. The incumbent of Clane was put in by the Chancery scheme; the fact that the incumbents of the adjoining parishes got notice when there was a vacancy gives them no locus standi to become governors. We ought not to extend the principle of appointing *ex-officio* governors beyond what the interests of the charity require; we could not appoint the whole six; there is no reason why one should be preferred to another, and therefore it becomes a question of who is to select. The scheme gives power to the trustees to select, not only from the incumbents, but from all suitable persons in the neighbourhood, those whom they think most likely to be of advantage to the charity. We will consider what you have said, but our impression is that we should not go beyond the present provision.

Rev. Mr. *Cotton*.—Upon the conscience clause there is a gentleman here whom I would wish to offer as evidence, on the importance of giving parents the privilege of selecting the religious instruction that shall be given to their children. Upon that point I wish to give evidence as to the objection which many Protestants have conscientiously to their children attending the present parish church of Clane, built by the liberality of Mr. Cooke-Trench, a real gem in its way, but not by any means a Protestant church. I have evidence in the room upon the point of the church being objectionable for young Protestants to attend, and that it would entirely contravert the intentions of the founder who willed that the children were to be brought up Protestants. I maintain that the children going to this new church would be in great danger of ceasing to be Protestants.

6465. Lord Justice FITZGIBBON.—Is it not the parish church?

Rev. Mr. *Cotton*.—It is recognised as the parish church.

6466. Lord Justice FITZGIBBON.—What do you mean by "recognised"?

Rev. Mr. *Cotton*.—A great many parish churches that I have seen in England are very much opposed to Protestant teaching.

6467. Lord Justice FITZGIBBON.—I am asking a question of fact—is the Clane church a parish church of the Church of Ireland?

Rev. Mr. *Cotton*.—There is no use in disputing that it is so.

6468. Lord Justice FITZGIBBON.—Then if so, we must recognise it as such. We are not a theological Commission, and if this or any other parish church is not conducted according to the law of the Church, we are not the tribunal to interfere, but there is a remedy open to any one aggrieved. We are bound to recognise the legal status of parish churches, and we have no jurisdiction to inquire, nor do I think we should hear evidence about the manner in which they are conducted.

Rev. Mr. *Cotton*.—Are you going to retain the conscience clause with regard to parents who are not members of the Church of Ireland, so that the children of parents who are not members of the Church of Ireland will be excluded from attending religious worship in the parish church of Clane, or receiving instruction from the clergyman, while you withhold this privilege from members of the Church of Ireland who may conscientiously object to sending their children to the parish church of Clane? July 6, 1888

6469. Lord Justice FITZGIBBON.—No child can be compulsorily taken to this school; the question is one of voluntary attendance. If a parent belonging to the Church of Ireland sends his child to the school, he sends it to a school which he knows to be under the charge of the incumbent of the parish, the legally authorised clergyman of his church; he wants no conscience clause, and we have never before been asked to insert one for children of the denomination to which the governing body exclusively belongs. But when children of other denominations are admitted there, we are obliged to put in a conscience clause binding the governors not to give religious instruction to such children against the parents will.

Rev. Mr. *Cotton*.—You are forcing now the members of the Church of Ireland to enter their children, either as Presbyterians or Methodists, to take advantage of the conscience clause.

6470. Lord Justice NAISH.—Has there ever been any objection by the parents of children to the Protestant instruction given in the school?

Mr. *Cooke-Trench*.—I have never heard of such.

6471. Rev. Dr. MOLLOY.—Do you want a conscience clause to protect the Protestant children from the clergyman of their own church?

Rev. Mr. *Cotton*.—Exactly, and to prevent Protestant children from going to a half Protestant church. I have evidence in the room, if the Commissioners would hear it.

6472. Lord Justice FITZGIBBON.—I have told you why I think we should not take that evidence. The church, like everything else, must be governed by law, and the law is open where anything illegal is done. We must assume that each church is conducted according to law; if it is not, we have no power to administer the necessary correction.

Rev. Dr. MOLLOY.—There is a remedy for you in this, that children need not go to the school; they are not compelled by our scheme to go.

Rev. Mr. *Cotton*.—The desire for education in Ireland now is dominant, and, therefore, it is a very hard case that a Protestant, a member of the Church of Ireland, should have to say—"I am forced to send my child to a good school, and also to a school that my conscience does not approve of."

6473. Professor DOUGHERTY.—Is it not a Protestant church?

Rev. Mr. *Cotton*.—I will give you evidence that it is not.

Mr. *Cooke-Trench*.—I ask you on page 11 to introduce a clause in the qualification of the child. "(a). He shall be a member of the said church." It is a Protestant school.

6474. Lord Justice NAISH.—There is no obligation on you to take any pupils except members of your own church, but if you think fit to take in others, then we think it fair that they should be protected against any teaching to which their parents object.

Lord Justice FITZGIBBON.—In defining the qualification of the free pupils you are right; for example, in the Presbyterian Orphan Society the qualification is, "he shall belong to the Presbyterian Church." But, besides the free pupils, the school is open to others.

Mr. *Cooke-Trench*.—It is not prepared to take them to service.

6475. Lord Justice FITZGIBBON.—But the conscience clause deals with more than divine service. Besides the free boarding pupils there may be other boarders.

Rev. Mr. *Sherlock*.—But don't you think it would be unjust to allow other pupils than members of the Church

Lord Justice FitzGibbon.—We express no opinion on that point; that is for the trustees to make up their minds upon. You may have Methodists or Presbyterians, or even as we have seen in some parts of Ireland—where there is no other good school in the neighbourhood—Roman Catholics going to the school for intermediate education, but the trustees may refuse them.

6476. Lord Justice Naish.—Would it not be a hard thing to prevent your trustees from receiving, say a Methodist or Presbyterian boy?

Rev. Dr. Molloy.—The scheme allows them a discretion to receive pupils of different religious denominations; but if they do so, they must submit to a conscience clause.

Mr. Goode-French.—We are rather afraid of this clause. This has been hitherto a strictly denominational school, and if this takes effect it ceases to be a denominational school.

6477. Lord Justice FitzGibbon.—We could put in, if you like, an express provision that the governors shall not be under any obligation to receive any pupil who does not belong to the Church, but that is merely expressing what the law is already.

Lord Justice Naish.—And providing that every free pupil shall be a member of the Church.

Rev. Dr. Molloy.—Yes, there is no difficulty about that.

6478. Lord Justice Naish.—That does not turn your school into an open school, but makes it a purely denominational school. Why should you go further? If the scheme leaves it a purely Church school without any right whatever on the part of any child who does not belong to that Church, of having any privilege or advantage out of it, why would you object to have power to take any child of another denomination if you thought fit yourselves?

Mr. Goode-French.—I think this clause might be used in this way. A child might be committed to our care as a member of the Church of Ireland. Six months afterwards perhaps the parents might say, "We have turned Presbyterians; we wish our child to be a Presbyterian." There is a clause that no child is to be deprived of the benefits of the school on this ground; our answer, under existing things, would be, "This is a Church school; if you have a conscientious objection to your child being brought up here you had better remove him;" but we are precluded from that by a subsequent clause.

6479. Lord Justice FitzGibbon.—We must make it perfectly clear that that is not the intention of the clause. It is not intended to oblige the trustees to receive any pupil whatever; it is left to their discretion whether they will take or refuse any child that does not belong to their denomination. The whole scope of this clause is that if they do take or retain a child of any other religious denomination it shall not receive religious instruction which is objected to.

Rev. Mr. Cotton.—If you allow that conscience clause, very justly, to the day scholar, why not extend the same protection to the boarders?

6480. Lord Justice FitzGibbon.—It extends to all pupils who are not members of the Church.

Rev. Mr. Cotton.—These boys, I believe, contrary to the will of the founder, are used now as choir boys of the parish of Clane, and are dressed in cassocks and surplices.

6481. Professor Dougherty.—I am not a member of your Church, but it seems to me that that is a very common thing in your churches.

Rev. Mr. Cotton.—In England.

6482. Professor Dougherty.—And Ireland, too.

Rev. Mr. Cotton.—A surpliced choir is a sign of a very remarkable movement in England.

6483. Lord Justice Naish (to Mr. Sherlock).—Would you wish to be restricted under no circumstances to take in any child who is not a member of the Protestant Episcopalian Church?

Rev. W. Sherlock.—No, because we might find it advantageous to go under the National Board, and then we shall have a conscience clause provided.

6484. Lord Justice FitzGibbon.—Even now, supposing if you had in your parish Methodist or Presbyterian farmers, they might wish to send their children, and you to take them. We don't want to prevent you, or to force you, but if you do admit children of other denominations, and their parents object to their receiving religious instruction, we have introduced that clause to cover the objection to be supported.

Rev. Mr. Cotton.—Are the Commissioners going to enforce the surplices and the cassocks as part of the education under the will of the testator? Supposing a parent said, "I want the education of this excellent school, but I don't wish my child to go into the choir and wear this cassock and surplice," will the child be expelled by the trustees?

Professor Dougherty.—Don't you wear a surplice yourself?

Rev. Mr. Cotton.—I do, but that is a very different thing from these boys—they are not privileged.

6485. Lord Justice FitzGibbon.—It is the same as if the parent was to object to the child's receiving instruction in some secular matter—he has the alternative, if he objects, and the trustees insist, he can take the child away. You want us to do what we have no right to do in dealing with this school, to involve ourselves in matters of church discipline connected with the conduct of divine service in the parish church.

Rev. Mr. Cotton.—With all respect I am asking whether parents sending their son to this school, for which £200 a year was left by this good man, object to him appearing in this choir and wearing the surplice and cassock, would the child be expelled.

6486. Lord Justice FitzGibbon.—There is nothing in the scheme to sanction his being expelled. If a parent objects to anything in the treatment of the child he can take him away.

Rev. Mr. Cotton.—Would he be expelled by the Governors?

6487. Lord Justice FitzGibbon.—The Governors need not keep any pupil they don't like, and no child can be kept except with the goodwill both of the parent or guardian and of the trustees, and whether it be singing in the choir or learning the Latin grammar, if there be an objection on either side there is no remedy except to take the child away.

Rev. Mr. Cotton.—And supposing the managers go further, and direct the children to wear crosses, harmless emblems in the opinion of some people, but harmful in the opinion of others, do you maintain that the child must do that or be expelled?

6488. Lord Justice Naish.—We don't like to meddle with these unfortunate differences in your Church.

Rev. Mr. Cotton.—It is unfortunate, for it was not the will of the testator. The children are starving for education, and these people won't give it except with a certain clog around the neck of the children.

6489. Lord Justice FitzGibbon.—Is there any objection to clause 16, with the limitation we suggest, that it should be within the discretion of the trustees whether they should receive any pupils who are not members of the Church, but if they do that the conscience clause should prevail?

Rev. Mr. Sherlock.—I think not.

Mr. Goode-French.—I think this ought to be a Church school.

6490. Rev. Dr. Molloy.—You can keep it so, if you choose.

Lord Justice Naish.—If you don't choose yourselves to keep it absolutely so; it is a very small restriction that is put on you.

Mr. Goode-French.—I don't press it with that limitation.

6491. Lord Justice FitzGibbon.—In order to get

all of the exclusive clauses you should limit the admission both of boarders and day pupils to pupils belonging to the church, and if you do that those clauses can go out altogether. You can either say "we won't take these children at all, or we will admit to an arrangement which is accepted by all schools which send children to the Intermediate Examinations?"

Rev. Mr. Cotton.—If it is put under the National Board then the day pupils would have certain privileges which I apprehend will not be accorded to the boarders.

6492. Lord Justice FitzGibbon.—No boarding school, so far as I know in Ireland, is conducted without religious instruction, and the privilege of a day pupil at a National Board school is to attend during the hours for secular instruction only.

Mr. Cooke-Trench.—We come now to page 10,—election of free boarders. There are a number of clauses which, in the opinion of the governors, would become a dead letter. In section 13 we propose to omit the special notice to governors of every election. In Poor Law Boards and other places where such notice is given, it becomes very much a habit to attend at the time of elections and at no other times. We think that the governors ought to attend upon all occasions that they can, and that they should not be specially invited to attend on these occasions.

6493. Lord Justice Naish.—Would your idea be that a boy, if there is a vacancy, should be capable of being elected at any meeting?

Mr. Cooke-Trench.—At any quarterly meeting.

6494. Lord Justice Naish.—Would you restrict the election to the time of the quarterly meetings?

Mr. Cooke-Trench.—Yes.

6495. Lord Justice Naish.—I don't think there is much objection to that, otherwise we might leave it open to two of the trustees to come together and elect pupils without any regular meeting.

Mr. Cooke-Trench.—Let us elect at the quarterly meetings only.

Lord Justice FitzGibbon.—There is no objection to that.

6496. Lord Justice Naish.—Does the notice of meeting as a matter of business contain the agenda?

Mr. Cooke-Trench.—There is a notice of the meeting; there is not an "agenda." We cannot afford to pay a secretary. I send out these notices, and I don't want to have more writing than is necessary.

6497. Lord Justice FitzGibbon.—Some of these provisions are required for large institutions, but yours is a small one and we need not put it in so many details, but you ought to give notice of vacancies and of the form in which application is to be made.

Mr. Cooke-Trench.—That we do as a matter of routine by sending it out to the adjoining incumbents.

6498. Lord Justice Naish.—Say "notice shall be given in such manner as the governors shall determine."

Mr. Cooke-Trench.—That will do. Then the clause "all candidates shall present themselves at the school upon the day of election," never has been the case; the committee have a large number of applications, and some from a distance, these are poor children, and it would be a great hardship on them.

6499. Lord Justice FitzGibbon.—I would strongly advise you to insist upon somebody representing the governors seeing every child before election. Either the children should come, or some one named by the Governors should give a personal report.

Mr. Cooke-Trench.—As soon as the applications are sent in they are submitted to the incumbent of the parish; he makes personal inquiries from the incumbents of the parishes to which the children belong. We require a doctor's certificate that the candidate is physically in a proper state to take advantage of the school, and we have found that to work very well.

Rev. Mr. Sherlock.—Perhaps we might draw up rules as they have done before.

6500. Lord Justice FitzGibbon.—The form for the Presbyterian Orphan Society, with three thousand children, is "all candidates for admission shall present themselves to, and be seen by the governors, or by some person appointed for the purpose by the governors, or by a local committee, or auxiliary society." That is the very smallest precaution you ought to insist upon; you should some one actually to see the child; personal inspection is the only way to find out the truth through the mists created by written testimonials and certificates.

Mr. Cooke-Trench.—Then perhaps we may say that all children shall be seen by the governors, or by some persons appointed by the governors. Of course that precludes the idea of competitive examination.

6501. Lord Justice FitzGibbon.—Of course. Now, what do you say about admitting girls?

Rev. Mr. Cotton.—The testator contemplated the education of girls as well as boys, and it was a very strange thing that girls were excluded when the mothers of the nation require education just as much, if not more, than the boys.

6502. Lord Justice Naish.—Would you have them brought up with the boys in the same building?

Rev. Mr. Cotton.—The former school of Kellaghtown was amply large enough to have two separate school-rooms, the boys in one and the girls in another. I, for the last twenty years, have had a somewhat similar school where the boys and girls are under the superintendence of a matron, with a separate staircase, in a smaller house, and there could be no objection on the ground of morality. I call the attention of the Commissioners to the report made ten years ago. There was £350 a year available for this charity.

6503. Lord Justice Naish.—I had no idea that there was anything like that.

Mr. Cooke-Trench.—Mr Cotton almost doubles it.

Rev. Mr. Sherlock.—£250 we make it out.

Rev. Mr. Cotton.—It was referred to as £350 by the Commissioners ten years ago.

6504. Lord Justice FitzGibbon.—Landed incomes have varied in the last ten years. At Clane we get the exact figures—about £250 a year. However, the present building would not hold both boys and girls, and I believe the experiment of keeping both boys and girls at Kellaghtown was not successful. We were told that the school was suspended altogether for years at one time owing to the difficulty of managing it.

Rev. Mr. Cotton.—The will of the testator should not be altogether neglected, especially when there is actually a school-house in the village of Clane, near the former church, which is at present unoccupied, and if that school was made available and was made a National school, there would be ample funds.

6505. Lord Justice FitzGibbon.—That is provided for by these statutes. The day pupils are to be male or female, the question arises only as to boarders. We can hardly think it practicable to propose female boarders in the school as it stands.

Rev. Mr. Cotton.—Because the house is too small; it cost £1,500, and it is too small; the other house was amply large enough.

6506. Lord Justice FitzGibbon.—If they established a second school for girls in another house where would they find the money for it?

Rev. Mr. Cotton.—There is a house at present vacant.

Mr. Cooke-Trench.—This was all brought before the Court of Chancery.

Rev. Mr. Cotton.—Nearly £300 a year has been spent on the maintenance of eleven or twelve boys.

6507. Lord Justice FitzGibbon.—We can insert a discretionary clause if the endowment should ever permit to extend it to girls.

Mr. Cooke-Trench.—There is not the slightest possibility of it.

6508. Professor Dougherty.—The power would do you no harm.

6509. Lord Justice FitzGibbon.—Somebody might give you a legacy.

July 5, 1888.

Mr. *Cooke-Trench*.—Mr. Cotton might give us a legacy.

Rev. Mr. *Cotton*.—Do you make any ruling about the education of girls?

6510. Lord Justice FitzGibbon.—We have made provision for the education of girls as day pupils. Is there the slightest chance of girl boarders?

Rev. Mr. *Cotton*.—Not in the present school, certainly not.

6511. Lord Justice FitzGibbon.—It is with the present school we are dealing.

Rev. Mr. *Cotton*.—I have tried to impress on the Commissioners that there is a school-house at present vacant near the old church in Clane.

Mr. *Cooke-Trench*.—It does not belong to the charity.

Rev. Mr. *Cotton*.—No, but belonging to the parish of Clane, where the former day school was held.

6512. Lord Justice FitzGibbon.—We are only dealing with the Hewetson endowment, the income of which, in 1881, was under £300.

Rev. Mr. *Cotton*.—That is difficult to believe.

6513. Lord Justice FitzGibbon.—It is unfortunately easy to be believed by anybody who knows how rents have fallen in Ireland during the past ten years, and this estate was particularly unfortunate. Here are the receipts:—1883, £354; 1884, £283; 1885, £374, including some arrears; 1886, £277; 1887, £190; 1888 to March 25, £100. One year with another in round numbers it is an income of £300.

6514. Professor Dougherty.—Is that diminution a result of the reduction in the rental?

Mr *Cooke-Trench*.—Yes.

Lord Justice FitzGibbon.—The trustees tried to sell the estate in 1885 under Lord Ashbourne's Act; they offered to take twenty per cent. off the rental, and that was refused by the tenants. If the estate was sold at twenty years purchase and the proceeds invested at 3½ per cent., the income would be about £300.

6515. Lord Justice Naish.—Have the tenants gone into the Land Court, or has a reduction been allowed outside?

Mr. *Cooke-Trench*.—We have given them a reduction outside.

6516. Lord Justice Naish.—Have you given them a larger reduction than they would get in the Land Court?

Mr. *Cooke-Trench*.—I don't know that we have.

6517. Professor Dougherty.—Is it a permanent reduction?

Mr. *Cooke-Trench*.—No, a reduction varying according to the seasons.

6518. Lord Justice FitzGibbon.—You may take it for granted that they are not likely to get much more than £300, and with that amount it would be only holding out false hopes to imagine that they could have a boarding school for girls as well as for boys.

Rev. Mr. *Cotton*.—For the last twenty years there has been a gross misapplication of the funds. Of that I don't accuse the gentlemen here present—they are coming in new to the management; but there have been £300 of income and only twelve boys maintained.

6519. Lord Justice FitzGibbon.—We can only deal with the estate as it is now, and I think you are under a misapprehension about the value of these lands.

Mr. *Cooke-Trench*.—At clause 14 I believe you took a note to introduce "member of said Church," clause (A.) I would ask to omit, and (c.) is a disabling clause not contemplated by the original will, and I don't quite see the object of it. For instance, it precludes the possibility of our taking a foundling.

Rev. Mr. *Sherlock*.—It precludes the possibility of our taking any but the children of paupers. It says, "both of whom shall be incapable of earning a livelihood."

6520. Lord Justice FitzGibbon.—The testator's will is for "poor boys and girls."

Rev. Mr. *Sherlock*.—But the child of a labourer or of a small farmer would be eligible, yet we could not take him in, because his father could earn a livelihood.

Mr. *Cooke-Trench*.—And we should be bound to get the marriage certificate of the parents. There might be cases in which it was desirable to take an illegitimate child, and I don't know why we should disable ourselves from doing so. A foundling is brought up according to law in the religion of the person who finds it, and one of these children—very often very nice children—might be a very pressing case.

Rev. Mr. *Sherlock*.—There is a case in the neighbourhood of a child whose parents have deserted him.

6521. Lord Justice FitzGibbon.—The will hardly contemplated the case of foundlings. I suppose you never had a child whose parents you did not know. We can provide that the children shall be in poor circumstances. The ages are right, I suppose?

Mr. *Cooke-Trench*.—I don't know whether it is right to introduce those limitations?

6522. Lord Justice FitzGibbon.—For your own protection you ought to do so, or you will have applications from children of all ages, and those proposed are the very widest limits for suitable pupils.

Mr. *Cooke-Trench*.—We don't press that. The latter part of (a.) "the names of the governors voting upon every election shall be recorded in the minutes," may be struck out. "In every such election preference shall be given to the qualified candidates (if any) belonging to the parish of Clane, or the adjoining parishes." I object to that, although it was inserted on my suggestion. I see now that it may work in a manner the very opposite of what was intended.

6523. Lord Justice Naish.—What did the testator himself say on the subject?

Lord Justice FitzGibbon.—Nothing.

Rev. Mr. *Sherlock*.—Mr. Trench thinks that it would pledge us to take a boy whose circumstances were less urgent, provided he came from one of these parishes.

6524. Rev. Dr. Molloy.—It only means that you are to give him a preference, if in other respects the claims are equal.

Mr. *Cooke-Trench*.—I submitted that clause to a very able solicitor, and his opinion was that if there was a candidate from one of the adjoining parishes just qualified, and a most urgent case from just outside, that we should be bound under the clause to take the one just qualified in preference.

6525. Lord Justice Naish.—Supposing we made it that where all circumstances are alike a preference should be given?

Mr. *Cooke-Trench*.—I think so.

6526. Lord Justice FitzGibbon.—I have in my mind a case in Dublin, the Blue-coat School, that was originally a Dublin municipal charity. The governors now nominate boys in rotation, there is no locality restricted, and the result is that the great majority of the pupils are from the country. Here is your own observation:—"Hewetson in his will showed so much desire to benefit the parish of Clane, where he resided, that it has been always held that children of that parish should have a preference. Residents in the adjoining parishes should be also held to have a claim in a minor degree. It would be well to introduce a clause to that effect." I think you ought to show on the face of the scheme that you ought to consider those people first.

Rev. W. *Sherlock*.—Archdeacon de Burgh feels that very strongly, and I think so too.

Mr. *Cooke-Trench*.—If words to the effect "caeteris paribus" are introduced I don't object.

6527. Lord Justice FitzGibbon.—We will introduce a provision that regard shall be had to the claims of candidates from Clane and the adjoining parishes.

Rev. Mr. *Cotton*.—The three adjoining parishes.

6528. Lord Justice FitzGibbon.—There are six adjoining parishes, and we will not leave any of them out.

Mr. *Cooke-Trench*.—With reference to clause 15, why limit it to the parish of Clane and the adjoining parishes? One parish that does not adjoin us comes very near us.

Rev. Mr. *Cotton*.—I have another amendment with reference to the appointment of officials. It refers to the appointment and duties of the teacher. My amendment would be that the officials be paid sufficient salaries, and be not permitted to fill any posts of emolument in connection with any place of worship. The present teacher is organist of the church and leader of the boys choir, and he is paid a very good salary of £160 a year for both these duties. This being organist of the church places him directly under the control of the incumbent and select vestry, and I maintain that the teacher of the school, especially if it be a National school, should occupy an independent position.

6329. Lord Justice FitzGibbon.—Instead of discouraging we should encourage having the teachers of schools with limited funds engaged in anything that increases their emolument without interfering with their duty. Even the National Board allows teachers to act as organists. In my old parish of [illegible] the only way we could keep the school up at all was by paying £20 a year to the teacher as organist.

Mr. *Cosby-French*.—Under the scheme passed by the Chancellor it was provided that in consideration of the contribution from the parish of [illegible] the teacher might act as organist of the church.

6330. Rev. Dr. Molloy.—He won't be a less efficient teacher because he plays the organ on Sundays.

Rev. Mr. *Cotton*.—He may volunteer to play the organ if he pleases.

6331. Lord Justice FitzGibbon.—He will play better if he is paid.

Rev. Mr. *Cotton*.—I would ask that his position be defined as a teacher with a fixed salary.

6332. Lord Justice Naish.—They can only pay him as teacher. If they paid anything out of the fund to an organist they would be responsible for breach of trust.

Rev. Mr. *Cotton*.—That is a very excellent remark, if you would allow me to say so; but they pay him £80 a year, and I would like to know what he is paid for?

Mr. *Cosby-French*.—Under the scheme passed by the Court of Chancery it was part of his duty, in consideration of the sum subscribed by the parish. The parish subscribes £20 a year, which goes into the school fund.

6333. Lord Justice FitzGibbon.—What is your next point?

Rev. Mr. *Sherlock*.—Clause 21. To allow meetings elsewhere than at the school.

6334. Lord Justice FitzGibbon.—Do you object to the provision that one or more of the governors is to visit once a month?

Rev. Mr. *Sherlock*.—I go there once a day, or at least once a week.

6335. Lord Justice FitzGibbon.—[illegible] was not visited at all.

Mr. *Cosby-French*.—But is not that a provision that will fall a dead letter, unless there is somebody like Mr. Sherlock there?

6336. Lord Justice FitzGibbon.—You will appoint a visiting governor.

Mr. *Cosby-French*.—We will appoint Mr. Sherlock, and at a meeting we may happen to ask for his book; the book will be produced, and there are no entries in it. Then what is to happen?

6337. Lord Justice FitzGibbon.—Whatever happens where people don't do what they are bound to do. Very frequently a clause of the kind prevents such things from occurring.

Mr. *Cosby-French*.—I only object to it because I don't like putting in clauses that are not likely to be observed.

Rev. Mr. *Sherlock*.—You always appoint the incumbent; the manager, and the trustees appointed me immediately after I was instituted.

6338. Lord Justice FitzGibbon.—As manager you visit the school?

Rev. Mr. *Sherlock*.—I do, every week.

6339. Lord Justice FitzGibbon.—You don't want to have the quarterly meetings at the school?

Mr. *Cosby-French*.—Not necessarily; we have several times found it necessary to have them in Dublin, to suit the convenience of the Primate.

6340. Lord Justice FitzGibbon.—You ought to meet at the school at least half-yearly.

Mr. *Cosby-French*.—Certainly.

6341. Lord Justice FitzGibbon.—Then let two of the meetings in each year be held at the school. You have no idea of the number of schools we have met with which the governors have never seen. You must go there twice a year, and you may meet where you like otherwise.

Mr. *Cosby-French*.—"Three clear days' notice, specifying the object thereof." I would only ask that to be omitted.

6342. Lord Justice FitzGibbon.—That is only for special meetings, and it is a protection against your being officially summoned for insufficient reasons.

Mr. *Cosby-French*.—In page 14, clause 22, the last line but one after the word "employment," introduce the words "and to the circumstances of the endowments."

6343. Lord Justice FitzGibbon.—Certainly.

Mr. *Cosby-French*.—These are all the points.

6344. Lord Justice FitzGibbon.—Is there anything else, Mr. Cotton?

Rev. Mr. *Cotton*.—No, my lord. I am very much obliged for the hearing you have given me.

Lord Justice FitzGibbon.—I wish there was money enough to give you a girls school.

The sitting terminated.

July 11, 1889.

PUBLIC SITTING—THURSDAY, JULY 11, 1889.

At the Office, [illegible], Dublin.

Present:—The Right Hon. Lord Justice FitzGibbon, and the Right Hon. Lord Justice Naish, Judicial Commissioners; and the Rev. Gerald Molloy, D.D., D.Sc., Anthony Traill, Esq., LL.D., M.D., F.T.C.D., and Professor Dougherty, M.A., Assistant Commissioners.

The Secretary, Wm. Edward Ellis, LL.B., and the Assistant Secretary, N. D. Murphy, were in attendance.

*RAINEY'S SCHOOL, MAGHERAFELT, AND THE PROPOSED EDUCATIONAL ENDOWMENTS OF THE SALTERS COMPANY.

The Right Rev. *William Clarke* (the Moderator), Rev. *John H. Orr*, D.D. (Clerk of Assembly), Rev. *H. B. Wilson*, D.D., Cookstown, Rev. *J. M. Hamilton*, M.A., Donore, and the Rev. *Wm. Reid* attended as a deputation from the General Assembly of the Presbyterian Church. The Rev. *George Gillespie* represented the Presbytery of Magherafelt.

6345. Lord Justice FitzGibbon.—We appointed to-day to meet a deputation in answer to the letter of 20th June last from the Clerk of the General Assembly, in reference to the Draft Scheme for Rainey's School, Magherafelt. You will understand that in receiving a deputation from any one denomination, we cannot, in the absence of others who are interested, come to any definite conclusion as to the settlement of the Scheme; but we shall be very glad to hear the views of the General Assembly in reference to this Endowment, in which the Presbyterians have an interest.

The *Moderator*.—Perhaps you will permit me to read the resolution which was passed at the last meeting of the Assembly:—

"It was further resolved—That whereas the Act of Parliament appointing the Educational Endowments (Ireland) Commission requires that in all their schemes dealing with endowments, they shall have regard to the will of the founders, the General Assembly claims that the Commissioners shall amend the Draft Scheme for the Rainey Endowment at Magherafelt, and give the only control over the funds and the school to the Presbyterians of that locality as officially represented by the Presbyteries of Magherafelt and Tyrone; and that the Clerk of Assembly be instructed to send a copy of this resolution to the Secretary of the Commission, and request them to receive a deputation consisting of the Right, the Moderator and the Clerk of Assembly, Dr. H. B. Wilson, Dr. W. Todd Martin, Dr. Lynd, John M. Hamilton, and William Reid, who are appointed to submit to the Commissioners the views of the Assembly."

We object to this Draft Scheme because we believe the intention of the testator was disregarded, and because the private Act of Parliament was fraudulent; it was obtained for selfish purposes by the executors and successors of the testator, retaining the larger sum, and giving no more than the original sum—that is to say, £151 per annum—to the charity. The object in obtaining the Act of Parliament was, I believe, to further their own selfish interests, and it was obtained without any regard to the welfare of the institution. Then there was another endowment of £5 to be paid to the Presbyterian Minister of Magherafelt, in accordance with the terms of the will, but that sum of £5 has not been paid within living memory; it was withheld entirely from the party to whom it ought to have been handed over from year to year. Then we maintain that the testator intended the religious [illegible] of the boys to be under the control of his own Church—that is to say, the Presbytery of Ulster, which occupied the same position in reference to the Presbyterians in those days that the General Assembly does now. Rainey was an elder of the Presbyterian Church, he discharged the active duties of the eldership in the congregation of Desertmartin, now Castledawson, and we have evidence of that in the records of that congregation.

6346. Lord Justice Naish.—I think there is no doubt he was a Presbyterian, and his will shows it.

The *Moderator*.—Then we have evidence, I think, clear enough to show that the testator wished the institution to be a Presbyterian institution. For instance, when any one of the "old grave and good men," who had to read with the people and pray with them, was found incompetent, or [illegible] to discharge the duties of that office, the executors were to write to the Presbytery of Ulster to appoint some one to replace him. Then we find that the management of the school was handed over largely to the Archbishop of Armagh; there was no mention made of that in the will.

6347. Lord Justice FitzGibbon.—Rainey's will directed his trustees to apply for an Act of Parliament to carry out his intentions. They got an Act of Parliament, but a very peculiar one, for it did not affect the trusts at all; it merely vested the property in the Primate, but gave him no power of management over the school whatever. The management apparently—for the history is rather obscure—was not transferred to the Primate until 1844 or thereabouts, when the last representative of the testator's family disappeared.

The *Moderator*.—But the Primate was not mentioned prior to that Act.

6348. Lord Justice FitzGibbon.—No, but that Act merely made him an official trustee of the property. It directed that the school should continue to be managed in conformity with Rainey's will.

The *Moderator*.—That Act gave him no administrative power, neither did the will. He was simply, as I take it, a receiver of rents. Then we object to the constitution of the Board, as it will always give, if this Draft Scheme becomes law, a preponderance to the other church, as the Archbishop will have a casting vote, and it therefore deprives us of what we consider to be our just rights and privileges. The Scheme instead of removing what we consider almost simply confirms them, and keeps us in that unenviable position in which we have been placed hitherto. We want to get out of that position, and to have sole control of the school as a Presbyterian school.

6349. Dr. Traill.—Do you propose to give up the Salters grant?

The *Moderator*.—Well, I don't know how to deal with the Salters grant, as it does not come before us under the present circumstances.

6350. Dr. Traill.—Yes, it does, because the Salters make it a condition that their grant is to go to the Rainey school under the Scheme as we have prepared it.

* See generally, Report and Evid., 1885–87, pp. [illegible], [illegible]; supra, pp. [illegible] et seq.; infra App. B, No. [illegible] to [illegible] (cd.), pp. [illegible].

The *Moderator*.—Then they have changed front, and ran away—they have broken faith. We claimed a share of that endowment, and instead of that they have divided it, giving part to another denomination.

6351. Dr. Traill.—Yes, that is very shabby, but a portion of the grant ought to go to the Rainey School. How could you claim an exclusive managing body for the Presbyterians?

The *Moderator*.—The Company got a quid pro quo from their endowment.

6352. Professor Dougherty.—I suppose you are prepared to work the school on the existing Rainey endowment, and let the Salters do what they like with theirs.

The *Moderator*.—That is so.

6353. Lord Justice FitzGibbon.—We cannot account back any of the property that by this Act of Parliament was appropriated to the family. We have jurisdiction only over the property that was bound by an educational trust at the passing of our Act in 1885. The amount converted what was intended by Rainey to be a share of his estate into a fixed rentcharge, which was assigned to the Primate, to be thenceforward applicable for the educational purposes of the will. The Act recites:—

"Whereas the rents are more likely to be duly created if the same are made payable to the Archbishop of Armagh."

and they are vested in the Archbishop for the purpose of meeting them—that is his only trust under the original Act—and, when created, the rentcharge was to be applied in accordance with the trusts of the will; that fixed the endowment at £175 Irish, per annum, for ever. Rainey intended a boarding school for boys who were to be maintained, clothed, and taught trades: that has long since disappeared, in fact I don't think it existed efficiently at any time; but neither the Salters money with Rainey's, nor, *a fortiori*, Rainey's endowment by itself, would be enough to maintain an institution of that kind. Then the Court of Chancery introduced a totally different school, a day school, under the management of the Primate. What does the Assembly now suggest, that the old boarding school shall be re-established or that the day school shall be continued?

The *Moderator*.—We are satisfied that the day school should be continued, but we want the management of it.

6354. Lord Justice FitzGibbon.—If then it is to be a day school, if we give it this £175 Irish of Rainey's, as a single endowment, we deprive the charity of the Salters money. The present day school was never efficiently maintained by Rainey's money alone, it always had the Salters grant also. The Salters grant has never under any circumstances been an exclusively Presbyterian endowment, and at Magherafelt, with Rev. Mr. Lynd's objection before us, the only point that appeared to be raised—the Presbyterians apparently admitted that the Government should be half and half—was that they objected that the chairmanship being given to the Archbishop would put them in a minority. Therefore I think we ought to know distinctly from you now, whether you desire that this school should be under a mixed governing body, or under an exclusively Presbyterian body?

The *Moderator*.—We wish it under an exclusively Presbyterian body.

6355. Lord Justice FitzGibbon.—Then are we to separate Rainey's rentcharge from the subscription which was provided by the Salters Company, and from their endowment?

The *Moderator*.—But they were recouped for that; they got more land.

6356. Lord Justice FitzGibbon.—They took up some land from the old school, not as an equivalent, but as a term of their agreement to aid the school when established under the Chancery Scheme.

The *Moderator*.—We look upon that as a quid pro quo, but besides we are not prepared to sell our rights and privileges for £65 a year.

6357. Lord Justice FitzGibbon.—I think you are a little sanguine in calling them "rights and privileges," because whatever claims you have under Rainey's will are very much modified by the fact that you have never been in possession under Rainey's will.

The *Moderator*.—But it was through no default of ours that we were put into that position. You will easily understand the difference between the position occupied by the Primate of Armagh at that time with reference to our Church and the relative positions now. We hold we did not get the rights to which we were entitled, but times have changed, and we are now prepared to stand upon our rights and assert them.

6358. Lord Justice Naish.—The Act provides that instead of having a moiety of the lands there was to be a rentcharge of £175 a year vested in the Archbishop of Armagh for this purpose:—

"The supporting, maintaining, educating, and placing out as apprentices twenty-four boys under the trusts, and subject to the administration in and by the said will declared and provided."

Dr. Traill.—But these children were not to be all Presbyterians.

The *Moderator*.—There is nothing said about any other denominations.

6359. Lord Justice Naish.—That apparently contemplated that as to the £175 given to the Archbishop all the trusts of the will were to take effect, and the Archbishop was to follow it.

The *Moderator*.—It was a matter of convenience at the time.

6360. Dr. Traill.—How is it you changed your principles? Here is the objection, signed by Mr. Lynd:—

"We are pleased to find that the scheme is based upon the principle of equality as between the Presbyterian and Episcopalian Churches."

How have you made this discovery since the Salters Company acted so shabbily?

The *Moderator*.—I have not changed my mind.

6361. Dr. Traill.—The objection is signed by four gentlemen. How is it that principle was so suddenly changed?

The *Moderator*.—I am quite satisfied with the principle of the scheme, in so far as equality. I want nothing more, but it takes from us the power we believe we are entitled to; it transfers the entire power to the Primate of Armagh.

6362. Dr. Traill.—If you say you are satisfied with the principle of equality, how is that consistent with the demand that you should get the whole management?

The *Moderator*.—It is not equality placing the Archbishop as chairman.

Dr. Traill.—I am ready to give that up entirely to you—I said so in Magherafelt—but I don't see how you can say you accept the principle of equality when you ask the whole governing body.

Professor Dougherty.—There is no doubt the principle of equality was accepted as satisfactory, because we have it under the hand of the Moderator and of the Minister of the First Magherafelt Presbyterian Congregation; but at that time it was understood that the Salters Company was supplementing the Rainey Endowment by an equal amount; the circumstances have now changed.

Dr. Traill.—I don't see how that can change a principle.

6363. Lord Justice FitzGibbon.—Some interest is being taken now about the sale of the London Companies estates, and this is a very remarkable instance. "The Salters Company told us from the beginning that they wanted to endow the Rainey school with the property that remained unsold in Magherafelt. We find—although it may have been looking a gift horse in the mouth—went to see this property, and found that it consisted of some unsold houses and a yard which had been used for market purposes. The above produced a varying rental,

July 14, 1888 [illegible]

* [illegible] Report, 1886-7, pp. [illegible]; [illegible] App. B., p. [illegible]

July 11, [illegible]

being occasionally hired for storing corn and flax. We found there was no patent for the market, and therefore all that could be got out of this property was whatever people might voluntarily pay for bringing their goods into this yard, with whatever rents could be got for the stores. We found a feeling strongly expressed in Magherafelt that, if the markets were placed under a Protestant denominational body, the Catholics would go against the markets, or if they were placed under an Episcopalian denominational body, the Presbyterians would do likewise. Besides, managing stores and markets was unsuitable work for the governing body of a school, and accordingly the constitution of the school board raised the question whether that body would be able to enforce any market dues, or to make anything of the property offered by the Company. We represented that to the Company, and they substituted a proposal that this property should be put into the hands of a representative market board at a fixed rent, which should represent their endowment, but was still offered as an endowment for Rainey's school. We also had a long correspondence with them as to what they meant when they told us they wanted Rainey's school as endowed by them to be available for all denominations, and we at last brought them to this, that all Protestant denominations were to be represented on the governing body, and the school was to be open to all denominations, including Roman Catholics, but they would not say whether they wanted the board to include Roman Catholics as well as Protestants. We then told them that this amounted to offering the endowment for all denominations on conditions which we knew one denomination would not take, and we declined to call it an endowment open to Roman Catholics if they placed it exclusively under Protestant management. They then changed their minds to this extent, and only to this extent, that they divided the money and said, "we will give a fixed part of it to the Roman Catholics, and another part to the Protestants." But it never was suggested that the Protestants were not all to join in taking one share, and it is very unfortunate, but it is the fact, that the whole of this "endowment" as they call it, is not worth, in any possible view of the case, at all so much as the Company used to give to the Protestant share. But all through it was understood by everybody, that the Protestant share was to go to Rainey's School, which was to be placed under a mixed Board of Presbyterians and Churchmen. Undoubtedly the Salters Company are still under the impression, as we were until now, that whatever they gave to Rainey's School was to go to all denominations of Protestants, and there was to be no further subdivision. That makes your present proposal a matter of very serious consideration, because it amounts to this, that we should give up the Salters endowment altogether. We cannot ask them to give that endowment to Presbyterians only. Further, I find that at Magherafelt Mr Minnis and Mr. Brown represented the Magherafelt Presbytery, and Lord Justice Naish asked the question:—

"[illegible]. Do you object to representatives of the late Established Church being placed on the governing body?"

Mr. Minnis said:—

"No, in these days of religious equality we do not wish to raise objections, and for the sake of that peace and harmony which Dr. Jordan so much desired we are willing to overlook the serious injustice that has been done."

I said:—

"[illegible]. We must make a scheme that will work. The proposed Board is half and half, and if there is no provision for a casting vote a tie will bring matters to a deadlock."

Mr Minnis said:—

"Supposing that at one meeting a Presbyterian presides, and that at the next there is an Episcopalian chairman, we could hold our own."

I pointed out that that would result in one meeting nullifying what had been done by another. Then Dr. Traill asked:—

"[illegible]. Would you be content if we left it to the present Primate, who is now a Governor, for his lifetime only, and then remove both Primate and Moderator from the future governing body?—I would most certainly object to such an arrangement as that; I consider that it would put the power altogether in the hands of the Governors who represent the Episcopal Church."

We all through went on the assumption that all denominations of Protestants were to work together in managing Rainey's school, and then the only question was how they were to be relatively represented. That they were to be on a joint body seemed to be the wish of every one except Dr. Wilson, who was in favour of separating the endowment, and he was asked whether he put it forward as other than his own view.

Rev. Dr. Wilson.—It was my own opinion.

The Moderator.—With your permission I shall call upon Mr. Wilson to make some remarks.

Rev. H. B. Wilson, B.D.

6444. At that meeting at Magherafelt you stated in your opening statement, that the Rainey foundation was Protestant in character, that under his will the governing body was Presbyterian, that under the subsequent Act of Parliament the Primate was made sole trustee of the property, and that under the existing Chancery Scheme he obtained the exclusive management of the school; all that we accept as correct. Well, now, what I want you to do at this Commission is just to brush aside that Act of Parliament, and that Scheme of Chancery, which you have the power to do, and go back to the will and carry out the intention of the founder. You have very naturally raised the objection to our Moderator. "How is it such a change of opinion has taken place?" My explanation of that is we have got more light on the subject, the matter has been looked into, and the conclusion arrived at by the people of Magherafelt, and everyone interested in it, is that the right course is to ask you as a Commission to deal solely with the foundation of Rainey, not to touch the Salters grant in any way whatever in the transaction; let it be a separate transaction, and we will go in as Presbyterians, and claim the sole representation on the Rainey board. We don't ask, as Dr. Traill has referred to it, that the twenty-four boys, if they were to be boys, should be Presbyterians, but we ask that the Governors shall be Presbyterians—in fact we simply ask that the scheme shall adhere to the founder's intentions, and if we were to act like Dr. Traill's friends, and take others than Presbyterians among the twenty-four, we would try and send them out Presbyterians.

6445. Dr. Traill.—But you always objected to that before; do you propose to carry out the same policy now?

Dr. Wilson.—I only say if we acted on the example we would turn them out Presbyterians.

6446. Dr. Traill.—Was not your great objection that the ancient governing body was Episcopalian; you are now asking that the same grievance should extend to the opposite side?

Dr. Wilson.—I ask to adhere to the rules laid down by Mr. Rainey. He was most scrupulously anxious that the money of the £400 should go to plant one, and he took special precautions that no deviation should take place with reference to the application of that money. I much regret that you have not the power to go back and see that more than a mere change should come to this bequest—but you have not the power and we need not lose sight of it—it would amount to £2,000 a year at least; so that we have suffered great abuse in every way. It was his object that it should be under Presbyterian government. Well, we have very little in the way of bequests made to us; what little we had in old times we were not able to retain. Happily we are now living under [illegible] condition when Presbyterians can not only exist but hold property, and I think, now, as you are armed with power to give us this property you ought to give it to us on the conditions that the owner has laid down. I would be anxious that we should adhere to the will as far as possible, and that you should adopt a scheme carrying that out. Now, the present action of the Salters Company has only had a partial influence with us; we are satisfied that the other endowment from the Salters Company should be separated from the Rainey; the thing has been discussed in our Assembly, and looked at in our educational committees, and that is our unanimous opinion now.

6667. Dr. Traill.—Would you give up the house too?

Dr. Wilson.—We are perfectly prepared to give up the house if they give us the twelve acres of land they took.

6668. Dr. Traill.—That was their property?

Dr. Wilson.—No, it was not.

6669. Lord Justice FitzGibbon.—It was part of the townparks of Magherafelt; it has been now sold and cannot be got back, for the Salters Company have nothing left in Magherafelt but the stores and market place.

Professor Dougherty.—The original schoolhouse was built by Rainey's executors.

Lord Justice FitzGibbon.—That was a different schoolhouse.

Rev. Mr. Orr.—It was the substitution of one schoolhouse for another.

Dr. Wilson.—If they come in and take the twelve acres, and take the schoolhouse, and build another schoolhouse in return for it, they have no right to take it from us.

6670. Professor Dougherty.—I remember putting the question to a gentleman of local knowledge at Coleraine, whether the Salters had got a *quid pro quo* for the old schoolhouse, and he stated that they had.

Dr. Traill.—Although, perhaps, it was an immoral transaction of theirs to resume that land if they did not give any equivalent for it, it was still their own property, and the Presbyterians had no claim to the twelve acres.

Dr. Wilson.—They acknowledged our right by saying that if they got the twelve acres they would build the school.

Dr. Traill.—For all denominations.

6671. Lord Justice Naish.—Were the twelve acres part of the Rainey endowment?

Dr. Wilson.—Yes.

6672. Dr. Traill.—No, no, it did not come from Rainey.

Lord Justice FitzGibbon.—The twelve acres appear from the Chancery scheme to have been taken as a farm in connexion with the school from the Salters Company at a rent, and though the tenant right might be Rainey's property, it appears that notice to quit had been served.

6673. Dr. Traill.—There was no tenant right in townparks.

Dr. Wilson.—We dispute that.

6674. Dr. Traill.—Morally there should have been, of course.

Dr. Wilson.—It is within my own time that the distinction of townparks not being sold was raised. I bought townparks and hold them now, and the twelve acres are good value for £40 an acre or £75 in Magherafelt. I have sold them at Cookstown at £100 per acre.

6675. Rev. Dr. Molloy.—Did the Rainey School pay a rent for those twelve acres?

Dr. Wilson.—Yes.

Dr. Traill.—It was £24 a year.

6676. Rev. Dr. Molloy.—I understand you would be content to get whatever was your interest in those twelve acres in case the Salters wish to take back their buildings?

Dr. Wilson.—Quite so.

6677. Lord Justice FitzGibbon.—We can not undo what was done in 1862 under the order of the Court of Chancery as to those twelve acres. The order recites that there were only seven boys in the institution, that the house—the old Rainey schoolhouse—was in a state of decay; that the instruction given to the scholars was inferior to that which they could obtain at other schools in the country. It further found that the existing schoolhouse—that was Rainey's schoolhouse—should be surrendered to the Salters Company, on whose property it stands, and that the farm—that is the twelve acres held in connexion with it from the said Company—should no longer be retained, and that the Salters Company had offered to defray the expenses of erecting a suitable building for the school on an eligible site in the town of Magherafelt, and to execute a declaration of trust or otherwise to secure the use of such building for the objects of the charity so long as the same should be administered in accordance with the scheme prayed for in the petition, or any altered scheme to which the Company would give their concurrence. We have throughout gone on the principle that, under that scheme the Company are trustees of the existing premises, now occupied by the school, although notwithstanding all that was done and spent in Chancery, the declaration of trust was never executed.

Dr. Traill.—But they gave their money on the faith that the school should be managed as settled by the Court of Chancery.

Dr. Wilson.—They got full value for their money; it came out in the evidence of Mr. Kinnaird at Magherafelt that when he came over he had to go to the Primate, and he was asked the question, did he belong to the Church of England, it was an essential to his getting the appointment. The people that attend there have always been attached to the Episcopal Church service, and the fact is they could not do more, according even to all that Dr. Traill would ask for, in the way of proselytism.

6678. Dr. Traill.—I would not proselytise any person. I am as much a Presbyterian as a Churchman for all you know; but you want to do the very thing now.

Dr. Wilson.—I do not; I only say it would come up to your standard.

6679. Dr. Traill.—I thought you asked to have it put under an entirely Presbyterian body?

Dr. Wilson.—I do, because it is Presbyterian money.

6680. Dr. Traill.—Won't the grievance be the same to the Church children?

Dr. Wilson.—You will establish a conscience clause, of course, and let no one go there who has any fear that the conscience clause will not sufficiently protect them.

6681. Rev. Dr. Molloy.—You want to get back for the Presbyterian body an endowment which was left by a Presbyterian, with instructions to have it placed under Presbyterian management, and your grievance is that the endowment so left was got possession of by another denomination and used by them for their own purposes.

Dr. Wilson.—Could not be better expressed. The Primate writes: "We have made a concession with a view to a settlement, and if I am deprived of my position in the Rainey School, an endowment for a sacred trust will be free from desecration." I hold that at the time he wrote that he was guilty of a desecration of the trust. I ask you to restore to us the Rainey trust; we will apply to the Salters for a share, and you may have a scheme for the Salters Company, of which we can have a share.

6682. Dr. Traill.—Is this a new principle that the Churchmen and Presbyterians in the North of Ireland cannot work together?

Dr. Wilson.—It may be a new principle, but it is not new in practice. When we have a purely Presby-

[illegible] terian endowment, what have the Churchmen to do with it?

6583. Dr. Traill.—Don't you take into consideration the length of time they have had it in their hands?

Dr. Wilson.—If you had the power, I would like to ask you to refund that money with interest. Our ancestors had to live in caves and dens at that time.

6584. Dr. Traill.—None of us are responsible for what our ancestors did. Don't you think it is a great hardship that the people who are at present in possession should be asked to walk out?

The Moderator.—We are suffering the consequences of their act, and must try to remedy its effect.

6585. Dr. Traill.—Would it not be much fairer to see whether you could not always work together?

Dr. Wilson.—We are willing to do so.

6586. Dr. Traill.—How can they when you won't allow the Churchmen to have any voice in the management?

Dr. Wilson.—If it was national property in that case we would work together, but we have heard in the Royal Schools that where there is a benefaction from an Episcopalian, they contend it should only be to Episcopalians.

6587. Dr. Traill.—If we were framing a scheme immediately after Rainey's death it would be a different thing; then the arguments you put forward would be unanswerable.

Dr. Wilson.—I think they are unanswerable any way.

6588. Dr. Traill.—No; I think possession is nine points of law.

Dr. Wilson.—You are here to take it out of the robbers' hands, and restore it to the rightful owners.

6589. Dr. Traill.—If you call them robbers it was done by Act of Parliament and by the Court of Chancery.

Rev. Dr. Molloy.—All the Act of Parliament did was to make the Archbishop of Armagh the trustee for this endowment, and your case is he has not carried out the trusts.

Professor Dougherty.—And it is only fair to say it does not appear to have been the act of the Archbishop of Armagh, but of Rainey's relatives.

The Moderator.—We are making no charge against the Archbishop.

6590. Dr. Traill.—He is an unwilling instrument, no doubt.

Dr. Wilson.—I don't know that.

6591. Dr. Traill.—He cannot give up the power entrusted to him by an Act of Parliament or a Chancery scheme.

The Moderator.—We are trying to relieve him of it.

6592. Dr. Traill.—But in every other case where we have had Presbyterians and Church people mixed up, it has always occurred to us to have a mixed body. In the Bernard case, where the Church people are ten to one over the Presbyterians who want to that endowment, we made the governing body half and half.

Dr. Wilson.—Where we have a purely Presbyterian endowment we want it ourselves.

6593. Rev. Dr. Molloy.—You would be willing to have a mixed body where there is a mixed endowment.

Dr. Wilson.—Quite so. And as to Mr. Kinnaird's pension, it is quite right that the man should have a pension, but it was the Salters Company that brought him here and had him appointed; it was through the Primate they did it, but they selected the man and sent him over here, and I think the pension should come out of the Salters Company.

Rev. Dr. Molloy.—If you get the endowment you will give Mr. Kinnaird to the Salters Company and the Primate.

6594. Dr. Traill.—Do you hold, then, the principle that where the Governing Body belonged originally, and was Protestant, or of any one denomination, even though it should be open to all denominations as regards the beneficiaries, that the Governing body should still belong to the original denomination?

Rev. Mr. Kerr.—Could we get an instance of an Episcopalian endowment being managed by a mixed body of Presbyterians and Episcopalians?

The Moderator introduced Rev. Mr. Orr.

Rev. *J. B. Orr*, B.A.—I don't wish to detain you after what has been said by the Moderator and Dr. Wilson. Our contention is that the founder of this charitable bequest had only in his eye one religious body. The Roman Catholic Church was beside him in his day; he makes no reference to it in his will. The Episcopalian Protestant Church was in existence in his day, and he makes no allusion to it in his will. But right in the centre of the will, when he is defining the arrangements with regard to the boys' clothing and maintenance in the school, and defining also the allowance—"the encouragement," he terms it—to be given to the schoolmaster, right in the centre of these provisions he specifies £5 to the Presbyterian Minister of Maghera, which was as much, we submit, a permanent grant unto his successors, as the payment to the schoolmaster, or to the two poor old men. Well, then, in addition to that, Rainey provides that whenever the two governors and men, I would term them overseers—they were very important men in connection with the establishment—when any of these proved unsuitable for the office the executors, or the persons holding the property in lieu of the executors were to apply to the Presbytery of Ulster. I am sure, my lord, you know that that was the old description of the chief court of the Presbyterian body in Ireland.

6595. Dr. Traill.—The Synod of Ulster.

Rev. Mr. *Orr*.—No, it was first known as the Presbytery of Ulster, and then the Synod of Ulster, and then by the Union of the Synod of Ulster forty-nine years ago, and the Secession Synod, we became the General Assembly. Rainey was a Presbyterian Elder, that is to say he held an office which we say is equivalent to that of the ministry; it is the same office as that of the ministry, we rule and teach, but he was simply a ruling elder. He attended the Courts of the Church, and the Synod of Ulster. Well, looking at the fact of his being a Presbyterian, and making this arrangement regarding the Presbyterian Minister getting £5 per annum—I think he had the idea that the minister was to do something in connection with the charity for the Presbyterians—and that he makes no allusion to any denomination of Christians but Presbyterians, we hold, therefore, it is a Presbyterian endowment, and should be so regarded. Contrary to this intention of the founder, the whole management has been given to another denomination, and you and your coadjutors propose by this draft scheme to perpetuate that. You make us simply equal on the governing board to the other denomination.

6596. Dr. Traill.—That is not perpetuating one religion.

Rev. Mr. *Orr*.—Yes, I will show you how. We are man for man on the governing board, and then you give the chairman a casting vote besides his own vote, and you secure the preponderance of that denomination to which the chairman belongs, and that perpetual chairman you make the Archbishop of Armagh. I quite take it both churches had been named in the will, if the Episcopalian Church had been expressly named, and it made the same terms as the Presbyterian, then the scheme, even on that supposition, would be unjust, because you would have given to one denomination a preponderance when they were both equally divided. But it is monstrous when the Presbyterian Church alone is named that you should hand over the practical government of the charity to another denomination, even though that denomination is Protestant, and a denomination with which we wish to live in peace.

If it is said that the Scheme of 1863 in Chancery—Master Litton I believe was the person who drew it up—if it is said that that scheme has settled that the Protestant Episcopalian Church should have the nomination of the boys, and also have the appointment of the teacher, and the control of the school, I reply that that scheme departed from the intentions of the founder—it had not regard to his intentions. I hold that no Scheme of Chancery is to be held as infallible, no more than an Act of Parliament. You have been told already that the Act was a fraud. The Act sanctioned a fraud; I don't say that the framers of the Act intended to defraud anyone. The Court of Chancery certainly had no regard to the intention of the founder, but you can go behind the Court of Chancery. You say, "After the date of this scheme, it shall be held, governed, managed, and applied for the purposes, with the powers, under the conditions and provisions, and in the manner hereinafter set forth, and not otherwise, any previous Act of Parliament, or, to the contrary notwithstanding." We ask you, my lords and gentlemen, to recast the scheme entirely and put aside the Act of Parliament, and set aside the Scheme in Chancery which has departed from the intentions of the founder. Now, in regard to the Salters endowment, I think I may say that those who sanctioned this scheme when you met in Magherafelt or expressed their agreement with it, were of course under the impression that the Salters Company were giving as much as they had been giving—£180 per annum, lately £150—but they had been originally giving on an average £180. Well, that was more than the Rainey endowment was yielding—£161 per annum—and the Presbyterians thought, in all fairness, "If the Salters are doing so much more than the Rainey foundation now does, and doing it for all denominations, why should we claim sole control." I think the representatives of the Presbyterian Church acted fairly and in a straightforward manner, and under the same conditions we might do the same. But the conditions are altered, the Salters propose now to give one-third of their original grant—£66—and since in Magherafelt the Presbyterians are as numerous as the Episcopalian Protestants, I think more numerous, we should at least get £33 per annum from the Salters Company. I have no doubt they will give it to us, and you have a provision here that whenever they in the Governors they are empowered to accept supplemental grants. If you give us a separate scheme, a different scheme from this, give us a scheme under the sole control of the Presbyterians, I guarantee we shall get the endowment. There are members of our congregation who will give endowments, and with the help of the Salters Company——

6597. Dr. Traill.—But the Salters have made it a condition of their grant that the governing body of Rainey's School shall be partly Presbyterian and partly Episcopalian.

Rev. Mr. Orr.—The Salters Company, their past action shows, very frequently change their mind. First of all they were to give their endowment to all denominations; they have now divided the endowment between the Romanists and the Protestants, and I am quite prepared to hear that they will divide their endowment between the two denominations of Protestants and Episcopalians. This school, even under our sole control, would be open to all denominations. We conduct our schools, whether they be primary or intermediate, on the principles of the National Board, that is to say, we observe strictly a conscience clause; no child is ever asked in a Presbyterian school to receive any religious instruction to which his parent or guardian does not give consent. Let me just say that, unless the school be ours, the Presbyterians could not accept a scheme like this.

6598. Dr. Traill.—They said they were delighted to accept a scheme based on the principle of equality.

Rev. Mr. Orr.—Let me say it was not the General Assembly that spoke.

6599. Dr. Traill.—"R. J. Lynd, M.A., Moderator of the General Assembly of the Presbyterian Church in Ireland; A. Montgomery, Minister of the First Presbyterian Congregation, Magherafelt; Alexander Nimmo, Presbyterian Minister, Saltersland; and Andrew Brown, Magherafelt."

Rev. Mr. Orr.—Well, they spoke for themselves, but we speak for the Presbytery of Ulster.

6600. Dr. Traill.—Mr Lynd was the Moderator at that time.

Rev. Mr. Orr.—But the Moderator must be guided by the resolutions of the General Assembly; and the Moderator was, I have no doubt, guided by this, that he believed the Salters endowment was as large as the Rainey's.

6601. Dr. Traill.—The amount of money could not alter the principle that you could work in harmony.

Rev. Mr. Orr.—Certainly, if two parties give me money I will hold their joint contributions on different terms from those on which I would hold simply the contribution of one. Dr. Traill, you do that yourself.

6602. Rev. Dr. Molloy.—That is to say you would be prepared to have a mixed Board to administer a mixed endowment, but you wish to have a Presbyterian Board to administer a Presbyterian endowment?

Rev. Mr. Orr.—Certainly.

6603. Dr. Traill.—But this endowment is not a purely Presbyterian one, because the Salters money is given you on a special trust.

Rev. Mr. Orr.—We want to make it what it was originally.

6604. Dr. Traill.—But we find it a working concern with which the Salters' money is mixed up.

Rev. Mr. Orr.—We wish you to have regard to the intention of the founder.

6605. Dr. Traill.—At present the endowment consists of two parts, one belonging to the Salters, and the other to the original founder.

Rev. Mr. Orr.—We are willing to give up the Salters endowment.

Rev. Mr. Reid.—Mr. Nimmo ought to be here, and I am sorry he is not, but his opinion has entirely changed.

6606. Rev. Dr. Molloy.—What is the amount of the Rainey endowment in money?

Rev. Mr. Orr.—£161, English.

6607. Rev. Dr. Molloy.—If the Protestant Episcopalians were to contribute an equal sum to the Rainey school, would you then be ready to work the Rainey school with a mixed Board?

Rev. Mr. Orr.—Certainly, but we would not give them a preponderance.

6608. Dr. Traill.—Not if the Salters grant was made up to £178.

Rev. Mr. Orr.—We would accommodate ourselves to the altered circumstances.

6609. Dr. Traill.—The Moderator, the local ministers, and the local laity all agreed at that time. If the contribution of the Salters was equal you would not have brought forward your present objection?

Rev. Mr. Reid.—That is a hypothetical case.

Dr. Wilson.—Mr. Reid is Clerk of the Magherafelt Presbytery, and is here to represent it. Our minister at Magherafelt, Mr. Montgomery, is dead, and he has been succeeded by Mr. Gillespie, if you would kindly hear them.

Rev. Mr. Reid.

6610. We had a special meeting convened to consider this matter, and when we understood this Salters Endowment was such a trifling thing, we preferred to accept the Rainey Foundation fund, and let the Salters grant go, claiming, at the same time, our share as Presbyterians, knowing that the Presbyterian farmers are the great majority of the farmers around the company from whom the Salters get their money, and believing we have a good right to get at least half of the £66. So the Magherafelt

July 11, 1890.

Presbytery passed a resolution saying, "We will not accept any scheme that does not give us control." Of course if the Episcopalians give an equal sum of money they must have an equal representation, but not a preponderance. But if it is said, "If the Salters contribute an equal amount!" Certainly not, we will ask for our proportion. The feeling in Magherafelt has become intense over this, and the school has been a failure and will be a failure I prophesy, unless the Presbyterian people are somehow or other satisfied that this Rainey School Endowment is restored to its original intention. We only want what is right and fair. Mr. Minnis was acting on the supposition that the endowment of the Salters Company was far larger than even the Rainey, but he objected very strongly at the same time to the casting vote of the Archbishop.

6611. Lord Justice FitzGibbon.—Nothing could be more distinct than the information we gave at Magherafelt with respect to the amount of the endowment offered by the Salters. We took a quantity of evidence, in Mr. *Minnis'* presence, showing everybody exactly what this endowment was, that it was a lot of buildings, the rental of which was extremely doubtful, and a number of premiums, [illegible]. Ultimately, after a great deal of discussion, we arrived at the conclusion that the school would be very lucky if it could make £110 to £160 a year out of it, but at that time it is right to say the idea of dividing it, and giving a separate share to the Roman Catholics was not thought of.

Rev. Mr. *Reid*.—Mr. Minnis was acting under great difficulties. He had a telegram from Dr. Todd Martin, convener of the Intermediate Education Committee, telling him to accept the proposal with modifications.

Dr. Traill.—It was to Dr. Wilson the telegram was.

6612. Lord Justice FitzGibbon.—It would be very unjust to throw any responsibility on Mr. Minnis. On all sides at Magherafelt the only question was as to the majority. I lay no blame on any one, we were all alike; we were all proceeding on the assumption that you were to have a mixed governing body to manage Rainey's school, with the help of the Salters' endowment, as a Protestant school.

Dr. M'Kane.—There is no doubt about it.

Rev. Mr. *Orr*.—As the Primate has held the chairmanship for so many years now, even if there was a Board with both denominations upon it, I think some Presbyterian ought to hold the chairmanship for an equal term.

Rev. Mr. Gillespie.

I am only locally acquainted with this case for the last two months, but I have given a good deal of attention to the question since I came there, and I find it absorbing a good deal of local interest, and I find a very decided opinion exists in the minds of the Presbyterians on the matter in regard to the action of those who gave evidence at Magherafelt at your sitting in October, both publicly and privately in the Presbytery. It was said by those who gave evidence that they were under a misapprehension. When they spoke before and gave evidence they were under the impression that your scheme was about to embody the Rainey endowment, and a large endowment from the Salters Company; they understand now that that is not so, and they have changed their positions.

6613. Lord Justice FitzGibbon.—I am afraid I must correct you in that. We were at Magherafelt on October 21, 1889, we had published our scheme on August 12, the two months were up, all the objections were before us, and it was on the scheme and the objections that the discussion took place. The draft scheme dealt exclusively with the Rainey endowment, but it was proposed to insert a provision for taking over what they could get from the Salters Company.

Rev. Dr. Molloy.—I tried to make it clear. Question 5560, I said:—

"Our scheme does not deal with the Salters endowment; it deals only with the Rainey endowment. The Salters Company then comes in, and seeing our scheme they say they will, under certain conditions, give to the governing body an additional endowment."

Rev. Mr. *Gillespie*.—Whatever precautions may have been taken I feel sure from what I have heard from those who gave evidence, that they laboured under a misapprehension. I am only sorry that the members appointed by the Presbytery to be here are not able all to be here. Mr. Brown telegraphed this morning that he missed the train.

6614. Lord Justice FitzGibbon.—Mr. Brown was the gentleman who put forward Mr. Todd-Martin's telegram, "he recommends we should adopt the scheme having equal powers of voting." There may have been a misapprehension as regards what they were to get from the Salters Company, for the proposal to divide had not yet been made; but there could be no misapprehension as to what our proposal was. Everybody went on the assumption that even if the Rainey endowment alone were included in the scheme, the school should be governed by a mixed body.

Rev. Mr. *Gillespie*.—The matter has been made very much clearer since, and I can assure you it has taken firm hold of the minds of the people there now, who understand their ground, as they think, and they see they are dealing with the Rainey endowment alone, and have claimed it and will not feel satisfied if it is not granted. The public opinion is that the Presbyterians have been badly treated in the past. It has been asked why Presbyterians and Episcopalians would not work together; they never got an opportunity of working together. The Episcopalians worked alone for the past 150 years, and the Presbyterians had no control over it, and looking over the past history they have no confidence in the school, and I am afraid the school will work with considerable friction.

6615. Dr. Traill.—Are not all the successful schools in the North of Ireland worked by a mixed board?

Rev. Mr. *Gillespie*.—I don't know that.

Rev. Mr. *Orr*.—The Belfast Methodist College is not mixed.

Rev. Mr. *Gillespie*.—The Presbyterians feel they have a moral right and a legal right to have the Rainey endowment managed solely by themselves. Having that opinion I don't think they would ever kindly be harmonious with a body who had it so long.

6616. Dr. Traill.—Could you tell what is the proportion of the poor of the two religious bodies in Magherafelt?

Rev. Mr. *Gillespie*.—I have seen a census but I have no confidence in it.

6617. Lord Justice FitzGibbon.—We were given these figures:—*Town of Magherafelt*, Roman Catholics, 681; Church, 411; Presbyterians, 838; Methodists, 72. *Salters estate*, Roman Catholics, 3,781; Church, 3,373; Presbyterians, 3,075; Methodists, 115. These were Dr. Jordan's figures.

Rev. Mr. *Reid*.—I know a large proportion of the farmers are Presbyterians.

6618. Dr. Traill.—But they are not poor people.

Rev. Mr. *Orr*.—This school was not intended for persons in absolute poverty, but the children of reduced persons, and the fact of their getting broadcloth clothing at 6s. a yard in those days, shows that they were the sons of decent people, sons of parents "who were of good repute and reduced to poverty."

6619. Dr. Traill.—They are not Presbyterians generally.

Rev. Mr. *Orr*.—Sometimes the world goes hard against them.

[illegible]. Lord Justice FITZGIBBON.—Having heard your views, I think we should tell you how the matter strikes us at present. The proposal that you have brought before us today is to separate from all other endowments the Rainey endowment which you claim as consisting of the rent-charge and the existing school buildings, to go back to Rainey's will, and to frame a scheme for what is now held under Rainey's will upon the terms that he himself originally laid down. That claim deserves careful consideration, and we will give it our best consideration. We must have regard to the spirit of the founder's intention in all cases, but we must also have regard to the present circumstances of the trust. There are considerations affecting us now in the final settlement of our scheme, which would not necessarily affect other people, namely the whole course of our proceedings and our dealing with the Salters Company. When our scheme goes before the Privy Council, that tribunal will not be affected by some circumstances that influence us; and if our way of dealing with the case does not give satisfaction to the Primate on the one side, or to you on the other, either or both of you can appeal to the Privy Council, or to either House of Parliament, who can decide whether the Rainey endowment is now to be treated as an exclusively Presbyterian endowment, or whether the two endowments are to be put together, or whether the Primate's rights which he has enjoyed for so many years, ought to override the original foundation. As you are a deputation from one side only, I should like, without indicating any final opinion, which of course I cannot now do, to mention some of the complications that you do not see so vividly as we do. I referred Dr. Wilson, in Magherafelt, to the judgment of Solomon as a test for the scheme which he was bringing forward. He asked us to cut this child in two in order to present the Presbyterians with half of it. It was our distinct opinion that the Rainey Endowment alone was not sufficient to keep up the school that Rainey intended, nor the school as it now exists. The school is not now kept up by the Rainey Endowment alone, but jointly by the Rainey Endowment and the Salters Endowment. Can we now divide these endowments? Again, we are greatly entangled with the Salters Company by what has taken place, for we have been for nearly three years carrying on with them a longer and more complicated correspondence than we have had in any other case, endeavouring, first, to induce the Salters Company to recognise the claim this school had on them for a continuance of the aid given for so many years since 1862. All through that correspondence, while we were fighting as hard as we could to get the Salters Endowment for the Rainey School,—and the only matter of controversy was their attempt to satisfy the claims of the Roman Catholics by what they were to give towards Rainey's School—we were trying to induce the Salters Company to give the Roman Catholics what we thought they had a fair claim to, such an endowment as they had been previously getting for their own schools, and to continue to Rainey's School the full amount that it had been getting while it was really a Protestant school. We were defeated in that, and the Salters divided their school endowment, giving, no doubt, the larger part for the Protestant School—the Rainey School—but giving, in all, less than they had for twenty-five years given to that school alone. We were discussing the matter all through on the basis, which everyone adopted, that whatever we got for Rainey's School should be placed under a mixed Governing Body, in which, at least, all Protestants should have a share. The reduction or division of the Salters Endowment has altered the proportion which that endowment bears to the Rainey Endowment, but it has left the principle of the school substantially the same. If we were now, as you ask, not only to wipe out the Act of Parliament and the Chancery Scheme, but also to disregard all our correspondence with the Salters Company, I think the necessary result would be that the Salters Endowment would be lost. We could frame a separate scheme for it, because it was offered on terms which were departed from. That is a great deal to ask us to do at this time of day, particularly where the Presbyterian authorities, who appeared at Magherafelt, formally accepted the principle on which we acted. We have the document here, signed by Rev. Mr. Lynd, the Moderator of the General Assembly of the Presbyterian Church in Ireland, Mr. Montgomery, Minister of the First Presbyterian Congregation; Mr. Mitchell, the Presbyterian Minister of [illegible], and Mr. Brown, of Magherafelt. I am not blaming them; we were all acting with the same object, trying to get as much money as we could from the Salters Company for a school, the advantage of which, it was expected, would meet the claims of all denominations of Protestants. We could not now ask the Salters further to divide that money, or to treat it as no longer claimed on behalf of all. I agree that it is open to consideration what the proportions of the governing body should be, but, even as to Rainey's Endowment, you must bear in mind that the will is 172 years old, and, however it happened, the Presbyterians never wakened up to put forward their claims until this Commission had been tried to do something for them in connection with this School. In 1862 the condition of this Endowment was as bad as could be. The School was reduced, there were only a score boys. A change was necessary, and the Salters Company took up the dilapidated schoolhouse and the farm of which they had given notice to determine the yearly tenancy. This took place in 1862, nine years before tenant-right was legalised. The Company provided a suitable building, and they have ever since been contributing varying but large amounts, under an arrangement sanctioned by Chancery in 1862, by which the School has been continuously managed by Episcopalians, with the Primate at their head. During all this time no claim was put forward on the part of the Presbyterians even to a share in the management. They did put forward a claim before us in 1886. They objected to our giving a casting vote to the Episcopalians; but, on the other hand, Dr. Jordan, who appeared for the Primate, objected even to the limited representation which we for the first time provided for the Presbyterians. All these things we cannot ignore in the history of the case. It is as difficult a case to deal with as one possibly be; and the object we had in view, up to the present, of establishing a mixed school under a fairly constituted governing body, available to all Protestants, and enjoying the two endowments, is one quite different from what you are for the first time bringing forward today—an exclusively Presbyterian School, having Rainey's Endowment only. It is difficult for us to turn round, as some have done, in the middle of the stream; that is a dangerous place for changing your mode of operation, and I think the result would be to upset the Salters Endowment into the river.

Mr. Orr.—We will get the Salters Endowment or our full share, and as to the Presbyterians not awakening, I may say we could only have awakened to any effect between 1787 and 1797.

[illegible]. Lord Justice FITZGIBBON.—I am bound to tell you as a lawyer that was [illegible]. The trusts were never [illegible] until 1862, and at any time after the [illegible] representatives disappeared, which was about 1848, anybody could have come into Chancery to have a scheme settled for the management of the Charity in accordance with the will. It was left wholly derelict until the petition of 1862 was presented by Lord O'Hagan, who was then Attorney-General. He was acting in the public interest to have the school made efficient, and even at that time no person came forward to represent the Presbyterian claims. However, there is no use in expatiating on that now. It is one of the most difficult cases we have had to deal with. It is additionally complicated by the sale

July 22, 1889.

of the Salters' Company, and by the nature of this remnant of property which they offer as an endowment. We will give our best consideration to it, and if we should not see our way to change our minds as quickly as you have done, it will be open to you to try to induce the Privy Council to adopt your own principle. If the Privy Council adopt that principle, we will at once endeavour legally to carry it out; but you are putting a hard task on us in asking us to throw over all that has passed between the Salters' Company and ourselves, while we were coming to arrangement with all Presbyterians and Churchmen, who had come before us.

Dr. Wilson.—I quite appreciate the industry and care you have shown in this matter, but I want to say that living in the neighbourhood of Magherafelt I know well the feeling that prevailed at the time of the Chancery Suit, the Presbyterians were thoroughly disgusted with the fact that it was entirely in Episcopalian hands, they felt a curse rested on it, and they would not send a child to it or touch it.

6622. Lord Justice FitzGibbon.—If they carried on the same course now Dr. Traill would be satisfied.

Dr. Wilson.—It is simply where we see a Commission here with power to follow the opinion of the men we come here.

6623. Dr. Traill.—Would you not go to Mr. Lea's Parliamentary Committee; on his motion a commission has been appointed to look into these matters.

Dr. Wilson.—We won't let Mr. Lea alone, I know him very well, and we will try and see what we can do.

6624. Lord Justice FitzGibbon.—Don't say we sent you there.

Dr. Traill.—You may say I suggested it.

Dr. Wilson.—I will only say Dr. Traill advised it. But my position is, I think, that you as a Commission ought to do what we ask. If we are allowed to appear before the Privy Council we will ask them to carry out our views, and if they don't we won't have anything to do with it.

The Moderator.—I think you have furnished us with the best argument in favour of our contention, namely, that they stand self-condemned of having mismanaged the school for 150 years. Give it to the Presbyterians and you will find that they will manage it and carry it.

6625. Dr. Traill.—But these people are all dead.

Dr. Wilson.—There is a great power in inheritance.

6626. Lord Justice FitzGibbon.—I am very slow to think that schools in the North of Ireland will not prosper in the future as in the past under mixed governing bodies. You see the difficulties in the case. We fully recognise, and I hope you have seen that we have done so from the beginning, and were the first to do so, that the Presbyterians have a large, if not the largest, claim on this endowment; the extent of their claim is the only thing in doubt.

The Moderator.—There is considerable interest in the Presbyterian mind over this matter, we take it as a crucial case and are determined to follow it out to the bitter end.

6627. Lord Justice FitzGibbon.—We will try to act fairly in the matter, and you can follow it up as you think right if you are not satisfied.

The Moderator. I beg leave to express our hearty thanks to you and the other members of the Commission for the kind way you have received us, and the great attention you have paid to the remarks we thought fit to make.

Lord Justice FitzGibbon.—We only hope that after all the Rainey School may yet flourish, which it can't do if you make it a bone of contention.

The sitting terminated.

July 23, 1889.

PUBLIC SITTING—TUESDAY, JULY 23, 1889.

At the Schoolhouse, Anahilt.

Present:—Rev. Gerald Molloy, D.D., D.Sc., Anthony Traill, Esq., LL.D., M.D., F.T.C.D., and Professor Dougherty, M.A., Assistant Commissioners.

The Assistant Secretary, N. D. Murphy, was in attendance.

THE ANAHILT ENDOWED SCHOOL (JAMESON'S ENDOWMENT).

Professor Dougherty made an introductory statement.

David W. Shaw, Secretary of Anahilt Endowed School, sworn and examined.

Mr. David W. Shaw.

6628. Professor Dougherty.—How long have you been Secretary of Anahilt Endowed School?—I have occupied that position for about two years.

6629. How are the members of the committee appointed?—They are appointed every year—on the first Monday of the year by the householders, or any of the householders who attend.

6630. By a meeting of the householders called for the purpose of appointing a committee?—Yes, in accordance, I believe, with the testator's will.

6631. Do you keep a record of these meetings of the householders?—Yes. Since I was appointed secretary I have kept a record of the meetings.

6632. Rev. Dr. Molloy.—How many members are on the committee?—Two members for each townland; there are twenty members.

6633. Professor Dougherty.—Do the persons coming from each townland vote for the representatives of that particular townland?—Any of the householders present that are not on the committee usually propose the re-election of the committee for the ensuing year.

6634. Has the committee been re-elected from year to year?—That is the usual course, but from 1881 until about 1886 there were no meetings of committee.

6635. Was any meeting of parishioners held?—No.

6636. And no committee was in fact existing?—No. Mr. Greer was the administrator then, and from 1881 until 1886 no record was kept.

6637. In 1886 you began again to hold meetings?—Yes. There was a committee meeting on the 7th of June, 1886. It was the first meeting held for several years.

6638. When was that committee elected?—It was [illegible]

the old committee on the books that met together, but it was not re-elected. The annual meeting of parishioners was held on the 3rd of January, 1887.

6639. What are the functions of that committee?—Before that time they had all the power; now they meet, and if any repairs are required they attend to them, and any other business that is to be done they transact.

6640. Do they administer the funds?—They have not done that since the Rev. Mr. Greer's death.

6641. In whom are the funds now vested?—Mr. Miller and Mr. Moorhead.

6642. And the committee has nothing to do with the administration of the funds?—No. The Commissioners of Charitable Donations and Bequests left the money entirely in the hands of the administrators who paid the salaries of the teachers but would not give anything for repairs.

6643. Do the committee visit the school from time to time?—Not usually, except at quarterly meetings.

6644. Are these meetings held at the school?—Yes.

6645. Are they held during school hours?—No, at seven o'clock in the evening.

6646. Then the committee do not interest themselves personally in the way of visiting the school?—In fact the committee have had little to say in the matter, and that is why they do not attend.

6647. What is the nature of the business discharged at the quarterly meetings; perhaps you can give us some of your records?—Well, here is one:—

"4th February, 1879.—The quarterly meeting was held here this evening at seven o'clock. Mr. A. Boyd in the chair. Members present:—Rev. J. W. Moorhead, Rev. J. Mitchell, Dr. Thomson, J.P., D. W. Shaw, Robert Gillespie, J. Dornan, J. M'Kelvey, Samuel Gillespie, Joseph Harris, John Ross, J. Patterson. It was proposed by Mr. Mitchell and seconded by Mr. Gillespie, that the secretary write to the administrators to know the amount of money at last half-yearly balance. It was moved by the Rev. J. Moorhead and seconded that the secretary write to the Commissioners of Charitable Bequests, and ask if we, as a committee appointed in accordance with the will of the testator, have any power to ask, for repairs of school premises, the surplus after paying teachers the annual amount of their salary. The secretary was instructed to write to the Board confirming Dr. Thomson's appointment, as correspondent, to the Board."

6648. That is the National Board?—Yes.

6649. Rev. Dr. Molloy.—When was the committee first constituted?—I do not know.

6650. When did the committee resume its annual meetings?—On the 3rd of January, 1887.

6651. When had it previously held any meetings?—About 1881.

6652. Then for a period of six years it did not meet at all?—I think for about five years.

6653. Are there any ex-officio members on that committee?—There are the vice-presidents—all the ministers, and Mr. Graham of Larchfield.

6654. All the ministers are ex officio?—Yes.

6655. How is Mr. Graham an ex-officio member?—He was appointed at one of the meetings of the committee.

6656. And once appointed he remains so permanently?—Yes.

6657. Have you a copy of your constitution?—I do not think it exists in writing.

6658. It is handed down by tradition?—Yes.

6659. How many, as a rule, attend your meetings of committee?—From three or four to half-a-dozen.

July 25, 1888.

Mr. David W. Shaw.

6660. Are the Committee satisfied with the power they have with regard to the school?—No, they are not satisfied.

6661. What power would they like to have?—The committee have now no power in the management of the funds, and when we want repairs done to the school we cannot get money to carry them out.

6662. Do you mean since 1857?—Since the money was put into the hands of the Charitable Commissioners. I think that was about 1878.

6663. Prior to that where were the funds invested?—In Lord Downshire's office, and Mr. Greer paid the teachers. Mr. Greer was Presbyterian minister of Anahilt, and he was paid by the agent of the Downshire estate.

6664. Can you give any explanation of the committee not meeting at all for a number of years?—Well, Mr. Greer was secretary and treasurer and all together, and did away with the committee; he received the money and spent it, and the committee thought there was nothing for them to do.

6665. When did Mr. Greer die?—March 25, 1885.

6666. You would like to have something to do with the administration of the funds?—Yes, we would like to have some of the funds for the repairs of the building.

6667. Who appoints the head master?—The committee; it was always the committee did so. The committee put in Mr. Clements, the present headmaster.

6668. Professor Dougherty.—I understand your complaint is that the committee is ignored by the Commissioners of Charitable Donations and Bequests?—Yes.

6669. You want to get for the committee the status assigned to them in the will of the late Thomas Jamieson?—Yes. £975 is the amount which the Charitable Commissioners hold. The original amount was invested in a mortgage on the estate of the Marquis of Downshire. And the sum I have mentioned came back into the hands of the Commissioners.

6670. Mr. Greer was appointed to manage the school in 1873 and continued to do so up to the time of his death?—Yes.

6671. Who succeeded him?—Mr. Miller.

6672. How soon after Mr. Greer's death was Mr. Miller appointed?—I cannot say.

6673. Was Mr. Mitchell chosen as Mr. Greer's successor as minister of Anahilt Presbyterian Church before then?—I think not.

6674. Is the Rev. Mr. Moorhead's congregation within the bounds of the parish?—It is.

6675. Rev. Dr. Molloy.—Are the two present administrators members of the committee?—They are vice-presidents.

6676. Who appointed these administrators?—The Commissioners of Charitable Donations and Bequests.

6677. Professor Dougherty.—How much land is attached to the school?—I think about four Irish acres.

6678. How is it held?—Under the Marquis of Downshire, at a nominal rent.

6679. Rev. Dr. Molloy.—Have you any lease?—No, we have just possession.

Robert Gillespie sworn and examined.

6680. Professor Dougherty.—You are a member of this committee?—I have been a member of the committee for between thirty and forty years: I was on the committee of repairs.

6681. Can you explain how it was that the committee did not meet during this long interval we have heard of?—I cannot explain it in any way except that Mr. Greer was the administrator, and the people had confidence in him. He had charge of the money, and when the committee met and saw what repairs the

Robert Gillespie.

July 23, 1880. Robert Gillespie.

school needed, the work was sanctioned by the committee. They then looked after the matter and Mr. Greer paid the accounts.

6681. The business of the committee was to look after the repairs of the school?—Yes.

6682. And they had very little else to do?—Very little else when it came under the National Board.

6683. Rev. Dr. Molloy.—When was it put under the National Board?—I could not say; it was under the National Board before the present master was appointed.

Mr. Andrew Clements (Master of the School).—It was about 1867.

6684. You are not satisfied with the present management of the endowment?

Witness.—No. The committee was always elected by the parishioners. It was the business of the parish to elect the committee, and reappoint them, and if one of the members died to put one in his place. The committee used to meet and visit the school regularly. After it went under the National Board they did not do so.

6685. Have you ever made a representation to the Commissioners of Charitable Donations and Bequests, on the subject of the Committee being ignored?—I do not know.

Dr. Thomson, J.P.—Oh, yes, it is in the minute book of the committee.

6686. Professor Dougherty.—What you desire is, that the committee should be recognised in future in the management of the funds?

Witness.—Yes, and that we should have the power, when we see the necessity for alterations or repairs, to manage the money.

6687. You think the money is sufficient to pay for improvements and repairs in addition to paying the schoolmaster and schoolmistress?—Yes, there always was money for that, and the buildings would not go out of repair if not kept up.

6688. Rev. Dr. Molloy.—When was the committee first constituted?

Witness.—I think it was in 1834.

6690. By whom?—By the parish.

6691. Dr. Traill.—How many heads of families used to meet together to appoint this committee?—There were generally a good many of the parishioners who met on the first Monday of the year, and they appointed two from every townland.

6692. Professor Dougherty.—Is there anything you would like to add?

Witness.—No, only that we would like the committee to have some of the management of the money, so that we could draw from the funds what would be over the teachers' salaries.

6693. I see on the minutes a letter from the Commissioners of Charitable Donations and Bequests. It is as follows:—

"Thomas Jackson's Charity.

"4th May, 1880.

"Sir,—With reference to the letter of the 16th ult., signed by you as Secretary to the Committee of the Annahilt Endowed School, inquiring whether the surplus income of the endowment after paying teachers' salaries can be expended in repairs to the school premises, I am directed to inform you that the Board having appointed local administrators of the endowment, who have not joined in the present application, my Commissioners do not feel called upon to express any opinion upon it."

The letter was signed "Arnold F. Graves." In consequence of that communication, had you any interview with the local administrators appointed by the Commissioners?

Mr. Shaw.—There was a mistake in that. The Rev. J. N. Moorhead was present, and joined in that application.

6694. Did you ever make any application to the other local administrator to join in this application?—I am not sure about that.

6695. Is he a member of the committee?—He ought to be a Vice-President.

6696. Has he attended the meetings?—No, never since he was appointed.

6697. How long has he resided in the parish?—I cannot say how long.

6698. I suppose he was appointed to the parish before Mr. Greer's death?—Yes.

6699. Rev. Dr. Molloy (to Witness).—I think you say that the wish of the committee is that the administration of the funds should be in their power so that they could expend them as they think fit for the good of the school?—They think that they should have some at least of the power.

6700. If the committee were put in the place of the administrators, would that meet their views?—They do not want that, they want to act with the administrators.

6701. Dr. Traill.—Would you make the administrators members of the committee?—They are members of the committee.

6702. Do you want to turn them out?—No, but that they should work together with the committee.

6703. Rev. Dr. Molloy.—What was the meeting at which administrators were first appointed by the Commissioners of Charitable Donations and Bequests?—I do not know.

Mr. Shaw.—There was a meeting of committee at which four names of ministers were sent forward to the Commissioners of Charitable Donations and Bequests. Of the four ministers named only two were appointed.

6704. Dr. Traill.—Was that after Lord Downshire had paid off the mortgage?—Yes.

6705. Rev. Dr. Molloy (to witness).—Would it meet your views if the whole power were vested in the committee appointed by the parishioners, the money to be paid to them and spent as they may think best in the interest of the school?

Witness.—Yes.

Rev. James Mitchell (Presbyterian minister of Annahilt).—I do not think they want so much as that.

6706. Rev. Dr. Molloy.—Do the committee think there is an advantage in having two bodies—one administering the funds and another managing the school; which would they prefer, having one body only, or two?

Dr. Thomson, J.P.—I think the committee would rather act in conjunction with the Rev. Mr. Moorhead and the Rev. Mr. Miller.

6707. Is there any advantage in keeping up two bodies to manage £30?—I do not know. At the present time the committee are not satisfied.

6708. If they had a body selected by themselves to receive the money from the Commissioners of Charitable Donations and Bequests with power to spend it themselves would that satisfy them?—Yes.

Rev. *Alexander Miller*, Rector of Annahilt, sworn and examined.

Rev. A. Miller.

6709. Professor Dougherty.—When were you appointed Rector of Annahilt?—In October, 1878, as successor to the Rev. John Gordon.

6710. Did you, in succeeding him, become one of the local administrators of this endowment?—No, not as a local administrator.

6711. You did not hold the office of administrator until after Mr. Greer's death?—No.

6712. Was he, up to his death, the sole administrator?—He was.

6713. After his death you and Mr. Moorhead were appointed?—Yes.

6714. Have you the letter of appointment?—I have, but I have not got it with me.

6715. Do you remember the terms of it?—Well, it was in very few words—a printed form with a seal attached to it.

6716. You can send it to us?—Yes, I can look it up.

6717. Had there been parish meetings or anything of that kind at that time?—Not that I am aware of.

6718. Was there no previous communication with the Commissioners on the subject?—There may have been. I do not know how it came that I was appointed, further than that I was in conversation with the secretary of the Charitable Commissioners, and I told him that the people of the parish were very much dissatisfied as to how the funds were administered. He asked me would I work with Mr. Greer, and I said I would not. That was in the office of the Commissioners. Again he asked me on the street, and I said "I will not, simply for the way in which the funds are administered." Said he, "You know, Mr. Millar, you will have to prove this," and I said, "No, for the people who raised this may not come forward."

6719. What was the complaint?—That the money was not accounted for.

6720. Did not the Commissioners ask Mr. Greer to account for the money they had given him?—They did not.

6721. And do you mean to convey that he never accounted for it?—Yes.

6722. Was there an allegation that the money given was not spent upon the school?—Yes, it was reported currently, and I said that to the Commissioners in their office, and told them that they would have to investigate the matter, but that I could not bring anyone forward to substantiate the charge. Their reply was, "We have not power to do that: we would have to apply to the Government for greater power than we have in order to do that."

6723. Do you think there is greater satisfaction now than there was?—There is no charge made now about misappropriation.

6724. Still we have evidence that the people are not pleased with the management of the endowment?—They have applied to me to give money for the payment of the rent of the place and repairs, and I consider that "Jameson's Charity" was for the free education of children. Accordingly I did not feel justified in giving money for any other purpose.

6725. Was not the payment of the rent part of the proper expenditure?—That question may be looked upon in different ways.

6726. But surely the maintenance of the fabric in which the children are taught was a proper payment?—I thought that while there were children not receiving education, the money might go to educate them.

6727. No matter what became of the children who were being educated here? Did you render an account to anybody for the money you spent?—No.

6728. So you did very much what Mr. Greer was in the habit of doing?—No; I lodged the money in bank to the credit of the charity, and it cannot be drawn except by myself and my co-administrator, Mr. Moorhead, who has the bank-book, and who is not here today.

6729. Mr. Moorhead is a Presbyterian Minister?—Yes, but I think that Mr. Greer could never be considered the Presbyterian Minister of this parish.

6730. Is not this Annahilt?—Yes, but his residence and place of worship are not in this parish.

6731. Dr. Traill.—In the will which was made in the year 1787, and proved 1797, the person mentioned is "The Minister of the Congregation of Protestant Dissenters"; probably that was Mr. Greer's predecessor. The will was proved in 1819?—Mentioned by name his predecessor was the Rev. Dr. Wright.

6732. Rev. Dr. Molloy.—How much money do you receive each year from the endowment?—About £33.

6733. How do you spend that?—We spend it in paying the salaries of the schoolmaster and schoolmistress.

6734. What salaries do you pay?—The schoolmaster could tell that. It is paid quarterly to them.

6735. Is the whole of the £33 spent on the salaries of the schoolmaster and schoolmistress?—No, their salaries do not amount to that.

6736. Can you send us your accounts?—Mr. Moorhead has the cheque-book.

6737. Dr. Traill.—And is there a balance accumulating in the bank?—There is; I cannot tell how much.

6738. Why is Mr. Moorhead not here today?—I cannot say; from his letter I think he intended to be here today.

6739. Professor Dougherty.—You stated your objection to giving anything for repairs was that you wish to provide free education for children who are not receiving it at present. Can free education be helped by this accumulating balance at the bank?—No, unless it is spent on the free education of the children in other schools. Might I suggest that as this school is used for political purposes that those people who attend such meetings might contribute.

6740. Dr. Traill.—Is the school vested in you?—No.

6741. Rev. Dr. Molloy.—You get £33 a year, and you have an unknown amount in bank. We want to find out how much money there is, and turn it to account for the people of Annahilt?—That is all right.

6742. How can we get information as to the state of your funds. Can you send us the accounts up to Dublin?—We can send up a memorandum of what has been spent.

6743. What is the rent of the school premises.

Mr. Allen.—About three shillings a year.

6744. Professor Dougherty.—Has there been any proposal to apply part of this endowment to any other school in Annahilt?

Witness.—No.

6745. No application has been made to the Commissioners?—Not that I know of.

6746. Rev. Dr. Molloy.—Do you say, on the part of the administrators, that they have no objection that the funds should be administered here by a local body, and that the same body should administer the funds and the school?—I can only speak for myself; I would be inclined to hand the whole thing over to them. The parishioners would vote against them.

6747. It is a waste of power to have two bodies; should you have any objection to having one compact body which would receive the money from the Commissioners in Dublin, and would spend it for the benefit of education in Annahilt?—I would have no objection, but I would not consider it necessary to remain on the Board.

6748. Dr. Traill.—The Rector of the parish is mentioned in the will?—Yes.

6749. Was Jameson a Presbyterian?

Mr. Gillespie.—He was; he was a far out relative of mine; of course I can only know by my forefathers.

6750. Dr. Traill (to Witness).—What are the relative numbers in the parish; how would you propose that the bodies of families should be represented if we were making a new governing body; what proportion of the children are Presbyterians or Episcopalians or Methodists?

Mr. *Gillespie*.—The schoolmaster could give you an idea as to how many Presbyterian children are here. It is a Presbyterian parish almost entirely.

6751. (*To Witness*).—Have you a separate church school?—No.

6752. And your own children come here?—A few of them come here, and a few of them go to other parishes.

6753. Professor Dougherty.—Is there anything you would wish to add to your evidence?—The money was given for the free education of children in the parish, but children outside the parish are getting the benefit of it. Is that right? May not the parents of those who get the benefit of it outside the parish contribute something to the repairs of the school or pay the rent. That is not an unreasonable proposition, I think.

6754. Dr. Traill.—Are there children coming here whose parents would be able to pay?—I think so.

6755. The teachers you have here get this endowment, in addition to their salary from the National Board?—Yes.

6756. Professor Dougherty.—We should feel obliged for a copy of your bank account, showing what amount you have received, what your payments have been, and what is the balance at the present moment?—We would have to write to the bank for that. I can send you the document from the Commissioners appointing myself and Mr. Moorhead as administrators.

Rev. Dr. Molloy.—Let us know the sum of money you have received each year for the last three years, the money you spent during that time, and the money now lodged in bank.

Rev. *James Mitchell*, Presbyterian Minister, Annahilt, sworn and examined.

6757. Professor Dougherty.—You are successor of the late Mr. Greer?—Yes; I became minister of Annahilt about a year after his death.

6758. And before your appointment, Mr. Moorhead had been appointed as local administrator of this endowment?—Yes.

6759. Are you well acquainted with the views of the people of Annahilt?—Yes.

6760. Is the evidence we have received today as to their dissatisfaction with the present state of affairs well founded?—There is no doubt of that; the people are very much dissatisfied; they have no power over the financial part of the endowment. They have sought in their accounts frequently to the present administrators for maps and such things, and they emphatically refuse to pay for maps for the school.

6761. What is the ground for their refusal?—Mr. Miller has already expressed it; he says he does not consider that any of these funds were allowed for repairs, or anything else, simply for the teachers.

6762. Do you think it unreasonable that well-to-do people deriving benefit from this school should contribute to some extent to the maintenance of the school fabric, and to what we might call the plant of the school?—We are simply wishing to have the will adhered to; we would have no objection in asking the children to pay fees.

6763. What you claim is that the people of Annahilt should have the power which the testator evidently intended?—Nothing more. In the will of Thomas Jameson I find these persons mentioned in connexion with the endowment, viz., the rector, the minister of the congregation of Protestant Dissenters, and the majority of an assembly of the heads of families. I say that I am "the minister of the congregation of Protestant Dissenters" at Annahilt.

6764. Do you know Mr. Moorhead?—Yes; he is minister of the Seceders Congregation at Loughaghery.

6765. And yours is a congregation belonging to the old Synod of Ulster?—Yes; and we have a bequest of £100 from the same Thomas Jameson. The will states:—

"I give and bequeath to the poor of the parish of Annahilt one hundred pounds, to be put out to interest by the minister, and elders, and heads of families of the congregation of Protestant Dissenters."

The terms as to the congregation are exactly the same in connexion with the two trusts, and after litigation was gone into the congregation of Annahilt maintained their rights.

6766. With whom was the litigation?—With, I think, Mr. Moorhead's father.

6767. Does he not belong to the Presbyterian Church?—Yes.

6768. What is the meaning of the word "Dissenters" here?—Well, I could hardly say. We are all now members of the General Assembly; Mr. Moorhead is now a member of the Assembly.

6769. You complain that the Presbyterian minister is deprived of his position, and that Mr. Moorhead is not the proper minister for the office?—What I wished to do was to bring out the fact that my congregation is the oldest in the neighbourhood. We have no other Presbyterian congregation called Annahilt.

6770. And this was the one referred to by Jameson?—Yes.

6771. You established your right to the £100 left to the "congregation of Protestant Dissenters" at Annahilt, by Thomas Jameson?—Yes. My predecessor, Mr. Greer, was administrator of the school fund.

6772. How long was he administrator?—There was never any person but himself and the rector as administrators.

6773. Dr. Traill.—There were four names sent up—Rev. John F. Gordon, Rector of Annahilt, Rev. Thomas Greer, Rev. Robert Moorhead, and Rev. R. S. Irwin?—Mr. Gordon and Mr. Greer were appointed.

Rev. Mr. Miller.—I think Mr. Gordon and Mr. Greer did not act.

Mr. Gillespie.—Oh, they did act, but they did not act long.

6774. (To Rev. Mr. Miller).—You were only elected along with Mr. Moorhead?—Yes.

6775. Rev. Dr. Molloy (to Witness).—What you claim is that besides being a member of the committee you also should be administrator?—Yes.

6776. Do you make that claim under the will?—Yes.

6777. The will states that the school is to be conducted—

"Upon such a plan and subject to such regulations as the rector, the minister of the congregation of Protestant Dissenters, and the majority at an assembly of the heads of families of said parish, shall adopt for the good and prosperity of said institution."

That body is the committee?—Quite so.

6778. The will does not give you a right to be appointed administrator?—It is strange that the rector of the parish and another gentleman were appointed. I thought they always tried to act in accordance with the will.

6779. But the will does not mention an administrator at all. Do you see any advantage in having administrators to manage the funds, and a committee to manage the school, or do you not think it would be better to have one body only?—We would wish the one body as it has been in the past.

6780. The only time you had one body was when Mr. Greer had matters in his own hand?—Before that.

6781. Should you be satisfied with one corporate body that would have the right to receive the money from [illegible] Commissioners and spend it for the benefit of education here?—Certainly.

[illegible]. Professor DOUGHERTY.—How would you propose to form it?—The congregations have been talking [illegible], and I have been trying to preserve our rights [illegible] congregation, but I think we would be satisfied if all the ministers of the various congregations in the parish and the rector of the parish were considered as administrators, and met here at the quarterly meetings of the committee, and, in conjunction with the committee, dispensed the money.

[illegible]. Could you not get rid of the administrators altogether, and have one body to receive and administer the money?—Certainly.

[illegible]. What is your opinion as to how that local body should be formed?—I would put the three Presbyterian ministers and the rector on it.

Rev. Mr. Miller.—There is a Covenanting body also at Ballie's Mill.

Witness.—Oh, yes; I believe there is.

[illegible]. Rev. Dr. MOLLOY.—That would be five clergymen?

Witness.—Yes.

Mr. Gillespie.—At present, on the committee, there are the representatives of eleven townlands—two out of each.

Witness.—The time might come when we would require to raise money through the country for the schools.

[illegible]. Professor DOUGHERTY.—Would you be prepared to allow the subscribers to elect a certain number on the managing committee?

Dr. TRAILL.—I suppose there would be few subscribers when there is an endowment?—I would have no objection on the matter.

Mr. Gillespie.—I don't think very many.

[illegible]. Rev. Dr. MOLLOY.—The bodies we usually appoint are from seven to eleven in number. Now, if you had five clergymen, and six representatives from the heads of families elected to act with them, you would have a body of eleven. Would not that be quite large enough?

Mr. Gillespie.—Quite large enough.

[illegible]. Dr. TRAILL.—That will comprise only two clergymen. What do you think of a body with only two clergymen on it? How many laymen are on it?

Mr. Gillespie.—Twenty-two—two out of every townland.

67[illegible]. Rev. Dr. MOLLOY.—The reason they did not attend is because there are so many. The Commissioners of Charitable Donations and Bequests now give the whole of the money to Mr. Moorhead and Mr. Miller, and therefore you must have Mr. Moorhead, Mr. Miller, and also Mr. Mitchell.

Professor DOUGHERTY.—And there is Mr. Wilson here.

67[illegible]. Rev. Dr. MOLLOY.—If the heads of families had six lay representatives on the board, with power to administer the funds, which they never yet have had, do you think it would be unreasonable to have five clergymen on the board?

Witness.—I would not say that any reasonable objection could be made to the arrangement.

6791. Professor DOUGHERTY.—Is the educational work done by the school satisfactory?

Witness.—Very satisfactory.

67[illegible]. What is the feeling as to having this free; is such education appreciated as much as if it was paid for?—Nothing is so highly appreciated as what is paid for. The attendance is good, and our master has sent several students to the University with high honours.

67[illegible]. Rev. Dr. MOLLOY.—I should consider the attendance small for the average on the roll; what is the percentage?

Dr. FLEMING, J.P.—This is the time of the hay harvest, and we have had a little disease.

6794. I looked over your list last night, and I found that the attendance was lower than what we find in schools of this class; when I came in here to-day I thought it was the same, and I wanted to give you an opportunity of explaining that. The number is not very large compared with the numbers on the roll?—These later years the children have been imposed upon.

67[illegible]. Dr. TRAILL.—What do you mean by the children being imposed upon?

Witness.—They are out weeding and engaged at other work that children can do.

Mr. Gillespie.—The labourers went away, and the children were called upon to do their work.

Andrew Clements, Head Master, sworn and examined.

[illegible]. Professor DOUGHERTY.—How long have you been master here?—For twenty-one years.

[illegible]. Who appointed you?—The committee.

[illegible]. Is there any record of your appointment?—Yes, it is recorded in the minute book.

[illegible]. I think at the time of your appointment the money was not in the hands of the Commissioners?—No, it was in the Downshire office.

[illegible]. And how was the money paid?—Always through the Treasurer of the committee.

[illegible]. And the repairs were paid for?—Yes.

[illegible]. Were you trained?—Yes, in Marlborough Street.

[illegible]. What class did you hold when appointed?—Third Division of First.

[illegible]. What class do you hold now?—First of First.

[illegible]. I think you are also a graduate of the Royal University?—Yes, B.A. and LL.B.

[illegible]. Practically, the children of the parish are educated in this school?—The great bulk of them are.

[illegible]. And the majority are farmers' children?—Yes.

[illegible]. The education is entirely free?—Yes, we receive nothing in the way of school-pence from them.

[illegible]. What endowment do you receive?—£[illegible] a year, paid quarterly.

6810. What do you receive from the National Board?—£[illegible] a year and results fees.

6811. What have your results fees been on the average?—About £[illegible] on the average; it varies from £[illegible] to £[illegible].

6812. You have conducted classes in connection with South Kensington?—Yes.

6813. What do you receive from these classes?—About £[illegible].

6814. There is some land attached to the school?—Yes, four acres.

6815. Do you cultivate that land?—Yes.

6816. Do you live in the house connected with the school?—I occupy the house connected with the school.

6817. Rev. Dr. MOLLOY.—Does anybody ask you for rent?—No, but I was in the office lately and a clerk told me that there were three years rent due, and I thought it as well to pay the amount. It came to about [illegible] altogether.

6818. Who paid the rent before?—Mr. Greer of late years.

6819. Dr. TRAILL (reading from the minute book).—I see that on the 1[illegible]th of October, 18[illegible], there was a meeting. It was largely attended, and—

"Mr. and Mrs. Clements were elected on the understanding that they would be ready to commence duties on the first week in November; six months' notice to be given on either side—at 1st of November or 1st of May."

Then at another meeting on November 6th, 1882, it is mentioned:—

"The Rev. Thomas Given and Captain Cody, as appointed at the last meeting, attended here this day, and received possession of the school premises from Mr. Clements and handed them over to Mr. Clements, who, in conjunction with his wife, signed the following agreement:—

"'We, the newly-appointed teachers in the Annish Free Endowed National Schools, do hereby bind ourselves to give up quiet and peaceable possession of these school premises and school appliances on giving or receiving six months' notice.

Andrew Clements—Mary Clements.'"

6820. Professor Dougherty.—How many children have you on the roll?

Witness.—Ninety-four.

6821. What is the average attendance?—For the last year it was fifty-two.

6822. For the whole year?—Yes, for the year.

6823. Fifty-two out of ninety-four?—Yes, about ninety-four. It was sixty-four in the first quarter of 1882, fifty-four in the second quarter, forty-three in the third quarter, and forty-four in the last quarter. The third and fourth quarters are always bad.

6824. To what do you attribute that?—The labourers have left the neighbourhood and the children are required on the farms.

6825. Have you formed any opinion as to the effect of free education upon the attendance of the children?—I have a very strong idea that free education is useless unless there is compulsion with it.

6826. You think they do not value it?—I think free education without compulsion would be a very bad thing for Ireland.

6827. Dr. Traill.—You think they would be paying you a compliment by going?—Yes.

6828. Are the parents of many of the children able to pay if asked?—They are, but they have always had a free school here, and I would not like to be the first to introduce the payment system.

6829. Do many children come from outside the parish?—Some, and I have power to charge fees to such children, but have never done so.

6830. Is the school visited by the clergymen of the parish?—Yes.

6831. Do the local administrators come?—Yes, they visit occasionally. Mr. Miller used to be our best visitor here.

6832. Professor Dougherty.—Did he ever give religious education here?—Yes.

6833. You are a Presbyterian?—Yes.

6834. You can give us, I presume, the religious denominations of those at present on the rolls?—Yes; fifteen of the late Established Church, and seventy nine Presbyterians—ninety-four in all.

6835. You have no Methodists?—No.

6836. What subjects do you teach in your evening classes connected with the Science and Art Department?—I had nearly a dozen at one time or other, but generally mathematical subjects.

6837. What class of pupils had you?—Principally the boys of the sixth class, with a few outsiders who do not attend the day school.

6838. How many boys of the school attended the evening classes?—There were eight out of the sixth class.

6839. And what was the total number in attendance at the Science and Art classes?—Twelve.

6840. Who is the recognised manager of the school under the National Board?—Dr. Thomson.

6841. Rev. Dr. Molloy.—Were you able to read your university course while attending to the school here?—Yes.

6842. In what course did you take your B.A.?—The course read was Jurisprudence, Political Economy, and Constitutional History.

6843. Dr. Traill.—How is religious instruction given in the school?—By myself. It is given from 10 to 10.30 o'clock.

6844. Is there any arrangement in existence for a minister if he came?—No, Mr. Miller was the last who came.

6845. Did the Presbyterian minister come?—No.

6846. Professor Dougherty.—What teachers have you here?—Two monitors both appointed from the 1st of July, 1882; they had passed their examination as monitors of the first year.

6847. Dr. Traill.—Do you give the entire religious education yourself?—Yes.

6848. Have you a catechism?—No, simply the Scriptures.

6849. Could not the parents of some of the pupils pay fees?—The parents have been so long accustomed to a free school, that I would not like to be the teacher who would try the experiment of charging fees. The action of the National Board in establishing new schools where they are not required has a great injurious effect on all the surrounding schools. Such a school was recognised in this neighbourhood some years ago; the new school drew its pupils from the three surrounding schools, and two of these were unable to keep up the average required for an assistant, while one of them, could hardly keep up the average required for one teacher, so that instead of two good schools with an assistant to teach needlework, &c., in each, there are now three miserable schools, in at least two of which there is a constant struggle for existence, as the average attendance is on the verge of reducing the schools to the capitation system. In such circumstances the teachers can demand no fees, and if such are paid it is only, I believe, on paper, as each school must return a certain amount of local aid in order to qualify for the second moiety of the results fees [illegible].

6850. Rev. Dr. Molloy.—You have no difficulty in keeping up your class average?—No. I may state that one time I lent £10 here and I never got it repaid.

6851. What did you lend it for?—I lent it to the committee to get them out of a difficulty. The place was all out of repairs at the time, and I understand they laid out £200.

Mr. Gillespie.—We got £200 from Lord Downshire's office. He presented £100, and the other £100 was to be paid back. This £100 that was borrowed was to be paid back in instalments of £10 a year; two instalments were paid, when we were told that if £20 were paid, it would settle the matter. When raising the £20 we got this loan.

6852. Dr. Traill.—Was it borrowed from the master.

Mr. Gillespie.—Yes.

Mr. Shaw (Secretary).—That was on November 6, 1871.

6853. Professor Dougherty. — And do you not think that if there is money the master should be paid?

Mr. Gillespie.—Oh, I think he should be paid.

6854. Dr. Traill.—Was it agreed that the £10 should be borrowed from the master?

Professor Dougherty.—The minutes say:—

"It was also arranged that Mr. Clements should lend over to the treasurer, to make up his present loan, the sum of £10 for the repayment of which the committee hereby make themselves responsible, and that he is to receive interest for the same at the rate of five per cent. The treasurer is to be requested on the receipt of the £10 from Mr. Clements, to make it a sum of £20, and hand it over to Lord Downshire's agent and get a clear receipt from him for the sums we were to pay annually in liquidation of the loan kindly made to us by the late Marquis for the repairs to these premises."

6855. Dr. Traill.—Who was Captain Cody?

Witness.—He was treasurer for the committee, but he has ceased to reside here.

Maria Harding, Teacher, sworn.

6656. Professor Dougherty.—How long have you been teacher here?—I have been teacher here since 1881. I was appointed by the committee.

6657. What is your classification as teacher?—First of First.

6658. Did you hold that position at the time of your appointment?—Yes.

6659. Were you trained?—Yes; in Marlborough-street, Dublin.

6660. And besides your class salary, how much do you receive?—£15 a year from the endowment; no fees from the pupils.

6661. How many children are on the roll?—Eighty-nine.

6662. And what is the average attendance?—Fifty-six. There was diphtheria in the district which frightened some of the children this season, but the attendance in the first two quarters of the year is generally very good. They are kept at home in the other quarters to assist their parents.

6663. Do you think the freedom from liability to pay school fees is a benefit?—I think they value it less, because they do not pay, but I would not like to introduce the payment system. If I were going away, I think the committee should enforce it. I had two monitresses up till 1st of July, when the time of one of them expired. The Inspector was not able to give me another in her place. I will therefore only have one monitress during the ensuing year.

6664. You do not live on the premises?—No.

6665. And you have no interest in the land?—None, whatever.

6666. Rev. Dr. Molloy.—How much do you get in results fees?—The amount varies from £27 to £35. When the attendance was satisfactory, the amount of course was larger.

Mr. Clements.—About £30 is the amount of my results fees.

William Thomson, Esq., M.D., J.P., Manager of the School, sworn.

6667. Dr. Traill.—When were you appointed Manager?—Shortly after the Rev. Mr. Greer died, the Rev. R. S. Irwin was appointed, and before his appointment was sanctioned he died. I was afterwards appointed.

6668. Is there any entry about that here in the minutes?—I think there is.

6669. Professor Dougherty.—Is the committee recognised by the National Board in any way?—Well, I do not know.

6670. Rev. Dr. Molloy.—Have you the appointment of the teachers?—No.

6671. In the case of a vacancy who would make the appointment?—The committee.

6672. The minutes of June 7, 1886, say:—

"Rev. R. S. Irwin, was requested to act as correspondent with the National Board [illegible] and Mr. Moorhead was directed to notify the Board of this arrangement. Mr. Moorhead was requested to notify the Board of Charitable Commissioners, that owing to the death of Rev. Thomas Greer, there was no administrator of Anderson's Charity. It was agreed that the annual meeting should be called for the first Monday in January, 1887."

There is no mention here about your appointment?—The Rev. Mr. Irwin, was appointed at the next meeting to correspond with the National Board, and shortly afterwards he died.

6673. It was part of the endowment that went to the payment for repairs?—Yes.

6674. The minutes of 21st February, 1887—that is two and a half years ago, say:—

"Dr. Thomson was requested to correspond with the National Board of Education, till the regular quarterly meeting in May next."

Was that done?—Yes. I would have like to add a word about the Rev. Thomas Greer. The treasurer's book is here, and it is correct up to a certain date. Mr. Greer's book is here, and you will see the items—what he paid to the teachers and what for repairs, up as I said to a certain date. After he was appointed administrator he transacted his business greatly by cheque, and he died so suddenly that he had not time to get the accounts made up. We had the whole thing investigated here, and the committee said that about £20 would square up the whole thing, and that has been done.

6675. Professor Dougherty.—I did not understand that Mr. Miller made any charge against Mr. Greer when he said that that gentleman did not account for the money which he received, as that is precisely the course which is adopted by the administrators now; they do not give any account at present.

6676. Rev. Dr. Molloy.—Was there a period when the treasurer was a member of the committee?—Yes. The money was then in Lord Downshire's office and the treasurer got the money and paid for the repairs which the committee had got carried out.

6677. Professor Dougherty.—And this Board of Administrators was created by the Commissioners of Charitable Donations and Bequests after the money came into their hands?

Witness.—Yes.

Rev. Mr. *Mitchell*.—There is a balance in the bank, and it is not given now either to the teachers or for the repairs of the school.

Mr. *Gillespie*.—And we have accounts yet to settle.

6678. Do you take much interest in the practical working of the school?—I do.

6679. You visit it occasionally?—I do.

6680. To what cause do you attribute the irregularity of attendance?—I attribute it to the labourers' children being kept at home.

6681. What is your opinion as to the effect of free education?—Oh, really I think it would be better they should pay unless you had compulsory education. We thought the children of Annahilt had no right to come here and receive education without paying. At a meeting we decided to charge them so much a quarter. I sent letters to the parents and I got in reply nothing but a 'no', and I then stopped the whole business.

Rev. Dr. Molloy.—It would seem desirable that those who are able should pay fees.

Professor Dougherty.—But in Annahilt there is nobody willing to do so.

6682. Dr. Traill (to Witness).—You know the difference between a vested and non-vested school?—I do.

6683. Would you wish that the school should be on the lines of a vested school, with all denominations equal?—I would not like to give an opinion.

6684. Practically there are only two ministers in Annahilt?—Yes.

6685. And you would not deny them the right to come in and instruct their children?—No.

6686. Have you made any regulations about religious instruction?—No, I have not.

6687. Professor Dougherty.—What are your ideas as to the constitution of a local governing body?—As to the Covenanting minister named, I do not know whether he is in the district or not.

6688. Do you wish to have all the ministers in the parish?—I would. Then we have ten townlands, and two from each would be twenty; that would be too large. If we could give the same number of lay and

July [illegible], 18[illegible]. Dr. Th[illegible], [illegible]

clerical members I would be satisfied, but I do not know how that would satisfy the people here.

6589. Could you not elect them at the annual meeting in this school?—Yes; I think it would be a very good thing to elect five instead of twenty.

6590. Dr. Traill.—Would you require them to be people with children?—Well, I would not care about that; I would have respectable people.

6591. Do you think Jameson intended to include the Covenanters?—I could not say.

6592. Professor Dougherty.—As the Covenanters make no claim I do not think we need go into that. (To Witness).—Would you give any privilege to subscribers?—I am quite satisfied that matter could be settled at the annual meeting in January. I am also satisfied that twenty would be rather large a body. I would include some members of the present committee in a small committee.

6593. What do you think should be the size of the committee?—About twelve altogether.

6594. Dr. Traill.—Are you satisfied with so many clergymen on it?—I am well satisfied.

6595. Professor Dougherty.—Do you think that clergymen as educated men should be at the head of the proposed body?—Yes.

Rev. Mr. Miller.—I wish to make a statement in addition to what I have already said. I consider the school is for the free education of all the children of the parish, but I found that while the Presbyterian children were taught the Presbyterian Catechism, the Church Catechism was not taught to the Church children. I requested that it should be taught, and the manager or patron refused. I wrote to the Commissioners of National Education asking could I not, as it was a free endowed school, insist on the Church children getting the same privileges as the other. What I meant by that was that they should be taught their own catechism by a teacher as the Presbyterian children were.

6596. Dr. Traill.—Or by a clergyman if he came in?

Witness.—Well, I did not say as to that.

Dr. Traill.—That is the reason why I asked about a vested school.

6597. Professor Dougherty.—I understand that the teacher is a Presbyterian; would you be satisfied with the teaching of your catechism by a teacher belonging to another church?

Witness.—I would.

6598. You never made any claim yourself to teach your own catechism in the school?—Yes, I came and taught them for a while, and I asked the mistress to teach the girls, and she told me she would if Mr. Greer allowed her, and afterwards she told me Mr. Greer would not allow her.

6599. Dr. Traill.—Have you agreed with Mr. Moorhead about this?—I applied after Mr. Greer's death, either to the master or someone else, but the matter was brought before the committee, and it was agreed that the Church Catechism might be taught. I asked that what was granted for one should be given to all. I attended here to give religious education, but when I found the catechism was not taught I became lukewarm. There is only this one room. It was filled up to a point with the ordinary scholars. The master was giving religious instruction to the Presbyterians, and I could not hear a word where I was. I then said to myself, "What is the use of my coming here as I am doing, seeing that I am doing no good."

Mr. Clements.—Mr. Miller was rather under a false impression about religious instruction. The Board issued a rule a number of years since that the two denominations could not receive religious instruction in the same room. Two catechisms could not be taught here unless one party was turned out while the other was being taught. Mr. Miller could not come now to teach the catechism.

6600. Dr. Traill.—He could do it after two o'clock.

Witness.—I thought I could do it during the time appointed for religious education.

Mr. Clements.—We have now no catechism taught. If we taught either catechism one party would have to go out.

6601. Professor Dougherty (to Witness).—What do you think of the mistress to teach the catechism?—I would rather it was taught.

Dr. Traill.—The master is perfectly competent to teach the children the Scriptures, and let them all read the Bible together; at the Sunday Schools they can be taught the catechism.

This concluded the inquiry.

APPENDIX B.

DOCUMENTS

IRISH SOCIETY'S SCHOOLS, COLERAINE.

No. 1.

MEMORIAL OF THE CLERGY AND LAITY OF THE PARISHES OF COLERAINE AND KILLOWEN.

Referred to in the Evidence of the Rev. F. O'Hara, p. [illegible].

TO THE GOVERNOR AND ASSISTANTS OF THE HONOURABLE THE IRISH SOCIETY OF LONDON.

GENTLEMEN,

After all the trouble you have taken about your two schools in this town, it is with great reluctance that we, the members of the Church of Ireland in Coleraine, again approach you on the same subject.

We only do so from the conviction that the interests of our children, as well as the peace and harmony of the community, are suffering from the present system of management by a mixed committee.

By the last census the members of the Church were more numerous than those of any other denomination living within the municipal boundary of Coleraine—the numbers being, Church of Ireland, [illegible]; Presbyterians, [illegible]; Roman Catholics, [illegible]; all others, [illegible]. Total, [illegible].

The Managing Committee and the Teaching Staff is mainly Presbyterian, and the majority of the children attending are of the same persuasion. The number of Church children, who are mostly of the poorer class, is yearly getting less, especially in the boys' school.

The Managing Committee has not for many years past worked smoothly, and many disputes have continually been arising in it. In proof of this we refer to the records of the Society, the experience of your general agent, and the recollections of such members of the court as visited Coleraine in 18[illegible].

We have no hope that under the new constitution of the committee this state of things will improve. In confirmation of which we may state that the Commissioners of Irish National Education absolutely refuse to recognise the existence of any such committee, and that we are not aware of any other case in Ireland where such a system of primary school management exists.

We, therefore, respectfully but earnestly beg of you to remove the evils we complain of by the following measures:—

1. By dispensing with the services of the present committee.

2. By allocating [illegible] per cent. of the total sum now granted by your honourable court for the support of primary education in Coleraine to the maintenance of Church of Ireland National Schools in the borough under the management of the local clergy. That being the proportion which our numbers bear to the entire population.

3. By granting for the use of such Church children one of your three schoolrooms in Beresford place.

4. By extending similar privileges to the members of other religious denominations.

Should you be pleased to comply with our request we will undertake:—

1. To conduct the schools according to the rules of the Irish National Board of Education.

2. To keep the fabrics of such schools in repair.

3. To offer a *free education* to every Coleraine child attending, unless otherwise ordered, with the approval of your court.

4. To furnish yearly to the court an account of the expenditure of all sums received from you, and also the report of the Inspector showing the work and progress of the schools.

5. To present the children for inspection, if desired, at the annual visit of the Society to Coleraine.

The practical effect of these changes, if adopted, will be—(1) that, as in most towns in Ireland, all religious denominations in Coleraine will be on exactly the same footing as regards educational advantages, (2) where the discord arising from the present mixed committee will cease, a healthy rivalry will exist between the different schools, and (3) to the Honourable Irish Society will be due the credit of providing for every poor child in Coleraine the advantages of a free education—a fact which we shall be proud and happy to acknowledge by describing every school, assisted as above-mentioned, as one of the "Irish Society of London's Free Schools." Other minor points which may arise in connection with the above changes are, we believe, easily capable of satisfactory arrangement.

THE RAINEY SCHOOL, MAGHERAFELT, AND THE PROPOSED EDUCATIONAL ENDOWMENT OF THE SALTERS COMPANY.

CORRESPONDENCE AND DOCUMENTS.

See Evid., pp. [illegible] et seq.

No. II. (a).

MEMORIAL OF THE ROMAN CATHOLICS OF MAGHERAFELT TO THE COMMISSIONERS.

Magherafelt,
December 18, 1887.

GENTLEMEN,—Some time ago your Commission sat in Coleraine, and took evidence concerning the Rainey School Foundation, Magherafelt. You will remember that you were there informed that the Foundation, as at present existing, consists in part of a bequest of a H. Rainey of lands and houses, and in part of a grant by the Worshipful Company of Salters, London.

Then, as you remember, from the will or charter of H. Rainey, the bequest did not specify its use to any religious denomination. You were also informed that the said bequest of H. Rainey was improved and liberally increased by the said Worshipful Company of Salters, by the erection of new schools and a dwelling for the head master, and also that they increased the annual amount of the Foundation, and that they did not set the interest apart for any religious denomination, and paid their scholarship to the people irrespective of creed or class. Briefly then, you see Rainey's Foundation consisted of school and houses from lands of H. Rainey; and now consists of new schools and master's house with an income from the Worshipful Company of Salters, made up in part by themselves and in part from the proceeds of the bequest of H. Rainey.

Now, in these foundations there is nothing to show that any particular class or creed was to be excluded from them. Nay, as stated already, they all shared in them, and although the Established Church came into the management of it, by an Act of the Irish Parliament, yet this did not convey any special right to the exclusion of others.

Now, most of the chief religious denominations have not been satisfied with the school as already existing. You may remember the evidence given by the Presbyterians showing how it did not satisfy them (see evidence given by Rev. A. Montgomery and J. Glover, Esq., Solicitor). The Roman Catholics, as could then be stated in evidence and as can still be testified, had and have still greater reasons for not approving of it as at present existing.

They have no share in its management, and the course of instruction given do not meet the wants of their children, nor satisfactorily prepare them for the pursuits in which in after-life these children are to be engaged. The results of the Intermediate Examinations bear this out.

We, the Roman Catholics, consider and advise that a division of the Foundations and Endowments would be the most satisfactory to the various religious denominations.

OUR PROPOSAL.

Our proposal consists of two alternative schemes, each based on the division of the Foundations and Endowments, one for girls, the other for boys.

Scheme A (for girls' school).—We assume here that the Foundations and Endowments as at present existing are divisible to girls' as well as boys' schools; for although the original Foundation may be said to primarily regard boys, yet as increased by the Worshipful Company of Salters it is not so hampered. Yes, we think it would be carrying out the Company's intentions more perfectly, because it would be extending the blessings of education to all classes of the community.

The Roman Catholics will carry on the work of education of girls by devoting the grant made to the maintenance in part—(a) of a poor or primary school, and (b) of a high-class school. The poor primary school will be erected at a cost of about £300; and the high-class school will be held at the Manor House, lately purchased for that purpose at a cost of about £3,[illegible]. Both will be conducted by an efficient and highly-accomplished body of teachers. The fact that there is no high-class school for girls in County Derry, except in Coleraine, leads us to believe that, with the railway facilities to Magherafelt, our proposed Scheme would prove highly beneficial to the surrounding districts as well as to Magherafelt. Of course it is needless to state that these schools, so far as secular instruction is concerned, will be open to all creeds and classes. We think the poor schools would secure an average attendance of over 100; and the high-class school between thirty and fifty.

Scheme B (for boys' school).—We are about building a new boys' school, and could, if grant were obtained, build there to suit both poor and high-class school. The poor or National school could be conducted by our Brothers [illegible] assisted by two monitors, and the high school by a special professor assisted by a[illegible] first-class teacher.

We would prefer the adoption of the Scheme for girls' school as it is the more necessary and useful under the circumstances, and would, we think, find favour with the Company, and be in keeping with their intentions.

Mode of Division.—There are in the locality three leading religious denominations:—Protestant, Presbyterian, and Roman Catholic. According to the Census of 1881 there were on the Salters' estate:—

Protestants, ...	[illegible]
Presbyterians, ...	[illegible]
Roman Catholics, ...	[illegible]

Now, inasmuch as the substantial portion of the Endowments has been made by the Salters' Company, we think that a division based on the proportion of population would be equitable. Then a value could be set upon the premises, and the denomination or denominations not occupying them should receive suitable compensation; or suppose any two denominations combine to form a Board to carry out their joint views, let these remain in possession of the premises and the third receive an increased endowment by way of compensation, which compensation, we would suggest, could be made at the rate of three or four per cent. on their estimated interest in the premises.

In conclusion we may state that it is possible—nay, highly probable, that the Protestants and Presbyterians will unite to form a joint Scheme, in which case the Catholics would be satisfied to receive their due proportion of the Foundations and Endowments to be employed in carrying out whichever of the above-mentioned Schemes may meet with your approval.

(Signed),

PATRICK CANON DONNELLY,
Chairman, P.P.

JOSEPH J. QUINN, } *Hon. Secs.*
JOHN DONAGHY, }

No. II. (b).

The Commissioners to Very Rev. Canon Donnelly, Magherafelt.

December 22, 1887.

Rev. Sir,—I am directed by the Commission, in reply to your Memorial, dated the 16th instant, to state that the matters therein stated will receive full consideration in the preparation of the Draft Scheme for the future government of the Endowments therein referred to, so far as the provision of the Educational Endowments Act requiring the Commissioners to have regard to the spirit of the founder's intentions will admit; and that on the publication of the Draft Scheme all parties interested, including the Memorialists will have a period of two months during which they may put forward objections or suggest amendments, after which the Commissioners can, if necessary, hold a further public inquiry on the subject. A copy of the Draft Scheme, whenever published, will be sent to the Chairman and Honorary Secretaries of the Memorialists.

(Signed), Wm. Edward Ellis,
Secretary.

No. II. (c).

Messrs. Maxwell and Son to the Commissioners.

16, Stephen's-green, North, Dublin,
24th February, 1888.

Dear Sir,—I enclose herein copies of letters received by me from the Secretary of the Salters' Company. . . . Perhaps the Commissioners would allow you to inform me when the Draft Scheme is prepared. The letters enclosed appear to render some immediate step necessary to secure the supplementary endowments proposed to be given by the Salters' Company and the School Buildings for the benefit of the Charity.

(Signed), John Maxwell.

Letters referred to by Messrs. Maxwell.

No. II. (d).

The Salters Company to Messrs. Maxwell and Son, Solicitors to the Representative Church Body.

14th February, 1888.

Gentlemen,—I have submitted to the Court of Assistants of the Salters' Company your letter of the 25th January, 1888, and I am directed to inform you that they have resolved that, under all the circumstances referred to by you, they will advance the salaries of the Head and Second Masters of the School for the quarters to Christmas, 1887, and Lady Day, 1888, upon condition that the rentcharges due 1st November, 1887, which you state are in course of collection are transmitted to the Company without deduction. But I am at the same time to intimate to you that these advances by the Company on behalf of the Charity will be final.

The Company wish me to point out to you that the Educational Endowments (Ireland) Commissioners have been for several months in possession of the Company's proposal for the future endowment of the school apart from the income derived from the rentcharges, and I am directed to inform you that the proposal referred to has recently been again under the Company's consideration and that they have confirmed their decision, except that in the interests of the Charity as well as of the town of Magherafelt they propose to cast the property in the town, subject to an annual rentcharge of £100 in favour of the new Governing Body of the School; this proposal is conditional on the creation of a Local Board under the Towns Improvement Acts, which the Company are desirous to promote.

(Signed), Edwd. Lawford Scott,
Clerk, Salters' Company.

No. II. (e).

The Salters Company to Messrs. Maxwell and Son.

18th February, 1888.

Dear Sirs,—I beg to acknowledge receipt of your letter, dated 17th inst., with enclosure, which I will lay before the Court of Assistants of the Salters' Company in due course. In the meantime allow me to remind you that the rentcharge proposed to be created in favour of the school upon certain property in Magherafelt is contingent upon the consent of the inhabitants of that town to be incorporated. See my letter to you dated 14th inst.

(Signed), Edwd. Lawford Scott, Clerk.

No. II. (f).

The Salters Company to Messrs. Matthews and Son.

25th February, 1886.

Gentlemen,—I am in receipt of your letter of the 24th inst., and I have to point out that you are under a misapprehension regarding the meaning of my communication of the 14th inst. on the above subject.

It is the intention of the Salters' Company to adhere to the original promise of supplementing the existing endowment of the Charity to the same extent and on conditions set forth in my letter to Sir Henry Cartwright, dated 6th March, 1857, so long as the Town of Magherafelt remains unincorporated (under the Town Improvement Acts). But as soon as the town is incorporated it is their intention that the endowment shall constitute a fixed charge on the annual rental of the gardens, flax stores, grain stores, &c., which property will in that contingency be presented by the Company to the town.

(Signed), Edwd. Lewis Scott,
Clerk of Salters' Company.

No. II. (g).

Messrs. Matthews to the Commissioners.

15, Stephen's-green, North,
Dublin, 24th June, 1886.

Re Rainey's Charity.

Sir,—We beg to enclose herewith copy of a letter received by the Reverend T. Jordan, D.D., from the Clerk of the Salters' Company, from which you will see that the Salters' Company decline to make any further advance for the support of the School pending the preparation of a draft scheme for the future government of the Rainey School Endowment.

We beg to refer you to the letter from the Clerk of the Salters' Company to H. E. Cartwright with reference to a proposed additional endowment for these Schools, which is printed, page 312, Appendix B, to the Report of your Commissioners for the year 1886–7. The proposal contained in this letter has been somewhat modified by the Salters' Company. They propose to dedicate the premises and property mentioned in that letter for the benefit of the Rainey Schools until Town Commissioners are appointed for Magherafelt under the Towns Improvements (Ireland) Acts. When or if such Commissioners are appointed, the property in question is to vest in such Commissioners subject to a yearly rent-charge of £150 to be applied as an additional endowment for the Rainey Schools.

We have been in communication with the Solicitors of the Salters' Company with a view to having the proposed endowment put into such a condition that it will come within the operation of the Educational Endowments (Ireland) Act, 1885. We have in accordance with their instructions prepared a draft deed of declaration of trust with respect to the property proposed to be given by the Salters' Company as an additional endowment for Rainey Charity. By this deed the Salters' Company will declare that they hold the property in trust for the School until Town Commissioners are appointed for Magherafelt, and when such Commissioners are appointed, in trust to vest same in such Commissioners subject to a perpetual yearly rentcharge of £150, such rentcharge to be applied as an additional endowment for the School. This deed will enable the Commissioners to deal with the additional endowment in any scheme they may frame as it will dedicate the endowment for the benefit of the Charity. We enclose a copy of the draft.

We feel greatly obliged if you will bring the matter before the Commissioners with a view to having a draft scheme prepared for this Charity with the least possible delay.

(Signed), Matthews & Son.

No. II. (h).

The Commissioners to the Salters Company.

9, Kildare-street, Dublin,
July 14, 1889.

Sir,—The Commissioners propose to publish the Draft Scheme for the future government and management of Rainey School, Magherafelt, on the 15th prox., and intend to propose the appointment of either three or four Governors to represent the endowment derived from the Salters Company. They are anxious that, in the first instance, these Governors should be named by the Company with due regard to the wish of the Company to prevent the exclusion of pupils of any denomination.

It would be desirable to avoid giving any preponderance to members of the late Established Church over the members of the Presbyterian Church in Ireland in connexion with the General Assembly or vice versa, representation of these denominations being provided for by Governors whom it is proposed to appoint to represent the original Rainey's endowment.

Under these circumstances I am to request that your Company will be good enough—if possible not later than this day fortnight—to let me have the names of three or four suitable Governors whose names may be inserted in the scheme and who will represent other religious denominations than those which I have mentioned or will include an equal number of members of each of these denominations.

(Signed), Wm. Edward Ellis,
Secretary.

No. II. (j).

THE SALTERS COMPANY to the COMMISSIONERS.

London, E.C., 24th July, 1888.

SIR,—I have submitted to the Salters' Company your letter of the 13th instant, in which you invite the Company to nominate three or four Governors to represent the supplementary endowment which the Companies at present remaining interested in the Manor of Sal in the above county have decided to grant from their corporate estate in Ireland for the benefit of the above school, and I am directed to inform you that the Company, while appreciating the wish of the Commissioners that these Governors should in the first instance be named by them, respectfully decline the offer as they prefer to leave the nomination entirely in the hands of the Commissioners.

(Signed), EDWD. LAWRENCE SCOTT,
Clerk of the Salters' Company.

No. II. (k).

THE COMMISSIONERS to the SALTERS COMPANY.

24, Nassau-street, Dublin,
13th August, 1888.

SIR,—I am directed to transmit herewith copy of the Draft Scheme published by the Commissioners for the above-named endowment, and to say that, as the proposals of the Salters Company were not sufficiently definite, with respect to the endowment which they offered, to enable the Commissioners to frame a scheme for its administration which would make it available for all denominations, they thought it better to confine the scheme to Rainey's endowment, leaving the administration of any property which the Company may hereafter devote to the purposes of the school, to be settled by the Company.

(Signed), N. D. MURPHY, JUN.,
Assist. Secretary.

No. II. (l).

DRAFT SCHEME PUBLISHED BY THE COMMISSIONERS FOR RAINEY'S SCHOOL.

Note.—The additions and amendments proposed by the Salters Company are given in *italics*, and the parts of the original scheme proposed by the Salters Company to be struck out appear in special type.

No. 48. *County of* LONDONDERRY.

EDUCATIONAL ENDOWMENTS (IRELAND) COMMISSION.

DRAFT SCHEME, under the Educational Endowments (Ireland) Act, 1885, for the future government and management of the Educational Endowments of and belonging to "RAINEY'S SCHOOL, MAGHERAFELT," in the County of Londonderry.

WHEREAS Hugh Rainey, of Magherafelt, in the County of Londonderry, by his Will dated April 11, 1707, gave, devised, and bequeathed to his executors therein named all his worldly concerns, upon trust, to lay out the same upon the purchase of a freehold estate of the value of £400 per annum, of which estate he left the one moiety to certain of his kindred, in the manner and subject to the conditions and upon the limitations in the said Will mentioned; and the other half or moiety of the same estate he devoted and set apart for pious uses, for ever, as follows:—He directed that a suitable Schoolhouse should be prepared in the town of Magherafelt, as in the said Will specified, and he ordered that his executors should put into the house, in the month of November, in the year 1712, and in each succeeding year, eight boys, sons of persons who were of good repute, and reduced to poverty, and that the boys so admitted should be clothed and fed in the house appointed for that purpose for three years, and that in the month of November, in the year 1715, and in each succeeding year, eight of the said boys should each be bound to such trade or occupation as should be judged most fit for his genius; and should be given a suit of new clothes, and for an apprentice fee fifty shillings in money, and should be put into a family of good repute; eight boys so qualified to be still put out, and eight put in, by his executors, at November in every year, for ever; and further, that if the income of the one moiety of the said estate should not be a sufficient fund for the support of so many poor boys, then their number should be reduced to so many as could be decently brought up; and the said testator further directed that two old grave and good men, known Christians, such as really feared God, well qualified to read the Scriptures, sing psalms, and pray morning and evening, and who should take pains to instruct the boys, and make them also to pray apart morning and evening, should be also maintained; and that if any of such old men should be found defective, or unable to perform such duties, he should be turned, and another wrote for to the Presbytery of Ulster, who should be found very capable, and fit to be an instructor of youth; and the said testator further directed that an allowance should be made to the old men aforesaid for clothes, and that they should diet with the boys, and be over them, as in the said Will provided; and the said testator also bequeathed to the poor of the Parish of Magherafelt the sum of five pounds yearly; and to the Presbyterian Minister that should have the oversight of Magherafelt, the sum of five pounds yearly; and for the encouragement of a schoolmaster to teach the poor orphans, or such as should not be able to pay, the sum of five pounds yearly; and further, that if it should happen that either the old men or boys did not behave as above expected, then it should be in the power of his executors, or such as were only life renters of his estate, to turn them out, and put in such as should be deserving; and the testator recommended that his executors should take proceedings for confirming his Will by a short Act of Parliament, in order that it might be put out of the power of any that should be interested with his property to misapply the same:

And whereas the said Hugh Rainey died shortly after the date of his said Will, and probate thereof was on May 19, 1708, granted to Thomas Ash and John Rainey, the executors therein named:

And whereas in or about the year 1718, in execution of the trusts of the said Will, a Schoolhouse was built, and a School was founded and established, at Magherafelt, upon certain lands, part of the estate of the Worshipful Company of Salters of the City of London; and a farm of land containing twelve acres or thereabouts was acquired for the purposes of the said School, which farm was held at a rent from year to year under the said Company:

And whereas the executors aforenamed died without fully carrying out the trusts of the said Will, and one Thomas Ash, a nephew of the testator, afterwards purchased, partly with the means of the testator and partly with borrowed money, certain freehold lands in the County of Down, of the value of £400 per annum, but subject to a mortgage to secure the sum of £2,441, borrowed as aforesaid:

And whereas by a private Act of Parliament, 11 Geo. II., cap. 2, intituled "An Act for rendering the Charity devised by the Will of Hugh Rainey, late of Magherafelt, in the County of Londonderry, Gentleman, more effectual," it was recited that one William Ash Rainey was then in possession of the said lands, and had enjoyed same; and certain provisions were made for the management and letting of the said lands; and it was enacted that, in lieu of the moiety of the estate of the testator applicable to the said Charity, the lands mentioned in the said Act and in the Schedule hereto, Part II., should stand charged with the yearly rentcharge of £173, late Irish currency equivalent to £161 10s. 9d., present currency, payable to His Grace Hugh Lord Archbishop of Armagh and Primate of all Ireland, and to his successors for ever, by two even portions on every 1st day of May and 1st day of November, for the supporting, maintaining, educating, and placing out to trades or occupations twenty-four boys, under the trusts and subject to the nomination in and by the said Will declared and provided:

And whereas, for many years after the passing of the said Act, the School founded as aforesaid was carried on and maintained, in the buildings and in connection with the farm aforesaid, by means of the said rentcharge, but the Schoolhouse was permitted to fall into decay, and became unsuitable for the reception of pupils, and the number of pupils became greatly reduced:

And whereas, in the year 1850, the said Company of Salters offered to vest a site situated in the town of Magherafelt, together with such ground and appurtenances as the Company should appropriate for the purposes of the said School, in Trustees, or otherwise legally to secure the same, for the use of the School, and at their own cost to build a new Schoolhouse, and to assist in maintaining the School therein, upon certain terms to be embodied in a Scheme to be settled and approved in Chancery, and upon the further terms that the former Schoolhouse and premises, and the said farm connected therewith, should be surrendered to the said Company:

And whereas, by an Order of the Lord Chancellor of Ireland, dated January 21, 1852, a Report of Edward Litton, Esquire, Master in Chancery, was confirmed, whereby it was, amongst other things, reported that the last male representative of the testator's executors died in the year 1847, that the estate of the testator, then worth about £4,800 per annum, was vested in different persons, subject to the said rentcharge of £161 10s. 9d. for the support of the said Charity; that the entire management of the said Charity had devolved upon the Archbishop of Armagh, who was in receipt of the said rentcharge as Trustee under the said Act, and who had committed the local oversight of the School to the Rector of Magherafelt, by whose advice the said Archbishop, by reason of none of the descendants of the said testator being in possession of the said estate, had, for many years, nominated the boys for admission to the said School; that a schoolmaster was appointed instead of the "poor old men" mentioned in the said Will; that the change in the value of money had rendered it impossible to feed, clothe, educate, and apprentice twenty-four boys out of the funds produced by the said rentcharge, and that the Charity could not, therefore, be conducted in the manner intended by the testator; that there were then only seven boys in the institution, and that the house was in a state of decay; that the existing Schoolhouse should be surrendered to the Salters' Company, and the said farm should be no longer retained, and that the foregoing offer of the said company should be accepted; and by the same Order a Scheme was confirmed, whereby it was, amongst other things, provided that the building proposed to be erected by the said Company, with such grounds and appurtenances as the said Company should appropriate for the purposes of the School, should be legally secured for the use of the School in perpetuity; that the rentcharge of £161 10s. 9d. should be applied for the use of the School, under the direction and control of the Archbishop of Armagh; that a well-qualified schoolmaster should from time to time be appointed by the Archbishop of Armagh for the time being; that the general direction and control of the School should be vested in the Archbishop of Armagh for the time being, who should have power to dismiss or discontinue the schoolmaster or other teachers; that the School should be open to day boys only; that the pupils should receive elementary education as in the said Scheme mentioned, and as the said Archbishop should from time to time direct, and should be regularly instructed in the Holy Scriptures; that instruction should be given gratis to thirty boys, fifteen of whom should be from time to time nominated by the Archbishop of Armagh for the time being, and fifteen by the Salters' Company; and that the School should be open to such boys of good conduct as might desire to attend it:

And whereas, in the year 1854, a new Schoolhouse and Teacher's residence were erected by and at the cost of the Salters' Company, upon the site described in the Schedule hereto, Part I. II., and the School was established and has since been carried on, as a School for Intermediate Education, upon the said premises, which are vested in the said Company, under the name of "Rainey's Foundation School, Magherafelt," and the said School has been maintained partly by means of the said rentcharge, and partly by means of contributions from the said Salters' Company, amounting for some years past to the annual average sum of £160 or thereabouts:

And whereas the Salters' Company, having in the year 1857 sold their estates in the neighbourhood of the said School, and having aided in making other provision for the maintenance of schools for the elementary education of pupils, male and female, of all religious denominations in and near the town of Magherafelt, and being desirous of discontinuing their contributions to the maintenance of Rainey's Foundation School, have proposed determined to make permanent provision in connection with the said School for the intermediate commercial and technical education of pupils of all religious denominations, but the said proposal has not yet been carried into effect, and for carrying out such determination they have, by a deed poll, dated 27th September, 1858, under their Common Seal, declared that they, the Salters' Company, their successors and assigns, would thenceforth stand seised and possessed of the lands, buildings, hereditaments

ments and premises specified in the first Schedule hereto, being the premises described in the Schedule hereto, Part I., but subject, as in such deed mentioned, upon trust, to apply the rents and profits thereof for the support, maintenance, and benefit of Rainey's Foundation Schools, as an Endowment therefor, in addition to the hereinbefore mentioned rentcharge, and by the same deed the Salters' Company declared that they, their successors and assigns, would thenceforth stand seised and possessed of the schoolhouse, buildings, and premises specified in the second Schedule thereto, being the premises described in the Schedule hereto, Part II., subject as therein, as therein mentioned, upon trust, for the accommodation, use, and benefit of the said schools in the same manner as theretofore, and as a perpetual Endowment:

And whereas certain accumulations of the said rentcharge of £101 10s. 9d., received by the Most Reverend Marcus Gervais, Lord Archbishop of Armagh, now deceased, were in or about the year 1844 invested by him in the purchase of the sum of £348 17s. 8d., Government New Three per Cent. Stock, which was afterwards sold, and the proceeds of the sale have since been paid by the representatives of the said Archbishop to the Most Reverend Robert Knox, D.D., now Lord Archbishop of Armagh, for the purposes of the School:

And whereas all the properties, funds, securities, and moneys now held or appropriated in trust for or applicable to the purposes of the said School, constitute Educational Endowments within the meaning of "The Educational Endowments (Ireland) Act, 1885," and the said Act applies to the same:

And whereas it has appeared to the Commissioners under the said Act, after due inquiry, that, in order to extend the usefulness of the said Endowments, provision should be made for the future government and management thereof in manner hereinafter appearing:

Therefore, from and after the date of this Scheme, being the day upon which the Lord Lieutenant shall by Order in Council declare his approbation thereof, the said Endowments shall be held, governed, managed, and applied for the purposes, with the powers, under the conditions and provisions, and in the manner hereinafter set forth, and not otherwise, any previous Act of Parliament, Letters Patent, Statute, Charter, Scheme, Will, Deed, Instrument, Trust, or Direction, relating to the subject-matter of this Scheme, to the contrary notwithstanding.

Preliminary.

1. For the purposes of this Scheme, unless the context otherwise requires, the following terms shall be interpreted as follows:—

Interpretation of Terms.

"The Act" shall mean the Educational Endowments (Ireland) Act, 1885.

"The Governors" shall mean the Governing Body of "Rainey's School, Magherafelt," hereby incorporated.

"The School" shall mean the educational institution heretofore existing at Magherafelt, and known as Rainey's Foundation School, and shall include any other school for the time being managed, maintained, or aided by the Governors under this Scheme.

"The Endowments" shall mean and include the lands, buildings, hereditaments, and premises mentioned in the Schedule hereto, Part I., also the site, buildings, land, and other premises occupied by the School and Teacher's residence in connection therewith, mentioned in the Schedule hereto, Part I. II., and all furniture, appliances, goods, and chattels thereunto belonging, and shall also include the rentcharge of £101 10s. 9d., mentioned in the Schedule hereto, Part II. III., and all sums due or accruing on account of the said rentcharge, and all arrears or accumulations or investments thereof, and so much of the proceeds of the abovementioned sum of £348 17s. 8d., Government Stock, as shall not have been applied to the purposes of the School, and all other property, real and personal, held or possessed or recoverable by any person or body, under the provisions or upon the trusts of the hereinbefore recited Will of Hugh Rainey, or of the hereinbefore recited Act of Parliament, or Scheme, or otherwise applicable to the purposes of the School; and all other property, real and personal, which may hereby or hereafter become or be vested in the Governors for all or any of the purposes of this Scheme.

"The General Synod" shall mean the body known as "The General Synod of the Church of Ireland," or other the supreme legislative authority for the time being of the Church formerly established by law in Ireland and in the "Irish Church Act, 1869," referred to as the Church of Ireland, hereinafter referred to as the said Church, and shall include any authority duly empowered to represent or act for the General Synod in that behalf.

"The Diocesan Council" shall mean the body known as the Diocesan Council of the Diocese in which the School shall be situated for the time being, constituted in accordance with the constitution of the said Church, and shall include any authority duly empowered to perform the functions now performed by such [illegible].

"The Select Vestry" shall mean the body known as "The Select Vestry of the Parish of Magherafelt," appointed in accordance with the constitution of the said Church, and shall include any authority duly empowered to perform the functions now performed by such Select Vestry.

"The General Assembly" shall mean the body known as "The General Assembly of the Presbyterian Church in Ireland," or other the supreme authority for the time being of the said Presbyterian Church, constituted in accordance with the laws of the said Presbyterian Church, and shall include any authority duly empowered to represent or act for the General Assembly in that behalf.

"The Presbytery" shall mean the body known as the Presbytery of Magherafelt in connection with the General Assembly, constituted in accordance with the laws of the said Presbyterian Church, and shall include any authority duly empowered to perform the functions now performed by such Presbytery.

"The Subscribers" shall mean the Subscribers to the funds of the School qualified as hereinafter provided.

"Intermediate Education" shall mean education in such subjects as are or may be included in the programme of examinations of the Intermediate Education Board for Ireland.

"Elementary Education" shall mean such education as may be given in the National Schools which are aided by grants from the Commissioners of National Education in Ireland.

"Technical Industrial and Commercial Education" shall mean and include all such theoretical and practical instruction and training as may directly tend to fit pupils for any trade, handicraft, or industrial or commercial pursuit or employment.

Governing Body.

2. From and after the date of this scheme, a Governing Body shall be formed for the future government and management of the School and of the Endowments, in manner following:—

It shall consist of four ex-officio Governors, of four Representative Governors, and of so many additional Governors as may from time to time be elected or co-opted as hereinafter provided.

The ex-officio Governors shall be the Protestant Archbishop of Armagh, the Moderator of the General Assembly, the Incumbent of the parish of Magherafelt, and the Minister, or the senior Officiating Minister if more than one, of the First Presbyterian Church at Magherafelt, in connection with the General Assembly.

The four Representative Governors shall be elected, as hereinafter provided, one by the Diocesan Council, two by the Presbytery, and one by the Select Vestry.

The Governors shall constitute a Body Corporate, by the name of "The Governors of Rainey's School, Magherafelt," with perpetual succession and a common seal, and power to acquire and hold property, real and personal, for the purposes of this Scheme.

Election of Representative Governors.

3. The Representative Governors shall, in the first instance, be such and so many of the following persons as, at the date of this Scheme, shall be able and willing to act, namely:—

Representing the Diocesan Council.

The Venerable W. E. Meade, Archdeacon of Armagh.

Representing the Presbytery.

The Reverend Alexander Minnis, Sufficient.
Andrew Brown, Esq., The Cottage, Magherafelt.

Representing the Select Vestry.

John Smyth, Rainey-street, Magherafelt.

The above-named Representative Governors shall hold office until the thirty-first day of December first happening more than twelve months after the date of this Scheme, and in the said month of December, or in the preceding month of November, and in the month of November or December in every year thereafter, the Diocesan Council and the Select Vestry, respectively, may each elect one qualified person, and the Presbytery may elect two qualified persons, to be Representative Governors for the calendar year commencing on the first day of January after the election.

If and whenever any of the said electing bodies shall fail to elect a Representative Governor within the period hereinbefore appointed, the other Governors may co-opt a qualified person to fill the vacancy, and each person so co-opted shall hold office so long as the Governor who might have been elected might have held the same. Unless and until additional Governors shall be elected or co-opted as hereinafter provided, the ex-officio Governors and Representative Governors aforesaid shall constitute the Governing Body.

Election of additional Governors.

4. If and whenever and so long as the Subscribers shall be not less than six in number, an Annual Meeting of the Subscribers shall be held at the School, upon a day to be appointed by the Governors, and the Subscribers present or represented by proxy or voting by voting papers, being not less than six in number, may elect one qualified person for every six Subscribers so present, represented or voting, to be an additional Governor representing the Subscribers, and to hold office until the next Annual Meeting. The number of additional Governors elected by the Subscribers shall not at any time exceed four in all.

Qualifications of Subscribers.

5. The following persons shall be qualified to act as Subscribers for the purposes of this Scheme:—

(a.) Persons who, at any time after the date of this Scheme, shall subscribe not less than £10, in one sum, to the funds of the School.

(b.) Persons who, at any time after the date of this Scheme, shall subscribe not less than £5, in one sum, to the funds of the School, and who shall also have paid to the School for the education therein of a pupil or pupils, sums amounting in all to not less than £10.

(c.) Past pupils of the School, who, having been educated therein for not less than three Academical years, and having attained the age of twenty-one years, shall, after the date of this Scheme, subscribe not less than £5, in one sum, to the funds of the School.

(d.) Persons who, after the date of this Scheme, shall annually subscribe not less than £1 to the funds of the School. Provided that no annual subscriber shall be qualified to act or vote as such until a period of six months shall have elapsed from the date of the payment by him of his first annual subscription.

The Governors shall prepare and keep a list of the Subscribers, and such list, certified to be correct by the Secretary or other officer appointed for the purpose by the Governors, shall be conclusive evidence that the persons named therein, and none others, are duly qualified as Subscribers; provided that such list may be corrected from time to time as occasion may require by the Chairman of any meeting of the Governors or of the Subscribers, acting under a resolution of such meeting.

6. No person shall be qualified for election as a Representative or Additional elected Governor who is not resident in the County of Londonderry or County of Antrim. Every outgoing Governor, if otherwise qualified, shall be eligible for re-election, if he shall have attended one-fourth of the meetings of the Governors held during his term of office, but not otherwise. Every vacancy among the Governors, with the cause thereof, and every appointment of a Governor shall be recorded in the minutes of the Governors.

General vacancies.

7. If at the date of this Scheme any of the above named Representative Governors shall be unable or unwilling to act, and whenever thereafter any Representative or Additional elected Governor shall die, or resign by writing under his hand, or become bankrupt, or refuse to act, or become incapable of acting, or shall cease to reside in the County of Londonderry or County of Antrim, his office shall thereupon become vacant, and the fact of such vacancy, with the cause thereof, shall be recorded in the minutes of the Governors; and, as soon as conveniently may be after the occurrence of such vacancy, the remaining Governors shall co-opt a duly qualified Governor to fill the vacancy. Every Governor so co-opted shall hold office only so long as the Governor in whose place he shall have been co-opted might have held the same.

Additional Co-opted Governors.

8. The Governors may from time to time, if they shall so think fit, co-opt one or more persons of experience in education, not exceeding three in all, to be additional co-opted Governors, and such additional co-opted Governors shall hold office for such period, and upon such conditions, as the other Governors shall from time to time determine.

Alteration of Governing Body.

9. At any time and from time to time after the date of this Scheme the General Synod and the General Assembly, respectively, may alter the constitution of the Governing Body hereby constituted, in such manner as such General Synod, or such General Assembly, shall deem expedient, so far as regards the ex-officio Governors and the Representative Governors belonging to or elected by bodies belonging to the said Church, and to the said Presbyterian Church, respectively; and may define the qualification and provide for the election, co-option, or appointment of such ex-officio and Representative Governors, and may declare and define the offices which shall

qualify such ex-officio Governors, and the body or bodies by which such Representative Governors may be elected; provided that the total number of such Governors, in each case respectively, shall not be altered, and that no existing Governor shall be removed without his own consent.

The Endowments.

10. From and after the date of this Scheme, the endowments and all rights, powers, and remedies for the recovery or collection thereof, shall, without any new conveyance or instrument, be transferred to and vested in the Governors, and shall be thenceforth held by them and their successors for ever, upon and for the trusts and purposes of this Scheme, and subject to the conditions and provisions herein contained, and to all such rents, charges, rights, easements, and liabilities as at the date of this Scheme may lawfully affect the same. From and after the date of this Scheme, all property, securities, goods, chattels, and moneys held or payable by any person or persons in trust for, or applicable to the purposes of the School, or recoverable or payable on account of the endowments, shall be delivered, transferred, and paid by the person or persons possessed thereof, or bound to pay the same, to the Governors, and the receipt of the Governors, duly executed as hereinafter provided, for any transfer, delivery, or payment hereby directed, shall be a good discharge for the person or persons making the same, and he or they shall not thenceforth be answerable for the application thereof.

11. The Governors may receive and hold donations, devises, bequests, subscriptions and other additional endowments, real or personal, and apply the same for all or any of the purposes of this Scheme. They may also receive and hold donations, devises, bequests, subscriptions, and other endowments, real or personal, and apply the same for any object connected with all or any of the purposes of this Scheme, which shall not be inconsistent with, or calculated to impede, the efficient working of the provisions hereof. Upon the occasion of any grant or donation of land by the Company of Salters, whereby any additional endowment, of the annual value of one hundred pounds or upwards, shall be obtained for the purposes of the School, the Governors with the concurrence of the said Company, may provide for the administration of the said additional endowments, and for the appointment of additional Governors representing such additional endowments, not exceeding four in all, upon such terms and in such manner as may be agreed upon, in writing, by and between the Governors and the said Company. All additional endowments so received or applied shall be included in the accounts to be kept by the Governors under this Scheme.

Trusts of Endowments.

12. From and after the date of this Scheme, and subject to the conditions and provisions herein contained, and to any special trusts or conditions lawfully affecting any part thereof, the endowments and all or any other property of or belonging to the Governors, or available for the purposes of this Scheme, shall be received and held by them upon trust to maintain, or to aid in maintaining, in or near the town of Magherafelt, a School to be called "Rainey's School, Magherafelt," in which boarders or day pupils, or both, may be received, and in which instruction shall be given in such branches of intermediate, technical, industrial, or commercial education as the Governors shall, from time to time, think best suited to the wants of the locality and the requirements of the pupils.

Application of Endowments.

13. All moneys received by the Governors under or for the purposes of this Scheme, shall, subject to the other provisions herein contained, and to any special trusts or conditions upon which any part thereof may be received, be expended and applied by them for the following purposes, or for such and so many of them as the Governors for the time being shall deem expedient:—

(a.) To maintain the school buildings, furniture, appliances, and premises in good order and condition, and to make such additions thereto and improvements therein as may be required from time to time.

(b.) To pay all rents, rates, taxes, cost of insurance, and other charges necessarily or properly payable out of or for the school premises, or the endowments, and to defray the necessary working expenses of the school, and the cost of managing the school and the endowments.

(c.) To maintain an efficient teaching staff; for this purpose the Governors may supplement the salaries and emoluments of such teachers and assistants as may be entitled to salary, fees, or emoluments from any other sources, and may employ and pay all such teachers as they may deem it expedient to employ for the instruction of the pupils attending the school, or any evening classes connected therewith, including teachers qualified to give instruction in natural and experimental science, drawing, handicraft, husbandry, and such other special subjects of intermediate, technical, industrial or commercial education as the Governors shall deem suitable or useful for any sufficient number of the pupils.

(d.) To maintain a sufficient household and domestic staff; to provide suitable board, lodging, and accommodation, for such pupils, if any, as shall be admitted to board in the school; and to provide clothing for pupils requiring such assistance.

(e.) To provide exhibitions and prizes for the most deserving pupils; such exhibitions and prizes may be awarded in such manner as the Governors may deem best calculated to benefit the pupils, and may be so given as to enable or encourage deserving and capable pupils who require such assistance, to continue their education at the school longer than they would otherwise do, or to obtain special instruction or more advanced education elsewhere.

(f.) To provide free scholarships to be granted and held upon the conditions of this Scheme.

(g.) To advance in life deserving pupils whose circumstances are such that they need assistance on leaving school. Such assistance shall, in each case, be given with due regard to the circumstances and needs of the pupil receiving the same, and may be given as or towards outfits or apprenticeship fees, or in such other mode, and subject to such conditions, as the Governors may consider most advantageous.

(h.) To defray the expenses of giving effect to the other purposes of this Scheme.

Education.—Maintenance of School.

14. Unless and until the Governors shall otherwise provide, the school shall be maintained in the buildings hitherto occupied thereby, or in such other buildings as the Governors may acquire, as hereinafter provided. The Governors may, if and when they shall so think fit, remove the school to some other convenient site or sites, or may acquire additional school premises, in or near the town of Magherafelt; any buildings and premises vacated upon any such removal shall be sold, let, or otherwise disposed of to the best advantage; provided always that no such removal shall take place, nor shall any agreement for the same, or for any letting, sale, or disposal of the existing school premises, be made or entered into by the Governors, or become binding upon them, without the previous sanction of the Commissioners of Charitable Donations

and Bequests for Ireland, and such sanction shall not be given unless and until the said Commissioners shall have satisfied themselves upon due inquiry that such removal is for the benefit of the school.

Boarders and Female Pupils.

15. Unless and until the Governors shall otherwise provide, the school shall continue to be maintained as a day school for the intermediate, technical, industrial, and commercial education of male pupils only; but if and whenever the funds at the disposal of the Governors shall suffice, and the Governors shall think fit, they may provide for the admission of boarding pupils; and they may upon such terms and subject to such conditions as they shall from time to time think expedient, admit female pupils to the school, or to any of the classes or departments thereof, or to the competition for free scholarships under this Scheme, or they may establish and maintain a separate school, or separate classes or departments, or additional free scholarships for female pupils.

Evening Schools and Classes.

16. The Governors may maintain an evening school or schools, or evening classes, for the education of pupils who are engaged during the day at trade or business, and who are desirous of carrying on their education in the evening. The course of instruction in the evening school or classes shall be arranged with special regard to the requirements of pupils obliged to maintain themselves by commercial or industrial pursuits, and, in addition to the usual subjects of Intermediate Education, may comprise instruction in Practical and Experimental Science, Drawing, Modelling, Shorthand, Book-keeping, and any other subjects of industrial, technical, or commercial education which the Governors may deem suitable or useful for any sufficient number of the pupils.

Aid from Public Sources.

17. The Governors may make all arrangements from time to time necessary to enable them to obtain for the school from the Education Board, from the Commissioners of National Education, from the Science and Art Department, from the Commissioners of Public Works, or from any other public body, such aid, by way of teachers' salaries, results fees, prizes, provision for technical or other special education, and grants or loans for building or other purposes as may at any time be available for or open to like schools, or the pupils thereof; and they may, notwithstanding anything herein contained, place any or all of their classes or pupils in connexion with or under the inspection of any such public body as aforesaid, and may comply with any rules and regulations for the time being in force respecting schools or pupils receiving such aid; all money and other aid which the Governors may so receive shall, subject to such rules and regulations, be applied by them in accordance with the provisions of this Scheme, and accounted for accordingly.

Religious Instruction.

18. The Governors may from time to time make such provision for the religious instruction of the pupils as they shall think fit, provided that no pupil attending the school shall at any time be permitted to receive or be present at any religious instruction which his or her parents or guardians shall not have sanctioned, and that the times for and mode of giving religious instruction shall be so fixed that no pupil shall be thereby in effect excluded, directly or indirectly, from any of the other advantages afforded by the school.

Free Scholarships.

19. The Governors shall establish and maintain free scholarships in the school, to be awarded from time to time by public competition, and to be held in the manner and subject to the conditions hereinafter provided.

(a.) The competition shall be by examination, to be held once in each year, and to be conducted under the directions of the Governors, at a time and in a course to be appointed and published by the Governors not less than six months previously.

(b.) The subjects of examination shall be those of elementary education only, and not below the standard of the Fourth Class, as defined by the rules and regulations of the Commissioners of National Education for the time being.

(c.) The examination shall be held at the School, and shall be conducted by an Examiner or Examiners appointed by the Governors, whose report as to the merit of the candidates shall be final.

(d.) Four free scholarships at the least shall be open for competition at each examination.

Qualifications of Candidates.

20. Every candidate admitted to compete for a free scholarship shall be qualified as follows:—

(a.) He or she shall have made one hundred attendances at the least as a pupil at an elementary school or elementary schools in or within ten miles of the town of Magherafelt, in each of the two years next preceding the examination, and shall be in circumstances to require the assistance to be obtained from free education in the School.

(b.) He or she shall be of good character and conduct, and physically and intellectually fitted to take full advantage of the education given in the School.

(c.) He or she shall, upon the day of election, be not less than eleven or more than thirteen years of age: provided that, in any case of exceptional urgency or necessity, the Governors may, by special resolution, extend either of the above limits of age by not more than one year.

(d.) All candidates shall, if required, present themselves to the Governors, and shall produce such evidence, and may be submitted to such preliminary examination, as the Governors may consider necessary to ascertain that they are qualified as aforesaid. If any question shall arise as to the qualifications of any candidate, the same shall be inquired into and determined by the Governors, whose decision shall be final.

(e.) No candidate shall be permitted to compete more than twice.

(f.) All candidates of the same sex shall be examined together, in the same course, and under the same conditions and regulations.

Every pupil to whom a free scholarship is awarded shall be entitled to free education, as a day pupil, in all subjects taught in the School until the end of the half year in which he or she shall attain the age of sixteen years; in any case of exceptional urgency or necessity, or where further education or training appears likely to prove of permanent advantage, the Governors may, by special resolution, permit any such pupil to continue to receive free education until he or she shall have attained the age of seventeen years. The Governors may deprive any pupil of a free scholarship, or may remove any pupil from the School, at any time, if he or she shall fail to make satisfactory progress, or for any other cause which they shall deem adequate, and the sufficiency of such cause shall be in the sole discretion of the Governors. The Governors may decline to award a free scholarship to any candidate who, in the opinion of the Examiner or Examiners, shall not have shown sufficient merit.

School Fees.

21. The Governors may from time to time authorise the charge of such school fees as they may think reasonable, provided that, so far as the funds at their disposal will allow, the Governors may permit the children of poor parents resident in or near the town of Magherafelt, to receive education in the School free of charge, or at reduced fees, if the Governors be satisfied that they are unable to pay the ordinary fees. All the pupils, free and paying, shall be educated together, and in the same manner.

General Provisions as to the Governors and Subscribers.—Chairman, Quorum, and Honorary Officers.

22. The Archbishop of Armagh shall be the Chairman, and the Moderator of the General Assembly shall be the Vice-Chairman of the Governors. The Chairman, or in his absence the Vice-Chairman, shall preside at the meetings of the Governors and Subscribers, and in the absence of both, the Governors, or the Subscribers, as the case may be, shall elect one of their number to act as Chairman for the occasion. Three Governors present, or six Subscribers present or represented by proxy, as the case may be, shall constitute a quorum, and all matters and questions shall be determined by the majority of the Governors present, or of the Subscribers present or represented by proxy, as the case may be. In every case of equality of votes, the Chairman of the meeting shall have a second or casting vote. The Governors may appoint out of their number an Honorary Secretary and such other Honorary Officers as they shall think fit.

Meetings.

23. Within one calendar month after the date of this Scheme, and once at the least in every three months thereafter, the Governors shall meet at the School, and they may also meet at such other times and places as they may from time to time appoint. At each meeting held at the School, the Governors shall take the opportunity of examining for themselves into the condition of the School premises, and the efficiency of the education given therein. Notice of every meeting of the Governors shall be given to each Governor by the Honorary Secretary, or other officer appointed in that behalf, three clear days, or such other time as the Governors may direct, before the meeting. The Chairman, or the Vice-Chairman, or any three other Governors, may at any time summon a special meeting of the Governors, giving notice to each Governor six clear days, or such other time as the Governors may direct, before the meeting, specifying in such notice the object thereof. The Chairman, or the Vice-Chairman, or any six Subscribers, may at any time convene a special meeting of the Subscribers, sending notice, by post or otherwise, to the last known address of each Subscriber, ten clear days at the least before the meeting, specifying in such notice the object thereof. Every meeting of Governors or Subscribers may adjourn for the completion of its business to such time and place as those present may appoint. No business other than that mentioned in the notice shall be transacted at any special meeting.

Minutes, Deeds, and Documents.

24. Minute books shall be kept by the Governors, in which all their proceedings, and those of every meeting of the Subscribers, shall be duly entered. All deeds and other documents, sealed with the common seal, and signed at any meeting by the Chairman of the meeting and two other Governors, shall be held to be validly executed on behalf of the Governors. Every Governor shall, at or before the first meeting which he attends, sign a declaration, in a book to be kept for that purpose, of his acceptance of the office of Governor, and until he shall have signed such declaration he shall not be entitled to act as a Governor.

Committees.

25. The Governors may, from time to time, appoint a Committee or Committees, consisting of any two or more of their number, to visit the School, to superintend and carry into execution any orders, rules, or directions of the Governors with respect to the purposes of this Scheme, or to manage such business as the Governors may deem it expedient to depute to such Committee or Committees. The Governors may, if they think fit, appoint a Ladies Committee to aid in the domestic management of the School, or in the education of the female pupils. The Governors may fix the quorum, define the duties, and regulate the proceedings of every Committee as they may think fit.

By-Laws and Annual Report.

26. The Governors may from time to time make such by-laws and regulations as they shall consider convenient and needful for the good management of the School, for summoning and regulating the meetings of the Subscribers, for carrying out the competition for free Scholarships, and for effectuating the other purposes of this Scheme, provided that no such by-law or regulation shall be inconsistent with the provisions of this Scheme, and that the same may be repealed, altered, and amended by the Governors as they may from time to time think fit. They shall present to the Subscribers at each annual meeting a report upon the condition of the School and the progress of the pupils during the preceding year, with the last reports of the Auditor and Inspector, and such further information as they shall think fit, or as the Subscribers shall require.

Powers of Governors.

27. Subject to the provisions of this Scheme, the Governors shall have and exercise general supervision and control over the School; they shall determine the various branches of education to be taught therein; they may from time to time fix the terms upon which boarders shall be received, and shall make such provision as they shall think fit for the care of the pupils, for the management of the Endowment, and for the maintenance of order and discipline in the School. Subject to the provisions hereinafter contained as to the vested interests of individuals holding office at the date of the passing of the Act, every Head Master, Teacher, Officer, and other person employed in the service of the School, shall be removable by the Governors for such cause as they shall deem adequate, or upon reasonable notice, or upon payment of a reasonable sum, not exceeding six months' salary, in lieu of notice; provided that no Head Master shall be removed except upon a resolution of the Governors, passed at a special meeting summoned on due notice, at which not less than one-half of the number of Governors for the time being shall be present, and confirmed at a subsequent meeting of the Governors held at an interval of not less than one week or more than five weeks after the first meeting, and at which not less than one-half of the Governors for the time being shall be present, and that an opportunity of being heard at each meeting shall be given to the Head Master concerned. No person appointed after the date of this Scheme to any paid office or employment under the Governors, or becoming entitled under

any such appointment to any salary or emolument out of the Endowments, shall be capable of becoming or shall continue to be a Governor.

Accounts and Audit.

28. The Governors shall cause to be kept regular accounts of all their receipts and disbursements, in such manner and form as may be from time to time prescribed or approved by the Local Government Board, and the accounts for each year ending the thirty-first day of December, or such other day as the Board may appoint, or an abstract thereof in such form as the Board shall prescribe or approve, shall be submitted for audit on or before the first day of March following, or such other day as the Board may appoint, to an Auditor of the Local Government Board, or to some other competent authority to be appointed or approved by the Board. The Local Government Board may fix, and the Governors shall pay, such reasonable sum as shall be necessary to defray the cost of audit. The Governors shall keep an account with such bank as they may from time to time select, and all moneys receivable or payable by them (except petty cash) shall be lodged to or drawn from such account, and every cheque shall be signed by two Governors, at the least, thereto authorised.

Inspection.

29. The Inspector to be appointed by the Lord Lieutenant in pursuance of the Act, section 17, shall inspect the School once at the least in each year, and as much oftener as the Lord Lieutenant may direct, and shall present his report thereon to the Lord Lieutenant; the remuneration of such Inspector, as fixed by the Lord Lieutenant, shall be defrayed by the Governors out of the Endowments.

Head Master and Assistant Teachers.

30. Subject to the provisions of this Scheme, the Governors shall appoint from time to time, upon such terms as they shall think fit, and at such salary and with such emoluments as they may deem sufficient, a Head Master of the School. Whenever a vacancy shall occur in the office of Head Master, or shall be about to occur in consequence of notice given either by the Governors, or by the Head Master, the Governors shall give public notice of the vacancy, and thereupon, at a meeting specially summoned for the purpose, they shall proceed to elect a Head Master by open voting. In the election of the Head Master a preference shall be given, if a suitable candidate can be found, to a Graduate in Arts or Science of one of the Universities of the United Kingdom.

Assistant Teachers.

31. After conference with the Head Master, the Governors shall from time to time determine the number of Assistant Teachers to be employed in the School, and shall fix their salaries and the mode of payment thereof. The Head Master shall appoint the Assistant Teachers, subject to the approval of the Governors, to be recorded in their minutes; and every Assistant Teacher shall be removable by the Head Master, or by the Governors, for such cause as he or they shall deem adequate.

Management of Property.

32. The Governors shall from time to time, make such arrangements as they may deem expedient for the custody of all deeds and documents belonging to the Endowments, for the management of the property vested in them, for keeping proper maps and records of holdings and tenancies, for the appointment of an agent or agents, and for the employment of a solicitor or solicitors and of such bailiffs and other officers as they shall find it expedient to employ to assist in the management of the Endowments. Every agent shall be required to give sufficient security for the faithful performance of his duties, and to furnish an account to the Governors once at the least in each year, and in such account to include all rents and other income due and payable up to the gale day next preceding the date of furnishing the account.

Lettings.

33. The Governors may make agricultural or occupation leases and lettings of land from year to year, or for any term of years not exceeding forty years, and leases of buildings from year to year, or for any term not exceeding ninety-nine years, and leases for building or improvement for any term not exceeding two hundred years, so that every such lease and letting shall take effect in possession upon or within three years after the making thereof, and shall be made at the highest rent that may fairly and reasonably be obtained, and without fine.

Sale, Exchange, and Fines.

34. The Governors may, in such manner as they, with the consent of the Commissioners of Charitable Donations and Bequests, shall deem most expedient, sell, exchange, let upon fine in fee farm or for any term, mortgage, or otherwise dispose of, all or any part or parts of the lands and buildings not being required for the purposes of the School, which may be vested in them, so that every such dealing shall be carried out to the best advantage, and that all money obtained thereupon, other than current rents, shall be treated as part of the capital of the Endowments, and shall be invested or otherwise disposed of in accordance with the provisions hereof.

Investments.

35. The Governors may from time to time sell any of the personal property, other than lands or buildings, funds, and securities vested in them, and invest the moneys arising therefrom, or other the capital of the Endowments, and may also invest and accumulate any surplus or residue of income not required in any year for the purposes of the School, in any of the public stocks, funds or securities of the United Kingdom, or of any colony or dependency thereof, or in the stock of the Bank of England or of the Bank of Ireland, or upon freehold or leasehold securities in the United Kingdom, or in the purchase of perpetual rents or rentcharges, or upon the bonds, debentures, or mortgages of any municipal, commercial, or other joint stock company or corporation, carrying on business or constituted for any purpose, in the United Kingdom or any colony or dependency thereof; and the Governors may from time to time vary such investments, and they may from time to time resort to the accumulations of income from any previous year, and apply the same for the purposes of this Scheme; they may retain in their existing state of investment, so long as they shall think fit, all or any of the securities which may from time to time be received by them for the purposes of this Scheme, provided the retention of such securities does not involve the Governors or the Endowments in any pecuniary liability.

Provision for Vested Interests and Superannuation.

36. Every individual who at the date of the passing of the Act held, and at the date of this Scheme shall continue to hold, any office, place, employment, pension, compensation, allowance, or emolument under or arising out of the Endowments here by transferred to and vested in the Governors, shall continue to hold and be entitled to receive the same from the Governors, upon the same terms and in the same manner in every respect as he or she held and en-

entitled to receive the same on the date of the passing of the Act, and every such individual shall remain bound to perform the same and all like duties for the Governors, so long as his or her employment shall continue, as he or she would have been bound to perform for his or her existing employers if this Scheme had not passed; and his or her employment may be determined by the Governors at any time after the date of this Scheme by dismissal for the like cause, or on the same notice or payment in lieu of notice, by the Governors, for or on which such existing employment might have been determined if this Scheme had not passed.

Superannuation.

37. The Governors may grant to any existing officer, or to any officer appointed after the date of the passing of the Act, who otherwise than from misconduct shall become incapable of further duty, or whose services shall no longer be required, such retiring allowance or gratuity, to be fixed by the Governors with due regard to length of service and to the circumstances of his or her employment, as the Commissioners of Charitable Donations and Bequests shall approve.

Payment of Expenses.

38. The Governors shall, subject to the other provisions of this Scheme, pay out of the Endowments all charges which under the provisions of the Act shall be properly and necessarily payable by the Governors, for the taxed costs and expenses of this Scheme, or for audit or inspection, or for other purposes.

Discharge of existing Governors.

39. Immediately after the date of this Scheme the Most Reverend Robert Knox, D.D., Lord Archbishop of Armagh, or other the existing Governors or Trustees of the School, shall proceed to pay and discharge out of the moneys in his or their hands all the salaries, outgoings, and liabilities due or payable by him or them up to the date of this Scheme, including his or their costs, if any, of and incidental to the preparation of this Scheme (such costs to be taxed and certified by the proper officer of the High Court of Justice in Ireland), and shall prepare a final account of all his or their receipts and disbursements on account of the Endowments, and shall submit the same for audit to the Local Government Board, or to some other competent authority to be appointed or approved by the Board. Upon such audit the net cash balance remaining in the hands of the said Archbishop, or other existing Governors or Trustees, or of his or their bankers or of any other person on his or their account, shall be ascertained and certified, and thereupon the same and all securities held by the said Archbishop, or other existing Governors or Trustees, shall be forthwith transferred or paid to the Governors, to be by them held and applied for the purposes of this Scheme, and accounted for accordingly. The said Archbishop, or other existing Governors or Trustees, and any other person or persons having custody thereof for him or them, shall, at the same time, deliver to the Governors all books, documents, and other chattels and effects belonging to the Endowments, and thereupon the said Archbishop, and other existing Governors and Trustees, shall be discharged. All debts and other sums then accruing or payable to or recoverable by the said Archbishop, or other existing Governors or Trustees, shall thereupon and thenceforth accrue and become payable to or recoverable by the Governors, and all sums then payable by or recoverable from the said Archbishop, or other existing Governors or Trustees, and all contracts and liabilities then binding upon him or them in respect of the School or of the Endowments, shall thereupon and thenceforth be payable by and recoverable from and binding upon the Governors.

Printing of Scheme.

40. The Governors shall cause this Scheme to be printed, or shall procure printed copies thereof, and shall keep the same for sale at a reasonable price.

Alteration of Scheme.

41. This Scheme may be altered from time to time by the Commissioners of Charitable Donations and Bequests for Ireland, in any matter whatever, upon the application of two-thirds in number of the Governors for the time being, or upon the joint application of the General Synod and General Assembly, or of the Diocesan Council and the Presbytery, but except upon such application no alteration shall be so made, and no alteration shall be made contrary to anything contained in the Act; provided that the Governors shall not be deemed to have made such application, unless the resolution authorising the making thereof shall specify the nature of the alteration required, and shall have been adopted by two-thirds in number of the Governors for the time being, at a meeting specially convened for the purpose.

SCHEDULE REFERRED TO IN THE FOREGOING SCHEME.

(Fee) Part I.

First, all those several plots of ground situate on the north side of Rainey-street, in the town of Magherafelt, together with the several buildings and other erections thereon, known respectively as the old and new Grain Store and the Market Yard; secondly, all that piece of ground situate on the north-east side of Queen-street, in the town of Magherafelt aforesaid, together with the buildings and other erections thereon, known as the Butter Market; and thirdly, all that piece of ground situate on the northeast side of King-street, in the town of Magherafelt, with the several buildings and other erections thereon, known as the Flour Store; and also, all that triangular piece of ground at the rear thereof now used as a yard in connection with the said stores; all which said premises are situate in the Parish of Magherafelt, Barony of Loughinsholin, and County of Londonderry, and are more particularly delineated in the plan drawn on the above-mentioned deed poll, dated 17th September, 1908, and therein surrounded with a red colour, and are respectively numbered 16, 17, and 17a (Rainey-street), 72, 78 (Queen-street), and 107 (King-street) of the Salters' Company's map of the town of Magherafelt.

Part II.—The School Premises.

All that piece of ground situate on the north side of Rainey-street, in the town of Magherafelt and *Parish of Magherafelt*, Barony of Loughinsholin, and County of Londonderry, together with the school buildings, master's house, and other erections thereon, known as "*The Rainey's Foundation Schools*"; which premises are more particularly delineated on the *Salters' Company's map drawn on the above mentioned Deed of Poll, dated 17th September*, 1908, of the town of Magherafelt, and are therein surrounded with a green colour, and are numbered 31 (*Rainey-street*) on *the Salters' Company's map of the town of Magherafelt.*

Part III.—The Rent-charge.

All that perpetual yearly rent-charge of £175, late Irish currency, equivalent to £161 10s. 9d., present currency, mentioned in the hereinbefore recited Act 11 Geo. II., cap. 2, and payable to the Lord Archbishop of Armagh for the time being, together with all arrears due and accruing on account thereof; issuing and payable out of the town and lands of Lower Ballyneane, Ballygahan, Granagevalle, [illegible], the Mill of Grange-hans, Ballyheenen, Lower Ballyclonder, Upper Ballyclonder, Ballyvarna, Tobermoney, with the mill and tolls thereunto belonging, and the quarter of Balle, in the said Act more particularly described; all which lands, tenements, and hereditaments are situate in the Manor of Desertmartin and County of Derry.

Draft Scheme, prepared and published by the Commissioners, in pursuance of the Act, sec. 21.

Wm. Edward Ellis, *Secretary*.

August 13, 188[illegible].

Objections and Amendments to Draft Scheme.

Referred to, Evid. p. 89 et seq.

No. II. (a).

1.—By Andrew Brown

The Cottage, Magherafelt,
30th August, 188[illegible].

Sir,—I am in receipt of Draft Scheme for management of Rainey's School, Magherafelt, which appears (generally) to meet the requirements of that institution. There are two points which appear to the writer to require further consideration:—

1st. The present arrangement for the reasonable balance of voting power which now exists may be upset by the appointment of Governors which may be made by the Worshipful Salters' Company. Such a condition of things should be guarded against, and not handicap the school unfairly, so that the best may be made out of this new start—that is may be less remodelling, and more reforming.

2nd. The admission of a Pensioning Clause—from what appears to be a slender support for the School, as disclosed in the expected Endowment by the Salters' Company, taken with the income already attached to the School—the management would be driven to a more cautious use of the funds for present purposes, and thus cripple the benefits to be derived from a well-paid staff of teachers, if a reserve fund were established for pensioning purposes. The School may grow in public estimation, and in course of time be so supported that the consideration of the Pensioning Clause might be taken up; but in giving it a fair start under present conditions, and with its very slender Endowments, I respectfully suggest the advisability of cancelling the Pensioning Clause.

(Signed), Andrew Brown.

No. II. (a).

2.—By the Existing Governing Body.

Sir,—We beg to object to the principle of the proposed Scheme, as it removes the Archbishops of Armagh from their very ancient and acknowledged position as sole Governors and Trustees of the charity.

This position was given to the Archbishops of Armagh by Act of Parliament, and has been held by them in succession since Primate Boulter's time, say for the last 150 years. When, in the lapse of time, the Archbishops found it necessary to modify the arrangements of the School, to meet the wants of the times, the Court of Chancery confirmed their position as sole Trustees, and this was done with the full concurrence of the Worshipful the Salters' Company, on whose estate the School was situate, and who were then and have been since the patronal friends of the School. The action of the Court of Chancery in A.D. 1863–4 was in response to the concurrent application of the then Primate and of that Company, and as a carrying out of the Chancery Scheme the present School premises were erected in A.D. 1864 by the Salters' Company.

Under this Scheme the advantages of the School were open to all *Protestant* denominations, who freely availed themselves of them, while the religious liberty of the scholars was guarded by a stringent Conscience Clause, and was universally respected. As an example of the desire to extend the advantages of the School we may mention that when the Salters' Company lately founded an Exhibition of the yearly value of £20, the first scholar of the School to hold it was a Protestant Churchman and the second was a Roman Catholic.

We are most strongly of opinion that the Primate should have the appointment of the Head Master of the School; should be President of meetings of the Governing Body to be appointed, with a second or casting vote, in cases of equal voting.

II. We beg to object to the position assigned in Draft Scheme (page 7) to the Governing Body.

While we would preserve the position of the Archbishops of Armagh as stated above, we would have under them a Governing Body for the School. This we think would give due weight to the historical requirement of the case, without sacrificing a venerable and acknowledged position, and at the same time would hold out attractions for the popular support of the School. The Governing Body might consist of eight—four of these being members of the Church of Ireland, and four of the Presbyterian body—to be elected as in Draft Scheme.

With regard to this Governing Body, we would propose that the School premises should be vested in them: that the Primate should, through his agent, pay over to them from time to time the proceeds of Rainey Trust, and that the Salters' Company should pay their contributions—in whatever form they may take—to the same body. We would also give this Governing Body power to appoint all officials except the Head Master (in which appointments the Head Master should have a vote), and to make such other arrangements as may seem good for the management and conduct of the School.

III. We beg to object to mode proposed (page 8) of electing additional Governors as calculated to lead

No. II. (n)—continued.

to rivalry among the religious denominations, and to produce a continual contest for which party should control the School. We would give every facility to the friends of education to found Exhibitions (bearing their names, and with their own conditions attached) to encourage the School, and to help struggling scholars to obtain higher education. This latter plan we would offer instead of that of "additional Governors," as we believe this would not interfere with a settled finality of government for the School; whereas the mode of "election of additional Governors," as leading to a continual rivalry of sects, would prevent the securing of efficient teachers, and would in many ways mar the success of the School.

(Signed),

Robt. Armagh, Primate.
Thomas Jordan, Visitor
Rainey School.

No. II. (o).

5.—By the Head Master.

Magherafelt, 5th October, 1888.

My Lord and Gentlemen,—As Clause 37 makes no provision for superannuation in my case and that of my assistant master, I beg respectfully to draw your attention to the fact that I have been here and have held this appointment for nearly twenty-four years. Had the Salters' Company still been the Governors of the school, I would have been entitled to a retiring pension in a very short period, and although I am willing to work as long as my health will permit, I feel it a duty to myself to ask you to fix a scale to which I would be entitled should circumstances compel me to ask for superannuation. My income has been about £240—viz., salary £150, house and grounds £30, fees £40, allowances £15, [illegible] £5. My assistant gets salary £30, and one-third [illegible].

(Signed), H. S. Kinkaid.

No. II. (p).

6.—By the Salters Company.

Salters' Hall, St. Swithin's Lane,
London, E.C., 5th October, 1888.

Sir,—Referring to your letter of the 13th August, 1888, I am directed by the Salters' Company to transmit herewith the Draft Scheme published by the Commissioners for the above-named endowment, together with the alterations and amendments suggested on the part of the Company, which alterations, you will observe, are necessary in view of the fact that the Company have executed a declaration of trust, dated 27th September, 1888, in respect of the premises in the Town of Magherafelt, which the Company intend to be vested in the new Governing Body of the school, as a Supplementary Endowment, provided that the Draft Scheme, as altered by the Company, is ultimately adopted.

I am also directed to inform you that the Company passed the following resolution with regard to this matter, viz.:—

"Resolved,—That this Company hereby records that they executed the Declaration of Trust with reference to certain premises in Magherafelt, dated 27th September, 1888, with the object of the property comprised therein being forthwith vested in the new Governing Body of Rainey's Foundation School, and they do not desire to nominate any person to be of such Governing Body, nor to participate in any way in the future management of such school."

(Signed),

Edwd. Lionel Scott,
Clerk of Salters' Company.

No. II. (q).

7.—By the Presbyterian Governors proposed in the Draft Scheme.

We who have been nominated as Presbyterian Governors under the "Scheme" for the future management of the Rainey School in Magherafelt, would respectfully desire attention to the following statement.

We are pleased to find that the Scheme is based upon the principle of equality as between the Presbyterian and Episcopalian Churches. In the provisions of the Scheme, however, there is one matter which would seem to endanger that equality. The Archbishop of Armagh will be Chairman at meetings of the Governors. The Scheme provides that the Chairman will have two votes.

We would desire that it would be so arranged that at every alternate meeting of the Governors there should be a Presbyterian Chairman. We consider that such an arrangement would render it secure that the dual voting power could not become a matter which either party could use to the detriment of the interests of the other.

It is also our opinion that the privilege of granting or withholding pensions should be left altogether in the discretion of the Governors.

Dated this 6th day of October, 1888.

R. J. Lynd, B.A., Moderator of the General Assembly of the Presbyterian Church in Ireland.
A. Macmeekin, Minister of the First Presbyterian Congregation, Magherafelt.
Alexander Meeke, Presbyterian Minister, Ballaghy.
Andrew Brown, Magherafelt.

No. II. (r).

6.—By the Intermediate Education Committee of the General Assembly.

Objection is lodged in regard to the following provisions of the above Scheme.

1. The Salters Company having "proposed to make permanent provision in connexion with said school," it is in their power under par. 6 to qualify subscribers, and so give undue preponderance to one denomination on the Governing Body. It is therefore proposed that the paragraph in question shall be so amended as to provide against such use of amount to be received from the Salters' Company.

2. Exception is taken to the arrangement [par. 12] constituting the Archbishop of Armagh, chairman of the Governors, and the Moderator of the General Assembly, vice-chairman.

It is proposed that the Scheme be amended, by providing that the Archbishop and Moderator shall fill the office of chairman alternately, or that the selection of chairman and vice-chairman be left to the Board of Governors.

W. Todd Martin,
Convener, Intermediate
Education Committee.

Assembly's Offices, Belfast,
12th October, 1888.

No. II. (s).

7.—By John Glover.

Magherafelt,
10th October, 1888.

Sir,—I feel greatly interested in the establishment of a school here for Intermediate Education, and I am glad to see that clause 15 of the Commissioners' scheme provides for education in this school on even a broader basis than Intermediate.

I observe that there are to be

4	Ex-officio Governors	}	clause 2.
4	Representative "	}	
4	Subscribers	"	clause 4.
3	Coopted	"	clause 6.
—			
15	in all.		

That these Governors may make a quorum—clause 23.

I venture to suggest that the quorum should be three, so long as the Governors consist of the eight ex-officio and representative ones.

That as soon as and after the subscribers have elected one Governor, and one other Governor be coopted, the quorum should be four, and that after the subscribers shall elect more than one Governor, and there shall be more than one coopted Governor, the quorum shall be five members.

By clause 23 the compulsory meetings are four each year, and by clause 5 attendance at one meeting is one of the qualifications for re-election of a Governor.

I venture to suggest that any Governor [except the Archbishop and Moderator] who attended the meetings only once in the year ought to be disqualified from re-election, and that the attendance of other Governors to qualify for re-election ought to be two compulsory meetings and two other meetings, if such be appointed.

This would displace gentlemen who took no interest and allow in others who might take an interest, and it would prevent stagnation.

I am sorry I have to take objection to the constitution of the Presbyterian Governors, for the following reasons:—

There are two Presbyterian churches and two Presbyterian congregations in Magherafelt. One of the churches is in the Presbytery of Magherafelt and the other is under the Presbytery of Tyrone, but both are under the General Assembly. There is another Presbyterian church (Lecumpher) very near Magherafelt, which is also in the Presbytery of Tyrone, and as the members of both these congregations in the Tyrone Presbytery are deeply interested in the success of this school, they ought, I think, to be represented in the Governing Body.

I therefore propose that one of the Representative Governors ought to be elected by the Presbytery of Magherafelt and one by the Presbytery of Tyrone, and I name the Rev. Samuel M'Cann, the minister of Union-road Presbyterian Church, Magherafelt, as representing the Presbytery of Tyrone in the first instance.

If the Commissioners see their way to adopt this proposal, I am certain the Scheme will receive much greater local support in the way of subscription, and that the prosperity of the school will be more likely to succeed. I am certain that if this modification be not complied on behalf of the Presbyterians of Magherafelt and neighbourhood will take no interest by subscription in the school, and very little otherwise.

(Signed), J. Glover.

No. II. (t).

8.—By the Roman Catholics of Magherafelt.

Gentlemen,—We, the undersigned, on behalf of the Roman Catholic School Committee, as representing the Roman Catholics of Magherafelt and district, beg to state, in reference to the above-mentioned foundation and the published Scheme and amendments:—

1. That we object to the fundamental principle of the Scheme, which totally exclude Roman Catholics from a participation in the endowment.

2. That we repeat our former Scheme already sent you before publication of draft Scheme.

3. That we consider the Salters Company's amendments to the Scheme unfair, if not unjust, to the Roman Catholics, as well as prejudicial to the social well-being of the town and the future revenues of the Rainey School.

Signed on behalf of the said R. C. Committee,

P. Canon Donnelly, *Chairman*.
James Harrison, J.P., *Vice-Chairman*.
Joseph J. Quinn, }
John Dougherty, } *Secretaries*.

Magherafelt, 12th October, 1888.

No. H. (u).

Referred to p. [illegible].

MAUNSELL and SON to the COMMISSIONERS.

16, Stephen's-green, North,
Dublin, 19th October, 1888.

RAINEY'S CHARITY.

DEAR SIR,—With reference to the objections filed on behalf of the Salters Company to this Scheme, we think it right that the Commissioners should be informed of the exact terms upon which we hold the deed of trust of 27th September, 1888. We, therefore, enclose a copy of the letter of the solicitors for the Salters' Company which accompanied the deed. We believe you have a copy of the deed, the trust as to the additional endowments being upon trust for the accommodation, use, and benefit and for "*the purposes of the said Schools in the same manner as heretofore*," and as a perpetual endowment thereafter.

We may add that on receiving this letter from the solicitors of the Salters Company of the 8th instant, we wrote, asking the Company to forego their claim to the arrears of dividend and rentcharge mentioned in their amendments to the Scheme, and on 17th of October we received a reply, dated 16th, of which we also send copy.

(Signed) MAUNSELL AND SON.

To the Secretary,
Educational Endowments Commissioners.

P.S.—Perhaps, under the circumstances, the Commissioners would allow us to have a print of the Scheme before same is finally settled and signed, so that we may submit it to the Salters Company, and obtain their instructions as to the delivery of the new deed of trust.

Letters referred to in Messrs. Maunsell's Letter, 19th October, 1888.

No. H. (v.)

MESSRS. THOMPSON and DEBENHAM to MESSRS. MAUNSELL.

Salters' Hall Court, London, E.C.,
8th October, 1888.

SALTERS' COMPANY.—RAINEY'S SCHOOL.

DEAR SIRS,—Herewith we hand you deed of declaration of trust executed by the Salters Company, in duplicate, together with memorial thereof, which please have stamped at your early convenience. The Salters Company have executed this deed on the condition that the property comprised therein should be vested by the Scheme of the Schools Endowment Commission in the Governors about to be appointed for the School.

The deed, consequently, is an escrow, and we must request you to hold it as such, on behalf of the Company, until we learn that the Commission accept the Company's condition, and the deed should not be registered at present.

Your charges for stamping and registering the deed we shall be prepared to pay.

We enclose print of the Schools Endowment Commission Scheme, with the Salters Company's suggested alterations and additions shown in red ink.

We shall be glad to know the present position of the action, The Church Representative Body v. Drury and Bell, and what probability there is, in your opinion, of recovering from the defendants the year's rentcharge due 1st November, 1888.

Yours faithfully,
THOMPSON AND DEBENHAM.

Messrs. Maunsell.

Salters' Hall Court, London, E.C.
16th October, 1888.

RAINEY [illegible] SCHOOLS.

DEAR SIRS,—We laid your letter of the 9th inst. before the Committee of the Salters Company, and, although we are not in a position to reply definitely thereto, we think it probable that the Company will comply with the request contained in your letter of the 9th inst., and waive all claim to the arrears of dividend and rentcharge now in the hands of the Representative Church Body.

We understand that Mr. [illegible], the clerk of the Company, intends writing to the Educational Endowments Commission, withdrawing the paragraphs inserted by the Company in the draft scheme dealing with the [illegible].

Yours truly,
THOMPSON AND DEBENHAM.

Messrs. Maunsell and Son,
16, Stephen's-green, N., Dublin.

No. H. (w).

REV. JOSEPH QUINN to the COMMISSIONERS.

Re Proposed New Convent Schools, &c., Magherafelt.

To the Secretary.

DEAR SIR,—In the event of not being called on by any of those making grants to the above proposed school, we are anxious to have the Trustees of same constituted a corporate body, and would feel greatly obliged if you would suggest to us the course we are to follow in asking the Commission to accede to our desire.

(Signed) JOSEPH QUINN, C.C.,
Sec. to R. C. S. Committee.

No. II. (x).

Very Rev. Canon Donnelly to the Commissioners.

Canon Donnelly very much regrets that, owing to an attack of illness, he was unable to personally appear before the Commissioners at their sitting at Magherafelt on the 22nd of October last.

He intends to communicate in a few days with the Commissioners on the two obstacles that stand in the way of the Roman Catholics being fairly heard at that sitting, namely:—(1) The decision that the Commissioners have practically arrived at that the Rainey Endowment, according to the founder's intention, should be Protestant in its management; and (2) that your Commission had no discretion in regard to the Salters' Company Endowment.

But lest the Commissioners should hold a sitting tomorrow he sends you the enclosed letter from the Clerk of the Salters Company, showing that the Company throws upon your Commission the responsibility of doing what is "*just and fair to all.*"

When you have done with this letter I wish you to return it.

(Signed), Joseph P. Quinn, C.C.,
for Canon Donnelly.

[Copy.]

Salters' Hall, St. Swithin's-lane,
London, E.C., 7th November, 1888.

To the Very Rev. Canon Donnelly, P.P.,
Magherafelt.

Dear Sir,—I have laid before the Court of the Salters Company your and the Rev. Father Quinn's letters, and I am directed to inform you that the Company have executed a Declaration of Trust, under which they have assigned certain premises in the town of Magherafelt to the Governing Body of Rainey's Foundation School, when constituted under the Scheme of the Educational Endowments (Ireland) Commissioners, with the intention that the rents and profits of the said premises shall be applied by way of supplementary Endowment for the benefit of the school. The Company cannot alter or vary the terms of this Deed, and have, after mature deliberation, and full consideration of your and Father Quinn's letters, resolved to adhere to their determination not to interfere in any way in the future government of the school, and to leave it to the responsibility of the Commissioners to draw up such Scheme as they may deem just and right, having regard to all the facts and circumstances of the case; but it is not the intention of the Company (as Father Quinn seems to imply) to exclude Roman Catholics or any other religious denomination from the benefits of the Endowment.

I am, dear sir, yours faithfully,

Edwd. Lawton Scott,
Clerk of Salters Company.

No. II. (y).*

Circular Letter from the Commissioners to all Persons interested in the Rainey School and the Salters' Endowment.

23, Nassau-street, Dublin,
14th January, 1889.

I am directed by the Commissioners to enclose a print of the evidence taken by them at Magherafelt on October 22, 1888, and which all those interested requested should be furnished to your Company before the final settlement of the draft scheme published by the Commissioners.

I am directed to call your attention in the first instance to the evidence relating to the Head Master (Mr. Kinnaird), who appears to have a strong claim upon your Company in respect of the salary which has hitherto been paid to him by the Company, and which the Rainey endowment alone would be inadequate to provide in future. I am also to invite your serious attention, on his behalf, to the statements contained in the evidence as to the circumstances of his appointment, and as to his recent communications with the late agent of your Company concerning his position.

Secondly, I am directed by the Judicial Commissioners to say that having carefully considered the present position of the school and the proposal of your Company to utilise the market premises of Magherafelt, as a future endowment for its benefit, they find great difficulty in giving effect to that proposal by the scheme. The compulsory jurisdiction of the Commission extends only to the Rainey endowment and the school premises, and with respect to this property the scheme must give effect to the intentions of the founder by preserving the exclusively Protestant character of the governing body. The trusts of any endowment given by your Company must be declared by themselves, unless the Company should think fit to allow the Commissioners to declare such trusts as they should consider just. This, your Company has not done.

Further, the evidence taken at Magherafelt, strongly supports the conclusion that, if the premises be vested in the denominational governing body of the school, opposition to the markets will arise, the school will be involved in difficulty, and the pecuniary value of the proposed endowment will be most precarious, while the governing body of a school would seem quite unfitted to undertake the management of public markets for the town. The Commissioners entertain serious doubts of the expediency of attempting to employ property so situated as an educational endowment, unless the markets and their management could be placed in the hands of some independent body, competent to conduct them with efficiency and paying a fixed rent for them which might be applied to educational purposes.

I am further to point out that the execution by your Company by way of escrow of the deed of September 22, 1888, has placed an additional difficulty in the way of dealing with the property comprised in that deed, for the escrow appears to be inoperative until the scheme comes into force, the deed seems framed so as thereupon either to take effect irrespective of the provisions of the scheme, or to fail altogether unless the scheme is framed so as to perpetuate the recent administration of Rainey's Charity, which the Commissioners are not prepared to hold to be in accordance with the founder's intentions. Under these circumstances the execution of the deed has rendered it impossible to deal with the market property by a scheme.

* No. II (y) to No. II. (aa).—See Draft, p. [illegible]

No. II. (y).—*continued.*

On the whole, subject to any observations which your Company may desire to submit, the safest course for the Commissioners would seem to be that they should settle the scheme for the future management of the Rainey endowment with due regard to the founder's intentions, leaving your Company subsequently, by deed or otherwise, to make such further provision as they may think fit for Rainey's School, and for meeting the educational claims of the various religious denominations on their late grants.

The Commissioners will await for a reasonable time such further proposals for the amendment of the Draft Scheme as the various parties interested may desire to submit. They hope, however, that all communications on the subject will be made to them not later than the 1st March next.

(Signed), Wm. Edward Ellis,
Secretary.

No. II. (z).

The Salters Company to the Commissioners.

Salters' Hall, St. Swithin's-lane,
London, E.C., 8th February, 1889.

Sir,—I have laid before the Salters Company your letter received the 15th January, 1889, and enclosed copy of evidence taken at Magherafelt, 22nd October, 1888.

With regard to the first point mentioned by you as to Mr. Kincaid, I am to state that the Company cannot admit any claim on his part as against them, and I am to point out that any advantage which he obtained from the voluntary subscriptions of the Company was derived from the supplementary assistance given by them in the interests of the School generally and not specially in his behalf. His appointment was made by the Archbishop of Armagh, three gentlemen having been recommended to His Grace by the Salters Company, they (the Company) being anxious in the interests of a school on their estate to obtain an efficient master.

With regard to the printed evidence as revised by Mr. Kincaid, that Sir H. E. Cartwright made an "express promise" to him that the Company would provide for him, Sir H. E. Cartwright denies in the most explicit terms that he ever said anything to Mr. Kincaid that could have even suggested to him a promise either expressed or implied that the Company would do so.

With regard to the second point mentioned in your letter, viz., the difficulty which the Commissioners have had in dealing with the supplementary Endowment proposed to be given to the School by the Salters Company as set forth in their Declaration of Trust of the 27th September, 1888, the Company desire me to point out that the condition which seems to have proved an obstacle to the Commissioners was, in the opinion of the Company's legal advisers, necessitated by their original proposal (communicated to the Commissioners by Mr., now Sir, Henry Cartwright, in March, 1887) to vest in the future School Authorities, properly constituted by a Scheme:—

(1.) The school buildings, the master's house, &c.

(2.) The market and grain stores in Rainey-street, the market and stores in Queen-street, and the flax stores in King-street, Magherafelt; and therefore it was also necessary to accompany the Declaration of Trust (forwarded through Messrs. Mansell and Son) with the condition that that Deed should only take effect upon the approval of a Scheme by the Commissioners, for until that event should happen, it appeared to the Company that there was no properly constituted authority to receive the gift. It was, however, very far from their intention to place any additional difficulty in the way of the Commissioners, and they have consistently declined, as you will see on reference to my letters of the 17th and 26th July, 1887, and 24th July, 1888, to nominate governors, preferring to leave such nomination entirely in the hands of the Commissioners.

The Company's intended grant of a supplementary endowment, was not—as Lord Justice FitzGibbon seems to imply—conditional upon the appointment of Governors of any particular denomination, and would have been carried out irrespective of the nature of any Scheme which the Commissioners, in the exercise of their jurisdiction, might have seen fit to approve, the alterations in the draft made by the Salters Company being purely technical in their character and necessary, in order to make the Scheme correspond with the actual form of the case. Moreover, the Company would not have raised any objection if the Commissioners had declared that the Supplementary Endowment (consisting of the markets, &c.) was held in such trusts, as they might think just, nor did they contemplate that the new Governors would become managers of the markets, but would be landlords in place of the Salters Company, receiving the rents from such persons as they might decide from time to time should be the lessees or tenants.

I am directed to state, in conclusion, with respect to the property offered by the Company to form an additional Endowment for the School, that in the hope that their offer will obviate all difficulties, they are prepared to allow the Commissioners to declare such trusts of the property as they (the Commissioners) may consider just in the interests of the inhabitants of the town of Magherafelt generally, irrespective of creed and of any limits of the original Trusts of Rainey's Foundation (as settled by the Act of Parliament passed in the last century), provided that the Company be thereby divested of all estate and interest in the property. It now rests with the Commissioners to accept or decline what was and is considered by the Company, a liberal further Endowment of the School, and the Company will expect a definite answer as to whether their offer be accepted or declined by the Commissioners, not later than the 7th March, 1889, so that the matter may be finally disposed of at their next Court.

(Signed), Edw. Lawrie Barry,
Clerk of the Salters Company.

No. II. (aa).

The Commissioners to the Lord Primate.

23, [illegible],
Dublin, February 14th, 1889.

My Lord Primate,—I am directed to send your Grace herewith copy of a letter dated 8th inst., received by the Commission from the Clerk of the Salters Company respecting the proposed endowment, originally offered by the Company for Rainey's School, Magherafelt.

Your Grace will observe that the Company are now prepared to allow the Commissioners to declare such trusts of the property as they, the Commissioners, may consider just in the interests of the inhabitants of the town of Magherafelt generally, irrespective of creed or of any limits of the original trust of Rainey's Foundation, provided that the Company thereby be divested of all estate and interest in the property.

The evidence taken by the Commissioners at Magherafelt on October 23, 1888, suggests much difficulty in vesting the property, the chief revenue of which is derived from public markets, in any educational or denominational body, and as at present advised, the Commissioners are inclined to think that it would be for the Company to constitute a satisfactory market authority as lessee, and then to deal with the rent only as an educational endowment, but they are desirous to invite your Grace's opinion and suggestions upon this letter, in addition to the subject of my former letter of January 11th. Your Grace's reply to both communications should reach this office not later than the 1st March.

Your Grace will understand that this communication relates exclusively to the property offered for educational purposes by the Salters Company, and that in dealing with the endowment derived from Hugh Rainey, the Commissioners are required to have regard to the intentions of the founder.

(Signed), Wm. Edward Ellis,
Secretary.

[illegible]—A similar letter, of same date, was also sent to Messrs. [illegible] and Son, H. E. Kinnaird, Very Rev. Canon [illegible], Campbell Gausen, and Andrew Brown.

No. II. (bb).

Campbell Gausen to the Commissioners.

[illegible] House,
[illegible], 20th February, 1889.

Sir,—In reply to your communication of the 14th instant, I would beg leave to inform the Commissioners that (with the exception of their treatment of Mr. Kinnaird) I quite approve of the arrangements which the Salters Company propose making for the future endowment of the Rainey School, as I believe it is the only one which would be practical under existing circumstances in Magherafelt, and I have not any doubt that such Governors as may be appointed under the proposed Scheme will not have any difficulty in easily finding solvent parties to become their lessees of the market, at rates which would be much above any which were ever realised by the Salters Company, or which could be obtained at any sale under their authority; and, as already mentioned in my former letter to the Commissioners, if they can see their way to include me (as the lineal representative of the founder) amongst such Governors, I can only promise that, as long as I am spared, the interests of such school should always have my best attention, and also that of my eldest son (Percival Gausen, [illegible]) on my decease.

(Signed), Campbell Gausen.

No. II. (cc).

Rev. Thomas Jordan to the Commissioners.

The Rectory, Magherafelt.

Dear Sir,—I beg to mention that Messrs. [illegible] and Son have kindly forwarded to me your letter of 14th February with regard to the proposed endowment offered by the Salters Company for Rainey School.

After the most careful consideration of the subject, my opinion is that for the sake of harmony in the future management of the School—which is so absolutely necessary—there are only two ways likely to conduce to this:—1. Let the Company hold still the markets as the landlords or lessors, allocating the rent as an educational endowment on the school.

Let the Company sell the markets and settle the proceeds on the school.

Either of these courses ought to be followed by some way of commemorating the generous conduct of the Company in this matter.

Possibly the school could be called in future the Rainey and Salters School. There is a memorial—in the gable of the house—of their having generously built the present house and school residence, when the joint action of Rainey Trust and of the Company was formulated in the [illegible] Scheme.

I quite feel that if the Company were kindly to do this generous act of theirs in such a way as to produce harmony among us here, something of this nature would be well deserved and ought to be done.

(Signed) Thomas Jordan.

No. II. (dd).

H. E. Kinnaird to the Commissioners.

Magherafelt, 22nd February, 1889.

To the Secretary,
Endowed School Commission.

Sir,—I have to acknowledge receipt of copies of two letters from Endowed School Commission, viz., one of the 14th February in reply to a former letter of 15th January, 1889, as forwarded to the Salters Company.

In the first place, I beg to thank the Commissioners for the great trouble they have had on my behalf, and for which I feel very grateful.

As the first paragraph in the letter of the 8th of February refers to me, I take it first. I cannot see why I should be treated differently to Mr. Spotswood, the former agent. Mr. Taylor, who was not their servant, but paid by the agent, and Sir H. Cartwright himself—these three were compensated more or less

No. II. (dd.)—continued.

Whether I have a legal claim or not, I certainly think I have a moral claim after twenty-four years service, longer than any of those except Mr. Taylor, the clerk.

I have never had, and never will have, recourse to any other means than I have done.

I have already stated that I have met with much consideration, but "necessity is a sharp taskmaster," and compels me to urge my request under present circumstances.

If the Company should refuse to allow me anything, either as a small annuity or in a lump sum, I have no alternative but to ask the Commissioners to apply a portion of the endowment they are about to have from the Salters Company to that purpose, and as I feel quite sure the Commissioners will see me fairly treated, I leave the matter in their hands.

With regard to Mr H. Cartwright's denial, it will be borne in mind that I was on my oath when giving evidence, and am now prepared to give the day of the month and hour as entered in my diary within an hour after.

The Commissioners have been good enough to ask for my opinion and suggestions respecting the Trust proposed to be handed over by the Salters Company.

The most satisfactory arrangement would be for the Salters Company to place £150 a year at the disposal of the Commissioners, and sell their markets to the highest bidders. The competition will be keen, and they will have no difficulty in selling them for such a sum as would produce £200 a year, and if desirous of making a grant to the Roman Catholic body; they would have £50 a year out of it to do so.

If this cannot be done, the only means (to my mind) which they could adopt would be, to constitute a body composed of two Churchmen, two Presbyterians, two Roman Catholics, and one Nonconformist, viz.:

T. S. Taylor, J.P.;
S. Porter, Presbyterian;
Dr. Vesey or H. Gaffikin,
H. M'Laughlin,
James Mackenzie, R.C.;
John Dempsey,
W. Steven, Clonconry;

or a similar body. These are men who have an interest in the markets, and (I think) would be very suitable. They would take over the Trust and pay to the governing body of the school, as now constituted, the sum of £150 a year by half-yearly payments, as fixed down, and if they had a surplus it could be applied for the benefit of the town.

I say, if they had, because I consider they would have, if they were properly managed, and I deduce my arguments from the following figures:—

	£	s.	d.	
Market Lower (Loan) let at	16	0	0	per annum.
„ quarterly tenancy	25	0	0	„
Butter Market, yearly	5	0	0	to charge.
Grass	22	0	0	yearly
Fair	[illegible]	0	0	„

these make up £101, and could be increased to £200.

I have no doubt other proposals will be placed before the Commissioners. I hope, however, what may be done will be for the benefit of the school, and with the intention of doing away with that bitter feeling which has existed for so long.

(Signed) H. E. Kincaid.

No. II. (ee)

Andrew Brown to the Commissioners.

Magherafelt,
20th February, 1889.

Sir,—In reply to yours of the 14th inst., I beg to state that those men who have the markets at present stated at a public meeting held at Magherafelt a short time ago that they were willing to take a private letting of the Markets from the Governors of the Rainey School.

Referring to evidence taken before the Commissioners at Magherafelt you will observe my strong objection to a private letting of the markets (I may add) to the present lessees, because the whole difficulty in settling the scheme of the Commissioners has been created by their fear of a public letting of the markets, or that they should fall into other hands than theirs.

I have heard that the Salters' Company make an offer—to give the markets and money into the hands of nine trustees, three Catholics, three Episcopalians, and three Presbyterians—the revenue to be divided equally to the three denominations for educational purposes. My friends and I consider that this arrangement would be reasonably fair, and would safeguard the people's interests, so that there be no less than nine trustees.

As Presbyterians claiming a Presbyterian bequest, I respectfully submit that Rainey's School with Rainey's endowment should be handed over to the Presbyterian Church, and I feel very confident that such an act of justice would commend itself to all men, while the school would flourish as it has not done heretofore. I refer you to the evidence of Mr. Kincaid at Magherafelt as proof that Presbyterian influence is paramount at Magherafelt as regards education.

(Signed) Andrew Brown.

No. II. (ff).

Very Rev. Canon Donnelly to the Commissioners.

Magherafelt,
27th February, 1889.

To the Secretary
Educational Endowments
(Ireland) Commission.

Dear Sir,—Your letters of the 14th January, 1889, and of 14th February, 1889, were duly received.

Relative to them I submit a few remarks:—

I. On the evidence of October 23rd, 1888; and

II. The reasons why the Roman Catholics will have nothing to do with Rainey School, as present or otherwise constituted;

III. The reasons why the Roman Catholics claim a division of the Salters proposed endowment; and finally,

IV. A suggested Scheme for the management of the markets, &c.—Yours truly,

P. Canon Donnelly, P.P.,
Magherafelt.

No. II. (27).—continued.

I.

Relative to the evidence of 22nd October, 1888, I may say that there are grounds on the Roman Catholic side for that statement of Rev. Mr. Wilson, namely, of tampering with the faith of the pupils. There is in my own memory a case of perversion of a Roman Catholic boarder, a simple-minded young Englishman. There is also another case of a town's boy (Roman Catholic). Our people did not like speaking of these publicly, both for the sake of peace, and to not annoy the parties concerned.

There is another statement quoted twice during the sitting from a letter of Mr., now Sir H. Cartwright's, of 12th December, 1884, that he had "given over to them (Roman Catholic) schools—male and female—of their own."* I really do not know what was here meant, as there was nothing of the sort then handed or given to us. Later on I asked the Company for grounds to build new schools, as the old ones were worthless, and in April, 1885, they granted the site on certain conditions, and saying that they would not contribute to the building of the new schools. Subsequently I was told that when the new schools would be built that the old ones would have to be pulled down. On selling out of the estate, however, the site, &c., were purchased at a small nominal cost, and paying certain expenses.

I attach Sir H. Cartwright's letter:—

Letter of Sir H. Cartwright referred to by Canon Donnelly.

Manor Office, Magherafelt,
20th April, 1885.

Dear Sir,—I am instructed by the Salters Company to inform you that your application for a site whereon new schools may be erected, as set forth on the diagram which accompanied the application, was laid before them, and that the Court have resolved to accede to the request of the Roman Catholic congregation by granting them the site asked for at a nominal rent of one penny per annum, for a term of 99 years, the said site to be conveyed to Trustees for school purposes, upon condition that the plans and elevations of the buildings to be erected are approved of by the Company and the National Board of Education, and that the schools are completed to their satisfaction, and the land occupied by the school and playground properly fenced in at the rear and sides as well as the front as proposed. I am also directed to intimate to you that although the Company are happy to grant the site, they must not be expected to contribute to the cost of the schools, nor to make any arrangement with the tenant or tenants occupying the land required should they have unexhausted interests or crop on the ground.

To assist your object in getting possession I shall be ready to have legal notice served upon the present occupiers to terminate their tenancy, if you give me timely notice to obtain it, as, of course, it must be served prior to 1st May, and it cannot be done at the last moment, so that you should inform me of your decision as to this on or before the 25th instant.—I beg to remain, dear sir, your faithful servant,

H. B. Cartwright.

The Very Rev.
Canon Donnelly, P.P.,
Magherafelt.

II.

The Roman Catholics will have nothing to do with Rainey's School as present or otherwise constituted:

1. Because of the history of the school. The history of the school shows that it is not such as Roman Catholics would have confidence in. The two cases already mentioned show this clearly.

(Again, your Commission has decided that the Rainey endowment as such, according to the founder's intention, is Protestant in its management, to the exclusion of others. Yet, although my people will have nothing to do with the school, they think that Rainey's will is not so exclusive, for in it, it is his executors or those having a life interest that were to have the power of governing, "putting in," "putting out," "trying," and "writing to Presbytery of Tirone," there being nothing apparently to exclude them in case they were Roman Catholics). Another reason why respectable parents oppose sending their children to it is the class of poor children with whom their children should associate.

2. At a meeting of the Roman Catholics held about 20th January, 1888, it was resolved that even in the event of a further plan that they would have no fair representation on it, and consequently that they would repudiate and reject it.

3. In this they were following out the advice of His Grace the Lord Primate (Dr. Logue), who said that a share, i.e., a division, in the Salters endowment was fairly due to the Roman Catholics.

III.

The Roman Catholics claim a fair and just proportion of the Salters Company's proposed endowment, namely, of the market, shares, etc.

1. In the first place this appears the only possible way in which the intentions of Rainey and the Company can be carried out. Because, it would be hard to carry out Rainey's intention, and the Company's intention, by putting both endowments all together—Rainey's (as your Commission says) to have an exclusively Protestant governing body, and the Salters Company, intending all to be fairly treated—to do which Roman Catholics should have a representation on the Board. But, by keeping Rainey's School Protestant, and their fair share of the Salters Company's grant, the Board can still be Protestant, and by giving the Roman Catholics their "just" share of the Salters endowment they can endow their own school. Thus the intentions of both would be carried out, and all be better pleased, except those who wish for all.

2. Again, we think a mixed Board would not give satisfaction in the locality.

3. We believe a division of the endowment to be in keeping with the intentions of the Salters Company. In their letter of the 5th instant to your Commission they allow you to declare such trusts of the property (i.e., the endowments), as you may consider just in the interests of the inhabitants of the town of Magherafelt, generally irrespective of creed, or of Rainey's trust. Thus, they leave you free to do what is just to the inhabitants of Magherafelt generally. Now, we say that no other scheme than a division of the endowment can be just to the Roman Catholics; and secondly, no other to the inhabitants "generally," because if all were centred on Rainey School no girls would benefit by the Salters Company, but by a division it will benefit the inhabitants generally. Besides, in a letter to me, and sent you on 17th November, 1888, you see that they leave it to you to draw such a scheme as may be "just and right."

* If the quoted expression meant anything, it might mean that when the Salters' Company would grant a site for the new schools they would grant the old schools, which they required should be pulled down when the new schools would be completed—certainly no great concession.—P. Canon Donnelly.

No. II. (F)—continued.

4. The endowment itself would be much improved by a division, because all would then have an interest in managing it, so that practically it might be as much as the Rainey School after division as without division.

5. At the meeting alluded to the Roman Catholics, after considering all the aspects of the question, declared that they would not consider themselves fairly treated except that they got their just and fair share of the Salters' proposed endowment, and their fair and just share in its management.

6. Having consulted His Grace the Primate, Dr. Logue—he said that he considered such a proposal fair.

Finally, the numbers of the Roman Catholics, as stated at the Commission, show that they are an important section of the community. Their means would also show the same.

I see that the Salters' Endowment is "for the inhabitants of Magherafelt generally." This, I presume, furnishes the basis of the division—thus a fair division would be that in proportion to the numbers of each denomination. But even on the basis of school going children the Roman Catholics would, I believe, have more. According to Dr. Jordan's statistics the Roman Catholics are 45 per cent.; the return per parish made in 1881 gives [illegible]—taking population, the Roman Catholics should get 45 per cent. of the net revenue of the markets, etc.

IV.

A Scheme for the management of the Property or Endowment.

1. Managed by a Board.
2. Constitution of the Board; mode of appointing; term.
3. Duties; powers, etc.

1. The property being public markets and stores, as you are already aware, except all are fairly treated as regards division and management, it would be the cause of dissension. But I am almost certain that if all are fairly represented on a Board of Management, and the fair and just division above named made of the revenues, that all would take an interest in them, and their revenues would be much increased, I should say by one-third.

2. The proposed Board might be made to consist, e.g., of seven members, divided thus:—Two Protestants, two Presbyterians, and three Roman Catholics. This would give the Protestants and Presbyterians combined a little more than their proper representation, and the Roman Catholics a little less than their due. If seven were considered too small, then, in the same proportions, let the number be doubled.

The mode of appointing the members of the Board could be either by each denomination of ratepayers electing their own representatives, or by the Protestant School Governors appointing theirs, and the Roman Catholic School Governors their representatives. The qualification of the members should be a medium high rating. Election, I think, the preferable.

The property being (as I suppose), vested for the Protestants in the trustees of Rainey School as to the Protestant share, and for the Roman Catholics in the trustees of the Roman Catholic School, as to the Roman Catholic share, whose names are about to be submitted to be constituted a corporation for educational properties, the Board would simply be a Board of Management, and not trustees.

Their duties would be in keeping therewith. Appointing officers, and seeing to the proper [illegible], if necessary, of the markets, repairing what is needed, but not undertaking any new work without the joint authority of the trustees of the Rainey and Roman Catholic Schools.

Their term of office, I think, should be about three years; should any die in the meantime the remaining members of his denomination could co-opt one in his place.

Now, this scheme, I think, should find favour with all; it gives all a fair share of the Salters' Endowment, and a fair share in the management thereof. And I think that all having an interest in the same, that the property would be made thus much more productive, while satisfying all.

Any other alternative will only lead to dissension, and to the property becoming depreciated in value, if not ruined.

We do not consider that it would be the better plan to get the Salters' Company to appoint market trustees. We consider the above plan to be the best arrangement, and the only one that could give satisfaction to all. Harmony will prevail if all are fairly and justly treated.

(Signed), P. Canon Donnelly, P.P.,
Magherafelt.

Roman Catholic School Trustees or Governors.

At present, it is proposed to have the following with perhaps one or two additional persons constituted governors:—

1. Dr. Logue, R.C. Primate, and his successor in office.
2. The Very Rev. Dean Byrne, V.G., and his successor in office.
3. The Very Rev. P. Canon Donnelly, P.P., Magherafelt, and his successor in office.
4. The [illegible] of the Convent School for the time being.

Joseph J. Quinn, C.C.

1st March, 1890.

No. II. (G).

Very Rev. Canon Donnelly to the Commissioners.

Magherafelt, 4th March, 1890.

To the Secretary, Educational Endowments (Ireland) Commission.

Dear Sir,—I still adhere to the statement I made and you on 1st March, per Rev. J. Quinn, namely, that division of the Salters' Endowment is the only way of dealing fairly to all, and again, that the only way of settling the management of the property is that by such a board as therein on the said paper indicated, namely, vesting the Protestants and Presbyterian part in the Governors of Rainey school, e.g., 55 per cent. (and therefore them receiving 55 per cent. of the net revenue), and the Roman Catholic share in the Governors of the Roman Catholic school, e.g., 45 per cent. going on the basis of population.

I feel still more confident that the Board of Management would work satisfactorily to all, because all that is sought throughout is that all be treated fairly.

Having just now seen a letter from Sir H. Cartwright, in which it is stated that he, in an interview with Professor Dougherty during last week in Dublin, and he (Sir H. Cartwright) says that he is still of opinion that the Company's plan is the better, and that he asked Professor Dougherty to get the Commissioners

No. II. (gg)—continued.

to recommend it, and to ask the Salters Company to make some other endowment for the Roman Catholic school, &c., &c.

Now, in reference to this action of Mr H. Cartwright, I think you will bear in mind that not having any interest in Magherafelt, his views can't be received on that head. You will also bear in mind that he is not now in the employment of the Company.

I think, from your own information, you can judge the effect of carrying out the old plan of the company.

We have no objection to the Company doing as much as they like for education. We would like even if they'd increase what they are giving. But what our people are firmly determined on, is that if they are to be treated fairly they must get a fair share of the market revenues, and a fair share in their management. This all consider fair. If an additional grant be made over and above this for the Roman Catholics, we will divide it with them.

We don't believe that selling the markets is wise; owing to no person they bring nothing worth. It would take a prophet to speak of the incorporation of the town.

We believe our plan practicable, fair, feasible, and the one that will take most money for education out of the property, and give most satisfaction to all classes.

I'd like you'd send me by tomorrow a copy of the suggestions, &c., you received from others, and any suggestion you may think useful, as I am about writing the Salters Company on Wednesday.

(Signed) P. Canon Donnelly, P.P.,
Magherafelt.

No. II. (hh.)

R. H. Todd, Solicitor to Magherafelt Markets Committee, to the Commissioners.

Waterloo-place, Londonderry,
8th March, 1888.

Re Rainey's School, Magherafelt.

Sir,—I am requested by the Committee of Management of the Magherafelt Markets to put certain suggestions of theirs before the Endowments Commission with the view of providing for the proper management and improvement of the Markets, and of thereby carrying out in a practicable form the intended endowment of the Rainey School by the Salters Company, and of securing a permanent and definite endowment for the School.

The Markets Committee are of opinion that the Trustees of the Rainey School are wholly unsuited for the management of the markets and other property with which it is proposed to endow the School, and they are apprehensive that if the control of the markets were vested in a purely sectarian body, it would lead to opposition and complications which would seriously depreciate the value of the property, endanger the value of the endowment, and injure the commercial prosperity of the town.

It was proposed some time ago that in case the town were incorporated, the Salters Company should vest the markets and stores in the Town Commissioners subject to an annual fixed payment to the Rainey School Trustees. A number of the inhabitants, however, opposed the incorporation on the ground that it might lead to increased taxation. The Markets Committee are anxious to obviate the difficulty, and now propose that in case the property be vested in them, subject to the annual payment to the Rainey Trustees hereinafter stated, they and each of them will enter into any covenants that may be required to become personally responsible for such payment; and also that they will hand over the property and any profits that may arise in the course of its management to the Town Commissioners in case the town should become incorporated at any time in the future; and that they will in the meantime devote any profits that may arise, to the maintenance and development of the property and the improvement of the town.

The present lettings of the property are as follows:—

	£	s.	d.
Net Rent of Markets,	70	0	0
Large Grain Store,	22	0	0
Small Grain Store,	16	0	0
Flax Store,	56	0	0
	£164	0	0

It seems that there are usually some of the stores empty, and it is considered that it would take about £50 per year to keep the premises in repair and cover the losses arising from vacant premises, &c. This would leave a net profit rent of £114. The Markets Committee, however, are willing to take the property charged with an annual payment of £120 to the Rainey Trustees on the terms above set out more fully. The names of the surviving members of the Committee willing to act are as follows:

Dr. Anderson, J.P.
James Harbison, J.P.
Saml. Porter, J.P.
T. S. Taylor.
John Dempsey.
Alexander Johnston.

I should, perhaps, say that all of these are gentlemen of considerable means, that they have at present and have had for many years back the control and management of the markets with the sanction and approval of the Company and of the town, and three of these gentlemen being Catholics and three of them Protestants, there is security that no reasonable objection can be made to their appointment by the people of the district, and that the popularity of the markets under their management will continue.

I am sending a copy of this letter to the Salters Company.

(Signed) R. H. Todd.

No. II. (i.)

THE COMMISSIONERS TO THE SALTERS' COMPANY.

23, Nassau-street,
Dublin, March 2nd, 1889.

SIR,—In reply to your letter of the 8th ult., stating, with respect to the property offered by your Company to form an additional endowment for the School, that your Company are "prepared to allow the Commissioners to declare such trusts of the property as they may consider just in the interests of the inhabitants of Magherafelt generally, irrespective of creed and of any limits of the original Trust of Rainey's Foundation," and asking a definite answer whether this offer be accepted or declined by the Commissioners; I am to point out that the offer does not appear to the Commissioners to be consistent with itself. In the opinion of the Commissioners, it was the intention of the founder that the Rainey Endowment should be administered by an exclusively Protestant body, and accordingly, in the scheme already published, a governing body of that character is constituted.

If your Company desire to give an additional endowment to the Rainey School, the Commissioners cannot regard such an endowment as really available in the interests of the inhabitants of Magherafelt generally, irrespective of creed, inasmuch as the Roman Catholics would have no voice in its management, nor would it be administered irrespective of the limits of the original trust of Rainey's foundation.

If, on the other hand, your Company intend the property offered by them to be administered "in the interests of the inhabitants of Magherafelt generally, irrespective of creed," it must be so administered by a governing body differently constituted from that of the Rainey School, and on which all denominations shall be fairly represented.

In either case, the Commissioners can exercise jurisdiction over any endowment offered by your Company only upon the written consent of the Company as the founders, given in accordance with the 7th Section of the Act, distinctly stating to which of the above purposes they desire their endowment to be applied, and accepting the responsibility of so applying it.

(Signed), N. D. MURPHY,
Assist. Secretary.

No. II. (k.)

THE SALTERS' COMPANY TO THE COMMISSIONERS.

Salters' Hall, St. Swithin's-lane,
London, E.C., 12th April, 1889.

SIR,—I am directed by the Salters' Company to inform you that they have given careful consideration to your letter of the 2nd March, 1889, as well as to Dr. Todd's letter of the 8th March, 1889, a copy of which that gentleman forwarded to the Company, and that they have decided to adopt his suggestion regarding the future management of the Markets, Flax Stores and Grain Stores at Magherafelt. The Company are therefore prepared to vest the property in the Markets Committee of Magherafelt, subject to an annual payment of £120 by way of rentcharge, to be secured upon the premises, the members of the Markets Committee entering into covenants by which they are made individually and collectively responsible for the payment of this rentcharge. They shall further covenant to hand over the property, subject of course to this rentcharge, and any profits that may accrue in the course of its management, to the Town Commissioners, if and when constituted, and in the meantime they shall devote any such profits to the maintenance of the property and improvement of the town. Having regard to the Company's wish that the Commissioners should declare such trust of the property as they may consider just in the interests of the inhabitants of the town, irrespective of creed and of any limits of the original trust of Rainey's Foundation, I am directed to state that the Company are prepared to consent to avail themselves of the jurisdiction to which you refer in your letter of the 2nd March, 1889, and I am therefore to request the Commissioners to take the necessary steps for the application of the rentcharge proposed to be secured upon the markets, &c., as hereinbefore described, to the undermentioned purposes, namely:—

£66 per annum to be applied to Rainey's Foundation School.

£54 per annum to be applied to the educational requirements of the Roman Catholic body of the town and neighbourhood.

The Company are given to understand that the above figures represent the proportion, as thereabouts, of Protestants to Roman Catholics on their late estate.

The Company hope that they have now removed all obstacles to the settlement of this matter.

(Signed), EDW. LAWLEY SCOTT,
Clerk of the Salters' Company.

No. II. (ii).

The Intermediate Education Committee of the General Assembly to the Commissioners.

Assembly's Offices, Belfast,

April 24, 18[illegible].

Dear Sir,—I am instructed to lay before the Commission the accompanying extract from the minute of proceedings of the Intermediate Education Committee of the General Assembly:—

(Signed) W. Todd Martin.

The Intermediate Education Committee of the General Assembly having before them the Rainey School Scheme, and the report of the Rev. Dr. H. B. Wilson, who had attended the court held by the Educational Endowments Commission to hear objections thereon, and who had taken exception to the Scheme on the part of the Assembly's Committee, resolved to call the attention of the Commission to the fact that under the proposed Scheme the Presbyterian Church would be placed in a position of inferiority, and must suffer manifest injustice. The Committee further resolved to urge that the Scheme be amended, so as to accord with the intention of the founder, and undo the wrong effected by Act of Parliament, when the trustees were handed over to the Archbishop of Armagh. The Committee cannot acquiesce in any arrangement that withholds from the Presbyterian Church control of a private charitable bequest, which is clearly Presbyterian; they therefore claim on behalf of the Assembly,—

1. That the Scheme be so framed as to carry out the founder's intention, and treat the Rainey Endowment as a Presbyterian foundation.

2. That the income derivable from the Rainey estate, together with the school buildings and premises now standing in lieu of lands and buildings provided under the will of Hugh Rainey, be dealt with as a Presbyterian foundation, and therefore placed under Presbyterian management.

3. That in so far as funds have been or may be received from a public company, or for the benefit of all without denominational distinction, an equitable share of such funds be allocated to the Presbyterian School Board created to administer the Rainey Endowment, in addition to the income received from the Rainey bequest.

W. Todd Martin, Convener.

No. II. (iii).

The Presbytery of Magherafelt to the Commissioners.

At a meeting of the Magherafelt Presbytery, specially convened on the 25th instant, to consider the whole question of the Rainey Endowment, in relation to the Scheme about to be formulated by the Educational Endowments (Ireland) Commission, the Presbytery had before them indisputable evidence of the following facts:—

1. That the Endowment was intended by the founder, Hugh Rainey, to be under the sole control of the Presbyterian Church.

2. That it was taken from under such control by Act of Parliament in the reign of George II., and placed under the exclusive authority of the Archbishop of Armagh, and from the passing of said Act till the present time the revenues derived from the Rainey Endowment have remained under the management of the Protestant Episcopal Church in direct contravention of the expressed intentions of the founder.

The Presbytery, after mature deliberation, unanimously resolved:

"That no Scheme or modification of Scheme will satisfy, or be accepted by, them that falls short of restoring the Rainey Endowment to the Presbyterian Church, to be managed solely by them as was intended by the founder. This they consider but simple justice, and they will be satisfied with nothing less; and they respectfully press upon the Commissioners the necessity of giving effect to this resolution in order that this long-standing and evident wrong may be redressed."

(Signed), Alexander Miller, Moderator of the Presbytery of Magherafelt.
W. Ross, Clerk of the Presbytery at Magherafelt.

At Magherafelt,
This 25th day of May, 18[illegible].

No. II. (iv).

Memorial from the Presbyterians of Magherafelt and neighbourhood to the Commissioners in relation to the Rainey Foundation School in Magherafelt.

We, the Presbyterians of Magherafelt and neighbourhood, respectfully beg to memorialize the above-named Commissioners on the matter of the "Rainey Foundation School," Magherafelt.

We base the prayer of our memorial on the following facts, which we hold to be indisputable:

1. The Endowment, as constituted by the will of Hugh Rainey, dated 1707, was purely Presbyterian, and placed solely under Presbyterian control and management. And it is clearly evident from the terms of said will that the founder of the Endowment intended it to continue under the management of the Presbyterian Church for all time to come.

2. By an Act of Parliament in the reign of George II. the Endowment was placed under the sole control of the Episcopal Church in Ireland, the management being placed in the hands of the Archbishop of Armagh. From the time of said Act till the present Presbyterians have been excluded from all control or management of the School and endowments. This control by the Episcopal Church through the Archbishop of Armagh, we believe to be in direct contravention of the intentions of the founder of the Endowment, and we feel it to be a grievous injustice, not only to the Presbyterians of this town and neighbourhood, but to the whole Presbyterian Church in Ireland.

Therefore the prayer of the Memorialists is:—

That in constructing a Scheme for the future management of that Endowment the Commission will have regard to the intentions of the founder, and place the Rainey Foundation School, with all the income accruing to it from the Rainey Endowment, under the sole control and management of the Presbyterian Church in Ireland.

In urging this prayer upon the attention of the Commission the Memorialists feel that they are asking for nothing more than that a long-standing wrong be now set right, and that after years of perversion of this Foundation justice now be done to the Presbyterian Church in the matter of this School.

And by granting the prayer of this Memorial your Petitioners, as in duty bound, will ever pray.

Dated at Magherafelt this 1st day of June, 18[illegible].

[Here follow 1[illegible] signatures.]

No. II. (xx).

The General Assembly to the Commissioners.*

Manse, Antrim,
[illegible] June, 1889.

Dear Sir,—According to the instructions of the General Assembly of the Presbyterian Church, specified in the accompanying extract minute of its proceedings, I beg to send you, as Secretary of the Educational Endowments (Ireland) Commission, copy of a resolution unanimously adopted by the General Assembly on the 12th inst., and request the Commissioners to receive the deputation appointed by the Assembly on the subject of the Draft Scheme for that Endowment.

The deputation will be prepared to wait upon the Commission at whatever time they may appoint, and I shall notify to the members the day and hour fixed on hearing from you.

(Signed), John H. Orr.

Secretary, Educational Endowments (Ireland) Commission.

Extract referred to in the foregoing Letter.

"At Belfast, the Twelfth day of June, One Thousand Eight Hundred and Eighty-nine years, which day the General Assembly of the Presbyterian Church in Ireland being met and constituted,

"Professor Leitch, in the absence of the Convener, Professor Todd Martin, brought up the report on Intermediate Education.

* * * *

"It was further resolved—That whereas the Act of Parliament appointing the Educational Endowments (Ireland) Commission requires that in all their schemes disposing of endowments, they shall have regard to the will of the founder, the General Assembly claims that the Commissioners shall recast the Draft Scheme for the Rainey Endowment at Magherafelt, and give the sole control over the funds and the school to the Presbyterians of that locality as officially represented by the Presbyteries of Magherafelt and Tyrone; and that the Clerk of Assembly be instructed to send a copy of this resolution to the Secretary of the Commission, and request them to receive a deputation consisting of the Revs. the Moderator and the Clerk of Assembly; Dr. [illegible] Wilson, Dr. W. Todd Martin, Dr. Leitch, John M. Hamilton, and William Reid, who are appointed to submit to the Commission the views of the Assembly.

"Extracted from the records of the General Assembly of the Presbyterian Church in Ireland by

"John H. Orr, [illegible]
"Clerk of Assembly."

ULSTER ROYAL SCHOOL ENDOWMENTS.

Correspondence and Documents.

See Evidence, pp. 140–180 and 183–191.

Nos. III. (b.) to III. (p.) refer to the valuation of the Royal School Buildings.

Nos. III. (r.) to III. (dd.) refer to the Revised Draft Scheme and the objections thereto, and to matters connected therewith, and to the Vested Interests of Dr. Steele and Dr. Moore Morgan.

No. III. (ee.) to III. (rr.) set out the correspondence relating to the proposal to form denominational Boards for Armagh and Tyrone.

No. III. (a.)

Referred to in Evidence, pp. 177, 184–6.

The Clerk of the Monaghan Union to the Commissioners.

Monaghan Union, Monaghan,
9th day of October, 1889.

Sir,—In compliance with your letter dated 30th September, 1889, I have gone over carefully the valuations of this union, and I believe the numbers of Roman Catholics and Protestants in the union rated at the amounts specified below correct.

(Signed), James Mitchell,
Clerk of the Union.

—	[illegible]	[illegible]	[illegible]	[illegible]
Protestants,	[illegible]	[illegible]	[illegible]	[illegible]
Roman Catholics,	[illegible]	[illegible]	[illegible]	[illegible]

Royal School Buildings.

Enniskillen.

No. III. (b.)

The Commissioners to the Rev. S. Cuthbert Mitchell.

15, Kildare-street, Dublin,
October 4, 1889.

Rev. Sir,—Referring to your * communication of 18th ultimo, I am directed to call your attention to an omission to supply the Commissioners with the figures at which, according to the estimate of your committee, the (a) buildings and (b) the lands of Portora should be valued by way of annual rent and also of capital value. As these figures are required to enable the Commissioners to consider the question of the fair distribution of the Endowment of which the buildings and lands form part, an early reply will oblige.

(Signed), Wm. Edward Ellis,
Secretary.

No. III. (c.)

Rev. S. C. Mitchell to the Commissioners.

Enniskillen,
8th October, 1889.

Dear Sir,—In reply to your letter of 4th inst., I am instructed by the Committee to say that, as we have already stated in our resolution of 18th September last, we consider the school buildings and lands attached ought to go together and be treated as a whole. While we cannot therefore suggest any sepa-

* See Report, 1889–90, p. [illegible]

rate valuation, we believe the fair letting value of the whole premises for educational purposes is two hundred pounds per annum.

We do not think it necessary to discuss the question of capital value at present, as the Commissioners have better means for forming an opinion on that point than we possess.

(Signed), S. Cuthbert Mitchell,
Hon. Secretary, Local
Protestant Committee.

*No. III. (d.)

The Commissioners to Rev. S. Cuthbert Mitchell.

1st December, 1888.

Rev. Sir,—I am directed to acquaint you with the enclosed proposal for the purchase of the existing buildings and land of Portora Royal School, and to invite the observations of your Committee thereon; it would be understood that the Commissioners would propose to treat the purchase-money of the premises, if sold, as portion of the endowment to which the Local Boards would be entitled in equal shares, and to make it available for the acquisition of suitable school premises or other local purposes of Intermediate Education.

(Signed), Wm. Edward Ellis,
Secretary.

[*The Letter above referred to.*]

The Colonel Commanding R. E. in Ireland to the Commissioners.

Very Pressing.

Dublin Castle,
29th November, 1888.

Sir,—I am directed by his Serene Highness the Commander of the Forces in Ireland to inform you that he has received a very pressing letter from the War Office, dated 26th instant, requesting him to communicate with the Educational Endowments Commission for Ireland, with a view to their inserting in the Act for regulating Endowments, which they are preparing, a proviso to the effect that the future trustees of the endowments should sell the existing buildings of Portora Royal School, and the ground belonging to the school, about fifty-four acres, more or less, with the existing buildings thereon, to Her Majesty's Principal Secretary of State for War for the sum of £7,000 (seven thousand pounds), if called upon to do so within the extreme limit of two years from the passing of the Act by the Privy Council.

(Signed), W. D. Marsh, Colonel,
Commanding Royal Engineer, Ireland.

No. III. (e.)

The Rev. S. Cuthbert Mitchell to the Commissioners.

Enniskillen,
4th December, 1888.

Sir,—The Local Committee having met and considered your communication, dated 1st December, 1888, direct me to say that until they see the amended Educational Scheme they are not in a position to express any opinion on the subject of your letter.

(Signed), S. Cuthbert Mitchell,
Hon. Sec. of Local Protestant
Committee.

No. III. (f.)

Rev. P. M'Glone (for Bishop Donnelly) to the Commissioners.

St. Macartan's Seminary, Monaghan,
December 22, 1888.

Sir,—The Most Rev. Dr. Donnelly, who is at present in Italy, has directed me to state, in reply to your letter of the first inst., that he "considers the Portora property—land and buildings—worth more than £7,000," and that he "objects to be bound to give the property to Government at that price"; but that he "consents that the Commissioners should insert in the Scheme a clause permitting the Local Boards or the Head Committee to sell to the Government at that price if they wish and think it wise to do so."

(Signed), Peter M'Glone.

Raphoe.

No. III. (g.)

Bishop O'Donnell to the Commissioners.

Letterkenny,
12th October, 1888.

Gentlemen,—After looking over the buildings and premises as carefully as I could, I beg to state what I consider to be the letting value of the Raphoe Royal School. I think it should be worth eighty-five pounds per year. Accordingly I offer £85 annually on behalf of the Roman Catholic body. Should it fall to us, the house would require some changes in the interior; but these could be executed under the eye of the Commissioners' surveyor or inspector.

(Signed), ✠ Patrick O'Donnell,
Bishop of Raphoe.

No. III. (h.)

The Commissioners to Bishop O'Donnell.

1st December, 1888.

My Lord,—The Commissioners have under immediate consideration the revision of the scheme for the Royal School Endowments with respect to the disposal of the school premises, and referring to your lordship's letter of October 12, 1888, offering "£85 annually on behalf of the Roman Catholic body, should the Raphoe Royal School fall to them," I am to inquire (1) Whether it is intended that the offer should be subject to the condition of using the premises for the purposes of Intermediate education in connection with

* Note.—A similar letter, of same date, was written to the Most Rev. Dr. Donnelly, Bishop of Clogher.
Nos. III. (d.) to III. (f.) are referred to in Evidence, pp. 138, 139.

the Raphoe Roman Catholic Local Board under the scheme. (2.) Whether, in estimating the amount, it was taken into consideration that nine acres of the school lands, held for a lease of 999 years, are subject to the rent of £23 11s. 2d.

Will you kindly let me know, as soon as convenient, a reply to the above queries.

(Signed), WM. EDWARD ELLIS,
Secretary.

No. III. (l.)

Bishop O'Donnell to the Commissioners.

Letterkenny, 3rd December, 1885.

Sir,—I am in receipt of your letter dated the 1st inst., relative to the Raphoe Royal School.

(1.) The offer of £85 a year on behalf of the Roman Catholic body was not made subject to the condition of using the institution for Intermediate education. It was made as an estimate of the general letting value, without any such restrictions as to use.

(2.) This sum of £85 was offered as being the value annually of the building, what is contained, and what is annexed to it. It is a moderate estimate of the whole amount the tenant should pay who gets the house and lands. Hence in my proposal the head rent of £23 11s. 2d., would not be an additional charge, but part of the £85.

I may add that purchase would be more convenient for the Catholic body than renting.

(Signed), ✠ PATRICK O'DONNELL.

Cavan.

No. III. (k.)

Rev. A. B. Baker to the Commissioners.

The Rectory, Cavan,
November 17, 1885.

Royal School Buildings, Cavan.

Dear Sir,—Being naturally interested in the above buildings and the securing of them for the use of the Protestants of Cavan for educational purposes, I have inquired of some twelve representative parishioners what they considered the *fair letting value* of the house and ten acres (Irish) would be; the result of such inquiries was as follows:—

I. The outside letting value was considered to be £60 per annum.

II. Several stated that owing to the kind of house it was, its position, its large schoolrooms and dormitory, so useless for letting purposes and so expensive to keep in repair, they would put no value on the *house*, but only on the *land*. Further, that while there may be ten acres altogether, so much is occupied by house, yards, garden, out-offices, shrubberies, and plantations, there would be scarcely more than six acres left for valuation.

III. Another stated that he believed an *offer*, for the purposes of *residing*, would give £50 per annum.

IV. At the present time there is a *good house* vacant, with some six (6) acres of land attached to it, beside the railway station, and the owner cannot get £40 per annum for it.

V. The fact of £3 per annum having to be paid to Rev. W. P. Moore, together with the fact that the avenue may be destroyed at any time through cabins being built upon it, greatly reduces the letting value of the place.

I thought the above facts, gathered from a number of residents of Cavan, might aid the Commissioners in arriving at an impartial judgment as to the value of the buildings.

(Signed), A. B. Baker, D.D., Rector.

Dungannon.

No. III. (l.)

The Commissioners to Very Rev. Dean Byrne.

3rd December, 1885.

Rev. Sir,—Referring to the suggestion made at the recent public sitting, that the Tyrone Local Board might possibly be able to arrange by agreement for the disposal of the lands and buildings of the Dungannon Royal School, utilizing them for the purpose of Intermediate Education in connexion with the Local Boards and under the conditions of the Scheme, I am to say that the Commissioners would be obliged if you could communicate with any one of the members of the proposed Roman Catholic Board resident in or near Dungannon, whom you may desire to select, and in conjunction with him confer with Colonel Lowry and James Brown, Esq., to whom I am writing on the same subject, with a view to informing the Commissioners whether such an arrangement is in your opinion practicable, and if so, as to the terms and conditions most likely to be acceptable to all concerned.

As the Draft Scheme is now under revision, early attention to this matter would be important.

(Signed), WM. EDWARD ELLIS,
Secretary.

Note.—A similar letter was sent to Colonel Lowry and James Brown, Esq.

No. III. (m.)

Dean Byrne to the Commissioners.

Dungannon, December 11th, 1885.

Dear Sir,—In accordance with the request conveyed in your letter of the 3rd inst., I had the pleasure of meeting the Rev. Lewis Richards, Rector of Drumglass, who had been deputed by Colonel Lowry as his representative, and James Brown, Esq., with both of whom I made a careful inspection of the Royal School. I am happy to say we were quite unanimous in the opinion that the buildings and lands were capable of division, and when divided could be used as Intermediate Schools for the different denominations under the conditions of the Scheme. The details, I believe, could be safely left to the future Boards to be appointed under the revised Scheme.

(Signed), P. J. Byrne.

No. III. (n.)

Rev. Lewis Richards to the Commissioners.

The Rectory, Dungannon,
12th Dec., 1885.

Dear Sir,—In accordance with Colonel Lowry's suggestion I met Dean Byrne, Rev. J. M'Cartan, and Mr. James Brown, to confer about the disposal of the Royal School buildings and grounds.

There is a strong feeling here among the members of the Church of Ireland, and other Protestants, in favour of retaining the buildings for school purposes.

The Roman Catholic party do not seem to care much for buildings, but would not object to getting a portion of the ground.

It was suggested at the conference that the building might be divided so as to give the north wing to the Roman Catholics, and the south wing to the Protestants. The idea seemed to meet with some favour, but in my opinion, and that of others whom I have consulted, such an arrangement would not be likely to work well.

It might, perhaps, fall in with the wishes of the Roman Catholic party that they should get possession of the garden, which lies opposite their chapel, and is bounded on two sides by the public road. The rest of the land, owing to its lie, goes of necessity with the great portion of the building—the garden might be cut off without inconvenience.

(Signed), Lewis Richardson, Clk.

No. III. (o.)

James Brown, Esq., to the Commissioners.

Donaghmore, Tyrone, 11th Dec., 1888.

Sir,—I beg to acknowledge the receipt of your favour of the 3rd inst. In conformity with the request made therein, I went to the Royal School in Dungannon yesterday, and met the Rev. Dean Byrne, and the Rev. Mr. Richards (who took the place of Colonel Lowry, he being unable to attend). We went over the school buildings and found them in good order. The question how best to dispose of them is a very difficult one, as they are too large to be continued as a single school for either the Roman Catholics or the various Protestant denominations.

The hope of selling them for other purposes, at a fair price, I look upon as very faint indeed. We, therefore, came to the conclusion that the best plan would be to divide the buildings and grounds into two shares, and give one to the Roman Catholics and the other to the Protestant denominations.

I am strongly of opinion that the Scheme as printed by the Commissioners is, in its main features, the very best that can be set forth for settling this question, and I would recommend that it should be adhered to.

(Signed), James Brown.

Armagh.

No. III. (p.)

The Commissioners to Archbishop Logue.

3rd December, 1888.

My Lord Archbishop,—With a view to revising the provisions for the disposal of the buildings and land of the Armagh Royal School, the Commissioners would be obliged if your Grace would be good enough to give the Commissioners your estimate of the annual letting value of the premises, with such observations as your Grace may desire to submit, with regard to the claim in respect of private benefactions.

As the draft scheme is now under revision, early attention to this matter would be important.

(Signed), Wm. Edward Ellis, Secretary.

Note.—The answer to this letter, dated March 5th, 1889, will be found *infra*, "Objections and Amendments," No. VII.

No. III. (q.)

Two Letters from James Greer and T. O. Johnson, Assistant Masters, Royal School, Raphoe.

Raphoe Royal School, 22nd April.

To the Judicial Commissioners.

We, the assistant masters of the Raphoe Royal School, have seen that, according to your scheme as in its present state, no provision is made for any compensation or gratuity in our case. All the principals and assistants in the other schools have had their claims considered and allowed. We do not understand whether this distinction has been made in our case because we did not bring our claims under your notice at the sitting of the Commission last August, or whether you consider us debarred from any compensation on the ground that we were not in our present posts until after the passing of the Educational Endowments Act. On this point we may call your attention to the fact that at the disestablishment of the Irish Church, even those who had been in preparation for the ministry received compensation.

If we receive any appointment under the Local Boards created by the scheme, or if Dr. Weir should decide to carry on the school, our interests are to a certain extent preserved. In the event, however, of the head master's resignation within the prescribed period of six months, we shall (if not appointed by any of the Local Boards) be deprived of our situations without any compensation.

We may also remark that on this point the scheme is scarcely consistent, as by the provisions of section 53 we would each seem to be entitled to a year's salary for three years' completed service. In conclusion we would ask either to be put on the same footing as the assistant masters in the other schools, or at least to be allowed the gratuity of a year's salary to which we are fairly entitled under section 53.

(Signed), James Greer.
T. O. Johnson.

Raphoe Royal School,
30th April.

To the Educational Endowments Commissioners.

We beg to acknowledge receipt of your letter of 25th instant. In reply we wish to state that your objection to our claims is founded on a total misapprehension of the facts. You state that we do not draw our salaries from any of the endowments over which the Commission has control, but that we are paid by the head master, Dr. Weir. If this were so we should not of course consider ourselves to have any claim whatever. Our salaries are respectively £60 and £40 per annum, and of this we do not receive one penny from the head master, but out of the funds of the estate through the Secretary, Mr. MacDowell. In this respect we are on precisely the same standing as the assistants in the other schools or as the head masters themselves, and at each half yearly payment have to give our receipt to the "Commissioners of Education in Ireland." You can easily verify the correctness of this statement by referring to Mr. MacDowell. The letter which you have addressed to us practically admits that our claims are well founded, and that we would not have been excluded from the scheme if the Commissioners had known that we were on the same footing as the other masters. The sum which we would receive would be very small, either a year's salary each in accordance with section 53, or the capitalized value of a very small annuity amounting on the whole to a trifling sum, not more than £150.

(Signed) James Greer.
T. O. Johnson.

Revised Draft Scheme, and Objections and Amendments thereto.

No. III. (F.)

Referred to in Evidence, pp. [illegible].

PORTIONS of the REVISED DRAFT SCHEME to which OBJECTIONS and AMENDMENTS were received.

This draft was submitted to the various parties interested as being the Scheme which the Judicial Commissioners proposed to sign.

On June 25, [illegible], a Scheme was framed and signed by the *Judicial Commissioners* and submitted to the Lord *Lieutenant* in Council.

To this Scheme objections were lodged with the Clerk of the Privy Council.

The Portions of the Scheme submitted to the Lord Lieutenant to which the objections lodged with the Privy Council refer will be found supra, p. xxii.

The objections lodged with the Privy Council and the observations of the Commissioners thereon will be found supra, p. xxxi.

Recitals—

The Ulster Royal Schools.
Cavan Royal School.
Banagher Royal School.
14 & 15 *Charles II.*, c. 10.

Commissioners of Education in Ireland:

53 *George III.*, c. 107.
3 *George IV.*, c. 79.
17 & 18 *Vic.*, c. 34.

Preliminary.

Interpretation of Terms, section 1.

PART I.—*The Commissioners of Education in Ireland.—Reconstitution of the Commissioners.*

2. From and after the date of this Scheme, "The Commissioners of Education in Ireland" shall be constituted in manner hereinafter provided, and as so constituted shall continue to be a Body Corporate, with perpetual succession and a common seal, and power to acquire and hold property, real and personal, for the purposes of this Scheme, and shall, for the purposes of this Scheme, continue to have, hold, exercise, and enjoy all the powers, jurisdiction, privileges, and authority which at the date of this Scheme shall be vested in or capable of being exercised or enjoyed by the Commissioners, under the hereinbefore recited Acts or otherwise howsoever.

From and after the date of this Scheme, subject to the provision hereinafter contained as to the continuing Commissioners, the said Body Corporate shall consist of the members following, that is to say—

(a.) Ten Commissioners appointed by the Lord Lieutenant as hereinafter provided.

(b.) Ten Commissioners elected by the Local Boards as hereinafter provided.

(c.) Two Commissioners elected by the Council of the University of Dublin as hereinafter provided.

(d.) Two Commissioners elected by the Senate of the Royal University of Ireland, as hereinafter provided.

(e.) Two Commissioners elected by the Governing Body of the Institution known as "The Catholic University of Ireland," as hereinafter provided.

(f.) Two Commissioners elected by the Intermediate Education Board for Ireland as hereinafter provided.

(g.) One Commissioner elected by the Council of Studies of the Royal College of St. Patrick, Maynooth, as hereinafter provided.

(h.) One Commissioner elected by the Faculty of The Magee Presbyterian College, Londonderry, as hereinafter provided.

From and after the date of this Scheme no person shall be entitled to be, to continue, or to become a Commissioner by virtue of any office whatsoever.

Continuing Commissioners.

3. In the first instance, such and so many of the existing Commissioners as at the date of this Scheme shall be able and willing to act, and shall have attended not less than one-fourth of the meetings of the Commissioners held during their tenure of office within three years next before the date of this Scheme, shall continue to be members of the Body Corporate, and shall be deemed to be Commissioners appointed by the Lord Lieutenant, and shall hold office as if they had been so appointed. The existing Commissioners so qualified are hereinafter referred to as the continuing Commissioners. All the existing Commissioners not so qualified shall, at the date of this Scheme, cease to be members of the Body Corporate, but shall be eligible for appointment or election as Commissioners under this Scheme. From and after the date of this Scheme, the continuing Commissioners, with such and so many Commissioners as shall have been appointed or elected as herein provided, shall constitute the Body Corporate, and shall and may have, hold, exercise, and enjoy all the property, powers, jurisdiction, privileges, and authority of the Commissioners for the time being; provided that every act done by the Commissioners during the period of two months next after the date of this Scheme shall be subject to confirmation by the Commissioners at their first meeting held after the expiration of that period.

Appointment of Commissioners by Lord Lieutenant.

4. The Commissioners appointed by the Lord Lieutenant shall be appointed in manner following, and shall hold office during the pleasure of the Lord Lieutenant. Immediately after the date of this Scheme, and from time to time thereafter, as occasion shall require, the Lord Lieutenant shall appoint such and so many persons resident in Ireland to be Commissioners as, with the continuing Commissioners, shall make up the number of ten Commissioners so appointed.

In the appointment of Commissioners, the Lord Lieutenant shall provide, so far as is consistent with the retention of office by the continuing Commissioners, that of the ten Commissioners appointed by the Lord Lieutenant, five shall be Protestants and five shall be Roman Catholics, and of the five Protestants, one at the least shall be a member of the said Church, one at the least shall be a Presbyterian, and one at the least shall be a Methodist.

Whenever any continuing Commissioner or Commissioner appointed by the Lord Lieutenant shall die, or resign by writing under his hand, or become bankrupt, or refuse to act, or become incapable of acting, or shall cease to reside in Ireland, or shall for the space of one year fail to attend any meeting of the Commissioners, or shall be removed from office by the Lord Lieutenant, his office shall thereupon become vacant, and the fact of such vacancy, with the cause thereof, shall be recorded in the minutes of the Commissioners, and, except in the case of removal by the Lord Lieutenant, shall be notified by the Commissioners to the Lord Lieutenant.

Immediately after the date of this Scheme, the Secretary of the Commissioners shall prepare from the minutes of the existing Commissioners, and shall forward to the Lord Lieutenant, a list of the existing Commissioners, with the dates of their appointments, and a return of their attendances at the meetings held within three years next before the date of this Scheme, distinguishing those qualified as continuing Commissioners under the provisions hereinbefore contained.

Election of Commissioners.

5. At a meeting of each Local Board, to be held after due notice, and within two months after the date of this Scheme, the members present shall elect one person to be a Commissioner. Each Commissioner so elected shall hold office until the last day of the calendar year first ending more than twelve months after the date of this Scheme. At a meeting of each Local Board to be held in the month of November or December in such year and in every year thereafter, the members present shall elect one person to be a Commissioner. Each Commissioner so elected shall enter upon office on the first day of January following his election, and shall hold office until the thirty-first day of December next ensuing, or until the election of his successor, whichever shall last happen.

Vesting of Endowments and Continuance of Powers.

6. From and after the date of this Scheme, subject to the provisions of this or any other Scheme or Schemes framed under the Act, all the Endowments then held by or vested in the existing Commissioners shall remain vested in the Commissioners as hereby constituted, who shall thenceforth hold, receive, and apply all the Endowments, except the Ulster Royal School Endowments, in the same manner as if this Scheme had not passed, and shall thenceforth hold, receive, and apply the Ulster Royal School Endowments, and the rents, issues, dividends, and produce thereof, and all other property and moneys applicable to the purposes of the Ulster Royal Schools, and receivable by the Commissioners, in the manner hereinafter prescribed. All powers, jurisdiction, privileges, and authority, at the date of this Scheme vested in the Commissioners, or capable of being exercised or enjoyed by them, shall continue to be vested in and may be exercised and enjoyed by the Commissioners as hereby constituted. All existing enactments and provisions then affecting, concerning, or relating to "The Commissioners of Education in Ireland," shall thenceforth apply to the Commissioners as hereby constituted, save so far as may by this or by any other Scheme or Schemes framed under the Act be otherwise provided.

General Provisions as to the Commissioners.—Chairman, Quorum, and Honorary Officers.

8. The Commissioners at their first meeting. . . . Five Commissioners shall constitute a quorum, and all matters and questions shall be determined by the majority of the Commissioners present; in every case of equality of votes the Chairman of the meeting shall have a second or casting vote. The Commissioners may, from time to time, appoint such honorary officers as they shall think fit, and may define the duties of such honorary officers.

9. *Committees.*

10. *Meetings.*

Minutes, Seals, and Documents.

11. . . . All deeds and other writings, sealed with the common seal and signed at any meeting by the Chairman of the meeting and two other Commissioners, and by the Secretary, shall be held to be duly executed on behalf of the Commissioners.

12. *By-Laws.*

Accounts and Audits.

13. The Commissioners shall cause to be kept regular accounts. . . . The Commissioners shall keep an account with such bank as they may from time to time select, and all moneys receivable or payable by them (except petty cash) shall be lodged to or drawn from such account, and every cheque shall be signed by two Commissioners, at the least, thereto authorised, and by the Secretary.

14. *Annual Report.*

15. *Inspection.*

16. *Additional Endowments.*

17. *Management of Estates.*

18. *Leasing Powers.*

19. *Powers of Investment.*

PART II.—*The Ulster Royal Schools.*

20. *Ulster Local Boards of Education.*

21. *Functions of Local Boards.*

Constitution of Local Boards.

22. Each Local Board shall consist, in the first instance, of nine members to be appointed as hereinafter provided. The members of each Local Board so appointed, may from time to time, by resolution passed at a meeting specially convened for the purpose, and supported by not less than seven such members, co-opt so many additional members, not at any time exceeding six in all, as they shall think fit. Each additional member so co-opted shall hold office, in the case of the Protestant Boards, until the next election of the Local Board; and in the case of the Roman Catholic Boards, for the same period as if he had been appointed to be a member of the Board under this Scheme.

The Protestant Local Boards.—Armagh Protestant Board.

23. Five members of the Armagh Protestant Board of Education shall be elected by the Diocesan Council of Armagh; three shall be elected by the General Assembly; and one shall be elected by the Methodist Conference.

Tyrone Protestant Board.

Two members of the Tyrone Protestant Board of Education shall be elected by the Diocesan Council of Armagh; one shall be elected by the Diocesan Council of Derry and Raphoe; five shall be elected by the General Assembly; and one shall be elected by the Methodist Conference.

Fermanagh Protestant Board.

Five members of the Fermanagh Protestant Board of Education shall be elected by the Diocesan Council of Clogher; three shall be elected by the General Assembly; and one shall be elected by the Methodist Conference.

Cavan Protestant Board.

Three members of the Cavan Protestant Board of Education shall be elected by the Diocesan Council of Kilmore; two shall be elected by the Select Vestry of the parish of Cavan; three shall be elected by the General Assembly; and one, representing the other Protestant Denominations of the District, shall be elected by the other members of the Board as hereinafter provided.

Donegal Protestant Board.

Three members of the Donegal Protestant Board of Education shall be elected by the Diocesan Council of Derry and Raphoe; five shall be elected by the General Assembly; and one, representing the other Protestant Denominations of the District, shall be elected by the other members of the Board as hereinafter provided.

General Vacancies.

24. If at the date of this Scheme any of the first members of the said several Protestant Local Boards hereinbefore named shall be unable or unwilling to act, and whenever thereafter any member of any of the said several Boards shall die, or resign by writing under his hand, or become bankrupt, or refuse to act, or become incapable of acting, or shall cease to reside in the District, his office shall thereupon become vacant, and the fact of the vacancy, with the cause thereof, shall be recorded in the minutes of the Board; and as soon as conveniently may be after the occurrence of such vacancy, the electing body amongst whose representatives the vacancy shall have occurred, or the remaining members of the Local Board to which such member belonged, as the case may be, shall elect a duly qualified person to fill the vacancy; each member so elected shall hold office so long only as the member in whose place he shall have been elected might have held the same.

Election of Members.

25. The first members of the several Protestant Local Boards shall hold office until the thirty-first day of December first happening more than twelve months after the date of this Scheme, or until the election of their respective successors, whichever shall last happen. Before the said thirty-first day of December, and once in every year thereafter, each of the several bodies entitled to elect representatives upon the said several Boards may elect such representatives. The elections shall be held, once in each year, at such times as the several bodies entitled to elect representatives shall respectively prescribe from time to time. The members so elected shall hold office until the election of their respective successors. Every outgoing member, if otherwise qualified, shall be eligible for re-election.

At the first meeting in each calendar year commencing more than twelve months after the date of this Scheme, the Protestant Local Boards of Cavan and Raphoe shall each elect one suitable person resident in the District and willing to act, who shall be a member of a Protestant Denomination not otherwise represented upon the Board, and each person so elected shall hold office as a member of the Board until the election of his successor. Every such outgoing member, if otherwise qualified, shall be eligible for re-election, provided he shall have attended at the least one-third of the meetings of the Board held during his term of office, but not otherwise.

The Roman Catholic Local Boards.

26. Each Roman Catholic Board of Education shall consist of the Roman Catholic Archbishop or Bishop hereinafter mentioned for the time being, with eight other members, of whom four shall be ecclesiastics and four shall be laymen.

Tyrone Roman Catholic Board.

The Tyrone Roman Catholic Board of Education shall consist in the first instance of such and so many of the following persons as at the date of this Scheme shall be able and willing to act:—

1. The Most Rev. Francis Kelly, D.D., Bishop of Derry, or other the Roman Catholic Bishop of Derry for the time being.

Representing the portion of the District in the Diocese of Armagh and County of Tyrone.

2. The Very Rev. Peter James Byrne, V.G., P.P., Dungannon, Dean of Armagh.
3. The Very Rev. Thomas Canon Rice, P.P., Cookstown.
4. William James Reynolds, Esq., M.P., Dungannon.
5. Henry Tohall, jun., Esq., Moy.

Representing the portion of the District in the Diocese of Armagh and County of Londonderry.

6. The Very Rev. Patrick Canon Donnelly, P.P., Magherafelt.

Representing the portion of the District in the Diocese of Derry.

7. The Rev. Bernard M'Namee, P.P., Omagh.
8. James Glenlon, Esq., Crown Solicitor, Omagh.

Representing the portion of the District in the Diocese of Clogher.

9. Michael MacMackin, Esq., Fintona.

Appointment of Ecclesiastical Members.

27. If at the date of this Scheme any of the abovenamed ecclesiastical members of the several Roman Catholic Boards, other than the Archbishop or Bishop for the time being, shall be unable or unwilling to act, and whenever thereafter any ecclesiastical member shall die, or resign by writing under his hand, or become bankrupt, or refuse to act, or become incapable of acting, or shall cease to hold an ecclesiastical appointment in the District or portion of a District represented by him, or shall fail to attend at the least one-third of the meetings of the Board held in any one year, his office shall thereupon become vacant, and the fact of the vacancy, with the cause thereof, shall be recorded in the minutes of the Board; and as soon as conveniently may be after the occurrence of such vacancy, the remaining ecclesiastical members of the Board shall co-opt a duly qualified person to fill the same.

Appointment of Lay Members.

28. If at the date of this Scheme any of the abovenamed lay members of the several Roman Catholic Boards shall be unable or unwilling to act, and whenever thereafter any lay member shall die, or resign by writing under his hand, or become bankrupt, or refuse to act, or become incapable of acting, or shall cease to reside in the District or portion of a District represented by him, or shall fail to attend at the least one-third of the meetings of the Board held in any one year, his office shall thereupon become vacant, and the fact of the vacancy, with the cause thereof, shall be recorded in the minutes of the Board; and, as soon as conveniently may be after the occurrence of such vacancy, the remaining lay members of the Board shall co-opt a duly qualified person to fill the same.

General Provisions as to Local Boards.—Chairman, Quorum, and Honorary Officers.

29. Each Local Board shall appoint a chairman. . . Each board may from time to time appoint an Honorary Secretary and such other Honorary Officers as they shall think fit, and may define the duties of such Honorary Officers.

30. *Meetings.*

31. *Minute Books and Documents.*

32. *Byelaws and Regulations.*

33. *Accounts and Audit.*

Committees.

34. Each Local Board may from time to time appoint a Committee or Committees, each consisting of two or more of their number, to carry into execution any orders, rules or directions of the Board with respect to the purposes of this Scheme, or to manage such of their business as the Board may deem it expedient to depute to such Committee or Committees. Any two or more Local Boards may in like manner appoint a Joint Committee or Joint Committees, each consisting of equal numbers of their members, for the transaction of any business in which the Boards may be jointly interested. The Board or Boards appointing such committee may for the purpose, define the duties, and regulate the proceedings of the Committee, as they may think fit.

35. *Estates Committees.*

36. *School Committees.*

Powers of Local Boards.

37. Subject to the provisions of this scheme, each Local Board, directly or through a School Committee, shall have and exercise general supervision and control over every school sharing in the endowments administered by the Board, shall appoint the masters and other members of the teaching staff, shall determine the various branches of education to be taught, shall regulate the fees to be charged in the school, shall fix the terms and vacations, and shall make such rules and regulations for the maintenance of order and discipline, as to the Local Board or School Committee, as the case may be, shall seem expedient. Subject as aforesaid, each Local Board, directly or through a School Committee, shall from time to time fix the number, salaries, and emoluments of the masters and other members of the staff to be employed in and about each school, and shall define their several and respective duties, and shall provide for the appointment of such domestic staff and other officers and servants as may be required.

Power to Protestant Local Boards to allocate Endowments.

38. Any Protestant Local Board may, with the sanction of the Commissioners, form a Committee or Committees for the purpose of allocating the endowments administered by the Board among the different Protestant denominations of the District, upon such terms and subject to such conditions as may be agreed upon. Each Committee shall consist of three or more members of the Board, and shall have, with respect to any school or schools placed under their control, all the privileges, powers and functions, which the Local Board might otherwise have under the provisions of this Scheme. The Local Board may, with the sanction of the Commissioners, allocate to any school or schools placed under the control of a Committee formed as aforesaid, so much of the Endowments administered by the Board as, having regard to the relative numbers of the members of the several Protestant denominations entitled to benefit from the endowments of the District, shall seem just.

Any two or more Protestant Local Boards, for the purpose and in manner aforesaid, may join in forming a Committee or Committees, and in allocating endowments, and in exercising the other powers conferred by this clause, as if for the purposes of this clause the said Boards had been one Local Board, and their several Districts and the endowments thereof had been united and amalgamated.

Provided that every appointment of a Committee, and every allocation of endowments under this clause, shall be made by resolution passed at a meeting specially convened for the purpose, and supported by not less than two-thirds of the full number of members of each Local Board concerned; provided also that all endowments allocated under this clause shall be administered in accordance with the provisions of this Scheme, which shall apply to each Committee formed as aforesaid as if the Committee were a Local Board.

Distribution of Ulster Royal School Endowments.

39. Subject to the other provisions of this Scheme, and after providing for all proper and necessary outgoings, charges and liabilities, the annual income received by the Commissioners from each of the Ulster Royal School Endowments during the period from the date at which this Scheme shall come into operation with respect to the said endowments respectively until the end of the second complete calendar year next following, which period is hereinafter called the first three years, shall be paid by the Commissioners, in equal shares, to the two Local Boards of the District, and the moneys so paid shall be applied by the several Local Boards for the following purposes, or for such and so many of them as the said Boards respectively shall deem expedient:—

(a.) To aid, maintain, or improve any existing Intermediate school or schools situated in the District, and managed by the Local Board, in accordance with the provisions of this Scheme;

(b.) To establish, or aid in establishing, in the District, any Intermediate school or schools to be managed as aforesaid;

(c.) To invest and accumulate a capital fund, of which the principal and interest may from time to time be applied by the Local Board, as they shall deem expedient, in aiding, maintaining, improving, or establishing any Intermediate school or schools in the District, to be managed as aforesaid;

(d.) To make provision, in such other manner as the Local Board shall deem expedient, for promoting Intermediate education in the District, so as to enable the Local Board after the first three years to avail themselves of the provisions of this Scheme.

Provided that if any Local Board shall think it more advantageous to apply the moneys paid to them under this clause, in aid of any Intermediate school or schools managed by another Local Board, they may, with the sanction of the Commissioners, so apply the same.

Application of Endowments after First Three Years.

40. Subject to the other provisions of this Scheme, and after providing for all proper and necessary outgoings, charges and liabilities, the annual income received by the Commissioners after the expiration of the first three years, from the several Ulster Royal School Endowments with respect to which this Scheme shall have come into operation, shall be distributed by the Commissioners among the several Local Boards, and shall be applied by the Local Boards for the purposes of Intermediate Education as hereinafter provided.

Minimum Grants.

41. For each calendar year commencing after the expiration of the first three years, the Commissioners shall in the first instance pay to each Local Board a minimum grant calculated as follows:—

To each of the Armagh Local Boards, twenty-five per cent. of the net income received during the year from the Armagh Royal School Endowments, other than the School premises.

To each of the Tyrone Local Boards, twenty-five per cent. of the net income received during the year from the Dungannon Royal School Endowments, other than the School premises.

To each of the Fermanagh Local Boards, twenty-five per cent. of the net income received during the year from the Enniskillen Royal School Endowments, other than the School premises.

To each of the Cavan Local Boards, thirty per cent. of the net income received during the year from the Cavan Royal School Endowments, other than the School premises.

To each of the Donegal Local Boards, fifty per cent. of the net income received during the year from the endowments of the Raphoe Royal School, other than the School premises.

Distribution of Residue among Local Boards.

42. After payment of the above-mentioned minimum grants, the residue of the annual income received by the Commissioners from the several Ulster Royal School Endowments with respect to which this Scheme shall have come into operation, during each calendar year commencing after the expiration of the first three years, shall be treated as a common fund, out of which the Commissioners shall first pay the amounts necessary to provide the free places hereinafter required to be provided by the Commissioners, and they shall then distribute the remainder in the manner set forth in the First Schedule hereto, among the several Local Boards for the benefit of the Intermediate Schools qualified as hereinafter provided.

Qualified Schools.

43. The conditions to be fulfilled by a School in order that it shall be qualified to receive benefit from the minimum grant of any Local Board, or from the above mentioned residue of the Ulster Royal School Endowments, shall be as follows:—

(a.) The School shall be conducted in accordance with the provisions of this Scheme, and shall be managed by the Local Board of the District in which it is situated, either directly or through a School Committee established appointed or recognised as hereinbefore provided.

(b.) Instruction shall be given in the School in the following subjects, at the least:—

In a School for Boys—Latin, Greek, English, French or German, Ancient and Modern History, Geography, Arithmetic, Algebra and Euclid.

In a School for Girls—Latin, English, French or German, Ancient and Modern History, Geography, Arithmetic, Algebra or Euclid, and Music or Drawing.

In a School for Boys and Girls.—Latin, Greek, English, French or German, Ancient and Modern History, Geography, Arithmetic, Algebra and Euclid, and Music or Drawing.

(c.) The School shall, during each school year for which a payment is claimed, have afforded Intermediate Education to not less than twenty pupils, each of whom shall have made one hundred attendances at the least in such school year, and not less than seven of these pupils shall, during such school year, have passed the examinations of the Intermediate Education Board for Ireland in the subjects specified in the First Schedule hereto at the least. The date at which the school year shall terminate for the purposes of this clause shall be fixed by the Commissioners; the attendances of the same pupil shall not be counted at more than one School in the same school year, and no pupil shall be included in the required number who on the last day of the school year shall be less than twelve or more than nineteen years of age.

(d.) The Inspector appointed by the Lord Lieutenant shall be satisfied, and shall report and certify, that, during each school year for which a payment is claimed, the buildings premises and appliances of the School have been sufficient and suitable for an efficient Intermediate School, and have been in good order, that a competent staff for the efficient teaching of the required subjects has been employed in the School, and that Intermediate Education has been afforded therein to the required number of pupils of the prescribed age.

Provided that in any case in which a School may be prevented, by any temporary or accidental cause, from fulfilling the conditions aforesaid during any school year, the Commissioners may for such year dispense with the fulfilment of any one or more of the said conditions, upon being satisfied that the School is likely to fulfil the same in the next succeeding year, but such a dispensation shall not be made for the same School for two consecutive years.

The Schools which fulfil the foregoing conditions are hereinafter referred to as qualified Schools.

Claims to Residue.

44. For each school year ending after the first three years, each Local Board may claim, in such manner as the Commissioners shall prescribe, a share of the residue of the income of the Ulster Royal School Endowments for any qualified School or Schools in their District, and the whole amount of such residue, after providing the free places hereinafter required to be provided by the Commissioners, shall be divided by the Commissioners among the several Local Boards for the benefit of the qualified Schools for which such claims shall have been made and established to the satisfaction of the Commissioners, in proportions to be calculated by results in accordance with the provisions contained in the First Schedule hereto.

Each Local Board may in the first instance select, according to their own discretion, the qualified School or Schools for which they will claim a share of the said residue, but the Governing Body of any School claiming to be qualified, or to be qualified in all respects save being managed by the Local Board, and for which the Local Board shall not have made a claim, may appeal to the Commissioners, who shall thereupon inquire and determine whether it is for the benefit of Intermediate Education in the District that the School should be admitted to share in the said residue, and may admit the School accordingly. Provided that, in every such case, the Commissioners shall require, as a condition of admission, that the School shall be placed under the management of the Local Board, either directly, or through a School Committee which shall be constituted as hereinbefore prescribed, and shall be established, appointed, or recognised by the Local Board of the District or by the Commissioners; and the Commissioners shall also satisfy themselves that the School is, in all other respects, qualified as hereinbefore prescribed.

45. *Free Places provided by Schools sharing Minimum Grants.*

(f.) Each candidate to whom a free place shall be awarded shall be entitled, subject to removal for misconduct or failure to make satisfactory progress, to receive Intermediate Education as a day pupil at a School sharing in the minimum grant received by the Local Board offering the free place, in all the subjects taught in the school, free of charge, for the two school years next following the examination; or, if admitted as a boarding pupil, shall, subject as aforesaid, be entitled to a reduction of ten pounds per annum in the fee usually charged in the school for a boarding pupil of the same age.

46. *Free places provided from Residue.*

47. *Application of the Endowments by the Local Boards.*

48. *Aid from Public Sources.*

49. *Religious Instruction.*

School Buildings and Premises.

56. The buildings of each of the Ulster Royal Schools, and the lands held and occupied therewith at the date of this Scheme, described in the third schedule hereto, and hereinafter called the school premises, shall be regarded as part of the Royal School Endowments of the District in which they are situated, and from and after the date at which this scheme shall come into operation with respect to each of the said endowments respectively, the school premises, and the value and produce thereof, shall be held and disposed of as hereinafter provided, and shall in each case be applied exclusively for the educational benefit of the District, and, subject to the provisions as to private endowments hereinafter contained, shall be treated as belonging in equal shares to the two Local Boards of the District, and as applicable to the same purposes as the said seven grants hereinbefore mentioned, in addition to the said grants.

Armagh School Premises.

As soon as conveniently may be after the date at which this Scheme shall come into operation with respect to the Armagh Royal School Endowments, the Commissioners shall proceed, on notice to the Armagh Local Boards, to ascertain and declare the proportion, if any, of the then value of the Armagh School premises which may be proved to be attributable to the expenditure of private moneys on the said premises, by any Protestant benefactor or benefactors. When such proportion has been declared, the Commissioners shall offer the said premises to the Armagh Protestant Local Board, to be used for the purposes of a school managed by the Board in accordance with the provisions of this scheme, at a rent fixed by estimating the fair competition rent of the whole of the said premises at £300 per annum, and deducting from that sum, as belonging exclusively to the said Board, the proportion attributable to the expenditure of the private moneys aforesaid. If the said Board shall take the said premises on the said terms, the Commissioners shall deliver the possession thereof to the said Board, and shall permit them to occupy the same on the said terms so long as they shall be used for the purposes aforesaid. If the said Board shall not take the said premises upon the terms aforesaid, or having taken them, shall at any time cease to use them for the purposes aforesaid, the Commissioners shall sell or let the said premises to the best advantage, and shall dispose of the proceeds thereof as herein provided.

Cavan School Premises.

As soon as conveniently may be after the date at which this Scheme shall come into operation, with respect to the Cavan Royal School Endowments, the Commissioners shall offer the Cavan School premises to the Cavan Protestant Local Board at the estimated capital value of £3,000. If the said Board shall take the said premises on the said terms, the Commissioners shall deliver the possession thereof to the said Board, and shall permit them to occupy the same so long as they shall be used for the purposes of a school managed by the Board in accordance with the provisions of this Scheme. The Commissioners shall, at the same time, invest or set apart from the capital of the Cavan Royal School Endowments a sum of Government Stock equivalent to £3,000, and shall thenceforth hold and apply the same as a building fund, for the purposes of the Cavan Roman Catholic Local Board, as hereinafter provided. If the Cavan Protestant Board shall not take the said premises upon the terms aforesaid, or, having taken them, shall at any time cease to use them for the purposes aforesaid, the Commissioners shall invest or set apart from the same capital, and shall thenceforth hold and apply, a further sum of Government Stock equivalent to £3,000, as a building fund, for the purposes of the Cavan Protestant Local Board, and shall sell or let the said school premises to the best advantage, and shall dispose of the proceeds thereof as herein provided.

Dungannon School Premises.

As soon as conveniently may be after this Scheme shall come into operation with respect to the Dungannon Royal School Endowments, the Tyrone Local Boards shall meet and consider, or shall appoint a Joint Committee to meet and consider, whether it would be more advantageous to employ the Dungannon School premises for the purposes of education, or to dispose of them by sale or letting, or to dispose of certain portions by sale or letting and to employ other portions for the purposes of education. They shall also consider whether it would be desirable, if the premises should be employed for the purposes of education, that they should be taken jointly or in several portions by the two Local Boards or by School Committees established, appointed, or recognised by them, or should be taken wholly or partly by one Board or School Committee for the purposes of a school or schools to be managed by such Board or Boards, or by such Committee or Committees, in accordance with the provisions of this Scheme, and they shall consider the terms and conditions on which the said premises may be most advantageously and justly dealt with, having due regard to the interests of both Local Boards therein, and treating any proportion of the value of the said premises which may be proved to be attributable to the expenditure of private moneys on the said premises, by any Protestant benefactor or benefactors, as belonging exclusively to the Tyrone Protestant Local Board.

In considering these questions the Local Boards or Joint Committee may submit any matters of difference to the decision of the Commissioners, or to the award of any arbitrator or arbitrators appointed by the Local Boards or Joint Committee.

If, having duly considered the matters aforesaid, the Local Boards, or Joint Committee shall agree upon a Scheme for the disposal of the Dungannon School premises, they may submit the same to the Commissioners, who shall confirm the same if satisfied that it is for the benefit of education in the Tyrone district so to do, or, if not so satisfied, may remit it for further consideration to the Local Boards or Joint Committee. Upon confirmation of any Scheme submitted as aforesaid, the Commissioners shall dispose of the School premises in accordance therewith.

If, within six calendar months after the date aforesaid, the Tyrone Local Boards shall not have submitted a Scheme to the Commissioners for the disposal of the Dungannon Royal School premises, or if any Scheme so submitted shall, after full consideration, be declared by the Commissioners not to be for the benefit of education in the district, the Commissioners shall sell or let the said premises to the best advantage, and shall dispose of the proceeds thereof as herein provided.

Enniskillen School Premises.

As soon as conveniently may be after this Scheme shall come into operation with respect to the Enniskillen Royal School Endowments, the Commissioners shall give public notice of their intention to dispose of the Enniskillen School premises to the best advantage, and shall invite tenders for the same within a limited time. Special notice of the intention to dispose of the said premises shall be given to Her Majesty's Secretary of State for War, and also to the Fermanagh Local Boards, who may offer to take all or any part of the said premises to be used for purposes of education. So soon as the time limited for receiving tenders shall have expired, the Commissioners shall consider the tenders received, and shall determine whether it would be more advantageous to sell or let the said premises, or to permit all or any part of them to be used by either or both of the Fermanagh Local Boards for purposes of education, and shall dispose of the said premises accordingly; provided that if a sum of £2,000 or upwards can be obtained upon a sale of the whole of the said premises to Her Majesty's Secretary of State for War, or to any other purchaser, they shall be sold in preference to retaining them to be used for purposes of education.

Raphoe School Premises.

As soon as conveniently may be after this Scheme shall come into operation with respect to the Raphoe Royal School Endowments, the Commissioners shall invite tenders within a limited time from each of the Donegal Local Boards to take the said premises to be used for the purposes of a school managed by the Board in accordance with the provisions of this Scheme. So soon as the time limited for receiving tenders shall have expired, the Commissioners shall proceed, on notice to the Donegal Local Boards, to consider and determine whether it would be more advantageous to accept any tender which may be received from either Local Board, or to dispose of the premises by public sale or letting. In determining this question the Commissioners shall have regard to the interest of both Local Boards in the said premises, and shall treat any proportion of the value thereof which may be proved to be attributable to the expenditure of private moneys on the said premises by any Protestant benefactor or benefactors, as belonging exclusively to the Donegal Protestant Local Board. The Commissioners shall also take into account—

(c.) The requirements of each of the Local Boards and of the Denominations represented by them, with respect to Intermediate School accommodation, and the accommodation available for each of the said Boards, for Intermediate Education, in the neighbourhood of the School premises.

(d.) The amount of capital or income likely to be made available for promoting Intermediate Education in the District by the sale or letting of the School premises.

If, having duly considered the matters aforesaid, the Commissioners shall be satisfied that it is for the interests of Intermediate Education in the District so to do, they shall accept the most advantageous tender, and dispose of the School premises accordingly. If no tender shall be received from either of the Local Boards, which the Commissioners think advantageous, they shall sell or let the said premises to the best advantage, and shall dispose of the proceeds thereof as herein provided.

Upon every sale letting or other disposal of School premises under the foregoing provisions, either or both of the Local Boards of the District directly or through a School Committee established appointed or recognised by them, may become the occupiers tenants or purchasers of the School premises or any part thereof, upon such terms as may be agreed upon, or as the Commissioners shall deem reasonable.

Every sale or letting or other disposal of School premises, and every dealing with moneys received from the same, or with the value thereof, shall be subject to the following provisions:—

(a.) The fair value of any School premises taken by a Local Board, if not hereby fixed, shall be ascertained or estimated, by way of annual occupation rent or of purchase-money, as the case may require, and the value of all premises so taken shall be charged against the Local Board taking the premises, and they shall in each case be bound to pay the amount hereby fixed, or ascertained or estimated as aforesaid, or to account for the same.

(b.) Any proportion of the value of any School premises which may be proved to be attributable to the expenditure of private moneys thereon by any Protestant benefactor or benefactors shall be treated as belonging exclusively to the Protestant Local Board of the District.

(c.) Any Local Board taking School premises, directly or through a School Committee, may account for the value thereof either by paying the same out of any Endowments at their disposal, or by charging the same, by way of annual occupation rent or of purchase-money as the case may require, against an equal amount of the income or capital of any moneys otherwise payable by the Commissioners to such Local Board under this Scheme.

(d.) Subject to the provisions of this Scheme as to private endowments, all moneys received or charged by the Commissioners by way of income or annual rent upon any sale, letting, or other disposal of School premises, shall be paid or credited by them to the two Local Boards of the District in equal shares, and shall be applicable to the same purposes as the minimum grants payable to the said Boards, in addition to the said grants.

(e.) Subject to the provisions of this Scheme as to private endowments, all moneys received or charged by the Commissioners by way of purchase-money or fine upon any sale, letting, or other disposal of School premises, shall be invested and held by them for the benefit of the two Local Boards of the District in equal shares, and the income thereof shall be applicable to the same purposes as the minimum grants payable to the said Board, in addition to the said grants. The capital thereof may in each case be applied from time to time, with the sanction of the Commissioners, as a Building Fund belonging to the District, in manner hereinafter provided.

61. *Building Funds.*

Vested Interests.—Head Masters.

62. The vested interests of the several Head Masters of the Ulster Royal Schools named in the Second Schedule hereto shall be saved, and this Scheme shall not take effect or come into operation with respect to any such vested interest, nor with respect to the Endowments of any of the Ulster Royal Schools in which any of the said Head Masters shall continue to hold office, until his vested interest shall be determined.

The Commissioners shall grant to the several Head Masters of the Royal Schools of Cavan, Dungannon, Enniskillen, and Raphoe, respectively, who shall resign, or shall be removed as hereinafter provided for any cause other than wilful misconduct or culpable neglect, retiring annuities equal in amount to the annual salaries payable to them respectively out of the Royal School Endowments at the date of the passing of the Act. The Commissioners shall, in like manner, grant to the Head Master of the Armagh Royal School, if he shall resign, or shall be removed as hereinafter provided for any cause other than wilful misconduct or culpable neglect, a retiring annuity equal in amount to one-thirtieth part of the annual salary payable to him as aforesaid, for each completed year during which he shall have held office. Such retiring annuity shall commence upon the date at which the Head Master shall retire or shall be removed, and shall give up the clear possession of the School premises to the Commissioners.

In addition to the retiring annuities aforesaid, the Commissioners may raise and pay, out of the Endowments of each of the Royal Schools, the Head Master of which shall resign his office, and give up the clear possession of the School premises to the Commissioners, within six calendar months after the date of this Scheme, but not afterwards, the several sums following, by way of consideration for the surrender of the School premises to the Commissioners for the purposes of this Scheme:—

To the Head Master of Armagh Royal School, the sum of £[illegible].

To the Head Master of Cavan Royal School, the sum of £[illegible].

To the Head Master of Dungannon Royal School, the sum of £[illegible].

To the Head Master of Enniskillen Royal School, the sum of £[illegible].

To the Head Master of Raphoe Royal School, the sum of £300.

If any of the said Head Masters shall neglect, refuse, or become unable to perform the duties of his office, the Commissioners, after due inquiry, may order that such Head Master be removed from his office, which shall thereupon determine; provided that any Head Master may, within one calendar month, appeal against the order of removal to the Lord Lieutenant in Council, who may confirm, discharge, or vary the order of removal, and whose decision shall be final.

Assistant Masters and others.

53. From and after the date at which this Scheme shall come into operation with respect to each of the Ulster Royal School Endowments, the services of the Assistant Masters and all other persons then employed in the Royal School, and receiving any salary or emoluments out of the Endowments thereof, shall be discontinued. Upon such discontinuance, each of the Assistant Masters and other persons named in the Second Schedule hereto, if then still holding the same office which he held at the date of the passing of the Act, and if not appointed by a Local Board to an office involving duties the same as or analogous to those previously discharged by him at a salary not less than that received by him out of the Royal School Endowments at the date of the passing of the Act, shall be entitled to receive from the Commissioners, during his life, a retiring annuity equal in amount to one-thirtieth part of the amount of the salary payable to him out of the said Endowments at the date of the passing of the Act, for each completed year during which he shall have held office at the date of the discontinuance of his services, not exceeding two-thirds of the amount of the salary aforesaid. Any of the said Assistant Masters or other persons who shall at any time decline to accept any such office as aforesaid, when offered to him by any Local Board, or, who, when appointed to any such office, shall fail to perform his duties with reasonable diligence, shall thereupon forfeit his retiring annuity, but unless dismissed for wilful misconduct or culpable neglect, he shall be entitled to receive from the Commissioners, in full satisfaction of all claims in respect of his office, a gratuity equal to one year's salary for the first three completed years, and one additional year's salary for every five subsequent completed years, during which he shall have held office as aforesaid, not exceeding in all a sum equal to three years' salary.

Any of the said Assistant Masters or other persons may, within three months after the discontinuance of his office for any cause other than his own voluntary resignation, wilful misconduct, or culpable neglect, but not afterwards, claim and receive from the Commissioners, instead of a retiring annuity, a gratuity to be calculated and paid as aforesaid.

Payment of Retiring Allowances.

54. Every retiring annuity payable by the Commissioners under this Scheme shall, for the purposes of apportionment, accrue from day to day, and shall, during its continuance, be payable quarterly out of the annual income and produce of the Endowments of the Royal School in which the annuitant held office at the date of the passing of the Act, but not out of the Endowments of any other Royal School. The said annuities shall be payable out of such income and produce accruing during the continuance of the annuity, but not afterwards, in priority to all other payments and charges under this Scheme, except as next hereinafter mentioned, but shall not be payable out of the capital or corpus of the Endowments, nor shall any deficiency of the annual income and produce of the Endowments in any year to meet the amount of the said annuities for such year, be made good out of any previously accrued income or produce. Every sum payable by the Commissioners under this Scheme by way of consideration for the surrender of School premises, or of gratuity, as hereinbefore mentioned, shall be charged upon the capital and corpus of the Endowments of the Royal School in which the recipient held office at the date of the passing of the Act, but not upon the Endowments of any other Royal School, and may be raised and paid by the Commissioners out of the Endowments charged therewith by sale or mortgage, or by such other means as they shall think proper, in priority to all other payments and charges under this Scheme.

If any annuitant under this Scheme shall, during the continuance of his annuity, be employed in any School managed by a Local Board, the amount of the retiring annuity paid to him during such employment shall be treated by the Commissioners as paid on account of any minimum grant which would otherwise be payable to the said Board during the same period, but no excess of the annuity above the amount of the minimum grant shall be charged against the Local Board or any moneys otherwise payable to them under this Scheme. If the Local Board employing any such annuitant shall belong to a different District from that upon whose Endowments the annuity is charged, the amount deducted from the minimum grant otherwise payable to the said Local Board shall be credited to the income and produce of the Endowments upon which the annuity is charged.

Exhibitions and Scholarships.

55. Every person who, at the date of this Scheme, shall hold any exhibition or scholarship payable out of the Ulster Royal School Endowments, shall be entitled to receive the emoluments of the same from the Commissioners, for the same period and upon the same terms and out of the same funds as if this Scheme had not passed, in priority to all payments and charges under this Scheme, but subject to the saving of all vested interests, and subject also to the retiring annuities, payments by way of compensation for the surrender of school premises, and gratuities aforesaid. If after the date of this Scheme any pupil of an Ulster Royal School who was such at the date of the passing of the Act, and who would, if this Scheme had not passed, have been entitled to compete for any Exhibition or Scholarship under like regulations to those which were in force in and for the year 18[illegible], shall so compete, and shall be awarded such an Exhibition or Scholarship, he shall be entitled to receive the emoluments of the same from the Commissioners for the same period and upon the same terms, and out of the same funds, as if this Scheme had not passed, in the same priority and subject to the same charges as if the same were an Exhibition or Scholarship held at the date of this Scheme.

56. *Payments by Commissioners.*

PART III.—*General Provisions.*

57. *Other Endowments administered by Commissioners.*

58. *Payment of Expenses.*

59. *Printing of Scheme.*

69. *Alteration of Scheme.*

This Scheme may be altered from time to time by the Commissioners of Charitable Donations and Bequests for Ireland, in any manner whatsoever, upon the application of Her Majesty's Attorney-General for Ireland, or upon the application of the Commissioners founded upon a resolution specifying the alteration required, which resolution shall be passed by a majority consisting of not less than two-thirds of the Commissioners present at a special meeting convened on due notice for the consideration thereof, and shall be afterwards confirmed by a like majority of the Commissioners present at a subsequent special meeting to be held after six days notice at the least. Except upon such application as aforesaid, no alteration shall be so made, and no alteration shall be made contrary to anything contained in the Act.

SCHEDULES REFERRED TO IN THE FOREGOING SCHEME.

FIRST SCHEDULE.—*Distribution of Residue.*

The residue of the annual income of the Ulster Royal School Endowments to be distributed under clause 42 of the foregoing Scheme, shall be annually divided among the several Local Boards in proportion to the number of marks obtained by the several qualified Schools for which claims shall have been made and established in accordance with the provisions of clause 44 of the foregoing Scheme.

(1.) One mark shall be allowed for every pupil who, during the School year for which the payment is claimed, shall have received Intermediate Education in a qualified School, in the subjects hereinafter prescribed at the least, and who shall have made not less than one hundred attendances as a pupil at the School within the School year aforesaid, and who, on the last day of the School year aforesaid, shall not be less than twelve nor more than nineteen years of age.

(2.) One additional mark shall be allowed for every pupil included in the foregoing number, who, during the same School year, or within one calendar month after its expiration, shall have passed the Examinations of the Intermediate Education Board for Ireland, in any Grade, in the several subjects hereinafter prescribed.

(3.) No mark shall be allowed for any pupil in more than one School in the same School year.

Before allowing a mark for any pupil, the Commissioners shall satisfy themselves that the pupil has received education, or has been examined and has passed, as the case may be, in the following subjects at the least:—

For Boys.—English; Latin; Greek or French or German; Arithmetic; Euclid or Algebra or Drawing.

For Girls.—English; Latin; French or German; Arithmetic; Euclid or Algebra or Drawing or Music.

The Commissioners may accept the certificate of the Inspector appointed by the Lord Lieutenant as sufficient evidence in the case of any pupil or pupils that the prescribed conditions have been fulfilled, or they may require such further or other evidence as they may think necessary.

The Commissioners may prescribe the manner and form in which claims shall be made and established under the provisions of the foregoing Scheme, and their decision upon every question arising in respect of any such claim, or of any pupil or examination, shall be final.

SECOND SCHEDULE.—*Vested Interests.*

ARMAGH ROYAL SCHOOL.

Name.	Office.	Date of Appointment.	Annual Salary at date of Act.
			£ s. d.
Rev. William [illegible], M.A.,	Head Master,	[illegible]	[illegible]
Thomas [illegible],	Assistant Master,	[illegible]	[illegible]

CAVAN ROYAL SCHOOL.

Name.	Office.	Date of Appointment.	Annual Salary at date of Act.
Rev. William [illegible], M.A.,	Head Master,	November [illegible]	[illegible]
[illegible]	Assistant Master,	February [illegible]	[illegible]
W. [illegible],	Assistant Master,	February [illegible]	[illegible]

DUNGANNON ROYAL SCHOOL.

Name.	Office.	Date of Appointment.	Annual Salary at date of Act.
Rev. [illegible], M.A.,	Head Master,	August [illegible]	[illegible]
W. [illegible],	Assistant Master,	August [illegible]	[illegible]
[illegible],	Assistant Master,	February [illegible]	[illegible]
[illegible],	Assistant Master,	February [illegible]	[illegible]
[illegible],	[illegible]	August [illegible]	[illegible]

ENNISKILLEN ROYAL SCHOOL.

Name.	Office.	Date of Appointment.	Annual Salary at date of Act.
Rev. William [illegible],	Head Master,	April [illegible]	[illegible]
W. [illegible],	Assistant Master,	November [illegible]	[illegible]
[illegible],	Assistant Master,	February [illegible]	[illegible]

RAPHOE ROYAL SCHOOL.

Name.	Office.	Date of Appointment.	Annual Salary at date of Act.
Rev. James A. [illegible], M.A.,	Head Master,	June [illegible]	[illegible]

No. III. (a.)

OBJECTIONS AND AMENDMENTS

MADE AND PROPOSED TO THE

REVISED DRAFT SCHEME for the re-constitution of the COMMISSIONERS of EDUCATION, and the FUTURE MANAGEMENT of the ULSTER ROYAL SCHOOL ENDOWMENTS.

These objections and amendments were heard and considered at a Public Meeting held in the Four Courts, Dublin, on May 21, 18[illegible].

List of Bodies and Persons

From whom OBJECTIONS have been received or by whom AMENDMENTS have been proposed.

N.B.—The objections and amendments follow the order and bear the numbers given in this List.

The existing Governing Body.

I. The Commissioners of Education in Ireland.

Bodies representing Religious Denominations.

II. The General Synod of the Church of Ireland.

III. The Diocesan Councils of Armagh, Derry and Raphoe, Kilmore and Clogher.

IV. The Intermediate Education Committee of the General Assembly of the Presbyterian Church in Ireland.

V. The Presbytery of Raphoe.

Persons representing Religious Denominations.

VI. The Most Rev. Dr. Logue, Lord Archbishop of Armagh.

VII. The Most Rev. Dr. Donnelly, Lord Bishop of Clogher.

VIII. The Most Rev. Dr. M'Gennis, Lord Bishop of Kilmore.

IX. The Very Rev. S. M'[illegible], P.P., V.F., Omagh.

X. Very Rev. Dean Byrne, P.P., Dungannon.

XI. Very Rev. Canon Donnelly, P.P., [illegible].

Local Bodies, Public Meetings, &c.

XII. The Local Committee of Protestant Denominations in the County of Fermanagh.

XIII. Raphoe proposed Local Boards (Protestant and Catholic).

Schoolmasters' Association.

XIV. The Schoolmasters' Association.

Vested Interests.

Head Masters of the Royal Schools:

XV. Rev. W. M. Morgan, LL.D., Armagh.

XVI. Rev. F. H. Ringwood, LL.D., Dungannon.

XVII. Rev. W. Steele, D.D., Enniskillen.

XVIII. Rev. J. A. Weir, LL.D., Raphoe.

XVIII. (a.) Do. do.

XIX. Rev. W. P. Moore, B.A., Cavan.

Assistant Masters in the Royal Schools:

XX. T. Gordon, Esq., B.A., Armagh.

XXI. W. H. Cumming, Esq., B.A., Dungannon.
M. Beckett, Esq., B.A., Dungannon.
T. C. Chambers, Esq., Dungannon.
C. Hewig, Esq., Enniskillen.

XXII. W. J. Vaughan, Esq., Enniskillen.

XXIII. W. Brown, Cavan.

Other Persons.

XXIV. A. Nairne, Armagh.

XXV. Rev. John Knox Leslie, The Manse, Cookstown.

Objections and Amendments.

I. The Commissioners of Education in Ireland.

SIR,—I am directed by the Commissioners of Education in Ireland to suggest, in the Revised Draft Scheme transmitted by the Endowments Commission, the introduction in sections 11 and 13, after the word "Secretary," of the words "or, in his temporary absence, by the person for the time being appointed by a resolution of the Commissioners to act in his place." Without such amendment, the absence of the Secretary would prevent the execution of deeds and the signature of cheques. They also suggest that it may be more clearly stated in section 44 (*f*) that the power of removal of a pupil is, like all other powers of a similar character, given to the Local Board.

(Signed) JEFFREY M'DOWELL,
For ROBERT M'DOWELL, Secretary.

21, Molesworth-street, Dublin.
April 26, 1889.

II. The General Synod of the Church of Ireland.

SIR,—We have to inform you that at its meeting yesterday the following resolution was adopted by this Synod, viz. :—

"That this Synod protests against the Revised Draft Scheme for the Ulster Royal School Endowments, and, among other reasons for so doing, specifies the following objections :—

"1. That it gives the Roman Catholic Church a share of the Endowments, which the statistics of Intermediate Education prove to be most excessive.

"2. That it assigns to the Church of Ireland a wholly inadequate representation on the proposed Local Boards which will deal with Protestant Endowments.

"3. That of the gross Endowments, it proposes to distribute the greater part in so-called 'Result Fees,' in the allocation of which, Results will be entirely outweighed by mere numbers.

"4. That while the Scheme recognises a right to compensation created by the expenditure of private moneys upon school premises, this compensation is, nevertheless, charged in the General Revenues of the Protestant Local Board, instead of going to the denomination to which the donor belonged."

We have also to inform you that a deputation has been appointed to wait on your Commissioners on Saturday next at 11 o'clock, to bring this resolution under their notice, and to express the views of the General Synod thereon, if the day and hour named are suitable to the Commissioners.

(Signed)
MORRAY W. JELLETT, } Hon. Secs. to the
CHAWORTH J. FERRIER, } General Synod.

Christchurch-place,
Dublin, May 1, 1889.

The Secretary,
Educational Endowments Commission.

III.—The Diocesan Councils of the Dioceses of Armagh, Derry and Raphoe, Kilmore, and Clogher.

1. We object to the constitution, in each district of one mixed Protestant Board instead of giving to each denomination a separate Board with its own share of the endowments and with power to co-operate or to unite. A separate board, while refused to our wishes, has been conceded to the Roman Catholics, and, being equal to us in number, but superior as being homogeneous, it will overpower us in the decision of common questions unless a final division of the endowment is now made.

We claim in the first instance a separate board in each district for the Church of Ireland, with the bishop as its chairman *ex-officio*.

2. We further object that, in the constitution of the mixed boards, the representation of the Church of Ireland is wholly inadequate from every point of view, whether regard be had to her gross population, or to their educational status, as proved by the last census.

In some of the districts in question in the Church of Ireland in a numerical minority, yet in the Boards of Tyrone and Donegal she is outweighed in the proportion of two to one; and from this disparity the utmost practical injustice may result in the election of committees for the allocation of endowments (vide section 38) and in the treatment of competing schools in the various districts, and also from the hopeless minority in which the Church would find herself in negotiating with Roman Catholic Local Boards.

3. We are strengthened in our conviction that a final division of the endowments upon equitable principles is the only satisfactory mode of treating them, by finding that the first proposal for the distribution of result fees has been abandoned, but is replaced by a scheme which in our opinion is at least as objectionable. The residue still professes to be divided "in proportions to be calculated by results" (section 44). But the first schedule by which these payments are regulated now only allows one mark for the passing of the Intermediate Examination by any pupil, even in the senior grade. There is no other educational test in the scheme, and no matter how seven pupils passed than it bestows another similar mark upon every pupil in the same school who shall have been under instruction in the prescribed subjects. Provided he has credit for a hundred attendances at the school, it matters nothing that all this time, with the exception of one solitary hour, may have been devoted to the study of the English alphabet. It is not asked how effective, how incompetent, or how brief may have been his instruction in the prescribed subjects or how far from deserving payment for any "result" whatever. The consequence will be that by far the greater part of the payments will be swallowed up by large elementary schools in which a handful of pupils will succeed in passing, and many others will get themselves counted, without even such an examination by a State Inspector as the National Board requires. And even if the local boards should refuse to admit such schools, an appeal is provided to the Commissioners in Dublin; whereas no appeal is allowed even to the other local board of the district, against the admission of schools not truly Intermediate (section 44).

4. We draw attention to the fact that the scheme now deals with Ulster Endowments alone, and that, in the cases of Navan and Clonmel it has been arranged that Intermediate Endowments, before vested

in the Commissioners of Education, should be transferred to local trustees. And we are of opinion that in the present case the governing body should meet and the supreme control of all affairs should be situated in Ulster.

5. We continue to hold the opinion that the representation of universities and other educational bodies can be sufficiently obtained by the Lord Lieutenant's appointments, and that the proposed arrangements for this object may, and probably will, seriously disturb the equipoise of religious representation.

We earnestly protest against the admission of formal representatives of Roman Catholic and Presbyterian Divinity Schools (Maynooth and Magee College), while the only provision for the Church of Ireland is that the Lord Lieutenant shall nominate one clergyman among his ten commissioners, of whom five must be Roman Catholics, one a Presbyterian, and even the Methodists are put upon an equality with us, although we outnumber them in Ulster ten times over (sections 2 and 3).

6. We repeat that in our opinion the scheme is inconsistent with itself, the local boards being denominational with regard to one promotion, but in regard to all the rest, mixed in strictly defined proportions (sections 26, 33), and again the Central Board being mixed but here in uncertain and varying proportions (sections 2 and 3). Moreover the claim has been conceded to the uttermost which Roman Catholic witnesses put forward, to an exclusive administration of their schools, but no attention has been paid to the evidence given in Dublin by the authorised representatives of all the Protestant denominations, claiming the same independent control of the education of their children for themselves.

This evidence was also practically unanimous in desiring a final distribution of the endowment, but to this also no attention has been paid.

7. In section 30 we object to the equal distribution of the endowments between the two Local Boards, as being unjust to the Protestant population, especially of the County Armagh.

8. In the same section we object to the provision that the gifts of our private benefactors shall be merged in the general property of the Protestant Local Boards, instead of being recognised as the property of the Church of Ireland. And we claim the fulfilment of the pledge given by Lord Justice Fitzgibbon in his opening statement at the public sitting of the Commission, on August 2nd, 1886, that such money should "be regarded as a private and denominational endowment, and taken into account as such," because "it would be unfair to divert the property so created from the denomination to which the donor belonged, and to the faith of the school continuing to belong to which, he spent his money."—(Blue Book Report of Endowments Commission, 1887-8, p. 337.) These words occur in the course of a statement, made at the request of the full Commission, "of those facts that appear undisputed, and which form the necessary condition of any settlement that may be arrived at."—*Ibid*., p. 333.

We also urge that the value of such gifts should be ascertained by the present Commissioners, as their successors will not possess the same legal training to set against the manifest interest which the larger number will have in reducing our claims to as low a point as possible.

9. In the same section we strongly object to the provision that on the mere motion of Her Majesty's Attorney-General for the time being (and no longer, as in the first draft, only upon the request of a large majority of the Commissioners themselves) the Commissioners of Charitable Donations and Bequests may alter the scheme "in any matter whatsoever," and therefore may possibly reconstruct it from the foundation. In our opinion this change will deprive the present Scheme of all stability and public confidence, and make these schools and their endowments the perpetual battle-field of factions.

10. We consider that a quorum of five Commissioners out of thirty is inadequate for the satisfactory decision of the weighty and disputed questions, with which they will have to deal. (Section 8.)

11. We object to the large powers given to a mixed Local Board in delegating its functions to a Committee; and we point out that even if the requirement in section 34 of a majority of two-thirds in the election of a Committee apply to section 34, yet there are two Boards upon which such a Committee, practically omnipotent, might be elected against the unanimous vote of the representatives of our Church, although as we have already asserted, we have in these very districts a demonstrable right to an actual preponderance upon the Board.

(Signed,) HENRY T. DIX and SONS,

Solicitors for said Diocesan Councils of Armagh, Derry, Raphoe, Kilmore, and Clogher, 61, Upper Sackville-street, Dublin.

IV. The Intermediate Education Committee of the General Assembly of the Presbyterian Church in Ireland.

1. The retiring annuity payable by the Commissioners under the Scheme to the present head master of the Raphoe Royal School should be made payable out of the General Endowment, and any compensation of the residue of the Endowments and not out of the annual income of the Raphoe Estate, which is already too small to maintain two efficient schools.

2. The condition required for a qualified school in section 43 (c) should be modified by substituting "five" for "seven" as the number of pupils passing the Intermediate Education Examination in each year, and by substituting for "twenty" "fifteen" as the number of pupils in attendance.

3. The Committee are of opinion that the provisions of the first Schedule as to the distribution of the residue should be modified so as to give more marks for efficiency and fewer for mere size of the schools. They propose to add to clause (1) "Provided that the number of marks allowed to any school under this clause shall in no case exceed four times the number of the pupils from the same school, who in the same year have passed one of the examinations of the Intermediate Education Board." They further propose to modify clause (2) by providing that one additional mark shall be allowed for every pupil who shall have passed the Junior Grade Examination, two additional marks for every pupil who shall have passed the Middle Grade, and three additional marks for every pupil who shall have passed the Senior Grade. They propose further to add an additional clause in the following terms:—

4. "No mark shall be allowed for any pupil whose parents (if alive) do not reside, or (if dead) did not at the time of their death reside within one or other of the districts to which this Scheme applies."

Signed on behalf of the said Committee, this 14th day of May, 1888.

JAMES HENRY, Solicitor.

(V.) *The Presbytery of Raphoe.*

The Presbytery of Raphoe having had under its consideration the Revised Draft Scheme for the future management of the Royal Schools, observes with regret that a change has been made which is calculated to have a disastrous effect on the interest of Intermediate Education in the district of Raphoe, viz., clause 58, which provides that in the event of the retirement of the head master, his pension shall be paid out of the endowment of the school of which he has been master.

Since there seems to be little prospect of deriving from the *Donegal School Estate* a larger yearly income than £200, the Presbytery believes that the payment of the pension of the head master of the Raphoe School out of the Donegal Endowment would leave a balance totally inadequate, when divided between the two local boards, to aid in the maintenance of an Intermediate school.

The Presbytery requests the Commission to reconsider this clause, and if possible provide for the payment of the head master's pension from some other source.

(Signed), A. G. Lecky,
Clerk of Presbytery.

Raphoe, May 14th, 1889.

VI. *His Grace the Most Rev. Dr. Logue, Lord Archbishop of Armagh.*

In conformity with the request of the Educational Endowments Commissioners I have had the Royal School buildings at Armagh and the land attached valued by a competent valuator. After making very considerable deductions from his valuation, which probably put the premises at the highest market value, I have come to the conclusion that the Armagh Royal School buildings, as they stand, *and in their present state of repair*, together with all the land attached to the Royal School, are good value for £4,000. I estimate the annual letting value at £200 per annum, which is something about the Government valuation of buildings and land.

Though I do not stand in need of the Royal School premises, still I would utilise them, and am quite prepared to take them, either at the capital sum of £4,000, or at an annual rent of £200. However, this offer is to be understood as applying to the buildings as they stand at present. Should some time elapse before they are disposed of, and the buildings get into a state of disrepair, I could not, of course, be held as bound by this offer.

I may state that, though prepared to take the school buildings and land at the above valuation, I would be very glad that the Protestant Body should take them on these terms, if they had any hope of continuing the school in an efficient state. Indeed it was, to some extent, for the purpose of making this as easy as possible for them, without depriving the endowment of the fair value of the school premises, that I put the estimate so much below the valuation of Mr. Hagan, architect, whom I employed, and who put the fair value of the Royal School buildings and the land attached at £7,[illegible].

Another question proposed to me by the Commissioners had reference to the allowance to be made for private benefactions.

1st. There is the question of fact as to the existence and amount of such benefactions. I think the existence and amount of such benefactions should be established by sufficient evidence, documentary or otherwise, and not taken on the strength of mere hearsay. I mention this because I think there is a very fair presumption against some of the benefactions alleged.

2nd. I take it as a matter of course that the Protestant Body should get full credit for the present value of such private benefactions as may be duly established.

3rd. I think the present value of such benefactions should bear the same proportion to the present value of the building that the sum originally contributed from private sources bore to the original cost of the buildings. To make the matter clear by an example: suppose the original cost of the buildings was, as alleged, £12,000, and the private benefactions contributed for their erection, as likewise alleged, was £3,000, the private contributions would be one-fourth of the original cost. This supposition being in accordance with fact, I would give the Protestant Body credit for one-fourth of the present estimated value of the buildings. In making this allocation, I think the value of the buildings alone should be taken into account, as any sums contributed from private sources were expended in the erection of the buildings, not in the acquisition of the land.

I believe this is the fairest and most reasonable solution of the whole question which I could suggest.

(Signed), ✠ Michael Logue,
Archbishop of Armagh, Primate of All Ireland.

Morrison's Hotel, Dublin,
20th March, 1889.

VII. *The Most Rev. Dr. Donnelly, Lord Bishop of Clogher.*

I have carefully considered the Revised Draft Scheme for the management of the Ulster Royal Schools Endowments, and I gratefully acknowledge that I find it to be, in many respects, an improvement on the former Draft Scheme. One or two remarks only do I think it advisable to make, and I regret I should have inadvertently allowed the month of April to pass over before making them.

1st. Touching the Fermanagh Roman Catholic Board of Education, one of the ecclesiastical members named in the scheme, as representing the portion of the diocese in the County Fermanagh, is the Very Rev. James Canon M'Quaid, P.P., [illegible], Enniskillen. This clergyman has ceased to reside in the County Fermanagh, having come to take charge of and reside in a parish in the County Monaghan. I would suggest as a substitute for him the Rev. [illegible] Maguire, P.P., Tempo, near Enniskillen.

2nd. It would appear that no Local Board will have power under the scheme to pay any remuneration to the person who may be employed by it as secretary. I apprehend that it will be difficult to find a person able and willing to act in that capacity without some small compensation at least. The office will be a troublesome one. The secretary must summon meetings of the Board, with statement of "agenda," record the minutes of Board meetings, keep accounts of receipts and disbursements, &c. Might not the Local Board be empowered to give some small remuneration, not greater, say, than £10 or £15 per annum, to the secretary? I throw out this suggestion, however, with great hesitation, and leave the matter to the wisdom of the Commission.

(Signed), ✠ James Donnelly,
R.C. Bishop of Clogher.

Monaghan, May 1, 1889.

VIII. *The Most Rev. Dr. M'Gennis, Lord Bishop of Kilmore.*

I have to propose certain changes in the Revised Draft Scheme.

Part I., section 4, first paragraph, to omit the words, "so far as it is consistent with the retention of office by the continuing Commissioners."

I consider it essential to a satisfactory arrangement that half the Commissioners to be appointed by the Lord Lieutenant be Catholics.

Part II., section 41, paragraph 6, to omit the word "thirty," and substitute "forty."

As the net income of Cavan School has been for past three years but £274 a year, and as provision for outgoings will considerably reduce this sum, it is plain that a minimum grant of 30 per cent. is quite insufficient. Armagh, Tyrone, and Fermanagh get 35 per cent. out of incomes more than treble that of Cavan.

Section 40, paragraph 2.

I object to the transfer of the Cavan School premises to the Protestant Local Board at an estimated capital value of £1,000. These premises are worth considerably more than twice that amount. I estimated the capital value at £4,[illegible], and calculating at 3½ per cent. I fixed a fair annual rent at £150 a year, expecting that the Catholic Local Board would get Government Stock to that amount.

Since the publication of the Revised Draft Scheme I employed a civil engineer to inspect and value the School buildings, and he valued them at £3,[illegible].

The land attached to the School, consisting of 16 acres 2 roods 18 perches statute measure, is beside the town of Cavan, and would set annually at between four and five pounds an Irish acre, according to the rent paid for land about the town. I think the Head Master of Cavan School, in his evidence before the Commission, valued this land at £5 an acre. This land is held in fee-simple. The fee-simple of land is now selling at from seventeen to twenty years purchase. The tenant right goes with the fee-simple in this case, and should bring up the selling value to 25 years purchase. I submit that the capital value of the land alone is beyond £1,[illegible].

I am willing that the Protestant Local Board get the School premises on moderate terms, but I cannot regard £3,[illegible] Government Stock as a fair equivalent for them. I would suggest that the Commissioners send a valuer to value them, or that it be left to the Local Boards to come to an agreement about them hereafter, or that they be sold.

In the Second Schedule of Revised Draft Scheme the salaries of the Masters of Cavan School are put at £[illegible].

I desire to know were these salaries paid this year, and if so, from what source, as the net income of the School for past three years was put by the Commissioners last year at £274.

I should like to know where the salary of Mr. F. J. Anderson was fixed at £[illegible] a year.

What is to be done with the money that has accumulated out of incomes of Cavan School, and which is now beyond £3,000? There is no explicit reference to it in Draft Scheme.

(Signed), ✠ EDWARD M'GENNIS,
Bishop of Kilmore.

IX. *The Very Rev. R. M'Namee, P.P., Omagh.*

I beg again to renew my protest against your Amended Scheme in reference to Royal Schools for Tyrone—firstly, because you include a portion of County Derry; 2ndly, because you give the Diocese of Derry only three representatives.

(Signed), R. M'NAMEE, V.F. and P.P.

Omagh, 24th April, 1889.

X. *The Very Rev. Dean Byrne, P.P., Dungannon.*

I beg to suggest the following amendment to clauses 27 and 28 of Revised Draft Scheme:—

To add to clause 27, "In the case of the Tyrone Roman Catholic Board of Education, in the filling of any vacancy, due regard will be had to the present proportion of representatives of the respective dioceses having jurisdiction in the county of Tyrone."

My object in writing in the above lines is to provide that our diocese shall always have secured to it the proportion of five to nine of the Board, as at present.

(Signed), P. J. BYRNE.

XI. *The Very Rev. Canon Donnelly, P.P., Magherafelt.*

Kindly note, at page 22, sections 17 and 18—I would suggest to add to those two paragraphs the following words:—

"Having regard to the district, or portion of the district, in which the vacancy exists."

I suggest this addition, so that all districts and parts of districts may retain the representation they now have—otherwise it would be possible in time to have all the members of the School Board from one district.

(Signed), P. CANON DONNELLY.

April 20, 1889.

XII. *The Local Committee representing the various Protestant Denominations of the County Fermanagh.*

We strongly object to clause number 65, in so far as it relates to the compulsory sale of Enniskillen School premises to any purchaser except the Fermanagh Protestant Board, which has already proposed, and still intends to take them as part of its Endowment.

We wish to point out that the savings which in our case now exceed £8,000 belong in a special sense to the party we represent, having been accumulated when the school was under Protestant management. We therefore maintain that as a matter of equity they belong exclusively to us; nevertheless, by way of compromise, we make the following proposal:—To hand over the school buildings and lands attached to the Fermanagh Protestant Board free of all charges, and if necessary a sum not exceeding £1,400 can then be allocated to the Fermanagh Roman Catholic Board for building purposes out of the accumulated savings. We also desire that a sum of £500 be placed at the disposal of the Fermanagh Protestant Board out of the above savings, for the purpose of repairing and equipping the premises here, which are not at present in a fit state to receive boarders.

Besides getting these premises it will be necessary for us to have an annual endowment sufficient to maintain the school in an efficient state, and we beg to point out that this has not yet been provided for—especially after "*the first three years*"—if the pensions amounting to about six hundred pounds (£600) shall then be a charge upon the current income. We therefore suggest that the term "*two complete calendar years*" (section 39) should be "*three complete calendar years*," and that the minimum grant should be not less than 33⅓ per cent. afterwards to our Local Board.

We further submit that in addition to the one uniform test of educational work done recognised by this Scheme, other open public examinations of an equivalent kind should in all fairness be added. As this town is not a centre for the Intermediate Examinations, considerable difficulty might be experienced, and heavy expense incurred in case our pupils were compelled to travel long distances to attend these examinations.

We fear the Commissioners did not catch the precise force of our objection to the annual election of the members of our Local Board. Our contention is, that men who undertake the heavy responsibility of this Trust should have a more permanent position on the Board than this Scheme gives them. Their tenure of office should be, we think, either for life or for a term of years subject to such conditions as may be necessary.

Signed for and on behalf of the Committee,

Charles T. Ovenden, Chairman.
S. Oughterson Mitchell, Hon. Sec.

Enniskillen,
17th April, 1889.

XIII. *The proposed Raphoe Local Boards (Protestant and Catholic).*

On behalf of the two Local Boards, and in conference as recommended, to consider how the Royal School premises might be advantageously disposed of, we beg to state that the amended Scheme contains a provision which, if continued, would seriously imperil the prospects of Intermediate education in this district, and which, in consequence, throws a great obstacle in the way of tenders from either Board. According to the amended Draft Scheme, a retiring annuity of £100 will be payable to Dr. Weir out of the income of the estate, and a further sum of at least £8 a year will be required to meet the interest on £200, to which Dr. Weir, if he resigns, is also entitled out of the Raphoe property, for surrendering possession of the school premises. In the previous draft all such charges were put upon the Compensation Fund, and unless this arrangement be ratified, in preference to the alteration now proposed, we respectfully submit that the principle of minimum grants falls to the ground in this district. The Commissioners in their second Report (p. xv.), say:—"To each Governing Body we propose to secure, in the first instance, a minimum annual grant from the endowment of its own locality, which ought to be sufficient to enable it to maintain at least one school." Now, under the change to which we refer, this excellent purpose cannot be attained, and we venture to think the Commissioners were of this opinion, when, in the previous draft, which made the Compensation Fund liable for such charges, they kindly allowed each of our Boards 40 per cent. of the local revenue as a minimum grant. Apart from school premises it would seem hazardous to count on an annual revenue of more than £200 a year. But even £100 annually to each Board would be considerable encouragement, when supplemented by the return from its interest in the school premises. If, however, the sum fall as low as £45 a year, as it would under the amended Draft Scheme, at the very time when a great effort must be made to get the Intermediate school of each Board into thorough working order, to qualify permanently for a minimum grant, and deserve a large share of the general results, it is obvious both Boards should remain without those educational advantages which the Commissioners by their Report signified their intention to confer, and which are certainly required to enable the Boards to gather such fruits in the field of education as will be a fair justification to the public for their corporate existence. In these circumstances we deem it a duty to appeal to you to apply the principle of minimum grants, so as to relieve any local annual revenue from the charges to which we have referred, and until we learn the result of your deliberations on this matter, we are of opinion we have not sufficient data to go upon in fixing the annual value of the Raphoe Royal School premises for Intermediate education purposes, and making suggestions as to their disposal.

(Signed), ✠ Patrick O'Donnell.
William Lowry Berkeley.

Letterkenny, 27th April, 1889.

Resolution passed at Letterkenny, Friday 26th April, 3 o'clock, P.M.

A Conference of the Protestant and Roman Catholic Boards, in connexion with the Raphoe Royal School Endowment, was held this day, the Right Rev. Dr. O'Donnell in the chair. There were present Rev. Joseph Boyle, P.P., Raphoe; Rev. P. J. [illegible], Seminary, Letterkenny; P. [illegible], J.P., Strabane; M. M'Fadden, J.P., Glenswilly, of the Roman Catholic Board; and W. H. Porter, Esq., J.P., Ballymacool; Rev. H. F. Macdonald, [illegible]; Rev. W. L. Berkeley, Raphoe; Rev. J. A. Hale, Raphoe; T. Hamilton, Esq., Raphoe; G. Wilson, Esq., Raphoe; and Rev. R. M'Mann, Manorcunningham, of the Protestant Board. The Chairman stated that this Conference has been convened at the request of the Endowed Schools Commissioners "with a view to submitting some definite suggestions . . . which would enable the Commissioners to make a satisfactory disposition of the Raphoe School premises."

It was unanimously resolved:—That inasmuch as by the amended scheme, the retiring annuity and bonus to the head master are to be paid out of the annual income of the school, and inasmuch as the probable income will be below £200, even in the event of the proposed purchase of the estate being carried out, and inasmuch as the sum available for Intermediate educational purposes would then be below £90, or a maximum sum of £45 to each Board, which would be obviously inadequate to ensure or aid an Intermediate school, the conjoined Boards request the Chairman and Rev. W. L. Berkeley to bring these facts under the consideration of the Commissioners, and urge on them the necessity of having all existing charges on the Raphoe Royal School Fund paid out of the Compensation Fund, as proposed in the Draft Scheme of April 20th, 1888.

(Signed) ✠ Patrick O'Donnell, Chairman.
R. M'Mann, Secretary, pro tem.

XIV. *The Schoolmasters' Association.*

I beg to submit some observations on the above in behalf of the Committee of the Schoolmasters' Association.

First Schedule, page 99—(1). No mark should be allowed without an examination test—the Intermediate if possible.

(2.) The Grades of the Intermediate should not have equal value. If the Junior Grade counted one mark, the Middle should count for two, and the Senior for three.

Section 30, p. 98, confers more extended powers on the Attorney-General than on a majority of the Commissioners. Such powers would appear to be without reason, and dangerous.

Section 43 c.—A School might from unavoidable causes, drop down to a roll of nineteen, who might all be Intermediate Exhibitioners. It might be better to require an average of twenty for a term of years, than twenty in any second year.

Section 57, final paragraph, &c. The Association expressed its views very fully on this section last June, in the paper of which I enclose copy [Report and Evidence, 1887–88, p. 684]. I am encouraged to refer to this matter by the Commissioners' inviting observations on the draft.

(Signed), William Wilkins,
Vice-Chairman, and Convenor of Committee.

The High School, Dublin,
17th May, 1889.

XV. *Rev. Wm. Moore Morgan*, LL.D., *Head Master, Royal School, Armagh.*

The Reverend William Moore Morgan objects to the revised Scheme of the Educational Endowments Commissioners on the ground that while it is proposed by the 62nd Clause of such Scheme that the vested interests in the several Head Masters of the Ulster Royal Schools therein named shall be saved, yet the whole scope and effect of the scheme is in the case of Armagh School effectually to destroy such vested interests; amongst other instances it deprives him in the event of resignation or retirement of a portion of his salary.

The sum of £800 thereby, in the events mentioned, specified to be paid to him, is wholly inadequate.

The Scheme does not take into account his vested interest in the lands and emoluments connected therewith, to which he is entitled. A new board of management, with new and different powers, is placed in authority over him to the prejudice of his position. The effect of the scheme is to deprive him of pupils and situations which would induce pupils to join his school, and upon other grounds appearing in said scheme.

Dated this 16th day of May, 1889.

[illegible],
Solicitors for Rev. William Moore Morgan,
Head Master of Armagh Royal School,
8, Clare-street, Dublin.

XVI. *Rev. F. H. Ringwood*, LL.D., *Head Master, Royal School, Dungannon.*

I beg to submit to the Commissioners that the sum of £800 does not appear to be an adequate consideration for surrendering my vested interest in the school residence and the lands appertaining thereto in Dungannon.

With regard to the acreage of the lands, I admit its being less than that attached to the Armagh and Enniskillen schools, but the following circumstances are to be weighed:—

When I was appointed, and for some subsequent years, what is now the playground formed three fields and a lane. One of these fields, which was about a third, or less, of all the ground at the rere of the school buildings, was surrounded by a high wall, and alone formed the playground of those days.

The other fields were appropriated to the master's use only. I threw the three fields into one for the use of the boys, and levelled one of them for a cricket ground, and rented other land for my own use from Lord Ranfurly. Again I took down a six-foot stone wall which divided a small paddock from the old garden, and enlarged and improved the latter, and also made tennis grounds adjacent to the garden, planting hedges, &c., &c. It is to be remembered, too, that I advanced about £3,000 for the new buildings, on which advance I received no interest.

My expenditure on the improvement of the buildings and grounds, all of which are of a permanent as well as of a very apparent character—in fact, "unexhausted improvements"—combined with my right to enjoy both in the terms conveyed by Letters Patent, seems to entitle me to a larger compensation than £800 for giving up possession of said premises and lands.

I submit this, while limiting my view of the subject to that of the present standpoint of the Commissioners, reserving, of course, my own judgment as to the general question of the scope of the Act of Parliament.

Considering, however, the shortness and uncertainty of life, I hereby offer my resignation on the terms of the Commissioners—(1) if the "consideration" be raised to £8[illegible]0; and (2) if I be released from duty (after thirty-nine years' service) at the end of this half year, i.e., on the 1st of August, or before that date, should the Commissioners prefer it.

(Signed), F. H. Ringwood.

April 9, 1889.

XVII. *Rev. W. Steele*, D.D., *Head Master Royal School, Enniskillen.*

I have been for some time more than willing to retire from the Head Mastership of this school, but the terms offered in the revised scheme come so far short of my necessities, and of what I consider just and reasonable, that I cannot but enter a strong but respectful protest against them.

There are two exceptional features in my case which give me, I think, a superior claim on your attention in adjusting the scale of compensations, one, that a large quantity of excellent land, rent free, is attached to the school-house, from which for the last six years I have derived an income of £150 a year; another, that £4,420 of my money has been sunk in valuable additions and improvements to the school buildings, pronounced to be "necessary and substantially executed." If an adequate pension, which I could convert into an equivalent bulk sum, were granted to me, I would at once gladly retire and surrender the school premises. I must therefore object to the Revised Draft Scheme, and press upon your kindly consideration its further amendment in the sense above indicated.

(Signed), W. Steele.

Portora Royal School,
May 16, 1889.

XVIII. *Rev. J. A. Weir*, LL.D., *Head Master, Royal School, Raphoe.*

With reference to your offer to me, as head master of Raphoe Royal School, of my present salary for life and £300 in hand in case I resign within six months, I venture most respectfully to urge the following considerations on the attention of your Commission. I do so in the hope that you may think there a ground for granting, in my case, a somewhat larger retiring allowance than my present salary. Though it might be complained to do so, I think there are exceptional circumstances in my case.

Raphoe School is the only Royal School which has no assistant masters requiring retiring allowances.

The allowance of endowment granted to the school has been always conspicuously small.

The success of the school in preparing pupils for the Universities, for the Civil Service, for the Professions, has been very great.

I spent my whole salary, and much besides, in maintaining assistant masters. I was obliged to work hard myself in the school; I believe much more so than is usual with head masters.

This was absolutely necessary if the school was to be successful with so small an endowment.

I do not expect a large addition to your present offer, but I trust it will not seem unreasonable to grant an enlargement of it. I could lengthen this letter by many details, but I will not trouble your Commission by a longer statement.

As I cannot, after forty years' work in the service of "The Commissioners of Education in Ireland," expect to enjoy the annuity for a long term, this may, perhaps, be added to the above.

(Signed), JAMES A. WEIR, Clk., LL.D.

Raphoe Royal School,
April 24, 1889.

XVIII (a.) *Rev. James A. Weir*, LL.D., *Head Master, Royal School, Raphoe.*

The said James Alexander Weir, as head master of said school, claims to be entitled as such head master, to the undermentioned vested interests which he had at the date of the passing of the said statute.

1. His salary as head master—admitted.
2. His residence as such head master, with use of land, appurtenances or usually enjoyed therewith, and all fixtures thereon respectively.

This has to a certain extent been recognised.

3. A right to have the said buildings and appurtenances kept in a substantial state of repair by the [illegible].
4. A right to receive pupils, day boys and boarders, and to receive fees therefrom.

This has been practically destroyed by the operation of the Scheme.

4a. A right to have the salaries of masters to assist objector in such education.

It is submitted that the compensation of £300 proposed for his surrender of the school premises is arbitrary and unconscientious, and absolutely inadequate, considering that objector is now only sixty-two years of age, and of good constitution, and that it ought to be left to arbitrators, mutually selected to value his life interest in the school premises in the event of a surrender to meet the policy of the Act.

Signed on behalf of James A. Weir, as such head master.

A. COLLEY, Solicitor.

May 18, 1889.

XIX. *Rev. Wm. Prior Moore*, M.A., *Head Master, Royal School, Cavan.*

The Reverend William Prior Moore objects to the revised Scheme of the Educational Endowments Commissioners, on the ground that while it is proposed by the final clause of such Scheme, that the vested interests of the several head masters of the Ulster Royal Schools therein named shall be saved, yet the whole scope and effect of the Scheme is in the case of Cavan School, effectually to destroy such vested interests.

The sum of £300 thereby, in the events mentioned, specified to be paid to him, is wholly inadequate.

The Scheme does not take into account his vested interest in the house, and emoluments, connected therewith, to which he is entitled.

A new Board of Management with new and different powers is placed in authority over him, to the prejudice of his position. The effect of the Scheme is to deprive him of pupils, and attractions which would induce pupils to join his school, and upon other grounds appearing in said Scheme.

Dated this 15th day of May, 1889.

KELLY and LLOYD,
Solicitors for Rev. William Prior Moore, M.A., Head Master of Cavan Royal School, 2, Clare-street, Dublin.

XX. *W. H. Gowring, M. Beckett, T. C. Gardner, and Curt Hennig, Assistant Masters, Royal Schools.*

We, the undersigned Assistant Masters of the Royal Schools, while thanking the Commissioners for the patient consideration they have given to our vested interests, beg respectfully to submit the following observations on the proposals contained in section 51 of the Revised Draft Scheme.

In the first place, we renew the objection, previously made by us, that no account whatever is taken of any emoluments except the portion of our salaries paid by the Commissioners of Education. This restriction of our vested interests we believe to be inequitable, and it involves a further, and in some respects graver, injustice. We refer to the proposal to give to a Local Board or any district over either religious denomination the power at any time to deprive us of the proposed annuities by offering us appointments at salaries of £80 per annum, which it would, of course, be impossible to accept. Moreover, if a Local Board were to offer an Assistant Master employment at such remuneration as he would be willing to accept, the offer might be made at a time when, owing to his being bound by other engagements, he would be compelled to decline it thereby forfeiting his annuity. The hardship of having our future depending on such contingencies is, we think obvious.

In conclusion, we would respectfully suggest that the tenure of these small annuities should not be made dependent on the action of the Local Board; though we admit that during such time as we may hold office under them, the payments of the annuities should either cease, or the amounts be deducted from the minimum grants otherwise payable to the Boards.

Permit us to call the attention of the Commissioners to the fact, that our scholastic year ends on 1st of February.

(Signed), W. H. GOWRING, B.A.
M. BECKETT, B.A.
T. C. GARDNER.
CURT HENNIG, B.A.

April 29, 1889.

XXI. *W. J. Valentine, Assistant Master, Royal School, Enniskillen.*

With reference to the Compensation Clause of the Revised Draft Scheme for the Ulster Royal Schools, as an Assistant Master I beg to observe:—

(1) That in taking as the basis of calculation salary merely, and not residence also, which I estimated at an additional £30 per annum, the Revised Draft Scheme does not appear to me to satisfy the terms of the Act, which directs that compensation be made for "emoluments," and that by the word emolument something other or wider than salary is meant, the Revised Draft Scheme itself recognises, when in section 37, p. 23, it empowers the Local Board to "fix the salaries and emoluments of the staff in each school."

(2) That while the amount of annuity awarded under the Revised Draft Scheme to me comes very near the estimate in my late objections, I should prefer to have the choice between annuity and gratuity left to myself, and that it should not be put in the power of a Local Board (i.e., any Local Board) to convert my annuity into gratuity by offering me at any time, possibly with that very object, a salary not less than my present. In this particular there is a departure from the principle of insisting the endowments of each of the schools. But I should prefer to exercise the choice independently of even the Fermanagh Protestant Board.

(3) That the expression "instead of retiring annuity," section 53, p. 34, suggests the inference that an Assistant Master who accepts office at "not less salary," can be retired on annuity at any time by a Local Board, but this important point is not directly stated to be so.

(4) That as our salaries are payable on 1st August and 1st February, they should be secured to us for the half year in which disendowment takes effect, and that it would be advantageous to both pupils and masters that disendowment under the Scheme should take effect on either of these days, as it would allow of arrangements for the reopening of school, and re-engagement of masters being made during the ordinary school holidays, without unusual loss of time.

(Signed), W. J. VALENTINE,

Royal School, Portora, Enniskillen.

April 25, 1889.

XXII.—*W. Browne, M.A., Assistant Master, Royal School, Cavan.*

As one interested I desire to object to the compensation offered to assistant masters in the Revised Draft Scheme for the future government and management of the Ulster Royal Schools.

By that Scheme I see that if the Cavan Local Board offer me a post with the munificent salary of £25 per annum attached, and if I do not accept the offer I am then debarred from all compensation. Naturally they will take advantage of this, and will make the offer knowing that it cannot be accepted.

I wish to protest against this, considering that my present salary is equivalent to about £120 per annum.

(Signed), WILLIAM BROWNE, M.A.

May 17, 1889.

XXIII. *A. Nelson, Armagh, as to Scholarships and Exhibitions.*

With reference to clause 55, p. 37, dealing with Scholarships and Exhibitions, I trust the Commissioners will see their way to make the following slight, but very important, alterations as regards some of the existing pupils, viz.:—strike out the words "If after the date of this scheme" in first line, and also the words "the Act," in third line, and substitute for latter the words "this scheme," so that the clause would read thus—"Any pupil of an Ulster Royal School who was such at the date of the passing of this scheme, and who would," &c.

There are many boys who have entered these schools since the passing of the Act with the sole object of competing for a Royal Scholarship in T.C.D., but who, by reason of their age, or from some other cause, are still ineligible to do so, and I respectfully submit that such boys have claims which should be taken into consideration by the Commissioners.

I may add that the Dean of Armagh informed me he would also write to you on this subject.

(Signed), A. NELSON,

District Registrar,

Probate Court.

April 27, 1889.

XXIV.—*Thomas Gordon, Assistant Master, Royal School, Armagh.*

I, Thomas Gordon, assistant master, Royal School, Armagh, beg to state that I object to Clauses 53 and 54 of the Revised Draft Scheme No. 34, on the ground that they neither save nor make due compensation for my vested interests in accordance with the provisions of the Educational Endowments (Ireland) Act, 1885.

(Signed), THOMAS GORDON.

Armagh, May 16, 1889.

XXV.—*Rev. John Knox Leslie.*

It seems to me that the rule in your Draft Scheme, making it compulsory for at least seven pupils to pass in the Intermediate examinations, will be most unfair to the schools in my neighbourhood.

As a rule boys who pass the junior grade are very unwilling to enter for the middle or senior, and those who are reading for the University or Civil Service absolutely refuse to present themselves for any grade of the Intermediate; and, in addition to this, the parents of such boys will not allow them to be put forward at all. I would suggest that a pass in the matriculation of the Royal University or Trinity College, Dublin, should take the place of a pass in the Intermediate—always, of course, supposing the pupil to be under the age, and to be examined on the subjects specified in your Scheme.

This would obviate the difficulty.

(Signed), JOHN KNOX LESLIE.

The Manse, Cookstown,

May 17, 1889.

No. III. (1).

Referred to in Evidence, p. [illegible].

Archbishop Walsh to Lord Justice FitzGibbon.

4, Rutland square, E., Dublin,
[illegible] June, [illegible].

Dear Lord Justice,—I wrote to Father Delany, Dr. Henry (St Malachy's), Father [illegible] (Castleknock), and Father [illegible] (Blackrock), for information as to the proportion of passes to the number of boys sent in for the Intermediate Examination.

I enclose their replies.

The figures, so far as I have looked into them, seem to show that 1 in 4 may be a fair proportion if we speak of passes in the sense of the Intermediate Board, but that 1 in [illegible] comes nearer to the mark when we deal with passes in the stricter sense of your Scheme.

One of my correspondents makes the judicious remark that the effect of the Scheme will be to direct the attention of the schools to the advantage of passing in the subjects enumerated in your Schedule.

In fixing upon the proportion to be assigned in the Scheme, it is also to be kept in view that a school engaged in the proper school work of preparing its boys for the University Matriculation is obliged, to a large extent, to withdraw them from the school examinations of the Intermediate Education Board.

I remain, my dear Lord Justice,

Most faithfully yours,

✠ William J. Walsh,
Archbishop of Dublin.

SUMMARY

Of Returns from Roman Catholic Intermediate Schools, showing Percentages of Pupils Passing Intermediate Examinations.

[illegible]	Year.	Pupils [illegible] Intermediate Education.	Pupils [illegible] Intermediate Examinations.	Percentage.	Pupils passing in Five specified Subjects.	Percentage.
Clongowes,	1887,	[illegible]	79	[illegible]	31	14·4
Do.,	1888,	[illegible]	[illegible]	[illegible]	[illegible]	[illegible]
Belvedere,	[illegible]	[illegible]	[illegible]	[illegible]	[illegible]	[illegible]
Limerick,	[illegible]	[illegible]	[illegible]	[illegible]	[illegible]	[illegible]
St. Malachy's, Belfast,	1887,	[illegible]	[illegible]	[illegible]	[illegible]	[illegible]
Do.,	1888,	170	[illegible]	[illegible]	[illegible]	[illegible]
		1,[illegible]	[illegible]	[illegible]	[illegible]	[illegible]

Returns from St. Vincent's College, Castleknock.

Year.	Pupils passing Intermediate Examinations.	Percentage of Total Pupils.	Papers passing in five specified Subjects.	Percentage of Total Papers.
1887,	[illegible]	[illegible]	[illegible]	[illegible]
1888,	[illegible]	[illegible]	[illegible]	[illegible]
	[illegible]	[illegible]	[illegible]	[illegible]

Returns from Blackrock College.

—	1887.		1888.	
	Sent in.	Passed.*	Sent in.	Passed.*
Senior,	[illegible]	[illegible]	[illegible]	[illegible]
Middle,	[illegible]	[illegible]	[illegible]	17
Junior,	[illegible]	[illegible]	[illegible]	[illegible]
	[illegible]	[illegible]	113	[illegible]

* Passed in the five prescribed subjects.

No. III. (u.)

Referred to in Evidence, p. 171.

Letter of Mr. Wilkins to the Commissioners.

High School, Dublin,
1st June, 1889.

Sir,—At the sitting of the Commission on yesterday it was suggested that an efficient school should pass one-fourth of its boys in a given year at the Intermediate Examinations. Below I give my experience on the subject from the records of this school.

Year.	Boys on Roll in June Quarter.	Boys passed at Intermediate Examinations.	Per cent.
[illegible]	[illegible]	[illegible]	[illegible]

Of course the conditions of passing have varied from year to year, growing for the most part harder, but the percentage of our boys passed never rose to twenty-five. This school must be taken as above the average, especially in 1888, when we stood first, as regards distinctions, of Protestant schools. (We were tabulated second to the Methodist College, Belfast, by the *Freeman* and *Irish Times*, but subsequent awards of the Commissioners placed us first).

The percentage of passes would be further reduced by the fact that the proposed standard will be higher than that of the Intermediate. Out of the [illegible] boys we passed in 1888, your standard would reject [illegible], reducing the percentage of passes down to 14.

I give below particulars of the passes in various subjects of the 43 boys whom we passed in 1888. It is unnecessary to consider any candidates who failed, for though nearly all did well in English and Mathematics, not one passed in a language other than English.

Subject.	Entrance on Roll.	Passed.
English,	[illegible]	[illegible]
Latin,	[illegible]	[illegible]
Arithmetic,	[illegible]	[illegible]
Algebra,	[illegible]	[illegible]
[illegible]	[illegible]	[illegible]
[illegible]	[illegible]	[illegible]
Drawing,	[illegible]	[illegible]
[illegible]	[illegible] (about)	[illegible]
[illegible]	[illegible]	[illegible]
[illegible]	[illegible]	[illegible]
	—	—

In compiling above table I treated a pass in Arithmetic and Algebra (senior grade), as a pass in both subjects, and similarly for a failure.

It would not be easy for me to get similar information from other schools for the Commissioners, certainly not within the prescribed limits of time.

(Signed), W. Wilkins.

No. III. (v.)

Archbishop Walsh to Lord Justice FitzGibbon.

4, Rutland-square, E., Dublin,
7th June, 1889.

My dear Lord Justice,—There was a matter about which I undertook to send you a suggestion before to-morrow—the reference to the persons to be named by the Lord Lieutenant as Commissioners of Education.

I do not yet how the matter can be arranged by the insertion of words definitely restricting the choice of the Lord Lieutenant to persons "having the confidence" of the religious denominations in question respectively. The Privy Council might very fairly say that the insertion of any such words would have the effect of throwing on the Lord Lieutenant an obligation which it would be impossible for him to fulfil.

I see, then, only two courses open: (1) to confine the freedom of the Lord Lieutenant in selecting his nominees from a list calculated in such a way as to ensure that it should consist only of persons having the confidence, &c.; and (2) to provide for the matter indirectly, by the insertion of a clause by way of preamble, such as the following: "With the view of ensuring that the Commission shall be persons having the confidence" of the religious denominations, &c., five of the persons so nominated shall be Roman Catholics, &c., &c.

This latter course would, I think, go very far to solve the difficulty.

(Signed). ✠ William J. Walsh,
Archbishop of Dublin.

No. III. (w.)

Referred to Evidence pp. 151, 163, 173.

Return of the Number of Students who Passed the Intermediate Examinations in the years 1886, 1887, 1888, and 1889, from the Schools in the Royal Schools Districts.

Whole of the Royal Schools Districts.—Summary.

—	1886.		1887.		1888.		1889.	
	Number of Passes.	Percentage of Total Passes.	Number of Passes.	Percentage of Total Passes.	Number of Passes.	Percentage of Total Passes.	Number of Passes.	Percentage of Total Passes.
Protestants,	[illegible]	[illegible]	[illegible]	[illegible]	[illegible]	[illegible]	[illegible]	[illegible]
Roman Catholics,	[illegible]	[illegible]	[illegible]	[illegible]	[illegible]	[illegible]	[illegible]	[illegible]
Total,	[illegible]	[illegible]	[illegible]	[illegible]	[illegible]	[illegible]	[illegible]	[illegible]

The [illegible] District.

The [illegible] District.

The Fermanagh District.

Schools.	[illegible]				[illegible]				[illegible]				[illegible]			
	Prot.		R.C.		Prot.		R.C.		Prot.		R.C.		Prot.		R.C.	
	Boys.	Girls.	Boys.	Girls.	Boys.	Girls.	Boys.	Girls.	Boys.	Girls.	Boys.	Girls.	Boys.	Girls.	Boys.	Girls.
[illegible]	...	[illegible]	...	...	...	...	...	...	...	...	...	...	...	...	...	...
[illegible]	...	...	...	[illegible]	...	...	...	...	...	...	...	...	[illegible]	...	...	...
[illegible]	[illegible]	...	...	...	[illegible]	...	...	...	[illegible]	...	...	...	...	...	...	...
[illegible]	...	...	...	...	...	...	[illegible]	...	...	...	[illegible]	...	...	...	[illegible]	...
[illegible]	...	...	[illegible]	...	...	...	[illegible]	...	...	...	[illegible]	...	...	...	[illegible]	...
[illegible]	[illegible]	...	...	...	...	...	...	...	...	...	...	...	[illegible]	...	...	...
[illegible]	...	...	...	[illegible]	...	...	...	[illegible]	...	...	...	[illegible]	...	...	...	[illegible]
[illegible]	...	[illegible]	...	...	...	[illegible]	...	...	...	...	...	...	...	...	...	...
[illegible]	...	[illegible]	...	...	...	[illegible]	...	...	...	...	...	...	...	...	...	...
[illegible]	...	[illegible]	...	...	...	...	...	...	...	...	...	...	...	[illegible]	...	...
Totals—Protestants and R.C.'s,	[illegible]		[illegible]		[illegible]		[illegible]		[illegible]		[illegible]		[illegible]		[illegible]	
Percentages of Total Passes,	[illegible]		[illegible]		[illegible]		[illegible]		[illegible]		[illegible]		[illegible]		[illegible]	
Private Addresses,	[illegible]				[illegible]				[illegible]				[illegible]			

The Cavan District.

Schools.	Prot. Boys.	Prot. Girls.	R.C. Boys.	R.C. Girls.	Prot. Boys.	Prot. Girls.	R.C. Boys.	R.C. Girls.	Prot. Boys.	Prot. Girls.	R.C. Boys.	R.C. Girls.	Prot. Boys.	Prot. Girls.	R.C. Boys.	R.C. Girls.
[illegible]	...	...	...	...	...	...	...	...	...	...	...	...	...	...	...	...
[illegible]	...	...	[illegible]	...	...	...	[illegible]	...	...	...	[illegible]	...	...	...	...	...
[illegible]	...	...	...	...	...	...	...	...	...	...	[illegible]	...	...	...	[illegible]	...
[illegible]	...	...	...	...	...	...	...	...	...	...	[illegible]	...	...	...	...	...
[illegible]	...	...	...	...	[illegible]	...	...	...	[illegible]	...	...	...	[illegible]	...	...	...
[illegible]	...	[illegible]	...	...	...	...	...	...	...	...	...	...	...	...	...	...
Totals—Protestants and R.C.'s,	[illegible]		[illegible]		[illegible]		[illegible]		[illegible]		[illegible]		[illegible]		[illegible]	
Percentages of Total Passes,	[illegible]		[illegible]		[illegible]		[illegible]		[illegible]		[illegible]		[illegible]		[illegible]	
Private Addresses,	[illegible]				[illegible]				...				...			

The Donegal District.

Schools.	Prot. Boys.	Prot. Girls.	R.C. Boys.	R.C. Girls.	Prot. Boys.	Prot. Girls.	R.C. Boys.	R.C. Girls.	Prot. Boys.	Prot. Girls.	R.C. Boys.	R.C. Girls.	Prot. Boys.	Prot. Girls.	R.C. Boys.	R.C. Girls.
[illegible]	[illegible]	[illegible]	...	...	[illegible]	[illegible]	...	...	[illegible]	[illegible]	...	...	[illegible]	[illegible]	...	...
[illegible]	...	[illegible]	...	...	...	...	...	...	...	...	...	...	...	...	...	...
[illegible]	[illegible]	...	...	...	[illegible]	...	...	...	[illegible]	...	...	...	[illegible]	...	...	...
[illegible]	...	...	...	...	[illegible]	...	...	...	[illegible]	[illegible]	...	...	[illegible]	...	...	...
[illegible]	...	...	[illegible]	...	...	...	...	...	...	...	...	...	...	...	...	...
Totals—Protestants and R.C.'s,	[illegible]		[illegible]		[illegible]		...		[illegible]		...		[illegible]		...	
Percentages of Total Passes,	[illegible]		[illegible]		[illegible]		...		[illegible]		...		[illegible]		...	
Private Addresses,	[illegible]				[illegible]				[illegible]				[illegible]			

Vested Interests.

Head Master of Royal School, Enniskillen.

No. III. (x.)

Rev. W. Steele to the Judicial Commissioners.

Portora Royal School,
25th May, 1889.

My Lords Justices,—As I find it impossible to [illegible] the public [illegible], I venture to say that to me it is a matter of great moment that I should be permitted under the final Scheme, as all were under the Draft Scheme of April, 18[illegible], to commute my pension into an equivalent bulk sum. My reason for asking this permission is simply the following: Owing to my very large outlay on the school buildings, which Mr. M'Curdy, the Commissioners' architect, in his evidence before Lord [illegible] Commission, said increased their value, followed as it was a few years after by the falling off in the number of boarders, arising from causes over which I had no control, I was involved in serious financial embarrassment, which the commutation of my pension would relieve. I, therefore, pray your lordships to grant me this indulgence, for which I shall feel thankful.

(Signed), W. Steele.

No. III. (y.)

Rev. W. Steele to the Judicial Commissioners.

Portora Royal School,
June 1[illegible], 1889.

My Lords Justices,—My letter was intended to convey that I am sincerely desirous to retire if the Commissioners would grant me such compensation as would enable me to do so. After much anxious thought, then, I have come to the determination of retiring within six months after the date of the Scheme, if the commutation of my pension be computed at three per cent.; trusting, however, that your lordships may make some moderate increase to the pension offered me in the Draft Scheme, in consideration of the £110 a year I derive from a portion of the land attached to the house coming to me as directly from the Endowment as the salary paid by the Board. According to the Carlisle Tables, a person sixty-nine years of age commuting a pension of £300 a year at three per cent. would receive £2,7[illegible] 1[illegible]s. This sum, added to the £[illegible] for [illegible], would amount to £[illegible], a sum not equal to my outlay on the school buildings, which, although constituting a claim which may not be legally enforced, yet, as no law forbids a certain amount of liberal and generous treatment in matters of [illegible] agreement, may well give me an equitable claim to favourable consideration.

(Signed), W. Steele,
Head Master of Portora Royal School.

No. III. (z.)

Rev. W. Steele to the Judicial Commissioners.

Portora Royal School,
21st June, 1889.

My Lords Justices,—In your letter of the 6th inst., you asked me to state at what rate of interest I should expect the commutation of my pension to be computed, and what would be the total amount. I replied that I expected it to be computed at three per cent., and that a person sixty-nine years of age would, according to the Carlisle tables, receive for a pension of £300 a year a bulk sum of £2,7[illegible] 10s. In your reply, dated 11th inst., you do not say that my demand is excessive, but, for other reasons which I shall not enter here, you do not consider it consistent with your duty to accede to it.

Nothing remains for me now but to ask your lordships what is the [illegible] under which you would consider yourselves justified in granting by way of commutation of my pension.

(Signed), W. Steele,
Head Master of Portora.

Head Master of Royal School, Armagh.

No. III. (aa.)

Rev. W. Moore Morgan to the Judicial Commissioners.

Royal School, Armagh,
June 3rd, 1889.

My Lords,—Before the Royal Schools Scheme is signed by your Lordships, I venture to submit some important facts bearing on my vested interests, and especially on the selection of thirty years (in clause 34) as the term of my full service, without prejudice to my serious objections on other grounds to the treatment of these interests in the Scheme.

1. In the new Schemes for English Endowed Schools, the retiring allowance clause uniformly lays down twenty years as the period of full service. The subjoined extract gives the provision there adopted:—

"*[illegible]. The Governors of the [illegible] School may, if they think fit, and the [illegible] at their disposal suffice for the purpose, agree with the Head Master for the formation of a fund in the nature of a Pension or Superannuation Fund, the main principle of such agreement being that the Head Master and the Governors of the [illegible] School respectively shall contribute annually for a period of twenty years such sums as may be agreed on; that these contributions shall accumulate at compound interest; that in case the Head Master accept his office for twenty years he shall on his retirement be entitled to the whole accumulated fund; that

*The same clause [illegible] is used for Head Masters. No contribution is made by the Governing Body [illegible] the twenty years are passed.—W. Moore Morgan.

in case she retires earlier on account of permanent disability from disease she shall also be entitled to the whole of the same fund; that in all other cases she shall, on ceasing to be Head Mistress, be entitled to the amount produced by her own contributions. If any question shall arise upon the construction or working of this provision, the same shall be referred by the Governors of the Girls' School to the Charity Commissioners, whose decision thereon shall be final and conclusive."

If the twenty years limit is thus accepted by the English Charity Commissioners as their rule for the *future*, it seems very reasonable that it should be adopted in a case so special as mine, and where such personal loss and hardship are involved.

2. In your revised Draft Scheme the Assistant Masters of the Royal Schools can obtain their *full* retiring allowance (two-thirds of their entire vested interests) *after twenty years service*.

I need scarcely point out the difference in tenure and emoluments between their position and mine. Also several of these are younger than myself.

3. The fact that I am the only "Ulster Royal School" Head Master with less than thirty years service is purely accidental. Had the service of one or more of the other Head Masters been only twenty or twenty-five years, might not this more opportune accident have lowered the full term accordingly? Also, does not clause 53 virtually treat my full service as twenty years by its offer to me for the surrender of the school premises "within six months of the date of the Scheme?"

Either this limit of six months is inequitable in my case or my full service should be fixed at twenty years.

4. A retiring allowance of £[illegible] a year is offered to each of the Head Masters of Dungannon and Enniskillen. Probably it has escaped notice that their salaries of £[illegible] a year each are both liable to payment of taxes on the full valuation of their respective school premises, whereas in my case the corresponding taxes are paid by the Commissioners of Education. To place me on equal terms in this particular, my salary should be treated as £[illegible] a year, the annual average of these taxes being £[illegible].

As in the above matters the proposals of the revised Draft Scheme differ in my case from the principle elsewhere adopted, even in the Scheme itself, I venture respectfully to hope that your Lordships will so far modify these provisions as to place me on at least as favourable a footing as other holders of vested interests.

(Signed), W. Moore Morgan.

No. III. (bb.)

The Commissioners to Rev. W. Moore Morgan.

[illegible],
June 6, 188[illegible].

Rev. Sir,—I am directed . . . . . to state that the minimum grants are subject in every case to the provisions for vested interests contained in the Scheme, and that it is not in the power of the Commissioners to bring the School into operation simultaneously in two districts unless the Head Master should retire.

(Signed), Wm. Edward Ellis,
Secretary.

No. III. (cc.)

Rev. W. Moore Morgan to the Commissioners.

Royal School, Armagh,
June 7th, 188[illegible].

Dear Sir,—In reply to your letter of yesterday, I beg to state that in urging my claim for treatment, "*at least equal* to that of the other Head Masters," I did not admit that a life annuity of £430, with a payment of £300 for the surrender of the school premises within six months of the date of the Scheme, could be regarded as adequate compensation on my retirement. I merely expressed a hope that the final Scheme would not leave me at a disadvantage, when compared with the other Head Masters. The above provision was in fact no more than I could reasonably claim had the Act of 18[illegible] found Armagh School in the same condition, as regards pupils, as *e.g.* Cavan or Dungannon Schools.

It is undeniable that the injurious effect of the above Act on emoluments outside salary and free residence is, practically speaking, confined to my case; and I am entitled to regard my claim under this head as altogether exceptional. In proof that such emoluments are "vested interests," I need only refer to the statements of Lord Justice FitzGibbon (Q. [illegible] in your last Report):—"We quite agree that *all the profits of his office* should be taken into account in estimating a retiring allowance;" and again (Q. [illegible]) in my own case, "We agree that he is to be compensated for his interests as a whole, and you must not suppose that we proposed to give the salary to the Head Masters on any different principle from their other emoluments."

If Mr. Moore's interest, at eighty years of age, in premises valued at £[illegible] a year, is placed at £[illegible] in the Scheme, how can my interest, at forty-[illegible] years of age, in premises valued in Clause 50 at £[illegible] a year, be limited to £[illegible]?

These and other like considerations will, I hope, justify my statement that, on a comparison of my case with those of the other Head Masters, I should be entitled to very much larger compensation than that above named.

However, to remove obstacles, and especially to facilitate the acceptance of the latest proposals of the Judicial Commissioners with regard to the Armagh and Tyrone Endowments, I am prepared to retire on a life annuity of £430, and on receipt of a capital sum of £3,[illegible] for the surrender of all my interest in the school premises, within six months from the date of the Scheme, and I wish it to be clearly understood that this is the very lowest compensation for which I could consent to retire as proposed. It is also conditional on more satisfactory provision being made in the Scheme for the payment of my retiring annuity, as I maintain that the latter should be a first charge, not merely on the Armagh Endowment, but also on the residue of the other Royal School Endowments, as guaranteed by the Act 3 George IV., c. 79, and as I object to the special limitation imposed by clause [illegible] to the obligation to pay these allowances.

(Signed), W. Moore Morgan.

No. III. (dd.)

Rev. W. Moore Morgan to the Commissioners.

Royal School, Armagh,
June 19, 188[illegible].

Dear Sir,—In reply to your letter of yesterday, I am to observe that there has been no misapprehension on my part of the proposals of the revised Scheme for the Royal Schools, but only of the object of your letter of the 6th instant.

I naturally thought that it proceeded on the assumption that the endowments could bear the charge therein referred to. I may remind you that in that letter, the annuity of £430, with the payment of £600, was designated "a retiring allowance on my resignation within six months of the date of the Scheme," and not in any respect as "compensation on abolition of office." I am, therefore, quite unable to understand how my reply to that letter can have been taken in the latter sense, and I cannot feel that my meaning was open to doubt.

I can only repeat my respectful but emphatic protest of the 3rd inst. against the revised Scheme, as being inconsistent with,

1. Its own provisions for the other Head Masters, especially those of Dungannon and Enniskillen;

2. Its own provisions for Assistant Masters; and

3. The provisions for Head Masters' pensions in recent Schemes for English Endowed Schools.

(Signed), W. Moore Morgan.

Denominational Boards for Armagh and Tyrone.

No. III. ([illegible])

Circular Letter of the Commissioners regarding the formation of Denominational Boards in Armagh and Tyrone.

Note.—This letter was addressed to the twelve members of the Local Boards for Armagh and Tyrone, and also to the ecclesiastical authorities of the various denominations interested.

13, Nassau-street, Dublin,

June 1st, 1888.

Armagh and Tyrone Districts.

Rev. Sir,—In the course of consideration of objections to the above Draft Scheme, the representatives of "The General Synod of the Church of Ireland," and of the "Diocesan Councils of Armagh, Clogher, Derry, and Kilmore," have pressed a claim to have separate Local Boards for the administration of such portions of the Ulster Royal School Endowments as may be applicable for the education of members of their Church.

The proposed Fermanagh Protestant Board have stated their intention of working as a mixed board, and the Commissioners have no reason to apprehend that the Cavan Protestant Board will find any difficulty in carrying out the provisions of the Scheme.

The amount of the Raphoe Endowment is too small for subdivision.

The Commissioners think it most desirable that opportunity should be given to the members of the several Protestant denominations in Armagh and Tyrone of entering into the arrangements best suited to the wants of their several localities. With this object the Commissioners invite an expression of opinion from those interested upon a suggestion made to the deputation of the Synod on May 4, 1888 (see Report attached, No. [illegible]), and at the public sitting yesterday, that the Armagh and Tyrone districts should, so far as the Protestants are concerned, be specially dealt with, so as to enable the leading denominations to determine for themselves whether to act separately or together.

The Commissioners think the following proposals worthy of consideration:—

That for the purposes of the Protestant Boards the Armagh and Tyrone Districts should be treated as one, and that two boards should be formed to administer the endowments of both districts for Protestant education, one board to consist of eight Church members, with one Methodist member, and the other to consist of eight Presbyterian members, with the second Methodist member. If such an arrangement should be made, the Protestant interest in the Armagh School premises, as defined in the Scheme, would be assigned to the Church Board and that in the Dungannon School premises to the Presbyterian Board; provision should be made to enable each board to maintain or aid qualified schools connected with its own denomination throughout the joint district, and the Protestant [illegible] grants, and share of the united Tyrone and Armagh Endowments, which are shown equal in value, would be equally divided between the two boards. The schools connected with each board would receive their own share of the residue of the Ulster Royal School Endowments, as provided in the scheme, section 43, and schedule I.

An alternative may be considered of placing both the Methodist representatives on one of the boards, giving it the administration of an additional share of the endowments, proportioned to the claim of the members of the Methodist Church.

These proposals, to a great extent, leave it to the determination of those interested whether mixed Protestant boards or separate boards are more for the advantage of education in the districts, and their adoption might enable the Armagh and Dungannon Schools, instead of being, as hitherto, competing schools, to be conducted under governing bodies, specially constituted to secure the confidence and meet the requirements of the two denominations largely interested. This would accord with one of the proposals made by the "Commissioners of Education" (the Protestant Commissioners) in their Draft Scheme.

The determination of the matter ought, in the opinion of my Commissioners, to be largely influenced by the wishes of those most directly interested, and in order to elicit their views, I am directed to forward a copy of this communication to each member of the Armagh and Tyrone Protestant Boards and to those who have represented the denominations concerned before the Commission, viz.:—The Standing Committee of the General Synod, the Presbyterian Intermediate Education Committee, the Methodist Conference, the Raphoe and Dungannon Local Committees, and the Commissioners of Education, with the Diocesan Councils.

The Very Rev. the Dean of Armagh, and the Rev. Hamilton B. Wilson, D.D., Cookstown, have been specially requested to favour the Commissioners, by convening a conference or by other means, with their assistance in obtaining an expression of opinion which may be a guide to the Commissioners in dealing with the subject.

You will oblige by communicating, through the gentlemen above named, or directly to this office, such observations as you may think desirable.

The matter is very urgent, but it is of such importance, that the Commissioners feel justified [illegible] deferring the final revision of the Scheme for a few days to give an opportunity for its discussion, but they must ask that any observations to be submitted to them shall be forwarded to me not later than next Tuesday week, the 12th inst.

(Signed), N. D. Murphy,
Assistant Secretary.

No. III. (ff.)

Rev. William Moore Morgan to the Commissioners.

Royal School, Armagh,
June 8, 1886.

Dear Sir,—As some doubt is still felt by those interested with regard to the exact working of the "minimum grant" clause of the Scheme, I shall be much obliged if you will kindly let me know, if possible, on Monday next (for the information of our Diocesan Council on Tuesday), which of the following interpretations is correct:—

Taking the Dungannon Endowment for argument sake, at £1,100 a year net (after deducting extra charge), and assuming that the vested interests will absorb £500 of the above, will the "minimum grant" for each Local Board, during the continuance of the full retiring annuities, be only £125 a year? or will it even then be £275 a year, subject to a deduction of £25 a year (to provide for vested interests), so long as these [sic] annuities last?

You will see that this is a serious question in connection with the proposal for the rental and maintenance of the Armagh and Dungannon school buildings. If the second of the above interpretations be correct, it would practically mean that the "minimum grant" should not be affected by the provision for vested interests until the "residue" (that would ultimately provide the "pension" fund), should have been first exhausted for that purpose. This residue, in the case of Dungannon, would be £250 a year, almost enough to cover the entire charge for "vested interests," should this charge continue in full beyond the "first three years." The "minimum grants" would thus start at almost their full figure, and would not be reduced to a figure which would render it almost impossible to maintain the present school buildings.

(Signed), W. Moore Morgan.

P.S.—You will see the ambiguity of the phrase "the minimum grants are subject to the provision for vested interests." On the first of the above hypotheses, the obligation or deductions would be £300 a year in all, whereas in the second it would amount to only £50 a year (£25 from each board)—a very serious difference.

No. III. (gg.)

Rev. W. M'Mullen to the Commissioners.

18, Leinster-road, Rathmines,
June 8, 1886.

Dear Sir,—On my return from London yesterday, I found awaiting me your communication of the 1st June, containing the suggestions of the Commissioners on the subject of the Local Boards for Armagh and Tyrone districts.

I found also awaiting me letters from the gentlemen named in the Draft Scheme, as the Methodist Representatives on the Local Boards of these districts. These gentlemen are, I find, very unfavourable to the proposal to divide the Protestant Local Boards into two—one Episcopalian, and the other Presbyterian.

I have given the proposal careful consideration, and I cannot see that it is desirable in itself or likely to serve any important educational purpose. As I leave home on Monday in order to attend the sittings of our Conference in Cork, I have no opportunity of consulting other members of our committee, but I am tolerably sure that they would agree with me in saying that the proposed change would not be an improvement on the Draft Scheme.

(Signed), Wallace M'Mullen.

No. III. (hh.)

Very Rev. James Byrne to the Commissioners.

Ergenagh Rectory, Omagh,
June 9, 1886.

Sir,—In answer to your circular inviting the expression of opinion on the proposal that the Armagh and Dungannon districts for endowed schools should be treated as one, and administered by two denominational boards, I beg leave to say that I think this would in practice come to a Presbyterian Board for Dungannon, and a Church board for Armagh, and that to such an arrangement I should prefer the mixed boards proposed by the Commissioners.

The establishment of exclusive boards would seem to assume that the Church and other Protestants could not beneficially work together a system of intermediate education, and the assumption seems to me an exaggeration of religious difference which does not correspond to the actual sentiments which prevail between the religious bodies themselves.

It would, I think, be a hardship on the Armagh Presbyterians, and on the Tyrone Church people to have the school in their own neighbourhood marked with this character of sectarian exclusiveness hostile to themselves. And though for boarders both the schools would be sufficiently near to any part of the two districts, the religious difference would tend to limit each religious body to one school instead of their having a choice of two. For, however willing they might each be to meet the other body in education on the large ground common to both, subject to a united administration; they would, I fear, be repelled by the total exclusion, from the government of their own religious body. Both schools would, I think, have more pupils under mixed boards, and would in consequence be more vigorous and efficient in every way, and it would in my view, be matter for deep regret that sectarianism should be stamped on the higher education of the country, to which we would rather look for a liberalising influence.

(Signed), James Byrne.

No. III. (ii.)

James H. Stronge, member of proposed Armagh Protestant Board, to the Commissioners.

Hockley Lodge, Armagh,
June 11, 1886.

Sir,—I was asked, as a member of the proposed Protestant Board of Intermediate education for the county of Armagh, to attend a conference at Portadown yesterday. At the conclusion of that conference I requested Dr. Wilson to inform the Commissioners that I preferred the proposal contained in their letter of June 1st to the Draft Scheme. I think, however, that it is only respectful to the Commissioners that I should state my reasons for so doing.

My preference for that proposal is very largely due to my desire to maintain boarding schools in Armagh and Dungannon, where buildings suitable for such institutions exist. I hold that there are advantages to education in its widest sense which are to be had at a boarding school and not at a mere day school.

The Royal Schools of Armagh and Dungannon have both had their periods of success in the past, and it is probable that in the future there will be a greater demand for such institutions than hitherto. Many of our class, which has hitherto sought education for its sons in England, will be obliged to seek cheaper education nearer home; and I think that there is another class, which at present has its sons educated at day schools, but which, as it rises in importance, will wish to obtain for them the advantages of public school training.

If it is, as I believe, to be wished that the schools at Armagh and Dungannon should be maintained as boarding schools, I think it follows that they should be managed by denominational rather than by mixed boards. The master in a boarding school must, to a very great extent, represent the absent parent; and I think that there are very many parents who would object to sending their sons to a boarding school unless they felt sure that they would be under a master of their own denomination.

I think also that it would be easier to maintain boarding schools at Armagh and Dungannon if each school offered special inducements to one denomination than it would be if the two schools competed with each other on identically the same ground.

In view of the great advantage which these boarding schools ought to be to the education of the district, I think that the compensation for vested interests should be paid out of the "surplus fees" rather than out of the "minimum grant."

In the event of the proposal embodied in the letter of June 1st not being adopted, I would venture to suggest that the Draft Scheme should be amended so as to give the Church of Ireland minority in Tyrone as full a representation on the Tyrone Board as the Presbyterian minority is given on the Armagh Board.

I further think that if the two boarding schools are to be under the management of mixed boards, it should be provided that the head master of Armagh school should belong to the Church of Ireland and the head master of Dungannon to the Presbyterian Church, and that in each case there should be an assistant master of the other denomination who should keep a house for boarders.

(Signed), JAMES H. [illegible]

No. III. (ii.)

Archdeacon Meade to the Commissioners.

Ardtrea Rectory,
Stewartstown,
June 11, 1892.

Sir,—In reply to your communication of the 1st inst., I beg to inform you that the following resolution was this day adopted by the Armagh Diocesan Council:—

"We welcome the proposal of the Educational Endowments Commission with respect to the division of Armagh and Tyrone, as a partial recognition of the principle for which we contend; but, being convinced that the proper maintenance of the premises and teaching staff of the present Royal Schools depends upon a fixed disposal of the endowments without any deduction for 'outside' payments, we regret that this fixed division will transfer so large a part of our claim.

We also observe with regret the proposal that the Methodist representatives should carry with them a share of the endowment disproportionate to the claim of the Methodist Church, as an admission of the principle for which we contend.

Lastly, we submit that, since our Episcopalian population in the two counties is 10,154, while that of all other Protestant denominations is 68,375, the proposal that we should pay any compensation, when granted a separate board, is at variance with the figures of the Commissioners themselves.

We assume that 'the Protestant interest' in school premises does not include any new private endowments, and we record our protest against the proportion given to the Roman Catholics in the division of the revenues."

(Signed), WM. E. MEADE, D.D.,
Archdeacon of Armagh and
Secretary of the Council.

P.S.—I am directed to add that the resolution was unanimously adopted.

No. III. (iii.)

William Paul, member of proposed Armagh Local Board, to the Judicial Commissioners.

Portadown,
11th June, 1892.

My Lords Justices,—I beg to acknowledge the receipt of a copy of the circular letter and enclosure supplied to each member of the proposed Provisional Local Boards for Armagh and Tyrone, and to present to you my views.

Constitution of Local Boards.

I am strongly opposed to the appointment of virtually denominational boards, and decidedly in favour of mixed boards, as provided for in the original Draft Scheme, for two reasons:—

Firstly.—Because I am convinced that it will need the united effort of the Protestant communities in each district to establish or continue successfully one school, qualified to give to the Protestant youth of the district who can avail themselves of it, intermediate and higher education (such a school as the Royal School at Armagh for County Armagh, and of Dungannon for County Tyrone); and the confidence which a mixed board would impart is the best security for such support being rendered.

Secondly.—Because the principle of your Scheme is involved if denominational be substituted for mixed boards. Since it is provided that the Commissioners of Education in Ireland shall be representative of all denominations and interests concerned, it follows that the Protestant Local Boards ought to be correspondingly representative.

What is good for Fermanagh and Cavan and Raphoe ought to be had for Armagh and Dungannon.

Therefore I object to the union of the districts of Armagh and Tyrone, and adhere to the constitution of the Local Board of Armagh, as specified in section 10, revised Draft Scheme.

Results:—

I cannot see how efficient education can be secured unless your Inspector be required to examine each candidate. The schools are not so numerous nor so difficult of access as to render such an examination impracticable, and the work to be done would not be so arduous as that of an Inspector of Elementary Education.

I am strongly opposed to paying result fees for instruction imparted to candidates for the Intermedate Examinations who have been unable to pass, because—

Firstly.—It will be calculated to promote [illegible] education, as it does away with the stimulus of competition.

Secondly.—Provision made in any school for a competent staff of teachers is not an equivalent for successful teaching.

The position of the efficient teaching staff of a qualified school who have instructed a large number of pupils in the intermediate course for the year, when they find but a few successful, is not an enviable one. Teachers of private schools are often similarly disappointed, while the records of such schools prove that with perseverance in another year or two they reap the results of their labours. I would prefer a declared standard, even though it were some degrees lower than the Intermediate test, to payment by heads.

Alteration of Scheme, sect. 68, Revised Draft Scheme.

I object to the introduction in the Revised Draft Scheme of the words—"Upon the application of Her Majesty's Attorney-General for Ireland, or," and recommend their omission, because the Attorney-General for the time being is an active member of some political party, and in my opinion the Scheme should be protected from party interference.

I approve of the remaining part of section 68, in which provision is made for alteration of the Scheme, "upon the application of the Commissioners," under certain conditions.

Committees:—

I find in section 33, Revised Draft Scheme, that in the election of committees provided for by that section the rights of minorities are appropriately guarded by the words—

(1.) "With the sanction of the Commissioners."
(2.) "Provided that every appointment . . . . as if the committee were a Local Board."

But in section 34 no such safeguards exist, and I would therefore ask your Lordships to insert similar provisions in that section for the protection of minorities, as without them it appears to me that any majority can depute all business to their own denominational colleagues on the board, destroying the principle of mixed boards.

(Signed), William Park.

No. III ([illegible])

Dean Chadwick and Archdeacon Meade to the Commissioners.

The Deanery, Armagh,
10th June, 1889.

Sir,—Dr. Wilson will forward to you, on my behalf and his own, the individual opinions of those members of the proposed "Mixed Boards" for Armagh and Tyrone, who today conferred upon the subject of your communication to us.

I enclose the qualifications, subject to which some of us then expressed our opinions. But I wish to add that, while perfectly friendly in its tone, this conference conclusively refuted the argument that our wish for separation could be met by an appeal to the Mixed Boards themselves. There we could only appeal to the members of other denominations to relinquish for our benefit the advantage of an undue representation given to them at our expense, and to restore to us the sole use of our private endowments, which you have cast into a common purse. To-day, naturally enough, they gave a solid vote against doing anything of the sort.

(Signed), Geo. A. Chadwick.

1. Our opposition of the proposed change is largely due to the desire to maintain the large schools of Armagh and Dungannon, which can only be kept up as boarding schools, and therefore (in our judgment) only by one denomination. But since their maintenance would require larger revenues than would remain after the payment of small fees to a number of minor schools, we connect our approval of the proposal with a repetition of our consistent claim for a fixed distribution of the funds. Failing this, we are convinced that the Commissioners will prove to have destroyed the centres of education contemplated by the founder, the spirit of whose intention they are instructed to respect.

2. Since the estimated members of the Church of Ireland in the two counties exceed, according to the tables of the Commissioners, those of all other Protestant communions in number, we consider that upon receiving the separate Board, which we have always claimed, we should rather receive compensation for this [illegible] excess than pay it to the other Board for receiving the Methodist representatives.

3. We assume, as a matter of course, that the proposed division of the Protestant interest in the school buildings is wholly independent of our claim to the greater value of private benefactions.

Geo. A. Chadwick, D.D.
William R. Meade, D.D.
Benjamin Wade, A.M.

June 10, 1889.

No. III. ([illegible])

Rev. H. B. Wilson, D.D., to the Commissioners.

Belfast,
June 11, 1889.

I have the honour to report that in the endeavour to ascertain opinion regarding the proposal to unite the Armagh and Tyrone Districts, I first convened the Intermediate Education Committee of the General Assembly; then on Friday, 7th inst., the non-Episcopal members of the Armagh and Tyrone Boards met in Belfast at my request. Again, on 10th inst., the joint Boards of Armagh and Tyrone Districts met at Portadown—Dr. Chadwick having convened the Armagh and I the Tyrone members; and, finally, a [illegible] meeting of the Intermediate Education Committee was held to-day.

The majority in each case prefer the revised Draft Scheme. But there is a minority who would prefer to see the two districts united, provided the funds were equally divided between Armagh and Tyrone. To that minority I belong. The Armagh members of the Board—I mean the Presbyterian members—are strongly opposed to the proposal to have denominational boards, as they think injury would be done thereby to the Armagh School mainly, but also to Dungannon in a less degree.

I send herewith the Minutes of the joint meeting

of the Boards at Portadown yesterday. It will be seen that the majority there were in favour of the revised Draft Scheme, and that the clerical members of the Episcopal Church prefer the proposal to unite the districts, subject to modifications which they did not reveal at the conference.

Personally, I prefer the new proposal without modifications, on the understanding that the funds shall be equally divided, subject to such modification as the action of the Methodist members might necessitate.

(Signed). H. B. Wilson,

Minutes referred to by Dr. Wilson.

The members of the proposed Protestant Local Boards of Armagh and Tyrone having been summoned by Dr. Chadwick and Dr. Wilson to meet at Portadown, in the Institute, on Monday, the 10th day of June, 1889, at 3.30 o'clock, the following gentlemen attended:—

Armagh Board.

The Very Rev. George A. Chadwick, D.D., Dean of Armagh.

The Rev. Benjamin Wade, M.A., Chancellor of Armagh.

James Henry Strange, Esq., Hockley Lodge, Armagh.

Rev. Jackson Smyth, D.D., Armagh.

Rev. John Elliott, Armagh.

William M'Crum, Esq., Milford, Armagh.

William Paul, Esq., Portadown.

Tyrone Board.

The Ven. William E. Meade, D.D., Archdeacon of Armagh.

Colonel J. G. J. Lowry, D.L., Rockdale, Dungannon.

Rev. H. B. Wilson, D.D., Cookstown.

James Brown, Esq., Donaghmore, Tyrone.

William Wilson, Esq., Coalisland.

Thomas H. Aiken, Esq., Dungannon; and

William J. Vernables, Esq., Cookstown.

Dr. Chadwick was unanimously requested to occupy the chair, and Dr. Wilson acted as secretary.

After a lengthened conference, in which opinion was freely expressed in reference to the question submitted, whether in their opinion the revised Draft Scheme should be adhered to, or the two districts be treated as one endowment, with two Protestant Boards, each denomination taking a school.

Mr. Venables submitted a series of resolutions, but the general opinion was that each member should state which he preferred—the revised Scheme or the proposal to unite the districts—and let the answers be sent forward to the Commissioners. This plan was adopted, and the following is the answer given by each member:—

Dr. *Chadwick*.—"I prefer the new proposal, with modifications, which I will write about."

Dr. *Meade*.—"I give the same answer."

Rev. Mr. *Wade*.—"I give the same."

Mr. *Strange*.—"I prefer the new proposal to the Scheme."

Mr. *James Brown*.—"Believing strongly in united education, I object to anything that would interfere with it."

Mr. *Aiken*.—"I am in favour of mixed boards."

Mr. *Venables*.—"I am opposed to the union of the two districts, and to the constitution of separate denominational boards, and in favour of the revised Draft Scheme."

Mr. *William Wilson*.—"I am in favour of mixed boards, and opposed to denominationalism."

Mr. *William Paul*.—"I give the same answer as Mr. Elliott."

Mr. *William M'Crum*.—"I prefer mixed boards."

Colonel *Lowry*.—"Having considered the proposed new Scheme of the Commissioners, I am of opinion that it is to be preferred to the original Scheme, because I would prefer two boards entirely denominational to two nominally united, but really denominational, as in the first Scheme; but as I believe that these schools will be guided in the future as they may do, they having failed as boarding, I would prefer mixed boards in both Tyrone and Armagh, composed of Churchmen and Presbyterians in equal numbers."

Dr. *Smyth*.—"I accept the revised Scheme, which provides for mixed boards, and reject the proposal for the union of the districts of Armagh and Tyrone with denominational boards."

Dr. *Wilson* was not asked, and gave no opinion.

(Signed), Geo. A. Chadwick, Chairman.
H. B. Wilson, Secretary.

No. III. (pp.)

Opinion of the Intermediate Education Committee of the General Assembly.

Belfast,
11th June, 1889.

The Intermediate Education Committee of the General Assembly having considered the proposal of the Educational Endowment Commissioners to treat the Armagh and Tyrone districts as one, assigning the Armagh School to an Episcopalian Local Board, and the Tyrone School to a Presbyterian Local Board, express their preference for the revised Draft Scheme on the following grounds:—

1. The majority of the members of the Protestant Local Boards on whom the chief responsibility of administration devolves are in favour of mixed Protestant Boards.

2. As a matter of fact, the mixed schools in Ulster have been, as a rule, the most successful.

3. While appreciating this proposal as an earnest attempt to avoid friction between the Protestant denominations in the working of these schools, they consider that the administration by mixed Protestant Boards will, on the whole, better subserve the educational interests of the country.

Matthew Leitch,
Convener, pro tem.

No. III. (p).

W. VENABLES, member of proposed Tyrone Board, to the COMMISSIONERS.

Having carefully considered the objections of the Representatives of the Protestant Episcopal Church to the Draft Scheme referred to in the circular letter of the Secretary of the Educational Endowments Commission, and the reasons advanced in favour of those objections, and having also carefully considered the suggested amendment of the Commissioners as to the union of the districts of Tyrone and Armagh, are of the opinion—

1. That it would not be for the benefit or advantage of education generally that the District of Tyrone and the District of Armagh should be united.

2. That it is not desirable, and would not be in the interest of education generally, that there should be separate Protestant Local Boards, our opinion being that the Educational Scheme could be and would be more advantageously worked for the general good by mixed boards, and we therefore decide against the proposal to constitute separate Protestant Local Boards.

3. In our opinion the constitution of separate boards would militate against the smaller and weaker Protestant denominations, and unduly and unfairly [illegible] in favour of the larger and stronger denomination, as in our opinion the [illegible] as to the minority being able to dictate its own terms in case a union with the majority were sought, is contrary to common experience, and we think that the minority would be at the mercy of the majority, and would have to submit to whatever terms the majority should choose to impose.

4. We desire to express our opinion that while the Draft Scheme may not be all that could be desired, if viewed from each different standpoint, and in particular because in our opinion the Methodist Church has not sufficient representation, still we are ready to accept the Scheme as it stands, and endeavour to work it fairly and equitably, with the object of the general good of all Protestants.

(Signed), W. VENABLES.

HEWETSON'S SCHOOL, CLANE—OBJECTIONS AND AMENDMENTS.

No. IV. (a.)

By the Reverend SAMUEL GEORGE COTTON, Rector and Vicar of Clane Parish.

The present position and status of the school, with its management, all of which it is contemplated in the proposed scheme to continue, are subversive of and antagonistic to the will and intentions of the testator, Patrick Hewetson, by whose bequest the endowments became available.

Patrick Hewetson, by his will, dated July 22nd, 1779, bequeathed certain property for the support and maintenance of a charity school to be built on the lands of *Betaghstown*.

That the present schoolhouse built recently, near Clane, on the *lands of Millicent*, and which the scheme proposes should be continued as a school, does not carry out the wishes of the testator.

That no sufficient reason was given in 1879 for the removal of the school from Betaghstown, when the Vice-Chancellor sanctioned a scheme for its removal.

That the report of Mr. Hugh Kaye Moore, Inspector of Primary Schools, states, Endowed Schools Commission, Ireland, Vol. I., p. 378, states as follows:—

"Betaghstown.—The house is large and rambling but still in sound repair and quite suitable for the accommodation of the teacher and his eleven pupils.

"The Rev. Mr. Cooke and some others are anxious to remove this school and amalgamate it with the Clane Parochial School, but I fear the advantages gained by such a union would never repay the amount of money spent on it."—[illegible] Sept., 1879.

That the testator further willed that in this school at Betaghstown, there should be maintained, so many poor boys and girls as the trustees should think fit and convenient.

That in accordance with this provision, as I have heard and believe, 13 boys and 16 girls were maintained in Betaghstown School in or about the year 1814, and some were apprenticed with fees to Protestant masters and mistresses, as the testator willed—and this when the income of the charity was considerably less than it afterwards became.

This statement is supported by the evidence of the late Rev. Mr. Cooke, before the Commission of Endowed Schools (see Report 1881, Vol. II., p. 285, question and answer 8727) in which he admits that he heard there had been girls there at one time, and [illegible] the records of the school are available.

However, in 1834 a scheme was approved of by the Court of Chancery, which provided that 15 boys only should be maintained and apprenticed. But it is remarkable that the Commission of 1857 particularly noticed the neglect of applying this endowment for the education of girls. See Report, Endowed Schools Commission, 1881, Vol. II., p. 287, question 8679.

But notwithstanding the decree of 1831, only 12 boys were maintained from 1836, with an income of about £300 a year, or £25 a head; and many of these boys were sent into the world, and not apprenticed (see replies of Rev. Mr. Cooke, Report Endowed Schools Commission, 1881, p. 286, questions and answers 8844 and 8845).

"After they have been educated do you do anything for them?—We used to apprentice them, but I have always been told we have not had money.

"I understand you have not funds to support more than twelve boarders?—We have not had boarders."

That it would appear from the Rev. Mr. Cooke's answer, 8726, p. 285, Vol. II., Report Endowed Schools Commission, 1881, that the reception of girls by the Charity was discontinued, "because it was not found suitable to have the girls in the same building with the boys."

That I have gone over the whole of the former schoolhouse at Betaghstown, and I believe it amply sufficient to accommodate fifteen boys and fifteen girls; that two separate houses might be constructed, and that with ordinary care no association, whatever could take place between the male and female pupils; but I do not think that the present schoolhouse, although costing £1,500, either from its construction or site could be made suitable for boys and girls.

That the will of Mr. Hewetson further provides that "the said boys and girls are to be lawfully instructed in the principles of the Protestant religion," and I charge that this provision has been and is neglected in a very marked way, and I object to the continuance of this regime as sanctioned by the proposed Scheme.

In Report of Endowed Schools Commission, 1881, p. 272, question and answer, 8331, Lord Justice Fitz-Gibbon asked the Rev. Mr. Cooke:—

"There is not come to this, that you want to bring the school nearer to the church?" Reply. "That is a very important reason."

It must therefore be explained that Mr. Cooke Trench, the owner of the land on which the present schoolhouse stands, has recently built a church for Clane parish in his own demesne, and very close to the present schoolhouse, both being built in or about the same time. This new church is a very handsome little building from an artist's point of view, a gem in its way, but very much opposed in its internal decoration to Protestant teaching.

The windows are stained with painted figures, one of these being that of Mary, the mother of our Lord, named underneath the figure, B. V. Mary.

There are besides two half-length figures of angels in mosaic over the communion table, especially [illegible] to Protestant teaching, and there is in front of the pulpit a beautifully carved figure of St. Peter holding keys, most repugnant to the spirit of Protestantism, which maintains that St. Peter never was Bishop of Rome, has no power of "the keys," and is not Christ's vicegerent on earth, all of which is symbolized by this figure; that, moreover, some of the boys of Stevenson's Endowed School are dressed in cassocks and surplices on Sundays and form part of the choir, led by the teacher of the school, also in a surplice, and I object to the boys of the school being so employed as contrary to the intentions of the testator, for although they might be good Protestants and wear surplices, yet it is well known that a surpliced choir is one of the works and practices of the High Church party in England, so many of which have joined the Church of Rome.

And further, these boys, as I am informed and believe, are taught to turn to the Communion Table at certain portions of the Service, and bow their heads, implying by such turning that the Almighty is present in one place more than another, and inculcating the idea of a "real presence," at the (so called) altar, also very much opposed to Protestant teaching.

And I object to the removal of the school from Betaghstown, which was carried out by an order of the Vice Chancellor of Ireland, dated July 15th, 1867, and which removal was in direct opposition to the will of the testator, and done to carry out a whim of Mr. Conyngham Trench and the late Rector of Clane and teach the people hybrid Protestantism or rather anti-Protestantism.

And I therefore propose as amendments, that the governing body shall consist of the three ex-officio governors named in proposed scheme p. 7. One governor to be nominated by the Bishop of Kildare, and instead of three co-opted governors, these should be the rectors of the three adjoining parishes of Kill, Ballymadagh, and Caragh, who now receive notice when each vacancy occurs to send in applications.

This would give a governing board of seven—the Archbishop of Armagh (or governor nominated by him), the Bishop of Kildare, and the governor appointed by him, the Rector of Clane, and the rectors of the three adjoining parishes.

That the clauses nominating the Venerable Maurice T. de Burgh and Thomas Cooke Trench, Esq., be struck out, these gentlemen however being eligible to be nominated by the Primate, as his representative, or as additional governor by the Bishop of Kildare.

That the governors so appointed shall hold office as long as they retain the different preferments, which entitle them to election, except in the case of the governor nominated by the Archbishop of Armagh, who shall hold office until he die or resign, or until his nomination be revoked by the Archbishop in writing under his hand, or until the said Archbishop shall himself act as governor.

That inasmuch as it is contemplated by the proposed scheme to admit girls as day scholars to the present school, I propose as an amendment, that twelve girls at least shall be received as boarders under the provisions of the will, there being about £301 a year available for the charity, and as the present schoolhouse would be inadequate and unsuitable for the reception of boys and girls, that the whole school founded by the charity be moved back to Betaghstown, that locality being especially named by the testator, and from its retirement and land adjoining for instruction in agriculture most suitable for such a school. That the building at Betaghstown formerly used as a school is in the parish of Clane and not more than about two Irish miles from the parish church.

That the founder never contemplated the reception of day scholars, but would appear from the provisions of his will to have their exclusion in his mind. And moreover, the £30 yearly, guaranteed to the present school by the Select Vestry of Clane, would be amply sufficient to maintain a good day school, either in the present schoolhouse, or in the village of Clane, where there is a building near the old church for the purpose, especially if such school were placed in connexion with the National Board, as is contemplated.

That as regards religious instruction, I propose as an amendment, that the boarders at said school shall not be required to attend at Clane Parish Church or receive religious instruction from the clergyman thereof if his or her father, or mother—father being dead, guardian or next of kin, object in writing to such attendance or such instruction, and that facilities be allowed for pupils so objecting to attend Divine worship and receive religious instruction elsewhere as the parents, guardians, or next of kin may direct.

That the officials connected with the school be paid sufficient salaries, and be not permitted to fill any post of emolument in connexion with any place of worship.

Dated this 17th day of April, 1889.

R. O. Cowen,

Rector and Vicar.

Caragh Glebe House, Naas.

No. IV. (h.)

By the Existing Governing Body.

1. The Governors doubt the expediency of so largely increasing the number of the Board. They anticipate considerable difficulty in finding three co-opted, one nominated, and possibly one additional governor qualified and willing to take a real share in the management of the school, besides the two appointed by name. They therefore propose to make it optional to fill all the vacancies, and with that view to substitute "may" for "shall" in the second line of page 6 and elsewhere as necessary.

2. They think it inexpedient to encourage the attendance of governors at elections who do not attend for the business of the school.

They think it inexpedient to overload the trust with obligations, which in practice are pretty sure to become obsolete.

And they think it inexpedient to impose restrictions in the choice of candidates, which were not imposed by the founder or found necessary by the experience of the past.

They therefore suggest the omission of the greater part of Nos. 10 and 14.

3. In 16 they propose to omit the words "belonging to the parish of Clane or the adjoining parishes."

4. As this is strictly a denominational school they object to the introduction of a conscience clause in No. 11. They also think that this might be quoted against them as evidence, that it was contemplated by the scheme that this should be a mixed school. It is also directly opposed to the simple condition laid down by the will of the founder. No. 21 again "at school."

5. Omit clause as to visiting school, which the governors have no power to enforce and would certainly become obsolete—omit "specifying in each notice the object thereof"—see above (2).

CORRESPONDENCE AND DOCUMENTS.

No. V. (a).

The COMMISSIONERS to LORD EMLY.

[illegible], Dublin,
13th January, 1888.

MY LORD,—I am directed by the Commissioners to forward your lordship the enclosed valuation which has been made of the buildings and lands of Mungret College, and which represents their estimated value at the time the latter was made.

I am to add that the Commissioners would be glad to receive any suggestions or amendments upon the scheme already laid before them on the part of the trustees, which your Lordship may think it desirable to make in view of the valuation which has been made.

(Signed), WM. EDWARD ELLIS,
Secretary.

Right Honorable Lord Emly,
Tervoe, Limerick.

NOTE.—Similar letters were sent to the Most Rev. Dr. O'Dwyer, Bishop of Limerick; the Very Rev. Thos. [illegible], S.J., President; and James G. Barry, esq., Secretary to the Trustees of Mungret College.

No. V. (b).

Dr. O'DWYER to the COMMISSIONERS.

The Palace, Corbally, Limerick,
14th January, 1888.

DEAR SIR,—In reply to your letter of 13th instant, enclosing valuation of Mungret house and lands, and inviting any comment in reference thereto on the scheme of the trustees; may I trouble you to thank the Commissioners for their courtesy, and to inform them that until I know how the valuation will affect the scheme I cannot meet their wishes, and for the present can only venture to suggest that twenty and twenty-eight years respectively, for lands and houses, seem to be a high price by which to ascertain their capitalized value.

(Signed), ✠ E. T.,
Bishop of Limerick.

No. V. (c).

JAMES G. BARRY, esq., to the COMMISSIONERS.

[illegible], George's-street, Limerick.

SIR,—In reply to your communication of the 13th instant, enclosing a valuation which had been made of the buildings and lands of Mungret College, I have to say in reply that the trustees have not been informed as to the purpose for which the valuation has been made.

They see no reason for making a change in the rough scheme which they have laid before the Commissioners. The valuation of the lands appears fair, but the trustees are of opinion that the value of the buildings to a solvent tenant is nil.

I am, sir, your obedient servant,
JAMES G. BARRY.

16th January, 1888.
W. Ellis, esq.

No. V. (d).*

MEMORANDUM of the COMMISSIONERS.

*This Memorandum was transmitted, by order of the Commissioners, to all persons concerned in the above-named Endowments.

Rep. 1887-8, pp. [illegible] to [illegible], and [illegible]. The Commissioners are engaged in the consideration of the above-mentioned Endowments, which were the subject of a Public Inquiry held at Limerick on October 10 and 11, 1887, and of subsequent correspondence. Before preparing any Draft Scheme for the future management of these Endowments, the Commissioners think it desirable to direct attention to the following statement, and to give the several parties interested a further opportunity of expressing their views.

The Endowments with which the Commissioners have to deal are—

I. The Mungret Endowment, consisting of land, buildings and money.

II. The Leamy Endowment, consisting of buildings and money.

III. The interest of "The Commissioners of Education" in the site and buildings of the Limerick Diocesan School.

The following circumstances appear to the Commissioners to be material in dealing with these original Endowments.

I. THE MUNGRET ENDOWMENT.

The origin of the Mungret Endowment was a sum of £4,078 8s. 1d., appropriated to charitable purposes or objects of public utility in the County of Limerick, out of the Reproductive Loan Fund, and vested in Trustees appointed by the Lord Lieutenant, for the establishment of an Agricultural School and Model Farm in the County of Limerick, for the promotion of agricultural science.

The Trustees applied a sum of £1,000 in purchasing the lands of Mungret, containing 71a. [illegible] statute measure, held in fee-simple, which they demised in 1852 to the Commissioners of National Education, for ninety-nine years, at an annual rent of £2[illegible] [illegible]s. 6d., for the purposes of an Agricultural School and Model Farm. They retained and invested a further sum of £1,000, to the end that the dividends might be applied for current expenses, and they paid over the balance of the trust fund, £2,078 8s. 7d., to the Commissioners of National Education, to aid in erecting the necessary buildings and offices of the School.

The Commissioners of National Education, with the aid of the Board of Public Works, erected extensive buildings upon the lands, including a residence for teachers and pupils, school-rooms, and a farm-steading, at an original cost of £7,[illegible], supplied from the trust fund, and from moneys provided by Parliament. The School was opened in 1853, upon trusts which were afterwards declared by deed dated December 10, 18[illegible], and was maintained, by the Commissioners of National Education, out of moneys provided by Parliament, until 1876. The School was never very successful, and ultimately failed; the number of pupils in attendance never exceeded twenty-three, and sometimes fell to three or four; the Commissioners finally closed the School on September 17, 1876, and, in pursuance of a power contained in their lease, surrendered the School and Farm, with all the buildings, to the Trustees.

The Trustees, from March, 1877, to the present time, have been Lord Emly, Sir Stephen E. de Vere, Sir David V. Roche, Edward W. O'Brien, and James O. Barry.

On August 13, 1879, a Local Act was passed "to enable the Lord Lieutenant, with the consent of Her Majesty's Treasury, to vary the Trusts of the Mungret Agricultural School and Model Farm": it enabled the Lord Lieutenant, with the consent of the Treasury, to direct that the lands, buildings, and premises, should be occupied or let on the best rent that might reasonably be had for the same, and that such lands, buildings, and premises, and the produce, profits, or rents thereof, and all trust funds then under the control of the Trustees, should from thenceforth be used and applied, under the control and direction of the Trustees, to such purposes of instruction, including the instruction in and the promotion of agricultural science, as to the Lord Lieutenant, with such consent as aforesaid, should seem meet.

The Act further enabled the Lord Lieutenant, with like consent, to provide a site for a Male National School, and to give the use of a house for a Female National School, on the premises.

In accordance with this Act, the Lord Lieutenant (Earl Cowper), with the consent of the Treasury, made an Order dated June 17, 1880, containing provisions to the following effect:—

That it should be lawful for the Trustees for the time being, from time to time thereafter, to demise all the said premises, except the School-house and buildings, other than farm buildings, and such portion of the lands adjoining thereto, not being less than [illegible] [illegible] acres, as the Trustees might think fit expedient to have occupied and used in connection with the School (which last mentioned premises were thereinafter termed the School premises), at the best rent and rents that could be reasonably had for the same, for any term with or without power of surrender, to any person or persons (including the Head Master as he appointed by the Trustees as thereinafter mentioned), who might be willing to become lessee or lessees thereof; provided that the lessees should not be made dispunishable for waste, and should covenant for payment of the rent, and also not to assign or sublet without the consent in writing of the Trustees, and that every lease should contain a proviso enabling the Trustees to determine the same on twelve calendar months' notice; and that the School premises not included in any such lease should be occupied and used for the purpose of carrying on therein a School affording such education and instruction as was prescribed in the Schedule annexed to the said Order.

The said Schedule contained provisions to the following effect:—

That, in addition to instruction in Classics and Science, instruction should be afforded in French and English suitable to an Intermediate School of the class contemplated by the Intermediate Education Act, 1878, and also in the Science and Practice of Agriculture.

That no pupil should be permitted to remain in attendance during the time of any religious instruction which his parents or guardians should not have sanctioned, and that the time for religious instruction should be so fixed that no pupil not remaining in attendance should be excluded, directly or indirectly from the advantages of the secular instruction given in the School.

That the School should be open to boys, without religious distinction, but inhabitants of the City and County of Limerick should have a preference in obtaining admission, and boys other than such inhabitants should not be admitted if there were a sufficiency of such inhabitants to fill the vacant places.

That the Fees to be paid by the pupils, and the maximum number of pupils, both Boarders and Day Scholars, should be fixed by the Trustees.

That the Head Master might be appointed and removed from time to time by the Trustees, who should make such arrangements for his remuneration as they might think fit; the number of other Masters, Teachers, and Monitors to be from time to time fixed by the Head Master, with the consent of the Trustees, and that all such other Masters, Teachers, and Monitors might be appointed and dismissed by the Head Master.

That every person employed in the School as Head Master should, at the time of his appointment, sign a document to the effect that he had read the Scheme, and the by-laws of the School, and accepted his appointment subject thereto, and that he should be held responsible for the observance thereof.

That the Trustees might from time to time make by-laws for the management of the School, not in any way inconsistent with the Scheme.

That the Trustees should be Visitors of the School, and should hold a visitation once a year, upon a day to be fixed by them, in addition to a special visitation whenever they deemed fitting, and that such Trustees should at all times have authority to visit and inspect the School, and to inquire into all the details of its management.

That the net annual income at the disposal of the Trustees should be applied by them in giving to pupils Bursaries or Prizes, to be awarded after competitive examination by such subjects as the Trustees should from time to time determine, but that no such Bursary or Prize should be awarded to any pupil who should not have passed an Examination in Agricultural Science.

That if the Trustees should think fit, they might apply a portion of the income of the trust funds, excluding rents and profits, to the payment of an Agricultural Teacher, and for the purchase of Scientific Apparatus, in precedence of the application towards Bursaries and Prizes.

That these rules might at any time be rescinded or varied by the Lord Lieutenant, with the consent of the Treasury.

The foregoing Order and Schedule do not appear to authorise a demise of the School buildings.

[illegible] On July 5, 1880, the Trustees appointed the Rev. Joseph Bourke to be Head Master, and by Lease dated August 11, 1880, reciting the foregoing Order, the lands were demised to him for the purposes of a School, at the rent of £79 [illegible], for a term of twenty-one years, determinable on twelve months' notice. This rent was calculated for the land only.

[illegible] The Rev. Joseph Bourke opened a School for Intermediate Education, literary and scientific, with the theory and practice of Agriculture; but on September [illegible], 1881, the Trustees, having ascertained that he had closed the [illegible], served notice upon him, as lessee of the lands, that they would require possession from him on or before September [illegible], 1882, and on March [illegible], 1882, they directed that he should be served with notice determining his appointment as Head Master in three months. On the same day they accepted a proposal from the Rev. W. [illegible] to become lessee of the lands and buildings, subject to approval, by the Lord Lieutenant and the Treasury, of certain alterations of the Scheme.

[illegible] On April 13, 1882, the Trustees authorised arrangements for the immediate surrender of the premises by the Rev. Joseph Bourke, and the following Lease, under which the premises have since been held, was executed.

[illegible] The Lease was dated April 13, 1882, and was made between the Trustees of the Mungret Agricultural School and Model Farm of the one part, and Rev. William [illegible], of [illegible] House, Limerick, Rev. Thomas A. Finlay, of Tullabeg College, Tullamore, and John White, of [illegible], Limerick, [illegible], of the other part. It recited the Act 42 & 43 Vic., cap. [illegible]; and stated that under the said Act the Lord Lieutenant and Treasury, as approved by the Order of June 17, 1880, had sanctioned [illegible] a "Scheme" enabling the Trustees to demise the lands and buildings; it further recited a resolution of the Trustees that the School premises should consist of the entire of the premises formerly known as the Mungret Agricultural School and Model Farm (except the Female National School, and the site for the Male National School) and should be let on lease for 500 years at the best rent that could reasonably be had for the same; that the lessees had agreed to take a lease of the said lands and buildings for such term at the annual rent of £70, for the purpose of carrying on a School therein in accordance with the said recited Scheme, upon the conditions thereinafter mentioned, and that the said rent was the best rent that could be reasonably had for the said premises upon the conditions aforesaid. The Trustees demised the lands and premises accordingly to the Lessees for 500 years from January 1, 1882, provided the interest of the Trustees should so long continue, at the yearly rent of £70. The Lessees covenanted to pay the rent; to keep the premises and all [illegible] thereon in good repair; to cultivate, manure and manage the lands according to the most approved course of husbandry; not to assign, sublet, or part with the possession of any part of the premises, or their interest therein, without the previous written consent of the Trustees; not to erect any additional building, or make any addition to the buildings already erected, upon the premises, without the previous licence in writing of the Trustees. The Lessees further covenanted that they would upon the premises establish a School as defined by the rules annexed to the Intermediate Education Act, 1878; and that such School should be conducted, managed, and carried on, in the manner prescribed in the Scheme set forth in the Schedule annexed to the Lease, with any alterations to be thereafter approved of by the Lord Lieutenant; and further that [illegible] of the premises at the least should each year be kept in tillage and be used for the purposes of Agriculture and the giving practical instruction therein. The Lease was made upon the express condition that, in case it should appear to the Trustees that the School was not being carried on in accordance with the regulations contained in the said Scheme, a copy of which was thereto annexed, or if such School should in their opinion fail as a useful Intermediate School, it should be lawful for the Trustees on any gale day to determine the demise and re-enter, upon twelve months' previous written notice under the hands of any two or more of the Trustees. The Lessees further covenanted that they would not at any time whatever make or be entitled to make any claim whatever under the Landlord and Tenant (Ireland) Acts, 1870 and 1881, for buildings, improvements, disturbance, or other cause whatever, and that the Lease and this covenant should be a bar to any such claim both at law and in equity; and that on any breach of the covenants therein contained the Trustees might re-enter upon the premises, and immediately thereupon the Lease should determine. The Lease contained a power of surrender on six months' notice; a covenant for quiet enjoyment; a proviso that all Trustees thereafter appointed by the Lord Lieutenant should have the same powers as the Lessors; and that, whereas the Lessees were also Trustees for the purpose of establishing and carrying on the School thereby intended to be provided, any persons thereafter nominated to any vacancy by the surviving or continuing Lessees or Lessee, or the executor or administrator of the last surviving or continuing Lessee, by deed, should be entitled to the benefit and subject to the liabilities of the lease, as if therein named as Lessees; and that upon any such nomination it should be lawful to increase or diminish the number of such Lessees to the number of five, all of whom should be resident within the United Kingdom.

[illegible] The "Scheme" annexed to the said Lease contained provisions which differed in several important respects from the Schedule to the Order of June 17, 1880. It does not appear that this Scheme was ever sanctioned by the Lord Lieutenant or Treasury.

[illegible] The rent of £70 reserved by the Lease was calculated on the land only. The Lessees entered into possession under the Lease, and the Trustees were afterwards sanctioned [illegible] Order, dated July 24, 1882, signed by the Lord Lieutenant (Earl Spencer), with the concurrence of the Treasury, to the following effect:

[illegible] After reciting the Act 42 and 43 Vic., cap. [illegible], the Order declared that it should be lawful for the Trustees for the time being, from time to time thereafter, to demise the Lands, Buildings, and Premises known as the Mungret Agricultural School and Model Farm, at the best rent and terms that could be reasonably had for the same, for any term, with or without power of surrender, to any person or persons willing to become Lessee or Lessees thereof, so however that the said Buildings, and at least [illegible] of the said land to be held therewith, should be so demised for the purposes only of carrying out therein a School, for the purposes, and under the rules and limitations, thereinafter specified, and that such School should be conducted, managed, and carried on in the manner prescribed in the Scheme set forth in the Schedule annexed to the Order, which should be enforced to its and interspersed with every house of the School Premises. It also directed that the rents and profits of the Lands, Buildings, and Premises, and the Trust Funds under the control of the Trustees, should thenceforth be used and applied, under the control and directions of the Trustees, for the purposes of instruction in the said School, including the instruction in and promotion of Agricultural Science as organised in the said Scheme.

[illegible] annexed to Order of July [illegible]

The Scheme annexed to the Order contained provisions to the following effect:—

That no pupil should be permitted to remain in attendance during the time of any religious instruction which his parents or guardians should not have sanctioned, and the time for giving religious instruction should be fixed so that no pupil not remaining in attendance should be excluded, directly or indirectly, from the advantages of the secular instruction given in the School.

That the School should be open to boys without religious distinction, but inhabitants of the City and County of Limerick should have a preference in obtaining admission to the School, and boys other than such inhabitants should not be received if there was a sufficiency of such inhabitants to fill the vacant places.

That the fees to be paid by Boarders or Day Scholars should be fixed by the Manager, with the consent of the Trustees.

That the Head Master of the School might be appointed and removed from time to time by the Trustees, who should make such arrangements for his remuneration as they might think fit. That the number of other Masters, Teachers, and Monitors should from time to time be fixed by the Head Master, with the consent of the Trustees, and all such other Masters, Teachers, and Monitors might be appointed and dismissed by the Head Master.

That the maximum number of pupils, both as boarders and day pupils, respectively, should be fixed from time to time by the Trustees.

That every person employed in the School as Head Master should, at the time of his appointment, sign a document to the effect that he had read over the Scheme, as well as the By-laws of the School in force for the time being, and accepted his appointment subject to them, and should be held responsible for the observance of the said Scheme, and By-laws, by the [illegible] Teachers.

That the Manager, with the consent of the Trustees, might make By-laws for the Management of the School, not inconsistent with the Scheme.

That the Trustees should be Visitors of the School, and should hold a Visitation once a year upon a day to be fixed by them; they might hold a special Visitation whenever they should deem fitting, and each one of them should at all times have the authority to enter and inspect the school, and inquire into all the details of its management.

That the net annual income at the disposal of the Trustees should be applied by them in giving such bursaries or prizes to pupils as they might determine, such bursaries or prizes should be awarded after competitive examination in such subjects as the Trustees and Manager should conjointly determine.

That if the Trustees should think fit, they might apply portion of the income of the Trust Funds, including rents and profits, to the payment of an Agricultural Teacher, and for the purchase of scientific apparatus, in precedence of the application towards bursaries and prizes.

That all powers thereby conferred upon the Trustees should be exercisable by a majority present at a meeting duly summoned.

That those Rules might at any time be rescinded or varied by the Lord Lieutenant, with the consent of the Treasury, upon receiving an application asking for such rescission or variation, from a majority of the Trustees for the time being.

[illegible] The Rev. William Ronan was appointed Head Master, and from 1883 to the present time the Institution known as Mungret College, conducted by the Jesuit Order, has been carried on under the foregoing Lease of April 18, 1882, and the Scheme of July 24, 1882. On September 27, 1884, the Trustees approved of the erection of a

[illegible]

Chapel, and on January 4, 1888, the Rev. J. Read was recognised by them as "Proctor Rector" of Mungret College. On October 4, 1897, the very meeting recorded in their Minutes, the Trustees resolved that, the Rev. W. Ronan having resigned the Head Mastership of Mungret College, the Rev. John R. Read should be appointed to that office; that the additional buildings then in course of erection, in execution of plans previously approved by the Trustees, should be sanctioned; that it was advisable that the energies of Mungret College should be exclusively directed to the preparation of Scholars for University Examinations; and that the Annual Visitation should be, for the future, held in the first week of October. [illegible]

On the same day the Rev. J. R. Read, S.J., formally accepted the appointment of Head Master under the Scheme of 24th July, 1882. [illegible]

In October, 1884, the managers of Mungret College began the erection of new buildings, and the alteration of the existing buildings, and they have since continued the works, including the erection of a Chapel, Class-Rooms, and Dormitories for pupils and the staff. A sum of about £12,000 was stated to have been thus expended by the Jesuit Order, and it was also stated by Lord Emly that he had expended £2,000, for which he was responsible, but it did not clearly appear whether this sum was in addition to the £12,000, or was included in that amount. [illegible]

Mungret College is principally devoted to University Teaching. The teaching staff includes ten Professors, who do work of the Classes of the Royal University. Nearly all the Professors are members of the Jesuit Order, appointed in accordance with the rules of the Order, but with the sanction of the Trustees. None of the pupils study Agriculture; there is no demand for practical instruction in that subject. The Managers wish it to be a College exclusively for students already in the Royal University; the greatest number of the students are clerical students for foreign and home missions, some are preparing for Medicine and other branches, but all must follow the course of the University. None but Roman Catholics have asked to be admitted, but the Head Master holds himself bound to admit any one without distinction of religion. After leaving Mungret College, a small proportion of the students go to Maynooth and join the secular clergy in Ireland, the greater number become Missionary Priests, about an average of about ten out of eighty go to lay professions. [illegible]

The number of students has varied from seventy to ninety, all boarders. The majority have come from the County of Limerick. They belong generally to the farming class; all pay fees at the rate of £30 per annum, some with the help of bursaries. [illegible]

In addition to their interest in the lands and buildings, the Trustees hold £1,[illegible] 13s. 2d. Government Stock, and £[illegible] 4 per cent. Preference Stock of the G.S.W. Railway. These funds were derived from the portion of the original fund reserved for expenses, with accumulations of interest, a sum of £[illegible] paid by the Commissioners of National Education on the surrender of their lease, and a sum of £[illegible] 3s. 4d. transferred to the present Trustees by Sir Stephen E. de Vere. This sum of £[illegible] 3s. 4d. was part of a fund standing in the Provincial Bank, Limerick, to the credit of the original Trustees of the Mungret Model Farm, and was transferred to the present Trustees on the condition that it should be reserved for the use and benefit of the Mungret Model Farm, and that, if it should cease to be conducted as a Model Farm, then the fund should be employed in the same manner and on the same trusts as the other funds of the Mungret Model Farm. Sir Stephen E. de Vere stated he was not aware of the source from which the fund arose, but, looking that the original depositors had all been Trustees of the Model Farm, he assumed that there was some trust, unknown to him, for that institution. This fund amounted on February [illegible], 1860, to £1,[illegible] 14s. [illegible] then standing in the names of the Right Rev. William Higgin, Lord Bishop of Derry and Raphoe, Thomas Lord Monteagle, Sir David Roche, William Monsell, and Stephen E. de Vere, who afterwards made the transfer as surviving trustees.

It has been stated to the Commissioners that in the first instance this last-mentioned fund came from profits of an Agricultural Show, supplemented by private subscriptions collected for Mungret Model Farm, but that no positive evidence is forthcoming as to these subscriptions.

Out of these Trust Funds, the Trustees have made occasional payments for repairs, and grants for scientific apparatus. They agreed to give the students of the rent of £[illegible] per annum payable under the Lease of April 12, 1882, for prizes; they "exchange receipts" for this rent; except a balance to their credit, they have expended the income of the Trust Funds in paying rates and taxes, in grants for scientific apparatus, and in payments to the College.

The Commissioners obtained from the Valuation Office a valuation of the lands of Mungret, and of the buildings which were upon the premises at the date of the Lease of April 12, 1882. The valuer was directed to proceed upon the assumption that the Lessees had not erected any new buildings, or removed any of those existing at the date of the Lease.

On the foregoing basis, and as between a willing seller and a willing buyer, the fair letting agricultural value of the land was, on December [illegible], 1887, estimated by the Valuation Office at £[illegible]; the fair letting value of the buildings at £[illegible]; the fair selling price of the land at £[illegible],[illegible]; and the fair selling price of the buildings at £[illegible].

II.—The Leamy Endowment.

The Leamy Endowment is derived under the Will of William Leamy, dated in 1814. He left the residue of his estate to his executors, "to be by them applied to the education of the poor in Ireland, principally those in and about Limerick City; or as they, my executors, in their better judgment, shall deem most to give this bequest the most extensive efficacy." The executors did not act; the estate was administered in Chancery, and on June 16, 1842, a Scheme was approved by the Lord Chancellor for the administration of the trust; a further Scheme was approved on July 4, 1874; and a sum of £[illegible] was expended in erecting school buildings at Hartstonge-street, Limerick, on a site held for [illegible] years. The original Scheme provided that in the school the English language, reading, writing, and arithmetic should be taught, and that, if the funds would permit, the Governors should have power to provide a more extensive system of education, subject to the approval of the Lord Chancellor. Under the Scheme of 1874, provision was made for giving instruction in elementary drawing, the elements of chemistry, the elements of mathematics, the elements of natural science as applied to the arts, French, and other subjects to fit boys for employment in trading, mercantile, and manufacturing pursuits. Part of the daily instruction, under the original Scheme, is to consist in reading the Holy Scriptures, without note or comment; and for this purpose it is directed that the scholars are to be placed, for an hour each day, the Protestants in one room and the Roman Catholics in another, "the Protestants to read the Holy Scriptures without any restriction, and the Roman Catholics to read such portions of the Holy Scriptures as are contained in four small books published by the National Board."

The present Governors—appointed by the Court of Chancery—are Lord Emly, the Right Rev. Dr. Graves (Protestant Bishop of Limerick), Dean Bunbury, the Ven. Archdeacon Hamilton, Dr. Kane, Sir James Spaight, Robert Hunt, Colonel Maxwell, Captain Vandeleur, and Lord Clarina. The Roman Catholic Governors have ceased to attend. Though the school is open to all denominations, it does not appear to have ever been taken advantage of by the Roman Catholic population to any considerable extent. The Inspector appointed by the Commission of 1878–80 found 43 boys and 65 girls in attendance, of whom 4 boys and 4 girls were Roman Catholics. In 1887 there were [illegible] girls and 45 boys on the roll, of whom 7 girls and 1 boy were Roman Catholics. The Roman Catholic Bishop does not allow Roman Catholic pupils to attend a mixed school. There is provision for the free education of [illegible] boys and [illegible] girls. At present there are 16 boys and [illegible] girls enjoying free places. The remaining pupils pay fees at the rate of £[illegible] a year.

The school buildings include four school-rooms, each large enough for 100 pupils, of which only two are now in use; they would afford accommodation for about four times the present number of pupils. Before 1874 "the school had been for several years altogether closed, and after it was re-opened, under the Scheme of 1874, the Roman Catholic Bishop withdrew from the management, as Protestant head teachers were appointed." At that time, although the Governors had made every exertion to get applications for the free places, the number had never been filled. There were but very few Protestant applicants, and no Roman Catholics. The number of pupils at present on the roll is 110; the average attendance [illegible]. As regards the circumstances of the pupils, the evidence goes to show that the free pupils are the children of the poor, but that the others are not children of the poor, but include children of the gentry, shopkeepers, and the respectable middle class.

The Leamy Endowment now consists of the following property:—

(A.) The School Buildings.

(B.) The Trust Fund, now in Chancery, consisting of £10,[illegible] 11s. 6d., Government Stock, with a current Cash Balance in the Governors' hands.

III. *The Limerick Diocesan School.*

The *Limerick Diocesan School* was established in 1857 at Roxborough Road, *Limerick*, upon a site containing 1 acre [illegible] roods and 10 perches, held in fee-simple, and purchased for £[illegible], and in buildings erected at a cost of £1,[illegible] [illegible]s. [illegible]d., provided by Grand Jury presentment. The School failed, the premises became dilapidated, and there were no pupils for ten years before 1874. The Master, the Rev. Dr. Hall, remained, until his death in 1874, in occupation of the premises, which are vested in "The Commissioners of Education." The Rev. Dr. Hall, in 1873, commuted and compounded the stipend to which he was entitled as Diocesan Schoolmaster, receiving £1,[illegible]; the remainder, £[illegible] 10s. [illegible]d., of the commutation money was retained by the Representative Church Body under the Irish Church Acts; the provision for the stipend of the Master was thereupon extinguished, and the School was discontinued.

In 1874 the Rev. James FitzGerald Gregg, Incumbent of Trinity Church, Limerick, entered into negotiations with the Rev. Dr. Hall for the possession of the schoolhouse, and applied to the Commissioners of Education to let or sell the school premises to him; but while the negotiations were still pending, the Rev. Dr. Hall died, leaving Mary Anne Hall, his widow and personal representative, in possession, and by deed dated November 5, 1874, in consideration of £30 paid to her, and of £7 10s. paid for rates due for the premises, Mary Anne Hall granted all her interest, and gave up the possession of the school premises, to the Rev. J. F. Gregg, who, with the knowledge of the Commissioners, entered into possession of the buildings, which were in a state of dilapidation, repaired them, and opened a Charity Boarding and Daily School for Girls therein, which he has since carried on with the aid of voluntary subscriptions.

From January 1, 1880, the Rev. J. F. Gregg became tenant of the premises, from year to year, to the Commissioners, at a rent of £30 per annum, under an accepted proposal in writing dated December 18, 1879, and he has expended a sum of £300 and upwards upon the premises in repairs and improvements; but for such expenditure the said premises would have become ruinous.

The School maintained by the Rev. J. F. Gregg is known as the Roxborough Road School; all the pupils are received and educated as Protestants, and the School is under the exclusive control of the Rev. J. F. Gregg.

The Commissioners of Education have hitherto expended the amount of the rent in repairs of the buildings.

PROPOSALS MADE AT THE PUBLIC SITTING.

At the Public Inquiry held on October 10, 1887, the Very Rev. Thomas Bunbury, Protestant Dean of Limerick, attended on behalf of the Governors of Leamy's School, and stated that they were satisfied with their existing Scheme and did not desire that it should be altered, although his own opinion was that Leamy's School ought not to be kept up as a Primary School, but should be established as a purely Intermediate School, as there were plenty of Primary Schools, but there was a great want for a Protestant Intermediate School in Limerick, not only in the city but for the district around.

As regarded Mungret, he stated that at present he was quite willing that the Roman Catholics, "who had it practically under their control, should so continue"—but, against that, he proposed that the Protestants of all denominations in Limerick should have the exclusive and entire control of Leamy's School and fund.

On the other hand, the Most Rev. Dr. O'Dwyer, Roman Catholic Bishop of Limerick, as regards Leamy's Endowment, stated that he thought the present marketable value of the School ought to be ascertained, and divided, together with the money invested, between the Catholics and Protestants of the City. At the same time he thought the Protestants, on their own showing, had hardly any claim to the Endowment, because "witness after witness had said they did not want poor schools—they had poor schools enough,"—and as long as there were poor in Limerick to whom Leamy's money could be applied, he did not think it ought to go to the rich; but he also stated that though he believed, on their own showing, the Protestant body had no claim to a share of the Endowment, he had no objection to their getting a share, but he thought it ought to be applied to the education of the poor. He further stated that, putting the value of the buildings at £3,000, and making a division of the entire Endowment between the Catholics and Protestants of Limerick, the buildings alone would very nearly exhaust any share that could, on any reasonable principle, be given to the Protestants. Q. [illegible]

He said that if the buildings, and a substantial part of Leamy's Endowment, were to go together, the School would make a first-rate Catholic Model School; a further portion of the Endowment could be given to the Christian Brothers; and Protestant and Catholic Boards should be formed, each to receive their own share, being bound to expend it in a particular way. Q. [illegible] Q. [illegible] Q. [illegible]

As regards the Roxborough Road School, the Most Rev. Dr. O'Dwyer objected to its being maintained for its present purpose, but he had no objection to the premises being devoted to the purposes of a Protestant Classical or Intermediate School. Q. [illegible]

As regards the Mungret Endowment, the Most Rev. Dr. O'Dwyer suggested that it would be better to allow the present Trustees, the representatives of the Jesuits, and himself, to confer, and to come before the Commission with their opinion matured upon the matter. Q. [illegible]

Mr. Barry stated it as his opinion that it would be better to have the Mungret Endowment denominational, otherwise the School would fail. Q. [illegible]

Lord Emly stated that he wished Mungret to be a College exclusively for students already in the Royal University, who should receive their collegiate education in Mungret. Q. [illegible]

Several other witnesses were examined, and practically the Roman Catholics and Protestants appeared to agree that the Educational Endowments to which they might be severally entitled should be placed under their own exclusive control.

SUBSEQUENT PROPOSALS—MUNGRET.

On October 27, 1887, the Commissioners received from Sir Stephen E. de Vere "Suggestions for a New Scheme for Mungret College," stated to have "the entire approval of the Trustees, the Bishop, and the Jesuit Body," "for the purpose of giving a permanent existence to a great Catholic College, serving as a feeder to the Royal University." Ev. 1887-8, p. [illegible]

These Suggestions were to the following effect:—

That the Trustees should necessarily all be Catholics, the Bishop of the Diocese and the Rector of the College, as ex-officio Trustees, taking the place of the present Protestant Trustees, Sir David V. Roche and E. W. O'Brien.

That the object of the College should be to prepare Students for degrees in Arts in the Royal University, and that no pupils should be prepared for the Intermediate Examinations.

That the Rector should be the sole authority to admit and dismiss Students; that all buildings for future Students, and any additions thereto, should be reserved for the education and accommodation of Students in training for Foreign Missions.

That the Students' fees should be fixed, and the bye-laws for the management of the College should be made by the Rector, who should be appointed and removed by the Head of the Order of which he professed to be a member, the appointment being subject to the approval of the Trustees.

That the lease should be amended so as to give full security to the Lessees, and be made, if possible, in the names of the Lessees as an Incorporated Body.

That the financial administration of the College should be entirely in the hands of the Rector.

That in the event of the Lessees seriously and persistently violating and refusing to comply with the rules laid down in the Scheme, the Governing Body should have power to determine the lease, subject, in this or any other question between the Governing Body and Lessee, to an appeal to the Lord Lieutenant in Council.

That in the event of the determination of the Lease, the Lessee might tender to the Trustees the full sum expended upon Mungret land and buildings up to January 1, [illegible], such value to be ascertained as agreed on; the Lessee, on payment of such estimated sum, to enter upon the full enjoyment of all the Mungret lands and buildings, and the Trustees to hold such sum subject to such Trusts for educational purposes as the Lord Lieutenant in Council should appoint.

The Commissioners have received from the present Managers of Mungret College, "Objections to the existing Scheme and Lease," making suggestions to the following effect:—

That the Managers should be freed from the obligation to teach Agriculture; that they should be relieved from the obligation of giving both an Intermediate and a University Education; and that they should be bound only to give such an education as would be a fair equivalent for the endowment.

That it should be clearly expressed that the College was to be a Roman Catholic College.

That the preference to be given to Limerick boys should not extend beyond a very limited number.

That the Trustees should have no power of interfering with the pupils' fees, unless considerably exceeding what would be fair for a middle class school.

That the right of appointing a Head Master should be transferred from the Trustees to the Superiors of the Body to which the Managers belong.

That the Trustees should have no right of fixing the maximum number of pupils, so long as the Managers were not overcrowding the College.

That the Rector should have the power of making by-laws, not inconsistent with the Scheme, independently of the consent of the Trustees.

That the authority of each Trustee at all times to inspect the School, and inquire into all the details of its management should be omitted.

That the Lessees should have the option of buying out the Trustees at a fair valuation of the lands and old buildings, but that if the Trustees preferred to put the lessees out of the College, they should get compensation for the buildings they had erected, and the improvements they had made.

That the [illegible] a year rent should still be given in prizes to the Students of the College, and the collection of philosophical instruments belonging to the Trustees should be permanently annexed to the Managers.

The Managers regarded the valuation put upon the buildings as far too high.

The Managers proposed that the new Lease should be made as simple and as short as possible; that the only essential obligation should be to conduct an educational establishment for young men such as would be a fair return for the value of the buildings, and also of the farm, in case the rent continued to be returned to them, as at present, for prizes; that all those clauses in which the objectionable portions of the Scheme were repeated should be expunged, also the clauses prohibiting the Lessees from erecting new buildings, or cutting down timber, without the consent of the Trustees; that a clause should be introduced, giving to the Lessees the right of compensation, in case of disturbance, for their improvements, including the new buildings, and giving them the right of buying out the place at a fair valuation, fixed according to what the old building and the farm would really sell for; that the Lessees of the new Lease should be chosen exclusively from the members of the Jesuit Body, and that all the Trustees should be Catholic; the Rector of Mungret being ex-officio one of them.

Leamy's School.

The Commissioners have received the following paper respecting Leamy's Endowments, from a meeting of the clergy of all Protestant Denominations in Limerick, and the present Governors, summoned to meet at the "Diocesan Offices," Limerick, on October 25, 1887:—

Leamy's School.

Inasmuch as Leamy's School is an Institution where a good, and, so far as funds permit, a free education can be obtained by the children of all classes and denominations, it, therefore, while capable of improvement, has met a want which no institution in our city could supply.

The history of the School has been already given in the Report of Evidence of the Endowed Schools Commissioners, 1858. It is therefore only necessary to state that the School was founded in [illegible], and was then, and has continued to be, open to Protestants and Roman Catholics on equal terms. Since its foundation Roman Catholics have availed themselves of the educational advantages of the institution. The number of Roman Catholic pupils at present is small, forming only nine per cent. of the total attendance, whilst, at the close of 1884, they formed twenty-five per cent. The diminution was caused by the withdrawal in a body of [illegible] Roman Catholic pupils in February, 1885, consequent upon an order issued by the authorities of the Roman Catholic Church in the city. It is not stated that this order was issued in consequence of any change in the constitution or working of the School. Both have remained, and still remain, in accordance with the Scheme under which the School was originally established. The withdrawal of so many pupils necessitated the reduction of the teaching staff at a time when, according to the report of the Examiner, the circumstances of the School were such that the teaching body required to be strengthened.

We do not consider that the refusal, under such circumstances, of a minority of the pupils to avail themselves of the advantages of the Institution supplies just grounds for affecting injuriously the rights of those who remain, or for alienating any portion of an endowment which at present is barely able to maintain the School efficiently.

While suggesting some changes and modifications in the present Scheme, the Protestants of all denominations in Limerick desire to maintain the principles upon which the School has been worked since its opening, and whilst claiming that their own rights be maintained, have no desire to limit, or infringe upon, the rights of others. They do not wish that any change should be made which would in any way have the effect of excluding the Roman Catholics of Limerick from availing themselves, as they hitherto have done, of all the advantages that Leamy's School may afford them.

The Commissioners of Educational Endowments having suggested that the Board of Governors should consult with the Protestant Clergy of all denominations in Limerick, for the purpose of extending more widely the advantages secured to the poor of Limerick by Leamy's Endowment, a meeting was accordingly held. The clergy of all Protestant denominations in Limerick, and all the members of the Board of Governors were duly summoned to meet at the Diocesan Offices, 97, George-street, Limerick, on Tuesday, 25th October, 1887.

At the meeting it was unanimously resolved to suggest to the Commissioners the advisability of modifying the existing Scheme in the following manner:—

That, as clauses 1, 2, and 4 restrict unnecessarily the number of teachers and the salaries to be paid to them, it was considered advisable that freedom be given to the Governors to act as they think fit in these details.

That, instead of clause 3, the following be adopted:—In addition to the subjects of instruction prescribed according to the Scheme of 1857, instruction may be given in such branches of intermediate, commercial, or technical education as the Governors shall from time to time think best suited to the wants of the locality and the requirements of the pupils.

For clause 4.—That the Governors be given discretionary powers to regulate the scale of fees and the number of free pupils, with a view to increasing the number of free pupils.

That for clause 7 be substituted:—That the total of free pupils in both Schools be limited to sixty, the Governors having, nevertheless, the power to increase the number if the funds derived from paying pupils permit it.

That in clause 8, the word "forty" be altered to "sixty."

(*Application of Endowment.*)—All moneys received by the Governors under or for the purposes of this Scheme shall be expended and applied by them for the following purposes:—

(1) To maintain the Schools, furniture, appliances, and premises, in good order and condition, and to make such additions thereto and improvements therein, as may be required from time to time.

(2) To pay all rents, rates, charges, costs of insurance and other outgoings and expenses, and to defray the necessary working expenses of the Schools and the cost of management.

(3) To provide for the education of the pupils. For this purpose the Governors may employ and pay such teachers as they may deem it necessary to engage for the instruction of the pupils in the Schools.

(4) To provide prizes for the most deserving pupils. Such prizes to be awarded as the Governors may see fit.

The Governors may from time to time make such provision for the religious instruction of the pupils attending the School or resident therein as they shall think fit, provided that no pupil attending the School shall at any time be permitted to receive or be present at any religious instruction to which his or her parents or guardians shall object, and that the times for, and the mode of giving, religious instruction shall be so fixed that no pupil shall be thereby in effect excluded directly or indirectly from any of the other advantages afforded by the School.

The Governors may also maintain an evening school or schools, or evening classes, for the education of boys who are engaged during the day at trade or business, and who are desirous of carrying on their education in the evening. The course of instruction in such evening school or classes shall be arranged with special regard to the requirements of the pupils obliged to maintain themselves by commercial or industrial pursuits.

That the following constitute the new Board of Governors, with such of the present Governors as wish to attend:—

The Lord Bishop of Limerick The Dean of Limerick Rector of St. Michael's Incumbent of Trinity and St. Lawrence Rector of St. Munchin's Presbyterian Minister Minister of the Methodist Church Congregational Minister of Baptist Church [illegible] Diocesan Inspector of Schools One Clergyman chosen by Diocesan Council	For the time being.

That the Diocesan Council select five suitable laymen, to be accepted by the Governors.

That the Presbyterian Church name one layman.

That the Methodist Church name one layman.

That the Congregational Church name one layman.

That a Committee of Management consisting of five or seven be elected from the above.

At this meeting there were present:—Very Rev. the Dean in the chair; The Archdeacon of Limerick, Rev. J. F. Gregg, Rev. E. Gabbett (Croom), Rev. G. G. [illegible], Rev. T. A. F. [illegible] (Kilmallock), Rev. W. J. Browne, Rev. J. W. Clarke, Rev. R. Wilson, B.D. (Presbyterian), Rev. W. [illegible] (Independent), Rev. W. C. Price (Wesleyan), Major-General Lord Clarina, Colonel Macleod, Captain Vandeleur, Mr. R. Hunt; Rev. J. Dowd, Hon. Secretary.

III.—The Limerick Diocesan School Endowment.

The Commissioners, on March 16, 1887, published a Draft Scheme for the future management of the Roxborough Road School, by which they proposed to form an exclusively Protestant Governing Body for its management, to continue the tenancy of the premises now held by the Rev. J. F. Gregg, so long as they should be used for educational purposes under the Scheme, and to apply the rent of £20, payable to the Commissioners of Education, for the purposes of Intermediate Education of pupils belonging to the City or County of Limerick, in such manner as the Commissioners of Education should deem expedient, or as might be directed by any further Scheme to be framed under the "Educational Endowments (Ireland) Act, 1885." *Draft Scheme, No. 51.*

Objections have been received to this Scheme from the Rev. J. F. Gregg, who claims that the rent of £20 should, as hitherto, be applied to the repairs of the buildings, or reduce his outgoings; and from the Most Rev. Bishop O'Dwyer, who claims that the Endowment, so far as of public origin, should be dealt with for the benefit of all denominations.

Under the foregoing circumstances the Endowments with which the Commissioners have now to deal appear to consist of:—

(*a.*) The Mungret Endowment, consisting of land and buildings, valued at £200 per annum, and Trust Funds, consisting of £1,100 13s. 9d. Government Stock, and £100 Four per cent. Preference Stock of the Great Southern and Western Railway.

This Endowment is subject to the rights of the present tenants under the lease of April 12, 1882, and to the claims of the tenants in respect of their expenditure upon the premises. The Endowment is also liable to a claim put forward by Rev. Thomas Brown, Parish Priest of Mungret, to provide accommodation for male and female National Schools upon suitable portions of the premises.

(*b.*) The Leamy Endowment, consisting of the site and buildings of the Leamy Free School, and Trust Funds, consisting of £10,844 11s. 4d. Government Stock.

(*c.*) The site and buildings of the Limerick Diocesan School, subject to the rights of the present tenant, and to his claims in respect of his expenditure upon the premises.

The Commissioners found, when they came to deal with these Endowments, that several questions presented themselves, to which it appeared that the attention of the several parties interested should be specifically directed, before any attempt was made to frame a Scheme or Schemes under the Act.

Among the questions to be determined are the following:—

(1.) What are the just claims of the several religious denominations on each of the Endowments, to which the Commissioners can and should give effect; and how can such effect best be given to them, with due regard to the rights of the present tenants of the Mungret and Roxborough Road premises, founded on the expenditure of private money?

(2.) Is it desirable that the Schemes under which the Mungret and Leamy Endowments are now at present administered should be altered, and if so, what should the alterations be?

(3) Is it desirable that the several Endowments should be dealt with separately; and, if so, how far should the disposal of each Endowment be taken into account in dealing with the others?

(4) What should be the nature and constitution of the bodies to be entrusted with the administration of the several Endowments?

The Commissioners would also desire to have the observations of the several parties interested upon the proposals and suggestions above stated.

The Commissioners request that, after consideration of the foregoing statement, the parties interested will, not later than October 1, next, furnish the Commissioners with a written summary of the views which they desire to present for consideration, upon which the Commissioners propose to appoint a further public sitting, to be held in *Limerick* in the month of October, for the discussion of the foregoing questions. Due notice will be given of this intended sitting, at which all parties interested may be heard.

By order of the Commissioners,

Wm. Edward Ellis,
Secretary.

Office of the Commission,
23, Nassau-street, Dublin,
August 10, 188[illegible].

No. V. (e.)

Sir Stephen E. de Vere to the Commissioners.

Monare, Foynes,
August 23, 188[illegible].

Sir,—On examining the memorandum of the Commissioners of Educational Endowments, bearing date 10th August last, I find several inaccuracies which demand correction.

I request that you will be so good as to place the following observations before the Commissioners.

At page 7 of the memorandum it is stated, with respect to the sum of £766 3s. 4d. transferred to the Trustees of Mungret by Sir Stephen E. de Vere, March 6, 1877, that "this sum of £766 3s. 4d. was *part of a fund* standing in the Provincial Bank to the credit of the original trustees of the Mungret Model Farm."

This sum originally consisted of £529 7s. 10d., lodged on deposit in the Provincial Bank, Limerick, to the credit of Bishop Higgin (now deceased), Lord Monteagle, Sir David Roche, William Hawley (all now deceased), and Stephen E. de Vere, now Sir Stephen E. de Vere, and the survivor or survivors of them. Being informed by the Manager of the Provincial Bank, on the 21st April, 1871, that this sum, together with interest then due, amounting in the whole to £646 1[illegible]s. 8d., was standing in my name as sole survivor, I directed that a new deposit receipt should be issued in my name, and made careful and long continued inquiries in order to ascertain the trusts or purposes for which the money had been originally deposited, but without success.

On 6th March, 1877, I stated the foregoing facts at a meeting of the Trustees held at Mungret, and handed over to the Trustees the sum of £766 3s. 4d., which included all interest upon the original deposit from the period of the money being lodged in Bank up to the time of its transfer to the Trustees.

The memorandum of the Commissioners is therefore incorrect in stating that this *sum of £766 3s. 4d.* was "*part of a sum of £1,066 14s. 10d.*, standing to the credit of Bishop Higgin, Lord Monteagle, Sir David Roche, William Hawley and Stephen E. de Vere in 18[illegible]," the fact being that that sum of £1,066 14s. 10d. was the original capital invested by the Trustees in Consols, out of the dividends of which the current expenses of the establishment were to be paid, and that the sum of £529 7s. 10d. deposited on deposit receipt, with its accrued interest, formed no part of the above sum of £1,066 14s. 10d.

Again, the memorandum of the Commissioners is incorrect in stating that "this sum of £766 3s. 4d. was transferred by me to the present trustees on the condition that it should be reserved for the use and benefit of the *Mungret Model Farm*, and that if it should cease to be conducted *as a model farm* then the fund should be employed in the same manner and on the same trusts as the other funds of *Mungret Model Farm*."

This is an entirely incorrect statement, and would lead to the opinion that my intention was that the fund was to be exclusively devoted to the purposes of the Farm. The memorandum states that the Mungret School in the hands of the Commissioners of National Education "was never successful and ultimately failed; the number of pupils in attendance never exceeded twenty-three and sometimes fell to three or four; the Commissioners (of Education) finally closed the school on September 17, 1878, and surrendered the school and farm with all buildings to the Trustees." The maximum number of pupils is understated. It never exceeded fourteen.

I had no intention to devote the fund, transferred by me, to the special use of a *moribund model farm* which even money provided by Parliament, and all the powers and energy of the Commissioners of National Education, failed to sustain.

The exact words of the condition, as extracted from the minutes of the meeting,* are as follows:—"That this money shall be reserved for the use and benefit of the Mungret Model *Farm and School* so long as it shall continue to be conducted as such, and if it should cease to be so, then this sum is to be employed in the same manner and on the same trusts as other funds of *Mungret Farm and School*."

The words "Mungret Model Farm and School" were used as the usual designation of the whole establishment. The minutes detailing the transaction have been in the hands of the Commissioners.

(Signed), Stephen de Vere.

No. V. (f.)

Lord Emly to the Commissioners.

Tervoe, Limerick,
August 2[illegible]th, 188[illegible].

Sir,—The trustees have received the memorandum of the Commissioners, and regret to observe in it many inaccuracies which require correction.

In page 3 it is stated that "the school was opened in 1852 . . . . . it was never very successful, and ultimately failed; the number of pupils in attendance never exceeded twenty-three, and sometimes fell to three or four." By a return in the report of the Commissioners for 1857-8, Appendix B, page 45, it appears the number never exceeded fourteen. In

* March 6, 1877.

page 5 it is asserted that the Scheme annexed to the lease made to the present lessee does not appear to have been ever sanctioned by the Lord Lieutenant or Treasury. The Commissioners omit to add that before the lessee entered into possession under their lease that the Scheme had been approved of by the Lord Lieutenant and Treasury, by order dated July 24th, 1852, and that this new Scheme is the one under which the college has been carried on since.

In page 7 reference is made to the sum transferred to the trustees by *Sir Stephen E. de Vere, Bart.*, in March, 1857. We annex to this document a letter of Sir Stephen's, of which we entirely approve. A far more serious misrepresentation than those we have already dealt with occurs on page 11. The trustees regret to find that by the suppression of a part of a paragraph in their suggestions for a new Scheme for Mungret College their views have been entirely misrepresented. This is the more extraordinary as the paragraph in question is correctly printed in the Blue Book, containing a report of the proceedings of the Commissioners in Limerick (page [illegible]).

The Commissioners' Memorandum, page 11, represents them as suggesting "that all buildings for lessee students, and any additions thereto, should be reserved for the education and accommodation of students in training for foreign missions."

If the Commissioners will refer to their own "Blue Book," page [illegible], they will find this paragraph to be quoted to be as follows:—

"Whereas considerable sums have been expended by the lessees on buildings for [illegible] students, all such buildings and any additions thereto shall be reserved for the education and accommodation of students in training for foreign missions."

The trustees asked that all moneys subscribed for foreign missionaries should be applied according to the intentions of the donors. The Commissioners represent them as asking that money, given not for ecclesiastical purposes, but for lay education, should be so applied. Unfortunately this misrepresentation has been widely circulated by the Commissioners.

The present condition of Mungret will show the necessity for carrying out the suggestions of the trustees.

The valuation of the buildings at Mungret devolved to the present lessee is £[illegible], a valuation which appears to the trustees excessive.

The sum subscribed for missionary purposes and expended by the lessees—exclusive of £[illegible] for the College Chapel—is £11,[illegible]; adding these sums together they amount to £1[illegible]. So that in regard to [illegible] three-fourths of the present buildings at Mungret should be appropriated to missionary, and one-fourth to lay education.

Last year there were forty missionary and twenty-four lay students. This year there are, we are informed, sixty missionary and fifty lay students.

It appears, therefore, that so far from any part of the original endowments being expended on missionary purposes through the union of missionary and lay students, the latter have largely benefited by the union, and that money subscribed for missionary has been diverted to secular education. This would be shown even more strongly if account were taken of the large annual sum subscribed for providing a missionary teaching staff, which staff, entirely provided by the present lessee, is used for the instruction of the lay students. The trustees therefore repeat their recommendation that all sums subscribed for missionary purposes should be strictly appropriated to those purposes, as, when Mungret College was new and unknown, it was impossible that it could have had many lay students; the [illegible] we insisted on might have appeared to be unnecessary, but the statistics we have given show that the appropriation of moneys given for missionary purposes, according to the intention of the donors, cannot legally be secured without it.

The only answer we think it necessary to make to the first questions put on page 15 is, that we adhere generally, without pledging ourselves to every detail, to the suggestions forwarded by Sir Stephen E. de Vere, Bart., to Lord Justice FitzGibbon, on the 11th October, 1886, and any approval of those suggestions, which maintain in principle the present constitution of the college, has been confirmed by the signal success since we made them.

(Signed), [illegible].

No. V. (g.)

REV. JAMES DOWD, Secretary to Meeting of Protestant Denominations in Limerick, to the COMMISSIONERS.

97, George-street, Limerick,
[illegible] Sept., 1886.

To the Secretary,
Educational Endowments (Ireland) Commission.

DEAR SIR,—I have been directed to send you the enclosed resolutions from a meeting of the clergy and laity of all Protestant denominations held in Limerick on Friday, [illegible] September.

Faithfully yours,
JAMES DOWD.

RESOLUTIONS unanimously adopted at a MEETING of CLERGY AND LAITY of all PROTESTANT DENOMINATIONS of LIMERICK, in answer to the Queries of the Educational Endowments (Ireland) Commission.

No. 1.—As the Endowments of Mungret and Leamy's School were and are strictly undenominational, we think that they should continue to be treated as such. In order that effect may be given to the various claims upon these Endowments, we are of opinion that the suggestion of the present Managers of the Mungret Trusts, viz.:—"That the Lessee should buy out the Trustees at a fair valuation of the lands and old buildings" be adopted; that the Trustees be then ordered to carry out their trust with the funds so realised; that the same principle be applied to the Residuary Land premises, viz.:—That the present lessees should have the first offer of purchasing it at a valuation based upon the condition in which the premises were when the present tenant got possession; and that the funds arising from this source be applied to the purposes of General Undenominational Education.

No. 2.—In reply to this query, we are of opinion that Leamy's Endowment should continue to be administered on the same undenominational principles as heretofore and at present, with such modifications as the Commissioners may deem desirable. As regards Mungret, we refer to answer to query No. 1.

No. 3.—We are of opinion that the several Endowments should be dealt with separately on their merits; but that the disposal of the value of each Endowment should be taken into account in dealing with the others. We would also urge the importance of not breaking up the existing educational centres.

No. 4.—In reply to this query, we have, at the request of the Commission, made suggestions in a previous letter with regard to Leamy's School. With reference to the constitution of the bodies to be entrusted with the administration of the other funds, we are of opinion that they should be Undenominational.

Limerick,
Friday, September 27, 1886.

No. V (a).

Most Rev. Dr. O'Dwyer to the Commissioners.

Boherbuoy Road School, Limerick.

I have already submitted my views on this school to the Commissioners, and have now only to add, that, while I shall resist to the utmost its continuance as a proselytising establishment, I shall be very glad to see it restored to the uses for which it was originally built, and made a high-class school for the Protestants of Limerick and its neighbourhood.

The evidence of the most representative Protestant clergyman in Limerick, given before your Commission, shows that they desire to have such a school, and for my part I cannot see by what right, in face of such a demand, a house and land, that were originally obtained by public moneys for that purpose, and for many years most unsuccessfully devoted to it should now, because, by the chicanery of the officials of the Commissioners of Education, they have passed temporarily into other hands, for other uses, be permanently alienated from it. And I would say that if the Protestant body in Limerick acquiesce in this alienation of the endowment of their own, "Diocesan school," it should be borne in mind, in case they claim a share in other endowments for the purpose of founding a similar school.

Leamy's School.

My evidence before the Commission puts my claim on this endowment plainly enough. It is, by the terms of Leamy's will, (a) an undenominational endowment, and (b) it belongs to the poor of Limerick, and I maintain that it is the duty of the Commission, as they can, to give effect literally to these two conditions.

(a.) With regard to the first, I think the Commissioners will recognise the fact that we, Catholics cannot and will not accept a system of Protestant or mixed education; and consequently if Leamy's School is worked under such a system it is only an indirect way of excluding us from it. If then the Catholics of Limerick—and above all, the poor of Limerick are not to be deprived of all benefit under Leamy's will, they must get an equitable share of the endowment to maintain an educational system in accordance with their religious convictions.

(b.) It seems to me to have been clearly established in evidence, that this second intention of Leamy, has been defeated from the first, and the school has never been worked in the interest of the poor of Limerick. At this very moment some of the Protestant clergy, who desire to have it maintained as it is, unless I am misinformed, are having their own children educated in it. Is that what Leamy meant by "the poor of Limerick"? In fact "the poor of Limerick," are practically all Catholics, the number of Protestant poor is inconsiderable, and consequently if this school is worked on Protestant or secularist principles, it will, by that very fact, shut its doors against those for whom it was intended.

I think then that this endowment substantially belongs to the Catholic body of Limerick, or if it is to be divided between them and the Protestants, the division ought to be in proportion to the numbers of their respective poor. And under this head I should wish to direct the attention of the Commissioners to the fact that more than one educational endowment has been diverted by the Protestant body in Limerick to other benevolent purposes, on the grounds that they had not pupils to avail of them.

Mungret College.

This too is clearly an undenominational endowment in which all religious bodies have rights, and I must admit that it is clearly within the power of the Commissioners to deal with it on such a basis.

I would observe, however, that in the original purpose it was more a rural than an urban school, and therefore the value of the endowment ought to be made available for the county rather than the city. Secondly, the extent of the interference of the Commissioners ought to be the value of the buildings and lands at the time they passed into the hands of their present occupants. Thirdly, that, as I have already informed the Commissioners, that value is very much less than the amount fixed by the official valuer. Fourthly, that it is only reasonable to take into account the very large sum of money which the Jesuits have expended on the place, seeing that they made that expenditure under the eyes of the Trustees, and in the conviction that they were not to be disturbed.

As far as their failure to teach agriculture goes, it may be observed that under the new scheme it was but a very small and secondary part of their duty—the simple fact that one half acre of land was to be kept for that purpose, and that they were at liberty to set the whole farm except two acres, shows that it was regarded as almost nominal, while the rest of their programme, which consisted of teaching either for the Intermediate examinations or for the Royal University, has been very satisfactorily discharged.

Finally, I wish to be understood with regard to this as well as the other endowments with which the Commission has to deal, as demanding that the present occupants get the consideration to which they are in justice and equity entitled, having regard to all the circumstances under which they came into occupation, and the way in which substantially they have fulfilled their trusts, and the rights which they have acquired by their outlay, made in good faith, and as they esteemed with valid title.

In conclusion, I would suggest that the Commission gather into one sum all the proceeds of these endowments, and divide it between the Catholic and Protestant bodies, to be administered by them under schemes to be sanctioned by the Commission. Should the suggestion be adopted, I shall be prepared to submit to the Commissioners names for the constitution of a Catholic Board, and, if it is thought desirable, the outlines of a scheme by which our share of the endowments may be made widely and effectively available for the purposes of education.

✠ Edward Thomas,
Bishop of Limerick.

29th September, 1879.

No. V. (b).

Rev. Thomas Head, S.J., to the Commissioners.

Mungret College, Limerick,
September 24.

Sir,—Fr. Ronan, S.J., has just got printed a pamphlet, entitled the "Case of Mungret College," addressed to the Endowed Schools Commissioners. As he is at present engaged in missionary work in a distant part of the country, he has directed me to send copies to the Commissioners. As I do not know their addresses with certainty, I send a dozen copies to you by this post. Will you kindly send one to each of the Commissioners, and keep the rest for the use of the office. Fr. Ronan is the principal trustee of Mungret College and the founder of the Apostolic School, now established there. As the Commissioners wish to get all communications of this sort about Mungret, before the 1st of October, I am anxious that you get the pamphlets soon. You will oblige me very much therefore if you acknowledge the receipt of them.

(Signed), Thomas Head, S.J.,
Rector of Mungret.

THE MUNSTER DAIRY SCHOOL AND AGRICULTURAL INSTITUTE.

No. VI. (a.)

[illegible] A. [illegible], Esq., Secretary of the Institute to the Commissioners.

Ashgrove, Queenstown,
Co. Cork, May [illegible], 18[illegible].

I have the honour to forward by this post copies of Draft of Charter of proposed Agricultural Institute for Munster, which has been drawn up by the Committee of the Munster Dairy School for the consideration of the Educational Endowments Commissioners, in accordance with a suggestion made, I understand, by your lordship to Dr. W. K. Sullivan, President, Queen's College, Cork.

I regret exceedingly to say that Dr. Sullivan is in such a critical state of health at present that he is unable to attend to business of any kind, and that therefore we must lose the advantage of having the objects we have in view stated and explained by him.

It has consequently devolved upon me as hon. secretary to the school to bring the subject under the notice of the Commission.

The idea in drawing up the Draft of the proposed Charter was to allow such scope in its wording that, should circumstances prove favourable, an Agricultural College for Munster might be established much on the lines of that of *Hohenheim in Würtemberg*, where everything connected with the science and practice of agriculture might be taught. At present the want of a separate farm for male agricultural pupils is much felt, as without it it is impossible to give the continuous education which is absolutely necessary to qualify a boy for practical work. Were this part of the school properly developed, so that the education there given would be such as to fit a boy of fair ability and industry for the post of bailiff or foreman on a farm, I believe there would soon be almost as large an attendance of male pupils as there has been of girl students, as there would then, in all probability, be the same likelihood of obtaining remunerative employment for the boys as at present exists for the girls.

I think it was suggested by some of the Commissioners that an arrangement might be made by which under a Charter the Committee or Governing Body of the School might be placed in an *independent position*, so as to be in a certain sense its own master, and not necessitate a *constant reference to Dublin for authority to make any particular expenditure*, or to alter any detail in the course of training given at the school.

I believe if this change could be effected it would have the best results.

Trusting that our proposed Draft of Charter may receive the approval and support of your lordship and the other members of the Commission.

(Signed), L. A. [illegible],
Hon. Sec.

No. VI. (b.)

Draft of Charter, Objects of Proposed Agricultural Institute for Munster.

To obtain powers to carry out all or any of the following proposals, viz.:—

1. To afford a means of imparting a thoroughly practical and theoretical knowledge of agricultural and dairy farming to the sons and daughters of the farming class, and to all other persons who are desirous of receiving instruction in agriculture, forestry, veterinary science, and cognate subjects.

2. To purchase, take, and hold land for the purposes of dairy stock, and tillage farms, and also with the object of illustrating the management of peat bogs, the manufacture of peat fuel, litter, &c., the reclamation of land, and for any other purpose within the scope of the Institute.

3. To establish at the dairy farm, a herd of pedigree milking cattle, with carefully kept records of the butter and milk yields of each animal, so as to illustrate the advantages to be derived from the intelligent selection of the best specimens of the type of animal required, and to bring within the reach of working dairy farmers, bulls calculated to get really good dairy cattle. Also to maintain small herds of pigs of the most approved types, and a stock of good poultry, with the view of supplying specimens of each kind of stock, to farmers at reasonable prices; and to establish at the dairy show or elsewhere a stud of breeding animals, of such kind as the requirements of the country may demand.

In addition to the foregoing, which shall be considered the principal and fundamental objects for which the Institute is founded, it shall have for its objects:—

(a.) To obtain powers to found a veterinary school, in view of the ultimate establishment of a veterinary college.

(b.) To establish a seed testing and experimental station, where experiments, of all kinds, relating to agriculture, may be carried out; and to obtain an agricultural laboratory, library, and museum.

(c.) To collect information, with regard to the management of woods, plantations, forests, and peat bogs, the preparation of peat, and the reclamation of land, and to make arrangements for providing both practical and theoretical instruction in these subjects.

(d.) To embody in reports such information contained in agricultural publications, and in other scientific works, as has been proved by practical experience, to be useful to the cultivators of the soil.

(e.) To correspond with agricultural, horticultural, and other societies, or with individuals, both at home and abroad, and to select from such correspondence all information which, according to the opinion of the Executive Committee, may be likely to lead to practical benefit, in the cultivation of the soil, or in the management of stock, dairy or other agricultural produce.

(f.) To communicate any occupier of land, or any other person, for any loss which he may incur by experiments undertaken at the request of the Executive Committee for the purpose of testing how far such information leads to useful results in practice.

(g.) To appoint one pay travelling instructors, who shall from time to time, visit the several districts of Munster, for the purpose of imparting information on agricultural subjects, by lectures or otherwise, to the occupiers of land, or to public institutions, and to report on the state of agriculture in each district.

(h.) To promote the comfort and welfare of labourers, and to encourage the improved management of their cottages and gardens.

(i.) To hold exhibitions of and to offer prizes for agricultural stock, produce, and machinery.

(j.) To embody the results of the working of the Institute in periodic reports

To perform such other acts, and incur such expenditure as may be considered necessary for the objects of the Institute.

The exclusion of all political subjects from the proceedings of the Institute to be a condition of the Charter.

CONSTITUTION AND GOVERNMENT OF INSTITUTE.

The Institute shall consist of subscribers and of such other persons as shall be appointed in the manner hereinafter detailed.

The governing body of the Institute, shall consist of a council of 47 members; of this number 12 shall be elected by the county grand juries, county boards, or similar public authorities, of the province of Munster, 2 from each county, 5 shall be nominated by the Commissioners of National Education (Ireland), 21 shall be elected from the general body of subscribers, at a general meeting, and the remaining 9 shall be elected by the Committee of the existing Munster Agricultural and Dairy School from amongst their own body.

In consideration of the work done by the Committee of the Munster Agricultural and Dairy School in furthering agricultural education, the 9 members of council elected by them shall be life members; but on each occasion that a vacancy is created by death or resignation, such vacancy shall be filled by election by the general body of subscribers at the general meeting, next following such death or resignation.

With the exception of the 9 original life members and the 5 members nominated by the Commissioners of National Education, who may be changed from time to time at the pleasure of the said Commissioners, one-third of the council, shall retire annually and shall not be eligible for re-election for twelve months.

The members who are to retire in each year shall be determined as follows, viz.:—

In the case of the 12 members elected for the several counties of Munster, the representatives of two counties, shall retire annually, commencing with the counties of Cork and Kerry, and followed in successive years, by the representatives of Limerick and Clare, and those of Tipperary and Waterford, in the order named.

In the case of the members elected by the general body of subscribers to the Institute, the one-third worst attending members shall retire in each year; should there be an equal number of worst-attending members, which number exceeds the above-mentioned one-third, then the members to go off shall be selected by lot from among these tie.

In the event of the number of members to be elected by the subscribers being increased by the death or resignation of any of the life members elected by the Committee of the Munster Agricultural and Dairy School, and that the number thus increased is not exactly divisible by three, then the number to retire shall be the number nearest under one-third.

After the members of council have been appointed, the members of the Institute, shall annually elect from amongst the council, a president and hon. secretary, or hon. secretaries.

The president or chairman to have a casting vote.

Five to form a quorum of the council.

The council shall have power to appoint such officers or servants as may be considered necessary for the proper conduct of the Institute, and shall allot the salaries or other remuneration for their services.

They shall also have power, subject to confirmation by a general meeting, to make such by-laws for the furtherance of the purposes for which the Institute is established as they may consider necessary, and to revoke or alter any of the said by-laws and to fix the amount of subscription to be paid by the members of the Institute.

The council shall meet twice each year, or oftener if necessary.

At the first meeting of the council in each year, they shall elect an executive committee of 11, to whom the administration of the Institute shall be handed over for the current year, and who shall be required to submit at least two reports annually, to the council on the work done at the Institute.

The members of the executive committee may be selected from the general body of members of the Institute. They should be chosen with a view to their special fitness for the duties devolving on them, and they should undertake to devote a reasonable amount of time, in a regular manner, to the work of the Institute.

The executive committee shall have power to delegate to such sub-committees of their own body as they may deem fit, with power temporarily to co-opt for special purposes such qualified persons as they may deem advisable, the practicable superintendence of the working details of the Institute, subject to the control of the whole committee.

The executive committee shall retire at the end of each year, but each member shall be eligible for re-election.

A record of the attendance of each member of the executive committee, either at the meetings of the full committee or of sub-committees, shall be kept, and shall be read out at the meeting of council, before proceeding to elect the new executive committee.

The president and hon. secretary, or hon. secretaries, shall be ex-officio members of the executive committee.

Three to form a quorum of the executive committee, the chairman to have a casting vote.

There shall also be a ladies' committee for promoting instruction in cookery, needlework, &c., among the female residents, and for the general supervision of the household arrangements of the dairy school, subject to the control of the executive committee.

No. VI. (a)

ABSTRACT of the HISTORY of the FORMATION of the MUNSTER AGRICULTURAL and DAIRY SCHOOL, supplied by L. A. BEAMISH, Esq., Secretary.

In consequence of the District Agricultural Schools in Ireland proving a failure, or rather yielding results totally inadequate to the expenditure, the Treasury decided "on the gradual abandonment of the system of maintaining these model farms out of public funds," and, in accordance with this decision, the Commissioners of National Education were making arrangements to give up the Munster Model Farm, Cork, and advertised it for sale, when the County of Cork Agricultural Society, early in 1880, made strong representations to the Commissioners of Education (Ireland) on the injurious effects to the agricultural community of the south of Ireland, if the school was closed up, and proposed that it should be continued, as an agricultural school, and in addition, that instruction should be given in dairy management to females.

The Agricultural Society offered to undertake the management of the school, and to raise sufficient funds to meet the increased expenditure.

The proposal met with the cordial support of the Board of Education (Ireland), who submitted to the Treasury the names of the Committee of the County of Cork Agricultural Society, as a guarantee that the project would be properly carried out, which was approved of by the Treasury.

The County of Cork Agricultural Society appointed

a sub-committee under the name of the "Munster Dairy and Agricultural School Committee," to carry out the scheme; this committee succeeded in raising in 1880–1, £[illegible] 6s. to meet the necessarily heavy outlay in erecting a new [illegible], the expense of which was further increased by the local committee being obliged to pay to the Treasury in first three years £[illegible] 14s. [illegible]d., being three years rent for a residence in Cork for the male teacher of the Munster Model Schools, Cork, who had hitherto resided at the farm, but whose removal was absolutely necessary, to admit of the reception of the female pupils.

The Board of Education still continued to be responsible for the administration of the public funds, leaving the local committee free to dispose the funds raised by them, and to arrange the details of management of farming operations and school.

The first session of four weeks for dairy pupils (girls) commenced on 10th August, 1880, when nine attended, a second session opened on September 13, with six pupils (girls), and a third session on 17th November, 1880, since then twenty-one sessions have been held, making twenty-four sessions in all, and [illegible] individual pupils have passed through the school, the first terms for 1880–1 lasted four weeks each, in 1882 the time was extended to six weeks, and to meet the growing demand it was decided in 1884 to further extend the term to eight weeks, to have three terms in the year to run consecutively, with an interval of two weeks between each, so as to give the pupils an opportunity, which has been largely availed of, of remaining on for two or three terms.

The fees of dairy pupils for the early classes were nearly altogether paid by landowners or patrons of the subject; now, in nearly every instance the fees are paid by the pupils or their parents.

The classes for agricultural students (young men) are still maintained; two terms of four months each were held in 1881, six attended each; two terms were also held in 1882, and three since then; in consequence of the increased number of girls' sessions, one session for male pupils has only been held each year; there have been, in all ten sessions for young men, and the total attendance has been [illegible].

The local committee provide qualified lecturers in agricultural chemistry and veterinary science, award prizes, &c.

The total funds raised by the local committee have been:—

	£	s.	d.
1880–1, ...	[illegible]	[illegible]	[illegible]
1881, ...	[illegible]	10	0
1882, ...	[illegible]	11	0
1883, ...	[illegible]	6	0
1884, ...	[illegible]	[illegible]	0
1885, ...	[illegible]	[illegible]	0
1886, ...	[illegible]	7	0
1887, ...	[illegible]	[illegible]	0
	[illegible]	17	0

There is also a ladies' committee who raise about £[illegible] per annum, which is expended in prizes, &c., to the dairy pupils for cookery, needlework, cleanliness, &c.

In 1887 the Treasury made a grant to the Dairy School Committee of £[illegible] without further condition than that it should be used for the furtherance of agricultural education. This sum has been invested in 2¾ consols, and has purchased a sum of £1,[illegible] [illegible]s. 7d. There is also a half year's dividend of £[illegible] 17s. 10d. on deposit receipt in the Provincial Bank, Cork.

No. VI. (d.)

PORTIONS of the DRAFT SCHEME referred to in the OBJECTIONS and AMENDMENTS of the ELECTED GOVERNING BODY.

Recitals.

1. *Preliminary.—Interpretation of terms.*

The Governing Body.

2. From and after the date of this Scheme a Governing Body shall be formed for the future government and management of the School, and of the Endowment, in manner following:—

It shall consist of (I.) eighteen Governors to be elected by the Subscribers, qualified as hereinafter provided; (II.) twelve Governors to be elected by the several Grand Juries of the Counties of Munster, as hereinafter provided; and (III.) such additional Governors as may be elected by the Council of the Royal Dublin Society, and by the Commissioners of National Education, respectively, under the provisions hereinafter contained.

Of the eighteen Governors representing the Subscribers, nine shall be Life Governors, and nine shall retire by rotation as hereinafter provided.

Of the twelve Governors representing the Grand Juries, two shall be elected by the Grand Jury of each of the Counties hereinafter mentioned, provided that in the case of the County of Tipperary one Governor shall be elected by the Grand Jury of each of the two Ridings of that County.

The Governors, in the first instance, shall be such and so many of the following persons as, at the date of this Scheme, shall be able and willing to act as Governors:—

I.—Representing the Subscribers.

(A.) *Life Governors:—*

1. W. H. Barry, Esq., Ballyadam, County Cork.
2. Richard Barter, Esq., St. Anne's Hill, Blarney.
3. William K. Sullivan, Esq., [illegible], President, Queen's College, Cork.
4. James Byrne, Esq., Wallstown Castle, Shanballymore.
5. T. J. Clanchy, Esq., W[illegible], Cork.
6. A. Ferguson, Esq., Belvidere, Cork.
7. Colonel [illegible], Castlelyons, County Cork.
8. James M'Kenzie, Esq., Cork.
9. Captain R. R. F. [illegible], D.L., [illegible], County Cork.

(B.) *Governors retiring by rotation:—*

10. W. R. Meade, Esq., D.L., Ballymartle, Ballinhassig, County Cork.
11. Captain R. P. [illegible], D.L., Ashbourne, Glounthaune, County Cork.
12. R. E. Longfield, Esq., D.L., Waterloo, Mallow.
13. R. U. Penrose Fitzgerald, Esq., M.P., D.L., Corkbeg House, Whitegate, County Cork.
14. Captain J. H. Bainbridge, [illegible], Frankfield, County Cork.
15. Colonel F. Heard, J.P., [illegible] House, County Cork.
16. Ludlow A. [illegible], Esq., J.P., Ashgrove, Queenstown.
17. James [illegible], Esq., Warren's place, Cork.
18. Edward Gibson, Esq., Caddingrove, Douglas Glanmire, Cork.

II.—Representing the Grand Juries.

County of Clare:—

1. Francis [illegible], Esq., Springfield, Sixmilebridge.
2. James Frost, Esq., Ballymorris, Cratloe.

County of Cork:—

3. William Ross, Esq., [illegible], Blarney.
4. Daniel Gibson, Esq., The Highlands, Glanmire.

County of Kerry:

5. Samuel M. Hussey, Esq., Edenburn, Tralee.
6. George F. Trench, Esq., Abbeylands, Ardfert.

County of Limerick:

7. John White, Esq., Nantenan, Askeaton.
8. Edward Croker, Esq., The Grange, County Limerick.

County of Tipperary:

9. North Riding.—Hon. G. Trench, Sopwell Hall, Cloughjordan.
10. South Riding.—Richard Bagwell, Esq., M.A., Marlfield, Clonmel.

County of Waterford:

11. Capt. W. Percival Maxwell, Moore Hill, Tallow.
12. H. Villiers-Stuart, Esq., M.A., Dromana, Cappoquin.

Additional Governors.

If and so long as the Council of the Royal Dublin Society shall contribute fifty pounds a year to the funds of the School, the said Council shall be entitled, if it shall think fit, to elect two additional Governors to represent the said Society; and so long as the School remains in connection with the Commissioners of National Education, the said Commissioners shall be entitled, if they shall think fit, to elect two additional Governors to represent the said Commissioners. The Governors representing the Royal Dublin Society and the Commissioners of National Education shall be elected in such manner, and shall hold office for such term, as the said Council and the said Commissioners respectively shall determine.

The said Governors shall be a Body Corporate, by the name of "The Munster Dairy School and Agricultural Institute," with perpetual succession and a common seal, and power to acquire and hold property, real and personal, for the purposes of this Scheme.

Life Governors.

3. Whenever any Life Governor shall die, or resign by writing under his hand, or become bankrupt, or refuse to act, or become incapable of acting, or shall cease to reside in the Province of Munster, his office shall thereupon become vacant, and the fact of the vacancy with the cause thereof shall be recorded in the minutes of the Governors; and, as soon as conveniently may be after the occurrence of such vacancy, the Subscribers shall, at a meeting specially convened for the purpose, elect a duly qualified person to fill the same. If, at any time, the number of Subscribers on the register should be less than fifty, the power of electing Life Governors shall not be exercised by them, but vacancies among the Life Governors shall be filled by co-option by the remaining Governors.

4. *Governors Retiring by Rotation.*

5. *Election of Governors by Grand Juries.*

Casual Vacancies.

6. Whenever any Governor other than a Life Governor, shall die, or resign by writing under his hand, or become bankrupt, or refuse to act, or become incapable of acting, or shall cease to reside in the Province of Munster, his office shall thereupon become vacant, and the fact of the vacancy with the cause thereof shall be recorded in the minutes of the Governors; and shall be communicated by the Governors to the body among whose representatives the vacancy has occurred; and as soon as conveniently may be after the occurrence of such vacancy, the Grand Jury, the Subscribers, the Council of the Royal Dublin Society, or the Commissioners of National Education, as the case may be, among whose representatives the vacancy has occurred, shall elect a duly qualified person to fill the same, and the Governor so elected shall hold office so long only as the Governor in whose place he shall have been elected might have held the same.

The Subscribers.

7. The following persons shall be qualified as Subscribers for the purposes of this Scheme:—

(1.) Every person who before or after the date of this Scheme shall have contributed £10 in one sum to the funds of the School.

(2.) Every Subscriber of £1 per annum to the funds of the School; but no annual Subscriber shall be entitled to the privileges of a Subscriber, in any year, until his or her subscription for that year shall have been paid.

An Annual meeting of the Subscribers shall be held in the month of November or December of each year, at a time and place to be fixed by the Governors from time to time, and of which notice shall be given by advertisement or otherwise as the Governors shall prescribe.

8. *Vesting and Transfer of the Endowments.*

9. *Additional Endowments.*

10. *Aid from Public Sources.*

11. *Trusts of the Endowments.*

Application of the Endowments.

12. All moneys received by the Governors under or for the purposes of this Scheme, shall, subject to the other provisions herein contained, and to any special trusts or conditions upon which any part thereof may be received, be expended and applied by them for the following purposes, or for such and so many of them as to the Governors, for the time being, shall seem expedient:—

(a.) To maintain, or assist in maintaining, an Agricultural and Dairy School for the sons and daughters of farmers and other persons, in which shall be taught the theory and practice of agriculture, dairy farming, and stock farming, and in which practical training shall be given in the management of farms, in the management of dairies, in the rearing and management of live stock, including poultry, and in garden farming, bee-keeping, and spade industry.

(b.) To purchase or rent pasture or tillage land for the purposes of the School, also peat bogs, or other land suitable for reclamation.

(c.) To provide or aid in providing a sufficient teaching staff in the various branches of agricultural education aforesaid, also in chemistry, forestry, veterinary science, and any other cognate subjects which the Governors may, from time to time, consider to be suited to the wants of the country, and the requirements of the pupils.

(d.) To aid in providing the necessary staff for the working of the farm and the dairy, and for the training of the pupils.

(e.) To carry out experiments in matters connected with the cultivation of the soil, the rearing of stock, the management of farms, and the other purposes of the School, and to make grants in aid of such experiments.

(f.) To establish, or to aid in establishing, an agricultural laboratory, library, and museum.

(g.) To provide, or to aid in providing the necessary equipment for the purposes of the School, including agricultural implements, stock, workshops, and machinery.

(h.) To defray the other expenses incurred in carrying out the purposes of this Scheme.

13. *General Provisions as to the Governors—Chairman, Quorum, and Honorary Officers.*

14. *Meetings.*

15. *Minutes, Books and Documents.*

Committees.

16. The Governors may, from time to time, appoint a Committee or Committees, each consisting of two or more Governors, to visit the School, to carry into execution any orders rules or directions of the Governors with respect to the purposes of this Scheme, or to manage such of the business of the School as the Governors may deem it expedient to depute to them. They may also appoint a Committee of Ladies to promote instruction in cookery, needlework, and domestic economy, and to supervise the household arrangements of the Dairy School, subject to the control of the Governors. The Governors may fix the quorum, define the duties, and regulate the proceedings of every Committee as they shall think fit.

By-Laws and Regulations.

17. The Governors may, from time to time, make such by-laws and regulations as they shall consider convenient and useful for the good government and management of the School, for keeping a Register of the qualified Subscribers, for regulating the election of Governors, and for otherwise effectuating the purposes of this Scheme; provided that no such by-law or regulation shall be inconsistent with the provisions of this Scheme, and that the same may be repealed, altered, and amended by the Governors, from time to time, as they shall deem expedient; provided also that unless and until the Governors shall make other by-laws and regulations as aforesaid, the by-laws of the School in force at the date of this Scheme shall, so far as the same are consistent with the provisions of this Scheme, remain in force.

18. *Accounts and Audit.*
19. *Inspection.*
20. *Annual Report.*
21. *Powers of Governors.*
22. *Religious Instruction.*
23. *Exhibitions and Scholarships.*
24. *Management of Property—Sales, Exchanges, and Lettings.*

Investments.

25. The Governors may, at any time, subject to any special trusts or conditions affecting any part thereof, sell any of the stocks, funds, and securities which may be vested in them for the purposes of this Scheme, and may invest the moneys arising from any such sale, or from sale or mortgage, or for equality of exchange of or upon any dealing with land or buildings, and also any residue of income not required for the purposes aforesaid, in any of the public stocks, funds, or securities of the United Kingdom, or of any Colony or Dependency thereof, or upon freehold or leasehold securities in the United Kingdom, or in the purchase of perpetual rents or rent-charges, or upon the bonds, debentures, or mortgages of any municipal commercial or other Joint Stock Company or Corporation, carrying on business or constituted for any purpose in the United Kingdom, or any Colony or Dependency thereof, or in any other securities for the time being sanctioned by law, or by the practice of the High Court of Justice, for the investment of trust funds, or may apply the same for the purpose of building or permanent improvements, and the Governors may from time to time vary such investments, and may have recourse in any year to the accumulations of income from any previous year or years.

Payment of Expenses.

26. The Governors shall, subject to the other provisions of this Scheme, pay out of the Endowments all charges which under the provisions of the Act shall be properly and necessarily payable by the Governors, or out of the Endowments, for the taxed costs and expenses of this Scheme, or for audit and inspection, or for other purposes.

27. *Provision for Vested Interests and Superannuation.*
28. *Discharge of existing Committee.*
29. *Printing of Scheme.*
30. *Alteration of Scheme.*

SCHEDULE REFERRED TO IN THE FOREGOING SCHEME.

Property comprised in the Endowments.

PART I.—*Lands, Buildings, and Premises now occupied by the School.*

All that and those the lands of Ballygaggin, now in the possession of the Commissioners of National Education in Ireland, situate in the barony of Cork and County of Cork, containing 126 acres 3 roods and 11 perches, statute measure, or thereabouts, with the buildings thereon, known as the Cork Model Farm, held by the said Commissioners for 99 years from January 1, 18[illegible], under Indenture dated December, [illegible], 18[illegible], subject to the yearly rent of £[illegible].

PART II. *Trust Funds.*

The sum of £[illegible] [illegible]s. [illegible]d. Government Stock standing in the books of the Governor and Company of the Bank of Ireland in the names of William Horatio Crawford, Lismore, Gabriel [illegible] Ambrose [illegible], William K. Sullivan, President, Queen's College, Cork, as Trustees for the School.

OBJECTIONS AND AMENDMENTS

Made and Proposed to the Draft Scheme

No. VI. (a).

1. By the [illegible] GOVERNING BODY.

At a meeting of the Governors, named in the Draft Scheme recently issued by the Educational Endowments Commissioners for the Munster Dairy and Agricultural Institute, held on [illegible] June at the Munster Dairy School Farm, for the purpose of considering the provisions of the Scheme, it was, after careful deliberation, decided to send forward to the Educational Endowments Commissioners the following suggestions for alterations in the details of the Scheme, viz:—

1st. That the following clauses shall be added to the Draft Scheme or clauses conveying the same meaning, viz:—

(a.) But it is distinctly provided and understood that no person who shall consent to act as a Governor of the proposed Institute shall incur any pecuniary liability by accepting the office, and that the funds at the disposal of the Institute shall alone be liable in any suit against the latter.

(b.) That immediately after the date of the Scheme the farm and buildings at present used for the purposes of the Munster Agricultural and Dairy School, together with all live-stock, implements, appliances, and fodder, shall be handed over to the Governors to be used by them for the purposes of the Scheme, subject to the approval of the Commissioners of National Education, who shall, however, still remain liable for the rent and rates payable out of the said farm and buildings.

(e) That in the event of the Governors finding that the funds at their disposal are inadequate for the proper working of the Institute, then they shall have power, having first obtained the consent of the majority of the subscribers to the Institute expressed at a General Meeting specially summoned to consider the question, to hand over the farm or farms, stock, implements, &c., to the Commissioners of National Education, and relinquish all powers and obligations vested in them by the Scheme, the Commissioners of National Education, in consideration of receiving any land, money, or other property that may at the time be vested in the Governors, undertaking to be responsible for the debts or other obligations contracted by the Governors on behalf of the Institute.

8. That the following alterations and additions be made in the Scheme:—

That the name be altered to "Munster Agricultural and Dairy Institute."

Par. 2.—Under the head of "*Governing Body*," to read—(II.) Eighteen Governors to be elected to represent the counties of Munster, twelve to be elected by the Grand Juries of Munster as hereinafter provided, and six to be members of Parliament of said counties to be selected as hereinafter provided.

" Sec. 3 to read—Of the eighteen Governors representing the counties of Munster two shall be elected by the Grand Jury of each of the counties hereinafter mentioned, provided that in the case of the county of Tipperary one Governor shall be elected by the Grand Jury of each of the two ridings of that county, and six shall be members of Parliament for the counties of Munster, one for each county, to be selected by the members of Parliament for the respective counties.

" In list of Governors—

Life Governors:

1. Savage French, Cuskinny, Queenstown, county Cork; in place of W. H. Barry, deceased.

Governors retiring by rotation:

11. Christopher Dunn, Watergrasshill, Cork, Chairman, Cork Butter Market Trustees; in place of Captain R. P. Beamish, resigned.

17. Richard H. Beamish, Ashbourne, Glounthaune, Cork; in place of James Ogilvie, resigned.

" The heading "Representing the Grand Juries" to read—"Representing the counties of Munster."

" After the list of Grand Juries Representatives, the names of the six selected members of Parliament to be inserted.

Par. 3.—Read after "become Bankrupt"—"or compound with his creditors."

" Read after "fill the same"—"but in the case of the Governors elected by the Commissioners of National Education, and by the Council of the Royal Dublin Society, residence in the province of Munster shall not be compulsory."

Par. 4.—Read after "election of the Governors"—"but the obligation to reside in the province of Munster shall not apply to the Governors elected by the Commissioners of National Education or by the Council of the Royal Dublin Society."

Par. 6.—Strike out the words—"The Council of the Royal Dublin Society or the Commissioners of National Education."

Par. 7.—Add to list of persons qualified as subscribers—(3.) "Every *bona fide* working farmer who shall subscribe ten shillings per annum."

" Add to paragraph (7)—"But a Special General Meeting of the Subscribers may be summoned at any time either at the instance of the Governors or on the requisition of ten subscribers."

Par. 12.—Sub-section (a.)—Insert the word "breeding" before "rearing" in fifth line.

" Sub-section (e.)—Insert the words "breeding and" before "rearing" in second line.

" Sub-section (f.)—add the words "and seed testing station."

" Call sub-section (h.) sub-section (k.); and insert the following, viz.:—

Sub-section (h.)—To appoint and pay travelling instructors, who shall from time to time visit the several districts of Munster for the purpose of imparting information on agricultural subjects by lectures or otherwise to the occupiers of land.

" Sub-section (i.)—To promote the comfort and welfare of labourers, and encourage the improved management of their cottages and gardens.

" Sub-section (j.)—To hold exhibitions of, and to offer prizes for, agricultural stock, produce, and machinery.

Par. 16.—Read after "to depute to them"—and "also co-opt on such committees for special purposes, such qualified persons as they may deem advisable."

Par. 17.—Read after "deem expedient"—"and the Governors shall submit such by-laws to the next general meeting for the approval of the members of the Institute."

Par. 23.—Power to be given to the Governors to purchase land in fee-simple or to invest in land out of the capital of the Trust.

Par. 26.—Add—"The Governors may also defray the actual travelling expenses of any of their number who may apply for them, out of the Endowment."

Pars. 28, 29, 30, to be numbered 29, 30, 31, respectively.

Par. 28.—New clause—The exclusion of all political subjects from the proceedings of the Institute to be a condition of the Charter.

And I have been requested to forward these suggestions to you for the consideration of the Commissioners.

I have also been directed to state that unless full and clear provisions can be introduced into the Scheme by which the Governors shall be absolutely freed from all pecuniary liability in the administration of the Trust beyond the Endowments or funds coming to their hands, and that power be given them, with the consent of the majority of the subscribers, to divest themselves of the obligations proposed to be placed on them by the Charter should they find the means at their disposal inadequate for carrying on the Institute in a suitable manner, then the Governors named in the Scheme respectfully decline to undertake the responsibility of acting as the Governing Body of the proposed Institute, as they feel that unless a sufficient grant or endowment is provided by the State, in addition to any subscriptions that may be received, for carrying out the Trusts detailed in the proposed Scheme, they would be powerless to effect the objects contemplated therein, and that therefore, should it unfortunately happen that the Government declined to grant the necessary funds, they feel that power should be given them to relinquish the Scheme and free themselves from all obligations created by the proposed Charter.

(Signed), L. A. Beamish,
Hon. Sec. M. A. & D. School.

No. VI. (f)

II. By the Commissioners of National Education.

Sir,—The Commissioners of National Education had under consideration at their meeting yesterday the "Draft Scheme under the Educational Endowments (Ireland) Act, 1885, for the future government and management of the educational endowments of and belonging to the Munster Dairy School and Agricultural Institute," and they have directed me to forward to you the enclosed statement, setting forth certain statistics and facts bearing on the case, and embodying the objections entertained by them to the scheme.

I am to request you will be good enough to submit the statement to the Educational Endowments Commissioners.

(Signed) John E. Sheridan.

June 26, 1889.

Statement setting forth certain statistics and facts bearing on the case of the "Draft Scheme for the Munster Dairy School and Agricultural Institute," and embodying the objections entertained by the Commissioners of National Education to the Scheme.

1. The Commissioners of National Education hold and administer the Munster Model Agricultural and Dairy National School under the powers of their Charter, and obtain the funds for its annual support from the votes of Parliament.

2. The farm contains 1[illegible] acres, and is held under lease from the Duke of Devonshire for [illegible] years from January, 18[illegible], at a rent of £[illegible] per annum. There is a six months clause of surrender in the lease on condition that all buildings erected on the farm shall, on such surrender, pass over to the Duke of Devonshire, without any compensation or allowance to the Commissioners.

3. Upon the erection of the buildings of the farm, the Commissioners, with the sanction of the Lords of Her Majesty's Treasury, have expended £1[illegible].

4. The last annual valuation of the cattle, implements, &c., was £1,6[illegible].

5. Irrespectively of the cost of repairs, fuel, light, &c. (about £[illegible] a year on the average) borne by the Board of Works, the net cost of the school from the Parliamentary grant has been in each of the last three years:—

	£
[illegible],	[illegible]
[illegible],	[illegible]
[illegible],	[illegible]

6. As set forth in the Board's rules, page [illegible], a local committee organized in 18[illegible], "co-operates with the Commissioners of National Education and their officers in watching over the interests of the school, in collecting funds, and in applying these funds to objects which they think best calculated to promote agricultural education in Munster."

This local committee in the same period of three years provided—

	£
[illegible],	[illegible]
[illegible],	[illegible]
[illegible],	[illegible]

7. In addition to the funds raised by the local committee, the Royal Dublin Society, in each of these three years subscribed £[illegible] towards the school, and in the same three years there was a total amount of £[illegible] subscriptions from other sources.

8. In accordance with the policy recommended by the Royal Commission of 18[illegible]–70, and the Treasury Departmental Committee of 1874, and repeatedly urged by the Lords of Her Majesty's Treasury, the Commissioners from time to time surrendered some of their Model Farms and sold others.

In 1877 they resolved to sell their interest in the Munster Farm but owing to the course pursued by the Duke of Devonshire who made no reply to their application for authority to sell, they were unable to do so.

In the meantime the Grand Jury of Cork petitioned the Government to continue the operation of the Munster Farm, and the upshot of this and other proceedings was the constitution of the Committee with the functions above described, as published in the Board's Rules.

This happened at a time when the Commissioners had under consideration the desirability of extending their Dairy Department, and they, accordingly, welcomed the co-operation of the Committee, whose main purpose was the promotion of dairy farming.

9. The Treasury consented to the continuance of the farm on the new basis on the understanding that the responsibility for its management would rest as before with the Commissioners of National Education, and that the connection of the Committee with the Farm would involve no extra charge upon the vote of Parliament.

10. The Treasury also required as a condition of continuing the Parliamentary Grant that a special report on the Munster Farm should each year be forwarded to their Lordships by the Commissioners along with the Estimates.

This special report has been made from year to year, and has been uniformly of a most satisfactory character. The number of dairymaids trained in the school since 1880 is 576.

11. On June 23rd, 1888, the Commissioners received from Mr. L. A. Beamish, Honorary Secretary of the Committee, a printed copy of a Draft Charter for a proposed Agricultural Institute, with a request that the Commissioners might afford the Committee their co-operation in founding such an Institute, and should they approve of the Scheme might nominate two members to represent them on the Council of the proposed Institute.

Upon this application, the Board at their meeting of 3rd July, 1888, made the following order:—

"That the Honorary Secretary be informed that the Commissioners of National Education are at present wholly unprepared with what would be the relations of their Model Agricultural and Dairy National School to the proposed Agricultural Institute, and that until they are fully informed on this subject they would not feel warranted in considering the question of nominating two members to represent them on the Council of the proposed Institute. The Commissioners will await information of any further progress that may be made in the preparation of the Scheme."

12. The functions of the Commissioners in the administration of the school and the management of their

property as it appears under the provisions of the Draft Scheme to be conferred upon the new governing body, subject only to certain vesting powers reserved to the Board.

15. Under their obligations to Parliament and their responsibility as a department of the public service, the Commissioners have no power to give their assent to any such Scheme.

16. But were the Commissioners otherwise free to entertain this Draft Scheme they find themselves bound to keep in view the following correspondence as to the nature and conditions of the Treasury ear-marked grant of £2,000 which constitutes the Educational Endowment referred to in the Draft Scheme.

"Irish Office,
"4th August, 1887.

"Dear Sir Patrick,—The Treasury and the Chief Secretary have agreed to give, or ask the House of Commons to give to the Munster Agricultural and Dairy Farm a special grant of £2,000. If the Committee of the School buy a farm, therefore, they will be able to stock it, and start it well, but they have been given most distinctly to understand that the Treasury will not support the Farm, or allow this grant to be made the ground of any future claim, and in order to make the position more clear they have been given also to understand that the money will be voted simply as a grant in aid of the school generally—so if they carry out the idea of buying the Farm they will do it at their own risk. The enclosed copy of a letter written to Mr. Barter gives you some further details. It is officially recorded at the Treasury, and I have been desired by the Chancellor of the Exchequer and the Chief Secretary to send you a copy so that you may know how the matter stands.

"Yours very faithfully,
"(Signed), T. Ramsden [illegible]

"The Right Hon. Sir P. J. Keenan, K.C.M.G."

"Treasury Chambers, Whitehall, S.W.,
"4th August, 1887.

"Sir,—With reference to the communications which have passed between us on the subject of the proposed grant to the Munster Agricultural and Dairy School, I am directed by the Chancellor of the Exchequer to inform you that the Government is prepared to ask Parliament to give £2,000 to that institution as part of the £20,000 which are to be devoted to the improvement of the industrial condition of Ireland.

"Before doing so, however, the Government is anxious to be assured that it is understood by your Committee that this grant will not be allowed to entail on the Exchequer any new liability in respect of the school. The £2,000 is an out-and-out gift of an entirely exceptional character and the Government can only ask Parliament to sanction it upon receiving the distinct assurance of your Committee that it will not hereafter be made the ground of any appeal for increased contributions from public funds towards the maintenance and expenses of your institution.

"I am further directed to say that in order to give the widest scope for the beneficial expenditure of the money, and at the same time to avoid any risk of involving the Committee in future liabilities which they might find it difficult to meet, the House of Commons will be asked to vote the sum of £2,000 as a grant in aid of the school generally, leaving it to the Committee to determine in what way it may be most advantageously applied.

"I have to request that you will be good enough to lay this matter before your Committee without delay, and to express the Chancellor of the Exchequer's hope that he may be favoured with an early reply from them, as the details of the £20,000 must be definitely settled at once.

"Believe me, your obedient servant,
"(Signed), Alfred Milner.

"E. Barter, Esq.,
Secretary, Munster Agricultural
and Dairy School."

17. In addition to the condition referred to in Mr. Milner's letter to Mr. Barter that "the grant of £2,000 will not be allowed to entail upon the Exchequer any new liability in respect of the school," it is important to observe that within the last week the Commissioners have received from the Secretary of the Local Committee at Cork the following communication:—

"Munster Dairy and Agricultural School
Committee, Cork, 17th June, 1889.

"Dear Sir,
"In re Draft Scheme of Charter, Munster Dairy Agricultural Institute.

"The Committee of the Munster Dairy School have given the above careful consideration, and I now have the pleasure to enclose copy of certain proposed alterations which the committee recommend should be made therein.

"It has been decided to summon a meeting of the Governors named in the Scheme to be held in Cork at the School Farm on Thursday, 20th inst., at 3 o'clock, p.m., to consider the general provisions of the Scheme together with the suggested alterations, and to determine whether the Governors shall accept the responsibility proposed to be placed on them by the Charter unless, first receiving an assurance from the Government that an adequate endowment will be provided for the proper working of the Institute.

"As it will be necessary that any proposed changes in the Draft Scheme shall be lodged with the Educational Endowment Commissioners not later than the 24th instant, it is hoped that all the Governors named in the Scheme will be able to attend the meeting on Thursday next.

"I am, dear sir, yours truly,
"(Signed) L. A. Beamish."

18. Of the result of this meeting the Commissioners have not received any official intimation.

John E. Sheridan, Secretary.

Office of National Education,
Marlborough-street, Dublin,
25th June, 1889.

No. VI. (g.)

III. By certain persons of influence in the City and County of Cork.

We, the undersigned, do hereby express our objection to the Draft Scheme prepared in this matter by the Educational Endowments Commissioners, bearing date the 29th April, 1889, on the following grounds, that is to say:—

1. That the County of Cork Agricultural Society and the funds at their disposal do not constitute an Educational Endowment within the meaning of the said Act.

2. That the establishment of the proposed "Munster Dairy School and Agricultural Institute" is not at present desirable or for the public advantage.

3. That the said Draft Scheme has been adopted without adequate notice to persons interested in same, and without sufficient publicity having been given to the proposal embodied in it.

4. That the constitution of the governing body of the proposed "Munster Dairy School and Agricultural Institute," as provided by said Draft Scheme, is objectionable:—

(a.) As appointing a considerable number of Governors holding office for life.

(b.) As permitting a disproportionately large number of Governors to be appointed by the subscribers without regard to the proportion between the amount of the funds of the Institute contributed by private subscriptions and the amount contributed from public sources.

(c.) As vesting the election of Life Governors solely in the subscribers, and as permitting Life Governors to be co-opted in certain cases.

(d.) As providing for no popular representation amongst the body of Governors, notwithstanding that the bulk of the Endowment comes from public sources.

(e.) As vesting the election of a considerable proportion of the Governors in the Grand Juries of Munster, these bodies having no power to contribute to the funds of the Institution, and being entirely unpopular in their constitution.

(f.) As making an objectionable selection of persons appointed to hold office as Governors in the first instance.

4. For other reasons which will be stated at the public inquiry.

Daniel Ryan, Mayor of Cork.
R. A. Atkins, High Sheriff of Cork.
Maurice Healy, M.P., Cork City.
J. William J. Lane, M.P., East Cork.
Jas. G. Flynn, M.P., N. Cork.
John Horgan, Alderman, Cork.
D. J. [illegible], [illegible].
James Byrne, Wallstown Castle.

No. VI. (h.)

IV. By the Grand Jury of the County of Kerry at the Kerry Summer Assizes, 1888.

Resolution adopted by the Grand Jury.

Proposed by J. G. Kellgan, seconded by Major Hewson, and

Resolved—That, in the opinion of this Grand Jury, the Governing Body of the New Munster Agricultural Institute and Dairy School should take steps to provide that, unless a grant or endowment can be obtained for the equipment and maintenance of the Institution, the present position of the Farm and School should not be interfered with, and that in that case the proposed Scheme should be rejected and the new Governing Body dissolved.

(Signed), E. De Moleyns, Foreman.

No. VI. (i.)

Letter of the Commissioners of National Education with regard to their Objections.

(See No. VI. (f), supra p. 381.)

Dublin, 22nd August, 1888.

In reference to my letter of the 29th June last, in which the Commissioners made a statement of the cost of the Munster Model Farm for the years 1884–7, 1887–8, and 1888–9, I am directed to acquaint you that the buildings of the Munster Agricultural School were constructed to accommodate not only the agricultural students, but the male pupil teachers of the Cork District Model School.

The agricultural students were resident only during the short agricultural sessions; but the pupil teachers of the model school were resident throughout the whole of the model school year.

When it was proposed to introduce classes of dairymaids resident in the intervals between the sessions of the agricultural students, it was found to be necessary, for obvious reasons, to remove the male pupil teachers from the farm buildings, and the board [illegible], accordingly, undertook to pay the rent for three years to provide a domicile for them elsewhere.

These years were 1881–2, 1882–3, and 1883–4.

Since then the Board had to pay this rent—£50 a year—but as the lodging of the pupil teachers from the beginning was a charge upon the model farm the annual payment had to be debited to the farm. The Commissioners, however, for the year 1888–9, obtained the sanction of the Treasury to transfer this item to the charge of the Model School.

Accordingly the item in my letter of 29th June last, setting forth the expenditure upon the farm for 1888–9, strictly represents the cost of the agricultural department for that year, but for the reasons now stated the amounts for the two preceding years, in the same light, should be diminished by £50 each year.

(Signed), John E. Sheridan, Secretary.

The Secretary,
Educational Endowments Commission,
22, Nassau-street, Dublin.

No. VI.

Ludlow A. Beamish to the Commissioners.

Ashgrove, Queenstown, co. Cork.
September 7th, 1888.

Sir,—I regret to have to enclose the accompanying resolution passed by the Committee of the Munster Agricultural and Dairy School at their last meeting on 31st ult., which I request you will be kind enough to lay before the Educational Endowments Commissioners, and by which they will see that the Committee have come to the conclusion that under existing circumstances they do not feel justified in proceeding with the proposed Scheme for an Agricultural Institute for Munster.

I have postponed forwarding the resolution in question until I had an opportunity of communicating with those of the Governors named in the proposed Scheme, who attended the meeting last June, to consider its provisions, and who are either not members of the Dairy School Committee or who were not present at last Saturday's meeting.

I have now received replies from all, but two, and they are unanimous in approving of the resolution passed by the Committee of the Munster Dairy School—one gentleman, Mr. Geo. Trench, in addition to writing to express his own concurrence therewith, has forwarded to me a copy of a resolution passed by the County Kerry Grand Jury at the last Assizes, which, as you will see from the accompanying enclosure, has anticipated the action of the School Committee.

Regretting extremely that the trouble to which the Educational Endowments Commissioners have been put in formulating a Scheme which, I believe, would have been of great service to the country, should have been wasted in consequence of want of adequate support from the Government.

(Signed), L. A. Beamish, Hon. Sec.

ALPHABETICAL LIST

OF

WITNESSES AND OTHERS WHO HAVE GIVEN EVIDENCE OR MADE STATEMENTS.

N.B.—The names of persons who have given evidence or made statements not on oath are given in italics.

INDEX.

www.ingramcontent.com/pod-product-compliance
Lightning Source LLC
Chambersburg PA
CBHW020449270326
41926CB00008B/536
9783742811141